Archibald Alison

History of Europe

From the fall of Napoleon in MDCCCXV to the accession of Louis Napoleon in

MDCCCLI. Vol. 1

Archibald Alison

History of Europe
From the fall of Napoleon in MDCCCXV to the accession of Louis Napoleon in MDCCCLI. Vol. 1

ISBN/EAN: 9783337350307

Printed in Europe, USA, Canada, Australia, Japan

Cover: Foto ©ninafisch / pixelio.de

More available books at **www.hansebooks.com**

HISTORY OF EUROPE

FROM THE

FALL OF NAPOLEON
IN MDCCCXV

TO THE

ACCESSION OF LOUIS NAPOLEON
IN MDCCCLII

BY

SIR ARCHIBALD ALISON, BART.

Author of the "History of Europe from the Commencement of the French
Revolution, in 1789, to the Battle of Waterloo," &c. &c.

VOL. I.

NEW YORK:
HARPER & BROTHERS, PUBLISHERS,
329 & 331 PEARL STREET,
FRANKLIN SQUARE.
1875.

PREFACE.

During a period of peace the eras of history can not be so clearly perceived on a first and superficial glance as when they are marked by the decisive events of war; but they are not on that account the less obvious when their respective limits have been once ascertained. The triumphs of parties in the Senate-House or the Forum are not, in general, followed by the same immediate and decisive results as those of armies in the field; and their consequences are often not fully developed for several years after they have taken place. But they are equally real and decisive. The results do not follow with less certainty from the movements which have preceded them. It is in tracing these results, and connecting them with the changes in legislation or opinion in which they originated, that the great interest and utility of the history of pacific periods consist.

The periods which have passed over during the thirty-seven years of European *national* peace—from the Fall of Napoleon, in 1815, to the Accession of Louis Napoleon, in 1852—are not so vividly marked as those which occurred during the wars of the French Revolution, but they have a distinctness of their own, and the changes in which they terminated were not less important. The resumption of cash payments in England in 1819 was not, to outward appearance, so striking an event as the battle of Austerlitz, but it was followed by results of equal permanent importance. The Reform Bill was not the cause of so visible a change in human affairs as the battle of Wagram, but it was attended with consequences equally grave and lasting. Without pretending to have discerned with perfect accuracy, as yet, the most important of the many important events which have signalized this memorable era, it may be stated that it naturally divides itself into five periods.

The First, commencing with the entry of the Allies into Paris after the fall of Napoleon, terminates with the passing of the Currency Act of 1819 in England, and the great creation of peers in the democratic interest during the same year in France. The effects of the measures pursued during this period were not perceived at the time, but they are very apparent now. The seeds which produced such decisive results in after times were all sown during its continuance. It forms the subject of the first volume, now submitted to the public.

The Second Period is still more clearly marked; for it begins with the entire establishment of a Liberal government and system of administration in France in 1819, and ends with the Revolution which overthrew Charles X. in 1830. Foreign transactions begin, during this era, to become of importance; for it embraces the revolutions of Spain, Portugal, Naples, and Piedmont in 1820; the rise of Greece as an independent state in the same year, and the important wars of Russia with Turkey and Persia in 1828 and 1829; and the vast conquests of England in India over the Goorkhas and Burmese empire. This period will be embraced in the second volume of this history. The topics it embraces are more various and exciting than those in the first, but they are not more important: they are the growth which followed the seeds previously sown. England and France were still the leaders in the movement; the convulsions of the world were but the consequence of the throes in them.

The Third Period commences with the great debate on the Reform Bill—of two years' continuance—in England in 1831, and ends with the overthrow of the Whig Ministry, by the election of October, 1841. The great and lasting effects of the change in the Constitution of Great Britain, by the passing of the Reform Act, partially developed themselves during this period; and the return of Sir Robert Peel to power was the first great reaction against them During the same time, the natural effects of the Revolution in France appeared in the government, unavoidable in the circumstances, of mingled force and corruption of Louis Philippe, and the growth of

PREFACE

discontent in the inferior classes of society, from the disappointment of their expectations as to the results of the previous convulsion. Foreign episodes of surpassing interest signalize this period; for it contains the heroic effort of the Poles to restore their national independence in 1831; the revolt of Ibrahim Pacha, the bombardment of Acre, and the narrow escape of Turkey from ruin; our invasion of Afghanistan, and subsequent disaster there. This period, so rich in important changes and interesting events, will form the subject of the third volume.

The Fourth Period, commencing with the noble constancy in adversity displayed by Sir Robert Peel and the English Government in 1842, terminates with the overthrow of Louis Philippe, and consequent European Revolutions in February, 1848. If these years were fraught with internal and social changes of the very highest moment to the future fortunes of Great Britain, and of the whole civilized world, they were not less distinguished by the brilliancy of her external triumphs. They witnessed the second expedition into Afghanistan and capture of Cabul; the conclusion of a glorious peace with China under the walls of Nankin; the conquest of Scinde, and desperate passage of arms on the Sutlej. Never did appear in such striking colors the immense superiority which the arms of civilization had acquired over those of barbarism, as in this brief and animating period.

The Fifth Period commences with the overthrow of Louis Philippe in February, 1848, and terminates with the seizure of supreme power by Louis Napoleon in 1852. It is, beyond all example, rich in external and internal events of the very highest moment, and attended by lasting consequences in every part of the world. It witnessed the spread of revolution over Germany and Italy, and the desperate military strife to which it gave rise; the brief but memorable campaign in Italy and Hungary; and the bloodless suppression of revolution in Great Britain and Ireland by the patriotism of her people and the firmness of her government. Interesting, however, as these events were, they yield in ultimate importance to those which, at the same period, were in progress in the distant parts of the earth. The rich territories of the Punjaub were, during it, added to the British dominions in India, which was now bounded only by the Indus and the Himalaya snows. At the same time, the spirit of republican aggrandizement, not less powerful in the New than in the Old World, impelled the Anglo-Saxons over their feeble neighbors in Mexico: Texas was overrun—CALIFORNIA conquered—and the discovery of gold mines, of vast extent and surpassing riches, hitherto unknown to man, changed the fortunes of the world. The simultaneous discovery of mines of the same precious metal in AUSTRALIA acted as a magnet, which attracted the stream of migration and civilization, for the first time in the history of mankind, to the Eastern World; and now, while half a million Europeans annually land in America, and double the already marvelous rate of Transatlantic increase, a hundred thousand Anglo-Saxons yearly migrate to Australia, and lay the foundations of a second England and another Europe, in the vast seats provided there for their reception.

Events so wonderful, and succeeding one another with such rapidity, must impress upon the most inconsiderate observer the belief of a great change going forward in human affairs, of which we are the unconscious instruments. That change is THE SECOND DISPERSION OF MANKIND; the spread of civilization, the extension of Christianity, over the hitherto desert and unpeopled parts of the earth. It is hard to say whether the passions of civilization, the discoveries of science, or the treasures of the wilderness have acted most powerfully in working out this great change. The first developed the energy in the breast of civilized man, which rendered him capable of great achievements, and inspired him with passions which prompted him to seek a wider and more unfettered situation for their gratification than the Old World could afford. The second, in the discoveries of steam, furnished him with the means of reaching with facility the most distant parts of the earth, and armed him with powers which rendered barbarous nations powerless to repel his advance; the third presented irresistible attractions, at the same time, in the most remote parts of the earth, which overcame the attachments of home and the indolence of aged civilization, and sent forth the hardy emigrant, a willing adventurer, to seek his fortune in the golden lottery of distant lands. No such powerful causes, producing the dispersion of the species, have come into operation since mankind were originally separated on the Assyrian plains; and it took place from an attempt, springing from the pride and ambition of man, as vain as the building the Tower of Babel.

That attempt was the endeavor to establish social felicity, and insure the fortunes of the species, by the mere spread of knowledge, and the establishment of democratic institutions, irrespective of the moral training of the people. As this project was based on the pride of intellect, and rested on the doctrine of human perfectibility, so it met with the same result as the attempt, by a tower raised by human hands, to reach the heavens. Carried into execution by fallible agents, it was met and thwarted by their usual passions; and the selfishness and grasping desires of men led to a scene of discord and confusion unparalleled since the beginning of the world. But it terminated in the same result in Europe as in Asia: the building of the political tower of Babel in France was attended by consequences identical with those which had followed the construction of its predecessor on the plains of Shinar. The dispersion of mankind followed, in both cases, the vain attempt; and after, and through the agency of a protracted period of suffering, men in surpassing multitudes found themselves settled in new habitations, and forever severed from the land of their birth, from the consequences of the visionary projects in which they had been engaged.

Views of this kind must, in the present aspect of human affairs, force themselves upon the most inconsiderate mind; and they tend at once to unfold the designs of Providence, now so manifest in the direction of human affairs, and to reconcile us to much which might lead to desponding views if we confined our survey to the fortunes of particular states. An examination of the social and political condition of the principal European monarchies, particularly France and England, at this time, and a retrospect of the changes they have undergone during the last thirty years, must probably lead every impartial person to the conclusion that the period of their greatest national eminence has passed, and that the passions by which they are now animated are those which tend to shorten their existence. But we shall cease to regard this inevitable change with melancholy, when we reflect that, from the effect of these very passions, the British family is rapidly increasing in distant hemispheres, and that the human race is deriving fresh life and vigor, and spreading over the wilds of nature, from the causes which portend its decline in its former habitations.

As the history of a period fraught with such momentous changes, and distinguished by such ceaseless and rapid progress, as that which is undertaken in this work, of necessity brings the author in contact with all the great questions, social and political, which have agitated society during its continuance, he has deemed it essential invariably to follow out the two rules which were observed in his former publication. These were, to give invariably at the end of every paragraph the authorities, by volume and page, on which it is founded; and never to introduce a great question without giving as copious an abstract as the limits of the work will admit, of the facts and arguments brought forward on both sides. The latter, especially, seemed to be peculiarly called for in a work which is more occupied with social and political than with military changes, and which is occupied with a period when the victories were won in the Forum or the Senate-House, not the field. The author has made no attempt to disguise his own opinions on every subject; but he has not exerted himself the less anxiously to give, with all the force and clearness in his power, those which are adverse to it; and he should regret to think that the reader could find in any other publication a more forcible abstract of the arguments in favor of Parliamentary Reform, a Contracted Currency founded on the retention of gold, or Free Trade in corn and shipping, than are to be met with in this.

In making this abstract, he has adopted two rules, which seemed essential to the combining a faithful record of opposite opinions with the interest and limits necessary in a work of general history. The first is to give *one* argument only on each side, and not attempt to give separate abstracts of the speeches of different men. Felicitous or eloquent expressions are occasionally preserved; but, in general, the argument given is rather an abridgment of the best parts of the arguments of many different speakers than a transcript of the oration of any one. That this is necessary, must be obvious, from the consideration that the author is often called on to give the marrow of an argument in three or four pages, which is expended over some hundreds of Hansard or the *Moniteur*; and it is surprising how effectually, where the attempt is made in sincerity and good faith, it proves successful. The second is, when a subject has been once introduced, and the opposite arguments fully given, to dismiss it afterward with a mere statement of the fate it met with, or the division on it in the Legislature. As the same subject was constantly debated in both Houses of Parliament, both in France and England, for many consecutive years, any attempt to give an account of each year's debate would both lead to tedious repetition and extend the work to an immoderate length.

For a similar reason, although the History is a general one of the whole European states, yet no attempt has been made to bring forward, abreast in every year, the annals of each particular state. On the contrary, the transactions of different countries are taken up together, and brought down separately, in one or more chapters, through several consecutive years. Thus the first volume is chiefly occupied with the internal annals of France and England, from 1815 to 1820, when all the great changes which afterward took place were prepared; the second, besides the annals of France and England, with the foreign wars or revolutions of Russia, Spain, and Italy, or the distant conquests of the English in India during the next ten years. In no other way is it possible to enable the reader to form a clear idea of the succession of events in each particular state, or take that interest in its fortunes which is indispensable to success or utility, not less in the narrative of real than in the conception of imaginary events.

One very interesting subject is treated of at considerable length in these volumes, which could not, from the pressure of warlike events, be introduced at equal length into the author's former work. This is an account of Literature, Manners, the Arts, and social changes in the principal European states during the period it embraces. An entire chapter on this subject, regarding Great Britain, has been introduced into the first volume; similar ones relating to literature and the arts in France, Germany, and Italy, will succeed in those which follow. This plan has been adopted from more than an anxious desire—strong as that motive is—to relieve the reader's mind, and present subjects of study more generally interesting than the weightier matters of social and political change. During pacific periods, it is in the literature, which interests the public mind, that we are to find the true seat of the power which directs it; and if we would discover the real rulers of mankind, we shall find them rather in their philosophers and literary men than either their statesmen or their generals. The only difference is, that it is a posthumous dominion, in general, which the author obtains: his reign does not begin till he himself is mouldering in the grave.

By steadily following out the rule of dismissing every subject of political debate when it has once been fully laid before the reader, the author has no doubt of his being able to comprise the history of the whole period in five volumes. The last volume will be accompanied by a copious Index.
A. ALISON.

POSSIL HOUSE, LANARKSHIRE,
October 8, 1852.

CONTENTS OF VOL. I.

CHAPTER I.

GENERAL SKETCH OF THE WHOLE PERIOD FROM THE FALL OF NAPOLEON TO THE ACCESSION OF LOUIS NAPOLEON.

Resumé of the War just concluded.—The second Drama was one springing out of Social Passions.—Causes which rendered it so Violent.—Governments now aimed at Peace, and the People clamored for War.—Causes in France which predisposed to the Revolution of 1830.—Causes which made England share in the Convulsion.—Great effects of the Revolution in both Countries.—Political Alliance between France and England which followed this Change.—Effects of the Change upon the Colonial Empire of England.—Still greater Results of the Free-trade Policy of England.—Vast Extension of the United States of America.—Vast Increase of Russia during the same Period.—Continued Increase of Russia from the Revolutions of 1830 and 1848.—Simultaneous Conquests of the English in India, and their Origin in necessity.—Their great Frequency and Extent.—Revolution of 1848 in Paris.—Causes of the Fall of Louis Philippe.—Calamitous effects of the Revolution of 1848 in Europe.—Extreme Violence of the Revolution in Germany.—Successful stand against the revolutionary Spirit in England and France.—Restoration of military Power in Austria.—Restoration of military Despotism in France by Louis Napoleon.—Great Increase of external Dangers from the Effects of the Revolution of 1848.—Disastrous Effects of this Revolution on the Cause of Freedom.—Dangers of Great Britain in particular.—Causes which have rendered the Condition of Great Britain so precarious.—Extraordinary Change in the national Mind in this respect.—Dangers springing from the Free-trade System.—Dangers arising from the Change in our foreign Policy.—Gold Mines of California and Australia.—Tendency to augment Influence of Wealth in the later stages of Society.—Way in which this is brought about.—Influence of Contraction and Expansion of the Currency on Rome, and on Europe in the sixteenth Century.—Vast effects of the Expansion of the Currency during the War.—Great Distress over the World from the Contraction of the Currency since the Peace.—Amount of that Contraction.—Hopeless prospects of Industry in Great Britain.—Vast effect of the Discovery of the Californian Gold.—What if California had not been discovered?—Vast blessings which its Discovery has introduced.—Immense Effect of the application of Steam to mechanical Labor and Importance of its being inapplicable to Agriculture.—Proof of this from statistical Considerations.—What if the Case had been otherwise?—Influence of this Law on the Fate of particular Nations.—Great effect upon the Fortunes of the Species.—Effect of general Education on general Morality.—Proof of this from various Countries.—Reasons of this peculiarity in human Nature.—General Power of Thought over Mankind.—Great consequent Influence of Mind on human Affairs.—Ease with which the Press may be perverted to the purposes of Despotism.—Great effect of the discovery of Steam and Electric communication.—Increased corresponding Activity in the principles which counteract Evil.—Way in which this was brought about.—General longing after representative Institutions.—Doubts which their general Failure has excited among Men.—Effect of representative Institutions in Britain.—Its effects in America.—Rise of Divisions and Passions of Race.—Great error in supposing national Character depends on Institutions.—Wars of Races are the great passion of Eastern Europe.—Doubts as to the wisdom of representative Institutions.—Real Character, good and evil, of representative Institutions.—Great effect of the Social Passions of Europe in propelling its Inhabitants to the New World and of the discovery of the Gold Mines of California and Australia.—What if the Case had been otherwise?—Increasing Influence of Russian Conquest.—Migratory propensities of Men in the youth of Civilization.—Corresponding moving propensities in the maturity of Civilization.—Necessity of republican Institutions to Colonial Settlements.—Adaptation of the Sclavonic and Anglo-Saxon Character to the parts assigned them in their Progress.—Destiny of the race of Japhet in reference to Christianity.—Increasing influence of Religion in Europe.—Differences of the era of this History and that of the Last.

CHAPTER II.

HISTORY OF ENGLAND FROM THE PEACE OF PARIS, IN 1815, TO THE END OF THE YEAR 1816.

Commanding Position of Great Britain at the close of the War.—Statistical Facts proving the general Prosperity of the State.—Warm and general Anticipations of general Prosperity on the Peace.—Universal disappointment of these Hopes, and general Distress.—Beginning of the Distress among the export Merchants.—Its spread to the Agriculturists.—Severe scarcity of 1816.—Distress among the Manufacturers, and Causes to which it was owing.—This general suffering was not owing to the transition from War to Peace.—Diminished supply of the precious Metals from South America.—Simultaneous and rapid Contraction of the Paper Currency of Great Britain.—Important Discussions on the Property Tax and other topics.—Argument against the Property Tax by the Opposition.—It was specifically a War Tax.—Not necessary as a general measure of Finance.—Argument on the other side by the Ministry.—No breach of Faith in its continuance.—The Petitions for its repeal not unanimous.—Necessity for its Continuance.—Abolition of the Tax.—Reflections on this Subject.—Vital Considerations on the Question, which were overlooked at this Time.—Remission of the War Malt Tax.—Reduced Estimates formed by Government.—Argument for a Reduction of Expenditure by the Opposition.—Argument on the other side by Ministers.—Establishments ultimately voted.—Debates on Agricultural Distress.—Argument of the Opposition on the subject.—Argument on the other side by the Ministry.—Measures of Government in regard to the restriction of cash Payments and a Loan from the Bank.—Argument of the Opposition against the continuance of the Bank Restriction Act.—Answer of the Ministry.—Reflections on this Subject.—Extraordinary Insensibility to right Conclusions which then prevailed.—General errors on the Subject which then

CONTENTS.

prevailed.—Consolidation of the English and Irish Exchequers.—Reflections on this Subject.—Motion respecting the Holy Alliance by Mr. Brougham.—Bail for the detention of Napoleon.—Marriage of the Princess Charlotte of Wales.—Votes for public Monuments.—Monuments to Sir T. Picton and others.—Grants to the Officers and Men employed in the War.—New Coinage.—Reflections on the preceding parliamentary Narrative.—Efforts of the factious to stir up Sedition.—Spafield Riots.—Expedition to Algiers.—Outrages which led to it.—Description of Algiers.—Lord Exmouth's Preparations for an Attack.—The manning and fitting out of the Fleet.—Departure of the Fleet and Voyage to Algiers.—Preparations of the Algerines.—Arrival of the Fleet off Algiers.—Commencement of the Battle.—Continuance of the Action, and Positions taken by the Ships.—Destruction of the Enemy's Ships and Flotilla.—The Fleet moves out of the Bay.—Results of the Battle, and killed and wounded.—The Algerines submit, and Peace is concluded.—Honors bestowed on Lord Exmouth and the Fleet.—Reflections on this Battle, and the commencement of the ascendant of Christianity over Mohammedanism.—Progressive ascendant of Christianity over Mohammedanism.

CHAPTER III.

HISTORY OF FRANCE FROM THE SECOND RESTORATION OF LOUIS XVIII. TO THE ORDINANCES OF SEPTEMBER 7, 1816.

Extraordinary Difficulties of the Government of France after the Battle of Waterloo.—Difficulties arising from the changeable disposition of the French People.—Important effects this produced in 1815, and Causes of the violence of Opinion.—Unbounded Humiliation and Sufferings of France at this time.—Which occasions a universal Reaction against Napoleon and his adherents.—Difficulties which these feelings threw in the way of the new Government.—Difficulties of Louis XVIII. in the choice of his Ministers.—Talleyrand and Fouché are appointed to the Ministry.—Formation of the Ministry, and Retirement of Chateaubriand.—The King's Proclamation from Cambray.—His entry into Paris.—Violence of the Royalists, and difficulties of Louis.—Difficulty in regard to the Convocation of the Chambers, and Debates on it.—The King issues an Ordinance, changing the mode of Elections, of his own authority.—Royal Ordinance, changing the Modes and Rules of Election.—Disunion between the King and the Duke d'Angoulême and Count d'Artois as to the Prefects.—The Freedom of the Press is restored in all but the Journals.—Reasons which rendered the Punishment of the leading Napoleonists necessary.—Lists of Persons to be accused, prepared by Fouché, and sanctioned by a royal Ordinance.—Ordinances regarding the Chamber of Peers.—The Peerage is declared hereditary.—Arrival of the allied Sovereigns in Paris.—Army of the Loire.—Its Submission.—Disbanding of the Army of the Loire.—Reorganization of the Army into departmental Legions.—Breaking up of the Museum.—Desperate state of the Finances.—Settlements of the allied Troops in France, and their Exactions.—Reaction in the South.—Massacre at Marseilles.—Departure of Marshal Brune for Paris.—He is murdered at Avignon.—Further Massacres in the South.—Atrocities at Nimes and the surrounding Country.—Persecution of the Protestants by the Roman Catholics.—Temper of France during the Elections.—Their ultra-Royalist character.—Dismissal of Fouché from the Ministry.—Fall of Fouché, and his Death.—Fall of Talleyrand, and his Ministry.—Ministry of the Duke de Richelieu.—Life of the Duke de Richelieu.—His Character.—Biography of M. Decazes.—Difficulties of the Negotiations with the allied Powers.—Exorbitant Demands of Austria and the lesser Powers.—Treaty of Paris.—Convention of 20th November, between the allied Powers, for Exclusion of Napoleon and his Family from the Throne of France.—The Holy Alliance, and Causes which led to it.—Terms of the Holy Alliance.—Treaties regarding the Ionian Isles, a Russian Subsidy, and Napoleon Bonaparte.—Reflections on these Treaties.—Violent Temper and Disposition of the Chamber of Deputies.—Composition and Parties in the Chambers—The extreme Royalists and their Leaders.—The Provincial Deputies.—The Opposition and its Leaders.—Composition of the Chamber of Peers.—Opening of the Chamber, and Speech of the King.—Manner in which the Speech was received by the Chamber.—Difficulties at taking the Oath of Fidelity.—Answer of the Chamber of Deputies.—Law against seditious Cries.—Law suspending individual Liberty.—Discussion on it in the Chambers.—Vehement Discussion on the Law against seditious Cries.—Law establishing Courts-martial for political Offenses.—Proposal for rendering the inferior Judges removable during a Year.—Discussion on the Acts in the Peers.—Answer of M. de Fontanes and M. de Brissac.—Argument against the Law on seditious Cries.—Speech of Chateaubriand on the Subject.—Reflections on the Deaths of Ney and Labedoyère.—External Influences exerted against the Government.—Considerations which weighed with the Court.—Measures of the Government to give the accused Persons the means of Escape.—Treachery of Colonel Labedoyère.—His Arrest.—His Trial and Condemnation.—His Death.—Trial of Marshal Ney.—His treacherous Conduct.—His Departure from Paris, and Arrest at Bessonis.—His Trial before the Chamber of Peers.—His Defense and Condemnation.—Appeal to the Capitulation of Paris.—He is found guilty, and sentenced to Death.—His Death determined on by the King.—His Execution.—Reflections on this Event, and on the Duke of Wellington's share in the Transaction.—Trial of Lavalette.—The King's pardon is applied for in vain.—He escapes by the aid of his Wife, and in her Dress.—Sir Robert Wilson, Mr. Hutchinson, and Mr. Bruce enable him to escape.—Mode in which they effect his Escape, and their Trial.—Adventures of Murat after the Battle of Waterloo.—He embarks, and lands in Corsica.—His arrival at Ajaccio, and descent on Naples.—The King lands.—Where he fails, and is arrested.—He is condemned by a Court-martial.—His Death.—Reflections on this Event.—Death of Mouton-Duvernet and General Chartrand.—A general Amnesty, which is coldly received by the Chamber.—Modifications with which it is passed into a Law.—Proposals for a new Law of Elections.—M. Vaublanc's Argument in favor of the ministerial Project on the Elections.—Project of the Royalists.—The Project of the Royalists is carried in the Deputies and rejected in the Peers.—The Budget.—Ministerial Plan on the Subject.—Proposition of the Chamber regarding the Clergy.—Argument in favor of an Endowment of the Church.—Answer of the Ministers, and their counter Project.—Argument of M. Bonald against the Law of Divorce.—Changes in the Administration.—Conspiracy of the Liberal Party.—Outbreak, headed by Didier, at Grenoble.—Exaggerations of General Donnadieu, and needless Severities.—Conspiracy in Paris.—Conspiracy at Lyons.—Preparations of the Government for a Change in the Electoral Law, and its difficulties.—Speech of M. Decazes in favor of a Coup d'État.—Adoption of these Principles by the King, and Preparations for carrying them into Execution.—Ordinance of Sept. 5, 1816.—Consternation of the ultra-Royalists, and Dismissal of Chateaubriand.—Great effects of this Ordinance.—The whole Chambers were elected by royal Ordinance.—Reflections on the Reaction of 1815, which was forced by the Nation on the Govern ment.—The greatest Iniquities of the Period were committed by Juries.—Expedience of abolishing entirely the Punishment of Death in purely political Offenses.—Banishment is its proper Punishment.

CHAPTER IV.

DOMESTIC HISTORY OF ENGLAND, FROM THE COMMENCEMENT OF 1817 TO THE REPEAL OF THE BANK RESTRICTION ACT IN 1819.

Vicissitudes and ceaseless Chain of Events in human Affairs.—Exemplifications of this Vicissitude in the History of France and England after the Revolution.—Consoling Features even in the Ruin of the Old World. — Fundamental Cause which has led to Disaster in France.—What has done so in England.—The mercantile Aristocracy pursue Measures for their peculiar Interests.—Which, in Ignorance, are supported by the operative Manufacturers.—Reason of this frequent Disappointment of general Wishes.—Continued Distress and Discontent in the Country.—Plan formed of a general Insurrection.—Meeting of Parliament, and Attack on the Prince-Regent.—Report of the Secret Committee in both Houses.—Suspension of the Habeas Corpus Act, and passing of the Seditious Meetings Act.—Measures of Government to suppress the Insurrection, which breaks out at Derby.—Extension of the Suspension of the Habeas Corpus Act.—Restoration of Confidence and improved Prospects toward the close of the Year. —Finance Accounts of 1817, compared with 1816. —Mr. Peel's Irish Insurrection Act.— Trial by Jury in civil Causes in Scotland.—Its entire Failure.—Acquittal of Watson and Hone.—Reflections on this Subject.—Error at that Period in the English Law.—Good effects of the Suspension of the Habeas Corpus Act.—Motion of Mr. Brougham regarding the Trade and Manufactures of the Country.—Establishment of Savings Banks, and diminished severity of Punishment in criminal Cases.—Return of Mr. Canning from Lisbon, and Death of Mr. Ponsonby and Mr. Horner.—Mr. Horner's Life and Character.—His Character as an Orator and political Philosopher.—Death of the Princess Charlotte.—Universal Grief of the Nation at this Event.—Improved Condition of the Country in the end of 1817 and Spring of 1818.—Cause of this increased Prosperity.—Steps of the Bank toward Cash Payments.—Argument for the resumption of Cash Payments by the Opposition.—Answer by the Ministers.—Bill of Indemnity for Persons seized under the Suspension of the Habeas Corpus Act.— Military and Naval forces voted, and Revenue.—Expenditure, and Increase of Exports, Imports, and Shipping, in 1817 and 1818.—Grant of a Million to build new Churches. —Treaty with Spain for the abolition of the Slave Trade.—Alien Bill, and Mr. Brougham's Committee concerning Charities.—Efforts of Sir Samuel Romilly to obtain a relaxation of our Criminal Code.—Death of Sir Samuel Romilly.—His Character.— Death and Character of Lord Ellenborough.—Death of Warren Hastings and Sir Philip Francis.—Sir James Mackintosh: his early Life. —His Character as a Statesman and Writer.—His Character as a parliamentary Speaker.—Death and Character of Queen Charlotte.—Favorable aspect of Affairs at the opening of 1819, and Disasters at its close.—Commencement of the Debates on the Currency Question.—Petition from Bristol against the too speedy Resumption of Cash Payments.—Its tenor.—First Speech of Mr. Peel on the Subject.—Petition of the Merchants and Bankers of London in favor of continuing the Restriction; which is presented to the House of Commons by the first Sir R. Peel.—His Speech on the Occasion continued.—Argument of Mr. Peel in favor of the Resumption of Cash Payments.— Argument on the other side.—Decision of Parliament on the Subject.—Reflections on this Decision.—Mr. Vansittart's Finance Resolutions.—Mr Vansittart's Finance Plan and new Taxes.—Sir James Mackintosh's argument in support of Criminal Law Reform.—Answer of Lord Castlereagh. —Sir James Mackintosh's Motion is carried.—Reflections on this Subject.—Results of Experience on the Subject.—What has caused the apparent Anomaly?—True Principles on the Subject.—Clandestine Succors sent by the English to the South American Insurgents.—Argument of Ministers in favor of the Foreign Enlistment Bill.—Answer by the Opposition.—The Succors to the Insurgents still continue.—Reflections on this Subject.—Vast Extent of the aid thus afforded to the Insurgents. — Punishment which England has received for this Injustice.—Dreadful Losses arising from our Interference with South America.

CHAPTER V.

PROGRESS OF LITERATURE, SCIENCE, THE ARTS, AND MANNERS, IN GREAT BRITAIN AFTER THE PEACE.

Great Impulse given to Literature and Science after the War.—Way in which War produces this effect. — Rapid Progress of Steam Navigation in Britain, and of the Cotton Manufacture. — Progress in other branches of Manufacture. — Brilliant Eras in Literature which generally succeed those of great public Dangers.—Literary Character of Sir Walter Scott. — Peculiar Character of his Writings.—Their elevated moral Character.—The Defects of his later Writings.—Lord Byron.—His Merits and Defects.—His Dramas and Don Juan. —Moore as a lyric Poet.—His Oriental turn and satirical Verses.—Campbell: his vast and noble Genius.—His lyrical Poems.—Rogers' Pleasures of Memory.—Southey: his peculiar Character.—His Merits as a Historian and Moralist.—Wordsworth: his Character as a Writer, and great Fame.—Parallel between him and Goethe.— Coleridge: his poetic Character. — Mrs. Hemans.— Crabbe.—Joanna Baillie.—Tennyson.—Character of the prose Compositions of the Period.—Dugald Stewart. — His want of original Thought. — Dr. Brown.—Paley.—Malthus: what led to his Doctrines.—Great Influence and rapid spread of his Doctrines.—His Errors, and subsequent Demonstration of them.—His Character as a political Philosopher.—Ricardo, M'Culloch Senior, and Mills. — Davy: his philosophical Discoveries. — Herschel, Playfair, D'Israeli, Alison. — Modern Geology: Buckland, Sedgewick, Sir Charles Lyell, and Sir David Brewster.—Rise of the learned Reviews and lengthened Essays. — Rise of the Edinburgh Review, Quarterly Review, and Blackwood's Magazine. — Jeffrey. — Brougham. — Sir James Mackintosh.— Sidney Smith.— Macaulay. —Lockhart.— Wilson.— Change in the Style of History.—Hallam.—Sharon Turner and Palgrave. —Lingard: previous Prejudices of the Historians of the Reformation.—His Merits and Defects as a Historian.—Tytler: his impartial Character.—His Merits and Defects.— Napier.— Lord Mahon.— Macaulay's History.—Miss Strickland.— Mitford. —Grote.—Arnold.—The new School of Novelists. —Miss Edgeworth.—Mr. James.—Sir Edward B. Lytton.—His Merits as a Poet and dramatic Writer. —Disraeli. — Dickens. — Thackeray and the Dickens School. — Miss Austin.— Mrs. Norton.— Mr. Warren.—Carlyle. — Dr. Croly. — Hazlitt.— Bentham.—Chalmers.—Monkton Milnes and Aytoun.— L. E. L., Warburton, and the Author of Eothen. — The Fine Arts — Architecture. — Sir Thomas Lawrence.— Turner.— Copley Fielding, Williams, Thomson.—Grant, Pickersgill, Swinton. —Landseer.— Wilkie.— Chantrey.— Flaxman. — Marochetti.—Mrs. Siddons.— John Kemble.— Miss O'Neil.—Kean.—Miss Helen Faucit.—Decline of the Drama in England, and its Causes.—The exclusive System in Society: its Causes.— Its great Effect on Society.—Increasing Liberalism of the higher Ranks.—Influence in Society of the great

CHAPTER VI.

HISTORY OF FRANCE FROM THE COUP D'ETAT OF SEPTEMBER 5, 1816, TO THE CREATION OF PEERS IN 1819.

Effects of the Coup d'Etat of 5th September, 1816.—Democratic Basis on which the elective Franchise was founded.—The Elections of 1815, and Measures taken to secure them.—Efforts of the Royalists and Liberals.—Result of the Elections.—Internal government after the Coup d'Etat of 5th September.—Great Distress in France in the Winter of 1816-17.—Opening of the Chambers.—State of Parties in the Chamber of Deputies.—Centre and Left.—Law of Elections of 5th February, 1817.—Argument of the Ministers in support of the Measure.—Answer by the Royalists.—It is passed.—Reflections on this Law.—Laws on personal Freedom and the Liberty of the Press.—Projects of Laws regarding the Liberty of the Press and personal Freedom.—Argument against the Law on the Liberty of the Press by the Opposition.—Answer of the Ministerialists.—Extreme Scarcity, and Measures of Government in consequence.—More liberal System in the Army.—Concordat with Rome.—Extreme Difficulty regarding the Finances.—Efforts of the Emperor Alexander and the Duke of Wellington to obviate these Difficulties.—Convention of 11th February, 1818, for the Diminution of the Army of Occupation.—The Budget of 1817.—Law regarding Bequests to the Church.—Arguments for a proprietary Clergy.—Answer of the Ministerialists.—Result of the Debate.—Modification of the Ministry.—Biography and Character of Count Molé.—Gouvion St. Cyr.—The Elections of 1817.—State of public Opinion.—State of public Opinion, and of the Press.—The Orleanists.—Measures of the Session: the Law of Recruiting.—The Law of Recruiting proposed by Government.—Argument in support of the Project by Ministers.—Argument on the other side by the Royalists.—The Bill is passed into a Law.—Law regarding the Liberty of the Press.—Expiry of the Laws against personal Freedom and the Prévôtal Courts.—Failure of the Law for establishing the new Concordat.—The Budget.—Conclusion of an Arrangement regarding the Indemnities.—Aix-la-Chapelle and its Concourse of illustrious Foreigners.—Embassadors there, and Instructions of Louis to the Duke de Richelieu.—Brilliant Concourse of Strangers at Aix-la-Chapelle.—Conversation of Alexander with Richelieu.—Conclusion of the Treaty of Aix-la-Chapelle.—Secret Treaty with the Allies.—Answer of Louis XVIII.—Secret Protocol.—Secret military Protocol.—Military Arrangements.—Secret Royalist Memoir presented to the allied Sovereigns at Aix-la-Chapelle.—Evacuation of the French Territory by the Allies.—Noble Conduct of the Duke of Wellington on this Occasion.—Attempted Assassination of the Duke of Wellington.—Visit of Alexander to Louis XVIII. at Paris.—Elections of 1818.—Financial Crisis.—Difficulties of the Duke de Richelieu.—Divisions in the Cabinet, and break-up of the Ministry.—Formation of the new Ministry.—Recompense voted to the Duke de Richelieu, and declined by him.—Measures of the new Ministers.—General promotion of the Liberals in the civil Service.—Movement against the Electoral Law in the Peers.—Argument of M. Barthélemy for a Change in the Law of Election.—Answer on the part of the Ministerialists.—The Proposition is carried, and vast sensation throughout France.—Measures of the Cabinet, and Liberals in the Chamber of Deputies.—Argument in support of M. Barthélemy's Proposal.—Argument of the Ministers on the other side.—Adoption of M. Barthélemy's Proposition, and Defeat of Ministers on the fixing of the financial Year.—Measures of the Government.—Great Majority in the Chamber of Deputies for Ministers.—Great and Lasting Results of the Changes already made in France.—Repeated Coups d'Etat in France since the Restoration.—The Coups d'Etat were all on the popular side.—Causes of this Peculiarity.

CHAPTER VII.

SPAIN AND ITALY FROM THE PEACE OF 1814 TO THE REVOLUTION OF 1820.

Analogy of the early History of Spain and England.—The Colonies were not a Source of Weakness to Spain.—Colonies are always a Benefit to the Parent State.—Support which Colonies afford to the Mother Country.—What the Colonial Policy of the Parent State should be.—Inevitable Loss to the Parent State from the Separation of the Colonies.—Tyrannical Rule of old Spain over her Colonies.—The Trade of Spain was all with foreign Manufactures.—Want of Industry in the national Character.—The Physical circumstances of Spain favored Commerce, but not Manufactures.—Effect of the long-continued Hostility with the Moors.—Impolitic Laws of Spain in regard to Money.—Important Effect of the Romish faith.—Difference of the Towns and Country in respect of Political opinion.—Disposition of the Army.—The Church.—State of the Peasantry.—State of the Nobility.—Huge gap in the Revenue from the loss of the South American Colonies.—Constitution of 1812: how it was Formed.—Its extreme Democratic tendency.—Utter unsuitableness of the Constitution to the generality of Spain.—Universal unpopularity of the Cortes and Constitution.—Influence of the Cortes on South America.—Situation of Portugal: effect of the Removal of the seat of Government to Rio Janeiro.—Its general Adoption of English Habits and Ideas.—Character of Ferdinand VII.—Ferdinand's arrival in Spain, and Treatment by the Cortes.—Universal unpopularity of the Cortes.—Decree of Valencia.—King's Declaration in favor of Freedom, and Promise to convoke a legal Cortes.—Universal transports in Spain at this Decree, and the King's return to Madrid.—Reflections on this Event, and the obvious Courses which lay open to the King.—Ferdinand's despotic Measures.—Re-establishment of the Inquisition.—Discontent in various Quarters.—Revolt of Mina in Navarre.—Fresh arbitrary Decree of Ferdinand.—Farther violent Proceedings of the King, and Porlier's revolt.—Its Failure, and his Death.—Invasion of France, and Retreat of the Spaniards. Fresh tyrannical Acts of the King.—Change of Ministers, and Policy at Madrid.—Restoration of the Jesuits, and other Despotic Measures.—Double Marriages of the Royal Families of Spain and Portugal.—Creation of the kingdom of Brazil.—Insurrection in Valencia.—Abortive Conspiracy in Barcelona, and Death of General Lacy.—Papal Bull regarding the Contribution by the Spanish Church.—Treaty regarding the Queen of Etruria.—Treaty for the Limitation of the Slave Trade.—Miserable state of Spain: its Army and Navy.—Extreme penury of the Finances of Spain. Decree, April 3, 1818.—Death of Queen Maria Isabella of Spain.—Disastrous fate of the first Expedition to Lima.—Fresh Revolt at Valencia, which is Suppressed.—Causes of the Revolt in the Isle of Leon.—Efforts of the Cadiz Liberals to promote it.—Insurrection at Cadiz.—The Conspiracy is at first arrested by d'Abisbal.—D'Abisbal is deprived of the Command of the Expedition.—Additional Measures of Severity on the part of the Government.—Yellow Fever at Cadiz.—Sale of Florida to the Americans.—Marriage of the King.—Revolution attempted by Riego.—Vigorous Measures adopted against the Insurgents.—Capture of the Arsenal, and Expedition of Riego into the Interior.—Its Defeat and Failure.—Perilous position of Quiroga in the Isle of Leon.—Insurrection at Corunna, and in Navarre.—Revolution at Madrid: the King accepts the Constitution.—Reflections on this Revolution.—Rapid advances of the Revolution.—Reception of the Revolution at Barcelona, Valencia, and Cadiz.—Massacre at Cadiz.—New Ministry at Madrid.—First Measures of the new Government.—Establishment of Clubs in Madrid, and other Revolutionary Measures.—Legislative Measures.—Meeting of the Cortes: its Composition.—Disorders in the Provinces.—Murder of one of the Body-guard, and Reward of the Murderers.—Opening of the Cortes.—Report on the State of the Army.—Majority of the Cortes: its Leaders.—Suppression of the Jesuits, and Measures regarding Entails.—Financial Measures.—Tumult at Madrid, and Dismissal of Riego.—Closing of the Session, and Rupture with the King.—Reception of the Decree against the Priests in Spain.—Illegal Appointment of General Carvajal by the King.—Return of the King to Madrid.—Victory of the Revolutionists.—New Society for Execution of Lynch Law.—Identity of recent History of Spain and Portugal.—Revolution at Oporto.—Which is followed by a Revolution at Lisbon.—Establishment of a Joint Regency at Lisbon.—Return of Marshal Beresford, who is forced to go to England.—Effect of the Banishment of the British.—Reaction, and Adoption of more Moderate Measures.—Commencement of Reforms in Italy.—Breach of the King's promise of a Constitution.—Progressive but slight Reforms already introduced.—Origin of Secret Societies.—Their Origin and previous History.—Commencement of the Neapolitan Revolution.—Defection of General Pepe and the Garrison of Naples.—The King yields, and swears to the Constitution.—Causes which prepared Revolution in Sicily.—Revolution in Palermo.—Frightful Massacre in Palermo.—First Measures of the new Junta.—Failure of the Negotiations with Naples.—Suppression of the Insurrection in Palermo.—Renewal of Hostilities.—Meeting of the Neapolitan Parliament.—Insurrection of the Galley-slaves in Civita Vecchia.—Commencement of the Revolution in Piedmont.—Revolt in Alessandria and Turin.—The King yields, and accepts the Constitution.—Resignation of the King, and Proclamation of the Prince of Carignan as Regent, and the Spanish Constitution.—General Character of the Revolutions of 1820.—What caused their speedy Overthrow.—What should the Military do in such circumstances?

CHAPTER VIII.

RUSSIA AND POLAND, FROM THE PEACE OF 1815 TO THE ACCESSION OF NICHOLAS IN 1825.

Vast Growth and Extent of Russia, America, and British India in recent Times.—Increase of Russia by the Treaties of 1814 and 1815.—Important Acquisition of Russia in the Grand-duchy of Warsaw.—Statistics of the Grand-duchy of Warsaw.—Establishment of the Kingdom of Poland.—Biography of the Grand Duke Constantine.—His Character.—His first Acts of Administration, and Training of the Army.—Great Advantage to Poland from its Union with Russia.—Great Increase of its Military Strength.—Failure of the Representative System in Poland.—Great Influence of Russia.—Great Wisdom of its External Policy.—Their Unity of Purpose.—Statistics of the Empire: its Population.—Great Rapidity of Increase of the Russian Population.—Great Room for future Increase in its Inhabitants.—Unity of Feeling in the whole Empire.—Reason of this Unity. Their Asiatic Habits and Religious Feelings.—Unity of Interest in the Empire.—General Insufficiency of the Schools to produce Enlightenment.—The Clergy.—Rank in Russia: the Tchinn.—Great Power given by the Tchinn.—Caste of the Nobles.—Of the Bourgeois and Trading Classes.—The Serfs: their Number and Condition.—Privileges and Advantages they enjoy.—The Tieglo: its Advantages and Evils.—Way in which it is carried into Effect.—Contrast of English and Russian Cultivators.—Opinion of M. Haxthausen on the Serfs and their Enfranchisement.—Evils of the Russian Serf System.—Foreign Conquest ever forced upon Russia by its Climate.—Fear the universal Principle of Government in Russia.—General use of Corporal Chastisement.—Character which these Circumstances have imprinted on the Russians.—Causes which have led to this Character.—Great Effect of the Distances in Russia.—Civilization depends entirely on the Higher Ranks.—Strong Imitative turn of the Russians.—Military Strength of Russia.—The Military Colonies.—The Cossacks.—The admirable Discipline and Equipment of the Army.—Russian Navy.—Revenue of Russia.—Positions of the principal Armies.—General Corruption in Russia.—Enormous Abuses which prevail.—Striking Instances of this Corruption.—Emigration in Russia is all Internal.—Great Impulse to Agricultural Industry in Russia from Free Trade.—What is the Destiny of Russia?—Two different People in Russia.—Liberal Ideas with which the Troops returned from France and Germany.—First steps of Alexander on his Return to Russia in 1814.—His beneficent Measures.—Marriage of Alexander's sister to the Prince of Orange, and of the Grand Duke Nicholas to the Princess of Prussia.—Incessant Travels of Alexander from 1815 to 1825.—Various beneficent Measures introduced by him.—His arrival at Warsaw in 1818.—Alexander's memorable Speech to the Diet.—Journey of Alexander to his Southern Provinces.—His Efforts for the Enfranchisement of the Peasants.—Transactions of 1819.—Expulsion of the Jesuits.—Great Changes in the Emperor's mind from the Revolution of 1820.—Violent Scene, and Dissolution of the Polish Diet.—Congress of Troppau.—Congress of Troppau: its Resolutions.—Congress of Laybach.—Reflections on the Division among the Allied Powers.—Limits of the Right of Intervention.—What Share had the Holy Alliance in this?—Attitude taken by England on the occasion.—War declared against the Revolution in Naples.—Unresisted March of the Austrians toward Naples.—Subjugation of Naples, and Return of the King.—Movement of the Insurgents in Piedmont.—Meeting of the Allies, and fresh Revolution in Genoa.—Increasing Difficulties of the Insurgents.—Total Defeat of the Insurgents at Agogna.—Submission of the Capital, and Termination of the War.—Violent Reaction in Italy.—Reaction in Piedmont, and Treaty with Austria.—Revolt in a Regiment of Guards at St. Petersburg.—Alexander refuses to Support the Greeks.—Extension of the Russian Empire in North America.—Suppression of Freemasons and other Secret Societies.—General Failure of the Emperor's Philanthropic Projects.—Dreadful Flood at St. Petersburg.—Description of the Situation of St. Petersburg.—Great Inundation of St. Petersburg.—Noble Charity of the Emperor and Nobles.—Internal Measures of 1824, and Settlement of the Boundaries of Russian America.—The Empress of Russia: her Birth, Parentage, Marriage, and Character.—Amours of the Czar.—Death of Alexander's Natural Daughter.—Reconciliation of the Emperor and Empress.—Solemn Service in the Cathedral of Notre Dame de Kazan.—His Departure from the Cathedral.—His Arrival at Taganrog.—His last Illness.—And Death.—And Funeral.—Death and Burial of the Empress.—

His Character.—His Failings.—State of the Succession to the Throne.—Constantine refuses the Throne.—How this came about.—Constantine's previous Renunciation of his Right of Succession.—Nicholas refuses the Crown, and proclaims Constantine.—Contest of Generosity between the two Brothers, and Nicholas mounts the Throne.—Account of the Conspiracy against him.—Details of the Conspiracy.—Information given of the Conspiracy to Alexander.—Plans of the Conspirators.—A Revolt is decided on by the Conspirators.—Commencement of it.—Heroic Conduct of Nicholas on the occasion.—Nicholas advances against the Rebels.—Forces on both Sides, and Irresolution of the Chiefs of the Revolt.—Death of Miloradowitch.—The Archbishop also fails in subduing the Mutineers.—The Emperor gains the Victory.—Seizure of the Leaders of the Conspiracy, and generous conduct of Nicholas to the Prisoners.—Appointment of a Commission of Inquiry.—Its Composition and Report.—Leaders of the Revolt in the Army of the South.—And in that of the West.—Arrest of the Mouraviells, and others.—Of the Conspiracy in the Army of Poland.—Its Suppression.—Sentences on the Conspirators.—Their conduct on the eve of Death.—Their Execution.—Reflections on this Event.—Noble Conduct of the Princess Troubetzkoi and the other Wives of the Convicts.—Condition of the Exiles in Siberia.—Generous Conduct of the Emperor to the Relatives of the Convicts.—Expiatory Ceremony on the Place of the Senate.—Great Reforms in all Departments introduced by the Emperor.—Great legal Reforms of the Emperor.—Crime of the Insurgents.—Coronation of the Emperor and Empress at Moscow.—Character of the Emperor Nicholas, and parallel between him and Peter the Great.—He is essentially Russian.—His personal Appearance and Failings.

CHAPTER IX.

ROYALIST REACTION IN FRANCE.

FRANCE FROM THE COUP D'ETAT OF 5TH MARCH, 1819, TO THE ACCESSION OF THE PURELY ROYALIST MINISTRY IN DECEMBER, 1821.

Great Evils of France at the Close of 1816.—Rapid Flow of Prosperity which succeeded them in the next Year.—Brilliant appearance of Paris.—Exports, Imports, and Revenue of France during this Period.—Thorough Establishment of Representative Institutions in France.—Which have no Effect in conciliating the Liberal Party.—Popular Acts of the New Ministry.—Return of Marat and many other of the Proscribed to France.—Increasing Strength of the Liberals, and Resistance to the Government.—Law regarding the Press.—Debate on the Return of the Proscribed Persons.—Speech of M. de Serres on the Subject.—Immense Sensation produced by this Debate.—Increasing Violence and Exasperation of the Press.—Budget of 1819.—Preparations for the Election of 1819.—Their Result: Election of the Abbé Grégoire.—Biography of the Abbé Grégoire.—General Foy.—His Biography.—M. de Serres.—His Character.—Conversation of Louis XVIII. and the Count d'Artois on the Election.—Change in the Ministry.—Violent Attacks on the new Ministry by the Press.—King's Speech at Opening the Session.—Comparative Strength of Parties in the Chamber.—Designs of the Liberals in Paris.—New Electoral Law proposed by the Government.—Electoral Law finally agreed on by the Government.—Violent Opposition of the Liberals.—The Duke de Berri.—His Biography.—Louvel, his Assassin.—Assassination of the Duke de Berri.—His last Moments.—His Death.—Immense Sensation which it produced.—Chateaubriand's Words on the Occasion.—General Indignation against M. Decazes.—The King resolves to support him.—He at length agrees to his Dismissal.—Resignation of M. Decazes, and the Duke de Richelieu sent for.—The King's Inclination for Platonic attachments.—The Countess Du Cayla.—Her first Interview with Louis, which proves successful.—Character of M. Decazes.—Merits of his Measures as a Statesman.—Division of Parties in the Assembly after M. Decazes' fall.—Funeral of the Duke de Berri, and Execution of Louvel.—Ministerial Measures of the Session: Argument against the First.—Answer by the Government.—Censorship of the Press: Argument against it by the Opposition.—Answer by the Ministerialists.—Result of the Debate.—Reflections on this Subject.—Alarming State of the Country, and defensive Measures of Government.—Denunciation of the Secret Government.—Ministerial Project of a new Electoral Law.—Argument against it by the Opposition.—Answer by the Ministerialists.—Camille Jourdan's Amendment carried.—The Amendment of M. Boin is carried by Government.—Disturbances in Paris.—Which become serious.—Loud declamation on the Subject in the Chamber of Deputies.—Their Suppression.—The Budget.—Military Conspiracy, headed by Lafayette.—Their Designs, and Efforts to corrupt the Troops.—Which fails by Accident.—Lenity shown in the Prosecutions.—Birth of the Duke of Bordeaux.—Universal Transports in France.—Congratulations from the European powers, and Promotions in France.—Rupture with the Doctrinaires.—Views of the Doctrinaires.—Views of the Royalists.—Disturbances in the Provinces.—Internal Measures of the Government.—Changes in the Household.—New Organization of the Army.—Ordonnance regarding Public Instruction.—The King's Circular to the Electors.—Result of the Elections favorable to the Royalists.—Effect of the Change in the Assembly.—Accession of Villèle, &c., to the Ministry.—Speech of the King, and Answer of the Chambers.—Measures of the Session, fixing the Boundaries of the Electoral Districts.—Law for additional Ecclesiastical Endowments.—Modifications in the Corn-laws.—Law for the Indemnity of the Imperial donataires.—Law regarding the Censorship of the Press.—Speech of M. Pasquier on the Occasion.—Increasing Irritation of Parties, and Difficulties of the Ministry.—Rupture with the Royalists, and Fall of the Richelieu Ministry.—The new Ministry.—Reflections on this Event.—Great Effects of the Change in the Electoral Law.—Defects of the Representative System in France.—Undue Ascendency of the Parti-Prêtre.—Cause of the Reaction against Liberal Institutions.—Death of Napoleon.—Reflections on his Captivity.—Great Exaggeration regarding the English Treatment of him.—Lamartine's Account of his Exile.—Irritation between him and Sir Hudson Lowe.—All Parties were wrong regarding his Treatment at St. Helena.—Change on Napoleon before his Death.—His Death.—His Funeral.—Immense sensation it excited in Europe.—He was the last of the Men who Rule their Age.

CHAPTER X.

DOMESTIC HISTORY OF ENGLAND, FROM THE PASSING OF THE CURRENCY ACT OF 1819 TO THE DEATH OF LORD LONDONDERRY IN 1822.

Difference of the Objects of the Liberal Party in France and England.—Difference in the Causes which produced Discontent in the Two Countries.—Great Effects of the Change in the Monetary Laws.—Mr. Smith's Views on this Subject.—Great Effects of any Variation in the Value of the Standard of Value.—Examples of this from former Times.—Discovery and wonderful Effects of a Paper Currency.—Advantages of a Paper Circulation, duly limited.—What is the Standard of Value?—Vast Effect of Variations in the Currency.—When this Effect takes place.—Vast Importance of an inconvertible Currency as a Regulator of Prices.—A Currency based on the precious Metals is always liable to Fluctuations.—Concurring Causes which brought about the Bill of 1819.—Danger of a Currency entirely rested on a Metallic Basis.—True System.—Peculiar Dangers with which the Resumption of Cash Payments was attended.—Strain on the Money Market, from the immense Loans on the Continent.—Great Prosperity of England in End of 1818 and Spring of 1819, from Extension of its Currency—Great Internal Prosperity of the Country.—Disastrous Contraction of the Currency.—Its Effects on the Bank Issues.—And on Prices of all Commodities.—Rapid Increase of Disaffection in the Country.—Meeting at Peterloo.—Great Excitement, and Objects of the Meeting.—Its Dispersion by the Military.—Noble Conduct of Lord Sidmouth on the Occasion.—Result of Hunt's Trial.—Reflections on the Impolicy of allowing such Meetings.—And on the Conduct of the Magistrates.—Seditious Meetings in other Quarters.—Augmentation of the Chelsea Pensioners.—Meeting of Parliament, and Measures of Government.—Lord Sidmouth's Acts of Parliament.—Impression Lord Sidmouth and Lord Castlereagh made on the Radicals.—Death of the Duke of Kent.—Death of George III.—Deep Impression which his Death made on the Country.—Birth of Queen Victoria.—Alarming Illness of George IV.—Ominous Questions regarding the Omission of Queen Caroline's Name in the Liturgy.—Remarkable Speech of Mr. Brougham.—Cato Street Conspiracy.—Thistlewood's previous Life.—Design of the Conspirators.—Their final Plans.—Conflict in the dark in the Cato Street Loft.—Execution of the Conspirators.—Disturbances in Scotland and North of England.—Insurrection in Scotland.—Outbreak of the Insurrection, and its Suppression.—Death and Character of Mr. Grattan.—His Character as a Statesman and Orator.—Increase of the Yeomanry Force.—The Budget for 1820.—Important Subjects of Debate in this Session.—Statistics on Education in England and Wales by Mr. Brougham.—Difficulties of this Subject, and Necessity of an Assessment.—Its Difficulties, and Attempts at their Solution.—Probable mode of solving it.—What is to be done with the Educated Classes?—Effect of Education in leading to the Dispersion of Mankind.—Disfranchisement of Grampound, and transfer of its Members to Yorkshire.—Rise of Free-trade Ideas among the Merchants, and Lord Lansdowne's Declaration on the Subject.—Lord Liverpool's memorable Speech in reply.—Appointment of a Committee to Inquire into Agricultural Distress.—Opinion of Mr. Brougham on this Subject.—Answer by Mr. Ricardo.—Additional Facts since discovered on this Subject.—Commencement of the Troubles about the Queen.—Sketch of her Life prior to this Period.—Her Conduct abroad, and Proceedings in consequence of it.—Omission of the Queen's Name in the Liturgy, and her Return to England.—Her Landing in England, and enthusiastic Reception.—Views of the Radical Leaders on the Occasion.—Enthusiastic Reception of the Queen at Dover and in London.—Failure of the Negotiations, and Commencement of the Inquiry.—Scene which ensued on the Trial.—Progress of the Trial, and its Difficulties.—Peroration of Mr. Brougham's Defence.—Queen's Defense, and Failure of the Bill.—General Transports of the People.—Rapid Reaction of Public Opinion.—Consternation of the Ministry, who resolve to remain at their Posts.—Return of Popularity of Government, and Causes of it.—Meeting of Parliament, and first Proceedings.—Debates on Foreign Affairs.—Sir James Mackintosh's Efforts to Improve the Criminal Law.—Mr. Canning's striking Speech on Catholic Emancipation.—Answer by Mr. Peel.—Which is carried in the Commons, and lost in the Peers.—Lord John Russell's Motion for Parliamentary Reform.—Appointment of a Committee to Inquire into Agricultural Distress.—Bank Cash Payment Bill.—Mr. Baring's Speech on the Subject.—Vehement Demand for a Reduction of Taxation.—Agricultural Committee Reports, and State of the Consumption of Articles of Luxury.—Increase of the desire for Reform among the Agriculturists.—Coronation of George IV.—Ceremony on the Occasion.—Aspect of Wellington, Londonderry, and George IV.—The Queen is refused Admittance: her Death.—King's Visit to Ireland.—Funeral of the Queen.—Dismissal of Sir R. Wilson from the Army.—Changes in the Cabinet.—Retirement of Lord Sidmouth, who is succeeded by Mr. Peel as Home Secretary.—Lord Wellesley appointed Viceroy of Ireland, and Change in the Government there.—Cause of the Wretchedness of Ireland.—What would have relieved the Country, and its Neglect.—Ruinous Effect of the Contraction of the Currency upon Ireland.—Progress of the Agrarian Disturbances in Ireland.—Lord Wellesley's able Conduct and Impartiality.—Dreadful Examples in the Disturbed Districts.—Dreadful Famine in the South and West of Ireland.—Suspension of the Habeas Corpus Act, and Insurrection Act.—Divisions on the Catholic Claims.—Increasing Strength of the Minority on Parliamentary Reform.—Peroration of Mr. Canning's Speech.—Sir James Mackintosh's Motion regarding the Criminal Law.—Great fall in the Price of all sorts of Produce.—Measures for the Relief of the Agricultural Classes.—Detailed Measures of Government for the Relief of the Agriculturists.—Motion of Mr. Western on the Currency.—Mr. Huskisson's Arguments in Support of the Existing System.—Reply by Mr. Attwood.—Repeated Defeats of Ministers in the House of Commons.—Great Reductions of Taxation introduced by Ministers.—The Budget.—Reduction of the 5 per cents.—Equalization of the Dead Weight, and Military and Naval Pensions.—Details of the Measure.—Important Small Notes Bill.—Its Provisions.—Six Acts relating to Commerce and Navigation.—Visit of the King to Edinburgh.—Particulars of the Royal Visit.—Death of Lord Londonderry.—His Character.—Its indomitable Firmness.—His Policy in Domestic Affairs.—Political Changes in progress, from the Resumption of Cash Payments.—Internal Changes arising from the same Cause.—Lord Londonderry was the last of the real Rulers of England.—Increased ascendant of the Rulers of Thought.—Simultaneous Outbreak of the Revolutionary Spirit in Different Countries.—Different Characters of the Revolts in the different States.

CHAPTER XI.

ENGLAND, FRANCE, AND SPAIN, FROM THE ACCESSION OF VILLELE IN 1819 TO THE CONGRESS OF VERONA IN 1822.

Divergence of France and England in regard to the Spanish Revolution.—Peculiar Causes which augmented this Divergence.—Character of Mr. Canning.—His peculiar Style of Eloquence.—His Defects.—Viscount Chateaubriand.—His Merits as an Orator.—His Character as a Statesman.—His Defects.—M. de Villèle.—His peculiar Turn of Mind, and Course of Policy.—M. de Corbière, M. Mathieu de Montmorency, M. de Peyronnet, Victor.—Law regarding the Press.—Its Stringent Provisions.—Discussion on it.—Rise of the Carbonari and Secret Societies in

France.—Rise of Carbonarism in France.—Abortive Conspiracy at Belfort.—Berton's Conspiracy at Thoüars.—Conspiracy at La Rochelle.—Their Trial and Execution.—Reflections on these Events.—Insurrections at Colmar, Marseilles, and Lyons.—Budget of 1822.—Favorable Result of the Elections to the Royalists.—State of Public Opinion.—Attempted Restoration of the Royal Authority at Madrid.—Opening of the Cortes, and Dismissal of the Ministers.—Conduct of the Cortes, and Appointment of a New Ministry.—Effect produced in Spain by the Crushing of the Revolution in Italy.—Extraordinary Outbreak of Revolutionary Fury in the East of Spain.—Revolutionary Laws passed by the Cortes.—Barbarous Murder of the Priest Vinuesa.—Institution of the Order of the Hammer.—Insurrection in Navarre, and Appointment of Murillo at Madrid.—Proceedings of the Cortes.—Deplorable State of the Finances, and Measures regarding them.—Fresh Tumults in Madrid.—Resignation of General Murillo.—The Secret Societies, or Communeros.—Riego's Plot at Saragossa, and his Arrest.—Suppression of the Tumults thence arising at Madrid.—Yellow Fever at Barcelona.—Fresh Agitation.—Refusal of Cadiz and Seville to receive the King's Governors, and Revolt at Corunna.—Opening of an Extraordinary Cortes.—Contradictory Resolutions of the Cortes.—Irresolute Conduct of the King, and Royalist Insurrection in the North.—Proposed Laws against the Press and Patriotic Societies.—Riots in Madrid on the passing of a Bill against the Press.—Composition of the new Cortes.—New Ministry.—Opening of the Cortes, and disastrous State of the Finances.—General Disturbances in Spain.—Proceedings of the Cortes, and Progress of the Civil War.—The Trappist: his Appearance and Character, and Followers.—Desperate Assault of Cervera.—Defeat of Misas.—Severe Laws passed by the Cortes.—Great Extension of the Civil War.—Deplorable State of the Spanish Finances.—Riot in Madrid, and Death of Landabura.—Commencement of the Strife between the Guard and the Garrison.—Departure of the Royal Guard from Madrid.—Progress of the Negotiations with the Insurgents.—Attack of the Guards on Madrid, and its Defeat.—Destruction of the Royal Guard.—Defeat of the Insurgents in Andalusia and Cadiz.—Change of Ministry, and complete Triumph of the Revolutionists.—The New Ministry, and Provincial Appointments.—Murder of Geoffreux.—Second Trial, and Execution of Elio.—Civil War in the Northern Provinces.—Vigorous Measures of the Revolutionary Government.—Capture of Castelfollit, and Savage Proclamation of Mina.—Continued Disasters of the Royalists, and Flight of the Regency from Urgel.

CHAPTER XII.

CONGRESS OF VERONA—FRENCH INVASION OF SPAIN—DEATH OF LOUIS XVIII.

Great Effect produced by these Successes of the Liberals.—Effect of these Events in France and Europe.—Lamartine's Observations on the Subject.—Opposite Views which prevailed in Great Britain.—Repugnance to French Intervention.—Danger of a Renewal of the Family Compact between France and Spain.—Influence of the South American and Spanish Bondholders.—Immense Extent of the Spanish and South American Loans.—Views of the Cabinet and Mr. Canning on the Subject.—Congress of Verona agreed on by all the Powers.—Members of the Congress there.—Description of Verona.—Views of the Different Powers at the Opening of the Congress.—Brilliant Assemblage of Princesses and Courtiers at Verona.—Treaty for the Evacuation of Piedmont and Naples.—Resolution of the Congress regarding the Slave Trade.—Note of England regarding South American Independence.—Instructions of M. de Villèle to M. de Montmorency regarding Spain.—Mr. Canning's Instructions to Duke of Wellington.—Measures adopted by the Majority of the Congress on the Subject.—Questions proposed by France, and Answers of the Continental Powers and England.—Views of what had occurred in this Congress.—Views of M. de Villèle and Louis XVIII.—Secret Correspondence of M. de Villèle and M. de Lagarde.—Debate on it in the Cabinet, and Resignation of M. de Montmorency, who is succeeded by M. de Chateaubriand.—The Warlike Preparations of France continue.—Failure of the Negotiations at Madrid, and Departure of the French Embassador.—Speech of the King at the Opening of the Chambers.—King of England's Speech at Opening of Parliament.—Reply of the Spanish Government.—M. Hyde de Neuville's Address in Reply to the Speech of the King.—Speech on the War in the House of Commons by Mr. Brougham.—Mr. Canning adopts the Principle of Non-interference.—M. de Chateaubriand's Reply in the French Chambers.—Immense sensation produced by this Speech.—M. Talleyrand's Speech on the War.—Vote of Credit of 100,000,000 francs.—Affair of M. Manuel in the Chamber of Deputies: his Speech.—Storm in the Chamber.—Expulsion of M. Manuel.—Dramatic Scene at his Expulsion.—General Enthusiasm excited by the Spanish War.—Preparations of the Liberals to sow Disaffection in the Army.—Feelings of Mr. Canning and the English people at this Crisis.—Views of Mr. Canning at this Juncture.—Portrait of Mr. Canning, by M. Marcellus.—His Opinion as to the probable Duration of the War.—Views of George IV. and the Duke of Wellington on the Subject.—Difficulties of the French at the entrance of the Campaign.—Which are obviated by M. Ouvrard.—Forces, and their Disposition on both Sides.—The Spanish Forces.—Theatrical Scene at the Passage of the Bidassoa.—Progress of the French, and their rapid Success.—Advance of the Duke d'Angoulême to Madrid.—Advance of the French to Madrid.—Entry of the Duke d'Angoulême into Madrid.—Advance of the French into Andalusia.—Proceedings of the Cortes, and Deposition of Ferdinand VII.—Violent Reaction at Seville, and over all Spain.—State of Affairs in Cadiz.—Advance of the Duke d'Angoulême into Andalusia, and Decree of Andujar.—Its Provisions.—Violent Irritation of the Royalists in Spain.—Progress of the Siege of Cadiz.—Assault of the Trocadero.—Operations of Riego in the Rear of the French.—Defeat and Capture of Riego.—Resumed Negotiations at Cadiz, and Assault of Santa Petri.—Deliverance of the King, and Dissolution of the Cortes.—Scene at his Deliverance.—First Acts of the New Government.—Loud calls on Ferdinand for Moderation and Clemency.—Sentence of Riego.—His Execution.—Entry of the King and Queen into Madrid.—Distracted and miserable State of Spain.—State of Portugal during this Year. Royalist Insurrection.—Royalist Counter-revolution.—Triumphant Return of the Duke d'Angoulême to Paris.—Offer of Assistance by Russia to France rejected.—Views of Mr. Canning in Recognizing the Republics of South America.—Mr. Canning did not give Independence to South America, but only acknowledged it.—Recognition of the South American Republics by Mr. Canning.—Effects of this Measure on British Interests.—M. de Chateaubriand's Designs in regard to the South American States.—Speech of Mr. Canning at Plymouth.—The Elections of 1824, and Strength of the Royalists.—Great Effect which this had on the future Destinies of France.—Meeting of the Chambers, and Measures announced in the Royal

Speech.—Law of Septenniality: Considerations in favor of it.—Argument on the other Side.—Law for the Reduction of Interest of the National Debt.—Which is passed by the Deputies, but thrown out by the Peers.—Reflections on this Decision. Difference of the English and French Funds.—Splendid Position of M. de Chateaubriand.—His Dismissal, and that of Marshal Victor.—Statistics of France in this Year.—Reign of Louis XVIII. draws to a Close.—His declining Days.—His great Powers of Conversation.—His Religious Impressions in his Last Days.—His Death.—Character of Louis XVIII.—His Private Qualities and Weaknesses.—Political Inferences from the Result of the Spanish Revolution.—Great Merit of the French Expedition into Spain in 1823.—It had nearly established the Throne of the Restoration.—The French Invasion of Spain was justifiable.—Was the English Intervention in behalf of South America justifiable?—Its ultimate Disastrous Effects to England.

HISTORY OF EUROPE.

CHAPTER I.

GENERAL SKETCH OF THE WHOLE PERIOD FROM THE FALL OF NAPOLEON TO THE ACCESSION OF LOUIS NAPOLEON.

THE fall of Napoleon completed the first drama of the historical series arising out of the French Revolution. Democratic ambition had found its natural and inevitable issue in warlike achievement; the passions of the camp had succeeded those of the forum, and the conquest of all the continental monarchies had for a time apparently satiated the desires of an ambitious people. But the reaction was as violent as the action; in every warlike operation two parties are to be considered—the conqueror and the conquered. The rapacity, the insolence, the organized exactions of the French proved grievous in the extreme; and the hardship was felt as the more insupportable, when the administrative powers of Napoleon gave to them the form of a regular tribute, and conducted the riches of conquered Europe in a perennial stream to the Imperial treasury. A unanimous cry of indignation arose from every part of the Continent; a crusade commenced in all quarters, from the experienced suffering of mankind;—from the east and from the west, from the north and from the south, the liberating warriors came forth, and the strength of an injured world collected, by a convulsive effort at the heart, to throw off the load which had oppressed it. Securely cradled amidst the waves, England, like her immortal chief at Waterloo, calmly awaited the hour when she might be called on to take the lead in the terrible strife; her energy, when it arrived, rivalled her former patience in privation, her fortitude in suffering; and the one only nation which, throughout the struggle, had been unconquered, at length stood foremost in the fight, and struck the final and decisive blow for the deliverance of the world.

¹ Resume of the war just concluded.

But the victory of nations did not terminate the war of opinion; the triumph of armies did not end the collision of thought. France was conquered, but the principles of her Revolution were not extirpated: they had covered her own soil with mourning, but they were too flattering to the pride of the human heart to be subdued but by many ages of suffering. The lesson taught by the subjugation of her power, the double capture of her capital, was too serious to be soon forgotten by her rulers; but the agony which had been previously felt by the people, had ended with a generation which was now mouldering in the grave. It is by the last impression that the durable opinions of mankind are formed; and effects had here succeeded each other so rapidly that the earlier ones were in a great measure forgotten. The conscription had caused the guillotine to be forgotten; grief for the loss of the frontier of the Rhine had obliterated that for the dissolution of the National Assembly. Men did not know that the first was the natural result of the last. There was little danger of France soon crossing the Rhine, but much of her reviving the opinions of Mirabeau and Sièyes. The first drama, where the military bore the prominent part, was ended; but the second, in which civil patriots were to be leading characters, and vehement political passions excited, was still to come; the Lager had terminated, but the Piccolomini was only beginning, and Wallenstein's Death had not yet commenced.

² The second drama was one springing out of social passions.

Every thing conspired to render the era subsequent to the fall of Napoleon as memorable for civil changes as that era itself had been for military triumphs. Catherine of Russia had said at the commencement of the Revolution, that the only way to prevent its principles spreading, and save Europe from civil convulsion, was to engage in war, and cause the national to supersede the social passions. The experiment, after a fearful struggle, succeeded; but it succeeded only for a time. War wore itself out; a contest of twenty years' duration at once drained away the blood and exhausted the treasures of Europe. The excitement, the animation, the mingled horrors and glories of military strife, were followed by a long period of repose, during which the social passions were daily gaining strength from the very magnitude of the contest which had preceded it. The desire for excitement continued, and the means of gratifying it had ceased: the cannon of Leipsic and Waterloo still resounded through the world, but no new combats furnished daily materials for anxiety, terror, or exultation. The nations were chained to peace by the immensity of the sacrifices made in the preceding war: all governments had suffered so much during its continuance, that, like wounded veterans, they dreaded a renewal of the fight. During the many years of constrained repose which succeeded the battle of Waterloo, the vehement excitement occasioned by the Rev-

³ Causes which rendered it so violent.

Vol. I.—A

olutionary wars continued; but, from default of external, it turned to internal objects. Democratic came instead of military ambition; the social succeeded the national passions; the spirit was the same, but its field was changed. Meanwhile the blessed effect of long-continued peace, by allowing industry in every quarter to reap its fruits in quiet, was daily adding to the strength and energy, because augmenting the resources, of the middle class, in whom these feelings are ever the strongest, because they are the first to be promoted by a change; while, in a similar proportion, the power of government was daily declining, from the necessity of providing for the interest of the debts contracted during the preceding strife, and reducing the military forces which had so long averted its dangers or achieved its triumphs.

4. Governments now aimed at peace, and the people clamoured for war.

The change in the ruling passions of mankind clearly appeared in the annals of nations, in the thirty years which followed the fall of Napoleon. Governments had often great difficulties to contend with—not, however, with each other, but with their subjects; many of them were overturned, not by foreign armies but by their own. Europe was often on the verge of a general war, but the danger of it arose, not, as in former days, from the throne, but from the cottage; the persons who urged it on were not kings or their ministers: they were the tribunes of the people. The chief efforts of governments in every country were directed to the preservation of that peace which the collision of so many interests, and the vehemence of such passions endangered: war was repeatedly threatened; but by the people, not by sovereigns. The sovereigns were successful; but their being so only augmented the dangers of their position, and increased the peril arising from the ardor of the social passions with which they had to contend; for every year of repose added to the strength of their opponents as much as it diminished their own.

5. Causes in France which predisposed to the Revolution of 1830.

The preservation of peace, unbroken from 1815 to 1830, was fraught with immense blessings to Europe, and, had it been properly improved, might have been so to the cause of freedom throughout the world; but it proved fatal to the dynasty of the Restoration. From necessity as well as inclination—from the recollection of the double capture of Paris, as well as conscious inability to conduct warlike operations, Louis XVIII. remained at peace; and no monarch who does so will long remain on the French throne. Death, and extreme prudence of conduct, alone saved him from dethronement. The whole history of the Restoration from 1815 to 1830, was that of one vast and ceaseless conspiracy against the Bourbons, existing rather in the hearts and minds, than in the measures and designs of men. No concessions to freedom, no moderation of government, no diminution of public burdens, could reconcile the people to a dynasty imposed on them by the stranger. One part of the people were dreaming of the past, another speculating on the future: all were dissatisfied with the present. The wars, the glories of the Empire, rose up in painful contrast to the peace and monotony of the present. Successive alterations of the elective constituency, and restrictions on the press, had no effect in diminishing the feelings thus excited in the minds of men, and which only became, like all other concealed passions, more powerful from the difficulty of giving it expression. France was daily increasing in wealth, freedom, and material well-being, but it was as steadily declining in contentment, loyalty, and happiness—a strange combination, though one by no means unknown in private life, when all external appliances are favorable, but the heart is gnawed by a secret and ungratified passion. At length the general discontent rose to such a pitch that it became impossible to carry on the government; a *coup d'état* was attempted, to restore some degree of efficiency to the executive, but it was conducted by the "feeble arms of confessors and kings;" the army wavered in its duty; the Orleans family took advantage of the tumult, and the dynasty of the elder branch of the Bourbons was overthrown.

6. Causes which made England share in the convulsion.

That so great an event as the overthrow of a dynasty by a sudden urban insurrection, should have produced a great impression all over the world, was to have been expected; but it could hardly have been anticipated it would have been attended by the effects which actually followed in Great Britain. But many causes had conspired, at that period, to prepare the public mind in England for change; and, what is very remarkable, these causes had arisen mainly from the magnitude of the successes with which the war had been attended. The great aristocratic party, whether in land or money, had been so triumphant that they deemed their power beyond the reach of attack; compromise, concession, or even consideration for their opponents, was out of the question. They neither considered their interests in legislation, nor had regard to their feelings in manner. The capital which had been realized during the war had been so great, the influence of the moneyed interest so powerful, that the legislature became affected by their desires. The Monetary Bill of 1819, before many years had elapsed, added fifty per cent to the value of money, and weight of debts and taxes, and took as much from the remuneration of industry. Hence a total change in the feelings, influences, and political relations of society. The territorial aristocracy was weakened as much as the commercial was aggrandized; small landed proprietors were generally ruined from the fall of prices; the magnates stood forth in increased lustre from the enhanced value of their revenues. Industry was querulous, from long-continued suffering; wealth ambitious, from sudden exaltation. Political power was coveted in one class, from the excess of its riches; in another, from the depth of its misery. The emancipation of the Roman Catholics severed the last bond, that of a common religion, which had hitherto held together the different classes, and imprinted on the minds of a large and sincere class a thirst for vengeance, which overwhelmed every consideration of reason. The result of these concurring causes was that the institutions of England were essentially altered by the earthquake of 1830, and a new class elevated to supreme power by means, bloodless indeed, but scarcely less violent than the revolution which had overturned Charles X.

The revolution of 1830 elevated the middle

class to the direction of affairs, and the Reform Bill in England vested the same class in effect with supreme power in the British empire. Vast consequences followed this all-important change in both countries. For the first time in the history of mankind, the experiment was made of vesting the electoral franchise, not in a varied and limited class as in old England, or in the whole citizens, as in revolutionary France or America, but in persons possessed only of a certain money qualification. The franchise was not materially changed in France; but the general arming of the national guard, and the revolutionary origin of the new government, effectually secured attention to the wishes of the burgher aristocracy. In England they were at once vested with the command of the state, for the House of Commons was returned by a million of electors, who voted for 658 members, of whom two-thirds were the representatives of boroughs, and two-thirds of their constituents shopkeepers, or persons whom they influenced. Thence consequences of incalculable importance, in both countries, and effects which have left indelible traces in the future history of mankind.

7. Great effects of the Revolution in both countries.

The first effect of this identity of feeling and interest, in the class then for the first time intrusted with the practical direction of affairs in both countries, was a close political alliance between their governments, and an entire change in the foreign policy of Great Britain. To the vehement hostility and ceaseless rivalry of four centuries succeeded an alliance sincere and cordial at the time, though, like other intimacies founded on identity of passion, not of interest, it might be doubted whether it would survive the emotions which gave it birth. In the mean time, however, the effects of this alliance were novel, and in the highest degree important. When the lords of the earth and the sea united, no power in Europe ventured to confront them; the peace of Europe was preserved by their union. The Czar, in full march toward Paris, was arrested on the Vistula; he found ample employment for his arms in resisting the efforts of the Poles to restore their much-loved nationality. Austria and Prussia were too much occupied with the surveillance of the discontented in their own dominions to think of renewing the crusade of 1813; nor did they venture to do so when the forces of England were united to those of France. The consequence was that the march of revolution was unresisted in Western Europe, and an entire change was effected in the institutions and dynasties on the throne in its principal continental states. The Orleans family continued firmly, and to all appearance permanently, seated on the throne of France; Belgium was revolutionized, torn from the monarchy of the Netherlands, and the Cobourg family seated on its throne; the monarchies of Spain and Portugal were overturned, and a revolutionary dynasty of queens placed on their thrones, in direct violation of the Treaty of Utrecht; while in the east of Europe the last remnants of Polish nationality were extinguished on the banks of the Vistula. Durable interests were overlooked, ancient alliances broken, long-established rivalries forgotten in the fleeting passions of the moment. Confederacies the most opposite to the lasting policy of the very nations who contracted them were not only formed, but acted upon. Europe beheld with astonishment the arms of Prussia united with those of Russia to destroy the barrier of the Continent against the Muscovite power on the Sarmatian plains; the Leopards of England joined to the tricolor standard to wrest Antwerp from Holland, and secure the throne of the Netherlands to a son-in-law of France; and the scarlet uniforms blended with the ensigns of revolution to beat down the liberties of the Basque provinces, and prepare the heiress of Spain for the arms of a son of France, on the very theatre of Wellington's triumphs.

8. Political alliance between France and England, which followed this change.

Novel and extraordinary as were the results of the Revolution of 1830 upon the political relations of Europe, its effects upon the colonial empire of England, and, through it, upon the future destinies of the human species, were still greater and more important. To the end of the world, the consequences of the change in the policy of England will be felt in every quarter of the globe. Its first effect was to bring about the emancipation of the negroes in the West Indies. Eight hundred thousand slaves in the British colonies, in that quarter of the globe, received the perilous gift of unconditional freedom. For the first time in the history of mankind, the experiment was made, of extending the institutions of Japhet to the sons of Ham. As a natural result of so vast and sudden a change, and of the conferring of the institutions of the Anglo-Saxons upon unlettered savages, the proprietors of those noble colonies were ruined, their affections alienated, and the authority of the mother country preserved only by the terror of arms. Canada shared in the moral earthquake which shook the globe; and that noble offshoot of the empire was alone preserved to Great Britain by the courage of its soldiers, and the loyalty of its English and Highland citizens. Australia rapidly advanced in wealth, industry, and population during these eventful years; every commercial crisis which paralyzed industry, every social struggle which excited hope, every successful innovation which diminished security, added to the stream of hardy and enterprising emigrants who crowded to its shores. New Zealand was added to the already colossal empire of England in Oceania; and it was already apparent that the foundations were laid in a fifth hemisphere of another nation destined to rival, perhaps eclipse, Europe itself in the career of human improvement. For the first time in the history of mankind, the course of advancement ceased to be from East to West; but it was not destined to be arrested by the Rocky Mountains;—the mighty day of four thousand years was drawing to its close; but before its light was extinguished in the West, civilization had returned to the land of its birth; and ere its orb had set in the waves of the Pacific, the sun of knowledge was illuminating the isles of the Eastern Sea.

9. Effects of the change upon the colonial empire of England.

Great and important as were these results of the social convulsions of France and England in the first instance, they sank into insignificance compared to those which followed the change in the commercial policy, and the increased stringency of the monetary

10. Still greater results of the Free-trade policy of England.

laws of Great Britain. The effect of these all-important measures, from which so much was expected, and so little, save suffering, received, was to augment to an extraordinary and unparalleled degree the outward tendency of the British people. The agricultural population, especially in Ireland, were violently torn up from the land of their birth by woes, suffering; a famine of the thirteenth appeared amid the population of the nineteenth century; and to this terrible, but transient, source of suffering, was superadded the lasting discouragement arising from the virtual closing of the market of England to their produce, by the inundation of grain from foreign states. When the barriers raised by human regulations were thrown down, the eternal laws of nature appeared in full operation; the old and r l. state can always undersell the young and poor one in manufactures, and is always undersold by it in agricultural produce. The fate of old Rome apparently was reserved for Great Britain; the harvests of Poland, the Ukraine, and America, began to prostrate agriculture in the British Isles as effectually as those of Sicily, Libya, and Egypt had done that of the old Patrimony of the Legions; and after the lapse of eighteen hundred years, the same effects appeared. The great cities flourished, but the country decayed; the exportation of human beings, and the importation of human food, kept up a grateful traffic in the seaport towns; but it was every day more and more gliding into the hands of the foreigners; and while exports and imports were constantly increasing, the mainstay of national strength, the cultivation of the soil was rapidly declining. The effects upon the strength, resources, and population of the empire, and the growth of its colonial possessions were equally, important. Europe, before the middle of the century, beheld with astonishment Great Britain, which, at the end of the war, had been self-supporting, importing ten millions of quarters of grain, being a full fifth of the national subsistence, and a constant stream of three hundred thousand emigrants annually leaving its shores. Its inhabitants, which for four centuries had been constantly increasing, declined a million in the five years from 1846 to 1850 in the two islands, and two million in Ireland, taken separately; three millions of quarters of wheat ceased to be raised in the British Islands;—but the foundation of a vast empire were laid in the Transatlantic and Australian wilds; and the annual addition of three hundred thousand souls to the European population of the New World, by immigration alone, had come almost to double the already marvellous rapidity of American increase.

11. Vast extension of the United States of America.

While this vast transference of the Anglo-Saxon and Celtic population to the embryo states of America and Australia was going forward, the United States of America were rapidly increasing in numbers and in extent of territory. The usual and fearful ambition of republican states there appeared in more than its usual proportions. During ten years, from 1840 to 1850, the inhabitants of the United States increased six millions they had grown from eighteen to twenty-four millions. But the increase of its territory was still more extraordinary; it had been extended, during the same period, from somewhat above 2,000,000 to 3,300,000 square miles. A territory nine times the size of old France was added to the devouring Republic in ten years. The conquests of Rome in ancient, of the English in India in modern times, afford no parallel instance of rapid and unbroken increase. Every thing indicates that a vast migration of the human species is going forward, and the family of Japhet in the course of being transferred from its native to its destined seats. To this prodigious movement it is hard to say whether the disappointed energy of democratic vigor in Europe, or the insatiable spirit of Republican ambition in America, has most contributed; for the first overcame all the attachments of home, and all the endearments of kindred in a large—and that the most energetic—portion of the people in the Old World; while the latter has prepared for their reception ample seats—in which a kindred tongue and institutions prevail—in the New.

12. Vast increase of Russia during the same period.

While this vast and unexampled exodus of the Anglo-Saxon race, across a wider ocean than the Red Sea, and to a greater promised land than that of Canaan, was going forward, a corresponding, and, in some respects, still more marvelous increase of the Sclavonic race in the Muscovite dominions took place. The immense dominions and formidable power of the Czar, which had received so vast an addition from the successful termination of the contest with Napoleon, was scarcely less augmented by the events of the long peace which followed. The inhuman cruelty with which the Turks prosecuted the war with the Greeks awakened the sympathies of the Christian world; governments were impelled by their subjects into a crusade against the Crescent; and the battle of Navarino, which, for the first time in history, beheld the flags of England, France, and Russia side by side, at once ruined the Ottoman navy, and reft the most important provinces of Greece from the dominions of Turkey. The inconceivable infatuation of the Turks, and their characteristic ignorance of the strength of the enemy whom they provoked, impelled them soon after into a war with Russia; and then the immeasurable superiority which the Cross had now acquired over the Crescent at once appeared. Varna, the scene of the bloody defeat of the French chivalry by the Janizaries of Bajazet, yielded to the scientific approaches of the Russians; the bastions of Erivan to the firm assault of Paskewitch; the barrier, hitherto insurmountable, of the Balkan, was passed by Diebitch; Adrianople fell; and the anxious intervention of the other European powers alone prevented the entire subjugation of Turkey, and the entry of the Muscovite battalions through the breach made by the cannon of Mahomet in the walls of Constantinople.

13. Continued increase of Russia from the Revolutions of 1830 and 1848.

Great as were these results to the growth of Russia of the forced and long-continued pacification of Western Europe, still more important were those which followed its intestine convulsions. Every throe of the revolutionary earthquake in France has tended to her ultimate advantage, and been attended by a great accession of territory or augmentation of influence. The Revolution of 1789, in its ultimate effect s brought the Cossacks to Paris; that of 1830 extinguished the last remains of Polish nationality, and established the Muscovites in a lasting way on the banks of the Vistula. The revolt of Ibrahim Pacha, and the victory of Koniah, which brought the Ottoman empire to the verge of destruction, advanced the Russian battalions to the shores of Scutari—and thus averted the subjugation of the Porte by a rebellious vassal, only by surrendering the keys of the Dardanelles to the Czar, and converting the Black Sea into a Russian lake. Greater still were the results of the French Revolution of 1848 to the moral influence, and, through it, to the real power of Russia. Germany, torn by revolutionary passions, was soon brought into the most deplorable state of anarchy; Austria, distracted at once by a Bohemian, Italian, and Hungarian revolt, was within a hair-breadth of destruction; and the presence of 150,000 Russians on the Hungarian plains alone determined the Magyar contest in favor of Austria. Immense was the addition which this decisive move made to the influence of Russia; no charge of the Old Guard of Napoleon at the close of the day was ever more triumphant. Russia now boasts of 66,000,000 of men within her dominions; her territories embrace an eighth of the habitable globe; and her influence is paramount from the wall of China to the banks of the Rhine.

14. Simultaneous conquests of the English in India, and their origin in necessity.
Great as the acquisitions of the Muscovite power have been during the last thirty years, they have almost been rivaled by those of the British in India. The latter have fairly outstripped every thing in this age of wonders; a parallel will in vain be sought for them in the whole annals of the world. They do not resemble the conquests of the Romans in ancient, or of the Russians in modern times; they were not the result of the lust of conquest steadily and perseveringly applied to general subjugation, or the passions of democracy finding their natural vent in foreign conquest. As little were they the offspring of a vehement and turbulent spirit, similar to that which carried the French eagles to Vienna and the Kremlin. The disposition of the Anglo-Saxons, practical, gain-seeking, and shunning wars as an interruption of their profits, was a perpetual check to any such disposition—their immense distance from the scene of action on the plains of Hindostan, an effectual bar to its indulgence. India was not governed by a race of warlike sovereigns eager for conquest, covetous of glory; but by a company of pacific merchants, intent only on the augmentation of their profits and the diminution of their expense. Their great cause of complaint against the Governors-General, to whom was successively intrusted the direction of their vast dominions, has been that they were too prone to defensive preparations; that they did not sufficiently study the increase of these profits, or the saving of that expenditure. War was constantly forced upon them as a measure of necessity; repeated coalitions of the native sovereigns compelled them to draw the sword to prevent their expulsion from the peninsula. Conquest was the condition of existence.

Yet such was the vigor of the Anglo-Saxon race and the energy with which the successive contests were maintained by the diminutive force at the disposal of the Company, that marvelous beyond all example were the victories which they gained, and the conquests which they achieved.

15. Their great frequency and extent.
The long period of European peace which followed the battle of Waterloo, was any thing but one of repose in India. It beheld successively the final war with, and subjugation of, the Mahrattas by the genius of Lord Hastings, the overthrow of the Pindaree horsemen, the difficult subjugation of the Ghoorka mountaineers; the storming of Bhurtpore, the taming of "the giant strength of Ava;" the conquest of Cabul, and fearful horrors of the Coord Cabul retreat; the subsequent gallant recovery of its capital; the conquest of Scinde and reduction of Gwalior; the wars with the Sikhs, the desperate passage of arms at Ferozeshah, and final triumphs of Sobraon and Goojerat. Nor was it in the peninsula of Hindostan alone that the strength of the British, at length fairly aroused, was exerted; the vast empire of China was wrestled with at the very moment when the strength of the East was engaged in the Affghanistan expedition; and the world, which was anxiously expecting the fall of the much-envied British empire in India, beheld with astonishment, in the same Delhi Gazette, the announcement of the second capture of Cabul in the heart of Asia, and the dictating of a glorious peace to the Chinese under the walls of Nankin.

16. Revolution of 1848 in Paris.
While successes so great and bewildering were attending the arms of civilization in the remote parts of the earth, a great and most disastrous convulsion was preparing in its heart. Paris, as in every age, was the centre of impulsion to the whole civilized world. Louis Philippe had a very difficult game to play, and he long played it with success; but no human ability could, with the disposition of the people, permanently maintain the government of the country. He aimed at being the Napoleon of peace; and his great predecessor knew better than any one, and has said oftener, that he himself would have failed in the attempt. He owed his elevation to revolution; and he had the difficult, if not impossible, task to perform, *without foreign war*, of coercing its passions. Hardly was he seated on the throne, when he felt the necessity in deeds, if not in words, of disclaiming his origin. His whole reign was a continued painful and perilous conflict with the power which had created him, and at length he sank in the struggle. He had not the means of maintaining the conflict. A successful usurper, he could not appeal to traditionary influences; a revolutionary monarch, he was compelled to coerce the passions of revolution; a military chief, he was obliged to restrain the passions of the soldiers. They demanded war, and he was constrained to preserve peace; they sighed for plunder, and he could only meet them with economy; they panted for glory, and his policy retained them in obscurity.

17. Causes of the fall of Louis Philippe.
Political influence—in other words, corruption—was the only means left of carrying on the government, and that state engine was worked with great industry, and for a time with great success. But although gratification

passions must always, in the long run, be the main foundation of government; men are not entirely, and for ever, governed by their reason. "C'est l'imagination," said Napoleon, "qui domine le monde." All nations, and most of all the French, occasionally require aliment to the passions; and no dynasty will long maintain its sway over them, which does not frequently gratify their ruling dispositions. Napoleon was so popular because he at once consulted their interests and gratified their passions: Louis Philippe the reverse, because he attended only to their interests. Great as was his influence, unbounded his patronage, immense his revenue, it yet fell short of the wants of his needy supporters, he experienced ere long the truth of the well-known saying, that every office gives away made one ungrateful and three discontented. The immediate cause of his fall, in February, 1848, was the pusillanimity of his family, who declined to head his troops, and the weakness of his counselors, who counseled submission in presence of danger; but its remote causes were of much older date and wider extent. Government, to be lasting, must be founded either on traditional influences, the gratification of new interests and passions, or the force of arms; and that one which has not the first will do well to rest, as soon as possible, on the two last.

18. Calamitous effects of the Revolution of 1848 in Europe.

Disastrous beyond all precedent, or what even could have been conceived, were the effects of this new revolution in Paris on the whole Continent; and a very long period must elapse before they are obviated. The spectacle of a government esteemed one of the strongest in Europe, and a dynasty which promised to be of lasting duration, overturned almost without resistance by an urban tumult, roused the revolutionary party every where to a perfect pitch of frenzy. A universal liberation from government, and restraint of any kind, was expected, and for a time attained, by the people in the principal Continental states, when a republic was again proclaimed in France; and the people, strong in their newly-acquired rights of universal suffrage, were seen electing a National Assembly, to whom the destinies of the country were to be intrusted. The effect was instantaneous and universal; the shock of the moral earthquake was felt in every part of Europe. Italy was immediately in a blaze; Piedmont joined the revolutionary crusade; and the Austrian forces, expelled from Milan, were glad to seek an asylum behind the Mincio. Venice threw off the German yoke, and proclaimed again the independence of St. Mark; the Pope was driven from Rome; the Bourbons in Naples were saved from destruction only by the fidelity of their Swiss Guards,—Sicily was severed from their dominion; and all Italy, from the extremity of Calabria to the foot of the Alps, was arraying its forces against constituted authority, and in opposition to the sway of the Tramontane governments. The ardent and enthusiastic were every where in transports, and predicted the resurrection of a great and united Roman republic from the courage of modern patriotism; the learned and experienced anticipated nothing but ruin to the cause of freedom from the transports of a people incapable of exercising its powers, and unable to defend its rights.

19. Extreme violence of the Revolution in Germany.

Still more serious and formidable were the convulsions in Germany; for there were men inspired with the Teutonic love of freedom, and wielding the arms which so long had been victorious in the fields of European fame. So violent were the shocks of the revolutionary earthquake in the Fatherland, that the entire disruption of society and ruin of the national independence seemed to be threatened by its effects. Government was overturned after a violent contest in Berlin. It fell almost without a struggle, from the pusillanimity of its members, in Vienna. The Prussians, especially in the great towns, entered, with the characteristic ardor of their disposition, into the career of revolution; universal suffrage was every where proclaimed—national guards established. The lesser states on the Rhine all followed the example of Berlin; and an assembly of delegates, from every part of the Fatherland, at Frankfort, seemed to realize for a brief period the dream of German unity and independence. But while the enthusiasts on the Rhine were speculating on the independence of their country, the enthusiasts in Vienna and Hungary were taking the most effectual steps to destroy it. A frightful civil war ensued in all the Austrian provinces, and soon acquired such strength as threatened to tear in pieces the whole of its vast dominions. No sooner was the central authority in Vienna overturned, than rebellion broke out in all the provinces. The Sclavonians revolted in Bohemia, the Lombards in Italy, the Magyars in Hungary; the close vicinity of a powerful Russian force alone restrained the Poles in Galicia. Worse, even, because more widely felt than the passions of democracy, the animosities of RACE burst forth with fearful violence in Eastern Europe. The standard of Görgei in Hungary—whom the Austrians, distracted by civil war in all their provinces, were unable to subdue—soon attracted a large part of the indignant Poles, and nearly the whole of the warlike Magyars, to the field of battle on the banks of the Danube. Not a hope seemed to remain for the great and distracted Austrian empire. Chaos had returned; society seemed resolved into its original elements; and the chief bulwark of Europe against Muscovite domination appeared on the point of being broken up into several separate states, actuated by the most violent hatred at each other, and alike incapable, singly or together, of making head against the vast and centralized power of Russia.

20. Successful stand against the Revolutionary spirit in England and France.

The first successful stand against the deluge of Revolution was made in Great Britain; and there it was withstood, not by the bayonets of the soldiers, but by the batons of the citizens. The 10th of April was the Waterloo of Chartist rebellion in England;— a memorable proof that the institutions of a free people, suited to their wants, and in harmony with their dispositions, can, in such felicitous circumstances, oppose a more successful barrier to social dangers than the most powerful military force at the command of a despotic chief. Rebellion, as usual when England is in distress, broke out in Ireland, but terminated in ridicule, and revealed at once the ingratitude and impotence of the Celtic race in the Emerald Isle. But a far more serious and bloody conflict awaited the cause of order in the streets of Paris; and society there narrowly escaped the restoration of the Reign of Terror and the government of Robespierre. As usual in civil convulsions, the leaders of the first successful revolt soon became insupportable to their infuriated followers; a second 10th August followed, and that much more quickly than on the first occasion;—but it was met by very different opponents. Cavaignac and the army were not so easily beat down as Louis, deserted by all the world but his faithful Swiss Guards. The contest was long and bloody, and, for a time, it seemed more than doubtful to which side victory would incline; but at length the cause of order prevailed. The authority of the Assembly, however, was not established till above a hundred barricades had been carried at the point of the bayonet, several thousands of the insurgents slain, and eleven thousand sentenced to transportation by the courts-martial of the victorious soldiers.

21. Restoration of military power in Austria.

Less violent in the outset, but more disastrous far in the end, were the means by which Austria was brought through the throes of her revolutionary convulsion. It was the army, and the army alone, which in the last extremity saved the state; but, unhappily, it was not the national army alone which achieved the deliverance. So violent were the passions by which the country was torn, so great the power of the rival races and nations which contended for its mastery, that the unaided strength of the monarchy was unequal to the task of subduing them. In Prague, indeed, the firmness of Windischgratz extinguished the revolt; in Italy the consummate talents of Radetsky restored victory to the Imperial standards, and drove the Piedmontese to a disgraceful peace; and, in the heart of the monarchy, Vienna, after a fierce struggle was regained by the united arms of the Bohemians and Croatians. But in Hungary the Magyars were not so easily overcome. Such was the valor of that warlike race, and such the military talents of their chiefs, that, although not numbering more than a third of the population of Hungary, and an eighth of that of the whole monarchy, it was found impracticable to subdue them without external aid. The Russians, as a matter of necessity, were called in to prevent the second capture of Vienna; a hundred and fifty thousand Muscovites ere long appeared on the Hungarian plains;—numbers triumphed over valor, and Austria was saved by the sacrifice of its independence. Incalculable have been the consequences of this great and decisive movement on the part of the Czar. Not less than the capture of Paris, it has fascinated and subdued the minds of men. It has rendered him the undisputed master of the east of Europe, and led to a secret alliance, offensive and defensive, which at the convenient season will open to the Russians the road to Constantinople.

At length the moment of reaction arrived in France itself; and the country, whose vehement convulsions had overturned the institutions of so many other states, was itself doomed to undergo the stern but just law of retribution. The undisguised designs of the Socialists against property of every kind, the frequent revolts, the notorious imbecility and trifling of the National Assembly, had so discredited republican institutions, that the nation was fully prepared for a change of any kind from democratic to monarchical institutions. Louis Napoleon had the advantage of a great name, and of historical associations, which raised him by a large majority to the Presidency; and of able counselors, who steered him through its difficulties;—but the decisive success of the *coup d'état* of December 2, was mainly owing to the universal contempt into which the republican rulers had fallen, and the general terror which the designs of the Socialists had excited. The nation would, though perhaps not so willingly, have ranged itself under the banners of any military chief who promised to shelter them from the evident dangers with which society was menaced; and the vigor and fidelity of the army insured its success. The restoration of military despotism in France in 1851, after the brief and fearful reign of "liberty, equality, and fraternity" in that ever changing country, adds another to the numerous proofs which history affords, that successful revolution, by whomsoever effected, and under all imaginable diversity of nation, race, and circumstances, can end only in the empire of the sword.

22. Restoration of military despotism in France by Louis Napoleon.

But although the dangers of revolutionary convulsion have been adjourned, at least, if not entirely removed, by the general triumph of military power on the Continent, and its entire re-establishment in France, other dangers, of an equally formidable, and perhaps still more pressing kind, have arisen from its very success. Since the battle of Waterloo, all the contests in Europe have been *internal* only. There have been many desperate and bloody struggles, but they have not been those of nation with nation, but of class with class, or race with race. No foreign wars have desolated Europe; and the whole efforts of government in every country have been directed to moderating the warlike propensities of their subjects, and preventing the fierce animosities of nationality and race from involving the world in general conflagration. So decisively was this the characteristic of the period, and so great was the difficulty in moderating the warlike dispositions of their subjects, that it seemed that the sentiment of the poet should be reversed, and it might with truth be said—

23. Great increase of external dangers from the effects of the Revolution of 1848.

"War is a game, which, were *their rulers* wise,
The people should not play at."

But this has been materially changed by the consequences of the great European revolution of 1848; and it may now be doubted whether the greatest dangers which threaten society are not those of foreign subjugation and the loss of national independence. By the natural effects of the general convulsions of 1848, the armies of the Continental states have been prodigiously augmented; and such are the dangers of their respective positions, from the turbulent disposition of their own subjects, that they can not be materially reduced. In France there are 385,000 men in arms; in Austria as many; in Prussia, 200,000; in Russia, 600,000. Fifteen hundred thousand regular soldiers are arrayed on the Continent ready for mutual slaughter, and awaiting only a signal from their respective cabinets to direct their united hostility against any country which may have provoked their resentment. Such have been the results of the French Revolution of 1848, and the rise of "liberty, equality, and fraternity" in the centre of European civilization.

24. Disastrous effects of this Revolution on the cause of freedom.

Disastrous beyond all precedent have been the effects of this revolutionary convulsion, from which so much was expected by the ardent and enthusiastic in every country, upon the cause of freedom throughout the world. Not only has the reign of representative institutions, and the sway of constitutional ideas been arrested on the Continent, but the absolute government of the sword has been established in its principal monarchies. Austria has openly repudiated all the liberal institutions forced upon her during the first throes of the convulsion, and avowedly based the government upon the army, and the army alone. Prussia is more covertly, but not less assiduously, following out the same system;—and in France, the real Council of State, servile Senate, and mock Assembly of Deputies of Napoleon, have been re-established; the National Guard generally dissolved; and the centralized despotism of Louis Napoleon promises to rival in efficiency and general support the centralized despotism of Augustus in ancient days. Parties have become so exasperated at each other, that no accommodation or compromise is longer possible; injuries that never can be forgiven have been mutually inflicted; the despotism of the Prætorians, and a Jacquerie of the Red Republicans, are the only alternatives left to continental Europe; and the fair form of real freedom, which grows and flourishes in peace, but melts away before the first breath of war, has disappeared from the earth. Such is the invariable and inevitable result of unchaining the passions of the people, and of a successful revolt on their part against the government of knowledge and property.

25. Dangers of Great Britain in particular.

Still more pressing, and to ourselves formidable, are the dangers which now threaten this country, from the consequences of that revolt against established institutions, from which the reign of universal peace was anticipated four years ago. Our position has been rendered insecure by the very effects of our former triumphs; we are threatened with perils, not so much from our enemies as from ourselves; it is our weakness which is their strength; and we owe our present critical position infinitely more to our own blindness than to their foresight. Insensibility to future and contingent dangers has in every age been the characteristic of the English people, and is the real cause why the long wars, in which we have been engaged for the last century and a half, have been deeply checkered in the outset with disaster; and to this is to be ascribed three-fourths of the debt which now oppresses the energies and cramps the exertions of our people. But several causes, springing from the very magnitude of our former triumphs, have rendered these dispositions in an especial manner powerful during the last thirty years, and it is the consequence of their united influence, which now renders the condition of this country so precarious.

26. Causes which have rendered the condition of Great Britain so precarious.

The Contraction of the Currency introduced in 1819, and rendered still more stringent by the acts of 1844 and 1845, has changed the value of money fifty per cent.; coupled with Free Trade in all the branches of industry, it has doubled it. In other words, it has doubled the weight of taxes, debts, and encumbrances of every description, and at the same time halved the resources of those who are to pay them. Fifty millions a year raised for the public revenue, are as great a burden now as a hundred millions a year were during the war; the nation, at the close of thirty-five years of unbroken peace, is in reality more heavily taxed than it was at the end of twenty years of uninterrupted hostility. The necessary consequence of this has been, that it has become impossible to maintain the national armaments on a scale at all proportionate to the national extension and necessities; and it has been exposed, on the first rupture, to the most serious dangers from the attacks of artless and contemptible enemies. Our Indian empire, numbering a hundred millions of men among its subjects, has been brought to the verge of ruin by the assault of the Sikhs, who had only six millions to feed their armies; and the military strength of Great Britain has been strained to the uttermost to withstand the hostility at the Cape of Good Hope of the Caffres, who never could bring six thousand men into the field. In proportion to the extension of our colonial empire, and the necessity of increased forces to defend it, our armaments have been reduced both by sea and land. Every gleam of colonial peace has been invariably followed by profuse demands at home for a reduction of the establishments and a diminution of the national expenses, until they have been brought down to so low a point that the nation, which, during the war, had a million of men in arms, two hundred and forty ships of the line bearing the royal flag, and a hundred in commission, could not now muster twenty thousand men and ten ships of the line to guard Great Britain from invasion, London from capture, and the British empire from destruction.

27. Extraordinary change in the national mind in this respect.

Still more serious, because more irremediable in its origin, and disastrous in its effects, has been the change which has come over the public mind in the most powerful and influential part of the nation. This has mainly arisen from the very magnitude of our former triumphs, and the long-continued peace to which it has given rise. The nation had gained such extraordinary successes during the war, and vanquished so formidable an opponent that it had come to regard itself, not without a show of reason, as invincible; hostilities had been so long intermitted that the younger and more active, and therefore influential, part of the people, had generally embraced the idea that they would never be renewed. Here, as elsewhere, the wish became the father to the thought, the immediate interests of men determined their opinions and regulated their conduct. The pacific interests of the empire had increased so immensely during the long peace; so many fortunes and establishments had become dependent on its continuance; exports, imports, and manufactures, had been so enormously augmented by the growth of our colonial empire, and the preservation of peace with the rest of the world, that all persons interested in those branches of industry turned with a shudder from the very thought of its interruption. To this class the Reform Bill, by giving a majority in the House of Commons, had yielded the government of the State. To the astonishment of every thinking or well-informed man in the world, the doctrine was openly promulgated, to admiring and assenting audiences in Manchester and Glasgow, by the most popular orators of the day, that the era of war had passed away; that it was to be classed hereafter with the age of the mammoth and mastodon; and that, in contemplation of the speedy arrival of the much-desired Millennium, our wisdom would be to disband our troops, sell our ships of the line, and trust to pacific interests in future to adjust or avert the differences of nations. A considerable part of the members for the boroughs—three-fifths of the House of Commons—openly embraced or in secret inclined to these doctrines; and how clearly soever the superior information of our rulers might detect their fallacy, the influence of their adherents was paramount in the Legislature, and Government was compelled, as the price of existence, in part at least, to yield to their suggestions.

28. Dangers springing from the Free Trade system.

The danger of acting upon such Utopian ideas has been much augmented, in the case of this country, by the commercial policy at the same time pursued by the dominant class who had come to entertain them. If it be true, as the wisest of men have affirmed in every age, and as universal experience has proved, that the true source of riches, as well as independence, is to be found in the cultivation of the soil, and that a nation which has come to depend for a considerable part of its subsistence on foreign states has made the first step to subjugation, the real patriot will find ample subject of regret and alarm in the present condition of Great Britain. Not only are ten millions of quarters of grain, being a full fifth of the national consumption, now imported from abroad, but nearly half of this immense importation is of wheat, the staple food of the people, of which a third comes from foreign parts. Not only is the price of this great quantity of grain—certainly not less than fifteen millions sterling—lost to the nation, but so large a portion of its food has come to be derived from foreign nations, that the mere threat of closing their harbors may render it a matter of necessity for Great Britain to submit to any terms which they may choose to exact. Our colonies, once so loyal, and so great a support to the mother country, have been so thoroughly alienated by the commercial policy of the last few years, which has deprived them of all the advantages which they enjoyed from their connection with it, that they have become a burden rather than a benefit. One-half of our diminutive army is absorbed in garrisoning their forts to guard against revolt. Lastly, the navy, once our pride and glory, and the only certain safeguard either against the dangers of foreign invasion or the blockade of our harbors and ruin of our commerce, is fast melting away; for the reciprocity system established in 1823, and the repeal of the Navigation Laws in 1849, have given such encouragement to foreign shipping in preference to our own, that in a few years, if the same system continue, more than half of our whole commerce will have passed into the hands of foreign states, which at any day may become hostile ones.

29. Dangers arising from the change in our foreign policy.

To complete the perils of Great Britain, arising out of the very magnitude of its former triumphs and extent of its empire, while so many causes were conspiring to weaken its internal strength, and disqualify it for withstanding the assault of a formidable enemy, others, perhaps more pressing, were alienating foreign nations, breaking up old alliances, and tending more and more to isolate England in the midst of European hostility. The triumph of the democratic principle, by the Revolution of 1830 in France, was the cause of this; for it at once induced an entire change of government and foreign policy in England, and substituted new revolutionary for the old conservative alliances. Great Britain no longer appeared as the champion of order, but as the friend of rebellion; revolutionary dynasties were, by her influence, joined with that of France, established in Belgium, Spain, and Portugal; and the policy of our Cabinet avowedly was to establish an alliance of constitutional sovereigns in Western, which might counterbalance the coalition of despots in Eastern Europe. This system has been constantly pursued, and for long with ability and success, by our Government. Strong in the support of France, whether under a "throne surrounded by republican institutions," or those institutions themselves, England became indifferent to the jealousy of the other Continental powers; and in the attempt to extend the spread of liberal institutions, or the sympathy openly expressed for foreign rebels, irritated beyond forgiveness the cabinets of St. Petersburg, Vienna, and Berlin. While the French alliance continued, these powers were constrained to devour their indignation in silence; they did not venture, with the embers of revolt slumbering in their own dominions, to brave the combined hostility of France and England. But all alliances formed on identity of feeling, not interest, are ephemeral in their duration. A single day destroyed the whole fabric on which we rested for our security. Revolutionary violence every day worked out its natural and unavoidable result in the principal Continental states. A military despotism was, after a sanguinary struggle, established in Austria and Prussia; the 2d December arrived in France, and that power in an instant was turned over to the ranks of our enemies. Our efforts to revolutionize Europe have ended in the establishment of military despotisms in all its principal states, supported by fifteen hundred thousand armed men; our boasted alliance with France, in the placing of it in the very front rank of what may any day become the league of our enemies.

When so many causes for serious apprehension exist, from the effect of the changes which are now going on, or have been in operation for the last quarter of a century in European society, it it is somewhat easy to think that there are some influences of an opposite tendency, that some of and which tend obviously and immediately to the increase of human happiness, or the elevation of the general mind. In the very front rank of this category we must place the discovery of the gold mines of California and Australia, which promise, in their ultimate effects, not only to obviate many of the greatest evils under which society has long labored, but to bring about a new balance of power in every state, and relieve industry from the worst part of the load which has hitherto oppressed it. This subject is neither so generally appreciated or understood as its paramount importance deserves; but it is every day forcing itself more and more on the attention of the thinking part of mankind, and, through them, it will ere long reach the vast and unthinking multitude.

31. Tendency to the undue influence of wealth in the later stages of society.

Whoever has studied with attention the structure or tendencies of society, either as they are portrayed in the annals of ancient story, or exist in the complicated relations of men around us, must have become aware, that the greatest evils which in the later stages of national progress come to afflict mankind, arose from the undue influence and paramount importance of *realized riches*. That the rich in the later stages of national progress are constantly getting richer, and the poor poorer, is a common observation, which has been repeated in every age, from the days of Solon to those of Sir Robert Peel; and many of the greatest changes which have occurred in the world—in particular, the fall of the Roman Empire—may be distinctly traced to the long-continued operation of this pernicious tendency. The greatest benefactors of their species have always been regarded as those who devised and carried into execution some remedy for this great and growing evil; but none of them have proved lasting in their operation, and the frequent renewal of fresh enactments sufficiently proves that those which had preceded them had proved nugatory. It is no wonder that it was so; for the evils complained of arose from the unavoidable result of a stationary currency, co-existing with a rapid increase in the numbers and transactions of mankind; and these were only aggravated by every addition made to the energies and productive powers of society.

32. Way in which this is brought about.

To perceive how this comes about, we have only to reflect, that money, whether in the form of gold, silver, or paper, is a commodity, and an article of commerce; and that, like all similar articles, it varies in value and price with its plenty or cheapness in the market. As certainly and inevitably as a plentiful harvest renders grain cheap, and an abundant vintage wine low-priced, does an increased supply of the currency, whether in specie or paper, render money cheap, as compared with the price of other commodities. But as money is itself the standard by which the value of every thing else is measured, and in which its price is paid, this change in its price can not be seen in any change in *itself*, because it is the standard: it appears in the price of every thing else against which it is bartered. If a fixed measure is applied to the figure of a growing man, the change that takes place will appear, not in the dimensions of the measure, but the man. Thus an increase in the currency, when the numbers and transactions are stationary, or nearly so, is immediately followed by a rise in the money price of all other commodities; and a contraction of it is as quickly succeeded by a fall in the money price of all articles of commerce, and the money remuneration of every species of industry. The first change is favorable to the producing classes, whether in land or manufactures, and unfavorable to the holders of realized capital, or fixed annuities; the last augments the real wealth of the moneyed and wealthy classes, and proportionally depresses the dealers in commodities, and persons engaged in industrial occupations. But if an increase in the numbers and industry of man co-exists with a diminution in the circulating medium by which their transactions are carried on, the most serious evils await society, and the whole relations of its different classes to each other will be speedily changed; and it is in that state of things that the saying proves true, that the rich are every day growing richer, and the poor poorer.

33. Influence of contraction and expansion of the currency on Rome, and on Europe in the sixteenth century.

The two greatest events which have occurred in the history of mankind have been directly brought about by a successive contraction and expansion of the circulating medium of society. The fall of the Roman Empire, so long ascribed, in ignorance, to slavery, heathenism, and moral corruption, was in reality brought about by a decline in the gold and silver mines of Spain and Greece, from which the precious metals for the circulation of the world were drawn, at the very time when the victories of the legions, and the wisdom of the Antonines, had given peace and security, and, with it, an increase in numbers and riches to the Roman Empire. This *growing disproportion*, which all the efforts of man to obviate its effects only tended to aggravate, coupled with the simultaneous importation of grain from Egypt and Libya at prices below what it could be raised at in the Italian fields, produced that constant decay of agriculture and rural population, and increase in the weight of debts and taxes, to which all the contemporary annalists ascribe the ruin of the Empire. And as if Providence had intended to reveal in the clearest manner the influence of this mighty agent on human affairs, the resurrection of mankind from the ruin which these causes had produced was owing to the directly opposite set of agencies being put in operation. Columbus led the way in the career of renovation; when he spread his sails across the Atlantic, he bore mankind and its fortunes in his bark. The mines of Mexico and Peru were opened to European enterprise: the real riches of those regions were augmented by fabulous invention; and the fancied El Dorado of the New World attracted the enterprising and ambitious from every country to its shores. Vast numbers of the European, as well as the Indian race, perished in the perilous attempt, but the ends of Nature were accomplished. The annual supply of the precious metals for the use of the globe was tripled; before a century had expired, the prices of every species of produce was quadrupled. The weight of debt and taxes insensibly wore off under the influence of that prodigious increase in the renovation of industry; the relations of society were changed; the weight of feudalism cast off; the rights of man established. Among the many concurring causes which conspired to bring about this mighty consummation, the most important, though hitherto the least observed, was the discovery of the mines of Mexico and Peru.*

34. Vast effects of the expansion of the currency during the war.

The ruinous effects which would inevitably have ensued from the simultaneous increase in the transactions and expenditure of all nations, and abstraction of the precious metals for the use of the contending armies during the Revolutionary war, were entirely prevented by the introduction of a paper currency in 1797, not convertible into gold, and therefore not liable to be withdrawn, and yet issued in such moderate quantities as satisfied the wants of man without exceeding them. It can not with truth be affirmed that this admirable system was owing to the wisdom and foresight of Mr. Pitt, or any other man. Like many other of the greatest and most salutary changes in society, it arose from absolute necessity; it was the last resource of a State which, after its specie had been drained away by the necessities of Continental warfare, had no other means of carrying on the contest. Such as it was, however, it proved the most important and decisive measure ever adopted by this or perhaps any other country. Like a similar step taken by the Roman government during the necessities of the second Punic war, it brought England victorious through the contest; and in the vast stimulus given to every branch of industry, it laid the foundation of those changes in the relations of society, and the ruling power in the State, which, in their ultimate effects, are destined not only to determine the future fate of England, but of the whole civilized world.

35. Great distress over the world from the contraction of the currency since the Peace.

That Great Britain, and every state largely concerned in industrial enterprises, has suffered grievous and long continued distress since the peace, is unhappily too well known to all who have lived through that period, and will be abundantly proved in the course of this history. It is hard to say whether England, France, or America has, in their industrial classes suffered the most. In this country, indeed, this long period of peace has been nothing but a protracted one of suffering, interrupted only by fitful and transient gleams of prosperity. In France the condition of the working classes, and the ceaseless exactions made from them by the moneyed, have been so incessant, that they were the main cause of the Revolution of 1830, and have produced that tendency to Socialist and Communist doctrines which has subsequently taken such deep root, and produced such disastrous consequences, in that country. In America such has been, during the same period, the distress produced by the alternate expansion and contraction of the currency, that it has exceeded any thing recorded in history, swept four-fifths of the realized capital of the country, away, and at once reduced its imports from this country from twelve to three millions and a half annually. The thoughtful in all countries had their attention forcibly arrested by this long succession of disasters, so different from what had been anticipated during the smiling days of universal peace, and many and various were the theories put forward to account for such distressing phenomena. The real explanation of them is to be found in a cause of paramount importance, and universal operation, though at the time unobserved—and that was the simultaneous contraction of the monetary circulation of the globe, from the effects of the South American revolution, and of the paper circulation of Great Britain, from the results of the act imposing the resumption of cash payments on the Bank of England.

36. Amount of that contraction.

The first of these causes, in the course of a few years, reduced the annual supply of the precious metals from the Mexican and South American mines, which, anterior to the commencement of the troubles in that quarter of the globe, had been, on an average, about £10,000,000 sterling, to considerably less than half that amount; and at this reduced rate the supply continued for a great many years.* The second, at the very same time, reduced the paper circulation of the British empire, which, including Ireland and Scotland, had been, during the last years of the war, above £60,000,000 annually, to little more than half that amount. The effect of this prodigious contraction in the circulating medium of the world in general, and of this country in particular, was much enhanced by the state of affairs, and the circumstances of society in all the principal countries of the earth, at the time when it took place. Universal repose prevailed almost unbroken during the whole period; and the energies of men in all nations, violently aroused by the excitement and passions of the contest, were generally turned into the channels of pacific industry. As a necessary consequence, population increased, and the transactions of men were immensely multiplied; and as this occurred at the very time when the circulation by which they were to be carried on was reduced to less than a half of its former amount, the necessary result was a great and universal reduction of prices of every branch of produce, whether agricultural or manufactured, which, before the lapse of thirty years, had every where sunk to little more than half of their former amount.†

---

* See "The Fall of Rome," *Alison's Essays*, iii. 418, where the author has endeavoured to trace out in detail, and from authentic materials, this most momentous subject.

* See Humboldt's *Nouvelle Espagne*, iii. 328; and Alison's *Europe*, chap. lxvii. § 18, note.

Year	Money raised in S. America.	Year	Bank and Bank of Notes, England.	Year	Prices of wheat per quarter.
	£		£		s. d.
1805	7,101,136	1814	47,501,080	1814	85 0
1806	6,502,142	1815	46,272,650	1815	76 0
1807	5,356,152	1816	42,109,620	1816	82 0
1808	6,169,038	1819	40,928,128	1819	78 0
1809	6,997,853	1820	34,145,295	1820	76 0
1819	3,838,350	1821	30,727,630	1821	71 0
1820	3,557,236	1829	28,301,437	1829	55 4
1821	2,887,187	1830	28,501,154	1830	64 10
1822	2,560,000	1831	26,945,094	1831	59 3

—Alison's *Europe*, chap. xcvi., Appendix.

Great Britain, as the richest country in the globe, and the one in which the largest amount of industry was carried on, was the one of course in which this reduction of prices was most sorely felt; and it came to affect the well-being of the largest portion of the people. It was not merely the reduction of prices on an average of years which was felt as so grievous an evil, but the vacillation from year to year, with the fluctuations of a currency since 1819 rendered mainly dependent on the retention of gold. The parliamentary proceedings during the whole period are filled with petitions complaining alternately of agricultural and manufacturing distress, which were regularly referred to committees, and as regularly followed by no alleviating measures. In truth, the evil had got beyond the reach of human remedy; for it arose from the confirmed ascendency in the legislature of a class which had gained, and was gaining, immensely by the general suffering with which it was surrounded. It was hard to say whether the manufacturing aristocracy engaged in the export trade gained most by the general reduction in the price of commodities, and, as a necessary consequence, in the wages of labor, or the moneyed from the commercial catastrophes which brought interest up to a usurious rate, and enabled them to accumulate colossal fortunes in a few years. Every thing turned to the profit of capital and the depression of industry; and so strongly were the interests magnified by these changes intrenched in the legislature, that the cause of humanity seemed hopeless. Every effort of industry, every triumph of art, every increase of population, tended only to augment the general distress, because it enhanced the disproportion between the decreasing circulation and increasing numbers and transactions of mankind; and prophetic wisdom, resting on the past, and musing on the future, could anticipate nothing but a decline and fall, precisely similar to that of ancient Rome, for modern Europe.

37. Hopeless prospects of industry in Great Britain.

But Providence is wiser than man; and often when human effort is inadequate to arrest the current of misfortune, and nothing but disaster can be anticipated for the future of mankind, a cause is suddenly brought into operation which entirely alters the destinies of the species, and educes future and unlimited good out of present and crushing evil. At the close of the fifteenth century the working classes over all Europe were sunk in a state of debasement, from which extrication seemed hopeless, from the strength of the position occupied by the feudal aristocracy by which they were oppressed. Providence revealed the compass to mankind, the Almighty breathed the spirit of prophetic heroism into one man—Columbus spread his sails across the Atlantic, the mines of Mexico and Peru were discovered, and the destinies of the world were changed. Less oppressed in appearance, but not less depressed in reality, the laboring poor were generally struggling with difficulties in every part of the civilized world, after the termination of the great strife of the French Revolution; the moneyed had come instead of the feudal aristocracy; and so strongly was the commercial class, which had grown up into importance during its continuance intrenched in the citadels of power that relief or emancipation from evil seemed alike out of the question. Even the terrible monetary crash of 1848 failed in drawing general attention to the subject, or making the suffering classes aware of the source from which their difficulties proceeded. Financial difficulties induced by that very monetary pressure drove the Americans into the career of conquest; repudiation of debts was succeeded by aggression on territory; Texas was overrun by squatters. CALIFORNIA conquered by armies, the reserve treasures of nature opened up, and the face of the world was changed.

38. Vast effect of the discovery of the California gold.

To appreciate the immense and blessed influence of this event upon the happiness and prospects of mankind, we have only to suppose that it had not taken place, and consider what would, in that event, have been the destinies of the species? America, with twenty-four millions of inhabitants, is now doubling its numbers every twenty-five years; Russia, with sixty-six millions, every fifty years; twenty-five millions are yearly added to the inhabitants of Europe, west of the Vistula; and the British colonies, in Australia, are rising at a rate which promises ere long to outstrip the far-famed rapidity of Transatlantic increase. Great and unprecedented as is this simultaneous growth of mankind in so many different parts of the world, it is yet outstripped by the increase of their industry and transactions. The enhanced activity and energy, springing from the development of the democratic passions in Western Europe; the multiplied wants and luxuries of man, arising from the long continuance of peace, and growth of realized wealth; the prodigious change effected by steam, at sea and land, in their means of communication, have all conspired to multiply their transactions in a still greater ratio than their numbers. In these circumstances, if the circulating medium of the globe had remained stationary, or declining, as it was from 1815 to 1849 from the effects of South American revolution and English legislation, the necessary result must have been that it would have become altogether inadequate to the wants of men; and not only would industry have been every where cramped, but the price of produce would have universally and constantly fallen. Money would every day have become more valuable—all other articles measured in money, less so; debts and taxes would have been constantly increasing in weight and oppression; the fate which crushed Rome in ancient, and has all but crushed Great Britain in modern times, would have been that of the whole family of mankind. The extension and general use of a paper currency might have alleviated, but it could not have removed these evils; for no such currency, common to all mankind, has ever yet been found practicable; and such is the weight of capital, and the strength of the influences which, in an artificial state of society, it comes to exercise on the measures of Government, that experience gives no countenance to the belief that any necessities of mankind, however urgent, would lead to the adoption of measures by which its realized value might be lessened.

39. What if California had not been discovered?

All these evils have been entirely obviated, and the opposite set of blessings introduced, by the opening of the great reserve treasures of nature in California and Australia. As clearly as the

HISTORY OF EUROPE.

basin of the Mississippi was prepared by the hand of nature to receive the surplus population of the Western World, were the gold mines of California provided to meet the wants of the Western, those of Australia of the Eastern Hemisphere. We can now contemplate with complacency any given increase in mankind; the growth of their numbers will not lead to the aggravation of their sufferings. Three years only have elapsed since Californian gold was discovered by Anglo-Saxon enterprise, and the annual supply has already come to exceed £25,000,000 sterling. Coupled with the mines of Australia and the Ural mountains, it will soon exceed thirty, perhaps reach forty millions! Before half a century has elapsed, prices of every article of commerce will be tripled, enterprise proportionally encouraged, industry vivified, debts and taxes lessened. A fate the precise reverse of that which destroyed Rome, and so sorely distressed England, is reserved for the great family of mankind. When the discovery of the compass, of the art of printing, and of the new world, had given an extraordinary impulse to human activity in the sixteenth century, the *silver* mines of Mexico and Peru were opened by Providence, and the means of conducting industry in consistence with human happiness was afforded to mankind. When, by the consequences of the French Revolution, the discovery of steam conveyance, the improvement of machinery, and the vast extension of European emigration, a still greater impulse was given to the human species in the nineteenth century, the *gold* mines of California and Australia were brought into operation, and the increase in human numbers and transactions was even exceeded by the means provided for conducting them! If ever the benevolence of the Almighty was clearly revealed in human affairs, it was in these two decisive discoveries made at such periods; and he who, on considering them, is not persuaded of the superintendence of an ever-watchful Providence, would not be convinced though one rose from the dead.

40. Vast blessings which its discovery has introduced.

41. Immense effect of the application of steam to mechanism, labor.

Coexistent with this boundless capability of increase afforded to the circulating medium of the globe, are the vast additions which the powers of art have made to the resources of industry and the means of human communication. It is hard to say whether the application of STEAM has acted most powerfully, by the almost miraculous multiplication it has produced of the powers of mechanical invention, or the facilities it has afforded to the communication of mankind with each other, and the mutual interchange of the produce of their labor. When we contemplate the effect of the steam-engine on machinery, and the conducting of nearly all the branches of manufacturing industry, as it has been exemplified in Great Britain for the last eighty years, we seem to have been entering on a career to which imagination itself can assign no limit. All that is told of the wonders of ancient art, all that is imagined of the fabled powers of genii or magicians, has been exceeded by the simple experience of the capabilities of that marvelous agent. It has multiplied above a hundred-fold the powers of industry; it has penetrated every branch of art and carried its vast capabilities into the most hidden recesses of mechanical labor. It has overturned constitutions, changed the class in which the ruling power was vested, saved and conquered nations. It outstrips the wonders figured by the fancy of Ariosto; it almost equals the marvels of Aladdin's lamp; it seems to realize all that the genius of Æschylus had prophesied for mankind, when Prometheus stole the fire from heaven.

Great as are the things which the steam-engine has done for mankind, it may be doubted whether what it has left undone are not still more important to human happiness and the moral purity of the species. Its marvels are confined to *manufacturing* industry: it is incapable of application to the cultivation of the soil. It enables one man to do the work of two hundred men, in providing dress or luxuries for mankind; but it has not superseded even the arm of infancy or old age in furnishing them with the means of subsistence. Behold that boy who tends his flocks on the turf-clad mountain's brow: he is as ignorant of art as his predecessors were in the valleys of Arcadia; but will the steam-engine ever encroach on his blessed domain? Listen to the song of the milkmaid, as she trips along yon grassy mead; is that gladsome note to become silent in the progress of civilization? Observe that old man who is delving the garden behind his cottage; the feebleness of age marks his steps, the weakness of time has all but paralyzed his arms; yet art, in all its glory, will not equal his labor in the production of food for man. Cast your eyes on that orchard, which is loaded with the choicest fruits of autumn—on that sunny slope, which seems to groan under the riches of the vintage—on that garden, which realizes all that the soul of Milton has figured of the charms of Paradise—and say, will these primeval and delightful scenes ever, in the march of improvement, be lost to mankind? The powers of steam, the inventions of mechanism, the division of labor, have done wonders in all the branches of handicraft and art; but they have left untouched the marriage of industry with nature in the fields; and in the last days of mankind, as in the first, it is in the garden of Eden that man is to find his earthly paradise.

42. And importance of its being inapplicable to agriculture.

The proof of this is decisive; it is to be found not less in the figures of the statist than in the dreams of the poet. The old state can always undersell the young one in manufactures, but it is as uniformly undersold by it in subsistence. England can produce cotton goods cheaper than any other nation, from a material grown on the banks of the Mississippi, and it is the consciousness of that ability which makes her now advocate the doctrines of Free Trade; but she is unable to compete with the harvests of Poland, the Ukraine, and America, just as ancient Italy was with those of Libya and Egypt. At this moment she exports sixty-five millions' worth of manufactures; but she imports ten millions of quarters of grain, of which nearly the half are of wheat, being a full third of that staple food of our whole people. Grain is never raised so cheap as in those places where the soil is rich, the people poor, and civilization, comparatively speaking, in a state of infancy.

43. Proof of this from statistical considerations.

The reason is, that in the old state, being the richer of the two, money is more abundant, the wages of labor higher, and the consequent cost of raising food greater than in the poorer state, where wages are low because money is scarce. Machinery obviates, and more than obviates, this moneyed inequality in the production of manufactures, but it has no influence in cheapening that of food. This is a fixed, eternal, and unchangeable law of nature—the same in the last stages of society, and ages of the world, as in the first—against which the genius, the inventions, and the industry of man are alike unable to strive. As such, it exercises a great and lasting influence upon the fortunes of the species. It was the main cause of the overthrow of Rome in ancient, and of the decline of Great Britain in modern times: it imposes, at one time, an impassable bar to the progress of a particular nation; and prevents, at another, the undue multiplication of mankind in a particular locality. It is the great means provided by Providence for arresting the corruption of aged societies, and securing, when the appointed time arrives, the general dispersion of the species.

44. What if the case had been otherwise?

To be convinced of this, and of the vast influence of this law of nature upon the destinies of mankind, we have only to consider what would have been their situation if the case had been otherwise—if subsistence, like manufactures or minerals, could be raised by huge factories in particular places, and fire had been capable of working the same prodigies in the production of food for man, as it is in that of cotton or iron goods. Would the world, in such circumstances have been worth living in? Could any human power have prevented the universal corruption of the species; could the progress, even, and increase of mankind, have been secured, when it is recollected that manufacturing districts, so far from increasing, are never able to maintain their own numbers; and that, but for a constant immigration from rural localities, they would constantly decline in population? If the husbandmen of the fields, the shepherds of the mountains, had become daily, in the progress of society, more and more collected in huge manufactories, where subsistence was rolled out of mills like cotton goods from the steam-power looms, or iron from the furnaces, what would have become of the human race? If, in the progress of society, the growth of wealth, and the extension of mechanical invention, one man became capable in these immense *food-mills* of producing subsistence for two hundred men, what could stand in infant states against such competition with the more advanced ones? And would not the inevitable result have been, that the human species, instead of following out the precept of the Almighty, and extending over the earth and subduing it, would have been all collected together round a few early-peopled districts where manners were corrupted, happiness blighted, and the multiplication of the race rendered impossible?

45. Influence of this law on the fate of particular nations.

The influence which this law of nature exercises upon the fate of particular nations is great and decisive. It has for ever rendered impossible that pressure of population upon the limits of subsistence, which, in the beginning of the present century, was so much the object of dread among political economists. When a country becomes rich and densely peopled, a considerable part of its inhabitants invariably take to manufacturing pursuits; and when this is the case, not only is the increase of that section of the community from its own resources immediately arrested, but the passions and desires which arise in the urban population and manufacturing districts lead to the stoppage of all increase in the agricultural. The cry for cheap bread is heard; and as it can never be raised as cheap in the old state as the young one, the consequence is, that free importation is first called for, and at last admitted. The moment this takes place, to any great extent, the limits of national progress have been reached, population declines, emigration increases, and the sinews of the state are transferred to distant lands. How clearly is the operation of this law of nature exemplified in the recent history of Great Britain, where the nation has been convulsed with the fierce demand for free trade in corn, first raised in the manufacturing towns; and, as a consequence of its concession, it now finds ten millions of quarters of foreign grain annually imported, three hundred thousand cultivators annually exported, and the chief market for its manufactures in the inhabitants of its own fields daily declining.

46. Great effect upon the fortunes of the species.

But if this law of nature, acting as it does upon the selfish dispositions and grasping propensities of mankind, has thus affixed an everlasting bar to the progress of particular nations, it is attended with very different results upon the general fortunes of the species. If the first leads to melancholy, the last inspires the most consolatory reflections. It is constantly to be recollected, that the designs of Providence are not limited to the growth of any particular people, but extend to the general extension and dispersion of the species. To people the earth and subdue it is the first duty, as it was the first command to mankind, in the last ages of the world as in the first. When, from the causes which have been mentioned, the progress of a particular state is arrested by the indulgence of the selfish passions of its own people, the sinews of its strength, the seeds of its greatness, are not lost; they are only transferred to distant realms, where a wider field is prepared for their reception, and the means of safe and unbounded multiplication are afforded. Sometimes this great migration of mankind takes place from the lust of foreign conquest, sometimes from the impatience of internal passion. In one age it appears in the fierce tempest of Scythian conquest; in another, in the ceaseless inroad of pacific immigration; at one time it implants the Gothic swarm in the destined fields of European enterprise; at another, spreads the Anglo-Saxon race over the boundless regions of Transatlantic or Australian freedom.

47. Effect of general education on general morality.

"Knowledge," says Lord Bacon, "is *Power*." He has not said it is either wisdom or virtue. In this respect a capital mistake has been committed both by the speculative and active part of mankind of late years; and, what is very remarkable, by the religious teachers, whose principles should have led them most to distrust the efficacy of intellectual cultivation in arresting the corruption of mankind. They forgot that it was eating of the fruit of the tree of knowledge which expelled our first parents from Paradise—that the precept of our Saviour was to preach the gospel to all nations, not to educate all nations. Experience has now abundantly verified the melancholy truth so often enforced in Scripture, so constantly forgotten by mankind, that intellectual cultivation has no effect in arresting the sources of evil in the human heart; that it alters the direction of crime, but does not 'ter its amount. The poet has said—

"Dedicisse fideliter artes,
Emollit mores, nec sinit esse feros."

And that is undoubtedly true. But observe, he has not said, "nec sinit esse *pravos*." Education and civilization, generally diffused, have a powerful effect in softening the *savage* passions of the human breast, and checking the crimes of violence which originate in their indulgence; but they tend rather to increase than diminish those of fraud and gain, because they add strength to the desires, by multiplying the pleasures which can be attained only by the acquisition of property. Then is indeed experienced the truth of the saying of the wise man, that "the love of money is the root of all evil."

This is a melancholy truth; so melancholy, indeed, that it is far from being generally admitted even by the best informed persons; and it is so mortifying to the pride of human intellect, that it is probably the last one which will be generally admitted by mankind. Nevertheless, there is none which is supported by a more widespread and unvarying mass of proofs, or which, when rightly considered, might more naturally be anticipated from the structure of the human mind. The utmost efforts have, for a quarter of a century, been made in various countries to extend the blessings of education to the laboring classes; but not only has no diminution in consequence been perceptible in the amount of crime and the turbulence of mankind, but the effect has been just the reverse; they have both signally and alarmingly increased. Education has been made a matter of state policy in Prussia, and every child is, by the compulsion of government, sent to school; but so far has this universal spread of instruction been from eradicating the seeds of evil, that serious crime is *fourteen times* as prevalent, in proportion to the population in Prussia, as it is in France, where about two-thirds of the whole inhabitants can neither read nor write.* In France itself, it has been ascertained, from the returns collected in the "Statistique Morale de la France," of commitments for crimes tried at the assizes, and the number of children at school, that the amount of crime in all the eighty-three Departments is, without one single exception, in proportion to the amount of instruction received; and accordingly, in the very curious and interesting tables constructed by M. Guerry, the lightest Departments in the map showing the amount of education, are the darkest in that showing the amount of crime.* By far the greater proportion of the ladies of pleasure in Paris come from the districts to the north of the Loire, the most highly educated in France. In Scotland, the educated criminals are to the uneducated as 4½ to 1; in England, as 2 to 1 nearly; in Ireland they are about equal.† In America, the educated criminals are in most of the States of the Union three times the uneducated, and some double only; in all, greatly superior in number.‡ These facts, to all persons capable of yielding assent to evidence in opposition to prejudice, completely settle the question; but the conclusion to which they lead is so adverse to general opinion, that probably more than one generation must descend to their graves before they are generally admitted.

And yet, although the pride of intellect is so reluctant to admit this all-important truth, there is none which in reality is so entirely conformable to the known dispositions of the human mind, or which is so frequently and loudly announced in Scripture. That the heart is "deceitful above all things, and desperately wicked," we know from the very highest authority; and probably there is no man whose experience of himself, as well as others, will not confirm the truth of the saying. But education has no tendency to weaken the influence of these secret tempters which every one finds in his own bosom; on the contrary, it has often a tendency to increase their power, by inflaming the imagination with pictures of enjoyment, which is not to be attained, at least in any short-hand method, but by crime or injustice. Discontent with our present lot is too often the result of highly-wrought, and often exaggerated pictures of the lot of others; thence the experienced and increasing difficulty of maintaining government, restraining turbulence, and preserving property from spoliation in the states and cities where instruction is most generally diffused. The common idea, that education, by rendering the pleasures of intellect accessible to the multitude, will provide an antidote and counterpoise to the seductions of sense, though plausible, is entirely fallacious. The powers of intellect—the capacity of feeling its enjoyments—is given to a small fraction only of the human race: the vast majority of men in every rank, are, and ever will be, hewers of wood and drawers of water. Physical excitement, animal pleasure, the thirst for gain, to be able to enjoy them, constitute the active principles of nine-tenths of mankind, in all ages and ranks of life. Increase their material well being, multiply their means of obtaining these enjoyments, render them, so far as possible, easy and comfortable in their circumstances, and you make a mighty step in adding to the sum of human felicity, because you open avenues to it from which none are excluded. Augment to any conceivable extent their means of instruction; establish schools in every street,

---

* In France and Prussia there were respectively in 1826,

	Prussia.	France.
Crimes against the person	1 in 31,122	1 in 32,411
Do. property	1 in 597	1 in 9,392
On the whole	1 in 587	1 in 7,285

See Alison's *Essays*, i. 558.

* See "Statistique Morale de la France," par M. Guerry, Paris, 1831—a most interesting work, the results of which are well abridged in Bulwer's "France," vol. i. p. 173–178.

† 1841—

	England.	Scotland.	Ireland.
Uneducated	9,220	696	8,735
Educated	18,111	2,831	7,152

—Porter's *Progress of the Nation*, and *Parliamentary Tables*.

‡ See Buckingham's "Travels," vol. i. pp. 472, 515.

libraries in every village, and you do infinite things, indeed, for the thinking few, but little for the unthinking many.

But this very circumstance of the extreme narrowness of the circle to which literary pleasures can by possibility be extended, and of the limited sphere over which its direct enjoyments spread, only renders the greater and the more enduring the sway of intelligence and intellect over mankind, and the permanent direction of human destinies by the power of thought. However much men, in troubled times, may aspire to self-government—however long and fiercely they may contend for it—there is nothing more certain, than that they can never enjoy it, not even for an hour. They are disqualified for it by the decided inferiority of the general mind. The first and most urgent necessity of mankind is to be governed. Man can exist for days together without food, for months without shelter; but not for an hour without a government. The first act of successful insurrection, as of victorious mutiny, invariably is to appoint a new set of rulers, who shall discharge the duties, and who never fail to render more stringent the powers of the old ones. Mankind does not by revolution escape from government; it only changes its governors. Monarchy was as really established in France under Robespierre, Napoleon, Louis Philippe, and Louis Napoleon, as ever it was under Louis XIV.: the only difference was in the person or party who wielded the sovereign powers. The English soon discovered whether the executive was less stringent or easily under the Long Parliament, Cromwell, or William III., than it had been under the princes of the Stuart line. Rousseau has affirmed, that the origin of government is to be looked for in the social contract; other political dreamers have sought it in the ruthless power of primeval conquests; but its real source is to be found in a cause of more general and lasting operation than either. It consists in the *experienced inability of mankind to govern themselves.*

It is this circumstance which has so immensely extended the influence of mind, and augmented, in so fearful a degree, the responsibility of those who direct its powers. The thinking few govern the unthinking many; and they are themselves directed by the still smaller number to whom Providence has unlocked the fountains of original thought. If we would discover the real rulers of mankind in civilized states, and in this age, we must look for them, not in the cabinets of princes, but in the closet of the sage. There is only this difference between them, that the sway of the latter does not arise till long after he has been mouldering in his grave. It does not commence till the third or fourth generation. That time is required for thought to descend from the pinnacles where it is first evolved, to the inferior regions, where it must spread before it is carried into effect. But though slow, the effect is not the less certain. Who brought about the French Revolution, and all the countless changes and convulsions to which it has given rise? It was neither Calonne nor Brienne, Necker nor Mirabeau; they only moved with the stream when put in motion: it was Voltaire and Rousseau that unlocked the original fountains; it is genius alone that can unlock the cavern of the winds. Who was the real author of free trade, and of a change of policy, the effects of which are incalculable upon the British empire? It was neither Sir Robert Peel nor Mr. Huskisson; it was not Cobden nor Bright: it is Adam Smith and Quesnay who stand forth as the authors of this mighty innovation. All that the subsequent statesmen did was to elaborate and carry into execution what they had announced and recommended. Even the reaction against innovation, and the frequent return, after an experience of the storms of revolution, to the stillness of despotism, or the sternness of military power, is owing to the powers of thought. It is they which enforce the lessons of experience, because they point out to what cause prior suffering had been owing. What a vail dropped from before the British eyes, when the *Icon Basilike* appeared! And even the arms of the Allies were less efficacious than the genius of Chateaubriand in procuring the restoration of the Bourbons.

It is generally supposed that the powers of thought, if allowed free expression, are the best guarantee against the encroachments of despotism; and that the loss of freedom is never to be apprehended as long as the liberty of the press is preserved. But though that is often, it is by no means always true; on the contrary, the selfish measures of class government, and the destruction of free privileges by military power, are never so effectually secured as by the support of a corrupted or hireling press. Beyond all question, the rude despotism of Cromwell in England, the nicely-constructed chains of imperial power in the hands of Napoleon in France, never could have existed, but for the cordial and interested support of an impassioned press in both countries. The utter ruin of the West India colonies—the deep depression of agricultural industry in Great Britain and Ireland, in consequence of the free-trade system—the general and long-continued distress of the whole class of producers in both countries, from the monetary laws—never could have been effected, if these measures had not been advocated by able and indefatigable journals in the interest of the moneyed class and the consumers. Those who lay the flattering unction to their souls that genius is the eternal enemy of oppression, and that liberty is safe if its expression is secured, would do well to look at the condition of Rome, when every successive emperor was lauded in the eloquent strains of servile panegyrists; of England, when the mighty genius of Milton was devoted to defending the measures of the regicide and Long Parliament; or of France, when the sonorous periods of Fontanes celebrated, in graceful flattery, the despotism of Napoleon.

The communication of thought over the whole world, and the consequent interchange of ideas and feelings between nations, has become infinitely more rapid since the powers of steam were applied to the means of conveyance by sea and land. That marvelous discovery, which has quadrupled the powers of industry and halved the distance of empires, has been greatly enhanced by the still more wonderful powers of the electric telegraph, which will soon, to all appearance, render all the civilized world one great community, over which the communication of intelligence and thought will be as rapid as over the streets of a single capital. With what important effects these great discoveries will be hereafter attended, may be judged of by the rapidity with which the electric shock, communicated from Paris, spread over Europe in 1848. Great consequences must inevitably result from this prodigiously enhanced rapidity of communication; but it is hard to say whether the consequences will be for good or for evil. Vigor of thought, spread of ideas, interchange of knowledge, have been immensely enhanced; but is it quite certain that these powers will be exclusively applied to good ends? Are the powers of evil not capable of taking advantage of the means of enhanced rapidity of communication thus put into their hands? Is not the spread of evil, and falsehood, and exaggeration, in the first instance at least, more rapid and certain than that of reason and truth, just in proportion as works of imagination are more eagerly sought after than those which depict reality? And is not the unexampled rapidity with which Europe took fire in 1848, a decisive proof that the increased rapidity in the communication of thought among nations tends to convert society into a huge powder-magazine, liable to blow up on the first spark falling into it?

54. Increased corresponding activity in the principles which counteract evil.

That there is much truth in these apprehensions, it is in vain to deny; but, happily for mankind, the remedy is as swift as the disease. "Experience," says Dr. Johnson, "is the great test of truth, and is perpetually contradicting the theories of men." Suffering, we may add, is the great, and perhaps the only effectual monitor of nations. In vain do men seek to elude its admonitions, to forget its lessons; it comes with unerring certainty when the paths of evil have been trod; and not now, as of old, on the third and fourth generation, but upon the very generation which has committed the forfeit. So swift is the communication of thought, that changes produce their inevitable results with unheard-of rapidity; and the cycle of excitement, folly, crime, and punishment is run out in a few years. Decisive proof of this has been afforded within the memory of many of the present generation; if the records of the past are referred to, the illustrations of it are innumerable. Eighty years elapsed, in ancient Rome, from the time when democratic ambition was first excited by the proposals of Tiberius Gracchus, till the period when the wounds of the Republic were stanched, and its peace restored, by the despotism of Augustus Cæsar; eleven years passed away, in modern times, before the passions of France, in 1789, were stifled by the sword of Napoleon; ten years marked the interval between the commencement of the troubles in England, and the confirmed military government of Cromwell. But in France, in recent times, before four years had elapsed, the dreams of "Liberté, Egalité, Fraternité" were superseded by the general demand for a strong government, and the establishment of the rude but effective military despotism of Louis Napoleon; and before the cry for Italian nationality, German unity, and Hungarian independence had ceased to resound on the banks of the Rhine, the Po, and the Danube, the ominous sounds were hushed by the force of arms on the Hungarian plains.

55. Way in which this was brought about.

The reason of this superior rapidity, both in the transmission of danger and the extrication of its remedies, in modern times, is very apparent. The laws of nature, in all ages and under all circumstances, are adverse to crime, iniquity, and injustice; they are calculated to foster only justice, industry, charity. But there is now no special interposition of Divine power, to enforce the laws of the Divine administration; the agents in this mighty system of wisdom, folly, crime, retribution, and punishment, are men themselves. The extension of the power of reading, the enhanced rapidity in the communication of thought, bring the lessons of experience more swiftly home to mankind: they cause both the seeds of evil, and the principles of good, to bring earlier forth their appropriate fruits. Such is the rapidity with which ideas are now communicated, that it resembles rather an electric shock than any of the ordinary means by which thought was formerly diffused; and as thought is directed by experience and suffering, not less than by passion and desire, the eradication or limitation of evil has become as rapid as its extension.

56. General longing after representative institutions.

The desire of all civilized nations, during the last half-century, has been for representative institutions; every attempted convulsion has had this object—every successful revolution has immediately been followed by its accomplishment. The examples of England and America, where they have been found to have been attended by rapid increase of wealth and population, a vast development of intellectual power, and a proportional extension of political influence, have been deemed decisive; and other nations considered themselves secure of the same advantages, if they obtained the same form of government. At different periods—in 1820, 1830, 1831, and 1848—their efforts proved successful, their desires were accomplished. Piedmont, Naples, Spain, Portugal, Belgium, France, Austria, Prussia, have successively obtained this much-coveted blessing; and the sequel of this history will show whether it has immediately, or generally been followed by the advantages which were anticipated. Certain it is, that at this moment (February, 1852) representative institutions are, with a few trifling exceptions, virtually extinguished on the Continent, and the despotic power of sovereigns re-established and supported by 1,500,000 armed men. And in South America, where royalty has been every where abolished, and republics established in its stead, the consequences have been so dreadful that population has generally declined a third, in some places a half, during the last thirty years, and a series of revolutions have succeeded each other, so rapid and destructive that history, in despair, has ceased to attempt to record their thread.

These disastrous results, so different from what were anticipated from the spread of institutions under which England and America have risen to such an unexampled pitch of prosperity and glory, have diffused a very general doubt among thoughtful men, whether the whole representative system is not a delusion, and whether its general establishment would not be one of the greatest curses which could be inflicted on mankind. They have been weighed in the balance, it is said, and found a-wanting. Men do not every where concur in abolishing institutions which are really beneficial in their tendency, or in recurring to those which are pernicious. The example of Spain and Portugal, reduced to political nullity by the action of representative institutions; of Piedmont, driven into august and ruinous aggression by the same cause; of the splendid regions of South America, rendered desolate by their effects, are sufficient to demonstrate to what they lead in states not fitted for their reception, and the wisdom of the effort so generally made in continental Europe by military power to counteract their tendency. It is in vain to say that this reaction has been owing to the interposition of an armed force, which has stifled the expression of the public voice, and arrested the march of human improvement. Armed men are but the executors of the national will; in all ages, but more especially in civilized and enlightened, they do not control, but express it. The stifling of the revolution of 1848, in France, was accomplished in the first instance by the soldiers, and by as rude an exercise of power as the dispersion of the Council of Five Hundred by the bayonets of Napoleon;—but the deed was approved by seven millions and a half of Frenchmen; and the forces of the Czar never could have re-established despotic power in Austria, if the brief experience of revolutionary anarchy had not made it generally felt that it was preferable to the storms of faction.

In truth, the present effects of representative governments in the two countries where they have been longest established, and been most successful, may well suggest a serious doubt whether, in their pure and unmixed form, they do not induce more evil than they remove. We must not confound with such governments the rule of a patrician senate watched by a plebeian democracy, as in ancient Rome; or of an aristocracy of land and commercial wealth controlled by an energetic commonalty, such as obtained under the old constitution of Great Britain, when all classes were adequately represented, and the House of Commons was equally the guardian of Colonial industry and British manufactures, of English land and native shipping, of territorial influence and urban ambition. Probably no candid inquirer into human affairs will ever hesitate in the opinion that, during the period, probably brief, when such a system of government endures, it affords the best guarantee for social felicity and national progress that human wisdom has ever devised. But though that is the representative system, as it grew up in most of the states of modern Europe, and as it has produced the wonders of British greatness, it is not the representative system as it is now understood by the popular party all over the world. That system consists in the representation of *mere numbers*; in the vesting supreme power in the delegates of a simple majority of the whole population. The near approach made to such a system by the Reform Bill of Great Britain, gives in its practical result, no countenance to the idea that such a system of government affords the best guarantee either for national security or social progress; on the contrary, it leads to the conclusion that its probable result is the selfishness and injustice of class government. Some one interest gets the majority, and it instantly makes use of its power to gain a profit to itself at the expense of every other class. Corporations, it is well known, have no consciences, for which proverbial fact an English Lord Chancellor has assigned a very sufficient reason;[*] and the experience of the last twenty years of English legislation, affords too clear evidence that an interest vested with political power is not likely to be behind its neighbors in selfish aggrandizement. Certain it is, that the ruin of industry and destruction of property effected in Great Britain, since the manufacturing school obtained the ascendency in Parliament, much exceeds any thing recorded in the history of pacific legislation, or that could have been effected by the most violent exertions of despotic power; and the melancholy fact stands proved by the records of the Census, that the population of the empire, which had advanced without intermission during five centuries, for the first time declined during the first five years of free-trade legislation.[†]

America, where republican institutions and universal suffrage have from the foundation of the state been established, affords an equally decisive proof of the tendency of such institutions to produce class government and unjust external measures. The principal States of the Union have, by common consent, repudiated their State debts as soon as the storms of adversity blew; and they have, in some instances, resumed the payment of their interest only when the sale of lands they had wrested from the Indians afforded them the means of doing so, without recurring to the dreaded horrors of direct taxation. The measures of Congress have been so generally directed by self-interest that they have, in more than one instance, brought the confederacy to the verge of dissolution; and the threatened separation of South Carolina was only prevented from breaking it up by the quiet concession of the central legislature. Subsequently, the selfish career of unbridled democracy has been

---

[*] In a case pleaded before Lord Thurlow, on the Woolsack, one of the counsel, who was stating the case against an incorporation, said that his client's opponents had no conscience. "Conscience!" said Thurlow, "did you ever expect a corporation to have a conscience, when it has no soul to be damned, and no body to be kicked."

[†] Population of Great Britain and Ireland
in 1841 26,831,105
Increase to 1846, one-half of ten preceding years 1,210,338

Total population in 1846....... 28,041,443
Actual population by census of 1851 27,435,313

Decrease in five years 606,128
— Census, 1851.

still more clearly evinced. Without the vestige of a title they have seized on Texas, and annexed it to their vast dominions; by concealing their title, which negatived their claims, they have obtained from Great Britain the half of Maine; they have done their utmost to revolutionize Canada; they have only been prevented by a melancholy tragedy from revolutionizing Cuba; and when the Mexicans took up arms to avenge the spoliation of their territory, they invaded their dominions, and wrested from them the half of all that remained to them, including the gold-laden mountains of California. During the last ten years they have, though attacked by no one, made themselves masters, by fraud or violence, of 1,300,000 additional square miles of territory, being nine times the area of France; already the *multis utile bellum* has become so popular among them, that the very children in all parts of the Union play at soldiers; democratic passions have found their usual and natural vent in foreign aggression; and America has added another to the many proofs which history affords, that republican, so far from being the most pacific, are the most warlike and dangerous of all states.[1]

[1] Tremenheere's Notes on America, 157, 224.

The last and memorable revolution in Europe — that which broke out in 1848 — has evolved a new element in social troubles, hitherto but little attended to, but which promises, ere long, to equal the most violent social passions in disturbing the peace and agitating the minds of men. This is the attachments and longings of RACE, which, even more than those of democracy, arouse the strongest feelings of our nature, and create divisions which the lapse even of the longest time is unable to heal. Experience has now abundantly proved in every age, and in every part of the world, that nature has imprinted an original and distinctive character upon the different families of mankind, alike in their minds as their persons, which remains the same from first to last, and which change of climate, situation, occupations, and political institutions, is alike unable to modify in any considerable degree. The Arab is the same now, and wherever he wanders, as when it was first said of the children of Ishmael, that "his hand is against every man, and every man's hand against him;" the Jew, albeit dispersed through every land, is alike unchanged in feature and disposition; the Gaul has not varied since his distinctive features were drawn with graphic power by the hand of the dictator; the Anglo-Saxon has carried into the wilds of America the enduring energy and patient perseverance which in Europe have produced the wonders of British greatness; the Hun is fiery, proud, and impetuous, as in the days when the squadrons of Attila swept over the earth; and the Celt, gay, ardent, and careless, incapable of self-direction or social improvement, is the same in Ireland, the Hebrides, Brittany, and America, as when the dark-haired hordes of his ancestors first approached the Atlantic Ocean.

60. Rise of divisions and passions of race.

Immense is the effect which this distinctive and indelible distinction of race has produced, and is producing, upon the destinies of mankind. More, perhaps, than any other cause, it has tended to bring discredit upon the principles of the French Revolution; because it has practically demonstrated their inapplicability to nations descended from a different stock from those in which corresponding principles first originated. The uniform doctrine of philosophers, and, after them, of statesmen and politicians, in the end of the eighteenth century, was, that institutions were every thing, and the character of nations nothing; that men were entirely formed by the government under which they lived; and that, if you extended to all the same institutions and civil privileges, you would produce in all the same character, and secure the same social progress. It was on this principle that the French republicans acted in surrounding the great parent commonwealth with the Batavian, Cisalpine, Helvetian, and Parthenopeian republics; it is on this principle that Great Britain has since acted in supporting revolutionary thrones in Spain, Portugal, Belgium, and Piedmont, and encouraging, by all the means in her power, the establishment of the South American republics. It is hard to say which of the two attempts has proved the greatest failure, or has led to the greatest confusion, disorder, and suffering among mankind. Their result has conclusively demonstrated that it is not institutions which form men, but men which form institutions; and that no calamities are so long continued and irremediable as those flowing from the establishment in one country of the form of government suited to another, or the awakening passions in a part of the people inconsistent with the interests or wishes of the remainder.

61. Great error in supposing national character depends on institutions.

Out of the mingled passions of democracy and race has arisen, especially in Eastern Europe, a strife more widespread and terrible than has yet desolated the face of nature in modern times. The former is found chiefly in towns; it is felt with most intensity in urban multitudes, among whom numbers, closely aggregated together, have awakened a feeling of strength, and increasing wealth has engendered the desire for independence. But the last burns most fiercely in the rural population; it acts with most force in the solitude and seclusion of country life. It is there that hereditary characteristics are most strongly marked, that ancient traditions are religiously preserved, and that the past stands forth in the brightest colors, from being undisturbed by any countervailing influences of the present. The war of races is often commenced by the impulse communicated by urban revolt; because it is that which first disturbs the peace of society, violently excites the public mind, and awakens the idea of provincial independence, by weakening the power of the central government. But the contest which begins with the ambition of towns does not expire with their short-lived fervor; the passions of the tent are more durable than those of the forum. When the shepherds of the hills, the cultivators of the plains, assemble in arms, it may in general be concluded that a serious struggle, a prolonged contest, is at hand. The fervor of the French Revolution excited the revolt of 1793 in Warsaw; but the storming of Prague has not extinguished the hopes of Polish nationality; it burns with undiminished force in the breasts of the peasantry; it has burst forth unweakened in subsequent

62. Wars of races are the great passion of Eastern Europe.

wars, and seriously weakened even the colossal strength of the Muscovite Empire. The animosity of the Celt against the Saxon is undiminished by five centuries of forced amalgamation; and when independence had become visibly hopeless, the bulk of the race fled across the Atlantic, and sought in the wilds of the Far West that independence of which they despaired amidst European civilization. The revolution in Paris, in 1848, spread the seeds of revolt to the Austrian capital; but the wars of races did not expire with the capture of Vienna: the Magyar continued in arms against the Sclave, the German against the Italian; and the dominion of the house of Hapsburg would have been torn in pieces by the passions of its own subjects, if it had not been rescued from ruin by the arms of the united Sclavonic race.

63.
Doubts as to the wisdom of representative institutions.
These facts, which have been so clearly brought forth by the events of late years, have awakened a very general doubt among reflecting men, in every part of Europe, whether representative institutions are the form of government best calculated to insure general felicity; or whether, at any rate, they can exist for any length of time among any people, but one of a homogeneous race and temperate practical character. Certain it is, that, though generally established in Europe by its northern conquerors, amidst the ruins of the Roman Empire, they every where fell into decay except where they were sustained by the mingled energy and slowness of the Norman and Anglo-Saxon race; and that, when re-established in our times by the influence of English Anglomania, or the united force of French and English arms, they have either speedily perished, or produced such disastrous results that, by common consent, they were very soon abolished. Certain it is, that they are evidently and universally inapplicable to any nation in which, like the Austrian, several distinct and hostile races are mingled together in not very unequal proportions; and probably the most enthusiastic supporter of representative institutions would hesitate before he would affirm they could have flourished in the British empire, if the Celtic race in both islands had existed in nearly equal numbers. If the present annual migration of above two hundred thousand from Ireland should continue a few years longer, and there is any truth in the assertions now generally made, that there are two millions of native-born Irish in the United States, and four millions of Irish descent, the Celtic race may acquire such a preponderance there as may ultimately render the maintenance of representative institutions impossible in some parts of the Union.

64.
Real character, good and evil, of representative institutions.
That the constitutional form of government is now on its trial, both in the Old and New World, is a common observation on both sides of the Atlantic; and it will be not the least important part of this History to trace its working in the different countries where it has been established. Such a survey will probably damp many ardent aspirations and hopes on the one side, and demonstrate the fallacy of many gloomy predictions on the other. That many evils have been found to flow from the representative system when it is really, and not in form merely, established; that selfishness often directs its measures, and corruption stains its members, is no real reproach to that form of government—it is only a proof that its powers are wielded by the sons of Adam. No one need be told that the same vices and weaknesses attach to other institutions; the page of history unhappily teems with too many proofs that sovereigns often rule only for the gratification of their passions and pleasure; and aristocracies, to farm out the industry of the people for their own profit or advantage. The real question is, whether greater scope is not given for the indulgence of these selfish propensities under the representative form of government than any other; whether it does not end in the establishment of a class government, more unscrupulous in its measures, and oppressive in its effects, than the rule of a single sovereign could possibly be; and whether the hope of checking iniquity in the administration, by admitting numbers to participate in it, is not, in fact, expecting to extinguish sin by multiplying the number of sinners. Perhaps future ages may arrive at the conclusion that it is the representation of *interests*, not *numbers*, which is the true principle; that the former, if duly balanced, is always safe, the latter always perilous; and that it is the extreme difficulty of preserving the equilibrium for any length of time which justifies the observation of the Roman annalist, that it is slow to come, swift to perish.*

65.
Great effect of the social passions of Europe in propelling its inhabitants to the New World.
But whatever ideas may be entertained on this speculative point, upon which experience has not yet warranted the forming of a decided opinion, one thing is perfectly clear, that the contending passions of the Old World, the mingled hopes and fears, wants and desires, expectations and disappointments, of ancient civilization, all tend powerfully to promote the settlement and peopling of the New. Already the emigrants who landed at New York alone, from Europe, have come to approach 300,000, of whom 163,000 are from Ireland, and 69,000 from Germany—the two countries perhaps most violently agitated by political and social passions of any in the Eastern Hemisphere. The total emigrants from Europe to America now exceed 500,000 annually.† In ten years, if the present rate continues, they will amount to 5,000,000, and, with their descendants, more than double the already far-famed marvels of Transatlantic increase. It is hard to say, in this wonderful transposition of the human race, whether the spread of knowledge or the passions of democracy exercise the most powerful sway over the minds of men, or are the most powerful and visible agents in carrying into effect the objects of Divine administration; for the last is perpetually leading to the indulgence of visionary and chimerical expectations of social felicity, from political change

---

* "Tarde veniens; cito peritura."—TACITUS.
† Landed at New York in 1851—

Irish	163,256
English and Welsh	30,742
Scotch	7302
Germans	69,883
Other nations	18,478
Total	289,661

—*Emigration Commissioners' Report,* 1851—New York

and the extension of popular power; while the former is as generally diffusing better founded expectations as to the real felicity and well-being to be attained by a settlement in the distant colonies of the world. The perpetual disappointment of the first, and the as uniform realization of the last, are the great means by which the *unmovable* character of civilized man is overcome; and the human race is as powerfully impelled into distant countries in the old age of civilization, by political passions, as it is in its infancy by the roving disposition of pastoral, or the lust of conquest in warlike tribes. No human foresight can foretell whether the passions which now so violently agitate Europe will terminate in the general establishment, *for a time*, of republican institutions, or their entire extinction by the rude arm of military power. But this much may with confidence be predicted, that in either case a vast propelling of the European race into the wilds of America, or Australia, will infallibly take place;—in the first, by the disappointment experienced by the partisans of political change; in the last, by the extinction of their hopes.

66. And of the discovery of the gold mines of California and Australia.

In this point of view, the influence is great of the discovery of the gold mines in California and Australia, not merely upon the general industry and well-being of the whole earth, but upon the attraction exercised by those richly-endowed regions upon its inhabitants. When gold is found scattered broadcast over whole countries, when valleys are discovered in which the whole alluvial deposit is impregnated with gold particles, and mountains where it is found in great quantities enclosed in veins of quartz, or embedded in fields of clay, it is impossible to over-estimate the influence which this exercises upon the desires and ambition of men. The idea of independence, it may be fortune, brought within the reach of mere manual labor, and falling to the lot, not so much of the most diligent as the most fortunate, is irresistible. The golden magnet draws votaries from all quarters; multitudes hasten to take their chance in the rich lottery where every one trusts that he himself will draw a prize and his neighbors the blank. Many doubtless perish, or are disappointed in the exciting chase; but some succeed, and their success, like the honors of war, or the fortunes of commerce, are sufficient permanently to attract mankind into the dazzling and perilous career. When twenty or thirty millions sterling are annually raised by human hands, and those the hands of *freemen*, who are themselves enriched by their toil, there is enough to rouse every where the spirit of the adventurous, to tempt the cupidity of the covetous. Californian gold has only been worked to any extent for two years, and already that State boasts 167,000 inhabitants; and a regular passage for European emigrants has been opened, both over the Rocky Mountains and the Isthmus of Panama. Among the means employed by Providence to insure, at the appointed season, the dispersion of mankind, one of the most powerful is the mineral treasures, which, long hid in distant regions in the womb of nature, are at length brought forth when the minds of men are prepared for their attraction, when the utmost facilities are afforded for the migration of the species, and when the influences of home are alike overcome by the disappointments of the Old World and the hopes of the New.

67. What if the case had been otherwise?

To appreciate justly the unbounded influence of these concurring moving powers, political passions in the Old World and gold regions in the New, we have only to suppose that it had been otherwise arranged, and consider whether mankind would ever have left their native seats. It might have been that the progress of civilization and the spread of knowledge were not to be the destined agents in moving mankind: that the attractions of wealth and the comforts of home were to become daily more powerful with the growth of nations, and that their roving propensities were to be confined to the earliest ages, when the first settlements of mankind were formed. It might have been that the gold treasures of California and Australia were to be found in the mountains of Switzerland or Bohemia, in the centre of Europe, and amid the multitudes of aged civilization. In such an event, could the European race, and with it the blessings of freedom, of knowledge, and of Christianity, ever have been diffused among mankind? Would not the inhabitants of Europe, under such circumstances, have clung forever to their homes, and the bones of their fathers, and left the distant parts of the earth alike unknown, unheeded, and uncultivated? We are not driven to speculation to figure to ourselves the consequences of such a state of things. China and Hindostan, with their civilization of four thousand years, exist to inform us what they would have been. They have had for thousands of years the knowledge, the education, and the mechanical arts of Europe, and teemed with a population of 500,000,000 souls; but they had none of its political passions. Society, from the earliest ages to the present time, has existed always under a pure and unmitigated despotism, and what has been the result? That mankind in those aged communities have an invincible repugnance to migration, and unconquerable attachment to their native seats, and have never spread beyond them. Every thing announces that Japhet will one day dwell in the tents of Shem, but unquestionably Shem will never dwell in the tents of Japhet. To the European race, endowed with intellect, and gifted with energy beyond the other families of mankind, has been predestined the duty of peopling the earth and subduing it; it is in the midst of the passions which lead to its accomplishment that we are now placed. In the last ages of the world, as in the first, the words of primeval prophecy shall prove true: "God shall enlarge Japhet and he shall dwell in the tents of Shem; and Canaan shall be his servant."

68. Increasing influence of Russian conquest.

But it is not to these agents alone that the great designs of Providence for the dispersion of the species have been intrusted. The original moving powers are still in full and undisturbed operation. The roving passions of pastoral life, the lust of barbarian conquest, are as active in impelling mankind from the wilds of Scythia, as ever they were in the days of Alaric or Attila: the Tartar horse have lost nothing of their formidable character, by being linked to the Russian horse-artillery. Still the wines and women of the south attract the brood of winter to the regions of the sun: still the pressure of barbarian valor upon the scenes of civilized opulence is felt with undiminished force. It will be so to the end of the world; for in the north, and there alone, are found the privations which insure hardihood, the poverty which impels to conquest, the difficulties which rouse to exertion. Irresistible to men so actuated is the attraction which the climate of the south, the riches of civilization, exercise on the poverty and energy of the native wilds. Slowly but steadily, for two centuries, the Muscovite power has increased, devouring every thing which it approaches; ever advancing, never receding. Sixty-six millions of men, doubling every half century, now obey the mandates of the Czar, whose will is law, and who leads a people whose passion is conquest. Europe may well tremble at the growth of a power possessed of such resources, actuated by such desires, led by such ability; but Europe alone does not comprise the whole family of mankind. The great designs of Providence are working out their accomplishment by the passions of the free agents to which their execution has been intrusted. Turkey will yield, Persia be overrun by the Muscovite battalions; the original birthplace of our religion will be rescued by their devotion; and as certainly as the Transatlantic hemisphere, and the islands of the Indian Sea, will be peopled by the self-acting passions of Western democracy, will the plains of Asia be won to the Cross by the resistless arms of Eastern despotism.

It would appear that, at stated periods in the history of nations, the passion for migration seizes upon the minds of men; and these periods are at the opposite ends of their progress—at its commencement and its termination. We read of the first in the wandering habits of the Helvetii, of whom Cæsar has left so graphic a picture; in the irruption of the Cimbri and Teutones, whom it required all the vigor of Rome and all the talents of Marius to repel; in the successive settlements of the Celts, the Franks, the Saxons, and the Normans, in the decaying provinces of the Empire; in the perpetual inroads of the pastoral nations of Central Asia, into the adjoining plains of Muscovy, Persia, Hindostan, and China. We see proof of it at this time in the ceaseless movement of the European population of America toward the Pacific, and the ardor with which the semi-barbarous pioneers of civilization plunge into the forests of the Far West. It is by the force of these passions that the first settlements of mankind were effected, and that the human race has been impelled by a blind instinct, of which it can neither see the objects nor withstand the effects, into the most distant parts of the Old World. It was thus, too, that the whole continent of America was originally peopled by its savage inhabitants; and the tales of tradition, as well as the more certain evidence of language, point alike to the period when the hunters of Kamtschatka, cast by accident, or impelled by restlessness, on the western slope of the Rocky Mountains, spread over the adjoining forests, and their descendants gradually penetrated the boundless wilds of North and South America.

69. Migratory propensities of men in the youth of civilization.

But an insurmountable difficulty checks all these early migrations of mankind; the ocean restrains their incursions. The Tartar horse, as Gibbon tells, incapable of being resisted by the whole forces of civilization, found an impassable barrier in the narrow channel of the Hellespont. The maritime incursions of the Saxons and Danes were confined to the neighboring coasts of Britain and Gaul, no distant settlements were formed by the sea-kings of the north. The Atlantic can be bridged only by the powers of civilization; but these powers are equal to the undertaking, and they are called into action at the time when the necessities and passions of aged societies require their operation. Multitudes nursed by the industry and opulence of former times, but now crowded together, require a vent, and eagerly look for new fields of settlement: the powers of steam furnish them with the means of migration; the passions of democracy render the transportation an object of desire. As strongly and irresistibly as the nomad tribes are impelled into the regions of opulence, and the daring hunter into the wilds of nature, is the civilized European urged to commit himself and his family to the waves, the ardent republican to seek the realization of his dreams on the other side of the Atlantic. Insensibly, under the influence of those desires, the frontiers of civilization are extended, the seats of mankind changed; and a new society is formed in regions unknown to their fathers, in which the different members of the European family find a cradle for future generations of their descendants.

70. Corresponding moving propensities in the maturity of civilization.

"For here the exile met from every clime,
And spoke in friendship every distant tongue.
Men from the blood of warring Europe sprang
Were but divided by the running brook;
And happy where no Rhenish trumpet sung,
On plains no sieging mine's volcano shook, [hook.
The blue-eyed German changed his sword to pruning-
....
And England sent her men, of men the chief,
Who taught those sires of Empire yet to be,
To plant the tree of life—to plant fair Freedom's tree!"*

Not only is the democratic passion in this way the great moving power which expels, as by the force of central heat, civilized man into the distant parts of the earth, but it is the most effective nurse of energy, progress, and civilization, when he arrives there. The pastoral tribes, whose passion is conquest, require a military chief to direct their movements; but the agricultural colonists, whose warfare is with Nature, invariably pant for democratic institutions. Left alone in the woods, they early feel the necessity of relying on their own resources; self-government becomes their passion, because self-direction has been their habit. All colonies which have flourished in the world, and left durable traces of their existence to future times, have been nurtured under the shelter of republican institutions: those of Greece and Rome, on the shores of the Mediterranean—those of Holland and England, on the wider margin of the ocean, attest this important fact. The colonies of Great Britain at this time, though nominally ruled by Queen Victoria, are for the most part, practically speaking, self-directed; and where the authority of the central govern-

71. Necessity of republican institutions to colonial settlements.

* Gertrude of Wyoming.

ment has made itself felt, it has generally been only to do mischief, and weaken the bonds which unite its numerous offspring to the parent state. Wherever democratic institutions do not prevail, colonial settlements, after a time, have declined, and at length expired; and it seems to be impossible to engraft republican self-direction upon original subjection to monarchical institutions. It must be bred in the bone, and nurtured with the strength. The Portuguese settlements in the East are almost extinct, and exhibit no traces of the vigor with which Vasco da Gama braved the perils of the stormy Cape; the attempt to introduce republican institutions, after three centuries of servitude, into the Spanish colonies of South America, has led only to anarchy and suffering; and the decisive fact, that the republican states of North America, though settled a century later, have now more than double the European population of the monarchical in the South, points to the wide difference in the future destinies of mankind of these opposite forms of government. Certain it is that, great as the British military empire in India now is, it will leave no settlements of Europeans behind it among the sable multitudes of Hindostan; and possibly future times may yet verify the saying of Burke, that, if the Englishman left the East, he would leave no more durable traces of his existence than the jackal and the tiger.

Observe, in this view, how the character of the races to whom the development of this mighty progress has been intrusted, and of the institutions which they have created for themselves, is adapted to the parts severally destined for them in it. It might have been otherwise. The character of the two great families of the race of Japhet might have been reversed, or the place assigned them on the theatre of existence different from what it is. The Anglo-Saxon, impelled by a secret impulse to effort, to commerce, to freedom, and to colonization, might have found himself in the plains of Muscovy or Siberia; the Selavonian, with his submissive habits, roving propensities, and lust of conquest, might have been located in Germany and the British isles. What would have been the result? Could the European family have spread the European influence as it has done? Could the race of Japhet have performed his destined mission, to replenish the earth and subdue it? No: by this simple transposition of race, the whole destinies of mankind would have been changed; the accomplishment of prophecy rendered impossible; the spread of Christianity arrested. The Anglo-Saxon, with his maritime inclinations, his aspirations after freedom, his industrious habits, would have been swept away in Scythia by the squadrons of the Crescent; the Selavonian, with his roving propensities, his thirst for conquest, his aversion to the ocean, would have been forever arrested by the waves of the Atlantic. Crushed in all attempts at colonization or settlement beyond his native seats, the Anglo-Saxon would have pined in impotent obscurity in the plains of Muscovy; restrained by the impassable barrier of the ocean, the Russian would have been forgotten in the forests of Britain. Placed as they have been respectively, by Providence, on the theatre of existence, each has been provided with a fitting stage for the exercise of his peculiar powers, and found around him the elements in nature adapted for their development. The Anglo-Saxon found in the forests of England the oak which was to give to his descendants the empire of the waves; the coal which was to move the powers of steam; the iron which, in a future generation, was to renew the age of gold. The Selavonian found in Central Asia the redoubtable horsemen who were to add strength and speed to his battalions; the naked plains, where they could act with resistless force; the enameled turf, which every where provided them with the means of subsistence and migration. The free aspirations of the first impelled him into the career of pacific colonization; the ocean was his bridge of communication; the despotic inclinations of the last prepared him to follow the standards of conquest; the steppe stretched out before him, to facilitate the migration of his conquering squadrons.

When Providence gave the blessings of Christianity to mankind, their diffusion at the appointed season was intrusted to the acts of free agents; but a particular race was selected by whose voluntary co-operation its design might be carried into effect. Beyond all question, the race of Japhet was the one to which this mighty mission was intrusted. The energy and vigor, the intelligence and perseverance, which have so long rendered it pre-eminent among men, bespeak its fitness for the undertaking; and it may be doubted whether any other family of mankind will, for a very long period, be fitted for the reception of the faith which it bears on its banners. Experience gives little countenance to the belief that the race of Shem and Ham can be made to any considerable extent, at least at present, to embrace the tenets of a spiritual faith. Christianity, as it exists in some provinces of Asia, is not the Christianity of Europe; it is paganism in another form; it is the substitution of the worship of the Virgin and images for that of Jupiter and the heathen deities. If Christianity had been adapted to man in his rude and primeval state, it would have been revealed at an earlier period; it would have appeared in the age of Moses, not in that of Cæsar. Great have been the efforts made, both by the Protestant and Roman Catholic churches, especially of late years, to diffuse the tenets of their respective faiths in heathen lands; but, with the exception of some of the Catholic missions in South America, without the success that was, in the outset at least, anticipated. Sectarian zeal has united with Christian philanthropy in forwarding the great undertaking; the British and Foreign Bible Society has rivaled in activity the Propaganda of Rome; and the expenditure of £100,000 annually on the enlightening of foreign lands has afforded a magnificent proof of devout zeal, and British liberality. But no great or decisive effects have as yet followed these efforts—no new nations have been converted to Christianity; the conversion of a few tribes, of which much has been said, appears to be little more than nominal; and the durable spread of the gospel has been every where co-extensive only with that of the European race. But that race has increased, and is increasing, with unexampled rapidity; its universal growth, and wide extension, bespeak the evolutions of a mighty destiny; and it has now become apparent, that the Anglo-Saxon colonist bears with his sails the blessings of Christianity to mankind.

74. Increasing influence of religion in Europe.

The influence of Christianity is obviously increasing in all the nations of Europe, and to nothing has this increase been so much owing as to the irreligious spirit which occasioned the French Revolution. Voltaire was the author of the second great crusade, he was the Peter the Hermit of the eighteenth century; without intending it, he, in the end, roused all nations in behalf of religion. He conferred one blessing of inestimable importance on mankind—he brought skepticism to the test of experience. He forever revealed its tendencies, and demonstrated its effects to the world. The Reign of Terror is the everlasting commentary on his doctrines; Robespierre is at once the disciple and the beacon of those of Rousseau. Nowhere has this reaction been more apparent than in France, the very country where infidelity was first triumphant. The increasing spirit of devotion in its rural districts has long been a matter of observation to all persons acquainted with French society; and the proof of this is now decisive—universal suffrage has brought it to light. Louis Napoleon has seized supreme power; but he seized it by the aid of the clergy. His first step was a solemn service in Nôtre Dame, the theatre of the orgies of the Goddess of Reason; and the votes of seven millions of Frenchmen demonstrated that the vast majority of the people coincided with his sentiments. In England, the influence of religious opinion has increased to such a degree as to become in some measure alarming; it begets, in the thoughtful mind, the dread of a reaction. Christianity, in Russia, is the mainspring both of government and national action: the Cross is inscribed on his banners; it is as the representative of the Almighty that the Czar is omnipotent. In no country in the world is religious zeal warmer, religious impressions more general, than in America, though unfortunately they have not had the effect of restraining their public actions. These appearances are decisive as to the future progress of the Christian faith, and its diffusion by the spread of the European race. When France and England, America and Russia, differing in almost everything else, combine in this one impression, it needs no prophet to announce the future destinies of mankind.

Such are the views which occur to the reflecting mind, from the contemplation of the eventful period in the history of Europe which it is proposed to embrace in this work. Less dramatic and moving than the animated era which terminated with the fall of Napoleon, it is, perhaps, still more important; it contains less of individual agency, and more of general progress. There are some incidents in it second to none that ever occurred, in tragic interest: the Affghanistan disaster, the passage of arms in the Punjaub, the revolutions of 1848 in Europe, will forever stand forth as some of the most heart-stirring events in the annals of mankind. But these are the exceptions, not the rule. The general character of the period is one of repose, so far as relates to the transactions of nations; but of the most fearful activity, so far as the thoughts and social interests of the people are concerned. The heroes of it are not the commanders of armies, but the leaders of thought; the theatre of its combats is not the tented field, but the peaceful forum. It is there that the decisive blows were struck, there that the lasting victories have been gained. The volumes of this History, therefore, will differ much from those of the one which has preceded it; they will be less dramatic, but more reflecting; they will deal less with the actions of men, and more with the progress of things. In the former period, individual greatness determined the march of events, and general history insensibly turned into particular biography; in the present, general causes overruled individual agency, and the lives even of the greatest men are seen to have been mastered by the progress of events. It is a common complaint in these times, that the age of great men has departed; that the giants of intellect are no longer to be seen; that no one impresses his signet on the age, but every one receives the impression from it. But the truth is, that it is the strength of the general current which has swept away particular men; the stream, put in motion by greatness in a former age, has been so powerful that it has become impossible for individual strength in this to withstand it; it is not that the age of great men has departed, but that of general causes has succeeded. But the ascendant of intellect is not thereby diminished: its triumphs are only postponed to another age; its sway begins when the body to which it was united is mouldering in the grave. The prophet is even more revered in future times than the lawgiver; when time has placed its signet on opinions, they carry conviction to every breast; and he who has had the courage to defend the cause of truth against the prejudices of one age, is sure of gaining the suffrages of the next.

CHAPTER II.

HISTORY OF ENGLAND FROM THE PEACE OF PARIS, IN 1815, TO THE END OF THE YEAR 1815.

1. Commanding position of Great Britain at the close of the war.

So great had been the success, so glorious the triumphs of England, in the latter years of the war, that the least sanguine were led to entertain the most unbounded hopes of the future prosperity of the empire. Prosperity unheard of, and universal, had, with a few transient periods of distress, when the contest was at the worst, pervaded every department of the state. The colonial possessions of Great Britain encircled the earth; the loss of the North American colonies had been more than compensated by the acquisition of a splendid empire in India, where sixty millions of men were already subject to our rule, and forty millions more were in a state of alliance; the whole West India islands had fallen into our hands, and were in the very highest state of prosperity; Java had been added to our Eastern possessions, and had been only relinquished from the impulse of a perhaps imprudent generosity; and the foundation had been laid, in Australia, of those flourishing colonies which are, perhaps, destined one day to rival Europe itself in numbers, riches, and splendor. How different was this prospect from that which, a few years before, the world had exhibited! There had been a time when, in the words of exalted eloquence, "the Continent lay flat before our rival; when the Spaniard, the Austrian, the Prussian, had retired; when the iron quality of Russia had dissolved; when the domination of France had come to the water's edge; and when, behold, from a misty speck in the west the avenging genius of these our countries issues forth, grasping ten thousand thunderbolts, breaks the spell of France, stops in his own person the flying fortunes of the world, sweeps the sea, rights the globe, and retires in a flame of glory."* Nor had the domestic prosperity of this memorable period been inferior to its external renown. Agriculture, commerce, and manufactures at home had gone on increasing, during the whole struggle, in an unparalleled ratio; the landed proprietors were in affluence, and for the most part enjoyed incomes triple of what they had possessed at its commencement; wealth to an unheard-of extent had been created among the farmers; the soil, daily increasing in fertility and breadth of cultivated land, had become adequate to the maintenance of a rapidly-increasing population; and Great Britain, as the effect of her long exclusion from the Continent, had obtained the inestimable blessing of being self-supporting as regards the national subsistence. The exports, imports, and tonnage had more than doubled since the war began; and although severe distress, especially during the years 1810 and 1811, had pervaded the manufacturing districts, yet their condition, upon the whole, had been one of general and extraordinary prosperity.

* Grattan.

2. Statistical facts proving the general prosperity of the state.

Facts proved by the parliamentary records sufficiently demonstrated that this description was not the high-flown picture of imagination, but the sober representation of truth. The revenue raised by taxation within the year had risen from £19,000,000, in 1792, to £72,000,000, in 1815; the total expenditure from taxes and loans had reached, in 1814 and 1815, the enormous amount of £117,000,000 each year. In the latter years of the war, Great Britain had above 1,000,000, of men in arms in Europe and Asia; and besides paying the whole of these immense armaments, she was able to lend £11,000,000 yearly to the Continental powers; yet were these copious bleedings so far from having exhausted the capital or resources of the country, that the loan of 1814, although of the enormous amount of £35,000,000, was obtained at the rate of £4 11s. 1d. per cent, being a lower rate of interest than had been paid at the commencement of the war. The exports, which in 1792 were £27,000,000, had swelled in 1815 to nearly £58,000,000, official value; the imports had advanced during the same period from £19,000,000 to £32,000,000. The shipping had advanced from 1,000,000 to 2,500,000 tons. The population of England had risen from 9,400,000 in 1792, to 13,400,000 in 1815; that of Great Britain and Ireland from 14,000,000 in the former period, to 18,000,000 in the latter. Yet, notwithstanding this rapid increase, and the absorption of nearly 500,000 pairs of robust arms in the army, militia, and navy, the imports of grain had gone on continually diminishing, and had sunk in 1815 to less than 500,000 quarters. And so far was this prodigious expenditure and rapid increase of numbers from having exhausted the resources of the state, that above £6,000,000 annually was raised by the voluntary efforts of the inhabitants to mitigate the distresses and assuage the sufferings of the poor; and a noble sinking fund was in existence, and had been kept sacred during all the vicissitudes of the struggle, which already had reached £16,0000,000 a year, and would certainly, if left to itself, have extinguished the whole public debt by the year 1845.[1]

[1] See Table in History of Europe, App. C. xcvi where the figures are all given.

3. Warm and general anticipations of general prosperity on the peace.

When such had been the prosperity and so great the progress of the empire, during the continuance of a long and bloody war, in the course of which it had repeatedly been reduced to the very greatest straits, and compelled to fight for its very existence against the forces of combined Europe, there seemed to be no possible limits which could be assigned to the prosperity of the state when the contest was over, and the blessings of peace had returned to gladden our own and every other land. If the industry of our people had been so sustained, their progress so great, during a war in which we were for a long period shut out from the Continent, and for a time from America also, what might be expected when universal peace prevailed, and the harbors of all nations, long famishing for the luxuries of British produce and manufactures, were every where thrown open for their reception? Views of this sort were so obviously supported by the appearances of the social world, that they were embraced not only by the ardent and enthusiastic, but the prudent and the sagacious, in every part of the country. The landholders borrowed, the capitalist lent money, on the faith of their justice. The merchant embarked his fortune in the sure confidence that the present flattering appearances would not prove fallacious; and the eloquent preacher expressed no more than the general feeling when he said—" The mighty are fallen, and the weapons of war have perished. The cry of freedom bursts from the unfettered earth, and the standards of victory wave in all the winds of heaven. Again in every corner of our own land the voice of joy and gladness is heard. The cheerful sounds of labor rise again in our streets, and the dark ocean again begins to whiten with our sails. Over this busy scene of human joy the genial influences of heaven have descended. The unclouded sun of summer has ripened for us all the riches of harvest. The God of nature hath crowned the year with his goodness, and all things living are filled with plenteousness. Even the infant shares in the general joy; and the aged, when he recollects the sufferings of former years, is led to say, with the good old Simeon in the Gospel, 'Lord, now let thy servant depart in peace, for mine eyes have seen thy salvation.'"¹

¹ Sermon on the Thanksgiving, Jan. 13, 1814, by the Rev. Archibald Alison—Sermons, i. 450.

Such were the expectations and feelings of the people at the termination of the war. Never were hopes more cruelly disappointed, never anticipations more desperately crossed. No sooner was the peace concluded than distress, wide-spread and universal, was experienced in every part of the country, and in every branch of industry. It was felt as much by the manufacturers as the agriculturists; by the merchants as the landlords; and, ere long, the general suffering rose to such a pitch that, while the table of the House of Commons groaned under petitions from the farmers, complaining of agricultural distress, the Gazette teemed with notices of the bankruptcy of traders; and disturbances became so common and alarming in the manufacturing districts, that special commissions had to be sent down, in this and the following year, to Ely, Derby, and the principal seats of the outrages, by whom the law was administered with unsparing but necessary rigor. The farmers, as usual with that class, bore their distresses with patience and resignation; but the manufacturers, always more excitable and tumultuous, were not so easily appeased. In the southern part of Staffordshire the distress was felt as peculiarly severe, and the working people in the populous village of Bilston were reduced to such a degree that they all fell upon the parish, the funds of which were inadequate to preserve them from absolute starvation. The iron trade in particular was every where suffering under great distress: large bodies of workmen, dismissed from their forges, paraded the country, demanding charity in a menacing manner; and at Merthyr-Tydvil, in South Wales, the disorders were not appeased without military interference. To excite public commiseration, great numbers of these dismissed workmen fell upon the expedient of drawing loaded wagons of coals to distant towns; and a division of these wandering petitioners approached the metropolis, and were only turned aside by the resistance of a powerful body of police."¹

¹ Ann. Reg. 1816, p. 93, 94; Memoirs of Lord Sidmouth, iii. 149, 151.

It was with the merchants engaged in the export trade that the distress, which soon became universal, first began; and in them it appeared even before hostilities had ceased. Possessed with the idea that the inhabitants of the Continent were languishing for British colonial produce, from which they had so long been excluded, and inflamed by the prospect of the sudden opening of their ports to our shipping, the English merchants thought, and acted upon the opinion, that no limits could be assigned to the profitable trade which might be carried on with them, especially in that article of merchandise. So largely was this notion acted upon, that the exports of foreign and colonial produce from Great Britain and Ireland, which in 1812 had been £9,533,000, rose in 1814 to £19,365,000. The necessary effect of so prodigious an increase of the supply thrown into countries impoverished to the very last degree by the war, and scarcely able to pay for any thing, was that the consignments were, for the most part, sold for little more than half the original cost, and ruin, wide-spread and universal, overtook all the persons engaged in the traffic. The eastern ports of the kingdom, in particular London, Hull, and Leith, suffered dreadfully by the extensive and disastrous shipments to the north of Europe. England then began to learn a lesson which has been sufficiently often taught since that time—namely, how fallacious a test the mere amount of exports is of the flourishing condition of the country in general, or even of the branches of trade in which the greatest increase appears in particular. That increase often arises from a failure of the home market, which renders it necessary to send the goods abroad, or from absurd and ruinous speculation, which terminates in nothing but disaster. The year 1814, during which foreign and colonial produce to the extent of £19,500,000 was exported, was far more disastrous to the persons engaged in that trade than the three succeeding years,* in which the exports of that description sank to little more than a half of that amount.

¹ Annual Reg. 1814, 219; 1815, 144

5. Beginning of the distress among the export merchants.

This distress, however, was not long of spreading to the agriculturists, and among them it

---

* Exports of foreign and colonial produce:
1814 .... £19,365,981
1815 15,748,554
1816 13,480,781
1817 10,292,684
—ALISON's Europe, Appendix, chap. xcvi

assumed a more formidable, because settled and irremediable form. Notwithstanding the protection to British agriculture which had been afforded by the corn law passed in 1814, of which an account has already been given,[1] it had already become apparent that the opening the harbors of America and Northern Europe for supplies of grain, coupled with the cessation of the lavish expenditure of the war, would seriously affect the prices of every species of agricultural produce. Already, they had fallen to little more than *two-thirds* of what they had been during the five last years of the war.* Although the prices which they still fetched may seem high to us, who have been accustomed to the much greater reduction which has since taken place, yet the fall from 120s. in 1813, to 76s. in 1815, and 57s. in the spring of 1816, for the quarter of wheat, was sufficiently alarming, and struck a prodigious panic into the minds of all persons engaged in agricultural pursuits. The rise in the price of rural produce had been so steady and long-continued, and the affluence in consequence arising to all persons connected with land, or depending either on the sale of its produce or the purchases flowing from its prosperity, so great, that all classes had come to regard it as permanent, and they had all acted accordingly. The landowners had borrowed money or entered into marriage-contracts on the faith of its continuance: present expenditure, provisions to children, had been regulated by that standard. The tenantry, in those parts of the country where leases were common, had entered into lasting contracts, in the belief that the high prices would continue; and they could now anticipate nothing but ruin if they were held to their engagements. A general despondency, in consequence, seized upon the rural classes; numbers of farms were thrown up in despair; and the universal suffering among that important class not only spread a general gloom over society, but seriously affected the amount of manufactured articles taken off by the home market, by far the most important vent for that species of industry.[2]

Before the close of the year 1816, these causes of distress assumed a different, but a still more alarming form. The summer of that year was uncommonly wet and stormy, insomuch, that not only was the quantity and quality of the grain every where rendered deficient, but in the higher and later parts of the country the harvest never ripened at all. So stormy, melancholy a season had not been experienced since 1799; the consequence of course was, that the price of grain rapidly rose, and the average for the year was 82s. a quarter. But it was much higher than this average in the latter months; indeed, in some places in the north of England, wheat in October was at a guinea a bushel.† The effect of this, of course, was to admit foreign importations duty free—the prices having surmounted that of 86s., fixed by the sliding scale as the turning point at which free foreign importation was to commence. This happy circumstance had the effect of checking the rise in the price of provisions, which, but for that circumstance, would doubtless have reached the level of a famine. The importation of wheat in that year amounted to 225,000 quarters; but in the next, when the effect of the scarcity of 1816 was felt, it rose to 1,620,000 quarters, and in 1818 to 1,593,000.[3] But from this circumstance sprang up a new cause of distress to the farmers, which was felt with the utmost severity in this and the two succeeding years. The importation kept down prices, but it did not restore crops; it deprived the farmer of a remunerating price for what remained of his produce, without making up to him what had been lost. And the nation, on comparing its present condition with what it had been during the last years of the war, began to feel the truth of Adam Smith's remark—"High prices and plenty are prosperity; low prices and want are misery."[4] *

When such general distress pervaded the whole classes depending upon land—then, as now, by far the largest and most important part of the community†—it was not to be supposed that the manufacturing interests were not also to be laboring under difficulties. The distress among them, accordingly, was universal—and equally among those who toiled for the foreign, as with those who supplied the home market. In some branches of industry which went directly to the supplying of arms and stores of war, the depression, on the cessation of hostilities, was immediate and excessive. England had for several years past been the great armory of the world, and could not but suffer severely in several branches of its industry on the return of peace. It is to this cause, chiefly, that the rapid reduction in the price of copper and iron was to be ascribed—the former of which had fallen from £180 to £80, the latter from £20 to £8 per ton.[5] But the depression was not confined to those branches of industry which were directly employed on warlike stores; it was universal, and felt as severely in those which were devoted to the supplying of pacific wants, as in those

---

* Average price of wheat per Winchester bushel:—

	Shillings.		Shillings.
1809	105	1813	120
1810	112	1814	85
1811	108	1815	76
1812	118	1816	82

— Alison's Europe, Appendix, chap. xcvi.

† On 8th October, the Earl of Darlington wrote to Lord Sidmouth, then Home Secretary:—"The distress in Yorkshire is unprecedented; there is a total stagnation of the little trade we ever had; wheat is already more than a guinea a bushel, and no old corn in store; the potato crop has failed; the harvest is only beginning; the corn being in many parts still green, and I fear a total defalcation of all grain this season, from the deluge of rain which has fallen for several weeks, and is still falling."—Earl of Darlington to Lord Sidmouth, 8th Oct. 1816. *Life of Sidmouth*, iii. 150.

* "If we think we are to go on smoothly without the effectual means of repressing mischief, and large means too, we shall be most grievously mistaken. I look to the winter with fear and trembling. In this island our wheat is good for nothing; barley and oats reasonably good. As a farmer I am ruined here and in Durham. So much for peace and plenty."—Lord Chancellor Eldon to Lord Sidmouth, 8th Oct. 1816. *Sidmouth's Life*, iii. 151.

† The classes directly or indirectly dependent on land are now (1852), in round numbers, 18,000,000; on manufactures and towns, 10,000,000.—Spackman's *Tables*, 1852.

which were immediately connected with hostilities. All were suffering, and apparently with equal severity. Distress was as great among the cotton-spinners of Manchester or Glasgow, the silk-weavers of Spitalfields, or the glove-manufacturers of Nottingham, as among the hardware-men of Birmingham, or the iron-moulders of Merthyr-Tydvil. The home market was soon found to be reduced to a half of its former amount; and the manufacturers, finding their usual vents for their produce failing them from domestic wants, sent them in despair abroad; but with so little success that the entire exports of British produce and manufactures, which in 1815 had risen to £42,875,000, sank in the succeeding year to £35,717,000.[1]

<small>[1] Alison's Europe, c. xcvi. App. Sid-mouth's Life, iii. 151, 152.</small>

9. Depression so severe and wide-spread could not be explained by the mere transition from a state of war to one of peace, to which the partisans of Government at that period, and for long after, constantly ascribed it. Every impartial and thinking person saw that, although that might explain the depression in some particular branches of industry which had been connected with hostilities, it could not account for the universal depression in *all* branches of industry, alike agricultural and manufacturing, for the home trade and the export sale. Still less could it explain the fact that the depression was universal in all markets, and even greatest in those connected with pacific employments, which might have been expected to have taken an extraordinary start on the termination of war expenditure. As little could the reduction be accounted for by the reduction of taxation, and diminution of the expenditure of governments in general, and that of Great Britain in particular; for that only altered the direction of expenditure, without lessening its amount; if it put less into the hands of Government to spend for the people, it left more in the hands of the people to spend for themselves. The Whigs and Radicals had a very clear solution of the question: the difficulties all arose from excessive taxation, and the measures of a corrupt oligarchy; and the remedy for them was to be found in parliamentary reform, and an unsparing retrenchment in all branches of the public expenditure. A vehement outcry, accordingly, was raised for these objects, which was supported with equal eloquence and ability both in and out of Parliament.*

<small>This general suffering was not owing to the transition from war to peace.</small>

soon demonstrated the fallacy of all hopes of a relief to the public suffering from these appliances. Retrenchment was, by the voice of the country and the anguish of general suffering, forced upon the Government; the income and malt taxes, amounting to £17,000,000 a year, were abolished; the public expenditure was reduced from £102,000,000 to £82,000,000 nearly 300,000 men were disbanded in the army and navy; and still the distress went on constantly increasing, and was greater than ever in the close of the very year 1816, in the course of which these immense reductions had been carried into effect. It is evident, therefore, that some more general and lasting cause was in operation than those to which the adherents of either party at that period ascribed it; and without denying altogether the influence of some of these subordinate ones, it may now safely be affirmed that the main cause was the following:

10. The annual supply of the precious metals for the use of the globe, derived from the South American mines, had been, for some years prior to 1808, about ten millions sterling; and of this, about a half was coined in South America, and the remainder for the most part found its way to Europe in the form of bullion.[1] The rapid rise in the price of commodities all over Europe, during the latter years of the war, was in part owing to the increased supply of the precious metals, obtained in consequence of the great rise in their value from the necessities of the belligerent powers. Gold, in consequence of this, had in 1813 and 1814 risen to £5, 8s. an ounce, from £4, which it had been in the beginning of the century. But the long and desolating wars in which the whole Spanish provinces of South America had been involved since 1809, in consequence of their calamitous revolution, soon put an end to this auspicious state of things. The capitalists who worked the mines were ruined during these disastrous convulsions; the mines themselves ceased to be worked, the machinery in them went to destruction, and they were in many places filled with water. So complete did the ruin become, that the population of the city of Potosi, in Peru, from whence the celebrated silver mines of the same name were worked, which in 1805 contained 150,000 inhabitants, had sunk in 1825 to 8000.[2] The only supplies of the precious metals which were obtained during these disastrous years, were from the melting down of their gold and silver plate by the wealthy proprietors of former days, who had been reduced to ruin, and from turning over the heaps of rubbish which had been turned out of the mines in the days of the r prosperity. But so diminutive and precarious were the supplies thus obtained

<small>Diminished supply of the precious metals from South America.</small>

<small>[1] Humboldt's Nouv. Esp. iii. 398.</small>
<small>[2] Miller's Mem. ii. 319; Alison's Eu rope, c. lxvii. § 65.</small>

<small>* "From a struggle which appalled, I believe, the boldest among us, we have by the talents and firmness of our general, and the intrepid and patient courage of our troops, been blessed with glorious victory. By the art of Ministers we have, from a state of triumph and exultation, from hopes of security, justified by success, been left to contemplate the real result of all these things. Let us look around us and see the state of our country; let us go forth among our fields and manufactories, and let us see what are the tokens and indications of peace. Can we trace them among a peasantry without work, and consequently without bread?—among farmers unable to pay their rents, and *a fortiori* unable to contribute to that parochial relief on which the peasantry is rendered dependent?—among landowners unable to collect their rents, and yet obliged to maintain their rank and station as gentlemen in society? Let us listen to the cry of the country—it is poverty, from the proudest castle to the meanest cottage, poverty rings in our ears; it lies in our path whichever way we turn. It is not the congratulations of the noble lord opposite, it is not the song of victory that can drown this lamentable cry; it is not in the power of the noble lord, it is not in the power of this House or of Parliament, to stifle the cry of want, nor to brave the stroke of universal bankruptcy. There is but one means left to satisfy the country, to avert these evils, or to redeem the pledged faith of Parliament—Retrenchment, rigorous and severe retrenchment, in every branch and in every article of the public expenditure."—Lord NUGENT's Speech on Lord G. CAVENDISH's motion for reduction of expenditure, April 25, 1816, *Parl. Deb.* xxxvi. 1222</small>

that they rapidly declined from year to year; and in the year 1816, the whole amount raised and coined in South America was only £2,500,000, just a quarter of what the amount raised in all parts of the globe had been ten years before, and only a third of what had been raised and coined in South America in 1805.[1]*

> [1] Alison's Europe, c. lxvii. 66 84, 87 ; Humboldt's Nouv. Esp. iii. 396, 407.

11. Simultaneous and rapid contraction of the paper currency of Great Britain.

This great diminution in the supply of the precious metals for the use of the globe was necessarily attended by a general fall of prices over the whole world, and was one great cause of the poverty and suffering which every where prevailed. But its effect was most seriously aggravated, in the particular case of Great Britain, by the simultaneous and still more serious contraction in its paper circulation, and the credit afforded to its merchants, by the declared intentions of Government in regard to the resumption of cash payments by the Bank of England. By the existing law under which that establishment acted, it was provided that the restriction on cash payments should continue "for six months after the conclusion of a general peace, and *no longer*."[2] As the time had now arrived when it was necessary to come to some resolution on the subject, because the six months was on the point of expiring, Ministers proposed that the restriction should be continued till the 5th July, 1818, and the Opposition strenuously contended for its being continued only to 5th July, 1817. The former resolution was adopted; but the discussion of the subject, and the difficulty Government had in carrying the prolonged period, spread such a panic among bankers, that the commercial paper under discount at the Bank of England, which in 1810 had been, on an average, £20,070,000, sunk in 1816 to £11,416,400, and in 1817 to £3,960,000 ; and the country bankers' notes in circulation, which in 1814 had amounted to £22,700,000, had sunk in 1816 to £15,096,000. Nothing in so prodigious a contraction at once of the precious metals for the use of the globe, and of the paper accommodation and circulation of Great Britain in particular, saved the country from absolute ruin, but the continuation of the restriction on cash payments by the Bank of England, which enabled it to continue its circulation of £27,000,000 of notes undiminished, and the rapid return of the precious metals from the Continent, which, in defiance of all the predictions of the Bullion Committee, flowed back in such quantities to the centre of commerce, on the termination of the demand for them on the Continent for the operations of war, that the Earl of Liverpool said, in his place in Parliament,[3] that it had exceeded his most sanguine expectations; and the price of gold in the English market fell from £5, 8s. which it had been in 1814, to £3, 19s. in 1816.*

> [2] 41 Geo. III. c. 148.

> [3] Part. Deb. xxxiv. 573, 579; Alison's Europe, 2 xcvi. App.

12. Important discussions on the Property Tax and other topics.

The general distress and desponding feelings of the country, arising from the fearful contrast between the sad realities that had ensued on the return of peace and the sanguine expectations of felicity which had so generally been formed, naturally led, as might have been expected, to important discussions in Parliament, and material modifications on our military and naval establishments, and the whole system of British finance. These discussions and measures are the more important, that they form the basis, as it were, of the whole subsequent monetary and financial policy of the empire, and all the incalculable consequences which have flowed from it. The year 1816, the first year of peace, marks the transition from the old to the new system in these respects, and therefore its legislative measures are in an especial manner worthy of attention. Four subjects, each of paramount importance, were brought under discussion—the continuance of the Bank Restriction Act, the continuance of the Property Tax, Agricultural Distress, and the Army and Navy Establishment. The priority, in point of time, belongs to the debate on the property tax; but it is difficult to fix upon any particular occasion on which the discussion on it was brought to a point, as it was renewed almost every night, during two months, on the presentation of successive petitions from all parts of the country on the subject. But, without asserting that they were contained in any one debate, the principal arguments on the subject will be found to be contained in the following summary;

13. Argument against the Property Tax by the Opposition.

On the one hand, it was contended against the continuance of the tax, by Mr. Ponsonby, Mr. Baring, and Mr. Brougham—"The petitions against this tax are innumerable, and all couched in the strongest possible language. They state facts which are undeniable, they advance arguments which are unanswerable. They do not come from any one class or section in the community; they come from *all* sections and all classes, and complain of an oppression from the operation of this tax, which is universal and intolerable. The farmers complain that they are assessed, on an arbitrary rule, on property which does not exist. To pay it, they are consuming their capital; they can neither stock their farms, nor maintain their families, but by encroaching on their substance. How could it be otherwise, when the price of wheat had fallen from 110s. a quarter to 55s. in the last two years, and every other species of agricultural produce in the same proportion? The merchants and bankers are equally loud and emphatic in their denunciation of this iniquitous tax; the petition from the merchants

---

* Gold and silver coin annually raised and coined in South America :

1803...£5,032,227		1810...£5,807,972
1804... 5,058,211		1811... 5,748,584
1805... 7,104,436		1812... 3,619,352
1806... 6,562,142		1813... 3,784,700
1807... 5,356,152		1814... 3,687,219
1808... 6,169,038		1815... 3,161,565
1809... 5,997,853		1816... 2,528,008

—Alison's *Europe*, Appendix, chap. xcvi.

* "Many of the speculations published in the Report of the Bullion Committee had been completely falsified by events. The restoration of peace in 1814, and last year, had had the effect, by stopping the foreign expenditure, of bringing back the specie even more rapidly than ever he had contemplated. But after so long a foreign expenditure as that since 1808, it was not a favorable exchange of a few months which would bring things back to their former level. This would require a considerable time."—Earl of Liverpool's Speech, May 17, 1816, *Parl. Deb.* xxxiv. 571.

and bankers of the city of London is perhaps the most numerously signed and important that ever was presented to Parliament from that or any other city. The impost is peculiarly vexatious and alarming to that class, because it implies an inquisition into their private affairs, at all times hazardous, but doubly so in a period of general gloom and contracted credit such as the present. The landed proprietors, over the whole length and breadth of the land, are equally unanimous on the subject; and it is no wonder it is so — for from their incomes being universally known, and the tax paid, in the first instance, by their tenants, escape or evasion are alike impossible; while from the weight of their debts, and the rapid decline of their rents, the tax, if longer continued, will in all cases essentially diminish, in some entirely sweep away, the residue which may remain to maintain their families, pay the jointures and interest of mortgages with which they are burdened, and enable them to maintain their position in society.

It is in vain to say that Parliament was bound,
14. in keeping faith with the public
It was specially a war creditor, to continue this tax longer. It never was impledged in security of loans; it was the indirect taxes alone which were so impledged. The property tax had been, from first to last, a war tax, and a war tax alone; it was so expressly denominated, both by Mr. Pitt, on his first introduction of it in 1799, and by Lord Henry Petty, on its being raised to ten per cent. in 1806; and the statute imposing it bears evidence of the same understanding, for it is laid on till the 6th of April next, after the conclusion of "a general peace, *and no longer.*"* If any thing could add to the force of these last words, it would be the cunning device adopted of *omitting* them in the hurried renewal of the statute, on the return of Napoleon from Elba last year. It is true, that the faith of Parliament stands pledged to the country on this subject; but it stands pledged to the removal of the tax, not its continuance. The country is now agitated from one end to the other; and it is universally felt that any renewal of the tax, even at the reduced rate of five per cent., and for a single year, is a direct breach of the public faith with the nation, which is little deserved, after the patience with which the tax was borne during the years when it really was unavoidable.

"Equally vain is it to assert, that the continu-
15. ance of the property tax is necessa-
Not necessary ry as a general measure of finance,
as a general and to uphold the credit of the
measure of country. The Chancellor of the
finance. Exchequer says, if it is not continued, there will this year be a deficit of ten millions, which will render it necessary for him to go into the money market and borrow to that amount, which would depress the Funds, and raise the interest of money. But supposing this to be the case; supposing that it is impossible, by economy, and reducing our establishments, to avoid a considerable loan, what is the inconvenience thence arising to that which may be anticipated from the continuance, even for a single year, of this most odious and grinding tax? Nothing whatever. Ministers have told us of the prosperous state of the finances of the country, and adverted to the fact, which is undoubtedly very remarkable, that the Sinking Fund, though trenched upon since 1813, is still twelve millions. What would it take from the efficiency of this fund, to take the interest of the whole loan which may be required, which at the very utmost will not exceed £600,000 a year from that fund? Is not such a measure better than continuing a burden on the country which it is wholly unable to bear, and which threatens, if longer continued, to drain away the resources of the people, and cripple Government most seriously in future years, by preventing the ordinary taxes from continuing productive? What would a loan of nine or ten millions be, which would perhaps be melted in one week into the general transactions of the country? Nothing whatever. And was the House, for so inconsiderable an advantage as avoiding placing the interest of such a loan on the Sinking Fund, to turn a deaf ear 1 Parl. Deb. to the prayers, and shut their eyes to xxxiii. 1210, the distresses of the country, and ruin 1226; and their character in the opinion of their xxxiv. 439, constituents?"¹ 442.

On the other hand, it was contended by Lord Liverpool, Lord Castlereagh, and
16.
the Chancellor of the Exchequer— Argument on "The principle on which the prop- the other side erty tax was originally proposed by by the Ministry.
Mr. Pitt, and subsequently extended
by Lord Lansdowne, was not merely to avoid the inconvenience of a large loan. The principle was, that it is important to provide a large supply within the year, in preference to the indefinite extension of permanent taxation by the indefinite accumulation of debt, as had been the case, and thereby to provide for the vigorous prosecution of the war, and for the future relief of the nation in peace. These objects had both been gained; and by the unswerving prosecution of this system, and the patience with which it had been borne by the nation, we had now nine millions less of permanent taxes to pay than we should have had if the opposite system had been continued. The burdens laid on during the war had been, upon the whole, collected with so much wisdom and success, that now the Consolidated Fund had a greater surplus than in the year 1791, or than was even hoped for by the Finance Committee of that year. We had now a surplus of £2,500,000, with a Sinking Fund of £11,000,000—in other words, £13,500,000 annually applicable to the reduction of debt. Could such a favorable state of things have arisen, had not the vigorous measure of a large property tax been adopted; and now that its fruits were beginning to be reaped, is it to be abandoned?

"To show that there is no breach of faith with the nation in proposing the con-
17.
tinuance of the property tax for two No breach of years longer, it is only necessary to faith in its recollect, that when the property continuance tax was raised to ten per cent by the Whig Administration in 1807, and when a permanent system of war expenditure, estimated at £32,000,000, was adopted, it was contemplated that

* "Be it enacted, that this Act shall commence and take effect from the 5th of April 1806, and that the said Act, and the duties thereof, shall continue in force during the present war, and until the 6th of April next, after the definitive signature of a treaty of peace, *and no longer*."— 1 *Property Tax Debate.*

the loans which would be necessary should be secured by mortgage of *all* the war taxes, including the property tax. It was no doubt said by the noble Marquis (Lansdowne), then Chancellor of the Exchequer, that if the war continued only seven years, it would not be necessary to mortgage the property tax; and it was also true, that instead of the war expenditure being on an average £32,000,000, it had been £52,000,000 since that time, and the contest had lasted more than seven years; but that only showed the more clearly, that the mortgage of all the war taxes was contemplated by those who extended the property tax, and that the outcry now raised as to a breach of faith with the public, in proposing its continuance, is entirely without foundation, seeing the very event has occurred which was always looked to as rendering its prolongation necessary.

18. The petitions for its repeal not unanimous.

"Nothing but an imperious sense of duty could have induced his Majesty's Ministers to propose the continuance, even for a short period, of a burden in opposition to the general reluctance which it was foreseen would be felt to submit to heavy taxation after the conclusion of the war, more especially when very severe distress was at the same time experienced from extraneous and temporary causes. But Government would be shrinking from its first duty, if it did not persevere in the course they had adopted. The utmost deference was due to the public voice on the subject; but, numerous as the petitions against the tax had been, they are not so expressive of general opinion as might at first sight appear. They are in all 400, of which one-third come from the two counties of Devon and Cornwall. Manchester, Liverpool, Glasgow, and all the great commercial towns, are divided on the subject. When this is considered, and the great popularity of any reduction of taxation is kept in view, it is not going too far to assert, that the strength of the demand for the remission of the tax has been much overrated, and that all that can be said is, that the nation is strongly agitated, and much divided on the subject.

19. Necessity for its continuance.

"But supposing the popular demand on the subject to be as strong as is represented on the other side, there are considerations connected with the financial situation of the country which render it the painful but necessary duty of Government to withstand it. In round numbers, the expenses for the present year may be calculated at £30,000,000, exclusive of the permanent expenditure arising from the interest of the debt. There is good reason, however, to hope that this large sum would be reduced next year by a third, or to about £20,000,000. All the retrenchments proposed by the gentlemen opposite, even if carried with unflinching rigor into full effect, would not reduce this sum by more than £2,000,000 annually. This, then, being our necessary expenses, what are our resources to meet them? Much has been said about borrowing on the credit of the Sinking Fund, or even applying a large part of that fund at once to the current expenses of the year. But as that fund does not now much exceed £11,000,000 a year, after what has been taken from it during the last three years, if it is to be applied in whole or in part to meet the current exigencies of the year, the country will soon be in the situation of having a debt of above £700,000,000, without any fund whatever to look to for its redemption. It is upon that ground that Government feel themselves imperatively called upon by the duty they owe to the country to resist the abolition of this tax. If it is withdrawn, Government, as a matter of necessity, must go into the market and borrow this year twelve, next year six or seven, millions: what effect will this have upon the price of the Funds, and, through it, on the rate of interest in the country? And if capital is kept locked up, or advances rendered costly by this cause, how are country gentlemen, how are merchants and traders, to obtain the accommodation necessary to carry on their undertakings, or overcome the difficulties with which they are surrounded? Would the British people, with the good sense and spirit which animated them, now shrink from the exertion which was necessary for their own preservation?—would they, in fact, be so infatuated as to turn their backs upon themselves?"[1]

1 Parl. Deb. xxxiii. 1217. 1222; xxxiv. 447, 450.

20. Abolition of the tax.

Notwithstanding the manliness of this appeal, which came with so much weight from the Ministers who had brought the contest to a triumphant issue, and the cogent nature of those arguments, such was the weight of the public voice that it proved irresistible. Upon a division, the motion for the entire abolition of the tax was carried by a majority of 37—the number being 201 and 238. The division was received with rapturous cheering in the House, which continued for several minutes; and the joyous sound being heard in Palace Yard, the huzzas soon spread through the dense crowd there assembled, and in a few minutes over all London. Never, since the battle of Waterloo, had such general joy been felt through the nation as was on this occasion; nothing like it occurred again till the second capture of Cabul and the conclusion of the Chinese war were announced in a single Delhi gazette. We must not estimate the universal transports felt on this occasion by what would be felt if the modified income-tax of seven-pence in the pound, introduced in 1842 by Sir R. Peel, was now abolished—for his was a light burden in comparison, and it extended to persons enjoying an income of £150 and upward alone; whereas the former was a tax of two shillings in the pound, and extended to all incomes of £50 and upward. As the heavier tax, when it was taken off, was producing at ten per cent. £15,000,000 a year, the assessable income of Great Britain must have been, at that period, £150,000,000 a year. And when we take into consideration the innumerable evasions generally practised, especially among the manufacturing and trading classes, where such were so easy and difficult of detection, it is within bounds to conclude, that the aggregate incomes of persons in Great Britain above £50 must at that period have been at least £200,000,000; an astonishing fact, when it is recollected that the whole inhabitants of the island did not, at that period, exceed thirteen millions; and that the nation had just concluded a war of twenty years' duration, in the course of which £600,000,000 had been added to the public debt, and the sums annually raised by taxation progressively increased from £20,000,000 to £72,000,000.[1]

*Part. Deb.
xxx-xxi. Ann.
Reg 1816, 26.*

In considering this subject, which has been of such moment in the subsequent financial and social condition of the British empire, it will probably be found, as is generally the case in such questions, that there was some truth, and not a little error, in the opinions advanced on both sides. Lord Castlereagh was unquestionably in the right when he so strenuously contended for preserving inviolate the Sinking Fund, and not, by the remission of taxation, leaving the nation in the situation of having £700,000,000 of debt, without any provision for its redemption. The manly stand which he made against a loud public clamor on this ground, is one of the most honorable, as, unhappily, it is one of the LAST, recorded in British history. But he seems as clearly to have erred in the ground which he selected for making this stand. He should never have chosen it on the question of upholding a heavy and unpopular *direct* tax. The great and wise principle of English finance, so constantly acted upon by Mr. Pitt, was to provide for the interest of debt and the Sinking Fund for its redemption by indirect taxes, and to reserve direct taxes as an extraordinary war resource, to continue only to its termination. The emphatic declaration in the Property Tax Act, that it was to "continue till the 6th April next, after the conclusion of a definitive treaty of peace, *and no longer,*" proves that this was in an especial manner the case with that burden. In striving to uphold it after peace was concluded, Government was not less violating the pledge given to the nation, on its imposition, than departing from the true principles of finance on the subject. If loans for a year or two after the conclusion of the war were necessary to wind up its expenses, they should, without hesitation, have been contracted in preference to continuing an oppressive *direct* war tax. The real error, and it was a most fatal one, was the unnecessary and often uncalled-for remission of indirect taxation in after years, by successive administrations bidding against each other in the race for popularity, which at first crippled and at length extinguished the Sinking Fund; but that mournful topic belongs to a subsequent part of this History.

22.
Vital considerations on the question, which were overlooked at this time.

There is another observation on this subject, suggested by the tenor of these debates, which will frequently recur to the mind in the discussion of great and momentous questions in subsequent years. This is, that the most material parts of the argument, and the most vital consequences likely to flow from the measures under discussion, were not alluded to on either side in the course of the debate in Parliament. They were either unseen, or, if seen, were carefully concealed by both parties. Thus the most material points in any discussion upon the property tax, and those upon which public attention has been chiefly fixed when it was brought forward in after times, undoubtedly are,—the injustice of taxing income derived from precarious or perishable sources, at the same rate as that derived from land, or fixed and imperishable investment—the extreme severity of direct taxation, when it is at all considerable, compared with indirect, when it is most productive; and the injustice of levying a heavy direct tax upon a small class of society—viz., that possessing an income above a certain level—from which all the rest of the people are exempt. Yet these topics are never once alluded to, in the course of the almost daily discussions which took place on the subject, in presenting petitions in this year, during two months! They are the topics, however, upon which most stress should always be laid, when this subject is again brought forward in future times, for they lie at its very foundation. They touch the all-important subject of the ability of the people to bear the burden—a topic far more momentous to them than interesting to their rulers. Yet, in reality, it is a topic which eventually must touch their rulers as much as themselves; for no taxes can long be levied by Government which trench deep upon the resources, and seriously abridge the comforts, of the people. Of these, however, direct taxes are, beyond all question, the most oppressive, and felt as most severe, for they always fall upon a limited class, generally not more than a thirtieth part of the community, in whose hands, however, they arrest the funds which maintain the whole; and, not being mixed up with the price of articles of consumption, their whole weight is made palpable to the people. Indirect taxes are so blended with the cost of articles that their existence is not perceived; and they are spread over so wide a surface, that their burden is not felt. No nation was ever seriously injured by taxes on luxuries consumed, because the very fact of their being consumed proved that they could be afforded, and had been paid for; but many have been utterly destroyed by direct taxation, because it seizes upon income, or eats in on capital before it is expended; and ruins the poor, when they imagine they do not pay the tax, by checking the growth of capital, and draining away the funds which should purchase the produce of their industry.

It was generally supposed at the time that Ministers would have resigned, upon Parliament having negatived a proposal forming so important a part of their financial system; but, instead of doing so, they equally surprised the House of Commons and the country, by voluntarily proposing, two days afterward, the entire remission of the war duty on malt—a tax producing at that time £2,700,000 a year. The reason assigned by them for this unlooked-for boon was, that as the abolition of the income tax would render it indispensable for them to go into the money market to meet the exigencies of the year, it was of little moment whether they borrowed a few millions more or less; and, therefore, that it was deemed advisable to give a material relief to the agricultural interest, which was laboring under a severer depression than any other class. There can be no question that there was much truth in this observation, although there were not wanting shrewd observers, who remarked that the boon would never have been heard of, if Ministers had not received a shake, and that this showed that the best way to inspire Government with philanthropic feelings was to make them afraid. Be this as it may, the remission of the tax was hailed with delight by the leaders of the agricul-

23.
Remission of the war Malt Tax. March.

tural interest in Parliament; and being levied on a beverage which the people in great part prepared for themselves, there can be no doubt that it was felt as a relief by the people generally, contrary to what too often obtains with the remission of indirect taxes, which only swell the profits of the dealers in the articles, without lessening their cost to the consumers.¹

¹ Parl. Deb. lxxxiii. 436; Ann. Regist. 1816, 26.

As the abolition of the property tax, and the remission of the war duty on malt, occasioned a loss to the Exchequer of fully £17,000,000 a year, it became necessary for Ministers to revise entirely their estimates for the year, and reduce the expenditure in proportion to the large defalcation in their resources. This was accordingly done, and with a success beyond the most sanguine expectations of the country: £3,000,000 was borrowed from the Bank; and this, with the issue of Exchequer bills to the amount of as much more, supplied the deficiencies of the Exchequer. The reduction of the estimates gave rise to warm debates in both houses of Parliament, which are important as evincing the ideas then afloat in the country, and forming the basis on which the whole pacific expenditure of the nation since that time has been bunded. The reduction effected was very great, for the expenditure, irrespective of the debt, was reduced from £62,000,000 to £25,000,000, and the loan for England and Ireland together was only £8,900,000. But the debates are peculiarly valuable, as evincing the temper of the nation on this all-important subject.¹ *

24. Reduced estimates formed by Government.

¹ Ann. Reg 1816, 70.

On the part of the Opposition, it was contended by Mr. Ponsonby, Mr. Tierney, and Lord Cavendish—"War is only borne because it is hoped it may lead to peace; and warlike expenditure, because it may pave the way for pacific reductions. But, according to the system now pursued, we are to have the evils and burdens of war without the blessings and reductions of peace. When we con-

25. Argument for a reduction of expenditure by the Opposition.

---

* The following Table, exhibiting the national expenditure for 1815 and 1816, as estimated, will show the great reductions effected in all branches of the public expenditure in the latter year:

Supply. 1815.		Supply. 1816.		
Army	£13,876,757	Army	£9,665,666	
Extraordinaries	23,983,061	Deduct troops in France	1,234,596	£8,431,070
Barracks	99,000			
Navy	18,644,209	Extraordinaries		1,500,000
Ordnance	4,431,643	Commissariat	480,000	
Miscellaneous	3,000,000	Deduct in France	75,000	
				405,000
	£62,135,030	Barracks		178,000
		Stores		50,000
Loans to foreign powers	11,035,247	Navy		9,431,440
		Ordnance	1,882,188	
Permanent Burdens.		Deduct in France	186,003	
Interest of debt Funded, and Sinking Fund	£41,015,527			1,696,185
Do. of Unfunded	3,014,003	Miscellaneous		2,500,000
		Indian debt		945,491
	£117,199,816			£25,140,186
		Permanent Burdens.		
		Interest of Funded debt and Sinking Fund		43,410,059
		Interest of Exchequer Bills		2,196,177
		Foreign loans	£1,731,139	
		Ireland	2,581,148	
				4,312,287
				£75,558,709

The expenditure for 1816, however, in reality reached £80,185,828, as various articles of outlay exceeded the estimate.—See Ann. Reg. 1816, 70, 71; and 1817, 256, 257.

To meet this expenditure, which even in the last of the two years was immense, the following were the receipts for the two years:

WAYS AND MEANS.

1815. Ordinary Revenue, nett.		1816. Ordinary Revenue, nett.	
Customs	£9,070,554	Customs	£8,169,780
Excise	25,539,098	Excise	19,013,630
Stamps	6,139,585	Stamps	6,181,288
Land and assessed	7,604,016	Land and assessed	7,257,906
Post-office	1,755,830	Post-office	1,659,854
Lesser resources	189,352	Lesser resources	67,240
Ordinary and hereditary revenue	£45,197,368	Permanent ordinary	£42,370,130
		Hereditary revenue	165,270
Extraordinary.		Extraordinary.	
Customs	£2,280,634	Customs	£1,067,810
Excise	6,537,628	Excise	4,581,637
Property-tax	14,078,248	Property-tax last year	12,039,120
Lottery	304,651	Lottery	231,080
Paid by Ireland	3,981,783	Interest of loans for Ireland	4,558,558
Irish expenditure	6,107,986	Ireland's share of expenses	1,181,099
Loans	39,121,950	Unclaimed dividends	333,536
Lesser heads	417,211	Lesser heads	131,000
Total	£119,370,629	Total without loans	£66,579,420
		Loan, including Ireland	8,939,802
		Total	£75,519,222

—"Finance Statement," Ann Reg 1816, 420; and 1817, 210.

VOL. I.—C

sider the enormous amount of our national debt, and the complete triumph of our arms which was purchased by it, nothing can be more evident than that at no former period were large reductions in our peace establishment both more loudly called for, or more safe and practicable, than at the present moment. What is the value of our boasted victories, if, after they have been gained, we are obliged to remain armed at all points, as before the contest in which they were achieved commenced? Some reductions, it is true, have been made, but on a scale by no means proportioned to the necessities of the case; and if our financial situation is considered, it will at once appear that, unless the expenditure is reduced on a very different scale from what has hitherto been attempted, the empire will be involved in inextricable difficulties.

26.
Continued.
"The total sums required to be provided for the service of the year amount, according to the statement of the Chancellor of the Exchequer, to £31,683,000, of which the establishments of the country formed upward of £28,000,000. In addition to this, by the Treaty of Union, two-seventeenths of the joint expenditure of the empire was to be charged to the account of Ireland; and such was now the financial situation of that country, that its finances were not equal even to the payment of the interest of its debt—so that, instead of its contributing any thing at all to the joint expenses of the United Kingdom, Great Britain would have to advance £997,000 to make up its deficiencies. Thus the whole sum we have to provide for the service of the year is about thirty-two millions and a half. To meet this sum, the surplus in the hands of the Chancellor of the Exchequer, according to his own account, is £12,700,000, leaving a deficiency in the first year of peace of no less than £19,981,000! It would be some consolation if we could flatter ourselves that this immense deficit was owing to winding up the expense of the war, and that any considerable reduction of it could be hoped for if our present establishment continued in future years. But this was very far from being the case. When the items of the expenditure are looked into, it appears that they are all permanent, arising from the current expenses of the year; and so far from there being any prospect of a reduction in future, it is evident that next year the charges of the nation must be increased £1,000,000, and that for ever, to meet the interest of the sum to be borrowed in this very year, to meet its excess of expenditure above income. If that is our condition in time of peace, and with all the security derived from the greatest triumphs, can any thing be so deplorable as our financial situation?

27.
Continued.
"If the establishment maintained in the different parts of the empire at this time be compared with what it was in 1792, the difference is prodigious, and wholly unaccounted for by any increased necessities of our situation. On the contrary, if there is any difference, it should be found in the diminished force now required, from the enhanced security which our commanding situation and unparalleled victories have now procured for us. Nevertheless, Government propose just the reverse; the establishment they have submitted to the House is more than double of what it was in 1792. The two years stand thus:

	1792.	1816.
	Men.	Men.
Great Britain	15,919	32,000
Old Colonies	16,848	27,000
Ireland	16,000	28,000
New Colonies	—	25,000
	48,767	112,000

Exclusive of troops in France and India.

"If to these forces be added the troops in France and India, which are maintained by their respective countries, and comprise at least 50,000 men, it follows that we have now above 160,000 men in arms in a period of profound peace, and immediately after the conclusion of a war which is boasted of as having given us unexampled security. All that we have gained, if the statement of Ministers be correct, by a war which has quadrupled our public debt, is, that we have incurred a necessity of tripling our military establishment." 1 Parl. Deb. xxxii. 1194, 1202.

28.
Argument on the other side, by Ministers.
On the other hand, it was contended by Lord Liverpool, Lord Palmerston, and Lord Castlereagh—"Much of the embarrassments and difficulties of the country during war have always arisen from our establishment in peace having been brought to so low an ebb that, on the first breaking out of hostilities, we were either absolutely powerless, or, if we attempted any thing, were constantly, for some years, involved in disaster. This was particularly the case during the first years of the American and the late war —on the last of which occasions Mr. Pitt, by whom the reductions were made, expressed bitter regret that he had been instrumental in reducing the establishment, during the previous peace, to so low an ebb that the fairest opportunity of bringing the war to an early and successful termination was lost. It was to the liberty we enjoyed that the industry and exertion which happily distinguished England from many of the Continental powers were to be ascribed; and to these advantages, which a free people only could possess, we owed all our superiority, which would not be in the smallest degree affected by the magnitude or diminution of our peace establishment.

29.
Continued.
"It is a very easy matter to compare our peace establishment in 1816 with what it was in 1792, and to ask, how, when we have been successful in the war, an additional and much larger military force is requisite. Is it not well known—has it not passed into a maxim in history—that success only multiplies the demand for increased means of defense, by widening the circle from which hostility may be apprehended? Our empire in the colonies has been more than doubled during the war; and are we to be told that, after having been won with so much difficulty, they are not worth preserving, but must be abandoned, for want of a protective force, to the first enemy who chooses to grasp them? Look around upon the colonies, and say whether there is any one of them for which a supply of soldiers has been voted larger than is absolutely necessary. The fact is notoriously the reverse; they are all so under-garrisoned that the men stationed there will be over-worked, and fall

victims to fatigue and the diseases of tropical climates. The new colonies obtained during the war were proposed to be garrisoned by 22,000 men, of whom not more than 15,000 could be reckoned on as effective; whereas the aggregate of effective soldiers who marched out of them, when they were taken, was upward of 30,000. In some of the old colonies—as Jamaica and Canada—it was proposed to station a force considerably larger than had been there before the war; but that was because America had become a considerable military and naval power, in consequence of the events of its later years.

"In regard to the home stations, the number allotted for Great Britain is 25,000, being about 7000 more than the quota of 1792. But is that an excessive addition, when the increase which during the war has taken place in our population and resources is considered? The first has increased a fourth; the last, if measured by our exports, imports, and shipping, have more than doubled. The augmentation of the army at home was by no means in the same proportion. In proportion as our colonial force is augmented, the troops at home, by whom they are to be fed or relieved, must be increased also. Then if, in addition to all this, the vast additions made to the armies of the Continental powers during the war, and the magnitude of their peace establishments, be taken into consideration, it must become at once apparent that not merely our respectability, but our very existence as an independent nation, was involved in resisting the reduction now proposed. The question at issue is not whether, by reductions in our establishment, we can get quit of the income-tax or loans in its stead, for by no possible reduction can that object be effected. It is, whether we shall compel the Crown to abandon all our colonial possessions, fertile sources of our commercial wealth, and whether we should descend from that elevated station which it had cost us so much labor, blood, and treasure to attain.

30. Continued.

"It is unfair to charge the whole expense of the army being £9,800,000 proposed this year, to the account of our present establishments: £2,000,000 of it is absorbed in pensions to those gallant men, now for the most part retired, who have borne us through the perils of the contest; £1,600,000 is applied to the forces embodied at present, which will be disbanded in the course of the year—particularly the regular militia and foreign corps, which are to be entirely reduced. Let it be recollected, too, that since the year 1792 the pay of the soldiers had been doubled—it had been raised from sixpence to a shilling a day, which added at least a third to the total expense of our military establishment. If these things are taken into consideration, it will be found that the proposed military establishment, so far from being excessive, is in reality extremely moderate, and could not be reduced in the present circumstances of Europe, the empire, and the world, without serious detriment to our national character, and the most serious danger to our national independence."¹

31. Concluded.

- Parl. Deb. xxxiii. 813, 872; and xxxiv. 1204, 1210.

Notwithstanding the force of these arguments, and the obvious inexpedience of too rapidly reducing the national establishments, from the pernicious effect which throwing a vast number of idle hands at once upon the labor market would have, such was the strength of the public cry for economy, and such the necessities of Government after the great resource of the property tax was withdrawn, that very great reductions became necessary in the army, against which the chief complaints were directed. The establishment was ultimately fixed at 111,756 men, deducting the foreign corps disbanded in the course of the year, and the troops in France and in the East India Company's territories. Including them, the number was 196,027.* The regular militia, 80,000 strong, and about 50,000 of the regular army were disbanded in the course of the year. For the navy 33,000 men were voted—a great and immediate reduction from 100,000, who had been voted in the preceding year. Great part of these copious reductions did not take effect till the succeeding year, and so had little effect in lessening the expenditure of this; but the disbanding of so large a number as 200,000 men from the two services, including the regular militia, however unavoidable, had a most prejudicial effect upon the labor market, and tended much to augment the suffering so generally felt by the working classes, from the diminution of employment, and the distressed condition both of the agricultural and manufacturing population.¹

32. Establishments ultimately voted

¹ Parl. Deb. xxxii. 812, 817. Ann. Reg. 816, 9, 10.

Agricultural distress, as might well have been expected, from the difficulties so generally experienced by that important class of the community who were engaged in the cultivation of the soil, holds a very prominent place among the subjects of parliamentary discussion in this year. The debates of course terminated in nothing effective being done for the relief of the landed interest; for the causes of this distress were either altogether beyond the reach of remedy on the part of Government, or they arose from measures connected with the currency, which the legislature was inclined to render more stringent rather than the reverse. But they are not, on that account, the less valuable in a historical point of view, as tending to indicate the commencement of the operation of those causes of a general nature which, ere long, had so important an influence on British prosperity, and came to exercise so decisive an effect on the legislation and destinies of the empire.

33. Debates on agricultural distress.

On the part of the Opposition, it was contended by Mr. Brougham, Mr. Tierney, and Mr.

---

* Army estimate for 1816

Land forces, including corps intended to be	Men.	Cost. £
reduced	111,756	4,702,611
Regiments in France	34,031	1,234,596
Regiments in India	28,491	906,601
Foreign corps	21,404	370,069
Recruiting Staff	344	20,835
	196,027	
		11,123,577
Deduct in	with lesser charges,	
France	34,031	£1,234,596
Do in India	28,491	906,604
	62,522	2,141,190
Remains	133,505	£8,982,387

—Parl. Deb. xxxii. 842.

Western:—" It is superfluous to say any thing on the amount and universality of the distress which exists in the country at this time. That, unhappily, is matter of notoriety, and is universally admitted. If any doubt could exist upon the subject it would be removed by the petition presented this very night from Cambridgeshire, in which it is stated that every single individual in a parish in that county, with one exception, has become bankrupt or a pauper, and that that one, in consequence, has fallen from a state of affluence to ruin, from the rates all falling upon him. The real point for consideration is, to what is this universal and overwhelming distress owing? In 1792, the average price of wheat was 47s. a quarter, now (April 9) it is 57s.—almost twenty per cent higher; yet no complaint of ruin from low prices was heard before the war. On the contrary, such a state of things was with reason hailed as the greatest possible blessing, as the first fruits of peace and plenty. We must seek for other causes, therefore, for the present distress, than in the mere fact of low prices; and those causes seem to be chiefly the following:

"The years 1796 and 1799, it is well known, were years of very bad harvests, and they, of course, raised the price of agricultural produce, and gave a temporary stimulus to cultivation. This was increased by the profuse expenditure of the war, which, not confined to income, lavished in single years the accumulated hoards of previous generations. But the great circumstance which tended to raise prices in a lasting way, was the suspension of cash payments by the Bank of England. This gave such a stimulus to that establishment, and also to all the country banks, that prices not only rose, but were retained at a high level. The consequence was, that the banks were encouraged to advance money to cultivators from the certainty of their obtaining a remunerating price for their produce, and thence a prodigious impulse was given to agriculture in all its branches. Nor is the effect of the vast increase of our colonial possessions to be overlooked, which has operated not merely by increasing our exports and imports, but, in a far more important degree, by promoting enterprise in the cultivation of our own soil. This appears from the great amount of riches which was remitted from these colonial possessions to purchase or improve land in Great Britain; and the source from which that wealth has come may be distinctly traced in the names of estates and farms, especially in Scotland, which are in many places taken from that of places—as Berbice, Surinam, or the like—in the East or West Indies. Lastly, among the causes which gave so great an impulse to agriculture during the war, we must assign a very prominent place to Napoleon's Continental blockade, which not only gave our cultivators, during the last seven years of its continuance, an almost entire monopoly of the home market for agricultural produce, but, by throwing the whole foreign commerce of the world into our hands, powerfully promoted the prosperity of our seaport and manufacturing towns, and through them reacted upon that of the most distant parts of the country.

"In consequence of this combination of circumstances, most of which were of a casual or temporary nature, there has occurred in this country what may without impropriety be called an *over-trading in agriculture*, and consequent redundance of agricultural produce. Inclosure bills to the amount of twelve hundred have been passed during the last ten years, and the number of acres thereby brought into cultivation has been estimated at two millions. Certain it is that, between the newly inclosed land and the improvement of that which was formerly under cultivation, at least the produce of two millions of acres, which may be taken at six millions of quarters of grain, has been added to the national supply. But the population of the island has only increased two millions during the war, and taking a quarter of grain for the average consumption of each individual, it follows that two millions of quarters only have been added to the demand, and six millions to the supply. This sufficiently explains the glut of agricultural produce, and consequent fall of prices, and the distress which now universally prevails among the cultivators and landed proprietors.

"Supposing, as is perhaps the case, that these calculations of political arithmetic are not altogether to be trusted, we may rely on a much safer testimony, the evidence of our own senses, to be convinced of the extraordinary advance which our agriculture has made of late years. The improvements in most parts of the country have been so great that the most careless observer must have been struck by them. Not only have wastes for miles and miles disappeared, giving place to houses, fences, and crops; not only have even the most inconsiderable commons, the very village greens, and little stripes of sward by the wayside, been subjected to division and exclusive ownership, but the land which formerly grew something has been fatigued with labor and loaded with capital until it yielded much more. The work both of men and cattle has been economized, new skill has been applied, and a more dexterous combination of different kinds of husbandry practiced, until, without at all comprehending the waste lands wholly added to the productive territory of the nation, it may be safely said, not, perhaps, that two blades of grass now grow where only one grew before, but certainly that five now grow where only four used to be; and that this kingdom, which foreigners were wont to taunt as a mere manufacturing and trading country, inhabited by a shopkeeping nation, is in reality, for its size, *by far the greatest agricultural state in the world.*

"It is since 1810 that these causes have in an especial manner come into operation, as appears in the price of wheat which, on an average, has been above 100s. the quarter since that time—a striking contrast to the woeful depression which has taken place since the peace. What is very remarkable, this depression is the very reverse of what took place on former pacifications; for on the peace of Paris, in 1763, wheat rose from 36s. to 41s. a quarter, and to 42s. 6d. on an average of five years ending 1767; and on the peace of Versailles, in 1784, it rose 5s. a quarter. In the present contest, however, the battle of Leipsic, which induced the hope of a speedy peace, at once lowered the price from 120s. to 86s., and before November 1813, wheat was at 68s. No man who attends to these figures and dates, can doubt that the fall of prices was connected with the prospect of an approaching termination of the war. Nor is it difficult to see how it is that this effect took place. A sudden diminution of expenditure, to the extent of £50,000,000 annually by the Government of this country alone, could not take place without immediately affecting the market both for manufactured and rude produce; and a derangement in the former is sure, sooner or later to be followed by distress in the latter. The commercial and manufacturing difficulties of 1811 and 1812, which are yet fresh in all our recollections, contributed powerfully to increase the dangers of our mercantile situation; for after the cramped and almost blockaded situation in which we had been kept for several years, a sudden rush into speculations and adventures took place on the reopening of the European harbors, which was so violent that it seized all classes of the community, and induced unheard-of losses. English goods were soon selling cheaper at Buenos Ayres and in the north of Europe, than either in London or Manchester. All this reacted, and that quickly, too, on agriculture; for the commercial interests of the country can never suffer without its being felt, and that right speedily, by the cultivators of the soil, who mainly live on their expenditure.

"Excessive taxation is the last, and perhaps the most powerful cause to which the present depressed condition of the agriculturists is to be ascribed. During the last twenty-five years, our revenue has increased from £15,000,000 to £66,000,000—our expenditure in one year exceeded £125,000,000; in this year of peace it is to be £72,000,000, and no hopes are held out of its being permanently below £65,000,000. These figures sound immense, and convey an idea of apparently interminable resources; but if we descend into detail, and examine how, in so short a time, so prodigious an increase of revenue has been effected, the illusion will be dispelled, and it will at once appear that it is owing to excessive and grinding taxation. Not only has the direct taxation risen to a most enormous amount—certainly not less, while the income-tax lasted, than 15 per cent. on the income of all persons liable to that tax—but the most ordinary and indispensable necessaries of life have come to be taxed with a severity which almost amounts to a prohibition. The duty on salt, which in 1792 was 10d. a bushel, had been raised, previous to 1806, to 15s., its present amount. The tax on leather has been doubled within the last four years. The duty on malt has been raised from 10s. 7d. a quarter to 31s. 6d., of which 16s. is war duty; that on beer from 5s. 7d. (in 1802) to 9s. 7d.; that on spirits from 7d. to 1s. 9d. Sugar is taxed 30s. per cwt., instead of 15s., the rate in 1792.

"Add to all this, also, the excessive inequality and injustice of our mode of levying and rating for the poor-rate. The whole burden of maintaining the poor is laid upon the land; and this reduces the price of labor below its natural level, at the sole expense of the cultivator. The money raised for the relief of the poor is, in direct opposition to the intention of the 43d Elizabeth, from a defect in the Act, laid entirely upon the land. Manufacturers and merchants are rated only as owners of large houses. In this way it often happens that a man who has an income of £10,000 a year from trade, is rated no higher than one who derives £500 a year from land. The gross injustice of this is rendered more glaring from the fact—the manufacturer creates the poor, and leaves the farmer to maintain them. The farmer employs a few hands only, the manufacturer a whole colony; the former causes no material augmentation in the number of paupers, the latter multiplies them wholesale; the first creates the poor, leaving it to the last to maintain them. In addition to this injustice, which is glaring enough, the custom has spread widely, and become almost universal, of 'making up,' as it is called, wages to a certain level out of the poor-rates; a system which has just the effect of compelling the land to bear, not only its own burdens, but part of the wages of all employed by the rest of the community. The magnitude of this burden may be estimated from the fact, that the total sum levied for the use of the poor, which before the American war was under £2,000,000, now exceeds £8,000,000. When, in addition to this huge burden, it is considered how large a proportion of the taxation of £66,000,000 annually is paid by the land, the price of the produce of which has sunk within eighteen months to half its former amount, it will cease to be surprising that the agricultural interest should be suffering, and evident that no substantial relief can be expected, as long as these burdens continue to oppress it."[1]

On the other hand, it was maintained by Lord Liverpool, Lord Castlereagh, and Mr. Vansittart—"It is so far consolatory to find that the Bank Restriction Act of 1797, which has been so often held out as the cause of all our calamities, is now admitted, not only to have had no such effect, but to have produced in some part at least, great prosperity. In fact it has been the main-spring of our strength; and no reasonable man can now deny that, had it not been for that measure, this country must long since have sunk in the conflict, and we have become a province of France. It is now seen, and admitted on the other side, by whom the system had so long and vehemently been condemned, that it was not only by this wise measure of Mr. Pitt's that the country has been saved, but that under this artificial circulating medium the prosperity of the country, even during war, had increased to an unparalleled degree.

"The existing distress is to be ascribed entirely to the simple fact, that during the last two years, and particularly during the last year, the great and necessary articles of human consumption have been depreciated at least a half. Every one knows what effect so great a change must produce on any interest in the community. What, then, must it be upon the farming property of the empire—that great interest which creates,

---

* The above is a mere skeleton of the able and instructive speech of Mr., now Lord Brougham, on this important subject.

notwithstanding all the increase of our manufactures, at least nine-tenths of the entire wealth of the empire? Then how has this great depreciation been brought about? It began, as has been correctly stated, in 1813, and the cause to which it was then owing was very obvious. It was the prospect of the opening of the Baltic harbors, and the letting in of the great harvests of Poland on our markets, coupled with the fine season of that year, which produced the fall. The farmers of this country, who, from the effects of war had long enjoyed a monopoly in the home market, were suddenly exposed to the competition of great grain-growing countries, where corn could be raised at a third of the cost at which alone it can here be reared. It was to mitigate this danger, one of the most appalling which could befall any nation, that the corn law of 1814 was passed, without which the depression, great as it has been, would have been far greater.* It is consolatory to find that that measure, which, at the time it was introduced, was the subject of such unmeasured condemnation by the gentlemen opposite, is now admitted to have not only been a necessary measure in our own defense, but the only effectual antidote to the still greater difficulties in which we are now involved.

"Corn, which in 1812 was selling at 120s. or 130s. the quarter, has now fallen to 56s. Nothing more was requisite to explain the agricultural distress which every where prevailed. It induced that most fearful of all contests which can agitate a community, the contest of *class with class* in the struggle to shake the burden off upon each other. But there is no reason to believe that this alarming contest will continue long. Shut out as this country is, in a great measure, from foreign supply, there is no reasonable room for doubt that the price of wheat will gradually rise to an average of 80s. and, with it, the profits of agricultural industry again reach a remunerative level. Great pressure is unhappily now felt, and some land has probably been brought into tillage which had better have been left in pasturage. There was no reason to suppose that the paper circulation was excessive, or would produce any very dangerous convulsion; still less that the great mass of agriculture was in a tottering state. It is secured against the only enemy who can beat it down—foreign; it is also secure from domestic competition, arising from other modes of employing capital; this being so, it must in the end attain remunerative prices.

"Coincident with the fall in the price of corn has been a great reduction in the amount of the circulating medium, and with it unhappily has departed the confidence which had existed before. Beyond all question, this is the principal cause of the distress which now generally prevails. But this diminution of the circulating medium is not founded on causes of a permanent nature. The return of peace must eventually lead to the return of old maxims—to the return of those common principles on which the circulation of every country ought to be regulated. All must see that the time is fast approaching when the country will again possess a large circulating medium, and, with it, the means of carrying on

* See *History of Europe*, chap. xcii. §§ 22, 29.

43. *continued.*

44. *Concluded.*

industrial operations of all sorts. The Bank Restriction Act will expire in two years;¹ and before that time comes, the return of the precious metals to the country will have rendered it a safe measure to resume cash payments. But, above all, let it never, under any circumstances, be proposed to trench upon the Sinking Fund, the sheet-anchor of the country, and any serious diminution of which will render its financial affairs altogether desperate."

¹ Parl. Debat. xxxiii. 1119, 1127.

No legislative measure did, or could, result from this debate, how interesting or important soever, for it related to a subject altogether beyond the reach of human remedy. But it was otherwise with another subject closely connected with the former, on which the measures of Government had a great and decisive effect on the future condition and ultimate destinies of the country. The proposal of Government, on this point was, that the Bank should lend the Treasury £6,000,000, and, in return, receive a prolongation of the suspension of cash payments for two years subsequent to 4th July, 1816. In this way, it was thought, the double object would be gained, of providing a supply adequate for the necessities of the state, the resources of which had been so much impaired by the repeal of the property tax, and giving time for the Bank to make the necessary arrangements for the resumption of cash payments. This proposal gave rise to animated and important debates in both Houses of Parliament, which are of the highest importance, as indicating the views entertained at that period on this all-important subject on which subsequent experience has thrown such a flood of light.¹

45. Measures of Government in regard to the restriction of cash payments and a loan from the Bank.

¹ Parl. Debat. xxxiii. 719.

On the part of the Opposition it was contended by Mr. Horner, Mr. Ponsonby, and Mr. Tierney—"If any thing is to be regarded as fixed in the legislation, or to which the Government of the country is pledged, it is that the restriction on cash payments is to continue till the conclusion of a general peace, and no longer. The proposal now made to continue this restriction for two years longer has already had this pernicious effect, that it has thrown a doubt upon the sincerity of all the former professions of Ministers on this subject. The Bank directors had declared, time out of mind, that they were most anxious to resume the system of cash payments; but it now appears that they eagerly grasp at the first opportunity of postponing that happy consummation. They have no objection to continue the system of over issue from which they have so long derived such exorbitant profits. The conduct of the Bank directors evinces such an example of rapacity on the part of a corporate body, and of acquiescence on the part of Government, as stood unrivaled in the financial history of any country of Europe. It is evident that Government have no settled ideas at all upon the subject, but that they have a confused notion that the longer the present system continues the better; and that by mixing up present measures of finance with its prolongation, it may be continued for an indefinite period.

46. Argument of the Opposition against the continuance of the Bank Restriction Act.

"Even when first introduced, and when the fatal principle of making the restriction last as long as the war continued was adopted, it was universally understood, and most solemnly declared, that it was to cease within six months after the conclusion of a general peace. Last year when the prospect of a durable peace was not nearly so favorable as at present, the prolongation was only made to the 5th July in the present year. Now, however, it was to be prolonged for two years longer, for no reason that can possibly be assigned but that it has become mixed up with a loan from the Bank, and is thought to be connected with the general agricultural distress. But if the Bank restriction is to be continued to uphold the profits of the farmers, why is it to be limited to two years? Why not render it perpetual? If the prospect of resuming cash payments is the cause of the agricultural distress, will it not recur, perhaps, with additional force whenever cash payments are resumed? If this view be well founded, we are only postponing the dreaded evil, not averting it.

"Are there no evils arising from the system now going on of indefinitely postponing the resumption of cash payments? During the war we borrowed money when it was of small value, and we are now obliged to pay it off when it is of high value; and this evil is every day increasing with the postponement of cash payments. This is by far the greatest danger which now threatens the country; for the debt was for the most part contracted in one currency, and the taxes, which come in from year to year, are paid in another. A greater and more sudden contraction of the currency has never taken place in any country than in this since the peace, with the exception, perhaps, of France, after the failure of the Mississippi scheme. This sudden contraction has been the cause of all our distresses; it is, and will long continue to be, the cause of all our difficulties. It arose from the previous fall in the price of agricultural produce. This had occasioned a destruction of the country bank paper to an extent which would not have been thought possible without more ruin than had ensued. The Bank of England had also reduced its issues. The average amount of its currency during the last year had not exceeded £25,000,000, while, two years ago, it had been £29,000,000, and at one time was as high as £31,000,000. But we must consider the vast reduction of country bank paper as the main cause of the vast fall of prices which had ensued.

"A fluctuating currency is the greatest curse which can by possibility befall an opulent and commercial community. At all times, and to all classes, it is pregnant with disaster; at one time unduly elevating the creditor at the expense of the debtor; at another as unjustly benefiting the debtor at the expense of the creditor. This is a state of things so fraught with ruin, first to one class and then to another, that it never can too much occupy the attention of a wise and paternal Government. As long as we have no standard, no fixed value of money, but it is allowed to rise and fall like quicksilver in the barometer, no man could conduct his property with any security, or depend upon any certain profit. If prices were fixed and steady, it is immaterial what is to be assumed as the standard. Last year, though it was for the most part one of peace, gold was never below £4, 8s. the ounce; this year, as so great a contraction of the country bankers' notes has taken place, it has fallen to nearly the Mint price of £3, 17s. 10d. the ounce. This, however, all took place in consequence of the impending resumption of cash payments, which, by the existing law, was to begin on July 5, 1816. If, however, a further suspension of cash payments takes place, the banks will begin issuing in all directions as before; prices will again rise, and we shall, a second time, enter upon that fatal mutation of prices from the effects of which we are just escaping. This is openly announced in certain publications. It is said if the restriction on cash payments is continued, and the issue expands again, prices may be run up to 100s. a quarter of wheat. Are the gentlemen opposite prepared to support this measure on such grounds? If not, now is the time to stop short, and avoid entering on a cycle flattering in the outset, but fraught with ultimate ruin."¹

On the other hand, it was contended by Lord Liverpool, and the Chancellor of the Exchequer—"The Bullion Committee themselves were of opinion that cash payments should not be resumed for two years after the return of peace, so strongly were even they impressed with the dangers to property and existing engagements which would result from the sudden contraction of paper credit. The difference between the two parties is not so great as would at first sight appear; it is a difference in point of time only, not of principle. There is no man on this side of the House who contends for the eternity of the restriction; none on the other who pleads for its instant termination. Is not two years a fair compromise between them? Preparations on the part of the Bank were indispensable before facing so great a change; one of the most necessary would be the permitting the Bank to issue £2 and £1 notes after the restriction ceased, as they had so long formed the staple of the circulation of the country. No reason had been assigned why two years was an unadvisable period; and although it did seem rather long, yet it was better to delay than precipitate important changes.

"It is a mistake to say prices have been forced by the copious issue of the currency; on the contrary, the increased issue was the effect of the previous high prices. The rise of prices preceded the increase of the currency; and it has now been proved, that the fall has not proceeded from its contraction, for it is admitted on the other side that it preceded that contraction. It is no doubt true that, when the prices of all articles of consumption began from the great importation to fall, the country banks, seized with panic, drew in their advances, and thereby augmented the general distress; but what did this prove? Nothing, but that paper currency could not be extended beyond what the circulation required. The variations in the price of gold showed they were unconnected with the price of grain. In the beginning of 1813, wheat was at 120s. 7d., in the end of the same year it was

¹ Parl. Deb. xxxiv. 139, 147.

82s. 4d.; while the price of gold in the beginning of that year was £5, 0s. 6d. an ounce, and in the end £5, 10s. This showed distinctly that the price of gold arose from the demand for itself, arising from causes abroad, and was wholly irrespective of the amount of paper issued at home. To the eternal credit of this country, it will be recorded in history, that the Bank restriction, though perhaps originally forced upon the country by necessity, and having forced up the price of gold, had proved the salvation of Europe, by enabling us to carry on a system which could not otherwise have been supported.

"The opinions of those who would uphold prices by a continued and lavish issue of paper, are as much condemned on this side of the House as the other. Nothing is farther from the intentions of Government than to make the restrictions on cash payments permanent. It is merely a question of time when they are to cease. The Bullion Committee had recommended two years from the conclusion of peace—all he asked for was two years and seven months. It was not till December last that the ratifications of the definitive treaty were interchanged. Several of the most eminent members of the Bullion Committee had concurred in this opinion. The restoration of the old state of the currency must obviously be done gradually, and with ample time for preparation; for it was to be recollected the Bank of England would be called upon to furnish cash for demands, not only on the Bank of England, but those of Ireland and Scotland." Upon a division, Mr. Horner's motion, which was for a select committee to inquire into the resumption of cash payments, was negatived by a majority of 146 to 73.¹

52. Concluded.

¹ Parl. Deb. xxxiv.139,166.

These debates on agricultural distress and the currency are almost as memorable for what was left unsaid, as what was said in the course of their discussion. Both parties were to a certain degree right, and to a certain wrong, in the opinions they advanced. Lord Liverpool was unquestionably right when he affirmed that the nation, and through it Europe, had been saved by the suspension of cash payments during the war; for but for it the armaments never could have been produced which brought it to a successful issue; and that the rise in the price of gold, which took place in its latter years, was owing to the increased demand for that article of commerce to meet the exigencies of war on the Continent, where hostilities on a great scale were going on. On the other hand, Mr. Horner, who had thought and written more profoundly on the subject of the currency than any other person then in existence,* was equally right when he observed, that the extensive issue of paper during the war was the cause of the rapid and extraordinary enhancement of prices which then took place in every article, whether of rude or manufactured produce, while it lasted; that the still more rapid and disastrous fall of prices which had taken place since the peace, was the result of the great contraction of the currency, especially of country

53. Reflections on this subject

* Several of that most able and lamented gentleman's papers on the subject in the *Edinburgh Review*, as well as his speeches on it in Parliament, are models of clear and forcible reasoning.

bankers, which had ensued from the prospect of immediately resuming cash payments in terms of the existing law on the termination of hostilities; and that by far the greatest evil which impended over the country was the necessity of paying off in a contracted, and therefore dear, currency during peace, the debts, public and private, which had been contracted during the lavish issue of a plentiful, and therefore cheap, currency during the war.

The extraordinary thing is, that when so many of the true and undeniable views on the subject were entertained by the ablest and best-informed men in the country, the obvious conclusions which flowed from them were, by common consent, rejected on both sides. Mr. Horner saw clearly that we had been so prosperous, and done such mighty things during the war, because we had possessed a currency adequate to our necessities, and had languished and suffered since the peace, because it had been suddenly and violently contracted from the prospect of immediately resuming cash payments. He saw also that interminable disasters impended over the country in the attempt to pay off war debts, public or private, in a peace currency. But neither he nor his opponents on the Treasury Bench perceived, what is now evident to every reasonable person who, apart from interested motives, reflects on the subject, that all those difficulties and dangers might have been averted, without either risk or detriment, by the simple expedient of taking the paper currency, like the metallic, at once into the hands of Government, and issuing, not an unlimited amount of notes, like the French assignats, not convertible into the precious metals, but such a *limited* amount as might be adequate to the permanent and average wants of the community. He saw clearly that oscillations in the value of money, and consequently in the price of every article of commerce, were among the most grievous evils which can afflict society, and rendered property and undertakings of every kind to the last degree insecure; and he thought that he would guard effectually against them, by fixing the entire currency on a gold basis—forgetting, what he himself at the same time saw, that gold itself is an article of commerce, and, like every other such article, is subject to perpetual variations of price; and that, from its being so portable and valuable, and every where in request, it is subject to more sudden and violent changes of value than any other article in existence.

54. Extraordinary insensibility to right conclusions which then prevailed.

He saw clearly that the great contraction of the currency was owing to the prospect of the resumption of cash payments; but he could see no remedy for the evils thence arising but in the immediate adoption of such payments. He saw the impossibility of paying off war debts in a peace currency; but it never occurred to him that the whole difficulty might be avoided by extending the war currency, under adequate safeguards against abuse, into peace. He was as much alive as any man to the perils of a sudden contraction of the currency; but it never occurred to him how fearfully these dangers must be aggravated by the contraction of paper going on at the very time when a still greater contraction of the annual produce of the treasure mines for

56. General errors on the subject which then prevailed.

the use of the globe was going on, from the disasters consequent on the South American revolution. The truth is, that, as generally occurs in human affairs, men's attention was fixed exclusively on the *last* evils which had been experienced; and as these had been the ruinous rise of prices, and destruction of realized property which had resulted from the frightful abuse of the system of assignats in France, the eyes of a whole generation were shut to the still more serious and lasting evils resulting from the undue contraction of the currency, and the fixing it entirely on a metallic basis, of which Great Britain was ere long to furnish so memorable an example.

A measure, of great importance to both countries, passed both Houses in this session of Parliament, for the consolidation of the English and Irish Exchequers. It appeared from the statement of the Chancellor of the Exchequer, that the unredeemed debt of Ireland was £105,000,000; the Sinking Fund, £2,087,000; and the whole charge of the debt, interest, annuities, and Sinking Fund, £5,900,000. On the other hand, the entire permanent revenue was only £2,681,000 a year, having risen to that amount from £847,000 in 1797. The entire gross revenue of the island was £7,000,000; but the clear produce, after deducting the expense of collection, was £5,752,000; and as it was stipulated in the union that two-seventeenths of the expenditure of the United Kingdom should be defrayed by Ireland, the result was that the clear revenue of Ireland was unable to defray the interest of its own debt, without contributing any thing at all to the joint expenses of the United Kingdom, which for several years past had been entirely provided for by Great Britain. In these circumstances, a consolidation of the two Exchequers had become a matter of absolute necessity, and it was accordingly unanimously agreed to.[1]

<small>56. Consolidation of the English and Irish Exchequers. May 29, 1816.</small>

<small>[1] Parl. Debat. xxxiv.588,615.</small>

This was undoubtedly a very great improvement; for, as matters stood before, the confusion arising from the separate charges for Ireland had been such as to occasion very great difficulty in arriving at a clear idea of the revenue and financial condition of the United Kingdom. Unhappily, however, the state of Ireland has ever since been such that it has been found impracticable to carry into execution the declared intentions of Government, in bringing forward the consolidation, of subjecting both countries to a similar measure of taxation. Ireland has from first to last been most generously treated by England in the article of assessment. It never paid the income-tax or assessed taxes, nor, till within these few years, any poor-rates. With the exception of a trifling hearth-tax, no man in Ireland has ever paid any direct tax to Government. Yet such has ever been the improvidence and want of industry of its inhabitants, that although possessing triple the population, and more than triple the arable acres of Scotland, Ireland has never paid its own expenses; while Scotland has yielded, for half a century, above five millions a year of clear surplus to the Imperial Treasury; and in the great famine of 1846, while Ireland received £8,000,000 from the British Exchequer, Scotland, great part of which had suffered just as much, got nothing

<small>57. Reflections on this subject.</small>

In a very early period of the session, Mr. Brougham, moved for a copy of the treaty concluded at Paris on the 26th September, 1815, entitled "The Holy Alliance," of which an account will hereafter be given. This treaty he stigmatized as nothing but a convention for the enslaving of mankind, under the mask of piety and religion. Lord Castlereagh, without denying the existence of such a treaty, which he stated had been communicated to the Prince-Regent, and of the principles of which he entirely approved, added that it had not received his royal highness's signature, "as the forms of the British Constitution prevented him from acceding to it." This being the case, the rules of Parliament forbade the production of any treaty to which this country was not a party. The House, upon a division, supported the latter view, the numbers being 104 to 30. There can be no question of the wisdom of this determination on the part of the British Government; for however sincere and philanthropic were the feelings which undoubtedly prompted the Emperor Alexander to bring about that celebrated Alliance, they were such as could be acted on only by absolute governments, omnipotent for good or for evil, and never could be rendered palatable to a popular government such as great Britain, divided by the passions, political and religious, of a whole people, and ruled by a legislature chiefly intent upon the present necessities and practical wants of its subjects.[1]

<small>58. Motion re specting the Holy Alliance by Mr. Brougham.</small>

<small>[1] Parl. Debat. xxxiii. 350, 363.</small>

A warm debate also ensued on another topic of foreign policy, a bill for the detention of Napoleon in St. Helena. This bill was strongly opposed by Lord Holland and Lord Lauderdale, who stigmatized the detention as illegal, unjust, and ungenerous; while it was defended by Earl Bathurst and Lord Castlereagh as a measure for the general security of the world, agreed to by the whole allied powers, and rendered unavoidable by his breach of all his engagements, and open declaration of war against the Allies, by returning from Elba and dethroning Louis XVIII. The debates on this subject, which terminated in the bill being passed in both Houses without a division, are of little historical value; for if the detaining Napoleon in captivity was illegal, it could not be validated by any British Act of Parliament—if legal, it required no such authority for its support. But it must always be a matter of regret to every generous mind in Britain that the conduct of so great a man, in breaking his engagements, had been such as to render his detention a matter of absolute necessity; and of gratification to every British subject, that necessary as that detention was, it excited so strong a feeling of commiseration and regret in the breast of a large portion of the English people.[1]

<small>59. Bill for the detention of Napoleon.</small>

<small>[1] Parl. Debat. xxxiii. 1014. 1019.</small>

Another topic was soon brought forward of still more general interest, and which passed both Houses of Parliament without a dissentient voice, as it excited a universal feeling of joy throughout the country. On the 14th March, Lord Liverpool,

<small>60. Marriage of the Princess Charlotte of Wales. March 14</small>

in the House of Lords, and Lord Castlereagh in the House of Commons, respectively presented a message from the Prince-Regent to the effect that he had consented to a marriage of his daughter, the Princess Charlotte Augusta, to Prince Leopold of Saxe-Cobourg. The announcement of this auspicious union was received with the utmost satisfaction by both Houses of Parliament, and universal joy by the country; and on the next day the House of Commons fixed the provision of her royal highness at £60,000 a year, of which £10,000 was to be for her own privy purse, and £50,000 for the support of their establishment. The like sum was settled as a provision for the Prince of Cobourg, in the event of his surviving his august spouse. These provisions were independent of £60,000 for the outfit of the royal pair, and were all agreed to without a dissenting voice. The marriage, from which so much was hoped, took place on the 2d May following, and ere long the situation of her royal highness gave hopes of an heir to the monarchy. The Prince and Princess fixed their residence at Claremont, near London, now an object of melancholy interest to every British heart, where their simple, unostentatious life, their fervent and mutual attachment, their kindness and affability of manner, won the affections of all who approached them, as the noble example of domestic virtue and purity which they exhibited in their conduct commanded the respect of the whole nation.¹

March 12.

¹ Parl. Debat. xxxiii. 37e, 3×2; Ann. Reg. 1816, 96.

The heart of the nation still beat violently at the recollection of the glorious events of the war; and the chill of indifference and economy had not yet paralyzed the expression of it by public grants. At an early period of the session a monument at the public expense was unanimously voted for the battle of Waterloo, to which, soon after, one was also agreed to for the battle of Trafalgar. These graceful tributes of a nation's gratitude to the gallant men by which it had been brought through the perils of the war, gave universal satisfaction, and great expectations were formed of the magnificence of the monuments which would thus be added to the growing splendor of the metropolis; for it was understood that £250,000 would be expended on each monument. Unfortunately, however, although the monuments were unanimously voted, their cost did not enter the estimates for the year, and thus nothing was done toward their commencement at that time. In subsequent times, the national ardor cooled, or the national necessities had increased; and the result has been, that two sterile votes of the House of Commons remain as the only national monument for the greatest and most glorious triumphs which ever immortalized the history of a nation in modern times.¹

61. Votes for public monuments.

¹ Parl. Debat. xxxi. 1049; xxxiii. 311.

To the memory of individual heroes who had died in the contest, however, the public gratitude was evinced in a more satisfactory way. Monuments were voted to Sir Thomas Picton, Sir Edward Pakenham, and Generals Hay, Gore, Skerrett, Gibbs, and Gillespie, and the requisite funds set apart for their completion. They were

62. Monuments to Sir T. Picton and others.

with great propriety placed in St. Paul's, at Westminster Abbey was so full that space could scarcely be found for any additional structures, and began that noble circle of sepulchral sculpture which now adorns that sublime cathedral, and which, having been commenced at a period when taste was comparatively pure, and the finest monuments of antiquity were accessible to artists, is in a great measure free from that painful exhibition of conceit and bad taste by which, with a few exceptions, those of Westminster Abbey are characterized. A great impulse was given to sculpture in this year, and the only secure foundation laid for national eminence in that art, by the grant from Parliament of £35,000 for the purchase from Lord Elgin of the Friezes, which he had by the permission of the Turkish Government brought from the Parthenon of Athens. Certainly, however much the traveler who sees the chasms which their removal has made on the still exquisite remains of that inimitable edifice may regret the spoliation, no Englishman can fail to feel gratification at beholding them arranged with so much taste and effect as they now are, in the noble halls of the British Museum; and not only forming the last stage in the historic gallery, beginning with the Nineveh sculptures, which are there preserved, but laying the only sure foundation, in the study of ancient perfection, of the desire to emulate it, in the only nation perhaps now in existence capable of approaching it.²

² Parl. Deb. xxxiv. 1027, 1029; xxxi. 913; and xxxii. 822.

Magnificent grants, bespeaking the nation's gratitude, were bestowed by Parliament on the officers and men engaged in the war. A vote of thanks was proposed and carried with enthusiastic cheers, in the Houses of Lords and Commons, to the Duke of Wellington, Prince Blucher, the Prince of Orange, and the officers and men engaged in the Waterloo campaign. An additional grant of £200,000 was bestowed on the Duke of Wellington—making, with former grants, £500,000 which he had received from the justice or gratitude of his country. On this occasion, Mr. Whitbread, who had always been a vigilant opponent of Government, and had more than once condemned in no measured terms the military conduct of the Duke of Wellington, made an *amende honorable* to both, which can not be read without emotion by any generous mind, and which is not less honorable to the party making than to those who received it.* Finally, the sacrifices of the war

63. Grants to the officers and men employed in the war.

* "He had always been one who watched with an eye of extreme jealousy the proceedings of Ministers; but their conduct in the prosecution of the war, waiving for the moment all consideration of its necessity or policy, was such as extorted his applause; and he had no hesitation in saying, that every department of Government must have exerted itself to the utmost, to give that complete efficiency to every part of the army which enabled the genius of the Duke of Wellington, aided by such means, to accomplish the wonderful victory he had achieved. It was gratifying to the House to hear the traits of heroism which have been mentioned of that noble Duke, especially that of his throwing himself into one of the British squares when charged by the enemy. To see a commander of his eminence, distinguished above all the commanders of the earth, throw himself into a hollow square of infantry, as a secure refuge till the rage and torrent of the attack was passed, and that not once only, but twice or thrice during the course of the battle proved that his confidence was placed not on one par

were wound up by a grant of £800,000 to the troops engaged in the Peninsula from 1807 to 1814, for the stores and munitions of war captured by them during its campaigns. And although this grant rather fell short of, than exceeded, the value of the captures made by the army, yet it must always be considered an honorable trait of the English Parliament that they agreed to so considerable a payment to their gallant defenders after the contest and the danger were alike over, and the nation was laboring under the accumulated evils of general distress and a fearfully diminished revenue.[1]

[1] Parl. Debat. xxxi. 978, 999.

64. New coinage.

A measure of less thrilling interest, but great practical importance, was passed in this session of Parliament, the benefit of which the nation has ever since experienced. This was the formation of a new silver coinage. The old coins which had been for above half a century, some a whole century, in circulation, had become extremely worn out and debased, and a new issue, especially of shillings, was loudly called for—the more so as, from the contemplated return to cash payments, it was evident that the entire currency of the country would ere long be rested on a metallic basis. An act passed accordingly, authorizing a new silver coinage, and the calling in and remoulding of the old one. This great improvement was carried into execution with entire success—the new coins were elegant in design, and substantial in material; and to such an extent did the issue take place, that in the following year no less than £6,711,000 was thrown off at the Mint and sent forth to the public.[2]

[2] Parl. Debat. xxxiv. 1018, 1027; Alison's Europe, c. xcii. App.

65. Reflections on the preceding Parliamentary narrative.

Long as the preceding abstract of the parliamentary proceedings in the year 1816 has been, it will not by the reflecting mind be deemed inordinate. During peace, it is the national thought and social interests which are the real objects of historic portraiture; its battles and sieges are to be found in the debates of the legislature. There is no period of repose, in this view, which is so interesting and important both in England and France, as this year; for not only was the transition then made from war to peace, but the great questions then emerged which have distracted the later period, and still divide the opinions of the world. The great fall of prices then began, which has ever since, with a few intervals, been felt as so serious an impediment to British industry. The sudden contraction of the currency, from the prospect of a speedy resumption of cash payments, then involved one-half of the farmers and traders of the United Kingdom in bankruptcy. The evils of an excessive importation of the principal articles of consumption reacted by forcing on a ruinous export of our manufactures, in search of a market which general cheapness had so much injured at home. The Exchequer shared in the universal embarrassment, and the demand for a general remission of taxation was so loud and general, that Government were reluctantly compelled to abandon at once above a fourth of the revenue, and thereby, for the time at least, completely to nullify the action of the Sinking Fund. The difficulties of peace rose up in appalling magnitude in the very first year of its endurance; and it is not the least important part of history to unfold their origin, trace their effects, and portray the contemporary ideas which they awakened in the general mind.

66. Efforts of the factious to stir up sedition.

When so many causes contributed to produce, in an unexampled degree, general distress and suffering through the country, it was not to be expected that the efforts of faction were to be awanting to inflame the general discontent, and direct it to the demand for a great and theoretical change in the government. This accordingly was in a very remarkable manner the case in Great Britain at this period; and perhaps at no time in its long annals was discontent more general, or were the efforts of faction more systematically directed to inflame it into sedition, or involve it in overt acts of high treason, than in this and the three succeeding years. Persons unknown before, unheard of since, suddenly shot up into portentous celebrity with the manufacturing classes, by magnifying their sufferings, inflaming their passions, and ascribing all the public distresses to the measures, the corruption, and the oppression of their superiors. According to these men, the reckless prodigality of Government, supported by a corrupt majority in Parliament, and sustained by fictitious paper credit, was the source of all our distresses; it was this which made provisions high, wages low, imports ruinous, and want of employment universal. The only remedies for these evils were a great reduction of expenditure, reform in Parliament, and a return to a metallic currency. The Common Council of London, that faithful mirror of the feelings of the *populace* of the metropolis at this juncture, presented a petition to the Prince Regent, which as a picture of the capacity of that body for the duties of legislation in peace, deserves a place beside the celebrated specimen of their fitness for the duties of war, afforded by their diatribe against the Duke of Wellington after the battle of Talavera.* It is remarkable that the measures which they recommended as likely to alleviate the public distress —viz., a sudden reduction of expenditure, and return to a metallic currency—are the very ones which experience has now proved were best calculated to increase them.[†]

[†] Ann. Regist. 1816, 95; Hughes' History of England, vi. 314, 315.

---

* Vide *History of Europe,* chap. lxii. § 67.

† "We forbear to enter into details of the afflicting scenes of privations and sufferings that every where exist; the distress and misery which for so many yet rs has been progressively accumulating, has at length become insupportable. It is no longer partially felt, nor limited to one portion of the empire; the commercial, manufacturing, and agricultural interests are equally sinking under its irresistible pressure; and it has become impossible to find employment for a large mass of the popula-

When ideas so extravagant, and language so intemperate, were adopted by the
67. Spafield riots, first incorporation of the kingdom,
Dec. 2. with the Lord Mayor of London at their head, in addressing the Sovereign, it may readily be conceived that inferior functionaries and demagogues were still more intemperate and violent in their measures. An example of this soon occurred in the metropolis. On December 2, a mob, collected by hand-bills plentifully dispersed over the whole manufacturing districts of London, and roused by the speeches delivered at a seditious meeting held in the same place a fortnight before, assembled at Spafields to hear the answer to a petition they had voted at the former meeting to the Prince-Regent. They waited some time for Mr. Henry Hunt, the leading orator, who was expected to address them; and as he did not make his appearance, they proceeded with tri-color flags and banners, and entering the city, headed by a man of the name of Watson, they attacked a gunsmith's shop, whom they shot when defending the entrance; and having rifled the shop, and loaded the guns they got, they marched on in military array to the Royal Exchange, where they were met by the Lord Mayor, Alderman Shaw, and a strong body of police; but notwithstanding their resistance, the rioters forced their way into the building, when three of the ringleaders were seized and made prisoners. The mob upon this fired over the rails, which had been closed upon the magistrates, and moved off to the Minories, where they broke into two other gunsmiths' shops, and remained for a considerable time in possession of that part of the town. Strong bodies of police and military, however, now rapidly arrived and surrounded the insurgent district; and the mob, finding themselves overmatched, by degrees dispersed. Two of the persons seized were condemned and executed; but the greatest criminal, Watson's son, escaped to America. This tumult, as is generally the case with such disorders, when promptly and firmly met by those in authority, was in the end attended with beneficial effects, by awakening the vigilance of the Government, by whom such meetings were afterward carefully watched, and showing the people
¹ Ann. Regist. with what danger they are attended, what were the real objects of Chronicle. their leaders, and how thin is the Hughes, vi. partition which separates seditious 316, 317. assemblages from general pillage.¹

One glorious exploit, second to none which has graced the annals of the British Navy, illustrated this year. It had long been a matter of reproach to the Christian powers
68. that the piratical states of Barbary Expedition to were still permitted, with impunity, Algiers. to carry on their inhuman warfare against the states of Europe, and that their prisons exhibited captives of every nation, who were detained in hopeless slavery, and exposed to the most shocking barbarities. In one instance, fifty out of three hundred prisoners died of harsh usage, at Algiers, on the very day of their arrival. Neither age nor sex was spared; and one Neapolitan lady of rank was rescued by the British, in the thirteenth year of her captivity, having been carried off with her eight children, six of whom had died in slavery! Notwithstanding these enormities, such had been the jealousies of the European powers, and their animosity against each other, that these audacious pirates had in an unaccountable manner been allowed to carry on their hostilities against the Mediterranean states with impunity, and it was suspected that the British connived at these depredations, as their flag, being the only one which was respected, gained an advantage
¹ Ann. Reg. in navigating that inland sea.¹ The 1816, 97; piracies were renewed on a more ex- Hughes, vi. tended scale with the revival of com- 317. merce after the peace, and the only check which the corsairs received was from the Americans, who, in the year 1815, in a very spirited manner, vindicated the honor of their flag, which had been insulted by these ferocious attacks.

At length, however, the general system of piracy which the Dey of Algiers 69. had adopted, brought him into con- Outrages tact with the subjects or allies of which led to it. Great Britain; in particular the inhabitants of the Ionian Islands, and of Naples and Sardinia. LORD EXMOUTH,* accordingly, who commanded

---

tion, much less to bear up against our present enormous burdens.

"Our grievances are the natural effect of rash and ruinous wars, unjustly commenced and pertinaciously adhered to, when no rational object was to be attained; of immense subsidies to foreign powers to defend their own territories, or to commit aggressions on those of their neighbors; of a delusive paper currency; of an unconstitutional and unprecedented military establishment in time of peace; of the unexampled and increasing magnitude of the civil list; of the enormous sums paid for unmerited pensions and sinecures; and of a long course of the most lavish and improvident expenditure of the public money throughout every department of Government—all arising from the corrupt and inadequate representation of the people in Parliament, whereby all constitutional control over the servants of the Crown has been lost, and Parliaments have become subservient to the will of Ministers."—*Address of the Lord Mayor and Council of London*, Dec. 9, 1816. *Ann. Reg* 1816, 417. *State Papers*.

* Edward Pellew, afterward Lord Exmouth, was born at Dover on April 18, 1757. His father was commander of the Post-office Packet on the Dover station; his mother a daughter of Edward Saughton, Esq., of Herefordshire, a woman of extraordinary spirit and determination of character. Early difficulties drew forth young Edward's energies. His father, who was a most exemplary man, died in 1765, leaving six children; and a subsequent imprudent marriage of their mother having deprived them of the support of their surviving parent, they were thrown on the world with scarce any resources. Edward entered the navy in 1771, in the Juno, Captain Stott, in which he was sent to the Falkland Islands. Soon after he sailed in the Blonde, Captain Pownall, an officer of the kindest and most elevated character. There he soon showed both his daring and humane disposition. On one occasion, in 1775, when the vessel was taking General Burgoyne out to America, the general was horrified at seeing a midshipman on the yard-arm standing on his head; but Captain Pownall quieted him by saying, it was one of the usual frolics of young Pellew, and that he need not be uneasy, for if he felt, he would only go under the ship's bottom, and come up on the other side. What was then spoken in jest by the captain was actually realized by young Pellew; for on an occasion soon after, a man having fallen overboard when the ship was going fast through the water, he actually sprang from the foreyard of the Blonde and saved the man. Captain Pownall reproached him for his rashness, but never spoke of it again without tears in his eyes. After the American war broke out, a party from the Blonde, of whom young Pellew was one, was sent across to Lake Champlain, where he was employed in the Carleton, and distinguished himself so much by his gallantry in performing a service of extreme danger, which no other man would execute; that it drew forth a letter of strong commendation from his commander, Sir Charles Douglas, and a holograph letter, appointing him lieutenant, from Lord Howe, the First Lord of the Admiralty. He was afterward attached with a party of seamen to General Bourgoyne's expedition, which terminated in such disaster at Saratoga; but even here

the British squadron in the Mediterranean, received orders to proceed to Tunis, Tripoli, and Algiers, and insist upon the inhabitants of these states being included in the same pacification as Great Britain, and, if possible, obtain a general abolition of Christian slavery. To these demands the beys of Tunis and Tripoli at once agreed; but the Dey of Algiers refused to consent to the last, on the ground that, being a subject of the Ottoman Porte, he could not do so without the consent of that government. He agreed, however, to dispatch a messenger to Constantinople in a frigate, to obtain instructions on the subject, and actually did so. Satisfied with these concessions, which attained all that he could reasonably expect, Lord Exmouth returned with his squadron to Great Britain. In the mean time, however, an outrage took place, which broke off the negotiation, and rendered immediate hostilities unavoidable. At Bona, on the coast of Algiers, on the festival of the Ascension, on 23d May, as the crews of a number of Italian, Corsican, and Neapolitan vessels were preparing, under the shelter of the British flag, to hear mass and join in the solemnities, they were, on the signal of a gun fired from the castle, suddenly assailed by a body of two thousand Turks and Moors, who cut the greater part of them to pieces, tore to pieces the English flag, broke into and pillaged the English consul's house, and thrust him into prison. Upon receiving intelligence of this outrage, the English Government, in a worthy spirit, not only resolved on demanding entire satisfaction, but on seizing the opportunity of destroying the nest of pirates who had so long inflicted their barbarities on the whole states of Christendom. Lord Exmouth was informed any force he might deem requisite would be placed at his disposal, and the equipment of the necessary squadron proceeded with the utmost activity.¹

The city of ALGIERS, which had so long been an object of terror and curiosity to the Christian powers, and has been the theatre of so many memorable actions by the principal states of Europe, is, like Genoa, built on the declivity of a steep hill, with its lower part washed by the ocean. It is in a triangular form, the sea being the base, and the apex high up on the hill; and as it is entirely inclosed within walls, and the buildings are of a white color, rising one above another, its appearance from a distance, when first descried by the mariner, is that of a huge sheet stretched out upon the dusky slope. Its fortifications are very strong, being surrounded by walls of immense thickness, which, like those of Genoa, run to the summit of the hill behind the town; and toward the sea, especially, the defenses are of the most formidable description. A broad straight pier, 300 yards long, projects into the sea from a point about a quarter of a mile from the seaport of the town. From the end of this pier a mole is carried, which bends round in a southwestern direction toward the town, forming in its course nearly a quarter of a circle. Opposite the mole-head is another smaller pier, and between the two is the entrance of the harbor, which is about 120 yards wide. The mole is constructed on a ledge of rock, which stretches out about 200 yards toward the northeast, beyond the angle at which it unites to the pier. All the points commanding the entrance

April 4.

May 23.

¹ Ann. Regist. 1816, 97, 99; Hughes, vi. 317, 318.

70. Description of Algiers.

he contrived to distinguish himself, for he recovered a vessel, containing provisions, with such skill and gallantry, that General Bourgoyne thanked him in a letter written with his own hand. When the capitulation was proposed, Pellew, who was the youngest officer in the council of war, earnestly entreated to be allowed to fight his way back with his handful of sailors, alleging he had never heard of seamen capitulating; and it was with great difficulty that Bourgoyne succeeded in dissuading him from making the attempt, by representing it would lead to a general ruin and violation of the capitulation. He returned to England in 1777, and was immediately promoted. He had already acquired such extraordinary skill in rowing and swimming, that he often ran the greatest risk by the dangers incurred, from his confidence in his own powers, and the fearless courting of danger which he constantly exhibited. In 1780, when on board the Apollo, still with Captain Pownall, he fell in with the Stanislaus, of heavier calibre, and Captain Pownall was badly wounded early in the action. "Pellew," he said, "I know you won't throw the ship away," and died in his arms. He continued the action an hour longer, and drove the enemy dismasted ashore, but was disappointed of his prize, by her claiming protection from a neutral harbor. His gallant conduct on this occasion led to his being appointed to the command of the Hazard sloop in July, 1780, and afterward to the Pelican, in which he performed many important services. When the war of the French Revolution broke out, he was appointed to the Nymph frigate, in which, after a desperate action, in which the commanders and crews of both vessels displayed the utmost skill and courage, he captured the French frigate Cleopatra, for which he was knighted. He was next appointed to the Arethusa frigate, in which, on 23d August, 1794, he took La Pomone, French frigate. After this he nearly lost his life in attempting to save two of his crew who had been washed overboard; and signalized himself in the most distinguished way at the wreck of the Dutton, near Plymouth, when he boarded the vessel as it was lying a wreck on the coast, took the command, and, by his energy and skill in running a hawser to the shore, succeeded in saving the whole crew, who would otherwise infallibly have perished. For this extraordinary act of heroism he was created a baronet. He was next appointed to the Indefatigable frigate, and by his great skill and admirable seamanship not only rendered most important service off the west coast of France, but by his admirable seamanship saved his own vessel when all but wrecked, in company of the Amazon which perished. The mutiny, which proved so formidable in 1797, broke out twice on board his vessel, and was only quelled by his undaunted conduct in twice arresting the ringleaders with his own hand, and ordering his officers to cut down the first man who resisted. When, on another mutiny, three of the ringleaders, on board the Prince at Port Mahon, were brought up for execution, Sir Edward, addressing the men who had followed him from the Indefatigable, said—"Indefatigables, stand aside; not one of you shall touch the rope; but ye who have encouraged your shipmates to the crime by which they have forfeited their lives, it shall be your punishment to hang them." The men of the Prince felt it as such; they wept aloud, but obeyed. These were terrible days; more terrible than any conflict with the enemy to the British navy; and it was Sir Edward Pellew's firmness, in a great degree, which brought it through the crisis. During the Peace of Amiens he obtained a seat in Parliament for the borough of Barnstaple, and he made a short but powerful speech in defence of the Admiralty, in a debate which ensued when the war broke out again. He was then appointed to the Tonnant of 80 guns, and soon obtained the command of the squadron blockading Ferrol; after which he was made commander-in-chief on the Indian station, where he remained till 1808, and rendered the most essential service, both by the destruction of several of the enemy's ships of war, and the protection afforded to British trade. In 1811 he proceeded as commander-in-chief to the Mediterranean, which position he held to the close of the war, anxiously watching for a general battle with the Toulon fleet, which the caution of the enemy caused them to avoid. He died on 23d January, 1832 with the calm serenity of a Christian. "Every hour of his life," said an officer who was much with him at that time, "is a sermon: I have seen him great in battle, but never so great as on his deathbed." See OSLER'S *Life of Lord Exmouth*, p. 1-361, a most interesting work; and which, with the *Life of Collingwood*, by G. L. COLLINGWOOD, should be studied by all who would learn the spirit, at once courageous and humane, simple and noble, pious and patriotic, which animated the British navy.

to the harbor were covered with the strongest fortifications. At the pier-head stood the lighthouse battery, a large circular fort, mounted by fifty heavy guns, in three tiers, exactly like those of a three-decker. At the outer extremity of the rock was another battery of thirty heavy guns and seven mortars, arranged in two tiers. The mole itself was also lined with cannon in two tiers, like the sides of a line-of-battle ship; but the eastern end, near the lighthouse, had an inner fortification with a third tier of guns, making sixty-six in the mole alone. On these batteries, at the entrance of the harbor, were mounted 220 guns, almost all thirty-two or twenty-four pounders. On the sea-wall of the town were nine batteries, the strongest of which was the fishmarket battery, in three tiers. Altogether there were nearly 500 guns defending the sea approaches of Algiers; and as the ramparts were admirably constructed of hard stone, and in the very best order, a more formidable object of attack could hardly be imagined.[1]

¹ Ostler's Life of Lord Exmouth, 307, 309; Ann. Regist 1816, 101; Hughes, vi 310.

Nelson, in a conversation with Captain Brisbane, on a former occasion had said that Algiers could not be successfully attacked by less than twenty-five ships of the line. Great, therefore, was the surprise of the Admiralty when Lord Exmouth proposed to attack it with five sail of the line, five frigates, and as many bomb-vessels; and many of the most experienced officers at the Board considered the works so strong, that the place was altogether unassailable. The opinion of that gallant and experienced officer, however, was founded on actual observation, which Nelson's was not, and it proved entirely correct. The truth is, that not one-half of the ships which Nelson spoke of could have found room abreast of the Algerine batteries; and being of necessity crowded one behind another, they would only have augmented the confusion, and presented an additional mark to the enemy's fire. He explained his plans accordingly to the Admiralty, showing the position which each ship was to occupy, and the works it was intended to rake; and they very wisely allowed him to act on his own judgment, though they entertained serious apprehensions as to the result; and there were not wanting those who predicted that the undertaking could terminate in nothing but disaster. His own confidence, however, never wavered. "All will go well," he said; "at least so far as depends on me. If they open their fire when the ships are coming up, and cripple them in the masts, the difficulty and loss will be greater; but if they allow us to take our stations,[2] I am sure of them, for I know nothing can resist a line-of-battle ship's fire."

71. Lord Exmouth's preparations for an attack.

² Ostler's Life of Exmouth, 310.

Scarcely was Exmouth appointed to this perilous service, when officers in crowds, tenfold greater than could be accepted, came forward to offer their services. He left the entire selection to the Admiralty, and refused all his own relations, though many were anxious to accompany him. An entirely new squadron was fitted out, none of the ships which had just returned from the Mediterranean being sent back.

72. The manning and fitting out of the fleet.

It was thought best that a fleet which was going to fight a severe battle should be manned entirely by volunteers. No difficulty, however, was experienced in getting sailors for the squadron; as soon as it was known it was going on a service of danger, the volunteers came forward in crowds. The ship's company of the Leander, then on the point of sailing for the North American station, where it was to be the flag-ship, volunteered to a man. Among them were a great number of smugglers, who had been taken on the west coast and sentenced to five years' service in the navy; they implored to be allowed to share in the perils of the expedition, and Lord Exmouth acceded to their request, and took them into his own ship the Queen Charlotte. His confidence was not misplaced: they behaved with such gallantry in the action which ensued, that Lord Exmouth applied to the Admiralty after his return, and obtained their discharge. Rear-Admiral Milne, a noble veteran, who had just got the command on the North American station, obtained permission to go out with the Leander; and as Sir Charles Penrose did not join at Gibraltar, he hoisted his flag on board the Impregnable, as second in command. Before Lord Exmouth sailed, he made every arrangement, as if for immediate death. Among the rest he wrote a long letter to his eldest son, detailing the duties which would devolve upon him as a British nobleman, which was found among his papers after his death.[1] He felt that he was setting out on what might truly be deemed a holy war: his feelings were those of Godfrey of Bouillon, or Raymond of Toulouse, when they mounted the breach of Jerusalem.

¹ Ostler's Life of Exmouth, 310, 312.

Lord Exmouth hoisted his flag on board the Queen Charlotte of 100 guns. His fleet consisted of five line-of-battle ships, of which two were three-deckers, three large frigates, and two smaller ones; four bomb-vessels, and five gun-brigs. His plan of attack, which was fully explained to all the officers in the fleet, was, that four of the line-of-battle ships were to breast the fortifications on the mole; a fifth cover them from the batteries of the town on the one side, while the heavy frigates did the same on the other; and the bomb-vessels, aided by the ships' launches, fitted up as rocket and mortar boats, were to keep up an incessant fire on the ships in the harbor, arsenal, and town. The fleet left Portsmouth on 25th July, and on the 28th was off Falmouth, where Lord Exmouth parted with his brother, at the very place where, three-and-twenty years before, he had sailed to fight the first battle of the war. From that place the Minden of 74 guns was sent on to Gibraltar, to provide supplies, and thither the whole fleet arrived on the 9th August, the evening after the Minden. On the voyage, the crews of all the ships were sedulously trained to their guns and ball practice; and on Tuesdays and Fridays, the whole were cleared for action, and each fired six broadsides. On board the Queen Charlotte, the captains of guns were constantly trained by firing a twelve-pounder at a small target hung from the fore-topmast studding-sail boom; and to such expertness did they soon arrive, that after a few days' practice the target was never missed.

73. Departure of the fleet, and voyage to Algiers.

though it was only three feet square, and ten or twelve bottles were hit every day. By these means, and by the effect of the mental excitement arising from the noble enterprise on which they were proceeding, the crews of all the vessels were highly elated, and kept in the best possible spirits. Not a doubt of their success was entertained by any one on board any of the vessels; and such was the effect of this mental excitement on the health of the men, that scarce a name was on the sick list; and when the Queen Charlotte was paid off on her return, only one man had died, excepting those slain in action, out of a thousand who had joined her three months before.[1]

[sidenote: 1 Ostler, 316, 317.]

[sidenote: 74. Preparations of the Algerines.]

At Gibraltar the fleet was joined by Vice-Admiral the Baron Von Capellan, with a Dutch squadron of five frigates and a corvette, who, on learning the noble object of the expedition, solicited and obtained leave to join it. On the 13th, every vessel was furnished with a plan of the fortifications and the place assigned to each in the attack. To the Dutch ships was allotted the attack of the fort and batteries toward the south of the town, a duty formerly allotted to the Minden and Hebrus, which were now brought up among their comrades on the front of the mole. On the same evening the Prometheus arrived from Algiers, bringing the wife, daughter, and infant child of Mr. MacDonnell, the English consul, the consul himself and fourteen of the crew of the Prometheus being detained in prison. The two former had escaped disguised as midshipmen; the last was detected by its crying as it passed the gate, and arrested; but the Dey sent it on board next morning—"a solitary instance of humanity," said Lord Exmouth, "which ought to be recorded." The Prometheus brought the most formidable accounts of the preparations made at Algiers to resist the attack. Forty thousand troops had been collected in the town, all the Janizaries called in from the distant garrisons, and the fortifications and batteries put in the best possible state of defense. The whole naval force of the regency, consisting of four frigates, five large corvettes, and thirty-seven gun-boats, were assembled in the harbor, manned by their most experienced and daring sailors.[2]

[sidenote: 2 Ostler, 318, 319.]

This intelligence, instead of daunting, contributed only to animate the sailors on board the British fleet, by showing the importance of the service on which they were bound, and the magnitude of the blow against the enemies of Christendom they were about to strike.

[sidenote: 75. Arrival of the fleet off Algiers. Aug. 27.]

On the morning of the 27th August, at daybreak, the fleet was off Algiers; Lord Exmouth immediately dispatched a flag of truce to the Dey, with the terms dictated by the Prince Regent, which were the entire abolition of Christian slavery and liberation of all captives, and full compensation to the British consul, and the sailors of the Prometheus, who had been imprisoned. An answer was promised by the port-captain in two hours, and meanwhile the fleet stood into the bay and anchored within a mile of the town. At two P.M. the boat was seen returning with the signal that no answer had been given. Lord Exmouth immediately made the signal, "Are you ready?" And the affirmative being returned from every vessel, the signal to advance was given, and every ship bore up for its appointed station. The Queen Charlotte headed the line, and made straight for the mole-head. It was Lord Exmouth's intention not to have opened his fire unless that of the enemy became very galling, and the guns on the upper and lower deck, accordingly, were not primed till the ship had anchored. But the Algerines, confident in their defenses, and hoping to carry the principal vessels by boarding, after they had taken their stations, allowed the Queen Charlotte to bear in without molestation, until she anchored by the stern, just half a cable's length from the mole-head, and was lashed by a hawser to the mainmast of an Algerine brig that lay at the harbor's mouth. Meanwhile the other vessels, in silence and perfect readiness, moved slowly forward under a light sea-breeze to their appointed stations. Not a word was spoken in the vast array; every eye was fixed on the enemy's batteries, which were crowded with troops, with the gunners standing with lighted matches beside their pieces.[1]

[sidenote: 1 Lord Exmouth's instructions. Ostler's Memoirs, App. p. 319, 320.]

"There was silence deep as death
As they drifted on their path,
And the boldest held his breath
For a time."

[sidenote: 76. Commencement of the battle.]

The mole-head at this time presented a dense mass of troops, whose turbans and shakos were distinctly seen crowding on the top of the parapets. Standing on the poop, Lord Exmouth waved with his hand to them repeatedly to get down, as the firing was about to commence. When the ship was fairly placed, and her cables stoppered, the crew gave three hearty cheers, which were answered from the whole fleet. The Algerines answered by three guns from the eastern battery, one of which struck the Superb. At the first flash Lord Exmouth gave the word "Stand by;" at the second, "Fire;" and the report of the third gun was drowned in the roar of the Queen Charlotte's broadside. So terrible was the effect of this discharge, that above five hundred men were struck down on the mole by its effects. In a few minutes, and before the action had become general, the fortifications on the mole-head were ruined and its guns dismounted; upon this the Queen Charlotte sprang her broadside to the northward, and brought her guns to bear upon the batteries round the gate which leads to the mole and the upper tier of the lighthouse battery. With such accuracy were the shot directed, that the lighthouse tower was soon in ruins, every successive discharge bringing down some of the guns; and when the last fell, a Moorish chief was seen springing up on the fragments of the parapet, and with impotent rage shaking his scimitar at the giant of the deep which in so brief a space had worked such fearful devastation.[1]

[sidenote: 1 Lord Exmouth's Disp. Ostler, 320, 324, 426; Ann Reg. 1816, 101.]

[sidenote: 77. Continuance of the action, and positions taken by the ships.]

Meanwhile the Algerines were not idle; a tremendous and well-sustained fire was kept up from every battery and gun on the ships as they approached and cast anchor; every bastion and battlement streamed with flames, and the roar of above a thousand can-now on the two sides, within a space not more than half a mile in breadth, exceeded any thing, since the battle of Copenhagen, heard in naval war. The Leander closely followed the flag-ship, and anchored astern of her; next came the Superb, which took her station two hundred and fifty yards astern of the Leander; the Minden anchored about her own length from the Superb. Astern of the Minden lay the Albion, the former passing her stream cable out of the larboard gunroom port to the Albion's bow, and lashing the two ships together. The Impregnable came in last, and was anchored astern of the Albion in a situation very much exposed to the enemy's batteries. The three large frigates and the Dutch squadron went into action with a gallantry which never was surpassed, and took their stations amid a tremendous fire, with the utmost accuracy. The Leander was placed athwart the Queen Charlotte's bows, her starboard broadside bearing upon the Algerine gun-boats with the after-guns, and on the fishmarket battery with the others. The Severn lay ahead of the Leander with all her starboard broadside also bearing on the fishmarket battery. Beyond her the Glasgow was stationed, and brought her larboard guns to bear on the batteries of the town. The Dutch took their position with great steadiness in front of the works to the south of the town. The two smaller frigates, the Hebrus and Granicus, were left to come into the line wherever they could find an opening. The former pressed forward to get next the flag-ship, but being becalmed, she was obliged to anchor on the Queen Charlotte's larboard quarter. Captain Wise, of the Granicus, steered straight for where Lord Exmouth's flag was seen towering above the smoke, and with a skill equal to his intrepidity, succeeded in placing his vessel in the open space between the Queen Charlotte and the Superb; thus taking a position, as Lord Exmouth justly said, which a three-decker might have been proud to occupy.[1]

Eastward of the lighthouse, at the distance of two thousand yards, were placed the bomb-vessels, the shells from which were thrown with admirable precision by the marine artillery; while the flotilla of gun, rocket, and mortar boats, distributed in the openings of the line, kept up an incessant and destructive fire on the ships in the harbor. Soon after the battle became general, the Algerine flotilla, under cover of the smoke, advanced, with true Mussulman intrepidity, to board the Queen Charlotte and Leander, and they were very near before they were descried; but when they were so, the fatal precision which the British gunners had acquired appeared conspicuous. The Leander brought her broadside to bear upon them, and, by a few discharges, thirty-three out of thirty-seven of the gun-boats were sent to the bottom. The thick smoke round the Queen Charlotte prevented the admiral from seeing the vessels as they came in and took up their position; but he soon received joyful proof of their presence, and the accuracy of their fire, by the yawning breaches and crumbling ruins which appeared, when the smoke for a few seconds cleared away, in the walls opposite the positions assigned to them. At four o'clock, as a close

[1] Lord Exmouth's Disp. Ann. Reg. 1816, 232, Ap. to Chron.; Ost. ler, 322, 323.

78
Destruction of the enemy's ships and flotilla.

action of an hour's duration had produced no signs of submission, Lord Exmouth determined to attempt the destruction of the Algerine ships. The nearest frigate was accordingly boarded by Lieutenant Richards in the Queen Charlotte's barge, accompanied by Major Gossett, of the marine artillery; and in a few minutes she was in a perfect blaze. When the frigate burst into a flame, he telegraphed to the fleet the animating signal, "Infallible;" and as the barge returned alongside, she was received with three cheers. The burning ship broke from her moorings, and drifted along the broadsides of the Queen Charlotte and Leander, and grounded ahead of the latter, under the town wall, so that the conflagration did not spread. Upon this the gunboats and barges opened a fire with bombs and carcasses on the largest frigate in the centre of the harbour, and she was soon in flames, from which the fire spread to the other ships around, which were all consumed with the exception of a sloop and brig. The arsenal also took fire, and, with all its stores, was totally consumed.[1]

[1] Lord Exmouth's Disp. Ann. Reg. 1816, 233; App. to Chron.; Ostler, 324, 326.

After sunset a message was received from Admiral Milne, in the Impregnable, which had suffered extremely from her position, exposed to the batteries and had lost 210 men killed and wounded, and requesting that a frigate might be sent to take off from her some of the fire under which she was suffering. The Glasgow immediately weighed anchor for that purpose, and gallantly stood forward into the thickest of the fire; but it was found impossible to reach the desired position, owing to the want of wind. An ordnance vessel was accordingly run ashore under the lighthouse battery, and blown up, which in some degree slackened the enemy's fire in that quarter. Toward night the fire of the Algerines slackened in all quarters, and at last entirely died away, except from the Emperor's Fort,* on the high ground, which, being above the range of the guns, continued firing with destructive effect to the very close of the action. On the side of the British, also, the fire slackened considerably; for the chief objects of the expedition having been gained, it became necessary to husband their powder and shot, the consumption of which had been beyond all parallel.† A little before ten the Queen Charlotte's bow-cable was cut, and her head hauled round to seaward. Warps were run out to get out, but they were in part cut by shot from the Emperor's Fort, and the batteries south of the town, which had been only partially engaged. About half-past ten the land breeze, on which Lord Exmouth had calculated, sprang up, and by the aid of the boats towing, she, with the remainder of the fleet, was got out of fire.[2] Soon after the breeze freshened, and a tremendous storm of thunder and lightning came on, with torrents of rain, which lasted three hours, but could not extinguish the flames of the burning

79.
The fleet moves out of the bay.

[2] Lord Exmouth's Disp. Ann. Reg. 1816, 233, 234. App. to Chron.; Ostler, 229, 230; Van Capellan's Account, Ann. Reg. 242, 243.

---

* So called from having been built by the Emperor Charles V. when he besieged the town in 1557.
† They had fired 118 tons of powder, 50,000 balls, weighing above 500 tons of iron, and 960 thirteen and ten inch shells thrown by the bomb-vessels and launches

ships, arsenal and houses, which cast an awful light over the scene of ruin. Before it had subsided, Lord Exmouth assembled in his cabin all the wounded who could be moved, that they might unite with him and his officers in thanks to the Almighty Disposer of events for their victory and preservation.

80. Results of the battle, and killed and wounded.

Such was the battle of Algiers, one of the most glorious even in the resplendent annals of the British navy. It was, withal, one of the most bloody—the best proof of the desperate nature of the service, and the heroic courage requisite to render it successful. In the British squadron, 128 were killed and 690 wounded—in all, 818: a greater proportion to the number engaged than in any action during the preceding war; for in Copenhagen itself, the bloodiest of that contest at sea, there were only 1200 killed and wounded out of eleven line-of-battle ships engaged;* but here there were 818 in five ships. The loss fell chiefly on three ships; in the Impregnable, which bore Admiral Milne's flag, there were 50 killed; and in the Leander and Granieus, which also took up line-of-battle positions, the loss was very severe. In the other line-of-battle ships the entire loss was only 26 killed and 62 wounded. The Dutch squadron had 13 killed and 52 wounded. Lord Exmouth had several most narrow escapes: he was struck in three places; a cannon ball carried away the skirts of his coat, and a shot broke the spectacles in his pocket. On the side of the Algerines it was computed by Lord Exmouth that 7000 had perished; a fearful loss, but which is not improbable when the crowded state of the batteries and the extraordinary precision of the English fire are taken into consideration. The British loss would have been much greater but for the commanding position taken at the very commencement of the action, and maintained throughout by the Queen Charlotte, which swept by her broadsides the whole batteries on the mole, the most formidable in the enemy's defenses. Admiral Capellan estimated that 500 men were thus saved to the allied squadron, who otherwise would have been destroyed. During the action the Queen Charlotte was often in the most imminent danger of being burned, from the blazing Algerine vessels which floated close past her, which came so near that Lord Exmouth was almost scorched as he stood on the poop, and he was obliged to haul in the ensign to prevent its being consumed. But when Admiral von Capellan and the other captains, seeing his imminent danger, offered him the assistance of the boats of the fleet to haul him out, he replied, "that having calculated every thing, it behoved them by no means to be alarmed for his safety, but only to continue their fire with redoubled zeal for the execution of his orders, and according to his example."†

† Admiral Capellan's Disp., Ann. Reg. 1816, 242, 243; App. to Chron.; Ost. ter, 336, 332; Lord Exmouth to Mr. Pellew, Sept. 8, 1816; Oster, 336, 337.

Next morning Algiers presented the most melancholy aspect. The mole, the lighthouse battery, and all the fortifications near them, were totally ruined; cannon, carriages, and dead bodies, lay one above another, intermingled with huge stones and masses of masonry, in one undistinguished mass to the water edge. In the walls of the town, huge gaps appeared opposite the broadsides of the vessels; and behind them, long lanes, cut in the houses as far as the horizontal shot could reach up the town, told how fatal the fire had been, and with what precision the shot had been directed. At daylight a flag of truce was sent in with the same demands as the afternoon before, the bomb-vessels at the same time resuming their positions, so as to renew the attack. This, however, was rendered unnecessary. The Dey at once submitted, and the conclusion of peace was announced by a salute of twenty-one guns. The terms were the abolition of Christian slavery forever; the instant delivery of the slaves of all Christian nations; the restitution of all money received for slaves since the commencement of the year; reparation to the British consul for the injuries he had received; and a public apology for the conduct of the Dey. These terms were all complied with, and on the following day twelve hundred slaves were embarked at Algiers, and restored to their country and friends. The total number liberated there and at Tunis and Tripoli, was 3003. The author was at Genoa when the Sardinian slaves, 62 in number, which had been delivered, were brought there in one of the English sloops which had shared in the action. The cheers of the people as they entered the harbor, and the thunder of the artillery which saluted the victors, still resound in his ears. It was one of those moments which make a man proud of his country and of the human race.¹

81. The Algerines submit, and peace is concluded.

¹ Lord Exmouth's Disp., Ann. Reg. 1816, 237, 239; App to Chron.; Ostler, 333, 335.

Lord Exmouth was deservedly made a Viscount for this glorious victory; and promotion on the usual scale was bestowed on the other officers engaged. Admiral Milne was knighted; and the achievement was noticed in the most flattering terms in Parliament, by whom thanks were cordially voted. "No one," said Lord Cochrane, who spoke on this occasion, "was better acquainted than himself with the power possessed by batteries over a fleet; and he would say, that the conduct of Lord Exmouth and the fleet deserved all the praise which that House could bestow. The attack was nobly achieved, in a way that a British fleet always performed such services; and the vote had his most cordial concurrence, for he never knew or had heard of any thing more gallant than the manner in which Lord Exmouth had

82. Honors bestowed on Lord Exmouth and the fleet.

was replied to, close under the massy walls of Algiers, will as little admit of description as the heroism and self-devotion of each individually, and Lord Exmouth in particular, in the action of this memorable day. Till nine o'clock he remained with the Queen Charlotte in the same position, in the hottest of the fire, encouraging every one not to give up the work begun till the whole was completed; and thus displayed such perseverance that all were animated with the same spirit: and the fire of the ships, against a brave and desperate enemy appeared to redouble."—Admiral CAPELLAN's Dispatch, August 30, 1816. Annual Register 1816, 242—Appendix to Chronicle.

* Alison's Europe, chap. lii. § 60.
† Admiral Capellan, who nobly seconded Lord Exmouth on this occasion, bore the following honorable testimony to Lord Exmouth's conduct during the battle:—"The Dutch squadron, as well as the British force, appeared to be inspired with the devotedness of our magnanimous chief in the cause of mankind; and the coolness and precision with which the terrible fire of the batteries

VOL. I.—D

laid his ships alongside the Algerine batteries."[1] These are noble words, such as the brave only can apply to the brave; rendered doubly striking, and not less honorable to the giver than the receiver, when it is recollected under what unmerited obloquy Lord Cochrane labored at that time, and the shameful ingratitude with which he had been treated by his country. There were not wanting, however, many who thought that, on such an occasion, honors and rewards might have been bestowed with a more liberal hand, and that Government would have acted more gracefully if they had seized this opportunity to bestow, perhaps, an unusual amount of the royal favor on a service which, during the last year of the war, had received so little of it, simply because the magnitude of its former victories had swept every enemy from the ocean. But the admiration and gratitude of the world was the real reward of the victors. Never, perhaps, since the fall of Jerusalem resounded through Christendom, had such a unanimous feeling prevailed every civilized state. Differences of race, of nations, of institutions, were forgotten in the common triumph of faith. The Roman Catholic grasped the hand of the Protestant, the Lutheran of the Greek. Through two hundred millions of human beings, one simultaneous burst of joy broke forth; the unity of feeling, which is the charm of love between two faithful hearts, was for once felt by an entire fifth of the human race.[2]

"Was ist Liebe, ich dir sage?
Zwei Seelen, ein Gedanke.
Zwei Herzen einer Schlag."[*]

§3. Reflections on this battle, and the commencement of the ascendant of Christianity over Mohammedanism.

The battle of Algiers was memorable in another point of view, still more important to the general interests of humanity. It was the first of the great and decisive triumphs of the Christians over the Mohammedans. Other victories had been gained in former days, but they were in defence only, or were obliterated in the consequences of subsequent disaster. The battle of Tours, in the days of Charles Martel, the deliverance of Vienna by John Sobieski, the victory of Lepanto by Don John of Austria, only averted subjugation from Christendom; the glories of Ascalon, the conquest of Jerusalem, the heroism of Richard Cœur-de-Lion, were forgotten in the disaster of Tiberias, the fate of Ptolemais, the expulsion of the Christians from the Holy Land. Even the more recent successes of the Russians over the Turks had been deeply checkered with disaster; the storming of Oczakow was balanced by the disaster of the Pruth; the Balkan had never been crossed by the followers of the Cross, and the redoubtable antagonists still exchanged desperate thrusts, with alternate success, on the banks of the Danube. But with the battle of Algiers commenced the decisive and eternal triumph of the Christian faith; the Cross never hereafter waned before the Crescent. Other triumphs not less decisive rapidly succeeded, and the Ottoman Empire was only saved from dissolution by the jealousies of the victors. Navarino wrenched Greece from its grasp; Acre saw the sceptre of Syria pass from its hands; Koniah brought it to the verge of ruin; Algiers delivered its sway over Africa to France; the passage of the Balkan rendered it tributary to Russia. Nor was the waning of the Crescent less perceptible in Asia. The bastions of Erivan gave the Muscovites the command of Georgia; the Cross was placed on the summit of Ararat, the resting-place of the Ark; the British standards were seen on the ramparts of Ghuznee, the cradle of the Mohammedan dominion of India.

These memorable occurrences, in a certain degree, lift up the vail which conceals the designs of Providence from mortal eyes. Whence proceeded this sudden and decisive superiority on the part of one of those antagonists, who for five centuries had struggled with each other with alternate success and equal resources? Evidently from the energy which a spiritual faith and unfettered thought had communicated to the Christian powers, and the vast development of military skill which had taken place in the principal European states from the wars of the French Revolution. And whence arose those memorable wars, disastrous to humanity at the time, but from which, as from the dragon's teeth, have sprung the armed men who are subduing the globe? From the efforts of Voltaire and the Encyclopedists to deride and destroy Christianity. Such is the system of Divine administration: it is hard to say whether it is most supported by the efforts of its enemies, or the sacrifices of its friends. That which all the devotion of the Crusaders could not effect, has been brought about at the appointed season by the agency of the infidels; the preaching of Voltaire has done that which that of Peter the Hermit had left undone. Humanity may cease, therefore, to deplore the ceaseless wars between civilized nations, when it perceives the superiority which they give to the arms of civilization over those of barbarism; it will discern in them the severe training by which the race of Japhet is prepared for its predicted mission to dwell in the tents of Shem, to overspread the earth and subdue it. Christianity, indeed, is destined to spread mainly by its winning the hearts of men; but in a world of selfishness and violence, it is not thus alone that mankind are to be converted even to their own blessing; the first entrance must be sometimes won by conquest; and he who bears even the olive branch and Cross in one hand, may often despair of success if he is not prepared, when necessary, to grasp the naked sword in another.

§4. Progressive ascendant of Christianity over Mohammedanism.

[*] GRILLPARZER, *Der Sohn der Wildniss.*

CHAPTER III.

HISTORY OF FRANCE FROM THE SECOND RESTORATION OF LOUIS XVIII., TO THE ORDINANCES OF SEPTEMBER 7, 1816.

1. Extraordinary difficulties of the Government of France after the battle of Waterloo.

If England, which had been victorious in the strife, and closed a conflict of twenty years with glory unprecedented in its annals, still found itself grievously straitened and reduced to the greatest difficulties on the return of peace, what must the condition of France have been, and what the difficulties of its Government, when, after having had the national passions excited to the very highest degree, by the long triumph of the Republic and the Empire, it was suddenly stript of all the fruits of victory, shorn of its conquests, humbled in its pride, with its armies defeated, its emperor a captive, its capital taken? To any nation such a series of reverses must have been a subject of deep humiliation and regret; but to the French it was doubly so from the warlike character of the people, their eager desire for military glory, and the unparalleled series of successes which, in the early wars of the Revolution, had fanned this desire into a perfect passion. Seven hundred thousand armed men, in the summer of 1815, invaded the territory of the Great Nation, from the Rhine, the Alps, and the Pyrenees; and spreading themselves, after the contest ceased, over its whole extent, systematically began the work of retribution on France for the innumerable evils and humiliations they had experienced from it in the days of its triumphs. England alone, which had experienced no such evils and humiliation, attempted no such retaliation; the state which had successfully withstood Napoleon in the plenitude of his power, now alone strove to appease the wrath of the conquerors, and restrain the uplifted arm of vengeance.

2. Difficulties arising from the changeable disposition of the French people.

To have founded a government and restored a dynasty with any prospect of success amidst such a whirlwind of disaster, would have been a matter of the utmost difficulty under any circumstances, and with any people. But in the case of the French, the difficulty was infinitely enhanced by the mobility of disposition, and extremes of passion by which they, beyond any other people recorded in history, have ever been characterized. Nations have their distinctive character as well as individuals, and what is first impressed on them by the signet-ring of nature as the peculiarity of the race, is rarely if ever changed in any subsequent period of their history. No one can have been acquainted with the men, and still more the women, of that highly intellectual and agreeable people, without being convinced that proneness to change, and readiness to pass from one extreme to another, is their great characteristic; and what individuals do in days, the nation as a whole does in years or centuries. "Emportée comme une femme" has in every age been their distinctive temperament. An eloquent French writer, who knew them well, and had himself experienced their mutability, has given the following graphic picture of the disposition of his countrymen:—"The people," says Lamartine, "are like individual men; they have their passions, their reactions, their exaltation, their depression, their repentance, their hesitation, their uncertainty. What we commonly call public opinion in free governments, is nothing but the moving needle on the compass, which marks the variations in the atmosphere of human affairs. That instability is more sudden and prodigious in France than in any other country in the world, if we except the ancient Athenian races. It has become a by-word in Europe. The French historian is bound to confess this vice in his country, of which he records the vicissitudes, and signalizes the virtues. That very mobility is allied to a noble quality of the great French race, Imagination; it forms part of their destiny. In war it is termed ardor; in the arts, genius; in reverses, despondency; in that despondence, inconstancy; in patriotism, enthusiasm. They are the people in modern times who have the most fire in their souls. It is the gales of that mobility which feed the flame. It is impossible to explain, but by this peculiarity in the character of the French race, the accessions of delirium which at times gain possession of the whole nation, and induce them unanimously to support, at only a few months' distance from each other, principles, men, and forms of government the most opposed to each other."[1]

[1] Lamartine, Histoire de la Restauration, v. 329, 330.

3. Important effects this produced in 1815, and causes of the violence of opinion.

Never did this extraordinary peculiarity of the French nation appear in more striking colors, or induce more important effects, than in 1815, after the return of Louis XVIII. from Ghent, and the re-establishment of the monarchy of the Bourbons in Paris. The passion for freedom, and the forms and privileges of a constitutional monarchy, which had burst forth so strongly at the opening of the Revolution, and been after suppressed by the blood of the Convention and the glories of the Empire, had broken out afresh, and spread immensely during the year of peace which followed the first restoration in 1814. Whatever had been the faults of the Bourbons during that period—and doubtless they were many—they had been against themselves and the cause of monarchical government alone; they had all redounded to the advancement and spread of liberal opinions. An opposition to the court, that invariable mark of a constitutional monarchy, had sprung up; and all the errors of the executive had only weakened its own respect and augmented the influence of the opposition. The days of sabre dominion were at an end; the access to power was to be sought by other means than the jingling of spurs in the ante-chambers of the palace. A powerful opposition had sprung up in the Chambers, and been supported by a large portion of the public press, in the free discussion of which the newly emancipated French people took the greatest delight. The nightmare of the Revolution, the dreams of the Empire, were past and in their stead the morning of freedom appeared to have dawned again, gilded with all the colors which, twenty-five years before, had lured the world by their brilliancy.[1]

[side note: 1 Lam. 1.St. de la Rest. v. 332, 334.]

These hopes and expectations had been alike dashed by the second return of Napoleon, and the sudden catastrophe by which it was terminated. The rule of constitutional government was at an end; the ambition which had turned into the channels of peace was at once blasted. The delusive colors with which the generosity or policy of the allied chiefs had disguised the first conquest of France had disappeared; the vail had been suddenly withdrawn, and subjugation, with all its bitterness, had fallen upon the people. There was no longer any semblance of moderation in the language or conduct of the conquerors; the stern law of retaliation— an eye for an eye, and a tooth for a tooth—had become the principle; the maxim *Væ victis* was not only in every mouth, but directed the movements of every hand. Requisitions, enforced by all the rigor of military execution, were every where made, and brought the anguish and weight of conquest home to every bosom. Already 790,000 armed men, and above 100,000 horses, were quartered in this manner on France; before autumn, their number amounted to nearly 1,040,000. The villages in the country, the small towns in the provinces, were all occupied by corps of Prussians, English, Austrians, or Russians; and every one had a story to recount of an indignity they had experienced, or a loss they had suffered. The general wrath, which had been restrained for a moment by the fascination of Napoleon's return, the terrors of the army, the vigor of the imperial police, and the hopes of a return of the days of glory, now broke out on all sides in loud complaints and lamentations; and it was no consolation to the suffering peasants to be told by the old soldiers that all this was only the fate of war, and that the blow which descended on their shoulders from the Prussian troops was no more than they had themselves inflicted on the Prussians ten years before.[2]

[side note: 4. Unbounded humiliation and sufferings of France at this time.]

[side note: 2 Capefigue, Hist. de la Restauration, iii. 6, 7; Lam. v. 334, 335.]

5.
Which occasions a universal reaction against Napoleon and his adherents.

Pride is the last weakness which can be conquered in the human heart. When either individuals or nations have undergone a great calamity, the first thing they think of is to find some individual or party on whom it can be laid; they will turn any way rather than ascribe it to its real cause—their own folies or sins. Great as may be the weight of external evils, it is as nothing to the sting of the secret mental reproach of having induced them. A scapegoat is invariably sought for to bear the burden of the sins of the nation, and take away the last and bitterest drop in the cup of misery, the consciousness of having deserved it. This scapegoat was found by the French at this disastrous epoch in Napoleon and his party. Great as had been the enthusiasm in 1789 in favor of the Republic, unbounded the exultation in 1806 at the glories of the Empire, they were equaled now by the unanimous burst of indignation at the same conqueror and his followers. All classes joined in it; all heads were swept away by the torrent. Royalists, liberals, proprietors, merchants, agriculturists, artisans, clergy Vendeans, Republicans, Catholics, Protestants, seaport towns, the provinces, the capital—all joined in one universal chorus against the fallen emperor. The mothers recounted their two or three sons who had been sacrificed in Spain or Russia to the ambition of the conqueror; the fathers, their fortunes or means of subsistence that had been wrested from them by the Continental blockade or the war contributions. All had a loss to lament a wrong to avenge.[1] They forgot that they themselves had been the first to swell the song of triumph when these bloody successes were gained. General opinion threw itself, without measure, without reflection, into indignation against one man and his military followers, and that universal transport seized men's minds which, be it right or be it wrong, the forerunner of blessings or the herald of disaster, is generally found to be for the time irresistible.

[side note: 1 Lam. v. 235; Cap. iii. 6, 7; Lacretelle, Hist. de la Restauration, i. 320, 322.]

6.
Difficulties which these feelings threw in the way of the new Government.

As this transport of indignation was all directed against the enemies of the Bourbons, it might naturally be supposed that it would have favored the return, and facilitated the government of Louis XVIII.; yet it was just the reverse, and, in truth, nothing augmented the difficulties of his position, in the first years of the second restoration, so much as the inconsiderate ardor of his party. Vengeance was the universal cry. The passions of the Revolution, the thirst for blood, again appeared, but directed against a different object. It was no longer against the royalists or aristocrats, but against the imperialists and revolutionists, that the persecution was directed. Misfortune had made them change sides. The people now loudly demanded the heads of those who had formerly been the objects of their idolatry. It was no easy matter for the Government, returning after so sad a calamity as the disaster of Waterloo, to moderate the vehemence of a nation torn by such violent passions, and demanding, with great semblance of justice, the sacrifice of such a multitude of delinquents. The rank, talent, and consideration, even the sex, of many who were loudest in the outcry, added to the difficulty of restraining it; for experience then again illustrated the truth, proved by so many passages in history, that when the passions are violently excited, it is in the softer sex that they appear with the most violence. Virgil never showed his knowledge of the human heart more than when he wrote the line—

"Gnarus, furens quid femina possit."

"Women," says Lamartine, "of the highest rank were implacable in their demands for blood. It would seem that generosity is the companion of force, and that the weaker the sex is the more is it pitiless. History is bound to say so in order to stigmatize it. Neither high birth, nor great fortune, nor literary education preserved in that crisis, more than it had done in many others, ladies of the aristocracy of Paris and of the court from the thirst for vengeance, and the sanguinary joys which had actuated women of the most abject condition under the Reign of Terror, and at the gates of the Revolutionary Tribunal."¹

¹ Lam v 429; Cap. iii. 4; Lac. i. 318.

7. Difficulties of Louis XVIII. in the choice of his Ministers.

Louis XVIII., as is always the case with sovereigns in similar circumstances, was the first to feel the pressure, and he did so even before he arrived in Paris from Ghent. The necessity of choosing his ministers as soon as the battle of Waterloo had reopened to him the path to the throne, at once brought it home to the monarch. Chateaubriand had held the portfolio of the Interior during the exile of the court at Ghent, and by his great abilities, evinced in many articles in the *Courier de Gand*, had powerfully contributed to aid the Royalist cause when it seemed desperate, and was all but deserted by the world. But experience has abundantly proved that the independence of real genius is in general but ill calculated for the address and suppleness necessary for success in courts; and that Lord North was right when he said, on being urged to bring Dr. Johnson into Parliament, where his great abilities, it was thought, might aid the Ministry—"Sir, he is an elephant; but he is as likely to trample down his friends as his enemies!" M. de Blacas was the Prime Minister of the fugitive monarch; but though Louis was very partial to him, his known unpopularity in France, owing to the violence of his royalist opinions, rendered it impossible for him to continue to hold that office when the court returned toward Paris. Pozzo di Borgo, the moment the news of the battle of Waterloo arrived, wrote to Louis to set out immediately, and travel quickly, or he might find his place taken before he arrived. T; that timely information Chateaubriand does not hesitate to say the king owed his restoration to the throne.² As M. de Blacas was of necessity dismissed, the office of Prime Minister was vacant, and Louis, who instantly set out from Ghent on receiving Pozzo di Borgo's letter, at first thought of offering it to M. de Chateaubriand, and even went so far as to say to him, "I am going to separate from M. de Blacas; the place is vacant, M. de Chateaubriand."³

² Chateaubriand, Mem. d'Outre Tombe, vii. 39, 40.
³ Ibid. vii. 44.

8. Talleyrand and Fouché are appointed to the Ministry.

But the monarch soon found that, in a constitutional monarchy, the sovereign has not in reality the choice even of his own ministers. Ere he had reached the French frontier, M. de Talleyrand had arrived; and though in the first instance coldly received by Louis, his great influence, and the important part he had played in the first restoration, in a manner forced him upon that monarch as the successor of M. de Blacas. A more serious difficulty arose soon after, from the proposal to take Fouché into the Cabinet, to which the king, as well he might, evinced the utmost repugnance. He was strongly supported, however, by the Count d'Artois and the whole extreme royalists, whom he had succeeded in persuading that without his co-operation the Restoration was impossible. Talleyrand also supported him, as did Marshal Macdonald and Hyde de Neuville; and the Duke of Wellington, who came up and had an interview with Louis at Mons, strongly urged him to submit to the cruel necessity A formal cabinet council was held at Gonesse on the 25th June on the subject, and Chateaubriand, with the utmost vehemence, maintained the opposite side. "The elevation," said he, "of such a man must produce one of two results: the abolition of the charter, or the fall of the ministry at the commencement of the session. Let us figure to ourselves such a minister on the 21st January,* interrupted every moment by a deputy from Lyons with the words, 'You are the man!' Men of that stamp can never be ostensibly beat with the mutes of the seraglio of Bajazet, or the mutes of the seraglio of Napoleon. What would come of the ministers if a deputy from the tribune, with a *Moniteur* of the 9th August in his hand, should demand the expulsion of Fouché from the ministry, as, in his own words, 'a robber and a terrorist, whose atrocious and criminal conduct reflected dishonor and opprobrium on any assembly of which he may be a member?'"¹

¹ Mém. de Chateaub. vii. 57, 58; Lac. i. 328, 329.

9. Formation of the Ministry, and retirement of Chateaubriand.

Strong as these considerations were, the necessity of the case was still stronger, and all the practical men about the king impressed upon him so urgently the impossibility of guiding the vessel of the state through the breakers with which it was surrounded, without the aid of so experienced a pilot, that he was obliged most reluctantly, at the eleventh hour, to give in. M. Talleyrand was named President of the Council and Minister of Foreign Affairs; Fouché, Minister of Police, with the superintendence of public opinion; Baron Louis resumed the seals of Minister of Finance; M. Pasquin became *Garde des Sceaux*; Gouvion St. Cyr, Minister-at-War; M. Jaucourt, of the Marine; the Duc de Richelieu, the Household of the King. M. Pozzo di Borgo was offered the Ministry of the Interior, but declined it. Chateaubriand retired, being resolved to take no part in a ministry of which Fouché was a member. The party of the Count d'Artois were in transports, not less at the retirement of the sturdy royalist, than at the admission of the dexterous regicide. "Without Fouché," they exclaimed, "there can be no safety for France. He alone has saved France; he alone can complete the work he has begun." Every consideration of principle, honor, loyalty, consistency, was forgotten in the universal joy at regaining their offices and emoluments by the aid of the arch-traitor. Many went so far as to assert that, if their heads were still on their shoulders, they owed it to Fouché. Louis XVIII. and Chateaubriand, though constrained to yield to the torrent, were not less decidedly of an opposite opinion; and before separating at St. Denis, on their advance to Paris, they had the following remarkable conversation: "Eh bien!" said Louis XVIII., when they were left alone. "Eh bien, sire," replied Chateaubriand; "you have taken the Duke of Otranto." "It was unavoidable," replied the monarch; "from my brother to the *bailli de coupon*, who at least is not suspected, all said I could not do otherwise. What think you of it?" "Sire," replied Chateaubriand, "the thing is done; I request permission of your

* The day on which Louis XVI was executed

Majesty to be silent." "No, no, speak out; you know how I have resisted ever since we left Ghent." "Sire, I only obey your orders; pardon my fidelity; I think it is all over with the monarchy." The king remained some time silent, and Chateaubriand began to fear he would have cause to repent his boldness, when at length he answered, "To say the truth, M. de Chateaubriand, I am of your opinion."[1]

10. The King's proclamation from Cambray. June 28.

Before leaving Cambray, the King, on the 28th June, issued a proclamation to the French people, which deserves a place in history, from the magnanimity which it breathes, and the spirit of moderation, in the most difficult circumstances, by which it was distinguished. "The gates of my kingdom," said he, "are opened before me; I hasten to collect my wandering subjects, to place myself a second time between the allied armies and the French, in the hope that the regard which I hope they feel for me may turn to the advantage of my subjects. That is the only part which I wish to take in the war; I have not permitted any Prince of my family to enter any foreign corps, and I have restrained the courage of my servants, who were desirous of ranging themselves in arms around my person. Returned to the soil of my country, I rejoice to speak to my people in the voice of confidence. When I first appeared among them, I found the minds of men carried away and agitated by passions, difficulties, and obstacles. Faults were scarcely to be avoided in such circumstances; perhaps they were committed. There are times when even the greatest purity of intention will not suffice; when sometimes it even misleads. Experience is then the only safe guide; it shall not be thrown away; I wish all that can save France. My subjects have learned by bitter proofs that the principle of legitimacy in sovereigns is one of the fundamental bases of the social order; the only one which can establish in the midst of a great people a wise and well-regulated liberty. That doctrine has been promulgated as that of entire Europe. I had consecrated it beforehand in my charter; and I have in view to add to it such guarantees as may secure its benefits. Much has been said, of late, of the restoration of titles and feudal rights: that fable, invented by the common enemy, has no need of being refuted. It is not to be expected that the King of France is to demean himself to reply to calumnies and lies. If the holders of national domains have conceived disquietudes, the charter should reassure them. Have I not myself proposed to the Chambers, and caused to be executed, sales of those properties? That proof of my sincerity is decisive; I do not intend to banish from my presence any but the men whose renown is a subject of grief to France, and terror to Europe. In the conspiracy which they have set on foot, I perceive many misled, some guilty; I promise, I who, as Europe knows, have never promised in vain, to pardon all the Frenchmen who have been misled, all that has passed from the day when I quitted Lille in the midst of so many tears, until that when I re-entered Cambray in the middle of so many acclamations. But the blood of my children has flowed from a treachery without example in the annals of the world. That treachery has brought the stranger into the heart of France; every day reveals to me a new disaster. I owe it then to the dignity of my throne, the interest of my people, the repose of Europe, to except from the pardon the instigators and authors of that horrible calamity. They shall be marked out for the vengeance of the law by the two Chambers whom I propose to assemble without delay. Frenchmen, such are the sentiments which he whom time can not change, nor misfortune exhaust, nor injustice depress, brings back into the midst of you. The King, whose ancestors have reigned over you for eight centuries, returns to devote the remainder of his days to your defense and consolation."[1]

11.

The King arrived at St. Denis on the 6th June, but he remained two days there, awaiting the occupation of His entry into the capital by the English and Paris. June 8. Prussian troops. They made their public and triumphant entry on the 7th July, and on the day following it was determined that the King should make his entrance. M. Decazes, dreading the Faubourg St. Denis, through which the cortege required to pass, and which was in a violent state of fermentation, advised Louis to postpone the entry till the night; but the King replied in a worthy spirit, in allusion to the nocturnal entry of Napoleon on the 20th March, "No, I will traverse Paris at mid-day, and in the middle of my people; when they see their King in France, conspirators disappear." Still the ministers insisted, and, as the King proposed to enter in an open carriage, they represented that a shot or a stone, thrown from one of the roofs in the Rue St. Denis, might prove fatal to France. "There is a misfortune," said he, "which I shall never know—that of fearing my people." In effect, the King made his entry at noon on the 8th. Though the utmost efforts were made by the police to put the people on a wrong scent, the crowd was immense on the passage; from the Porte St. Denis, where the procession entered the capital, to the Tuileries, where the King alighted, the streets seemed paved with human heads. Ever passionately fond of theatrical display, the Parisians on this occasion had a still more pressing motive for crowding to see the entry; they sought a momentary distraction to their thoughts —they hoped to see in the pacific monarch the dove with the olive branch, which returned with the glad tidings that the deluge was retiring. The National Guard in full uniform every where lined the streets, and evinced for the most part, with perfect sincerity, the utmost enthusiasm on the occasion. The applause was universal; white flags were generally hung out from the windows or suspended from the roofs, and the cheers of the multitude resembled rather the exultation felt at the sight of a triumphant conqueror, than the feelings awakened by the return of a fugitive monarch in the rear of foreign bayonets. The partisans of Napoleon, few in number, humiliated in feeling, and execrated by their countrymen, had retired with the army behind the Loire, or sheltered themselves in obscure corners of the metropolis. The feelings of all present were unanimous; tears flowed down many cheeks; the extremity of disaster had reconciled many enemies—caused many feuds to be forgotten; cries of "Vive Henri IV.!"—"Vive Louis XVIII.!" were heard on all sides; and in the midst of unparalleled difficulties and public disasters, the monarch experienced a few minutes of heart-felt joy as he re-entered the palace of his fathers.[1]

But the pleasing illusion was of short duration; and Louis soon experienced the bitter truth, that the worst possible foundation for a dynasty is conquest by foreign arms. It is impossible to imagine the violence of the victorious Royalists, or the urgency with which they besieged the sovereign for vengeance, speedy, general, and unrelenting, against the authors of all their calamities. An entire purification of the Chamber of Peers, of the magistracy, of the army, and of the ministry; the restoration to the provinces of the power of the clergy, and of the noblesse, were the conditions held out as indispensable by such of the Royalists as were most moderate, and least inclined to sanguinary measures. Argument was out of the question; there was no discussion or division of opinion in the saloons of the Faubourg St. Germain; universal transport gave vent to the universal fury. But in the midst of these dangerous excesses, the king had a very difficult part to play; for there were perils, and no light ones, on the other side; and the ministry contained men who were themselves the chief objects of popular reprobation, and yet whose aid could not be dispensed with in the critical state of public affairs. Talleyrand and Fouché, on their part, as strongly inculcated the extreme danger of any violent reactionary movement, and represented the strength of the party in France which was attached to the principles of the Revolution, enriched by its spoils, and resolute not to be stripped of any of its acquisitions. To add to the general difficulties, the allied cabinets loudly demanded some guarantee for the peace of Europe, by the punishment of the most guilty among those who had disturbed it; while the French, on all sides, as loudly complained of the dreadful exactions of the allied troops, and insisted that the first care of the sovereign should be to endeavor to procure some mitigation of the sufferings of his subjects.[2]

But there was a question of still greater nicety, and attended with more lasting consequences, which remained behind, and that was the convocation of the legislature, without the aid of which it was evidently impossible that any of these objects could be attained, or even the government be carried on for any length of time. Two plans here suggested themselves; but each was attended with very great difficulties. The one was to convoke the deputies of 1814, who were the existing legislature at the period of the return of Napoleon from Elba; passing over the Hundred Days entirely, as a usurpation of no legal effect, and entitled to no consideration. The second was, to have a new election. It was impossible to go on with the Chamber recently elected under Napoleon, as it was of so extremely democratic a character that even his firm hand had proved unable to guide it. To an Englishman, accustomed as the people of this country have been to the vicissitudes of a constitutional monarchy, there could be no doubt what course in these circumstances should have been pursued. This was to convoke simply both Chambers as they stood at the departure of the king for Ghent, as was done in this country on the restoration of Charles II. in 1661. But the French cabinet decided otherwise, on the ground that the first requisite of a representative legislature is to be in harmony with the feelings of the people; that the events which had passed since the preceding March were equivalent to an ordinary century; and that no unity of feeling could be expected between the representatives of the first and the people of the second restoration.[3]

But another question was wound up with the first, and upon its decision the future fate of France in a great measure hinged. By what laws were the elections to be regulated? By those of the Empire, or of preceding times during the Revolution? The Acte Additionnel. passed by Napoleon during the Hundred Days, was felt to have contained some important modifications of the charter in this respect; and it had been determined at Ghent to adopt some of them, if a second restoration should take place. In particular, the reduction in the age requisite for a seat in the Chamber of Deputies, an increase in their number, and the power of proposing laws or resolutions, seemed desirable, and in harmony with the spirit of the age. In the absence of any existing legislature, there was no authority from which these changes could emanate but that of the king in council; and the 14th article of the charter, which reserved power to the king of introducing such modifications in the charter as the interests of the state required, seemed to give sufficient authority for such a proceeding. In conformity with these views, an ordinance was issued, which stated in the preamble: "It was his Majesty's intention to have proposed to the two Chambers a law for the regulation of election of deputies for the departments. His wish was to have modified, in conformity with the lessons of experience and the well-understood wishes of the nation, many articles of the charter, especially those touching the conditions of eligibility, the number of deputies, the initiative in laws, and the mode of deliberation. The misfortunes of the times having interrupted the sitting of the Chambers, the king still felt that at present the number of deputies in the departments was much too small to render the nation sufficiently represented. It seemed in an especial manner to be necessary that the national representation should be numerous; that its powers should be periodically renewed; that they should emanate directly from the electoral colleges; in fine, that the elections should be the expression of public opinion at the moment. As no act of the legislature can authorize these changes, any more than the modifications intended to be introduced into the charter, the king thought it was just that the nation should, in the mean time, enjoy the advantages it would derive from a legislature at once more numer ous and less restricted in the conditions of eligibility. Wishing, at the same time, that any modification of the charter should not be considered as definitive until it had received the constitutional sanction, the proposed ordinance will be the first object in the deliberations of the Chambers. Thus the legislature will jointly enact on the law of election, and the changes to be made in the charter in that particular; and the king only takes the initiative in them so far as they are indispensable and urgent, and under the obligation to follow as closely as possible the charter and the forms already in usage."¹

¹ Moniteur, July 12, 1815; Cap. iii. 13, 14.

15. Royal ordinance, changing the modes and rules of election. July 12.

In pursuance of these motives, the Chamber of Deputies, elected in 1814, was dissolved, and a new one summoned on an entirely new basis, which rested only on the royal ordinance. The electoral colleges were divided anew into Colleges of Departments, and Colleges of Arrondissements. The latter presented the candidates, among whom the colleges of departments chose the half of the deputies. The electors were permitted to vote at twenty-one, instead of twenty-five, the time fixed by the charter. The deputies were declared eligible at twenty-five, instead of thirty, the former age. The number of deputies was increased from 262 to 395; and all members of the Legion of Honor were admitted, on that qualification alone, to the suffrage. The payment of direct taxes to the amount of 300 francs (£12) was the general basis of the qualification for voting. It is particularly worthy of observation, that this great change in the constitution of the country, introducing an entire new class of voters, drawn from the army, and adding no less than 133 new members to the Chamber of Deputies, was introduced by the *sole authority of the king*, without the concurrence of any other branch of the legislature, and by a royal ordinance alone. But being for the most part a concession in favor of the democratic party, the thing passed without objection, and they silently acquiesced in an exercise of the royal power which, in this instance at least, was in their favor. The chamber was convoked for the 24th September.¹

¹ Ordinance, July 12, 1815; Moniteur, July 12, 1815; Cap. iii. 15, 16.

16. Disunion between the King and the Duke d'Angoulême and Count d'Artois as to the Prefects.

By this ordinance an immense deal of power was thrown into the hands of the prefects of departments, who were, especially in the south, almost entirely in the hands of the Royalist committees, composed of the most ardent and vehement Royalists. The Duke d'Angoulême had, in the first tumult, and amid the first necessities of the restoration, received from the King the most unlimited power for the organization of the royal authority in the southern provinces, which he had traversed in their full extent, and where he had rendered the most important services. He was intrusted in them all with the nomination of new prefects in lieu of those placed by Napoleon, subject to the approbation, however, of the king in council. As he was entirely ignorant of the proper persons to be nominated, he necessarily followed the advice of the Royalist committees; and they proposed persons so violent that great part of his nominations were not confirmed by the King. As soon as the Duke d'Angoulême was informed of this, he hastened to Paris to lay his complaints before the King; but he was without difficulty brought to see that, in so important an affair, and one on which the ensuing elections would in a great measure depend, it was indispensable that the prefects should be in entire harmony with the cabinet. It was not so easy a matter, however, to deal with the Count d'Artois, and the Royalist Committees in the north, which were under his direction; and such was the resistance experienced in many places by the royal prefects, that Talleyrand went so far as to propose in the cabinet that that Prince should be exiled from the kingdom. This strong measure was not gone into, but every effort was made to strengthen the interior administration. M. DE BARANTE was appointed Secretary to the Minister of the Interior, and M. GUIZOT Minister of Justice; and a circular equally eloquent and judicious, soon after issued by the Government to the prefects, which had the happiest influence, revealed the pen of the former of these accomplished writers.¹* But it augured ill for the harmony of administration, and the future fate of the monarchy, when schisms so serious took place so early in the royal family. At length matters came to such a pass that, after a few days' deliberation, an ordinance was issued, withdrawing the powers of the extraordinary commissioners, and restoring the whole power in the kingdom to the prefects appointed by the King.†

¹ Ordinance, Moniteur, July 19; Cap iii. 21, 23.

Ere there was time for the royal authority to obtain the benefit of these judicious ordinances, in calming, to a certain degree, the passions

---

* "Faites sentir aux habitans de votre département, combien le cœur du Roi souffre surtout de ne pouvoir empêcher les désastres que la guerre entraîne à sa suite, mais que les désastres seraient plus grands encore, que notre avenir serait pour ainsi dire sans espérances, si un gouvernement honorable et toujours esclave de sa foi, ne donnait à l'Europe une garantie, que rien ne pourrait suppléer ni remplacer. Nos malheurs sont grands aujourd'hui, mais il y a quatre mois que tous les bons Français en gémissaient d'avance, et les voyaient venir à la suite du destructeur de notre patrie. En exposant nos maux je viens de tracer vos devoirs, c'est en ne vous écartant jamais de la ligne constitutionelle que suit le gouvernement du roi, en vous occupant sans relâche de tous les détails de vos fonctions, en portant vos soins sur la conduite et l'expédition des affaires, en rendant, à tous une justice exacte et bien faisante que vous pourriez apaiser quelques esprits encore exagérés et inquiets. L'appui et les avantages individuels que chaque citoyen recevra d'un régime de liberté, et d'une administration régulière, sont le meilleur et même le seul moyen de conciliation entre tous les partis."—*Circulaire aux Préfets, du Ministre de l'Intérieur*, 17th July, 1815; *Moniteur*, 18th July.

† "Les circonstances extraordinaires dans lesquelles s'était trouvée la France depuis trois mois, et l'impossibilité de la faire gouverner par les magistrats royalement institués, avaient obligé de déléguer, soit par sa Majesté elle même, soit par ses ministres, des pouvoirs extraordinaires à quelques sujets dévoués qui tous avaient servi avec zele et courage, et qui presque toujours avaient agi avec succes pour faire reconnaitre l'autorité legitime. Aujourd'hui que le Roi avait repris les rênes de son gouvernement, que le ministère était organisé et en correspondance avec les administrateurs nommés par sa Majesté; les fonctions des commissaires extraordinaires devenaient superflus et même nuisibles à la marche des affaires en détruisant l'unité d'action qui est le premier besoin de toute administration régulière. Le Roi voulait donc que les fonctions des commissaires extraordinaires cessassent sur le champ."—*Ordonnance de 18me Juillet, 1815; Moniteur, 19me July*; and CAPEFIGUE's *Hist. de la Restauration*; 23, 24.

which distracted the country, a new subject of difficulty of the most urgent nature presented itself, and that was in regard to the press. Talleyrand and Fouché strongly urged on the cabinet the necessity of some great relaxations in this respect, as bringing the administration more in harmony with public opinion, which passionately longed for the consolation to be derived amid all their distresses from the liberty of complaining. The liberty of the press had, by means of the censorship, been totally extinguished under Napoleon; and though restored at the first restoration in 1814, it was soon found to be so dangerous an arm that it was deemed indispensable to impose some check upon it. Accordingly, the law of October 21, 1814, subjected all pamphlets or journals of less than twenty leaves to the censorship. Now, however, when public opinion was declaring itself so strongly in favor of the restoration and against the Napoleonists, it was thought that the journals alone were to be considered as dangerous, and that works of thought and reflection in the form of pamphlets, however brief, would favor the government rather than the reverse. Louis did not share that opinion, and kept the ordinance several days beside him before it received his sanction; but at length, on the pressing solicitation of his ministers, he affixed his signature to the ordinance, removing the censorship from every publication except the journals.¹

17.
The freedom of the press is restored in all but the journals. July 15.

¹ Ordinance, July 15, 1815; Moniteur, July 16; Cap. ii 25, 26.

A still more hazardous subject, because one more immediately affecting the passions, required next to be considered, which was the selection of the delinquents who were to be capitally proceeded against or banished for their accession to the rebellion of 1815. Fouché was intrusted with the preparation of the lists—ostensibly as the Minister of Police—really as the person in France best acquainted with the threads of the conspiracy, and most qualified, by his familiarity with traitors, to trace them out and mark them out for public justice on this occasion. Many circumstances rendered it indispensable to select and proceed against the delinquents, and that without delay. The universal opinion at the Court, and among the Royalists, was, that it was a deep-laid conspiracy which had brought back Napoleon; that the army, under the guidance of its leading officers, was the principal agent in it; and that, if the chief conspirators were only convicted and punished, the delusion would be almost entirely eradicated in the country. The great majority of the nation, grievously wounded in their feelings by the presence, and injured in their purses by the exactions of the Allies, loudly called for the punishment of the authors of these disasters; while the representatives of the allied sovereigns at Paris, in a voice less loud, but still more decisive, insisted that a great example was necessary, and that the leaders of a revolution which had involved Europe again in the flames of war, compelled a million of armed men to enter France, and cost the allied powers at least £100,000,000 sterling, must be brought to condign justice. Clemency and generosity had been tried at the first restoration,

18.
Reasons which rendered the punishment of the leading Napoleonists necessary.

and failed; firmness and decision were the qualities which had now become indispensable Louis was not ignorant with what perils any measures of severity against the marshals or generals of the army would be attended; but the circumstances left him no alternative, and orders were given to Fouché to prepare the lists of proscriptions.¹

¹ Cap. iii. 26 27; Lac.i.330, Lam. v. 226 227.

The veteran traitor drew up two lists, embracing a great proportion of the survivors of those who had been linked with himself in his innumerable treacheries and treasons during his long career; and he put the crowning act to the whole by countersigning the ordinance which marked them out for punishment.¹ As originally prepared by him, the lists were much larger than was finally agreed to. The number of those ordered to leave Paris within twenty-four hours, which at first contained sixty names, including two ladies,* was reduced, by the humanity of Louis, or the intercession of his ministers, to thirty-eight; and nineteen were ordered to be arrested and delivered to the proper military tribunals for immediate trial. The number, considering the magnitude of the conspiracy, and the terrible results which had flowed from it, was not great; but it had a melancholy interest from the celebrity of many of the names, immortal in history, which were contained in it, and the great and glorious deeds in French annals with which they had been connected. The names were—"Marshal Ney, Labedoyère, the two brothers Lallemand, Drouet, D'Erlon, Lefebvre Desnouettes, Ameile, Brayer, Gilly, Mouton, Duvernet, Grouchy, Clausel, Deville, Bertrand, Drouot, Cambronne, Lavalette, Rovigo." To all who are acquainted with the history of the revolutionary wars, many of these names are as household words.² The second list containing the names of those who were to be banished forty leagues, was more numerous, and contained names not less illustrious; but it has not the absorbing interest of the former, from none of the persons contained in it having met with the same tragic fate.†

19.
Lists of persons to be accused prepared by Fouché, and sanctioned by a royal ordinance. July 21.

² Ordinance, July 24, 1815; Moniteur,July 26; Cap. iii. 30, 24; Lac. i 330, 331.

Before any person could be brought to trial under this ordinance, two other ordinances appeared, regarding the Chamber of the Peers. By the first of these, issued on the same day as the fatal lists prepared by Fouché, it was declared that all those of the former Chamber of Peers sitting under the monarchy, who had accepted seats in the one convoked by

20.
Ordinances regarding the Chamber of Peers, which is declared hereditary. July 21, and Aug. 17, and Aug. 20.

---

* Mesdames Hamelen and De Souza.
† "Les individus dont les noms suivent—Lavoye, Maréchal Soult, Alex. Excelmans, Bassano, Marbot, Felix Lepelletier, Boulay de la Meurthe, Mehul, Toussaint, Gen Lamarque, Lobau, Harel, Pierre Barrère, Arnault, Pomereul, Regnault de St. Angely, Arrighi de Padoua, Dessau (fils), Garreau, Réal, Bouvier, Dermiusard, Merlin de Douai, Durbach, Dirat, Defermont, Bory St. Vincent, Felix Desportes, Garnier de Saintes, Mellinet, Hullin, Cluys, Courtin, Forbin, Jancon (fils aîné), Letorgne, Dideville—sortiront dans trois jours de la ville de Paris, et se reuriront dans l'intérieur de la France, dans le lieu que notre Ministre de la Police-Générale leur désignera, et où ils resteront sous sa surveillance, en attendant que les Chambres statuent sur ceux d'entre eux qui devront ou sortir du royaume ou être livrés à la poursuite des tribunaux."—Ordonnance, 24th July, 1815; Moniteur, 25

Napoleon during the Hundred Days, should be held to have, *ipso facto*, vacated their seats in the former assembly, and be now erased from the list of its members. By another ordinance, dated 17th August, no less than eighty-two members were added to the peerage. This large addition was anxiously considered both by the king and his cabinet; and many names, after being inserted, were erased, and again inserted. The list, as finally arranged, contained many illustrious names, then for the first time elevated, or restored to that dignity, and exhibited a curious proof of the various and contending interests which had been at work in its formation. The king invested with the peerage M. de Blacas, the Count de la Chatres, the Dukes d'Enars, d'Avaray, and d'Aumont, the Count d'Artois, Viscount Chateaubriand, Count Mathieu de Montmorency, Jules de Polignac, and the Marquis de Rivière, the Duke d'Angoulême, General Mounier, Admiral Ganthenume, the Duke de Berri, the Count de la Guiché, and the Count de la Ferronnays, M. de Talleyrand, the Abbé de Montesquieu, the Marquis d'Ormond, the Duke d'Alberg, and several others.[1] To these were afterward added the sons of the Duke of Montebello, of Marshal Berthier, and Marshal Bessières.

[1] Ordinance, Aug. 17, 1815; Moniteur, Aug. 18; Cap. iii. 41, 42.

A still more momentous change took place by an ordinance which appeared a few days after, on August 19, making the seat in the Peers hereditary, which was the subject of long and anxious discussions during four days in the cabinet. Louis argued strongly that, in agreeing to this change, he was stripping the crown of one of its most important prerogatives, and of nearly all its influence in the Chamber of Peers. "With the cessation of ambition," said he, "my influence over the peerage is at an end. When it becomes a family inheritance, I have no power over it: I can no longer put a ring on the finger of one of my own household." Talleyrand insisted vehemently for the hereditary succession: "We must have," said he, "stability: *we must build for a long future*." At length it was carried for the hereditary right; and the preamble of the ordinance bore—"The king being desirous to give to his people a new pledge of his anxiety to establish in the most stable manner the institutions on which the government reposes, and being convinced that nothing insures more the repose of states than that inheritance of feeling which is created in families, by being called to the exercise of important functions, which creates an uninterrupted succession of persons in high stations, whose fidelity to their prince and devotion to their country are guaranteed by the principles and examples they have received from their fathers." There can be no doubt that these observations are well founded, but unfortunately something more is required to render a hereditary House of Peers either useful or influential—either a rampart to the crown, or a barrier against its encroachments—and that is, a corresponding succession of fortune to support the dignity, which can only be secured by territorial aristocracy, and the right of primogeniture. Both were swept away in the very commencement of the Revolution, and with them the possibility of reconstructing society in France on the basis of European freedom, in which a powerful hereditary aristocracy is an essential element. Without it there remains to society only the choice of Oriental despotism, or American equality; the tyranny of pachas and agas, or prefects in the Old World, or the imperious commands of a numerical majority in the New.[1]

21. The peerage is declared hereditary. August 19.

[1] Cap. iii. 42, 43; Ordinance, August 19, 1815; Moniteur, Aug. 20.

In the midst of these important discussions, the allied sovereigns returned to Paris. The importance of the negotiations of which it had become the theatre rendered their presence indispensable. But their entry was very different from what it had been the year before: the melodramatic display of generosity was at an end, the reality of vengeance was to commence. They came without external pomp or parade, and after their arrival were entirely occupied with the important negotiations which were going forward. If they appeared at all, it was attended by a single footman, and driving in a traveling caleche with a pair of horses. They had no need of the pomp of royalty in the metropolis; their attendants were sufficiently numerous through the country. They extended from the British Channel to the Pyrenees. Never had such an inundation of armed men poured over a single country. Eight hundred thousand warriors in the highest state of discipline and equipment had already entered, and the stream still continued to flow on without any visible abatement. The eastern provinces could no longer contain the armed multitude; already they extended over the central parts of the country, and were even approaching those which were washed by the Atlantic waves. A certain district behind the Loire, occupied by the troops which had retired from Paris,[2] and the wreck of the army which had fought at Waterloo, alone remained in the hands of the French, surrounded by the innumerable multitude of their enemies; but even this last relic of nationality was ere long swept away.

22. Arrival of the Allied Sovereigns in Paris, July 8 and 11.

[2] Cap. iii. 44, 45; Lam. v. 189, 190.

The army which had retired under the command of Marshal Davoust behind the Loire was still 45,000 strong, with 120 guns; and as it was for the most part composed of the corps of Marshal Grouchy, which had, comparatively speaking, suffered little during the brief campaign in the Netherlands, it presented a very imposing appearance. The peasants in the departments in which it was cantoned, seeing those dense battalions, splendid regiments of cavalry, and long trains of artillery and caissons, still in the finest possible order, could not be persuaded that the army had suffered any serious reverse, and loudly demanded to be incorporated in its ranks, and led against the enemy. The soldiers, and nearly all the colonels and inferior officers, shared the same sentiments; insomuch that it was with no small difficulty that they were restrained within the bounds of discipline, and prevented from breaking into open revolt. The chiefs of la Vendée had entered into correspondence with them, and offered to array the whole strength of the western provinces round the sacred standard of national independence. But noble as these sentiments were, and honorable to the men who in

23. Army of the Loire.

this extremity forgot their former feuds in the common desire to save their country, they were far from being shared by the superior officers, and generals of the army, Marshal Davoust, General Haxo, General Gerard, and Kellerman, who were at its head. Without undervaluing their own resources, they were more aware of the strength of the enemy opposed to them. It was in vain to expect that 45,000 or 50,000 men could maintain a contest with 400,000 or 500,000, who could be brought to bear upon them.¹ Davoust accordingly issued a proclamation to the soldiers on the 14th of July, in which he called on the troops to unite themselves to the king; and, however unpalatable to them the stern realities of their situation, it carried conviction to every breast.*

¹ Lam. v. 182, 183; Cap. iii. 49, 50.

24. Its submission. July 13.

So general was the feeling of the absolute necessity of these sentiments, that on the day following Davoust was enabled to present to the king the unqualified submission of the troops. "Sire!" said he, "the army, full of confidence in your generosity, and determined to prevent, by uniting itself to you, civil war, and to bring back, by their example, such as may be estranged from you, flatters itself that you will receive its submission with kindness, and that, throwing a vail over the past, you will not close your heart to any of your children." On the day following, Davoust ventured on the still more decisive and perilous step of causing them to hoist the white flag. "Soldiers!" said he, "it remains for you to complete the act of submission you have just made, by a painful but necessary sacrifice. Hoist the white flag! I know that I demand of you a great sacrifice; during twenty-five years we have gloried in the colors which we bear. But, great as it is, the good of our country demands that sacrifice. I am incapable, soldiers, of giving you an order which is contrary to your honor: preserve for your country a brave and numerous army."¹

¹ Moniteur, July 17, 1815; Lam. v. 183, 184.

25. Disbanding of the army of the Loire.

But although the army of the Loire had thus hoisted the white flag, and submitted to the royal authority, it still formed a formidable body, and its dissolution was justly deemed by the allied sovereigns an indispensable condition of a general peace. The Emperor Alexander in particular, was in an especial manner urgent upon that point, and through his minister, Nesselrode, demanded, in peremptory terms, its immediate disbanding. Several secret notes had been presented to that sovereign, which painted in strong but not exaggerated colors the danger of allowing a powerful body of turbulent men, trained by twenty years of war and license, to remain as a nucleus for the disaffected in the heart of the country.* No sooner was the formal demand for the dissolution of the army of the Loire presented by the allied sovereigns to the French Government, than they took the most effective means to enforce compliance with the requisition. 225,000 men rapidly defiled toward the Loire, and took up positions around it in every direction, which rendered resistance or escape alike impossible. The king made no opposition to the demand, too happy to have the powerful armies of the Allies to enforce a measure, indispensable alike for the stability of his throne and the peace of his kingdom. No new ordinance was promulgated; the ordinance of 23d March, 1815, which proclaimed the disbanding of the army on Napoleon's return, was only officially published, and ordered to be acted upon by the authorities. Thus France was spared the mortification of seeing her army disbanded by an ordinance emanating directly from the Allied head-quarters.¹

¹ Moniteur, July 24, 1815; Cap. iii. 45, 47; Lam. v. 192, 193.

26. Reorganization of the army into departmental legions.

Marshal Gouvion St. Cyr, as war minister was intrusted with the regulations for the reorganization of the army. The great object in view, in that measure, was to extirpate the *esprit de corps* which attached so strongly to particular regiments from the memory of glorious deeds, and substitute in its room the attachments and associations connected with the provinces. For this purpose the whole army was not only disbanded, but entirely broken up, the officers and men detached from each other, and rearranged in new battalions formed after a totally different manner. Eighty-six departmental legions, of three battalions each, were formed, and fifty-two of cavalry and artillery. Every soldier, conscript or recruit, was enrolled in the legion of the department where he had been born; and the old soldiers of the Empire were so scattered through the different legions that not only was their spirit broken, but their numbers rapidly declined, and their ascendency was at an end. This plan, the execution of which was intrusted to the experienced hand of Marshal Macdonald, was admirably calculated to extinguish the military *esprit de corps* in the army, which had proved so fatal to France and to Europe; but it was likely to induce hazards of a different kind if serious internal troubles arose again, and the ardent Royalist legions of la Vendée and Provence came to be arrayed against the sturdy republicans of Burgundy or Alsace.¹

¹ Cap. iii. 49, 51; Lam. v. 193; Lac. i. 313, 314.

---

* "Les commissaires donnent l'assurance qu'une réaction ne sera pas à craindre, que les passions seront domptées, les hommes respectés, les principes sauvés; qu'il n'y aura point de destitutions arbitraires dans l'armée, que son honneur sera à couvert. On en a pour gage la nomination du Maréchal St. Cyr au ministère de la guerre, celle de Fouché au ministère de la police. Ces conditions sont acceptables. L'intérêt national doit rendre franchement l'armée au roi. Cet intérêt exige quelques sacrifices; faisons les avec une énergie modeste. L'armée, l'armée unie deviendra au besoin le centre de ralliement des Français et des Royalistes eux-mêmes! Unissons-nous, serrons-nous, ne nous séparons jamais, soyons Français! Ce fut toujours, vous le savez, le sentiment qui domina mon âme. Il ne me quittera qu'avec mon dernier soupir." — *Proclamation du Maréchal Davoust*, 4 July, 1815; *Moniteur*, 15 July, 1815.

* "Vingt années de guerre et de licence ont formé en France une population militaire qui se refuse à toute ordre et à toute soumission. L'armée voulait la chance des hazards, les dotations, et les avancements dans les grades. Elle ne les voyait que dans le rappel de son chef, et elle y était décidée avec rage. L'armée Française rappelle à tous les souvenirs des Mameluks en Egypte, de la Garde Prétorienne à Rome, des Arabes fanatiques sous Mahomet. Pour servir à l'époque de la paix, cette armée doit être décomposée, moralisée, si on ne parvient pas à en détruire les trois quarts. Il faut donc l'attaquer sans perdre de temps. Il n'y a pas à hésiter; il faut que cette armée soit attaquée de toutes, les prisonniers conduits en Russie doivent y rester assez longtemps pour s'accoutumer comme les déportés à Botany Bay."—CAPE. iii. 1. k. 45, 46.

Another mortification, not so great in reality, but more galling, because more visible to the senses, awaited the Parisians in the breaking up of the great museum, and the restoration of those glorious works of art which had been carried off by the French from all the countries which they had conquered. This important event, which has been already noticed as closing the great drama of the French Revolution,¹ requires to be again mentioned in this place, as commencing the new drama which was to succeed it; for such is the ceaseless succession of human events, and the connection between the chains which unite them, that what appears to terminate with poetic justice one epoch, is found to have been only the commencement of a new one. Among the many difficulties which beset the government of the Bourbons during the first years of the Restoration, not the least arose from the ulcerated feelings which this great act of retributive justice awakened in the breasts of the French people. They were incapable of appreciating the dignified self-restraint which led the Allies, when they had the power, to abstain from following their bad example, and to confine the abstraction to the restitution of the works of art which they had reft from the European states. They saw only in the breaking up of the museum a convincing proof of the reality of their subjugation, and themselves experienced the anguish which they had so often inflicted on others. No one could deny the justice of their doom—

27.
Breaking up of the Museum.

Hist. of Europe, c. xcv.

"Neque enim lex æquior ulla,
Quam necis artifices arte perire sua."

But no one need be told that, however much the justice of this rule may satisfy the feelings of others, it is any thing but a consolation to the sufferers under it; and that, of all the aggravations of the pains of punishment, there is, perhaps, none so great as the secret consciousness of having ourselves induced it.¹

¹ Lac. i. 338, 339; Lam. v. 185, 186.

The state of the finances of the kingdom was so desperate that nothing could well exceed it; and if some breathing time had not been given by the Allies in their requisitions, utter ruin must have overtaken the French nation. Baron Louis, the new finance minister, had entered upon the duties of his office on the evening of the 10th of July. He found the coffers empty, credit ruined, the revenue forestalled by the requisitions in the provinces, or dried up by the impossibility of collecting any taxes. In the general despair, every one looked only to his own security; and the most obvious and efficacious way of doing that appeared to be for every person to hold fast by his own property, and cease altogether the payment of any demand by another. Revenue there was none; for the bayonets of the Allies, who had overspread three-fourths of the territory of France, forced payment of their scourging requisitions without leaving a sous to meet any other demand. Several measures to raise a supply for the immediate necessities of the state were adopted, as the sale of woods, and certain properties belonging to municipalities, which the Crown had a right to dispose of. But this was a trifling and temporary relief only; the material thing was to get

28.
Desperate state of the finances.

some modification in the grinding requisitions of the Allies, which rendered all collection of the revenue for the internal necessities of the kingdom hopeless. The capitalists, who had great confidence in the good faith of the Government and credit of the country, made this an absolute condition of any advances on their part to meet the necessities of the state; and at length, on the urgent representations of Baron Louis, an arrangement was concluded which in some degree alleviated the distress of the treasury. It was agreed that, in consideration of the sum of 100,000,000 francs (£4,000,000 sterling), instantly paid down, the requisitions should cease for two months. This sum was raised by forced loans laid on the chief towns, in payment of which the Government agreed to take bills payable at distant dates, which the treasury discounted on reasonable terms. The measure was violent, but the public necessities left no alternative;* and to the credit of the French capitalists it must be added that they came liberally forward, and aided the municipalities powerfully in providing for the sums assessed upon them. So successful were their efforts, that the crisis was surmounted better than could have been expected. The deficit for the year was only 35,000,000 francs (£2,200,000), the income being 876,318,232 francs, (£35,000,000), and the expenditure 931,441,104 francs, or £37,200,000.¹

¹ Cap. iii. 51, 52; Stat. de la France, Art. Finances, pp. 7, 8.

Notwithstanding this convention, which afforded great relief when it was once fully acted upon, and the regular payments begun, the exactions of the Allies continued without intermission; and on all sides fresh bodies of armed men were continually pouring into the devoted country. There seemed no end to the crusade: large as France is, it seemed almost incapable of containing the prodigious multitude which poured into its territory. The Allies divided its provinces between them, and the districts they severally occupied were deemed ominous of an approaching partition of their country. The English, Hanoverians, and Belgians, 80,000 strong, were quartered in the provinces between Paris and the Flemish frontier. The Prussians were encamped in a mass round Paris, and stretched from thence to

29.
Settlements of the Allied troops in France, and their exactions.

* The following table exhibits the income and expenditure of France for the last years of the war, and first of the Restoration:

RECEIPTS.
Francs.
1812 .... 1,070,000,000 or £42,800,000
1813 .... 1,150,000,000 " 46,000,000
1814 .... 637,432,000 " 25,500,000
1815 .... 876,318,232 " 35,000,000
1816 .... 1,036,604,534 " 41,400,000

EXPENDITURE.
Francs.
1812 .... 1,076,014,000 or £43,000,000
1813 .... 1,171,418,000 " 46,800,000
1814 .... 709,394,626 " 28,260,000
1815 .... 931,411,404 " 37,200,000
1816 .... 1,055,854,028 " 42,250,000

—*Statistique de la France*—Finance, p. 12.

During the reign of Napoleon, nearly half the expenditure of France was levied on foreign states, and did not appear in the finance accounts at all. From 1814 downward it was reduced to its own resources. The great expenditure of 1816 was owing to the war-contributions to the Allies.

the Loire and the Atlantic Ocean: their insolence and overbearing manner, as well as exactions, the requital of six years of French bondage, excited universal indignation. The Austrians, Bavarians, and Wirtemburgers, were scattered over Burgundy, the Nivernois, the neighborhood of Lyons, and Dauphiné. The Piedmontese and Austrians from Italy occupied Provence and Languedoc; the numerous corps of the Russians overspread the plains of Lorraine and Champagne; the Saxon and Baden troops, Alsace; the Hungarians were spread out along the shores of the Mediterranean. "Pour comble de malheur," as the French historians say, 40,000 Spaniards crossed the Pyrenees, and inundated Roussillon and the roots of the Pyrenees, not to engage in the conflict, for it was entirely over, but to share in the expected booty. The Duke d'Angoulême, by hastening to the spot, and by great personal exertions, succeeded in persuading this uncalled-for and unruly body of invaders to retire. Never before—not even in the days of universal mourning, when the northern nations overthrew the Roman Empire, and, advancing like a resistless torrent, drove the whole native population before them—had such an inundation of armed men overwhelmed a country; and never had a people been so thoroughly subjugated, for already 800,000 foreign soldiers occupied their territory, and their native army was disbanded. The moderation of the conquerors was their last remaining hope.[1]

¹ Cap. iii. 167, 16 ; Lam. v. 189, 190 ; Lac. i. 345, 346.

30. Reaction in the south. June 25.

This dreadful accumulation of evils produced its usual result in ulcerating the minds of men. In the south, especially the effect appeared with extraordinary vehemence, for not only were the inhabitants of its provinces all of a warm and ardent temperament, but the party feuds of centuries' duration between the Roman Catholics and Protestants, and subsequently between the Royalists and Republicans, had inspired them with the most violent hatred against each other. Disorders there were already seen to be inevitable during the month of June, when the Imperial armies were collected on the frontier, and few armed men remained in the provinces to suppress the general effervescence, when, on the 25th of that month, the news of the battle of Waterloo arrived, and the telegraph brought to General Verdier, the commander of the district, at the same time the intelligence of the abdication of Napoleon. The news arrived at Marseilles on Sunday at noonday, when the people were just leaving church, and instantly spread like wildfire through the city and the adjoining districts. Being all ardent Royalists, the intelligence excited them to the very highest degree. The transports were universal—the enthusiasm unbounded. General Verdier had a regiment of infantry, a battery of artillery, and several squadrons of horse, at his command, and with military instinct they arranged themselves round their commander on the commencement of the crisis; and the firm countenance of the troops, who shouted incessantly "Vive l'Empereur," for a time restrained the ardor of the people, among whom the cry of "Vive le Roi" was on the point of breaking out. But the Royalists got possession of the church steeples, and sounded the tocsin; and its well-known clang, with the flying rumors already in circulation, soon brought a prodigious concourse of peasants from the country into the streets. This accession of strength rendered the transports of the Royalists uncontrollable. Cries of "Vive le Roi" burst from all sides. The troops were soon enveloped by an insurgent and menacing multitude; and Verdier, despairing of the possibility of maintaining himself in his posts, though there were two forts commanding the city, and dreading the responsibility of commencing a civil war, while as yet uncertain what authority was to obtain the ascendency at Paris, evacuated the town in the course of the evening, and retreated with all his forces to Toulon.[1]

¹ Lam. v. 401, 406 ; Cap. iii. 171, 173 ; Lac. i. 317, 318.

31. Massacre at Marseilles. June 25 and 26.

This retreat was the signal for the commencement of the massacre; and never did the violent passions and savage disposition of the inhabitants of the south of France appear in more frightful colors. The effervescence was so great, the people so violent, that the troops had considerable difficulty in making their way through the multitudes which thronged around them on every side; but after they were gone, all order ceased, and the reaction burst forth with ungovernable fury. It began with the murder of a few Mamelukes, with their wives, who had followed the army of Napoleon back from Egypt. They were cut down without mercy, many on the harbor's edge, where they had fled in hopes of finding barks to escape from their murderers. The whole, with their wives and children, were slaughtered, and thrown into the water. A few who had swam out to sea were dispatched by musket shots after they had gained a considerable distance. Having once tasted of blood, the multitude was as fierce as maddening wolves in pursuit of their prey. During the whole night, and the day following, they sought out the old officers and soldiers of the Imperial army, and bayoneted them without mercy. Among the victims was M. Angles Capefigue, a man of eminence and respectability, the friend of Massena, and many of the leading men of the Empire; his body was pierced in a hundred places with pikes. Powerless, and passed by their followers, in the strife, the Royalist Committee remained passive spectators of the massacre. At length, after two days of tumult and bloodshed, and the loss of above a hundred lives, a sort of urban guard was assembled, and messengers dispatched to some English vessels in the bay, and by the aid of succor sent by them an end was put to the massacre. Marseilles proved on this occasion the satanic wisdom with which the chiefs of the Gironde had sent for and awaited the arrival of the Fédérés de Marseilles, to head the insurrection on the 18th August, 1792.[1]

¹ Cap. iii. 174, 176 ; Lam. v. 405, 406 ; Lac. i. 319, 350 ; History of Europe, c. vii. § 90.

32. Departure of Marshal Brune for Paris. July 31.

Marshal Brune was at this time intrusted with the general command in the south of France; and he was at Toulon when Verdier arrived with the troops from Marseilles, followed soon after by intelligence of the frightful atrocities committed in that city. Uncertain at first which party was to gain the ascondency at Paris, he temporized for a few weeks, but in the end of July, finding the authority of the king firmly established in the capital, and generally recognized throughout France, he hoisted the white flag, and sent in his adhesion. The Royalists had no fault to reproach him with but his ready recognition of Napoleon, and tardy return to the colors of the monarchy. To explain his conduct in these particulars, the marshal set out on the 31st for Paris by land. His friends, who dreaded the catastrophe which followed, in vain besought him to change his route, and embark at Toulon for Havre de Grace. The old soldier revolted at such a proposal as an imputation on his courage, and, only the more resolute to brave the dangers from the representations of their reality, persevered in his intention of proceeding by land.¹

¹ Lam. v. 467; Cap. i. 177; Lac. i. 351.

33.
He is murdered at Avignon. Aug. 2.

On the 2d August he arrived at Avignon, whither the rumor of his approach had preceded him. He stopped in the morning at a hotel near the Rhone to change horses; his countenance was recognized, and a crowd immediately assembled, in which the ferocious passions and vehement spirit of the south were soon conspicuous. A rumor, as false as it was certain to be believed, spread rapidly through the crowd, that he had been actively concerned in the massacres of September, 1792, in Paris, and had actually carried the head of the Princess of Lamballe, affixed to a pike, to the windows of the king. His friends in vain represented that he was not in Paris at all, but on the frontier with the army, on the occasion. That statement, though true, did not produce the slightest impression. It was added, that he was not going to Paris, but to the army of the Loire, to aid in leading the troops and renewing the war. Twice he set out from the hotel under the escort of the prefect, M. de St. Chamont, the mayor of Avignon, and a handful of intrepid citizens, who, though Royalists, had hastened with generous devotion to save the life of their opponent at the hazard of their own; and twice he was forced to return, from the experienced impossibility of forcing a passage. At length the people became so furious that all resistance was in vain; they violently assaulted the principal gate of the hotel, and while the prefect and mayor, with a handful of troops, bravely made good that post, a few dastardly assassins got in by a back window, and, breaking into the room where the marshal was, laid him dead at their feet by two shots from carbines. Ferocious shouts, as from the demons of hell, immediately followed the bloody deed; the body was dragged by the heels through the streets, and cast into the Rhone. That rapid stream quickly floated it down to the sea, by the waves of which the body was cast ashore in a deserted haven between Arles and Tarascon, where it was descried amid the sea-weed by the vultures, which in those warm climates never fail to discover their prey. Their concourse attracted the attention of a poor fisherman, who approached the spot and discovered the corpse. He retired at the moment for fear of danger to himself, for, being an old soldier, he recognized the features of him who had once been his general; but returned at night, and with his own hands gave it a decent sepulture in the sands of the shore—as if to prove that the most renowned tragedies of antiquity were to find a parallel in those which arose out of the French Revolution.¹*

¹ Lam. v. 466, 411; Cap. iii. 178, 179; Lac. i. 351, 352

Such was the impotence, not merely of the constituted authorities, but of the Royalist committees, who were supposed to direct the public movement, that the official gazette announced that Marshal Brune, menaced by the populace of Avignon, had committed suicide. It was not for a considerable time after that the real facts became known—so powerful is popular passion, not merely in instigating to the most atrocious deeds, but in concealing their enormity, or misrepresenting their character. The horrid example was not long in being followed in the adjoining provinces. Bands of assassins, issuing from Avignon, Nimes, and Toulouse, devastated the houses of the suspected persons wherever they could be found, and perpetrated cruelties on the unhappy inmates, which recalled the memory of the worst atrocities of the Revolution. After sacking the chateau of Vaquerville, the wretched inhabitants were burnt alive in its flames. At Toulouse, General Ramel, commander of the department, was murdered in his own hotel in open day. A band of assassins burst into the room where he was sitting. "What do you wish?" said he. "To kill you, and in you, an enemy of the king," was the reply of one, pointing his musket at his breast. A sentinel sprang forward and turned aside the muzzle. Ramel drew his sword and advanced, determined to sell his life dearly; but while he did so, a fresh shot pierced him through the breast, and he fell mortally wounded beside the faithful sentinel, who had been already slain by his side. The dying general was carried up to his room and stretched on his bed; but soon the assassins burst in, and although the surgeon on his knees besought them to spare the last minutes of a dying man, they hacked him with sabres, and plunged pikes in his body, till he was literally cut to pieces. When this was done, the frightful multitude defiled regularly in, and went round the bed singing songs of triumph, and dipping their pikes in the blood of his mangled remains.¹

34. Further massacres in the south. Aug. 15

¹ Lam. v. 447, 448; Cap. iii. 181, 182; Lac. i. 353, 464.

These atrocities were but a specimen of what went on during the whole of August in the south of France. At Nimes, the brave General Lagardt was severely wounded, while endeavoring at the head of his troops to suppress a sedition in the public square, which had arisen from no other cause but his having had the courage to arrest Trestaillon, the chief of the assassins. This open contempt of the law produced a great impression on the king, who ordered an unlimited number of troops to be quartered on the town till the guilty parties were given up. But this act of firmness produced no result. Justice, as usual in such cases, was impotent in the midst of crime; the tyrant majority was alike guilty and secure of impunity. Unable to

35. Atrocities at Nimes and the surrounding country.

---

* The classical reader need not be reminded of the freedman and old soldier of Pompey celebrating the funeral obsequies on the shores of Egypt after the battle of Pharsalia.

make head against such a universal *débâcle* of violence, the prefect of the department, M. Darbaud de Jouque, a moderate but firm man, selected for that perilous office for his known ability to discharge its duties, entreated the Duke d'Angoulême to come to Nîmes, in the hope that the presence of a deservedly beloved prince of the blood would tend to calm the effervescence of his impassioned adherents. He arrived accordingly, and for a time succeeded in overawing the violence of the Royalists. When pressed by numerous influential bodies, especially among the Roman Catholic clergy, to order the liberation of Trestaillon, he replied, "No! I will never screen assassins and incendiaries from the law." Trestaillon accordingly was brought to trial; but here the inherent weakness of jury trial amid the effervescence of the passions became apparent. Both he and Bovines, the assassin of Lagardt, were, in the face of the clearest evidence, acquitted unanimously by the jury, and immediately carried in triumph through the streets of the town which they had disgraced by their crimes.¹

¹ Lam. v. 413, 416; Lac. i. 352, 353; Cap. iii. 181, 182.

35. Persecution of the Protestants by the Roman Catholics.

The impunity with which these atrocious crimes were committed led to a fearful multiplication of similar deeds of blood. The passions of the moment became engrafted on those of centuries' duration, and the power of murdering without risk revived the frightful thirst for blood which in those regions had led to the crusade against the Albigeois, and all the savage deeds which have forever disgraced the Roman Catholic religion. The two most violent and dangerous passions which can inflame the human breast—political zeal and religious fanaticism—were aroused with the utmost violence at the same time, and for once pulled in the same direction. The Royalists held that they were entitled by their temporal wrongs to wreak their vengeance without restraint on the Napoleonists; the Roman Catholics deemed themselves secure of salvation, when they burned the temples or plunged their pikes in the bosom of the Protestants. The Crusade of the thirteenth was blended with the reaction of the nineteenth century. In vain the allied sovereigns interested themselves in the unhappy Protestants of the south; in vain the Duke of Wellington, with generous humanity, made the utmost efforts for their protection. The king issued a noble proclamation, denouncing these atrocities, and calling on the magistrates to bring the guilty parties to justice.* The prefects followed his example, and called on all good citizens to aid them in the discovery and prosecution of the assassins, who were a disgrace to society. It was all in vain; the guilty majority was omnipotent. The free institutions which France had won proved the safeguard of the criminals. The guilty were screened from arrest; if taken, witnesses were suborned, removed, intimidated; juries proved " the judicial committee of the majority,"* and acquitted in the face of the clearest evidence: and, to the disgrace of free institutions be it said, the whole of this long catalogue of frightful crime in the south of France passed over without *one single criminal being brought to justice*, while more than one judicial murder, on the other side, proved that the passions of the moment could direct the verdicts of juries as well as the pikes of assassins.¹ Tranquillity was not restored till, by orders from headquarters at Paris, the allied troops were spread over the disturbed districts, and the Imperialists and Protestants found that shelter under the bayonets of their enemies, which they could no longer look for in the justice of their countrymen.

¹ Lam. v. 419, 422; Cap. iii 55, 182, 184; Lac. i. 353.

36. Temper of France during the elections.

It was in the midst of this vehement effervescence of the passions that the elections took place over France, and never was evinced in a more striking manner the extreme danger of appealing to the people during a period of violent public excitement than on that occasion. Already the King and Council of State, who were resolutely bent on moderate measures, had become apprehensive of the violence of the current which was setting in in their own favor, and strove by every means in their power to moderate it. Secret instructions were sent down to the prefects and presidents of colleges, to favor as much as was in their power, or consistent with their duty, the return of members who might not by their violence occasion embarrassment to the Government. Fouché set all his agents and intrigues, and they were not a few, in motion, to support the Republican candidates, and form a respectable minority, at least, in favor of liberalism. But it was all in vain; and the elections of 1815 afforded the first indication of what subsequent events have so completely proved, that though France in general is entirely submissive to Paris, and follows with docility the mandates of the capital, yet its real opinion is often very different; and when an opportunity does occur, in which it can make its voice be heard, it does so in a way which can not be mistaken.¹

¹ Cap. iii. 185; Lam. v. 333, 335; Loc i. 354, 357.

38. Their ultra-Royalist character.

Public opinion in the provinces threw itself, without reflection and without reserve, into the very extremes of Royalist prejudice. Prudence, wisdom, foresight, moderation, justice, were alike disregarded; one only voice was listened to, and it was that of passion; one only thirst was felt—it was that of vengeance. A flood, broad and irresistible as the tides of the ocean, overspread France from the banks of the

---

* "Nous avons appris avec douleur, que dans les départements du Midi, plusieurs de nos sujets se sont récemment portés aux plus coupables excès; que sous prétexte de se faire les ministres de la vengeance publique, des Français, satisfaisant leurs haines et leurs vengeances privées, avaient versé le sang des Français, même depuis que notre autorité était universellement rétablie et reconnue dans notre royaume. Certes, d'infâmes trahisons, de grands crimes, ont été commis, et ont plongé la France dans une abîme de maux; mais la punition de ces crimes doit être nationale, solennelle, et régulière; les coupables doivent tomber sous le glaive de la loi, et non sous le poids de vengeances particulières. Ce serait bouleverser l'ordre social que de se faire à la fois juge et exécuteur pour les offenses qu'on a reçues ou même pour les attentats commis contre notre personne. Nous espérons que cette odieuse entreprise de prévenir l'action des lois a déjà cessé; elle serait un attentat contre nous et contre la France, et quelque vive douleur que nous passions en ressentir, rien ne servit épargné pour punir de tels crimes. C'est pourquoi nous avons recommandé par des ordres précis à nos ministres et à nos magistrats de faire strictement respecter les lois, et de ne mettre ni indulgence ni faiblesse dans la poursuite de ceux qui les ont violées."—*Moniteur*, July 26, 1815; CAPEFIGUE, i. 51

* DE Tocqueville in regard to America.

Rhine to the shores of the Atlantic. All attempts to stem it were in vain, or rather, by irritating, they tended only to inflame its violence. Even the presence of the allied troops, and their occupation of the cities and departments where the elections were going on, was no restraint upon the general fervor: on the contrary, they tended only to increase it; for who had brought that burden upon themselves—that disgrace upon their country? Mortified by defeat, humiliated by conquest, oppressed by contributions, irritated by insult, the French people had no mode of giving vent to their universal feelings of indignation, but by returning to the legislature members animated by the same sentiments; and so strong were their feelings, so universal their indignation, that they sent to Paris a Chamber of Representatives more counter-revolutionary than the allied sovereigns—more Royalist than the King.[1]

¹ Lam. v. 335, 236; Cap. iii. 186, 187.

39. Dismissal of Fouché from the ministry.

The known tendency of these elections, and the increasing vehemence with which extreme Royalist opinions were promulgated in the now unfettered pages of the Parisian press, rendered the position of the two leaders of the revolutionary party in the ministry every day more precarious. Fouché, in particular, against whom, from the bloody reminiscences connected with him, and his unparalleled tergiversations, the public indignation was in an especial manner directed, began to perceive that he would not be able much longer to maintain his ground. The party of the Count d'Artois daily insinuated to the King, that public opinion was now declaring itself so strongly that all attempts to withstand it were in vain, and that both Talleyrand and Fouché must be dismissed. The latter, conscious of the sinister eyes with which he was regarded, came now very rarely to the Tuileries; when he did so, a murmur always ran through the courtiers, "There is the regicide." The very persons who, a few months before, had joined in the chorus that he was the saviour of France, and the only man who could extricate it from its difficulties, because he was likely to favor their ambition, were now the first to exclaim against him, because he threatened to oppose it. In despair of being able to influence the affections of men, he appealed to their fears, and wrote with his usual ability several reports on the state of public opinion and of the country, ostensibly intended for the eye of the King, but which, from the extensive circulation surreptitiously given to them, were obviously intended to intimidate the Court. In them he portrayed in strong, even exaggerated colors, the dangers of the country, and the strength of the party, especially among the great body of the rural proprietors, who were still attached to the principles of the Revolution.* Notwithstanding the

* " Les villes sont opposées aux campagnes, dans l'ouest même, où l'on vous flatte de trouver des soldats. Les acquéreurs de domaines nationaux y résisteront à quiconque entreprendrait de les déposséder. Le Royalisme du midi s'exhale en attentats. Des bandes armées parcourent les campagnes et pénètrent dans les villes. Les pillages, les assassinats se multiplient. Dans l'est, l'horreur de l'invasion et les fautes des précédents ministères ent aliéné les populations. Dans la majorité des departements on trouverait seulement une poignée de Royalistes a opposer à la masse du peuple. Le repos sera difficile à l'armée, une ambition démesurée l'a rendue aventureuse.

"Il y a deux grandes factions dans l'état. L'une défend les principes; l'autre marche à la contre-revolution.

sinister appearances against him, he was nothing daunted. He married a young lady of good family, Madame de Castellane, whom he had met at Aix at the close of the Empire; and relying on his talents, his good fortune, the favor of the Duke of Wellington, and the political necessity which had compelled the King to get over his repugnance, he still hoped to overcome the difficulties with which he was surrounded. He now openly professed his adherence to the principles of monarchy.[1] "When one is young," said he, "revolutions please; they excite—they agitate, and we love to mingle in them; but at my age they have lost their charm: we sigh for repose, order, and security; we no longer wish to gain, but to enjoy."

¹ Cap. iii. 114, 115; Lam. v. 336, 341; Lac. i. 356, 357.

Talleyrand now saw that Fouché was no longer necessary to the maintenance of his power—that, on the contrary, the prejudice against him was so violent that it seriously impeded the Government. He consented, therefore, not unwillingly, to the instances of the Count d'Artois and his party, who urged his dismissal. To give a color to his downfall, he was in the first instance appointed minister at the court of Saxony. With his fall from power, Fouché's influence was at once at an end; and with such violence did the public indignation burst forth against him, that he was obliged, in crossing France on his way to the Rhine, to travel in disguise under a false name, and with a false passport. Within a few months after his arrival at Dresden, he was recalled from that office, forbidden to return to France, and exiled to Austria, where he spent the last days of his life in obscurity at Lintz, alike detested and despised by all parties in the world. His vote for the death of Louis XVI., and his atrocities at Lyons, had forever shocked the Royalists—his signature of the recent lists of proscription alienated the Republicans. His only consolation was in the kindness and tenderness of his young wife, who, with a true woman's fidelity, clung only the more closely to him from the desertion of all the rest of the world. Tormented to the last by the thirst for power, he never ceased to solicit M. Decazes, then minister to Louis XVIII., and Prince Metternich, for leave to reside at Paris or Vienna; but they both withstood his importunities. Cast away on the shore, he could not, like the seabird, live at rest on the strand, but ever threw a lingering look on the ocean on whose waves he had been tossed; and his last thoughts were in anticipation of the storms which were to succeed him.[1]*

40. Fall of Fouché, and his death.

¹ Lam. v. 345, 347; Cap. iii. 137.

D'un côté le clergé, les nobles, les anciens possesseurs des biens nationaux aujourd'hui vendus, les membres des anciens parlements, des hommes obstinés, qui ne veulent pas croire que leurs idées anciennes soient en défaut, et qui ne peuvent pardonner à une Révolution qu'ils ont maudite; d'autres qui fatigués du mouvement, cherchent le repos dans l'ancien régime; quelques écrivains passionnés flatteurs des opinions triomphantes. De côté opposé, la presque totalité de la France, les constitutionnels, les républicains, l'armée, et le peuple, toutes les classes des mécontents, une multitude de Français même attachés au Roi, mais qui sont convaincus qu'une tentative, et qui même une tendance à l'ancien régime, serait le signal d'une explosion semblable à celle de 1789."— Mémoire de Fouché, LAMARTINE, v. 329, 340.

* "J'ai signé l'ordonnance de la Proscription; elle était, et elle fut considérée alors comme le seul moyen de sauver le parti, qui m'en accuse aujourd'hui. Elle l'enlevait à la fureur des Royalistes, et le mettait à l'abri dans l'exil

Talleyrand and his ministry did not long survive the disgrace of the regicide Minister of Police, whom they had introduced into power. Many causes contributed to their downfall, and they were so powerful that, sooner or later, they must have led to that result. The demands of the allied powers in the negotiations for a general peace—of which an account will immediately be given—had become so exorbitant, that they recoiled from the thought of subscribing them, or even making them known to the public. The Emperor Alexander, who had so powerfully supported Talleyrand on occasion of the first restoration in 1814, was now cold and reserved toward him; he had not forgotten his opposition to the demands of Russia at the Congress of Vienna. The King of France, although fully sensible of the great ability and consummate address of the minister who had contrived to keep afloat through all the storms of the Revolution, was in secret jealous of his ascendency; he felt the repugnance of high birth at the guardianship of intellect and experience. Though so experienced a courtier, M. de Talleyrand could not avoid, on some occasions, letting fall expressions indicating his sense of his own influence with foreign powers, and services under the Empire. But most of all, the elections had now been decided in favor of the extreme Royalists, by a majority which it was hopeless to withstand. By the 20th September they were all concluded; and the result was such a preponderance on that side as left no doubt that the ministry could not maintain their ground. Unable to contend with a hostile majority in the Chambers, M. Talleyrand did not yet despair. He desired to engage the King in a contest with the legislature, and thought he had influence sufficient to effect that object. But he was much mistaken. When Talleyrand, at the conclusion of his speech in the cabinet council, tendered his resignation and that of his colleagues, if the proposed measures were not adopted, the King calmly replied—"You resign, then: very well; I will appoint another ministry," and bowed them out of the apartment.[1]

Along with M. Talleyrand, there retired from the ministry M. Louis, M. Pasquin, Jaucourt, and Gouvion St. Cyr. The ministry required to be entirely new modeled; and the king, who had long foreseen the necessity of this step, and was not sorry of an opportunity of breaking with his revolutionary mentors, immediately authorized M. Decazes, who had insinuated himself into his entire confidence, to offer the place of President of the Council, corresponding to our Premier, to the DUKE DE RICHELIEU. Independent of the high descent and personal merits of that very estimable man, there were peculiar reasons of the most pressing nature which pointed him out as the proper minister of France at that period. An intimate personal friend of the Emperor Alexander, and having acquired his entire confidence in the course of the important government with which he had been intrusted at Odessa, there was every reason to hope that his influence with the Czar would in some degree tend to moderate the severity of the terms which, as the conditions of peace, the allied powers were now insisting for. M. de Richelieu felt the painful position in which he would be placed by accepting office, the first step in which would be the signature of a treaty in the highest degree humiliating to France: but he was clear-sighted enough to perceive the necessity of the case, and too patriotic to refuse to serve his country even in the worst crisis of its fate. He accepted office accordingly, and with him the ministry underwent an entire change. M. Decazes was appointed Minister of Police, an office which, in those critical times, was of the very highest importance; the seals were intrusted to M. Barbé-Marbois; the Duke de Feltre (Clark) was appointed Minister at War; M. Vaublane, Minister of the Interior; while the Duke de Richelieu discharged the duties at once of President of the Council and Minister of Foreign Affairs.[1]

ARMAND, DUKE DE RICHELIEU, grand-nephew by his sister of the cardinal of the same name, was grandson of the Marshal de Richelieu, so celebrated in the reign of Louis XV. as the Alcibiades of France. When called to the ministry in 1815, he was forty-nine years of age. Consumed from his earliest years, like so many other great men, by an ardent thirst for glory, he had joined the Russian army in 1785, and shared in the dangers of the assault of Ismael under Suwaroff. When the French Revolution rent the nobles and the people of France asunder, he hastened from the Crimea to join the army of the emigrant noblesse under the Prince of Condé, and remained with it till the corps was finally dissolved in 1794. He then returned to Russia, where he was at first kindly received by, but soon after shared in the caprices of, the Emperor Paul. On the accession of Alexander, the conformity of their dispositions, with the known abilities and illustrious descent of Richelieu, endeared him to that benevolent monarch, and he selected him to carry into execution the philanthropic views which he had formed for the improvement of the southern provinces of his vast dominions. During ten years of a wise and active administration, he more than realized the hope of his illustrious master. The progress of the province intrusted to his care was unparalleled, its prosperity unbroken, during his administration. To his sagacious foresight and prophetic wisdom Russia owes the seaport of Odessa, the great export town of its southern provinces, and which opened to their boundless agricultural plains the commerce of the world. The French invasion of 1812 recalled him from his pacific labors to the defense of the country and he shared the intimacy and councils of Alexander during the eventful years which succeeded, till the taking of Paris in 1814. Alternately at Paris, at Vienna, or at Ghent, he represented his sovereign, and served as a link between the court of Russia and the newly established throne of Louis XVIII.[1]

41. His character. His character qualified him in a peculiar manner for this delicate task, and now for the still more perilous duty to which he was called—that of standing, like the Jewish lawgiver, between the people and the plague. He was the model of the ancient French nobility, for he united in his person all their virtues, and he was free from their weaknesses. He was considered, alike in the army and the diplomatic circles at home and abroad, as the most pure and estimable character which had arisen during the storms of the Revolution. His fortunate distance from France during so long a period, at once preserved him from its dangers, and caused him to be exempt from its delusions; he had studied mankind in the best of all schools, that of real practical improvement, and neither in that of theoretical speculations nor of military ambition. His physiognomy bespoke his character. His talents were not of the first order, but his moral qualities were of the purest kind. A lofty forehead bespoke the ascendant of intellect; an aquiline nose and high features, the distinctive mark of family; but the limpid eye and mild expression revealed the still more valuable qualities of the heart. It would seem as if a sad and serious revolution had passed over the hereditary lustre of his race, and impressed upon it the thoughtful and melancholy character of later times. He was adored by his sisters, the Countess of Jumilhac, and the Marquise de Montcalm, the latter of whom was one of the most charming women in France; but it required all their influence, joined to the entreaties of the king and the representations of the Emperor Alexander, to overcome his natural modesty, or induce him to take the helm in this crisis of the fortunes of his country.[2]

45. Biography of M. Decazes. M. DECAZES, who at the same period commenced his brilliant career under the Restoration, had not the same advantage of family as the Duc de Richelieu; but this deficiency was compensated by his natural abilities, and still more by the address and tact which in so peculiar a manner fitted him to be the minister of a pacific sovereign. He rose to greatness neither in the cabinet nor in the field; the bureau of the minister of police was the theatre of his first distinction.[*]

He had already become remarkable for the zeal and activity with which he had discharged the duties of prefect of police at Paris, when the skill with which he withdrew its funds from the rapacious hands of the Prussians had excited general attention. But what chiefly attracted the confidence of Louis was his natural repugnance to and distrust of Fouché, and yet the experienced necessity of having some one in the police on whom he could rely, and who might supply information directly on the state of public opinion, and any designs which might be in agitation. In short, he desired a spy on Fouché, who had spies on every one else; and the address and intelligence of M. Decazes answered this object so completely, that he had already come to be in intimate daily communication with the sovereign, before the change of ministry opened to him the situation of minister of police. His great talent consisted in his knowledge of mankind, and his ready insight into the prevailing dispositions or weaknesses of the principal personages with whom he was brought in contact. Thus he early divined that the ruling passion of Louis was a love of popularity, his prevailing inclination a love of ease, and his favorite amusement hearing and retailing little anecdotes and scandalous reports, which the agents of police could of course furnish to him in sufficient abundance. By these means, joined to his fidelity to the interests of his sovereign, as well as the indefatigable zeal with which he attended to the duties of his station, he not merely won the confidence of his sovereign, but the esteem of the nation, and the support of a steady majority in the Chambers, which enabled him to conduct the administration during several years, amidst very great difficulties, with surprising success.[1]

46. Difficulties of the negotiations with the allied powers. The new ministry had need of all their skill and influence with foreign powers to weather the difficulties with which they were surrounded, for never did embarrassments to appearance more insurmountable overwhelm any government. But here the benevolent views of the Emperor Alexander, and personal influence of the Duke de Richelieu with that monarch, aided by the moderation of England and the justice and firmness of the Duke of Wellington, came to the timely aid of the French administration. The principal difficulty was with the lesser powers: the great states, farther removed from the scene of danger, and having more extensive resources to rely on, were more easily dealt with. But in appearance, at least, the Allies were entirely united; all their deliberations were taken and answers given in common; and the last answer of M. de Talleyrand, before he went out of office, had only called forth an *ultimatum* of the most desperate severity. Not only were enormous pecuniary sacrifices required of France, but large portions of its territory on the frontier were reclaimed for Flanders, Prussia, and the lesser German states. The Duke de Richelieu, in accepting the head of the administration, had not disguised from the Emperor Alexander that he did so in reliance on his moderation and

---

[*] "He was the son of a magistrate of Libourne, in the department of the Gironde, the district of all others in France which has given birth to the greatest number of eminent political men, and made the greatest figure since the Revolution in the civil government of the country. He was at this time in his thirty-fifth year. He had come to Paris in the last days of the Empire, to prosecute his legal studies, when his elegant manners and talent in conversation attracted the regard of the daughter of M. Muraire, the President of the Court of Cassation, who bestowed upon him her hand. This led to his obtaining employment under the Imperial Government, but he did not share in its fall, and, both during the first Restoration and Hundred Days, made himself conspicuous by his steady adherence to Royalist principles, insomuch that he was banished to a distance of forty leagues from Paris by Napoleon. This was the making of his fortune: upon the return of Louis he was immediately selected by Fouché and Talleyrand to fill the situation of Prefect of the Police, in which capacity his zeal, activity, and devotion soon attracted the regard of Louis XVIII."—LAMARTINE, v. 214, 216; and *Biographie Universelle*—Suppl. (Decazes.)

friendship; and, in a secret interview, the Czar had assured him that he should not do so in vain. "I have no other interest," said the monarch, "in this negotiation, but to secure the repose of the world, and the stability of the system which we are establishing in France." With that very view, however, he was easily brought to see the necessity of moderating the demands of the allied powers, and not exacting conditions which would prove an *arrêt de mort* to the dynasty, the stability of which appeared the only guarantee for the peace of Europe. But so keen were the feelings of the allied sovereigns that it required all his influence, joined to the energetic co-operation of the Duke of Wellington, to obtain any considerable modification of the demands; and as it was, the Duke de Richelieu said, at the time he signed the treaty, and only on the earnest entreaties with tears of the king, that he did so "more dead than alive."* The Emperor Alexander gave him at the time a map containing the provinces marked which had been reclaimed by the allied powers, and which he had prevailed on them to waive their claims to. "Keep it," said the Czar; "I have preserved that one copy for you alone. It will bear testimony in future times to your services and my friendship for France, and it will be the noblest title of nobility in your family." It is still in possession of his successors.¹

_{¹ Cap. iii. 219, 223; Lam. v. 354, 366; Lac.}

47. Exorbitant demands of Austria and the lesser powers.

It is remarkable that Austria was the great power with which there was most difficulty in coming to an accommodation. She openly demanded the cession of Alsace and Lorraine, the first inheritance of her family; and in order to induce Prussia to concur in the spoliation, she offered to support the demand for that power of any fortresses on the frontier from Condé and Philipville, in the Low Countries, to Joux and Fort Ecluse on the borders of Switzerland. Finding Prussia too much under the influence of Russia and England to acquiesce in these demands, the cabinet of Vienna addressed itself to the lesser German powers, and conjointly with them prepared a plan by which France was to be shorn of great part of its frontier provinces, and nearly all its strong places on the Rhine. They even went so far as to demand the demolition of the fortifications of Huningen and Strasbourg. When this project was submitted to the Emperor Alexander, he communicated it to the Duke de Richelieu, who exclaimed, "They are determined on another war of twenty-five years' duration; well, they shall have it! In a few days the army of the Loire could be recalled to its standards and doubled; la Vendée will join its ranks, and monarchical France will show itself not less formidable than Republican." Louis XVIII. declared that there was no chance of war so terrible or disastrous, which he would not prefer to a treaty so ignominious. But these were vain

_{* "Tout est consommé! J'ai apposé plus mort que vif mon nom à ce fatal traité. J'avais juré de ne pas le faire, et je l'avais dit au Roi. Ce malheureux Prince m'a conjuré, en fondant en larmes, de ne pas l'abandonner. Je n'ai plus hésité! J'ai la confiance de croire que personne n'aurait obtenu autant. La France, expirant sous le poids de calamités qui l'accable, réclamait impérieusement une prompte délivrance."—M. le Duc de RICHELIEU à Madame la Marquise de MONTCALM, sans date.—LAMARTINE, v. 365.}

menaces; eight hundred thousand armed men were in possession of the French capital, fortresses, and territory; its army was disbanded and it had no resource but in the moderation of policy of the conquerors. At length, by the united efforts of the Emperor Alexander, Lord Castlereagh, and the Duke of Wellington, the demands of Austria and the lesser German powers were abated, and a treaty was concluded, which, although much less disastrous than might in the circumstances have been expected, was the most humiliating which had been imposed on France since the treaty of Bretigny closed the long catalogue of disasters consequent on the battle of Agincourt.¹

_{¹ Lac. i. 360, 361; Lam. v. 366, 367; Cap. iii. 220, 223.}

48. Treaty of Paris, Nov. 20, 1815.

By this treaty the limits of France were fixed as they had been in 1790, with the following exceptions: the fortresses of Landau, Sarre-Louis, Philipville, and Marienbourg, with the territory annexed to each, were ceded to the Allies; Versoix, with a small district around it, was ceded to the canton of Geneva; the fortifications of Huningen were to be demolished; but the little territory of Venaisin, the first conquest of the Revolution, was preserved to France. Such was the moderation of the Allies, that after so entire an overthrow she lost only twenty square leagues of territory, while, by the retention of the Venaisin, she gained forty square leagues. But the payments in money exacted from her were enormous, and felt as the more galling because they were a badge of conquest. A contribution of 700,000,000 francs (£28,000,000) was provided to the allied powers, as an indemnity for the expense of their last armaments, to be paid regularly day by day. In addition to this, France agreed to pay 735,000,000 francs (£29,500,000) as an indemnity to the allied powers for the contributions which the French troops had, at different times during the war, exacted from them; besides 100,000,000 francs (£4,000,000) to the lesser powers who subsequently joined the Alliance—in all, 1,535,000,000 francs, or £61,500,000;—probably the greatest money payment ever exacted from any one nation since the beginning of the world.* In addition to this, it was stipulated, as a measure alike of security to Europe and protection to the newly-

_{* The proportions in which this sum was claimed by the Allies, and agreed to be paid by France, were as follows:}

	Francs.	£.
Austria	189,000,000 or	7,360,000
Prussia	100,000,000 "	4,240,000
Netherlands	88,000,000 "	3,520,000
Sardinia	73,000,000 "	2,920,000
Hamburg	71,000,000 "	2,840,000
Tuscany	4,500,000 "	180,000
Parma	2,000,000 "	80,000
Bremen	3,000,000 "	120,000
Lubeck	4,000,000 "	160,000
Baden	1,500,000 "	60,000
Hanover	25,000,000 "	1,000,000
Hesse Cassel	1,500,000 "	60,000
Hesse Darmstadt, &c.	20,000,000 "	800,000
Mecklenburg-Schwerin	1,000,000 "	40,000
Denmark	17,000,000 "	680,000
Rome	29,000,000 "	1,160,000
Bavaria	72,000,000 "	2,120,000
Frankfort	3,000,000 "	120,000
Switzerland	5,000,000 "	200,000
Saxony	15,000,000 "	600,000
Prussian Saxony	5,000,000 "	200,000
	735,500,000	719,500,00

—CAPEFIGUE, 227.

established dynasty in France, that an army of 150,000 men, belonging to the Allies, was to be put in possession of the principal frontier fortresses of France—viz., Cambray, Valenciennes, Bouchain, Condé, Quesnoy, Maubeuge, Landrecies, Avennes, Rocroy, Givet, Sedan, Montmedy, Thionville, Longwy, Bitche, and Fort Louis—for not less than three, nor more than five years. This army was to be entirely maintained, paid, and clothed at the expense of the French nation. The contingent of Great Britain was 30,000 men; and the seal was put to its national glory, and the personal fame of its great General, by the allied sovereigns unanimously conferring the command of the whole upon the Duke of Wellington.¹

49. Convention of 20th Nov between the allied powers, for exclusion of Napoleon and his family from the throne of France.

On the same day on which this treaty was signed, another treaty was concluded between Russia, Prussia, Austria, and England, which afterward became of essential importance in the direction of European affairs. France was no party to this treaty; it was concluded, like that of Chaumont in 1813, as a measure of security for the allied powers among each other. By it the four allied powers renewed, in all its provisions, the treaties of Chaumont and Vienna, and in an especial manner those which "exclude forever Napoleon Bonaparte *and his family* from the throne of France." * It was declared that the occupation, during a limited number of years, of the military positions in France, was intended to carry into effect these stipulations; and, in consequence, they mutually engaged, in case the army of occupation should be menaced by an attack on the part of France, or if a general war should arise, to furnish without delay, in addition to the forces left in France, each their full contingent of 60,000 men. Should these prove insufficient, they engaged to bring each their whole forces into action, so as to bring the contest to an immediate and favorable issue, and in that event to make such pacific arrangements as might effectually guarantee Europe from a return of similar calamities. This treaty was communicated to the Duke de Richelieu, with a letter from the four allied powers, in which they expressed their entire confidence in the wisdom and prudence of the king's government, and his determination, without distinction of party, or lending an ear to passionate councils, to maintain peace and the rule of justice in his dominions. † Finally, it was determined to renew at stated periods these congresses of sovereigns, to arrange without bloodshed the affairs of Europe; and the first of these was fixed for the autumn of 1818.¹

50. The Holy Alliance, and causes which led to it. Nov 26, 1815.

On the same day on which these important treaties were signed, another one, which acquired still greater celebrity at the time, but was not destined to produce such durable consequences in the end, was concluded. This was the celebrated treaty of "THE HOLY ALLIANCE." Its author was the Emperor Alexander. This sovereign, whose strength of mind and knowledge of mankind, were not equal to the magnanimity of his disposition and the benevolence of his heart, had been in some degree carried away by the all important part he had been called on to play at the first taking of Paris and the Congress of Vienna, and the unbounded admiration, alike among his friends and his enemies, with which his noble and generous conduct on these occasions had been received. He had come to conceive, in consequence, that the period had arrived when these principles might permanently regulate the affairs of the world—when the seeds of evil might be eradicated from the human heart; and when the peaceful reign of the Gospel, announced from the throne, might forever supersede the rude empire of the sword. In the belief of the advent of this moral millennium, and of the lead which it was his mission to take in inducing it, he was strongly supported by the influence and counsels of Madame Krudener, a lady of great talents, eloquence, and an enthusiastic turn of mind, who had followed him from St. Petersburg to Paris, and was equally persuaded with himself that the time was approaching when wars were to cease, and the reign of peace, virtue, and the Gospel, was to commence on the earth. Alexander, during September and October of this year, spent whole days at Paris in a mystical communication of sentiments with this remarkable lady. Their united idea was the establishment of a common international law, founded on Christianity, over all Europe, which was at once to extinguish the religious divisions which had so long distracted, and the warlike contests which had desolated it. Sovereigns were to be regulated by the principles of virtue and religion, the people to surrender themselves in peace and happiness to the universal regen-

---

* "Les hautes puissances renouvellent et confirment particulièrement *l'exclusion à perpétuité de Napoléon Buonaparte, et de sa famille,* du pouvoir suprême en France, qu'elles s'engagent à maintenir en pleine vigueur, et, s'il était nécessaire, avec toutes leurs forces."—Act 2, Convention, 20th November, 1815; Schoell, xi. 563, and Martens' Sup.

† "Les Cabinets Alliés trouvent la première garantie de cet espoir dans les principes éclairés, les sentiments magnanimes, et les vertus personnelles de sa Majesté très chrétienne. Sa Majesté a reconnu avec eux, que dans un etat déchiré pendant un quart de siècle, par des convulsions révolutionnaires, ce n'est pas à la force seule à ramener le calme dans les esprits, la confiance dans les âmes, et l'équilibre dans les différentes parties du corps social; que la sagesse doit se joindre à la vigueur, la modération à la fermeté, pour opérer des changements heureux. Loin de craindre que sa Majesté ne prêtât jamais l'oreille à des conseils imprudens ou passionnés, tendant à nourrir les mécontentemens, à renouveler les alarmes, à ramener les haines et les divisions, les Cabinets Alliés sont complettement rassurés, par les dispositions aussi sages que généreuses, que le Roi a annoncées dans toutes les époques de son regne, et notamment à celle de son retour après le dernier attentat criminel. Ils savent que sa Majesté opposera à tous les ennemis de son bien public, et de la tranquillité de son royaume, sous quelque forme qu'ils puissent se présenter, *son attachement aux lois constitutionnelles* promulguées sous ses propres auspices, sa volonté bien prononcée d'être le père de tous ses sujets, sans distinction de classe ni de religion; d'effacer jusqu'au souvenir des maux qu'ils ont soufferts, et de ne conserver des temps passés que le bien que la Providence a fait sortir du sein même des calamités publiques. Ce n'est qu' ainsi que les vœux formés par les Cabinets Alliés, pour la conservation d l'autorité constitutionnelle de sa Majesté, pour le bonheur de son pays, et le maintien de la paix du monde, seront couronnés d'un succès complet, et que la France, *rétablie sur ses anciennes bases,* reprendra la place éminente à laquelle elle est appelée dans le système Européen."—*Lettres des Quatre Puissances a M. le Duc de Richelieu,* 20 Nov. 1815.—SCHOELL, xi. 565 566

eration of mankind. This treaty, from being concluded between the absolute monarchs of Russia, Austria, and Prussia, was long the object of dread and jealousy to the liberal and revolutionary party throughout Europe. But now that its provisions have become known, it is regarded in a very different light, and looked upon as one of the effusions of inexperienced enthusiasm and benevolence, to be classed with the dreams as to the indefinite prolongation of human life of Condorcet, or the visions of the Peace Congress which amused Europe amid universal preparations for war in the middle of the nineteenth century.[1]

¹ Cap. iii. 216, 217; Lam. v. 369, 370; Lac. i. 366, 367.

By this celebrated alliance, the three monarchs subscribing—viz., the Emperors of Russia and Austria, and the King of Prussia—bound themselves, "in conformity with the principles of the Holy Scriptures, which order all men to regard each other as brothers, and, considering themselves as compatriots, to lend each other every aid, assistance and succor, on every occasion; and, regarding themselves toward their subjects and armies as fathers, to direct them on every occasion in the same spirit of fraternity with which they are animated, to protect religion, peace, and justice. In consequence, the sole principle in vigor, either between the said governments or among their subjects, shall be the determination to render each other reciprocal aid, and to testify, by continued good deeds, the unalterable mutual affection by which they are animated; to consider themselves only as members of a great Christian nation, and not regarding themselves but as delegates appointed by Providence to govern three branches of the same family—viz., Austria, Prussia, and Russia; confessing also that the Christian nation of which they and their people form a part has in reality no other sovereign to whom of right belongs all power, because He alone possesses all the treasures of love, knowledge, and infinite wisdom—that is to say, God Almighty, our Divine Saviour Jesus Christ, the Word of the Most High, the Word of Life—they recommend in the most earnest manner to their people, as the only way of securing that peace which flows from a good conscience, and which alone is durable, to fortify themselves every day more and more in the principles and exercise of the duties which the Divine Saviour has taught to men. All the powers which may feel inclined to avow the sacred principles which have dictated the present treaty, and who may perceive how important it is for the happiness of nations too long agitated that these truths should henceforth exercise on human destinies all the influence which should pertain to them, shall be received with as much eagerness as affection into the present alliance. (Signed) Francis, Frederick-William, Alexander." There is no good Christian, and even no good man with a good heart, who must not feel that the principles recognized in this treaty are those which *should* act rate the conduct both of sovereigns and their subjects; and that the real millennium is to be looked for when they shall do so, and not till then. But the experienced observer of mankind in all ranks and ages will regret to think how little likely they are to be carried practically into effect,

51. Terms of the Holy Alliance. Nov. 20, 1815.

and class them with the philanthropic effusions of Freemason meetings, or the generous transports of a crowded theatre which melt away next morning before the interests, the selfishness, and the passions of the world.[1]

¹ See the treaty in Schoell, xi. 553, 554; Martens, xiii. 607.

This treaty, out of compliment to its known author, the Emperor Alexander, was ere long acceded to by nearly all the Continental sovereigns. But as it was signed by the sovereigns alone, without the sanction or intervention of their ministers, the Prince-Regent, by the advice of Lord Castlereagh, judiciously declared, that while he adhered to the principles of that Alliance, the restraints imposed upon him as a constitutional monarch prevented him from becoming a party to any convention which was not countersigned by a responsible minister. Several minor treaties, but still of considerable importance in future times, were also concluded in the usual way between the allied powers in this great diplomatic year. 1. The first of these regarded the seven Ionian Islands, which had been taken possession of by Great Britain during the campaign of 1813, with the exception of Corfu, ceded to them by the treaty of 1814, but the destiny of which had not hitherto been made the subject of a formal treaty between the allied powers. It was now provided that the Islands should form a separate state, to be entitled the "United States of the Ionian Islands," to be placed under the immediate protection of Great Britain, by whom its fortresses were to be garrisoned and governors appointed—all the other powers renouncing any pretensions in that respect. 2. In consideration of the vast efforts made by Russia during the preceding campaign, which, it was declared, had moved 100,000 men into the interior of France beyond what she was bound to have done by the existing treaties, of whom 40,000 were placed under the immediate command of the Duke of Wellington, besides a reserve force of 150,000, which had passed her frontier, and advanced as far as Franconia, Great Britain agreed to pay to that power an additional subsidy of 10,400,000 francs, (£416,666.) 3. A convention was concluded between the four allied powers on the 2d August, 1815, for the disposal of the person of Napoleon. By it he was declared a prisoner of the four allied powers which had signed the treaty of 25th March preceding, at Vienna. The custody of his person was in an especial manner intrusted to the British Government; but the three other powers were to name commissioners, who should reside at the place which the British Government should assign as his place of residence, without sharing the responsibility of his detention. The King of France was to be invited to send a commissioner, and the Prince-Regent of Great Britain pledged himself faithfully to perform the engagements undertaken by him in this treaty.[1]

52. Treaties regarding the Ionian Isles, a Russian subsidy, and Napoleon Buonaparte.

Nov. 5, 1815.

Oct. 4, 1815.

August 2

¹ Schoell, xi. 550, 552; Martens, xi. 627

Such were the treaties of 1815, for ever memorable as terminating, for a time at least, the revolutionary governments in the civilized world, and closing in a durable manner the ascendency of Imperial France in Europe. It is hard to say

53. Reflections on these treaties

whether the magnitude of the triumphs which had preceded it, or the moderation displayed by the victors in the moment of conquest, were the most admirable. France, indeed, was subjected to immense pecuniary payments, but that was only in requital of those which she had, in the hour of her triumph, imposed on others;—and they did not reach half their amount, for £61,000,000 sterling only was imposed on France, with its 30,000,000 of inhabitants; whereas Napoleon, after the battle of Jena, had imposed £24,000,000, in contributions and military exactions, on Prussia alone, which had only 6,000,000 of souls in its dominions.[1] But as regards durable losses, she not only had no ground of complaint, but the highest reason to be satisfied and grateful. After the most entire conquest and subjugation recorded in history, when her Emperor was a prisoner, her capital taken, her army disbanded, and 1,100,000 men were in possession of her fortresses and territory, she lost *only twenty square leagues* of territory, just half the area of the Venaisin, the first conquest of the Revolution, which she was permitted to retain! What did Napoleon do to Prussia after the battle of Jena?—Deprived her of half of her dominions.[2] What to Austria, after the battle of Wagram?—Cut off a sixth of the whole Austrian States from the house of Hapsburg.[3] If the allied powers had acted to France as France did to them in the hour of her triumph, they would have reft from her Lorraine, Alsace, Picardy, Franche-Comté, French Flanders, and Roussillon, and reduced the monarchy to what it was in the days of Louis XI. And England, in an especial manner, displayed the magnanimity in prosperity which is the true test of greatness of soul. She made no attempt to retaliate upon France in the moment of its sorrow the successful partition of her dominions by the accession of Louis XVI. to the American War, but when her ancient rival was prostrate at her feet, threw the whole of her weight in diplomacy to moderate the demands of the victors; and, when the treaty was concluded, took neither one ship nor one village to herself, and bestowed the whole of the war indemnity which fell to her share upon the kingdom of the Netherlands, to reconstruct the barrier which had been cast down by the philanthropic delusions of Joseph II. before the Revolution.[4]

[1] Hist. of Europe, c. 46, § 77.
[2] Hist. of Europe, c. xlvi. § 77.
[3] Hist. of Europe, c. ix. § 40.
[4] Hist. of Europe, c. ix. § 52.

54. Violent temper and disposition of the Chamber of Deputies.

It was 'n the midst of the negotiations which were to lead to these results that the Chambers met in France, and the strong feelings of the nation found a vent in the resolutions and measures of its representatives. It might have been anticipated, what experience soon proved to be the case, that the greatest difficulties of the Government in this crisis would be, not with the strangers, but with its own subjects, and that the violence of the legislature would call for measures which the wisdom and foresight of the executive would be fain to moderate. This is invariably the case. Great reactions in public opinion never take place from the force of argument, howsoever convincing, or the evidence of facts affecting others, how conclusive soever. Against all such the great majority of me, are always sufficiently fortified, if their passions are inflamed, or their interests, or supposed interests, are at stake. But this very circumstance renders the reaction the more violent, and the more to be dreaded, when these passions or interests are turned the other way, and men are taught by suffering, and, above all, by pecuniary losses, to themselves, the consequences of the course which they have so long pursued, and to the dangers of which they remained obstinately blind till those consequences were fully developed. That effect had now taken place in France; events had succeeded each other with more than railway speed; the last three years had done the work of three centuries. The forces which poured into France had gone on increasing till they had now reached the stupendous amount of *eleven hundred and forty thousand men.* The armed multitude was all fed and maintained by the French people; and exactions of an enormous and unheard-of amount were made upon the government, for the expenses which the putting such a crusade in motion had occasioned to the foreign governments. The truths which reason and justice would have striven in vain to impress upon the majority in France, were now brought home to every breast by the irresistible force of mortification and suffering; and, in despair of effecting any thing against the Allies, who were the immediate cause of their disasters, the only vent which the public indignation could find was against the party in France which had induced them.[1]

[1] Cap. iii. 187, 189; Lam. v. 373, 374; Lac. i. 409, 410.

55. Composition and parties in the Chambers.

Great as the dangers were which, under any circumstances, must have beset a legislature elected amid the fervor of such feelings, they were much aggravated in France by the peculiar situation of the provinces, from which a majority of the representatives had been drawn. The great addition of 133 members made to the Chamber of Representatives by the royal ordinance of July, which raised their number to 389, and the admission by the same ordinance of all the members of the Legion of Honor to the right of voting, joined to the general excitement and vehemently roused passions of the moment, had immensely increased the Royalist majority in the Chamber. So entire had been the defeat of the Imperial and Republican parties in the elections, that the regular opposition—that is, the persons attached to the Republican or Imperial Government—could never muster above forty or fifty votes. The majority was composed of persons about the court—emigrants, journalists, or pamphleteers on the side of the *ancien régime,* nobles from the provinces, or red-hot Royalists from the departments—men wholly unacquainted with business, in great part imperfectly educated, but all smarting under the intolerable sense of present wrongs, and conceiving themselves intrusted with one only duty—that of avenging on their authors the sins and sufferings of France. One universal feeling of indignation pervaded this body, and in the vehement passions with which it was animated the women of the highest rank connected with the members stood pre-eminent, and strongly excited all the men with whom they were connected, or whom they could influence. The human heart is the same at all times, and in all grades of society; and the same principle which causes two-thirds of the crowd at every public execution to be composed of the humbler part of the softer sex, now rendered many of the highest foremost in the demand for scaffolds which were to cover France with mourning.[1]

¹ Cap. iii. 187, 189; Lam. v. 373, 375; Lac. l. 402, 410.

Several men of unquestioned talent were to be found in the ranks of this formidable majority, and some acquired the lead of the several sections of which it was composed. The section of extreme Royalists, of whom the Count d'Artois, the heir-apparent to the throne, was the acknowledged head, and which was known in France by the name of the "Pavillon Marsan," from the quarter in the Tuileries where the apartments of that prince were situated, was mainly under the direction of M. de Vitrolles, a man of talent, activity, and the most agreeable manners, who had acquired an unlimited command over his royal master, and was looked forward to as his future prime-minister. Chateaubriand also, in the Chamber of Peers, at that period belonged to the same party, and lent it the influence of his great talents and literary fame; while M. de Bourrienne, with less genius, but superior talents for business, and all the zeal of a new convert from the Imperial *régime*, was a valuable ally, especially in matters of detail, and those connected with the public administration. Several of the old noblesse also, particularly M. Armand de Polignac, destined to a fatal celebrity in future times, M. le Vicomte Bruges, and Alexander de Boisgelin, were also numbered among their most warm adherents, and, without the aid of great talents, possessed considerable influence in the Chamber, from their high rank, and their known connection with the heir-apparent to the throne.[1]

56. The extreme Royalists and their leaders.

¹ Cap. iii. 180, 191; Lam. v. 207, 211.

Above half of the Chamber of Deputies was composed of persons who might be considered as representing with fidelity the provinces, the inhabitants of which formed a large majority of the people of France. It was to this class that the 133 new deputies, admitted by the royal ordinance of 24th July, 1815, chiefly belonged; and it was that ordinance which gave them a majority in the Chamber, and rendered it so difficult of management by the court. Their ideas were peculiar, antiquated, and, for the most part at variance with the settled ideas which the Revolution had impressed on the metropolis and great towns. Common hatred of the Napoleonists and suffering under the exactions and humiliations of the Allies, had for a time united them in common measures; but it was easy to foresee that this alliance could not long survive the catastrophe which had given it birth. They were at once impregnated with Royalist and Republican ideas—with the former, in so far as any measures for the support of the monarchy or the Church were concerned; with the latter, in so far as a career might be opened for the intelligence and ambition of the provinces, in the offices at the disposal of the central government. Jealousy of Paris and provincial ambition were the leading principles by which they were actuated; they hoped out of the departments to raise up a counterpoise to the long-established reign of the metropolis. The chiefs of this party were men of remarkable abilities, far superior to those of the Pavillon Marsan for the conduct of affairs, and accordingly ere long they acquired the direction of the country. M. de Bonald, M. de Villèle, de Corbière, and Grosbois, were the most remarkable of them, and soon acquired the lead in a large section of the Assembly. The first was a man of decided talent, inflexible integrity, and ready conversation, with the mildest manners, but the sternest and most uncompromising Royalist principles. M. de Villèle, as yet unknown, and a deputy from the south of France, soon gave proof in the committees of the Chamber of those great business talents, and prodigious command of details, which, like similar powers in Sir R. Peel, ultimately gave him the lead in the Assembly, and made him head of the Administration. M. de Corbière, formerly remarkable by the indolence of his disposition, was roused by ambition to different habits, and by his talent in drawing reports and capacity in business, soon became distinguished; while M. de Grosbois was universally respected from his energy, his eloquence, and the power which he evinced not less in business than debate.[1]

57. The provincial deputies.

¹ Cap. iii. 191, 192; Lam. v. 212, 214.

As is invariably the case after the decisive triumph of one party in a great political crisis, the minority, to all practical purposes, was entirely unrepresented. The liberal opposition in the Chamber could not at the utmost number above sixty persons in its ranks—not a sixth of the whole, which comprised 395 members; and it was rare on a division involving any vital question that they mustered more than forty-five. But the influence of a minority, and its chances of *ultimate* success, are not always to be measured by its numbers at the outset of a parliamentary contest; the history of England, especially in later times, affords numerous instances of courageous and united minorities, first commanding respect by their talents and consistency, and ere long acquiring power by the disunion of their opponents, or the general admiration which their qualities have awakened. The reason is that the minority are forced to evince courage and appeal to principle; and it is by these qualities that, in the long run, when the passions are excited, mankind are governed. The chiefs of this small party were M. Royer Collard, de Serres, Pasquier, and Braquey—men of lofty feelings, ardent minds, and persuasive eloquence, who never ascended the tribune without commanding attention, and seldom left it without having in some generous breast awakened sympathy, in some powerful intellect produced conviction. M. Royer Collard, and de Serres in particular, were gifted with such great powers of oratory, that though they could never win over any thing like a majority to their side, they seldom failed to awaken the unanimous admiration of the Chamber; and from admiration it is but a step to influence, not less in public assemblies than in affairs of the heart. Such was the power in debate of these very eminent men, that they insensibly won over several of the chief members on the other side to their opinions on

58. The Opposition, and its leaders.

many points; among whom may be named M. Hyde de Neuville, one of the ablest and noblest of the Royalists, whose subsequent career has sufficiently proved the elevation of his mind and purity of his principles,[1] and who has demonstrated, like Chateaubriand, that the warmest devotion to the throne, in generous breasts, is consistent with, and in truth proceeds from, the same principles as the most sincere attachment to public liberty.

59. Composition of the Chamber of Peers.

The Chamber of Peers deserves much less consideration, for unhappily the general want of great and independent proprietors in its ranks, the servility and frequent tergiversations by which it had invariably been distinguished in later times, and the recent creation of ninety-two new peers by the king, had nearly deprived it of all consideration in the country. The majority was decided on the Royalist side; indeed, the recent numerous creations were made with no other view but to effect that object. But it was less compact and decided than the majority in the Chamber of Deputies; for, being composed for the most part of men experienced in public life, it was more inclined to moderation—of those inured to revolutions, disposed to temporize. The leaders of the Royalist majority were the Count Jules de Polignac, the Dukes de Fitzjames, de Serent, d'Uzes, and de Grammont, and the Viscount de Chateaubriand. The great literary fame and splendid eloquence of the last would have rendered him beyond all question the most powerful man in the Assembly, had his reason been as powerful as his imagination, his consistency as his oratory. But unfortunately these qualities were by no means equally strong in his ardent mind; and he adds another to the numerous examples which go to prove that in public life the judgment is a more important faculty than even genius, and that it is not so much the pre-eminence of any one mental quality, as their happy combination, which is the secret of success. Ever energetic and eloquent, he was not always consistent; on reviewing his political life, it is hard to say what his opinions really were; and no better refutation can sometimes be sought for his arguments at one period than his speeches at another.[2]

60. Opening of the Chamber, and speech of the king. Oct 7.

The session was opened by the king in person, with great pomp, on the 7th October. The restoration of the Bourbons, the unparalleled misfortunes which had befallen the country, the still greater evils which it was feared were impending over it, all tended to invest the ceremony with a melancholy and absorbing interest. The sovereign appeared, surrounded by his brothers, his nobles, the marshals of the empire, and all the pomp of the monarchy; and the speech which he delivered is memorable, not only as an important state paper in an unparalleled crisis, but as known to have been his unaided composition.[*] He spoke as follows: "When, last year, I for the first time convoked the Chambers, I congratulated myself upon having, by an honorable treaty, restored peace to France. It was beginning to taste the fruits of it, all the sources of public prosperity were reopening, when a criminal enterprise, seconded by the most inconceivable defection, arrested their course. The evils which that ephemeral usurpation have caused to my country afflict me profoundly; but I must declare, that if it had been possible they could have reached me alone, I should have returned thanks to Providence. The marks of attachment which my people have given me, in the most critical moments, have been a solace to my personal distresses; but those of my subjects, of my children, press upon my heart. It is in order to put a period to that state of suspense, more trying than war itself, that I have felt it my duty to conclude with the powers who, after having overturned the usurper, occupy at present a great part of our territory, a convention which will regulate our present and future relations with them. It will be communicated to you without any reservation, when it has received the last formalities. You will feel, the whole of France will feel, the profound grief which I must have felt on the occasion; but the salvation of my kingdom rendered that great determination necessary; and when I took it, I felt the whole duties which it imposed upon me. I have directed that this year there should be transferred from my privy purse to the general exchequer a considerable part of my revenue; my family, the moment they heard of my resolution, have done the same. I have ordered similar reductions on the salaries of all my servants, without exception; I shall ever be ready to share in the sacrifices which mournful circumstances have imposed upon my people. The public accounts will be laid before you; you will at once see the necessity of the economy which I have prescribed to my ministers in all branches of the administration. Happy if these measures shall meet the exigencies of the state; but, in any event, I reckon on the devotion of the nation, and the zeal of the Chambers. But other, sweeter, and not less important cares await your attention. It is to give weight to your deliberations, and to obtain myself the advantage of greater light, that I have created new peers and augmented the number of the deputies. I hope I have succeeded in my choice; and the zeal of the deputies, in such a difficult conjuncture, is a proof alike that they are animated by a sincere affection for my person and an ardent love for our country. It is therefore with a sweet joy and entire confidence that I behold you assembled around me, certain that you will never lose sight of the fundamental basis of the felicity of the state, a cordial and loyal union of the Chambers with the King, and respect for the constitutional charter. That charter—on which I have meditated with care before giving it—to which reflection every day attaches me more—which I have sworn to maintain, and to which you all, beginning with my family, are about to swear obedience—is, without doubt, like all human institutions, susceptible of improvement; but I am sure none of you will ever forget that side by side with the advantage of amelioration is the danger of innovation. To cause religion to flourish, to purify the public morals, to found liberty on a respect for the laws,

---

[*] "J'ai eu ce discours tout entier écrit de la main du Roi, sur une petite feuille de papier à lettre, avec cette écriture si nette, qu'il employait à sa correspondance. Il se ressentait la rédaction claire et élégante de ses discours; il y mettait un soin infini; c'était pour lui une affaire littéraire à laquelle il attachait de l'importance, même sous le rapport du style."—CAPEFIGUE, III. 203.

to give stability to credit, reorganize the army, heal the wounds which have too much wounded our country, to secure internal tranquillity, and cause France to be respected without: these are the ends to which all our efforts should tend."¹

¹ Moniteur, Oct. 15, 1815; Lam. v. 376, 378; Cap. iii. 201, 203.

61. Manner in which the speech was received by the Chamber.

These were noble and dignified expressions, worthy of a king of France meeting the representatives of his people in a period of unequalled gloom and difficulty. Inexpressibly striking was the scene which the Chamber presented during their delivery. There was none of the enthusiasm usually exhibited on these occasions; none of the transports which in general attend the restoration of a monarch of an ancient race to the throne of his fathers. The Chamber was profoundly loyal, but the public misfortunes crushed every heart. It was known that a treaty of peace was in progress, that grievous exactions would be made by the Allies, and that probably a considerable portion of the territory on the frontier would require to be abandoned. Sadness, consternation, despair, were on every countenance as the words so prophetic of evil were pronounced by the king. The obscurity of the expressions rendered them more terrible; no one knew what the impending calamity would be, or on whom it would fall. The deputies of the departments which it was feared would be ceded on the frontier, shed tears at the thoughts of their approaching severance from their country. It was felt by all that a family long united was about to be broken up; the well-known halls would be deserted—the gladsome hearth become desolate.²

² Lam. v. 379, 380; Cap. iii. 203, 204.

62. Difficulties at taking the Oath of Fidelity.

The king, before even the session began, had a convincing proof of the thorns with which his path was to be beset. The oath of fidelity to the King and the Constitution required to be taken by the whole of the legislature, beginning with the peers of the blood-royal. But here a difficulty at once arose. The Count d'Artois at first refused to take the oath, and it was only after a long and difficult negotiation that his scruples were overcome. The Prince of Condé made similar difficulties, and feigned sickness to avoid taking it. M. Jules de Polignac and M. de la Bourdonnaye refused to take it altogether, though they were among the newly-created peers. The deputy of Montauban, when called on, insisted on making some reservations. These incidents were not material, but they indicated the strength of the prevailing feeling, and in what quarter it was that the principal difficulties of the session would arise. When the vote came to be taken for the president of the Chamber, the strength of the several parties was at once demonstrated. M. Lainé, the president during the former year, and whose intrepid conduct on more than one eventful crisis had won for him the esteem of all parties, was indeed called to the chair by a large majority; he had 328 votes out of 516. But the strength of the opposition was tried and appeared on the vote for the second candidates, or *supplians*. The Prince de la Tremouille, who represented the opinions, and was supported by the whole strength of the Count d'Artois' party, had 229 votes; while M. de la Rigaudie, who united the suffrages of the united Liberals and moderate Royalists, had only 169 votes.¹

¹ Moniteur, Oct. 15 and 17, 1815; Cap. iii. 206, 207; Lam. v. 384.

The answer of the Chambers, though upon the whole, as the speeches of the mover and seconder of the Address are in England, an echo of the speech from the Throne, yet gave proof of the profound feelings of indignation with which the representatives were animated. "The evils of the country," said M. de Lainé, "are great, but they are not irreparable. If the nation, albeit inaccessible to the seduction of the usurper, must nevertheless bear the burden of a defection in which it has taken no share, it will submit. But in the midst of our wishes for universal concord, and even to cement it, it is our duty *to solicit your justice* against those who have imperilled alike the throne and the nation. Your clemency, Sire, has been without bounds; we do not come to ask you to retract it; the promises of kings, we know well, should be held sacred. But we do supplicate you, in the name of the people, who have been overwhelmed by the weight of their misfortunes, to cause justice to march when clemency is arrested; and let those who, now encouraged by the impunity they have enjoyed, are not afraid to make a parade of their rebellion, *be delivered over to the just severity of the tribunals*. The Chamber will zealously concur in the passing of such laws as may be necessary to effect that object. We will not speak of the necessity of intrusting to none but pure hands the different branches of your authority. The ministers who surround you present sufficient guarantees in that respect. Their vigilance in its prosecution will be the more easily exercised that the events which have occurred, have sufficiently revealed every sentiment, and laid bare every thought."²

63. Answer of the Chamber of Deputies

² Moniteur, Oct. 17, 1815; Cap. iii. 207, 208.

The first measures proposed in the Chamber were nothing but an attempt to carry into execution these ulcerated feelings. They were chiefly three: a law against seditious cries; one suspending individual liberty, and investing Government with extraordinary power of arrest; and one establishing courts-martial for the summary trial of political offenders. The first was introduced by M. Barbé-Marbois, the Keeper of the Seals, who thus expressed the grounds on which Government proceeded in bringing forward the measure: "If great atrocities have been committed; if, to avoid his own destruction, the loyal citizen has been compelled to remain a passive spectator of the deeds of seditious mobs; if crime has enjoyed for some time fatal triumphs, these calamities are prolonged even when their success has been interrupted. Then it is that the insurgents endeavor, by the force of audacity, to recover their lost ground; the seditions mutually encourage each other, and exert themselves to be seen in every place, and at every hour, as if advancing to an assured victory. If they succeed in inspiring fear, they associate in their ranks all whom the army has expelled with indignation, and all the criminals whom their obscurity has screened from the

64. Law against seditious cries, Oct. 16.

vengeance of the laws. Should the force of the Government arrest their designs, they never think of renouncing them, but take refuge in libelous discourses, calumnious publications. Impunity encourages them. Many of them show themselves without disguise; and although their indiscretion reveals their weakness, it is not the less certain that their proceedings disturb the social order, and the public interest requires that their turbulent designs and detestable enterprises should be effectually repressed. There are some men whose sole morality is the fear of punishment. It is against culprits of that stamp that our laws are in many respects powerless. To the necessity of a positive law for such cases is joined that of a rapid procedure, and of a punishment inflicted immediately after the offense." In pursuance of these reasons, the proposed law, after defining what should be deemed seditious cries, punished them with imprisonment not below three months, nor exceeding five years. Severe as these penalties may appear for mere seditious *words*, irrespective of overt *acts* of treason, they fell so far short of the vindictive feelings of the Assembly that the proposal was very coldly received; and though it passed into a law, it by no means gave vent to the public indignation.[1]

[1] Moniteur, Oct. 17, 1815; Cap. iii. 278; Lam. v. 389, 390.

65. Law suspending individual liberty, Oct. 18.

The next law proposed (that on individual liberty) was much more favorably received, and may be considered as faithfully expressing the opinions and feelings of the majority of the Assembly. M. Decazes brought forward the proposition; and it was loudly applauded as "full of hatred at the Revolution." "The law proposed," said he, "had no other object but to reach the *great criminals*—to prevent the attempts of those men who are strangers to remorse, whom pardon can not conciliate, whom clemency offends, whom nothing can reassure, because their consciences will never permit it. These are men whom justice can not overtake, because its forms, salutary but slow, render it impotent to prevent, often even to repress; and because that species of delinquencies are executed by unseen springs, hidden even from their author. By the law now proposed, the weak will be reassured. They will range themselves with confidence under the shield of a strong Government, which has given proof of its resolution to defend others and itself. The people wish, above all things, to be saved. The impotence to which the factions have been reduced since the fall of the usurper, so far from moderating, has only increased their audacity. Like the evil spirit which inspires them, they ruminate on crime to shun oblivion." On this preamble the law proposed enacted that every individual, without exception, who had been arrested on any charge of being concerned in attempts against "the authority of the king, the persons of the royal family, or the safety of the state, might be detained in custody until the expiry of the law, the termination of which was to be the end of the next session of Parliament, if not then renewed." The execution of this law was committed to all the public functionaries to whom the constitution intrusted the cognizance of the crimes to which it refers.[2]

[2] Moniteur, Oct. 19, 1815; Cap. iii. 279, 280; Lam. v. 289, 299.

Disguised under an appearance of severity which might render it acceptable to the feelings of the majority of the Chambers, a humane feeling had really dictated the proposal of the law to the Government. It was brought forward at the time when popular murders had stained all the south of France with blood, and when there seemed no way of saving the victims but by subjecting them to a temporary confinement. It was desired, too, to legalize, in some degree, the numerous arrests which had taken place over the country during the last few months, and to secure the detention of a number of persons during a critical period, whose seditious intentions were beyond a doubt, but against whom it might be difficult to adduce complete legal proof. It met, however, with a much greater resistance than the law against seditious cries, because it threatened to affect a much superior class of persons. But if the resistance was determined, the support was still more impassioned, and at length it was carried by a majority of 294 to 56, amid cries and shouts resembling rather the enthusiasm of the theatre than the sober deliberations of a legislative assembly.[1]

66. Discussion on it in the Chambers, Oct. 17.

[1] Cap. iii. 283, 284; Moniteur, Oct. 23, 1815.

The discussion of the law on seditious cries revealed in a still more painful manner the impassioned feelings of the Assembly. It was moved as an amendment in committee, that the penalty of raising seditious cries, or hoisting any other flag but the white one, should be not imprisonment, but transportation, accompanied by confiscation of any public pension. Even this addition to the punishment did not seem to the majority to be adequate to the offense. M. Jossé de Beauvois exclaimed. "After what we have seen, is this the time for vain indulgences? Since the return of the king, we have been caressing crime rather than punishing it; I propose forced labor for life, in addition to transportation." "Death! death!" exclaimed M. Humbert de Lesmaiseons: "we must strike at the great culprits. The punishment of death seems to me the only penalty for those who hoist any other flag but the white one; and it should extend not only to the actors, but the instigators of that offense." "The pains of parricide," added M. Boin, "if the act has been begun to be carried into execution!" These vehement apostrophes in a manner secured the adoption of the amendments in the committee: the Government were too happy to avoid the extreme penalty by adopting the milder punishment of transportation, which was accordingly agreed to.[2]

67. Vehement discussion on the law against seditious cries.

[2] Moniteur, Oct. 23, 1815; Lam. v. 394, 395; Cap. iii. 284, 286.

The law for the establishment of Prévôtal Courts for the punishment of political offenses, which might dispose of cases summarily, without the intervention of a jury, came on on the 17th November. It was deemed essential by the Government, as it ever will be by right-thinking ministers in similar circumstances, to take the cognizance of political offenses entirely out of the hands of juries; for so completely was the country divided, and so vehement were the passions excited on both sides, that in some departments the guilty were

68. Law establishing courts martial for political offenses. Nov. 17

certain to escape, in others the innocent ran the greatest risk of being convicted. M. de Feltre brought forward the proposed measure, and the motives prompting to it were thus stated by him: "Those are unhappy epochs when society, assailed with violence, is obliged to treat as enemies those who, placed in its own bosom, have declared against it a sort of open law. It is to that imperious law of necessity that we owe the introduction of Prévôtal Courts, created by the genius of the greatest magistrates. Its object is to restore in the kingdom that tranquillity which similar establishments have produced in former times; to intimidate the wicked, and isolate them, in a manner, from the weak crowd whom they make their instruments." The law proposed, which was supported in the Chamber of Deputies by the eloquence of M. Royer Collard and the scientific fame of M. Cuvier, enacted that "every department was to have a provost-marshal and Prévôtal Court, composed of the provost and four assessors, chosen among the members of the Tribunals of the First Instance. It was to be competent to try all political crimes, seditious assemblages, cries, or attempts against the king or the royal family. It was empowered to apply all the criminal and correctional pains. The provost was the public prosecutor. The procedure was to be as brief as possible; the accused, in twenty-four hours after apprehension, was to be brought before the Prévôtal Court, which was to determine on the case, and pronounce sentence without separating. The sentence was to be instantly carried into execution, and not to be subject to the review of the Court of Cassation, or any superior court.[1]

Broad as were the powers conferred by these acts on the magistracy and the Government, they fell short of what the majority deemed indispensable for the necessities of the case. They feared that the judges in the inferior tribunals, holding their situations for life, should not be sufficiently pliant to the wishes of the Government, or of the majority in the Chambers. M. Hyde de Neuville, accordingly, proposed that a considerable part of the inferior tribunals should be suppressed, and that the whole judges in those which were retained should hold their situations during pleasure, only for the period of a year. Thus the reaction had become so violent that the Royalist Chamber was adopting the measures of the regicide Convention, and evincing that predilection for appointments *during pleasure*, which in every age and country has been the characteristic of tyranny, whether civil or ecclesiastical, alike in monarchs, aristocracies, democracies, or congregations. It was with considerable difficulty that Government succeeded in throwing out these extreme propositions, which went to destroy the very foundations of freedom in the land; and it is a striking proof of the danger of intrusting power during periods of excitement to popular assemblies, that such a man as M. Hyde de Neuville could be led to bring forward such a measure;—and the Assembly of representatives of the people, but for the interposition of the crown, would have adopted it.[2]

Thus these bills, as we should call them in England, having all passed the Lower House, the discussion of them began in the Chamber of Peers. That conferring the power of unlimited arrest was the first which came on. Then M. Lanjuinais, who had been created a peer by the king, evinced the same intrepidity in combating the encroachments on public freedom by the Royalists, which he had formally done in resisting the savage measures of the majority in the Convention. "The law proposed," said he, "is unjust, because it goes to elevate suspicion into proof, and render it a sufficient ground for arrest and detention; because it takes away from the accused the most important and sacred of all rights, that of being tried by the constitutional and immovable judges! What must be the effects of such a law? What but the law against 'suspected persons,' with all its terrors, and better combined even than that tyrannical enactment to enslave the imagination, extirpate the conscience? You have spoken of Rome and England; but what have they in common with this proposal?—the suspension of the Habeas Corpus Act, and the *Carcant Consulea*, with such a law as the present? I demand, at least, that it should be referred to a committee, to soften its more objectionable clauses. Doubtless the circumstances are imperious; perhaps some such law may be indispensable; but a thousand circumstances of detail, which require to be limited and defined, are unexplained by it. It is even uncertain by what functionaries it is to be executed; and what a host of doubts and difficulties will that single circumstance create! Every locality, every department, will execute it in a different manner; and possibly its execution may be mildest in the very places where rigor is most called for."[1]

"The proposed law," answered M. de Fontanes, "can alone give effect to the feeling of the Chamber, as expressed in the address to the King. That address recommended to the King to exercise his justice; it seemed to dread the excess of his clemency. Some say they will vote against it from feelings of humanity: I will vote for it from the same sentiment. We must inspire terror if we would avoid doing evil. Factions agitate and declaim against oppression only under a weak government; if it is strong, they are peaceable and silent. You can I know well, in the name of liberty, move every thing that is most profound in the human heart —its finest feelings, its noblest sentiments; but whatever may be said, it is not liberty, but order, which is the first necessity of society—the first end of its establishment. It is in the name of order that I vote for the simple and unmodified adoption of the law. The law proposed is a measure of indulgence. All that Government required to do was to take from a certain number of individuals the power of injuring themselves or others, without giving them the liberty which could lead only to their being seated on the accused bench, to enable all the rest to enjoy their freedom in peace and tranquillity." The law was passed by a majority of 52, the numbers being 167 to 112.[2]

The discussion of the law on the raising of

seditious cries excited a warm discussion in the Assembly, remarkable chiefly for the violence of the sentiments which it elicited. "What," said the Marquis de Frondeville, "are the offenses against which the law is directed? Are they not the most serious which can menace society? They comprehend menaces against the life or person of the king and royal family, provocations against the Government, incitement to take up arms to resist the Royal authority. Is the punishment of transportation an adequate mode of repressing such offenses? For what crimes is the punishment of death to be reserved, if Government fears to strike the miserable wretches who are trying to overturn the throne, the government, society itself? If transported, where are they to be taken to? Have we islands in distant seas, like the English, whither to send such monsters to league with their kind? They may, says the law, be banished from the European continent—that is to say, they may settle themselves within a few leagues of its shores, and there enjoy the tranquillity which they have wrested from us. Do you really suppose that by such means you can repress the conspiracies, of the existence of which we have received such frightful proof? It is in vain to say you must apply a different measure of punishment to provocations to crime and their actual commission. True; but the penal code has itself shown how this is to be done, by denouncing the simple penalty against an expression of intention, and the penalty aggravated by the pains of parricide against the completed act."¹

<small>72.
Argument against the law on seditious cries.</small>

<small>¹ Moniteur, Nov. 9, 1815; Cap. iii. 297, 298.</small>

"The proposed law," said Chateaubriand, "in the 5th article, denounces a penalty against any one who utters an expression which might excite alarm in the holders of national domains. The enactment is barbarous, for it menaces with the same penalty an excusable regret and a sacrilegious machination. It will reach the poor emigrant despoiled of his inheritance, whom a jealous acquirer of his property may surprise exhaling some regrets, shedding some tears over the tomb of his fathers. Dragged before the tribunal by calumny, he will be judged by passion; he will there lose his honor, the only possession which the Revolution has left him; and all that to calm apprehensions which should have been for ever set at rest, if any thing could do so, by the solemn promises in the charter. Wherefore is all this done?—to stifle those murmurs, the inevitable consequence of a great injustice—to impose a silence which, to be effectual, should ordain at the same time the demolition of the stones which mark the boundaries of the heritages of which you are so anxious to reassure the possessors." These extreme opinions did not influence the majority; and the law, as it was sent up from the Chamber of Deputies, as well as that establishing the Prévôtal Courts, was adopted in the Peers without alteration by large majorities—the latter with scarce any discussion.²

<small>73.
Speech of Chateaubriand on the subject.</small>

<small>² Moniteur, Nov. 9 and 10, 1815; Cap. iii. 301, 302; Lam. v. 394, 395.</small>

It is necessary to consider and reflect on these debates, if we would judge with impartiality the conduct of the French Government in the great tragedy in which the Hundred Days terminated—the deaths of Marshal Ney and Colonel Labedoyère. It is impossible to approach this subject without painful emotions; to an Englishman especially, who recollects that the former was a great and glorious enemy, and that his mournful fate is in some sort wound up with our triumphs, and could not have happened but for the conquest of Waterloo, it will always be the subject of the most poignant regret. How much more gladly would every generous heart in Britain have joined in celebrating the heroism of the bravest of the brave, and doing honor to his gray hairs, than in weaving the chaplet which is to express regret upon his tomb! The very circumstance of his having been our enemy, of his having combated Wellington in Portugal, headed the charge of the Old Guard at Waterloo, only augments the sorrow with which his fate must ever be regarded. Those who are most attached to principles will ever be most indulgent to individuals; and it is the glory of modern civilization to behold in an enemy only a friend, when he has ceased to combat in the hostile ranks. Yet this very feeling of equanimity should lead us to do justice to the Government upon whom those melancholy acts were imposed as a species of state necessity; we must consider its situation, measure the difficulties with which it was surrounded, and the weight of the influence, external and internal, which was brought to bear upon its deliberations. If any decided opinion results from these considerations, it will probably be against the system of public law under which those melancholy executions took place; and even the blood of Marshal Ney will not have been shed in vain if it leads, in all civilized nations, to the abolition of the punishment of death in all purely political offenses.

<small>74.
Reflections on the deaths of Ney and Labedoyère.</small>

External influences of no ordinary kind were exerted to impel the Government into measures of severity on this occasion. The opinion of the Allies and their sovereigns, not even excepting the mild and benevolent Alexander, was unanimous, that there could be no peace in Europe till the military spirit was checked in France; and that, in Wellington's words, "a great moral lesson" was more requisite for the French army than the French people. It was the insatiable ambition of the army which he commanded, more even than his own disposition, which had impelled Napoleon into the career of conquest; it was their rapacious and covetous desires which had rendered their ascendency so insupportably odious to every people they had come among. The Hundred Days had sufficiently demonstrated that no reliance could be placed on the fidelity of their chiefs; that their submission was merely forced, their loyalty feigned; and that the leopard would change his spots, the Ethiopian his skin, before they would be influenced by any other passion but the lust of conquest. It was for that reason that it was deemed indispensable to insist on the dissolution of the army of the Loire, the exile of the principal military leaders, and the change of the national colors of France: steps, and not unimportant ones, in the formation of a new national spirit. But, in addition to this, it was necessary to affect the imagination by great examples; to strike, and to strike boldly,

<small>75.
External influences exerted against the Government.</small>

and prove by decisive acts that if this had not hitherto been done, it was owing to humanity, not fear. "We must strike," said M. Gentz, "the chiefs of the conspiracy, or we have no security for the peace of Europe for a year."[1]

[margin: ¹Cap. iii. 315, 316.]

Still more exasperated was the Royalist party at the Court, and in the Chambers, which called out aloud for great examples. It was no wonder it was so, for they had humiliation to deplore, losses to revenge. If the feeling of the necessity of punishment was strong in the conquerors—in those to whom treachery had only opened the avenue to conquest—what might it be expected to be in the conquered—in those to whom it had opened only the gates of perdition?—among whom it had brought the disgrace of defeat, the tarnishing of glory, the overthrow of a dynasty, the loss of frontier towns, the oppression of a million of armed men, the imposition of humiliating and insupportable exactions? Generosity had been tried, magnanimity had had its day, and what had been the result? Nothing but a repetition on a still greater scale of treachery and treason. Not a head had fallen, not an estate had been confiscated, not a human being banished on the first restoration, and the only consequence had been the formation of a vast conspiracy to overturn the Government and destroy their benefactors. Humanity was, as usual in such cases, ascribed to fear; moderation considered as a proof of imbecility. The time had now come when it was necessary to undeceive the conspirators by great examples, and, after the manner of Napoleon, vindicate the authority of Government by the condign punishment of those who had alike insulted it, and all but ruined their country.[2]

[margin: 76. Considerations which weighed with the Court.]

[margin: ²Cap. iii. 306; Lam. v. 423, 424.]

Strong as these considerations in themselves were, and powerfully as they spoke to the feelings of a Government which had been overturned by a conspiracy, and only reinstated by conquest, they did not sway the humane breast of the king, or move the enlightened minds of his ministers. Louis XVIII., M. Talleyrand, M. Fouché, the Duke de Richelieu, and M. Decazes, were alike impressed with the necessity of a great act of amnesty, and of avoiding the most fatal of all inaugurations for the commencement of their government—the inauguration of blood. They did every thing in their power to furnish the accused persons with the means of escape, designedly in order to avoid the embarrassment of their trial. When the lists, prepared and signed by Fouché on the 24th July, appeared, the execution of the warrants of arrest was delayed for several weeks, purposely to give the accused persons an opportunity of escape. Passports were furnished to all, or nearly all, the proscribed persons; and not only were they earnestly entreated to withdraw, but large sums of money were placed at the disposal of the minister of police to enable them to do so. No less than 459,000 francs (£18,360) were expended by the minister of police in this humane attempt. But the benevolent and wise intentions of the Government were in some instances frustrated by the zeal of the provincial authorities, who

[margin: 77. Measures of the Government to give the accused persons the means of escape.]

arrested the proscribed persons as they were making their escape—in others rendered nugatory by the devotion of the persons endangered themselves, who in a heroic spirit preferred remaining at home, and undergoing all the risks of trial, to taking guilt to themselves by making use of the means of escape.[1]

[margin: ¹Lam. v. 423; Cap. iii. 316, 317; Lac. i. 422, 423.]

The first of the persons who was arrested from the latter cause, and forced upon the Government for trial, was COLONEL LABEDOYERE. This ardent and gallant young man, whose defection at Grenoble first opened to Napoleon the gates of France,[2] and whose subsequent fate has made his name imperishable in history, was connected with several of the first families of the Court, but had been involved in the meshes of the Napoleonist conspiracy by the influence of Queen Hortense, whose saloons in Paris, under the name of the Duchess de St. Leu, were the chief rendezvous of the Imperial party. Even so early as 8th February, 1815, he had assured M. Fleury de Chaboulon, then on his route to Elba, that the Emperor might reckon on him. Being in command of the 7th regiment at Grenoble, the first fortified town between Cannes and Paris, his defection was of the highest importance to Napoleon; and it was mainly from knowing that he might be relied on, that the Emperor had chosen the mountain road which lay through that town.[3]

[margin: 78. Treachery of Col. Labedoyère.]

[margin: ²Hist of Europe, c. iii § 60.]

[margin: ³Cap. iii. 318, 319; Lam. v. 425; Lac. ii. 4, 5.]

After the capitulation of Paris, Fouché sent for Labedoyère, and said to him, "I advise you to leave France; here are your passports: if you want money, here are 25,000 francs (£1000) in gold; but set off." He left Paris in pursuance of this advice, but repented before he had passed Clermont, where he stopped. The Paris police were aware of his residence, and Fouché repeatedly warned him of the necessity of remaining concealed; but, instead of doing that, he returned to Paris, resisting all the efforts of General Exeelmans and Count Flahault, who did their utmost to prevent him, and returned to Paris, and repaired to the house of a lady to whom he was attached His emotion at learning of the arrest of Lavalette, who had been seized shortly before, as well as his fine and martial figure, revealed him to an agent of the police who was in the carriage, who tracked him to the place where he had hoped to remain concealed,[4] screened by the vigilance, and guarded by the fidelity of love.

[margin: 79. His arrest]

[margin: ⁴Cap. iii. 318, 321; Lam. v. 430, 433; Lac. ii. 7, 8.]

The agent communicated the circumstance to the prefect; and as the Government could not overlook the return of so great a criminal to Paris, after he had been furnished with the means of escape, he was arrested in the night and conveyed to prison.

He was brought to trial before a council of war on the 14th August. There could be no difficulty in proving his guilt; it was notorious to all the world, and admitted in the most express manner by himself, in his declaration when brought before the police magistrate. It was established in the clearest manner that he se. out from Grenoble, at the head of the 7th

[margin: 80. His trial and condemnation.]

regiment of infantry, to meet Napoleon, notwithstanding all the instances of his commander, General Devilliers, who endeavored to dissuade him; that this was a premeditated act; that he had intimated his intention to his officers, harangued the soldiers, and prepared the tricolor cockades, which were concealed in a drum, and distributed when the period for action had arrived; that he had alike disobeyed the orders and resisted the supplications of his general, who remained faithful to his allegiance; and that when he met the Emperor, instead of attacking, he embraced him, and brought him back in triumph to the foot of the ramparts of Grenoble. The public prosecutor called on the judges, as these facts were clearly established, to pronounce the sentence of the law on so great a criminal, whose defection had drawn after it that of the whole army. Labedoyère did not controvert the facts proved; he only sought to vindicate his memory by explaining his motives. "If my life only was at stake, I would not detain you a moment: it is my profession to be ready to die. But a wife, the model of every virtue, a son as yet in the cradle, will one day demand of me an account of my actions. The name I leave them is their inheritance; I am bound to leave it to them, unfortunate but not disgraced. I may have deceived myself as to the real interests of France: misled by the recollections of camps, or the illusions of honor, I may have mistaken my own chimeras for the voice of my country. But the greatness of the sacrifices which I made, in breaking all the strongest bonds of rank and family, prove at least that no unworthy or personal motive has influenced my actions. I deny nothing; I plead only guiltless to having conspired. When I received the command of my regiment, I had not a thought that the Emperor could ever return to France. Sad presentiments, nevertheless, overtook me at the moment when I set out for Chambery; they arose from the weight of public opinion pressing on me. I confess with grief my error; I confess it with anguish, when I cast my eyes on my country. My fault consisted in having misunderstood the intentions of the king, and his return has opened my eyes. I shall not be permitted to enjoy the spectacle of the constitution completed, and France still a great nation united around its king. But I have shed my blood for my country; and I wish to persuade myself that my death, preceded by the abjuration of my errors, may be useful to France; that my name will not be held in detestation, and that when my son may be of an age to serve his country, he will not be ashamed of his father's name."¹

¹ Moniteur, Aug. 20 1815; Lam. v. 435, 437; Cap. iii. 321, 323.

§1. His death.

As a matter of necessity, he was condemned to death, though the judges themselves shed tears when sentence was pronounced. His relations offered 100,000 francs (£4000) to the keeper of the prison if he would favor his escape. As a last resource, his young wife threw herself at the feet of the King, whom she reached as he was descending the great stair of the Tuileries to enter his carriage. "Grace, grace!" exclaimed the unhappy woman, her voice broken by sobs. "Madam," replied the monarch with deep emotion, "I know your sentiments, and those of your family, for my spouse; I deeply regret being obliged to refuse such faithful servants. If your husband had offended me alone, his pardon would have been already given; but I owe satisfaction to France, on which he has induced the scourge of rebellion and war. My duty as a king ties my hands. I can only pray for the soul of him whom justice has condemned, and assure you of my protection to yourself and your child." At these words the suppliant fell in a swoon at his feet. Labedoyère's mother, clad in the deepest mourning, awaited the monarch on his return, but the strictest orders had been given to prevent her reaching the royal presence, and her cries alone reached his ears. Meanwhile Labedoyère, recalled by solitude and misfortune from the illusions which had misled him, had regained the sentiments of his youth. He received with gratitude the consolations of religion, and prepared in a worthy spirit to undergo his fate. When brought out for execution, his eyes met those of M. César de Nervaux, a faithful friend and companion in arms, who had come to support him in his last moments. They pressed each other's hands in silence. When the soldiers who were to perform the painful duty took their stations opposite the wall before which he was placed, he advanced a few steps, and took his station in the middle of the intervening space; then suddenly turning round, as if he had forgot something, he whispered for a few seconds to the priest who accompanied him. Then calmly resuming his place, he refused to have his eyes bandaged, and looking straight at the leveled muskets, exclaimed in a loud voice, "Fire, my friends!" He fell pierced by nine balls; and when the smoke of the discharge had passed away, the priest approached and steeped his handkerchief in the blood which flowed from his breast, which he took with him as a relic to the wife of the fallen officer.¹

¹ Lam. v. 442, 447; Cap. iii. 323, 324; Lac. ii. 3, 4.

§2. Trial of Marshal Ney. His treacherous conduct.

The next person selected for trial was Marshal Ney, who had at the head of his corps betrayed the royal cause as effectually as Labedoyère had done at the head of his regiment. His flagrant defection, and the decisive consequences with which it was attended, were too deeply impressed on the mind of the Royalists to give the Government any option in dealing with so great a criminal. He had said in the Chamber of Peers, before the departure of Napoleon for Rochefort, that he had every thing to fear from the resentment of the Royalists, and that he was about to set out for the United States. It was undoubtedly true that he had used the famous expression to the king, before he set out from Paris to take the command at Melun. "I will bring Bonaparte back in an iron cage." The remarkable expression had been overheard by the Prince de Poix and the Duke de Duras as well as his Majesty, who was surprised at them coming from a marshal who had risen so high in the Imperial service. He himself admitted in his judicial declaration that he had used the words "Cage de Fer."*

* "Je dis au Roi que la démarche de Bonaparte était si insensée qu'il méritait, s'il était pris, d'être conduit à Paris dans une cage de fer. On a prétendu que j'avais dit que je le conduirais moi-même, si je le prenais, dans

He admitted that, in a transport of Royalist enthusiasm, he had said, "If I see the least hesitation in the troops, I will seize the first grenadier's musket, make use of it, and give an example to others." He admitted having signed the fatal proclamation of the 14th March, in which the cause of Napoleon was openly espoused, and which was immediately followed by the defection of the whole army. He said in his declaration that it was written by Napoleon, and sent to him by means of his brother Joseph, who was at Prangin. Yet so strong had been his protestations of fidelity, that down to the very last moment the royal family had more confidence in him than in any man in France.[1] *

[1 Moniteur, Nov. 11, 1815, Sup.; Cap. iii. 339, 340; Lac. ii. 5, 6; Procès de Ney. 30.]

Ney was in Paris, though not employed with the army, when the capitulation with the Duke of Wellington and Marshal Blucher was signed—a circumstance which led to a painful difficulty, so far as this country was concerned, in the trial which ensued. He received passports under a feigned name from Fouché, which were indorsed by the Austrian and Swiss embassies at Paris, and by Count Bubna, the Austrian commander at Lyons. He was just leaving France in pursuance of Talleyrand's advice, and had reached Nantua, within a few leagues of the Swiss frontier, when he was seized, like Labedoyère, with a fatal desire to return to his own country. He was haunted by the idea of a sentence of death *par contumace*, which would weigh upon his memory and the interests of his relations. He returned accordingly, and took up his residence at the chateau of Bossonis, which belonged to his family. There he made no attempt at concealment, and was discovered by a magnificent sabre, with his name engraven on the hilt, which had been given him by the Emperor in the days of his glory. He was in consequence seized, without any instructions from head-quarters, by M. Locard, the prefect of the department, a zealous Royalist, and sent to Paris, where his arrival occasioned no small regret and consternation among the members of the Government.[1]

63. His departure from Paris, and arrest at Bessonis.

[1 Cap. iii. 310, 312; Lac. ii. 4, 5.]

But, once taken, it was out of the power of Government not to bring him to trial; for, if so great a traitor escaped, how could any inferior criminal be brought to justice? Great difficulty, however, was experienced in finding a court to undertake the responsibility of his trial. He was, in the first instance, sent to be tried by a military commission, presided over by Marshal Moncey; but that veteran recoiled from the idea of trying an old companion in arms, and declined the trial on the plea of having no jurisdiction over a peer of the realm. This refusal, which was considered by the Royalists a decisive proof of a general conspiracy in the army, gave profound mortification to the court, and was punished by three months' imprisonment, inflicted on the recusant marshal. Ney was next sent to the Chamber of Peers, which, how unwilling soever to undertake the painful duty, could find no pretext to evade it. The Duke de Richelieu, in introducing the accusation on behalf of the Government, observed—"It is not only in the name of the king that we discharge this duty—it is in the name of France, long indignant, and now stupefied: it is even in the name of Europe that we at once conjure and require you to undertake the trial of Marshal Ney. We accuse him before you of high treason and crimes against the state. The Chamber of Peers owes to the world a conspicuous reparation; and it should be prompt, if it is to be effectual. The king's ministers are obliged to say that the decision of the council of war has become a triumph to the factions. We conjure you then, and in the name of the king require you, in terms of the ordinance of his majesty, to proceed to the trial of Marshal Ney." The trial proceeded accordingly, the defense of the marshal being intrusted to the able hands of MM. Berryer and Dupin.[1]

64. His trial before the Chamber of Peers.

[1 Moniteur, Nov. 11, 1815, Sup.; and Nov. 25, 1815; Cap. iii. 300, 301; Lac. ii. 5.]

These able counselors could not deny the facts proved against him, the most important of which were admitted by himself in his judicial declaration. They confined themselves, therefore, to the plea that he was no longer a free agent when he signed the proclamation of the 14th of March, sent to him by Napoleon;* that he was carried away by the torrent, and that the cause of Napoleon had been by the soldiers so warmly embraced before it was issued, that to have taken any other course had become impracticable. But to this it was justly replied, that difficulty will never justify crime; that if he could not control his troops, he might at least have withdrawn from the command, and not employed the power confided to him by the king for the destruction of his authority. And the defense of being carried away, such as it was, was

65. His defense and condemnation.

---

* "Officiers, sous-officiers, et soldats—La cause des Bourbons est à jamais perdue! Le dynastie legitime que la nation Française a adoptée va remonter sur le Trône; c'est à l'Empereur Napoleon notre Souverain qu'il appartient seul de regner sur ce beau pays! Que la noblesse des Bourbons prenne le parti de l'expatrier encore, ou qu'elle consente à vivre au milieu de nous, qu'importe! La cause sacrée de la liberté et de notre indépendance ne souffrira plus de leur funeste influence. Ils ont voulu avilir notre gloire militaire, mais ils ne sont troupes; cette gloire est le fruit de trop nobles travaux pour que nous puissions en perdre la memoire. Soldats, les temps ne sont plus où on gouvernait les peuples en étouffant tous leurs droits; la liberté triomphe enfin et Napoleon notre auguste Empereur, va l'affermir à jamais! Que desormais cette cause si belle soit la notre et celle de tous les Français! Que tous les braves que j'ai l'honneur de commander se penetrent de cette grande verité. Soldats, je vous ai si souvent menés à la victoire, maintenant je veux vous conduire à cette phalange immortelle que l'Empereur Napoléon conduit à Paris, et qui y sera sous peu de jours, et là, notre esperance et notre bonheur seront à jamais égalaux. Vive l'Empereur!"—*Lamo-le-Saulnier, le 13 Mars, 1815.—LE MARECHAL DE L'EMPIRE, "PRINCE DE LA MOSKOUA."—Moniteur, 22d Nov. 1815.*

* "Tout dépend des premiers coups de fusil, car enfin il n'y en a pas encore de tirés. J'attends tout de Ney, puisque c'est le seul qui combattra cet homme. Ne perdez pas de temps à ce vilain Paris; mon beau frère est assez pour le contenir; mais vous, pourquoi n'êtes vous pas avec Oudinot ou Ney?"—*Madame la Duchesse D'ANGOULEME à M. le Comte D'ARTOIS, Bordeaux 29 Mars, 1815.—CAPEFIGUE, IV. 421—Appendix*

entirely overturned by the evidence of Generals Lecourbe and Bourmont, who were with him at the time of his defection—who concurred in stating, the one in oral testimony, the other in a deposition emitted before death, that Ney had himself said, in their presence, that it was all over; that *every thing had been agreed upon for three months*, and they would have known it, if they had been at Paris; that no violence was to be done to the king, but that he was to be dethroned, put on board a vessel, and conducted into England.[*] It appeared, from what fell from General Bourmont, that Ney's words led to the belief that, like many other of the most terrible catastrophes recorded in history, from the siege of Troy downward, his conduct on this occasion had been mainly instigated by female jealousy and mortifications.

Deposition de Bourmont; Procès de Ney, 87: and Moniteur, Dec. 6, 1815.

It now remained only to the counsel for the accused to appeal to the capitulation of Paris; and here, it must be admitted, they had a much stronger case to rest upon. By the twelfth article of the capitulation of that city, concluded at St. Cloud, it had been stipulated that no person then in Paris should be disquieted in his person or estate on account of his conduct during the Hundred Days; and by another article, that if any doubt arose concerning the interpretation to be put on any part of the convention, it should be construed in favor of the party capitulating.† Three witnesses of the highest respectability, who took part in the capitulation, Marshal Davoust, General Guillimont, and M. Bignon, concurred in deposing that this article was intend-

26. Appeal to the capitulation of Paris.

ed to cover the military as well as the ordinary inhabitants of Paris; and that had this not been agreed to, they would have broken off the negotiation. "I had," said Marshal Davoust, "25,000 cavalry, 400 or 500 guns; and if the French are ready to fly, they are not less ready to rally under the walls of Paris." Marshal Ney exclaimed upon this—"The article was so entirely protective, that I relied on it: but for it, can it be believed I would not have died sword in hand? It was in defiance of that capitulation that I was arrested, and on its faith that I re-entered France." The Peers, by a majority, held that they could listen to no defense founded on the military convention of July 3, concluded between foreign generals and a provisional government not emanating from the king, and to which he was so entire a stranger, that two-and-twenty days after he signed an ordinance, directing a certain number of individuals to be brought to trial, which was signed by the very minister who had been president of the provisional government. As a last resource, M. Berryer objected that Ney was no longer a Frenchman, or subject to the laws of that country; for, by the treaty of 20th November last, the place of his birth had been detached from France. But the marshal stopped that defense in a noble manner—"I am a Frenchman," exclaimed he, "and will die as such. Hitherto my defense has appeared free; it is no longer so. I thank my generous defenders, but I would rather not be defended than have the shadow only of a defense. I am accused in opposition to the faith of treaties, and I am precluded from appealing to them. I imitate Moreau—I appeal from Europe to posterity."[1]

1 Moniteur, Dec. 7, 1815; Cap. iii. 384, 386.

When the appeal to the capitulations was refused, the counsel for Ney had no longer any defense. He was accordingly found guilty—1st, By a majority of 107 to 47, of having, in the night of the 13th and 14th March, received the emissaries of the usurper; 2d, Unanimously, of having, on the 14th March, read a proclamation in the chief square of Lons-le-Saulnier, tending to excite his troops to rebellion, and immediately given orders to them to unite their forces with those of the usurper, and of having himself effected that junction; 3d, By a majority of 157 to 1, of having committed high treason. It remained to determine on the punishment to be inflicted, the determination of which the French law, in the case of that high tribunal, gives to the judges—viz., whether it would be that prescribed by the penal code or the military law 142 voted for death, according to the martial law, 13 for transportation, 5 declined voting. The sentence was pronounced in absence of the accused, the privilege of doing so having been given to the Peers by the royal ordinance directing the trial. In the majority who voted for death were found the names of Marmont, Serrurier, the Duke of Valmy, Latour, Maubourg, and many others of Ney's old companions in arms.[2]

27. He is found guilty, and sentenced to death.

2 Moniteur, Dec. 7, 1815 Cap. iii. 389, 401; Lac. ii. 11, 12.

The marshal himself supped calmly that night, and, after smoking a cigar, slept for some hours. He was wakened by M. Cauchy, who

---

* "C'est une chose absolument finie," dit le Maréchal. Je ne l'avais pas compris. Le Général Lecourbe entra; "je lui disais que tout est fini," dit-il au Général Lecourbe; celui-ci parut étonné. "Oui," ajouta le Maréchal, "c'est une affaire arrangée, il y a trois mois que nous sommes tous d'accord; si vous aviez été à Paris vous l'auriez su comme moi. Les troupes sont divisées par deux bataillons et trois escadrons, les troupes d'Alsace de même, les troupes de la Lorraine de même; le Roi doit avoir quitté Paris, ou il sera enlevé, mais on ne lui fera pas de mal; malheur à qui ferait du mal au Roi; on n'avait l'intention que de le détrôner, de l'embarquer sur un vaisseau et de faire conduire en Angleterre. Nous n'avons plus maintenant qu'à rejoindre l'Empereur." Je dis au Maréchal qu'il était très extraordinaire qu'il proposât d'aller rejoindre celui contre lequel il devait combattre. Il me répondit qu'il m'engageait à le faire, "mais vous êtes libre." Le Général Lecourbe lui répondit—"Je suis ici pour servir le Roi, et non pour servir Bonaparte. Jamais il ne m'a fait que du mal, et le Roi ne m'a fait que du bien. Je veux servir le Roi, j'ai de l'honneur." "Et moi aussi," répondit le Maréchal, "pareeque je ne veux pas être humilié. Je ne veux pas que ma femme retourne chez moi les larmes aux yeux des humiliations qu'elle a reçues dans la journée. Le Roi ne veut pas de nous, c'est évident; ce n'est qu'avec Bonaparte que nous pouvons avoir de la consideration; ce n'est qu'avec un homme de l'armée que pourra en obtenir l'armée." Une demi-heure après, il prit un papier sur la table—"Voila ce que je veux lire aux troupes." Et il lut la Proclamation. . . . Le Maréchal était si bien déterminé d'avance à prendre son parti qu'une demi-heure après il portait la décoration de la Légion d'Honneur avec l'Aigle, et à son grand cordon la décoration à l'Effigie de Bonaparte.—*Déposition du Général Bourmont—Moniteur, 6 Dec. 1815.*

† "Seront respectées les personnes et les propriétés particulières; les habitans, et, en général, tous les individus qui se trouvent dans la capitale, continueront à jouir de leurs droits et libertés, sans pouvoir être ni enquiétés ni recherchés, même relativement aux fonctions qu'ils occupent ou auraient occupées, à leur conduite et à leur opinion politique. S'il survient quelques difficultés sur l'exécution de quelques-uns des articles de cette convention, l'interprétation en sera faite en faveur de l'armée Française, et de la ville de Paris."—Arts 12 et 15. Capitulation de Paris—*Moniteur*, July 9, 1815; Cap. iii. 3, 6, 367

came to announce to him the decision of the House of Peers. "Marshal," said he, "I have a melancholy duty to perform." "Do your duty, M. Cauchy, we all have ours in this world." Then, as the preamble began, he said —"To the point, to the point." When the numerous titles of the accused—Prince of the Moskwa, Duke of Elchingen—began, he interrupted him again: "Say simply Michel Ney, soon a little dust; that is all." Never did execution succeed a sentence more rapidly. The king's ministers were in a state of extreme anxiety; the state of the metropolis was reported to them every quarter of an hour. In the evening a conference of the royal family was held, at which it was resolved by all that a great example was necessary; the Duchess d'Angoulême was particularly vehement in inculcating this opinion. At midnight the ministers had a meeting, at which it was determined, after anxious deliberation, to petition the king in favor of a commutation of the sentence to one of banishment to America. The Duke of Richelieu was, with some difficulty, brought to acquiesce in this resolution; but, having done so, he exerted himself to the utmost to carry it into effect, and besought the king to exercise his clemency by acceding to the wishes of the cabinet; but he found the monarch immovable. He had not courage enough to be magnanimous; the heroic only have such. It is those who could themselves confront death that can forgive it to others. It was doubtless a matter of extreme difficulty for the king to resist the unanimous voice of the European powers, who concurred in demanding the punishment of a great delinquent, and the impassioned feelings of the great majority of both the Chambers, who concurred in that requisition. But there is a voice in the human heart superior to that of public opinion, and that voice is the voice of God. Condemned by the great majority of men at the moment, the forgiveness of Ney, by one whom he had so deeply injured, would have been the noblest inauguration of the monarchy for all future times.[1]

58. His death determined on by the king.

[1] *Cap. iii. 401, 403.*

At three in the morning of the 8th, the palace of the Luxembourg, where Ney was confined, was taken possession of by M. de la Rochecouart with two hundred soldiers, chiefly gendarmes and veterans. At nine in the morning, the marshal, having drank a little claret, entered a carriage, accompanied by the Curé of St. Sulpice: two gendarmes occupied the front seat of the carriage. The vehicle drew up in the gardens to the left of the entrance, about fifty yards from the gate. Ney got out with a rapid step, and placing himself eight paces from the wall, said, addressing the officer in command, 'Is it here, sir?' "Yes, M. le Maréchal," was the reply. He refused to have his eyes bandaged. "For five-and-twenty years," said he, "I have been accustomed to face the balls of the enemy." Then taking off his hat with his left hand, and placing his right upon his heart, he said in a loud voice, fronting the soldiers. "My comrades, fire on me."[2] The officer in command gave the signal, and he fell

89. His execution. Dec. 8.

[2] *Moniteur, Dec. 9, 1815; Cap. iii. 403, 405; Lac. ii. 13, 11.*

without any struggle: death was instantaneous, three balls had penetrated the head, and four the breast. The place of execution may still be seen in the gardens of the Luxembourg, and no spot in Europe will ever excite more melancholy feelings in the breast of the spectator.

The death of Ney was one of the greatest faults that the Bourbons ever committed. His guilt was self-evident; never did criminal more richly deserve the penalties of treason. Like Marlborough, he had not only betrayed his sovereign, but he had done so when in high command, and when, like him, he had recently before been prodigal of protestations of fidelity to the cause he undertook. His treachery had brought on his country unheard-of calamities—defeat in battle, conquest by Europe, the dethronement and captivity of its sovereign, occupation of its capital and provinces by 1,100,000 armed men, contributions to an unparalleled amount from its suffering people. Double treachery had marked his career; he had first abandoned in adversity his fellow-soldier, benefactor, and emperor, to take service with his enemy, and, having done so, he next betrayed his trust to that enemy, and converted the power given him into the means of destroying his sovereign. If ever a man deserved death, according to the laws of all civilized countries—if ever there was one to whom continued life would have been an opprobrium—it was Ney. But all that will not justify the breach of a capitulation. He was in Paris at the time it was concluded—he remained in it on its faith—he fell directly under its word as well as its spirit. To say that it was a military convention, which could not tie up the hands of the King of France, who was no party to it, is a sophism alike contrary to the principles of law and the feelings of honor. If Louis XVIII. was not a party to it, he became such by entering Paris, and resuming his throne, the very day after it was concluded, without firing a shot. True, the magnitude of the treachery called for a great example; true, Europe in arms demanded his head as an expiation;—but what then? The very time when justice is shown in harmony with present magnanimity and ultimate expedience, is when a great crime has been committed, a great criminal is at stake, and a great sacrifice must be made to secure that harmony. Banished from France, with his double treason affixed to his name, Ney would for ever have been an object of scorn and detestation to every honorable mind. Slain, in defiance of the capitulation, in the gardens of the Luxembourg, and meeting death in a heroic spirit, he became an object of eternal pathetic interest; and the decoration of the Legion of Honor, which his sentence directed to be torn from his neck, was for ever replaced around it by the volley of the platoon which consigned him to the grave.

90. Reflections on this event.

During the trial, and when his counsel had appealed to the capitulation of Paris as protecting him, great efforts were made with foreign powers to save his life. Notes were addressed to all the foreign embassadors then at Paris, and the intervention of the military chiefs who concluded that convention was in an especial manner invoked. Madame

91. And on the Duke of Wellington's share in the transaction.

Ney applied for and obtained an interview with the Duke of Wellington on the subject, and in the most passionate manner invoked the protection of the 12th article. "Madam," answered the Duke, "that capitulation was only intended to protect the inhabitants of Paris against the vengeance of the allied armies; and it is not obligatory except on the powers which have ratified it, which Louis XVIII. has not done." "My Lord," replied Madame Ney, "was not the taking possession of Paris, in virtue of the capitulation, equivalent to a ratification?" "That," rejoined the Duke, "regards the king of France; apply to him." Wellington expressed himself in the same terms to Marshal Ney, in answer to a letter addressed to him by the marshal on the subject.* The whole case rests on both sides on this brief dialogue: all the wit of man to the end of time can add nothing to their force. Strictly speaking, the Duke of Wellington was undoubtedly right: the capitulation bound him, and had been observed by him; if the King of France violated it, that was the affair of that monarch and his ministers; and there was a peculiar delicacy in a victorious foreign general, in military possession of the capital, interfering with the administration of justice by the French government. In private, it is said, Wellington exerted himself much, though unhappily without effect, to save the life of his old antagonist in arms; but, in the face of the united opinion of the whole powers of Europe, he did not conceive himself at liberty to make any public demonstration in his favor. His situation was doubtless a delicate one, surrounded with difficulties on every side; but there is an instinct in the human heart paramount to reason, there is a wisdom in generosity which is often superior to that of expediency. Time will show whether it would not have been wiser to have listened to its voice than to that of unrelenting justice on this occasion; and whether the throne of the Bourbons would not have been better inaugurated by a deed of generosity which would have spoken to the heart of man through every succeeding age, than by the sacrifice of the greatest, though also the most guilty, hero of the empire.

Another trial took place at the same period before the ordinary courts of justice in Paris, which, although not terminating in the same mournful catastrophe, was attended with circumstances of perhaps greater romantic interest. M. Lavalette was in civil administration what Marshal Ney had been in military—the great criminal of the Hundred Days. Accompanied by General Sebastiani, he had taken forcible possession, in the name of the Emperor, of the important situation of Director-General of the Post-office, which he had formerly held under the Emperor, and had used the power thus acquired to the worst purposes. On the 20th March, before the entry of the Emperor into Paris, he had addressed a treasonable circular to the inferior postmasters, which had a powerful effect in tranquilizing the provinces, and facilitating Napoleon's peaceable resumption of the throne.* In addition to this, he had written to Napoleon at Fontainebleau, urging his immediate advance to Paris, and refused post-horses to several of the persons in the suite of Louis XVIII., in particular Count Ferrand, the former postmaster, on the departure of that monarch for Lille. His guilt, therefore, was self-evident; indeed, it has been confessed by himself;† but, like so many others of the persons implicated in the treason of the Hundred Days, he made no attempt at escape. He remained, on the contrary, at his own hotel, or the country house of his mother-in-law, near Paris, after the return of the king, and even after the fate of Labedoyère might have taught him the expedience of consulting his safety by flight, the more especially as he was not in Paris at the time of the capitulation, and could not appeal to its protection. He had even the extreme imprudence to disregard a significant hint sent him by Fouché, and remained at his mother-in-law's without concealment. The consequence was, he was arrested and brought to trial; and, as his treason was clearly proved, he was found guilty and sentenced to death.¹

The counsel of Lavalette, to gain time, advised him to apply to have the sentence reviewed by the Court of Cassation, and meanwhile applied, through the Duke de Richelieu, to the king for mercy. Louis answered: "M. de Lavalette appears to me to be guilty; the Chamber of Deputies demands examples, and I believe them to be necessary. I have every wish to extend mercy to M. de Lavalette; but recollect that, the day following, you will be assailed by the Chamber of Deputies, and we

---

* "I have had the honor of receiving the note which you addressed to me on the 13th November, relating to the operation of the capitulation of Paris on your case. The capitulation of Paris, on the 3d July, was made between the commander-in-chief of the allied British and Prussian armies, on the one part, and the Prince of Eckmuhl, commander-in-chief of the French armies, on the other, and related exclusively to the military occupation of Paris. The object of the 12th article was to prevent the adoption of any measures of severity, under the military authority of those who made it, toward any persons in Paris, on account of offices which they had filled, or their conduct, or their political opinions. But it never was intended, and could not be intended, to prevent either the existing French Government, or any French Government which might succeed it, from acting in this respect as it might deem fit."—WELLINGTON to Marshal NEY, 19th *. 1815; GURWOOD, xii. 694.

¹ Cap. iii. 321, 325; Moniteur, Nov. 21, 1815; Lavalette's Mém. ii. 150, 156.

93. The king's pardon is applied for in vain.

* "L'Empereur sera à Paris dans deux heures et peut-être avant. La capitale est dans le plus grand enthousiasme; et quoi qu'on puisse faire, la guerre civile n'aura lieu nulle part. Vive l'Empereur!—*Le Conseiller d'Etat, Directeur-Général des Postes,* Comte LAVALETTE."—*Moniteur,* 21st Nov. 1815.

† "En sortant de la Rue d'Artois pour entrer sur le boulevard, je rencontrai le Général Sebastiani en cabriolet. Il me donna la nouvelle du départ du Roi, mais il n'en avait aucune sur l'Empereur. 'J'ai bien d'envie,' lui dis-je, 'd'en aller chercher à la poste;' et je me plaçai à côté de lui. En entrant dans la salle d'audience qui précède le Cabinet du Directeur-Général, je trouvai un jeune homme établi devant un bureau, à qui je demandai si le Comte Ferrand était encore à l'hôtel. Sur la réponse affirmative je lui donnai mon nom, en le priant de demander pour moi quelques instans d'entretien à M. le Comte Ferrand. M. Ferrand se présenta, mais sans s'arrêter et sans m'écouter il ouvrit son cabinet. Je ne l'y suivis pas; et j'allai dans *une autre pièce où je trouvai tous les chefs de division réunis de me revoir,* et disposés à tout faire pour m'obliger. M. Ferrand, après avoir pris ses papiers, se retira, et laissa son cabinet à ma disposition. J'avais un vif désir de courir à Fontainebleau, pour embrasser l'Empereur; mais je voulais voir ma femme avant de partir, et pour concilier ces deux mouvemens de cœur, je pris la résolution d'écrire à Fontainebleau. On me donna un courrier, qui partit à l'instant. J'annonçai à l'Empereur la nouvelle du départ du Roi, et je lui demandai *des ordres pour la Poste,* puisque M. Ferrand avait abandonné l'administration."—*Mémoire de Lavalette,* ii. 152, 153

shall be in a fresh embarrassment." By the advice of the king, the intervention of the Duchess d'Angoulême was applied for, as it might support him in the course which his inclination prompted, and the princess shed tears at the recital, and recommended that Madame Lavalette should throw herself at the king's feet. She did so, having with great difficulty obtained entrance to the chateau by the assistance of Marshal Marmont; but though the monarch addressed her with kindness he promised nothing, and it was understood the law would be allowed to take its course. It was fortunate he did so, for it gave occasion to one of the most touching instances of female heroism and devotion that the history of the world has exhibited.[1]

¹ Laval. Mém 272, 275; Cap. iii. 331, 332.

The day of his execution was fixed, and the unhappy prisoner, despairing of life, had already begun to familiarize his mind with the frightful circumstances of a public execution. In this extremity every thing depended on the courage and energy of Madame Lavalette; and to her he owed his salvation. The evening before, being the 21st December, she came to have a last interview with him, accompanied by her daughter, a child of fourteen years; and, as soon as they were alone, proposed that he should escape in her dress. With much difficulty she persuaded him to accede to the proposal, and after their last repast, the change of apparel was effected with surprising celerity and address. The hope of success, the consciousness of heroism, had restored all her presence of mind to Madame Lavalette, and she was not only cheerful but animated on the occasion. "Do not forget," said she, "to stoop at passing through the doors, and walk slowly in the passage, like a person exhausted by suffering." He did so: the jailers did not, through the vail which he wore, perceive the change; the porters of the sedan chair in which Madame Lavalette arrived had been gained by twenty-five louis; and after passing four gates, and about twelve turnkeys in different places, he got clear off. When the jailer some time after entered the apartment, he found Lavalette escaped, and the heroine of conjugal duty seated in his place.[2]

94. He escapes by the aid of his wife, and in her dress.

² Laval. Mém. ii. 288, 291; Lac. ii. 22, 24.

But though the prison gates had been passed, much remained to be done, for the escape was soon discovered: the police were on the alert; the most active search was made in every direction; and the Government, held into to escape. to rigorous measures by the clamor raised in the Chamber of Deputies, where they were openly accused of having favored the escape, were compelled to direct every effort to be made to apprehend the fugitive. But fortune seemed never weary of accumulating romantic incidents around this memorable trial; and the escape of Lavalette from Paris, and into Germany, was effected by an intervention of all others the most unlooked for in such a case. Sir Robert Wilson, the determined antagonist of Napoleon, who had so vehemently denounced the massacre of the prisoners and the poisoning of the sick at Jaffa, who had commanded with distinction a guerilla party on the frontiers of Portugal, and who was the first man who entered the great

95. Sir Robert Wilson, Mr. Hutchinson, and Mr. Bruce, enable him to escape.

redoubt in the assault of Dresden, was then in Paris, and to him, with the aid of two courageous friends, Mr. Hutchinson and Mr. Bruce, Lavalette owed his escape. Endowed by nature with a heroic spirit and an ardent temperament, Sir Robert Wilson had, at the same time, the generosity of disposition which is so often the accompaniment of that character, and should make every equitable mind overlook many of the frailties to which it is in a peculiar manner subject. Allied to the Opposition in the English Parliament, with whom the French Emperor had always been an object of interest, his enmity to Napoleon was turned, since his fall, into ardent admiration; and his chivalrous disposition led him to lend himself to every project formed for the escape of the persons implicated in his restoration. He was privy to a design for the escape of his old antagonist Ney, which had been only prevented from taking effect by the tripling of the guards of his prison the evening before his execution;[1] and having failed in that, his next object was to aid in the escape of Lavalette.[1]

¹ Lac. ii. 26, 28; Laval. Mém. ii. 293, 296.

Lavalette, on escaping from the prison, took refuge, by the guidance of a friend, M. Baudin, who met him by appointment, in the apartments of M. Bressore, part of the hotel of the Minister of Foreign Affairs, then occupied by the Duke de Richelieu: a circumstance which warrants a suspicion that that generous nobleman was no stranger in secret to his escape. Meanwhile the court were in consternation, deeming the event the result of a deep-laid conspiracy which was on the point of breaking out; and, to their disgrace be it said, Madame Lavalette, who remained in prison in her husband's room, was in consequence subjected for six-and-twenty days to solitary confinement, so rigorous that, with the entire ignorance of her husband's fate in which she was kept, her mind became affected, and she did not entirely recover her sanity for twelve years. Lavalette remained three weeks in his place of concealment in the Hôtel des Affaires Etrangères, and at the close of that period, finding the search for him by the police every day becoming more rigorous, he succeeded in making his escape from Paris, and reaching Germany in safety, by the aid of Sir Robert Wilson, Mr. Hutchinson, of the family of Lord Hutchinson, and Mr. Bruce of Kennet, in Clackmannanshire, who, from motives of humanity, generously aided him in the attempt, and accompanied him beyond the reach of danger. They were discovered, however, and brought to trial for abetting his escape, and sentenced to three months' imprisonment, the lightest punishment prescribed by the French law for offenses of that description: a lenient sentence, if their undoubted infraction of the laws of that country is considered; but a severe one, if the motives of men, whose conduct had excited the admiration and interest of all Europe, is alone regarded.[2] *

96. Mode in which they effect his escape, and their trial

² Mém. de Lavalette, ii. 291, 327; Lac. ii. 26, 28, Ann Regist. 1816, 335; Moniteur, April 26, 1816.

* The indictment against Sir Robert Wilson, Mr. Hutchinson, and Mr. Bruce, charged them with having been accessory to a general conspiracy for overturning all established governments in Europe; but nothing was brought home to them, except some democratic papers

The fate of another paladin of the French Empire belongs to this period of history, though his fate was determined on the Italian shores. After the calamitous result of his vash attempt to raise Italy against the Austrians, recounted in a former work,* this illustrious chief had sought refuge in France, where he remained obscure and unemployed during the Hundred Days. Napoleon's confidence in his judgment was irrevocably shaken; his white plume was not seen surmounting the armor of the cuirassiers on the field of Waterloo. When that decisive battle had overturned the Imperial dynasty in France, he remained in Provence in concealment, and repeatedly escaped, almost miraculously, from the pursuit of the police. At length, after undergoing three months of anxiety and suffering, worn out with suspense, and determined to brave all hazards in preference to continuing it, he issued from his place of concealment, and with great difficulty succeeded in making his way down to the sea-coast, accompanied by the Duke of Rocca Romana and a few other faithful attendants; but there he was accidentally separated from his attendants, and wandered about for four days and nights on the sea-coast alone, anxiously looking for a bark, and supported solely by the ears of maize which he rubbed in his hands. At length,

₉₇ Adventures of Murat after the battle of Waterloo.

driven by hunger, he knocked at the door of an humble cottage, and was admitted and offered refreshment by an aged domestic. Soon after the master of the house came in, and, seeing a stranger of a noble air seated at table, he saluted him courteously, and took a place opposite to him at the repast. A sudden ray of the sun having illuminated the countenance of the King, who sat before in shade, the peasant knew him. He had the generosity, however, not only to conceal his surprise, lest he should betray his illustrious guest, but to offer to put his life and property at his disposal. In spite of all the precautions that could be taken, the rumor spread abroad that the King of Naples was concealed on the coast, and, on the night of the 13th August, the cottage in which he slept was surrounded by sixty armed volunteers from Toulon. The old servant, however, detained them so long in opening the door, that Murat, who always was dressed, and with his arms beside him, had time to escape by a back window, and conceal himself under a pile of vine fagots in the vineyard behind the house. As he lay there hidden, several of the party, with lanterns in their hands, passed within a few feet, and almost trode upon the concealed monarch.¹

¹ Lam. v. 210, 259; Lac. ii. 32, 33; Biog. Univ. xxx. 430.

Though this danger was escaped, yet as was known he was somewhere concealed in the vicinity, and a reward of 1000 louis was offered for his apprehension, it was justly deemed too great a hazard for him to remain longer in his present state of concealment. He embarked accordingly in an open boat attended by four persons; but was overtaken by a violent tempest, which carried away the sail and rudder, and caused a leak to be sprung in the frail bark. They were on the point of sinking, when the packet-boat from Toulon to Corsica came past, by which they were taken up, and where he found by accident a number of the partisans of Napoleon, who like him were flying from the dangers of the violent reaction in the south. On arriving in Corsica, he repaired to the house of Colonna Cecaldo, in the Place of Vescovato, the most considerable personage in that district, and, announcing his name, solicited hospitality. He was kindly received, and soon after was joined by a few of his partisans from Naples. The governor of Bastia, the chief place of the island, hearing of his descent at Vescovato, issued a proclamation declaring him a public enemy, and sent a detachment of four hundred men to arrest him; but Murat, having got intelligence of their approach, fled to the mountains, where the fame of his name speedily drew a thousand armed peasants to his standard, who presented amidst their defiles and precipices so formidable a front to the soldiers, that they did not venture to hazard an attack, and returned without having effected any thing. After this success, the enthusiasm in his favor in Corsica was such that the people solicited him to accept the crown of the island; and he was offered an asylum in Austria, with the title of count, though on condition that he renounced his claims to the throne of the two Sicilies. He was offered also by Lord Exmouth, to whom he dispatched a messenger, a secure passage to England on board his ship; but the admiral was not empowered to pledge himself

_{98.} He embarks and lands in Corsica.

---

found in Sir R. Wilson's repositories, and the actual aiding in Lavalette's escape, which they all admitted, and which was clearly proved. Sir R. Wilson said in his defense, and the words, coming from such a man, drew tears from the audience—" The appeal made to our humanity, to our personal character, and to our national generosity—the responsibility thrown upon us of instantly deciding on the life or death of an unfortunate man, and of an unfortunate stranger—this appeal was imperative, and did not permit us to calculate his other claims to our good-will. At its voice we should have done as much for an obscure unknown individual, or even for an enemy who had fallen into misfortune. Perhaps we were imprudent, but we would rather incur that reproach than the one we should have merited, by basely abandoning him who, full of confidence, threw himself into our arms. Those very men who have calumniated us, not knowing our motives, would have been the first to reproach us as heartless cowards, if, by our refusal to save M. Lavalette, we had abandoned him to certain death. We resign ourselves with confidence to the decision of the jury; and if you should condemn us for having contravened your positive laws, we shall not have at least to reproach ourselves for having violated the eternal laws of morality and humanity." Mr. Bruce said in a firm and manly tone— " Political considerations had no influence with me in the affair of M. Lavalette: I am moved solely by feelings of humanity; and you will see from my declaration that I scarcely knew him. I never was in his house, nor he in mine. I have never had the honor of seeing his wife, nor had I any previous communication with him, direct or indirect, since his arrest. It has been proved that in no respect was either I or either of my friends implicated in his designs. I respected the fetters and gates of a court of justice. I have not, like Don Quixote, gone in quest of adventures. An unhappy man, condemned by the laws, solicited my protection; he proved that he had confidence in my character—he put his life in my hands—he appealed to my humanity—what would have been said of me if I had gone to denounce him to the police? Should I not have deserved the death with which I have since been threatened? Nay, what would have been thought of me, if I had refused to protect him? Would I not have been regarded as a coward, without principles, without honor, without courage, without generosity, and deserved the contempt of every honorable mind?" These were noble words, which make us proud of our country; and they came with peculiar grace from Sir R. Wilson, the determined antagonist in so many bloody fields of Napoleon, and Mr. Bruce, who had stood at the head of his company in the front rank of the Foot Guards, which repulsed the last attack of the Old Guard on the field of Waterloo.—See *Ann. Reg.* 1816, 385—*App. to Chron.*; LAVALETTE, ii. 29; and *Moniteur*, April 16, 1816.

* *History of Europe*, chap. xciii. § 23, 24.

for any thing in regard to his ulterior destination. Fearing, however, that he would incur the fate of Napoleon, and still dreaming of his beloved Naples, he resolved to hazard all by attempting to regain its throne. In vain his most trusty followers represented to him the dangers of such an enterprise when Europe was in arms, and the Austrian troops in great strength occupied the Italian peninsula.[1] He was deaf to every thing that could be alleged, and so set upon carrying it into execution, that when his aid-de-camp, Colonel Macerone, arrived from Paris with a safe-conduct from the allied powers, and offer of an asylum in Austria, he declined the offers, and resolved in preference to brave all the hazard of the attempt.

[1] Colletta, Six Dernier Mois de Murat, 89, 92; Lam. v. 267,272; Biog. Univ. xxx. 431, 432.

He set out from Vescovato on the 17th September with 250 men, and entered Ajaccio, the chief town of the island, in triumph, amidst the acclamations of the inhabitants. It was a moment of illusion between the throne and the tomb, which recalled for a brief period the remembrance of his happier days. The conversation at dinner turned on the battle of Waterloo. "Ah!" exclaimed Murat, "if I had been there, I am convinced the destinies of the world would have been changed. The French cavalry was madly engaged; it was sacrificed to no purpose in detail, when its charge en masse at the close of the day would have carried every thing before it." His conversation was easy and varied, as if his mind was relieved from all anxiety. In the evening he wrote a letter to Colonel Macerone, intended for the allied sovereigns, in which he declared his resolution to decline their offers, and hazard all on the expedition he had undertaken.* Having delivered this letter to Macerone and retired to rest, a cannon discharged at one in the morning roused the party from their slumbers, and they embarked on board six small feluccas before sunrise on the 28th September, and after a tedious voyage arrived in sight of the mountains of Calabria near Paolo, on the evening of the 6th October.[2]

99. His arrival at Ajaccio, and descent on Naples.

[2] Lam. v. 274, 283; Colletta, 92, 96; Biog. Univ. xxx. 431.

The flotilla cast anchor, and Murat dispatched Colonel Ottaviani ashore to sound the inhabitants, and bring intelligence whether any thing had been prepared to oppose his debarkation.

Ottaviani and the sailor who accompanied him were arrested the moment they landed, and did not return. This was considered as a bad omen, and discouragement was already visible in the expedition. During the night the other vessels disappeared; and even Captain Conrand, who had been seven years a captain in his guard, slipped his cable during the night and made sail for Corsica. Disconcerted with these defections, Murat proposed to his captain, a man of the name of Barbara, to make sail for Trieste, for which place he had passports and the Austrian safe-conduct; but he declined, alleging he had no flour or provisions for so long a voyage, offering at the same time to go ashore and procure a larger vessel provided he got the passports. The king, fearing treachery, refused to part with them, upon which an angry altercation got up between them, which ended in his exclaiming to his officers—"You see he refuses to obey me; well, I will land myself! My memory is fresh in the hearts of the Neapolitans; they will join me." He then ordered his officers to put on their uniforms; and as the wind was fair, and the day fine, he steered into the bay of Pizzo, and cast anchor on a desert strand at a little distance from that town. His generals and officers, five-and-twenty in number, wished to precede him in going ashore; but the king would not permit it. "It is for me," he exclaimed, "to descend first on this field of glory or death; the precedence belongs to me as the responsibility;"—and with these words he leapt boldly ashore.[3]

100. The king lands.

[3] Colletta,117, 120; Lam. v. 286,289; Biog. Univ. xxx. 430, 431.

Already the shore was covered with groups of peasants, whom the unwonted sight of the barks in the bay, and the uniforms of the officers landing, had attracted to the spot. Among them was a detachment of fifteen gunners who came from a solitary guard-house on the shore. They still bore Murat's uniform. "My children," said he, advancing toward them, "do you know your king?" And with these words he took off his hat; his auburn locks fell on his shoulders, and the noble martial figure which was engraven on their hearts appeared before them. "Yes, it is I," he continued; "I am your King Joachim; say if you will follow and serve the friend of the soldiers, the friend of the Neapolitans." At these words the officers in Murat's suite raised their hats, and shouted "Vive le Roi Joachim!" and the soldiers mechanically grounded their arms; but a few only exclaimed "Vive Joachim!" Meanwhile the inhabitants of Pizzo, under the direction of the agent of the Duke del Infantado, who had great estates in the neighborhood, and who was ardently attached to the Bourbon family, assembled, and, while Murat was vainly awaiting a movement in his favor, declared against him. While still uncertain what to do, two peasants arrived, and, informing Murat of what was going on in the town, offered to guide him to Monteleone, where the garrison might be expected to be more favorable, and the possession of a fortified place would open to him the gates of his kingdom. This offer Murat accepted, and the party, consisting in all of forty persons, were soon seen in their brilliant uniforms wending their way over the olive-clad summits by which the road passed. They were soon met by a colonel of the royal gendarmerie, named Trenta Capelli, a noted chief of the Calabrian insurrection, and the fate of whose three brothers slain on the scaffold by the French, had inspired him with inextinguishable hatred toward them.

101. Where he fails.

---

* "I can not accept the conditions which Colonel Macerone has offered to me. They imply an abdication on my part; I am only permitted to live. In this the respect due to a sovereign in misfortune, known to all Europe, and who in a critical moment decided the campaign of 1815 in favor of the very powers which now pursue him with their hatred and their ingratitude! I have never abdicated; I am entitled to recover my throne, if God gives the power and the means of doing so. My presence on the soil of Naples can disturb no one: I can not correspond with Napoleon, a captive at St. Helena. When you receive this letter, I shall be already at sea, advancing to my destiny. Either I shall succeed, or I shall terminate my life with my enterprise. I have faced death a thousand times combating for my country; may I not be permitted to face it once for myself? I have but one anxiety; it is on the fate of my family."—MURAT to Colonel MACERONE, 27th September, 1815; LAMARTINE, v. 281, 282.

Murat knew him, and called him by name to join his cause. "My king," said he, pointing to the flag which waved on the towers of Pizzo, "is he whose colors wave over the kingdom."¹

Murat was deceived, or pretended to be so, in regard to Trenta Capelli's intentions, and, advancing toward him, they entered into conversation. But as soon as the crowd of armed men which advanced from Pizzo with the cannoneers arrived, Capelli joined them, and summoned the king to surrender. Seeing the intentions of the crowd to be evidently adverse, Murat addressed them in a few words, alleging that he had no hostile designs, and was only endeavoring to seek an asylum in the Austrian states, for which he had passports which their King Ferdinand himself was bound to respect. The Neapolitans answered only by confused cries and violent gesticulations, followed by a discharge of firearms, by which one captain in his suite was killed and several wounded. A second volley decimated his ranks; and Murat, seeing his party dispersed, endeavored to make his escape across the fields to the sea-coast. He there called aloud to his captain, Barbara, to steer in and come to his relief; but the perfidious wretch, instead of doing so, stood out to sea, carrying with him the arms, gold, ammunition, and all the effects of the unhappy monarch. At the same time the soldiers in Trenta Capelli's band were seen rapidly approaching from the land side. In this extremity, the king threw himself into a fishing-boat, moored at a little distance from the coast; but the bark, stranded on the sand, resisted all his efforts to set it afloat. He was soon surrounded by a furious crowd, which broke into the vessel, and dragged him, disarmed and bleeding ashore, where the soldiers had the barbarity to strike the wounded hero on the face with the butt-ends of their carbines, and tore from his breast the ensigns of his glory, which he wore in that hour of his fate. Such was the fury of the multitude, that twice, in going from the coast to the prison of Pizzo, the hatchet was suspended over his head; and it was only by the efforts of Trenta Capelli, and the agent of the Duke del Infantado, that he was saved from instant death.²

The moment intelligence was received by the Neapolitan general, Nunziante, who commanded in Calabria, of the descent and capture of an armed party on the coast, he sent Captain Stratts with a party of soldiers to secure and protect the prisoners, yet ignorant of the name and quality of their august captive. "Who are you?" said Stratts to the third who was brought forward for examination. "Joachim Murat, King of Naples," replied the monarch, with an intrepid air. Stratts bowed to heroism in misfortune, and courteously ordered him to be conducted to an apartment furnished with every comfort, and apart from the other prisoners, where his wounds were tended, and he had leisure to reflect on his approaching fate. On the following day, Nunziante arrived, and dined with the king in an apartment of the chateau to which he had been removed. The captive was more cheerful than the general, for the latter was already seized with disquietude as to the orders which he might receive from Naples regarding the disposal of the prisoner. So little was Murat aware of his approaching fate, that he conversed at table about an arrangement by which he might cede Sicily to the King of Naples, and be himself recognized as king in the continental dominions of the house of Bourbon. He was not long of being undeceived. After much perplexity, the court of Naples adopted the resolution of sending the prisoner to a military commission, to try him under a law which he himself had introduced against the Bourbon aspirants to his throne. So determined were the government on destroying him, that the same orders which directed him to be brought before a military commission, enjoined that he should only be allowed half an hour to receive the consolations of religion.* He was brought to trial accordingly, and, when the room was preparing for the court-martial, wrote a letter to his queen, Caroline, which is one of the most touching examples of the genuine pathetic of which history has preserved a record.† When brought before the tribunal, he refused to recognize its authority, or even to allow his counsel to plead for him, and, as a matter of course, was condemned to be shot within half an hour.¹

The priest who was sent for to administer the last consolations of religion happened to be one to whom, in the days of his greatness, he had made a considerable gift when in the course of a tour through his provinces: he said to him that that was a good omen for the intercession of his prayers in his behalf. He declared that he died a good Christian. He then heard without emotion the sentence of the court-martial which condemned him to death, and thanked General Nunziante, the priest, and officers, for the kindness they had shown to him during his short captivity; and himself led the way into a sort of fosse, where the execution was to take place, exactly similar to the one in the castle of Vincennes in which the Duke d'Enghien, whose delivery to a military commission had been countersigned by Murat,² had suffered ten years before. Twelve soldiers, with loaded muskets, awaited his approach; the

* "Le Général Murat sera traduit devant une Commission Militaire dont les membres seront nommés par notre Ministre de la Guerre.
"Il ne sera accordé au condamné qu'une demi-heure pour recevoir les secours de la religion.—FERDINAND."
—LAMARTINE, Histoire de la Restauration, v. 313.

† "Ma chère Caroline! Ma dernière heure est arrivée. Dans quelques instants j'aurai cessé de vivre; dans quelques instants tu n'auras plus d'époux. Ne m'oublie jamais. Je meurs innocent. Ma vie ne fut tachée d'aucune injustice. Adieu, mon Achille! Adieu, ma Laetitia Adieu, mon Lucien! Adieu, ma Louise! Montrez-vous au monde dignes de moi. Je vous laisse sans royaume et sans biens au milieu de mes nombreux ennemis Soyez constamment unis! Montrez vous supérieurs a l'infortune, pensez à ce que vous êtes et à ce que vous avez été, et Dieu vous bénira! Ne maudissez point ma mémoire! Sachez que ma plus grande peine, dans les derniers moments de ma vie, est de mourir loin de mes enfants! Recevez la bénédiction paternelle : Recevez mes embrassements et mes larmes. Ayez toujours présent à votre mémoire votre malheureux père." With truth does Lamartine observe, "L'adieu de Murat arrachera des larmes à la postérité la plus reculée. Si on n'y sent pas la victime et le martyr, on y sent l'amant, le père, et le héros. Il se rendait à lui-même un vrai témoignage."—LAMARTINE, Histoire de la Restauration, v. 317, 318.

space in the bottom of the ditch was so confined that the muzzles almost touched his breast. Looking at them with a steady eye, and a smile on his lips, he said—"My friends, do not make me suffer by taking bad aim; the narrowness of the space obliges you almost to rest the muzzles of your pieces on my breast; do not tremble; spare the face; straight to the heart." With these words he put his right hand on his breast, to mark the position of his heart, and in his left held a little medallion, which contained portraits of his wife and his four children. He was still gazing on the loved images when the discharge took place, and he fell pierced by twelve balls, his left hand still holding the medallion till it was relaxed in death. His remains were respectfully interred in the cathedral of Pizzo, which his gifts had enriched while on the throne, and a general amnesty was humanely pronounced on his companions in misfortune.[1]

[Lam. v. 321, 325; Colletta, 167, 174; Biog. Univ. xxx. 431.]

Such was the end, at the premature age of forty-eight, of Joachim Murat, King of Naples, one of the most distinguished of the heroes of that age of glory. His life, his character, and his death, approach more nearly to the visions of the poet than the events of reality; he belonged to the days of romance rather than the Revolution. Born in a humble station on the mountains of the Pyrenees, he cut his way to a throne by his good sword; he won the sister of an emperor by his chivalry, and the admiration of the world by his renown. Amadis de Gaul or Palmerin of England could not have exceeded him in the vigor with which he led his cavalry into the midst of the enemy's squadrons; he rivaled Rinaldo in the heroism of single combat, Tancredi in the fervor of chivalrous attachment. Murat's abilities were those of a knight rather than a general: no one ever exceeded him in the gallantry with which he headed a charge of horse; but he had no capacity for general combination, and in separate command never achieved any thing worthy of his reputation. As a king he was mild and benevolent in his conduct, and affable and conciliating in his manners; but he was destitute of political firmness, and, like many other men individually brave, vacillating to a surprising degree when a decisive crisis arrived. His death affords a memorable instance of the moral retribution which, even in this world, often attends great deeds of iniquity, and by the instrumentality of the very acts which appeared to place them beyond its reach. He underwent, in 1815, the very fate to which he himself, seven years before, had consigned a hundred Spaniards at Madrid, who were guilty of no other crime but that of having bravely defended their country; and by the application of a law to his own case, which he himself had introduced to check the attempts of the Bourbons to regain a throne which he had usurped.[2]

[105. Reflections on this event.]

[Hist. of Europe, c. iii. § 67.]

Happily these examples sufficed to appease the wrath of the Royalists, and the reaction which invariably, in civilized society, succeeds to deeds of severity, enabled the Government to act upon their decided inclinations in favor of a return to humane measures.

[106. Death of Mouton-Duvernet and General Chartrand.]

General Mouton-Duvernet was one of the last victims of the Royalist reaction. He was deeply implicated in the events of the Hundred Days, having commanded at Lyons during that period; and after the return of the Bourbons, he was for some months in the house of a Royalist, who generously sheltered him in his misfortune. At length, fearful of endangering his benefactor, or tormented by the torture of anxiety and suspense, he quitted his asylum and gave himself up. He was tried by a court-martial, condemned, and executed, evincing in his last moments the courage which in misfortune so often expiates error. The like fate attended General Chartrand, who had also held an important command in the south at the landing of Napoleon, and by his defection had much aided his cause. He was condemned by a council of war at Lille, and executed. But with these mournful examples, the blood shed by the reaction ceased to flow in France. Several persons—in particular General de Bello, General Gilly, General Clausel, and General Decaen—owed their salvation to the intercession of the Duchess d'Angoulême, to whom they had shown respectful regards during the brief struggle with that heroic princess at Bordeaux.[1] Others were acquitted, among rops, c. xciii whom was Admiral Linois, who § 6, commanded Guadaloupe, and for whom the feeble defense was sustained that his defection to Napoleon was done to prevent that colony from falling into the hands of the English; General Drouet, whom Marshal Macdonald, not without difficulty, succeeded in saving, by recounting the energetic manner in which the accused had exerted himself to prevail on the army of the Loire to submit to the royal decree directing its dissolution; and General Cambronne, who commanded a division of the Imperial Guard at the battle of Waterloo. It was evident that the tide was turning, and that Government, even after so vast a treason, and in the excited state of the public mind, might safely return to a system of mercy—happy distinction of an age of real civilization and under the influence of religion, which is soon satiated with blood, and, even under the greatest provocations, gladly returns to the sentiments of humanity.[2]

[2 Lac. ii. 16, 22; Lam. v. 342, 352; Cap. iii. 431, 438.]

Encouraged by these symptoms, the French Government resolved to venture on the great act of a general amnesty; and the time selected for bringing it forward was the day after the execution of Marshal Ney, when all hearts in Paris yet thrilled with that mournful event. Accompanied by all his colleagues, the Duke de Richelieu entered the Chamber, and said, with a faltering voice: "A great example of just severity has just been given; but the tribunals are still charged with those who belong to the first class designated in the ordinance of 24th July; and if some have escaped, sentence of death pronounced against them as contumacious will serve as an example in the mean time. His Majesty, by the proclamation of Cambray, has already published an amnesty which he is desirous of now extending; the right of forgiveness, after revolts and great political commotions, is the most precious right inherent in sovereignty. It is an additional satisfaction, on such a solemn

[107. A general amnesty.]

occasion, to obtain the concurrence of the other branches of the legislature. The King is rejoiced that a considerable part of the power which the new laws have bestowed upon him is temporary only; he will make use of it with justice. He will pursue with severity those whom nothing can correct, nothing conciliate; but extend mercy to such as have been only misled. The army has been decimated at Waterloo; some of its chiefs have since met the death which they would rather have found on the field of battle. Obedient to the wishes of the King—to the wishes of France—the army has yielded to the force of misfortune: it has been disbanded. Evils enough oppress France, which can not be avoided, without aggravating them by our own divisions. The testament of Louis XVI. is constantly present to the mind of the King; and his sacred word in maintaining one of the most important articles of the charter will inspire confidence as to the remainder. He will give the first example of a mutual reciprocal confidence, and has charged us to present the following law of a general amnesty." The amnesty was then read, which applied to all persons who had taken part in the insurrection of the Hundred Days, with the exception of those mentioned in the first article of the ordinance of 24th July; those in the second article were only required to leave France within two months, under pain of transportation if they returned without the leave of the king. The family or relations of Napoleon, and their descendants, to the degree of uncle and nephew, were forever excluded from the kingdom, and could hold no office, right, or property in it; but they were permitted six months to sell their possessions. The Duke concluded with these words—" The amnesty proposed to you is not new in our annals: Henry IV., whose acts ¹ Moniteur, I am proud to retrace, gave a Dec. 10, 1815; similar one in 1594, and France Cap. iv. 36, 43. was saved."¹

108. Which is coldly received by the Chamber.

The proposed act was listened to with profound attention by the Chamber; but it was soon evident that a much larger degree of severity was required to satisfy their highly excited passions, and that it would be no easy matter for the Government to carry through the amnesty which they were so anxious to introduce. On the contrary, the majority of the Chamber openly aimed at carrying a much more extensive proscription than the Government itself had at first thought necessary; and M. de Labourdonnaye, who was their mouthpiece, had prepared a list of *twelve hundred persons*, who were to be included in the first category, instead of the thirty-eight to which the ordinance of 24th July extended! It was particularly urged, that to include the relapsed regicides, or regicides who were involved in the treason of 1815, in the amnesty, was insupportable—a wish which struck at once in M. Fouché, and many of the most obnoxious of the Revolutionists. "Attend not," said M. Labourdonnaye, "to the sophisms of a spurious philanthropy, so skillfully made use of by our enemies. When did they ever practice it when they had the power? To hesitate to punish is to betray weakness. Divine Providence has delivered into your hands the murderers of your king, the assassins of your families,

as if the supreme justice had reserved them in the midst of all our disasters, to prove the vanity of human prudence, and the perfidy of hearts without remorse. These men, now vanquished and disarmed, invoke a clemency which they never showed in the days of their power; as if crime was to be forever assured of impunity. And you, pusillanimous magistrates, unforeseeing legislators, are you prepared **to see proved plots and treasons, the disgrace of the nation and of humanity, and to hesitate at punishing their authors?** What possible excuse can be alleged for those who, holding their offices or their commands from the sovereign, have turned against him, and used the power they had received to support to the destruction of the royal authority?" These words, which were supported by the genius and eloquence of M. de Chateaubriand, were warmly applauded in the Chamber, and by the whole Royalist party, now in a majority among the electors. They expressed so entirely the sentiments of the great majority of the Chamber, that the committee to whom, according to the usual form, the proposed law was referred, reported in favor of a much more extensive proscription; and, in particular, inserted a clause for the perpetual banishment of the regicides.¹ ¹ Moniteur, Jan. 3, 1816; Cap. iv. 43, 45; Lam. vi. 83, 84.

109. Modifications with which it is passed into a law. Jan. 14, 1816.

Louis XVIII. and his ministers were seriously alarmed at this impassioned resistance of the great majority of the Assembly; and it was then that the idea appears to have first struck them, that it was impossible to carry on the Government on the principles they had adopted with such a Chamber, and that a *coup d'état*, altering the composition of the legislature, had become indispensable. They made accordingly the strongest resistance to the amendments threatened to be forced upon them by the Assembly. "From the days of Tiberius," said the Duke de Richelieu, "to those of Bonaparte, confiscations have been presented under the name of amnesties. Let us not deprive the august family of the Bourbons of the glory of having abolished them, and annihilated that inheritance of penalties. How can you still insist upon the last amendment relative to the regicides, to which it is known his Majesty is opposed? It is not on the earth, it is not among men, that we are to seek the causes of this resolution of a sovereign who would wish to forget every thing but the first pardon. Is it inspired by the testament of the martyr king? Is it dictated by an inherited magnanimity, the noblest appanage of a sovereign? Be it as it may, such is the wish of the king; and who would gainsay it? Let me conjure you not to make of a law of mercy a subject of discord, but rather a great and touching image of the concord and reconciliation of all Frenchmen." These words produced a great impression: all the Government could do, however, was to prevail on the Chamber to abandon the most severe of its other amendments, but that providing for the perpetual banishment of the regicides was forced upon them by the almost unanimous voice of the Chamber, and passed with the act of amnesty into a law.² ² Moniteur, Jan. 9, 1816. Cap. iv. 69, 72; Lam. v. 82, 85.

The formidable opposition experienced

the Chamber on this occasion, and which it required all the personal influence of the king and his ministers to overcome, convinced the Government that a new law for the elections had now become indispensable. All parties concurred in this opinion. The ordinance of 13th July, 1815, under which the existing Chamber had been elected on a footing entirely different from that provided by the charter, had emanated only from the royal authority, and had never received the sanction of the legislature. A law sanctioned by the whole legislature was therefore imperatively called for; and the Government had become convinced that they could not go on with a legislature representing the furious animosities of the moment so faithfully as the present one did. So vehement had the passion of the Chamber become, that the President, M. Lainé, was publicly insulted in his chair by an outrageous Royalist—a circumstance which he felt so deeply that he resigned his situation, and was only prevailed on to resume it at the personal solicitation of the king, and from the prospect which he was encouraged to entertain of being admitted into the ministry at no distant period. Meanwhile the action of the Prévôtal Courts—especially in the southern provinces, where the Royalists had their entire direction—had become so violent, that serious apprehensions were entertained of an outbreak of civil war in that quarter; but how it was to be averted was not so apparent, when the Royalists had the majority in the Chamber, and had proved themselves disposed to support any measures, however stringent, against the party from which they had suffered so much. Both parties thus felt that a change was necessary; and both perceived, that whichever got the command of the elections would be in a situation to carry into execution their system of government. The preparation of a law on the elections, therefore, was eagerly undertaken by each. M. Vaublanc was intrusted with it on the part of the government, M. de Villèle undertook it on the part of the Royalist opposition. The subject became the object of important debates in the Chamber, which throw much light both on the state and views of parties at the time, and the working of the new representative system in France.[1]

[marginal: 110. Proposals for a new law of elections.]

[marginal: 1 Cap. iv. 114, 117; Lam. vi. 91, 92.]

"The situation of elector," said M. de Vaublanc, "having become a species of fixed function, it has been found necessary in later times to balance, by an extraordinary measure, the influence of some men, of whose principles you were not secure. But that expedient, to which the king is entitled to have recourse, ceasing with the circumstances which produced it, it has become necessary to recur to a fixed and stable law. Experience has proved that the electoral power was subject to grave inconveniences when all its exercises were not regulated. Formerly there were three steps—the Primary Assemblies, the Colleges of Arrondissements, and the Electoral Colleges of Departments. We intend to abolish entirely the Primary Assemblies, which are liable to be troubled by tumult and discord. It has been proposed to establish a system which has only one step, which was quite simple—namely, that the Colleges of Arrondissements, composed of citizens who pay each 300 francs of direct taxes, shall name the deputies. That system is plausible, but, when examined in detail, it will be found liable to insuperable objections. In some arrondissements the number of citizens who pay 300 francs of direct taxes is not more than twenty or thirty. The department of the Mouths of the Rhone, of which Marseilles is the chief place, would have only three deputies; that of the Rhone, of which Lyons is the head, only two; while those of the High and Low Alps would have six. For these reasons we have rejected the system of one degree, and are of opinion that two degrees, wisely combined, would suffice. We have selected sixty of the principal colleges of arrondissements, uniting them with the presidents of the colleges of the first instance, the procureurs-généraux, the presidents of the tribunals of commerce, the justices of the peace, the vicars-general and their curates. We must all agree that it is desirable, when the primary assemblies meet, that their choice should fall on such men.[1]

[marginal: 1 Cap. iv. 115, 116.]

"The same principles are applicable to the formation of the electoral colleges of the departments. We think they should be formed of the first ministers of religion, with the addition of sixty of the principal proprietors, ten of the chief merchants, and also, provided they implement the conditions required by the charter, the presidents of councils of the departments. When you consider this law, let me conjure you to reflect on what the interest of the French monarchy demands. Never, perhaps, was Assembly called on to decide such great questions. You are placed between that ancient monarchy, which has shone so long and with so brilliant a lustre, and that new monarchy, which has been inaugurated amidst so many storms, under the auspices of virtue seated on the throne. Unite these, the past and the future ages. It is to you that I address myself—you who have only witnessed in your childhood the evils produced by the social overthrow. Prepare the happiness—prepare for yourself the honor of being able to say to your descendants, We have arrested in its march the terrible chariot of the Revolution."[1]

[marginal: 112. Continued.]

[marginal: 1 Cap. iv. 117, 118.]

The object and evident tendency of this bill was to throw the whole electoral influence into the hands of the Government; and, composed as the ministry now was, the Royalists were not prepared to concede to them any such power. The fundamental principle of their policy was, "that it is not possible to arrive at a combination of popular and aristocratic liberty but in descending to the lowest step of the social hierarchy, and awakening its intimacy with the aristocracy." Proceeding on this basis, the Royalists had calculated, with great local knowledge and discrimination, the probable influence which might be supposed to become prevailing in each department. Above a month had been passed in these inquiries, and in preparing a measure based upon their results, the object of which was to secure the influence of the Royalists in the elections—to exclude equally the extreme democrats and the ministerial influence. By this project there was to be established an electoral assembly in each canton, composed of

[marginal: 113. Projet of the Royalists.]

all domiciled citizens aged 25 years complete, and paying 50 *francs of direct taxes annually.* The electoral list, prepared by a commission, at the head of which was the under-prefect, was to be published ten days before the meeting of the communal assemblies. The presidents of colleges were to be nominated by the king. The electoral colleges in the departments were not to be under 150, nor above 300; and the lists of these electoral colleges were to be formed of all the citizens of 30 years of age, paying 300 francs of direct taxes; and if an adequate number could not be got, the deficiency was to be supplied by citizens paying 300 francs between 25 and 30, or by citizens of 30 years, but not paying 300 francs. The number of the deputies was to be 402, and the lists were to be prepared by a commission drawn from the general council of the department, of which the prefect was president, which fixed the number of electors in the department, the list of the persons eligible for the electoral colleges, and of electors to compose the electors of the department. The prefect was to be ineligible in his department; the deputies were to be elected for five years, or until the king, before the expiry of that term, exercised his right of dissolution.[1]

[1] Moniteur, March 27, 29, 1816; Cap. iv. 120, 123.

114. The project of the Royalists is carried in the Deputies, and rejected in the Peers April 3, 1816.

These opposite projects were the subject of prolonged discussions in the Chamber of Deputies during the whole of March. The parties chose as their battle-ground, as usual in such cases, the details and separate points of the two measures; but that was done chiefly to conceal the real motives which influenced each. These were, on the part of the ministerialists, the desire to augment as much as possible the influence of the Crown, by admitting the numerous *employés* of administration in numbers to the right of voting; on the part of the Royalist opposition, to vest the influence in the small proprietors and nobles in the provinces, whose interests would lead them permanently to support the monarchical side, even when, as at present, necessity or delusion might cause the Government to incline to the Liberals. The ministry combated this project with all their power, but they were defeated by a majority of 48, the numbers being 180 to 132. The whole Liberal party voted with the Government against the project of the Royalist majority—so strangely were parties dislocated in less than a year after the Restoration.[2] The Government, seeing their project defeated, and that of an inflamed majority substituted in its stead, had no alternative but to get it thrown out by the Peers, which was done accordingly, after keen debates, on April 3, by a majority of 32, the numbers being 89 to 57.

[2] Lac. ii. 54; Cap. iv. 55; 120, 146.

115. The Budget.

As the popular branch of the legislature was now committed to open war with the Crown, on so important a point as the representation of the people, ministers began to suspect that it was impossible for the Government to go on; either they must resign, or a *coup d'état* to alter the composition of the Chamber of Deputies be attempted. The former would at once have been the course adopted in England, where the usages of a representative government have come, from long usage, to be thoroughly understood; but the latter was deemed the most advisable in France, where the nation had been so accustomed to acts of violence since the commencement of the Revolution, that all parties had come to regard them as a natural and unavoidable step in the conduct of affairs. But several subjects for discussion remained, which it was absolutely necessary to bring to a close before the termination of the session. The most important of these was the BUDGET, and that was a subject beset with difficulties, because the enormous sums due under the treaty of 20th Nov. 1815, rendered heavy taxes or extensive loans indispensable; and the impoverished state of the nation appeared to render it equally hopeless to attempt to levy the first, or to have recourse to the last. After a long period, however, and great efforts, the difficulties were surmounted; and the fact of their being so is the strongest proof both of the almost inexhaustible resources of France when enjoying peace, and the improved credit which its government had obtained from the restoration of its legitimate line of monarchs.[1]

[1] Cap. iv. 190 192; Lac. ii. 59.

116. Ministerial plan on the subject.

The budget was based on the following propositions. The receipts of the nine last months of 1815 amounted to 533,715,940 francs (£21,350,000); and the expenditure to 637,132,662 francs (£25,500,000); and for the whole year the receipts were taken at 814,567,000 francs (£32,600,000); and the expenditure at 954,000,000 francs (£37,800,000). The extraordinary tax of 100,000,000 francs (£4,000,000), laid on to commute the contributions in kind to the allied troops, was an additional burden to be made good by certain additional per-centages, to be levied monthly during the first eight months of 1816. Woods to the extent of 400,000 hectares, or 600,000 acres, were permitted to be alienated to meet the exigences of the state. The receipts of 1816 were taken at 800,000,000 francs (£32,000,000), and the expenditure at the same sum. The receipts, however, both years, fell short of what had been calculated, and the budget, which became the subject of vehement discussion and debate, both in the Chamber and in the public journals, was considerably modified before it was finally passed, on April 24, 1816. The total receipts of 1815, as actually collected, were 798,590,000 francs (£31,980,000), and the expenditure the same; the income being swelled by a loan of 100,000,000 francs (£4,000,000), and 54,760,659 levied in anticipation on the taxes legally due in 1817. The receipts of 1816 were 895,577,205 francs (£35,800,000), and the expenditure the same; but in the former were included nearly 200,000,000 francs (£8,000,000), of extra charges, which weighed with excessive severity on a country already wasted by enemies' contributions, and a harvest uncommonly scanty and deficient. It is greatly to the honor of the French government that, when weighed down by such an unparalleled load of difficulties, it honorably fulfilled its engagements both to foreign states and its own subjects,[2] and not less so to the nation, that when oppressed by such burdens, and only beginning to breathe after

[2] Moniteur, Dec. 21, 1815, and April 25, 1816; Archives Diplomatiques, v. 288, 300; Cap iv. 199, 201.

a war of twenty years' duration, it not only furnished its rulers with the means of making them good, but established a sinking fund of 20,000,000 francs, or £800,000 a year.*

117. Proposition of the Chamber regarding the clergy.

The Government had the utmost difficulty in carrying through the budget, so strenuous was the Royalist opposition, and so numerous and harassing the amendments they proposed. They were obliged to abandon the project of selling the woods of the state, from the Royalist opposition. But a variety of other subjects were at the same time broached in the Chamber, which convinced Louis XVIII. that the legislature had become unmanageable, and that another session could not be ventured upon without its dissolution. The ideas of the majority were firmly fixed on two objects, alike hostile to the spirit of the Revolution and the present frame of government, and these were to augment the influence of the clergy, and to supplant the action of the central government by local influences in the provinces. There can be no doubt that these were the only means by which the course of events which the Revolution had prepared could have been arrested; whether it was possible to introduce them after the entire destruction of the landed proprietors which the confiscations of the Convention and the new law of succession had effected, and the concentration of all power in the hands of the executive at Paris, which had thence necessarily resulted, was a different question, upon which the heated Royalists never bestowed a thought. Experience has shown that the object they followed was a vain illusion, impossible in the existing state of society; but it was not thought so at the time, and it is surprising with what perseverance it was pursued.¹ _{Cap. iv. 257, 259; Lac. ii. 39, 40.}

118. Argument in favor of an endowment of the Church.

The miserable condition in which the clergy had been left by the Revolution attracted, as well it might, the early attention of the Chamber. Bereft of all its possessions by the very first tyrannical act of the National Assembly, the once richly-endowed Church of France had ever since pined in indigence and obscurity, its clergy not elevated in circumstances or consideration above the parochial school

---

* The receipts and expenditure of 1815 and 1816 stood thus:—

1815. RECEIPTS.

Direct taxes, viz.:—

	Francs.	Francs.
Land Tax,	172,132,000	
50 per cent. additional,	86,066,000	258,198,000
Personal Tax,	27,289,000	
50 per cent. additional,	13,644,500	40,933,500
Doors and Windows,	12,892,000	
Additional,	1,289,000	14,181,000
Patents,	15,416,000	
Additional,	771,000	16,187,000
		329,499,500
Deduct cost of collection, &c.,		9,499,500
		320,000,000
Registrations and domains and woods,		167,763,000
Customs and salt,		70,615,000
Tobacco and wines and spirits,		80,117,000
Lottery,		7,857,000
Posts,		8,830,000
Salt Mines,		2,400,000
Miscellaneous,		8,993,000
Loan,		92,662,000
In advances on 1817,		54,760,000
Total,		798,598,859

EXPENDITURE.

	Francs.
Civil List,	25,000,000
Royal Family,	8,000,000
Peers,	1,263,500
Deputies,	2,575,240
Justice,	18,991,312
Foreign Affairs,	9,654,112
Interior,	53,557,000
War,	328,293,134
Navy,	39,646,699
Police General,	1,027,516
Finance Minister,	16,334,246
Interest of National Debt,	98,640,000
Cautionary Interests,	8,000,000
Negotiations,	10,000,000
Contributions to the Allies,	180,000,000
Total,	798,598,859

Archives Diplomatiques, v 258, 300.

1816. RECEIPTS.

	Francs.	Francs.
	172,132,000	
	75,779,280	223,174,000
	27,289,000	
	12,892,000	
	1,280,000	
	6,446,000	124,195,244
	15,416,000	
	17,805,000	
	771,000	
		346,618,000
Deducting cost of collection and insolvents,		
Registrations and domains and woods,		168,815,000
Customs and salt,		70,526,000
Additional,		35,000,000
Tobacco and wine and spirits,		95,291,000
Lottery,		9,171,000
Posts,		11,798,000
Salt Mines,		2,775,000
Miscellaneous,		3,371,000
Cautionary,		65,101,000
Tax on salaries,		12,051,000
Relinquished by King,		10,000,000
Do. by Royal Family,		1,000,000
Loan,		69,763,000
Forestalled of 1817,		17,998,000
Total,		895,577,205

EXPENDITURE.

	Francs.
Civil List,	25,000,000
Royal Family,	9,000,000
Peers,	2,000,000
Deputies,	700,000
Justice,	17,580,000
Foreign Affairs,	11,620,000
Interior,	51,400,000
Department Expenses,	23,923,760
War,	218,800,000
Navy,	48,000,000
Police General,	1,000,000
Finance Minister,	15,300,000
Negotiations,	16,142,780
Interest of National Debt,	119,120,000
Sinking Fund,	20,000,000
Cautionary Interests,	8,000,000
Treasury Bills,	1,122,000
First War-contribution to Allies,	140,000,000
Cost of 150,000 men,	138,000,000
Additional cost of Foreigners,	21,000,000
Interest on Advances,	6,369,886
Total,	895,577,205

masters in this country. The archbishop of Paris had only £600 a year; the ordinary bishops, £200; the parish priests from £15 to £50 a year. This state of things was strongly and pathetically insisted on in the Chamber. "Travel," said M. Castelbajac and M. St. Gery, "where you will in France, and you will shudder at the state of humiliation to which religion has been reduced. In many of the provinces, the temples, living monuments of the faith of our fathers, are abandoned, the bird of prey has established its abode where was formerly the tabernacle; and where formerly the holy strains resounded, is to be heard only the mournful exclamation of the pious inhabitant of the fields, who gazes on the ruins, and asks where is now the abode of the God of his fathers. This has all arisen from the confiscation of the property of the Church, and reducing its ministers to the condition of salaried dependents on the state. There is great inconvenience in lowering the income of ministers of religion, if you desire to re-establish the influence of morality and religion. Not to mention the invidious distinction between their salaries and those of the civil servants of Government, it is evident that, in the present state of society, influence and importance depend on property, so that the clergy can not resume the consideration which they ought to possess in society but by becoming proprietary. In principle, in a nation essentially proprietary, the clergy should be in the same situation.

119. Continued.

"In what respect has the spoliation of the clergy contributed to the well-being of the people? The wise administration of the ecclesiastics diffused ease and contentment in the lands which belonged to them; and never were they wanting to the state in its necessities. Let us restore to our descendants an institution which was the source of the happiness of their fathers. The Constituent Assembly, when it despoiled the clergy, came under an engagement to provide them with an income from the state of 82,000,000 francs (£3,280,000). What has been done as regards that engagement, and how has it been fulfilled? That income is the subject of a sacred promise; let us do what we can to redeem it. In many places, possessions, the rents of capitalists, have been withdrawn from the cupidity of the Revolutionists, and put into the hands of third parties as trustees. The successive governments down to the Restoration have employed fraud, or encouraged informations, to gain intelligence of these deposits, or get possession of them. Why not address yourselves to the consciences of the holders of these deposits, and encourage their application to the objects of the trusters, without requiring any accounting for the past? Without doubt, you must sustain the public credit, and meet all public engagements; but the evils described must cease if you would reconcile God with the earth, the Almighty with France. Already the judgment of Heaven appears upon us. What but the consequences of perjury have assembled us here in the midst of the mutilated remains of the monarchy? Is it not religion which restrains perjury? The army has wavered in its faith; can you therefore be surprised that the God of battles has deserted us? What has become of the glorious days when your standards left our temples to be carried into our camps, and returned charged with victories to adorn our altars?" In pursuance of these principles, it was proposed as a law, "That the bishops and curates shall be authorized to receive all donations of movables, heritages, and rents, made to them by individuals for the support of the ministers of religion, its seminaries, or any other ecclesiastical establishment, and possess them, they and their successors, for ever, under the obligation only of applying them to the purposes intended by the donors." In addition to this, it was proposed by M. Piet to restore to the clergy all the possessions belonging to the Church which had not been alienated, and that the keeping of the parish registers should be vested in their hands. Finally, a commission, of which M. Laboire was the organ, reported that an annual increase of 20,000,000 francs (£800,000) should be made from the funds of Government to the support of the Church.[1]

[1] Cap. iv. 260, 266, 269; Lac. ii. 40, 42; Moniteur, Dec. 22, 1815, Jan. 9, 1816, and Feb. 15, 1816.

Although these doctrines pointed not obscurely to an intention to resume at no distant period the possessions, and restore the influence and consideration of the clergy, yet they were so strongly rooted in the feelings and wishes of the majority, that it was no easy matter to combat them. The partisans of Government, however, adopted the most effectual means of doing so, which was to appeal to the selfish passions and fears of human nature, by identifying such extreme proposals with a great increase of the public burdens and an eventual national bankruptcy. "Such a system of reparation," they exclaimed, "is at variance with the interest of the state, the public credit, the engagements of the king, and the liberties of the people. If we subject ourselves in this manner to the influence of Rome, we shall find ourselves constrained to submit to all the encroachments and demands of the Papal See. Why create a new injustice, when we are straining every nerve to wipe away the effects of an old one? If we consider the new charges which it is proposed to impose upon France in favor of the clergy, and the enormous burdens fixed upon it by the Treaty of Paris, the uncertainty of its revenues, the nullity of its credit, what can be expected as the consequence of such ill-timed largesses?—a second bankruptcy—a bankruptcy under the Bourbons; a bankruptcy which will swallow up the last and only remaining third of the property of which two-thirds had been destroyed by the Revolution, and which will require a loan of at least a thousand millions. Shall the work of religion and bankruptcy be brought for the first time into so strange and unholy an alliance?" These considerations startled the Assembly; and the Chamber, as a compromise, adopted the principle which passed into law, that the clergy might receive gifts to the Church, but only to the extent of 1000 francs (£40) yearly, without the sanction of the king, but above that sum only with the royal authority.[2] This was but a feeble advantage to be gained; but it was a very important one, as demonstrating how the public opinion

120. Answer of the ministers, and their counter project.

[2] Cap.iv. 264, 269; Lac. ii. 41, 46; Moniteur, March 16, March 28, April 19, 1816.

was going; and ministers showed their sense of it by adding 10,000,000 francs (£400,000) a year to the funds of the clergy.

121. Argument of M. Bonald against the law of divorce.
The next and last important subject which occupied the attention of the Chamber, before the prorogation of the session was that of DIVORCE. The deplorable state of general license in which manners had been left by the Revolution, had long rendered it evident that some efficient remedy was required in this respect; but it was easier to see the evil than devise such a cure, so strongly did the feelings of the influential class in the metropolis and great towns run in favor of the unrestricted liberty which they had so long enjoyed. The ascendency of the clergy in the present Assembly, however, encouraged M. de Bonald, who had struggled against this abuse ever since the days of the Consulate, to bring forward a law for its entire abolition. "You must all regret," said he, "that the strictness of our regulations prevents us from paying a striking homage to public morals, by voting by acclamation the abolition of the power of divorce. You can not but lament that you are not at liberty to break that disastrous law, as those notorious criminals whom public justice puts *hors la loi*, and whom it condemns to a capital punishment as soon as their identity is established. Let us hasten, at least, to abolish that part of our weak and feeble legislation which dishonors it; that first-born of a philosophy which has overturned the world, and ruined France; and which its mother, ashamed of its excesses, does not venture any longer to defend. The ancients, in an imperfect state of society—more advanced in the cultivation of the arts than in the science of laws—may have said, 'Of what avail are laws without morals?' But when a state, arrived at the last stages of civilization, has obtained so great an ascendency over the family, we must reverse the maxim and say, 'What can morals do without laws which support them, or against laws which derange them?' Legislators, you have seen the facility of divorce introduce in its train all the excesses of democracy, and the dissolution of a family precede that of the state. Let that experience not be lost either for your happiness or your instruction. Our families demand morals, and the state demands laws. To reinforce domestic authority, the natural element of public power, and to consecrate by law the entire dependence of women and children, is the best security for the constant obedience of the people." So strongly were these ideas rooted in the minds of the majority of the Chamber, that no opposition was made, and the proposition to introduce the law passed unanimously. It was too late, however, for it to receive the sanction of all the branches of the legislature till the next session. Even then it failed to apply a remedy to the prevailing evils: so true is it that positive laws are nugatory, unless supported by general opinion.[1]

[1 Cap. iv. 269, 278; Lac. ii. 42, 46.]

122. Changes in the administration.
The hostility, now open and avowed, between the majority of the Chamber and the ministry, and the determination of the former to force measures on the government which they felt they could not carry into execution, in the existing state of the country, without inducing civil warfare, confirmed the leading members of administration in the opinion which, as already mentioned, they had long entertained, that a legislature elected on a different basis was indispensable to the existence of the monarchy. This could only be done by a *coup d'état*, because it was evident that the existing Chamber would never consent to a change which might weaken the influence of the ultra-Royalists in future legislatures. But it was necessary to be very cautious in the preparation of such a *coup d'état*, because a considerable part of the ministry, it was known, would be hostile to its adoption, and their opinion was sure to be embraced by the great majority of the Chamber. A modification of the ministry was therefore resolved on, in order to bring it more into harmony with the secret designs of the *Camarilla*, which took the lead in the cabinet. To effect this, M. Lainé, who had supported the ministerialist project for the elections, and incurred, in consequence, the vehement hostility of the majority of the Chamber, was advanced to the important office of Minister of the Interior in room of M. Vaublanc, who was permitted to retire. The only condition which this able and intrepid man made on joining the government, which was at once agreed to, was, that the basis of the electoral suffrage was to be *uniform*, and that it was to be the payment of 300 francs yearly of direct taxes. At the same time M. de Marbois was dismissed on the *pretext* of ill health, though, as he himself said, "The certificate of my physician attests that I am in a fair way of recovery; but the certificate of the king proves that I am daily getting worse." His office was not filled up, the seals being intrusted *ad interim* to the chancellor. The object was to leave a seat in the cabinet vacant for some influential member of the new Chamber which was in contemplation. M. Guizot, from fate reserved for higher destinies, went out of office with his chief, M. de Marbois, and did not re-enter it till an entire change ensued in administration. Posterity has no reason to regret his retirement from the labors and cares of office, for it led to his appointment as professor of history in the University of Paris, and the composition of his immortal historical works.[1]

[1 Cap. iv. 29*, 280; Lac. ii. 65, 66; Lam. vi. 95, 96.]

123. Conspiracy of the Liberal party.
While these modifications were in progress in the administration, with a view to the establishment of a legislature and system of government more in harmony with the prevailing tone of feeling which the Revolution, for good or for evil, had impressed upon the country, the ardent democrats and Napoleonists, impatient of inaction, were preparing more immediate and decisive measures. They could not brook the delays of Parliament, or the slow progress of changes in general opinion; instant action, immediate overthrow of the government, could alone satisfy their ardent aspirations. In their view the government of the Bourbons had been violently forced upon the country by foreign powers, and it was the duty of every friend to his country to concur without any delay in measures for throwing it off. In this they were all agreed; but very great disunion—the germ of future civil conflict—existed as to the government which was to succeed them. The disbanded officers of the army were for a restora-

tion of Napoleon II., and of the military régime; but the great majority of the civilians engaged in the conspiracy had different views. A republic constructed on the broad basis of universal suffrage, like that of 1793, was the object of their ambition, because every one hoped to have a lucrative place under such a government; and they joined the Bonaparte faction, in the mean time, only in order to get quit of a dynasty which was equally an impediment to the ambition of them all. The plan of the conspirators, who had their head-quarters at Paris, but their branches over all France, was to envelop the capital, where the faubourgs were not yet disarmed and great elements of revolution existed, in a vast net spread over all France, except the towns on the frontiers occupied by the allied troops, and, before the French army was reorganized, or any means of resistance existed, at once to overturn the monarchy.¹

¹ Cap. iv. 291, 292; Lam. vi. 98, 97; Lac. ii. 62, 63.

M. de Lafayette, and the heads of this conspiracy at Paris, though in their saloons and drawing-rooms they scarcely attempted any concealment of their designs, were too prudent to engage in overt acts before their preparations were complete, and the period of action had arrived. But, as often happens in such cases, the impatience of the inferior agents outstripped the more prudent designs of the chiefs: liberalism had its ultras, as well as loyalty. M. Didier, a fanatic of extravagant character and opinions, whose thirst for conspiracies had been such that, under Napoleon, he had engaged in them for the restoration of the Bourbons, and had recently been a *habitué* of the ante-chambers of the Duke of Orleans, where all the discontented of all liberal parties assembled together to exhale their common animosity against the government, set out from Paris in the end of April, and set up the standard of revolt in the neighborhood of Grenoble, where it was known Napoleon had many partisans, on the 14th May. Government had information of the design, and sent a legion that could be relied on to Grenoble, under the command of General Donnadieu, an able man and devoted Royalist, but, as the event proved, of an ambitious and exaggerating character. The revolt broke out on the night of the 14th May. The insurgents, to the number of two hundred, attended by another hundred of mere spectators whom curiosity brought together, marched on Grenoble, where they were promptly met by General Donnadieu, and totally defeated and dispersed, with the loss of eight killed on the spot, and sixty prisoners.²

124. Outbreak, headed by Didier at Grenoble. May 5, 1816.

² Lam. vi. 100, 101; Cap. iv. 293, 296; Lac. ii. 63, 64.

So far, General Donnadieu's conduct had been energetic and praiseworthy; and by the defeat of this, the first conspiracy which had broken out since the second restoration of the Bourbons, he had rendered an important service to the monarchy. But, either from misinformation as to the real nature and extent of the conspiracy, or from a natural tendency to exaggeration, he transmitted such inflamed accounts of what had occurred to the government, as not only diffused very general alarm, but led to measures of severity in the

125. Exaggerations of General Donnadieu, and needless severities.

circumstances unnecessary, and which were deeply to be regretted. According to his second dispatch, "the insurgents who attacked Grenoble were four thousand strong, and their dead bodies covered all the roads round the town;" whereas, in point of fact, they were only two hundred, and the slain eight in all. The result was, that a reward of 20,000 francs (£800) was offered by Government for the apprehension of Didier, dead or alive; and three prisoners, who had been taken during the nocturnal combat with arms in their hands, were shot two days afterward by the Prévôtal Court. Twenty-one were subsequently brought to trial, of whom fourteen were executed by the guillotine—a terrible example, and which the magnitude or formidable character of the insurrection by no means warranted. Didier himself, in the first instance, made his escape into the mountains on the confines of Savoy and Dauphiny; but the promised reward proved too strong for the virtue of the mountaineers. He was betrayed by the friends (two men and a woman) with whom he had sought refuge, brought to trial, and condemned to be executed. He behaved with firmness in his last moments, and seemed in the supreme hour to regain the attachment which he had originally felt for the Bourbons. His last words, addressed to General Donnadieu, were—"Tell the king that the only proof of gratitude which I can give him, for the kindnesses which I have received from him, is to advise him to remove from himself, from the throne, and from France, *the Duke of Orleans and M. Talleyrand*"—an advice which was of importance, as coming from one who had been intimate in the Orleans establishment, and which subsequent events rendered prophetic.¹

¹ Cap. iv. 296, 310; Lam. vi 109, 125; Lac. ii. 63, 64.

Paris is the centre of every movement in France; an explosion never takes place in the provinces that the train has not been laid in the metropolis. It was well known to the police that the heads of the Liberal party in Paris were privy to the designs which were on foot, and that the saloons of M. de Lafayette, M. d'Argenson, and M. Manuel, were the rendezvous almost every evening of discontented persons, by whom the project of overturning the government was discussed with scarcely any reserve. The police had full information of their designs, and strongly advised the arrest of M. Manuel; but the government hesitated to take a step which would at once commit them into open hostility with the whole Liberal party in France, while the evidence might prove insufficient to secure the conviction of the accused. Proceedings were adopted, however, against the subordinate agents. Tolleron, an engraver, Pleignier, a bootmaker, and Carbonneau, a writing-master, were apprehended on the charge of having prepared and circulated a treasonable proclamation;* and it

126. Conspiracy in Paris.

* "Français! nous sommes arrivés au terme du mal heur. Amis du peuple dont nous faisons partie, nous avons lu dans l'âme de nos frères. Nous nous sommes empressés de prendre mesures les plus sages et les plus certaines pour la chûte entière des Bourbons. Notre succès est certain: nous sommes impénétrables; on ne nous trouvera nulle part et nous sommes partout: nous pourrions même défier les Satellites de la plus odieuse tyrannie: nous ne supposerons jamais de traîtres parmi les compagnons de nos glorieux travaux: s'il s'en trou-

soon appeared that the designs of the conspirators were of a still more violent description. It was discovered that a small body of these desperadoes had formed a plan for surrounding and attacking the Tuileries during the night. To facilitate the operations, a mine was to be run under the palace, charged with twenty barrels of powder, lodged in an old sewer, which was to be exploded before the attack was made. The design of the conspirators was to destroy the royal family, establish a provisional government, and convoke a new Assembly. The treasonable proclamation was at once admitted by the accused, and they were all convicted by the jury, condemned, and executed—a deplorable result of civil dissensions, to cause the passions to descend to the lowest grades of society, where they tend to anarchy, conspiracy, and murder, and end in hideous judicial massacres.[1]

¹ Cap. iv. 313, 327; Lam. vi. 137, 146.

127. Conspiracy at Lyons, June 8.

A conspiracy, which proved abortive, was also discovered at Lyons soon after, which, though not in itself formidable, acquired importance from the time at which it was discovered, and its obvious connection with the treasonable plots, all emanating from Paris, which were elsewhere in operation. The outbreak was fixed for the 8th June, on which day the tocsin sounded in several of the villages around Lyons, and a body of conspirators advanced toward Lyons in the evening, where they were instantly dispersed by a body of gendarmes. Eight or ten persons were seized with arms in their hands; and the Prévôtal Courts were soon in such activity, that above two hundred prisoners encumbered the prisons of the department. But the government were satisfied with the advantage they had gained, and had come to regret the blood unnecessarily shed at Grenoble. Marshal Marmont and General Fabvier were sent to Lyons, by whose orders the prosecutions were suspended; and happily tranquillity was restored without any sacrifices on the scaffold.[1]

¹ Lam. vi. 146, 151; Moniteur, June 20, 1846.

128. Preparations of the government for a change in the electoral law, and its difficulties.

These repeated alarms confirmed the Duke de Richelieu, M. Decazes, and Count Molé, in their opinion that a dissolution of the Chamber, and changes in the electoral law, had become indispensable to the public tranquillity, and that the longer continuance of the system of government pursued by the majority of the Chamber was impossible. But very serious difficulties occurred in carrying this intention into execution. Under what law, supposing the Chamber dissolved, were the elections to take place? The project proposed by M. Vaublanc, on the part of the Government, had been rejected by the Deputies; and that of M. Villèle, which they had passed by a large majority, had been combated by the whole influence of the ministry in the House of Peers, and thrown out. The ordinance of 13th July, 1815, under which the existing Chamber had been elected, had been issued only by the royal authority, and was different in many important respects from that under which either the first Chamber or that of Napoleon, during the Hundred Days, had been elected. The first Chamber elected in 1814 had not been chosen under any legislative authority which the Bourbon government were bound to acknowledge. There was thus no legislative enactment in existence on the most important and vital point in a constitutional monarchy—the system under which the representatives of the people were to be elected. The entry of M. Lainé into the cabinet gave a majority to the party there which inclined to the opinion that, in a question surrounded with so many difficulties, the only safe course was to adhere to the charter granted by Louis XVIII. on his first restoration; and as there was no hope of getting the existing Chamber to alter the system under which itself had been elected, it was resolved to have recourse to a *coup d'état*, dissolve the Chamber, and regulate the election of a new one by the simple expedient of a royal ordinance.[1]

¹ Cap. iv. 328, 333; Lac. ii. 70, 76; Lam. vi. 144, 149.

129. Speech of M. Decazes in favor of a *coup d'état*.

"Sire!" said M. Decazes, in the cabinet, "it is necessary to dissolve the Chamber, for it thwarts the government of the king: it weakens his authority, usurps his power. At one time it endangers, at another openly attacks, the measures emanating from his profound wisdom; foments the angry passions which your Majesty would wish to calm; perpetuates, after the victory has been gained, the crisis of the Hundred Days; retards indefinitely the period of the evacuation of our territory—that time which can alone permit your Majesty to breathe, or give rest to your patriotic heart. It is necessary to dissolve without delay; at this very moment, M. de Villèle, M. de Castelbajac, and Calviens, are felicitating themselves on the triumphant reception which Toulouse and Nîmes have awarded to them. In the next session they will be emboldened to attempt every thing, from the interested eulogies passed on them by those who expect from them the restoration of their estates. By the effect of its turbulent combination, the present Chamber has caused the entire year to be lost, so far as regards the evacuation of our territory. By refusing to sanction the sale of part of the woods of the state, with the sole view of saving the woods of the clergy, they have deprived us of all means of borrowing, by withdrawing the security we might offer. They have, of their sole authority, broken an engagement undertaken toward the public creditors, and sanctioned by the law. The public debt is regarded by them in no other light but as a burden which they are at liberty to throw off at the expense of honor, morality, and religion. When we had no other resource left but credit, and no means of re-establishing it but a scrupulous good faith, they have let the infamous words of bankruptcy escape from their lips, or have supported propositions which were identical with it. Masters of the budget, with regard to which they have usurped the initiative, they have made it the vehicle of their prejudices and their passions. In presence of 150,000 men spread over our strong places, they have left us without an army, without national energy; while at the same time they give us every reason to apprehend a crisis, when that energy might revive from the effects of despair, and a return of the furious passions at which the universe has already shuddered.

vait un, malheur à lui son jugement est prononcé, tenez-vous prêts: dans peu vos bras seront nécessaires. Songez que rien ne doit nous manquer, armes, munitions."—CAPEFIGUE, iv. 316.

"If that moment has not arrived, sire! to what are we to ascribe it? Entirely to the system of moderation, firmness, and wisdom, which your Majesty has pursued in presence of a vindictive Assembly. In that honorable contest, the throne has for auxiliaries the entire nation, which has separated its cause from that of the proud and haughty privileged classes. That nation calls to you, sire! Maintain the charter—your work, your gift to the nation; we can only support by known facts alarms so general. Yes, contempt for the charter is every where professed by the envenomed majority; your Majesty is no stranger to the impassioned vehemence with which they declaim against the charter; why give that majority an opportunity of giving a new proof of its dangerous disposition? It would be safer, it is sometimes said, to postpone a dissolution till the majority has given a yet more decisive proof of its mischievous tendency. Is it then certain that the nation will submit to fresh insults? Or shall we wait till they have inflicted some new wound on the finances of the state? Three months lost for our liberation, three months wasted in civil discord; three months during which your Majesty has been controlled in the acts of clemency so dear to your paternal heart; three months of irresolution, of anarchy—these are what your faithful servants can no longer contemplate without horror. Beyond the concessions which the safety of the state have suggested to us, we can not make one. Your Majesty is aware with what patience we have borne repeated defeats, with an equanimity of which you alone know the secret motive; but to the public, by whom that motive is unknown, it can have no other aspect but that of weakness. We can not longer continue to play a part, which, if persevered in, would compromise the dignity of the crown. An immediate dissolution will re-establish that dignity, of which we are the jealous guardians, and will exhibit royalty in all its force. It will be in some sort a second gift of the charter, a new contract of love and peace. It is necessary to give that charter a character of immutability, which the ordinances of 13th and 14th July, 1815, have unhappily taken away, by declaring a revision of fourteen articles. It is desirable, therefore, that the ordinance of the dissolution should be preceded by a declaration that no article of the charter is to be altered. The Chamber should be reduced to 260, the number designed by the charter. Stability is the first wish of a people worn out by convulsions; it is the rein which is to restrain men consumed by the passion for retrograde changes; it is what Europe and its sovereigns demand. It is for us, or rather for the king to set the first example of an immutable order, in a country which has undergone so many revolutions within, and launched so many abroad."[1]

130. Continued.

[1] Lac. ii. 78, 80; Memorial of Decazes, Cap. iv. 352, 356.

Whatever may be thought of this speech, which, amid much exaggeration, contained some important truths, there can be but one opinion as to the skill with which it was prepared to work on the feelings and gratify the secret vanity of the king. The leading principle of his mind at this period was an anxious desire to get quit of the allied troops, and deliver his country from the humiliating vassalage to which it had been subjected; his secret vanity a pride in the charter, and in his own ability to wield the power of a constitutional monarch. Louis XVIII., accordingly, was easily persuaded to give in to these views; and the Duke de Richelieu and Count Molé had already embraced them. The whole month of August was passed in preparations by this trio for the dissolution, and in measures for increasing the popularity of the court. The Legion of Honor was reconstituted, with precautions against the undue multiplication of its honors; the Ecole Polytechnique re-established; measures adopted for advancing primary education; prizes given to agriculture; and the payments from the Treasury made with such regularity as went far to re-establish public credit, which had been severely shaken by the language of the majority in the Chamber. Circular letters were addressed to the prefects and heads of the Prévôtal Courts, recommending the greatest moderation in prosecutions. At the same time, the sentiments of the Emperor Alexander were asked on the subject, through the medium of Count Pozzo di Borgo; and the king had the satisfaction of receiving an autograph letter from that monarch, in which he said, that, "in the interest of the Government of the King of France, it appeared to him that a dissolution of the Chamber of Deputies would be attended by beneficial results."[1]

121. Adoption of these principles by the king, and preparations for carrying them into execution.

[1] Emperor Alexander to Duke de Richelieu, Aug. 5, 1816; Cap. iv 346, 357.

Fortified by such support, the famous ordinance of September 5 was prepared, and promulgated in the Moniteur, without any one but its immediate authors in the cabinet being aware of what was in contemplation. It was written out in the afternoon of the 4th, signed at eight in the evening, and immediately sent to the printing-office of the Moniteur, where it appeared to the astonished inhabitants of Paris the following morning. The Count d'Artois and the other members of the royal family were in entire ignorance of what was going forward. This important state paper, by the mere authority of the king, reduced the number of deputies from 394, their existing number, to 260, the number specified in the charter, and raised the age required in deputies to forty years. New electoral colleges were constituted, in terms of the ordinance of 21st July, 1815: those of arrondissements were directed to meet on the 25th September; those of departments on the 5th October. The presidents of colleges were named in the ordinance, and embraced Camille Jourdan, André de la Lozère, Royer Collard, and a number of others, all of the moderate or constitutional party, their appointment indicating, in the most unequivocal manner, the wish of the government that the Chambers should be elected of moderate men, equally removed from the extremes on either side. The Duke de Richelieu, though he acquiesced in the dissolution and ordinance, was yet not without his misgivings as to the influence of the new electoral system upon the future fate of France; and accordingly he said, in his circular to the prefects with the writ for the new election— "Do your utmost to prevent true Jacobins being returned in the new Chamber—that would alto-

132. Ordinance of Sept. 5, 1816.

gether defeat our intentions. No party men —that ought to be our object; but if they can not be avoided, ultra-Royalists are better than Revolutionists."[1*]

133. Consternation of the ultra-Royalists, and dismissal of Chateaubriand.

No words can describe the consternation of the royal family, the majority of the Chamber, and the extreme Royalists throughout France, when the sudden announcement of the dissolution of the legislative body, and the convocation of a new one, chosen under a different electoral system, fell upon them. The Duke de Richelieu undertook the difficult task of announcing it to the Count d'Artois; that prince was in despair at the intelligence, prophesied the fall of the monarchy, and openly accused M. Decazes of betraying the throne. The Duchess d'Angoulême positively refused to see any of the ministers on the subject; the duke, her husband, was more moderate; and the Duke de Berri testified satisfaction on the occasion. The court was in the deepest affliction at the intelligence; they could not have been more so if the monarchy had been swept away—which, indeed, was generally prophesied as the inevitable result of the measure. The Royalist press throughout France broke forth into the most violent invectives against the ministry, whom they represented as having usurped the royal authority, coerced the king, and delivered over France, bound hand and foot, to the Revolutionists. Chateaubriand gave vent to the general feeling of the Royalists in an eloquent and impassioned postscript to his celebrated pamphlet published at that time, in which, not content with violently assailing the measure, he threw doubts on the unrestricted consent of the king to it. Louis was extremely indignant at this imputation, which, in addition to an attack on the ministry, amounted to a reflection on his personal firmness; and the consequence was that a decree appeared next day in the *Moniteur*, by which the name of Chateaubriand was erased from the list of privy councilors. But this measure of severity against so very eminent a man only augmented his influence, and that of his pamphlet, which was immense, and materially affected the return of members for the next Chamber.[1*] He lost not only his situation in the privy council, but the salary attached to it, which reduced him to such straits, in point of finance, that he was obliged to sell his country house and books, reserving only a little Homer in Greek, on the margin of which were some translations he had made of the lines of the immortal bard. But he lost neither his spirit nor his influence from becoming poor, though he now walked to the Chamber of Peers, or went in a hackney coach when it rained. "In my popular equipage," says he, "under the protection of the mob which surrounded the carriage, I regained for myself the rights of the working class, to which I now belonged; from the height of my chariot I ruled the train of kings."[2]

1 Mon. Sept. 5, 1816; Cap. iv. 358, 360; Lac. ii. 81, 82.

1 Moniteur. Sept. 12, 1816. Cap. iv. 364, 365; Lac. ii. 63.

2 Chateaub. *Mémoires d'outre Tombe*, vii. 227.

134. Great effects of this ordinance.

The royal ordinance of 5th September, 1816, wrought so great a change in the electoral body and composition of the Chamber of Deputies in France, that it was equivalent in effect to a revolution, and is generally considered by the Royalist party as the main cause of the overthrow of the elder branch of the house of Bourbon. It will appear in the succeeding volumes of this work how this effect was worked out; but, in the mean time, there are two observations which are suggested by the tenor of that decree itself. The first is, that the great reduction in the number of deputies—from 394 to 260—operated to the prejudice of the rural districts, and proportionally augmented the influ-

---

* "Depuis notre retour dans nos états, chaque jour nous a démontré cette vérité, proclamée par nous dans une occasion solennelle, qu'à côté de l'avantage d'améliorer, est le danger d'innover. Nous nous sommes convaincus, que les besoins et les cœurs de nos sujets se réunissaient pour conserver intacte cette charte constitutionelle, base du droit public en France et garantie du repos général. Nous avons en conséquence jugé nécessaire de réduire le nombre des députés au nombre determiné par la charte, et de n'y appeler que des hommes de quarante ans. Mais pour opérer légalement cette réduction, il est devenu indispensable de convoquer de nouveau les collèges electoraux, afin de procéder à l'élection d'une nouvelle Chambre des Députés. A ces causes, nos ministres entendus, nous avons ordonné et ordonnons ce qui suit. 1. Aucun des articles de la charte ne sera cassé. II. La Chambre des Députés est dissoute. III. Le nombre des députés des départements est fixé conformément a l'Art. 33 de la charte, suivant le tableau ci-joint. Les collèges électoraux d'arrondissement et de département étant composés tels qu'ils ont été reconnus et tels qu'ils ont été complétés par notre ordonnance du 21 Juillet, 1815. Les collèges électoraux d'arrondissement se réuniront le 25 Septembre de cette année. Chacun d'eux élira un nombre de candidats égal au nombre de députés du département. Les collèges électoraux de département se réuniront le 4 Octobre. Chacun d'eux choisira au double la totalité des députés parmi les candidats presentés par les collèges d'arrondissement. Si le nombre des députés du département est impair, le partage se fera à l'avantage de la portion qui doit être choisie parmi les candidats. Toute élection ou l'assistera pas la moitié au moins des membres des collèges sera nulle. La majorité évidente parmi les membres présens est nécessaire pour la validité des élections des députés. Si les collèges d'arrondissements n'avaient pas complété l'élection des candidats qu'ils peuvent choisir, le collège du département n'en procédera pas moins à son opération; les procès verbaux des élections seront examinés à la Chambre des Députés, qui prononcera sur la régularité des élections. Les députés élus seront tenus de produire à la chambre leur acte de naissance constatant qu'ils sont âgés de 40 ans, et un extrait d'ordres dûment légalisé par le préfet constatant qu'ils payent au moins 1000 francs (£40) de contributions directes. La session de 1816 s'ouvrira le 4 Nov. de la présente année. Les dispositions de l'ordonnance du 13 Juillet 1815, contraires à la présente, sont révoquées."—*Moniteur*, 5th Sept. 1816.

* Chateaubriand's postscript commenced with these words: "La Chambre de Députés est dissoute! Cela ne m'étonne pas. C'est le système des intérêts révolutionnaires qui marche. Je n'ai donné rien à changer à cet écrit. J'avais prévu le dénouement, et je l'ai plusieurs fois annoncé. Cette mesure ministérielle sauvera, dit-on, la monarchie légitime. Dissoudre la seule Assemblée, qui depuis 1789 ait manifesté des sentimens purement Royalistes, c'est, à mon avis, une étrange manière de sauver la monarchie. . . . Et que veut d'ailleurs le Roi? S'il était perteus de pénétrer dans les secrets de sa haute sagesse, ne pourroit-on pas présumer, qu'en laissant constitutionellement toute liberté d'action et d'opinion à ces ministres *responsables*, il a porté ses regards plus loin qu'eux. Il a peut-être jugé que la France satisfaite lui renverserait les mêmes Députés dont il était satisfait; que l'on aurait une Chambre Nouvelle aussi Royaliste que la dernière bien que convaincue sur d'autres principes, et qu'alors il n'y aurait plus moyen de nier la véritable opinion de la France." The ordinance of the king was in these words: "Le Vicomte de Chateaubriand ayant, dans un écrit imprimé, élevé des doutes sur notre *volonté personnelle* manifestée par notre ordonnance du 5 du present mois, nous ordonnons ce qui suit.—Le Vicomte de Chateaubriand cessera, dès ce jour, d'être compris au nombre de nos Ministres d'État.—Louis."—*Moniteur*, 12 Sept. 1816. *La Monarchie selon la Charte* (Œuvres de Chateaubriand, xviii. 131, 140.)

ence of the towns. Nearly the whole of the members struck off had been elected for departments, chiefly in the south of France, and they were selected for destruction, because they had proved the most unmanageable. The second, that in the departments which still retained the privilege of sending members to Parliament, the right of voting was confined *to one class only*, and that a very limited one. By the ordinance of 13th of July, 1815, under which the dissolved Chamber had been elected, a variety of persons, as members of the Legion of Honor, and official functionaries, were admitted to the franchise; but by the ordinance of 5th September, 1816, these were all swept away; and the suffrage was confined to one single class, viz., persons paying 300 francs, or £12 of direct taxes. The direct taxes are so very heavy in France, that this payment implies a very different class from what it would in Great Britain; it denotes persons having from 2500 to 3500 francs (from £100 to £140) a year. The total number of persons entitled to the suffrage in France on this payment was about 80,000, of whom 60,000 paid from 300 to 500 francs (£12 to £20) of yearly taxes. Thus the government of France, under this electoral system, was devolved upon 60,000 persons of one description only—that is, small shopkeepers in towns, and small proprietors in the country. They, too, were for the most part holders of the national domains—persons enriched by the revolution, and resolute to support the gains it had brought them. The immense body of peasant proprietors, several millions in number, and the working classes in towns on the one hand, and the whole body of affluent or highly educated persons on the other, were, to all practical purposes, unrepresented. This is not the representative system; it is irresponsible class government of the worst kind. The representative system is founded on the entire representation, not of mere numbers, *but of classes of society*: mere numbers have no tendency to induce this, or rather they induce the very reverse, viz., class government of the lowest ranks of society. An unrestricted feudal aristocracy is a great evil; but an unrestricted burgher aristocracy is a still greater.

Another circumstance worthy of note, and which appears not a little strange to one accustomed to English ideas, is, that in all the changes made on the electoral system in France, the royal authority alone was interposed. The Chamber, which sat from July, 1815, to September, 1816, was elected under the royal ordinance of 13th July, 1815, which added 131 members to it; that of 1816 and 1817, and all the subsequent ones, under the royal ordinance of 5th September, 1816, which took them away. Supposing that a royal ordinance was a matter of necessity in the disastrous state of the country in 1815, when there was no legislature in existence, the same can not be said of the royal ordinance of 5th September, 1816, issued when a legislature was actually sitting, and the concurrence of the three branches of the legislature might have been obtained for any organic change which appeared necessary. It is remarkable, too, that all classes acquiesced without objection in this great stretch of the royal prerogative, so subversive of any thing like real constitutional government; and, with the Liberal party, in particular, it was the subject of the highest possible exultation and eulogium—a striking contrast to their conduct in July, 1830, when they made a similar exercise of the royal authority a pretext for overturning the throne.

135. The whole Chambers were elected by royal ordinance.

136. Reflections on the reaction of 1815.

The parliamentary and social history of France during 1815 and 1816 is worthy of particular attention from all who consider history, not merely as the amusement of a passing hour, but as a source of political instruction, and the subject of serious thought. Long as the preceding chapter has been, it could neither have been shortened nor divided, for it embraces one subject, and that one of the most fruitful in political lessons which history has preserved—THE REACTION OF 1815. The Revolution had worked out its inevitable and appropriate result; its sins had been visited by their natural consequences; and conquest, ignominy, and suffering, had closed a career commenced in selfishness, ambition, and crime. With the usual disposition of mankind to ascribe the punishment of their sins to any thing but those sins themselves, they now rushed into the opposite extreme; and the last leaders of the Revolution were as much the object of unanimous horror and detestation as the first had been of triumph and enthusiasm. All persons with right feeling must regret the measures of severity adopted on the second restoration, and the heroic blood shed on the scaffold in consequence of the treason previously committed; but, in truth, it was unavoidable. The people, by an overwhelming majority, demanded victims, as so many scapegoats to bear the sins of the community; and the legislature, which compelled the government to select them, was but the mouthpiece of a nation which, in a voice of thunder, demanded their punishment. In this terrible and tragic reaction, another circumstance is very remarkable. It was *forced* by the nation upon the sovereign. Louis XVIII. was constitutionally humane, and he was too much versed in revolutions not to know what violent reactions noble blood shed on the scaffold scarce ever fails to produce. Every one of the victims of 1815 were forced from the humanity of the government by the violence of the people. This is a very remarkable circumstance, and well worthy of consideration, for it points to the principal danger to be apprehended under a popular form of government. Those intrusted with power are invariably more inclined to moderation than those who only by their votes or their clamor seek to control their measures. The reason is, that the former feels its responsibilities, and are made acquainted with its difficulties; whereas the latter are actuated only by ambition or passion, unfettered by experience or a sense of duty. Paucity of number in the former case induces a sense of responsibility; in the latter it extinguishes it. Destructive measures—ruin to national security or freedom—are much more to be apprehended, in a popular government, from the legislature than from the executive. Responsibility checks the excesses of the last; the absence of it lets loose the passions of the first. It is a common saying that patriots generally become corrupted when they are taken into administration, and that there is nothing so like a Tory in power as a Whig in power; and the fact is certain, but the reason commonly assigned for it is not the true one. It is not so much that they are corrupted by the sweets of power, as that they are made aware of its duties and impressed with its responsibilities.

"Where," says M. de Tocqueville, "shall a person persecuted by the majority in America fly for redress? To the legislature?—it is elected by the majority. To a jury?—it is the *judicial committee of the majority.*"

138. The greatest iniquities of the period were committed by juries.

Impartial justice must confess that the year 1815 in France was no exception to this rule; nay, that it furnishes the strongest confirmation of it. The worst judicial acts which stained the Royalist reaction in that country were perpetrated by the agency of juries. It was juries who, in 1815, screened from justice every one of the criminals, however clearly proved to be guilty, who were implicated in the frightful Royalist excesses in the south of France in that year; it was juries who, in the next, terminated contemptible conspiracies with a long array of criminals executed on the scaffold. The truth is, juries are, and have been in every age, the judicial committee of the majority, and neither more nor less. As such they have frequently rescued persons, prosecuted for offenses interesting to the majority, from the hands of oppression; but they have in many more, when the majority itself was in power, committed the most atrocious judicial iniquities. In one year, juries perpetrated the long catalogue of judicial murders consequent on the Popish Plot; in another they were the instruments of the equally unjust and sanguinary vengeance of the Rye House. The whole state trials of England—the most appalling collection, as Hallam has observed, of judicial iniquities which the history of the world can exhibit—were conducted by means of juries. The whole murders of the Convention were sanctioned by the verdict of juries. No one in Great Britain need be told how little chance there is of justice being done in Ireland by a Catholic jury on a Catholic offender, or by an Orange jury on a Protestant. The reason in all these cases is one and the same, and it is this: Undivided responsibility is a check upon a single judge in a court composed of a *small* number of judges;—but there is no such check upon juries, the names of whose members are scarcely ever known, or, if known, speedily forgotten; and in whom, even at the moment of committing iniquity, numbers shelter the perpetrators. Jeffries himself would never have perpetrated the enormities which have forever blasted his name, if he had not been sheltered in the verdict, at least, by the concurring iniquity of his juries.

The treason for which Ney and Labedoyère suffered, was clearly proved, and it brought evils of an unexampled amount on France; and it was terminated by a list of capital convictions of unequaled paucity. Only six persons suffered on the scaffold over all France for a rebellion which dethroned the king, caused the conquest of the country, and fixed a debt of £64,000,000 on its inhabitants. The English historians justly congratulate themselves on the increasing humanity of the age, when the Jacobite rebellion of 1715, which was confined to Scotland and the northern counties of England, and never for one moment endangered either the country or the throne, was only chastised by the execution of two-and-twenty. There can be no doubt, therefore, that the rebellion of 1815 was, according to all the settled maxims of European law, not only clearly proved against all the persons who suffered for their participation in it, but, on the whole, most leniently dealt with. Yet we can not read the account of the execution of Ney and Labedoyère without deep regret; and that regret will be shared by the generous and the humane to the end of time. The reason is, that PURELY POLITICAL OFFENSES SHOULD NOT BE PUNISHED WITH DEATH; banishment or transportation are their appropriate penalties. Death should be reserved for great moral crimes, concerning which all mankind are agreed—as murder, fire-raising, or violent robbery—and not extended to acts such as those of treason, which originate, not in moral wrong, but in difference of political opinion, and are sometimes justified by necessity, or rewarded by the highest fortune or lasting admiration of mankind.

139. Expedience of abolishing entirely the punishment of death in pure ly political offenses.

The feelings of mankind have never stigmatized mere treason as a moral crime, so often has it arisen from noble though mistaken motives. Many families are proud of an ancestor who lost his head on the scaffold for his accession to a revolt, but none ever pointed with exultation to one executed for murder or house-breaking. Transportation to a distant country, under certification of death in case of return, is the true mode of dealing with acts which, without the intermixture of baser crimes or motives, tend only to change the government. The persons engaged in them should be considered as domestic enemies, to be made prisoners, and treated according to the laws of war, if in their insurrection they conform to its usages. If they do otherwise, and begin with pillage and conflagration, by all means treat them as pirates and enemies of the human race. To go farther, and shed their blood on the scaffold, though their conduct has not degenerated into such atrocities, but has been confined to the limits of legitimate warfare, is the same injustice and the same error as to burn for heresy. Opinion is not the proper object of punishment—it is acts only that are; and the appropriate punishment for acts tending to dispossess the government is to dispossess the person attempting it

140. Banishment is its proper punishment.

CHAPTER IV.

DOMESTIC HISTORY OF ENGLAND, FROM THE COMMENCEMENT OF 1817 TO THE REPEAL OF THE BANK RESTRICTION ACT IN 1819.

1. Vicissitudes and ceaseless change of events in human affairs.

THE study, and still more the composition of the history of an important and animating era in human affairs, is apt to induce the belief that the tale is to close when the principal actors have disappeared from the stage, and the curtain has fallen on the great catastrophe in which the drama has terminated. We are interested in it as we are in a novel or romance, which has a beginning, a middle, and an end; forgetting that in real life events grow in a perpetual chain, and share in the undying succession of the human race. No sooner are the transactions of one period brought to a close, and an apparent lull has crept over the busy scene by the exhaustion of the energies by which it had been sustained, than another set of causes comes into operation, at first scarcely perceptible, and often for a time unobserved, but which in the end act with resistless force, and induce an entire change on the fortunes of the world. The same vicissitude is conspicuous there, as in the affairs of private life: nothing is permanent, nothing unchangeable; joy succeeds to sorrow, sorrow to joy; and what is most earnestly desired at one period, as the highest object of ambition, is discovered at another to have been the commencement of ruin. Seeds sown in one age spring up, in the next, with an entirely different crop from what was anticipated, and the calculations of human wisdom are confounded by results diametrically opposite to those which had been looked for. To the affairs of nations, not less than those of individuals, the words of the poet are applied:

"Still where rosy pleasure leads,
See a kindred grief pursue;
Behind the steps that misery treads
Approaching comfort view.
The hues of bliss more brightly glow,
Chastised by sabler tints of woe,
And, blended, form with artful strife
The strength and harmony of life."*

2. Exemplifications of this vicissitude in the history of France and England after the Revolution.

Never was the truth of these beautiful words more clearly evinced than in the history both of France and England during and after the memorable contest of the Revolution. Both had gained what they contended for in the strife; both had been successful in the grand objects for which they had fought; and both have found in the attainment of these objects the termination of their greatness, the commencement of their ruin. The dreams of the Revolutionists were realized, the visions of the Girondists had come to pass; every thing they desired was accomplished, and what was the result? A monarchy without power, a nation without consideration, liberty precarious, loyalty extinguished, morals destroyed, religion discredited, the bulwarks of freedom ruined, and nothing but the calculations of selfishness to supply their place. The history of France, from 1815 to 1852, is nothing but the annals of the impotent efforts of a nation to recover what itself had destroyed; of wisdom to repair what madness had broken through; of selfishness to grasp what generosity had won or valor achieved. England had been as successful in the end, in the national, as France had been in the social strife; the Continent was arrayed under her banner, the sceptre of the ocean had passed into her hands; her enemy was vanquished, glory transcending all former glory, riches exceeding all former riches, had been won. What was the result? The commencement of a series of causes and effects, springing out of the very magnitude of these triumphs, which is destined to undo the fabric of British greatness, dissolve the magnificent British empire, and leave the fragments of its dominions scattered in separate independent states throughout the globe.

3. Consoling features even in the ruin of the Old World.

Yet even in this vast disruption there is much in which humanity must rejoice, in which patriotism must exult. The Consoling English empire may be rent asunder, but the enlightenment of English genius, the achievements of English thought, the bond of English associations, will never be lost. English will, beyond all question, be the language spoken by half the globe for interminable ages yet to come; and to English genius is opened a future of fame and usefulness, exceeding any thing yet conceded to mankind. In the noble words of a worthy scion of the British stem, albeit in Transatlantic realms, we may say, "Go forth, thou language of Milton and Hampden—language of my country! Take possession of the North American Continent! Gladden the waste places with every tone that has been rightly struck by the English lyre, with every English word that has been spoken for liberty and for man! Give an echo to the now silent and solitary mountains; gush out with the fountains that as yet sing their anthems all day long without response! Fill the valleys with the voices of love in its purity, the pledges of friendship in its fidelity; and as the morning sun drinks the dew-drops from the flowers all the way from the dreary Atlantic to the Pacific Ocean, meet him with the joyful hum of the early industry of freemen. Utter boldly, and spread widely through the world, the thoughts of the coming epoch of the people's liberty, till the sound that cheers the desert shall thrill through the heart of humanity, and the lips of the messenger of the people's power, as he stands upon the mountain, shall proclaim the renovating tidings of equal freedom to the race."[1]

[1] Bancroft's American Revolution, i. 520.

---

* GRAY—"Ode to Vicissitude."

The cause of the sudden bursting forth of the principles of decay, which took place in both France and England after the termination of the contest, is to be found in a very simple source—the general, it might almost be said universal, selfishness or human nature. So prone are mankind, in every rank, station, and situation, to use power mainly for the advantage of themselves or their adherents, that it scarce ever happens that, when one obtains it without control, a government does not ensue so oppressive as speedily to dry up the sources of national prosperity, and lay the foundation of ultimate ruin. In France this effect took place by the complete triumph of the popular party in the outset of the Revolution, and the entire destruction of all the powers or influences in the state which might be able to coerce their ambition or moderate their excesses. When the king was beheaded, the aristocracy ruined, the Church destroyed, the corporations extinguished, no power remained in the state but the force of numbers; and the tyranny of the majority soon became such, that the people, from sheer necessity, were constrained to abandon all their former principles, and take refuge from their own madness under the empire of the sword. The whole subsequent history of France has been nothing but a series of fruitless attempts to avoid this fatal necessity, and reconstruct the fabric of freedom, without the essential elements of which it must be composed.

4. Fundamental cause which has led to disaster in France.

In Great Britain, as it was not the democratic, but the aristocratic party which was victorious in the great contest of the Revolution, the causes which have induced disaster have been different, but springing at bottom from the same inherent selfishness of human nature. The aristocracy which gained the victory, and in whose hands the war left the direction of the state, was one of a very peculiar kind, and more dangerous to social prosperity than a mere body of wealthy territorial magnates would have been. Such a body is certainly never deficient in attention to its own interests; and if nations have often risen to greatness under the rule of such a body, it is not because its measures were more based on the general good than those of other men, but because its own interests, being based on production, were identical with those of the great body of producers throughout the state. But the aristocracy, which had gained the ascendency in England at the fall of Napoleon, was not entirely, or even principally, a territorial aristocracy. It was a mixed body, composed of merchants, manufacturers, bankers, colonial proprietors, ship-owners, and shop-keepers, even more than landholders, in Great Britain or Ireland. The House of Commons was the representative, not of one species of property, but of every species of property; and, although numbers were by no means unrepresented, yet the members elected by the popular constituencies were few in number compared to those who rested on the mercantile, landed, or colonial interests. It was in the undue ascendency of the mercantile interest in this mixed aristocracy—springing out of the vast riches they had amassed, and the influence they had

5. What has done so in England.

acquired during the war—that the remote cause of the whole subsequent difficulties of the British empire is to be found.

The reason of this is that—unlike a territorial aristocracy, whose interests, being founded on production, must always be the same as those of the laboring classes who cultivate their land—the gain of a moneyed aristocracy is often found chiefly in the depression and penury of the great body of the people. Manufacturers for the home market, indeed, can never, in the end, thrive on the ruin of their customers; but those for the export sale, who are generally the most enterprising and influential, often do so; because the cost of production is lessened by a fall in the wages of domestic labor, and that fall does not lessen the amount of foreign consumption. Thus the profits of manufacturers for foreign markets is often materially augmented by domestic suffering; and they would be greatest if, like the poor Hindoos, the persons they employ could be brought to subsist on three-pence a day. The moneyed classes, all possessed of fixed incomes, and all the holders of realized capital, gain immensely by the suffering of the producing classes, for that brings down the wages of labor, lowers the price of commodities of all sorts, and proportionally increases the value of money. Hence the efforts of those classes, when they have become so powerful as to have gained the command of the state, are always mainly directed to the introduction of measures which may augment their fortunes without any effort on their part, simply by enhancing the value of money by cheapening the cost of every thing else. These measures, by striking at the remuneration of industry, are in the long run of all others the most fatal to the working classes, and hence it was that Adam Smith said, "High prices and plenty are prosperity; low prices and want are misery."

6. The mercantile aristocracy pursue measures for their peculiar interests.

But unfortunately this effect is remote and circuitous, and therefore altogether beyond the vision of the great majority of men; while the advantages of a fall of prices, especially in articles of daily consumption, are immediate and obvious to every capacity. In the interval, too, which may often extend over years, between the fall in the price of subsistence and the inevitable subsequent decline in the consumption of manufactures by its producers, the operative manufacturers, as well as their employers, may be considerable gainers by the fall; because the gain to them has already come, the consequent loss has not. The producing classes are encroaching on their capital, or borrowing money, or living on credit, in hope of better times coming, rather than face the immediate discomfort of abandoning the consumption of luxuries, which to them have become necessaries. It need not be said that this can go on only for a time; that the decline in the resources of their rural customers must, in the end, tell with fearful effect on the welfare of the urban operatives. But in the interval, short as it may be, measures irreversible, when once introduced, though fraught with the most disastrous ultimate consequences, may be adopted—not only with the entire

7. Which, in ignorance, are supported by the operative manufacturers.

concurrence, but in consequence of the enthusiastic support, of the very classes who are in the end to suffer most from them. Hence it is, that it has always been found that the measures of domestic legislation or social change, which have produced the most wide-spread, lasting, and irremediable distress among the people, have been adopted at their suggestion, or carried on to gratify their wishes. If hell is paved with good intentions, this world is built up of delusive expectations.

8. Reason of this frequent disappointment of general wishes.

The reason of this frequent ultimate disappointment of the hopes most generally formed and ardently entertained by the people, is to be found in the moral law of Providence, which has forever doomed to retribution and suffering, even in this world, those who engage in measures calculated to elevate or benefit their own class, at the expense of the other classes of the community. Such measures are often attended with great *immediate* benefit to the class which introduces them; and it is the prospect of this immediate benefit which constitutes their great attraction, and renders them so fearfully alluring. But if their ultimate consequences are traced, it will invariably be found that they bore with them the seeds of retribution: the curse they bestowed on others has recoiled on themselves. The mutual dependence of all the interests of society on each other, and the indissoluble connection between social or national crime and social or national punishment, is not merely a vision of the philosopher, or a dream of the poet, but a practical principle of ceaseless operation among men, to the agency of which many of the greatest changes in human affairs are to be ascribed. No class can ever derive lasting prosperity but from measures which benefit equally every other class: if the one is for a time enriched by the ruins of the other, it will, in the end, be proportionally punished. The tracing out the operation of this moral law, in the effects of the victory of the popular class in France, and of the moneyed class in England, upon their country and themselves, during the five-and-thirty years which succeeded the fall of Napoleon, will form not the least interesting or instructive part of this History.

9. Continued distress and discontent in the country.

The seeds of evil sown by the violent contraction of the currency, and sudden termination of the war expenditure in the preceding year, had been too wide-spread, and had taken too deep root, to be speedily eradicated. The distress, indeed, was much alleviated in the rural districts by the rise in the price of provisions of all sorts which took place in the end of 1816, and continued through the whole of the succeeding year, in consequence of the very bad harvest of the first. Wheat, on an average, in 1817, was 116s. a quarter, while in the spring of 1816 it had been down at 57s. The harvest of 1817, though not so bad as that of the year before, was still very deficient both in quantity and quality. But though this great rise of prices, almost to the highest level they had attained during the war, was attended with immediate relief to the agricultural class, it aggravated in a most serious degree the sufferings of the manufacturers, who were suffering at the same time under the effects of the shake given to credit and general diminution of employment, in consequence of the contraction of the currency in the preceding, and which continued through this year. The country bankers' notes in circulation in England this year were only £15,894,000, while in 1815 they had been £22,700,000; the commercial paper, on an average, under discount at the Bank of England, was £3,960,000, while in 1810 it had been £20,070,000, and in 1815, £14,970,000.[1] So prodigious and sudden a contraction in the currency of the nation, and the accommodation afforded to the trading classes, was, of course, attended by a still more ruinous diminution of confidence and credit; and this, combining with the high price of provisions, produced an amount of distress in the great towns and manufacturing districts, which, ere long, occasioned overt acts and secret machinations of the most alarming description.

[1] Alison's Europe, c. xcvi. App. and Ann. Reg. 1817, 2, 5.

10. Plan formed of a general insurrection.

The effect of the continued contraction of the currency appeared strongly in the great falling off of the imports during 1817, which only amounted to £29,910,000, while in 1810 they had been £37,613,000, in 1814 £32,622,000, and in 1815 £30,822,000. This indicated a very great diminution in the means of consumption which the people enjoyed, and gave too much ground for the disaffected to represent the general distress as entirely the result of extravagance and waste on the part of Government. The real cause of the suffering, which was to be found in the sudden contraction of the currency, from the prospect of resuming cash payments at no distant period, was never once thought of. Every thing was set down to the oppression of Government and the unbearable load of taxation; and the remedies suggested were radical reform in Parliament, the disbanding of the army, and overthrow of the Government. A vast plan of insurrection was formed, having its centre in the metropolis, but extending widely also through the mining and manufacturing districts of the north of England and Scotland, the object of which was the overthrow of the monarchy and establishment of a republic in its stead.* Mr. Hunt, the leading demagogue of Spafields, commenced a tour through the western provinces, addressing the people every where in the most seditious and inflammatory language; and in the densely-inhabited districts of the north appearances were still more alarming, for there the people were meeting in large bodies, evidently under the orders of secret leaders, and an outbreak was daily expected by the local magistrates.[2]

[2] Sidmouth's Life, iii. 165, 166.

Parliament met on the 28th January, and the Prince-Regent, in the speech from the throne, lamented the distress which generally prevail

* "The lower orders are every where meeting in large bodies, and are very clamorous. Delegates from all quarters are moving about among them, as they were before the late disturbance; and they talk of a general union of the lower orders throughout the kingdom."—Mr. NADIN to LORD SIDMOUTH, Manchester, January 3, 1817. "A very wide and extensive plan of insurrection has been formed, and which might possibly have been acted upon before this time, but for the proper precautions used to prevent it."—DUKE OF NORTHUMBERLAND to LORD SIDMOUTH, March 21, 1817. –*Life of Lord Sidmouth*, iii. 165, 177

1817.

11. Meeting of Parliament and attack on the Prince-Regent. Jan. 29.

ed, and the consequent decline which had taken place in the revenue; but expressed a hope that these evils would be of temporary duration, and strongly condemned the factious efforts made to render them the foundation of attempts to overturn the Government. The Opposition, headed by Earl Grey in the Lords, and by Tierney and Brougham in the Commons, could find no other remedy for the existing evils but unflinching economy and a great reduction of expenditure—measures calculated to meet the diminished state of the public revenue, but of no effect upon the deep-rooted seats of evil that occasioned the distress in the country. The disturbed state of the public mind, and the acts by which the general suffering had been rendered the means of exciting disaffection against the head of the Government, were evinced when the Prince-Regent left the House of Lords, after delivering the speech from the throne. The carriage was surrounded by an insulting mob, which, from contumelious words, soon proceeded to acts of violence; and one of its glasses was broken by stones or balls from an air-gun aimed at his Royal Highness.¹

¹ Ann. Reg. 1817, 1, 2; Hughes, vi. 32.

12. Report of the secret committee in both Houses.

This open insult to the head of the Government, coupled with the alarming accounts of the progress of the disaffection which they received from all the manufacturing districts, determined ministers to apply to Parliament for extraordinary power. On the 3d February, a message from the Prince-Regent was communicated to both Houses of Parliament, stating the existence of a secret and wide-spread conspiracy against the Government, and upon its receipt a secret committee was moved for and appointed in both Houses. They made their report on the 19th February, and both contained the same information, which was of a sufficiently alarming character. The reports declared that a "general conspiracy had been formed to overturn the Government, which had its centre in London, but its ramifications through all the great towns and manufacturing districts of the country. The designs of the conspirators were to be carried into execution by a general rising in the metropolis, and liberation of all prisoners, whether for debt or crimes, to whom an address was already prepared; by setting fire to the barracks of the military, and by an attack simultaneously on the Tower, Bank, and other points of importance in the metropolis. The tricolor flag was to be the banner under which they were to assemble; and particular pains were to be taken to conciliate the soldiers, who were the brothers of the people. This project was intended to have been carried into execution at the meeting in Spafields on December 2, and it was only then prevented from being successful by accidental circumstances; but the design was only adjourned till after the meeting of Parliament, when the insurrection was to take place. Similar designs had been formed and matured in Manchester, Liverpool, Glasgow, and other great towns, and not a doubt was entertained by the conspirators of entire success. The number of the disaffected who might be expected to rise was estimated at several hundred thousand, chiefly in the great towns and manufacturing districts; and societies were every where formed, which, under the name of "Spencean Philanthropists," "Hampden Clubs," and the like, really regulated and directed their movements which were conducted with equal skill and secrecy, and almost entirely by the aid of signs and ciphers, without other written correspondence.

¹ Report of Lords and Commons Ann. Reg. 1817, 7, 13 and Parl. Deb. xxxv 411, 438.

Upon receiving these reports, which revealed the precipice on the brink of which the nation stood, ministers brought forward a bill for the suspension of the Habeas Corpus Act. It was introduced by Lord Sidmouth in the House of Lords, and Lord Castlereagh in the House of Commons, and met with the most violent and impassioned resistance in both Houses. The reports of the secret committees were ridiculed, and declared to be founded on falsehood, misapprehension, and terror; the measures proposed were pronounced tyrannical and oppressive. The public mind, however, was too strongly impressed with the reality of the danger, from the threatening demonstrations held in all the great towns, to render it a matter of difficulty for the Government to obtain the necessary powers. On the 24th February the bill for the suspension of the Habeas Corpus Act was introduced into the House of Lords by Lord Sidmouth, and on the same night one for the prevention of seditious meetings. This bill embodied into one act the provisions of the 35 Geo. III. c. 127, relative to tumultuous meetings and debating societies, and the 39 Geo. III. c. 37, regarding corresponding societies. The acts were to be only temporary, and have long since expired; but one clause in the latter act, which was strongly and justly objected to, declared it punishable with *death* if a meeting, being summoned by a magistrate to disperse, did not immediately do so. Sir Samuel Romilly and Sir James Mackintosh strenuously endeavored, but in vain, to get seven years' transportation substituted for that extreme penalty. After a violent opposition from the whole Whig and Radical party, the bills passed both Houses by very large majorities, that in the Commons being 162 — the numbers 265 to 103; and in the Lords by 113 to 30.²

13. Suspension of the Habeas Corpus Act, and passing of the Seditious Meetings Act.

Feb. 28. ² Parl. Deb. xxxv. 708, 822, and 1202, 1302; Ann. Reg. 1817, 28, 34.

Armed with these extraordinary powers, Government were not slow in taking the necessary steps to put a stop to the insurrection which was rapidly organizing in every part of the country. The information was daily more alarming, and proved that the conspiracy was more wide-spread and formidable than had been at first imagined. Among the rest, the particulars of an oath administered in Glasgow to a secret society composed of great numbers of persons were obtained, which, after binding the person taking it to entire secrecy, under the penalty of death, to be inflicted on him by any member of the society, bound him to do his utmost to obtain annual parliaments and universal suffrage, and to support the same "by moral or *physical* strength as the case may require." A

14. Measures of Government to suppress the insurrection which breaks out at Derby. June 9.

motion to omit the words "or physical" as leading to rebellion, was negatived by a large majority. Intelligence of an immediate rising being in contemplation was received at the same time from Manchester, Bolton, Birmingham, and all the principal manufacturing towns. On 27th March, Lord Sidmouth addressed a circular letter to the lord-lieutenants of counties, calling their attention to the numerous blasphemous and seditious publications which were circulating through the country, and stating that any justice might issue a warrant to apprehend a person circulating such publications upon oath, and hold him to bail. The legality of the opinion thus expressed was strongly contested at the time in both Houses of Parliament, but amply confirmed by the first legal authorities. Eight persons were apprehended on a charge of high treason at Manchester, and eight at Leicester. The whole of the latter were convicted, of whom six suffered the last penalty of the law. Severe as this example was, it had not the effect of checking the spirit of disaffection in the manufacturing counties; and on the 9th June an insurrection broke out in Derbyshire which bore marks of an extensive conspiracy. It was headed by a man of the name of John Brandreth, and ere long 500 men were assembled, who proceeded in military array to the Butterby iron-works near Nottingham, from whence, being deterred by the preparations made for defense, they advanced toward Nottingham. On the road to that place, however, they were met by Mr. Rolleston, an intrepid magistrate of the county, with eighteen of the 15th Hussars, under Captain Phillips, by whom they were stopped, pursued, and forty prisoners taken. The native cowardice of guilt, the power of the law, was never more clearly evinced. Brandreth escaped at the time, but was soon after taken, and a special commission having been sent down to Derby in autumn, he was capitally convicted, and suffered death with Turner and Ludlam, his two associates; while eleven others were transported for life, and eight imprisoned for various periods.[1]

Oct. 17.
[1] State Trials, xxxii. 327; Sidmouth's Life, iii. 179, 182.

15.
Extension of the suspension of the Habeas Corpus Act.

The menacing aspect of the manufacturing districts, and the intelligence which Government had now received of the designs and organization of the conspirators, induced them to apply to Parliament for an extension of the period during which the suspension of the Habeas Corpus Act, which had been originally limited to the sitting of Parliament, should be continued. The evidence was laid before the same select committee which had previously reported, by whom a second report was prepared and laid before both Houses in June. Their report stated that a plan of a general insurrection had been organized, which was to break out in the first instance in Manchester, on Sunday 30th March, and to be immediately followed by risings in York, Lancaster, Leicester, Nottingham, Chester, Stafford, and Glasgow. It was calculated that 50,000 persons would be ready to join them in Manchester alone by break of day, and with this immense force they were to march to attack the barracks and jails,

June 3.

liberate the prisoners, under the houses of all the nobility and gentry, seize all the arms in the gunsmiths' shops, and issue proclamations absolving the people from their allegiance, and establishing a republic. The outbreak in Derbyshire was a part of this design, which was only frustrated there and elsewhere by the vigilance and courage of the magistrates, and prompt appearance and steady conduct of the military. Upon this report, the truth of which was abundantly proved by the worst acts committed at the time by the conspirators in various parts of the country, the House of Commons, by a majority of 190 to 50, continued the suspension of the Habeas Corpus Act and the operation of the Seditious Meetings Act to the 1st March, 1818, when they finally expired.[1]

[1] Second Report, June 3, 1817; Ann. Reg. 1817, 74–82; Parl. Deb. xxxvi. 1198, 1251.

16.
Restoration of confidence and improved prospects toward the close of the year.

The effect of these vigorous measures was great and decisive, and it was much aided by the favorable harvest, which, though not very abundant, was greatly more so than the one of the preceding year had been. Prices in consequence rapidly fell, and in autumn confidence began to be generally restored, and industry to resume its wonted labors.* As the distress of 1816, and of the first half of 1817, had been mainly owing to the rapid contraction of the currency and consequent fall in the price of produce of every kind, agricultural and manufacturing, so the first symptoms of amendment appeared in the enlarged advances of the country bankers, encouraged by the suppression of the efforts of the disaffected, and the great rise, compared with 1816, which had taken place in the price of rural produce. Prosperity — and it is a markworthy circumstance — began with a *rise of prices*, even though that rise was owing to a scarcity in the preceding year. The importation of wheat in this year was considerable, compared with what it had been in former years: it amounted to 1,020,000 quarters; whereas the average for six years before had little exceeded 300,000.† The exports were above an average; they amounted to £40,911,000 — a clear proof that the distress among the manufacturing classes

* "In Devonshire every article of life is falling, the panic among the farmers wearing away, and, above all, that hitherto marketable article, discontent, is every where disappearing. I have every reason to unite my voice with my neighbors to say we owe our present peaceful and happy prospects to your firmness and prompt exertions in keeping down the democrats." — Lord EXMOUTH to Lord SIDMOUTH, 10th Sept. 1817. "We can not, indeed, be sufficiently thankful for an improvement in our situation and prospects, in every respect far exceeding our most sanguine, and even the most presumptuous hopes. A public and general expression of gratitude must be required in due season by an order in Council." — Lord SIDMOUTH to Lord KENYON, Sept. 30, 1817. *Sidmouth's Life*, iii. 198, 199.

† IMPORTATION OF WHEAT AND WHEAT-FLOUR, FROM 1811 TO 1818.

Years	Qrs.	Years	Qrs.
1811	238,366	1817	1,020,949
1812	244,385	1818	1,493,518
1813	423,599		
1814	681,333		
1815	none.		
1816	225,263		
	6,811,946		

Average of six years, 302,491
— PORTER's *Progress of the Nation*, 139.

was owing to the failure of the home market, even then at least double all foreign markets put together, from the effects of a contracted currency and general suspension of credit and ruinous fall of prices. Government acted alike with wisdom and liberality in proposing and carrying a proposal on 28th April, to advance £500,000 in Great Britain, and £250,000 in Ireland, by the issue of Exchequer bills, on proper security, to relieve the general distress—a measure which passed without opposition, and had a surprising effect both in alleviating distress by restoring confidence, and diminishing discontent by showing sympathy.[1]

¹ Parl. Deb. xxxvi. 27, 50; Ann. Reg. 1817, 15, 47; Sidmouth's Life, iii. 198, 199.

17. Finance accounts of 1817, compared with 1816.

This was a very trying year to the exchequer of the empire, for it had to contend at once with a diminution in the ordinary sources of revenue, in consequence of the general distress and the huge gap in the public income, arising from the taking off of the income-tax and war malt-tax in the preceding year. The total revenue, which in 1816 had been £62,264,000, in 1817 fell to £52,195,000; the war taxes amounted only to £14,365,000, instead of £16,665,000, as in the preceding year. The total produce of the taxes, irrespective of loans, was, in 1816, £57,360,000 for Great Britain alone; in 1817, £55,783,259 for Great Britain and Ireland together, even with the aid of arrears of war-taxes. On the other hand, the public expenditure of 1817 amounted to £68,875,000, of which no less than £44,108,000 was for the interest of the public debt and the sinking fund, being for the united kingdom of Great Britain and Ireland.[2] In these circumstances, a very considerable loan, in some form or another, became indispensable; and the Chancellor of the Exchequer provided for the deficiency by issuing Exchequer bills to the extent of £9,000,000, trusting to a gradual improvement in the revenue to make up the remainder. The sum applied this year to the reduction of debt was £14,514,000; so powerful did the sinking fund still continue, notwithstanding all that had been done to cripple its operations, so that after taking into view the sum borrowed, above £5,000,000 was really applied to the reduction of debt.[3]

² Finance Accounts, 1817; Parl. Deb. xxxvi. 2, App.; and xxxvii. 46, App. Porter's Parl. Tables, i. 4.

18. Mr. Peel's Irish Insurrection Act, March 11.

Ireland, being wholly an agricultural country, suffered, as might well be imagined, beyond any other, from the disastrous fall of prices produced by an artificial scarcity of money, and the subsequent rise, owing to a real scarcity in the supply, which had taken place in the last two years. So serious did the agrarian disturbances in that country become that, on the 11th March, Government brought forward a measure intended for their permanent coercion, and which has been attended by the very best effects. It was introduced by Mr. Peel, the Secretary for Ireland, afterward SIR ROBERT PEEL, whose measures will occupy so large and important a place in this history. His character, however, will come in more appropriately after the great changes which he introduced into our commercial policy, and their effects, are considered. The object of the bill was to establish a general police force capable of acting together in any county which the Lord-Lieutenant might direct, that officer having the power of determining what portion of the expense was to be laid on the inhabitants. The measure met with general approbation, and proved so efficacious that Government did not find it necessary to extend the suspension of the Habeas Corpus Act to Ireland, and were able to reduce the military force in that country from 25,000 to 22,000 men, and the artillery from 400 to 200 guns.[1]

¹ Parl. Deb. xxxv. 982; Ann. Reg. 1817, 42.

19. Trial by jury in civil causes in Scotland.

English legislation, in this instance, undoubtedly conferred a very great boon upon Ireland; but the same can not be said of a measure introduced by English influence into Scotland, and which came into operation in this year— viz., the extension of jury trial to civil causes Scotland, from the remotest period, has had laws, institutions, and courts of its own. Its inhabitants may well be proud of them, for the greatest improvements which, during the last eighty years, have been introduced into the law of England, or which its wisest legislators are now anxiously laboring to effect, are nothing but transcripts of the statutes which, a hundred and fifty years before, had been inserted on the statute-book of its northern and comparatively barbarous neighbors.[*] In 1816, however, the Anglomania was very ardent; and, partly to aid the progress of Liberal ideas and the Liberal party in Scotland, partly to procure a dignified and easy retirement for a very amiable man and agreeable companion,[†] who had long been on intimate terms with the Prince-Regent, a bill was passed introducing jury trial, without limitation, in all cases where oral evidence was required or might be anticipated, in Scotland, and establishing a court, specially with an English lawyer at its head, for the disposal of such cases. Great was the joy of the popular leaders in the northern part of the island at this change, which was an entire innovation; for though Scotland, from the earliest ages, had been familiar with jury trial in criminal cases, it had never been known or attempted in civil causes. Unbounded were the anticipations of the blessings to the country, and the training of its inhabitants to their social duties, which would result from the change. In every respect received fair play. The judges on the bench gave it every possible encouragement; the ablest counsel at the bar, and they were

---

* The expenditure of Great Britain and Ireland for 1817 was as follows:

Interest of debt and sinking fund	£44,108,233
Do. on Exchequer bills	1,815,926
Other charges on consolidated fund	2,303,602
Civil government of Scotland	130,646
Lesser expenses	451,403
Navy	6,473,062
Ordnance	1,435,401
Army, deducting troops in France	9,614,861
Foreign loans	33,272
Local issues	42,585
Miscellaneous	2,466,483
	£68,875,477

—Parl. Deb. xxxviii. 26, Parl. Rep.

* See Alison's Essays, vol. ii. 635, "The old Scottish Parliament," where this extraordinary fact is fully demonstrated.

† William Adam, Esq. of Blair-Adam, who was made the head of the new court.

many and powerful at that time, supported it by their energy, and adorned it by their talents; and a clause was introduced into a subsequent act, passed a few years after, authorizing the transference by simple motion of all actions involving parole proof from inferior courts, when the demand of the plaintiff was above £40 sterling.[1] Under these enactments, if the mode of trial had been suited to the people, nearly the whole legal business of the country should have been carried into the jury court.[1]

[1 46 Geo. III. c. 117; and Judicature Act for Scotland.]

Nevertheless, it turned out quite the reverse; and the attempt to introduce jury trial in civil cases into Scotland remains a lasting and instructive proof of the impossibility of transplanting institutions from one country to another without the greatest risk of entire failure, or ruinous disasters to the state into which they are introduced. Jury trial has been, and still is, a total failure in Scotland; and the opinion has become general among its most experienced practitioners, that it is one of the greatest curses that ever has been inflicted upon the country. The reason is, that it is totally at variance with the habits, institutions, and wishes of the people. Jury trial succeeds in England, because it is not the trial of the jury, but the trial of the judge; it has failed in Scotland, because it is not the trial of the judge, but the trial of the jury. Long habit, centuries of practice, have accustomed the English juries to follow the suggestions of the bench; and, except in a few cases which violently excite the public mind, those suggestions are never disregarded. In Scotland, where the native turn of the people is opinionative and pugnacious, and the great object of ambition with all is to get their own way, the first principle with juries has too often been to assert their independence by disregarding the bench, and show their superiority to others by throwing overboard the witnesses. Thus chance and prejudice have come so often to sway their verdicts, that it has passed into a common saying that the issue of a jury trial is as subject to hazard as the game of *rouge-et-noir*, and that nothing is certain in it but delay and expense. The popular leaders have not courage to admit in public the entire failure of their favorite system of training the national mind; but their sense of its unsuitableness to Scotland has already been evinced by an Act of Parliament giving litigants the means of escaping the much-dreaded ordeal;[*] and so strongly has the national feeling on the subject been declared, that after six-and-thirty years of training and bolstering up, the cases tried by jury in all Scotland have dwindled away to twenty or thirty in a year; and instead of the Court of Session being overwhelmed, as was expected, with hundreds of cases brought from the sheriff courts to obtain the blessings of jury trial, the sheriff courts are overwhelmed with as many thousand cases, brought before them to escape the certain expense and uncertain issue of that species of decision.[†]

[* The Act 10 and 11 Victoria, introduced by Lord-Advocate Rutherford, one of the ablest and most accomplished of the Scotch Bar, whom the author is proud to call his early and steady friend.]

[† The cases brought into the sheriff court of Lanark-]

21. Acquittal of Watson and Hone.

The uncertainty of jury trial, in cases which strongly excited the public mind, was strikingly evinced in England itself during this very year. Watson, the father of the culprit who had shot the gunsmith who defended his shop in the Spa-fields riot on December 2d, was tried for high treason at Westminster Hall, and acquitted by the verdict of a London jury. This decision is perhaps not to be regretted, as the acts with which they were charged, though amounting to sedition and riot of the most aggravated kind, could scarcely be held, in reason at least, what ever it might be in law, to amount to high treason, or a design to overturn the Government; and the indictment was brought for the heavier offense, mainly in consequence of the English law recognizing at that period no medium between riot or sedition, which were misdemeanors punishable only by fine and imprisonment, and high treason, which was chastised by death. The wiser and more humane Scotch law recognized transportation as the appropriate punishment for aggravated cases of riot, and sedition bordering on treason—a punishment which has since, by special statute, been introduced into England and Ireland for such offenses. But the same can not be said of another memorable trial, which took place in the same year in the Court of King's Bench—of Mr. Hone, for blasphemous libel. He was tried three times—once before Mr. Justice Abbott, and twice before Chief-Justice Ellenborough—and on all these occasions exhibited a union of self-possession, readiness, and talent, worthy of a better cause.[1] He was on all the three acquitted; on the two last chiefly in consequence of the overbearing manner of the presiding judge, who unfortunately was as remarkable for the haste of his temper as for the power of his intellect.

[1 State Trials xxxii. 471; Hughes 495; vi. 339, 340.]

22. Reflections on this subject. Error at that period in English law.

The contradictory nature of the verdicts obtained in three state trials in the same year, and in regard to crimes of substantially the same description, suggests considerations of the highest importance for the right government of mankind. Brandreth and twenty-three of his associates were sentenced to death at Derby for exactly the same crime for which Watson and his accomplices were acquitted in London. There can be no doubt that there was a great defect both in the law and institutions of the country, when at the same time, and on so momentous a crisis, the same criminals shared so different a fate. Nor is it difficult to see what this defect is. So far as the law is concerned, it consisted chiefly in the absurdity of the English law, which admitted no medium between high treason, punishable with death and its terrible penalties, and sedition, which could be coerced only by fine or imprisonment. It was to evade this difficulty that

shire alone, on written pleadings, are now about 7500 annually; in the small debt court, in the same county, which decides, on oral pleadings, cases under £8 6s. 8d. above 15,000. The county courts of England, which have become so popular, and risen to such importance in so short a time, have mainly succeeded by the suitors avoiding jury trial; and if their jurisdiction is extended, like that of the sheriffs in Scotland, to cases of debt and contract of any amount, it is easy to see they will drain away nearly all the business from Westminster Hall and the circuit assizes.

the astuteness of the English lawyers invented the doctrine of *constructive treason*, or the inference as to an intent to depose, kill, or levy war against the sovereign, from acts of a seditious tendency. But although this doctrine is firmly established in the decisions and *dicta* of the English judges, it has often been resisted by the common sense and just feelings of the English juries, and always combated by all the eloquence and ability of the English bar. It is next to impossible to persuade a jury that the leaders of a mob, which engages in the most outrageous acts of pillage, violence, and depredation, have a design to dethrone or assassinate the sovereign. To get drunk or fill their pockets is probably their ultimatum. It was this which led to Watson's acquittal, as it had done to the escape of Hardy, Thelwall, Horne Tooke, and many of the most dangerous state criminals recorded in English history. Indicted for sedition and riot, they could not by possibility have escaped; and if transported, they would have suffered a punishment suitable, and not excessive, for their crimes. In prosecution, the wisest course always is to select the minor offense, unless the major has, beyond all doubt, been incurred; in legislation, to affix no punishment to crimes but such as the general feelings of the country will permit to be carried rigorously into execution.

23. Good effects of the suspension of the Habeas Corpus Act.

The salutary effect of the suspension of the Habeas Corpus Act in this year, and the death-blow which it gave in a short time to the machinations and efforts of the disaffected, suggests the defect in our institutions to which this distressing uncertainty in the conviction of state crimes is to be ascribed. This is in the idea, so plausible and unhappily so prevalent, that their prosecution should be left to the unaided efforts of the common law. It no doubt sounds well to say that Government seeks for no extraordinary powers, and combats sedition and treason with no other weapons but those of the common and statute law; and loud cheers seldom fail to follow such an announcement in the House of Commons. Nevertheless, it is founded on an entire fallacy; and perhaps nothing has contributed so much to perpetuate disorder, distrust, and consequent misery, both in Great Britain and Ireland, as this miserable delusion. Extraordinary cases require extraordinary remedies; it is in vain to attempt to combat them with ordinary ones. Jury trial, and the trial by that means of subordinate criminals, does very well in common crimes, or passing local disorders; but it is wholly unsuitable to those more serious exigences, when a large party in the state is banded for some common political purpose which is to be brought about by violence and intimidation. To leave every thing to the ordinary remedies of the law in such cases, is to leave it to be worked by men liable to be influenced by prejudice or intimidation. It is, in effect, little else but proclaiming impunity to crimes even of the deepest dye; or wreaking the vengeance of the law upon miserable and deluded followers, while the selfish and guilty leaders, whom it is as impossible to reach by the verdict of a jury as it is easy to reach by an act of the executive, remain wholly untouched.

The suspension of the Habeas Corpus Act, which enables Government to apprehend such leaders upon grounds perfectly sufficient to justify their detention, though their weight would not be admitted by a jury in excited times, is the appropriate remedy. The true object of such apprehension should be, not to imprison the persons seized, but to send them out of the country, under pain of transportation if they returned before the expiration of a limited time. The ostracism of Athens, the banishment of Rome, were wise and humane institutions, had they not been often abused by a tyrant majority; and he has little reason to complain who is intercepted in his projects of revolutionizing his country, and sent, till quieter times return, to ruminate on social change on the banks of the Leman Lake, or dream of human perfectibility among the crowds of Paris.

24. Motion of Mr. Brougham regarding the trade and manufactures of the country.

Although the parliamentary season of 1817 was not distinguished by debates of the same surpassing magnitude and importance as that of the preceding year, yet there were one or two things deserving of notice, as indicating the silent march of thought, and, consequently, of future events which characterized it. The first of these was a motion by Mr. Brougham on the state of the trade and manufactures of the nation, the scope and aim of which will at once appear from the resolutions which he moved, and which were negatived by a majority of 55, the numbers being 118 to 63.* These resolutions, being by inference condemnatory of the neglect alleged to have been evinced by ministers in not securing for the country those commercial advantages which might have been obtained by treaty with foreign nations at the conclusion of the war, were in the main of a party character, and therefore of passing interest. But there were some remarks which fell from the able and inquisitive mind of the mover which were of lasting importance, and, like the first streaks of light in the eastern horizon, betokened the complexion of the day which was beginning to dawn. "The period," said he, "is now arrived when, the war being closed, and prodigious changes having taken place through the world, it becomes absolutely necessary to enter on a careful but fearless revision of our whole commercial system, that we may be enabled safely, yet promptly, to eradicate those faults which the lapse of time has occasioned or displayed; to retrace our steps where we shall find that they have deviated from the line of true policy; to adjust and accommodate our laws to the alteration of circumstances; to abandon many prejudices, alike antiquated and senseless, unsuited

---

* "1. That the trade and manufactures of the country are reduced to a state of such unexampled difficulty as demands the serious attention of this House. 2. That those difficulties are materially increased by the policy pursued with respect to our foreign commerce, and that a revision of this system ought forthwith to be undertaken by the House. 3. That the continuance of these difficulties is materially increased by the severe pressure of taxation under which the country labors, and which ought by every practicable means to be lightened. 4. That the system of foreign policy pursued by his Majesty's ministers has not been such as to obtain for the people of this country those commercial advantages which the influence of Great Britain in foreign courts fairly entitled them to expect."—Mr. Brougham's *Resolutions*, March 13, 1817 *Parl. Debates*, xxxv. 1014.

to the advanced age in which we live, and unworthy of the sound judgment which distinguishes the nation. In the Navigation Laws, in particular, some change is loudly called for. Whatever may have been the good policy of that law when it was first introduced, I am quite clear that we have adhered to it for a century after the circumstances which alone justified its adoption have ceased to exist."[1]

[1] Parl. Deb. xxxv. 1018, 1055

If these ideas of Mr. Brougham were descriptive of the germ of the doctrines, the fruit of Adam Smith's philosophy, which afterward so widely expanded, and occasioned so entire a revolution in the commercial policy of England, other acts of the Legislature at the same time indicated the setting in of an under-current destined to bring nothing but unmixed good to society. Almost unnoticed amid other parliamentary business, which at the time excited much more attention, a bill passed both Houses this year establishing SAVINGS BANKS —institutions which have since spread so widely, and prospered so immensely in all parts of the island, and which, by encouraging habits of prudence, frugality, and self-control among the working classes, and fostering the generous affections in preference to the selfish passions, have gone far to elevate the character of the most deserving of the poor, and to counteract the many causes of debasement which since that time have spread such ruin among them. In the same session, the increasing humanity of the general mind was evinced by strong statements in the House of Commons regarding military flogging, the barbarity of which was daily attracting more attention, so as to foreshadow its abolition at no distant period; and a bill brought in by General Thornton, for abolishing the degrading punishment of flogging in the case of females, received the unanimous assent of the same House.[2]

25. Establishment of Savings Banks, and diminished severity of punishment in criminal cases. May 23.

[2] Parl. Deb. xxxvi. 833, 294, 932.

26. Return of Mr. Canning from Lisbon, and death of Mr. Ponsonby and Mr. Horner.

The respective balance of parties in the House of Commons was materially affected this year by the return to the parliamentary arena of the most eloquent man on one side, and the death of two, not the least eminent, on the other. Mr. Canning—who, ever since his rupture with Lord Castlereagh in 1810, had been out of office, and since 1814 in a sort of honorable banishment as embassador at Lisbon—returned to England on the invitation of the Prince-Regent, and accepted the office of President of the Board of Control, vacant by the death of the Earl of Buckinghamshire. His name will occupy hereafter a prominent place; his deeds and speeches strongly arrest the attention in the course of this history. In June, 1816, Mr. Ponsonby, who had long discharged with zeal, ability, and straightforward honor, the arduous duties of leader of the Opposition, died; and his lamented loss was shortly succeeded by that of Mr. Horner, a much younger, but more rising and promising man, who expired at Pisa, whither he had gone on account of a pulmonary complaint, on 8th February, 1817.[3]

[3] Canning's Life, Works, i. 105; Horner's Life, i. 412.

Mr. HORNER was born in 1778, passed the bar in Edinburgh in 1800, was called to the English bar in 1807, and entered the House of Commons in 1806. The son of a respectable linen-draper in Edinburgh, he owed his elevation in no degree to aristocratic or parliamentary influences, so powerful at that period in procuring advancement for others into situations for which they were not fitted by nature. Like Mr. Canning, Sir S. Romilly, Lord Eldon, and many of the greatest men whom the country can boast, he was the architect of his own fortune, and entered on his public career from no other influence but that arising from his known and acknowledged abilities. His first seat was for a Treasury borough (St. Ives), for which, by the influence of Lord Kinnaird and the Whig Government then in power, he was elected in June, 1806; so that, like all the other great men of the day, he owed his entry into public life to the nomination boroughs. So great were his abilities, and so high the respect entertained for his character, that, had he lived, he would, beyond all doubt, have been the Chancellor of the Exchequer when the Whigs came into power in November, 1830, and possibly risen to still higher situations during the long continuance of that party in office for the next twenty years.[1]

27. Mr. Horner's life and character.

[1] Horner's Life, i. 379.

He was the most intellectual and profound of that remarkable school of eminent men who were educated and entered life together at that period in Edinburgh. Less eloquent and discursive than Brougham, less aerial and elegant than Jeffrey, he was a much deeper thinker than either, and brought more systematically the powers of a clear understanding and logical reasoning to bear upon a limited number of subjects, to which he directed his attention. These he mastered with consummate ability. Many of his papers on the corn-laws and the currency in the *Edinburgh Review*, as well as his speeches in Parliament on the same subjects, are models of clear and accurate reasoning. Yet must history confess with regret that he stopped short in the admirable career on which he had entered, and bequeathed to posterity a host of errors when he was on the very verge of the most important truths. He was on the edge of important discoveries in the most abstruse branch of political science, to which he had been led by the native vigor of his understanding and the clearness of his perception, when he was turned aside and riveted in error by the influence of party. He was the main author of the Bullion Report of 1810, and he bequeathed the adoption of its principles to the nation by the bill of 1819, restoring cash payments. What those effects were will abundantly appear in the sequel, and need not be here anticipated. It is sufficient to observe, as a curious proof of the warping even of the strongest intellects by the chain of party,[*] that while he clearly saw and has ably illustrated the obvious truths—that the great rise of prices during the war was owing to the copious issue

28. His character as an orator and political philosopher.

[*] He seriously complained to Mr. Jeffrey, then its editor, that the *Edinburgh Review* was too independent, and not sufficiently Whiggish—a charge which has never before or since, it is believed, been brought against that celebrated journal.—COCKBURN's *Life of Jeffrey*, i. 458.

of paper currency, and that the greatest danger to be apprehended on the return of peace was the impossibility of discharging the debts, public and private, contracted during a plentiful circulating medium, with the resources of a contracted one—he could discern no other mode of averting these dangers but by instantly rushing into the contracted currency; and that while he was well aware that variations in the amount of the circulating medium are the greatest calamity which can befall a mercantile nation, the only way in which he deemed it practicable to avert them was to base it entirely on gold, the most eagerly desired, easily transported, and therefore evanescent of earthly things.

29. Death of the Princess Charlotte, Nov. 6.

The close of this year was marked by a most melancholy event, which, more than any other in the recollection of man, wrung with anguish the heart of the whole nation. This was the death of the Princess Charlotte of Wales, who expired, after severe and protracted suffering, on the 6th November. This charming princess, whose beauty, high spirit, and amiable manners had endeared her to the whole people, had lived in domestic felicity, known only by never-failing deeds of kindness, since her marriage in May of the preceding year. She was understood to be in the way of giving an heir to the monarchy; and as the direct line of succession depended on the success of her accouchement, the attention of the nation was turned with the most intense anxiety to the coming event from which so much was hoped. It came at last, but the angel of death at the same time entered the bridal chamber. So long and severe were the sufferings of the princess, during a protracted labor of forty-eight hours, that it became necessary to sacrifice the infant—an uncommonly fine and healthy prince—to her preservation; and the painful sacrifice was made in vain. Such was the exhaustion of the royal mother, after the delivery was over, that she sank rapidly, and expired a few hours after. So great was his despair at this calamitous event, that the principal medical attendant of her Royal Highness, in a fit of insanity or despair, committed suicide a short time afterward.[1]

Ann. Reg., 1817; Chronicle, 109; Hughes, vi. 346.

30. Universal grief of the nation at this event.

No words can paint the universal consternation and grief which seized the entire nation on this calamitous event, which buried an illustrious princess, the sole daughter of England, and a royal posterity in a single tomb. Nothing comparable to it had been seen in the country since the head of Charles I. fell upon the scaffold. Then was seen how universal and deep-seated is the loyalty of the British heart, and how strong and indelible the chords which bind the people to their sovereign. Every house, from the ducal palace to the peasant's cottage, was filled with mourning; tears were seen in every eye; the bereavement was felt by all with the intensity of domestic affliction. Business was generally suspended; scarce a word was spoken even by the most intimate friends when they met in the streets—they pressed hands and went on in silence. The hum of men ceased; no sound was heard but the mournful clang of the church-bells, which from morn till night gave forth their melancholy peal; minute-guns were fired from all the batteries and ships—

"The flag was hoisted half-mast high,
A mournful signal on the main;
Seen only when the illustrious die,
Or are in glorious battle slain."

A royal proclamation ordered a general mourning. The injunction was unnecessary; every human being above the rank of a pauper spontaneously assumed the garb of woe. On the 18th November, when the funeral at Windsor took place with great solemnity, every church and chapel in the United Kingdom was opened and filled with mourning multitudes, whose grief could find no other alleviation but in its united expression. Those who consider loyalty as a merely instinctive feeling, which wears out and becomes extinct in the progress of society, with the enlightenment of the general mind, and the popularizing of institutions, would do well to contemplate this memorable event, and to search the annals of the world for a parallel to the grief which then wrung the British heart among rude and uneducated nations, the most remarkable for attachment to the throne.

31. Improved condition of the country in the end of 1817 and spring of 1818.

The social condition of the country and its general prosperity were much improved in the year 1818. The change had begun in the middle of the preceding year, and arose chiefly from prices of agricultural produce having so much risen, and the home market for our manufactures having in consequence so much improved from the increased ability of the rural population to purchase them. The Funds, that sure test of public prosperity, rose 30 per cent.; in 1817, the Three per Cents. ascended from 62, in January, 1817, to 83 in December of the same year. The bankruptcies in England, which in February, 1816, were 209, were reduced in September to 61: the total was 1575 in the year, being a decrease of 454 from the preceding year, when they had been 2029.[1] These unmistakable symptoms of general amelioration continued throughout 1818. The Funds maintained the level they had reached on the close of the preceding year; and the bankruptcies were 519 less; they sank to 1056, being only half of what they had been in the year 1816.[2] The revenue, without the imposition of any new taxes, rose above £1,700,000; and the money applied to the reduction of debt, which in 1817 had been £14,514,000, rose in 1818 to £15,339,000, being somewhat above the loans of the year.[3] Wheat, on an average of the year, sold at 96s.—a high price, indeed, but a considerable reduction from the preceding year, when it had been 116s.; and such was the affluence of the Bank of England, and the general confidence reposed in that establishment, that the Chancellor of the Exchequer, in the last discussion on the subject in 1817, boasted, not without reason, that the bank had begun voluntarily to resume payments in

[1] Ann. Reg. 1817, 258; App. to Chron.

[2] Ann. Reg. 1818, 365; App. to Chron.

---

* Net revenue of Great Britain in 1817....£52,055,913
          "   "   in 1818.... 53,747,595
—Porter's Parl. Tables.

cash;¹ that nothing would prevent the restriction of cash payments from expiring in July, 1818; and that even in foreign countries the notes of the bank were taken in preference to cash.

¹ Parl. Deb. xxxvii. 115; Hughes, vi. 237.

The cause of this great improvement in the affairs of the country, and, of consequence, of the Government, was the continued suspension of cash payments to the 5th July, 1818, according to the act of 1817, already noticed.² As the dreadful crash and distress of 1816 had arisen from the sudden and prodigious contraction of the country bankers' issues, which took place from the prospect of immediately being obliged to pay their notes in cash, which at once reduced their circulation from £22,700,000 in 1814 to £15,894,000 in 1816; so the postponement of cash payments by the bill of 1816 had a directly opposite effect. The circulation both of the Bank of England and the country banks increased rapidly with the period during which cash payments were postponed, and in 1818 it had become above £6,000,000 more than it had been in 1816.* The necessary effect of this increase in the circulation was a restoration of confidence, a general rise of prices, augmented undertakings by capitalists, and improved comfort among the laboring classes. The greater activity thus communicated to trade appeared in the increase of the exports, which rose in 1818 to £45,180,000 declared value, from £40,180,000 in the preceding year; but the vast addition made to the well-being of all classes was evinced still more clearly by the great increase of the imports, which rose from £27,000,000 in 1816 to £36,000,000 in 1818.†

32. Cause of this increased prosperity.

² Ante, c. ii. § 45.

33. Steps of the Bank toward cash payments.

So confident were the directors of the Bank of England in the continuance of these favorable circumstances, and of their ability to continue cash payments, that in January, 1817, they issued a notice that they were prepared to make payments in cash of outstanding notes of a certain description, amounting to about £1,000,000 sterling. Gold was so plentiful that it had fallen to £3 18s. 6d. an ounce, and very little of the cash at that rate was taken up. The success of this experiment induced the directors to issue a notice, in October, 1817, that they would pay cash for notes of every description issued prior to January 1, 1817. But the result of this experiment was very different, and gave a premonitory warning of what might be expected to ensue if the suspension of cash payments was permanently closed. The deficient harvest of the preceding year had caused a considerable importation of grain, amounting to above 1,500,000 quarters of wheat alone—a quantity unexampled in those days; and to meet the bills drawn for payment of their price, and also supply the wants of the numerous English who were flocking to the Continent in search of health, amusement, or economy, and pay up a French loan of £5,000,000, a very great drain for gold set in upon the bank, and the sum paid in cash for these notes before the end of the year amounted to £2,600,000. This alarming drain, and the total disappearance from the country¹ of the coin thus withdrawn from the coffers of the bank, at length convinced Ministers of the impolicy of enforcing the return to cash payments on 5th July, 1818, as it then stood regulated by law, and led to important debates in both Houses of Parliament, which threw increasing light on that all-important subject.

¹ Ann. Reg 1818, 68; Part. Deb. xxxviii. 1230, 1233.

On the part of Opposition, it was urged by Mr. Tierney, Lord Althorpe, and Sir H. Parnell: "We have now, at the close of the war, in round numbers, £800,000,000 of funded, and £40,000,000 of unfunded debt — rather an appalling prospect, against which it is futile to set off our Sinking Fund of £14,000,000, since, although we keep up that fund, it is done only by borrowing money annually, in Exchequer bills or otherwise, to nearly an equal amount. The advantageous terms on which it appears a loan could now be negotiated proves, indeed, the present prosperity of the country. But is there any man in his senses who would maintain that this prosperity should be based on a circulation not convertible into specie? On all sides it would be heard, God forbid! The suspension of cash payments was never defended but as a measure of necessity, justified by an unprecedented combination of circumstances. How, then, has it happened that, in the third year of peace, the same measure is necessary, which was only justified by the extraordinary pressure of a most extraordinary war? Why is the pledge given as to the return to cash payments in July, 1818, not to be redeemed? It may be true that British capitalists, from a superabundance of money, have engaged largely in foreign loans, and that seventy-nine thousand travelers were gratifying their desires by going abroad; but are such trivial circumstances to be gravely stated as grounds for an entire subversion of our monetary system? The suspension by Mr. Pitt in 1797 was expressly rested on the most overpowering necessity—a general run upon the bank, which brought it to the brink of ruin —a universal panic and hoarding in the country, and vast loans in specie to foreign countries. Can there be a more complete contrast than this state of matters affords, to the present time, when we are at profound peace with all the world, when there were no foreign subsidies, no threat of invasion, but increasing and apparently lasting prosperity?

34. Argument for the resumption of cash payments by the Opposition. May 1, 1818.

"Did not the House of Commons, two years ago, when there really was a panic and great distress in the country, even then enter into a solemn pledge

35. Continued

Years.	Bank of England Notes.	Country Banks.	Total.
1814	£24,801,080	£22,700,000	£47,501,080
1815	27,261,650	19,011,000	46,272,650
1816	27,013,620	15,096,000	42,109,620
1817	27,397,900	15,894,000	43,291,900
1818	27,771,070	20,507,000	48,278,070

—Alison's *Europe*, c. xcvi. Appendix.

† Years.	Exports, official Value, British, Irish, and Colonial.	Imports, declared Value.
1816	£49,197,850	£27,431,604
1817	50,404,111	30,834,299
1818	53,560,338	36,889,182

Porter's *Progress of the Nation*, third edition, 356.

that cash payments were to be resumed in next July! And have we not been told that such is the confidence in the bank, and the public confidence in its solidity, that cash payments to a certain extent have voluntarily been resumed on the part of that establishment! Is it expedient, is it decorous, under such prosperous circumstances, to violate a pledge given in such adverse ones? The bank directors profess their willingness to resume cash payments, and have evinced the sincerity of their declarations by their voluntary acts; where then is the necessity for violating the faith of Parliament! Is the House satisfied that all that has been advanced by the Bullion Committee should be set aside? Is there any one who doubts that an excessive issue of paper must have an effect on the price of gold? The market price of gold is at present four shillings an ounce above the Mint price; is not that difference to be ascribed rather to the excess of paper in circulation than the foreign loans now in course of payment? Supposing the loan to France is £10,000,000, and the money required by travelers and foreign indemnities £20,000,000 more, still a large part of this sum would be sent out in goods, and a still larger in advances by foreign capitalists. But even supposing the whole were sent out in gold—would that occasion a run upon the bank? Would it not soon improve the exchanges, and, by rendering gold dear in this country, quickly bring it back, and furnish the bank with the means of replenishing its coffers? On every ground, then, there is an urgent necessity for an inquiry into the circumstances of the bank; for if it can resume cash payments, it should be constrained immediately to do so; if it can not, the public should be informed to what cause the inability is owing, and what prospect there is of cash payments *ever* being resumed.

36. Continued.
"There are some persons in this country who anticipate all sorts of horrors from the resumption of cash payments— that nobody would receive rents, the funds be reduced to zero, and a general bankruptcy ensue. There is every reason to believe that these apprehensions are either altogether unfounded, or greatly exaggerated. If cautiously gone about, it would be attended with little or no disadvantage. But even if the evils represented were in a great degree well founded, would they not be preferable to the state of uncertainty in which mercantile speculations of all sorts are kept, by the uncertainty which exists as to the resumption of cash payments? It would be better to declare at once that the bank is never to resume payments in specie, than to go on every year, postponing the return from year to year, and, in consequence alternately fostering speculation by an excessive issue of paper, and ruining the speculators by its sudden contraction! The only criterion by which it can be known whether or not an issue of paper has become excessive, is its convertibility into cash. When the obligation to pay every note issued in specie is taken away, this criterion is entirely lost; there is no longer any restriction on the amount of issues; and the enormous profits accruing from them to the bank will soon render them excessive.

"Recent events have too clearly illustrated the reality of this danger. In 1816, the average circulation of the Bank of England was £26,500,000; in 1817 it was £28,200,000—so that there was an increase in that species of paper alone of two millions; although the resources and loans of 1816 were £82,000,000, and in 1817 only £69,000,000. The average circulation of country banks before 1816 was £21,000,000; it was reduced by fully a third during that year, but it had been increased by the same amount in 1817; so that, between the Bank of England and the country banks, there had been an increase in the circulation in one year of no less than £9,000,000! Was there any intelligible cause, any plausible excuse even, for such an excessive issue—the result evidently of the postponement of the obligation to pay in specie? Was there any man of common honesty who could deny, in these circumstances, that inquiry is necessary? What has become of all this money? Could it have any other effect but raising the price of every thing? Is not the great rise which has taken place in the Funds in the last year entirely to be ascribed to that circumstance? And what limit can be assigned to future danger, when in so short a time, and under circumstances so little justifying it, so excessive an over-issue has taken place?"†

37. Concluded.

† Part. Deb. xxxviii. 435, 454.

On the other hand, it was answered by the Chancellor of the Exchequer, Mr. Huskisson, and Mr. Thornton: "The grounds on which the appointment of a committee to inquire into the affairs of the bank are rested are entirely fallacious. The internal state of the country had never been so distressed as it was in 1816, and it had never revived so rapidly as it did in the last half of 1817 and first months of 1818. The issues of country banks had increased by at least £6,000,000 during that period; but why had they increased? Simply because the great impulse communicated to the agriculture, trade, and manufactures of the country during that period called for an enlargement of the issue to carry it on. The difference between the market and the Mint price of gold was erroneously considered as a test of the superabundance of paper in the home market; but it in reality arose from a very different cause—the gold which was sent out of the country to pay up foreign loans, and meet the wants of British travelers. The experience of late years decisively proved that the doctrine of the Bullion Committee in 1810, that the difference between the market and the Mint price of gold was owing to an over-issue of paper, and was measured by its amount, was decisively disproved by the facts which had since occurred. In 1814 the bank issues were £23,600,000, and the market price of gold was £5 10s. per ounce; in 1815 the bank paper was £26,300,000, and the price of gold had fallen to £4 6s. 6d. per ounce; proving that the price of gold was owing to the enhanced demand for it on the Continent to meet the exigences of foreign war, and not to any excess in the domestic circulation.

38. Answer by the Ministers.

"The immense loans which the French Government has been obliged to contract in the present year, amounting to no less than £30,000,000 sterling, most of which would be negotiated in this country, necessarily occasioned a very great drain of gold

39. Continued.

from this country, for which it behooved the directors of the bank to make provision. Add to it is a loan of £5,000,000, actually negotiating at this moment in London. These loans were eight times the amount of the Austrian loans, in 1796, of £1,500,000 which the directors at that period, by a solemn resolution laid before Mr. Pitt, declared would, if repeated, prove fatal to the bank. It is true the postponement of cash payments for a year is a deviation from what was formerly proposed and intended; but if circumstances change, must not the corresponding measures either for commercial transactions or foreign loans. No doubt, by an unlimited issue of gold from the bank, provided they could get it to issue, it might be possible to turn the present adverse exchanges in favor of this country. But where was the bank to find gold adequate to counterbalance the greater part of a loan of £30,000,000, all payable in specie, which was to go from this country?

"The proper time for resuming cash payments is when the exchanges are at or above par. The great danger of a paper circulation is its tendency to increase itself, from the profit with which such increase is attended to the issuers; and if the bank had been prepared with gold, it would have been desirable to have returned to cash payments last year; but this year the thing was impossible. The exchanges, from the large importations of foreign grain, and the immense foreign loans negotiated in this country, were so much against us, that to do so at this time was out of the question. The loans were for the most part remitted to the Continent in bills of exchange; and it is no doubt true that a considerable part of such bills may be paid in goods manufactured in this country. But they can not *all* be so paid, especially when loans to a very large amount have to be remitted; because the foreign recipients of the loans can not take an unlimited quantity of goods; they can take only so much as their inhabitants are willing to purchase and able to pay for. The balance, which is often very large, must all be paid in money; and the fact of the exchanges being now so much against us, proves that the foreign markets are already overstocked with our manufactures, and that the only thing they will take is our gold, for which there is a never-failing demand."*

_{40.} Concluded.

_{1 Parl. Deb. xxxviii. 435, 439.}

* On this occasion Mr. Huskisson used these expressions, which subsequent events have rendered prophetic: "The facility enjoyed by Great Britain of extending her paper circulation, has had the like effect that had been found to arise from the discovery of the mines of America; for, by *increasing the circulating medium over the world to the extent of forty millions*, it proportionally facilitated the means of barter, and gave a stimulus to industry. In proportion, however, as the bank found it necessary to purchase gold on the Continent to meet its engagements with the public here, the circulating medium of the Continent was diminished; and, as the Continental States did not enjoy the credit possessed by this country, and were thereby debarred from increasing their paper circulation, the result was discernible in the great confusion and deterioration of property that had taken place on the Continent during the last two years. Indeed, he had no hesitation in saying that *much of the distress that had prevailed upon the* Continent was fairly attributable to the purchase of bullion by the Bank of England. The increase of the circulating medium of this country has given a great stimulus to its arts and industry; it was only to be lamented that, while the general appearance of the country had so much improved, the comforts and rewards of the laborers had been much reduced. The population of the country had increased in proportion to the rapidity with which the circulating medium had advanced; but though there was an increased demand for labor, its wages, measured by the existing price of grain, were diminished. But the general improvement of the country, under the extended currency, is proved by facts beyond all dispute. From 1654 to 1750 there had not been one bill of inclosure—and this country imported corn; from 1754 to 1796, during which there had been a rapid increase of the circulating medium by imports from the mines of America, bills of inclosure to the number of 3500 had been passed, and this country had become an exporting country. *It is idle to talk of the resumption of cash payments producing any serious convulsion*; at the same time, nothing has tended more to create alarm than the clamor raised on the subject of the resumption of cash payments by the bank. It was notorious that in Scotland, even previous to the restriction upon cash payments at the Bank of England, the principal currency was in paper, and that there was very little gold currency in that country. Such, indeed, was the happy system of the chartered banks in Scotland, that, even in the years 1793 and 1796, when the pressure was felt as so distressing in England, no *inconvenience was felt in that country from want of a metallic currency.* Nevertheless, he felt that it was the duty of the bank to resume cash payments as soon as possible; and he was convinced that, by a gradual, temperate, and cautious conduct, the resumption might take place *without risking any material alteration in the affairs of the country.*"—Mr. HUSKISSON's *Speech*, May 1, 1818; *Parl. Deb.* xxxviii. 490, 491. It is hard to find a speech in which more valuable and decisive facts are adduced on one side, or more erroneous opinions, notwithstanding, adhered to on the other, than in this very remarkable oration.

Upon this debate the House of Commons supported Ministers by a majority of 65—the numbers being 164 to 99. The Committee moved for by Mr. Tierney was refused, and the suspension of cash payments was continued till 5th July, 1819.

Thus, like every thing relating to the currency and, in consequence, general credit and prosperity of the country, was by far the most important measure of this session of Parliament. But others deserving of mention also took place. Under the suspension of the Habeas Corpus Act a great number of persons had been arrested under warrants from the Home Office in the preceding year; and one of the earliest measures of the Government, in the session of 1818, was to move for a committee to report, with a view to a bill of indemnity to Ministers for their proceedings in regard to the persons who had been imprisoned without being brought to trial. In the debates which ensued on this subject, the most vehement attacks were made on Ministers, on the ground of their having been, in fact, the authors of the conspiracy in the preceding year, by the employment of spies to excite it. Lord Sidmouth, in reply, rested on the information transmitted to Government by the highest magistrates and functionaries in the kingdom; in particular, Earl Fitzwilliam, the Whig lord-lieutenant of the West Riding of Yorkshire, as to the disturbances being the result of a settled conspiracy to overturn the Government, and the impossibility of obtaining the requisite information to trace it out without the employment of agents who might get into the confidence of the disaffected. After very warm debates, the

_{41. Bill of Indemnity for persons seized under the suspension of the Habeas Corpus Act.}

bill of indemnity passed both Houses by large majorities—that in the Commons being 82 to 23—in the Lords, 93 to 27; the suspension of the Habeas Corpus Act was allowed to expire on the 1st March; and Lord Sidmouth communicated the gratifying information that any further continuance of it was no longer required, and that only two persons who had been apprehended under it remained still in custody.* The conduct of Lord Sidmouth during this trying time was the subject of vehement party condemnation at the time it was going on; but, like all other conduct which is at once judicious, necessary, and intrepid, it obtained in the end the applause even of its most impassioned opponents; and his biographer may well pride himself on the testimony borne to it, twenty-five years after, by one of the most determined of his parliamentary antagonists.¹†

¹ Parl. Deb. xxxvii. 338, 395; Sidmouth's Life, iii. 213, 215, 217, 221, 225.

42. Military and naval forces voted, and revenue.

The troops voted for the army in 1818 were 113,640 men, including those in France, being a reduction of 22,000 from those voted in the preceding year; and 20,000, including 6000 marines, only were proposed for the navy. The great reduction of these numbers, compared with the establishment which had been kept up at the conclusion of the war, which was 150,000 soldiers and 39,000 sailors, showed how much the resources of Government had been hampered by the distresses of the country, and how much the abolition of the income-tax—as Lord Castlereagh had predicted it would—disabled the country from maintaining the establishment called for by its multifarious and widespread dependencies. The average number of notes of the Bank of England, from January to June, 1817, had been £27,339,000; but from July to December it rose to £29,210,000, and continued above £28,000,000 through 1818. This considerable increase in the circulating medium was attended by a corresponding rise in the revenue, and increase in the prosperity of the kingdom. The entire income of the United Kingdom of Great Britain and Ireland for 1818 was £68,294,568, of which £10,850,000 was loans or advances on Exchequer bills, leaving £57,444,568 for the net revenue from taxation

—a great increase from the preceding year, when it had been £55,783,000 only.¹ The cheering effect of this change appeared in a still more decisive manner in the state of the Sinking Fund, which now, for the first time since the peace, began to exceed the loan borrowed during the year, and so to afford a prospect of a real reduction of the debt. The surplus of the Consolidated Fund this year was no less than £15,038,000, and the loans contracted £10,850,000, leaving a balance of £4,188,000 really paid off. In addition to this, £27,000,000 of Exchequer bills were funded this year, the money for which was borrowed at the very moderate rate of £4 per cent. In the course of his statement on the Budget, the Chancellor of the Exchequer mentioned that such had been the progress of the Sinking Fund, that since 1st November, 1815, and 1st June, 1818, it had paid off £50,000,000 of stock, and it was now above £15,000,000 a year. The entire sum paid off by the Sinking Fund, since its commencement by Mr. Pitt in 1786, was £347,119,000—a fact speaking volumes as to the wisdom of his finance system, and the wonders which it would have effected toward the extinction of the debt had it been adhered to by his successors.²

¹ Ann. Reg. iv. 18.

² Finance Accounts; Parl Deb. xl. 32, 39, App. and xxxiv. 212, 225.

The expenditure of 1818, as ascertained by the accounts laid before Parliament in 1819, amounted to £68,821,000, of which no less than £44,800,000 was for the interest of the debt and Sinking Fund. This was a trifling reduction since the preceding year, when the expenditure had been £68,875,000.* The accounts of exports, imports, and shipping exhibited a steady and gratifying increase since the year of woeful depression, 1816, which will best appear by comparing the returns for these different years together.† The increase of imports and shipping inward, it is to be particularly observed, in three years, is more than twice as great as that of the total exports, home and colonial; for the shipping had advanced from 17 to 26, and the imports from 30 to 40, but the exports only from 51 to 56. As this took place at a time when industry in all its branches at home was adequately protected by fiscal duties, this affords decisive evidence that the internal consumption

43. Expenditure, and increase of exports, imports, and shipping, in 1817 and 1818.

---

* "I can not conclude without calling to your recollection that all this tumultuous assembling, rioting, and so forth, is not the consequence of distress, want of employment, scarcity or dearness of provisions, but is the offspring of a revolutionary spirit; and nothing short of a complete change in the established institutions of the country is in the contemplation of their leaders and agitators."—Earl FITZWILLIAM to Lord SIDMOUTH, 17th Dec. 1817. Sidmouth's Life, iii. 211.

† "As I have been correcting the press of the third volume of our dear friend Lord Wellesley's memoirs, in the third volume of my 'Statesmen,' I thought your lordship would like to see the just, and most just, tribute which I have paid to your public conduct. I well know that nothing would have gratified more him who unceasingly ascribed so much of his success to your wise and generous support."—Lord BROUGHAM to Lord SIDMOUTH, Sept. 24, 1843. Sidmouth's Memoirs, iii. 222. The passage alluded to was in these words: "Lord Wellesley was only prevailed on to retain his position in India, at a most critical period of Indian history, by the earnest intercession of Mr. Pitt's Government, who gave him, as Lord Sidmouth did, with his characteristic courage, sagacity, and firmness, their steady support. Lord Wellesley always gratefully acknowledged the merits and services of Lord Sidmouth, to whom, through life, he had been much attached."—Statesmen of the Time of George III iii. 304.

* The items were as follow:

Interest of debt and Sinking Fund	£46,849,152
Civil List, &c.	2,336,079
Civil Government of Scotland	129,627
Other payments out of Consolidated Fund	483,472
Navy	6,521,714
Ordnance	1,467,807
Army	8,517,644
Foreign Loans	206
Local Issues	60,078
Miscellaneous	2,020,891
	£68,968,670
Deduct loan to East India Company	144,636
Total	£68,824,157

—Ann. Reg. 1819, 408—Parl. Accounts.

†

3 Years ending 5th January	Exports, official value, Home and Colonial, Great Britain.	Imports, official value, Home and Colonial, Great Britain.	Shipping onward.
1817	£51,243,574	£30,105,566	1,795,138 tons.
1818	53,123,202	33,965,232	2,070,132 "
1819	56,854,319	40,157,024	2,618,854 "

—Parl. Accounts, in Reg. 1819, 404, 407.

of the country had undergone even a greater increase than its manufactures for the export sale, and that agriculture and the staple branches of domestic industry had, in a great degree, recovered from the state of depression in which, from the ruinous effect of low prices, they were sunk in the first year after the war.

44. Grant of a million to build new churches.

Notwithstanding the still laboring condition of the finances of the empire, in consequence of the loss of the income-tax, Ministers had the courage to propose, and the House of Commons the virtue to vote, a grant of £1,000,000 sterling toward the building of new churches, chiefly in the manufacturing districts. The necessity of this was very apparent; for, in many counties, hundreds of thousands of persons had, within the last quarter of a century, been suddenly huddled together, for whom the old parish accommodation, calculated for perhaps an hundredth part of their amount, was wholly inadequate.* The necessary result of this was, on the one hand, a vast increase of dissent to meet the religious wants of such great and growing communities; and, on the other, a still greater increase of the profligate and sensual class, the parent of crime, which lived altogether without God in the world. The money was raised by Exchequer bills, and was aided, to the amount of above thirty per cent., by munificent subscriptions of private individuals; yet all fell lamentably short of the necessities of the case. There is no solid foundation for the objection that such grants, being for the promotion of a particular religion, should not come from the public funds, which are obtained by assessment from all sects. It is the duty of Government to provide for the religious instruction of the destitute poor who can not pay for it themselves, and the building of additional churches is the first step in the discharge of that duty. The religious accommodation provided should always be in the established faith of the country, being the faith of the majority of the whole inhabitants, and which the nation has deemed the true one—just as the defenders of the country should be arrayed under the national banners and in the national uniform, whatever their private opinions may be. For those who do not approve of it, and prefer the luxury of dissent, every possible facility, in the way of private establishment, should be given; but the state can, with propriety, from the public funds, support only its own spiritual militia.[1]

[1] Parl. Deb. xxxvii. 1118, xxxviii. 426, 430, 462.

45. Treaty with Spain for the abolition of the slave trade. Sept. 23, 1817

Another benevolent and most praiseworthy attempt was made in this session of Parliament, which, unfortunately, was not attended with the same beneficial results. This was a treaty with Spain, concluded on the 23d September, 1817, for putting an end to the slave-trade, which gave rise, in the next session, to interesting debates in both Houses of Parliament. By this treaty, in consideration of the sum of £400,000, to be paid by Great Britain on the 20th February, 1818, as an indemnity to the persons engaged in that traffic, the court of Madrid engaged, from and after the 30th May, 1820, that the slave-trade should be absolutely abolished; and that, from that date, "it shall not be lawful for any of the subjects of the crown of Spain to purchase slaves, or to carry on the slave-trade on *any part of the coast of Africa*, upon any pretext, or in any manner whatever." It was declared unlawful, from the *date of the treaty*, for Spanish ships to carry on the slave-trade on any part of the coast of Africa to the north of the equator; and a reciprocal right of search on the part of ships of war of both countries was expressly provided for. A similar treaty for the entire suppression of the slave-trade was concluded with the King of the Netherlands;[2] and tribunals, composed of judges from both countries, were appointed to adjudicate upon the seized vessels; and a bill passed establishing similar mixed tribunals for vessels seized belonging to Portugal, which had already consented to the abolition. It will appear in the sequel how these treaties, conceived in a noble spirit, were evaded, and how long, and with what cruelty, the slave-trade was afterward carried on by the merchants of every part of the Spanish peninsula. But it must ever be considered a glorious circumstance in the history of Great Britain that she took the lead in this great deliverance; that she set the example by first abolishing the odious traffic in her own dominions; that she contributed a large sum, when embarrassed in finance and overburdened with debt, to purchase its abolition in foreign states; and that, if it still continued to be carried on under their flags, it was in opposition to her example, and notwithstanding the utmost efforts on her part to prevent it.[3]

[2] May 11, 1818.

[3] Parl. Deb. xxxvii. 67, and xxxviii. 996, 1039.

46. Alien Bill, and Mr. Brougham's committee concerning charities.

The Alien Bill—which gives Government the power to apprehend and send out of the country foreigners residing in it, who may be engaged in machinations to disturb the public tranquillity in this or the adjoining states— was, notwithstanding the most violent resistance on the part of the Opposition, continued for two years longer. It was justly deemed unsafe and unwise to let a knot of foreign refugees make London their head-quarters for rekindling the flames of war on the Continent; and the recent example of the return of Napoleon from Elba afforded decisive evidence of the disastrous results to which the toleration

---

* It was stated by the Chancellor of the Exchequer, in proposing this grant, that the proportion of persons who could be accommodated in the existing churches and chapels, to the existing population in the under-mentioned towns and districts, stood as follows :

	Population in 1811.	Sittings in Churches.	Deficiency.
London	1,129,451	151,536	977,915
York diocese	720,091	139,103	720,091
Chester diocese	1,286,702	228,696	1,016,006
Winchester diocese	325,209	59,503	265,706
Liverpool	94,376	21,000	73,376
Manchester	79,459	10,950	68,509
Marylebone	75,624	8,700	66,924

—*Parl. Debates*, xxxvii. 1119, 1122.

See also a very interesting publication on church accommodation, by the Rev. M. Yates, replete with valuable information.

A parliamentary return in this year showed that there were in England and Wales—

Benefices .... 10,421 } for a population above
Churches and chapels 11,743 } 10,000,000.
Glebe houses fit for residence 5117
Benefices under £100 a year 2274
Do. under £150 a year 3503

—HUGHES, vi. 362, and *Parl. Rep.* No. 79, 1818.

of even a small body of such conspirators might lead. Mr. Brougham took an active part in opposing the bill, but it was carried by a majority of 65—the numbers being 94 to 29. Mr. Brougham found a much more worthy field for his talents in the report of a committee, which he had succeeded in getting appointed, on the charitable trusts and establishments of Great Britain for the education of the poor. The report, which was a most valuable and elaborate one, bore testimony to the great and increasing thirst of the poor in all situations for education, and the praiseworthy zeal with which the inquiries of the committee had been seconded by the clergy of all denominations in every part of the island; but stated, at the same time, "that a very great deficiency exists in the means of educating the poor, wherever the population is thin and scattered over country districts. The efforts of individuals combined in societies are almost all confined to populous places. Nothing, in such situations, can supply the deficiency but the adoption, under certain material modifications, of the parish-school system, so usefully established in the northern part of the island ever since the latter part of the seventeenth century." There can be no doubt of the justice of these observations; but it is a most extraordinary circumstance that, notwithstanding their undeniable weight, no provision for a general system of parochial education has yet been made in England, and still more extraordinary that it was fully established, and has ever since been acted upon with the best effects, in Scotland, above a century and a half ago.[1]

[1] By the Act of Scottish Parliament, 1696, c. xviii.; Report of Committee on Education, June 3, 1818; Parl. Deb. xxxviii. 814, 827, 1207.

Sir Samuel Romilly continued, through this session of Parliament, his humane and benevolent efforts to effect a mitigation of our criminal code, and succeeded in getting through the House of Commons a bill for abrogating the punishment of death for stealing under the value of £5 in shops. He introduced this measure in a luminous speech, in which he stigmatized excessive severity of punishment as the greatest of all promoters of crime, by discouraging prosecutions, and thus practically, in the majority of cases, leading to impunity. In these attempts he was seconded by a still abler man, Sir James Mackintosh, who, in the same session, obtained the appointment of a committee to examine into the most effectual means of preventing the forgery of bank-notes. The general concurrence of both sides of the House in this measure proved that the time was fast approaching when the cruel and excessive severity of our criminal law would yield to a more humane and enlightened system. When Sir Samuel's bill, however, was sent up to the House of Lords, the Chancellor, Eldon, succeeded in getting it thrown out, as he had already repeatedly done before. He was deterred by the effects which had followed the bill passed in the preceding session of Parliament, removing the punishment of death from theft from the person, forgetting that the only effectual way of repressing crime is by insuring its punishment; and that an increase of prosecutions may, and sometimes does, arise more

47. Efforts of Sir Samuel Romilly to obtain a relaxation of our criminal code.

from the guilty being more readily brought to punishment, than from their absolute number increasing.[1]

[1] Parl. Deb. xxxvii. 1180; Twiss's Life of Eldon, ii. 316.

The period had now, however, arrived when the great lawyer and humane legislator, with whom these reforms had first originated, was to be withdrawn from this earthly scene. The excessive labors of Sir Samuel Romilly's life, arising from the combination of the highest practice at the Chancery bar, with the late hours, continual excitement, and occasional efforts in debate in the House of Commons, came at length to unsettle a mind which, notwithstanding its powers, had a constitutional tendency to excessive sensitiveness. He had recently before been returned, without canvassing or solicitation, for Westminster, and was at the very zenith of his fortune, fame, and usefulness, when, on the 2d November, 1818, he was found with life extinct, having committed suicide in a fit of insanity. Lady Romilly, to whom he was tenderly attached, had died three days previously; and for some weeks before he had been in a very nervous state, having for many nights together lost the power of sleeping. The grief consequent on this melancholy bereavement so preyed on a mind naturally sensitive and nervous, and overwrought by excessive exertion, as to produce the melancholy catastrophe which deprived the bar of one of its brightest ornaments—the country of one of its most useful and philanthropic legislators.[2]

48. Death and character of Sir Samuel Romilly.

Nov. 2, 1818.

[2] Romilly's Life, iii. 307, 368; Hughes, vi. 360.

Sir Samuel Romilly was undoubtedly a very remarkable man: that is sufficiently proved by his having risen, without either family or official connections, to the head of the Chancery bar. His powers of reasoning were very considerable—his application immense—his memory retentive and ready. By adopting De Witt's maxim of doing every thing at its proper time, and putting every thing in its proper place, he succeeded in getting through a mass of business, both legal and parliamentary, which would have crushed any ordinary man. At the same time, he kept up with the whole literature of the day—devoted the evening of Saturday and the whole of Sunday to the enjoyment of his family in the country, and never allowed secular labor to interfere with the appointed seventh day of rest. He was eminently sincere and pious in his feelings, and humane in his disposition almost to a fault. It was the strength of these feelings which led him to engage with such warmth, and prosecute with such perseverance, the reformation of the criminal code of England, and the extirpation of the many sanguinary enactments which disgraced its statute-book. Humanity owes him much for having been the first to enter upon that glorious task. Yet is it, perhaps, not to be regretted in a general point of view, however grievous his loss was to his family and friends, that he was cut short when he was in his career of mercy, for his mantle descended upon a much superior man—a greater philosophic lawyer. He was by no means the equal, either in philosophy, oratory, or political wisdom, of Sir James Mackintosh, who follow

49. His character.

ed in his footsteps. His mind was essentially sensitive. "Impressionable comme une femme," might be said, with not less truth, of him than of Lamartine in after days. Hence he was a warm party man, and never rose to those lofty views by which Bacon, Burke, and Mackintosh showed themselves qualified to direct the thoughts of future times. His excessive sensibility and mental weaknesses did not appear in his public career, but have been prominently brought forward by the indiscreet zeal of his biographer, to whose amiable partiality they appeared as excellences.[1] He was in the highest degree amiable in private life, and beloved alike by his friends and opponents. When Lord Eldon first beheld the vacant seat within the bar where Sir Samuel used to sit, he was so affected that he burst into tears, and broke up the court.

[1] Twiss's Life of Eldon, ii. 324.

Another remarkable man died this year, second to none in intellectual vigor and capacity, although they were displayed rather in legal argument than the larger political arena. This was Lord Ellenborough, Chief-justice of the Court of King's Bench, who died, after a lingering illness, on 13th December. His health had long been declining. Like almost all the other great lawyers at the English bar, he was the architect of his own fortune. Of respectable origin, the fourth son of Dr. Law, Bishop of Carlisle, he was yet without either connection or patronage, and owed his elevation entirely to the uncommon vigor and force of his understanding. These were such that they in a manner forced him into greatness, and would have done so, like other great men, in any career, civil or military, upon which he might have entered. Nothing can surpass the force of the arguments which he delivered at the bar, or the lucidity and masterly analysis of the judgments he pronounced on the bench. They remain in the law reports enduring monuments of the clearness and power of his understanding. He was a Whig in politics; and one of the most unpopular acts of that party, when they came into power in 1806, was giving him a seat in the Cabinet—a step which, however palliated in his case by his great abilities, was justly regarded as of dangerous example in future times, as putting in hazard the independence of the bench. He continued throughout life a Whig, but a Whig of the old school—that is, one who inclined to the aristocratic, not the democratic, part of the Constitution. Hence, when he was made Chief Justice in 1802, it was a common subject of complaint that he was occasionally arrogant in his manner, and overbearing in his disposition; and great surprise was expressed at the same person evincing these qualities, who had been their most vehement opponent when at the bar in early life. But there is nothing at all surprising in the change; on the contrary, they are both symptoms of the same ruling disposition, and often make their appearance at different periods of life in the same individual. Resistance to opposition is the fundamental principle—a domineering disposition, the uniform characteristic, and it never changes. In early life, when 1e person actuated by it is among the govern-

50. Death and character of Lord Ellenborough.

Dec. 13.

ed, it appears in resistance to oppression; in mature years, when he has risen to the station of governor, in coercion of insubordination.[1]

[1] Ann Reg. 1818, 265; Chron.

It is remarkable that the same year which was marked by the death of Lord Ellenborough witnessed also the demise of Warren Hastings, of whom, during his long and vexatious prosecution, he had been the steady and intrepid advocate; and of Sir Philip Francis, who had been his not less relentless and energetic persecutor. The first of these remarkable men expired at his hereditary seat of Daylesford, in Worcestershire—lost by his ancestors, but regained by his exertions—on August 22, in the eighty-sixth year of his age. He belongs to a different period in the history of England—to that marvelous era when, in both hemispheres, the deep foundations of British greatness were laid. There were giants in the earth before the moral as well as the physical flood. His character has been drawn, the ingratitude he experienced depicted, in a former work.[2] Less distinguished in public life, his antagonist, Sir Philip Francis, has left a reputation hardly less enduring; for there seems to be no doubt that he was the author of the Letters of Junius, which, for a season, almost counterbalanced the influence of the sovereign on the throne. He died in London, on December 22, in the seventy-eighth year of his age. The uncompromising enemy of oppression, corruption, and despotic measures in both hemispheres, he, at one period of his life, shook the throne in England; at another, fought a duel with the Governor General of India, from whom he received a shot through the body in 1781. A moral courage which nothing could daunt—great abilities, and the energy which a consciousness of their possession seldom fails to inspire, were his characteristics. His style of composition, as it appears both in the Letters of Junius and in his speeches in Parliament, was condensed and epigrammatic in the highest degree; and it is their admirable force and brevity which, like the sayings of Johnson, recorded by the graphic pen of Boswell, have given the former their colossal and enduring reputation. But, like all other productions in the same style, they are one-sided, and often unjust. Unfortunately, however, it is these very blemishes which have rendered them so famous; for such is the admiration of mankind for talent, that falsehood and exaggeration, brilliantly arrayed, often carry the day, even in after times, against truth and justice, clothed in the silver robe of innocence. Tacitus would never have been immortal had he not been a party writer.[3]*

51. Death of Warren Hastings and Sir Philip Francis. Aug. 22, and Dec. 22.

[2] Hist. of Europe, c. xlviii. [3] 21, 25.

[3] Ann. Reg. 1818, 295; Chron.

This great celebrity of rhetorical ability, and its superiority to unadorned truth, however, is not universal; and every age presents numerous examples of men in whom justness of decision, wisdom of thought, and a

52. Sir James Mackintosh. His early life.

* The author has no doubt Sir Philip Francis was the author of the Letters of Junius. Identity of style in those celebrated letters with his acknowledged compositions, as well as numerous direct pieces of evidence, appear to place it beyond a doubt.—See Mahon's History of Eng. and, v. 274, 285.

philosophic turn of mind, lay the foundation of fame as great, and beneficence far more enduring, than the utmost brilliancy of one-sided eloquence. Of this Sir James Mackintosh, the able and philosophical follower of Romilly in the career of criminal amelioration, is an illustrious example. Of humble parentage, the son of a small landholder on the banks of Loch Ness, he owed nothing to early patronage or connections. What he became he owed to himself, and the blood he inherited, alone. But he was not without advantages in the latter respect; from the mother's side, the usual channel in which intellectual powers descend, he inherited the talents of his grandmother, Mrs. Macgillivray, a woman of uncommon powers and cultivation of mind. He was born on 17th October, 1765, and was educated at Edinburgh, and took part in the debates of the Speculative Society there, in which Brougham, Lansdowne, Jeffrey, Horner, and the many eminent men who afterward rose into fame in the Scottish metropolis, made their first essays in oratory. Subsequently he was called to the English bar, and became first known to the public by his *Vindiciæ Gallicæ*, published to defend the Revolution in France from the dreaded antagonism of Burke. In 1803 he sailed for India, having been appointed, by Lord Sidmouth, Recorder of Bombay; and there he spent, in no very agreeable banishment, the next nine years of his life. In 1812 he returned to England, with a moderate independence, and was soon after admitted to Parliament for the close borough of Weymouth. He was afterward made a privy counselor, but never held any Government appointment, and died in 1832,

¹ Mackintosh's Life, 2 vols. passim.

while still in the full vigor of his understanding, and without having done any thing in literature commensurate to the high expectations justly formed of his abilities.¹

53. His character as a statesman and writer.

These expectations were chiefly formed in consequence of its being known that he had engaged in the herculean task of continuing Hume's History of England down to recent times; a work in which he had made some progress, and for which he has left several splendid sketches, for the most part composed in his voyage home, but which he never brought to maturity. In fact, he had not perseverance adequate to the task. His powers of conversation were great, and the gratification he experienced from their exercise was so excessive that it led him to forego the main object of his life for its enjoyment.* He spent the forenoon

* The author once spent one of these forenoons in his society, from breakfast to two o'clock. Lord Jeffrey, and Mr. Earle Monteith, now sheriff of Fife, were the only other persons present. The superiority of Sir James Mackintosh to Jeffrey, in conversation, was then very manifest. His ideas succeeded each other much more rapidly; his expressions were more brief and terse—his repartee more felicitous. Jeffrey's great talent consisted in amplification and illustration, and there he was eminently great; and he had been accustomed to Edinburgh society, where he had been allowed, by his admiring auditors, male and female, to prose and expand ad libitum. Sir James had not greater quickness of mind, for nothing could exceed Jeffrey in that respect, but much greater power of condensed expression, and infinitely more rapidity in changing the subject of conversation. "Tout toucher, rien approfondir," was his practice, as it is of all men in whom the real conversational talent exists, and where it has been trained to perfection by frequent collision in polished society with equal or superior men, as

generally conversing with ladies or literary men, instead of writing, and it is not thus that great things are done. "Conversation," says Gibbon, "strengthens the understanding, but solitude is the school of genius." It was deeply regretted by his friends at the time that this distraction of the powers of so great a mind should be going on; and, undoubtedly, for ethical and political disquisitions, and essays on history, it can never be sufficiently lamented; for in these branches his mind appeared in its full lustre. There is nothing in the English language superior in wisdom to some of his political essays, which first appeared in the *Edinburgh Review*, and are now reprinted in his collected essays; in criticism, to his characters of the leading men of the eighteenth century, to be found in the very interesting memoir of him by his son. But there is no appearance in his writings of the qualities which indicate that he could ever have become great in narrating events. He was an admirable essayist on history, after the manner of Guizot; but he had not the talents requisite for a historian. His abbreviated History of England, and fragment of the History of the Revolution of 1688, are a proof of this. The former contains many admirable observations and reflections; but it gives no idea whatever of the thread of events, and the student will rise from its perusal without any distinct impression, if otherwise uninformed, of the history of his country. The latter is so dull, that it may be doubted whether any one, but from respect for the author, or for motives of party or reference, ever read it through. His mind was essentially philosophical; hence his powers were didactic rather than pictorial—instructive than dramatic; and that is a fatal peculiarity either for a statesman or a historian. Energy and fire are the soul of eloquence in the forum, as much as wisdom and moderation are of discourses in the academy; and there never yet was a great historian whose talents would not have led him to the first eminence as a painter or dramatic poet.

In Parliament, Sir James Mackintosh attained a high, but by no means the highest place. His speeches were all prepared: they were learned and admirable essays on the subject in hand; but they had not the force of expression, personal allusion, or stinging rejoinder, requisite for success in a mixed, not always learned, but always highly excited, assembly. His luminous and learned orations were always listened to with respect, and often spoken of, on reflection, with admiration; but, at the time, they were often delivered to empty benches, or, like Burke's, acted like a dinner-bell in clearing the House. But while these peculiarities precluded him from rising to the first rank as a parliamentary debater, they qualified him admirably for the great task to which his efforts in Parliament were directed—the reformation and humanizing of our criminal code. His philosophic mind threw a luminous radiance over that intricate subject, eminently calculated to make an impression on a popular

54. His character as a parliamentary speaker.

elegant and charming women. Jeffrey, in conversation, was like a skilful swordsman flourishing his weapon in the air; while Mackintosh, with a thin, sharp rapier, in the middle of his evolutions, ran him through the body assembly, in a large part of whom Liberal ideas were beginning to germinate. He took it up as a whole—generalized the infinite details in which it was involved, and deduced his conclusions from acknowledged premises and generous feelings. He thus obtained far greater success than Sir Samuel Romilly, working only on separate and detached points, ever could have done; and it is to his influence, acting in public and private, on the candid and convertible mind of Mr. Peel, that the great reformation which soon after took place in our criminal code is mainly to be ascribed.

This year witnessed the demise also of the Queen, who had so long shared with her husband the honors and cares of royalty, and whose latter years, during his mental aberration, had been so assiduously devoted to his comfort. Queen Charlotte expired at Kew, on the 17th of November, in the seventy-fifth year of her age. If the old observation be true that those women in any rank are most estimable of whom least in public is said, never was a more unexceptionable character than this lamented queen. She had no beauty, was not remarkable for talents, and had none of the charm of conversation or coquetry of manner which so often, in exalted stations, leads women to the perilous borders of captivation and corruption. Married early in life to a consort of religious principles, integrity of character, and domestic habits identical with her own, to whom she bore a numerous family, her life was rather remarkable for the regularity with which home duties were performed than the brilliancy by which public admiration or love is secured. Her sense of decorum bordered on austerity—her love of economy on parsimony. The Court, under her direction, was stiff and correct; very different from the brilliant scenes with which it is always clothed in imagination, and sometimes arrayed in reality. Yet must history ever acknowledge with gratitude the inestimable service which she rendered, not only to public morals, but to the stability of the Constitution, by the unvarying correctness of her private life, and the care which she took to preserve the Court from that contamination which, in so many other countries of Europe, was shaking at once the throne and the altar.[1] She was interred on the 2d December, in the magnificent vault of St. George's Chapel, Windsor, whither her bereaved lord was soon to follow her—ignorant now alike of his present loss or his approaching end.

55. Death and character of Queen Charlotte. Nov. 17.

[1] Hughes, vi. 361, 362.

The year 1819 commenced under more favorable auspices than had been known for several years. In the speech at the opening of Parliament, the Prince-Regent informed the nation that "there is a considerable and progressive improvement of the revenue in its most important branches; and that the trade, commerce, and manufactures of the country are in a most flourishing condition." Allowing for a certain amount of exaggeration on the favorable side in all such state documents, there is enough proved, by incontestable evidence, to leave no room for doubt that, in the first part of the year at least, a very considerable amelioration had taken place. The revenue afforded evidence of that; it exhibited a very considerable increase in the earlier months. But these appearances were short-lived and fallacious; and the distress of the latter part of the year was so great that, upon the whole, instead of an increase, it exhibited a falling off from the preceding year of above a million.* The exports fell off in the latter part of the year so immensely that they presented a decline of fully a fourth from the preceding year; the imports, a falling off of above a *fifth*.† Something must obviously have occurred in the interval, between the commencement and the end of the year, to produce so great and disastrous a change; nor is it difficult to perceive what that something was. In the interval, the act ESTABLISHING CASH PAYMENTS BY THE BANK OF ENGLAND was passed; and with it a series of embarrassments began, national and social, financial and political, which have never yet been got over, and have imprinted lasting effects upon the fortunes of the British empire.[1]

56. Favorable aspect of affairs at the opening of 1819, and disasters at its close.

[1] Ann. Reg. 1819, 3; Regent's Speech.

The period had now arrived when, after various postponements, it was deemed indispensable by the leading men on both sides of politics to revert to cash payments by the Bank of England. That was universally admitted; the only question was when, and under what limitation, if any, the new system was to come into operation. The debates on this subject are of the very highest interest, fraught as they were with the future destinies of Great Britain, and exhibiting one of the most curious instances recorded in history of the erroneous views entertained by the ablest men, and the general insensibility to impending dangers on the part of an entire community, the fortune of every individual in which was more or less dependent on the measures which were adopted. The subject was introduced on February 2, by a motion on the part of the Opposition, headed by Mr. Tierney, for the appointment of a committee to inquire into the effects of the Bank Restriction Act; which was met by an amendment on the part of the Chancellor of the Exchequer on the day following, to the effect that the committee be instructed to report to the House such information, relative to the affairs of the bank, as may be disclosed without injury to the public interests, with their observations thereon. The amendment of the Chancellor of the Exchequer was carried by a majority of 109, the number being 277 to 168. The secret committee was chosen by ballot, and its chairman, Mr. Peel, brought up its report on April 5.[2]

57. Commencement of the debates on the currency question.

[2] Parl. Deb. xxxix. 213, 280; Ann. Reg. 1819, 33.

As the Legislature were all but unanimous in support of the measure which was ultimately

---

* Total revenue, 1818 .... £53,747,792
  "   "   1819 52,648,847
—Porter's *Progress of the Nation*, 475, third edition.

Years.	Exports, British and foreign, at official Value.	Imports—declared Values.	Exports, British and Irish—declared Value.	Shipping. Tons.
1817	£53,404,111	£29,910,502	£40,349,233	2,564,906
1818	53,560,238	35,845,340	45,180,150	2,074,468
1819	42,438,989	26,681,640	34,252,251	2,666,396

—Porter's *Progress of the Nation*, 359, third edition. Alison's *Europe*, xcvi. Appendix, 311.

adopted on this all-important subject, it is essential, in order to record the arguments urged on the other side, to have recourse to what was stated beyond the walls of Parliament. With this view, nothing better can be adduced than the petition from the merchants, bankers, and traders of the city of Bristol, which was presented to the House of Commons on February 3. It affords another example of a truth, of which many illustrations have occurred, and will again occur, in the course of this history—that the truth on important political questions is often much more clearly perceived, and the practical effect of measures better discerned, out of the Legislature than in it; and that the powers of the acutest understandings are not in the latter situation to be relied on, in opposition to the influence of party connections or the sway of theoretical opinions.

58. Petition from Bristol against the too speedy resumption of cash payments. Feb. 3, 1819.

It was stated in this remarkable petition, which was, as it were, the opening of the great debate: "Your petitioners have heard, with much apprehension, that the design is entertained of proposing in Parliament the resumption of cash payments by the Bank of England. The petitioners have the utmost confidence in the resources of the national bank, and that its issues are fully warranted by the property which it holds in deposit; and they are firmly persuaded that, if this measure shall be forced upon the country before it shall, by a favorable state of its foreign exchanges, be fully prepared for its reception, not only the finances and revenue of the state must suffer, but even the stability of the bank itself be endangered, by the exportation of its bullion, and the depreciation of the property which it holds as a security for its issues. The petitioners conceive, also, that the present is a period peculiarly hazardous for an experiment of so important a nature, when loans of an unprecedented magnitude are in process of payment in Europe, and when the exchange with both the continents is greatly against this country. The petitioners confidently anticipate that, as the present state of our foreign exchanges may be justly attributed to causes which, although quite adequate to the effects, are not in themselves necessarily permanent, the period may reasonably be expected to arrive at which a resumption of cash payments may be made with safety, and without inconvenience. Awaiting, then, this period, the situation of the country can only be rendered alarming by a premature recurrence to measures which the petitioners are satisfied must cramp the commercial intercourse of England with foreign countries, contract its trade and manufactures, and be injurious to its best interests. The petitioners, therefore, most humbly pray that the House will reject every proposal which may be made for a hasty and premature adoption of such a measure."¹

59. Its tenor.

¹ *Bristol Petition, Feb. 3, 1819; Parl. Deb. xxxix. 276, 277.*

On the other hand, it was argued by Mr. Peel, who was the chairman of the committee, and moved the adoption of its report: "The present position of the bank calls, in the first instance, for an interim measure before the final measure is adopted. In consequence of the notes issued in 1816 and 1817 by the bank, with the very best intentions, in which they undertook to pay in specie all notes dated previously to January 1, 1847, a very large amount of treasure had been drawn from the bank. The whole which had been issued by the bank since January, 1816, had amounted to £5,200,000. The issue of that treasure had not been attended with any good to the nation; and he thought, indeed, it might have been foreseen that, unless their issue had been accompanied by a simultaneous reduction of the numbers of bank-notes, the gold would find its way to those places where there was a greater demand for it. There was little doubt, at present, as to the place of its destination; for, by a report of the minister of finance in France, it appeared that, within the first six months of the last year, 125,000,000 francs (£5,000,000) had been coined at the French Mint, of which it was understood three fourths had come from this country. In these circumstances, it was necessary to pass a bill restraining the payments in gold until the final measure shall pass; and the circumstances of the bank were such, that it had become necessary that the bill should go through its several stages that evening." The necessity of the case being evident, a bill continuing the restriction till the final measure was adopted, passed both Houses with very little opposition.¹

60. First speech of Mr. Peel on the subject.

¹ *Parl. Deb. xxxix. 1399, 1401.*

The grand debate on the final measure came on on May 24, and preparatory to it two petitions were presented to the House of Commons—one from the directors of the Bank of England, and another from the merchants and bankers of the city of London, in which the effects of the proposed measure are foretold with a clearness, and, as the event has proved, a truth, which render them among the most valuable and instructive documents recorded in history. That from the bank directors, with great propriety, disclaimed any interested view of the matter, but submitted to the Legislature what must be the effect of a return to cash payments in the existing financial, commercial, and monetary state of the country.* The petition of

61. Petition of the merchants and bankers of London in favor of continuing the restriction.

---

* The petition of the bank directors stated "That, in the view of the committee, the measure of the bank resuming cash payments on the 5th July next, the time prescribed by the existing law, is utterly impracticable, and would be entirely inefficient, if not ruinous. The two committees have arrived at this conclusion, at a period when the outstanding notes of the bank do not much exceed £25,000,000, or when the price of gold is about £4 1s. per ounce, and when there is great distress from the stagnation of commerce and the fall in the price of imported articles. It must be obvious that, so long as such a state of things shall last, or one in any degree similar, without either considerable improvement on one side, or growing worse on the other, the bank, acting as it does at present, and keeping its issues nearly at the present level, could not venture to return to cash payments with any possibility of benefit to the public or safety to its establishment. The proposal of the committee is, that the bank shall not resume payments in coin for four years, but shall be obliged, from 1st May, 1821, to discharge their notes in standard gold bullion, at Mint price, when demanded, in sums not amounting to less than thirty ounces; and that from 1st February, 1820, the bank should pay their notes in bullion, if demanded, in sums not less than sixty ounces, at the rate of £4 1s. per ounce; and from 1st October, 1820, to 1st May, 1821, at £3 19s. 6d. per ounce. The bank directors are obliged

the merchants and bankers of London went a step further, and prophesied the consequences of the proposed measure in the following remarkable terms: "Your petitioners have reason to apprehend that measures are in contemplation, with reference to the resumption of cash payments by the Bank of England, which, in the humble opinion of your petitioners, will tend to a *forced, precipitate, and highly injurious contraction of the currency* of the country. That the consequences of such a contraction will be, as your petitioners humbly conceive, to add to the burden of the public debt, greatly to increase the pressure of the taxes, to lower the value of all landed and commercial property, seriously to affect and embarrass both public and private credit, to embarrass and reduce all the operations of agriculture, manufactures, and commerce, and to throw out of employment (as in the calamitous year 1816) a great proportion of the industrious and laboring classes of the community. That your petitioners are fortified in the opinion thus expressed by the distresses experienced by commercial, trading, manufacturing, and agricultural interests of the kingdom, from the partial reduction of the bank issues which, it appears, has recently taken place. Neither the manner nor the time which, your petitioners have reason to apprehend, is intended to be proposed for the resumption of cash payments, is suited to avoid the evils they anticipate. The petitioners, therefore, humbly crave that the time, as at present fixed by law, for the termination of the restrictions on cash payments by the Bank of England, may be extended to a period which shall not tend to a forced and precipitate contraction of the circulating medium of the country, or to embarrass trade, or to injure public credit, agriculture, manufactures, and commerce.¹

These petitions from Bristol and London, coming, as they did from the first commercial men in England, and couched in such strong yet respectful language, showed how strongly the mercantile classes had taken the alarm at the proposed resumption of cash payments by the Bank of England, and how clearly their practical experience and native sagacity had detected the real tendency of a measure fraught with the most momentous consequences, but which it was known had obtained the assent of both branches of the Legislature. The petition was rendered the more remarkable by its being presented to the House of Commons by Sir Robert Peel, who had made a colossal fortune under the cash restriction system, and who now stood forward to oppose his eldest son, Mr. Peel, who was prepared to terminate it. The honorable baronet observed: "The petition he held in his hand came from a body of men entitled to the very first consideration—a body of men who, in times of public distress or calamity, were the very first to come forward to relieve the Government. The Bank Restriction Act could not have passed in 1797 if the merchants and bankers of London had not, at a similar meeting, expressed themselves strongly in its favor. The petition he now held in his hand was that of a great and important body, all of the first respectability, praying that the resolutions which were intended to be submitted to the House might not be carried into effect. They were the best judges of such a measure, for their whole fortunes were wound up with it. Although, also, they were the men in the country best qualified to give evidence, from their great transactions and connection with our manufactures and commerce, yet they had not been examined before the committee. He entreated, therefore, that before a measure so destructive of the commercial interests of the country, and, with them, of every other interest in the country, the House would pause, in order to collect that information which was so much wanted.

"At the meeting from which this petition originated, he was in company with many of the best friends of the country; but he should not do justice to two persons who attended there if he did not say that they behaved in a

---

1. Petition of the merchants of London, May 21, 1819; Parl. Deb. xl. 599, 600.

62. Which is presented to the House of Commons by the first Sir R. Peel.

To observe that, as it is incumbent on them to consider the effect of any measure to be adopted as operating upon the general issue of their notes, by which all the private banks are regulated, and of which the whole currency, exclusive of the notes of private bankers, is composed, they feel themselves obliged, by the new situation in which they have been placed by the bank restriction of 1797, to bear in mind not less their duties to the establishment over which they preside than their duties to the *community at large*, whose interests, in a pecuniary and commercial relation, have, in a great degree, been confided to their discretion. The directors being thus obliged to extend their views, and embrace the interests of the whole community in their consideration of this measure, can not but feel a repugnance, however involuntary, to pledge themselves in approbation of a system which, in their opinion, in all its great tendencies and operations, concerns the country in general more than the immediate interests of the bank alone. When the bank directors are now to be called upon, in the new situation in which they are placed by the Restriction Act, to procure a fund for supporting the whole national currency either in bullion or coin, and when it is proposed that they should effect this measure within a given period, by regulating the market-price of gold by a limitation of the amount of the issue of bank-notes, *with whatever distress such limitation may be attended to individuals or the community at large*, they feel it their bounden and imperious duty to state their sentiments thus explicitly, in the first instance, to his Majesty's ministers on this subject, that a tacit consent and concurrence at this juncture may not at some future period be construed into a previous implied sanction on their part of a system which they can not but consider as fraught with very great uncertainty and risk. They can not venture to advise an unrelenting continuance of pecuniary pressure upon the commercial world, of which it is impossible for them either to foresee or estimate the consequences. The directors have already submitted to the House of Lords the expediency of the bank paying its notes *in bullion at the market-price of the day*, with a view of seeing how far favorable commercial balances may operate in restoring the former order of things, of which they might take advantage; and with a similar view they have proposed that Government should repay the bank a considerable part of the sums that have been advanced upon Exchequer bills. These two measures would allow time for a correct judgment to be formed upon the state of the bullion market, and upon the real result of those changes which the late war may have produced, in all its consequences, of *increased public debt, increased taxes, increased prices*, and altered relations as to interest, capital, and commercial dealings with the Continent, and how far the alterations thus produced are temporary or permanent, and to what extent and in what degree they operate. The directors, therefore, feel that they have no right whatever to invest themselves, of their own accord, with the responsibility of countenancing a measure in which the *whole community is so deeply involved*, and possibly *to compromise the universal interests of the empire in all the relations of agriculture, manufactures, commerce, and revenue*, by a seeming acquiescence or declared approbation on the part of the directors of the Bank of England."—Petition of the Bank of England, 20th May, 1819. Parl. Debates, xl. 601, 604.

way not the least disorderly in the world, for they were in close alliance with his Majesty's ministers—they inveighed against any attempt at deferring the period of resuming cash payments. The circumstance so new, of these men being supporters of the administration, constituted the subject of a very good caricature; but, at the same time, it filled him with the most dismal forebodings. To see the noble lord and his honorable friend, on the one hand, and Messrs. Hunt and Wooller on the other, united in their attempt to pull down the mighty fabric erected by the immortal Pitt, was at once ludicrous and painful. He implored the House to pause before they engaged in any such attempt. It was true, in resisting it, he should have to oppose a very near and dear relation. But while it was his own sentiment that he had a duty to perform, he respected those who did theirs, and who considered them to be paramount. The gentlemen who opposed him at the meeting of which he had spoken were rather indignant at his mentioning the name of Mr. Pitt. His own impression was certainly a strong one in his favor; he always thought him the first man in the country. He well remembered one occasion, when that near and dear relation was only a child, he observed to some friends who were standing near him, that the man who discharged his duty to his country in the manner in which Mr. Pitt had, did most to be admired, and was most to be imitated; and he thought at that moment, if the life of his dear relation should be spared, he would one day present him to his country to follow in the same path."¹

63. His speech on the occasion continued.

¹ Parl. Deb. xl. 673, 674.

On the other hand, it was argued by Sir Robert Peel's son, Mr. Peel, who then made his first important step in public life, and was the chairman of the committee the resolutions of which were proposed to the House for adoption:* "He was bound to say that, in consequence of the weight and great respectability of the evidence laid before the committee, and the discussions which had ensued upon it, his opinion in regard to this question had undergone a great change. He was ready to avow, without shame or remorse, that he went into the committee with a very different opinion from that which he at present entertained; for his views of the subject were most materially different from what they were when he voted against the resolutions brought forward in the bullion committee in 1811 by Mr. Horner. After giving his best attention to the subject, he had no hesitation in stating, that though he should probably even now vote against the practical measure then recommended, yet he concurred in the fourteen first resolutions proposed to the House by that able and much lamented individual. He conceived them to represent the true nature and law of our monetary system. It was without shame or repentance he thus bore testimony to the superior sagacity of one with whose views he agreed on that point, although he differed so much from him on many other great political questions.

64. Argument of Mr. Peel in favor of the resumption of cash payments.

"After the repeated declaration of Parliament that it was advisable that the bank should, at the earliest possible period, resume cash payments, he had hoped that the only points necessary for them to proceed to that night, would be to fix on the period when the restriction should cease, and to adopt the most feasible mode of carrying their intention into effect. But it was impossible for him to conceal from himself that new and extraordinary opinions had been promulgated, which, if the House were prepared to act on them, must inevitably lead to an indefinite suspension of cash payments. When he recollected that the necessity of a resumption of cash payments was recognized in the preamble of several acts of Parliament, when he knew that no one objection was formerly made to the principle of so doing, he confessed he was not prepared to hear that a principle the very reverse was to be contended for. But judging from several publications by which he feared the public mind might be influenced, it did appear that the return to cash payments was viewed in some quarters with apprehension; and if weight and authority were given to the sentiments and principles contained in these works, the House must be prepared to legislate for an indefinite suspension. It is, therefore, absolutely necessary that Parliament should in the contest make up its mind whether a metallic standard of value should not be resorted to. After an experience of twenty-two years, during which it was abandoned, it did appear impossible that any considerate man could hesitate upon that question, or upon the expediency of returning to the ancient system of fixing upon some standard of value.

65. Continued.

"Upon the necessity of establishing such a standard, he could appeal to the opinion of all writers upon political economy, and to the practice of every civilized country, as well as our own, prior to the year 1717. All the witnesses examined before

66. Continued.

* The proposed resolutions were as follows:

"I. That it is expedient further to continue the restriction upon cash payments by the bank for a time, to be limited in such manner and on such conditions as shall be provided by Parliament, with a view to insure its final termination at the period to be fixed.

"II. That, previously to the resumption of cash payments by the bank, it is expedient that the bank should be required, at a time to be fixed by Parliament, to give in exchange for its notes gold duly assayed and stamped at his Majesty's Mint (if demanded to an amount not less than a number of ounces to be limited), valuing the same in such exchange at a price not exceeding £4 1s. per ounce.

"III. That at the expiration of a further period, to be also fixed by Parliament, the bank should be required to give in exchange for its notes, gold, so assayed and stamped, to an amount not less than a certain number of ounces to be limited, valuing the same in such exchange at the Mint price.

"IV. That at some time between the two periods above mentioned, the bank should be required to give in exchange for its notes, gold, so assayed and stamped, valuing the same at a price between £4 1s. and the Mint price; and that, after the price at which gold shall be valued in such exchanges shall have been once lowered, it shall not again be raised.

"V. That after the period shall have arrived at which the bank shall be required to give gold in exchange for its notes at the Mint price, a further period, to be fixed by Parliament, should be allowed, and a certain notice given before the bank shall be required to pay its notes in cash.

"VI. That it is expedient that all laws which prohibited the melting or exportation of the gold or silver coin of the realm, and the exportation of gold or silver bullion made of such coin, should be repealed."—*Gover nment Resolutions*, May 2, 1819; *Parl. Deb.* xl. 606.

the committee, with the exception of Mr. Smith, of Norwich, a very respectable man, recommended the establishment of this standard. Even he, when asked whether he would propose an indefinite suspension of cash payments without any standard of value, answered, 'No; the pound should be the standard.' Being asked what he meant by a pound, he answered, 'I find it difficult to explain it; but every gentleman knows it: it is something which has existed in this country for eight hundred years, three hundred years before the introduction of gold.' Mr. Locke, with all his powers of understanding, could not succeed in defining what he meant by a pound. Sir Isaac Newton himself was for a time misled on this subject; but at length he came back to the simple doctrine, that the true standard of value was a certain definite quantity of gold bullion. Every sound writer on the subject came to the same conclusion, that a certain weight of gold bullion, with an impression on it denoting that it was of a certain weight and of a certain fineness, constituted the only true, intelligible, and adequate standard of value; and to that standard the country must return, or the difficulties of our situation would be aggravated as we proceeded. These difficulties were universally known, and they would not be diminished by our declining to acknowledge their existence; and it is notorious that the restoration of a metallic standard of value is essential to our relief from these difficulties.

"The issues of the Bank of England were the foundation on which the whole superstructure of the country banks was raised, and those issues were made either in the purchase of gold, the discount of mercantile bills, or the purchase of Government securities. It is a delusion to say that the issues of the bank are regulated by the demands and necessities of the mercantile world. How can you distinguish between the advances it makes to Government in loans, or discounting Exchequer bills, and a paper circulation emanating directly from it? The bank, no doubt, is safe; the solvency of their establishment is beyond all doubt. But does it follow that, because the bank is able to discharge all its engagements, therefore there can be no over-issue of its paper? If solvency alone was a sufficient proof that there was no excess of circulation, the theory of Mr. Law was just, and the land as well as the funds might be made the basis of a circulating medium. There was, in fact, no test of excess or deficiency, but a comparison with the price of gold. This was not the conclusion of theory only; the last few years had afforded the most ample confirmation of it.

"In the year 1815 our commerce was in full activity; a great impulse had been given, speculation was at its height, and the exports were great beyond example. But 1816 and 1817 came—the natural result of those overstrained hopes and expectations. A languor proportionate to the degree of excitation succeeded. An immense accumulation of property had taken place, for which there was no demand. Prices fell—the country banks stopped their issues—and thousands were in a moment stricken to the ground, by a blow which they could not foresee, and against which it was impossible to provide. The Bank of England notes in circulation previous to 1814 were £23,000,000; in 1815, £25,000,000; 1816, £26,000,000; end of 1817, £29,000,000. At the latter period, trade revived, and importations were made from all parts of the world. Many were deceived by a nominal profit, which, in truth, resolved itself into an excess of currency; and the same scene of distress and embarrassment was renewed. Mr. Gladstone, the great Liverpool merchant, had stated before the committee that the value of grain and provisions imported into Liverpool, from Ireland, in 1817, was £1,200,000; and in 1818, £1,950,000. He added that, in 1816, 270,000 bales of cotton were imported into the same place; in 1817, 350,000; 1818, 457,000. The consequence of this prodigious excess in the supply was a fall in the price of cotton of 40 per cent. Mr. Gladstone added, that in 1818 goods to the value of £3,000,000 were stored in Liverpool beyond what had been done in the preceding year. All this overtrading was productive of no lasting advantage even to the parties engaged in it; but to the laboring classes it was attended with incalculable mischief. The unequal and fluctuating demands for labor deranged all the relations of humble life. The rapidity with which these changes succeeded one another defeated all private arrangements, discouraged the steady accumulation of savings, and frequently overwhelmed the laborer with want and misery.

"The only effectual check which can be imposed on these evils is a check on the over-issue in which they all originate, and this can only be applied by the establishment of a metallic standard of value; for the issue of paper has not, like the wise provisions of Providence, or the prudent regulations of man, any counteracting principle within itself. The paper system went on very well as long as the excitation lasted; but it was sure, on its relapse, to scatter distress and ruin. Private bankers, at first anxious to accommodate, no sooner perceived the symptoms of declining credit, than, in the eagerness to provide for their own security, they refused further aid, and increased the want of confidence. This is the great defect of the paper system; and the question the House has to consider is, whether a system fraught with so many evils is to be permitted to continue. Its evils in future are not to be measured by the past. Hitherto there has always been some check—the admonitions of Parliament had been respected; but if once a hope should be held out that the suspension might last for an indefinite time—that the amount of the circulating medium was to be left to the discretion of the directors—they would be controlled by no consideration but that of their own profits, and it is impossible to overestimate the mischief that would ensue. The committee had perceived that a mere declaration on the subject would be useless, and that mercantile transactions would continue in their present course, instead of being adapted to a return to the ancient standard. It would answer no good purpose to declare in favor of a return to cash payments without fixing upon some definite period for the resumption; for such a promise had already been made no less than five times, and every time proved delusive. The country, then, to be satisfied, must see that a serious resolution existed upon the subject.

70. Continued. "It was when engaged in the conquest of Wales, and amid his efforts to subdue Scotland, that Edward I. first turned his attention to the reformation of the coin; and the next great reformer on that subject was Queen Elizabeth. At her accession to the throne she found that the coin had been debased 400 per cent. in the reign of Henry VIII. and Edward VI.; when there should have been eleven ounces, there were only three. The price of every thing, in consequence, had risen greatly, and there were considerable commotions through the country. By the advice of Burleigh, she determined to restore the value of the coin; and when the difficulties of the attempt, in the distracted state of her dominions and precarious title to the throne, was represented, that able minister replied, 'So far should such considerations be from deterring your Majesty from the pursuit, they should rather be considered as the motives for perseverance, as in the end they must raise and establish the character of the country, increase the attachment of your Majesty's subjects, and command the respect even of your enemies.' Such a conduct was the proudest eulogium on her merits. The inscription on her tomb, after enumerating the queen's titles to distinction, concluded with these words: 'Gallia domata, Belgium sustentum, pax fundata, moneta in justum valorem reducta.' The glories of the present reign exceeded the glories of Elizabeth, and it was to be hoped the hour was near at hand when the triumphant parallel would be completed.

71. Continued. "It is a mistake to say that the country was indebted for all its military honor in the late war to an inconvertible paper currency. Had not the country enjoyed its full share of prosperity and military glory before 1797, when we were first blessed with an inconvertible paper currency! Let them adhere to that good faith in time of peace which they had shown with such magnanimity through all the dangers of war, and toward the foreigners whose countries were at war with them. Let them recollect that the fluctuations of price which an inconvertible paper currency occasioned were injurious to the laborer, who found no compensation in the rise of his wages at one time for the evils inflicted by their depression at another. Every consideration of sound policy, and every consideration of strict justice, should induce them to return to the ancient and permanent standard of value. It is a most delusive idea to suppose that the evils of an inconvertible paper currency will be obviated by obliging the bank, as has been proposed, to pay their notes in bullion at the current price it bore in the market at the time. He warned the House against the adoption of a measure so fatal—a measure fraught with destruction to the ends proposed—a plan which would remove gold to the standard of paper, instead of paper to the standard of gold, and inevitably lead to the interminable continuance, the total adoption, of a paper medium, and only multiply *ad infinitum* the difficulties with which the subject was at present surrounded.

"When people talked of gold rising in price, were they prepared to show it had risen in intrinsic value! Let them not talk of its price in paper, but in any other commodity of a real and fixed value.

72. Concluded. Did a given quantity of gold at present buy any more corn, or any more silver, than it would have done fifty years ago! Setting aside the fluctuations of seasons, which of course materially affected the price of grain, it would be found that gold did not within the period alluded to, through its increased price, command more of any fixed commodity than in former times. So far from that being the case, it positively commanded less than it did in former times; and on this account—because they had found a substitute for gold; and beyond that—because they had a greater stock of that metal, and consequently its value was less than it was fifty years ago. There could not, as long as the pound remained the standard, be any corresponding variation between the price of gold and the increase of taxation."[1]

[1] Parl. Deb. xl. 676, 709.

73. Argument on the other side. So general was the concurrence of the Houses of Commons and Lords in these opinions, that in searching for the leaders of the debate on the other side, we must recur to names unknown to fame; but not on that account the less worthy of attention, for they were practical men, who spoke from their actual experience of what would be the result of the proposed change. It was stated by Mr. Alderman Heygate and Mr. Gurney: "It was generally supposed, and in fact commonly assumed as an incontrovertible position, that our paper was depreciated to a certain extent. Great as the authorities and splendid as the names were which were cited in the report of the committee as supporters of that opinion, yet research and inquiry would convince every unbiased mind not only that no such depreciation did now exist, but that it never could exist. The preliminary point for inquiry is, Was our money depreciated or not! If it was, we were bound to devise a remedy; if it was not, Parliament should pause before they put in force enactments which could not but have the most distressing consequences. Can the circulation be called excessive! Is it not, on the contrary too small, when it is recollected that it is no larger now than it was in 1792! It could not be considered as excessive, if we considered the enormous increase of population, property, and taxes, in the intermediate period, during which the inhabitants of the empire had increased at least fifty per cent.; the revenue had risen from £16,000,000 a year to £54,000,000, and the National Debt from £240,000,000 to £800,000,000. Add to this the still greater increase of our colonies, commerce, docks, public buildings, agriculture, manufactures, and undertakings of all kinds, and no man can deny that, so far from our circulation being excessive, it is greatly within the wants of the community.

74. Continued. "The argument that the supply of gold is dependent on the paper circulation, and that it will always be driven out of the country when an over-issue of that takes place, is utterly erroneous, and is disapproved by the facts. In Nov., 1817, the notes in circulation exceeded £29,000,000, and the price of gold was £4 0s. 6d. the ounce. Since that period there had been a reduction of £3,000,000 in the notes in circulation, and yet the price of gold had been somewhat higher. Gold, in the last years of the war, was as high as £5 4s. an ounce; and, without any reduction in the amount of bank paper in circulation, it fell, in 1816, to £4 1s. the ounce. The truth was, gold was a valuable commodity, an article of commerce in universal request, and, like every other such article, it varied in price according to the varying demand for it in this or other countries. Nothing could be more dangerous than to make our entire circulating medium dependent on the supply of gold, and impose upon the bank the necessity of constantly referring to its price as the measure whereby to regulate the amount of their own issues. The circulation of the country banks is entirely regulated by the profuseness or caution of the issues of the Bank of England; and the whole circulation being in this manner dependent on that basis, in what situation shall we be if, the moment the price of gold rises, and it, in consequence, disappears from circulation, our whole paper is, at the same time, drawn in! This was exactly what happened in 1816. Gold was then on a par with paper; and yet such was the calamity, and so extensive the distress at that unfortunate period, that it pervaded every part of the country. The landed proprietor could get no rents, the manufacturer no market, the laborer no employment. Bankruptcy was universal. Even if next autumn the harvest should be abundant, the exchanges become favorable, and the price of gold fall, still every prudent banker must, if the proposed plan receives the sanction of Parliament, limit his issues, and every prudent merchant and manufacturer his undertakings; and thus, with all the elements of prosperity at our command, universal distress must again ensue. This anticipation was supported by all the evidence taken before the committee, and by none more than that of Mr. Baring, the individual, perhaps, in existence, best qualified to form an opinion on the subject. But if the price of gold should rise, and exchanges prove unfavorable, can imagination itself assign any limit to the disasters which must ensue!

"The right honorable mover of the resolutions had eulogized the conduct of Queen Elizabeth in restoring the purity of the coin; but were the circumstances of that period parallel! Were they not rather a contrast to the present? The country was not then burdened with a debt of £800,000,000, and the necessity of raising a revenue of £54,000,000 annually. What might have been wise and magnanimous in that princess, might now be the height of imprudence and infatuation. It is a most fallacious idea to suppose that, if the proposed plan were adopted, the price of gold would permanently remain at the present level. It might do so in so far as this country is concerned, but who can be sure that nothing is likely to occur abroad which will at once raise the price of gold, and occasion such a run upon the Bank of England as will seriously injure, if not wholly destroy credit? In such a case, the situation of the bank, and with it of every country bank, would be full of hazard. Their only chance of safety would be in an appeal to Parliament to relax the law, but it might not be sitting at the time; and, at all events, it would undoubtedly be reluctant to interfere till the very last extremity, and great distress had already been undergone. If, however, the recommendations of the report were adopted, every merchant, manufacturer, and banker would regulate his dealings with a view to the possibility of such an event; and if it occurred, where would be the employment of the poor? and how fearful the increase of the poor-rates! This is the expectation of a large portion of that part of our community engaged in carrying on agriculture, trade, and manufactures; and coming events are already foreshadowed by the great decline of confidence, and decrease of orders and employment, which has taken place since the secret committees were appointed in the present session of Parliament.

75. *Continued.*

"The avowed object of the new system is to establish a fixed standard of value; but although by its adoption you may confer steadiness on that of gold, at what price will that be purchased in the price of all other commodities? Can any man, if the resolutions are adopted, say what will be the condition or value of his property in February next? If a run upon the bank takes place at that time, it may be compelled to stop payment in a fortnight. The country, which had so cheerfully borne the burdens of the war, is at least entitled to be saved from the risk of losing its currency, and having the miseries to undergo consequent on a universal destruction of credit. The rise in the price of provisions has no natural or immediate effect on the wages of the laboring classes, but a cessation of employment has an instantaneous and destructive effect upon them. All we have suffered from the terrible fluctuation of prices since the peace is to be ascribed to the erroneous determination avowed by Government, that an ounce of gold should, under a debt of £800,000,000, happen what might, pass for no more than £3 17s. 10½d. an ounce—a determination which only fixes it at that price by destroying credit, ruining industry, and occasioning a frightful fluctuation in the prices of all other commodities. It is said by the supporter of the measure proposed (Mr. Ricardo) that *the variation of prices it will produce will not exceed 3 per cent.;* but it will be found that it will be above 20 per cent.; and if so, how are our farmers to pay their rents, or the nation its taxes, and the interest on its debts, public and private?

76. *Continued.*

"It is said that an alteration on the standard would be a fraud on the national creditors, and that, in justice to them, we must return to the old standard. But, to say nothing of the comparative amount borrowed since the restriction, it should be recollected there are two parties to a bargain. Has the national creditor called for this change? Had he thought the change would prove beneficial to him, the Three per Cents. would have risen to 100, instead of falling, as they have now done, to 66. But the national creditor saw, what was undoubtedly the fact, that increased pressure upon those who must pay him his interest less-

77. *Concluded.*

* "The difficulty is only that of raising the currency 3 per cent. in value (hear, hear); and who can doubt that, even in those states where the currency is wholly metallic, it often suffered a variation equal to this without inconvenience to the public?"—Mr. RICARDO's *Speech*, May 24, 1819; *Parl. Deb.* xl. 743.

ened his security, and he would gladly continue to take his share in a currency somewhat diminished in value, together with his neighbors, rather than incur the risk of being exempted from that which, in fact, had operated as a sort of property-tax on property of every description, and which had insured the regularity, if it had diminished the value, of the stockholders' dividends."[1]

[1] Parl. Deb. xl. 730, 762.

Upon this debate the resolutions were agreed to *without one dissentient voice*, the proposed amendment of Alderman Heygate being withdrawn. Mr. Canning stated "that he would take this as nothing less than a *unanimous determination* of Parliament that the country should return, as speedily as possible, to the ancient standard of value in the establishment of a metallic currency," which was accordingly done by the act which passed in terms of the resolutions.[2]*

78. Decision of Parliament on the subject.

[2] Parl. Deb. xl. 800.

On one occasion, counsel, pleading in the House of Lords before Lord Eldon, opened the case by saying, "My lords, this is an appeal from a *unanimous* judgment of the Court of Session." "So much the worse for you," observed the Chancellor, "for that renders it the more probable that the case was either not understood or not properly considered." When the question was put to the Convention whether Louis XVI. was guilty or innocent, they unanimously declared him guilty; the subsequent narrow division was on the nature of the punishment to be inflicted only. Posterity has reversed the sentence; it has unanimously declared him innocent. This is not the time to discuss the effects of this great measure, with which, for good or for evil, the future destinies of Great Britain, and, with it, of half the globe, are wound up. At present three things only are worthy of observation, and should be kept in mind in considering the ample commentary which subsequent events have furnished on this unanimous decision of the Legislature. The first is, that no allusion was made on either side to the great defalcation then going on, and which had been in progress for ten years before the discussion began, in the supply of the precious metals for the use of the globe from the South American mines, from the revolutionary convulsions raging in that quarter, although the effect of these convulsions had been to reduce the annual supply of the precious metals to little more than a *fourth* of its former amount. The second, that the ablest speakers who supported the resolutions—in particular, Mr. Peel and Mr. Ricardo—maintained that the change of prices, arising from this measure, would not exceed 3 per cent., and that its adoption was the only way to guard against the evils of great variations in prices. The third is, that these views were *unanimously* adopted by the Legislature—the opponents of the measure being too few in number to risk a division—at the very time when a contraction of the currency was so much to be deprecated from the great falling off in the supply of the precious metals from the South American mines, and the vast addition to the wants and transactions of the world which was daily taking place from the continuance of peace, the extension of commerce, and rapid increase of population, as well in Europe as in the States of North America, and the immense loans which at that very time required to be provided for, contracted by the French government.

79. Reflections on this decision.

The finances of the country underwent a very thorough discussion in this session of Parliament, both on occasion of a motion by Lord Castlereagh for a select committee to inquire into the income and expenditure of the country, and of a series of finance resolutions* which Mr. Vansittart brought forward on 3d June. These resolutions, and the report of the committee, are very valuable, as exhibiting the financial state of the country, and the resources it possessed at the time when the great change in its monetary policy was adopted. The results were extremely satisfactory—much more so than could have been anticipated, when it is considered what an enormous weight of debt, funded and unfunded, remained at the close of the year; that £18,000,000 of taxes were taken off in the first year of the peace, and the revenue that remained had been seriously impaired

80. Mr. Vansittart's finance resolutions.

June 3.

---

* The resolutions were:

"I. That it is inexpedient to continue the restriction of cash payments beyond the time at present limited by law.

"II. That it is expedient that a definite period should be fixed for the termination of the restriction on cash payments, and that preparatory measures should be taken to facilitate and insure, on the arrival of that period, the payment of the notes of the Bank of England in the current coin of the realm.

"III. That the debt of £10,000,000 due by Government to the bank should be provided for and gradually paid.

"IV. That it is expedient to provide by law, that from and after 1st February, 1820, the bank shall be liable to deliver on demand, gold of standard fineness, having been assayed and stamped at his Majesty's Mint, a quantity of not less than sixty ounces being required in exchange for such an amount of bank-notes of the bank as shall be equal to the value of the gold so required, at the rate of £4 1s. per ounce.

"V. That from 1st October, 1820, the bank shall be liable to deliver gold at the rate of £3 19s. 6d. per ounce, and from 1st May, 1821, at £3 17s. 10½d.; and that from 1st May, 1823, the bank shall pay its notes on demand in the legal coin of the realm.

"VI. That all laws prohibiting the melting and exportation of coin shall be repealed."—*Parl. Deb.* xl. 701.

---

* The income and expenditure of Great Britain and Ireland for the year 1819 stood as follows:

I. INCOME.

Customs	£11,592,664
Excise	25,565,640
Stamps	6,889,674
Post-office	1,790,199
Lesser Items.	
Lottery	665,300
Unclaimed dividends	237,312
Imperial moneys	371,905
Total revenue	56,010,108
Loans	18,756,087
Total	£74,796,195

II. EXPENDITURE.

Interest of National Debt and Sinking Fund	£46,467,997
Interest on Exchequer bills	779,992
Civil List, and charges on Consolidated Fund	2,538,666
Civil Government of Scotland	129,988
Lesser payments	380,161
Navy	6,395,552
Ordnance	1,538,209
Army	9,450,550
Local objects	55,101
Miscellaneous	1,855,918
Total	£69,595,576

—*Ann. Reg.*, 1820, 618.

by the repeated fluctuations of the currency, induced by the constant terror of resuming cash payments which hung over the bank; and that, with very few exceptions, and those of short periods only, general distress had prevailed in the country. It was stated in Mr. Vansittart's resolutions that, by the removal of the property and war malt taxes, the income of Great Britain had been reduced by £18,000,000 yearly; that the interest and charge of the debt, funded and unfunded, of Ireland, exceeded its revenue by £1,800,000 annually; that the income of the United Kingdom, for the year ending 5th January, 1818, was £51,665,458, while, for the year ending 5th January, 1819, it was £54,620,000, showing an increase of above £3,000,000, which, however, was reduced by arrears of war duties on malt and property to only £49,334,927 as the real income in 1817, while the income in 1818 included only £556,639 of these. The general result was, that there was, in 1818, a total surplus of £3,558,000, applicable to the reduction of the national debt; and if £1,000,000 was allowed as the interest of the loan required to keep the expenditure off the Sinking Fund, there would remain £2,500,000 of real surplus revenue, and really paid-off debt.¹

[margin: ¹ Mr. Vansittart's Finance Resolutions; Parl. Deb. xl. 914, 923.]

Mr. Vansittart stated, in reference to future finance measures of Government, "That in consequence of the extensive and searching investigations that had lately taken place into our finance situation, its strong and its weak points were now fully known both in this country and abroad; while, at the same time, by the return of our army from France, and the great reductions which had been made in our establishments, both by land and sea, we had arrived at what might be called our peace establishment, from which no material reductions were to be expected. At the same time, our currency had at length been restored to its proper basis; and as the military pensions, which constituted so large a part of the cost of the army, must soon yearly diminish, it becomes Parliament, at the same time, to take measures for putting our finance on a proper foundation. This can only be done, adverting to the magnitude of our public debt, by applying £5,000,000 at least annually to its reduction. The Sinking Fund is about £15,000,000 a year; and the loan his year will be £13,000,000. This leaves an excess of £2,000,000 really applicable to the reduction of debt; and, therefore, £3,000,000 additional taxes would require to be laid on, to make up the requisite annual surplus. The loan of the year I propose to devote one half in liquidation of the unfunded debt, and one half in repaying part of the £10,000,000 advanced by the bank." Parliament agreed to these proposals, which were obviously founded in statesmanlike wisdom, and the new taxes imposed were on foreign wool and tobacco, tea, coffee, and cocoa-nuts. This was a great step in the right direction; for not only was a considerable sinking fund secured, but it was obtained without recurring to the odious and unjust system of direct taxation, which falls with very unequal weight upon a small part only of the community; but by indirect taxation, chiefly on luxuries, which is in general so light, and spread over so large a surface, that it is no exaggeration to say the money is got without any one being sensible of the burden of its collection.¹

[margin: ¹ Parl. Deb. xl. 917, 927.]

[margin: §1. Mr. Vansittart's finance plan and new taxes.]

Sir James Mackintosh, in this session of Parliament, brought forward the subject of a reform of the criminal law in a speech replete with masterly statements and statesman-like views, which showed how little the cause had lost by the work of Romilly having been transferred to him. He observed: "I do not propose to form a new criminal code. Altogether to abolish a system of law, admirable in its principle, interwoven with the habits of the English people, and under which they have long and happily lived, is a proposition too extravagant to be for a moment listened to. Neither is it proposed to abolish the punishment of death. The right of inflicting it is a part of the right of self-defense with which all societies as well as individuals are endowed. Like all other punishments, the infliction of death is an evil, if unnecessary; but, like any other evil employed to remedy a still greater one, it is capable of becoming a good. Nor is it proposed to take away the power of pardon from the Crown. On the contrary, my object is to restore to the sovereign the real and practical enjoyment of that prerogative, of which usage in modern times has nearly deprived it. My object is to bring the letter of the law more near its practice; to make the execution of the law form the majority, its remission the minority of cases. It is impossible, indeed, to frame a system of law so graduated that it can be applied to every case without the intervention of a discretionary power; but there is good reason to complain of a system of law such as that which at present prevails in England, when the remission of the law forms the rule, and its execution the exception. The object of my reform is to transfer into the statute-book the exceptions to rigor, which the wisdom of modern times has introduced into its practice.

[margin: §2. Sir James Mackintosh's argument in support of criminal law reform. March 2.]

"It is said the progress of the country in manufactures is the principal cause of the great increase of crime which has taken place. But is our progress in wealth and manufactures to be arrested? Great cities are, without doubt, the hot-beds of crime; but can cities be prevented from becoming large in the later stages of society? It is to the causes of increase which arise from errors of legislation, and a pernicious code of laws, that the attention of Parliament should chiefly be directed, because it is there alone that the means of reformation are in our hands. The game-laws are, without doubt, in rural districts, a great source of demoralization; and the returns of commitments show a great increase since 1808, when our paper currency first became seriously depreciated. But the main ground for a reformation of the criminal law is, that it is not so efficacious as it ought to be in checking the increase of crime arising from these various causes, and that in consequence of its excessive severity. There are no less than two hundred felonies on the statute-book punishable with death; but, by the returns from London and Middlesex, from 1749 to 1819, a period of sev-

[margin: §3. Continued.]

enty years, there are only twenty-five sorts of felonies for which any individuals have been executed; so that there are a hundred and seventy-five capital felonies respecting which the law, during that time, has never been enforced! In the thirteen years since 1805 there are only thirty descriptions of felonies on which capital convictions have taken place in England and Wales; so that there are one hundred and seventy capital felonies which have practically gone into desuetude.

This extraordinary multiplication of crimes against which the sanction of death was pronounced, has arisen mainly from the Revolution of 1688—in other respects productive of so much good—by the facility which it afforded to every class to get any offense which trenched at all on them declared capital. It is inconceivable how heedlessly and recklessly this was done in former times. The anecdotes which are current of this extraordinary and shameful facility I am almost ashamed to repeat. Mr. Burke told me that on one occasion, when he was leaving the House, one of the messengers called him back. Mr. Burke said he was going on urgent business. 'Oh!' replied the messenger, 'it will not keep you a single moment; it is only a felony without benefit of clergy.' Mr. Burke added, that although, from his political career, he was not entitled to ask any favor of the ministry, yet he was persuaded he had interest enough at any time to obtain their assent to a felony without benefit of clergy. This unfortunate facility in granting an increase in the severity of the law to every proposer, with the most impartial disregard of political consideration, arose and was carried on at the very time when the humane feelings of the country were daily more and more refining under the influence of knowledge, and this it was which produced the final separation between the letter and practice of the law; for the Government and the nation alike revolted at executing laws which in moments of heedlessness the Legislature had sanctioned. Most justly did that great and good man, Sir William Grant, say that it was impossible both the law and the practice can be right; that the toleration of such a discord was an anomaly which could no longer be tolerated; and that as the law might be brought to an accordance with the practice, but it was impossible to bring the practice into accordance with the law, the law ought to be altered for a wiser and more humane system. The last century has exhibited a continual confederacy of prosecutors, witnesses, counsel, juries, judges, and the advisers of the Crown, to prevent the execution of the law.

"The crimes against which our penal code, as it at present stands, denounces the punishment of death, may be divided into three classes. In the first are numbered murder, shooting, stabbing, and such other offenses as endanger life, and on which the extreme sentence of the law is invariably executed. In the second class are included arson, highway robbery, piracy, and other similar offenses, in which the law, though not always, is very frequently carried into effect. On these two divisions I admit that at present it would be unsafe to make any alteration. But there is a third class—some connected with frauds of various kinds, but others of the most frivolous and fantastic description, against which the punishment of death is denounced in our statute-book, but never now carried into execution, and in which it never was executed, even in former times, without exciting the utmost disgust and horror in all good men—such as cutting down a hop-vine, or a tree in a gentleman's park; or cutting the head of a fish-pond, or being found on the high-road at night with the face blackened. These trifling, and even ridiculous capital felonies, are about a hundred and fifty in number; and although for the last seventy years they have in no one instance been carried into execution, yet there they stand, at this hour, a perpetual monument of savage barbarity, and an eternal proof of the difference between the written law and its practical execution. From the whole of this class of cases I propose to take away in law, as has long been done in practice, the capital sanction.

"But even in those cases where the punishment of death may still, without shocking our moral feelings, be inflicted, it seems expedient, in every point of view, that the extreme punishment of the law should, if not entirely removed, be at least extremely limited. I do not contend for the entire abolition of the punishment of death: in some crimes, and especially murder, it ought to be inflicted. The courts of law should, in such cases, be armed with the awful power of taking away the offender's life; and thus it may be seen that, in this country, that may be done by justice which may not be done by power. But in order to render that authority fully impressive, I am convinced that the punishment of death should be abolished in those cases where inferior punishments are not only applicable, but usually applied. Nothing can be more detrimental to the purposes of justice than the frequency with which the sentence of death is pronounced from the judgment-seat, with all the solemnities prescribed for the occasion, when it is evident, even to those against whom the sentence is pronounced, that it will not be carried into effect. The frequency of escape in such cases takes away the whole effect of capital sentence as an example. 'A single escape,' says Fielding, 'excites a greater degree of hope in the minds of criminals than twenty executions excite of fear.' The whole effect of punishment, as an example, is destroyed when the sympathy of the spectators is with the criminal when he is executed, or against the law when sentence is pronounced.

"In all nations, and in all stages of society an agreement between the laws and the general feeling of the people is essential to their efficacy. But this agreement becomes of unspeakable importance in a country in which the charge of executing the laws is in a great measure committed to the people themselves. God forbid that I should wish to throw any impediment whatever in the way of our civil government; on the contrary, it is my object to remove such as exist. My object is to make the laws popular, to reconcile public opinion to their enactments, and thus to redeem their character. It is to render their execution easy, their terror overwhelming, their efficacy complete, that I implore the House to gave to the subject their most serious consideration. The just and faithful administration of the law is the great bond of society—the point at which authority and obedience meet most nearly. If those who hold the reins of government, instead of attempting a remedy, content themselves with vain lamentations on the increase of crime—if they refuse to conform the laws to the opinions and dispositions of the public, that growth must contribute to spread a just alarm."¹

To these just and able arguments, it was replied by Lord Castlereagh. Mr. Canning also coinciding with him: "My own views do not differ materially from those which have been enforced by the honorable gentleman with so much learning and ability. The great point, however, is to proceed with due caution; for unless this is done, the cause of criminal reform itself will be endangered by the experienced failure of its effects. This result has already taken place in one instance. In the year 1815, Sir Samuel Romilly brought in a bill, which became law, taking away the punishment of death for stealing from the person. What was the result? Why, that the convictions for that offense increased four-fold;* that crime, the punishment of which had relaxed, had increased in a greater proportion than other crimes. The argument, therefore, that a relaxation of punishment would produce diminution of crime, was not in every instance well founded. This did not show that the parliamentary inquiry moved for should not be granted; but it was a warning how cautiously and deliberately it should be entered into. The committee moved for was not to be authorized to consider the question of secondary punishments. But how was it to bring about any practical good unless it did so? For if the punishment of death is to be taken away, is not the very first thing to be considered, what penalties are to be substituted in their room? Out of the 13,000 criminals with whom our jails are annually crowded, at least 10,000 are those to whom such secondary punishments are applicable.

"It is fortunate that the learned mover has not been led away by the theoretical innovations as to the abolition of the punishment of death in all cases. When was there a nation which had ever been able to dispense with that painful necessity? Indeed, the mover's speech is to be admired, not less for what is contained than what is omitted in it. It may be true that the great increase which has taken place in the crimes for which the punishment has been mitigated, has been owing to the increased number of prosecutions. But is it possible, with any consistency, to say first that the increase of crime has been owing to undue severity in its punishment, and then that a still greater increase has been owing to its relaxation? If there is truth in the argument on the other side, the diminished severity of punishment, and consequent increase of convictions, should have led to a decrease in the crimes committed. The committee already appointed, and now actually sitting, on the state of the jails in the kingdom, with a view not only to the safe custody, but to the reformation of prisoners, would have to consider much which should be embraced in the present motion; that on the punishment of transportation, another part. It was prudent to await the result of their labors, before engaging in any more extensive inquiry as to the general amendment of the criminal law; for what could be more dangerous than to abolish generally the punishment of death, without being prepared to say what secondary penalties could be inflicted in its stead?"¹

It was evident, from the feeble manner in which Sir James Mackintosh's motion for the appointment of a committee to inquire into our criminal laws was resisted, that Government felt that the case was indefensible, and that the sense of the House, as well as the nation, was in favor of the desired reformation. They only resisted the motion by a side-wind, in order to gain time, or bring forward a motion themselves, on which they might get a committee of their own appointment. In this, however, they were unsuccessful, for, on a division, Sir James's motion was carried by a majority of 19—the numbers being 147 to 128.²

This was the first decisive victory gained in the Legislature by the advocates of criminal reform, and as such it deserves consideration. It was the turning-point between two systems. For a hundred and fifty years before it, every successive session of Parliament had been marked by one or more additions to the catalogue of capital crimes, until at length they had reached the enormous number of two hundred. Since that time, the penal sanction has been taken away by statute in so many cases, and the mercy of the Crown exercised so liberally in others, that for ten years past no persons have been sentenced to death in Great Britain but for murder; and execution has never taken place, except in willful and cold-blooded cases of that crime. The number of persons who suffer the extreme penalty of the law is now never above fifteen or twenty in a year in England, and three or four in Scotland; and the melancholy spectacle of public executions does not take place a tenth part as frequently as it used to do, before Romilly and Mackintosh began their humane labors.* So far there is great cause for congratulation on the part of all the friends of humanity. But the subject is sur-

---

* CONVICTED FOR STEALING FROM THE PERSON.

Years	Convicted	Years	Convicted
1810	64	1815	131
1811	83	1816	224
1812	78	1817	257
1813	135	1818	262
1814	311		

* SENTENCED TO DEATH IN ENGLAND AND WALES.

Years	Sentenced	Executed	Years	Sentenced	Executed
1816	890	95	1845	49	12
1817	1302	115	1846	56	6
1818	1254	97	1847	54	8
1819	1314	108	1848	60	12
1820	1236	107	1849	56	15

Since 1839 no person has been executed in England but for willful murder; before the change in the law, the murderers were seldom more than a fourth of the number executed.—PORTER's *Progress of the Nation*, 635, third edition.

rounded with difficulties; and if there is good cause for rejoicing in this respect, there is equal ground for apprehension in another. The difficulty arises not from the argument, but the fact, and the results which have actually followed this great relaxation of our penal code.

It has been followed by a very great increase both of committals and convictions; the former, however, in a considerably greater proportion than the latter—indicating that, though the administration of the criminal law has become more regular, and there is an increased inclination on the part of injured persons to prosecute, and of juries to convict, yet no decrease, but, on the contrary, a very great increase of crime has taken place.* The increase of commitments, since the lenient system first began to be carried into effect in 1822, has been most alarming; for they have swelled in Great Britain and Ireland during that period from 27,000 to 74,000, or above 250 per cent.; while, in the same period, population has only advanced from 21,000,000, in the two islands, to 28,000,000, or about 33 per cent.; in other words, crime has increased about *eight times* as fast as the numbers of the people.† This is a sufficiently startling result, the more especially as the last year (1849) was undisturbed either by Irish famine or rebellion; and the free-trade measures, from which the most general blessings had been predicted for the empire, had been for three years in full operation in Great Britain. And as it is well known to all persons practically engaged in these matters that, so far from commitments for trial being of late years issued for more trivial crimes than formerly, the case is just the reverse; and cases are constantly now disposed of by the police magistrates, and chastised by a few weeks' imprisonment, for which, thirty years ago, sentence of death or transportation was pronounced.

In truth, however, this anomaly is more apparent than real; and this disheartening result, so far from disproving, only proves more clearly the justice of Sir James Mackintosh's principles. Crime has increased so immensely, chiefly because they were applied only to the punishment of death, and not followed out, as they should have been, through the whole ramifications of offenses, and the penalties attached to them. His fundamental principle was, that *certainty* of punishment is the only effectual mode of deterring from crime, and that this can never be attained unless the feelings of the people coincide with the law, and co-operate in its execution. No reasonable being can doubt the soundness of this principle; but, to be effective, it should be applied universally. When the capital sentence is taken away from a great variety of offenses, if *certainty* of secondary punishment is not imposed in its stead, the temptation to the commission of crime, from the hope of comparative impunity, is of course increased. Unfortunately, however, many causes have contributed to render secondary punishments in the British empire more uncertain and ineffective, at the very time when the punishment of death has in all cases, excepting wilful murder, been taken away. One class trusted to education to arrest the progress of crime; forgetting that in England the educated criminals were already double of the uneducated, and in Scotland four and a half to one.* Another rested their hopes on the effect of the improvement of prison discipline in reforming the criminals, an illusion of all others the greatest; for experience has now abundantly proved that neither solitary confinement, nor long imprisonment, nor any amount of moral and religious instruction within the walls of a prison, has the least effect in amending the lives of prisoners in their own country, when they are discharged from it. In the mean while, the great increase of prisoners transported, who swelled from a few hundreds to nearly five thousand annually, and the extremely injudicious step of sending them all, without any intermixture of untainted settlers, to Van Diemen's Land—the most remote colony of Great Britain, and the least accessible to free colonists—rendered transportation there so great an evil, and so much an object of dread to other colonies, that a general resistance to the reception of convicts was manifested, and for several years none, excepting young women, were removed to the colonies. Thus transportation, after being pronounced as a sentence, was not carried into effect; the jails soon became incapable of holding the multitudes crowded within their walls; government quietly let

---

* CONVICTIONS IN ENGLAND AND WALES PER CENT. OF COMMITTALS.

Years	Per Cent	Years	Per Cent
1805	60.13	1830	70.72
1810	61.35	1835	71.04
1815	62.16	1841	73.05
1820	67.23	1845	74.69
1825	69.01	1849	75.49

—PORTER's *Progress of the Nation*, 638, third edition.

‡ COMMITMENTS FOR SERIOUS CRIMES IN GREAT BRITAIN AND IRELAND.

Years	England	Scotland	Ireland	Total	Population of whole
1822	12,241	1,691	13,354	27,183	21,500,000
1823	12,263	1,733	14,632	28,628	
1824	13,698	1,802	15,258	30,748	
1825	14,437	1,876	15,515	31,828	
1826	14,164	1,999	16,318	31,481	
1845	24,303	3,537	16,696	44,536	
1846	25,107	4,069	18,492	47,668	
1847	28,883	4,635	31,209	64,677	
1848	30,349	4,909	38,522	73,780	
1849	27,866	4,357	41,902	74,169	28,000,000

—PORTER's *Progress of the Nation*, third edition, p. 8, 635, 637, 638, and *Parl. Returns*.

---

* Table showing the instruction of criminals over the British empire in 1844 and 1848:

	Neither read nor write	Imperfectly	Well	Superior	Total educated	Total uneducated
1844						
England	9,220	13,732	2,253	126	18,171	9,220
Scotland	696	2,048	554	42	2,831	696
Ireland	7,152	3,664	5,631	...	8,733	7,152
1848						
England	9,691	17,111	2,884	81	20,076	9,691
Scotland	...	...	...	...	3,985	911
Ireland	...	...	...	...	...	...

—*Parl. Returns*, 1844-8.

In France, it appears from M. Guerry's tables that in all the eighty-four departments, without exception, the amount of crime is in proportion to the amount of instruction; while in Prussia, where education is more general than in any other country in the world, being enforced by government on every citizen with a family, the proportion of serious crimes to the population is *twelve times greater* than in France, where half the people can neither read nor write.—See ALISON's *Essays*, i. 555

them go, after a year or two of imprisonment had been undergone; and they were soon back in their old haunts, committing new crimes, and giving their old associates the most encouraging accounts of the ease with which, by a little address, liberation from the severest sentence of transportation could be obtained.*

The true principles to follow in dealing with secondary punishments as with that of death, is to render them as certain as possible, and to consider imprisonment at home as only a preparation for, and means of teaching a trade to, those who are ultimately to be transported. For juvenile offenders, and trifling cases, a very short imprisonment, as of a week, or a flogging, should be inflicted, merely with a view to terror. For a second offense of any sort, or a first of more serious, a prolonged imprisonment, as of nine months or a year, should be the penalty, during which the convict should be carefully instructed in a trade. For the next offense, transportation should invariably be inflicted, and *as invariably carried into execution*. And if it be objected that the colonists will not receive the convicts, the answer is, that no such difficulty was experienced, till, by the abolition of the assignment system, and keeping convicts in gangs, and sending them all in overwhelming multitudes to one colony, it became an object of dread, rather than ambition, to all others; that this difficulty will at once be overcome by engaging, on the part of Government, to send three untainted colonists for one convict to any colony which will receive the latter; or establishing an entire new penal colony, to which all untainted persons emigrating at the expense of Government might be sent; a system which would at once convert all the refractory colonies into petitioners for a portion of the fertilizing stream; and that, if it should prove otherwise, Australia is large enough to afford room for the establishment of new penal colonies, regarding which no consent need be asked for thousands of years to come.†

<small>94 True principles on the subject.</small>

Another subject of general interest was discussed in Parliament this year, which was that of the succors clandestinely furnished by the British to the insurgents in South America. Ever since the contest between the splendid colonies of Spain and the mother country had begun in 1810, of which an account has been given in a chapter of the author's former work,¹ it had been regarded with warm interest in Great Britain; partly in consequence of the strong and instinctive attachment of its inhabitants to the cause of freedom, and sympathy with all who are engaged in asserting it; partly in consequence of extravagant expectations

<small>95. Clandestine succors sent by the English to the South American insurgents. ¹ Hist. of Europe, c. lxvii.</small>

formed and fomented by interested parties, as to the vast field that, by the independence of these colonies, would be opened to British commerce and enterprise. As long as the war in Europe lasted, this sympathy was evinced only by an anxious observance of the struggle; for the physical resources of the country were entirely absorbed in the terrific contest with Napoleon. But when peace succeeded, and the armies of all the European states were in great part reduced, the interest taken in the cause of South American independence began to assume a more practical and efficient form. Great numbers of officers from all countries, wearied of the monotony of pacific life, or tempted by the high rank and liberal pay offered them in South America, began to go over to the ranks of the insurgents, and ere long rendered their forces greatly more formidable than they had previously been. The English, prompted by the love of freedom, wandering, and adventure, which seems to be inherent in the Anglo-Saxon character, were soon pre-eminent in this respect; and the succors they sent over ere long assumed so formidable an appearance as attracted the serious notice of the Spanish government. Not only did great numbers of the Peninsular veterans, officers and men, go over in small bodies, and carry to the insurgents the benefit of their experience and the *prestige* of their fame, but a British adventurer, who assumed the title of Sir Gregor M'Gregor, collected a considerable expedition in the harbors of this country, with which, in British vessels and under the British flag, he took possession of Porto Bello, in South America, then in the undisturbed possession of a Spanish force, a country at peace with Great Britain. This violent aggression led to strong remonstrances on the part of the Spanish government, in consequence of which Government brought in a Foreign Enlistment Bill, which led to violent debates in both Houses of Parliament.¹

<small>¹ Parl. Deb. June 28, 1819, xl. 1381, 1382.</small>

On the part of Government, it was argued by the Earl of Liverpool, Lord Bathurst, and Lord Castlereagh: "As the law at present stands by the 9th and 29th Geo. II., and the 9th Geo. III., it is made felony, without benefit of clergy, to seduce subjects of this country to enlist in the service of foreign powers. These enactments are quite general, and apply to all foreign countries without exception, and have no special reference to the raising troops for the service of the Pretender, though they were probably conceived with that view. Soon after the late peace was concluded, it was discovered that several British officers had left this country to take service with the insurgents of South America. At first, while the number was inconsiderable, the Government did not consider it necessary to notice their engagements. When, however, the number increased, it was notified to officers on half-pay, that if they enlisted in foreign service they would lose their half-pay. This notice, however, had not the desired effect. The enlistment of recruits for South America went on openly: several large bodies embarked in British harbors for that country, and lawyers thought it doubtful whether the existing Acts of Parliament could

<small>96. Argument of Ministers in favor of the Foreign Enlistment Bill.</small>

---

* At the spring circuit at Glasgow, in April, 1848, out of 117 ordinary criminals indicted, there were 22 who had been convicted at that place within two years previously, and sentenced to various periods of transportation, none under seven years; and the previous sentence was stated in the indictment as an aggravation of the offense. The same was the case for several years, and obtains, though in a lesser degree, to this day.

† In the essay on "Crime and Transportation," in the author's *Miscellaneous Essays*, vol. i., p. 547, this very important and interesting subject is discussed more at length, and in detail, than is practicable in a work of general history.

reach them. It became necessary, therefore, to do something more efficient; and this was alike called for by our position as a neutral power, and by the special engagements under which we stood with Spain relative to the South American insurgents.

97. Continued.
"By the treaty of 1814 with the cabinet of Madrid, Great Britain had expressly become bound to furnish no succors to the Spanish insurgents, and the Government declared their resolution to observe a strict neutrality; and a proclamation, founded on this principle, was issued in 1817, warning his Majesty's subjects not to accept any military commissions from, nor give any aid to, either of the parties. This principle was strictly acted upon by the British Government; and although some British officers were serving by license in the Spanish army, it was understood they were not to act against the insurgents, and this understanding had been enforced in two instances. A change of the law, however, had become necessary, because the severity of the penalty denounced in it rendered it impossible to carry it into execution. It is proposed in the present act to take away the capital sanction, and declare persons enlisting in foreign service guilty of misdemeanor only, and to declare the supplying the belligerents with warlike stores, and equipping vessels for warlike purposes, the like offense. The law thus mitigated, in conformity with the spirit of the age, may be really carried into effect, so as to show that we are really in earnest in the neutrality we have declared.

98. Continued.
"Such a determination is one which is not to be regarded as a temporary, but a permanent resolution—a declaration of the policy which, in all similar circumstances, has regulated just and considerate neutral states, and which it is incumbent on this country in an especial manner steadily to adhere to. It is expressly provided for by the treaty with Spain in 1814; but, irrespective of that treaty, it is incumbent on us by the eternal principles of justice, and the acknowledged maxims of international law. It is impossible to say we are at peace or amity with a country, the subjects of which are entitled to make war at pleasure with the subjects of our own country. Such a species of hostility is war in its very worst form; for it is war without its laws, its restraints, its direction, or its objects. It is not national hostility directed to public purposes, but private piracy aiming at nothing but individual plunder. Can we permit armaments fitted out in this country to attack the peaceable colonies or possessions of another country, or to aid its insurgents in severing themselves from its dominion? This case has actually occurred in the recent seizure of Porto Bello, a town of New Spain, by an expedition commanded by a person who assumed the title of Sir Gregor M'Gregor. If this was sanctioned against Porto Bello, might it not equally be done against Corunna, Cadiz, or Madrid itself! Was this consistent with justice? Was it not, on the contrary, sanctioning the grossest injustice? Of all states in the world, Great Britain is the one which has the most decided interest to resist the promulgating of such doctrines; for not only is Ireland the perpetual field of domestic discontent and foreign tampering, but her colonies in every part of the world at once invite aggression, and render defense almost hopeless.

99. Concluded.
"The same case has occurred in former times with other countries, and been always met by the steady resistance for which we now contend. In 1792 a treaty was concluded between Great Britain and the United States, by which it was stipulated that the subjects of neither power should accept commissions in the service of any prince or state at war with the other. The government of the United States, when the war broke out between this country and France, immediately passed a law prohibiting the enlisting of their citizens in the service of any foreign prince or power, or furnishing them with ships or warlike stores; and this act, which punished any infringement of its provisions by fine or imprisonment, though at first temporary, was afterward made permanent. In 1818 the Americans extended this law to any power, whether recognized or not, expressly in order to meet the case of the succors sent to the Spanish insurgents in the southern parts of their continent. It is true that volunteering into foreign service was permitted in the reigns of Elizabeth, Charles I., and James II.; but then it was only because the services entered into were those of states at war with the avowed enemies of Great Britain, and at a time when the virulence of religious warfare rendered hostilities as ceaseless between Catholics and Protestants as ever they had been between Mussulmans and Christians. But can this be predicated of our old and faithful allies the Spaniards, who have stood by our side in the terrible Peninsular struggle during seven years with Napoleon? And are we prepared, as the first proof of our gratitude to them for the devoted fidelity with which they fulfilled their engagements toward us during war, to aid their enemies, 1 Parl. Deb. on the return of peace, in dismembering their dominions?"¹ xl. 1376, 1387.

100. Answer by the Opposition.
On the other hand, it was contended by Lord Holland, Lord Lansdowne, and Mr. Tierney: "The present bill has been brought forward, not on any general ground of policy, for it is directly contrary to the practice of England in its best days, but solely in consequence of a specific application from the court of Spain. Had, then, that power any right to make that demand, either upon the ground of the general law of nations, or the terms of any particular treaty; and if she had not, are there any reasons of justice or expedience which call upon us to depart from the undoubted law, and still more undoubted feeling, of this country for above a century back? Both questions must be answered in the negative. The German jurists, particularly Martens, say that it is perfectly consistent with neutrality to give every assistance to either of the belligerents, except warlike expeditions. This principle has been constantly acted upon in this country. It was done, and to a very great extent, in the reign of Elizabeth, when the Dutch were struggling for their independence; and in that of James, when Gustavus Adolphus was contending, on the plains of Germany, for the cause of religious freedom all over the world. Could it be said that the efforts of

individuals to support the cause of South American independence were warlike expeditions, in the sense of the German jurist.' 'Every state,' says Martens, 'has a right to give liberty of raising troops in its dominions, and marching them through the country, and may grant to one state what it refuses to another, without infringing its neutrality.' It is in vain to say this is a novel and unheard-of doctrine; it has been constantly acted upon in this country. Queen Elizabeth allowed her subjects to enlist to any extent in the service of the Dutch commonwealth, though never in that of Philip of Spain; and James I., a great jurist, though certainly no hero, allowed 2460 soldiers to be raised for the service of Gustavus Adolphus, while he remained undisturbed in his relations of amity with the Emperor, against whom they acted. It may be asserted, without fear of contradiction, that for four centuries, and down to the year 1792, when the Netherlands were engaged in a revolt against Joseph II., there never was a period in which British subjects were not engaged in giving succor, as individuals, to other states; and no instance can be shown in which government interfered in the manner now proposed to prevent them.

"But it is said the government of Spain is entitled to particular rights by the treaty of 1814, already alluded to. Not a hint on this subject had been given when the treaty was signed; but now, after the lapse of five years, they come forward and claim performance of certain stipulations in their favor. It is impossible to suppose that the clause in that treaty is to be understood in the sense now put upon it; for, if so, how is it possible to explain the silence of both governments in regard to it during the last five years? Nay, in the treaties with France, the subjects of the two countries are interdicted from issuing letters of marque; so that, according to the doctrine of Government, this country, not having the advantage of a treaty of commerce with Spain, was to be held as having incurred an obligation which only a treaty of commerce could have imposed. The strict interpretation of this treaty would bear very hard on the independent states of South America; for it is well known that arms are sent openly from this country to the government of Old Spain, to be used against the South American states; and, indeed, the public journals have publicly declared that the expedition from Cadiz was only delayed for that purpose. The execution of this treaty would not be preserving even the balance of a strict neutrality; it would be enabling the government of England to give assistance to the government of Old Spain, while it withheld succor from the states of South America, struggling for their independence.

"Much had been said as to the assistance given to the South American states by the half-pay officers who have entered their service from the army of this country; but there is much also to be said on the other side, on behalf of that gallant and meritorious body of men. It is easy to make rhetorical flourishes about soldiers retiring, and converting their swords into pruning-hooks; but every one knows that, though that sometimes took place in antiquity, it does not exist save in the dreams of the poets in modern times. A large body of men who have devoted themselves to war as a profession, and have spent the best part of their lives in its service, can not, in general, turn to any other profession; and if unable to maintain themselves in their proper rank in this country, it is the height of injustice to debar them from following out their profession in foreign states. The commercial interests of the country loudly call for the Government not to discourage a movement eminently calculated to extend and promote new fields for the enterprise of its merchants in the New World. This is a great and important consideration, which ought not lightly to be passed over. There is no man in England who can for a moment suppose that the colonies of Spain will ever return to the government of the old country, attached as they are to freedom by passion and inclination, as well as by the prospect of enjoying the blessings which Providence has so bountifully placed within their reach. After the long, painful, and bloody war shall have ended, and these countries have obtained those first of earthly blessings, liberty and independence, it would be painful to think that England, during its continuance, had been linked only with the cause of their tyrants; and that, not content with dealing out a fair measure of justice between the contending parties, Parliament had thought fit to invoke the aid of the common informer against those persons who devoted their abilities and energies to the cause of freedom in the New World."¹

On this debate the Lords determined in favor of Ministers by a majority of 53—the numbers being 100 to 47. On a debate on the same subject in the House of Commons, the majority was 61—the numbers being 190 to 129.²

It was evident, from the comparatively narrow majority in the Commons on this important subject, that a strong national feeling had come to prevail in the Legislature in favor of the insurgents in South America; and, in truth, this feeling was but the reflection of a still stronger one in the nation on the subject. The English people were all but unanimous in favor of the cause of South American independence. All classes joined in the desire to see the Spanish colonies emancipated from what was supposed to be the tyranny of the mother country. The philanthropic and enthusiastic saw a boundless career of happiness opened to those boundless regions, if they were extricated from the meshes of governors and priests, and blessed with Anglo-Saxon freedom and institutions. The democratic party rejoiced in the establishment of republican institutions all over the world. The half-pay officers, languishing in obscurity and poverty, were easily persuaded to enter the service of states which offered them high rank, liberal pay, and a grant of land at the conclusion of the contest. Not a few of the giddy youth were caught by the brilliant uniforms which were displayed at the shop-windows, and which, donned the moment they received their commissions, enabled them to figure at balls in London before they had undergone any of the perils of real warfare. The covetous and selfish—and they were by far the largest class—looked forward to an immense addition to our export trade, to the future extension of which no limits could be assigned, if the Spanish monopoly was broken down, and a colonial trade, which, before the war, amounted to above *fifteen millions sterling of exports* from Old Spain, was thrown open to British enterprise.[1] The two strongest principles in the Anglo-Saxon mind—the love of freedom and the love of gain—were so firmly enlisted in favor of the South American insurgents, that all attempts to check it were vain. The Act of Parliament passed remained a dead letter. The embarkation of troops, stores, and loans of money continued without intermission; and, as detailed in a former work, Spanish America was thereby rendered independent, and severed from the dominion of Old Spain.[1]

<small>[1] Humboldt, Nouvelle Espagne, iv. 153, 154.</small>

<small>[1] See Hist. of Europe, c. lxvii. §47-91.</small>

Yet, though success attended these efforts of Great Britain in favor of the Spanish insurgents, as it did those of France in support of the North American insurgents in the last century, there can be no doubt that in both cases the conduct was equally criminal, and equally a violation of the law of nations. Admitting that the doctrine of Martens, on which Lord Lansdowne so strongly rested, is well founded, and that it is in no violation of neutrality for one belligerent to be allowed to levy men in the dominions of a neutral power, that was a very different thing from the course which was now adopted in Great Britain in regard to the South American insurgents. There was no levying of men by isolated foreign agents, as in the wars of the Duke of Alva or Gustavus Adolphus. Joint stock companies were formed; loans to an enormous extent granted to the governments of the insurgent states, at a very high rate of interest, provided for by retaining twenty or thirty per cent. off the sum subscribed; and great expeditions sent out, which at last amounted to 8000 and 10,000 men, fully armed and equipped by the companies engaged in the undertaking, in order to secure for them the payment of their dividends. Never had the Government of England during the war, before the Spanish contest commenced, furnished such effective succors to its allies on the Continent, both in men, money, and arms, as were now sent out by private companies and individuals to aid the cause in which they were so deeply interested in the New World; and the success gained was proportionally great; for it, and it alone, prolonged the contest, and at length severed the colonies from the parent state.[2]

<small>104. Vast extent of the aid thus afforded to the insurgents.</small>

<small>[2] Hist. of Europe, c. lxvii. §§ 49-91.</small>

But immediate success is not always the test either of the wisdom or justice of national measures. God visits the sins of the fathers upon the children, but it is often on the third and fourth generations. From 1814 to 1824, England acted most iniquitously in aiding in the dismemberment of an allied state, with which she was in perfect amity at the time, and which had faithfully stood by her during her previous struggle, and, like France, for a similar faithlessness before, she has got her reward. By aiding the revolution in America, France brought on revolution upon herself a few years after; and the same result followed, though from a different series of causes, the English efforts to dismember the allied Spanish empire in the next century. The prolongation of the contest, which raged without intermission for fifteen years, from 1810 to 1825, utterly ruined the mines of South America, and brought down the annual supply of precious metals for the use of the globe from ten millions to three millions annually; thence, of course, ensued a general reduction of prices of every article over the whole world, and especially its work-shop and trading emporium, Great Britain. Actuated by a similar motive, the love of gain, and the desire of augmenting the value of realized capital, England at the very same time adopted the decisive step, by the Act of 1819, of contracting her paper currency, and rendering it entirely dependent on the retention of gold, beyond the limited amount of fourteen millions — an amount wholly inadequate to the wants of the nation. At the moment when, by its foreign policy, and the aid given to the cause of insurrection, the nation was so diminishing the supply of the precious metals over the globe, as to render their retention in this country in adequate quantities a matter of impossibility, it voluntarily cut off the resource of a domestic paper circulation, and dried up the springs of industry, by halving the currency by which it was to be maintained. Thence the terrible monetary crisis of 1825, the long-continued and widespread suffering which followed that catastrophe, the Reform revolution which that suffering induced, the total change in the commercial policy of the empire which ensued in the next twenty years, and the dissolution of those bonds which united her colonies to the parent state, and held together the magnificent fabric of the British empire. All this resulted from our own acts—was all the direct and immediate consequence of our own injustice. The year 1819 was the turning-point in our policy, both foreign and domestic; all the vast changes which have since ensued may be traced to the ascendency of the principles in the nation which were then brought into operation.

<small>105. Punishment which England has received for this injustice.</small>

And what gain has England won, even in the first instance, to compensate such wide-spread and lasting devastation! Admissions made by the ablest leaders of the new system, facts collected by its best statisticians, give the answer Lord Palmerston has told us, in his place in Parliament, that Great Britain, between 1820 and 1840, had advanced £150,000,000 in loans to the popular states and republics of Spain and South America, nearly the whole of which had been lost by the faithlessness or insolvency of the states which received them. If to this we add the dreadful losses consequent on the monetary crisis of 1825, the direct consequence, as will immediately appear, of the speculations entered into in 1824 by British capitalists in South America, at a time when the maintenance of our currency at home was rendered entirely dependent on our retention of the daily declining supplies of gold, we shall have a loss of three hundred millions sterling inflicted upon Great Britain, the direct consequence of her own selfish pur

<small>106. Dreadful losses arising from our interference with South America.</small>

suit of gain at the expense of other interests or states. Was, then, the gain from these unwise or iniquitous measures such as to compensate the direct and fearful loss with which they were attended! So far from it the export trade from Great Britain to South America, which embraces nearly all of European fabrics which the independent states can take off, had sunk to £1,290,000 in 1827, and in 1842 had only reached £2,300,000;* although the exports from Spain alone to these colonies before the war was £15,000,000, and the imports from them £17,150,000, the greater part of which immense trade was in the hands of British merchants.† As if to demonstrate, too, that it is to the Revolution, and it alone, that this prodigious decline is to be ascribed, our exports to Brazil, which has retained its monarchical government, have averaged about £2,500,000 for the last twenty years.‡ And our exports to America, exclusive of the United States, were in 1809, before the Revolution began, no less than £18,014,219; and in 1810, £15,640,166.§ Such have been the effects, even to the immediate interests of England, of her iniquitous attempt to dismember, by insidious acts in peace, the dominions of a friendly and allied power! Providence has a just and sure mode of dealing with the sins of men, which is to leave them to the consequences of their own actions.

* EXPORTS FROM GREAT BRITAIN TO SOUTH AMERICAN STATES.

Years.	Mexico.	Guatemala.	Columbia.	Rio de la Plata.	Peru.	Total.
	£	£	£	£	£	£
1827	692,800	1,948	213,972	154,895	228,466	1,292,076
1828	307,028	6,191	261,113	312,389	374,615	1,261,330
1829	303,562	..	232,703	758,540	300,171	1,542,048
1840	465,330	2,373	359,743	611,047	799,961	2,239,454
1841	434,901	21,265	158,972	989,466	536,046	2,140,440
1842	374,260	..	234,711	969,791	684,313	2,260,784

—Porter's Parl. Tables, xii. 114.

† IMPORTS FROM SPAIN, AND EXPORTS TO IT FROM THE SOUTH AMERICAN COLONIES IN 1809.

Imports from Spain.

	Piastres.	£
Porto Rico	11,000,000	2,750,000
Mexico	21,000,000	5,250,000
New Granada	5,700,000	1,450,000
Caraccas	8,500,000	2,150,000
Peru and Chili	11,500,000	2,875,000
Buenos Ayres and Potosi	3,500,000	875,000
	59,200,000	15,200,000

Exports to Spain.

	Agricultural Produce.		Precious Metals.		
	Piastres.	£	Piastres.	£	
Porto Rico	9,000,000	2,250,000			
Mexico	9,000,000	2,250,000	22,500,000	5,660,000	
New Granada	2,000,000	500,000	3,000,000	750,000	
Caraccas	4,000,000	1,000,000			
Peru and Chili	4,000,000	1,000,000	8,000,000	2,000,000	
Buenos Ayres and Potosi	2,000,000	500,000	5,000,000	1,250,000	
	30,000,000	7,500,000	38,500,000	9,650,000	

—HUMBOLDT's Essai Politique sur la Nouvelle Espagne, iv. 153, 154.

‡ EXPORTS FROM GREAT BRITAIN TO BRAZIL AND AMERICA, EXCLUDING UNITED STATES.

To Brazil.		To America, excluding United States.	
Years.		Years.	
1827	£2,312,109	1806	£10,877,968
1828	2,518,297	1807	10,439,423
1829	2,516,040	1808	16,591,871
1840	2,625,852	1809	18,014,219
1841	2,556,554	1810	15,640,166
1842	1,756,805	1811	11,939,680

—Porter's Parl. Tables, xii. 114.

§ Porter's Progress of the Nation, 159, third edition.

CHAPTER V.

PROGRESS OF LITERATURE, SCIENCE, THE ARTS, AND MANNERS, IN GREAT BRITAIN AFTER THE PEACE

1.
Great impulse given to literature and science after the war.

Those who consider war a universal and unmitigated evil, and fields of battle vast shambles, where human beings massacre each other without either object or pity, would do well to consider the progress of Great Britain and France in literature, science, and the arts, during the forty years which followed the close of the war, and compare it with any other epoch which is to be found in the annals of modern times. In none does so great an impulse appear to have been given to human genius, nor were such efforts made by human industry, nor such triumphs achieved by human exertion. Compared with this era, all preceding ones sink into insignificance. Science made splendid discoveries—literature a mighty stride—genius took lofty flights. The effect was the same in England, France, and Germany; the Augustine age of each was that which immediately succeeded the fall of Napoleon. The triumphs of art, the additions made to the power of man over the elements, were unparalleled during this period. Space was almost annihilated—time essentially abridged. The electric telegraph conveyed intelligence in a few minutes from Paris to London. Steam conveyed the emigrants in ten days from Britain to America, in six weeks to India. In proportion to the vehemence of the internal passions, the hidden fires which impelled mankind into the wilderness of nature, was the addition made to the facilities by which they were to reach, the powers by which they were to subdue it; and after the lapse of three thousand years, Fire vindicated the right of the poet to rank Prometheus as the greatest benefactor of the human species.

2.
Way in which war produces this effect.

It is not merely by the impulse given to energy, and the extrication of talent and vigor by the danger and necessities of war, that it acts in this decisive way, in great emergencies, upon the fortunes of mankind. A still more important effect takes place by the direction which it gives to the passions and the thoughts, by impelling them out of the narrow circle of selfish and individual objects, into the wider sphere of public and national interest. Selfishness is the upas-tree which invariably grows up and sheds its poisoned drops around during periods of tranquillity, because then there is no counter-attraction to the seductions of sense—the suggestions of interest. Every man sits under the shadow of his own fig-tree, but every man thinks of that fig-tree alone. In war, he is obliged, by the approach of danger, to extend his view to the furthest parts of the horizon—to become interested in remote and future events, to sympathize with the fortunes of men in distant lands. This, when extended to nations, is an immense advantage; for it is the application of a remedy to the greatest weakness and radical curse of humanity. The actors in war, indeed, are often selfish, rapacious, hard-hearted; though many among them are noble, generous, devoted. But the sufferers under it are actuated, in general, by the generous emotions. Among them is to be found the patience which endures suffering, the heroism which braves danger, the patriotism which sacrifices self to country. It is in these emotions that the spring is to be found of national greatness, even in the arts of peace; it is not less true in the moral than the material world, that "a nation makes the Past, the Distant, and the Future predominate over the Present—exalts us in the scale of thinking beings."

3.
Rapid progress of steam navigation in Britain.

If the period succeeding the war is one which is not rich in great events, it is fruitful in great men; if the triumphs of arms are awanting, those of philosophy, literature, and the arts were memorable and everlasting. It was distinguished by the first successful application of steam to the purposes of locomotion—a discovery of which the original honor is due to Scotland, but the first successful application to America; and of which the consequences, in their ultimate results, are destined to change the face of the moral world.* Like all the other changes which have made a great and lasting impression on human affairs, its importance was not at first perceived. It was decried by philosophy, and rejected by the French *savans*, to whom Napoleon remitted the consideration of it as a means of forwarding the invasion of Great Britain.† Practical men, however, were not long of discovering its importance; and within a few years of the time when the first steam-boat—the Comet—was launched upon the Clyde, several hundreds were sailing round the British islands. For long it was thought that steam could not be used for long voyages; and naval men generally declared that, from the fragility of the materials necessarily employed in generating it, it would make no material change in naval warfare. Time, however, has now enabled us to estimate at their true value these prognostications. The Atlantic has been breasted by the British steamers—the duration and expense of the voyage to New York have been halved—the journey to Bombay, by the Red Sea, is habitually performed in six weeks; and preparations are making for conveying emigrants in seven by the Isthmus of Panama or that of Suez to Australia. Already nearly the half of the British

---

* The first steam-boat ever constructed was built by Mr. Miller, of Dalswinton, in 1797. The author has seen it, as a curiosity, on the Forth and Clyde Canal. One of the workmen engaged in its construction carried the secret out to America, where it was eagerly embraced, and energetically carried into execution by Fulton in 1812. The first one which ever sailed in the British seas was the Comet, on board of which the author made a voyage in 1813. † See Alison's *Europe*, c. 24, § 67.

navy is composed of steam-vessels of war; and the principal security of England is founded on the belief that she could, on an emergency, fit out a greater number of those ocean giants than any other power.

1. Advance of the cotton manufacture.

Less striking in appearance, but not less important in reality, has been the progress of the cotton manufacture, the creature of steam, in the British islands, especially during the years which immediately succeeded the peace. Rapid as had been its advance during the war, its forward movement and the improvement in its machinery was still more marvelous since its termination; for British industry was then exposed to the competition of foreign nations in which labor was cheaper and taxes lighter, and superiority could only be maintained by a continued addition to the powers and simplification of the wheels of machinery. But here the coal and iron-stone of Great Britain came to the aid of its inhabitants; and great as had been the discovery of Watt, its powers were quadrupled by the additions made to it by subsequent geniuses. The marvels of the cotton manufacture, in Britain, have since that time exceeded all other marvels; and the vast development of native wealth and industry during the last thirty years has been mainly owing to its progress. From the accounts laid before Parliament, it appears that the official value of cotton goods exported, which in 1785 was £864,000, and in 1797 had risen to £2,580,000, had mounted in 1814, at the close of the war, to £17,655,000; and in 1833 had reached the enormous amount of £46,000,000!* So great and rapid an increase is, perhaps, not to be found in any single branch of manufacture; nor, perhaps, in all branches put together, since the beginning of the world. If these wonderful statistics afford a key to much of the strength exhibited in England during the war, those which follow are equally symptomatic of its weakness, and of the prolific seeds of distress which the resumption of cash payments and the contraction of the currency had implanted, in the period succeeding the peace, in the community. The

* COTTON MANUFACTURES AND YARN EXPORTED FROM GREAT BRITAIN.

Years.	Official Value.	Declared Value.
1697	£5,915	
1780	355,060	
1785	864,710	
1797	2,580,568	
1800	5,854,057	
1810	18,951,994	
1814	17,655,378	£20,033,132
1815	22,289,615	20,620,956
1816	17,564,464	15,577,392
1817	21,230,224	16,012,601
1818	22,589,130	18,767,517
1819	18,282,292	14,699,912
1820	22,531,079	16,516,758
1821	23,541,615	16,694,807
1822	26,911,043	17,218,801
1823	26,514,770	16,276,813
1824	30,155,904	16,376,515
1825	29,495,224	18,253,631
1826	25,191,270	14,013,675
1827	33,182,998	17,562,384
1828	33,467,417	17,140,114
1829	37,269,432	17,394,575
1830	41,050,969	19,335,971
1831	39,357,075	17,182,036
1832	43,756,233	17,344,676
1833	46,317,210	18,450,000

—*Parl. Paper*, 1831, No. 145; and *Finan's Accounts*, 1834.

official value, which indicates the *quantity* manufactured, had risen, between 1814 and 1832, from £17,600,000 to £46,000,000; the *declared* value, which indicates the price received for it, had sunk from £20,000,000 to £18,450,000. It is not surprising that this extraordinary diminution in the declared value of cotton goods exported took place at a time when so great an increase in the production was going forward, for such was the reduction in the cost of production, by the application and improvement of machinery, and contraction of the currency, that the price of cotton-yarn, No. 100, which in 1786 was 38s., had sunk in 1832 to 2s. 11d.; and a piece of calico, which in 1814 cost £1 4s. 7d., was selling in 1833 for 6s. 2d.! Whoever will consider these figures with attention, will have no difficulty in discovering the principal causes at once of the strength and weakness of the British empire during and subsequent to the war, and of the vast social and political changes which so soon after occurred in it.[1]

[1] Barnes's *History of Cotton Manufacture*, 350, 357; Parl. Papers, 1831, No. 145

5. Progress in other branches of manufacture.

The vast impulse given at this period to industry was not confined to the cotton manufacture; though it, as the greatest, was the most conspicuous, and has attracted most attention. In woollen goods, cutlery, hardware, and iron, the progress was nearly as rapid; the last, in particular, was in a manner a new creation in Great Britain since the peace. The total quantity of pig-iron wrought in Great Britain, in 1814, was 350,000 tons; in 1835 it had risen to 1,000,000 tons.* Generally speaking, however, it was in the useful arts only that this extraordinary growth was perceptible; in the more delicate and ornamental, and those which depended on the fine arts for their design and beauty, we were still greatly inferior to our Continental neighbors. Remoteness of situation, distance from the models of taste in the remains of ancient genius, was the cause of this inferiority. The necessity of studying them, the value of schools of design to diffuse and perpetuate a knowledge of their beauty and of the principles of art, was unknown. A quarter of a century had to elapse before the nation became sensible of its inferiority in these respects, and endeavored, by the general establishment of elementary schools for the study of the fine arts, to emancipate itself from the necessity of recurring to foreign artists for designs in all the ornamental branches of manufacture. Since that period its progress in the fine manufactures, and the designs requisite for them, has been great and rapid; but at the Great Exhibition of 1851 it was apparent that even then an equality with foreign taste had not yet been attained.

If the triumphs of British art and industry have been great during this memorable period,

* IRON MADE IN GREAT BRITAIN.

Years.	Tons.	Years.	Tons.
1796	124,000	1830	653,000
1802	170,000	1835	1,000,000
1806	250,000	1836	1,200,000
1814	350,000	1840	1,500,000
1823	442,000	1847	1,999,000
1825	581,367	1848	2,093,736
1828	702,584		

—PORTER's *Progress of the Nation*, 267, 269. 3d edition

those of its genius and thought have been not less remarkable, and still more lasting. This is generally the case, after a great and decisive national struggle: the energy and talent developed during its continuance by the urgency of the public dangers, is directed, on their termination, to pacific objects. Literature then assumes its noblest character, and is directed to its most elevated objects; for general have superseded individual desires, and the selfish passions have, by the pressure of common danger, been for a time extinguished by the generous. This appeared — and from the same cause — both in Greece and Rome, and in modern Europe: the age of Pericles and Euripides immediately succeeded that of Themistocles; the genius of Cicero and Virgil illuminated the era which had witnessed the contests of Cæsar and Pompey. The era of Michael Angelo, Ariosto, and Tasso threw a radiance over the expiring strife of the Crusades; that of Bossuet, Molière, and Racine over the declining glories of the Grand Monarque; that of Shakspeare, Bacon, and Milton soon followed the fierce passions of the Reformation. The period during which this transcendant union exists is generally as short-lived as it is brilliant; and the reason, being founded in the very causes which produced it, is of lasting influence. The vehement contests which awaken and draw forth the latent powers of the human soul are necessarily of no very long duration: one party or another is ere long vanquished in the strife; and alike to the conquerors and the conquered succeeds a period of constrained repose. It is at the *commencement* of that period, when the sway of the generous passions, awakened by former common danger, is still felt, and their direction only is changed, that genius appears in its brightest colors, and works destined for immortal endurance are produced. The lengthened duration either of the prosperity consequent on success, or the humiliation resulting from adverse fortune, does not extinguish genius, but misdirects it; in the first case, by directing effort to selfish objects—in the last, by depressing it through the extinction of hope.

6. Brilliant eras in literature which generally succeed those of great public dangers.

Sir WALTER SCOTT is universally considered as the greatest writer of imagination of this century; and his reputation has been so wide-spread and lasting, that it may reasonably be anticipated that it will not materially decline in succeeding times. Like most other great men, the direction of his genius was, in a great degree, determined by the circumstances in which he arose; but its character was exclusively his own. He rose to manhood during the heart-stirring conflict with the French Revolution; and his mind, naturally ardent, was early inflamed by the patriotic and warlike feelings which that contest naturally produced. A volunteer himself in the yeomanry ranks, his animated strains induced many to follow his example. The influence of those circumstances is very conspicuous in his writings, and many of the finest passages in his descriptions of Flodden and Bannockburn were suggested by the mimic warfare on Portobello Sands, near Edinburgh, where his corps exercised. This in

7. Literary character of Sir Walter Scott.

some degree directed the application, but t did not stamp the character of his genius. That was entirely his own. Close observation of nature, whether animated or inanimate, was his great characteristic; the brilliancy of fancy, the force of imagination, were directed to clothing with sparkling colors her varied creations. It is hard to say whether his genius was most conspicuous in describing the beauties of nature or delineating the passions of the heart; he was at once pictorial and dramatic. To this he owes his great success—hence his worldwide reputation. He was first known as a poet; but, charming as his poetic conceptions were, they were ere long eclipsed by the widespread fame of his prose romances. The novels of the author of *Waverley* caused the poems of Walter Scott to be for a time forgotten. But time has re-established them in their celebrity; and great as is still the fame of the Scotch novels, it is rivaled by the heart-stirring verses of *Marmion*, the enduring charm of the *Lady of the Lake*.

Sir Walter Scott commenced his career under very peculiar circumstances, singularly favorable for the portraiture of character at different times and under different aspects. Passing much of his childhood on the banks of the Tweed, his early fancy was kindled by the tales of the Border chivalry; educated in Edinburgh, he dreamed, in maturer years, in the grassy vale of St. Leonard's, of the knights of Ariosto and the siege of Jerusalem. But the charms of poetry, the creations of romance, did not detach his mind from the observation of nature. Mounted on a hardy Highland pony, he wandered over the mountains of Scotland, observing its scenery, inhaling its beauties, studying the character of its inhabitants. On the mountain's brow, by the glassy lake, he engraved the features of the land on his recollection; by the cottage fireside he stored his mind with the feelings and anecdotes of the peasantry; amid the castle ruins he realized, in fancy, the days of chivalry. The poetic temperament of his mind threw over the pictures of memory the radiance of imagination, without taking away the fidelity of the recollection. Thence the general admiration with which his works were received. The romantic found in them the realization of their imaginative dreams; the antiquarian, a reminiscence of the olden times; the practical, a picture of the characters they had seen around them, and with which they had been familiar from their infancy. Lord Jeffrey said, in one of the early reviews of his writings, that Scott had opened an unworkable vein, and that no human ability could make the manners of the olden time popular—a strange observation in a country in which the creations of Ariosto, the tenderness of Tasso, charmed every successive generation of men, and the error of which subsequent experience has abundantly demonstrated.

8. Peculiar character of his writings.

With these great and varied powers Scott might have been a most dangerous writer, if, like Voltaire, he had directed them to sapping the foundations of religion, or to the delineation of the degrading or licentious in character. But the elevated strain of his mind preserved

9. Their elevated moral character.

him from such contamination. It was on the noble, whether in high or low life, that his affections were fixed; the ordinary was delineated only as a set-off to its lustre. Thence his enduring fame—thence his passport to immortality. Nothing ever permanently floated down the stream of time but what was buoyant from its elevating tendency. The degrading, the licentious, the fetid, is for a time popular, and then forgotten. Alike in delineating the manners of feudal times, or the feelings of the cottage, the dignity of man was ever uppermost in his mind: he was the poet of chivalry, but, not less than the bard of nature, he never forgot that

"The rank is but the guinea stamp,
The man's the gowd for a' that."

No man ever threw a more charming radiance over the traditions of ancient times, but none ever delineated in a nobler spirit the virtues of the present; and his discriminating eye discovered them equally under the thatch of the cottage as in the halls of the castle. It has been truly said that the influence of his writings neutralized, to a certain extent, the effect of the Reform Bill; but it is not less true that none ever contributed more powerfully to that purification, without which all others are nugatory—the reform of the human heart; and perhaps he is the only author of numerous works of fiction of whom it may with truth be said that he never wrote a line which, on death-bed, he could wish recalled.

It is to his earlier writings, however, that this unqualified praise applies. *Waverley, Guy Mannering, The Antiquary, The Bride of Lammermoor, Old Mortality*, are the perfection of romantic pictures of later times; *The Abbot, Quentin Durward*, and *Ivanhoe*, of the days of chivalry. But these rich veins were at length exhausted, and the prolific fancy of the author diverged into other scenes and periods in which he had not such authentic materials to work with, and where his graphic hand was no longer to the same degree perceptible. Some of his later romances are so inferior to the first, that it is difficult to believe they have been composed by the same master spirit. It is on the earlier novels, which delineate the manners, feelings, and scenes of Scotland, and a few, such as *Ivanhoe, Kenilworth, The Talisman*, and *Quentin Durward*, which paint those of other lands, that his fame as a writer of romance will permanently rest; another proof among the many which the annals of literature afford, that it is on a faithful delineation of nature that the permanent reputation of works even of imagination must be founded, and that the Ideal can be securely rested on no other basis but the Real.*

10. The defects of his later writings.

LORD BYRON is the author who, next to Sir Walter Scott, has obtained the most wide-spread reputation in the world; and yet his character and the style

11. Lord Byron.

of his writings differ so widely from those of the Wizard of the North, that it is difficult to understand how, at the same time, they attained almost equal celebrity. He was not antiquarian in ideas, nor graphic in the delineation of character. He neither studied the days of chivalry in old romances, nor human nature in the seclusion of the cottage. He was in an especial manner the poet of high life. He has often delineated the Corsairs of the Archipelago and the maids of Greece; but it was to please the high-born dames of London that all his pictures were drawn. Born of a noble English family, but of a Scotch mother, and nursed amid the mountains of Aberdeenshire, his ardent temperament was first evinced in childhood by a precocious passion for a Scottish beauty, his poetic disposition awakened by the mist-clad rocks of Lochnagar. Thrown into the fashionable world in London at a very early age, he soon felt that satiety which genius never fails to experience from the excess of pleasure, and that dissatisfaction which real greatness generally feels amid the vanities of fashion. Wearied with the inanities of gay, the dissipation of profligate life, he sought change abroad; the rocks of Cintra, the beauties of Cadiz, the isles of Greece, successively rose to his view; and the brilliant moving panorama, seen through the eyes of genius, produced the poem of *Childe Harold*, which has rendered his name immortal.

It is on this splendid production, more than on his metrical romances, that his reputation will ultimately rest. The success of the latter was at first prodigious, but it arose from a peculiarity which is fatal to durable fame. They were so much admired, not because they were founded on nature, but because they differed from it. Addressed to the exclusive circles of London society, they fell upon the high-born votaries of fashion with the charm of novelty; they breathed the language of vehement passion, which was as new to them as the voice of nature, speaking through the dreamy soul of Rousseau, had been to the corrupted circles of Parisian society half a century before. As such they excited an immense sensation, and even more than the thoughtful and yet pictured pages of *Childe Harold*, raised the author to the very pinnacle of celebrity. But no reputation can be lasting which is not founded on the images and feelings of nature singularity, affectation, caprice, if wielding the powers of genius, may acquire a temporary celebrity, but it will be but temporary. With the circumstances which nursed the fashion which exalted it, it falls to the ground. It was ere long discovered that his Corsairs and Sultanas were all cast in one mould, and bore one image and superscription; their passions were violent and powerfully drawn, but they were all the same, and bore no resemblance to the diversified emotions of real life. They were like the trees of Vivarez or Perelle, so well known to the lovers of engravings—rich, luxuriant, and charming at first sight, but characterized by decided mannerism very different from the veracious outlines of Claude or Salvator.

12. His merits and defects.

In one class of readers the dramas of Byron have won for him a very high reputation; in another, *Don Juan* is his passport to popularity. But though characterized by ardent genius, and

* Sir Walter Scott had a prodigious fund of stories and anecdotes at command, both in regard to the olden and the present time, which he told with infinite zest and humor; and his conversation was always interspersed with those strokes of delicate satire or sterling good sense which abound in his writings. But he had not the real conversational talent; there was little interchange of ideas when he talked; he took it nearly all to himself, and talked of persons or old anecdotes, or characters, not things.

13. abounding with noble lines, his dramatic pieces want the elements of enduring fame. They are too wild for ordinary life, too extravagant for theatrical representation. They do not come home to our hearts; there is nothing in them which can be enjoyed by the cottage fireside. Applause from the humbler classes would never begin with their performance. They are addressed to, and calculated for, minds as high-strung and poetical as his own; and how many are they amid the multitude of ordinary readers! *Don Juan* is different: there is much in it which unhappily too powerfully rouses every breast. But although works of fiction, in which genius is mingled with licentiousness, often, at first, acquire a very great celebrity, at least with one sex, they labor under an insurmountable objection—they can not be the subject of conversation with the other. Works of fiction are chiefly interesting to both sexes, because they portray the feelings by which they are attracted to each other. When they are of such a description that neither can communicate those feelings to the other, the great object of composition is lost, and lasting celebrity to the author is impossible.*

His dramas and Don Juan.

14. The same objection applies in an equal degree to the earlier writings of Moore; but there is a much wider acquaintance with the human heart in his later poems, and a much more graphic, and therefore touching, delineation of human feeling than in the Corsairs and Medoras of Byron. In some respects he is the greatest lyric poet in the English language. Without the discursive imagination of Akenside, without the burning thoughts of Gray, without the ardent soul of Campbell, he has written more that comes home to the hearts of the young and impassioned of both sexes than any other author—if a few lines in Burns are excepted—in the whole literature of Great Britain. His Irish and national melodies will be immortal; and they will be so for this reason, that they express the feelings which spring up in the breast of every successive generation at the most important and imaginative period of life. They have the delicacy of refined life without its fastidiousness—the warmth of natural feeling without its rudeness. He is in an especial manner the poet of love; but it is the love of chivalry and romance rather than license, and embellished with all those images and associations with which pains in successive ages has heightened the warmth of natural feeling. Vast numbers of his lines are committed to memory by the young of both sexes; their charm is to many associated with the magic of song—the smiles of beauty; and their enduring celebrity may be anticipated by the wide-spread interest which they have already awakened.

Moore as a lyric poet.

The mind of Moore was essentially Oriental the images and ideas of the East sparkle in all his verses. His feelings were chivalrous—his soul turn, and sapenetrated with the refinements of Europe; but his thoughts were of the cloudless skies, and resistless genii, and bewitching maids of the land of the sun. So strong was this propensity, that it led to the composition of a poem of which the scene and characters were entirely laid in the East; and *Lalla Rookh* remains an enduring monument of the charm produced by the clothing of Oriental images and adventure with the genius and refinement of the Western World. But though charming to persons of general reading and varied information, it will never be so popular with ordinary readers as those lyric poems which express the feelings of the universal heart. The greatest defect of his compositions is a vein of conceit, which, even in nature years, he was never able entirely to overcome. His images are always sparkling, often brilliant; but they are as frequently far-fetched, and bespeak rather the conceit of fancy than the genuine effusions of passion. His earlier poems, published under the name of Little, though often beautiful, are so licentious that they are never now heard of but from the lips of the professed votaries of pleasure. Great part, in point of bulk, of his poems is occupied with subjects of a satirical cast or ephemeral character: they will share the usual fate of such productions; they will expire with the manners or characters which are satirized. There are many *lines* in the satires of Juvenal and Horace which are in every mouth, but the *whole poems* are *read* by none except school-boys, into whom they are driven by the force of the rod. Many persons are amused, some instructed, by the picture of the follies of their own age, but comparatively few by the absurdities of those which have preceded them; and although few are indifferent to the scandal of their contemporaries, fewer still take an interest in that of their great-grandmothers.*

15. *His Oriental lyrical verses.*

If the wide spread of his fame, and deep impression produced by his poems, is to be taken as the test of excellence, Campbell is the greatest lyric poet of England, and second to few in the general scale of poetic merit that Great Britain has ever produced. With the exception of Shakspeare and Gray, there is no author of whom so many ideas and lines have been riveted in the general mind of his country, or become, as it were, household words of the English in every land. It is not so much the

16. *Campbell: his vast and noble genius.*

---

* It was impossible that a man of Lord Byron's genius could converse for any length of time without some sparks falling; and his celebrity and rank rendered him a great favorite, especially of women of high rank. But he wounded nature in his ideas, and simplicity in his manner. He never forgot himself, and was constantly affecting the rose and man of fashion, rather than the poet or literary man. Don Juan was the picture of him in real life, much more than any of his heroes or Corsairs. The author met him only once at Venice in 1818, when he kindly entertained him in his hotel, and rowed him through the Grand Canal and the Lagunas to Lido in his gondola. The conversation was charming, chiefly from the historic anecdotes connected with the places which Lord Byron mentioned; but the impression left on the whole was rather lowering than elevating to that previously formed by the study of his writings.

* The author met Moore only once, but that was under very interesting circumstances. After an evening party at Paris, in the Rue Mont Blanc, in 1824, when he charmed every one by his singing of his own melodies, especially the exquisite one on genius outstripping wealth in the race for ladies' favor, they walked home together, and falling into very interesting conversation, walked round the Place Vendôme, in constant talk for three hours. They separated at three in the morning, with regret, at the foot of the Pillar of Austerlitz, and never met again. His conversation was very sparkling; and, as it abounded in the rapid interchange of poetical ideas, it impressed the author more than the more discursive and amusing anecdotes of Sir Walter Scott.

felicity and brevity of expression, though they never were surpassed, which have won for him this vast celebrity; it is the elevation and moral grandeur of his thoughts which have so generally fascinated the minds of men. He was in every sense the Bard of Hope. Undoubting in faith, untired in hope, he discerned the Rainbow of Peace amid the darkest storms of the moral world.* In the gloomiest disasters he never despaired of the fortunes of mankind, and was prepared to light

"The Torch of Hope at Nature's funeral pile."

The experienced in the ways of men will probably be inclined to regard many of his poems as Utopian and impracticable — the wise and reflecting, as better adapted to a future than the present state of existence; but the young, the ardent, and enthusiastic will never cease to turn to them as fraught with the noblest aspirations of our nature; and we may despair of the fortunes of the species when the admiration for *The Pleasures of Hope* begins to decline.

Great as is the reputation of that noble poem, that of his lyric pieces is still greater. They are at present, perhaps, the most popular poems of the kind in the English language; and there is no appearance of their fame diminishing. The *Rainbow*, the *Mariners of England*, the *Stanzas to Painting*, *Lochiel's Warning*, the *Ode to Winter*, the *Last Man*, *Hohenlinden*, the *Battle of the Baltic*, have become so engraven on the national heart that their impression may be regarded as indelible. They bear a very close resemblance to the ballads and poems of Schiller, and share in all the noble feelings, and yet simple and homespun images, by which those beautiful strains are distinguished. They have all the terseness and felicity of expression which have rendered Horace immortal, without any of the licentiousness which disfigures his pages. But his poems are very unequal; many, especially of the later ones, are so feeble and inferior, that it could hardly be believed they proceeded from the same hand as his earlier productions. No man was ever more felicitous in his images, or conveyed a beautiful idea in more pure and striking metaphor. His well-known image—

"'Tis the sunset of life gives me mystical lore,
And coming events cast their shadows before"—

is perhaps the most perfect and unmixed metaphor in the English language. His genius was brilliant, but it was precocious, and declined as life advanced; its flame rose up at once to a towering height, but it did not, like that of Burke, Bacon, and Rousseau, gather strength with all the acquisitions of life; and of him could not be said, as was done of ancient genius, "Materia alitur, motibus excitatur, et urendo lucescit."

If the *Pleasures of Hope* to the end of time will fascinate the young and the ardent, those of *Memory* will have equal charms for the advanced in years and the reflecting. Rogers has struck a chord which will forever vibrate in the human heart, and he has touched it with so much delicacy and pathos, that his poetry is felt as the more charming the more that the taste is improved and the mind is filled with the recollections of the past. His verses have not the vehemence of Byron's imagination, nor the ardor of Campbell's soul: "thoughts that breathe and words that burn" will be looked for in vain in his compositions. He was not fitted, therefore, to reach the highest flights of lyric poetry. He never could have written the "Feast of Alexander," like Dryden; nor the "Bard" of Gray; nor the "Stanzas to Painting" of Campbell; but he possessed, perhaps, in a still higher degree than any of them, the power of casting together pleasing and charming images, and pouring them forth in soft and mellifluous language. This is his great charm; and it is one so great that, in the estimation of many, particularly those with whom the whirl and agitation of life is past, it more than compensates for the absence of every other. To the young, who have the future before them, imagination and hope are the most entrancing powers, for they gild the as yet untrodden path of life with the wished-for flowers. But to the aged, by whom its vicissitudes have been experienced and its enjoyments known, memory and reflection are the faculties which confer the most unmixed pleasure, for they dwell on the past, and recall its most enchanting moments. Campbell had the most sincere admiration for Rogers, and repeatedly said that he was a greater poet than himself. Without going such a length, it may safely be affirmed that there is none more chaste, none more refined; and that some of his verses will bear a comparison with the most perfect in the English language.*

If ever two poets arose in striking contrast to each other, Rogers and SOUTHEY are the men; and yet they appeared in the same age, and flourished abreast of each other. Rogers is the poet of home; his charm consists in painting the scenes of infancy — portraying the endearments of youth; and he is read by all with such pleasure in mature life, because he recalls ideas and revives images which all have known, but which have been almost forgotten, though not destroyed, by the cares and anxieties of life. Southey embraces a wider sphere, but one less calculated permanently to interest the human heart. His knowledge was immense—his reading unbounded—his memory tenacious; and he availed himself of the vast stores these provided, with graphic power and scrupulous fidelity. He was a historian in poetry as well as prose; and narrated, with all the charm of diction, and embellished with the richest hues of nature, many of the most stirring events which have

---

* Witness his noble lines on the partition of Poland:

"Hope for a season bade the world farewell,
And Freedom shrieked as Kosciusko fell;
Yet thy proud lords, unpitied land! shall see
That Man hath yet a soul, and dare be free;
A little while along thy saddening plains
The starless night of Desolation reigns;
Truth shall restore the light by Nature given,
And, like Prometheus, bring the fire of Heaven.
Prone to the dust Oppression shall be hurled—
Her name, her nature, withered from the world."
Pleasures of Hope.

* As, for example, the Invocation to Memory:

"Hail, Memory, hail! within thy sparkling mine,
From age to age what boundless treasures shine!
Thought and her shadowy brood thy call obey,
And space and time are subject to thy sway!
Thy pleasures most we feel when most alone,
The only pleasures we can call our own!"
Pleasures of Memory.

occurred in the annals of mankind. But it is rare, indeed, to find a mind which can clothe reality in verse with the charms of fiction. Homer, Virgil, and Shakspeare, have alone done so since the beginning of time; and the secret of their success was not their graphic power, nor their brilliant imagination, so much as their profound knowledge of what is in all ages the same—the human heart. Southey's *Madoc*, *Don Roderick*, and the *Curse of Kehama*, are splendid metrical histories, but they do not contain the traits which speak at once to all mankind—they are addressed to the learned and studious, and these are a mere fragment of the human race. Admired, accordingly, by the well-informed, they are already comparatively unknown to the great body of readers; and the author's poetical fame rests chiefly on *Thalaba*, in which his brilliant imagination revelled without control, save that of high moral feeling, in the waterless deserts, and palm-shaded fountains, and patriarchal life of the happy Arabia.

If Southey's knowledge as a historian has impeded his success as a poet, his fancy as a poet has not less seriously marred his fame as a historian. He wrote several large historical works, of which the *Annals of the Peninsular War* and the *History of Brazil* are the most considerable; but though both possess merits of a very high order, and abound in passages of great descriptive beauty, they have never attained any high reputation, and are now well-nigh forgotten. He had not the patience of research and calmness of judgment indispensable for a trustworthy historian. His facts in many places will not bear investigation; he was credulous in the extreme, and gravely retailed statements on the authority of inflamed chronicles which subsequent inquiry disproved, and common sense at the moment might at once have discovered to be false. Living secluded and retired, he was entirely ignorant of the realities of life, and never had been brought in contact with men in their business transactions—the only way in which a thorough knowledge of their secret springs of action can ever be attained. The want of this is painfully conspicuous both in his historical and social writings; but though this deficiency must prevent them from permanently holding the place in general estimation which might have been anticipated from the genius and acquirements of the author, they must always command respect from the erudition they display, the reflection they evince, and the elevated moral and religious feelings by which they are always characterized.*

In all these respects, except the last, the neighbor of Southey in the mountains of Cumberland, WORDSWORTH, presents the most decided contrast. He had not his information—was not distracted by any prose compositions—and made no attempt to traverse the numerous and varied fields of thought or industry which Southey has tilled with so much zeal. But on that very account he was more successful, and has left a far greater reputation. He was less discursive than his brilliant rival, but more profound. Little attended to as works of that stamp generally are in the outset, they gradually but unceasingly rose in public estimation; they took a lasting hold of the highly educated youth of the next generation; and he now numbers among his devout worshipers many of the ablest men, profound thinkers, and most accomplished and discriminating women of the age. Indeed, great numbers of persons, whose mental powers, cultivated taste, and extensive acquirements entitle their opinion to the very highest consideration, yield him an admiration approaching to idolatry, and assign him a place second only to Milton in English poetry. He is regarded by them in much the same light that Goethe is by the admiring and impassioned multitudes of the Fatherland.

It may be doubted, however, whether, with all his depth of thought, simplicity of mind, and philosophic wisdom, Wordsworth will ever get that general hold of the English which Goethe has done of the German mind. The reason is, that he is not equally imaginative. He is a great philosophic poet; and, to minds of a reflecting turn, no writer possesses more durable or enchaining charms. But how many are the thoughtful or reflecting to the great body of mankind! Not one in twenty. "C'est l'imagination," said Napoleon, "qui domine le monde." Goethe, on the other hand, is not only simple and reflecting, but he is in the highest degree imaginative. His creative genius transports us alternately to the Chersonesian Taurus, the palace of Ferrara, and the cliffs of the Brocken. He is equally at home in the prison of Count Egmont, the wickedness of Mephistopheles, and the jealousy of Tasso. Wordsworth had nothing dramatic in his composition; he had an eye alive to the beauty, a soul responsive to the melody, of nature; but he had not the power of bringing the events of life with the colors of reality before the mind of the reader. His reflection was vast on the stream of human affairs, his sagacity great in detecting their secret springs; but he viewed them as a distant, unconcerned spectator, not an impassioned, energetic actor. Goethe had as little turn for action as Wordsworth, but he had incomparably more power of narrating its passions; he kept out of the whirl himself, but he lent the whole force of his mind to delineating the feelings of those who were tossed about by its billows. As the active bears so great a proportion to the speculative part of mankind, Goethe, who depicts the feelings of the former, will always be a more general favorite than Wordsworth, who delineates the speculations of the latter; but that very circumstance only enhances the admiration felt for the English poet by that small but gifted portion of the human species who, mingling with the active part

---

* The author met Southey only once, but he then saw much of him, under very interesting circumstances. Traveling through the Highlands of Scotland in autumn, 1819, with his friend Mr. Hope, the present Lord Justice-Clerk of Scotland, they were put into a room at Fort Augustus, the inn being crowded, with two other gentlemen, who proved to be Mr. Telford, the celebrated engineer, a very old friend of the author, and Southey. It may readily be believed the conversation did not flag in such society; it continued from nine at night till two in the morning, without a moment's intermission. Southey was very brilliant, but yet unassuming. He left an impression on the mind which has never been effaced; and the author was gratified to find, on sending him a copy of his *History*, that he had not forgotten the nocturnal meeting.

of the world, yet judge them with the powers of the speculative.

23. Coleridge's poetic character.
Coleridge, in some respects, bore a close resemblance to Wordsworth, but in others he was widely different. He was deep and reflecting, learned in philosophic lore, and fond of critical disquisition. He was less abstract than Wordsworth, but more dramatic—less philosophic, but more pictorial. Deeply penetrated with the genius of Schiller, he has transferred the marvels of two of the great German's immortal dramas on Wallenstein to the English tongue with the exactness of a scholar and kindred inspiration of a poet. His ode to Mont Blanc is one of the sublimest productions in that lofty style in the English language. But he is far from having attained the world-wide fame of Gray, Burns, and Campbell in that branch of poetry. The reason is, that his ideas and images are too abstract, and too little drawn from the occurrences or objects of common life. He was deeply learned, and his turn of mind strongly metaphysical; but it is neither by learning nor metaphysics that lasting celebrity, either in oratory or poetry, is to be attained. Eloquence, to be popular, must be in advance of the age, and *but a little* in advance. Poetry, to move the general mind, must be founded on ideas common to all mankind, and feelings with which every one is familiar, but yet educe from them novel and pleasing conceptions. It reaches its highest flights when, from these common ideas and objects, it draws forth uncommon and elevating thoughts; conceptions which meet with a responsive echo in every breast, but had never occurred, at least with equal felicity, to any one before.

24. Mrs. Hemans.
The genius of woman at this period produced a rival to Coleridge, if not in depth of thought, at least in tenderness of feeling and beauty of expression. Mrs. Hemans was imbued with the very soul of lyric poetry; she only required to have written a little less to be one of the greatest in that branch that England ever produced. A small volume, containing twenty or thirty of her best pieces—and these only such as "The Graves of a Household," "The Deserted Hearth," "The Cliffs of Dover," "The Voice of Spring," "The Ancestral Homes of England," and the like—would at once take its place beside the lyric poems of Collins, Gray, and Campbell. Melancholy had marked her for its own; she was deeply impressed with the woes of life, and it is in working up mournful reflections and images with the utmost tenderness and pathos that her great excellence consists. There she is, perhaps, unrivaled in the English language. She had undergone more than the usual share of the sufferings of humanity; for, married early in life, and, as it proved, unhappily, she was thrown, in some degree, for the support of herself and sons, upon the resources of her own genius. Thence at once her excellence and her failings: her sufferings made her portray grief with faithful power; her circumstances impelled her to do so in dangerous profusion. It is impossible to be a great *and voluminous* lyric poet: the fame of Horace and Pindar rests on as few great odes as Schiller, Gray, or Campbell have left to the world. The diamond, the brightest and purest of all substances, lies hid in the recesses of nature, and is drawn forth only in small portions, and distant intervals, to fascinate the world.

25. Crabbe.
Memorable, indeed, in poetic annals is the age which produced seven such poets as those who have now been considered; and immortal would be the British muse, if she never added another string to her lyre. But there were other poets at the same period whose talents adorned the poetic literature of the day, and whose genius would have conferred lustre on any preceding age. Crabbe was a writer of a totally different character from any of the preceding; but, nevertheless, of very high merit. He had nothing imaginative in his disposition—none of the spirit of chivalry, none of the ardor of romance. But he had a feeling, sensitive heart—warm sympathy with the sufferings of the poor, great power of delineating them. Living in a country village, and surrounded with distress, which his humanity prompted him to seek out, and affluence did not enable him to relieve, he endeavored to support the cause of the poor by painting their lives, their virtues, their sufferings, and thus enlisting the sympathy of the rich in their behalf. In this attempt he was eminently successful; and whoever wishes to obtain a faithful picture of the real condition of the rural population of England at that period, will do well to consult his graphic pages. But their reputation is sensibly on the decline: he is now seldom read, and still seldomer quoted; none of his lines have sunk into the public mind, and become as household words. The reason is that they want the lofty spirit, the elevating tendency, which is the only passport to immortality. Such a lofty spirit is perfectly consistent with the delineation of humble life. We see it in the lives of the patriarchs in Holy Writ—we see it in the poems of Burns—we see it in the tales of Sir Walter Scott. Gray has made the most popular poem in the English language out of the reflections on a country church-yard,

"The short and simple annals of the poor."

But the mere delineation of humble life, without the heroism which dignifies, or the magnanimity which rises superior to it, however popular for a season, never has a durable reputation. Time ever vindicates the immortal destiny of man; nothing can permanently float down its stream but what is buoyant from its elevating tendency.

26. Joanna Baillie.
Joanna Baillie is an authoress of a totally opposite character—of less graphic, but greater imaginative powers. In the seclusion of a Scottish manse were nurtured in her breast, in early life, the romantic visions of real genius: the past, with its heroes, its minstrels, its damsels, its tragedies, floated before her eyes; she aimed at delineating the passions, but it was the passions as they exist in noble breasts. Less stately and pompous than Corneille, less vehement and impassioned than Schiller, her dramas bear a certain affinity to both; they belong to the same family, and give token of the same elevated and heroic spirit. The great defect of her tragedies is, that they want those touches of nature and genuine pathos which go at once to the soul, and thrill

every succeeding age by the intensity of the emotions they awaken. Every thing is in sonorous Alexandrine verses; stately, dignified, and often beautiful; but sometimes tedious, and often unnatural, at least in impassioned scenes. She had no conception of stage effect; and on this account, as well as from the English being habituated to the rapid dialogue and strokes of nature in Shakspeare, her dramas have never succeeded in actual representation. But to minds of an elevated and sympathetic cast, they form, and will ever form, a charming subject of study in the library; and whoever reads them with a kindred spirit will acquiesce in the elegant compliment of Sir Walter Scott—

"And Avon swans, while rang the grove
With Basil's love and Montfort's hate,
Responsive to the vocal strain,
Deemed their own Shakspeare lived again."

27. Tennyson. TENNYSON belonged to a period in English annals somewhat later than the one with which we are now engaged; but the whirl of political events will not permit a recurrence to the inviting paths of poetry and literature—and he will, perhaps, not regret being placed beside his great compeers. He has opened a new vein in English poetry, and shown that real genius, even in the most advanced stages of society, can strike a fresh chord, and, departing from the hackneyed ways of imitation, charm the world by the conceptions of original thought. His imagination, wide and discursive as the dreams of fancy, wanders at will, not over the real so much as the ideal world. The grottoes of the sea, the caves of the mermaid, the realms of heaven, are alternately the scenes of his song. His versification, wild as the song of the elfin king, is broken and irregular, but often inexpressibly charming. Sometimes, however, this tendency leads him into conceit; in the endeavor to be original, he becomes fantastic. There is a freshness and originality, however, about his conceptions, which contrast strangely with the practical and interested views which influenced the age in which he lived, and contributed not a little to their deserved success. They were felt to be the more charming, because they were so much at variance with the prevailing ideas around him, and reopened those fountains of romance which nature has planted in every generous bosom, but which are so often closed by the cares, the anxieties, and the rivalry of the world.

28. Character of the prose compositions of the period. It was hardly to be expected that the same age was to be equally celebrated in prose compositions; it is rarely that the sober thought required in works of abstract reasoning, and the ardent temperament which is the soul of poetry, coexist in the same generation. Yet such a union, though unfrequent, is not unknown; and the ages of Sophocles, Socrates, and Thucydides—of Cicero, Virgil, and Livy—of Bossuet, Racine, and Molière, are sufficient to prove that, when it does occur, it leads to the very highest efforts of human intellect. It could not, in truth, be otherwise; for repetition and monotony of ideas are the bane of literature not less than of imagination; and the social convulsions, which lead to the most daring flights of the poetic muse, tend equally to cast down the barriers which restrain thought, and induce the collision of opinions, from which, as from the striking of flint and steel, the light of truth is elicited. It is not at once, however, that the bright illumination always appears; clouds and dust often, for a time, follow the shock; and it is only when they have rolled away that the pure flame at length shines forth.

29. Dugald Stewart. As a philosopher, DUGALD STEWART stands at the head of the writers of the age; but yet he belonged rather to the one which had preceded it. His writings are the efflorescence of the ideas which grew in the days of Montesquieu and Helvetius, of Reid and Hume. French philosophy and Scotch metaphysics met in his mind; but he arrayed the offspring of the marriage in brilliant colors. His learning was great, his taste exquisite: all the philosophy of mind, from the days of Plato, was present to his memory; all the images of poetry, from the time of Homer, floated in his imagination. The author is not afraid of exaggerating, either from the recollections of early friendship, or the reverence of academic instruction, when he places him at the head of the didactic orators of the age. His lectures were written, but always interspersed with long interludes of extempore effusion; and on these occasions the glow of his eloquence and the rich treasures of his memory were poured forth with a profusion which transported every one who listened to it. Philosophers may contest many of his opinions, statesmen search in vain for instruction in his writings; but none ever listened to his lectures without having an image engraven on the memory which no length of time can efface.

30. His want of original thought. Yet with these many and transcendent merits, Stewart had several wants; and hence his fame with posterity will be greatly less than it was with the age in which he lived. The very qualities which rendered him so great as a teacher to the young, disqualified him from being the leader of opinion to those engaged in active life; he lived in thought with the past, and therefore he failed to meet the wants of the present. He was the man of the past age, but not of the one in which he lived; he brought his pupils down the stream of time with admirable skill to the edge of the ocean on which they were to embark; but he there left them, without either rudder or compass, to the mercy of the waves. He did more; he imbued them with doctrines which, if carried out to their full extent, would lead to the most disastrous consequences. In metaphysics, he had corrected the errors of Locke and Hume, by the sound sagacity of Reid; but in politics, he was still guided by the visions of Turgot in the days of Napoleon; in political economy he was a follower of Quesnay and Smith, in the age which was resounding with the gloomy predictions of Malthus. He discoursed admirably on the thoughts of preceding times, but he drew little light from the events of his own; and his writings are distinguished rather by great learning, refined taste, and correct judgment, than original thought, or a just appreciation of the social changes in the midst of which he himself was placed.

The successor of Dugald Stewart in the chair of Moral Philosophy at Edinburgh, Dr. Thomas Brown, was a man, if not so cultivated, at least of a more original cast. His mind was of a very peculiar kind; it was a cross between the Scotch metaphysician and the German romancer. He had all the acuteness and analytical turn of Hume or Hutchinson, and all the ardor and tenderness of Goethe or Schiller. It is not often that such opposite qualities and powers coexist in the same mind; but, when they do, they seldom fail in producing a very great impression, and conferring durable fame. Rarity is not the least ingredient in earning permanent popularity; it is common minds, with their works, which are swept down the gulf of time. Inferior in learning to Stewart, Brown was more original; he drew less from the thoughts of others—more from the ideas of his own breast. He was extremely acute, and inferior to none in the masterly manner in which he analyzed the feelings, and detected the errors of former inquirers. But it was other qualities which gave him his great success. Himself of a poetical turn of mind, his taste was exquisite, and he adorned his lectures by those charming fragments of former genius which, often more than even original composition, contribute to the power of eloquence. The success of his published Lectures, accordingly, was immense; they have already gone through sixteen editions—by far the greatest number of any book on the subject in the English, or perhaps any other language. So vast a circulation proves that they had extended beyond the narrow circle of metaphysicians into the great sphere of general readers. A premature death, brought on in some degree by the intensity of his studies, cut him off in the flower of his age, and deprived Great Britain of one of the most eminent philosophers, and his friends of one of the most amiable men that ever existed.

If Scotland, in Brown, gave token of its national character, by exhibiting the combination of poetic genius with metaphysical acuteness, the practical and sagacious turn of the Anglo-Saxon mind was not less clearly evinced in PALEY. He belongs rather to the age of George III. than to that of his successor; but he is too eminent to be omitted in a survey of English literature at this period. His mind was essentially English, and English in its best mood. He was not remarkable for his learning, though far from being ill-informed; but the bent of his mind was not toward scholarship. He was eminently practical in his ideas; his thoughts, descending from the clouds, ever turned to some object of actual importance in real life. His mind was not of the most elevated cast, and accordingly he made *utility* the great object of life and measure of actions. He will never be a favorite, accordingly, with that handful of men who nevertheless alone do great things in the world, who aim at the noble and generous in all things, and let the useful take care of itself.* But, while his disposition precluded him from rising to the highest rank in literature, which never is to be attained but by the influence of lofty feelings within his limits, and in a lower sphere, he was very admirable, and eminently useful. His *Natural Theology* is the best work on the sublimest subject of human contemplation—the wisdom of God in the works of nature—that exists in our language; his *Moral Philosophy*, a clear exposition of the leading truths and most useful branches of ethics. That so very eminent a man, who had rendered such services to his country, should not have been raised to the highest dignities in the Church, to which so many inferior men were elevated, is the strongest proof of the narrow and timid principles on which patronage in those days was regulated. George III. said of him, "Paley is a great man—will never be a bishop, will never be a bishop;" words which at once mark the acknowledged superiority of his intellect, and the inferiority of those who are intrusted with the disposal of Church preferment.

If original views were awanting in this accomplished writer, they were not so in the great political philosopher of the age, Mr. MALTHUS. On him, at least, the experience of passing events was not thrown away; and the collision of thought struck out new and original ideas, which cast a broad light on political science. Action and reaction seems to be the law, not less of the moral than the material world; it is only after violent oscillations either way that the pendulum of thought takes its lasting position in the centre. From the earliest period of civilized history, it had been thought that the strength of a state depended mainly on the amount of its population; and it had passed into a maxim, both with statesmen and philosophers, that to increase the numbers of the people was the surest way both to augment the national resources, and add to the sum of human happiness. In the end of the eighteenth century, however, the aspect of things, both in the Old and the New World, led this original thinker to distrust these propositions. The social misery which had terminated in such convulsions in France—the increasing and alarming weight of the poor-laws in England—appeared to give no countenance to the idea that the oldest periods of social progress were the happiest; while the extraordinary rapidity with which population was advancing in America afforded the clearest indication of the capability of advance with which, under favorable circumstances, the human species was invested. Mr. Wallace had previously demonstrated that the rate of human increase, if unchecked, was that of a geometrical progression; and as that rapidity of progress had actually been realized for nearly two centuries in America, Malthus arrived at the conclusion that it would obtain universally, if the powers of human multiplication were not restrained by adverse external circumstances. These appeared to be, Moral Restraint—or a prudential abstinence from marriage till the means of providing for a family had been attained—and Vice and Misery; and so general and wide-spread did the operation of the two latter checks seem to be, compared to the limited sphere of the former, that he arrived at the melancholy conclusion that the great source of human suffering was to be found a

---

* "Paucorum civium egregiam virtutem cuncta patravisse, eoque factum, ut divitias paupertas, multitudinem paucitas superaret."—SALLUST, *Bell. Cat.* § 53.

the disproportion between the powers of human increase and those by which subsistence can be provided for the growing multitude. Population was capable of increasing in a geometrical, while, by the utmost efforts of industry, subsistence could not be made to advance in more than an arithmetical ratio: the former was thus constantly pressing on the latter; this pressure increased with the advancing age of society; and so severe did it at length become, that all other sources of misery were as nothing compared to the original and inherent causes of distress which arise necessarily and immediately from the constitution of our nature, and our position in the world.

34. Great influence and rapid spread of his doctrines.

To produce a great and immediate effect on general opinion, there is nothing so efficacious as some image which strikes the senses, or some terse expression of familiar illustration, which conveys in the clearest possible manner a simple idea to the mind. It is the most difficult thing in the world for reason or experience to combat such an influence. Government, for many a long day, was twitted with "the ignorant impatience of taxation," of which, in vexation at losing the income-tax, Lord Castlereagh spoke; and many convulsions which shook the most powerful states have arisen from the cry at the high price of provisions, or the exhibition of the big and little loaf. The celebrated paradox of Malthus was of this description. The idea he struck out was novel—the illustration by which it was conveyed, equally clear and felicitous. The geometrical and arithmetical progression were soon in every mouth. Men caught with alacrity at an expression which seemed to express with precision an idea which had been long floating in their minds, and which explained in the clearest possible way some of the most alarming anomalies in our social position. It was satisfactory to be able to lay upon Providence many evils which had formerly been supposed to have been induced by ourselves; and it was not the least agreeable consequence of such a doctrine, that the necessity of public and private charity was in a great measure removed by the obvious inadequacy of such remedies to close the real sources of human suffering.

35. His errors, and subsequent demonstration of them.

Political economy is not less certain in its conclusions than the exact sciences, when it is founded on a sufficiently broad deduction of facts, and the whole circumstances bearing on a particular result are carefully taken into view. But it is the most uncertain of all branches of thought, when conclusions are drawn from insulated or detached facts, and general inferences are deduced from partial premises. The geometrical and arithmetical progression is nothing more than a huge fallacy, only the more deceptive from its wearing an air of mathematical precision. There is no relation between the increase of population and subsistence, but that of cause and effect; if mouths increase fast, hands increase as fast also, and hands in a right governed state will never want employment. Population, it is mathematically certain, is capable, if unchecked, of advancing in a geometrical ratio; and it is equally certain that the earth, if unchecked

will fly to the centre of attraction, and the vision of the poet be realized:

"Suns sink on suns, and systems systems crush,
Headlong, extinct, to one dark centre fall,
And dark, and night, and chaos mingle all!"

But the centrifugal force averts the catastrophe, and forever retains the heavenly bodies in their orbits. It is the same in human affairs; there are centrifugal as well as centripetal forces in the moral as well as in the material world. The passions of men, the moving powers of mind, ruled by Omnipotence, hold the balance as even in the former as the opposite forces of attraction and repulsion do in the latter. Even in the age in which Malthus lived, this was demonstrated. While the attention of men, fascinated by the novelty of his doctrine, and the striking example of North American increase, was fixed on the alarming powers of human multiplication, the human race was disappearing in its original seats, and the most gloomy apprehensions were entertained of its entire extinction on the plains of Shinar, and in the Delta of Egypt. And within half a century of the time when the terrors of undue multiplication in these islands got possession of the British mind, a stop was put to British increase; for the first time in five centuries our numbers declined, and the annual exodus of 300,000 of our people proved that Providence, when the appointed season arrives, can transport the chosen race to the promised land.*

36. His character as a political philosopher.

Notwithstanding this fundamental error, Malthus was a great political philosopher, and the very promulgation of his error was an important step in the advance to truth. It is by slow degrees and frequent oscillations that the pendulum at length settles in the centre. His mind was vigorous and capacious—his understanding clear—his information immense. He cast a discriminating glance over the whole surface of the world, and compared the condition of mankind in all ages and countries, with a view to deduce the general laws of their social condition. His principles of population were a vast step in political science, and even greater in the method of investigation pursued than in the deductions drawn. He first applied on a great scale the method of induction to political science, and made the "Past, the Distant, and the Future" predominate over the Present. Hume had obtained a glimpse of the system, but he had not sufficient industry to carry it through. Malthus did not, like Adam Smith, dream, in the solitude of Kirkcaldy, of the doctrines of the Economists, and imagine a scheme of universal freedom from restraint, at variance alike with the wants, the necessities, and the selfishness of men. He was, in every sense, the man of the age—impressed with its wants—aware of its necessities—taught by its lessons. But it is not equally certain that he was the man of the next age. He first opened the eyes of men to the important truth that the mere multiplication of their numbers, though an important, is not the *sole* element in national prosperity; and that, though generally a source of strength,

---

* The population of Ireland had declined, between 1845 and 1851, above 2,000,000; that of the British islands, taken together, about 600,000 in the same period.—*Census of 1851.*

it may, under adverse circumstances, become a cause of weakness. He is a bold man who, with the example of Ireland before his eyes, attempts to gainsay that proposition. The result at which philosophy will probably ultimately arrive is, that the true test of social felicity is to be found in the *increase of mankind combined with their general felicity;* that the means of attaining this combination have been afforded by the bounty of Providence in every age to all; that the requisite limitations to population are as much a part of the human constitution as the principle of increase itself; and that nothing mars the harmony of their co-operation but the disturbing forces arising from the selfishness, the follies, and the vices of men.*

Adam Smith and Malthus were the two original men whose *idées mères* gave an entire new turn and direction on these subjects to human thought. But they were followed by other men of great talent and industry, who pushed their doctrines to their remotest consequences, and perhaps impaired their practical usefulness—certainly diminished their popularity—by laying down their results as abstract propositions of undoubted truth, to be carried into execution without any regard to the modifying circumstances of society. Immense is the influence which their principles have had, not so much with the majority of men in England as with the thinking few, who in every age regulate the opinions and determine the destiny of their countrymen. If the Economists, of whom Turgot was the incarnation, had a great share in producing the French Revolution, the political economists have had a still greater in inducing the alteration of opinion on commercial and monetary subjects, and with it the organic changes which have altered the Constitution, and the commercial policy which has been adopted by the councils of England. They have collected a great variety of statistical facts, relating to the present time, to support their opinions; but unfortunately have not, like Sismondi in France, been equally attentive to those on the other side, which the historical records of other states present. Mr. RICARDO, Mr. M'CULLOCH, Mr. SENIOR, and Mr. MILLS are the most eminent of this school of political philosophy in recent times; and they have brought to bear upon that important and interesting science intellectual powers and industry of the very highest kind. Even those who differ most —and they are many—from their abstract conclusions, or the expediency of applying them practically in these times, and our present complicated state of society, must be the first to admit their great ability, and the vast addition which the facts they have collected, and the ideas they have thrown out, have made to the sum of human knowledge, and eventually, by their establishment or overthrow, to the cause of truth.

If Malthus cast a broad and lasting light on political affairs, Davy, in the same age, gave an impulse almost as great to physical science.

27. Ricardo, M'Culloch, Senior, and Mills.

Endowed by nature with the intrepid and inquisitive spirit which is the very soul of discovery, he carried the torch of sagacious inquiry into the recesses of nature, and for the first time detected, in the physical world, mineral substances the existence of which had never before been even suspected by the most inquisitive observers. His powers of conversation were great, his temper mild, his disposition unruffled. He carried the spirit of "the last days of a philosopher" through the whole of life. Nor were his researches confined to abstract subjects. He applied science with success to its noblest purpose — human improvement; and had the happiness, which to a man of his benevolent mind was great, of reflecting, on his death-bed, that he had chained even the frightful violence of the fire-damp, and given the miner the means of securely pursuing his darksome toil, while the noisome blast, pregnant with death, played innocuous round the lambent flame that rested on his forehead.*

28. Davy: his philosophical discoveries.

Though not on a level with these illustrious philosophers, there were several other men in Great Britain who signalized themselves in different branches of science and literature at this period. Herschel, by multiplying with incredible labor and skill the powers of the telescope, was enabled to look further into space than man had ever done before, discover a world hitherto unseen in the firmament, and, in the Georgium Sidus, add a "new string to the lyre of heaven;" Playfair, illustrating with philosophic wisdom and chastened eloquence the thoughts of Hutton, developed the true theory of the earth, now universally admitted, and traced in the revolutions of our globe that mysterious system of action and reaction which pervades alike the moral and the material world; D'Israeli (the father), casting the glance of genius over its achievements in former days, illustrated the curiosities of literature, the literary character, the animosities and sufferings of authors, with the knowledge of a scholar, the zeal of an antiquarian, and the powers of an orator, at the same time that, in history, he threw a new and important light on the eventful reign of Charles I.; while Alison, inspired by a genuine taste for the sublime and the beautiful, resolved the beauty of the material world into the expression of mind, traced the influence of association in multiplying the links of the unseen chain which unites man to the Creator, and sought to represent "the world we inhabit as the temple of the living God, in which praise is due, and where service is to be performed."[1]

29. Herschel, Playfair, D'Israeli, Alison.

[1] Alison's Essays on Taste, concluding sentence.

* The author is profoundly impressed with the truth of the propositions contained in this paragraph, which he has endeavored to illustrate in his *Principles of Population;* but they are too much at variance with present opinions to render it possible for him to look for a general concurrence in them during his own lifetime.

* Sir Humphry Davy's powers of conversation were great, and the more charming from the entire freedom from vanity or ostentation, and almost boyish simplicity, by which they were distinguished. The author once supped with him at Rome, when the whole party consisted of Sir Humphry, Lady Davy—who was also brilliant in conversation—Canova, and his late lamented friend, Captain Basil Hall. The conversation turned on the deficiency, at that period, of the fine arts in England, and the author observed that it was very surprising, because in other countries, as Greece and modern Italy, the fine arts had advanced *abreast* of literature, philosophy, and the drama. Canova replied, "Sir, it is entirely owing to your free Constitution: it drains away talent of every sort to the bar and the House of Commons. If England had been Italy, Mr. Pitt and Mr. Fox would have been

One branch of knowledge may, in a manner, be said to have been created, and almost brought to perfection, during this period. This was the science of GEOLOGY, as based on the study of organic remains in the various strata of which the crust of the earth is formed. Werner, in Germany, and Hutton, in Scotland, had previously presented complete theories of geology, which still remain monuments of their genius and reach of thought, and from a combination of which the true theory of the earth has since been extracted; and Playfair had illustrated the subject with the spirit of philosophy and the graces of eloquence. But little was thought, or indeed known, by any of these great men, of the organic remains which were imbedded in the strata, the formation of which they considered, and which yet, like the relics of language in the strata of the human species, bespoke the successive revolutions of the globe. The study of these remains opened a new field of profound and interesting inquiry—so much the more valuable, that it was entirely based on facts and actual discovery—so much the more interesting, that it carried us back, by a certain clue, into the labyrinth of forgotten time. Mr. BUCKLAND, Professor SEDGEWICK, and Sir CHARLES LYELL, are the most eminent of the new school of geology which has sprung up simultaneously in France and England, and which, by a strict application of the Baconian method of philosophizing, has made earth reveal the secret of its formation anterior to the race of man, by the remains imbedded in its bosom. A more fascinating inquiry never was presented to the investigation of the philosopher; and it derives additional interest to the Christian believer, from the confirmation which it affords, at every step, of the Mosaic account of creation, and the truth of Holy Writ. Optics had made so great a stride under the genius of Newton that little remained to be gleaned by future observers; but yet BREWSTER has added much to the circle of our knowledge in the polarization of light, and added a new element in the production of harmonious beauty in the changes of the kaleidoscope.

40. Modern geology: Buckland, Sedgewick, Sir Charles Lyell, and Sir David Brewster.

In one particular a fresh walk in literature was opened up at this period, and cultivated with the most brilliant success. This was the new style of review and lengthened essay. Reviews, indeed, had long been established in Great Britain; and Addison, Steele, and Mackenzie had brought the *short* essay to as great perfection as was practicable in that limited species of composition. But the *Monthly Review* and *Gentleman's Magazine* were poor periodicals, distinguished by little talent, illuminated by no genius, containing scarcely more than meagre abstracts of, or interested eulogiums on books, and jejune records of transactions. Even the mighty genius of Burke, then unconscious of its own strength, had been unable to burst the fetters with which political narrative at that period was restrained; and his historical compositions in the *Annual Register* contain few symptoms of the vast conceptions which afterward shone forth and illuminated the world in his writings. No one need be told that the essays of Addison, Steele, and Johnson are charming compositions, distinguished by taste, embellished by fancy, adorned by imagination, in which the stores of learning are set off with all the decorations of modern genius. But their day has passed away; they are well-nigh forgotten. They are to be seen in every library, but are seldom taken down from its shelves. This oblivion is, no doubt, in part to be ascribed to the prodigious multiplication of works of imagination which has since taken place, and which renders it next to impossible for works of a former period to maintain their ground against the constantly-increasing tide. Yet this is not the sole cause of their neglect; works of superlative merit have no difficulty in maintaining their place. Poems innumerable have since appeared, but Virgil and Tasso are in no danger of being forgotten; our walls are every day decorated with new paintings, but we gaze with undiminished admiration on the works of Raphael and Claude. The true reason of the decline in the estimation in which our old essayists are held is to be found in their own defects. With a few brilliant exceptions, they are commonplace in thought, and feeble in expression; full of truisms, but wanting in originality; often distinguished by conceit, seldom by simplicity; remarkable more for taste than genius; and rather fitted for the thoughtless amusement of a vacant half hour than to be the charming companion of an evening fireside.

41. Rise of the learned reviews and lengthened essays.

It was in this state of the periodical literature of the country that the EDINBURGH REVIEW arose, and communicated a new character to its pages, a fresh impulse to its exertions. Discarding the feeble and irresolute criticisms of the *British Critic* and *Monthly Review*, its authors boldly dashed forward into the unoccupied arena of severe and caustic animadversion, and quickly secured general favor by indulging in general abuse. This is the most certain passport to extensive popularity. All, except the objects of attack, like to see others abused. Above all, it was refreshing to the great body of readers to see the oligarchy of authorship broken down, and the lash of criticism applied to a class who, even when in fault, had hitherto escaped without any adequate animadversion. The practical application of their motto, "Judex damnatur cum nocens absolvitur," gave universal satisfaction; for every one hoped his neighbor would fall under, and himself escape the chastisement. The vigorous talent and varied acquirements of its early contributors sustained and increased the reputation at first acquired by more questionable means; it was impossible that a journal where the talents of Jeffrey, Brougham, Sidney Smith, Mackintosh, Playfair, and Malthus were alternately exerted, could fail in attracting general notice and acquiring extensive popularity. Its reputation, accordingly, soon became very great, its circulation immense, its influence formidable even to the Government in power. To counteract it, a new journal was set up in London, which, under the title of the QUARTERLY RE-

42. Rise of the Edinburgh Review, Quarterly Review, and Blackwood's Magazine.

your artists; and then you would have had no reason to lament your inferiority in the fine arts."

view, under the direction, first, of Gifford, and then of Lockhart, with the aid of Sir Walter Scott, Southey, Canning, Ellis, Frere, and Rose, soon came to rival its northern competitor, and has ever since maintained its elevated position; while in Edinburgh itself a rude assault was made on the Whig oligarchy of the north by a still more sturdy antagonist, and the genius of Wilson, Lockhart, and their coadjutors soon elevated BLACKWOOD'S MAGAZINE to the lead in patriotic effort, independent thought, and varied criticism. These journals, each admirable in its way, but yet entirely different from each other, have given an entirely new tone to our periodical literature, and been the vehicles by which the most important thoughts on philosophical, political, and literary subjects have, during the last half century, been sent forth to the world.

43. Jeffrey.
JEFFREY, who took the lead in this great revolution in literature, was a very remarkable man, but more so from the light, airy turn of his mind, and the felicity of illustration which he possessed, than from either originality of thought or nervous force of expression. His information was far from extensive; he shared in the deficiency of his country at that period in classical knowledge; he was ignorant of Italian and German; and his acquaintance with French literature was chiefly confined to the gossiping memoirs of the day, and with that of his own country, to the writings of the Scotch metaphysicians or the old English dramatists. But these subjects he knew thoroughly; within these limits he was thoroughly master. He was fitted by nature to be a great critic. A passionate admirer of poetry, alive to all the beauties and influences of nature, with a feeling mind and a sensitive heart, he possessed at the same time the calm judgment which enabled him to form an impartial opinion on the works submitted to his examination, and the correct taste which, in general, discovered genius and detected imperfections in them. Kindly and affectionate in private life, he was equally indulgent and considerate in his public disquisitions; his long career as a critic foreshadowed on a great scale the uprightness and temperance of opinion, which rendered him in the highest degree popular and useful as a judge. His style of speaking in public was rather fascinating from quickness of fancy or felicity of illustration, than impressive from force of expression or elevation of thought. In conversation, his mind was rapid, discursive, and often very brilliant; but there was a constant straining after display, and a total want of that simplicity which always characterizes the greatest minds and constitutes their chief charm. His political essays contained nothing original or striking, and were so deeply imbued with the party views of the day, that they have long since been forgotten, and have not, in one single instance, been reproduced in his collected works.

44. Brougham.
A more striking contrast to Jeffrey, as an essayist, can hardly be imagined than BROUGHAM; for he possessed all that the former wanted, and wanted everything which he possessed. His writings, like his speeches, are varied, vigorous, and discursive, full of talent, replete with information, and often adorned by a manly eloquence. But they have none of the cool thought and temperate judgment which is essential for lasting influence in political science; they partake rather of the excitement of the bar, or the fervor of the senate, than the sober judgment of the academy. Many of them were much admired and talked of when they first appeared; none are now recollected, or have taken a lasting place in our literature. What is very remarkable, his style, both of speaking and writing, is precisely the reverse of what his taste approves, and what his judgment has selected as particularly worthy of admiration in others. He is a passionate admirer of the Greek authors, and peculiarly emphatic in his eulogies on the terseness of their expression, and the admirable brevity of their diction; and yet he himself, in his style of composition, is the most signal example of the danger of deviating from these precepts, and of the way in which the greatest talent may be in a manner buried under the redundance of its own expression. He illustrates an idea, and puts it in new forms, till the original impression is well-nigh obliterated. His knowledge is great, his acquirements vast, his mind capacious; but his fame is varied rather than great. He has marred his reputation by aiming at eminence in too many things; and he will be considered by posterity rather as a powerful debater and a skillful dialectician, than either a profound philosopher or consistent statesman.

45. Sir James Mackintosh.
MACKINTOSH has been already discussed in these pages as a senator; but his merits as an essayist, and as one of the original contributors to the Edinburgh Review, are too considerable to render any apology necessary for again making him the subject of discussion. His mind was essentially philosophical; his soul was imbued with principle, his memory stored with knowledge. He was fitted to have been a great teacher of men, rather than their powerful ruler. These characteristics are strongly apparent in his writings; and the English language can not present a more perfect example of philosophical disquisition than some of his political essays, particularly that on Parliamentary Reform, exhibit. He had candor enough, in his later years, to abandon many of the opinions which, with the hasty ardor of genius, he had at first embraced; the antagonist of Burke, and the apologist of the Revolution in the Vindiciæ Gallicæ in early life, he became the most ardent admirer of the former, and enemy of the latter, in his maturer years. He had great powers both of generalization and condensation—two qualities apparently dissimilar, but which, in reality, are counterparts of each other; for the former distills thought, the latter abbreviates expression. He was greatly improved as a philosopher, though perhaps injured as a debater, by his long residence in the solitude of the East: it is not in the arena of politics, or the busy whirl of party contention, that the fountains of wisdom are unlocked to mankind. His compositions on the voyage home are a proof of this; there is nowhere to be found a more brilliant series of characters of literary and political men than in those in the composition of which he relieved the solitude of the Atlantic

wave, and which appeared in his admirable biography by his sons. But his mind was philosophic, not dramatic; his style didactic, rather than graphic. He had no pictorial powers, and little poetic thought; he was a great discourser on history, but not a historian. He never could have carried on, in a style of equal popularity, the immortal work of Hume; and the absorption of his mind, and waste of his time in the attractions of London society, so much a subject of regret at the time to his friends, perhaps saved his reputation from the injury it must have sustained had he aimed at a higher flight, and failed in the attempt.

46. Sidney Smith. SIDNEY SMITH, so well known in his day as one of the most popular essayists in the *Edinburgh Review*, and of the most brilliant wits about London, had powers of an entirely different order, but more fitted for immediate popularity than Mackintosh. He had no philosophic turn, little poetic fancy, and scarce any eloquence, but a prodigious fund of innate sagacity, vast powers of humorous illustration, and a clear perception of the practical bearing of every question. Though bred to the Church, and holding considerable preferment, the Dean of St. Paul's had very little of the clerical in his disposition; his turn was rather for the humorous in thought, the brilliant in society, the felicitous in expression. He would have made a great *nisi prius* lawyer; his influence with juries, from the combined effect of wit and sterling good sense, would have been irresistible. In society he was very much sought after, from the fame of his convivial talents, and the real force of his colloquial expressions; but there was a constant straining after effect, and too little interchange of thought to raise his discourse to a very high charm. It is very seldom that the conversation of professed wits possesses that attraction; it sometimes amuses, seldom interests. It is in statesmen, diplomatic characters, and men of the world, where they are also well informed, that we must look for the true conversational talent, which consists in the rapid interchange of thoughts on interesting subjects, and which, when it occurs between persons of equal abilities, sympathetic minds, but opposite sexes, is perhaps the greatest enjoyment which life can offer. It is neither to be found in the prelections of professors, the vanity of artists, nor the sallies of wits. Sidney Smith's talents as an essayist were great; the success of his collected works, both in Great Britain and America, is a decisive proof of it. But their popularity was owing to force and felicity of expression, rather than depth of thought or power of eloquence; his name is linked with no great question, either in morals or politics, which is permanently interesting to mankind; and he will probably, in the end, afford another illustration of the truth of Sir Joshua Reynolds' observation. Posterity and present times are rivals; he who pays court to the one must reckon upon being discountenanced by the other."

47. Macaulay. MACAULAY, as a historian, belongs to a later period of this history; but, as an essayist, he early began to give tokens of the vast and deserved reputation which he afterward acquired. Nature had singled him out for a great man: she had impressed the signet mark of genius on his mind. Endowed with vast powers of application and an astonishing memory, an accomplished scholar and erudite antiquarian, he had, at the same time, the brilliant genius which can apply the stores of learning to useful purposes, and the moving eloquence which can render them permanently attractive to mankind. It is hard to say whether his poetry, his speeches in Parliament, or his more brilliant essays are the most charming; each has raised him to very great eminence, and would be sufficient to constitute the reputation of any ordinary man. That he was qualified to have taken a very high place in oratory, is proved by many of his speeches in the House of Commons, particularly those on the Reform Bill; that he was a brilliant essayist will be doubted by none who have read his reviews of Lord Clive and Warren Hastings, perhaps the most perfect compositions of the kind in the English language; that he was imbued with the very soul of poetry is sufficiently evinced by his "Battle of the Lake Regillus," and his moving "Legends of Rome." Rarely, indeed, does a single mind exhibit a combination of such remarkable and opposite qualities. But perfection was never yet given to a child of Adam, and the traces of the weakness common to all may be discerned in him in the very brilliancy of the qualities which render him so attractive. His imagination often snatches the reins from his reason; his ardor dims his equanimity. His views, always ingenious, generally eloquently supported, are not uniformly just; his powers as a rhetorician sometimes make him forget his duties as a judge; he is too often splendid, rather than impartial. The reader will never fail to be interested by his narrative; but he is not equally certain to be instructed: the impression left, however brilliant, is often fallacious; and the fascinating volume is often closed with regret that the first pleader at the bar of posterity has not yet been raised to the bench.

48. Lockhart. If the *Quarterly Review* can not exhibit such a splendid series of essays from one individual, as those of Macaulay in the *Edinburgh*, it has not the less taken a memorable part in English literature, and acquired no inconsiderable weight in the formation of English opinion. Supporting the principles of Conservatism in politics, of orthodoxy in religion, it has brought to the support of the altar and the throne a powerful phalanx of talent, and an immense array of learning. Its present accomplished editor, LOCKHART, who at a short interval succeeded Gifford in its direction, brought to his arduous task qualities which eminently fitted him for its duties. He is not political in his disposition, at least so far as engaging in the great strife of public questions is concerned; he is one of the light, not the heavy armed infantry, and prefers exchanging thrusts with a court rapier to wielding the massy club of Hercules.* But in the lighter branches of

---

* The expression was suggested by the distinction drawn by a lady of rank and genius, who was well acquainted with the talents of either, and at her splendid mansion of Newton Don had often received both Sir Walter Scott and Mr. Lockhart. "Sir Walter," said Lady Don (now Lady Wallace), "always puts me in mind, in conversation, of his own description of Richard Cœur-de-Lion; he lets fall a massy club: Lockhart is Saladin

literature he has deservedly attained the very highest eminence. As a novelist, a critic, and a biographer, he has taken a lasting place in English literature. His *Valerius* is the most successful attempt which has ever yet been made to ingraft the interest of modern romance on ancient story; its extreme difficulty may be judged of by the brilliant genius of Bulwer having alone rivaled him in the undertaking. But his fame with posterity will mainly rest on his *Life of Sir Walter Scott*, for which, as his near relation, he had no doubt great advantages, but which he has executed with so much skill, and in so admirable a manner, that, next to Boswell's *Life of Johnson*, it will probably always be considered as the most interesting work of biography in the English language.

WILSON, as the leading contributor, for a long series of years, to *Blackwood's Magazine*, has brought more vigor and genius into the field of periodical literature than any of his contemporaries. His mind is essentially poetical. The inspiration of genius is apparent in all his writings. Ardent in feeling, warm in temperament, impassioned in thought, he wants the calm judgment, patient research, and laborious industry requisite for success in political or historical literature; his fancy wheels in aerial flights through the heavens, without alighting or caring for the concerns of a lower world. He dwells in the regions of imagination, and there he soars on the eagle's wing. The whole literature of England does not contain a more brilliant series of critical essays than those with which he has enriched the pages of *Blackwood's Magazine*; and, what is rarer still, the generosity of feeling by which they are distinguished equals their critical acuteness and delicacy of taste. Himself a poet, and endowed with the very highest gifts of the muses, he is entirely destitute of that wretched jealousy which so often, in persons of a similar temperament, mars the greatest endowments, and disfigures the brightest genius. If his criticisms have any imperfections, it is that they are too indulgent. He is justly alive to faults, and, when obliged to notice, signalizes them with critical justice; but the generosity of his nature leads him rather to seek for excellences, and, when he finds them, none bestows the meed of praise with more heartfelt fervor. He is one of the most striking examples that ever existed of the important truths, that simplicity of thought and generosity of feeling are the surest characteristics of the highest class of intellect; that true taste is to be evinced by the appreciation of beauties, rather than the detection of blemishes; and that none are fitted really to criticise merit but those who could have rivaled it.

Historical literature, next to poetry, reflects most strongly the images of the time; the moving phantasmagoria of real events ere long kindles the imagination, and tinges the pictures of the narrative. The cold academic style of Robertson may suit the comparative calmness of the eighteenth century, but the fervor and animation of its close communicated itself to the historical works of the next. HALLAM was the first historian whose style gave token of the coming change; his works mark the transition from one age and style of literature to another. In extent and variety of learning, and a deep acquaintance with antiquarian lore, the historian of the Middle Ages may deservedly take a place with the most eminent writers in that style that Europe has produced; but his mind is more imaginative than those of his laborious predecessors, and a fervent eloquence, or poetic expression, often reveals the ardor which the heart-stirring events of his time had communicated to his disposition. His extensive and varied learning, alike in parliamentary transactions and general literature, has enabled him to throw an important light on our constitutional history, and illustrate, with happy discrimination, the literature of modern Europe. It is only to be regretted that he sometimes has not, in artistic style, sufficiently massed his lights and shadows. There is often a want of breadth in his pieces; the light is thrown too equally on all, and the mind of the reader, oppressed with an infinity of unimportant details or unknown names, sometimes loses the general thread of the composition, or misses the impression which the author himself desired to produce by his work.

SHARON TURNER, like Hallam, belongs to the antiquarian school, but, like him, he has enlivened the industry of unwearied compilation by gleams of fervent imagination. His *History of the Anglo-Saxons*, by far his best work, has thrown a new and important light on that interesting portion of English history; and illustrated, with equal truth and accuracy, the institutions, manners, and habits of the people who form so large a part of the stock of English ancestry. When we compare the meagre and often inaccurate accounts of our Saxon forefathers, which preceded the labors of this indefatigable antiquarian, with the broad light which has now been shed upon them, the step appears great indeed, and evinces how many treasures ardent zeal and indefatigable industry may often extract from mines which appeared well-nigh exhausted. Turner's *History of England*, though distinguished by the same research and acuteness, is not of equal merit; and, unfortunately, the peculiarities and uncouthness of its style, as well as a strange attempt to introduce novelty in spelling, has hindered the work from acquiring the popularity which it really deserves. No account of the historians of early England could be regarded as complete, if honorable mention is not made of Sir FRANCIS PALGRAVE, whose antiquarian lore is so great, and withal so accurate, that we not only have obtained the same light from his labors on the past which we enjoy on the present, but feel equal confidence in threading our way through the one which we do in treading the other.

LINGARD is a historian of great merit, whose labors have filled up an important blank in English literature. However much we may pride

---

who flies round him with a Damascus cimiter." It is impossible to characterize more happily the conversational character of these two near relatives and very eminent men; and the author trusts an early and highly-valued friend, whose great talents and charm in conversation—equal to that of either—so eminently qualify her to appreciate similar excellences in others, will forgive him for recording an expression which departs, more truly and faithfully than he could have done, the conversational talents of two men in whom posterity will always feel so warm an interest.

ourselves on the liberty of our Constitution, and the manner in which, under the influence of unbounded freedom of discussion, truth is elicited from the collision of opposite opinions, there is nothing more certain than not only that it is not immediately that this effect takes place, but that centuries may often elapse before the most important transactions are represented in their real colors. Violent convulsions, whether in religion or politics, so strongly move the passions, that the strongest partialities or prejudices are often perpetuated for a very long period; chains may be thrown over the human mind, as well by the tyrant majority as by the imperious despot. Emancipation is as slow, and often more difficult, from the prepossessions of the multitude, as from the dogmas of priests or the mandates of sovereigns. No one can now read the *History of the Reformation* without seeing that, for nearly three centuries, it had been represented in a great measure under false colors by Protestant historians. They did not, they could not, exaggerate the blessings of the liberation, but they represented in an entirely fallacious light the merit of many of the liberators. The emancipation from superstition was the work of Heaven; but the actors in the deliverance were not all imbued with heavenly virtues. Here, as elsewhere, human passions and iniquity mingled with the current; rapacity largely influenced the actors; ambition disgraced the leaders in the movement; and an extrication of the human mind, which was destined to spread in the end the seeds of freedom throughout the world, was impelled in the outset by the profligacy of passion or the cupidity of selfishness. It is the clearest proof of the salutary tendency of the Reformation, and the Divine influence which has protected it, that from such beginnings ultimate blessings have sprung.

52. Lingard: previous prejudices of the historians of the Reformation.

Dr. Lingard has taken the lead in the attempt to exhibit the other side of the question from that presented by the Protestant historians, and no man could have been found more fitted for the task. Acute, learned, and indefatigable, he possesses, at the same time, the caution and self-control which, in contests with the pen not less than the sword, are essential to lasting success. *Ars est celare artem* is his maxim; he is a partisan writer, but no one conceals his partialities more cautiously, or exhibits a greater appearance of candor in treating of the most delicate questions. He had too much tact not to be well aware that violence in language and intemperance in thought generally defeat their own object; and that, as future times always come to be divested of the passions of the present, no opinions can by possibility be durable but those which, founded in reason and supported by experience, are likely to command the assent of distant and unimpassioned generations. His prepossessions — and, like all sincere Roman Catholic writers, they are many — are all in favor of his own religion, and the sovereigns or statesmen who have supported it in the great contest with the Lutheran heresy; but his narrative wears no aspect of partisanship, and he trusts for impression rather to the views which, from the facts presented, will naturally occur to the reader's mind, than to any attempt vividly to force his own opinions upon him. His secret bias appears, not from what he tells us, but from what he conceals; the best informed critic will not easily detect him in a false allegation, but the most superficial will have no difficulty in discovering much that is known and true, but adverse to his side, that is kept out of view. He has not moral courage or confidence in his opinions sufficient to state them boldly and manfully; or perhaps he has yielded to the maxims of his persuasion, and never attempts openly what can be accomplished covertly. He is not eloquent, has no poetic imagination, and but slight dramatic or pictorial powers; and therefore his history, in general estimation, will never rival the immortal narrative of Hume. But he is skillful, ingenious, sagacious, and indefatigable; his history will ever be the text-book of English story with all of his own persuasion; and even with the candid of the other it will always be esteemed as containing the opposite side of the question, and disentangling historical truth from many errors with which the counter partialities of preceding historians had clogged it.

53. His merits and defects as a historian.

The influence of the increasing lights and information of the age, which absolutely required an enlarged impartiality in historians, is clearly evinced in the next great historical writer of this period, Tytler, whose labors have thrown so imperishable a light on Scottish history. Unlike his predecessors, who were contented with the meagre details of monkish annalists, or the fabulous compilations of imaginative historians, he went at once to the fountain-head, and founded his narrative mainly on the authentic correspondence preserved in the State-Paper Office. He was indefatigable in his endeavors to deduce from thence both an impartial estimate of character and a truthful narrative of events. As the success with which he has prosecuted this praiseworthy plan has been the principal cause of the durable and general reputation with all men of sense and information which his great work, the *History of Scotland*, has acquired, so it is the one which has, perhaps, most impeded its immediate popularity. When he went to the authentic records of private and confidential letters, he found much that had been either unknown to or concealed by preceding historians. Many a great reputation is lessened when the secret thoughts come to be revealed; not a few who were thought to have been saints, prove to have been sinners. Tytler, in bringing forward the truth founded on authentic documents, has undergone the fate invariably reserved for those who make such an attempt: he has incurred the rancorous hostility of those whose minds, steeped in error, or inflamed by party, whether in religion or politics, feel the utmost antipathy for all who attempt to unhinge their settled opinions. He will only on that account, however, be the more esteemed by posterity; and his fame with future times will be founded on the very circumstances which have impeded his popularity with the present.

54. Tytler; his impartial character.

He possesses in a very high degree many of the qualities of a great historian. Indefatigable in industry, accurate in detail, trustworthy in spirit, he

55. His merits and defects

unites with these qualities—which are the foundation of history—the poetic temperament and fervent spirit, which are essential to the superstructure. His mind was not philosophical; he had few general views, and little turn for the wide-spread glance with which Robertson and Guizot have surveyed the maze of human affairs. His disposition was rather for biography than general history; he interested himself, like a novelist, more in individual event or character, than in the progress or transactions of nations. On that very account, however, he was peculiarly fitted for the history of Scotland, which is little more, in all its phases, than a narrative of the deeds of the kings, queens, and nobles by whom its destinies have been ruled. His powers of narrative and description are great; he had both the eye of a painter, the soul of a poet, and the refinement of a scholar in his composition. His *Scottish Worthies* is, perhaps, the most interesting series of short biographies in the English language; his death of Queen Mary, in his great history, one of the most moving historical pictures that ever was presented to the world. The defect of his work, and it is one into which antiquarians, and those who found their narrative on accurate research, are peculiarly liable to fall, is that it contains too many quotations from original documents, or letters, *in the text*; a practice which, however clearly it may evince the industry and accuracy of the writer, is injurious to the continued interest, and consequent popularity, of the work. The information founded on original letters, or documents, is of inestimable importance, and the light they throw on character often of the very highest value. But it is rarely that they contain expressions so important or characteristic as to call for a place in the text; and the author who transfers them, as is too much the practice now, to the body of his work in great numbers, inevitably destroys the symmetry of its composition, and mars the unity of effect which in history, not less than any other of the fine arts, is indispensable to the highest success.

The next great historian who appeared in England at this period, General NAPIER, possesses merits and is marked by defects of a different description. As a describer of noble deeds and heart-stirring events, he is without a parallel in the English, or perhaps any other language. Himself a soldier, who had acted bravely and bled freely in the field, he possesses in a very high degree both the military ardor which prompts to glorious actions, and the scientific mind which qualifies him to judge of, and criticise, the conduct of others in military affairs. His great reputation has arisen chiefly from the fire and moving eloquence of his descriptions of battles; which are at once so true, so graphic, and so animated, that European literature, perhaps, can not present their equal. But, to professional men, his *History of the Peninsular War* possesses a still higher merit; and both the young and the experienced soldier will study with equal profit and delight the just and scientific observations with which he has enriched his work, on the military conduct both of his own countrymen and of their enemies. His candor as a military critic appears in the generous praise he has so often bestowed on Napoleon and his generals;

56. Napier.

although, perhaps, the natural indignation he felt at the exaggerated pretensions and vainglorious boasts of the Spaniards has led him sometimes not sufficiently to estimate the influence of their indomitable perseverance on the final issue of the contest. His great defect as an artist is, that he has not sufficiently studied the management of light and shade, and has brought a multitude of inconsiderable combats so prominently forward as to confuse the reader's recollection, and impair the unity of his composition. As a historian, the candid reader —amid all his admiration for the genius of the writer—will have frequent cause to regret the unfounded severity of his judgments, especially in civil transactions, and the occasional vehemence of his language. He would have been a perfect historian if he had wielded the pen with the same calmness that he did the sword, and recollected that in civil, not less than military conflicts, the observation of General Foy is applicable—"Le soldat Anglais possède la qualité la plus precieuse dans la guerre—le calme dans la colère."

Lord MAHON has brought to the arduous task of continuing Hume's History through the eighteenth century, the taste of a Lord Ma scholar, the liberality of a gentleman, hon. and the industry of an antiquarian. As he begins his narrative only with the Peace of Utrecht, the greater part of the period which he had to go over was pacific; and therefore his History of necessity became, in a great degree, for the most part a parliamentary one. But he has great powers of description; and, where an opportunity occurred for their display, he has made use of them with very great effect. His account of the Rebellion in 1745, the death of Wolfe, and of the principal events of the American war, is by far the best that has yet appeared of those interesting episodes; and he has interspersed his narrative with agreeable and instructive disquisitions on letters, manners, and scientific progress, which add so much to the value of history, and are so necessary, especially in pacific periods, to enhance its interest. His position as a nobleman, and the heir of an ancient house, rendered illustrious in one of the brightest periods of English story, has given him great advantages in the account of the formation of cabinets, the contests for power, and the secret causes of the rise and fall of Administrations; and his characters both of statesmen and heroes, are able, just, and discriminating. If these are not the most momentous or interesting topics for history, they are the most suitable for the period which his work embraced; for the eighteenth century was one of mental repose and social rest, midway between the religious contests of the seventeenth, and the political passions of the nineteenth centuries; and Lord Mahon's disposition and acquirements peculiarly qualified him for the elucidation of its secret springs of action.

57.

If Lord Mahon has left a chasm between the termination of Hume's and the commencement of his own narrative, that important period of English history was not long of being adequately illustrated. Mr. MACAULAY has brought to the task of developing that momentous epoch the same talents and acquirements which have rendered

58. Macaulay's History.

his essays so great an acquisition to English literature. Genius the most transcendent, eloquence the most captivating, graphic power the most brilliant, shine forth in all his pages, united to learning the most extensive, and research the most unwearied. It is this combination of the imaginative with the laborious qualities, of the flights of fancy with the solidity of information, which renders his works so remarkable, and in that respect unrivaled in modern literature. If their calmness of judgment and impartiality of statement were equal to their profusion of learning and brilliancy of style, they would be without a parallel in modern historical literature. His mind is not merely poetical but systematic, and where not influenced by the zeal of a partisan, no one can exhibit more of the wisdom of a statesman or the far-seeing glance of a philosopher. Unfortunately, however, the ardor of his mind has sometimes disturbed its equanimity; his learning is greater than his impartiality, his power of description than his equity of judgment. He has given, so far as he has yet gone, the most brilliant and fascinating, but not the most trustworthy or impartial history in the English language. It is not by the allegations of any thing which is erroneous or can be disproved by authentic evidence, so much as by keeping out of view what is equally true, but adverse to the side which he has espoused, that this is done. He is more a brilliant barrister than an upright judge. Instances of this disposition appear in many parts of his writings. His style, always condensed and pregnant, is sometimes labored; his ideas often succeed each other too rapidly; the mind of the reader can scarcely keep pace with the rapidity of thought in the writer. Filled to repletion with a succession of striking thoughts and brilliant images, the student of his History sometimes sighs for the repose, even the tedium of ordinary narrative. The immortal episodes of Livy owe much of their charm to the simplicity of the narrative with which they are environed; the fascination of Scottish scenery is heightened by the long tracks of dusky moor which separate its sequestered glens and glassy lakes.

If the reader of the splendid history of Macaulay sometimes regrets the want of the impartial charge of the judge in the brilliant oratory of the barrister, the student of Miss STRICKLAND meets with excellences and deficiencies of a somewhat similar description. The mind of this highly-gifted lady fitted her in a peculiar manner to write the *History of the Queens of England*; and probably no man, be his abilities what they may, could have executed a work on that subject equally suitable and entertaining. She possesses all the zealous industry and indefatigable research which characterize Macaulay, and, like him, she has her prepossessions and dislikes. A vail is sometimes drawn over the weak points of the favorite Princesses or Houses who form the subject of her narrative. But it is all done in a noble spirit: the foundation of her judgment is always admiration of the gallant in conduct, the chivalrous in disposition; and though the intensity of this feeling has often biased her judgment, it does not diminish the respect due to her motives. The reader may sometimes be misled in the estimate of individual character by her captivating pen, but he is sure never to be so on the side, whether of virtue or vice, which is the fit subject of praise or condemnation. Her work is conceived in the true spirit of chivalry, and a brighter record does not exist of its elevating tendency than in her varied and animated pages. Add to this, her habits and objects of interest as a woman have led her to enrich it with a variety of interests and details in regard to manners, customs, hospitalities, feasts, coronations, and dresses, which, perhaps, no man would have collected, but which, nevertheless, are invaluable as a record of the olden time, and as illustrating the moving diorama of her long and interesting narrative. What is principally to be regretted, in so very accomplished and fearless a writer, is that, with true womanly sympathy with misfortune, she espouses, in her history of Mary of Modena and Queen Anne, the cause of the Stuarts so strongly, and evinces such intense indignation against William III. and Marlborough, as not only renders her impartiality suspected, but weakens the effect of the original and important disclosures she has made in regard to that important period, with every unbiased mind. The style of her work is easy and flowing, often graphic and pictorial, at times rising into moving and dignified strains of eloquence. Its chief defect consists, not in what she has written, but in what she has inserted of the writings of others; but the undue loading of historical works with long quotations in the text, of original documents and letters, is the fault of the age in which she lives, and should not be visited on the head of any single writer, and, least of all, on that of a lady who stands at the head of her whole sex, in all ages, in historical literature.

Any account of the literature of the British empire, in the first half of the nineteenth century, would be imperfect, if the merits of the rival historians of Greece are not displayed. Mr. MITFORD is the first who brought to the arduous task of Grecian history the extensive research, accurate inquiry and profound reflection which characterize the scholars of recent times. Instead of compiling, as former historians had done, a pleasing narrative from the romances of Xenophon, or the credulity of Herodotus, he, like Niebuhr in the elucidation of Roman story, sought every contemporary authority, every authentic document, every line of poetry, which could elucidate, correct, or confirm their charming episodes, and extracted from the whole an elaborate and consistent account of the complicated transactions of the Greek republics. It is, perhaps, the most difficult task in the world to make such an account interesting; for, with the exception of the magnificent periods of the Persian invasion, the Syracusan expedition, and Alexander's conquests, it is nothing but the annals of the internal divisions and wars of a cluster of republics, the transactions of which are at once so insignificant and complicated that, if there is any thing more difficult than to make them intelligible, it is to render them interesting to the reader. The marvels of genius which were displayed in these diminutive states have done little to relieve the historian of this difficulty; for, unhappily, human annals are chiefly composed of the public transactions of nations, not the triumphs, however great, of philosophy or art. Nevertheless, Mitford has done much in this way; and his two volumes on the conquests of Alexander the Great combine the interest of the romance of Quintus Curtius with the authenticity and accuracy of Arrian. His great work was chiefly composed during, or shortly after, the French Revolution; and it was mainly intended to counteract the visionary ideas, in regard to the blessings of Grecian democracy, which had spread so far in the world from the magic of Athenian genius. With this view he has brought out a great many most important facts, concealed before amid the splendors of Grecian eloquence, which the republican party would willingly have buried in oblivion, and which, as they tended to unhinge many settled opinions, excited the most violent indignation among them. Perhaps he would have done more wisely if, like Lingard, he had concealed his object, and left facts to speak for themselves, without disclosing too openly the end in view in their compilation. But the cause of truth has been essentially aided by his exertions; and the experiences of the working of democracy in our own times have been such as to forbid a doubt as to the accuracy of the facts he has stated, whatever hesitation may be felt as to the wisdom of the expressions in which they are sometimes conveyed.

61. Grote.
If Mitford, notwithstanding his industry and abilities, is sometimes open to the reproach of having too keenly asserted the conservative, it is fortunate for the cause of historic truth that another distinguished writer of equal talent has recently illustrated Grecian history on the opposite side. A decided liberal, perhaps even a republican in politics, Mr. GROTE has labored to counteract the influence of Mitford in Grecian history, and construct a history of Greece from authentic materials, which should illustrate the animating influence of democratic freedom upon the exertions of the human mind. In the prosecution of this attempt he has displayed an extent of learning, a variety of research, a power of combination, which are worthy of the very highest praise, and have secured for him a lasting place among the historians of modern Europe. If his voluminous work, like that of Mitford, is often uninteresting, and it is felt to be a heavy task to get through it, that must be ascribed rather to the nature and complication of the subject than to any defect in the historian; and those only who have attempted the task can conceive the extraordinary difficulty of throwing a broad and steady light on such a multitude of minute transactions as Grecian story presents. A more serious, because better founded, charge arises against him from his adopting the Greek mode of spelling in the names of places and of the heathen deities, instead of the Roman, heretofore in use in modern Europe. The attempt is hopeless, and tends only to confuse the unlearned reader. Jupiter and Neptune, Venus and Mars, Vulcan and Diana are too much naturalized among us to admit of their names being ever changed; they may be so when the works of Virgil and Ovid, of Horace and Cicero, of Milton and Racine are forgotten, but not till then. It may appear strange to say that there is equal truth in the monarchical history of Greece by Mitford, and the republican by Grote, but, nevertheless, it is so. Both tell the truth, and nothing but the truth—but neither the whole truth. They each illustrate, truly and justly, the opposite working of the democratic principle on the greatness and sufferings of nations; but neither presents a picture of their *united* operations, which, nevertheless, was what really occurred, and occasioned the brilliant meteor of Grecian genius, with its simultaneous suffering and rapid fall.

62. Arnold
If the political events and anxieties of the time have caused the history of Greece to be learned in a very different spirit, and with much greater intelligence, than in any former period of modern times, a similar effect has appeared in regard to the history of Rome; and the world has too much cause to lament the premature death which interrupted the work which was in progress illustrative of this influence. ARNOLD possessed the chief qualities required to form a great historian. To profound scholarship, vast industry, and unwearied application, he united the rarer gifts of original genius, independent thought, an ardent disposition. Adopting from Niebuhr and the German scholars all that their prodigious labors had accumulated in regard to the early history of Rome and the adjoining states of the Italian peninsula, he arranged their discoveries in a more lucid order, and adorned them with the charms of a captivating eloquence. His mind was ardent in all things; patient, but yet imaginative—bold, but methodical—brilliant in conception, but laborious in execution. What genius had struck out, learning supported, industry filled up, and eloquence embellished. He had a strong bias on political subjects, and, like most men of an independent turn, inclined *at first* to the popular side; but he was essentially candid and trustworthy, and the philosophic student will nowhere find more important facts on the practical working of democracy than in his luminous pages. He had great graphic powers, a strong turn alike for geographical description, strategical operations, and tactical evolutions. His account of the campaigns of Hannibal—the best that exists in any language—proves that, like Livy, he was adequate to the history of the majestic series of Roman victories. A critical taste will probably condemn the strange style in which he has narrated the early and immortal legends of Rome, and regret that the charming simplicity of Livy was not imitated in translating his pages; but a generous mind will hesitate to condemn where there is so much to admire, and join in the general regret that the only man who has yet appeared in Britain capable of throwing over the rise and progress of the Roman Republic the same light which Gibbon has cast over the decline and fall of the Empire should have been cut short in the very threshold of his career.

63. The new school of novelists
If the historians of England, during the last half century, exhibit in a clear light the important influence of political convulsions on national literature, the working of the same causes is still more strikingly evinced in our writers of romance. Indeed, there the change is so great, and so striking, that there is nothing in the whole an

nals of English literature to compare to it. If we consider the novelists who had attained great, and, in some respects, deserved reputation, before the time of Sir Walter Scott—Richardson, Mackenzie, Mrs. Radcliffe, Mrs. Charlotte Smith—the magnitude of the step made by that great writer appears prodigious. It was not merely the length of the stride which he made that constituted its importance; the great thing was, that it was made in the right direction. Preceding writers of novels had considerable talents, great command of the pathetic, brilliant powers of description. Fielding and Smollett had delighted the world with their wit, humor, and graphic powers. But the sentimental school were entirely deficient in the most essential of all requisites for works of imagination—a thorough acquaintance with human nature in all its grades; and the humorous was devoted almost exclusively to middle or low life, and destitute of those elevated and chivalrous feelings which constitute at once the greatest charm and chief utility of works of imagination. It was reserved for Scott to combine both, and exhibit, in his varied and fascinating pages, alternately the noble spirit of chivalry, the dignified feelings of heroism, the charms of beauty, and the simplicity and virtues, without the vulgarity, of humble life.

Ere the wand of this mighty enchanter, however, had wrought an entire change in the lighter literature of the age, the reaction against the sentimental school had become very conspicuous; and what is remarkable, a female writer had led the way in the alteration. Miss EDGEWORTH possesses merits of a very high order; but they are of the solid and substantial, rather than the light and airy kind. Strongly impressed with the visionary and dreamy tendency of the romance writers who had immediately preceded her, she boldly struck out in the opposite direction, and delineated life, not in its romantic and poetical, but in its real and practical form. She aimed at portraying, not the sorrows of the heart, but the sad realities of life: "Out of Debt, out of Danger," was much more in her thoughts than "All for Love, or the World well Lost." She had a keen eye for the humorous, and has delineated Irish character with a skill which never was surpassed; but the chief merit of her compositions is her sterling good sense, sound judgment, and practical acquaintance with middle life which they exhibit. Her defects—since all have some, and the fair sex are not exempted from them—are the want of the noble and chivalrous sentiments which constitute the great characteristic of modern Europe, as contradistinguished from all the rest of the world, and the almost entire absence of any appeal to the feelings and influences of religion. There is no reason to suppose that she was skeptical or indifferent on this subject; indeed, those who enjoyed her friendship know it was very much the reverse; but still there is no allusion to it in her novels, and that has seriously impaired the value of her writings, and has already caused their popularity to decline. Neither the sensible, the practical, nor the humorous ever can suffice alone for the gratification of the human mind; other feelings must be roused, other aspirations satisfied; and the author who discards the influences of love and devotion has voluntarily cast away the chief means by which the human heart, in every age, is to be affected, or lasting fame attained.

Another writer, still more voluminous than Miss Edgeworth, soon after began to pour forth a periodical stream of novels with a prodigality which has not yet ceased to astonish the world. If Mr. JAMES's works have not all equal merit, and frequent repetition of images and scenes is to be found in them, they are entirely exempt from many of the blemishes which disfigure some of those of his contemporaries which, in the outset, have acquired greater popularity. There is a constant appeal in his brilliant pages not only to the pure and generous, but to the elevated and noble sentiments; he is imbued with the very soul of chivalry, and all his stories turn on the final triumph of those who are influenced by such feelings over such as are swayed by selfish or base desires. He possesses great pictorial powers, and a remarkable facility of turning his graphic pen at will to the delineation of the most distant and opposite scenes, manners, and social customs. His best novels—*Attila, Philip Augustus, Mary of Burgundy,* and the *Robbers*—must ever hold a very high place in English literature. In his works may be discerned the varied capabilities of the HISTORICAL ROMANCE of which Sir Walter Scott was the great founder, and which has so immensely augmented both the interest and utility of works of imagination, by at once extending the sphere of their scenes, and rendering them the vehicles of information as well as amusement. Not a word or a thought which can give pain to the purest heart ever escapes from his pen; and the mind wearied with the cares, and grieved at the selfishness of the world, reverts with pleasure to his varied compositions, which carry it back, as it were, to former days, and portray, perhaps in too brilliant colors, the ideas and manners of the olden time. But, with these great and varied merits, he can not be placed in the first rank of romance writers; he wants the chief qualities requisite for its attainment. He has no dramatic powers: his dialogue is seldom brilliant, often tedious, and totally deficient in the brevity and antithesis which is the very soul of conversational success. His mind is pictorial more than reflecting, his descriptions rather of external objects than internal feelings. It is in the last, however, that the greatest charm of romance is to be found; it is not so much by describing physical nature as by reopening the fountains of tenderness, which once have gushed forth in every bosom, that the wand of the intellectual magician, like that of Moses, refreshes the soul, wearied amid the wilderness of life, and carries it back, perhaps only for a few minutes, to the brightest moments on which memory can dwell.

If the romances of Mr. James are deficient in the delineation of the secret feelings that dwell in the recesses of the heart, the same can not be said of the next great novelist whose genius has adorned English literature. In the highest qualities required in this branch of composition, Sir EDWARD BULWER LYTTON stands pre-eminent, and entitled to a place beside Scott himself, at the very head of the prose writers of works of imagination in our country. Born of a noble family, the inheritor of ancestral halls of uncommon splendor and interest,* he has received from his Norman forefathers the qualities which rendered them noble. No man was ever more thoroughly imbued with the elevated thoughts, the chivalrous feelings, which are the true mark of patrician blood; and which, however they may be admired by others, never perhaps exist in such purity as in those who, like the Arab steeds of high descent, can trace their pedigree back through a long series of ancestors. In delineating the passion of love, and unfolding its secret feelings, as well in his own as the opposite sex, he is unrivaled in English literature; Madame de Staël herself has not portrayed it with greater truth or beauty. In that respect he is greatly superior to Scott, who cared little for sentiment, and when he did paint the tender feelings, did so from their external symptoms, and from the observation of others only. Bulwer would seem to have drawn his pictures from a much truer and wider source—his own experience. He describes so powerfully and so well because he has felt so deeply. There is no portrait so faithful as that which is drawn by a great master of himself. *Rienzi* is one of the most perfect historical romances—*Godolphin* and *Ernest Maltravers* among the most interesting and charming novels in the English language. Nor is he only remarkable as a novel writer—he is at the same time a successful poet and dramatist. He has inhaled the kindred spirit of Schiller in the translation of his ballads. His *Timon* is by far the most brilliant satire, his plays the most popular dramatic compositions, of the age in which he lives.

67. His merits as a poet and dramatic writer.

If some of his other works are not of equal merit, it is only the usual fate of genius to be more happy in some conceptions than in others. In all, the marks of deep reflection and profound thought are to be seen, as well as great observation of, and power in delineating character. A more serious defect is to be found in the occasional choice of his subject, and the charms with which his magic pencil has sometimes environed vice. The greatest admirers of his genius can not but feel surprised that he should have chosen as the heroine of one of his novels a woman who commits three murders, including that of her own husband and son; or regret that one so capable of charming the world by pictures of romance in its most elevated form should ever have exerted his powers on the description of low life, or characters and scenes of the most shocking depravity.

* The dining-room at Knebworth, in Hertfordshire, Sir E. Bulwer Lytton's noble family mansion, originally built by a Norman follower of the Conqueror, is fifty-six feet long and thirty high, hung round with the armor which the family and their retainers wore at the battle of Bosworth, and ended by the gallery in which the minstrels poured forth their heart-stirring strains: in the state-room is the bed, hung round with velvet curtains, in which Queen Elizabeth slept in the year of the Armada: in the library, the oak table at which Cromwell, Pym, and Vane concerted the Great Rebellion. The author had once the happiness of spending two days under Sir Edward's hospitable roof, with himself and his highly-valued friends Professor Aytoun and the late lamented Mr. Robert Blackwood; he must be forgiven if he adds that it is seldom, indeed, in life that such society is enjoyed amid such recollections.

It is true he never makes licentiousness in the end successful, and the last impression in his works, as well as innumerable exquisite reflections, are all on the side of virtue; but in intermediate stages it appears often so attractive that no final catastrophe can counteract the previous impression. Every one knows that this is no more than what occurs in real life; but that is just the reason why additional force should not be given to it by the charms of imagination. It is true, painting requires contrast, and the mixture of light and shade is requisite to bring out the forms and illustrate the beauty of nature; but the painter of the mind, not less than material objects, would do well to recollect the rule of Titian, that the greater part of every picture should be in mezzotinto, and a small portion only in deep shade.

68. Disraeli.

Disraeli, long known as a brilliant satirist and romance writer, before he was elevated to the lead of the House of Commons, is an author different from either Mr. James or Sir E. Bulwer Lytton, but with merits of a very high description. He is not feudal and pictorial, like the first—nor profound and tender, like the last; he is more political and discursive than either. He has great powers of description, an admirable talent for dialogue, and remarkable force, as well as truth, in the delineation of character. His novels are constructed, so far as the story goes, on the true dramatic principles, and the interest sustained with true dramatic effect. His mind is essentially of a reflecting character; his novels are, in a great degree, pictures of public men or parties in political life. He has many strong opinions—perhaps some singular prepossessions—and his imaginative works are, in a great degree, the vehicle for their transmission. To any one who studies them with attention, it will not appear surprising that he should be even more eminent in public life than in the realms of imagination; that the brilliant author of *Coningsby* should be the dreaded debater in the House of Commons—of *Vivian Grey*, the able and lucid Chancellor of the Exchequer. His career affords a striking example of the truth of Dr. Johnson's observation, that what is usually called particular genius is nothing but strong natural parts accidentally turned into one direction; and that when nature has conferred powers of the highest description, chance or supreme direction alone determines what course their possessor is to follow.

69. Dickens.

The strong turn which romance and novel writing, in the first half of the nineteenth century, took to the delineation of high life, with its charms, its vices, and its follies, naturally led to a reaction, and a school arose, the leaders of which, discarding all attempts at Patrician painting, aimed at the representation of the manners, customs, ideas, and habits of middle and low life. The field thus opened was immense, and great abilities were early turned to its cultivation. At the very head of this school, both in point of time and talents, must be placed Mr. DICKENS, whose works early rose into great, it may be said, unexampled celebrity. That they possess very high merits, is obvious, from this circumstance: No one ever commands, even for a time, the suffrages of the multitude, without the possess-sion, in some respects at least, of remarkable powers. Nor is it difficult to see what, in Mr. Dickens' case, these powers are. To extraordinary talent for the delineation of the manners and ideas of middle life, and a thorough acquaintance with them in all their stages below the highest, he unites a feeling and sensitive heart, a warm interest in social happiness and improvement, and most remarkable powers for the pathetic. To this must be added, that he is free from the principal defects of the writers who have preceded him in the same line, and which have now banished their works from our drawing-rooms. Though treating of the same subjects and grades in society, he has none of the indelicacy of our older novelists. We see in him the talent of Fielding, without his indecency—the humor of Smollett, without his grossness. These brilliant qualities, joined to the novelty and extent of the field on which he entered, early secured for him a vast circulation and wide-spread reputation. It was founded on more than the merit, great as it was, of the author—selfish feelings in the readers combined with genius in the writer in working out his success. The great and the affluent rejoiced in secret at beholding the manners of the middle class so graphically drawn. To them it was a new world; it had the charm of foreign traveling. They said in their inmost hearts, "How different they are from us!" The middle class were equally charmed with the portrait; every one recognized in it the picture of his neighbor—none of himself.

70. Thackeray and the Dickens school.

A host of other writers have followed in the same school, which has become so considerable as to have assumed an important place in the literature of the nineteenth century. Many of these writers are distinguished by great talent and graphic powers, among whom Mr. Thackeray stands conspicuous. The taste for compositions of that description has become so decided, that it has extended to our highest imaginative writers. It is not difficult to foresee, however, that it is not destined to be durable; and that, from the general reaction which will ensue, compositions in that style are, perhaps, likely to be sooner forgotten than their real merits deserve. Satirical or humorous works, founded on the ridicule of passing manners, however popular or diverting at the time, rarely attain any lasting celebrity. The reason is, that the follies which they ridicule, the vices which they lash, are in general only of ephemeral duration. Those only, as the works of Juvenal, Cervantes, Le Sage, or Molière, which dive deep into the inmost recesses of the soul, and reach failings universal in mankind, command the admiration of all ages. Profound insight into the human heart, condensed power of expression, are essential to success in such compositions; and they are given only to the greatest of mankind. Imagination is a winged deity; its flight, to be commanding, must ever be upward. Ridicule is valued only by those who know the persons ridiculed; elevation of thought is prized by all who feel generous sentiments, and they are the noble-hearted in all ages.

There are two writers of works of imagination, however, who belong to a different school, because their genius has led them to aim at different objects. Miss Austin and Mrs. Norton both possess merits of a very high order, and yet entirely different from the authors of the Dickens school. Miss Austin, whose career ended in 1817, aims chiefly at the delineation of the domestic life of England, which her sex, her turn of mind, and her opportunities of observation enabled her to do with peculiar effect. There is nowhere to be seen in our literature so correct and faithful a delineation of the manners, motives, and ideas of the middle classes of English society, that great class which is every day rising into greater importance, and is equally removed from lords and ladies on the one hand, and assassins or desperadoes on the other. She does not aim at representing either the lofty in character, the heroic in action, or the pathetic in feeling; it is the average events and emotions of every-day life which she portrays; and that she has done with a tact, delicacy, and truth which never were surpassed. Marivaux himself has not exceeded her in the delineation of the working of vanity in the female heart—Beaumarchais, in the truth with which she has portrayed the selfish impulses which, in general, actuate people of ordinary characters in this world. She is the Wilkie of novel-writing.

71. Miss Austin.

Mrs. Norton aims at a much higher object and has attained a distinguished place in romantic literature. Gifted with the true poetic genius, and imbued with that vein of romance which is the secret spring of every thing that is noble and elevated in this world, she has, at the same time, advantages which have fallen to the lot of few of her sex for the faithful picture of the very highest English society. Descended from the great Mr. Sheridan, she has inherited not only his talents, but his comic vein, while she has blended with it the romantic feelings which give a higher tone to their direction, and the delicacy which her sex seldom fails to show in the delineation of the softer feelings. Thrown from her earliest years into the most elevated circles, and having enjoyed the friendship of nearly all the eminent men of the age, she is better qualified than perhaps any other living person could be to exhibit, as in a mirror, at once their excellences, their ideas, and their follies. But her writings prove that the enjoyments of this elevated society, and the unbounded admiration which her personal charms and great powers of conversation have long secured for her, have not been sufficient to fill up the void of a refined and ardent mind; and that her life has been a long aspiration after an imagined felicity, which she has never yet attained. Melancholy is the prevailing tendency of her mind; and though we can not but regret that one whose society never fails to confer pleasure should have so often been disappointed in its search herself, we can not but rejoice that circumstances should have thrown her genius into that which was perhaps its natural channel, and enriched our literature, both in poetry and prose, with so many gems of the pathetic, which are indelibly engraven on the memory of all who are acquainted with them.

72. Mrs. Norton.

Very different in style from this accomplish

73. Mr. Warren.
ed authoress, Mr. WARREN has taken a lasting place among the imaginative writers of this period of English history. He possesses, in a remarkable manner, the tenderness of heart and vividness of feeling, as well as powers of description, which are essential to the delineation of the pathetic, and which, when existing in the degree in which he enjoys them, fill his pages with scenes which can never be forgotten. His *Diary of a Physician* and *Ten Thousand a Year* are a proof of this; they are, and chiefly for this reason, among the most popular works of imagination that this age has produced. Mr. Warren, like so many other romance writers of the age, has often filled his canvass with pictures of middle and humble life to an extent which those whose taste is fixed on the elevating and the lofty will not altogether approve. But that is the fault of the age rather than the man. It is amply redeemed, even in the eyes of those who regard it as a blemish, by the gleams of genius which shine through the dark clouds of melancholy with which his conceptions are so often invested; by the exquisite pathetic scenes with which they abound; and the pure and ennobling objects to which his compositions, even when painting ordinary life, are uniformly directed.

74. Carlyle.
CARLYLE is the object of impassioned admiration, not only to a large class of readers, but to many whose taste and acquirements entitle their opinions to the very highest respect. Nature has impressed upon his mind the signet-mark of genius. A sure test of it is that there is, perhaps, no writer of the age who has made so many original and profound remarks, or ones which strike you so much when transplanted into the comparatively commonplace pages of ordinary writers. But it is to his detached and isolated thoughts that this high praise chiefly applies; as a whole, his ideas are not calculated to command equal respect, at least with the generality of men. He is essentially a "hero-worshiper," and the defects as well as the merits of that disposition are strongly marked in his writings. He has made strenuous efforts to glorify several doubtful, and write down several celebrated characters recorded in history; and that is always a perilous attempt—for the voice of ages arising from the general opinion and experience of men is, in the ordinary case, founded in truth; and the author who attempts to gainsay it runs the risk, when "he meant to commit murder, of only committing suicide." Mr. Carlyle has great powers in the delineation of the terrible and the pathetic; numerous instances of both, in his history of the French Revolution, will immediately recur to the recollection of every reader. But his style, founded upon an unbounded admiration and undue imitation of the German idiom, appears often harsh and discordant to the reader; and this peculiarity will probably prevent his writings from ever acquiring the popularity of standard works with the great body of English readers.

75. Dr. Croly.
No similar blemish is to be found in Dr. CROLY, whose thoughts full of genius and lofty views, are conveyed in the purest and most classical English idiom. The ardent admirer of Burke, he has adopted his views, shared his fervor, and, in a great measure, imitated his style. But he has largely inhaled, also, the spirit, and profited by the lessons of the age in which he lived; the contemporary and observer of the French Revolution and its consequences, he has portrayed both in a philosophic spirit and with a poet's fire; and what Burke predicted from the contemplation of the Future, he has painted from the observation of the Present. His Life of that great man, written in a kindred spirit, is the best account of his mind and writings in our language: in many of his other writings there appear the style and thoughts of a prophet, not less than the pictures and colors of a historian. The ardent champion of Protestantism, he has met the zeal of the Romish Church with equal fervor, and been led sometimes, perhaps, with undue warmth into the defense of his own faith. It is only to be regretted that an author capable of such things should have devoted his talents so much to illustrating the ideas of others, and not inscribed his name on some great original work, at once a monument of his own genius and of the age in which he lived.

76. Hazlitt.
HAZLITT was prior in point of time to both these very eminent writers, and he differs materially from either. He was less political and historical in his disposition; his ideas were riveted on the realms of imagination, not on the transactions of men; it was on the world of thought, not the world of humanity, that his mind was fixed. Criticism, the drama, the theatre, poetry, the arts, alternately engaged his pen, and his ardent mind and deep reflection never failed to impress upon these subjects the marks of original thought and just observation. In critical disquisitions on the leading characters and works of the drama, he is not surpassed in the whole range of English literature; and what in an especial manner commands admiration in their perusal is the indication of refined taste and chastened reflection which they contain, and which are more conspicuous in detached passages than in any entire work. He appears greater when quoted than when read. Possibly, had his life been prolonged, it might have been otherwise, and some work emanated from his gifted pen which would have placed his fame on a durable foundation.

77. Bentham.
If a great work has been wanting to the fame of Hazlitt and Croly, the same may with still more justice be said of a very eminent man who has illustrated the age by his profound and original thoughts. BENTHAM has brought to the philosophy of law the vigor of an independent, and the views of a creative mind. He was not a practical lawyer, and therefore his views, how just and convincing soever, must often be essentially modified and most cautiously handled before they are introduced into practice; but there can be no doubt that they contain the germ of much useful legislation on the subjects they embrace. They are so because they contain the deductions of an acute and reflecting mind on the application of the principles of human nature, and especially the ruling principle of selfishness, to the principal situations and trials of character which emerge in the course of legal conflict or judicial decision. In this re-

spect his writings contain more original, and often just thought, than is to be found in any other writer. He was very indolent, and, notwithstanding the clearness and force of his understanding, had not the faculty of expressing his ideas in equally distinct or lucid language; hence his thoughts were often communicated to the world in a foreign language, to be collected by the friendly industry of Dumont, and are to be found rather scattered through a variety of works than contained in any one of superior condensation or excellence. He was a utilitarian in principle, an ultra-Liberal in politics, hence lofty views and generous feelings are not to be looked for in his writings; but that only renders the suggestions they contain the more worthy of consideration, in a practical point of view, in a world where selfishness or ambition so largely influences the actions of the great majority of men.

78. Chalmers. CHALMERS, though his name is attached to no work commensurate to the great fame he enjoyed during his life, has made a vast impression on the minds of his countrymen, and deservedly earned a high place in the bright assembly of Scottish worthies. He was gifted with very great natural powers, which had been scattered rather than condensed by the style of education then generally given in his country. He was not very learned; his information was various rather than extensive on any one subject; and we shall look in vain in his writings for those stores of erudition which, when brought forth by genius and arranged by philosophy, form the only true foundation for lasting fame in the mental or social concerns of men. But Chalmers, notwithstanding, was a great man. Within the limits which nature or education had prescribed to him, he did great things. The fervor of his mind, the brilliancy of his genius, overcame every obstacle, supplied every deficiency, at least for the purposes of present gratification to his audience or his readers. His oratorical powers were very great, greater perhaps than any of his contemporaries. No one so entirely thrilled the hearts of his audience, or swept away every mind in one irresistible burst of common emotion. His judgment, however, was not so strong as his fancy; his opinions are not to be so implicitly relied on as his genius is to be admired. If his writings, however, often do not materially inform the understanding, or safely regulate the judgment, they never fail to charm the imagination, and move the feelings by the fervent piety, benevolent spirit, and enlarged understanding which they evince, and the brilliant eloquence in which they are always couched.

79. Monkton Milnes and Aytoun. There would be no end to the present chapter if every writer of eminence in the British empire, in the present or past age, were to be separately noticed. But there are two who, albeit, from youth, not as yet at the zenith of their fame, have given such brilliant promise of future celebrity, that they can not be passed over in silence. Mr. MONKTON MILNES has presented to the world several volumes of poems abounding in such brilliant imagery, and containing such refined sentiments, that they have secured for him a very high place in the estimation of all to whom the beautiful or interesting in art or nature possess any charms. And Mr. WILLIAM AYTOUN, albeit bred to different habits, and educated in the thorny pursuits of the law, has evinced early in life the very highest talents for lyric poetry, and enriched the literature of his country with a volume of ballads, which exceed the strains of Tyrtæus in patriotic spirit, while they rival the odes of Dryden in fire and pathos. So great, indeed, is their merit, and so varied the talents and powers of their accomplished author, that no hesitation need be felt in predicting for him, if his life is spared, the highest destinies in the realms of poetry, as well as the less inviting fields of political discussion.

80. L. E. L., Warburton, and the author of Eothen. If the house of mourning, in real life, ever adjoins the house of joy, and the voice of gladness is ere long drowned in the wail of sorrow, the same vicissitude is not less conspicuous in literature. The cypress is ever mixed with the laurel in its verdant fields. If the brilliant author of EOTHEN has produced one of the most striking pictures of the East that ever was presented to the nations of the West, another author, whose pencil, like his, was "dipped in the orient hues of heaven," has been prematurely snatched from his admiring country. Mr. ELLIOT WARBURTON, whose glowing descriptions of the East, rivaling those of Beckford himself, are so indelibly engraven on the national mind, has been prematurely snatched by a mournful catastrophe from the country whose literature he was so well qualified to adorn; and not many years before, a female authoress, whose lyre, as melancholy and not less melodious than that of Sappho, had so deeply moved the British heart, breathed her last on the sombre shores of Cape Coast Castle. But the poems of L. E. L., of surpassing sweetness and pathos, rivaling those of Mrs. Norton herself in heart-rending sentiment, will long survive their unhappy author, and speak to the heart of generations to which her premature fate will be a lasting subject of commiseration.

81. The Fine Arts—Architecture. The impulse given to the FINE ARTS in Great Britain, by the animation and excitement of the war, was not so great as might, perhaps, have been expected, and suggests a painful doubt whether there is not something in the climate of England, or the character and consequent institutions of the Anglo-Saxon race, which is inconsistent with eminence in those noble departments of genius. ARCHITECTURE was the one in which our deficiency, during the war, was most apparent, and in which the greatest efforts were made, on the return of peace, to repair that deficiency. The numerous travelers who crowded to the Continent for several years after the peace, all returned with the greatest admiration of the noble edifices recently erected in Paris, or which attested the magnificence of former ages in Rome, Florence, and Venice, and with a painful sense of the inferiority of England in that particular. Her cathedrals, and many of her country churches, were the finest in the world; and St. Paul's is, in the interior, only second—in the exterior, superior—to the fane of the Vatican, the dome of St. Peter's. But if the streets of London were considered, being

entirely built of brick, and for the most part extremely narrow, they bore no proportion to the wealth or importance of the British metropolis. Vigorous efforts, however, were soon made to supply the defects. Regent Street, opened up through one of the densest parts of London, soon exhibited a splendid and varied scene of architectural decoration and mercantile opulence; Regent's Park showed long lines of pillared scenery surmounting its glassy lake and umbrageous foliage; and Waterloo, Southwark, and London Bridges bestrode the floods of the Thames, with arches second to none in the world in magnificence and durability. Unhappily, however, the other buildings of the metropolis, with very few exceptions, were all constructed of brick, with plaster fronts; and the facility of adding decoration with that plastic material has introduced a taste for gorgeous display at variance with every principle of good taste, and which painfully contrasts with the perishable nature of the materials of which it is composed. The noble freestone, and commanding situation of Edinburgh, have led to the prevalence there of a chaster and severer style of architecture, and rendered it by far the finest city in the British dominions, and one of the most striking in Europe. But having ceased to be the seat of government, and consequently lost the concourse of the nobility, it has sunk into a provincial town, and can never again be adorned by those sumptuous edifices which are raised by the national resources, and gathered round the centre of the nation's power.

It can not be said that the country of Sir Joshua Reynolds is destitute of the genius for painting; and yet this noble art has not, in the period when it might most confidently have been expected, risen to any distinguished eminence. There have been portrait-painters in abundance — some of very great merit; but placed beside the works of the great masters of the Flemish, Italian, and Spanish schools, theirs sink into insignificance. Valuable, often invaluable, to a single generation, from the fidelity of the likeness they have preserved, they cease to be considered when a new race succeeds to which that likeness was unknown. None of them will bear a comparison with the master-pieces of Vandyke or Rubens, of Titian or Velasquez. The details are unfinished, the still life is neglected, the attitude often stiff, the extremities ill drawn. It is easy to see that the whole effort of the painter has been thrown into the likeness of the countenance. The reason is, that the countenance only was an object of interest to the purchasers of the pictures; few of them had knowledge to understand, or taste to appreciate any thing else. The best pictures of Sir Thomas Lawrence are no exceptions to these observations. The likeness is generally good, the countenance powerful, the light and shade well disposed, the expression often angelic; but the picture, on the whole, is always unfinished — the coloring, except on the face, raw and inharmonious. Many of his most lovely female portraits often resemble an angel peeping out of the clouds. His best pieces, when put beside the master-pieces of Vandyke or Titian, appear so inferior that an Englishman turns aside with mortification. His fame was

82. Sir Thomas Lawrence.

great, the prices received for his paintings immense, during his life; but both have sensibly declined since his death, and his portraits have come to stand on their own merits as pieces of art, irrespective of the recognition of the likeness by the spectators.

TURNER, in landscape-painting, has attained a reputation more likely to be durable; for in genius he is equal, in variety of conception superior, to Claude himself. No one can study the *Liber Studiorum* of the former master, and compare it with the *Liber Veritatis* of the latter, without perceiving that the palm of originality and variety of imagination must be awarded to the first. There is none of his pictures as perfect as one of Claude's; none over which the glow of an Italian sunset is thrown with such magic over every object in the piece — the sky, the sea, the trees. But there is greater variety in his effects; his drawing from nature has extended over a much wider surface; his fancy is more discursive — his conceptions wilder, and more dissimilar. He has aimed at, and succeeded in awakening emotions of a far more varied kind than his great predecessor. Within his own limits Claude is perfection, but those limits are narrow. Turner's embrace the whole earth, and all ages of history. It is to the power of his conceptions, however, and the vigor of his imagination, that this unqualified praise applies; indelicacy of finishing, harmony of coloring, and minuteness of detail, combined with generality of effect, he is inferior to Claude, as indeed every subsequent painter has been, and perhaps ever will be. The latter pictures of Turner, when he indulged in a new and more vivid style of coloring, in which bright orange and saffron predominate, can hardly be considered as his productions; they would be more aptly designated as the works of genius run mad. There is only one consolation in reflecting on this running riot of so much talent, and that is, that it has elicited the genius, and displayed the taste and vivid powers of description of his accomplished advocate, Mr. Ruskin, who, in attempting to defend his extravagances, has only caused his ingenuity to be the more admired, that it has obviously been exerted in an indefensible cause. His great and varied genius and taste appear equally conspicuous in his *Seven Lamps of Architecture* — one of the most profound and original works of the kind in the English language.

83. Turner.

COPLEY FIELDING can not be said to be the equal of Turner in vigor of conception or variety of imagination; but in beauty of detail and polish of finishing he is sometimes his superior. Like Claude, his limits are narrow; but, like him, within them he is very perfect. He has two sets of pieces, and is essentially a mannerist in both; but in both a vivid eye for the beautiful in nature, and great powers of execution are conspicuous. No one ever excelled him in the representation of storms at sea, or of

84. Copley Fielding, Williams, Thomson

———"Ocean's mighty swing,
When, heaving on the tempest's wing,
It breaks upon the shore."

And in the delineation of sunsets at land, of the misty heat of a forenoon in the Highlands, or of the wild sweep of open downs in England, he is equally perfect. These are his limits, however; he never passes them; if he attempts to do so, he only repeats himself. WILLIAMS has thrown over the exquisite remains of Grecian genius the glow of a southern sun, enhanced by the richness of northern fancy; and permanently implanted into our collections the image of the most perfect architectural ruins in the world; while THOMSON, endowed with greater powers, and a more masculine turn of thought, has disdained to leave his own country in the search of the sublime or beautiful, and found, in its spreading pines, and misty mountains, and glassy lakes, the elements which only awaited the hand of genius to be moulded into the expression of perfect beauty. Like all the painters of the day, however, he is deficient in finishing; his pictures appear rough sketches when put beside those of Poussin or Salvator, to whose conceptions his bear a very close analogy. Neither portrait nor landscape painting will ever approach perfection in this country till our artists learn that minuteness of finishing is perfectly consistent with generality of effect; that accuracy of drawing is essential to give reality to the conceptions of imagination; and that unity of impression is not to be attained without a copious sacrifice of lesser details to the one prevailing emotion intended to be awakened.

85. Grant, Pickersgill, Swinton.
It was long before any portrait painters appeared in London upon whom the mantle of Sir Thomas Lawrence appeared to have descended; but at length two artists arose whose talents seemed to indicate that the Fine Arts could take root in the mountains of Caledonia as well as on the slopes of the Apennines. Mr. FRANCIS GRANT, albeit not originally bred to the art, and habituated at first to the most elegant and polished society, ere long showed that genius can overcome the want of early study, and that a thorough acquaintance with the most polished society only makes an artist better acquainted with the aerial graces and nameless charms which enter so largely into the composition of the Cestus of Beauty. No British artist ever excelled him in the delineation of female elegance; it is easy to see that he is a gentleman who has not only felt its influence, but felt in what it consists, and learned how it is to be perpetuated to future times. His early passion for the chase, also, has stamped the character of his works in another respect. His horses are admirable, and particularly remarkable for the spirit and accuracy of drawing they display. PICKERSGILL's portraits are often admirable, from the fidelity of the likeness and the brilliancy of the coloring; but there is generally a deficiency of shade in them, and, as in all modern pieces, a want of finishing of details. SWINTON is the rival of Grant, and in the same style; he represents female elegance so well, because, by living with it, he has learned in what it consists. Many of his portraits of the most lovely of our female nobility are beautiful pictures, as well as striking likenesses; but they are very unequal, and a want of drawing is sometimes conspicuous, even in his most careful productions. Nor is Scotland without her own honors in the Fine Arts; for REABURN was equal to any artist of his time in portrait painting; and ALLAN has left many paintings, especially of Eastern and Circassian scenes, of very great excellence; while in Sir JOHN WATSON GORDON she may still boast an artist, perhaps, superior to any of his contemporaries in the delineation of masculine power of countenance.

86. Landseer.
There is one painter of the age, however, who stands at the very head of the department of the art to which his genius has been directed, and has elevated it to a height which never was attained in any foreign state. It may safely be said that in the representation of animals LANDSEER is unrivaled. In truth, he has opened an entire new mine of surpassing richness in this branch of art. Schneider had represented, with the utmost skill, the painful scenes of boar hunts, and in vigor of design and power of execution, he never was surpassed; and Reinagle and Du Jardin had delineated the domestic life of animals with equal taste and fidelity. But Landseer has struck out an entirely new path; he has represented *the pathetic* in animals. He is not the painter of them when hunted, and either the enemies or the victims of man: he is one of themselves; he sympathizes with their terrors, shares their griefs, is inspired by their affections. His representations of the fawn seeking to obtain nourishment from its dead mother, of the herd striking into the wilderness on the approach of the hunters, of the devoted fidelity of dogs, of the monarch of the glen starting up from his heathery lair, and other similar subjects, are not merely admirable as pieces of art, but unrivaled in the expression of pathos and sentiment. He is the painter of Nature, and has studied her not merely in her wildest scenes, but in her most hidden recesses and secret habits. England may well be proud of having given birth to such a man; and he affords evidence that, if painting in its highest branches has not hitherto flourished as might have been expected in so brilliant an era in this country, the fault lies in the direction of the national taste, not in want of genius in its artists.

87. Wilkie.
WILKIE's name will be always associated with this period of English history; and, in many respects, he is equal, in his own style, to the greatest painters the world has ever produced. He did not aim at the expression of the pathetic in animals, like Landseer—nor the humorous in man, like Teniers—nor the vulgar in low life, like Ostade: he took counsel from his own genius, and struck out a new vein in the representation of mankind. He portrayed THE DOMESTIC in humble life—its joys, its interests, its amusements, its sorrows. He was the Burns of painting—inspired with his sentiment, penetrated with his ardor, gifted with his powers. In minuteness and delicacy of finishing, he was quite equal to Teniers, and, at the same time, without his occasional coarseness: so that his paintings, even of the humblest scenes, may be looked on by the most delicate female without pain. His drawing is admirable—his coloring brilliant, and yet harmonious. The great defect of his style —and it is a very serious one—is, that he does not sufficiently mass his lights and shadows; admirable in detail, there is a want of generality in effect. The light on each figure is admirably

done; but the light on the whole is too indiscriminately thrown. He has shaded well, according to Titian's simile, each individual grape; but he has forgot the shading of the whole bunch. By far too many of his figures are illuminated; he would have done well to have remembered the observations of Sir Joshua Reynolds, that, in Titian's painting, two thirds is in shade, and only one third in bright light.

If Landseer has struck out a new vein—the pathetic in animals, CHANTREY has equally illustrated himself by opening a fresh mine—the pathetic in sculpture. In this he is unrivaled—"above all Greek, above all Roman fame." The group of the Niobe family alone, in ancient sculpture, showed what powerful emotions might be awakened in that way; but Chantrey, in his monumental pieces, worked it out with deep feeling and admirable effect. Breaking off at once from the strange mixture of allegory and conceit with which the barbarous taste of former ages in England had deformed the glorious fane of Westminster, he boldly struck into a new line, and, with the materials of the Simple, aimed at the expression of the Pathetic. His success was prodigious and decisive; it raised him at once to the very head of modern art in this department. His Sleeping Children, in Lichfield Cathedral, which first gave him his colossal reputation, and several other monumental pieces in the same style, are unequaled in simplicity of thought and beauty of expression. Many of his busts — among which that of Sir Walter Scott may be cited as the most admirable—are as perfect and characteristic likenesses as ever were made. If to these powers and chaste designs this great artist had united the knowledge of drawing and command of the figure which Phidias and the first masters of antiquity possessed, he would perhaps have made the greatest sculptor that ever existed. But there he was obviously deficient; and perhaps no modern artist, without the advantage of the Palestra, can ever hope to rival the artists of antiquity in that respect. His entire figures are generally stiff—sometimes out of drawing; the attitudes are often constrained, the contour unpleasing, the horses unnatural. His fame will rest on his sepulchral pieces and portraits, not on his entire figures or public monuments.

FLAXMAN possessed a greater and more varied imagination than Chantrey, and more akin to the genius of ancient sculpture. He did not aim so much at the expression of one sentiment or feeling as at the delineation of incident or event of a critical or interesting nature, by means of the chisel; and there his powers were of the very highest order. The Metopes of the Parthenon, the contests of the Athenians and Amazons, constantly floated before his imagination; he was imbued with the very soul of Homer. His designs in illustration of the *Iliad* are the finest series of the kind which modern Europe has produced. If English taste or spirit had been adequate to the undertaking of a national monument to commemorate the deliverance of Great Britain from Gallic invasion, he would have produced a frieze worthy of being placed beside that of Phidias himself. His conceptions were grand—his attitudes varied and striking, his drawing truthful and accurate. He was less perfect, however, with the chisel than the crayon; his execution was not equal to his conception; he could hardly work out the beauty which he had imagined. In single figures he often failed, and in still life was sometimes inanimate; it was the vehemence and heat of battle which kindled his imagination and inspired it with the heroic spirit. His portraits of individuals, though often striking likenesses, were not equal to those of Chantrey; his power consisted in the representation of life in action rather than character in repose.

Albeit, born in Italy, and bred in France, Baron MAROCHETTI may be reckoned among British artists, and is entitled to a very high place among the highest of them. He has become naturalized among us; his genius has adorned our chief cities; and the statues of Richard Cœur-de-Lion in London, and the Duke of Wellington in Glasgow, have given him an enduring claim to the gratitude of his acquired countrymen. His genius is of the very highest order; it is a combination of that of Chantrey and Flaxman. In the expression of character he is equal to the former, in the delineation of incident he rivals the latter. By combining a frieze in alto-relievo, in which the figures are in action, round the pedestal of his statues, with the figures in an attitude of repose on its summit, he has succeeded in exhibiting his powers in both these lines in the same monument. So European has his reputation become, that, shortly after finishing his noble statue of Victor Emmanuel at Turin, he was engaged, at the same time, in the monumental figure of Napoleon for his tomb in the Invalides at Paris, in the formation of the equestrian statue of the Duke of Wellington in Glasgow, and that of the Duke of Orleans at Algiers. His drawing is, in general, accurate; he is a perfect master of the anatomy of horses, and his grouping is bold and striking; but in working out the details of his figures, he is not equal to the recent sculptures of the German school; and the prize at the Great Exhibition in London, in 1851, was worthily awarded to Kiss, for his inimitable representation of the combat of the Amazon and Lion.

In one art, nearly akin to sculpture, England at this period rose to the very highest eminence. If the drama is the efflorescence of epic poetry, the histrionic art is the efflorescence of sculpture.

"But by the mighty actor brought,
Creation's brightest fancies come;
Verse ceases to be airy thought,
And sculpture to be dumb."

In this noble and bewitching art the family of the KEMBLES stands pre-eminent; and Mrs. SIDDONS was the founder of the honors of the house. She was the Tragedy Queen personified. Endowed by nature with a commanding figure, a noble countenance, and stately air, with raven locks, a majestic carriage, and sonorous voice, she united all that the poets had prefigured of the lofty in character, the imposing in woman. She had nothing tender in her disposition—none of its expression in her countenance—none of the elements which awaken it, either in her character or person. She was made, not to be loved, but worshiped; she stepped forth, no amid her adorers, but her subjects. She could at times—in Juliet, Desdemona, and Belvidera—awaken the very soul of tenderness, and melt every spectator by the most harrowing touches of the pathetic; but that only showed the variety of her powers—it did not bespeak the bent of her disposition. It was the majestic, the noble, the devoted, the generous, which suited her character; and in the expression of them she was unrivaled. In Queen Constance, Isabella, Mrs. Haller, Lady Macbeth, and similar characters, her powers shone forth in their full lustre; and she produced an effect upon every class of spectators, which never has been, and probably never will again be equaled on the English stage.

<small>92.
John Kemble.</small> JOHN KEMBLE, brother to Mrs. Siddons, and the coinheritor with her of the genius of the family, was cast in the same mould and endowed with the same spirit; but he had not the same marvelous combination of physical advantages. His countenance had her Roman cast—his hair was of her raven hue; but he had not the same stately air, the same majestic figure. Seen off the stage, his height seemed under the middle size; and latterly he had a considerable stoop from the shoulders. His voice, never powerful, was at times husky, and plaintive rather than melodious. But these disadvantages, which, in a person less mentally gifted, would have been serious, if not fatal, were overcome, and more than overcome, by the ardor of his mind, the energy of his disposition, the lofty conceptions which filled his soul. In these he was fully equal to his sister, more highly gifted though she was, so far as personal advantages are concerned. His mind was filled with grand ideas; a Roman magnanimity was the characteristic of his disposition. He had great powers for the pathetic; but it was not ordinary grief which he represented; it was the Stranger mourning his faithless love—it was Cato preferring death to slavery—it was Brutus learning, on the eve of Philippi, the death of Porcia, which he represented with such admirable effect. He was learned, a great antiquarian, and studied the dress, armor, and costume of the olden time with the most assiduous care. His air was magnificent when he walked the boards as Brutus or Coriolanus, in the exact costume of the conquering republic: the line of the poet involuntarily recurred to the mind,

"Thou last of all the Romans, fare thee well!"

<small>93.
Miss O'Neil.</small> If Kemble overcame many personal disadvantages by the lofty tone of his mind, an actress who rose in his declining years, yet often appeared on the boards with him, Miss O'NEIL, had every gift of nature to aid a tender and impassioned disposition in melting the hearts of the spectators. A finely-chiseled Grecian countenance, dark glossy hair, a skin smooth as monumental marble, and beautiful figure, gave her every advantage which genius could covet for awakening emotion; but to these were added the very mental qualities which were fitted to bring them forth in full lustre. She was not majestic and queen-like, like Mrs. Siddons—nor stately and imposing, like Kemble; she was neither the tragedy queen nor the impassioned sultana. The tender woman was her real character, and there she never was surpassed. She had not the winning playfulness which allures to love, nor the fascinating coquetry which confirms it; but none ever possessed in a higher degree the bewitching tenderness which affection, when once thoroughly awakened, evinces in its moments of unreserve—or the heart-rending pathos with which its crosses and sufferings in this world are portrayed. In the last scenes of Juliet, Belvidera, and Desdemona, nothing could exceed the delicacy, power, and pathos of her performance. She was too young for Queen Constance—too innocent for Lady Macbeth; but in Mrs. Haller her powers, aided by her beauty, shone forth in the highest perfection; and when she appeared on the boards of Covent Garden in that character with John Kemble, whose older aspect and bent figure so well suited her deserted husband as the Stranger, a spectacle was exhibited such as no one ever saw before, as no one will ever see again, and which did not leave a dry eye in the whole audience.

<small>94.
Kean.</small> KEAN, although contemporary with Miss O'Neil, was an artist of an entirely different character. He had no advantages of figure or air; his stature was short—his voice far from powerful—his countenance, though very expressive, not handsome. But all these deficiencies were compensated, and more than compensated, by the fire and energy of his mind. "Sir, he is terribly in earnest," said John Kemble of him when he first appeared; and this was strictly true, and was the secret of his success. The vigor of his thoughts, the vehemence of his delineation of passion, bore down all opposition, and raised him to the very highest eminence in the histrionic art. He was not so commanding as Kemble in any one part, but he excelled in a greater number of parts: the former had more grandeur of conception—the latter more variety of execution. He was peculiarly admirable in the delineation of villainy and dissimulation, or of the mental conflicts of irresolute character. None could excel him in the representation of Iago or Richard III.; few in the conflicting passions of Jaffier or Hamlet. He would have made a perfect Jaffier to Kemble's Pierre; and if Miss O'Neil had at the same time played Belvidera, future ages might perhaps hope to rival, but assuredly they never could excel, the spectacle.

<small>95.
Miss Helen Faucit.</small> If powers of the very highest order united to fascinating beauty, and the most lofty conceptions of the dignity and moral objects of her art, could have arrested the degradation of the stage, Miss HELEN FAUCIT would have done so. But this highly gifted actress arose in the decline of the drama, and even her genius was unequal to the task of supporting it in the days of corrupted taste. She is a combination of Mrs. Siddons and Miss O'Neil; with the majestic air and lofty thoughts, but not the commanding figure of the former, and as great pathetic power, and not less winning grace, but without the regular features of the latter. Variety is her great characteristic, versatility her distinguishing feature. Like Garrick, she excels equally in tragedy or elegant comedy: it is hard to say whether her Rosalind is the more charming, or her Lady

Teazle the more fascinating, or her Juliet the more heart-rending. Dark raven locks, a fine figure, and singularly expressive countenance, bestow on her all the advantages which, in addition to the highest mental gifts, beauty never ceases to confer on woman; and a disposition marked by deep feeling, alternately lively and serious, sportive and mournful, playful and contemplative, gives her that command of the expression of different emotions, and that versatility of power, which constitute her great and unequaled charm. She has the highest conception of the dignity and moral capabilities of her art, and by the uniform chasteness and delicacy of her performances does the utmost to uphold it in its native purity; but it is all in vain. She has appeared in the days of the decline of taste, and, notwithstanding her great genius and celebrity, is unable to arrest it. The drama here, as elsewhere, has been in a certain stage of society succeeded by the melodrama; the theatre by the amphitheatre. Covent Garden has become an Italian, Drury Lane an English opera-house. Singing and dancing, stimulants to the senses, splendor for the eye, have come to supplant the expression of passion, the display of tenderness, the grandeur of character.

96. Decline of the drama in England, and its causes.

This progress has occurred so uniformly in rich and luxurious nations, that it may be considered as inevitable, and arising from some fixed and universal principle in our nature. Nor is it difficult to see what that principle is. It arises from the gradual rise, and ultimate ascendency, of a middle class in society, the minds in which are not so cultivated as to enable them to enjoy intellectual or moral pleasures, while their senses are sufficiently excited to render them fully alive to the enjoyments of the physical. Disguise it as you will, that is the real principle. When that class, which is ever a vast majority of mankind, becomes, in the progress of opulence, so rich and powerful that its patronage forms the main support of the theatre, the ruin of the drama is inevitable and at hand. This change was accelerated, and perhaps prematurely brought on in this country, by the well-meant and sincere but unfortunate prejudices of a large and respectable portion of society, which withdrew altogether from our theatres, from a natural feeling of indignation at the immorality of some of its dramas, and the license of many of its accessories. There can be no doubt it would be well if these abuses could be corrected; and it would also be well if corruption could be banished from literature, vice from the world. Unfortunately, the one is not more likely to happen than the other. Both spring from the universal corruption of our nature, and will cease when we are no longer children of Adam, but not till then. The only effect of this portion of society withdrawing from our theatres has been that their direction has fallen into the hands of the unscrupulous. Their support of the profligate, and the licentious character of their representations, have in consequence been greatly increased. We can not destroy the art of Æschylus, Shakspeare, and Schiller, but we may alter its character and degrade its direction; and the unhappy result of the respectable classes withdrawing from the theatre has been too often to convert what might be, at least occasionally, the school of virtue into the academy of vice.

Society in the higher classes underwent a great change in England during the year subsequent to the peace, and from the same cause which induced the decline of the drama. During the twenty years that the war had lasted, great fortunes had been made in agriculture, the law, trade, and commerce; and numbers of persons had risen to affluence and distinction in society, many of whom had been ennobled, who were not equal in birth, manners, or refinement, to those among whom they were now introduced. The glorious victories and unparalleled successes of the army in the latter years of the contest had led to numerous chivalrous honors being bestowed on its veteran commanders, some of whom, however gallant or able in the field, were rather saddle than carpet knights, and better fitted to wrest standards from the enemy than to win smiles from ladies fair in drawing-rooms. From this intermixture of society, and extensive introduction of a new class into its highest circles, arose another species of aristocracy—that of fashion —self-elected, but universally bowed to, which deserves mention even in a work of general history, from the important political consequences by which it was followed. Beyond all question, the *Exclusive System* was one of the remote causes of the Reform Bill.

97. The exclusive system in society; its causes.

It was very natural, and not to be wondered at, that the ancient aristocracy, who saw their hereditary and long-acknowledged domain invaded by a host of intruders, many of whom were better provided with wealth to dazzle than manners or accomplishments to adorn it, should endeavor to arrange themselves in an interior and more limited circle, to which the only passport should be the possession of some qualities which added to the lustre or enhanced the charms of society. It was like the garrison of a fortified town, driven from the external walls, taking refuge behind the ramparts of the citadel. The beauty, charms, and accomplishments of the ladies of high rank and distinction, who were at the head of this exclusive circle, soon rendered its attraction universal, their own influence irresistible. Mere wealth was wholly inadequate to procure admission to it; rank even the highest, if unaccompanied by other qualifications, as little; the carriages of duchesses were to be seen waiting at the doors of the ladies' patronesses of Almacks, where marchionesses and countesses presided over the distribution of the tickets. The highest fame and consideration in the other sex were equally unable to resist the ascendant of fashion—the Duke of Wellington and Lord Castlereagh bowed, perhaps not unwillingly, to its influence. Yet even here the changes which recent events had introduced into society were conspicuous; the ancient prerogatives of birth were often broken through from the influence of modern distinction, and genius obtained an entrance when hereditary rank was excluded. Literature was speedily influenced by this new power which had arisen in the metropolis, and a host of novels appeared, professing to paint the manners of the exclu-

98. Its great effect on society.

sives and the penetralia of that inner shrine, of which so many were the devout worshipers, but so few the initiated priesthood. Meanwhile its attractions were magnified, as is always the case, by the imaginations of those who were shut out from the magic circle; and discontent and jealousy spread widely through society from the injustice thought to have been committed upon many of its members. The important political effects of this feeling will abundantly appear in the sequel of this history.

99. Increasing liberalism of the higher ranks.
During the fifteen years which immediately followed the peace, the tendency became very apparent in young men of rank to adopt Liberal opinions, and range themselves in politics in opposition to the side which their fathers had adopted. So far did this tendency spread, that although during the war fully two thirds of the House of Peers had been of the Conservative party, before the Reform Bill was carried it had become doubtful whether they had a majority. This important change arose doubtless in part from the natural tendency to reaction in the human mind, against the strong bias to monarchical opinions which had been induced in Great Britain by the horrors of the Revolution in the neighboring kingdom. Opinion had been bent so far one way, that now, in the next generation, it inclined equally far the other. But it was in a great degree, also, owing to the influence of the foreign traveling which at that period prevailed so widely among the young men of this country. Long shut out from it by the war, the youth of Great Britain rushed in crowds to the Continent on the return of peace; and, being in great part recently escaped from college, or emancipated from parental control, they were just at the age when new ideas most easily find an entrance into the mind, and foreign influences are most powerful. Wherever they went, except in Vienna, they found Liberal opinions in a large portion of the higher ranks in the ascendant, and the most agreeable houses and charming society deeply imbued with them. These influences, with young men of ardent minds and generous dispositions, often proved irresistible; the new opinions only appeared the more attractive because they were new; and the sons of many sturdy peers, whose fathers had spent their lives in combating the democratic principle, gave way to its sway under the influence of French Liberalism or the smiles of Italian beauty.

100. Influence in society of the great Whig houses.
This tendency in so many of the younger part of the English aristocracy, at this period, was much increased by the extraordinary attractions presented by the society in several of the leading Whig houses. Holland House, Devonshire House, Lansdowne House, Woburn Abbey, and several other mansions of the Whig nobility, both in the provinces and the metropolis, collected a circle and exhibited attractions such as never before had been seen in English society. Intimate, from their rank and connections, with the highest aristocratic families, they did not, like the exclusives, confine their attentions to their members alone. They sought out and encouraged talent in every department, whether at the bar, the senate, in literature, science or art. They bestowed on the rising or eminent in their department the flattery which, of all others, is the most seductive to talent less favored by birth or fortune—a momentary equality with those to whom, in both respects, she had been most propitious. It was very difficult for young men, whose genius had raised them much above the position in society in which they had been born, to resist the attraction of a society in which Lady Holland and Sir James Mackintosh, Macaulay and Landseer, Jeffrey and Chantrey, were to be met at dinner; where Moore sang his bewitching melodies with still more bewitching right honorables in the evening, and the lustre of the most splendid assemblies or balls closed the scene of enchantment. Incessant were the efforts made by the Whig party, in the interval between the close of the war and the passing of the Reform Bill, to recruit their ranks with the most rising young men, of whatever side, by their attractions; and to the success with which they were attended, the progressive rise in the strength of the Liberal party in both Houses of Parliament, during that period, is in no slight degree to be ascribed. There are Armidas in the political as well as the military world; and the charms of genius, the smiles of beauty, by withdrawing the most stalwart knights from their own side in the conflict, have prolonged or decided many other contests besides those around the walls of Troy or the ramparts of Jerusalem.

101. Which was wanting on the Conservative side: causes of the difference.
The Tories at that period had no corresponding attraction on the other side to present; and to the want of this the decline in their numbers, and desertion of many of their adherents in Parliament, is in some degree to be ascribed. The same has long been observed in English society; for nearly a century, the principal houses where the aristocracy of rank and talent were united had been those of the great Whig nobility. The reverse has only begun to take place since the Tories were excluded from power by the effects of the Reform Bill, and they have been driven by necessity to the alliance with talent, from which their opponents had derived so much benefit. The reason is founded in the nature of things; and the relative position of the two parties will be found, in similar circumstances, to be of permanent influence. The Tories being the dominant party, which had been long in power, and rested on the support of the great bulk of the property in the kingdom, which at that period influenced the House of Commons through the nomination boroughs, they not only did not require the aid of genius, but they were averse to it. They dreaded the influence of a rival power, which they feared might one day wrest from them their exclusive domain. They desired the aid of talent, but it was of talent entirely subservient to their views and devoted to their purposes—that is, of talent emasculated and rendered incapable of permanently directing or influencing mankind.

102. and advantage of the Whigs in this respect.
The Whigs had no such jealousy or apprehensions. Out of power, they had no fears of being compromised by the imprudence of their supporters; in a minority in Parliament, they were fain to obtain the aid of

any power **which** could aid them in gaining a majority. Thence a long-continued alliance between the powers of intellect and the principles of liberalism, of which the effects will amply be unfolded in the sequel of this work. Both parties **felt** the benefit of a union into which both had **been** driven by necessity, and each was likely to experience the advantage. But the alliance was not destined to be perpetual; it ceased with the victory which their united strength had achieved. The revolution in France of 1830, in England of 1832, dissolved it in both countries. The reaction of the strength of mind against **the** despotism of numbers then **began on** both sides **of** the Channel; it was dis**covered** that the tyranny of numbers is even **more** oppressive than that of a monarch or an aristocracy. The cause of humanity and freedom was lost, if the powers of thought had **followed** the general bent, **and** flattered the ruling multitude as much as its sycophantish followers then did, or courtiers had done kings in former days. But, in that crisis, Mind remained true to itself, and reasserted its original destiny as the leader of mankind. Intellect ranged itself under its real standard—that of the human race. Genius, long a stranger to the cause of order, resumed her place by its side; she gave to a suffering what she had refused to a ruling power. It is this reaction of independence against oppression—the power of mind against the tyranny of strength—the force of intellect against the domination of numbers, which steadies the march of human events, and renders the misfortunes of one age the means at once of instructing the wisdom, correcting the errors, and mitigating the sufferings of those which succeed it.

CHAPTER VI.

HISTORY OF FRANCE FROM THE COUP D'ETAT OF SEPTEMBER 5, 1816, TO THE CREATION OF PEERS IN 1819.

The *coup d'état* of 5th February, 1816, which dissolved the Chamber of Deputies, and changed the electoral system, is generally considered as the commencement of constitutional government in France, because it altered the franchise, and remodeled the popular branch of the legislature, in conformity with the wish of the popular party, and gave them the means, by the annual retirement of a fifth of its members, and election of others in their stead, of permanently bringing the legislature into harmony with the majority of the electors. As such, it has received the most unqualified eulogium from the whole Liberal party of France. It is true, the number of electors, compared with the population, was small; it did not amount to 100,000, out of 30,000,000. But this was immaterial. It is the *class* from which the electors who return an assembly vested with supreme power which is the decisive circumstance. A *democratic oligarchy* of electors can return an assembly which will work out the purposes of Republicanism as effectually as the most numerous body of constituents: sixty thousand Liberals, intrusted with the election of the majority of the legislature, can mould the measures of its government to their will just as effectually as six millions. Nay, they are likely to do so more effectually, because, being a smaller body, they are more compact, more docile to the directions of their chiefs, and more likely to be swayed by personal ambition or class interests, than a larger and more heterogeneous multitude.

1. Effects of the coup d'état of 5th September, 1816.

The suffrage in France being founded on one basis only—viz., the payment of 300 francs direct taxes to Government—the direction of the legislature fell necessarily into the hands of a majority of that *single* class of society. This majority, it was known from the tax-office returns, was to be found in persons paying from 300 to 500 francs a year of taxes (from £12 to £20), and they formed, perhaps, the most dangerous class in the community, if lasting measures were looked to. They were not so likely to adopt violent measures, in the outset, as a body of electors embracing the inferior classes of society; but they were more likely to follow them out to the end: they were less hasty, but more persevering. The income of persons paying direct taxes to this amount was from £100 to £150 a year; and this class was invested with the entire direction of the state. They formed sixty out of the eighty or ninety thousand electors in France. A legislature the majority of which was composed of persons elected by such a body of small proprietors, was not so likely to be threatening to property as to power; there was no danger of their not attending to their own interests, but great risk that they would be regardless of the interests of others. The risk was not that they would support measures subversive of property, but that they would pursue a system which would be dangerous to the throne, and gratify their own ambition by establishing a republican form of government, in which they might divide the offices and emoluments among themselves. This accordingly was the result which actually took place; and the history of France during the next year is nothing but that of a continual struggle of the Crown with the Legislature which, by a violent stretch of the royal prerogative, itself had called into existence.

2. Democratic basis on which the elective franchise was founded.

Louis XVIII. had given a cordial assent to the ordinances of September 5, 1816.* He was more apprehensive at that period of the Ultra-Royalists than of the Democrats; he dreaded the Count d'Artois and the Pavillon Marsan more than either the Jacobins or the Napoleonists. Every thing, however, depended on the elections; for, as the Government had now unreservedly thrown itself upon the Liberal party, and entirely broken with the Royalists, if a Jacobin Chamber was returned it might at once lead to the overthrow of the monarchy. The greatest pains, accordingly, were taken to secure returns which might meet the views of the Government; and the King, both in circulars to the prefects, and in verbal audiences given to the heads of the electoral colleges, did his utmost to impress his views upon them, and, by their means, upon the electors. Concord and unanimity was the prevailing idea in the royal mind; he thought that the passions of the Revolution might be expected to subside when its convulsions had ceased, as the waves of the ocean subside after the storm has ceased to blow. "France," said he, to one of the electoral presidents, M. Raviz, "has unhappily undergone too many convulsions; it has need of repose. To enjoy it, what is required is a body of representatives attached to my person, to the cause of legitimacy, and to the charter; but, above all, moderate and prudent. The department of the Gironde, to which you belong, has already given me many proofs of its attachment and fidelity: I expect fresh ones in the elections about to take place. Tell them that it is a good old man who only asks them to make his last days happy for the felicity of his children."¹

3. The elections of 1815, and measures taken to secure them.

¹ Cap. v. 2, 7.

The Royalists, sensible of the danger which impended over the monarchy, and that every

---

* "Un des moments les plus heureux de ma vie a été celui qui a suivi la visite de l'Empereur de Russie en 1816. Non seulement il était entré dans toutes mes pensées, mais il me les avait dites avant que j'eusse eu le temps de les émettre. Il avait hautement approuvé le système de gouvernement et la ligne de conduite que je suis, depuis que je me suis déterminé à rendre l'ordonnance du 5 Septembre."—*MS. de Louis XVIII.*; Capefigue, iv. 369.

thing depended on the result of the elections, made the greatest efforts to secure a majority in their favor. They formed at that period a very powerful body; and acting, as they did, under the directions of a central committee of direction in Paris, their efforts were the more likely to be attended with success. In the south and west of France they were all-powerful, both from the feeling of the people, which was there monarchical to excess, and from nearly the whole official appointments having fallen into their hands during the period when the Count d'Artois, on the suggestion of the local Royalist committees, filled them up with the most determined men of their party. Secret societies were formed, which powerfully contributed to aid the same cause, and which government in vain endeavored to suppress. So strongly did general opinion, even in the towns, at this period run in favor of the Royalist party, that the Democratic party every where took refuge under the wings of the ministerialists; and the strange spectacle was exhibited of the Government functionaries generally supporting candidates who were avowedly banded together to overturn the throne! So true it is that the greatest and most durable popular revolutions receive their first impulse, in many cases, from the efforts of the executive. The reason is not apparent at first sight, but when once stated, its force becomes very apparent. The government for a time allies itself with the democrats, because, for a brief season, this relieves it of its opponents, and adjourns the inevitable conflict to a future time.[1]

4. Efforts of the Royalists and Liberals.

[1] Lac. ii. 89; Cap. v. 19, 12; Lam. vi. 140, 141.

The ordinance of 5th September, which divided the electoral colleges into two parts—the colleges of arrondissement, and the colleges of department—gave great advantages to the ministerial party. It was difficult to suppose that the Government would not obtain one or two names in each list of candidates, and that they should not have sufficient influence to get their candidates nominated for the colleges of department; and this accordingly, in a great many instances, took place. Nevertheless, so strong was the Royalist feeling in the majority of the rural districts, and so well organized and ably conducted their system of opposition, that in a great many instances they succeeded in throwing out the ministerial candidate. Nearly the whole leaders of the Royalist party re-entered the Chamber by the result of the elections, many of whom the ministers would have gladly dispensed with; and even in Paris and the great towns, where the ministerial action was the most powerful and most strongly exerted, several Royalists were returned. If the Chamber had been retained at its former number of 394, the majority would still have been Royalist, and it was turned the other way only by the great reduction of its members to 260. So skillfully had this reduction been effected, and so well-founded the local information on which it was rested, that the disfranchised places and classes of electors were for the most part those which were likely to return the most determined Royalists; and those on the Liberal side were, comparatively speaking, left untouched. The result was, that the ministerialists obtained a majority in the new Chamber, though not so considerable as they had expected. Those of the old Chamber re-elected were 171: 86 were new members, and 115 of the former legislature were thrown out, either by being defeated at the poll, or from having not attained the legal age of 40 years. Among the latter was M. Decazes, whom the king in consequence determined to raise to the peerage.[1]

5. Result of the elections.

[1] Lac. ii. 89, 90; Cap. v. 16, 17; Lam. vi 140, 141.

After the *coup d'état* of 5th September, the cabinet was completely united. The greatest efforts were made to sustain the revenue; and, by incredible exertions, all the stipulated payments to the allied sovereigns were made good; and the public creditors were made good; but it was done by such sacrifices as demonstrated the extreme financial embarrassment of the country. The Five per Cents were at 57 and 58; the exchequer bills were still negotiable, but at a very heavy discount. It was by means of loans, however, that the Treasury obligations could alone be made good, and the capitalists of Paris declared themselves unequal to the relief of the necessities of Government. In this extremity, recourse was had to foreign assistance; and, after great difficulties, a large loan was concluded with Messrs. Hope and Baring, by which the immediate necessities of Government were relieved, though at a heavy rate of interest. The cabinet unanimously agreed on the necessity of maintaining the laws restraining the liberty of the press, and establishing the Prévôtal Courts; but instructions were sent to the presidents and prefects to diminish the prosecutions, and lessen the severity of punishments. At the same time, a more liberal system was established in the army. The Duke de Feltre received instructions to be more indulgent in the granting of commissions: several were bestowed on the relatives of Liberal leaders; and the half-pay officers, recently the objects of so much jealousy, were cautiously re-admitted to the ranks. The princes of the blood vied with each other in endeavors to conciliate this important branch of the public service; and frequent reviews, and periodical visits to the barracks and hospitals of the troops, revealed their anxious desire to conciliate the affections of the men. A general order from the minister at war directed that each legion in succession should be called to the service of the capital; while the utmost pains were bestowed on the composition, both in officers and men, of the Guards. Every thing indicated that the Government was preparing for the time when the allied troops, which occupied the frontier fortresses, were to be withdrawn, and the Government was to be left to rest alone on the loyalty of the people, and fidelity of the army.[1]

6. Internal government after the *coup d'état* of 5th September.

[1] Lac. ii. 90, 91; Cap. v. 23, 24.

But in the midst of these useful and honorable labors, a new difficulty arose, which was the more hard to guard against that it arose not from the act of man, but the direct dispensation of the Almighty. The summer and autumn of 1816, beyond all precedent cold and rainy in all the northern parts of Europe, were in an especial manner unpropitious in France. Nearly incessant rains during the whole of July

7. Great distress in France in the winter of 1816-17.

August, and September, entirely flooded the low grounds adjoining the rivers, and almost destroyed the crops on their banks; and, even in dry situations, the harvest was essentially injured by the long continued wet. But for the potato crop, which fortunately in that year was very abundant, famine with all its horrors would have been superadded to the other ills of France. As it was, prices rose rapidly; and the holders of grain, anticipating a still greater advance of prices, kept up their stocks, and supplies in very insufficient quantities were brought to market. M. Lainé, upon whom, as minister of the interior, the duty of facing this dreadful calamity principally fell, did his utmost to assuage the public distress, and granaries were established in the most distressed parts of the kingdom, where corn was sold by Government to the most destitute of the people at a reduced price. But, in spite of every thing that could be done, the suffering was extreme: prices rose to more than double their average level, and in many parts of the kingdom numbers perished of actual want. In these distressing circumstances the beneficence of the king and the royal family shone forth with the brightest lustre: their names were to be seen at the head of all subscriptions in every part of the country; and such was their unwearied benevolence that it might have softened down many asperities, and extinguished many animosities, if, in a country heated by the fervor of a revolution, any thing could have this effect but the gratification of its passions.[1]

[1] Cap. v. 25, 26; Lac. ii. 95, 96.

8. Opening of the Chambers. Oct. 5.

The Chamber met on the 5th October, and the opening speech of the king was deeply tinged by the disastrous circumstances in which the country was placed. "Painfully affected," said he, "by the privations which the people are suffering in consequence of the inclemency of the season, the king feels still greater regret at being unable to hold out any prospect of an alleviation of the public burdens. He feels that the first necessity of the people is economy, and he has endeavored to introduce it into every branch of the public service. My family and myself will make the same sacrifices as last year; and to enable me to conduct the government, I rely on your attachment to my person and to our common country." He concluded by expressing his firm determination to uphold the charter, and never permit the smallest infringement of its fundamental provisions. "My ordinance of 5th September, 1816, says it sufficiently."[2]

[2] Moniteur, Oct. 6, 1816.

8. State of parties in the Chamber of Deputies.

When the Chamber was constituted and proceeded to business, the vast change made in the representation, effected by the ordinance of 5th September, was at once apparent. The Royalists, who composed so large a majority in the former Chamber, were now reduced to a minority of eighty members, who, however, were formidable, as all similarly constituted bodies are in a deliberative assembly, from their unanimity of opinion, their perfect discipline, and docile obedience to the voice of their chief. Having lost the command of the Chamber, and the direction of the Government, they had recourse to the people, and on every occasion advanced the opinions and supported the measures which were most likely to insure their popularity, even with the opponents of their general system of government. Their leaders in the Assembly were M. de Villèle and M. de Corbière, and none could be more skilful in the lead of such an opposition; but it was not there that their real strength was to be found. The real strength of the party was the press: its effective leaders the great writers. M. de Chateaubriand and M. de Frioce, powerfully supported their side by the united powers of genius and eloquence;[1] and so powerful are these weapons, and so overjoyed the people to see them ever ranged on their side against the Government, that they very soon acquired great popularity, and an influence in the Assembly altogether disproportioned to their numerical strength.

[1] Cap. v. 34.

10. Centre and Left.

The Centre, as it is called in French parliamentary language, was the most numerous and important body in the Assembly, because, by its inclining to the side of Ministers or the Opposition, it at once determined the measures of government and the fate of administration. It was divided into the Centre Droit and the Centre Gauche, according as its members inclined to the extreme royalist or democratic opinions; but, in general, it supported the measures of Government, partly from patriotic feelings, partly from an instinctive dread of any decisive measures which might be attended with important changes. M. Lainé was the most distinguished man of this party; and to insure its support, the chief members of Administration, among whom may be reckoned MM. Pasquier and Bignon, besides M. Lainé himself, were taken from it. The Centre Gauche was chiefly distinguished by M. Camille Jourdan, and M. de Courvoisier, whose abilities and eloquence caused them always to be listened to in the Assembly, though their practical acquaintance with business was not such as to cause their being taken into the Administration. In the extreme Left, which mustered about sixty votes, M. Laffitte, a great banker in Paris, who afterward became celebrated, and M. Royer d'Argenson, were the acknowledged leaders, but such was now the strange confusion of parties in the Assembly, that they were much more frequently acting in support of Ministers than in alliance with the Royalist opposition. The different parties came to a trial of strength on the choice of a president. MM. de Serres and Pasquier, who were supported by the Ministers and Centre, had respectively 112 and 102 votes; while the Royalist candidate, M. de Corbière, had only 76.[2]

[2] Cap. v. 36, 42, 43.

11. Law of election of 5th February, 1817.

The first important legislative measure of the session was an act brought forward by Ministers to legalize the preceding election, and obtain the sanction of all the branches of the legislature to the royal ordinance of 5th September, 1816. There was an obvious absurdity in an assembly, elected by a royal ordinance, proceeding, as its first act, to pass a law *legalizing its own appointment*, and declaring it to be the law in future; but so accustomed were the French to *coups d'état* that they saw nothing incongruous in this proceeding—and perhaps, in the circumstances, when a stretch on the part of the Crown had been committed, there was no other way of getting back to legal measures. To support the ministerial measures, returns were obtained from different departments of the number of persons entitled to the franchise under the ordinance of 5th September, and they amounted to 90,878, paying 300 francs of direct taxes; and 16,052, paying 1000 francs yearly. It was evident, therefore, that though the suffrage was very limited in point of numbers, yet the majority of that number was decidedly democratic; for out of the whole 90,000, no less than 60,000 were persons paying from 300 to 500 francs of direct taxes yearly (£12 to £20), which corresponds to incomes of from 2500 to 4000 francs (from £100 to £160); being, perhaps, the most democratic portion of the community. The ministerial project was, that every Frenchman aged thirty years, and paying 300 francs yearly of direct taxes, should be entitled to the suffrage; that the prefect was to prepare the electoral lists, and decide appeals against his judgment in his council, the courts of law determining such as depended on legal questions. Every department was to have one electoral college, which was to meet at the chief place of its bounds; it was to sit ten days to receive the votes, and to be presided over by a chairman appointed by the king; and if more than 600 electors required to vote at any college, it was to be divided into two or more sections. The debates on this project began on Dec. 26 and the 26th December, and elicited arguments of the highest historical importance.[1]

Moniteur, Dec. 26 and 27, 1816; Cap. v. 66, 68.

12. Argument of the ministers in support of the measure.

On the part of the Government it was urged by M. Royer Collard, M. de Serres, and M. Camille Jourdan: "The ruling principle of this project is to bring the electoral law into harmony, as nearly as possible, with the charter; unless we adhere to that landmark, we have no chance of avoiding being lost in a sea of speculation and innovation. Now, the charter leaves no doubt on the matter; it expressly declares that the electoral right shall be bestowed on every Frenchman paying 300 francs of direct taxes; that the elections shall be direct, and by one degree only. The double election—first by arrondissement, and then by department—is infinitely more complicated, and exposed to the action of corruption and intrigue. It is preposterous to suppose that a law which confines the suffrage to 90,000 out of 30,000,000 of inhabitants, is too democratic. At the same time, the electors by department will be sufficiently numerous to render bribery or undue influence impossible. In every point of view, therefore, the project is both safe and expedient—protective to liberty, and yet not endangering to monarchy.

13. Continued.

"Had the charter stopped short with laying down certain vague principles for the elections, some difficulty might have been experienced in the details of any measure intended to carry it into effect; but the charter has relieved us of this difficulty—for it has pronounced on all questions that can arise in their fullest extent. It has declared that there shall be deputies by department, and neither more nor less; that every Frenchman paying 300 francs a year of direct taxes, shall be admitted to the franchise. These are precisely the bases of the proposed law. The Elective Chamber is intended to represent the nation, its opinions, and its wants; and for that very reason, all those who fulfill the prescribed conditions are *ipso facto* electors. Nothing is said of primary elections, for this plain reason, that they are not mentioned in the charter. It has wisely closed that field of discord, so fatally ensanguined during so many years. The projected law, then, is the complement of the charter: it carries into execution, and brings out in detail, the principles which it has announced. It is its principle, its life, its movement: it should influence all our destinies. If a wider field were opened for our discussion—if we were not chained to the charter—much might perhaps be advanced in favor of a double degree of election, and the admission of an inferior number. The only danger of the proposed system is, that it reposes on too limited a base—that it does not sufficiently secure the interests of the masses. But to object to it on the ground of its not being sufficiently protective of the monarchy is, of all unfounded objections, the most untenable."[1]

[1] Moniteur, Jan. 1, and 2. 1817; Cap. v. 69, 71.

14. Answer by the Royalists.

To these arguments, which sufficiently demonstrated that the Centre was enlisted on the side of the ministerial measure, it was replied on the part of the Royalists, by M. Villèle, M. Decazes, and M. de Castelbajac; "It is an entire mistake to suppose that the circumstance of the electoral suffrage being confined to persons paying 300 francs of direct taxes is a sufficient security for the monarchy. The elections will be determined by the persons paying from 300 to 500 francs of direct taxes annually (£12 to £50), and they are the most democratic portion of the community. The great proprietors will have no influence; the immense body of the peasant proprietors and working classes as little. Is this a proper representation of a country at once agricultural and commercial; rich in great names and historical recollections—richer still in modern energy and glory? Such a law, instead of being imposed upon us by the charter, is only fit to destroy the institutions and the guarantees which it has given us. The charter has not intrusted the exclusive nomination of the legislature to a majority of electors paying from 300 to 500 francs of direct taxes, and yet that is the effect of this law. It virtually confines the suffrage to one class of society; and as it is necessarily the most numerous, it becomes master of the state, and may let in anarchy when it pleases. To obviate such dangers, it is necessary to establish an electoral system more extensive than that which is proposed. The king might, without danger, and in policy should, permit the citizens to group themselves around such interests as they have in common. Thus there should be established under the monarchy, councils of secondary administration, corporations, chambers of commerce, legal bodies, and fraternities of men of letters, and of all sorts. All these bodies should have representatives in the Chamber of Deputies, and not merely a single class of society.

15. Continued.

"Five-and-twenty years of revolution have influenced our destinies too powerfully not to render innovation repugnant when it is not absolutely necessary. We have gone on very well hitherto with the elections by double degrees; we owe to it the Chamber of 1814, which, on the return of our legitimate monarchs, showed itself so favorable to the sentiments of France; to it the Chamber of 1815, now the object of such undeserved calumny. The prefects, who have succeeded by their influence in removing as candidates the members of 1815, are the worst enemies of the monarchy. Party in a monarchy is necessarily adverse to the king; no absurdity can be so great as is implied in the words, 'the *Royalist Party.*' What! under the government of a king, can there be a royalist party? It is by such denominations that the way is prepared for revolution. We are called '*Ultra* Royalists:' do the Liberals hope by these words to efface the bloodshed, the services rendered, the heroic devotion? The ideas of monarchy, and of the influence of families, are inseparable; and every electoral law which does not rest upon these ideas will speedily become a weapon in the hands of the factious for the overthrow of the monarchy.[1]

All that we contend for is, to avoid the operation of a law which would deliver over the Chamber of Deputies, and with it the entire government of France, to a class of Frenchmen from whom we contend the electors should not be exclusively chosen.

[1] Moniteur, Jan. 4 and 10, 1817; Cap. v. 71, 72, 77; Lac. ii. 137.

16. Concluded.
"The proposed law is, in truth, more dangerous than the wildest conceptions of the Constituent Assembly. It receives no support from the charter. The charter merely says that 'the French, aged thirty years, and paying 300 francs of direct contributions, *shall concur* in the election of the deputies; the present law says that *they alone* shall name them. The whole question lies there: the charter says these persons shall form one class of the electors; the law says they shall constitute the *sole class*. The pretended worshipers of the charter, therefore, have reserved for themselves the privilege of altering and modifying it according to their interest or inclination, or their insatiable thirst for popularity. The unity of the College of Electors adds another scourge to that of the unity of the direct representation. We shall have armies of ten or twelve thousand electors assemble in a single great city for their votes—armies only a little less numerous than those with which Gustavus Adolphus shook the Austrian throne. By removing the higher college, and reducing every thing to a single college, you will overthrow the strongest barrier which Napoleon had constructed against the revolutionary spirit. Can the monarchy dispense with the support of the great proprietors? and how is it to be exercised in the midst of a crowd of uniform electors, paying 300 francs each, and enjoying, at an average, not 4000 francs a year each? If the great proprietors are not permitted to vote in a college apart by themselves, they will be virtually disfranchised, and every thing governed by a mob of small proprietors. What can be the consequence of this but new advances, fresh spoliations, and the ultimate overthrow of the monarchy?"[2]

[2] Moniteur, Jan. 19, and 21, 1817; Cap. vi. 71, 73; Lac. ii. 143, 144.

Various amendments were proposed in the Chamber, and the law became the subject of warm and able discussions in the public press, and in a host of pamphlets on either side. M. de Serres, one of the ablest men on the Royalist side, proposed an amendment, the object of which was, when there was only one member for a department, to establish a separate college for the urban and the rural electors. The discussion continued extremely animated, both in the Chamber of Deputies and in the public journals, during the whole of January; and the king every day become more infatuated in favor of his system of a uniform franchise, founded on the payment of 300 francs. As the majority of the Chamber of Deputies were known to be decisively in favor of the ministerial measure, without any amendment, M. Decazes took advantage of this delay to secure a majority in the Chamber of Peers. The king warmly seconded him in this attempt: he spoke constantly in favor of the uniform suffrage; and when an opposition of opinion appeared, he scrupled not to exert all his private influence, and even to make use of entreaties, to secure even a single vote. At length, by these means, and the most unscrupulous exertions of the whole influence of the Crown, the measure was adopted in both Houses, but by a larger majority in the Commons than the Peers. The majority in the former was 32—there being 132 votes for the measure, and 100 against it; in the latter it was only 18, the numbers being 95 to 77.[1]

17. It is passed.

[1] Moniteur, Feb. 10, 1817; Cap. v. 79, 83; Lac. ii. 141, 150.

On reviewing this debate and decision of the legislature, which, like all other decisions involving a great change in the electoral system, was decisive of the fate of the monarchy, one thing must strike every one as very remarkable. This is the opinion which was so generally expressed by the ministerial party, that no possible danger could be apprehended from the proposed change, because the number of electors would, under it, be so small in proportion to the whole population—not more than 100,000 out of 30,000,000. They forgot that it is not on the number of electors, but on the disposition and feeling of their majority, that every thing depends. A country may be as effectually revolutionized by 100,000 electors as by 10,000,000, sometimes more effectually, provided only that the majority of the 100,000 are of the democratic party, and invested with sufficient power to work out their designs. A convention of 1200 men overturned monarchy, extinguished the church, and divided property in France. 3,000,000 of electors placed Napoleon, 6,000,000 Louis Napoleon, on the imperial throne. The peril of the electoral law, in a manner forced upon France by the Crown, consisted in this, that it invested with supreme power a majority of electors drawn from a body of all others the most democratic—little proprietors—and virtually disfranchised the great proprietors, the men of cultivated education, and the laboring classes of the community. It is remarkable that this decisive law, fraught with the fate of the monarchy, originated with the king's ministers, was forced through the Commons by their influence, and through the Peers by the personal solicitation and efforts of the king himself.*

18. Reflections on this law.

* "La victoire paraissant incertaine, et les Ministres étaient menacés d'une défaite éclatante si le Roi, qui en-

The next important measures of the session were those relating to individual freedom and the liberty of the press. The violent restrictions on these, which had been obtained from the Chamber of 1815, had been introduced by M. Decazes, and carried through by the Royalist majority, then in close alliance with him, and they all expired at the end of the session, being limited to that period. Now, however, the Royalists, being in opposition, felt these restrictions oppressive, and by a natural consequence became desirous of their abolition. The press was the principal engine by which they hoped to succeed in shaking the Liberal party now in possession of power, and therefore they were desirous of securing its freedom: it was the chief enemy which the Liberals had to dread, therefore they were desirous of continuing its restrictions. Such a transposition of parties on a particular question is well known in the history of England, and, however strange in appearance, it arises from a very obvious cause, and is not likely ever to cease. It springs from the desire for power being stronger than the influence of principle, and individual ambition supplanting public consistency.

19. Laws on personal freedom and the liberty of the Press.

The ministerial project concerning the liberty of the press was short and simple. It was, "that the censorship of the press was to be continued till January 1, 1818." The proposal was based on the alleged necessity of the law, which was curious, as it was now to be applied against the very party for whose support it had originally been introduced. The proposed law on the liberty of the person was not so stringent as that of 1815, but still sufficiently dangerous to freedom. It was to this effect, that every person charged with a conspiracy or machination against the person of the king, or the security of the state, might be summarily arrested without the necessity of being immediately brought to trial. No extraordinary arrest could be made but on a warrant signed by the President of the Privy Council, and by one of the Secretaries of State. The jailer was to send an intimation of the name of the person imprisoned, with the charge against him, to the Procureur du Roi, by whom he was to be interrogated, and the charge and declaration transmitted to the Minister of Justice. It was almost identical with the suspension of the Habeas Corpus Act in England, and was to continue only to the first of January, 1818. This law underwent a most animated discussion in both Chambers, and was not passed into a law without the most violent opposition.[1]

20. Projects of laws regarding the liberty of the press and personal freedom.

1 Cap. v. 109, 112; Lac. n. 151, 152.

On the part of the Opposition, it was contended by M. de Villèle, M. Castelbajac, and M. de Labourdonnaye: "We are told that the stringent laws of 1815 have restored public tran-

trait dans leurs vœux avec ardeur, n'appuyait son influence personnelle de l'ascendant de son amitié sur de nobles Pairs qui faisaient partie de sa cour. Après avoir formé son humble cour de Mattan et Hartwell, ce fut le 30 Janvier 1817 que la Chambre des Pairs vota sur l'ensemble de la loi. Il fut adopté à la majorité de 95 voir contre 77. La soumission plutôt que la conviction donnait une majorité qui devant céder au premier choc, dès que deux épreuves peu favorables à l'espoir des Ministres ramenèraient ce débat."—LACRETELLE, *Histoire de la Restauration*. ii. 159.

quillity: if so, where is the necessity for still recurring to exceptional laws? In 1815 the French army was disbanded, the courts of justice disorganized, the heads of departments changed, the most violent and terrible political and external crisis just surmounted. These were the reasons assigned, and with justice, for the suspension of individual liberty at that time; but now the same measures are attempted to be justified by a state of things exactly the reverse—by the happy re-establishment of the influence of the Government in all branches of the administration. We have nothing to add to the picture of general improvement drawn by the partisans of Government except the corrollary naturally flowing from these —'the exceptional laws should cease.' What is our present position? The charter guarantees to us individual freedom and the liberty of the press, and we have neither the one nor the other. Has France any reason to apprehend a fresh revolution?—is royalty of new in peril? If it is so, let the king be invested with unlimited power. But if, thanks to Providence, France is peaceful, why not terminate the exceptional laws, justifiable only in periods of anarchy?

21. Argument against the law on the liberty of the press by the Opposition.

"All is favorable—all is well, exclaim the supporters of Government: the elections are free—the cries, 'Down with the nobles,' 'Down with the priests,' are no longer heard under the peaceful reign of the Bourbons; the deputies of the departments will, under the new electoral law, be chosen from the most estimable, the most esteemed, the most independent of their several districts; the bases of public instruction are to be love of God and fidelity to the king. The word legitimacy may well be very differently defined, if you adopt this project, from what it was lately by a member of the Government, when he said, 'Legitimacy is order—order is moderation.' You can not deny, indeed you yourselves boast, that the Jacobins are reduced to a dozen or two of individuals whom every one laughs at, and five or six insane fanatics; where then is the necessity, where the expediency of continuing, under these favorable circumstances, which the Government are themselves the first to proclaim, those exceptional laws, the fatal bequest of disastrous periods, which are alike subversive of public freedom and of all rational attachment to the throne?"[1]

22. Concluded.

1 Moniteur, Jan. 15, 17, and 18, 1817; Cap. v. 110, 114.

On the other hand, it was contended by M. Decazes, M. de Serres, and M. de Courvoisier, on the part of the Administration: "Anterior to the return of Napoleon on the 20th March, the respect for individual freedom was carried the length of absurdity. A law similar to that of 29th October, 1815, would have disconcerted the conspirators, and prevented all the ruinous consequences which have resulted from their success. This consideration alone is sufficient to engage us to support the project which has been brought forward by the Ministry. Laws of exception are made for extraordinary circumstances; and can it with reason be maintained that there are no extraordinary circumstances at this time? I see Frenchmen reject it by their country, and have they no interest to revi-

23. Answer of the ministerialists.

troubles and overturn the existing order of things? I see 150,000 allied soldiers in possession of our fortresses—is that not an extraordinary circumstance? In the interior there are a vast number of discontented persons, officers out of the service, employés without occupation—is it not for the public interest to deprive them of the means of creating fresh disturbances?

"The king measured with a judicious and discriminating eye the state of France when he published the ordinance of 5th September last. His words and deeds on that occasion alike afford fresh guarantees for liberty, security, and property. If he dissolved by a somewhat violent act the former Chamber, it was because, it must be said, the vehement exasperation of the great majority in it threatened the French with the destruction of their property and liberties. The Ministry are not to be deterred by declamations about a dictatorship; they know their position as consuls of the state, and they are not afraid of the Tarpeian rock. The circumstances are critical: distress generally prevails from the badness of the last harvest; the minds of the people are soured by misfortune; agitators are on the watch to convert the general discontent into measures of sedition and rebellion. Is this a time to relax the precautions taken to insure public tranquillity in circumstances, in truth, less alarming? The king relies on the love of his people; the people on the love of their king." The Chamber, by a large majority, supported the two measures of Government, suspending the liberty of individuals and that of the public press: in the former case by a majority of 43, the numbers being 130 to 87; in the latter by one of 39, the numbers being 128 to 89. In the Peers, in like manner, they passed by considerable majorities.¹

24. Concluded.

¹ Moniteur, Jan. 17 and 18, 1-17; Cap. v. 114, 121.

A more difficult task, however, remained behind, than that of contending with a powerful minority in parliament, and that was, making head against the distress which, from the extreme deficiency of the last harvest, had now come to press upon every part of France. Bread had risen in Paris to twenty-four sous for a loaf of four pounds, which was about 2½d. a pound—a frightful state of things, as it was nearly triple the usual price. Disturbances in consequence were general, both there and in every part of France; and although they did not, except at Lyons, assume a political character, yet they were very alarming, and called for the utmost vigilance on the part of Government and those intrusted with the administration. The carts of farmers bringing grain to market were, in many places, seized by the peasantry, and their contents distributed among famishing multitudes; and many granaries were broken open and openly pillaged. As a natural consequence, less grain was brought to market, and less imported and stored in the warehouses, which augmented the general distress. The riots were particularly formidable at Chateau-Thierry, Chatillon-sur-Seine, and in the department of Puys de Dôme. These excesses were vigorously repressed by the Government, but not without bloodshed in many places —a distressing state of things, and which more

25. Extreme scarcity, and measures of Government in consequence.

than any thing else justified the stringent laws introduced by the Ministers, to prevent the disaffected from taking advantage of the general distress to excite disturbances against the Government. A large vote of credit was passed by the Chambers to give Government the means of relieving the public distress; large purchases of grain were made in the Crimea, both by Government and private individuals; and a bounty was offered, on the importation of grain, of 5 francs a quarter. By these means, so plentiful a supply was obtained from Odessa and the fertile plains of Poland and the Ukraine, that in the spring of 1817 the price rapidly fell, and, before summer, was below its ordinary level.¹

¹ Moniteur, Jan. 27, and Feb. 11, 1817 Cap. vi. 122, 131.

A more liberal, and withal judicious, system was at the same time adopted in the army. The public necessities, and the enormous weight of the contributions made to the Allies, rendered considerable reduction of expense necessary in that department; but so judicious were the measures of the Duke de Feltre that, simultaneously with these reductions of expenditure, he was able to make a considerable increase in the effective strength of the army. A fifth squadron was added to each regiment of cavalry, and the strength of the legions considerably augmented. The repugnance to the old officers of the Imperial army, so generally felt in the first years of the Restoration, was rapidly giving way; and numerous officers on half-pay were every day readmitted into the ranks from the lists of half-pay, who at once increased the strength of the army and diminished the resources of the discontented parties in the state. At length the general rule was adopted, that all the officers on half-pay who had not been replaced in the ranks should be replaced in the last squadron and battalion formed. By this means the expense of the half-pay was diminished at the very time that the ranks of the army were recruited by experienced officers; and it was mainly by the adoption of this judicious system that the diminished expense of the army was accompanied by an increase of its numerical strength.²

26. More liberal system in the army.

² Cap. v. 128, 142.

Difficulties had arisen between the court of France and the papal see, on the subject of eternal discord between the Pope and the temporal princes —the extent of the interference of the former in ecclesiastical appointments. To obviate them, and negotiate a concordat, M. de Blacas, who had negotiated the marriage of the Duke de Berri with the Princess Caroline of Naples, was sent to Rome in the beginning of 1817. But, though not destitute of abilities, M. de Blacas was no match in negotiation for the Cardinal Gonzalvi, and the other skilful diplomatists who at that period conducted the foreign affairs of the court of Rome. His pious zeal led him to make concessions unauthorized by the Chambers, unsuitable to the age, and for the support of which no possible means remained of providing funds in the revolutionized realm of France. M. Gonzalvi skilfully represented to M. de Blacas, that Napoleon's former concordat in 1801, which had done so much to establish the independence of the Church of France, should be annulled, as a concession on the part of the

27. Concordat with Rome.

papal see to the revolutionary spirit justified only by necessity. To this M. de Blacas consented; and the effect of this was to revive, in full force, the concordat of Francis I., and annul all the concessions made by the Romish see since 1789. Among the rest, it revived a claim for the territory of Avignon, one of the first conquests of the Revolution from the Church; and this M. de Blacas agreed to take into consideration, or pay an indemnity. But a much more serious inconvenience resulted from this injudicious abandonment of the concordat of 1801, and that was the revival of the numerous bishoprics and other ecclesiastical benefices which at that remote period covered the soil of France, and were richly endowed from its territorial possessions; but for the support of which no funds whatever now existed but from a vote of the Chambers, who it was easy to see would not consent, in the present distressed state of the finances, to any addition, even for these pious purposes, to the public burdens. To render the risks of this concession still greater, by the concordat of Francis I., now revived, the sanction of the papal court was requisite for any appointment to a monastery, prebendary, or bishopric, and the right of excommunication of whole districts for notable offenses was recognized. It was easy to see how these powers would accord with the feelings of revolutionized France in the nineteenth century.[1]

Concordat, July 16, 1817; Archiv. Dip. v. 627, 629. (31; Bulletin, Nov. 24, 1817.

28. Extreme difficulty regarding the finances.

The main difficulty of the year, however, in France at this period lay in the finances, the embarrassments of which were only equaled by the pressing necessity of effecting as speedily as possible some adjustment of them. In truth, the difficulties in this department were such that they might fairly be considered as insurmountable; and they would have proved so, had not the allied sovereigns and their ministers met them in a liberal spirit, and abated in their demands founded on the treaty of 20th November, 1815, in order to facilitate the re-establishment of the king's government in France, and relieve it of the most pressing dangers with which it was surrounded. On the one hand were the allied sovereigns, armed with the severe clauses of the treaty of 1815, in possession of all the frontier fortresses, held by 150,000 of their troops, commanded by the Duke of Wellington, all of whom were paid, clothed, and fed at the expense of France. On the other hand was the realm of France, worn out by a war of twenty years' duration, scarcely able to meet its own engagements, and yet burdened with the payment, in a few years, of £61,000,000 of indemnities to the allied sovereigns or their subjects! The strongest head reeled, the most intrepid spirit quailed, under such a combination of difficulties; and yet, till they were overcome, no stable government could be erected in France, or the least prospect be afforded of a dynasty being firmly seated on the throne. The difficulties, great as they were, with the sums due to the governments under the treaty, yet yielded to those arising from the rapacity and exorbitant demands of the persons and bodies entitled to indemnity by its provisions,[2] which proved to be so

[2] Cap. v. 152, 153; Lac. ii. 155, 156.

prodigies that there appeared no possibility of their ever being liquidated.

Fortunately for France and the tranquillity of Europe, the mixed commission, to whom the adjustment of these claims was referred, was presided over by a man whose capacity, great in military, was not less conspicuous in civil affairs, and whose moderation and sense of justice, as well as good sense, were equal to his genius. M. Dudon was the nominal president of the mixed commission; but the Duke of Wellington was the person to whom all difficult points were referred, and he was its real head. The Duke de Richelieu, finding the demands for indemnity, especially on the part of the lesser German princes, so exorbitant, addressed a long memorial to his old patron and friend, the Emperor Alexander, on the subject; and he returned a noble answer, and a letter addressed to the Duke of Wellington, which deserves a place in history, as investing with fresh laurels the brow of conquest.* Instructions in the same equitable spirit were addressed by the Russian government to their embassador at Paris, which distinctly recognized the truth of the statement to the Duke de Richelieu, that such was the magnitude of the private indemnities demanded of France under the treaty, that it was wholly impossible for that country to make them good, and pointed to some equitable adjustment which might be within the bounds of possibility,† and lead to an eventual

29. Efforts of the Emperor Alexander and the Duke of Wellington to obviate these difficulties.

---

* Placé comme vous, êtes, M. le Maréchal, à la tête des forces militaires de l'Alliance Européenne, vous avez contribué plus d'une fois, par la sagesse et la modération qui vous distinguent, à concilier les plus graves intérêts: Je me suis constamment adressé à vous dans toutes les circonstances qui peuvent particulièrement influer sur l'affermissement de l'état heureusement rétabli en France par vos glorieux exploits: maintenant que la question de créance particulière à la charge de la France prend un caractère critique et décisif, à raison des difficultés que présente l'exécution littérale du traité du 8-20 Novembre, 1815, je n'ai pas cru devoir laisser ignorer mon opinion aux monarques mes alliés, sur le mode d'envisager cet engagement onéreux, de manière à en prévenir l'infraction et à le rendre exécutable. Les assertions du gouvernement Français vous sont connues, M. le Maréchal; mon Ministre à Paris reçoit l'ordre de vous communiquer le mémoire qui a été tracé sous très peu relativement à cette question importante. Je vous invite à porter toute votre attention sur l'enchaînement des motifs de droit et de convenance politiques qui se trouvent consignés, dans ce travail, à l'appui du principe d'accommodement présent, pour résoudre les complications inhérentes à l'acquittement des créances particulières, qui furent imposées à la France, alors qu'il n'était pas facile de prévoir leur énorme développment. Vous appuierez, M. le Maréchal, l'ensemble des considérations supérieures qui plaident à l'appui d'un système de conciliation équitable. Vous répandrez toute la lumière d'un esprit juste, la chaleur d'une âme élevée à la hauteur des circonstances, sur une question de laquelle dépendent peut-être le repos de la France, et l'inviolabilité des engagements les plus sacrés. C'est la modération et la bonne foi qui ont été de nos jours le mobile d'une force bienfaisante et réparatrice, et c'est à celui qui en a proposé et secondé le triomphe à faire entendre dans tous les momens critiques le langage de cette même modération et de cette même bonne foi. Dans cette conviction s'il me restait encore un vœu à énoncer, ce serait de vous déférer, par l'assentiment unanime de mes alliés, la direction principale des négociations qui pourraient s'ouvrir à Paris, sur la question des créances particulières, et sur le mode le plus équitable de la décider d'un commun accord. Recevez, &c. ALEXANDRE."
—CAPEFIGUE, Histoire de la Restauration, v, 297, 209.

† "Toutes les puissances sentent le besoin d'arriver à un résultat sans détruire le texte des conventions arrêtées. Le gouvernement Français ne conteste pas la dette qu'il a contractée en signant le traité du 20 Nov. Il en a déjà acquitté jusqu'à concurrence de 200 millions

shortening of the period of the occupation of its territory.¹ In consequence of this interposition, the presidency of the commission for liquidating the demands of private creditors was taken from M. Dudon, and bestowed on M. Mounier, who co-operated cordially with the Duke of Wellington on the subject. The latter general was appointed president of the diplomatic and finance committee charged with the same affair; and the result of their labors was a convention concluded, in February, 1818, by which the burdens undertaken by France, by the treaty of November, 1815, were sensibly abated, and a prospect was opened of the ultimate evacuation of its territory.

By this convention it was provided—1. That the strength of the army of occupation should be diminished by 30,000 men; that is, by a fifth of each corps of that army. 2. That this reduction should be carried into effect on 1st April next ensuing. 3. That from that date the 200,000 rations which the French government were bound to furnish daily for the support of the troops should be reduced to 160,000, without, however, any reduction being made in the 60,000 rations furnished daily for the horse. In communicating this convention, the embassadors of the allied powers observed—"In communicating so signal a proof of the regard entertained by their august masters toward his most Christian Majesty, the embassadors are, at the same time, desirous of declaring to his Excellency the Duke de Richelieu the sense they entertain of how much the principles of the ministry over which he presides have contributed to establish that mutual confidence and good understanding which, directed by justice, and a regard to existing treaties, has yet succeeded in arranging such delicate interests, and affording the prospect of a speedy and satisfactory definitive arrangement." The ease afforded to France by this arrangement was considerable, but it was rendered doubly valuable by the prospect which it afforded of a final and entire deliverance of the territory.² Such as it was, it was entirely to be ascribed to the magnanimous disposition of the Emperor Alexander, and the wisdom, moderation, and generosity with which his views were met and carried out by the Duke of Wellington and Count Pozzo di Borgo, to whom the French historians themselves entirely ascribed the relief thus obtained for their country.*

¹ Convention, Feb. 10, 1818; Archiv. Dip. v. 767; Cap. v. 169, 177; Martens, Sup. v. ii. 93

30. Convention 11th February, 1818, for the diminution of the army of occupation.

² See the Convention, Martens, Sup. vii. 93; Cap. v. 175, 177.

All the moderation and generosity of the allied sovereigns and their ministers, and all the wisdom of the Duke of Wellington, would have failed in obtaining the desired result, had the efforts of the French financiers not contributed, at the same time, to such regularity in the discharge of their engagements as enabled the Allies to meet their wishes without injuring the just claims of their own subjects. Never was a more difficult task undertaken by man, for, to meet the immense engagements under which France lay by the Treaty of 1815, there did not appear to be any available resources whatever. The utmost limits of taxation had been reached during the years 1815 and 1816; and experience had proved that any attempt to increase the amount levied on the country would fail by the imposts becoming unproductive. The sum to be raised in the year 1817 by loan, to meet the unavoidable expenses, amounted to 250,000,000 francs, or £10,000,000 sterling; and when the capitalists of Paris were applied to on the subject, they unanimously declared the impossibility, at any rate of interest, of their advancing so large a sum. Diminution of expenditure seemed impossible, for that had been carried to the utmost practicable length in the two preceding years, and any farther reductions would both increase the public discontent and render France altogether defenseless in regard to foreign powers. In this extremity the Duke de Richelieu applied to the capitalists of London and Amsterdam, and he was fortunate enough to obtain a loan from them of the required sum, though at a most exorbitant rate of interest. Not less than 9,090,000 francs of rentes were impledged for 100,000,000 of francs advanced, which was upwards of 9 per cent., in addition to which the creditors were allowed 2½ per cent. commission; and the first term of payment was postponed to 31st March, 1817. They contracted also for a second loan of 100,000,000 francs, at 58 francs advanced for 5 francs interest. These terms were so high that they gave rise to warm and able debates in both Chambers, in the course of which the financial and oratorical abilities of M. de Villèle shone forth with the highest lustre. But the answer of ministers, that the terms of the loan, however to be regretted, were unavoidable, as the requisite sum could not be got on any other terms, was justly deemed decisive; and the budget containing these loans passed both Chambers by very large majorities.¹ * (See Table in next page.)

31. The Budget of 1817.

¹ Moniteur, Jan. 2, and 29, 1817; Cap. v. 155, 182; Lac. ii. 154, 160.

A measure fraught with very important results, and which in its ultimate consequences was one of the causes of the overthrow of the elder branch of the house of Bourbon, was brought forward in this session of parliament, relative to bequests to the Church. Already, even before it was risen from its ruins, the aspiring disposition of the Romish Church had become apparent, and it was evident, from the measures which its clergy brought forward, that they aimed at nothing less than the re-establishment of its ancient hierarchy and splendor. Louis was by no means inclined to favor these pretensions. He felt warmly toward the clergy, but still more so toward the crown and he was by no means dis-

32. Law regarding bequests to the Church.

*ce total des reclamations qui subsistent encore s'élève a plus d'un milliard. Quelque diminution que cette somme puisse éprouver, il est impossible au gouvernement Français de l'acquitter; d'où résulte la question, 'Les principes du droit public, n'autorisent-ils pas le gouvernement de sa Majesté très chrétienne à proposer aux puissances alliées de modifier essentiellement ce traité?'"—Instructions au Ministre Russe à Paris, 1812. CAPEFIGUE, v. 209.

* "Je ne saurais trop rendre témoignage à la magnanime influence de l'Empereur Alexandre dans toute cette négociation. Le Czar se montra généreux envers la France comme il avait été lors du traité du mois de Novembre, 1815. Je le dirai également de l'action du Comte Pozzo di Borgo, sur les notes addressées à M. de Nesselrode, par un rapport personnellement soumis à l'Empereur de Russie sur la situation et des opinions en France; enfin les sentiments personnels du Duc de Wellington contribuèrent au grand résultat obtenu."—CAPEFIGUE, Histoire de la Restauration v. 177

posed to sacrifice any of its rights to the ambition of a rival establishment. The bill on the subject, which was brought forward by M. Lainé, provided that "every ecclesiastical establishment *legally authorized* might accept, but *with the sanction of the king*, all the goods movable and immovable which might be conveyed to it by donation *inter vivos*, or by bequest after death. The great object of this enactment was to reconstitute the clergy on the footing of separate proprietors, and put an end to the humiliating state of dependence in which they were now placed, on annual votes of the Chambers for a precarious and miserable subsistence. Vehement debates took place also on what was substantially the same question—a proposal by the Minister of Finance to alienate a portion of the woods yet belonging to the clergy to meet the exigencies of the state. The debates on this subject were of the highest importance, for they relate to one of the greatest wounds inflicted on society by the Revolution, and are of lasting interest to all future generations of man.[1]

On the part of the clergy it was contended by MM. Lainé, Bonald, and Villèle: "There is no footing on which the clergy can be established in a respectable and useful manner, but that of being separate proprietors. The proposal to alienate a portion of their woods for the necessities of the state, is brought forward by the same party who resist the re-acquisition of property by the church, from the munificence or bequests of individuals. Both are founded on the same basis—a dread of a beneficed and independent clergy, the greatest blessing which it is possible for society to receive, but on that very account the object of a superstitious dread on the part of the philosophers of the eighteenth century. They dreaded the independence of the clergy, because it tended to establish in society an interest and influence which might rival their own. Yet, how is it possible in any other way to render the clergy either independent, useful, or respectable? Since the woods of the clergy have escaped the hammer of atheism, the hatchet of cupidity, what right have we now in these days to wrest them from the clergy, or rather from religion itself? It is: mere mockery to say you propose to increase the vote for the clergy by 4,000,000 (£160,000)—a sum equal to the annual value of the woods sold. What comparison is there between a revenue forever derived from independent funds and a precarious annual vote from a democratic Assembly? Deep indeed have been the wounds religion has received in recent times; but was it ever anticipated that the most cruel blow should be struck in the name of a descendant of St. Louis?

"We tolerate religion now as we do a returned emigrant, on the condition that he is to make no claim to restitution. We tolerate the clergy on condition that they are never to become independent, and that they are to grow mercenary. Every year a vote of the Chamber is to determine the salaries of the clergy: it depends on whether or not they please the majority of the members whether their condition is to be comfortable or destitute. Is this a fit condition for the teachers of the people, the ministers of our holy religion, to be kept in? We are apparently awaiting the election of a thoroughly democratic Assembly, the worthy inheritors of the Constituent, which shall confiscate the whole remaining property of the church, and withdraw the miserable pittance which they have allowed instead of its once magnificent endowments.

"A proprietary clergy, the grand object of terror to the philosophers of the eighteenth century, seems to be equally the object of dread to the statesmen of the nineteenth. They lay their plans with more skill, disguise their motives with more address, embody their measure in a less revolting form; but the object is the same. That object is to render the clergy entirely destitute of property, and dependent for their subsistence on the votes of the Chamber. Nevertheless, it is to our proprietary clergy that we owe the greatest blessings we possess—the fertility of our fields, and the example of a vigilant and paternal administration. Is it to favor agriculture, that great branch of industry, the interests of which are incessantly invoked and incessantly betrayed, that this measure is adopted? It would seem that our rulers take a pleasure in consummating its ruin, by furnishing fresh fuel

* The Budget of 1817 was as follows:—

RECEIPTS.	Francs.	EXPENDITURE.	Francs.
Land Tax	258,141,667	National Debt	120,660,000
Stamps	154,170,000	Sinking Fund	40,000,000
Posts	12,475,000	Annuities	12,400,000
Lottery	6,250,800	Pensions—military, civil, and ecclesiast.	44,434,954
Salt tax	56,376,000	King, and Civil List	34,000,000
Indirect taxes	101,575,000	Peers Deputies.	2,630,000
Salt mines of the state	2,574,000	Justice	18,285,000
Miscellaneous	741,000	Foreign Affairs	55,300,000
Woods	16,819,200	Departmental expenses	28,727,000
Arrears of do.	8,843,800	Bounties on grain imported	22,200,000
Surrendered by King and Royal Family	5,000,000	Purchases of grain	2,500,000
Deducted from salaries	12,399,000	English indemnities	5,700,000
Loans	345,065,000	Cadastre	10,152,632
Do	7,024,033	Army	137,000,000
	1,118,532,500	Do of occupation	23,569,605
To meet arrears of former years	84,997,706	Navy	173,000,000
		Police	44,000,000
Revenue of 1817	1,033,535,706	Cautionary engagements	1,000,000
	(or £41,340,000)	Interest on do.	9,000,000
		Negotiating	22,700,000
		Fifth contribution to Allies	140,000,000
		Arrears of former contributions	23,000,000
		Miscellaneous to Allies	20,494,144
			1,036,810,582
			or £41,470,000

—*Archives Diplomatiques*, v. 201, 304.

to the flame which, ever since the Revolution, has never ceased to consume it—that is, the infinite subdivision of properties. Now that leveling fury is carried to such a length that it is desired to sacrifice to it the woods which the Revolution itself, in the midst of its furies and its extravagances, has left untouched. Despite the universal complaints on the state of our fields, supported by a thousand reasons, by a thousand facts, our present enlightened friends of agriculture propose to level with the ground those ancient forests which adorn our hills, shelter our plains, and constitute the sole fuel of our people. It has been reserved for an age boasting its intelligence and its wisdom to accomplish the prediction of Sully, that France would one day perish for want of woods. Pagan superstition has for useful purposes clothed these woods with superstitious reverence, to save them from the cupidity of the spoiler; but we, who pay so little respect to the laws of the living God, we insult alike the wisdom of the ancients, and the foresight of our ancestors, in order to lay the foundation of a sinking fund, destined to afford food for speculation on compound interest, the worthy bequest of an age of revolutions."[1]

[1] Moniteur, March 7 and 10, 1817; Lac. t. 163, 165.

"On the other hand, it was contended by M. Camille Jourdan, M. Courvoisier, and the Keeper of the Seals: "There is an essential difference between the property of an incorporation, and the property of an individual which descends to his heirs. The jurisprudence of every country has recognized this distinction; and it is founded on the obvious consideration that the heirs of an individual are known and designed by law, and therefore there is an obvious injustice done to them, if they are deprived of their inheritance; but no man can say who are to be the successors of an incorporation, and therefore no one can say he is injured by its property being applied to the service of the state. The pretensions now openly put forth by the clergy, and sought to be embodied in these enactments, clearly reveal the ambition of that aspiring body; and their determination, at all hazards, to regain that opulence and political power which they once possessed, and so much abused. Such an attempt, made in this age, is a greater absurdity than the worst extravagances of the Revolution; it is more calculated to inflict a wound on religion itself than the efforts of its worst enemies. For what object is the sacrifice of these woods, of which so much is said, required? Is it not to liberate our soil from the presence of the stranger, to emancipate our citadels from his hands? Is it to withhold such a blessing from France that so great an effort is now made to prevent any part of the woods of the church from being alienated for their redemption?

36. Answer of the ministerialists.

"What signify, in so grave a discussion, and when such weighty interests are at stake, the frivolous lamentations of our adversaries on the hardship of being deprived of the many recreations afforded by our forests; on beholding the trees fall which have sheltered our infancy, on their loss as depriving us of splendid appanages? Their hearts appear to have contracted for those noble trees a sort of chivalrous enthusiasm—one of them haven gone so far as to enter into a pathetic dialogue. The oak which inclosed the soul of Clorinda did not draw more tears from Tancredi, when prepared to strike it, than our menaced forests have caused to fall from the eyes of M. Piet, in the course of the speech which evinced that singular species of sensibility. To answer all that, is to say that it would be very allowable and very agreeable to abandon ourselves to all these fantasies, for trees, for gardens, for palaces, if our fortune would admit of it; but that when bankruptcy threatens us, the best direction which even the most poetical imagination can take—the best measure which this most chivalrous sensibility can adopt—is to endeavor to pay our debts not only by abandoning all useless superfluities, but even by retrenching some of our most cherished long-established necessities."[1]

37. Concluded.

[1] Moniteur, March 7, 1817; Lac. ii. 164, 167; Cap. v. 180, 187.

Upon this debate the Chamber, by a large majority, supported both the propositions of Government—that is, they admitted legal donations or bequests of property to the church, provided they were sanctioned by the king; and they voted the alienation of woods belonging to the church to the extent of 20,000,000 francs (£800,000). As an increased grant of 4,000,000 francs (£160,000) was voted to the clergy, there was no injury done to the church in the mean time; but the debates, nevertheless, are valuable, as bearing on a great question of state principle of lasting interest to mankind, and illustrating the indomitable firmness, strong vitality, and aspiring disposition of that church which had, to all appearance, been entirely crushed by the events of the Revolution.[2]

38. Result of the debate.

[2] Cap. v. 187, 194; Lac. ii. 167.

As the Chamber of Deputies was now decidedly Liberal, and the majority of the Ministry of the same way of thinking, Government felt the necessity of making it entirely so, and rooting out of the Cabinet the last remains of the Royalist party, of which, in the first instance, it had been almost entirely composed. The first change was made in the ministry of marine, in which M. Dubouchage was supplanted by Marshal Gouvion de St. Cyr, whose great abilities, as well as popularity with the veterans, seemed to point him out as the proper person to carry into execution the great changes in the composition of the army which were in contemplation. The appointment of St. Cyr to the ministry of marine, accordingly, was only temporary; and ere long a royal ordinance appeared, appointing Gouvion St. Cyr to the ministry at war and Count Molé to that of the marine. This was an important change; for both the dismissed ministers belonged to the Royalist party, and the Duke de Feltre was one of their ablest and stanchest supporters. All the pure Royalists were now rooted out of the Cabinet; its composition had become entirely Liberal or Doctrinaire, and in complete accordance with the majority of the Chamber of Deputies. Of its whole original members, the Duke de Richelieu, MM. Decazes and Corvetto, alone remained in it; and they, either from necessity or conviction, had embraced in their full extent the Liberal doctrines. Things were advancing swiftly in their natural course. For good or for evil, the *coup d'état* of 5th

39. Modification of the Ministry. May, 1817.

September, 1816, was producing its unavoidable fruits—it was either to prove the salvation or the ruin of the monarchy.[1]

_{40.}
Biography and character of Count Molé.

Count MOLE, who was now for the first time admitted into the Cabinet, was one of the most remarkable men of the Restoration. He enjoyed, in a very high degree, the confidence of the Duke de Richelieu; and his administrative talents fully justified his predilection. Endowed by nature with a firm and energetic mind, he had been early thrown into the school of Napoleon; but even the ascendant of that great man had not been able to modify the strong mould and distinctive marks of his character. He was better fitted to direct than to obey—to communicate than to receive impressions. No one in his grade possessed in a higher degree the confidence of Napoleon; and in the evening conversations in which the Emperor took such delight, and in which the talents of Cambacérès, Monge, Portalis, and M. de Fontanes, shone forth with so much lustre, he bore a most distinguished part. Had he possessed, with these brilliant qualities, perseverance and patience equal to his energy and determination, he would have been a first-rate statesman. But the defect of his character was a want, not of resolution, but of endurance; he was easily disconcerted and frequently led to abandon the most important objects and even retire into private life, rather than exert the resolute perseverance which so often, by wrestling with difficulties, overcomes them.[1]

_{1 Biog. Univ. Sup., voce Molé, lxxxv. 161; Cap. v. 198, 129.}

_{41.}
Gouvion St. Cyr.

Marshal GOUVION DE ST. CYR was one of those celebrated characters of the Empire whose name it is impossible to hear without a thrill of emotion. No one acquainted with the annals of those memorable years need be told of his achievements. On the Rhine and the Moselle, in Catalonia and Saxony, he was equally distinguished; and the military works he has left on those campaigns are not the least valuable of the monuments which remain of the astonishing talent and energy with which they were conducted. He was a decided Liberal in politics, and therefore eminently qualified to carry through the great task to which he was destined by the Government—that of remodelling and popularizing the army. This had now become in a manner a matter of necessity; for, as there was now a fair prospect of the allied troops being withdrawn from the frontier fortresses, the Government would be left to its own resources, and could not expect either to maintain its existence or independence but by the support of its own subjects. St. Cyr was a soldier of the Revolution; and he never got over the strong impression in favor of public freedom then made on his mind. But he was an honest and upright man; he was attached, like so many others, to the popular party, because he, in truth, believed it to be the only true foundation of constitutional freedom or social happiness. In command he was a strict disciplinarian, as persons of those principles generally are, and rigid in exacting the discharge of their duties by the officers; but he was beloved by the private men, for whose interests and comforts he was always ready to exert himself. His appointment to the important situation of War Minister was therefore a very important step and regarded as such by both parties. The Napoleonists and Democrats hailed it as an indication of the disposition of the Court to throw itself in sincerity and good faith on the nation, and, casting away foreign influence, to resume its proper place in the scale of European politics; the Royalists regarded it as a step which would probably be irrevocable in the overturning of the monarchy. The Count d'Artois said that, since the king was determined to destroy himself, he might do so, and that he would look out for his own interests.[1]

_{1 Cap. v. 199, 201; Biog. Univ. voce St. Cyr, Sup. lxxiv. 194.}

_{42.}
The elections of 1817.

The elections of 1817 for the fifth of the Chamber, who by lot vacated their seats, and were replaced by new members, were conduced peaceably, and without any external tumult; but their importance was not on that account less generally felt, and it was already foreseen by both parties, that in its ultimate results, the new electoral law would prove decisive of the fate of the monarchy. Eight new deputies were to be returned for Paris; they were all elected from the Liberal ranks, and more than a half were democrats, hostile even to the present Liberal government. MM. Lafitte, Delessert, Roy, and Casimir Perier, were among the returned; not one Royalist was among the number. Upon the whole, although as usual in such cases, the results were various, and success apparently nearly balanced, yet the Royalists sensibly lost lost ground, and the extreme Republicans gained it. Government might congratulate themselves upon the defeat of the three known leaders of the republicans, MM. Lafayette, Manuel, and Benjamin Constant; but they experienced a bitter alloy in seeing three extreme Liberals, Dupont de l'Eure, Chauvelin, and Beguin, admitted to the legislature. The Royalists, who were generally defeated, loudly declaimed against an electoral law which excluded from the king's service his most faithful servants, and predicted the ruin of the monarchy from its effects. The Doctrinaires, who had introduced that law, began in secret to dread its effects, but still in public defended it, and flattered themselves that, though in power, and exposed to the obloquy of office, they would be able to contend successfully in the elections with their democratic rivals.[2]

_{2 Lac. ii. 163, 184; Cap. v 214, 225.}

_{43.}
State of public opinion.

The circumstances of the country, however, were such that the democratic party however much in reality inclined to overturn the monarchy and revert to a republican form of government, were constrained to be circumspect in their measures. Notwithstanding the embarrassments of the Treasury, and the enormous weekly contributions which were paid to the allied powers, the country generally was rapidly increasing in prosperity. The wretched harvest of 1816 had been succeeded by one in 1817 which, although still below an average, was greatly better than that which had preceded it; and the blessed effects of peace and tranquillity appeared in a general, and, for so short a time, surprising revival of industry and increase of opulence. Paris, especially, had already attained an unprecedented degree of prosperity. Strangers arrived from all quarters to visit its monuments, its theatres, its galleries; its pleasures attracted the young, its historical interest and objects of art the middle-aged and reflecting. Those who had visited it in 1814 or 1815 and returned again in 1818—among whom the author may include himself—were astonished at the unmistakable marks of prosperity which were to be seen on all sides. Splendid streets had arisen or were in progress in many quarters; the Boulevards, the gardens of the Tuileries, the Champs Elysées, breathed, even on ordinary occasions, the air of happiness and joy; the streets were filled with elegant equipages; while the increasing brilliancy of the shops, and variety and beauty of the dresses of the women, proved that the bourgeois class shared in their full proportion of the general affluence and prosperity which the continuance of peace and the immense concourse of strangers had brought upon the metropolis. Among these strangers, the Russians and the English were particularly remarkable for the eagerness after works of art which they exhibited, and the immense sums which they spent. These sums, indeed, were so great as much to exceed the heavy weekly payments which the French were still compelled to make to the commissioners of the allied powers; and, like the Greeks of old, they might console themselves with the reflection that they had established a more desirable ascendant than that of conquest over the minds of their conquerors; and that, if they paid tribute to the rude barbarians of the North, they received a homage more lasting and flattering in the influence of their acknowledged superiority in taste and art.[1]

[1] Cap. v. 226, 227.

44. State of public opinion, and of the press.

In presence of so much material prosperity, and with the happy prospect of soon obtaining a definitive liquidation of their debts, and evacuation of their territory by the allied powers, the Liberal party did not venture openly to attack the government of the Bourbons. Too many real interests had flourished, too much undoubted prosperity prevailed, to admit of this being done at the moment, with any prospect of success. But they were not, on that account, the less determined nor the less able and energetic in the policy which they pursued. They prepared the ground for future operations by every means which prudence could suggest, or talent carry into effect. The press was the great engine of which they made use to agitate the public mind, and disseminate those alarms, or inculcate those principles, which might, at some future period, lead to the overthrow of the monarchy. Declamations against the ambition of priests and the intrigues of the Jesuits; alarms insidiously spread as to the resumption of the church property and the dispossessing of the holders of national domains; eloquent eulogies on the glories of the Empire, and the boundless career of fame and fortune then open to every Frenchman, formed the staple of their compositions. By a skilful use of these topics, and no small ability in the handling of them, they succeeded in attracting to their standard the large bourgeois class, who, in towns especially, are for the most part envious of Government, and desirous of humbling it; and it soon appeared that, on every successive election, the great majority of this class would vote for the Liberal candidate.[2]

[2] Cap. v. 229, 231; Lac. ii. 183, 184.

45. The Orleanists.

The partisans of the Orleans family still formed a considerable party, which was held firmly together by the skill and riches of the r chief, and the chances of eventually succeeding to the throne, which were evidently open to him in the divided state of the public mind. The immense estates of the family had, with perhaps imprudent generosity, been restored to them by Louis; he hoped to attach them by this act of liberality; but, although acts of kindness may sometimes conciliate an enemy, they seldom have any other effect but that of augmenting the alienation of a rival. It is the mortification to self-love which arises from being indebted to one whom it is desired to supplant which has this effect. The Duke of Orleans, however—who was gifted with uncommon penetration and powers of mind, and whose eventful career had made him acquainted with the secret designs of all the parties in the state—was fully aware of the difficulties of his position, and the still greater embarrassments he would encounter if he were to succeed to the throne. "I am too much a Bourbon," said he, "for the one, and not enough for the other,"—a very just observation, on which his future eventful career affords a striking commentary. Thus the different parties arrayed against the Government were held to their respective banners rather by a vague hope for the future than any definite projects for the present; and the only point on which they were all united, and to which their immediate endeavors tended, was that of resisting the measures, and augmenting to the utmost of their power, the unpopularity of the Bourbons.[1]

[1] Cap. v. 231, 236.

46. Measures of the session: the law of recruiting.

The general result of the elections had been so decidedly Liberal, that Ministers felt the necessity of both conciliating the Chambers and disarming their opponents by bringing forward measures in the interest, and likely to secure the suffrages, of the majority. The first and most important of these was the law of recruiting for the supply and future establishment of the army. This had now become a matter of necessity, for the negotiations with the allied powers left no room for doubt that the evacuation of the territory would take place at an earlier period than was originally contemplated, and the present strength of the army was not such as to enable the Government to stand alone, or maintain its position as an independent power. On the other hand, there were no small difficulties in the way of augmenting it. The rallying cry of the Bourbons, when they returned to France in 1814, had been—"*Plus de Conscription!*" and it was the extreme unpopularity of that mode of filling the ranks which had been the chief cause of the reluctance of the people to support Napoleon in the later years of the war which had occasioned his fall. The army had been recruited hitherto, since the peace, by voluntary enlistment; but that method brought a great number of loose characters about the royal standards, and it was very doubtful whether it would prove adequate to the support of the extended force which would become necessary upon the withdrawal of the allied forces. On the other hand, the conscription brought forth the very flower of the lation; but it ran the risk of becoming unpopular, it involved a breach of the royal word, and it could not, it was well known, be re-established without that progressive rise of privates to the rank of officers which was the great alleviation of its bitterness to the people, and was so direct an expression of the desires of the Revolution. This filling up of commissions from the ranks of the soldiers might be extremely agreeable to them, and so far obviate the objections to this mode of recruiting the army; but it involved the sacrifice of the most important part of the royal prerogative, and it might ultimately place the armed force in the hands of those upon whom, in a crisis, no reliance could be placed.¹

<small>Cap. v 240.
212 Lac. u.
183. Lam. vi.
122.</small>

47. *The law of recruiting proposed by Government.*
In a question surrounded by so many difficulties, the Government adopted the course usually followed in such cases; they brought in a measure in harmony with the inclination of the majority of the legislature. M. Gouvion St. Cyr, in a very able report, unfolded both the principles and the details of the proposed project. "All modes of recruiting," said he, "reduce themselves to two—voluntary enrolment and compulsory service; the latter will not be called into operation unless the first shall prove insufficient. The complement of the legions is fixed at 150,000 men; the number required yearly is 40,000. The proposed regulations are to be divided into three heads: those concerning the levying, the legionary veterans, and the promotion. The first are mainly founded on the old laws of the conscription—softened, however, in every particular in which it was practicable. The regulations concerning the legionary veterans are based on the principle that, in a free state, every man is bound to render service to maintain the independence of his country. Those regarding promotion, on the principle that, as a compensation for the sacrifices thus imposed upon the people, a regular and invariable system of promotion should be established in the army; that, beginning from the ranks, it should ascend to the highest grades;² that the regulations on this subject should have the fixity of laws, and the recompenses should be as widespread as the services, so that the common soldier might have the prospect of arriving at any rank, any employment, without any limit, or any other title but his talents or his services."

<small>¹ Rapport de M. Gouvion St. Cyr, Monvieur, Jan. 14 and 17, 1816; Cap. v. 276, 277.</small>

48. *Argument in support of the project by Ministers.*
A law fraught with such momentous, and it might be irreparable consequences, called forth, as well it might, animated debates in both Chambers. On the one hand, it was contended on the part of Ministers, by M.M. Courvoisier and Royer Collard: "The proposed law differs from the conscription in the most essential particular, for it fixes the *maximum* of the levy, whereas the main grievance of Napoleon's system consisted in this, that nothing was fixed absolutely; no amount of sacrifices secured the country against fresh demands. Under the monarchy, although voluntary recruiting was as much as possible encouraged, Government never lost hold of the important right of forced enrollment. The militia was constantly raised by levy; in remoter times the Ban and Arrière Ban were called forth. Forced levies were repeatedly had recourse to during the long and disastrous wars of Louis XIV. Look at England, that model of representative government does it not make use, in cases of necessity, of compulsory service? What else is the press, which mans the fleet which has given her the empire of the waves? Look around you in Europe, and you will see armies every where maintained by forced enrollments, which latterly have been pushed to a length that apparently knows no limits. Is it fitting for us, surrounded by so many powerful neighbors, decorated with so much glory, the object of such inextinguishable animosities, to rely for our defense only on the shadow of an army? Are we prepared to descend from the summits of military fame, to the condition and the reputation of a second-rate power? We have still within ourselves the elements of a military force capable of securing forever the independence of our country; shall we let them wither away for want of employment? Our misfortunes have not deprived us of the right to be proud, but they have imposed upon us the duty of being vigilant. Cast your eyes on our frontiers, on the garrisons of our citadels, and say if this is the time to slumber at our posts? We are accused of betraying the royal authority when, if we acted otherwise, we should be betraying the independence of our country; and the king, by surrendering that of his prerogative, has given a noble example of what the duty of his situation requires, the love of his people can effect.

49. *Continued.*
"The reserve of veterans which it is proposed to establish, under the name of 'legionary veterans,' is a measure at once called for by necessity, and justified by every noble and honorable feeling. We have to consider, in approaching this subject, if we shall again call to the defense of the country the soldiers who have created its glory, or if we shall forever stigmatize them as dangerous to its repose. Such a declaration would be at once rigorous and unjust, for our soldiers were admirable in the day of battle, and indefatigable ardor animated and heroic patience sustained them; never have they ceased to feel that they owed their life to the safety of France; and when they retired from their standards they were still prepared to offer to them immense treasures of force and bravery. Is it fitting that France should renounce the privilege of demanding them? Is it fitting she should cease to pride herself on those whom Europe is never weary of admiring? No! the thing is impossible; our safety is not placed in the oblivion of such services, in the distrust of such courage, in the abandonment of so secure a rampart. Empires are not founded on distrust. The king knows it; the king wishes that there should not exist in France a single national force which does not belong to him, a single generous sentiment of which he has not made the conquest. Our soldiers have expiated much, for they have suffered much; breathes there the man who would still repel them?

50. *Concluded.*
"We must say to those whom the phantom of the old army terrifies, that their prejudices are unjust, their alarms without foundation, and that in this, as in so many other cases, the dread of imaginary perils may induce real danger. After a crisis

such as we are emerging from, for evils such as we have endured there is but one remedy—and that is oblivion. It is oblivion alone which can heal the wounds of a state so long and violently agitated. Whoever refuses to sacrifice to oblivion prepares new tempests. What Frenchman has not need of oblivion, if not for himself, at least for his family, his brothers, his children? Error has been in all camps, within all walls, without all walls, under all banners. Our country has often seen rebels in both armies. All of us have faults more or less grave to expiate; and the king has given the best proof that he knows how to reign by his knowing how to forgive!"[1]

[1] Moniteur, Jan. 14 and 29, 1818; Ann. Hist. i. 54, 69; cap. v. 279, 284; Lac. ii. 189, 192.

51. Argument on the other side by the Royalists.

The last words, pronounced in a most emphatic manner by the Minister at War, produced a prodigious impression both in the Chamber and over France. They spoke too strongly to the most powerful passions of the people not to excite universal enthusiasm. They penetrated alike the camps, the towns, and the cottages; already the words were heard in the streets, "the Grand Army still exists." But the Royalists were not discouraged; and, without directly running counter to these noble and popular sentiments, they rested their opposition to the proposed measure chiefly on its tendency to despoil the Crown of the most important part of its prerogative, that of appointing officers to the army, and to establish an armed force, which could not be relied on under all circumstances, to support its authority. "The proposed law," said MM. de Villèle, de Chateaubriand, and Salaberry, "will renew what was most odious and oppressive under the Imperial regime—the forced levying of men by the conscription. Such a measure is repugnant to every idea of a tempered constitution or real freedom; it is unknown in England, where compulsory enrollment is known only in time of war, and then only for the militia, which can not be sent out of the country but with its own consent. Other kings have known how to conquer provinces, resist formidable leagues, with the aid of voluntary enrollment; are we less powerful than they? The conscription is the scourge of every country, but, above all, of an agricultural one; for what can replace the robust arms which are torn from the plow? It leaves, as in the last years of the Empire, none to conduct cultivation but widows and orphans. Why make such a display of hostile intentions at this time? Is it desired to awaken the jealousy of the sovereigns, to make them call to mind the exploits of the Grand Army, and dream of a second Waterloo? Is legitimacy so very firmly established, that it can with safety be abandoned to those who have so recently shown themselves its bitterest enemies? On the other hand, why oblige the veterans to come forth from their retreats, and persecute them by a compulsory service, under a government which there is too much reason to fear they are forever severed from in their hearts?

"'Promotion, promotion!' These are the magic words which are presented as the soul of the new law, as the secret destined to procure for us the restoration of our perilous glory. Promotion indeed! Is it already forgotten but frenzy was substituted

52. Continued.

for the noble sentiment of patriotism in the young élèves of Napoleon, and that to it are entirely to be ascribed the disasters of the Hundred Days? How is it proposed to regulate this promotion? Why, by despoiling the king of what is the very essence of the royal prerogative—the appointment of officers to the armed force! The charter expressly secures this important power to the king; and now the authors of the ordinance of 5th September, who were so loud in their assertion of the principle that not an iota of the charter should be changed, openly violate it, in order to secure the suffrages of a party the sworn enemies of legitimacy, and in order to humiliate the rural noblesse, who are the best supporters of the throne!

"It is not the law as a military institution which we are to consider. Possibly, in that view, it may be open to very few objections. It is its spirit, its tendency, that we are to consider. Its tendency in this view is perfectly plain—it is anti-monarchical. All its clauses are conceived in this spirit, that the impulsion and the movement shall no longer proceed from the throne. Under the monarchy, on the same principle, and for the reason that all judicial appointments and authority flowed from the throne, so the army, essentially obedient, recognized no other but the sovereign. It was his name, and his alone, which it bore on its arms, on its standards. The proposed law alters this entirely, for it takes the nomination and promotion of officers from the king; it violates the charter, which expressly recognizes that privilege as residing in him the formation of veteran legions is nothing but a decisive concession to those who have never ceased, and will never cease, to aim at the overthrow of the monarchy and the charter. There exists a flagrant conspiracy against both. The coup d'état of September 5 has rendered it omnipotent in civil matters, the present law will do the same with military. There was wanting to the Genius of Evil nothing but an army; when he has obtained one, he will seat himself on the ruins of a throne, at the foot of which fidelity and honor will fall in vain, too late recalled, too late appreciated."[1]

53. Concluded.

[1] Moniteur, Jan. 15, 1818; Ann. Hist. i. 70, 72; Cap. v. 278, 279; Lac. ii. 128, 199.

Various amendments were proposed, and some carried in both Chambers: but they related only to matters of detail, which were worked out with extreme care. The principle of the law was too strongly intrenched in the feelings and opinions of the majority of the Chamber of Deputies to be shaken; and although a majority of the Peers were inclined to the other side, the influence of Ministers, and the personal solicitations of the King, obtained for it success. On the final division, the law passed the Deputies by a majority of 55—the numbers being 147 to 92. In the Peers, the majority was less considerable—the numbers being 96 to 74. Thus passed this bill, which has ever since continued the charter of the French army, and has been successively adopted by all the governments which have succeeded to its direction. Its consequences were great—it may be said decisive—on the future fate of France and of Europe. It is remarkable that this important change in the composition of the French army—fraught,

54. The bill is passed into a law.

as the event proved, with such momentous consequences was carried through in presence of the European embassadors, and with their armies still occupying the French citadels; and there was as much truth as eloquence in the last speech of the Minister at War on the subject—"It is a spectacle unique in the history of the world to behold a free and national government discussing its military system in presence of the armies of Europe, still encamped on its territory."[1]

This was the great and decisive measure of the session. When this important victory was gained by the popular party, the lesser successes followed as a matter of course. The principal remaining struggle took place on the law proposed by government in regard to the liberty of the press. The provisions of the bill on this subject brought forward by M. Pasquier, the Keeper of the Seals, were these: The author of every writing published in France was to be primarily responsible for its contents; if the author was unknown, the publisher; and minute regulations were laid down for the seizure of works of an inflammatory tendency, and leading to revolt; and no journals or periodical works were to appear without the sanction of the censorship, before the 1st January 1821. This certainly was very far from being the liberty of the press, but still it was a step toward it, and indicated an intention on the part of Government, at no distant period, to remove all restrictions on it. The project, however, excited a great division in the Chamber; and a portion of the Centre, headed by Camille Jourdan, voted against it. This was an ominous symptom, and so the event proved. The bill was so altered by successive amendments—carried some against, some by the government—that in the end, neither party was very anxious for its passing into a law; and the result was, that after having passed the Chamber of Deputies by a majority of 34—the numbers being 131 to 97—it was thrown out by the Peers by a majority of 43—the numbers being 102 to 59. This result was obtained by the Royalists having to a man united with the extreme Left to throw out the bill;—a strange coalition at first sight, but natural in reality, when two parties—the most at variance on other points—are excluded from power, and both look to freedom of discussion as the only means of regaining it.[2]

The laws restrictive of individual liberty, and establishing the odious Prévôtal Courts, expired at the end of this year, to which period alone they stood extended, without either renewal or observation. In fact, they had become a dead letter; only four arrests had been under their authority in the course of the year. Thus the cause of freedom was sensibly advancing in France with the cessation of treason and sedition. Government no longer felt the necessity of exceptional laws, and were too happy to let them expire; the public feeling at once reprobated and rendered unnecessary their continuance. A great truth, interesting to all, and especially free nations, may be gathered from this circumstance—and that is, that the cause of real freedom never is promoted by sedition or revolt. A change of government may result, and often has resulted, from the success of such attempts; but the cause of liberty has never failed to suffer from them. If the treason is successful, none dare call it treason; its leaders are elevated to high stations, and liberty is in every mouth; but meanwhile the substance is lost, and the new government is both more powerful and oppressive than the old. If it is unsuccessful, the old government is only rendered the more powerful and vindictive, from the failure of an attempt to shake its authority. Freedom can not be won by rude violence, though a change of masters for the worse may: it is the result only of continued tranquillity and peace, and perishes in the first burst of civil dissension.[1]

A more serious difficulty awaited ministers in the establishment, in the realm of France, of the concordat lately concluded with the court of Rome. This could only be done by the consent of the Chambers, because, as the Church had been despoiled of all its inheritance by the Revolution, the new sees and establishments proposed could only be endowed from the funds of the state. It was no easy matter, with a Chamber, the majority of which was decidedly Liberal, to obtain such a grant; and yet, without it, the concordat would remain a dead letter. The Duke de Richelieu, to meet the difficulties, brought in a moderate bill, the purport of which was, that, in conformity with the concordat of Leo X. and Francis I., now again become the law of France, there should be seven new archbishoprics, and one hundred and thirty-five new episcopal sees established in France, the funds for the support of which should be taken from the public exchequer; that no bull or brief of the Pope should be published in France till it had received the sanction of the king; and that those concerning the Church in general, the interest of the state, or which modified its existing institutions, should be submitted to the Chambers. It was not likely that a bill which went, on the one hand, to impose so considerable a burden on the public funds, and on the other, abridged in such important particulars the authority of the Church of Rome, would meet with the support either of a Liberal Chamber, or of the Papal Government.[2] It experienced, accordingly, great opposition; and after being anxiously discussed in committee, and vehemently by the public press, it was withdrawn by ministers, and the matter referred again to the Duke de Richelieu, for farther negotiation with the Court of Rome.

The most important matter which remained for consideration was the BUDGET, and the greatest interests were wound up with it. On the success of the Ministry's measures of finance it depended whether France could make good its still onerous engagements to the Allies, and thereby effect an arrangement which might lead to the evacuation of the territory. This was a matter of the very highest importance, upon which the king's heart was most anxiously set, and upon the success of which the stability of his government might be considered as in a great degree dependent. Much consideration was requisite before a subject so surrounded with difficulties could be adequately handled, and the resources of France, equally with the capital of its moneyed men, were alike unequal to making good the engagements. But happily the CREDIT of its government stood high, and the honorable punctuality with which it had discharged its obligations, since the Restoration, had gone far to remove the effects of the confiscation of so large a part of its public debt during the Revolution. M. Corvetto, the Finance Minister, estimated the ordinary receipts at 767,778,000 francs (£30,710,000); and the expenditure was 993,244,022 francs (£39,700,000);—so that the deficit to be provided for by loan was no less than 225,465,000 francs, or £9,018,000. As the French capitalists were wholly unequal to the raising a sum so large, especially after the great loans of the preceding years, recourse was again had to foreign aid, and Messrs. Baring and Hope furnished the requisite assistance. The loan was obtained on more favorable terms than that of the preceding year, the Five per Cents being taken at 67 instead of 58, as in 1817; no less than 16,000,000 francs of rentes were inscribed on the *Grand Livre* for the interest of this loan;[1] the loan, with the extra charges of commission, &c., was contracted for at nearly 10 per cent.; and it must always be regarded as a most honorable circumstance for the French government and nation, that they discharged such enormous obligations with exactness and fidelity.*

[1] Ann. Hist. i. 195, 197; Cap. v. 285, 288; Moniteur, Dec. 17, 1817.

59. Conclusion of an arrangement regarding the indemnities.

This great difficulty having been surmounted, negotiation began in good earnest for the evacuation of the French territory. The great obstacle was the enormous amount of the indemnities claimed by governments or individuals for exactions made from them during the war, which had swelled to 1,600,000,000 francs, or £64,000,000. At length, however, by the indefatigable efforts of the commissioners, aided by the liberal and just views of the Duke of Wellington, who was at their head, the claims were so far adjusted that the interest of the new debt, to be created for this purpose, was fixed at 12,400,000 francs, or £482,000, a very small sum compared with what had been anticipated. "France," said the Duke de Richelieu, in announcing the conclusion of this arrangement to the Chamber of Peers, "should now reap the reward of her courageous resignation. Holding in her hands the treaties of which she has performed the most onerous conditions, she will not appeal in vain to Europe for the execution, in her turn, of such as are favorable to her. The treaty of 20th November, 1815, bears this clause: 'The military occupation of France may terminate at the end of three years!' That term approaches, and every French heart quivers at the thought of seeing on the soil of our country no other banner but that of France. The sovereigns are about to assemble, to deliberate on this great question. This assembly will not be one of the congresses of kings which history has often recounted as of sinister omen: that august reunion will open under noble auspices. Justice will preside over it—the august rulers of nations will yield to the wish of the king—to that wish which, after the example of its august family, entire France has pronounced with a unanimous voice. The most perfect tranquillity reigns in France—our institutions are developed and strengthened—the charter, thrown open to all parties, receives them, not to become their prey, but that they may be cherished and lost in its bosom. If, for a moment, they have seemed to revive, the wise firmness of the king has immediately disarmed them; and the experience of that has proved for us, as for all Europe, an evident demonstration of their impotence. Last year a cruel calamity, the most likely of any to agitate a people, made itself severely felt. If, in the midst of so many difficulties, the legitimate monarchy has displayed so much strength, what has it to apprehend for the future; and what alarm can Europe feel at the prospect of France, free under the beneficent sceptre of its sovereigns?" As a corollary to these cheering expressions, he proposed the inscription on the Grand Livre—in other words, the creation of

---

* The Budget of 1818 stood thus:—

I. INCOME.

	Francs.
Land tax,	259,034,937
Personal tax, patents, windows,	98,433,663
Registers and woods,	162,200,000
Customs,	80,000,000
Indirect taxes,	126,000,000
Posts,	12,000,000
Lottery and salt mines,	14,000,000
Given up by Royal Family,	3,000,000
Receipts by police,	5,900,000
Retained from salaries,	13,200,000
Total income,	767,778,600
Total expenditure,	993,244,022
Difference to be provided for by loan,	225,165,422
(or about £9,018,000)	

II. EXPENDITURE.

Ordinary.

	Francs.
Interest of National Debt,	140,782,000
Sinking Fund,	40,000,000
Annuities,	12,800,000
Pensions of all sorts,	65,968,000
Civil List,	31,000,000
Clergy,	22,000,000
Peers,	2,000,000
Deputies,	680,000
Various Ministries,	291,943,000
Departmental expenses,	31,976,000
Cautionary engagements,	8,000,000
Negotiation,	18,000,000
Cadastre,	3,000,000
Non Valeurs,	9,916,000
	680,975,000

Extraordinary.

Fifth war contribution,	140,000,000
Cost and pay of allied troops,	151,800,000
Arrears of do.	14,468,422
Miscellaneous,	6,000,000
	312,268,421
Total,	993,244,022

—Annuaire Historique, i. 196, 197, and Moniteur, 16th Dec. 1817.

stock—to the extent of 12,400,000 francs, to meet the demands of private parties, and 24,000,000 francs on rentes yearly (£960,000), to form a fund of credit wherewith to meet the demands of the foreign powers. Overjoyed at the prospect of obtaining a liberation of their territory by such sacrifices, these grants were agreed to without a dissenting voice in both houses.[1]

[1] Cap. v. 227, 228; Ann. Hist. i. 172, 176.

60. Aix-la-Chapelle and its concourse of illustrious foreigners.

AIX-LA-CHAPELLE, where it was determined that the Congress charged with such weighty matters of consideration should sit, is an old town in the German part of the Low Countries, long celebrated for its antiquities, and the memorable events of which it has been the theatre. Charlemagne fixed upon it as the capital of his extensive dominions, which, like those which a thousand years afterward were under the influence of Napoleon, extended far into Germany on the right bank of the Rhine. It contains the tomb of that illustrious man, and many objects of antiquarian interest; but, having ceased to be a metropolis when his mighty dominion fell to pieces, it had rapidly sunk from its ancient splendor, and for several centuries had been chiefly supported by the concourse of strangers, who assembled annually to drink its celebrated waters. Now, however, it received a passing but brilliant illustration from the momentous Congress which assembled within its walls, and on whose decisions the fate, not only of France, but of Europe, in a great measure depended. To those who reflect on the vicissitudes of time, and the mighty changes produced by the course of events, it will not appear the least remarkable coincidence of that memorable era, that the sovereigns charged with the consideration of when the French territory should be liberated from its thralldom, assembled after the lapse of a thousand years in the capital city of their former conqueror, and in the close vicinity of his tomb; and that a leading power in the conferences was that formed by the descendants of the heroic Witikind,[2] who had struggled as long and perseveringly against the first Charlemagne as his descendants had done against the second.

[2] Cap. v. 262, 263.

61. Embassadors there, and instructions of Louis to the Duke de Richelieu, September 20.

The concourse of strangers soon began in Aix-la-Chapelle. Prince Metternich arrived on the 20th September, and soon after M. Capo d'Istria, Prince Lieven, and Pozzo di Borgo, and Nesselrode; on the part of Russia, General Chernicheff, Count Woronzoff, General Jomini, and several others. Prince Hardenberg, Baron Bernstorff, and Baron Alexander de Humboldt, appeared on behalf of Prussia; Lord Castlereagh, the Duke of Wellington, and Mr. Canning, on that of Great Britain. Finally, Messrs. Hope, Baring, and Rothschild, were there as private individuals, but possessing more weight than many sovereigns, from being alone possessed of the capital requisite to carry into effect the vast financial operations which were in contemplation. The Duke de Richelieu attended on the part of France; he took an affectionate leave of Louis XVIII., whose last words to him on setting out were: "M. de Richelieu, make every sacrifice to obtain the evacuation of the territory; it is the first condition of our independence: no flag but our own should wave in France. Express to my allies how difficult my government will be so long as it can be reproached, with the calamities of the country, and the occupation of the territory; and yet you know, M. de Richelieu, it was not I, but Bonaparte, who brought the allies upon us. These are my whole instructions. Repeat to the Emperor Alexander that he has it in his power to render a greater service to my house than he has done in 1814 or 1815; after having restored legitimacy, it remains for him to reap the glory of having restored the national independence. Obtain the best conditions possible; but, at any sacrifice, get quit of the stranger."[1]

[1] Cap. v. 356, 357.

The king of Prussia, within whose territories Aix-la-Chapelle is situated, arrived on the 26th September, to receive his august allies, the Emperors of Russia and Austria, who arrived on the 28th. As the congress was expected to be short, there was not the same brilliant concourse of strangers which had met at Vienna in 1814; but still enough to throw an air of splendor over the august assembly. The Princess Lieven and Lady Castlereagh shone pre-eminent among the female diplomatists—not the least important personages in a congress of that description—and received all the illustrious persons who were assembled on the occasion. The splendid diamonds of the latter were the object of general admiration. Madame Catalani appeared there with the magnificent diamond brooch which had been given her by the Emperor Alexander; and the chief beauties of the opera at Paris added the influence of their charms to the gayety of the scene. Nor were there wanting some who aimed at attracting the notice of the Emperor Alexander by falling in with his peculiar and superstitious feelings; and Mademoiselle Lenormand, in the dress and with the pretensions of a sibyl, endeavored, though without the same success, to play the part which Madame Krudener had done in bringing about the Holy Alliance.[2]

62. Brilliant concourse of strangers at Aix-la-Chapelle.

[2] Cap. v. 365.

The Emperor Alexander gave several audiences to M. de Richelieu, with whom he conversed in the most unreserved manner on the affairs of France. "Your nation," said he, "is brave and loyal; it has supported its misfortunes with a patience which is heroic. Do you think, M. de Richelieu, that it is prepared for the evacuation: do you consider the government sufficiently established? Tell me the simple truth; you know I am the friend and admirer of your nation, and I wish nothing but your word on the subject." "Never," replied the Duke de Richelieu, "was nation more worthy and better prepared to receive the great act which the magnanimity of your Majesty is preparing for it. Your Majesty has seen with what fidelity it has discharged all its engagements; and I will answer for the results of its political system." "My dear Richelieu," rejoined the Emperor, "you are loyalty itself. I do not fear the development in France of liberal institutions; I am liberal myself—very liberal. I should even wish that your king should per

63. Conversation of Alexander with Richelieu.

form some act which should conciliate the holders of the national domains; but I fear the Jacobins—I hate them; beware of throwing yourself into their arms. Europe will have nothing more to do with Jacobinism. There is but one Holy Alliance of kings, founded on morality and Christianity, which can save the social order. We should set the first example." "You may rely on the King of France doing all in his power to extinguish Jacobinism; and the law of elections has produced satisfactory results." "I know it," replied the Emperor; "but let us await the next returns. In the name of Heaven, M. de Richelieu, let us save the social order. Prussia is very urgent for money; Austria, too, is very needy; I, for my own part, should have no objections to receive the sums due to me for indemnities as King of Poland. Come to an understanding with M. Baring; it is there that the key to all the arrangements we desire is to be found."¹

Cap. v. 369, 370.

64. Conclusion of the treaty of Aix-la-Chapelle, Sept. 30.

When sentiments of this sort were entertained by the principal parties at the Congress, it was not difficult to come to an understanding. The preliminaries were arranged on the 1st October, and a courier, the moment the signatures were attached, was dispatched to the King of France to announce the happy result. The conditions were—1. That the troops should retire from the strong places which they occupied on the territory of France, on or before the 30th November, which were to be immediately occupied by the French troops. 2. That the sums required for the pay, clothing, and maintenance of the troops, as regulated by the convention of December 1, 1817, should be paid down to the 30th November. 3. That, in consideration of this evacuation before the five years, to which it might have extended, had expired, France should pay to the allies the sum of 265,000,000 francs (£10,600,000), of which 100,000,000 were to be made good in inscriptions in the Grand Livre, dated 22d September, 1818, and taken at the current rate of 5th October. 4. The remaining 165,000,000 were to be settled by drafts on the houses of Hope and Baring, in nine monthly payments of equal amount each, the drafts to be delivered to the commissioners of the allied powers by the agents of the French treasury at the time of the final evacuation of the territory.²

² Treaty, Oct. 9, 1818; Monitcur, Oct. 10, 1818; Ann. Hist. i. 432, 433; Cap. v. 372, 373.

65. Secret treaty with the Allies.

Having accomplished this great object of the deliverance of the territory, the next object of the Duke de Richelieu was to obtain the admission of France into the European confederacy, by whom it had so long been an object of secret dread or open hostility. He addressed himself to this effect to the ministers of the allied powers, and the request was favorably received; but it was deemed better that the first diplomatic advance should come from the powers themselves. In consequence, a note signed by the ministers of the four great powers was addressed to the Duke de Richelieu, in which they stated that their sovereigns, after having maturely and anxiously weighed the state of France, and the chances of stability in its existing institutions, had come to a unanimous opinion that they had the happiness of thinking that the order of things established by the restoration of the Bourbon line, and the wisdom of his Most Christian Majesty, was now firmly rooted; that the French government had discharged its obligations with the most scrupulous fidelity, and, in consequence, the allied powers had determined to make the occupation of the territory cease on the 30th November. Animated by these sentiments, they indulged the hope that his most Christian Majesty would permit them to unite their counsels and efforts with his for the attainment of these objects; and they invite him to take part in their deliberations, present or future, for the maintenance of peace, and the mutual guarantee of the rights of nations.¹

¹ Ann. Hist i. 434, 435; Cap v. 377, 378.

This was a most important step, as it tended at once to readmit France into the European alliance: a matter of nearly as great importance to the stability of its government as the evacuation. M. de Richelieu, in the name of Louis XVIII., hastened to answer. "His Majesty the King of France has received with the most lively satisfaction this fresh proof of the confidence and friendship of the sovereigns who have taken part in the deliberations of Aix-la-Chapelle. In casting his regards on the past, and being convinced that at no other period no other nation could have discharged with equal fidelity the engagements France has contracted, the King has felt that this new species of glory was to be ascribed to the force of the institutions which rule it; and he perceives with joy that the consolidation of these institutions is regarded as not less advantageous to the repose of Europe than essential to its prosperity. Convinced that his first duty is to perpetuate, by every means in his power, the peace now happily established among the nations, that the intimate union of their governments is the surest pledge of its durability, and that France can not remain a stranger to a system the force of which arises from an entire unity of principles and actions, his Majesty has received with cordiality the proposition made to him, and has, in consequence, authorized the undersigned to take part in all the deliberations of the ministers and plenipotentiaries, in the view of maintaining the treaties and guaranteeing the mutual rights which they have established."²

66. Answer of Louis XVIII.

² Réponse de M. de Richelieu, Nov. 12, 1818; Ann. Hist. i. 435; Cap. v. 379, 380.

It soon appeared that the accession of France to the European alliance was not to be a mere formality. In a few days after a secret protocol was signed by the ministers of all the five powers, which bore—"1. That the sovereigns are determined never to deviate, neither in their mutual relations nor in those which unite them to other states, from the principles which have hitherto united them, and which form a bond of Christian fraternity which the sovereigns have formed among each other. 2. That that union, which is only the more close and durable that it is founded on no separate interests or momentary combination, can have no other object but the maintenance of the treaties, and the support of the rights established by them. 3. That France, associated with the other powers by the restoration of a Government at once

67. Secret Protocol, Nov. 15, 1818.

legitimate and constitutional, engages henceforth to concur in the maintenance and support of a system which has given peace to Europe, and can alone secure its duration. 4. That if, to attain these ends, the powers which have concurred in the present act should deem it necessary to establish particular reunions, either among the sovereigns themselves or their ministers, to treat of subjects in which they have a common interest, the time and place of such assemblages shall be previously arranged by diplomatic communication; and in the event of such reunions having for their object the condition of other states in Europe, they shall not take place except in pursuance of a formal invitation to those by whom those states are directed, and under an express reservation of their right to participate in it directly, or by their plenipotentiaries."[1]

[1] Protocol Nov. 15, 1818 Ann. Hist. 436. Cap. v. 382, 383.

This protocol was followed by another, which was of a more practical nature, and went directly to regulate the military arrangements which were to be adopted in the event of a fresh revolutionary outbreak in France. The ministers of the *four* great powers accordingly—on the urgent solicitation of the lesser states in Germany, who were more immediately threatened on such an event—met secretly, without the concurrence of France or the Duke de Richelieu. At this conference it was agreed—" 1. That all the engagements stipulated by the Quadruple Alliance of 20th November, 1815,[2] are reserved in their full force and effect with reference to the '*fœderis et belli casus,*' as it was foreseen and provided for by that treaty. 2. That for the *casus fœderis,* such as was provided for in the second paragraph of the said treaty, the high contracting parties to the present protocol, in pursuance of their existing engagements, agree to concert, in such an event, in particular reunions, either among the monarchs in person, or the four cabinets, on the most effectual means of arresting the fatal effects of a *new revolutionary overthrow with which France may be threatened ;* recollecting always, that the progress of the evils which have so long desolated Europe has only been arrested by the intimacy of the union, and the purity of the sentiments which unite the four sovereigns for the happiness of the world."[3]

68. Secret military Protocol.

[2] Ante, c. iii. § 49.

[3] Protocol Nov 19, 1818; Cap. v. 386, 387.

In pursuance of this agreement, it was provided that the *corps d'armée,* stipulated by the treaty of Chaumont, should simultaneously enter upon the campaign the day when the allied powers declared that the *casus fœderis* had arisen. The British corps was to assemble at " Brussels, the Prussian at Cologne, the Austrian at Stuttgardt, the Russian, after the lapse of three months, on account of its great distance at Mayence. The Duke of Wellington, who had been specially directed by the government of Great Britain, and that of the Netherlands, to overlook and report upon the fortifications of the Low Countries, has declared that he can certify that the quantity of works executed has been immense; and that a powerful defensive attitude would be taken in the next year, should circumstances demand it. The plenipotentiaries of the other powers have, in like manner, declared that they can give satisfactory assurances on the progress of the defensive preparations on the other countries adjoining the French frontier. In these circumstances, the plenipotentiaries of the four powers have considered the best means of providing for the garrisoning of these fortresses, in the event of a war breaking out and hostilities commencing in the Low Countries. These fortresses have not been constructed for the defense of any single country, but for the general protection of Europe ; and there are several in the second line which require to be occupied on the Dutch frontier. It has, therefore, been agreed to recommend to his Majesty the King of the Netherlands, in the event of the *casus fœderis* being declared, that the fortresses of Ostend, Nieuport, Ipres, and those on the Scheldt, with the exception of the citadels of Antwerp and Tournay, should be occupied by the troops of his Britannic Majesty, and the citadels of Huy, Namur, and Dinant, as well as the strong places of Charleroi, Marienburg, and Philippeville, by those of his Prussian Majesty."[1]

69. Military arrangements.

[1] Secret Protocol, Nov. 20, 1818 ; Cap. v. 387, 389.

It was not surprising that, amidst all this seeming cordiality with the French nation, the allied powers took these precautionary measures against a possible revolution in its government; for, in truth, they were inspired with very serious alarms on the subject. Although the new electoral law had been only two years in operation, the results obtained from the two-fifths of the Chamber which had been returned under it, were sufficient to inspire the most serious apprehensions that, when the whole Assembly was remodelled after the same fashion, the majority would be decidedly hostile to the Bourbon dynasty. A very able memoir had been drawn up by the Royalists at Paris, and secretly transmitted to the sovereigns at Aix-la-Chapelle, in which the Liberal policy of M. Decazes was violently arraigned, the certain overthrow of the monarchy predicted from its continuance, and the only remedy suggested in an entire change of men and measures.[2]* Without giving complete credit to these prognostications, which were evidently the offspring of vehemently excited and deeply chagrined party feelings, the allied sovereigns

70. Secret Royalist Memoir presented to the Allied Sovereigns at Aix-la-Chapelle.

[2] Cap. v. 348, 355; Lac. ii. 229, 230.

* " La révolution étend jusqu'aux dernières classes de la nation qu'elle agite partout avec violence, les principes destructeurs de notre monarchie proposés à la tribune par les ministres du Roi ; et l'on ne veut pour exemple que le discours du Ministre de la Guerre sur la loi du recrutement, et celui du Ministre de la Police sur la liberté de la presse ; des écrits audacieux sapent tous les fondemens de l'ordre social, et les lois répressives ne font obstacle qu'aux écrivains qui soutiennent la monarchie et la légitimité ; les jugements des tribunaux sont livrés aux diatribes les plus violentes ; tous les liens de l'état social sont relâchés ; le Gouvernement ne paraît marcher que par l'impulsion d'un pouvoir qui n'existe plus, et par la présence des forces étrangères ; enfin, tout se prépare à faire la guerre à l'Europe. Par quels moyens peut-on empêcher que la France, et par elle l'Europe entière, ne viennent encore la proie des révolutionnaires? Changer le système du gouvernement par le changement complet du Ministère qui le dirige. Le changement du Ministère est le seul moyen salutaire, le seul véritablement efficace, et en même temps qu'il est le seul loyal et admissible pour empêcher que la France ne redevienne encore un foyer de révolution, on ne tardera pas à embrasser l'Europe entière."—*Mémoire Secret Présenté aux Souverains à Aix-la-Chapelle, par M. le Baron Vermeul.* CAPEFIGUE, *Histoire de la Restauration,* v. 348, 355.

saw that there was sufficient foundation for some of them to render it advisable to make arrangements for an eventual renewal of the war.

But whatever might be the apprehensions which the allies in secret entertained in regard to the stability of the existing order of things in France, there was no want, so far as external appearances went, of the most entire confidence and cordiality between them. The allied sovereigns, and the Emperor Alexander in particular, considered it a point of honor to carry into execution all the arrangements for the evacuation of the territory, with the same scrupulous good faith and exactness with which the French government had discharged all the onerous engagements undertaken by it under the treaty of 20th November 1815. On the day stipulated, the 30th November 1818, the fortresses occupied by the Allies were every where evacuated by their troops, and handed over to the French corps under the Duke d'Angoulême, which were at the gates to occupy them. With speechless delight the French troops defiled through the gates of their ancient strongholds, reoccupied the well known quarters, and beheld, amidst thunders of artillery, the national standard again hoisted on their walls. The most scrupulous good faith and exactitude prevailed in all the arrangements, and the utmost courtesy and politeness between the officers of the retiring and the entering armies. As the allied troops had, in general, conducted themselves exceedingly well, under the firm and judicious direction of the Duke of Wellington, and had spent large sums of money in the cities which they occupied, their withdrawal was a matter of regret to many; but to the majority, whatever regard they entertained for them individually, it was a subject of unspeakable delight to see the foreign colors lowered, and the national ones again hoisted on their citadels. The Duke of Wellington, previous to the breaking up of the army of occupation, issued a touching valedictory address to the noble army, composed of so many nations, whom he had commanded for three years; and retired with cheerfulness into the comparative obscurity of English life, from the proudest situation "above all Greek, above all Roman fame," ever held by an uncrowned military commander.[1] *

71. Evacuation of the French territory by the Allies. Nov. 30.

1 Cap. v. 467, 469; Lac. ii. 213, 215; Ann. Hist. i. 473.

Justice requires that the course of the narrative should for a moment be suspended, to reflect on the conduct of the Duke of Wellington on this occasion. As commander-in-chief of the allied army of occupation, his appointments were immense; his expenses were all paid; and he held a situation which in point of dignity and importance, any conqueror might envy, and which far exceeded that enjoyed by any sovereign prince. He was at the head of the united armies of Europe, and he held in fetters the realm of Napoleon. Nevertheless, so far was he from endeavoring to prolong a situation of so much dignity and emolument to himself, that his whole efforts were directed to its abridgment; from first to last, he did every thing in his power to induce the Allies to shorten the stay of the army of occupation; and at last succeeded, very much by his personal efforts, in lessening it by two years. His situation as commander-in-chief, and still more, his vast personal reputation, rendered him in a manner the final arbiter in the many disputed points which arose between the French and the Allies regarding the pecuniary indemnities; and in that capacity his decisions were not only regulated by the strictest justice, and the most assiduous attention to the rights of the parties, but they were so liberal and indulgent toward the vanquished and unfortunate, that they have extorted the praise even of the French historians, the most envious of his great reputation.* In this conduct we discern another trait of that singleness of heart and disinterestedness of disposition which formed the leading features of that great man's character; and a memorable proof how completely a mind, actuated only, and on every occasion, by a sense of duty, can rise superior to the most powerful influence and greatest temptations of this world. The author has a melancholy pleasure in recording this tribute to the greatest man of the age, now no more; and when there remains only to his country

72. Noble conduct of the Duke of Wellington on this occasion.

* "Le Field-Maréchal Duc de Wellington ne peut prendre congé des troupes qu'il a eu l'honneur de commander, sans leur exprimer sa gratitude pour la bonne conduite qui les a fait distinguer pendant le temps qu'elles ont été sous ses ordres. Il y a près de trois ans que les souverains alliés ont confié au Field-Maréchal le commandement en chef de cette partie de leurs forces que les circonstances avaient rendu nécessaire de laisser en France. Si les mesures que leurs MM. avaient commandées ont été exécutées à leur satisfaction, le résultat doit être entièrement attribué à la conduite prudente et éclairée tenue dans les circonstances par leurs excellences les Généraux en chef, au bon exemple qu'ils ont donné aux autres Généraux et officiers leurs subordonnés, aussi bien qu'aux efforts de ceux-ci pour les seconder, et enfin à l'excellente discipline qui a été constamment observée dans les contingences. C'est avec regret qu'il a vu arriver le moment où la dislocation de cette armée allait mettre fin à ses rapports publics et privés avec les commandants et autres officiers des divers corps. Le Field-Maréchal ne peut assez exprimer combien ces rapports lui étaient agréables; il prie les Gouverneurs en chef de recevoir et de transmettre aux troupes qui sont sous leurs ordres, l'assurance qu'il ne cessera jamais de prendre le plus vif intérêt à ce qui les concerne, et que le souvenir des trois années durant lesquelles il a été à leur tête, lui sera toujours cher."—G. Murray, le Général en chef de l'Etat Major de l'Armée Alliée."—*Annales Historiques*, i. 437, 438.

* "On n'a point en général rendu assez de justice au Duc de Wellington, pour la manière large et loyale dont il protégea les intérêts de la France dans toutes les négotiations avec l'étranger. Je ne parle pas d'abord de l'immense service rendu par S. S. dans la fixation des créances étrangères. Le Duc de Wellington se montra arbitre désintéressé, et la postérité doit reconnaître, à l'honneur de M. de Richelieu, qu'il sortit pauvre d'une position où l'oubli de quelques devoirs austères de la conscience aurait pu créer pour lui la plus colossale des fortunes. Le Duc de Wellington fut très-favorable à la France dans tout ce qui touchait l'évacuation du territoire. Sa position de Généralissime de l'armée de l'occupation donnait un grand poids à son avis sur cette question; il fut chaque fois consulté, et chaque fois également il répondait par des paroles élevées qui faisaient honneur à son caractère. Le Duc de Wellington, par la cessation de l'occupation armée, avait à perdre une grande position en France, celle de Généralissime des Alliés, ce qui le faisait en quelque sorte membre du Gouvernement; il avait à sacrifier un traitement immense; de plus, le noble Lord connaissait l'opinion de Lord Castlereagh, et d'une grande partie des membres de l'aristocratie Anglaise, sur la nécessité de l'occupation armée. Tous ces intérêts ne l'arrêtèrent point; il fut d'avis que cette mesure de précaution devait cesser, car la France avait non seulement accompli les paiements stipulés, mais son Gouvernement semblait offrir le caractère d'ordre, et de durée: cette opinion fut très-puissante dans le congrès d'Aix la Chapelle."—CAPEFIGUE, *Histoire de la Restauration*, 351, 357.

the pride of his deeds and the example of his virtues.*

73. Attempted assassination of the Duke of Wellington. Feb. 11, 1818.

It was while engaged in these great and beneficent deeds, which came with such peculiar grace and lustre from the conqueror of Waterloo, that the hand of an assassin had all but cut short his career. On the 11th February, when the Duke was at Paris, actively engaged in endeavoring to reduce the enormous pecuniary indemnities claimed from the French, and the diminution of which was indispensable to any arrangement which might shorten the period of the occupation of their territory, an attempt was made to assassinate him. At one in the morning, as he was stepping out of his carriage at the door of his hotel, a pistol was suddenly discharged at him, though happily it missed the object. The assassin, who was seen by the servant behind the carriage, glided off in the obscurity, and escaped in the dark; but a man of the name of Cantillon, and another of the name of Marenit, both old soldiers, were afterward arrested, and brought to trial. But the evidence was deemed insufficient, and they were both acquitted. The calm attitude of Wellington was not in the slightest degree affected by this circumstance; he continued his diplomatic labors as if nothing had occurred; and felt only great gratification from the marked interest which the attempt excited over all Europe. Although the jury did not deem the evidence against Cantillon sufficient, yet there can be no doubt of his guilt;¹ for Napoleon, in his testament made not long afterward, left him a legacy of 10,000 francs (£400), expressly in consequence of his having attempted to murder the Duke of Wellington—a step as characteristic of the revengeful nature of his Italian disposition, as the noble conduct of the Duke, in striving at the very time to alleviate the burdens of France, was of his more elevated character.† The contrast between the two was the more remarkable, that the Duke had, during the advance to Paris after the battle of Waterloo, strenuously resisted, and succeeded in averting a proposal of Blucher's that, if taken, Napoleon should be instantly executed as a pirate, the enemy of mankind.²

¹ Lac. ii. 238; Moniteur, Feb. 13, 1818; Antommarchi's Derniers Moments de Napoleon.

² Muffling, Feldzug von 1815. App. No. 2. Gneisenau to Wellington.

After the conclusion of the congress of Aix-la-Chapelle, the Emperor Alexander adopted the resolution of paying a visit as a private individual to Louis XVIII. at Paris. He arrived accordingly, and remained but one day; and the King has told us, in an elegant memoir, given entire in Lamartine's *History of the Restoration*, that that day was the happiest of his life. The French monarch had felt the utmost solicitude for the evacuation of the territory, which he justly regarded as the great work, and only secure inauguration of his reign; and when it was finally arranged, he said to the Duke de Richelieu—"I have lived enough; I have seen the day when no standard but that of France waves over the French citadels." The joy which he felt at this great deliverance heightened the satisfaction he experienced at receiving the monarch whom he, with reason, regarded as his chief deliverer. Alexander opened his mind to him without reserve. "Your Majesty," said he, "has conducted your affairs with great wisdom. I approve of your ordinance of 5th September. It had become indispensable to get quit of a Chamber which dragged you back. See what I have done for Poland! Shall I be deceived in my fond desire to reconcile the two great principles of Peace and Liberty? The fermentation in Germany is alarming, but it is owing to the imprudent attempts of the Emperor of Austria and the King of Prussia to recede from the promises they have made to their people. Let us have no Revolutionists or Jacobins, but Christian freedom." He was made acquainted with M. Decazes, whom he commended in the highest terms to the king. The Grand-Duke Constantine arrived after the departure of the Czar, and was entirely absorbed with military ideas. At one of the reviews he had presented to him a private in the 1st regiment of grenadiers-à-cheval who had wounded him in single combat during the war in Russia. He paid him the highest compliments, and offered to take him into his service—an offer which the grenadier had the patriotism and the good sense to decline.³

74. Visit of Alexander to Louis XVIII. at Paris. Dec. 2.

³ Cap. v 463, 467; Lam. vi. 169, 192.

75. Elections of 1818.

The approach of the annual renewal of a fifth of the Chamber of Deputies threw France, as usual, into an agony of excitement, and awakened on all sides the most violent passions. It was worse than annual parliaments would be in the ordinary state of the British constitution; for the parties were so nearly balanced that it was generally felt that a few votes either way would cast the balance decisively in favor of one or

---

* Written on 18th September, 1852, the day after the intelligence of the Duke of Wellington's death was received in Scotland.

† "Je lègue 10,000 francs au sous officier Cantillon, qui a essuyé un procès comme prévenu d'avoir voulu assassiner Lord Wellington, ce dont il a été déclaré innocent. Cantillon avait autant le droit d'assassiner cet oligarque que celui-ci de m'envoyer périr sur le rocher de St. Hélène. Wellington, qui a proposé cet attentat, cherchait à le justifier sur l'intérêt de la Grande Bretagne. Cantillon, si vraiment il eût assassiné le Lord, se serait couvert et aurait été justifié par les mêmes motifs, l'intérêt de la France de se défaire d'un Général qui d'ailleurs avait violé la capitulation de Paris, et par là s'était rendu responsable du sang du martyr Ney, Labedoyère, &c., et du crime d'avoir dépouillé les Musées contre le texte des Traités."—Art. 5, *Codicil au Testament de Napoléon*, April 24, 1820.—Antommarchi, *Derniers Moments de Napoléon*, ii 233.

‡ "Un des moments les plus heureux de ma vie a été celui qui a suivi la visite de l'Empereur de Russie. Sans parler de la grace extrême qu'il a mise à venir me voir, et à retracer ainsi, mais bien mollement, ce que la plus basse flatterie fit faire au Duc de la Feuillade à l'egard de Louis XIV., il était difficile de ne pas être satisfait de son entretien. Non seulement il était entré dans toutes mes pensées, mais il les avait dites avant que j'eusse eu le temps de les émettre. Il avait hautement approuvé le système de gouvernement, et la ligne de conduite que je suis, depuis que je ne suis determiné a rendre l'ordonnance du 5 Sept. 1816. (Je ne puis m'empêcher de remarquer que c'était le moment des élections de Paris et que l'Empereur partit persuadé que Benjamin Constant serait élu.) Enfin, ce Prince m'avait fait l'éloge de mes ministres, et particulièrement du Comte Decazes, pour lequel je ne crains point d'avoir une amitié fondée sur les qualités à la fois les plus solides et les plus aimables et sur un attachement, dont il faut être l'objet pour en sentir tout le prix."—*Mémoires de Louis XVIII*, Dec 1818. Lamartine. *Histoire de la Restauration*, vi. 163

other party. Thus the whole efforts of party, the whole declamations of the journals, the whole anxieties of the people, were concentrated on the limited number of elections in which the struggle was to be maintained. As the contest drew near, the weakness of the Royalist party, and the progressive growth of the Liberal, became manifest. One journal only, the *Conservateur*, supported the white flag, while dozens poured forth daily declamations on the popular side. Few of the Royalists presented themselves as candidates for the vacant seats; when they did so, it was as martyrs rather than with the step of conquerors. So completely were they depressed, that the contest scarce any where took place between them and the Ministerialists; it lay between the latter and the extreme Democrats, and in most cases terminated to the advantage of the latter. M. Lafayette was returned for la Sarthe; M. Manuel, a popular leader, for la Vendée; and M. Benjamin Constant, after having run the Ministerial candidate very hard in Paris, was returned as another deputy for la Sarthe. As these districts were known to be Royalist, these returns spread great dismay in the Tuileries, and first suggested a serious doubt as to whether the new electoral law rendered the returns a true index of general opinion. It was evident it did not, for it threw them entirely into the hands of *one single class, the small proprietors,* who supported the Revolution, because they had been enriched by its spoils. The Royalists did not disguise their satisfaction at these results, and the verification of all their predictions. "We foretold it all," they exclaimed; "one or two more of the annual renewals, and a convention all complete will emerge from the new electoral law." Even [1 Lac. ii. 246, 253; Cap. vi. 1, 21; Duke de Richelieu to M. Decazes, Dec. 17, 1818. Ibid.] the Government shared in some degree these apprehensions.[1] "I see with pain," said the Duke de Richelieu, "that the law of elections is excluding all the Royalists from the Chamber. I fear we have gone too far to the other side; I would rather have Royalist exaltation than Jacobinism. In the name of Heaven, look out for a remedy. I see with terror the men of the Hundred days returning; they have destroyed our position in Europe: for God's sake let us avoid revolutions."

The difficulties of Government were much augmented in the close of the year by a severe monetary crisis, the natural result of the great financial arrangements concluded at Aix-la-Chapelle, and the immense sums which the contractors for the loans borrowed by the French Government had to raise to make good their engagements. The unavoidable effect of these circumstances was grievously aggravated at this period by the known determination of the English Government, in the next session of Parliament, to put a period to the paper credit, and resort to the system of cash payments. As this restricted credit and limited accommodation took place in both countries, at the very time when the aid of paper currency was most required, the consequence was a general run upon the Bank of France for cash, and an immediate and most serious contraction of its discounts. A severe monetary crisis, with all its alarming conse-

76. Financial crisis, Aix. Dec 1818.

quences, quickly followed; and so great did the pressure soon become, that the funds at Paris fell 10 per cent, and, in the middle of November, credit was almost annihilated in that capital. In this extremity, the Duke de Richelieu, on the advice of Messrs. Hope and Baring, made a proposal to the allied powers to prolong to eighteen months the heavy payments which were to be made in nine months, according to the convention of 9th October preceding. The ministers of the allied powers at Aix-la-Chapelle had several conferences on this subject, and it was no easy matter to come to an understanding, for they themselves, especially Prussia and Austria, were nearly as much pressed for money as the Bank of France. At length an arrangement, drawn up by Prince Metternich, was agreed to, by which the period of payment was prolonged to eighteen months, 5 per cent interest being stipulated for the postponed season, and a certain proportion of the payments were to be received in bills drawn upon places out of France. By this means, aided by the strenuous efforts of the Government and Bank of France, the crisis was surmounted, without any suspension of payments; but it had been so severe, and required such exertions to meet it, that it broke down the health of the able finance minister, M. Corvetto, who solicited and obtained leave to retire. He was succeeded by M. Roy, who had been one of the Chamber of Deputies during the Hundred Days, and who augmented the already preponderating influence of the Liberal party in the Cabinet.[1] [1 Convention, Nov. 19, 1818; Ann Hist i. 438, 439; Cap. vi. 22, 33; Lac ii. 246, 217.]

The known result of the last elections, and the certain majority which it was foreseen the Liberals would have in the Chamber of Deputies, rendered the situation of the Duke de Richelieu very difficult. He had given a somewhat reluctant consent to the *coup d'état* of 5th September, 1816, which shook the confidence the Royalists had hitherto reposed in him; and now he was threatened with a hostile majority in the Chamber of Deputies, composed of the very persons whom that measure had brought into the legislature. Threatened thus with a hostile vote in the Lower House, Richelieu had no resource but to strengthen himself in the Upper; and at his instigation, a party composing a majority of the Peers was formed, prepared to stand by the king in any emergency that might occur. At the same time, conferences were held with M. de Villèle, M. Molé, and the other Royalist chiefs, who promised a frank and loyal adhesion, provided only the Electoral Law was changed; but that was insisted on as an indispensable preliminary to any arrangement. M. de Richelieu was not averse to such a modification; and it was agreed, in the preparatory scrutiny of votes, to ascertain how the numbers of the Centre and Right united together in the Chamber of Deputies would stand. As, however, it was felt that a crisis was approaching, and that it would require all the influence and address of the Duke de Richelieu and his ministry to surmount it, the opening of the session was postponed to the 10th December, in order to give time for any arrangements which might be found necessary to meet it.[2]

77. Difficulties of the Duke de Richelieu. Dec. 10, 1818.

[2 Lac. ii. 254, Cap vi. 31, 34.]

As usual in such cases, the approaching conflict in the Legislature was preceded by a division in the Cabinet. Some of the ministers, among whom were the Duke de Richelieu, MM. Lainé, Molé, and Pasquier, were inclined to go into the terms proposed by the Royalists, and modify the Electoral Law; but the majority, headed by M. Decazes and Marshal Gouvion St. Cyr, deemed any change of policy unnecessary and hazardous, and decided otherwise. The opening speech of the king at the commencement of the session, on December 10th, which committed neither party, was agreed to without a division in the Cabinet; but two days afterward, various conflicts took place there between the two parties, and it soon became evident that their united operation was no longer to be relied on. When the king, who had hitherto been in a great measure ignorant of those ministerial divisions, perceived to what a length they had gone, and that a separation had become unavoidable, he prepared, though with great regret at losing M. Decazes, to support the premier, to whom his entire confidence had been given, whose ideas on every subject entirely coincided with his own, and whose wisdom had guided him in safety through the perilous period of the occupation of the territory. The anxiety which he felt, at the prospect of a break-up of the Cabinet, however, brought on a fit of the gout, which for some days prevented him from attending the state councils; and he was in the very worst crisis of his malady, when a meeting was held to consider whether any modification should be introduced into the Electoral Law. The votes in the Chamber for the president had shown a majority of 101 to 91, formed by the Centre Right and Right against the Liberals of all shades. Encouraged by this favorable result, the Duke de Richelieu supported the proposed modification; but at the close of the conference, the king rose and said—"Let us plant our standard on the ordonnance of the 5th September: let us continue to follow the line we have hitherto followed; but let us at the same time extend a hand to the right as well as the left, and say with Cæsar, 'He who is not with me is against me.'" The majority was of the same opinion, and the Cabinet council broke up without having come to any formal determination on the subject; but though the king hoped the division was healed, it had in reality become incurable, and next day he was thunderstruck by receiving letters of resignation from the Duke de Richelieu, MM. Lainé, Molé and Pasquier, which were soon followed by one from M. Decazes, who felt he could no longer remain in a cabinet from which so many of his old colleagues had seceded.[1*]

78. Divisions in the Cabinet, and break-up of the Ministry. Dec. 12.

[1] Mémoire de Louis XVIII.; Lam. vi. 175, 182; Cap. vi. 45, 55; Lac. ii. 255, 257.

Had a thunderbolt fallen on the king, he could not have been thrown into greater consternation than he was by the receipt of these resignations. It equaled that experienced on the return of Napoleon, for then the kingdom only was lost; but now, though the kingdom remained, the only means of governing it had disappeared. Richelieu had made it a condition of his retaining office, that M. Decazes should be sent on a foreign embassy to St. Petersburg or Naples—a stipulation which sufficiently revealed the real cause of the break-up of the ministry. At the earnest request of the king, however, and moved by the delicate situation of Madame Decazes, who was in her fourth month of pregnancy, he agreed so far to modify his demands as to remain at the head of the ministry if Decazes were removed only to Italy. He endeavored to form a ministry resting on the Centre Right and Right of the Chamber, and from which M. Decazes was to be excluded; but all his proposed arrangements proved ineffectual. The Electoral Law proved an invincible barrier to any united administration. Finding he could not form a ministry, M. de Richelieu simply resigned; and the king, driven thus to throw himself without reserve into the arms of the Liberals, sent, by the advice of the Duke de Richelieu, for M. Decazes accordingly, and by his advice a ministry purely Liberal was formed after the following manner: General Dessoles—a Liberal, but who had done great service to the Bourbons at the Restoration—was President of the Council and Premier; M. de Serres, Keeper of the Seals; Decazes, Minister of the Interior; Baron Portal, the Navy; Baron Louis, the Finance; Gouvion St. Cyr, Minister-at-War. These changes rendered the ministry entirely and exclusively Liberal.[1] Thus fell the ministry of the Duke de Richelieu—the victim of the measure it had adopted to conciliate its opponents and of the hostile party which it had introduced into power.

79. Formation of the new Ministry Dec. 28.

[1] Cap. vi. 42, 71; Mémoires de Louis XVIII.; Lam. vi. 185, 191; Lac. ii. 264, 267.

One of the first acts of the new ministry was to propose a national recompense to the Duke de Richelieu, whose great public services, during the three years he had held the reigns of power, well entitled him to some distinguished mark of the public gratitude,

80. Recompense voted to the Duke de Richelieu, and declined by him.

pays, et que ce sentiment qu'elle avait la bonté d'appeler hier modestie, n'est que le résultat d'une connaissance plus approfondie de moi-même: penser autrement ne serait pour moi qu'une misérable présomption. Votre Majesté sait si j'estime et aime M. Decazes: mes sentimens sont et seront toujours les mêmes. Mais d'un côté, outragé sans raison par un parti dont les imprudences ont causé tant de maux, il lui est impossible de se rapprocher de lui; de l'autre, il est poussé vers un côté dont les doctrines nous menacent davantage, tant qu'il ne sera pas fixé. Hors de France par des fonctions éminentes, tous les hommes opposés au Ministère le considèrent comme le but de leurs espérances, et il deviendra, malgré lui sans doute, un obstacle à la consolidation du Gouvernement. Je crois ce sacrifice nécessaire si je dois rester au Gouvernement. L'ambassade de Naples ou de Petersbourg, et un départ annoncé et exécuté dans une semaine, tels sont, suivant moi, les préliminaires indispensables, je ne dis pas au succès, mais à la marche de l'administration. Après avoir exprimé ma pensée, souffrez, Sire, que je me jette encore aux pieds de votre Majesté, pour lui demander avec les plus vives instances de m'accorder ma liberté."—*Duc de Richelieu au Roi Louis XVIII.*, Dec. 23, 1818. LAMARTINE, *Histoire de la Restauration*, vi. 183, 185.

while his private disinterestedness had left him without fortune at its close. The subject was introduced in the Chamber of Peers by the Marquis de Lalli, and seconded by General Dessolles; in the Chamber of Deputies by M. Decazes. No sooner, however, did the fallen minister hear what was in agitation than he addressed a noble letter to both Houses, in which he declined any public recompense, upon the ground that he could not bring himself to add to the public burdens at a time when so many heavy obligations already weighed upon France.* Notwithstanding this generous refusal, the project was persisted in, and General Dessolles, who was now created a marquis, after a brilliant picture of the great services of the Duke de Richelieu, proposed that an entailed estate of 50,000 francs (£2000) a year taken from the domains of the Crown, should be settled to descend to his heirs male with the peerage. Notwithstanding the great and acknowledged services of the duke, the proposal was seriously combated in both Houses; the opposition being chiefly rested on the magnitude of the public burdens, and the illegality of alienating any portion of the royal domains settled on the Crown by the law of 1814. It was carried, however, by large majorities in both Houses; the numbers in the Chamber of Deputies being 124 to 85—in the Peers, 83 to 45. The duke, however, persisted in his disinterested refusal; he accepted only the honor, and conveyed the property to an hospital at Bordeaux. When he did so, he had no fortune whatever either in land or money; and his sisters procured for him a slender competence of 8000 francs (£320) a year only, by selling the diamonds presented to him, according to diplomatic usage, on signing the many treaties to which his name was attached. Such conduct makes us proud of our species, and may well induce oblivion of the many baser acts which history is constrained to record. Certainly if, as the Scripture says, the love of money is the [1 Lac. vi. 267, 270; Cap. vi. 100, 115.] root of all evil, disinterestedness in regard of it is the index of all good.[1]

81.
Measures of the new Ministers.

The decisive change in the Government soon appeared in the system of administration pursued both in civil and military affairs. The first care of M. Decazes, as Minister of the Interior, was to erase from the list of proscribed persons nearly all the names which still stood on it. The king entered cordially into all these measures. "They have suffered much," said he, "but they should ascribe it less to me than to circumstances; but when we do resolve on acts of grace, let them be complete." So fully was this benevolent intention carried into effect, that the arrears of pay during the period of their exile were given to the officers restored. Marshal Soult received some hundred thousand francs in this way. At the War-Office, Marshal Gou-

vion St. Cyr pursued with more vigor than ever his system of oblivion and fusion. Not merely the subordinate officers, but the superior ones and generals—among the rest, General Foy, and others who had been attached to the fortunes of Napoleon during the Empire and the Hundred Days—received permission to return. To such a length was this system carried, that at last an ordinance opened to the officers and sub-officers of the army the entry into the Royal Guard of the King and the Count d'Artois. This excited, as well it might, the loudest complaints among the Royalists; but the system was nevertheless pursued with vigor and perseverance, and in a short time a majority of the officers in both services was composed of men known to be partial to the Liberal or Napoleon party. A still more vehement clamor was raised in the Royalist camp by an ordinance which gave certain colonels in the Guard rank and position in the army as marshals of the camp—a measure it was said, obviously intended to remove from the royal family the few faithful defenders which still remained to them.[1] [1 Cap. vi. 90, 92; Lac. ii 70]

The same system was pursued with equal, unflinching determination in the civil service of the State. The prefects, the sub-prefects, were all chosen from the Liberal party; even the Council of State was remodelled, so as to give a majority to that party. Among the many eminent men of that side who thus obtained admission into the Council of State, were MM. Siméon, Royer-Collard, Portalis, Mounier, and Camille-Jourdan, who were placed in the legislative section of that body; while the deliberative, a still more important section, contained MM. Cuvier, Degrando, Berenger, Raymond, the Prince de Broglie, Gen. Mathieu Dumas, Guizot, Barante, and a great many others, all Liberals of the first rank, station, and ability. In a word, the choice of Government in filling up appointments realized the fine saying of Louis XVIII.—"Whoever is faithful to me now has ever been so." To such a length was this system carried in subordinate officers, that one of the royal courts in the south of France, that of Nimes, was composed *entirely* of the magistrates who had held office during the Hundred Days—the Royalists who had succeeded them being entirely excluded. In a word, the Government threw themselves every where, and without reserve, into the arms of the Liberal party, hoping that they would thus found the monarchy upon the affections or interests of the majority of the nation.[2] [2 Cap. vi. 92, 270, 271; Lac. ii.]

82.
General promotion of the Liberals in the civil service.

No measure of moment was brought forward by the new ministers from their appointment on the 28th December till the beginning of February, and the Parisians, impatient of delay, and thirsting for excitement, were beginning to complain that the Liberal ministry were doing nothing; but, ere long, they had ample subject for meditation from what occurred in the Chamber of Peers. The Royalists had there a decided majority; and they were so convinced that the Electoral Law would terminate in the destruction of the monarchy, and before many years had elapsed would effect it, that they resolved, at all hazards, to attempt its modification. The great object was to neutralize in some way the

83.
Movement against the Electoral Law in the Peers.

---

* "Si dans le cours de mon ministère, j'ai eu le bonheur de rendre des services à la France, et dans ces derniers temps de concourir à l'affranchissement de son territoire, mon âme n'est pas moins attristée de savoir ma patrie accablée de dettes énormes; trop de calamités l'ont frappée, trop de citoyens sont tombés dans le malheur; et il y a trop de pertes à réparer, pour que je puisse voir s'élever un fortune en de telles conjonctures. L'estime de mon pays, la bonté du Roi, le témoignage de ma conscience me suffisent."—*Duc de Richelieu aux Chambres*, Jan. 27, 1819. *Moniteur*, Jan. 28.

majority of *small proprietors of the national domains*, who, at present, by the Electoral Law, had the means of returning a majority of the Chamber of Deputies, of persons attached to the fortunes of the Revolution. The person selected to commence the movement was M. Barthélemy, the veteran diplomatist, who, elected, contrary to his wishes, a member of the Directory, had been seized on occasion of the revolution of 11th Fructidor, in 1797, by his democratic colleagues, and transported to the burning deserts of Sinamari, from whence his escape seemed little short of a miracle. He was now old and infirm, but still in the full possession of his faculties; and being a living monument of the excesses of the Revolution, he seemed a fitting person to arrest its march.[1]

[margin: 1 Hist. of Europe, c. xxxv. §§ 48-51. Lac. ii. 271. Cap. vi. 115, 121; Ann. Hist. ii. 31. 32.]

81. Argument of M. Barthélemy, for a change in the law of election. Feb. 20, 1819.

"It is now two years," said the veteran orator, "since a change was introduced into our infant institutions by a change in the law of election. The advantages anticipated from it were maintained with so much warmth, the inconveniences foreseen were supported by reasons so plausible, that there was ample room for difference of opinion on the subject. The course of our discussions rendered that incertitude so natural, that it was in some degree shared by the orators of Government themselves; and, in the last debate, they declared that the new law was only an experiment, which would be open to revision if it should prove unsuccessful. That declaration fixed many of those who had hitherto hesitated; and I am not ashamed to confess myself one of those who was induced by it to vote in favor of the proposed law. Two years have since elapsed, two elections have taken place under it, and twice the Government has been thrown into an agony of apprehension from its results. I feel it, therefore, a duty to solicit the redemption of a pledge which determined my vote. I demand that the Chamber of Peers should adopt a resolution to petition the King to bring forward the project of a law which may introduce into the organization of the electoral colleges the requisite modifications."[2]

[margin: 2 Ann. Hist. ii. 33; Lac. ii. 271, 272.]

85. Answer on the part of the Ministerialists.

To this it was replied on the part of the Ministry by Decazes and Lally Tollendal: "Great stress has been laid on certain promises said to have been made by the Ministry when the law of elections was under discussion. No minister, in bringing forward such a law, could promise any thing but that it should be literally carried into effect; and, in fact, nothing more was promised by the ministers of that period. The Government is now persuaded that it can not so well discharge its duty as by repelling with all its strength a proposition which it, with sincerity, regards as the most dangerous that can emanate from this Assembly. This fundamental law, the principal spring of government, the faults or merits of which must have so decisive an influence on our destinies, was adopted, after a warm and long discussion —by a small majority it is true, but one as large as could be expected on such a subject in the circumstances. The result has fully answered our expectations. From the Rhine to the Pyrenees all is now tranquil and contented; will any man venture to predict that the same will be the case to-morrow if this proposition is adopted by the Assembly? From the agitation already arising in its bosom we may augur the commotion which the proposal will soon awaken over the whole of France."[1]

[margin: 1 Ann. Hist. ii. 34; Moniteur, Feb. 27, 1819.]

86. The proposition is carried, and vast sensation throughout France.

These words proved prophetic of the effect produced over France by the introduction of this measure. Leave was given to bring in the proposition by a majority of 80 to 53. Immediately the most violent agitation commenced in every part of France, much exceeding any thing which had been witnessed since the Restoration. The people are possessed of an instinct which seldom errs as to the probable effect upon their *immediate* interest of any measures that are brought forward, or the influence they may acquire over the government: it is in regard to their ultimate effects— which require foresight and reflection, to be appreciated—that they are so generally deficient. The agitation was universal, and reached far beyond the limited class to which the right of voting was at present extended. The whole body of holders of the national domains took the alarm. Conscience made cowards of them all; they felt the same dread of being dispossessed of their ill-gotten gains that the holder of stolen goods does when a police-officer enters the house. Hundreds of petitions were prepared in every part of the country, and eagerly signed by hundreds and thousands, praying the king to make no change in the Electoral Law; and, for the first time since the extinction of the fervor of the Revolution by the carnage of the Convention, France, from the Pyrenees to Bayonne, was convulsed by democratic passions.[2]

[margin: 2 Lac. ii. 120. Cap. vi. 121, 126.]

87. Measures of the Cabinet, and the Liberals in the Chamber of Deputies.

This open declaration of the Chamber of Peers, by so large a majority, against the Electoral Law, was rendered the more serious, from the weight and influence of the members of whom the majority was composed, which embraced the most respectable and enlightened of the peerage. The king was very much struck with this circumstance; he said that, in the estimation of the best defenders of his throne, it was no longer a question of party, but of the dynasty and the monarchy. M. Decazes had great difficulty in persuading him that it was necessary to persist in the support of the Electoral Law; which, however, he at length agreed to do, as the Cabinet, by a great majority, thought it should be made a condition of its existence. M. Lafitte, in the Lower House, made a motion for the deputies to present an address to the king, praying him to make no change in the Electoral Law; and although this proposal was negatived on the objection in point of form, that the matter had not yet come in regular course before them, yet it served to support the majority of the Cabinet in their resolution to permit no change in the existing law.[3]

[margin: 3 Cap. vi. 128, 129; Ann. Hist. ii 60.]

The discussion on the merits of the question came on in the Peers on the 26th February, when it was argued by MM. de Barthélemy, de Fontanes, and de Castellane: "We have supported the law of election, because we thought that little was to be apprehended from a democracy of eighty thousand electors in a country possessing twenty-seven millions of inhabitants; but experience has undeceived us. The opponents of the law have better than ourselves perceived its real tendency. What is the end which we should pursue?—to strengthen power by giving it the support of the nation. If history proves that the ministers of kings are in general more inclined to support the rights of the crown than those of the people, those who are now in power are free from that reproach. But have they always been equally confident in the merits of the law, to the maintenance of which they now attach their political existence? Have they had no misgivings as to its democratic tendency? Is it not equally open to abuse on the other side, should a ministry arrive at power sufficiently unscrupulous to make use of its powers in that respect? What is so easy as to multiply patents, and bestow them on persons in the interest of the Crown? To eschew these evils, we must recur to the great territorial aristocracy. There once was a man who terrified Europe by his ambition; however we may regard that man, no one can deny to him the knowledge of the science of power. One day he was preparing in the Council of State the Electoral Colleges, and I (M. de Fontanes) was present. Some of his confidential counselors suggested to him that his plan was not without danger: for several of the great properties still remained in the hands of the former proprietors, and that sooner or later the choice of the six hundred most considerable in each college, in whom the franchise was vested, would bring in the partisans of the ancient monarchy. Napoleon was no ways staggered by this observation; his answer was as follows, 'These men,' said he, 'are great proprietors—they do not wish, therefore, that the soil should tremble—their interest is mine.' Have the great proprietors any influence under the present Electoral Law? None whatever; for they are outvoted twenty to one by the small proprietors, who, having nearly all been enriched by the Revolution, are attached to its fortunes.

"What clearly proves that there is something fundamentally wrong about the present law is the fact, that although there are 130,000 electors in France, never more than 80,000 have taken part in any election. This is an evil of the very first magnitude, which loudly calls for a remedy. If, in the infancy of our institutions, and when the electoral franchise was by many to be exercised for the first time, so great a number of electors have not come forward, what may be anticipated in ordinary times? Is it not evident that the number of electors will constantly diminish; and as the law provides that, in such an event, the Electoral Colleges are to meet two or three times in the year, a burden will be imposed on the electors exceeding in weight that of their whole contributions to the state. The effect of this will be a progressive diminution in the number of electors, till they become quite illusory, and amenable to every species of influence or corruption.

"There is another consideration not less important. In the laudable intention of encouraging commerce and industry, patents (franchises derived from income-tax), have been assimilated and put on the same footing as those resting on direct taxes from land. But that extension, already sufficiently great, has become altogether monstrous, from the circumstance that, as this tax is paid monthly, it is held that the payment of one installment—that is, one-twelfth of three hundred francs—confers the franchise. Thus the right of voting is acquired by the payment once only of a tax of twenty-five francs. Is not this a manifest violation of the act—a departure alike from its letter and its spirit? The introduction of such a body of disqualified electors into the register of voters, is an act of manifest injustice to the holders of land. The latter, however, in every age and country, have constituted the strength of nations. They it is who are the guardians at once of our morals and institutions. In intrusting to them the enjoyment of political rights, our legislators have done no violence to natural justice; because civilization renders property always accessible to the persevering efforts of industry, and it is the sure recompense of labor and economy.

"Finally, there is an important defect in our Electoral Law, which requires amendment. The power of naming supplementary members, in the event of those named in the first instance failing, has been omitted; although it was in an especial manner required under the new Electoral Law, which so greatly restricted the number of deputies. As matters at present stand, it is not death or serious disease disqualifying the deputy, which renders necessary a new election; the same follows from a double return of the same individual for different places—an event which has very frequently occurred in recent times. This renders fresh elections necessary, and perpetuates the excitement, turmoil, and intrigue consequent on them. Even now, from this cause, the Chamber is incomplete; and it has been so ever since the commencement of the session. The necessity of these new elections not only entails a great additional expense and trouble on the electors, but perpetuates an agitation, which, in every point of view, it is desirable to avoid."

On the other hand, it was contended by the Marquis Dessolles, the Premier, M. Languinan, and M. de Larochefoncauld: "To attack the Law of Elections is to attack the charter—to menace our liberties—to commence the counter revolution. That in the execution of that law there may be some errors, negligences, and abuses, is very possible, and obtains in this as in all earthly things. The remedy for them, however, is in an ordinance of the King, or a circular of the Ministers, not a change of the law. The Law of Election is generally considered as good, and the best guarantee of our liberties. The people are attached to it as the chief safeguard given them by the charter. To propose to touch it now, is to sow the seeds of alarm; to attack the majority of the citizens in that which they cherish the most, to assail immediately the sentiments which are most deeply seated in their affections, to expose France to the anxieties, the passions, and the agitation, which we are all so anxious to avoid; to cast anew a firebrand into the nation; and God only knows when the conflagration thus raised will be extinguished. The Law of Election is our second charter; and the attack on it must be combated by facts rather than arguments.

_{93.}
Continued.
 "After four years of secret notes addressed to the allied powers; after the criminal, but still unpunished intrigue of Aix-la-Chapelle against our charter; after the attempt in December last to renew the evils which the King averted by the ordinance of 5th September, 1816, a nebulous point has again formed in the heavens—the forerunner of a dreadful tempest—and the cloud has first appeared in the House of Peers. That house was instituted to calm the passions, to avert storms, to establish harmony between the powers; and it is now in its name that vague innovations are proposed—the more alarming, that they are uncertain—the more to be deprecated, that they are unnecessary. Let us not deceive ourselves: a great faction, now very apparent, without the Chamber—the faction of privileges, of abuses, of sinecures, of prodigalities, of the oligarchy—agitates and disturbs us, in the hope of subverting the charter, which they have long undermined, or of reducing its effects to unmeaning ceremonies. The object of that league is to overturn the existing Ministry, which enjoys the confidence at once of the king and the nation, and which is distinguished alike by patriotism and unanimity. They would replace them by the most extravagant of the opposite faction, in order by their aid to annihilate the Electoral Law, which has cost two years of labor, and is so dear to the immense majority of Frenchmen. They would re-establish the double steps of election, so favorable to aristocracy, and restore the elections to those little places where their influence is predominant: an abuse so wisely provided against by the existing law. In a word, this is the first act of the counter revolution against the charter.

_{94.}
Concluded.
 "Already you see the effects of the proposition which has been entertained by the Chamber. You see it in the stagnation of industry, the decline of confidence, the indignation of the public, which exhales in the thousands of petitions which encumber your table, to one of which is attached three thousand signatures. If the proposition is not withdrawn, the result will be the re-establishment of the peers, who were excluded without judgment in 1815; a fatal step, but indispensable to bring back the House of Peers into a state of harmony with the other branches of the government. It is already too numerous compared to the limited number of the other Chamber. Is it in consequence to be dissolved, and a more numerous one convoked? If this step is not adopted, it will be necessary to change the Ministry, and seek their successors among those who will be willing to accept the new measures. What these measures are, it is not difficult to foresee. New elections in the interest of the oligarchy; the re-establishment of a packed Chamber, the entire ruin of a representative government; exceptional measures, which will be first tolerated, then execrated; universal discontent, national excitement, civil war, foreign invasion; dangers from all sides to the throne, the altar, the public liberty, the dynasty, the existing peers, and all other peers; in fine, an absolute despotism or liberty—a third time, and too dearly, purchased. Do you wish to count us? It is not in this assembly you must do so—it is in the midst of thirty millions of Frenchmen you must commence your calculation. There is but one way to avoid these dangers; it is by rejecting or withdrawing the proposition submitted to the Chamber. It is the unanimous opinion of the government to resist any change in the Law of Elections. The results of the proposal, even to make such a change have been sufficient to prove its danger, and to render it the first duty of the Government firmly to oppose it."[1]

¹ Moniteur, March 28, 1819; Ann Hist. ii. 3e, 58; Cap. vi 129, 133; Lac. ii 281, 283.

Notwithstanding these denunciations the majority of the peers remained firm in their resolution; and M. Barthélemy's proposition was adopted by a majority of 45—the numbers being 98 to 53. So elated were the Royalists with this victory that they proceeded immediately to another demonstration against the Government of a much more doubtful kind. It had been determined by the Ministers, and agreed to by the Chamber of Deputies, to make a change in the financial year. To accomplish this, there was but one method that appeared practicable, and that was to vote the supplies at once for eighteen months. This, however, was a violation of the charter, which declared that the supplies were to be voted for one year only; and on this ground it had been strongly opposed in the Chamber of Deputies. "When Bonaparte," said M. de Villèle in that Chamber, "came to disperse the National Assembly, they invoked their rights as established by the constitution. He answered, 'You have violated them.' Dread a similar answer. Dread it whether your blindness brings you to see a triumphant democracy demand the overthrow of the throne, and the dissolution of the Chamber of Peers—or a new soldier tries to consecrate in this hall a violation of the principle of legitimacy." The expedience of the case being on the other side, however, the Chamber of Deputies adopted the change; but it was at once rejected in the House of Peers, by a majority of 39—the numbers being 93 to 54.[2]

_{95.}
Adoption of M. Barthélemy's proposition, and defeat of Ministers on the fixing of the financial year.

² Ann. Hist. ii. 58, 59; Moniteur, March 6, 1819; Lac ii. 286, 287.

These repeated defeats convinced the Government that the time had now arrived when it was necessary to take a decisive step. M. Dessolles laid a memoir before the King, in which the state of the case was clearly set forth, and the courses which might be adopted were pointed out.* It was evident that it had become un-

_{96.}
Measures of the Government.

---

* "Les deux Chambres vont être en complète dissidence sur une question fondamentale, celle qui constitue le corps électoral, principe démocratique de la Constitution. Les députés veulent maintenir le système électoral, les Pairs veulent le modifier. Dans cette position, le Ministère de votre Majesté partageant l'opinion de la Chambre élective, il ne reste au Roi qu'un parti à prendre, c'est ou de dissoudre la Chambre élective et de composer un Ministère dans le sein de la majorité de la Pairie, ou de soutenir le Ministre et la Chambre des Députés et de

avoidable either to dissolve the Chamber of Deputies, and form a new Ministry in harmony with the opinions of the majority of the Peers, or to overcome the majority in the Peers by a great creation in that Assembly. It was at first proposed simply to repeal the ordinance of 15th August, 1815, which excluded from the House the peers who had taken an active part in favor of Napoleon during the Hundred Days; but the King objected to this. "I wish," said Louis, "that they should hold their seats from my single will, and that they should feel grateful for it." It was agreed, in consequence, to make a great creation of peers; and next morning the columns of the *Moniteur* revealed to the astonished Parisians the names of sixty-three persons; all of the Liberal party, or attached to the Liberal party, who were advanced to the peerage.¹ Among them were six of Napoleon's marshals—viz., the Dukes of Albufera, Cornegliano, and Dantzic, the Prince of Echmühl, Marshal Jourdan, and the Duke of Treviso; and many names known to fame—in particular, Rapp, Latour Maubourg, Reille, Dubreton, Maurice Mathieu, Claperede, Admiral Tonguet, and several others. The victory of the Liberals was now complete.

¹ Moniteur, March 8, 1819; Ann. Hist. ii. 59; Cap. vi. 136, 139.

97. Great majority in the Chamber of Deputies for Ministers.

By the *coup d'état* of September 5, 1816, they had revolutionized the Chamber of Deputies; by that of March 5, 1819, they had overcome the resistance of the Chamber of Peers. The king had thrown himself into their arms; the magistracy was filled with their adherents, the army guided by their generals, the press by their supporters. The whole powers of the state were wielded by their adherents. An astonishing revolution! to have been effected in so short a time, in a country in which the tide had set so violently the other way during the year 1815; but by no means without a parallel, both in the previous and subsequent history of that volatile and easily excited people, and not without parallels among their more sober neighbors on this side of the Channel. Nothing remained for the Government to consolidate its power but to demonstrate its ascendency in the Chamber of Deputies; and here the effects of the decisive blow struck in the Peers at once appeared, for, on a division on the Electoral Law in the Chamber of Deputies, Ministers were supported by a majority of 56 —the numbers being 150 to 94.¹

¹ Ann. Hist. ii. 82; Moniteur, Mar. 22, 1819.

98. Great and lasting results of the changes already made in France.

Although not five years had elapsed since the second restoration of the Bourbons, yet decisive events, fraught with the fate of futurity, had during that time taken place both in France and England. It is a mistake to suppose that important events pregnant with lasting consequences produce their effects in every instance immediately. This is, without doubt, sometimes the case; and of the reality of such sudden results the French Revolution affords ample evidence. But, in general, the lasting effects of the greatest political changes are only developed after a considerable period, and when they have had time to work, as it were, through all the strata of society. The great political alterations made in France during this period, the *coup d'état* changing the Electoral Law, the new ordinances for the regulation of the army, the great democratic creations of peers, rendered a revolution inevitable, but inevitable at a future period. The first fixed the representation upon a uniform and democratic basis of small proprietors and moderate intelligence, disfranchising practically the higher education and larger properties of the kingdom, by throwing them into a minority; the second deprived Government of the support, in any crisis which might arise, of a faithful and intrepid army, and rendered it next to certain that, in the decisive moment, it would side with the enemies of the monarchy; the third severed from the throne any aid it might receive from a body of peers whose interests were identified with its preservation. In like manner, the new monetary system adopted in England, in 1819, had rendered an entire change of government and alteration of policy inevitable at no distant period; for it had laid the foundation of such a prodigious alteration of prices as could not fail to change the ruling class in the country, and, by the general suffering with which it must be attended, shake even the stability and loyalty of the British character.

It is worthy of observation how early the French nation, after they had attained the blessing, had shown themselves unfitted, either from character or circumstances, for the enjoyment of constitutional government. Only five years had elapsed since it was for the first time established in France by the overthrow of Napoleon, and scarcely a year had passed which was not marked by some *coup d'état*, or violent infringement, by the sovereign, of the constitution. The restoration of the Bourbons in 1815 was immediately attended by the creation of sixty peers on the Royalist side, and the expulsion of as many from the Democratic; this was followed, within four years, by the creation of as many on the Liberal. The whole history of England prior to 1832 could only present one instance of a similar creation, and that was of *twelve* peers only, in 1713, to carry through the infamous project of impeaching the Duke of Marlborough. It was threatened to be repeated, indeed, during the heat of the Reform contest; but the wise advice of the Duke of Wellington prevented such an irretrievable wound being inflicted on the constitution. The French Chamber of Deputies was first entirely remodeled, and 133 new members added to its numbers, by a simple royal ordinance in 1815; and again changed—the added members being taken away, and the suffrage established on a uniform and highly democratic basis—by another royal ordinance, issued, by the sole authority of the king, the following year. Changes, alternately on the one side or the other, greater than were accomplished in England by the whole legislature in two centuries, were carried into execution in France in the very outset of its constitutional career, by the sole authority of the king, in two years.

99. Repeated *coups d'état* in France since the Restoration.

briser l'opposition qui s'est formée dans la Chambre des Pairs. Et je ne dissimule pas à votre Majesté que ce dernier parti est le plus populaire, et que dans les circonstances actuelles, c'est le seul qui puisse ramener le calme dans les esprits."—*Mémoire du Marquis Dessolles au Roi*, Mars 2, 1819. CAPEFIGUE, *Histoire de la Restauration*, i. 135.

What is still more remarkable, and at first sight seems almost unaccountable, every one of those violent stretches of regal power was done in the interest, and to gratify the passions, of the majority at the moment. The Royalist creation of peers in 1815, the Democratic addition of sixty to their numbers in 1819, the addition of 133 members to the Chamber of Deputies in the first of these years, their withdrawal, and the change of the Electoral Law by the *coup d'état* of September 5, 1816, were all done to conciliate the feelings, and in obedience to the fierce demand, of the majority. That these repeated infringements of the constitution in so short a time, and in obedience to whatever was the prevailing cry of the moment, would prove utterly fatal to the stability of the new institutions, and subversive of the growth of any thing like real freedom in the land, was indeed certain, and has been abundantly proved by the event. But the remarkable thing is, that such as they were, and fraught with these consequences, they were all loudly demanded by the majority; and the power of the Crown was exerted only to pacify the demands, which in truth it had not the means of resisting.

100. The coups d'état were all on the popular side.

A little reflection, however, will at once show how it happens that, in periods of crisis and violent public excitement, the people so frequently demand, and the government concede, what is certain in the end to prove fatal to the interests of both. It is that both are governed by present feelings or convenience, and neither is capable of either carrying their views into futurity, or, if they could do so, of incurring present risk or obloquy to avert the perils with which these views are fraught. Neither can make "the past or the future predominate over the present." The one party demand what appears at the time to them to be a most desirable object; the other concedes what they are probably reluctant to grant, but which is yielded to avoid the risk of present collision. Thus the power of the Crown is exerted to forward the advances of democracy; and the influence of democracy is directed to forward changes which, by destroying all intermediate influences, are in truth paving the way for future despotism. Tranquillity and peace are generally purchased at the moment by such concessions; but this advantage is gained at the expense of future safety; the danger is transferred from the streets to the legislature—from the turbulence of mobs to Acts of Parliament. The danger in such a case is, not so much that the Government will be overturned in a well-concerted urban tumult, as that, with the consent of all branches of the legislature, and the cordial support of the majority of the people, measures in the end destructive of the nation, and subversive of its liberties, will be adopted. Whoever has attentively considered the situation of a country in which a mere numerical majority has really, and not in form merely, acquired the direction, will see that this is the greatest social danger which threatens society; and as it arises from the most prevailing weakness of human nature—that of sacrificing the future to the present—it is the one which is least likely to be obviated by any efforts of human wisdom. Possibly it is one of the appointed means by which communities make their exit from the world; and as nations, like single men, were not destined for immortality, but intended, at the appointed season, to make way for their successors on this transitory scene, so it is by the growth of popular passions, which tend to shorten their duration, that the way is prepared for their removal from the theatre of existence, and the gates of the tomb opened to the most powerful and renowned of human societies.

101. Causes of this peculiarity.

CHAPTER VII.

SPAIN AND ITALY FROM THE PEACE OF 1814 TO THE REVOLUTION OF 1820.

1. Analogy of the early history of Spain and England.
DIFFERING from each other in climate, national character, and descent, there is a striking, it may be a portentous, resemblance in their history and political destinies between SPAIN and GREAT BRITAIN. Both were inhabited originally by a hardy race, divided into various tribes, which maintained an obstinate conflict with the invaders, and were finally subdued only after nearly a century's harassing warfare with the Legions. Both, on the fall of the Empire, were overrun by successive swarms of barbarians, with whom they kept up for centuries an indomitable warfare, and from whose intermingled blood their descendants have now sprung. The Visigoths to Spain were what the Anglo-Saxons were to Britain; and the Danes in the one country came in place of the Moors in the other. The rocks of Asturias in the first were the refuge of independence, as the mountains of Wales and the Grampian Hills were in the last. Both were trained, in those long-continued struggles, to the hardihood, daring, and perseverance requisite for the accomplishment of great things in the scene of trouble. In both the elements of freedom were laid broad and deep in this energetic and intrepid spirit; and it was hard for long to say which was destined to be the ark of liberty for the world. The ardent disposition of both sought a vent in maritime adventure, the situation of both was eminently favorable for commercial pursuits, and both became great naval powers. Both founded colonial empires in various parts of the world, of surpassing magnitude and splendor, and both found for long in these colonies the surest foundations of their prosperity, the most prolific sources of their riches. When the colonies revolted from Spain in 1810, the trade, both export and import, which she maintained with them, was exactly equal to that which, thirty years afterward, England carried on with its colonial dependencies. Happy if the parallels shall go no farther, and the future historian shall not have to point to the severance of her colonies as the commencement of ruin to Great Britain, as the revolt of South America, beyond all question, has been to the Spanish monarchy.

2. The colonies were not a source of weakness to Spain.
Historians have repeated to satiety that the decline of Spain, which has now continued without interruption for nearly two centuries, is to be ascribed to the drain which these great colonies proved upon the strength of the parent state. They seemed to think that the mother country is like a vast reservoir filled with vigor, health, and strength, and that whatever of these was communicated to the colonial offshoots, was so much withdrawn from the parent state. There never was a more erroneous opinion. No country ever yet was weakened by colonial dependencies; their establishment, like the swarming of bees, is an indication of overflowing numbers and superabundant activity in the original hive. As their departure springs from past strength, so it averts future weakness. It saves the state from the worst of all evils—a redundant population constantly on the verge of sedition from suffering—and converts those who would be paupers or criminals at home, into active and useful members of society, who encourage the industry of the parent state as much by their consumption as they would have oppressed it by their poverty.

3. Colonies are always a benefit to the parent state.
Every emigrant who is now landed on the shores of Australia, converts a pauper, whose maintenance would have cost Great Britain £14 a year, into a consumer who purchases £8 yearly of its manufactures. Rome and Athens, so far from being weakened, were immeasurably strengthened by their colonies; those flourishing settlements which surrounded the Mediterranean Sea were the brilliant girdle which, as much as the arms of the Legions, contributed to the strength of the Empire; and England would never have emerged victorious from her immortal conflict for European freedom, if she had not found in her colonial trade the means of maintaining the contest, when shut out from the markets of the Continental states. If it were permitted to follow fanciful analogies between the body politic and the human frame, it would be safer to say that the prolific parent of many colonies is like the happy mother of a numerous offspring, who exhibits, even in mature years, no symptoms of decline, and preserves the freshness and charms of youth for a much longer period than she who has never undergone the healthful labors of parturition.

4. Support which colonies afford to the mother country.
There is no reason, in the nature of things, why colonies should exhaust the mother country; on the contrary, the tendency is just the reverse. They take from the parent state what it is an advantage for it to lose, and give it what it is beneficial for it to receive. They take off its surplus hands and mouths, and thereby lighten the labor market, and give an impulse to the principle of population; while they provide the means of subsistence for those who remain at home, by opening a vast and rapidly increasing market for its manufactures. A colony for long is always agricultural or mining only. Manufactures, at least of the finer sort, can never spring up in it for a very long period. An old state, in which manufactures and the arts have long flourished, will nowhere find such a certain and growing vent for its fabrics as in its colonial settlements; while they will never find so sure and steady a market for their rude produce as in the wants of its in-

habitants. Similarity of tastes and habits renders the fabrics and productions of the parent state more acceptable to the young one than those of foreign lands. The certainty of not having their supplies of necessaries interrupted, is an inappreciable advantage to the mother country. Their identity of interest perpetuates the union which absolute dependence on one part had at first commenced. The connection between a parent state liberally and wisely governed, and its colonies, is founded on the surest of all foundations—a real reciprocity of advantages; and, as such, may long prove durable to the great benefit of both, and retain the infant state in the bonds of allegiance, after the time has arrived when it might aspire to the honors of separate dominion.

5. What the colonial policy of the parent state should be.

To preserve, however, this connection between the mother country and her robust colonies, a wise and liberal system of government is indispensable. If such be not adopted, they will, when they have attained majority, inevitably break off on the first serious difficulties of the parent state. Nothing can permanently retain them in their allegiance but a real reciprocity of advantages, and the practical enjoyment of the powers of self-government by the colonies. The reason is, that the rule of the distant old state, if unaided by colonial representation, direct or indirect, never can be founded upon an adequate knowledge of the necessities, or attention to the interests, of the youthful settlement. It will always be directed by the ideas, and calculated for the advantage of the society with which it is surrounded—generally the very reverse, in the first instance at least, of what the young state requires. The true colonial policy, which can alone insure a lasting connection between the mother country and her transmarine descendants, requires the most difficult of all sacrifices on the part of the former—that of her established prejudices and selfish interests. Yet it is the sacrifice of her *immediate* advantages only; for never will the interests of the old state, in the end, be so promoted as by the most liberal and enlarged policy towards its distant offspring. What that policy should be, has been written in characters of fire on the tablets of history. It should be the exact reverse of that which lost England North, and Spain, South America. It should be the government of the colonies, not for the interest of the mother country, but for the advantage of themselves—an administration which should make them feel that they would lose rather than gain by a severance of the connection. Rule the colonies as you would wish them to rule you, if the seat of government were in the colony, and you were the distant settlement, and it will be long indeed before they will desire to become independent. This is, perhaps, the last lesson of wisdom which will be learned by the rulers of mankind; yet is it the very first precept of the religion which they all profess; and the whole secret of colonial, as indeed of all other governments, is to do to others as we would they should do unto us.

There is no idea more erroneous than that which is entertained by many in this country, that it is for the interest of the old state to sever the connection with the colonies when they have arrived at a certain degree of strength; because by so doing, as it is said, you retain the advantages of mercantile intercourse, and get quit of the burden of providing for defense. Experience has proved that this opinion is of all others the most fallacious; because the very first thing which a colony does when it becomes independent, is to levy heavy import duties on the manufactures of the mother country, in order to encourage its own, and thus the benefit of its rising market is at first abridged, and at length lost to the parent state. The United States of America, accordingly, have imposed an import duty of 30 per cent. on all imports whatever; and the consequence is, that our average exports to them are not now so great as they were forty years ago, when their inhabitants were little more than a fourth of what they now are; and while our colonies consume, some £2 10s., some £2, some £6 or £8 a head of our manufactures, our emancipated offspring in North America do not, on an average of years, consume 12s. worth.* To the shipping of the parent state the change is still more disastrous, for, instead of being all on the side of one country, it becomes divided into two, of which the younger rapidly grows on its older rival. Witness the British trade to her North American colonies, with 2,600,000 of inhabitants, which employs 1,200,000 tons of British shipping; while that with the United States, with their 24,000,000, employs only 1,400,000, the remainder, about double that amount, having passed into the hands of the Americans themselves.† And while Spain, while she possessed her colonies,¹ carried on a traffic with them equal to what England has since attained with her settlements in all parts of the world, and fleets capable for long of maintaining an equal conflict with the mistress of the seas, since she lost them her foreign trade has sunk to nothing, and her fleet, the successor of the invincible Armada, has

6. Inevitable loss to the parent state from the separation of the colonies.

¹ See ante, c. iv. § 107, where the figures are given. Humboldt's *Nouvelle Espagne*.

---

* Exports from Great Britain in 1851 to

		Population.	Rate per Head.
Australia	£2,807,356	500,000	£5 16
British North Amer.	3,813,707	2,600,000	1 10
West Indies	2,201,032	970,000	2 10
South Africa	752,000	450,000	1 15
United States of Amer.	14,362,000	24,000,000	0 12

—*Parliamentary Paper*, Nov. 29, 1852.

† Shipping of Great Britain with

	British Tons.	Population.	For. Tons.
Brit. N. Amer.—1849	1,280,000	2,100,000	
United States, "	1,482,707	23,000,000	2,658,326

—Porter's *Progress of the Nation*, 1851, p. 392.

The great amount of the British tonnage to the United States of late years has been mainly owing to the prodigious emigration—on an average, 250,000 souls—from Great Britain to that country. Before this began, our tonnage with America stood thus:

Years.	British to U. States.	British to N. Am. Col.	America. Tons.	Exports to U. States.	Exports to Canada.
				£.	£.
1842	152,633	541,451	319,524	3,528,807	2,233,525
1843	200,781	771,905	306,186	5,013,510	1,751,211
1844	206,183	789,410	338,781	7,938,079	3,070,861
1845	223,676	1,090,224	444,442	7,142,839	3,555,950

—Porter's *Parl. Tables*, vi 43, vii. 43; iii. 50, 52, 518 —years 1839, 1840, 1841.

dwindled to two ships of the line and three frigates.*

7. Tyrannical rule of old Spain over her colonies.
Although the prosperity of the Spanish colonies had become such that they contained, when the Revolution severed them from old Spain, nineteen millions of inhabitants, and carried on an exportand import trade with it of above £16,000,000 sterling in all, yet this had arisen chiefly from the bounty of nature and the resources of wealth which they themselves enjoyed, and in no degree from the government of the parent state. Its administration had been illiberal, selfish, and oppressive in the very highest degree. It was founded mainly on three bases—1. The establishment of the Romish faith in its most bigoted form, and the absolute exclusion and refusal even of toleration to every other species of worship; 2. The exclusive enjoyment of all offices of trust and emolument in the colonies, and especially the working and direction of the mines of gold and silver, by persons appointed by the Spanish government at Madrid; 3. The entire monopoly of the whole trade with the colonies to the merchants and shipping of the mother country, especially those of Cadiz and Coruna, whom its immense profits had long elevated to the rank of merchant princes. Here the radical selfishness and shortsighted views of human nature appeared in their full deformity; and accordingly, as these were the evils which depressed the energies and cramped the efforts of the colonies, the prevailing feeling which produced the revolution, and the war-cry which animated its supporters, were for the opposite set of immunities. Liberation from Romish tyranny, self-government, and free trade with all the world, were inscribed on the banners of Bolivar and San Martin, and in the end proved victorious in the conflict. Happy if they had known to improve their victory by moderation, and exercise the powers it had won with judgment, and if the liberated states had not fallen under a succession of tyrants of their own creation, so numerous that history has not attempted to record their succession, and so savage that it recoils from the portrait of their deeds.

8. The trade of Spain was all with foreign manufactures.
Although, too, the trade which Spain carried on with her colonies was so immense anterior to the revolution in Spanish America, yet we should widely err if we imagined that it consisted of the manufactures raised or worked up in Spain itself; on the contrary, it consisted almost entirely of the manufactured articles produced in Holland, Flanders, Germany, and England, brought by their merchants to the vast warehouses of Cadiz and Coruna, and transported thence beyond the Atlantic. The government of Madrid was entirely swayed in these matters by the merchants of these great seaport towns; and their interest was wound up with the preservation of the monopoly of the *trade,* and by no means extended to the production of the *manufactures.* On the contrary, they were rather interested in keeping up the purchase of the articles which the colonies required from foreign states, for they enjoyed in that way in some degree a double transit, first from the seat of the manufactures in Britain or Belgium to Cadiz and Coruna, and again from thence to the American shores. Spain, notwithstanding the efforts of the Government to encourage them, had never possessed any considerable manufactures; and even if the merchants engaged in the colonial trade had wished it, they could not have found in their own country the articles of which their colonies stood in need. Thus the traffic with those colonies, great as it was, did little to enrich the country in general. It created colossal fortunes in the merchants of Cadiz and Coruna, of the Havana or Buenos Ayres, but nothing more—like the railway traffic from London to Liverpool and Manchester, which does much for the wealth of these great towns at either end of the line, but comparatively little for the intermediate country along the sides of the communication between them. The causes of this peculiarity are to be found in the peculiarities of its physical circumstances, national character, and long-established policy, which have deprived old Spain of nearly all the advantages of her magnificent colonies, and afford the true, though hitherto unobserved, key to her long decline.

9. Want of industry in the national character.
1. The first of these is to be found in the national character and temperament, the real source from which, here as everywhere else, more even than its physical or political circumstances, its fortunes and destiny have flowed. The races whose mingled blood have formed the heterogeneous population of old Spain, have none of them, excepting the Moors, been remarkable for their industrial habits. Tenacious of custom, persevering in inclination, repugnant to change, the original inhabitants of the country, with whom the Legions maintained so long and doubtful a conflict, were, like all the other families of the Celtic race, formidable enemies, indomitable guerrillas, but by no means either laborious husbandmen or industrious artisans. The Visigoths, who poured through the passes of the Pyrenees, and overspread the country to the Pillars of Hercules, added nothing to their industrious habits, but much to their warlike propensities: from them sprang Pelayo and the gallant defenders of the Asturian hills, but not either the cultivators of the fields or the manufacturers of the towns; from them sprang Pizarro and Cortes, and the conquerors of the New World, but neither a Penn or a Franklin, nor the hardy pioneers of civilization in its wastes. The Moors alone, who at one time had nearly wrested all Spain from the Christians, and established themselves for a very long period on the banks of the Guadalquivir, were animated by the real spirit of industry, and great was the wealth and prosperity of their provinces to the south of the Sierra Morena. But religious bigotry tore up from the state this source of wealth; and the banishment, three hundred years ago, of nearly a

---
* Imports and exports of Spain to her colonies in 1809:—
Exports .... 59,200,000 piastres, or £15,200,000
Imports .... 68,500,000 piastres, or £17,150,000
—HUMBOLDT, *Nouvelle Espagne,* iv. 153, 151. See also *sup.* c. iv. 107, where the details are given.

Exports of Great Britain to her whole colonies in
1847 ...... £11,912,000 | 1850 ...... £18,517,000
1848 ...... 12,833,000 | 1851 19,496,000
1849 ...... 15,090,000 |
—*Parl. Returns of these years.*

million of its most industrious and orderly citizens, deprived Spain—as a similar measure, at a later period, did France—of the most useful and valuable portion of its inhabitants, and with them of the most important advantages she could have derived from her colonial settlements.

2. The physical circumstances and peculiarities of Spain, and the pursuits to which its inhabitants were for the most part of necessity driven, were such as favored nautical and commercial, as much as they obstructed manufacturing pursuits. Placed midway between the Old and the New World, with one front washed by the waves of the Atlantic, and another by the ripple of the Mediterranean, with noble and defensible harbors forming the access to both, she enjoyed the greatest possible advantages for foreign commerce; and accordingly, even in the days of Solomon, the merchants of Tarshish rivaled those of Tyre in conducting the traffic of the then known world. But she had little natural advantages for interior traffic or manufactures. The mountainous nature of the greater part of the country rendered internal intercourse difficult; the entire want of roads, save the great chaussées from Madrid to Bayonne, Cadiz, Barcelona, Badajos, and Valencia, made it impossible. What little traffic there was off these roads, was all carried on on the backs of mules. Having little or no coal, and few of the forests which in France supply in some degree its want, she had none of the advantages for manufacturing industry which that invaluable mineral has furnished to northern Europe, enabling the inhabitants of Great Britain to reap the whole advantages of their own colonies, and great part of those of Spain, by supplying the former directly, and the latter by the merchants of Cadiz and Corunna, or the contraband trade in the West Indies, with the greater part of the manufactured articles which they required. Hence it was that the Spanish merchants sought the materials of their traffic in Belgium or Lancashire, and that the manufacturers of Flanders and England, not Spain, reaped the principal advantages arising from the growth of its colonial dominion.

10. The physical circumstances of Spain favored commerce, but not manufactures.

3. If the physical circumstances of Spain were such as almost to preclude the possibility of manufacturing industry arising among its inhabitants, its history had still more clearly marked their character and occupations. Their annals for five centuries are nothing but a continual conflict with the Moors. These ruthless invaders, as formidable and devastating in war as they were industrious and orderly in peace, spread gradually from the rock of Gibraltar to the foot of the Pyrenees. They were at last expelled, but it was only after five hundred years of almost incessant combats. These combats were not, for a very long period, the battles of great armies against each other, but the ceaseless conflicts of small forces or guerrilla bands, among whom success and defeat alternated, and to whom at length the predominance was given to Spain only by the perseverance and energy of the Spanish character. It was the wars of the Heptarchy

11. Effect of the long-continued hostility with the Moors.

or of the Anglo-Saxons with the Danes, continued, not till the reign of Alfred, but to that of Henry VII. Incalculable was the effect of this long-continued and absorbing hostility upon the bent and disposition of the Spanish mind. As much as eight centuries of unbroken peace, during which the southern counties of England have never seen the fires of an enemy's camp, have formed the English, have the five centuries of Moorish warfare stamped their impress on the Spanish character. Engrossing every thought, animating every desire, directing every passion in the country; uniting the fervor of the Crusader to the ardor of chivalry, the glow of patriotism to the thirst for conquest; penetrating every valley, ascending every mountain in the Peninsula, they have stamped a durable and indelible character on the Spanish nation. They made it a race of shepherds and warriors, but not of husbandmen and artisans. In the Cid we may discern the perfection of this character, when it was directed to the highest objects and refined by the most generous sentiments; in the indolent hidalgo, who spent his life in lounging under the arcades of Saragossa or in the coffee-houses of Madrid, the opposite extreme, when it had become debased by the inactivity and degraded by the selfishness of pacific life.

4. These circumstances would have rendered it a very difficult matter, if not an impossibility, for the manufacturers of Spain, had any such sprung up, to have maintained their ground against those of northern Europe, even in the supply of their own colonies. But, in addition to this, there was a very curious and decisive circumstance, which must at once have proved fatal to the manufacturers of Spain, even if they had begun to arise. This was the possession of the mines of Mexico and Potosi by the Government, and the policy, in regard to the precious metals, pursued with determined perseverance by the cabinet of Madrid. This was the policy of favoring the importation and prohibiting the exportation of the precious metals, in the belief that it was the only way to keep their wealth to themselves. The effect of this policy is thus described by the father of political economy: "That degradation in the value of gold or silver, which is the effect of the increased fertility of the mines which produce those metals, or the discovery of new ones, operates equally, or nearly so, over the whole commercial world; but that which, being the effect either of the peculiar situation or political institutions of a particular country, takes place *only in that country*, is a matter of very great consequence, which, far from tending to make any body really richer, tends to make every body really poorer. The rise in the money-price of all commodities, which is in this case peculiar to that country, tends to discourage, more or less, every sort of industry which is carried on within it, and to enable foreign nations, by furnishing almost all sorts of goods for a smaller quantity of silver than its workmen can afford to do, to undersell them not only in the foreign, but even in the home market. Spain by taxing, and Portugal by prohibiting, the exportation of gold and silver, load that exportation with the price of smuggling, and raise the value of

12. Impolitic laws of Spain in regard to money.

those metals in those countries much above what it is in other countries. The cheapness of gold and silver, or, what is the same thing, the dearness of all commodities, discourages both the agriculture and manufactures of Spain and Portugal, and enables foreign nations to supply them with many sorts of rude, and with almost all sorts of manufactured produce, for a smaller quantity of gold and silver than they themselves can either raise or make them for at home."¹

^{1 Wealth of Nations, b. iv. c. 5.}

5. The religion which obtains a lasting place in a country is often to be regarded as an effect rather than a cause. It is the consequence of a predisposition in the general mind which leads to the embracing of doctrines or forms which fall in with its propensities. We are apt to say that the Scotch are energetic and persevering because they are Protestants, the Irish volatile and indolent because they are Roman Catholic; forgetting that the adoption of these different creeds by these different nations was with both a voluntary act, and that it bespoke rather than created the national character. Had the English been of the turn of mind of the Spaniards, they never would have become Protestants; had the Spaniards been of the English, they never would have remained Catholic. But admitting that it is in the distinctive character of RACE that we are to look for the remote cause of the peculiar modification of faith which is to be durably prevalent in a nation, it is not the less certain that the reaction which it exerts upon its character and destiny is great and lasting. The fires of the Inquisition were not fed with human victims for three centuries in Spain, without producing durable and indelible effects upon the national character and destiny. Independence of mind, vigor of thought, emancipation from superstition, were impossible in a people thus shackled in opinion; adherence to the faith which imposed the shackles was not to be expected among the educated few, who had emerged from its restraints. Thus the Spanish nation, like every other old state in which the Romish faith is established, was divided in matters of religion into two classes, widely different in point of numbers, but more nearly balanced in point of political influence and power. On the one side were a few hundred thousand citizens in Madrid, Cadiz, Corunna, and Barcelona, rich, comparatively educated, free-thinking, and engaged in the pursuit of pleasure; on the other, twelve millions of peasants in the country, hardy, intrepid, and abstemious, indifferent to political privileges, but devotedly attached to the faith of their fathers, and blindly following the injunctions of their priests, and the mandates of the See of Rome.

13. Important effect of the Romish faith.

6. From these circumstances arose an important difference between the views of the citizens of the towns and the inhabitants of the country in political thought and desires. The former, placed within reach of political advancement, were animated, for the most part, by an ardent desire for freedom, and an emancipation from the fetters on thought and expression, which had so long been imposed by the tyranny of the priests and the tortures of the Inquisition; the latter, living in the seclusion of the country, and having nothing to gain by political change, were enthusiastically attached to the throne, and devotedly submissive to the mandates of the clergy. If the Basque Provinces alone, where important political privileges had from time immemorial been enjoyed by the peasantry, their loyal feelings were mingled, as in England, with attachment to their constitutional rights; in the other provinces of Spain, they were founded on their entire abandonment. "Viva el Rey apostolico!" was the cry which expressed at once their feelings and their wishes. From the small number of considerable towns in the Peninsula, the largest of which had not two hundred thousand inhabitants, while the generality had not more than thirty or forty thousand, the democratic section of the community was not a twentieth part of the immense mass of the rural population. But from their position in the great towns and fortresses of the kingdom, and their being in possession of nearly the whole of its available wealth and energetic talent, they had great advantages in the event of a serious conflict arising; and it was hard to say, in the event of civil war, to which side victory would incline.

14. Difference of the towns and country in respect of political opinion.

7. The apparent inequality of parties, from the immense preponderance of numbers on the country side, was more than compensated by the temper and feelings of the ARMY. This body, formidable and important in all countries, was more especially so from the peculiar circumstances of Spain, which had just emerged, on the accession of Ferdinand, from a desperate war of six years' duration, in the course of which nearly all the active energy of the country had been enrolled in the ranks of war, and the troops had at last, under the guidance of Wellington, acquired a tolerable degree of consistency. These men, and still more their officers, were for the most part democratic. During the long contest in the provinces, the generals had enjoyed nearly unlimited power in their separate commands, and they did not relish the thought of returning from the rank of independent princes to subordinate command. All of them had been brought in contact with the English, numbers of them, in a friendly way as prisoners, with the French troops; and from both they had imbibed the free spirit and independent thoughts by which both were characterized. Great, indeed, was the contrast between their extensive information and general knowledge of the world, and the narrow ideas of the spiritual militia who had hitherto been their sole instructors. The contrast was rendered the more striking, from the brilliant career which had attended at first the arms of France, then those of England, when compared with the almost uniform defeats which their own had sustained. Hence the armies of Spain, as indeed those of all the Continental monarchies, retired from the conflict deeply imbued with democratic principles; and the officers, especially, were generally impressed with the belief that nothing but the establishment of these was wanting to open a boundless career of prosperity to their country, of promotion and elevation to themselves.

15. Disposition of the army.

8. But if the army was an important, it might be a decisive ally to the democratic party in the towns, the royalists in

16. The Church

the country had a force for their support equally numerous, equally zealous, and still better disciplined and docile to their chiefs. The Curian was unanimous in favor of the crown, and the establishment of arbitrary power: an unerring instinct told them that freedom of thought would inevitably lead to freedom of action, and the termination of their long-established dominion. Their numbers were immense, their possessions extensive. A hundred thousand priests, doomed to celibacy in a country suffering under the want of hands, and capable of maintaining, with ease and comfort, at least double its number of inhabitants, were diffused over its whole extent, and in all the rural districts, at least, exercised an unlimited sway over the minds of their flocks. Essentially obedient to the voice of their spiritual chiefs, which was every where governed by the commands issuing from the conclave of the Vatican, the efforts of this immense body of spiritual militia were entirely devoted to one object—the re-establishment of despotic power, in its most unmitigated form, over the whole Peninsula. The policy of the court of Rome was directed to this object in Spain and Portugal, from the same motive which led it to support the democratic propensities of the Romish Church in Ireland. In both cases, regardless of the real welfare of the people of their persuasion, they were governed by one motive—the furtherance of the power and extension of the influence of their own establishment. In the Peninsula, this was to be done by aiding despotic power against democratic infidelity; in the British Islands, by supporting democratic ambition against heretical power. But when the vast influence and wide-spread possessions of the clergy are taken into consideration, and the absolute direction which they had of the minds and opinions of their followers in all the rural districts and many of the towns, it was a most formidable enemy with which the republicans had to contend, and it was doubtful whether, in a protracted struggle, victory might not incline to the side which it espoused.

9. This influence and importance, in a political point of view, of the clergy, was the more important, from, generally speaking, the comfortable and prosperous condition of the peasantry, and their entire submission to the voice of their pastors. If the clergy were a zealous and admirably trained phalanx of officers for the church militant, the peasantry composed an incomparable body of private soldiers. Sober, abstemious, regular, and yet ardent and capable of great things, the Spanish peasant is the one in Europe, with the exception, perhaps, of the Polish, who most readily forms a good soldier, and is most easily induced to undertake his duties. The five centuries of incessant warfare with the Moors had nurtured this tendency; the benignity of the climate, and absence of artificial wants among the peasantry, have rendered it easy of retention. The Castilian or Catalonian loses little by leaving his home and joining a guerrilla band in the mountains; his fare remains the same, his habits are little different, the sphere of his achievements is much extended. The roving adventurous life of partisan warfare, with its hairbreadth escapes and occasional triumphs, suits his taste and rouses his ambition.

17. State of the peasantry.

Unlike the peasant of Northern Europe, the Spanish cultivator is never worn down by the labors, or depressed by the limited ideas, of daily toil. Blessed with a benignant climate, tilling a fruitful soil, or wandering over vast downs after immense flocks, he can satisfy his few wants with a comparatively small amount of actual labor. The greater part of his life is spent in doing nothing, or in such exercises as nourish rather than depress his warlike disposition. "The Spaniards," says Chateaubriand, "are Christian Arabs: they unite the savage and the religious character. The mingled blood of the Cantabrian, the Carthaginian, the Roman, the Vandal, and the Moor, which flows in their veins, flows not as other blood. They are at once active, indolent, and grave." "Every grave nation," says Montesquieu, in discoursing of them, "is indolent; for those who do not labor consider themselves as masters of those who do. In that country liberty is injured by independence. Of what value are civil privileges to a man who, like the Bedouin, armed with a lance and followed by his sheep, has no need of food beyond a few acorn, figs, or olives?" The *dolce far niente* is as dear to the Spaniard as to the inhabitants of the Ausonian fields; but the precious hours of rest are not spent in listless inactivity: they are cheered by the recital of the ballads, or the recounting of the stories which recall the glories, the dangers, the adventures of war. There was scarcely one at this time who had not his musket suspended over his hearth, which had been used in the guerrilla warfare with the French, and his tale to recount of the indignities endured, or the vengeance taken, or the surprises achieved, in the conflict with those ruthless invaders. Mutual benefits and dependence, and a long series of kind actions and good deeds, performed by the parochial clergy to their flocks, had endeared them to the whole rural population;[1] and it was easy to see that if any civil warfare ensued they would take the side, whichever it was, which was espoused by their spiritual directors.

[1] Chateaub. Congr. de Verone, i. 12, 13.

10. So great was the influence of the clergy, and so loyal the feelings of the peasantry, that they would in all probability have enabled the king to resist all the efforts of the malcontents, had there been any body of efficient and united landed proprietors in the country. But none such existed in Spain. Generally speaking, the clergy were the sole leaders of the people. There were many nobles in Spain, and they were inferior to none in the world in pride and aristocratic pretension; but they had neither political power nor rural influence. Nearly all absentees, residing the whole year round in Madrid, they had none of that sway over the minds of their tenantry which is enjoyed by landed proprietors who have attached them by a series of kind acts during many generations: intrusted with no political power, they had no weight in national deliberations, or authority in the affairs of Government. The grandees of Spain, who cherished the purity of their descent as carefully as the Arabs do the pedigree of their steeds, and who would admit of, and indeed could contract, no marriage where sixteen quarterings could not be counted on both sides,

18. State of the Nobility.

had incurred the penalty prescribed by nature for such overweening pride and selfishness. They had become a worn-out and degenerate race, considerably below the usual stature of the human frame, and lamentably inferior in vigor, courage, and intelligence. Not one great man arose during the whole of the protracted Peninsular war: few of the generals who did distinguish themselves belonged to the class of grandees. Nevertheless, this selfish *fainéant* race possessed a great part of the landed property in the kingdom, and by the operation of the strict entails under which it was nearly all held, and the constant intermarriage of the nobility among each other, it was every day running more and more into a few hands. The greater part of the remaining landed property was in the hands of incorporations, municipalities, or the Church; so that there was perhaps no country in the world which, from its political situation, stood so much in need of an efficient body of rural proprietors, and yet was so entirely destitute of it.

11. It was scarcely possible that a monarchy so situated, distracted by such passions, and divided by so many opposite interests, could long escape the convulsions of civil war; but it was accelerated, and the means of averting it were taken away, by the peculiar circumstances in which, on the restoration of Ferdinan I in 1814 to the throne of his ancestors, the FINANCES of the country stood. From the causes which have been mentioned, the industry and resources of old Spain had declined to such a degree, that little revenue was to be derived from taxation at home; while, on the other hand, the gold and silver mines in the hands of Government in the colonies had become so prolific that the chief revenue of the state had long been derived from its transmarine possessions, and the principal attention of Government was fixed on their maintenance. The income derived by Spain from her colonies, anterior to the Revolution, amounted to 38,000,000 piastres, or £9,500,000 —fully a half of the whole revenue, at that period, of the Spanish crown. It is true, about £7,500,000 of this sum was absorbed in expenses connected with the colonies themselves, leaving only £2,000,000 available to the royal treasury at Madrid; but still it was by this vast colonial expenditure, and the establishment it enabled the king to keep up, that nearly the whole power and influence of Government was maintained. It was the gold of Mexico and Peru that paid the armies and civil servants, and upheld nearly the entire sway of the court of Madrid. Now, however, this source of influence was gone. The revolution in South America had cut off fully a half of the whole revenue of Spain; and how was revolution to be combated without armies, themselves the creatures of the wealth which had been lost! This is the true cause of the ceaseless embarrassments of finance, which have ever since distinguished the Spanish government; which led them, as will appear in the sequel, to hazard revolution at home in the desperate attempt to extinguish it in the colonies, and has since led them into so many acts alien to the old Castilian honor, and discreditable to subsequent administrations.

19. Huge gap in the revenue from the loss of the South American colonies.

¹ Humboldt, Nouvelle Espagne, iii. 301, iv. 153, 154.

12. While so many circumstances tended to prognosticate future and fierce dissension in the Spanish peninsula, the enormous defects of the Constitution of 1812, which was the ruling form of government at the time of the restoration, rendered it imminent and unavoidable. The circumstances under which that constitution was framed have been already explained, and the calamitous influence they exercised on the deliberations and temper of the Spanish Constituent Assembly.¹ That Assembly—convoked in 1811, at the most disastrous period of the contest with France, and when the Imperial armies occupied the whole country except a few mountain provinces and fortresses on the sea-coast—so far from presenting a faithful representation of the feelings of the majority of the nation, presented the very reverse. Galicia and Asturias alone—evacuated by Ney at the time of the advance of Wellington to Talavera—with the seaport towns of Valencia, Cadiz, and Alicante, were in the hands of the Spaniards: the whole remainder of the country was occupied by the French; and, of course, the election of members for the Cortes was impossible from the provinces they were masters of. Thus the Cortes was returned only by the seaports of Cadiz, Valencia, and Alicante, and the mountaineers of Galicia and Asturias; and as they were not a tenth part of the entire inhabitants of the country,² the remaining members were all selected by the *people of those provinces then in Cadiz*—that is, by the most democratic portion of the community. In this extraordinary and unconstitutional device, perhaps unavoidable under the circumstances, the real germ of the whole subsequent calamities of Spain, and of the south of Europe, is to be found.

20. Constitution of 1812: how it was formed.

¹ Hist. of Europe, 1789-1815, c. lxv. §§ 22, 23.

² Toreno, Histoire de la Guerre de la Revolution, iii. 349, 351; Marignac, Sur l'Espagne, 91, 95; Hist. of Europe, 1789-1815, c. lxv. §§ 13, 14.

As might have been expected, from its construction by the representatives of little more than the democratic rabble of three seaport towns, the Constitution of 1812, formed by the Cortes at Cadiz, was republican in the extreme. It preserved the shadow of monarchy, but nothing more. It did not establish a "throne surrounded with republican institutions," but a republic surrounded by the *ghost* of monarchical institutions. The Legislature consisted of a single Chamber, elected by universal suffrage; there was to be a representative for every 70,000 inhabitants in old Spain; and the American colonies were also admitted on similar terms to a considerable share in the representation. Every man aged 25, and who had resided seven years in the province, had a vote for the representation of his department in the Cortes. The king had a *veto* only twice on any legislative measure; if proposed to him a third time by the legislature, he was *constrained* to pass the measure, whatever it was. There was no House of Peers, or check of any kind on the single Chamber of the Cortes, elected, as it was, by universal suffrage; and the king's ministers, by becoming such, *ipso facto* lost

21. Its extreme democratic tendency.

their seats in the National Assembly. The Cortes was to be re-elected every two years; and no member who had once sat could be again returned to its bosom. The king had the appointment of civil and military officers, but only out of a list furnished to him by the Cortes, who could alone make regulations for the government of the army. The judges in all the civil courts were to be appointed by the Cortes. The king could declare peace or war, and conclude treaties in the first instance; but his measures in those particulars required, for their validity, the ratification of the Cortes. Finally, to aid him in the government of the kingdom, he was empowered to appoint a privy council of forty members, but only out of a list of a hundred and twenty furnished to him by the Cortes. In like manner all diplomatic, ministerial, and ecclesiastical appointments were to be made out of a list of three, presented to him by the same body; and, to perpetuate its power, a permanent committee was appointed, which exercised, during the intervals of its sessions, nearly the whole powers of the administration intrusted to the entire body.[1]

¹ Chateaub. Congrès de Vérone, i. 24, 25; Torene. iv. 328, 341; History of Europe, c. lxv. §§ 23, 25; Constitution of 1812; Archives Diplom. iii. l. 159.

This constitution was so thoroughly democratic in all its parts, that it could not by possibility coexist with a monarchical government in any country of the earth. Biennial parliaments, universal suffrage, the exclusion of the king's ministers from the legislature, a single chamber, the practical appointment to all offices, civil and military, by a Cortes thus popularly elected, and the eternal succession of new and inexperienced persons into the legislature, by the self-denying ordinances which they had passed, were amply sufficient to have overturned society in Great Britain—long as its people had been trained to popular institutions—in six months. What, then, was to be expected when such a constitution was suddenly imposed on a country inured to political nullity by centuries of absolute government—by a so-styled National Assembly, elected, during the whirl of the French war, almost entirely by the populace of Cadiz, when crowded to suffocation by all the most ardent spirits in the Peninsula refluent within its walls from the effects of the French invasion? It was impossible to imagine a constitution more at variance with the ancient institutions, or repugnant to the present feelings of nineteen-twentieths of the Spanish people. It was like a constitution for Great Britain formed by a parliament elected by the inhabitants of the Tower Hamlets, Marylebone, and Manchester, with a few returned from the mountains of Cumberland and Wales. But, unfortunately, in proportion to its utter unsuitableness for the entire inhabitants of the Peninsula, and the abhorrence of the vast majority of the people to its provisions, it was the object of impassioned attachment on the part of the democratic populace in the capital and a few seaport towns. It was so for a very obvious reason: it promised, if established in a lasting way, to put the whole power and patronage of the state at their disposal. Therein the seeds of a lasting division of opinion, and of a frightful civil war at no distant period in the Peninsula, in which it might be expected that 12,000,000 bold, hardy, and loyal peasants, scattered over the whole country, would be arrayed on one side; while 500,000 ardent and enthusiastic democrats concentrated in the capital and chief fortresses, and having the command of the army, were in arms on the other.

62. Utter unsuitableness of the constitution to the generality of Spain.

The proceedings of the Cortes, and the democratic character of the measures they were pursuing, was well known to the Duke of Wellington, and discerned by him with his wonted sagacity. He repeatedly warned the government of Great Britain, that while the spirit of the nation was anti-Gallican, not democratic, that of the Cortes and its narrow body of constituents was democratic, not anti-Gallican; and that it would be their wisdom, without sanctioning in any shape, or interfering at all with the proceedings at Cadiz, to turn their attention exclusively to the expulsion of the French from the Peninsula.* They did so, and with what effect need be told

23. Universal unpopularity of the Cortes and the constitution.

* "The natural course of all popular assemblies—of the Spanish Cortes among others—is to adopt democratic principles, and to vest all the powers of the state in their own body, and this Assembly must take care that they do not run in this tempting course, as the wishes of the nation are decidedly for a monarchy. By a monarchy alone it can be governed; and their inclination to any other form of government, and their assumption of the power and patronage of the state into their own hands, would immediately deprive them of the confidence of the people, and render them a worse government, and more impotent, because more numerous, than the Central Junta."—WELLINGTON to H. WELLESLEY, Nov. 4, 1810; GURWOOD, iv. 559.

"The Cortes are unpopular every where, and, in my opinion, deservedly so. Nothing can be more cruel, absurd, and impolitic than those decrees respecting the persons who have served the enemy. It is extraordinary that the revolution has not produced one man with any knowledge of the real situation of the country. It appears as if they were all drunk, thinking and speaking of any other subject than Spain."—WELLINGTON to H. WELLESLEY, Nov. 1, 1812; GURWOOD, ix. 524.

"It is impossible to describe the state of confusion in which affairs are at Cadiz. The greatest objection I have to the new constitution is, that in a country in which almost the whole property consists in land—and these are the largest landed proprietors which exist in Europe—no measure has been adopted, and no barrier provided, to guard landed property from the encroachments, injustice, and violence to which it is at all times liable, particularly in the progress of revolutions. Such a guard can only be afforded by the establishment of an assembly of the great landed proprietors—like our House of Lords, having concurrent power with the Cortes; and you may depend upon it there is no man in Spain, be his property ever so small, who is not interested in the establishment of such an assembly. Unhappily, in legislative assemblies, the most tyrannical and unjust measures are the most popular. I tremble for a country such as Spain, in which there is no barrier for the preservation of private property, excepting the justice of a legislative assembly possessing supreme power. It is impossible to calculate upon the plans of such an assembly; they have no check whatever, and they are governed by the most ignorant and licentious of all licentious presses—that of Cadiz. I believe they mean to attack the royal and feudal tenths, the tithes of the Church, under pretense of encouraging agriculture; and finding the supplies from these sources not so extensive as they expected, they will seize the estates of the grandees. Our character is involved in a greater degree than we are aware of in the democratical transactions of the Cortes, in the opinion of all moderate, well-thinking Spaniards, and, I am afraid, with the rest of Europe. It is quite impossible such a system can last; what I regret is, that I am the person who maintains it. If the king should return, *he will overturn the whole fabric*, if he has any spirit; but the gentlemen at Cadiz are so completely masters, that I fear there must be another convulsion."—WELLINGTON to DON DIEGO DE LA VEGA, Jan. 29, 1813; GURWOOD, x. 64, 65, 247; xi. 91.

to none; but though Spain marched under his guidance in the career of conquest, and, to external appearance, was enveloped in a halo of glory, the working of the democratic constitution was not the less felt, and it had become beyond measure repugnant to the vast majority of the inhabitants of the Peninsula. What chiefly excited their indignation was the selfishness and rapacity of the half-starving employés, who, issuing from Cadiz, overspread the country in every direction, like an army of locusts, and ate up the fruits of their industry, by exactions of every description, from the suffering inhabitants. The general abhorrence in which these rapacious employés were held, recalls the similar indignation excited in Flanders by the Jacobin commissioners sent down there by Danton, when the country was overrun by the republican armies in 1792.¹ It will be so to the end of the world, in all governments, monarchical and republican, where the executive and legislative functions are united in one person or assembly; for then there is no possible check upon the misdeeds of either. The only security which can be relied upon is to be found in their separation and mutual jealousy, for then they act as a check upon each other.²

¹ Hist. of Europe, c. x. § 55.
² Chateaub. Congrès de Verone, i. 16, 17; Martignac, 99, 109; Ann. Reg. 1812, 67, 68.

24. Influence of the Cortes on South America.

The proceedings of the Cortes, and the republican spirit with which they were animated, acted in a still more important way upon the destinies of the New World than those of the Old. The deputies from the Transatlantic provinces, to whom, in a liberal and worthy spirit, the gates of the national representation at Cadiz had been opened, came to the hall of the Cortes, in the Isle of Leon, with feelings wound up to the highest pitch, from the wrongs they had so long endured from the selfish and monopolizing policy of the mother country, and the free and independent spirit which the breaking out of the revolution in the Caraccas and elsewhere had excited in her transmarine possessions. They found themselves in a highly democratic and vehemently excited assembly, in which the noble name of liberty was continually heard, in which the sovereignty of the people was openly announced, the whole fabric of the new constitution was made to rest on that foundation, and in which the most enthusiastic predictions were constantly uttered as to the future regeneration and happiness of mankind from the influence of these principles. They returned to South America, under the restriction which had been adopted of each Cortes to two years' sitting, before these flattering predictions had been brought to the test of experience, or any thing had occurred to reveal their fallacious character.³ They instantly spread among their constituents the flattering doctrines and hopes with which the halls of the Cortes had resounded in Europe. Incalculable was the influence of this circumstance upon the future destinies of South America, and, through it, of the whole civilized world. To this, in a great degree, is to be ascribed the wide-spread and desperate resolution of the vast majority of the inhabitants in the revolutionary contest in those magnificent settlements; their frightful desolation by the horrors of a war worse than civil; and their final severance, by the insidious aid of Great Britain, from the Spanish crown.

³ Comte de Trequimont, de l'Angleterre et Lord Palmerston, ii. 265.

In all the particulars which have been mentioned, PORTUGAL was in the same situation as Spain; but in two respects the situation of that country was more favorable for innovation, and her people were more ripe for revolt than in the Spanish provinces. The royal family having, during the first alarm of the French invasion, migrated to Brazil, and dread of the terrors of a sea voyage having prevented the aged monarch from returning, he had come to fix his permanent residence on the beautiful shores of Rio Janeiro. A separation of the two countries had thus taken place; and the government at Lisbon, during the whole war, had been conducted by means of a council of regency, the members of which were by no means men either of vigor or capacity, and which was far from commanding the respect, or having acquired the affections, of the country. While the weight and influence of Government had been thus sensibly weakened, the political circumstances of Portugal, and the events of the war, had in an extraordinary manner diffused liberal ideas and the spirit of independence through a considerable part of the people.

25. Situation of Portugal: effect of the removal of the seat of government to Rio Janeiro.

Closely united, both by political treaties and commercial intercourse, with Great Britain, for above a century Portugal had become, in its maritime districts at least, almost an English colony. English influence was predominant at Lisbon: English commerce had enriched Oporto: the English market for port had covered the slopes of Tras-os-Montes with smiling vineyards. In addition to this, the events of the late war had spread, in an extraordinary degree, both admiration of the English institutions, and confidence in the English character, through the entire population. Thirty thousand Portuguese troops had been taken into British pay: they had felt the integrity of British administration: they had been led to victory by British officers. Unlike the native nobles who had held the same situations, they had seen them ever the first in the enemy's fire—the last in nets of domestic corruption. Immense had been the influence of this juxtaposition. Standing side by side with him in battle, they had learned to respect the English soldier in war, to admire the institutions which had trained him in peace. Even the hatred in which they had been bred of the heretic, yielded to the evidence of their senses, which had taught them his virtues. In daily intercourse with the British soldiers, they had learned to appreciate the liberty which had nurtured them; they had come to envy their independence of thought, and imitate their freedom of language. The mercantile classes in Lisbon and Oporto, almost entirely supported by British capital, and fed by British commerce, were still more strongly impressed with the merits of the political institutions, from intercourse with a nation governed by which they had derived such signal benefits. Thus a free

26. Its general adoption of English habits and ideas.

spirit, and the thirst for liberal institutions, was both stronger and more wide-spread in Portugal than in the adjoining provinces of Spain; and it was easy to foresee that, if any circumstances impelled the latter country into the career of revolution, the former would be the first to follow the example.

FERDINAND VII., whom the battle of Leipsic and conquest of France had restored to the throne of his ancestors, was not by nature a bad, or by disposition a cruel man; and yet he did many wicked and unpardonable deeds, and has, beyond almost any other of his contemporary princes, been the object of impassioned invective on the part of the liberal press in Europe. Placed in the very front rank of the league of princes, ruling a country in which the vast majority were decidedly monarchical—a small minority vehemently democratic—brought, the first of all the monarchs of Europe, in contact with the revolutionary spirit by which they were all destined to be so violently shaken, it was scarcely possible it could be otherwise. But the character of Ferdinand was, perhaps, the most unfortunate that could have been found to tread the path environed with dangers which lay before him. He had neither the courage and energy requisite for a despotic, nor the prudence and foresight essential in a constitutional sovereign: he had neither the courage which commands respect, the generosity which wins affection, nor the wisdom which averts catastrophe. Indolence was his great characteristic; a facility of being led, his chief defect. Incapable of taking a decided line for himself, he yielded easily and willingly to the representations of those around him, and exhibited in his conduct those vacillations of policy which indicated the alternate ascendency of the opposite parties by which he was surrounded. His inclination, without doubt, was strongly in favor of despotic power; but he had great powers of dissimulation, and succeeded in deceiving Talleyrand himself, as well as the liberal ministers subsequently imposed upon him by the Cortes, as to his real intentions. Supple, accommodating, and irresolute, he had learnt hypocrisy in the same school as the modern Greek has learned it from the Turk—the school of suffering.[1]

<small>27. Character of Ferdinand VII.</small>

<small>28. Martignac, 100, 106.</small>

The treaty of Valençay, as narrated in a former work,* restored Ferdinand VII. to liberty, and he re-entered the kingdom of his fathers on the 20th March, 1814, just ten days before the Allies entered Paris. This treaty had been concluded with Napoleon while the monarch was still in captivity, and it was a fundamental condition of it that he should cause the English to evacuate Spain. The subsequent fall of the Emperor, however, rendered this stipulation of no effect; and, after having been received with royal honors by the garrisons, both French and Spanish, in Catalonia, the monarch proceeded by easy journeys to Valencia, where he resided during the whole of April. The reason of this long sojourn in a provincial town was soon apparent. He was there joined by the Duke del Infantado, and the leading grandees of the kingdom, as well as many of the chief prelates. Meanwhile the Cortes, who had testified the greatest joy at the deliverance of the king, refused to ratify the Treaty of Valençay, as having been concluded without their consent—continued resident at Madrid, without advancing to meet their sovereign—and soon began to evince their imperious disposition, and to show in whom they understood the real sovereignty to reside. At the moment when Ferdinand re-entered his kingdom, they published of their own authority a decree, in which they enjoined him to adopt, without delay, the Constitution of 1812, and to take the oath of fidelity toward it. Until he did so, he was enjoined not to adopt the title, or exercise the power, of King of Spain; and they even went so far as to prescribe the itinerary he was to follow on his route to the capital, the towns he was to pass through, and the expressions he was to use in answer to the addresses he was expected to receive. It is not surprising that he turned aside from such taskmasters.[1]

<small>29. Ferdinand's arrival in Spain, and treatment by the Cortes.</small>

<small>1 Decree, March 20, 1814; Martignac, 107; Ann. Reg. 1814, 47, 68.</small>

Scarcely had the monarch set his foot in Spain when he received the most unequivocal proofs of the detestation in which the constitution was generally held, and the universal hatred at the subordinate agents to whom the Cortes had intrusted the practical administration of government. From the frontier of Catalonia, to Valencia—in the fortresses, the towns, the villages, the fields—it was one continual clamor against the Cortes: "Viva el Rey Assoluto," was the universal cry. The King was literally besieged with petitions, addresses, and memorials, in which he was supplicated, in the most earnest terms, to annul all that had been done during his captivity, and to reign as his ancestors had done before him. The constitution was represented—and with truth—as the work of a mere revolutionary junta in Cadiz, in a great measure self-elected, and never convoked either from the whole country or according to the ancient constitution of the kingdom. There was not a municipality which did not hold this language as he passed through their walls; not a village which did not present to him a petition, signed by the most respectable inhabitants, to the same effect. The generals, the army, the garrisons, besieged him with addresses of the same description. The minority of the Cortes, consisting of sixty-nine members, presented a supplication beseeching the king to annul the whole proceedings of their body, and to reign as his fathers had done. From one end of the kingdom to the other but one voice was heard, that of reprobation of the Cortes and the constitution, and prayers to the king to resume the unfettered functions of royalty.[2]

<small>29. Universal unpopularity of the Cortes.</small>

<small>2 Martignac, 108; 109; Ann Reg. 1814, 68; Chateaub. Congrès de Vérone, i. 26, 27.</small>

Impelled in this manner by the unanimous voice of the nation, not less than his own secret inclination, to annul the constitution, and grasp anew the sceptre of his ancestors, Ferdinand ventured on the decisive act. On the 4th May, 1814, appeared the famous decree of Valencia, which at once annulled the whole acts of the

<small>30. Decree of Valencia, May 4, 1814.</small>

<small>* History of Europe, 1789–1815, chap. lxxxvii. § 71.</small>

Cortes, and restored absolute government over the whole of Spain. In it the king, after recapitulating briefly the principal events which had occurred in the Peninsula since his treacherous seizure and captivity by Napoleon in 1808, declared that he had, by a decree of 5th May in that year, convoked the Cortes; but the French invasion prevented it from being assembled, and compelled the several provinces to elect juntas, and severally provide for their own defense. "An extraordinary Cortes," said the monarch, "was subsequently convoked in the island of Leon, when nearly the whole country was in the hands of the French, consisting of 57 proprietors, 104 deputies, and 47 supplementary members,* without either the nobles or the clergy being summoned to their deliberations, and convoked in a manner wholly illegal and without a precedent, even in the most critical and stormy days of the monarchy. The first step of this illegal assembly was to usurp the whole powers of sovereignty on the very first day of their installation, and to strip me of nearly my whole prerogatives; and their next, to impose on Spain the most arbitrary laws, and compel it to receive a new constitution, unsanctioned either by the provinces, the provincial juntas, or the Indies. By this constitution was established, not any thing resembling the ancient constitution, but a republican form of government, presided over by a chief magistrate, deprived alike of consideration and power, and framed entirely on the principle and form of the democratic French constitution of 1791. Force alone compelled the members to swear to the constitution: the Bishop of Orense refused to take the oath, and Spain knows what was the fate of that respectable prelate.

"Nothing has consoled me amidst so many calamities, but the innumerable proofs of the loyalty of my faithful subjects, who longed for my arrival, in the hope that it might terminate the oppression under which they groaned, and restore the true happiness of the country. I promise—I swear to you, true and loyal Spaniards—that your hopes shall not be deceived. Your sovereign places his chief glory in being the chief of a heroic nation, which, by its immortal exploits, has won the admiration of the whole world, and at the same time preserved its own liberty and honor. *I detest, I abhor despotism:* it can never be reconciled neither with civilization, or the lights of the other nations in Europe. The kings never have been despots in Spain; neither the sovereign nor the constitution of the country have ever authorized despotism, although unhappily it has sometimes been practiced, as it has been in all ages by fallible mortals. Abuses have existed in Spain, not because it had no constitution, but from the fault of persons or circumstances. To guard against such abuses in future, so far as human prudence can go, while preserving the honor and rights of royalty (for it has its own as well as the people have theirs, which are equally inviolable), *I will treat with the deputies of Spain and the Indies in a Cortes legally assembled,* composed of the one and the other, as soon as I can

31. King's declaration in favor of freedom, and promise to convoke a legal Cortes.

convoke them, after having re-established the wise customs of the nation, established with the consent of the kings our august predecessors. Thus shall be established, in a solid and legitimate manner, all that can tend to the good of my kingdoms, in order that my subjects may live happy and tranquil under the protection of our religion and our sovereign, the only foundation for the happiness of a king and a kingdom which are rightly styled Catholic. *No time shall be lost in taking the proper measures for the assembly of the Cortes,* which I trust will insure the happiness of my subjects in both hemispheres." The decree concluded with declaring the resolution of the king not to accept the constitution; to annul all the acts of the Cortes; and declaring all persons guilty of high treason, and punishable with death, who should attempt by word, deed, or incitement, to establish the constitution, or resist the execution of the present decree.[1]

[1] Decree, May 4, 1814; Arch. Diplom. iii. 64, 69.

No words can describe the universal transport with which this decree was received, or the loyal enthusiasm which the prospect of the re-establishment of the ancient constitution and customs of the monarchy excited in the nation. The joy was universal: it resembled that of the English when they awoke from the tyranny of the long Parliament and Cromwell to the bright morning of the Restoration. The journey of Ferdinand from Valencia to Madrid was the exact counterpart of that of Charles II. from Dover to London, a hundred and fifty-three years before. It was a continual triumph. In vain the Cortes assumed a menacing aspect, and, in a tumultuous and stormy meeting, adopted the most violent resolutions to resist the royal authority, and to declare traitors, and punish as such, all who should aid the king in his criminal designs. Physical force was awanting to support their resistance. The troops which they sent out to withstand the royal cortége were the first to array themselves in its ranks, amidst loud cheers and cries of "Viva el Rey Assoluto!" Every where the pillar of the constitution was overthrown and broken; enthusiastic crowds, wherever he passed on the journey to Madrid, saluted the returning monarch; and the Cortes, deserted by all, even their own ushers, in utter dismay fled across New Castile toward Cadiz. Some remained, and were thrown into prison. It was on the 13th May that the king, surrounded by a loyal and enthusiastic crowd, which, as he approached the capital, was swelled to above a hundred thousand persons, and amidst the universal and heartfelt acclamations of his subjects, entered Madrid, and reascended the throne of his fathers.[2]

32. Universal transports in Spain at this decree, and the king's return to Madrid, May 13.

[2] Martignac, 119, 121; Ann. Reg. 1814, 70, 71; Chateaubriand, Congres de Verone, i. 27, 28.

Thus fell the work of the Cortes—the Constitution of 1812, the victim of its own violence, folly, and injustice. Happy if it had never been revived, and become, in consequence of that very violence and injustice, the watchword of the revolutionary party all over the world! Hitherto the proceedings of the king had been

33. Reflections on this event, and the obvious course which lay open to the king.

---

* Members chosen in the Isle of Leon, to represent the provinces in the hands of the French.

entirely just, i.b.i and such as must command the assent of all the liberals, not only of order, but of freedom, throughout the world. The constitution which had been overthrown was not only an object of horror to the vast majority of the nation, but had been imposed upon it by a small minority, whose ideas and designs were not less threatening to the interests than repugnant to the habits of the people. It was the work of a self-elected knot of revolutionists at Cadiz, whose object was to secure to themselves the real government of the country, strip the Crown of all its prerogatives, and divide the whole offices and patronage of the country among themselves. The king had pledged his royal word that he would without delay assemble the Cortes, convoked according to the ancient laws and customs of the country, and with their aid commence the formation of laws and the reformation of abuses, which might secure the happiness of his subjects in both hemispheres. It was a matter of little difficulty in Spain, whatever it might be elsewhere, to effect such a reformation; for its ancient constitutions contained all the elements of real freedom, and its inhabitants could tread the path of improvement in the securest of all ways, without deviating into that of innovation.*

Chateaub. Congrès de Verone, 1. 18, 19.

34. Ferdinand's despotic measures. Re-establishment of the Inquisition.

But Ferdinand did not do this, and thence have arisen boundless calamities to his country, lasting opprobrium to himself. He resumed the sceptre of his ancestors and reigned as an absolute monarch; but he forgot all the promises, so solemnly made, to reign with the aid of a Cortes assembled according to the ancient laws and customs of the realm. He fell immediately under the direction of a camarilla composed of priests and nobles, who incessantly represented to him that there could in Spain be no constitutional government, and that the only way to secure either the stability of the throne or the welfare of the kingdom, was to restore every thing to the condition in which it was before the Revolution. He was not slow in following their advice. Disregarding a patriotic and moderate address from the University of Salamanca, in which he was prayed to follow up the gracious intentions professed in the declaration from Valencia, of convoking a Cortes, and establishing with their concurrence the laws which were to govern the kingdom, he re-established by a decree from Madrid *the Inquisition*, and as a natural consequence recalled the Pope's nuncio, who had left the country on its abolition by the

July 21.

* It is a curious and instructive circumstance how it was that the ancient elements of freedom were lost in Spain; Chateaubriand thus explains it: "Les premières auxquelles les députés du Tiers assistèrent, furent celles de Léon en 1188; cette date prouve que les Espagnols marchaient à la tête des peuples libres. Peu à peu les bourgeois fatigués laissaient le souverain payer leurs mandataires, et de signer les villes aptes à la députation. Douze cités seulement en obtinrent le droit. Charles V. tyran, naturellement ligué avec son collègue cet autre tyran, le peuple, éleva les villes représentées à vingt; mais en même temps, dans la réunion de Tolède, en 1585, il retrancha pour toujours des Cortès le Clergé et la Noblesse. Les rois, débarrassés du joug des Cortès, furent contraints de s'en imposer d'autres. Des conseils ou des conseillers dirigeaient la monarchie."—CHATEAUBRIAND, *Congrès de Verone*, tom. 19. See also *Historia d'España*, viii. 471. Madrid, 1851.

Cortes. The use of torture, however, in all the civil tribunals, was prohibited by a decree soon after; and in a memorial to the Pope by the Spanish government it was proposed to abolish it also in the dungeons of the Inquisition, and various regulations were submitted for mitigating the severity of that terrible tribunal. These proposals were carried into effect; and thereafter its proceedings were confined to a species of police surveillance over opinions, to check the progress of heresy, but without the frightful tortures which had characterized its secret, or the *Autos-da-fé* which had forever disgraced its public proceedings.[1]

Aug. 3.

[1] Ann. Reg. 1814, 71, 72; Moniteur, Aug. 1 and 15, 1814.

The open assumption of absolute power by the Government, the delay in convoking the Cortes, and, above all, the re-establishment of the Inquisition, excited the utmost alarm in the liberal party throughout Spain, and spread great dissatisfaction even among the officers of the army, by whose support alone they could be carried into effect. Symptoms of disturbance soon appeared in various quarters; for in Spain the habits of the people are so independent, and danger or life are so little regarded, that from dissatisfaction to hostility, as with the Bedouins, is but a step. The roads in the whole of Estremadura, the Castiles, Andalusia, Aragon, and Catalonia, were so infested by bands of guerrillas, who, long inured to violence and rapine, had now become mere robbers and bandits, that the captains-general of those provinces were enjoined to take the most effectual measures for their suppression; but they had no adequate armed force at their disposal to effect that object. A proclamation by the governor of Andalusia revealed the existence of more serious disturbances, having a decided political tendency, and threatened every person who should be found either speaking or acting against Ferdinand VII. with death, within three days, by the sentence of a court-martial. A great number of arrests took place soon after in Madrid—ninety persons were apprehended in a single night; and so numerous did the prisoners soon become that the ordinary places of confinement would not contain them, and the spacious convent of San Francisco was converted into a vast state prison, to embrace the increasing multitude.[2]

35. Discontent in various quarters.

Aug. 7.

[2] Ann. Reg. 1814, 73, 75; Moniteur des Es-poz y Mina, II. 166, 169.

These proceedings excited the greatest consternation among the liberals, and great numbers of persons who deemed themselves compromised fled across the Pyrenees into France. Among the rest, the famous ESPOZ Y MINA, who had gained such great celebrity as a partisan chief in Navarre in the war with Napoleon, fell under the suspicion of the Government, who sent him an order, on the 16th September, to fix his residence at Pampeluna, and place the troops he had formerly commanded under the orders of the Captain-general of Aragon. Regarding this injunction, as it certainly was, as a decided measure of hostility, this daring chief, at the head of the 1st Regiment of Volunteers, approached that fortress in the night of the 26th. They were provided with scaling-ladders, and acted in concert with the 4th Regiment, then in

36. Revolt of Mina in Navarre, Sept. 26.

garrison in the city, by whom Mina was admitted into the fortress, and with the officers of which he spent a part of the night on the ramparts, expecting a movement in his favor. Although the greater part of the officers, however, had been engaged in the conspiracy, the private soldiers nearly all remained faithful; and in Mina's own regiment of volunteers they sent information to the governor of Aragon of what was in agitation, and warned him to be on his guard. The consequence was, that the attempt proved abortive; Mina himself with difficulty made his escape, his troops nearly all deserted him, and he deemed himself fortunate in being able to retire to France by Puente la Reyna—thus seeking refuge among the enemies whom he had so strenuously combated, from the king he had so powerfully aided in putting on the throne.[1]

¹ Memorias del Espoy Mina, ii. 168, 169; Moniteur, Oct. 9, 1814; Ann. Reg. 1814, 75, 77.

This abortive insurrection, as is ever the case in such circumstances, strengthened the hands and increased the rigor of the monarch. It soon appeared that the restoration of the absolute government, and the chief privileges of the nobles, had been resolved on by the camarilla which ruled the State. Already, on 15th September, a decree had been issued restoring the feudal and seignorial privileges of the nobles, which had been abolished by a decree of the Cortes on 6th August, 1811; and this was soon followed up by the still more decisive step of reinvesting the council of the Mesta with its old and ruinous right of permitting its flocks to pasture at will over the downs in Leon, Estremadura, and the two Castiles, thus rendering the inclosure of the land or the improvement of the soil impracticable. On 14th October, on occasion of the king's going to the theatre of Madrid, an amnesty for State offenders was published, which professed to be general, but contained so many exceptions that in reality was little more than nominal; and the resolution of the Government to extinguish any thing like free discussion in the kingdom was evinced by the king in person arresting and committing to prison M. de Macanay, the Minister of Justice and of the Interior. Soon after, the state prisoners at Madrid were sentenced, some to ten, some to six, and some to two years of the galleys, or of imprisonment in strong castles; and they included the editors of, or contributors to, the *Redacta General*, and principal liberal journals published at Madrid.[2]

37. Fresh arbitrary decrees of Ferdinand. Sept. 15.

Nov. 7.

Dec. 17. ² Moniteur, Nov. 11, and Dec. 25, 1814; Ann. Reg. 1814, 77, 78.

Open war was now proclaimed by the Spanish Government against the liberals of all grades, and, unhappily, the violence of the Government kept pace with the increasing desire of the inhabitants of the great towns for constitutional privileges. As it had now become a matter of imminent danger to hazard such opinions in public, the liberal leaders had recourse to the usual resource of a zealous and determined party under such circumstances. Secret societies were formed under the direction of the chiefs of their party, and the ancient and venerable order of freemasons was laid hold of as a cover for designs against the Government.

38. Further violent proceedings of the king, and Porlier's revolt.

The Inquisition, in consequence, issued a proclamation denouncing these societies; and ere long it appeared that there was too much foundation for their apprehensions. On 18th September, General Porlier, who had greatly signalized himself in the Peninsula, assembled the troops stationed at St. Lucia without the gates of Corunna at night, and suddenly entering the city, the sentinels of which had been gained, put the Captain-general of Galicia, the governor of the town, and a few other persons, under arrest. No sooner was this done than he issued a proclamation, in which he proposed the reassembling of the Cortes, and dismissal of the Ministers; and another, purporting to be from the Provincial Junta of Galicia, under the "presidency of General Porlier, General-commandant of the Interior of the Kingdom."[1]

March 5.

¹ Moniteur, Sept. 29, 1815; Ann. Reg. 1815, 117.

In taking these bold steps, which at once committed him with the Government, the principal reliance of Porlier was on a body of grenadiers and light infantry stationed at St. Iago, which he had reason to believe would join him. Being informed, however, that they hesitated, and that his presence might probably determine them, he set out in haste from Corunna at the head of eight hundred men and four guns, and arrived at a village within four leagues of St. Iago, where he halted to rest his men, who were much fatigued by their march. While there, some emissaries from the convent of St. Iago introduced themselves in disguise among his men, and urged them to arrest their general by the promises of ample rewards in case of success. These promises proved successful. Porlier and his officers were suddenly surrounded and seized by their own men, while reposing in a cabaret in the heat of the day after their march; and the general, being taken back to Corunna, was condemned by a court-martial to be hanged, which sentence was immediately carried into execution. He wrote, on the eve of his death, a pathetic letter to his wife, with a handkerchief steeped in his tears, in which he exhorted her not to afflict herself on account of the species of death to which he was sentenced, since it was dishonorable only to the wicked, but glorious to the virtuous. He met his fate with dignity and resolution. Then began the days of tragedy in Spain, which ere long led to such frightful reprisals on both sides, and for many long years deluged the Peninsula with blood: the unhappy bequest of the insane liberals, who established a constitution utterly repugnant to the vast majority of the people, but eminently attractive to the ardent and generous among the educated classes.[2]

39. Its failure and his death.

Oct. 3.

² Moniteur, Oct. 10, 1815, Ann. Reg 1815, 117.

In the end of August, one Spanish army, under Castaños, crossed the frontier near Perpignan; and another, under the Conde d'Abisbal, the Bidasoa, with the professed design of aiding Louis XVIII. in his contest with the partisans of Napoleon. As that contest had been already decided by the battle of Waterloo and the presence of a million of the allied troops in

40. Invasion of France, and retreat of the Spaniards. Fresh tyrannical acts of the king

Vol. I.—O

France, it may readily be imagined that the presence of the Spanish auxiliaries was any thing but desirable, and accordingly the Duke d'Angoulême, as already mentioned, hastened to the Spanish head-quarters, where he had an interview with Castaños, whom he prevailed on to retire and his retreat on the eastern was soon after followed by that of the Conde d'Abisbal on the western frontier.[1] The people both in Pampeluna and Corunna had taken no part in the attempts of Mina and Porlier; the latter had been publicly thanked by the king for their conduct on the occasion. It was hoped, therefore, that no measures of severity would follow the suppression of these insurrections; and the dismissal, soon after the death of Porlier, of several of the ministers most inclined to arbitrary measures, led to a general hope that a more moderate system was about to be adopted, and that possibly a Cortes convoked according to the ancient customs might be assembled. But these hopes were soon blasted; and before the end of the year the determination of the king to act upon the most arbitrary principles was evinced in the most unequivocal manner. The trial of the liberals who had been arrested in Madrid, among whom were included several of the ministers of state, and most distinguished members of the late Cortes, began in November; but after long proceedings, and a transference of the cases from one tribunal to another, which it was thought might be more subservient to the royal will, the judges of the last reported that the evidence against the accused was not such as to bring them within the laws against traitors or persons exciting tumults and disturbances, which alone authorized severe punishments. Upon receiving this report the king ordered the proceedings to be brought to him, and pronounced sentences of the severest kind, and entirely illegal, on thirty-two of the leading liberals in Spain, which he signed with his own hand. Among these was one of ten years' service, as a common soldier, in a regiment stationed at Ceuta, on the celebrated Señor Arguelles, whose eloquence had so often resounded through the halls of the Cortes; and one of eight years of service *in chains*, in a regiment stationed at Gomera, on Señor Garcia Herreros, formerly Minister of Grace and Justice![2]

Notwithstanding these severities, the situation of the king was very hazardous at Madrid, and secret information soon after reached him, which convinced him that a change in the system of government had become indispensable. The extreme penury of the treasury, from the loss of nearly all the resources derived from South America, and the distracted state of society in Spain after the six years' dreadful war of which the Peninsula had been the theatre, rendered it impossible to maintain the national armaments on any thing like an adequate scale; and if it had been practicable, it was doubtful whether the danger of convulsion would not be thereby increased, since the whole revolts came from the army, and had been organized by its leading officers. The precarious condition of the royal authority was the more strongly felt, that the clergy, though possessed of unbounded influence over their flocks, and invaluable allies in a protracted struggle, had no armed force at their command to meet the rebellious bands of the soldiery, whom the liberal leaders had shown they could so easily array against the Government. The weight of these considerations ere long appeared in a partial change of the ministry. To the surprise of all, there appeared in the *Madrid Gazette* of 28th January, 1816, a decree appointing the celebrated and enlightened Don Pedro de Cevallos to his former office of First Secretary of State, and admitting that his dismissal, on the resumption by the king of the royal authority, had been founded on erroneous information.[*] By the same decree, the cognizance of state offenses was taken from the extraordinary tribunals, by which they had hitherto been tried, and remitted to the ordinary tribunals. This was a great step toward a more just system of administration; and the changed policy of the Court was at the same time evinced by the conferring of honors and offices on the ministers who had formed the cabinet of Don Pedro de Cevallos, though they were not reinstated in the ministry. These advances toward a liberal government, however, had no effect in checking the conspiracies, for one was soon after discovered at Madrid, chiefly among half-pay officers, who had flocked there in great numbers—which, however, was suppressed without any commotion.[1]

It soon appeared, also, that if the liberals were determined on continuing their conspiracies, the king was not less set on rushing headlong into the most arbitrary measures. A severe decree against all persons bearing arms after nightfall was issued on 20th March, and another on 4th December. The discovery of the conspiracy at Madrid was made the pretense for innumerable arrests in every town, and almost every village, in the kingdom, of persons who were found meeting after ten at night; and the utmost terror was struck into the persons apprehended, and their relations, by the information that, on the 19th July, the State prisoners at Ceuta, who embraced most of the members of the late Cortes, had been removed at dead of night, put in irons, and hurried on board a zebeeque, which set sail with them on an unknown destination. In fact, they were conveyed to Port Mahon in Minorca, where it was thought they would be more secure. And about the same time a decree appeared which revealed, in a still more decisive manner, the determination of Government permanently to destroy freedom of thought. Not content with enthralling the present, they aimed at throwing their chains over the future; and a decree issued in July, re-establishing the order

[*] "Considering as unfounded the motives which induced me to order your discharge from the office of my First Secretary of State and of the Cabinet, and being highly satisfied with the zeal, exactitude, and affection with which, in the cruelest times, you have served myself and the State, I reinstate you in the use and exercise of your office, of which you will immediately take charge."—Decree, 26th January, 1816.—*Madrid Gazette.*

of the Jesuits, restoring to them their possessions in so far as they had not been alienated, and intrusting them with the entire direction of education, both male and female, threatened to throw the same chains permanently over the souls of the people.[1]

¹ Decree, July 21, 1816; Moniteur, Aug. 1, 1816; Ann Reg. 1816, 130, 131.

43. Double marriages of the royal families of Spain and Portugal. Sept. 28.

An event occurred in the autumn of this year, which was fondly looked forward to by the persecuted liberals as a harbinger of rest, and that was a double union of the royal families of Spain and Portugal. Ferdinand, who, since the loss of his young and captivating consort in 1808, had been a widower, now resolved to afford a chance for the continuance of the direct line of succession, by entering into a second marriage, and, by the advice of his Council, he determined on making proposals to his niece, the Infanta Maria Isabel Francisca, second daughter of the King of Portugal. At the same time, proposals were made for an alliance between DON CARLOS, the King's younger brother, and the heir-presumptive to the throne, for whom so adventurous a fate was reserved, and the Infanta Maria Francisca de Acis, third daughter of the same sovereign. Both proposals were accepted; and as the princesses were at Rio Janerio, where the royal family of Portugal had been since their flight thither in 1808, when Portugal was first overrun by the French, the Duque del Infantado was sent with a splendid retinue to Cadiz, to receive the princesses on their landing from Brazil. The marriages were both celebrated with great pomp at Madrid on the 28th September; and on this occasion an amnesty, which professed to be general, was published. It contained, however, so many exceptions as practically left it in the power of Government to continue, with scarce any limitation, the oppression of the liberals, for it excluded all persons charged with the following crimes —"Lese majesty, divine and human treason, homicide of priests, blasphemy, coining false money, exporting prohibited articles, resisting the officers of justice, and mal-administration in the exercise of the royal powers." There were few crimes connected with the State which might not, with the aid of a little straining, be brought within some one of these exceptions.[2]

Sept. 28.

² Decree, Sept. 28, 1816; Moniteur, Oct. 5, 1816; Ann. Reg. 1816, 130, 131.

41. Creation of the kingdom of Brazil. Dec. 28, 1815.

An event connected with the Peninsula occurred in the close of the preceding year, and was heard of in Europe in this, strongly illustrative of the vast consequences which were to follow to the most distant parts of the earth from the events following on the French Revolution. On December 28, 1815, the Prince-Regent of Portugal, who had never, since the migration of the royal family, quitted the shores of Brazil, issued a decree, in which, after enumerating the vast extent and boundless capabilities of his dominions in the New World, and the benefits which would result from the entire union of the dominions of the house of Portugal in both hemispheres, he declared that the colony of Brazil should thenceforward be elevated to the RANK OF A KINGDOM; and directed that, in future, Portugal, the two Algarves, and Brazil, shall form one united kingdom, under the title of the "United Kingdom of Portugal, Brazil, and the two Algarves." Thus was monarchy, for the first time, erected by the European race in the New World—an event of the more importance that the immense territories of the house of Braganza in the New World, embracing above four times the area of Old France, were placed alongside of the newly emancipated republics, broken off from the dominions of Spain in the same hemisphere; and thus an opportunity was afforded of demonstrating, by actual experiment, the comparative influence of the monarchical and republican forms of government on the welfare of the species under the climate of South America, and with the Iberian or Celtic family of mankind.[1]

¹ Decree, Dec. 28, 1815; Moniteur, Feb. 16, 1816; Ann. Reg. 1816, 131.

The year 1817 commenced with an insurrection of a more serious character than had yet occurred in the Peninsula. Unlike the preceding, it began, not with the soldiers, but the citizens. A trifling tax on coals excited a tumult in Valencia on the 17th January, which ere long assumed the character of an insurrection. At first the populace were successful; and during the whole of the 17th the city was, with the exception of the barracks, in their possession. They immediately proclaimed the Constitution of 1812; but their triumph was of short duration. General Elio, who commanded the garrison, concentrated his forces; the troops continued faithful; the respectable inhabitants remained in their houses, and took no part in the insurrection; and the populace, meeting with no other support than what they could derive from their own numbers, were at length defeated, but not before much blood had been shed, and General Elio himself wounded. He immediately published a severe decree, denouncing the penalty of death against all persons, except those privileged as cavaliers to carry arms, found with weapons in the dark, and authorizing the patrol to fire upon them. This was soon followed by a decree prohibiting the importation of a great variety of books into Spain, among which the works of Voltaire, Gibbon, and Robertson, Benjamin Constant, and a great many others, are specially mentioned as "false in politics, and to the hierarchical order, subversive of the power of the church, and tending to schism and religious toleration, and pernicious to the state." It was easy to see what influence had been predominant in the preparation of this decree.[2]

45. Insurrection in Valencia. Jan. 17, 1817

March 2.

² Moniteur, Feb. 2, 1817; Ann. Reg. 1817, 117, 118.

Ere long another conspiracy broke out in Barcelona of a very extensive character, in which Generals Lacy and Milans, who had distinguished themselves so much in the late war, were implicated. The object of the conspirators, as of all the preceding ones, was the re-establishment of the Constitution of 1812, and the convoking of the Cortes. It was to have broken out on the night of April 5, and a great number of officers, besides a considerable part of the battalion of the light infantry of Tarragona, were

46. Abortive conspiracy in Barcelona, and death of General Lacy.

April 5.

engaged on the side of the conspirators. Castanos, the captain-general of the province, however, received intelligence of the plot, and arrested Lacy and three hundred officers who were implicated in his designs. He was immediately tried by a court-martial, and sentenced to be shot.¹ Being sent over, however, to Minorca, to have the sentence carried into execution, as it was deemed unsafe to attempt it in Spain, he attempted, when on the beach of that island, and attended only by a slender escort of prisoners, to make his escape. The soldiers pursued him, and in endeavoring to defend himself he was, fortunately for himself, accidentally killed.

<small>¹ Castaños' proclamation, April 12, 1817; Moniteur, May 7, 1817; Ann. Reg. 1847, 118, 123.</small>

A very important papal bull was issued in the same month, regarding the property of the church in Spain. Such had become the penury of the royal treasury, in consequence of the loss of the South American colonies, and the cessation of industry in Spain during the dreadful war of which, for six years, it had been the theatre, that it had become absolutely necessary to have recourse to some extraordinary resources, and the church, as the body which was most tractable and capable of bearing such a burden, was selected to make up the deficiency. A negotiation in consequence was opened with the court of Rome, to which the necessity of the case was fully represented, and the consequence was, that on the 16th April a papal bull was issued, which, on the narrative of the "enormous expenses at which we have had the satisfaction of seeing an extremely glorious victory gained, as well for religion as the monarchy, authorized Ferdinand to exact annually, during six years, the sum of 30,000,000 reals (£300,000) from the estates of the church, as well regular as secular." This was an immense relief to the treasury, but, great as it appears, it was not more than sufficient to fill up the annual deficit which had been constantly increasing since the restoration. Such as it was, however, it led to incalculable calamities, both to the nation and the monarchy.²

<small>47. Papal bull regarding the contributions by the Spanish Church, April 16.</small>

<small>² Moniteur, April 29, 1817; Ann. Reg. 1817, 120, 121.</small>

The King of Spain had certain claims on the part of the Infanta, Queen of Etruria, on the states of Parma, Placentia, and Guastalla, which had been made the subject of anxious claim and negotiation at the Congress of Vienna in 1815, and subsequently with the allied powers. Such were the difficulties with which the question was involved that it led to a very protracted negotiation, which was not brought to a conclusion till this year, when a treaty was concluded, by which, on the one hand, Spain was admitted into the European alliance and the treaties signed at the Congress of Vienna; and, on the other, the reversion of the duchies of Parma, Placentia, and Guastalla was secured to the Infant Don Carlos Louis, the Infanta's son; and until that reversion opened, the states of Lucca were assigned to her majesty the Queen of Etruria. It is in virtue of this treaty that the present Duke of Parma, who married the daughter of the Duke de Berri, now enjoys the duchy of Parma.¹

<small>48. Treaty regarding the Queen of Etruria.</small>

<small>¹ Treaty, May 5, 1817; Martens' Sup. vii. 122; Ann. Reg. 1817, 121.</small>

In the close of this year the negotiations, so long and anxiously conducted on the part of the British government, for the suppression of the slave trade, were brought to a successful issue with Spain. By it the King of Spain prohibited, absolutely and immediately, all purchase of negroes in Africa north of the line, and denounced ten years' transportation against whoever should infringe the present decree. Leave was to be given, however, to purchase slaves south of the line, to such as might apply for a license to that effect, until the 30th May, 1820, when it was to cease absolutely and for ever in the Spanish dominions in every part of the world. Foreign vessels trading to Spanish ports were to be subject to the same regulations, in every respect, as the Spanish. This decree was only extorted from Spain with great difficulty by the British government, by the engagement, as already mentioned, on their part, to pay to Spain £400,000 for the abolition, on 20th Feb. 1818, which was punctually done.¹ It is a singular circumstance, as creditable to the English as it was discreditable to the Spanish government, that the one consented to give and the other to receive so considerable a sum for an act called for by every consideration of humanity and justice.² It will appear in the sequel how entirely both parties to this treaty departed from the object it had in view, and how the one, by its fiscal policy, restored the slave trade to a frightful extent, and the other, by repeated evasions, continued to practice it until it arose to the enormous amount of from fifty to seventy thousand slaves annually sent into Cuba alone.

<small>49. Treaty for the limitation of the slave trade. Dec. 20, 1817.</small>

<small>¹ Ante, c. iv. § 45.</small>

<small>² Decree, Dec. 20, 1817; Moniteur, Jan. 5, 1818; Parl. Deb. xxxvii. 67, xxxviii. 666; Decree, Dec. 1817; Ann. Reg. 1817, 123.</small>

The internal situation of Spain had not sensibly ameliorated during the years the transactions of which have been now briefly enumerated. The Inquisition had spread its leaden arms over the kingdom, and crushed any approach to independent thought; the severance of South America had dried up the principal sources of its material industry. The army, in great part without pay, always long in arrears, was with difficulty held to its standards, and the effective strength of the regiments exhibited a very different return from the rolls on paper. So great had the dilapidation of the military force of the kingdom become, from the penury of the Exchequer, and discontent and desertion of the troops, that by a decree on June 1, its organization was entirely changed, and they were divided into forty-seven regiments of common and light infantry, twenty-two regiments of cavalry, five thousand artillery, two regiments of guards: in all, seventy thousand men, to which were to be added forty-three regiments of provincial militia, which mustered about thirty thousand combatants. As to the navy, it had fallen into such a state of decay, that the power which, two hundred and thirty years before, had fitted out the invincible Armada, and planted such magnificent colonies in the Indies, and even in later times had all but rivalled the power of England upon the seas, was unable to fit out a fleet to trans-

<small>50. Miserable state of Spain: its army and navy.</small>

<small>June 1.</small>

port the military succors which were so loudly called for to the New World. In this extremity the Government, with the money extorted the preceding year from the priests, *bought a squadron of old worn-out line-of-battle ships from Russia*, to which Alexander, out of pure generosity, added three frigates in a present. Such, however, was their state of decay that they took five months to make the voyage from Cronstadt to Cadiz, and had to put into Plymouth to refit.¹ At length the squadron arrived at Cadiz, on 21st February, and two thousand men were embarked on board of it for Lima.

¹ Ann Historique, i. 301, 302.

51. Extreme penury of the finances of Spain. Decree, April 3, 1818.

The extreme penury of the finances, in consequence of the loss of the mines of South America to the Government, and its commerce to the country, was the cause of this woeful state of decrepitude—a memorable proof of the straits to which even the greatest naval power may be reduced by the severance of its colonies. The government was overwhelmed with demands for payment of debts by foreign countries, when by no possible contrivance could they raise money to pay their own armaments. The most pressing part of the debt consisted of 1,500,000,000 reals (£14,500,000), composed of *vales*, a species of assignats issued in former times by the treasury. The Cortes had provided for the payment of the interest of this debt by assignation of the property of the Inquisition; but as the restoration of the property of that body left nothing for the creditors, the minister of finance, by a decree on 3d April, reduced the debts to a third of their amount, and made provision for the interest of that third from the estates of the Church. By another decree, Corunna, Santander, Cadiz, and Alicante were declared free ports—a vain attempt to restore the commerce to which the loss of the colonies had brought total ruin. A manifesto was prepared, and submitted in the end of the year to the Congress of Aix la Chapelle, to be addressed to the revolted colonies, which promised them an amnesty for the past, reformation of abuses, and a certain degree of freedom of commerce. It was approved of and published, but proved of no avail with men resolutely set upon asserting their independence.²

March 30.

Sept. 14.

² An. Hist. i. 306, 310; Ann. Reg. 1818, 129, 161.

52. Death of Queen Maria Isabella of Spain. Dec. 26.

An event occurred in the close of this year, which, in its final results, was attended with most important effects upon both kingdoms of the Peninsula. On 26th December, the young Queen Maria Isabella, who had arrived from Brazil in the autumn of 1817, to share the fortunes of the King of Spain, and who was very near her time, was suddenly seized with convulsions, and expired in twenty minutes. The infant was delivered after the mother's death by the Cæsarean operation, but it expired, after being baptized, in a few minutes after its mother. Being a female, it could not have succeeded by the existing law, sanctioned by all the powers of Europe at the treaty of Utrecht, to the crown of Spain;³ but this bereavement, by leaving the king to marry again, which, as will appear in the sequel, he actually did, was attended with consequences of the last moment to the Peninsula, and of general interest to the whole of Europe. This death was almost immediately followed by that of the old King, Charles IV., who had been forced to resign the crown at Bayonne in 1808, who expired at Naples on 20th January, 1819, a few weeks after his Queen, Louisa Maria Theresa of Parma, had died on the road to that place.¹

³ An. Hist. i. 310.

¹ Ibid. ii. 381, 382; Moniteur, Jan. 20, 1819.

53. Disastrous fate of the first expedition to Lima.

Meanwhile the preparations for the grand expedition to South America, which had been so long in preparation, went on without intermission; although the fate which befell the advanced guard of two frigates, with two thousand men, dispatched in the preceding year, was not such as to afford very encouraging hopes of its ultimate success. The soldiers and crew on board one of the frigates mutinied, threw the officers overboard, and sailed into Buenos Ayres, where they were received with open arms by the insurgents, whom they immediately joined. The other was captured off the coast of Peru by the insurgent squadron, and eight thousand muskets which it had on board were immediately appropriated to their use. Undeterred by these disasters, however, the Government continued their preparations for the grand expedition with the utmost activity; and by the middle of January fifteen thousand men were collected in the Isle of Leon, and six ships of the line, in a tolerable state of equipment for the voyage.²

² An. Reg. 1819, 179; Ann. Hist. i. 310, 311, ii. 382, 383.

54. Fresh revolt at Valencia, which is suppressed Jan. 21.

The disorganized state of all parts of Spain, however, still continued, and the repeated revolts which broke out, especially among the soldiery, might have warned the Government that a serious disaster was impending over the monarchy, and that the great armament in the Isle of Leon was not likely to sail without making its strength felt by the Government. On the 21st January a fresh conspiracy was discovered by General Elio in Valencia, the object of which was to assassinate him and his principal officers, and immediately proclaim the Constitution of 1812. At its head was Colonel Vidal, who made a vigorous defense against the soldiers sent to arrest him, and was only made prisoner after he had been run through the body. He himself was hanged, and his associates, to the number of twelve, shot from behind, the punishment reserved for traitors. This event had a melancholy effect upon the fate of the prisoners at Barcelona, who had been implicated in General Lacy's revolt in the preceding year. They were condemned to death to the number of seventeen, and executed without mercy. Disturbances at the same time broke out in New Castile, Estremadura, and Andalusia, the roads of which were infested by bands of old guerrillas, who formed themselves into bands of robbers, amounting to three hundred men. But all these disorders were ere long thrown into the shade by the great revolt which broke out among the troops in the Isle of Leon, which was attended with the most important consequences on both hemispheres.³

³ An. Hist. ii. 384, 385; Ann. Reg. 1819, 178, 179.

Such had been the penury of the exchequer, and the state of dilapidation into which the once magnificent arsenals and dockyards of Cadiz had fallen, that the fitting-out of the expedition, after two years' incessant preparation, was still incomplete. Two ships of the line and a frigate were dispatched on 11th May, to clear the coasts of America of the insurgent corsairs who infested them; but one of these—the Alexander—was obliged, a few days after, to return to Cadiz to refit. During the long delay occasioned by these difficulties, the troops collected for the expedition, which by the end of May amounted to twenty-two thousand men—a force perfectly capable of effecting the subjugation of South America, had it arrived in safety at its destination—were left concentrated and inactive in the island of Leon. During the leisure and monotony of a barrack life they had leisure to confer together, to compare the past and present condition of their country, and ruminate on the probable fate which awaited themselves if they engaged in the warfare of South America. A large number of veterans, who had served under Murillo in those disastrous campaigns, not a few of whom were in the public hospitals suffering under severe mutilations, gave the most dismal accounts of the dreadful nature of the warfare on which they were about to be sent, the ferocious enemies with which they had to contend—the English veterans trained under Wellington, who formed so large a part of the insurgent forces—the interminable deserts they had to cross, the pestilential gales, so fatal to European constitutions, with which the country was infested, and the frightful warfare, where quarter was neither asked nor given on either side, which awaited them on their arrival. A proclamation of the king, issued on 4th January, in which it was announced that no quarter would be given to any soldiers of foreign nations found combating in the insurgent ranks, rather increased than diminished these alarms, by proving the reality of one of the many, and not the least formidable, of the dangers which were represented as awaiting them.¹

To these considerations, already sufficiently powerful, were added the efforts of the merchants and revolutionists of Cadiz, who spared neither their talents nor their riches to induce the assembled troops to abandon their duty and revolt against the Government. They painted to them in the most gloomy colors the disastrous state of the country, with its colonies lost, its trade ruined, its exchequer bankrupt, its noblest patriots in captivity or in chains, its bravest generals shot, its liberties destroyed, the Inquisition restored, the public education in the hands of the Jesuits, an inconsistent camarilla, fluctuating in every thing except evil, ruling alike the monarch and the country. They professed the utmost respect for the king, and the firmest determination to protect his person and just authority: the only object was to displace a ministry, the worst enemy he had in his dominions, and restore the Cortes, the only security for their prosperity and just administration. To these considerations, in themselves sufficiently just and powerful, was added the gold of the Cadiz merchants, who hoped, by frustrating the expedition, to succeed in re-establishing peace with the colonies, and regaining the lucrative commerce they had so long enjoyed with them. The result was, that, before the time arrived when the expedition could by possibility set sail, the whole army was imbued with revolutionary ideas, and only awaited the signal of a leader to declare openly against the Government, and avert the much dreaded departure for South America.¹

The CONDE D'ABISBAL, formerly General O'Donnell, of Irish extraction, who had distinguished himself in Catalonia during the late war, was at the head of the expedition. He was a man of a bold and enterprising character, and possessed of such powers of dissimulation that those most entirely, as they thought, in his confidence, were not in the slightest degree aware of what he really intended. He had at first entered cordially into the designs of the conspirators, and their principal hopes of success were founded on his heading the enterprise. For a long time he adopted the views of the disaffected, and from the knowledge which they had of this, he gained unlimited influence over the minds of the soldiers. But when the decisive moment arrived, the deep dissimulation of the man became apparent. In the night of the 7th July, when the conspiracy was on the point of breaking out, the Conde d'Abisbal assembled the garrison of Cadiz, six thousand strong, which was entirely at his devotion, and without revealing to them what he intended to do, informed them that he was about to lead them on a short expedition, of which the success was certain, and which would entitle them to the highest rewards from their sovereign and country; but he required them to bind themselves by an oath to obey his orders, whatever they were. The soldiers, ignorant of his design, but having confidence in his intention, at once took the oath, and as soon as this was done he led them into the camp "des Victoires," where seven thousand men, destined to be first embarked, were assembled.²

These troops were ordered to assemble in parade order, and no sooner was this done than d'Abisbal stationed his men round them in such positions as to render escape impossible, and then, ordering the soldiers to load their muskets and the artillerymen their pieces, he summoned the men to lay down their arms, and deliver up the officers contained in a list which he had prepared. Resistance was impossible, as the men who were surrounded had no ammunition, and they were compelled to submit. A hundred and twenty-three officers, comprising the chiefs of the army, were put under arrest, a part of the troops sent out of the camp, and dispersed through villages of Andalusia, and three thousand compelled to embark and set sail they knew not whither. In fact, their destination was the Havana, where they arrived in safety six weeks afterward. Having by these extraordinary means gained this great success, succeeded in arresting his comrades, and crushing a conspiracy of which he himself had been the chief, D'Abisbal hastened to Madrid, where he took credit to himself for having at once defeated a dangerous conspiracy, and compelled a mutinous body of soldiers to obey orders,[1] and proceed on their destination. He was received with the greatest distinction at Court, decorated with the great ribbon of the order of Charles III.; and his second in command, General Saarsfield, who had powerfully seconded him in his enterprise, promoted to the rank of lieutenant-general.

[1] Martignae, i. 180; Ann. Hist. 389; Ann. Reg. 1819, 179, 180.

59. D'Abisbal is deprived of the command of the expedition.

But these flattering appearances were of short duration, and the discovery of the conspiracy proved entirely fatal to the expedition, with the exception of the three thousand who, in the first stupor of astonishment, had been hurried on board, and sent off to the Havana. The Government had become, with reason, so distrustful of the troops that they no longer ventured to keep them together, or in the neighborhood of Cadiz; and sinister rumors ere long reached Madrid as to the share which the Conde d'Abisbal had had, as well as his second in command, in the conspiracy. The consequence was that they were both called to the capital, under pretense of giving personal information on so dangerous an affair; and while there they were deprived of their commands, and the direction of the expedition intrusted to the Conde de Calderon, a veteran of seventy years of age. D'Abisbal was too powerful a man, however, to be brought to judgment; and, to the surprise of every one, this scene of dissimulation and hypocrisy on both sides was brought to a close by a decree, which, after reciting the great services he had rendered to his country, appointed him Captain-general of Andalusia, President of the Audience of Seville, and Governor of Cadiz.[2]

Aug. 6. [2] Ann. Hist. ii. 389, 390; Martignae, i. 181.

60. Additional measures of severity on the part of the Government.

But although every thing was thus smooth on the surface, D'Abisbal was far from having really regained the confidence of the Government, and they were daily thrown into greater consternation by the discoveries made as to the extent of the conspiracy, and the share which the new captain-general had had in fomenting it. Great numbers of officers were arrested; but the Government did not venture on the hazardous step of bringing them to justice. They took the opportunity, however, of acting with extreme severity in other quarters. Ten officers who had been arrested for their accession to Portier's conspiracy in Galicia in 1815, and had remained in prison ever since, were ordered to be executed *par contumace*, twenty were sent to the galleys, and twenty-five imprisoned for various periods. Additional levies of troops ordered in Galicia and Catalonia, the mountaineers of which provinces were deemed attached to the royal cause. General Elio adopted the most rigorous measures, and even made use of torture, to discover the traces of a conspiracy which was suspected to exist in Valencia, and to implicate a large number of the most respectable citizens; and every effort was made to prevent the introduction of French books across the Pyrenees, by which it was suspected the minds of the soldiers and people had been chiefly corrupted. But these measures of precaution proved ineffectual: the importation of foreign revolutionary books continued, and the concentration of the troops in the great towns, where the principal danger was apprehended, left the provinces open to the incursions of armed bands which infested the roads, and, in some instances, openly proclaimed the constitution.[1]

[1] An. Hist. ii. 391, 392; Ann. Reg. 1819, 180, 181.

61. Yellow fever at Cadiz. Aug. 20.

Still, however, the preparations for the expedition continued at Cadiz; but in the course of the autumn a fresh difficulty arose, which proved insurmountable. In the end of July, a dangerous epidemic broke out at Cadiz, which soon spread from the hospitals to the crews of the ships, and the troops in garrison, or in the adjoining camps in the Isle of Leon; and though the punishment of the galleys was, in the first instance, threatened to the physician who gave it its true appellation, on the 20th of August a proclamation of the commander *ad interim* of the expedition, Don Blaise-Foumas, announced the true character of the disease, which was the yellow fever, though it was disguised under the name of the *typhus icterodis*. In spite of all the precautions which could be taken, the progress of the malady was very rapid, especially among the indigent and crowded population of that great seaport. Ten thousand were soon seized with the disorder—the hospitals were full—the deaths rose to a hundred a day; and the soldiers, seized with a sudden panic, mutinied against their officers, burst through the barriers of the quarantine which had been established round the island of Leon, and, spreading to the number of nine thousand over the adjoining villages of Andalusia, carried the seeds of real contagion and the terrors of imaginary danger wherever they went. So far did the alarm spread that the most rigorous measures were adopted, to prevent any communication between Andalusia and New Castile; a sanitary junta of eighty persons was established at Madrid to prevent the contagion spreading to the capital; and a decree published, denouncing the punishment of death against any person who should enter the capital, without a certificate of health, from the infected province.[2]

[2] An. Hist. ii. 391, 392; Ann. Reg. 1819, 180.

62. Sale of Florida to the Americans. Feb. 22.

While these events, fraught with incalculable, and then unforeseen, consequences to both hemispheres, were in progress in Spain, its Government was actively engaged in diplomatic negotiations of the most important character. The extreme penury of the exchequer compelled them to have recourse to every imaginable device to replenish it: one thought of was the sale of the Floridas to the Americans, which was effected, under color of determining the limits of the two countries, by a treaty signed at Washington on 22d February. By this treaty the Americans acquired the whole territories known by the name of the Floridas, between the Mississippi and the Gulf of Mexico—a territory of vast extent, and in great part of surpassing fertility. The price, disguised under the name of discharging claims on the Spanish Government, was to be 5,000,000 dollars (£1,250,000). Some difficulties arose about the ratification of this treaty by the Spanish government, on the ground of a predatory expedition, alleged by the Spaniards to have been connived at by the American government, into the province of TEXAS. At length, however, these difficulties were adjusted, and the cession took place. Thus while Spain, in the last stage of decrepitude, was losing some of its colonies by domestic revolt, and others by sales to foreign states, the great and rising republic of America was acquiring the fragments of its once boundless dominions, and spreading its mighty arms into further provinces, the scene of war and appropriation in future times. One of the most interesting things in history is the unbroken succession of events which obtains in human affairs, and the manner in which the occurrences, apparently trivial, of one age, are linked in indissoluble connection with changes the most important in another.[1]

_{1 Treaty,
Feb. 22,
1819; Message to
Congress,
Dec. 7,
1819; Ann.
Hist. ii.
597, 601.}

Anxious, if possible, to continue the direct line of succession, the king, after the death of his former queen, did not long remain a widower. On 12th of August a proclamation announced to the astonished inhabitants of Madrid that the king had solicited in marriage the hand of the Princess Maria Josephine Amelia, niece of the Elector of Saxony, and been accepted. The marriage was solemnized by proxy at Dresden on the same day, and the young queen set out immediately for Spain. She arrived at the Bidassoa on 2d October, and at Madrid on the 19th of the same month, when she made her public entry into Madrid on the day following, amidst the discharges of artillery, rolling of drums, clang of trumpets, and every demonstration of public joy. But it was of bad augury for the married couple that the very day before an edict had been published, denouncing the penalty of death against any one coming in from the infected districts in the south. An amnesty was published on occasion of the marriage; but as, like the former, it excluded all persons charged with political offences, it had no effect in allaying the anxiety of the public mind.[2]

_{63.
Marriage
of the king.
Aug. 12.}

_{Oct. 19.}

_{2 Ann. Hist.
ii 395, 396;
Ann. Reg.
1819, 181.}

But the time had now arrived when an entire revolution was to take place in the affairs of the Peninsula, and those changes were to commence which have changed the dynasty on the throne, altered the constitution of the country, and finally severed her American colonies from Spain. The malcontents in the army, so far from being deterred by the manner in which the former conspiracy had been baffled by the double and treacherous dealing of the Conde d'Abisbal, continued their designs, and, distrusting now the chiefs of the army, chose their leaders among the subordinate officers. Every thing was speedily arranged, and with the concurrence of nearly the whole officers of the army. The day of rising was repeatedly adjourned, and at length definitely fixed for the 1st January, 1820. At its head was RIEGO,

_{64.
Revolution
attempted
by Riego.
January 1,
1820.}

whose great achievements and melancholy fate have rendered his name imperishable in history.[*] On that day he assembled a battalion in the village of Las Cabezas where it was quartered, harangued it, proclaimed amidst loud shouts the Constitution of 1812, and marching on Arcos, where the head-quarters were established, disarmed and made prisoners General Calderon and his whole staff; and then, moving upon San Fernando, effected a junction with QUIROGA, who was at the head of another battalion also in revolt. The two chiefs, emboldened by their success, and having hitherto experienced no resistance, advanced to the gates of Cadiz, within the walls of which they had numerous partisans,[1] upon whom they reckoned for co-operation and admission within it. But here they experienced a check. The gates remained closed against them—the governor of the fortress denounced them as rebels—the expected co-operation from within did not make its appearance, and the two chiefs were obliged to remain encamped outside, surrounded with all the precautions of a hostile enemy.

_{1 Martignac, i. 183;
Ann. Hist.
ii. 386,
390; Ann.
Reg. 1820,
222, 223.}

The intelligence of this revolt excited the greatest alarm at Madrid, and the Government at first deemed their cause hopeless. The next day, however, brought more consoling accounts—that Cadiz remained faithful, and a majority of the troops might still be relied on to act against the insurgents. Recovering from their panic, the Government took the most vigorous measures to crush the insurrection. General Freyre was dispatched from Madrid at the head of thirteen thousand men hastily collected from all quarters, upon whom it was thought reliance could be placed, and he rapidly reached the Isle of Leon, where the insurgent troops, to the number of ten thousand, lay intrenched. A part of them, however, joined the insurgents, the force of whom was thus raised to ten thousand men. By the approach of the royalist army, however, they found themselves in a very critical situation, placed between the fortress of Cadiz on the one side and the troops from Madrid on the other, and in a manner besieged themselves in the lines of the besiegers. They published

_{65.
Vigorous
measures
adopted
against the
insurgents.}

* "Raphael y Nunez del Riego was born in 1785 at Tuna, a village of Asturias. His father, a Hidalgo without fortune, placed him in the Gardes-du-Corps, which, ever since the scandalous elevation of the Prince of Peace, by the favor of the Queen, from its ranks, had been considered as the surest road to fortune in Spain. He was in that corps on occasion of the French invasion of that country in 1808 ; and when it was disbanded by the seizure of the royal family, he entered a guerrilla band, and was afterward promoted to the rank of an officer in the regiment of Asturias. He was ere long made prisoner, and employed the years of his captivity in France in completing his education, which he did chiefly by reading the works of a liberal tendency in that country. On the peace of 1814 he was liberated, returned to Madrid, and received the appointment of Lieut. Colonel in the 2d battalion of the Regiment of Asturias. That regiment formed part of the army under the Conde d'Abisbal, destined to act against South America ; and it was thus that Riego was brought to destruction and ruin."—*Biographie Universelle*, lxxix. 114, 115 (RIEGO).

† " Notre Espagne touchait à sa destruction, et votre ruine aurait entraîné celle de la Patrie : vous étiez destinés à la mort, plutot pour délivrer le Gouvernement de l'effroi que votre courage lui impose, que pour faire la conquête des colonies, devenue impossible. En attendant vos familles restaient dans l'esclavage le plus honteux, sous un Gouvernement arbitraire et tyrannique, qui dispose à son

proclamations and addresses in profusion, but without obtaining any material accession of strength beyond what had at first joined them;[1] and the defection and disquietude began to creep over them which invariably pervade an insurgent array when decisive success does not at once crown their efforts.

Unable to endure this protracted state of suspense, and fearful of its effect on the minds of the soldiers, Riego directed an attack on the arsenal of the Caraccas, an important station on an island in the bay of Cadiz, which was taken by a detachment under the command of Quiroga. By this success, a large quantity of arms and ammunition fell into their hands, as well as a seventy-four gun ship laden with powder; and they rescued from the dungeons of that place a number of liberals in confinement. Several attacks were afterward made on the dykes which led from the opposite sides of the bay to Cadiz, but they all failed before the formidable fortifications by which they were defended; and though several *émeutes* were attempted in the fortress, they all failed of success. Meanwhile Freyre's troops were drawn round them on the outside, and effectually cut them off from all communication with the mainland of Andalusia; and the troops became discouraged from a perception of their isolated position, and the long inactivity to which they had been exposed. To relieve it, and endeavor to rouse the population in their rear, Quiroga, who had been invested with the supreme command, detached Riego with a movable column of fifteen hundred men into the interior of the province. They set out on 27th January, and without difficulty passed the river near Chictana, and reached Algesiraz in safety, where they proclaimed the constitution amidst the loud acclamations of a prodigious concourse of inhabitants. After remaining five days, however, in that town, he found that shouts and huzzas were all that the inhabitants were disposed to afford; and leaving their inhospitable streets, he directed his march to Malaga, which he reached, after several combats, and entered on the 18th February, and immediately proclaimed the constitution. But although his little corps had been received with acclamations wherever he went, it had met with no real assistance; the people cheered, but did not join them; and, to use the words of Riego's aid-de-camp, "All applauded: none followed them."[2]

Meanwhile his associate, Quiroga, was the victim of the most cruel anxieties. Weakened by the detachment of the force under Riego, and besieged in his intrenched camp before Cadiz, he daily found his situation more critical, and his soldiers evinced unequivocal symptoms of discouragement from the inactivity in which they had been retained since their revolt, and the want of any succor from the troops with which they were surrounded. He sent, in consequence, orders to Riego to return to the lines in the island of Leon, but it had become no longer possible for him to do so. Riego was closely followed by a light column under the orders of O'Donnell; and finding that the population of the country were not inclined to join him, and that his corps was daily diminishing by desertion, he evacuated Malaga, and bent his steps toward the Cordilleras, with a view to throwing himself into the Sierra-Morena. He crossed the Guadalquiver by the bridge of Cordova, and directing his steps toward the hills, at length reached Bien-Venida on the 11th March with only three hundred followers, destitute of every thing, and in the last stage of exhaustion and discouragement.[1]

The intelligence of the disasters of Riego, which reached the Isle of Leon in spite of all the precautions which the generals of the revolutionary army there could take to intercept it, completed the discouragement of the troops of the revolutionary army there assembled. Mutually fearful of defection, Quiroga and General Freyre had long ceased to combat each other, but by proclamations and invitations to the soldiers on either side to abandon their colors and range themselves under the banners of their opponents. But in this wordy warfare the royalists had the advantage: the words of honor and loyalty did not resound in vain in Spanish ears, and although defection was experienced on both sides, it was soon apparent that the balance was decidedly against the liberal host. Their numbers were at last reduced to four thousand men; while their opponents, under Freyre, independent of the garrison of Cadiz, were three times that number; and this little band was so discouraged as to be incapable of attempting any of those bold steps which alone, in a protracted war of rebellion, can reinstate a falling cause.[2]

But while the cause of the revolution seemed to be thus sinking, and to have become well-nigh hopeless in the south, the flame burst forth simultaneously in several other quarters, and at length involved the whole peninsula in conflagration. The blow struck at Cadiz resounded through the whole of Spain. Every where the movement was confined to the officers of the army and a few citizens in the seaport towns; but in them it took place so simultaneously as to reveal the existence of a vast con-

---

gre des propriétés, de l'existence, et de la liberté des malheureux Espagnols. Ce Gouvernement devait détruire la nation, et finir par se détruire lui-même ; il n'est pas possible de la souffrir plus longtemps.—Vident et faible a la fois, il ne peut inspirer que l'indignation ou le mépris ; et pour que la Patrie soit heureuse, le Gouvernement doit inspirer la confiance, l'amour, et le respect. Soldats! nous allons employer pour notre bien, et pour celui de nos frères, les armes qui ont assuré l'indépendance de la nation contre le pouvoir de Buonaparte ; l'enterprise est facile, et glorieuse ! Existe-t-il un soldat Espagnol qui puisse s'y opposer ? Non ! dans les rangs même de ceux que le Gouvernement s'efforce de rassembler, vous trouverez des frères qui s'uniront à vous ; et si quelques-uns assez vils osaient tourner leurs armes contre vous, qu'ils périssent comme des satellites de la tyrannie, indignes du nom d'Espagnols."—ANTONIO QUIROGA, *Général-in-chef de l'Armée Nationale*, 5 Jan. 1820. *Annuaire Historique*, iii. 390, 391.

spiracy, directed by a central authority which embraced the whole Peninsula. On the 21st February, the day after Vanegaz, the new Captain-general of Galicia, had arrived at Corunna, an insurrection broke out among the officers of that fortress, who surprised Vanegaz, when disarmed and incapable of making any resistance; and on his refusal to place himself at the head of the movement, made him a prisoner, and conducted him with all his staff to the Fort of St. Antonio, where they were placed in confinement. The constitution of 1812 was immediately proclaimed, the gates closed, the drawbridges raised, and the revolution effected in an hour, without any resistance. A provisional junta was established; the prisons were broken open, and their inmates liberated; a sergeant named Chacon, who had denounced Porlier, massacred, and his widow, sobbing with grief, carried in triumph amidst revolutionary shouts through the streets. The insurrection spread to Ferrol, where the military revolted, and proclaimed the constitution on the 23d; Vigo declared on the 24th; Pontevedra on the 26th; and at the end of a week, with the exception of St. Iago, where the troops remained steady, the whole of Galicia had hoisted the standard of the constitution. Saragossa shortly after followed the example, and there the insurrection assumed a more serious aspect by being under the direction of Don Martin de Garay, the former Finance Minister, who had been disgraced. Mina, at the same time, reappeared on the frontiers of Navarre, which he entered with a few followers. He immediately proclaimed the constitution, and being joined by some soldiers, made himself master of the important cannon foundry at Aizzabal, and lent to the cause of insurrection the aid of a name which still spoke to the hearts of the patriotic throughout Spain.[1]

The intelligence of these repeated and general defections excited the utmost consternation in the Court of Madrid; and the conduct of the King and Cabinet evinced that vacillation which, as it is the invariable mark of weakness in presence of danger, so it is the usual precursor of the greatest public calamities. At first the most vigorous measures were resolved on. General Elio was recalled from Valencia to organize the means of defense in the capital, and a corps hastily assembled to move against the insurgents in Galicia, of which the Conde d'Abisbal was appointed commander. But vain are all attempts of government to make head against treason when their own officers and soldiers are the traitors. Unknown to them, the Conde d'Abisbal had already concerted with the chiefs of the conspiracy at Madrid, and with his brother, Alexander O'Donnell, who commanded a regiment stationed at Ocaña, the plan of a general insurrection, which was to embrace all the troops in Old and New Castile, and compel the king to accept the constitution. In pursuance of this plan, the Conde left Madrid on the 3d of March, to take the command of the troops destined to act against Galicia; but, like Ney in 1815, instead of doing so, he no sooner arrived at Ocaña, nine leagues from Madrid, where his brother's regiment was stationed, which had been prepared for the outbreak, than he harangued the troops, proclaimed the constitution, threw the magistrates into prison, and formed a Provisional Junta, subordinate to that of Galicia. The news of this defection at once brought matters to a crisis in Madrid. A general disquietude, which the police were no longer able to restrain, appeared among the lower orders in the capital. Many attempts were made to raise again the pillar of the constitution; the regular troops deserted by companies to the side of the populace, and the barracks became the scene of mutinous transport and revolutionary enthusiasm. The *Puerto del Sol*, since so famous in revolution, was filled with tumultuous mobs loudly demanding the constitution. Symptoms of disaffection even appeared among the Guards, and the officers of that chosen corps were among the first to attempt the raising the pillar of the constitution. In this extremity the cabinet sat permanently; and at length, seeing that no means of resistance remained, they resolved, on the advice of General Ballasteros, who was inclined to liberal opinions, to yield. On the 7th March, the Madrid Gazette contained a decree convoking the Cortes, and declaring the king's resolution to do every thing which the good and wishes of his people demanded, "who have given me so many proofs of their loyalty." This was followed the next day by a decree declaring that, "to avoid the delays which might arise in the execution of the decree pronounced yesterday for the immediate convocation of the Cortes, and the general will of the people (la voluntad general del pueblo) being pronounced, I have resolved to swear to the constitution promulgated by the general and extraordinary Cortes in 1812."

Thus fell the despotic government of Ferdinand VII. in Spain, the work of the nobles and the priests overthrown by the army and the populace. If little was to be expected of a government framed by the first, still less was to be augured of its overthrow by the last. Stained in its origin with treachery in the army, and treason by the officers even in the highest commands, the movement was brought about, and rendered for the time inevitable, by the revolt of the soldiery, and their abandonment of the oaths they had taken, and the sovereign under whose banners they were enrolled. History can find no apology for such conduct. The first duty of all persons in authority, whether civil or military, is to discharge the functions intrusted to them, and defend their sovereign with the powers which he has committed to their administration. If that sovereign has become despotic, and violated the rights of his subjects, that may be a good reason for throwing up their offices, and in extreme cases, where no other remedy is practicable, joining the ranks of the insurgents, but it is never for deserting a trust while still holding it. Even the splendid abilities of Marlborough, and the glorious career of Ney, have been able to wipe out the stain affixed by such treachery on their memory. Many honorable and noble men have suffered death for high treason, and their descendants have gloried, and shall glory, in their fate; but none ever pointed with exultation to success gained by breach of trust. We might well despair of the fortunes of the human race if the fair fabric of freedom was to be reared on such a foundation.

72. Rapid advances of the revolution.

Such as it was, however, the overthrow of the Spanish monarchy was too important an event not to rouse to the very highest degree the spirit of revolutionary ambition, not only in Spain, but over all Europe. Its effects are still felt in both hemispheres. Being the first instance in which democracy had gained a decided victory since its terrible overthrow in 1814 and 1815, it made a prodigious sensation, and every where excited the hopes and revived the expectations which had ushered in the French Revolution. The march of events at Madrid was as rapid as the most ardent partisans of innovation could desire. A Supreme Junta was immediately formed, to whom the king, two days after his proclamation of the March 9. 7th, took the oath to observe the constitution. The nobles and magistrates, obedient to the royal will, followed his example. In the midst of the ringing of bells, the discharge of artillery, and the cheers of the multitude, the guards, the soldiers, and all the civic authorities, took the oath, in the square of the Pardo, to the constitution. The whole prisoners confined for state offenses were liberated, and paraded through the streets amidst the shouts of the populace; many of them soon passed from their cells to the cabinet. In the evening a general illumination terminated the first day of the revolution, which hitherto had been one of unmingled joy.[1]

1 An. Hist. iii. 411; Ann. Reg. 1820, 225, 226; Martignac, i. 202, 203.

73. Reception of the revolution at Barcelona, Valencia, and Cadiz.

But the march of revolution is not always on flowers; the thorns soon began to show themselves. Some days before the constitution was accepted at Madrid by the king, it had been proclaimed at Saragossa and at Pampeluna, where Mina had already of his own authority supplanted Espalata, the royal governor. At Barcelona the garrison compelled Castaños to do the same, and March 10. soon removed that sturdy veteran to make way for General Villa-Campa, then in exile at Arons. He returned, ere long, liberated all the political prisoners, and burned the office of the Inquisition amidst general transports. At Valencia, General Elio, who had taken so decided a part against the former attempts at revolution, was only saved from death at the hands of the populace by being humanely thrown into prison; at Granada, General Eguia was displaced by the students, and Campo Verde installed in his stead. The revolution at Madrid was an unexpected godsend to Riego, who received it when wandering, almost alone, and destitute of every thing, in the solitudes of the Sierra Morena. From the depths of misery and despair he was suddenly elevated to fame and fortune, and brought back to Cordova, where he joined in proclaiming the constitution with General O'Donnell, and those who had lately pursued him with such unrelenting severity, and soon after made a triumphal entry into Seville.[1]

1 An. Hist. iii. 412,413; Ann. Reg. 1820, 225; Reg. Univ. Ixxxx. 120, 121.

74. Massacre at Cadiz, March 9, and 10.

A deplorable catastrophe at Cadiz first interrupted these transports, and revealed an alarming division of opinion even among the military, by whom the revolution had been effected. On the 9th March the people in Cadiz, accompanied by a part of the military, flocked to the square of San Antonio, and General Freyre, seeing no other way of extricating himself from his difficulties, published a proclamation, in which he engaged, on the following day, at ten o'clock, in the same place, to announce the acceptance of the constitution. The people, who looked upon this as a certain step to the pacification of the colonies, and the recovery of the lucrative commerce they had so long enjoyed with South America, were in transports, and flocked on the day following, at the appointed hour, to the Place San Antonio. But a dreadful fate awaited them. In the midst of the general joy, when the square was crowded with joyous multitudes, when every window was hung with tapestry, or filled with elegantly dressed females, and flags waved in every direction, bearing liberal devices, a discharge of musketry was suddenly heard in one of the adjoining streets, and immediately a disordered crowd, with haggard countenances and cries of horror, were seen flying into the square, closely pursued by the military. It was the soldiers of the regiments of the Guides and del Lealtad (of Fidelity), which, issuing from their barracks, had, without any orders, and by a spontaneous movement, commenced a fire on the people. Instantly, as if by magic, the square was deserted; the multitude, in the utmost consternation, dispersed on every side, and took refuge in houses or the casements of the fortifications, closely pursued by the soldiers, who massacred them without mercy, and abandoned themselves to all the atrocities usual in a town taken by assault. The deputies of the Isle of Leon, who were in an especial manner the objects of indignation to the soldiers, were only saved from destruction by being transported to Fort Saint Sebastien, where they were kept during three days, crowded in the casements, and almost starving. On the following day the same scenes of disorder were renewed; the soldiers issued from their barracks, and systematically began the work of plunder and extortion; and before order was restored, the killed amounted to four hundred and sixty, including thirty-six women and seventeen children, and the wounded to above a thousand.[2]

2 An. Hist. iii. 413,415; Ann. Reg. 1820, 226; Martignac, i. 203.

75. New ministry at Madrid.

While these frightful scenes were inaugurating the revolution at Cadiz, the new ministry was formed, and entered upon its functions at Madrid. It was composed, as might be expected, of the leading men of the liberal party, several of whom passed from a dungeon to the palace of the Government. It contained, however, many eminent names, which have acquired a lasting place in the rolls of fame. Senor Arguelles, whose eloquence in the former Cortes had acquired for him the surname of "the Divine," was Minister of the Interior; Don Garcias Herreras, one of the most violent orators on the liberal side, was appointed Minister of Justice; Canga Arguelles was Minister of the Finances; the Marquis Las Amarillas, of War; Perez de Castro and Don Juan Jabat, were appointed to the Exterior and the Marine.[1] Though the new ministers had all been leading orators on the liberal side in the Cortes, and many of them had suffered persecution and imprisonment from the king, yet, with the acquisition of office, they felt, as is generally the case, its difficulties and responsibilities. They endeavored, so far as in their power, to moderate the general fervor which had elevated themselves to office; but their views were by no means shared by their impatient followers, and it was soon apparent that their reign was not destined to be of very long duration.

[1] Ann. Hist. iii. 418, 419; Ann. Reg. 1820, 227; Martignac, i. 204, 205.

76. First measures of the new government. March 26.

The first measures of the new Government betrayed the external pressure to which they were subjected, and the extreme division of opinion which prevailed in the country on the recent changes. A decree was issued on the 26th March, declaring that every Spaniard who should refuse to swear to the new constitution, or who, in taking it, should qualify it with mental reservation, should, if a layman, be deprived of all honors, distinctions, and offices; if an ecclesiastic, his property was to be sequestrated. Another decree allowed the *Juramentados* or *Afrancesados*, as they were called, or Spaniards who had sworn fealty to Joseph Bonaparte, and who were estimated at six thousand, to return to Spain; but another, April 23. after they had in great part returned, compelled them to remain in Biscay or Navarre, provinces under the government of Mina, their implacable enemy. A third placed April 26. the sixty-nine members of the former Cortes, who had signed the petition to the king to resume the powers of an absolute monarch, under surveillance of the police in certain convents, till the pleasure of the new Cortes was taken on their fate. It augured ill of the cause of freedom when its inauguration was signalized by measures of such oppressive character or revengeful severity.[2]

[2] Martignac, i. 205, 206; Ann. Hist. iii. 419.

77. Establishment of clubs in Madrid, and other revolutionary measures.

The Cortes was convoked for the 9th July; but in the mean time the real powers of government resided, not in the King's Ministers, but in the Supreme Junta which sat alongside of them in Madrid. That body, elected by the populace in the first fervor of the Revolution, was composed of persons of the most violent character, and as they foresaw that their tenure of power would be of short duration, as it would be superseded by the meeting of the Cortes, their principal care was to organize the means of controlling that body, and subjecting it to the domination of the democrats in the capital. It was under the influence of this body that the severe decrees which have been mentioned had been passed. Nothing could be done without their sanction—nothing could withstand their control. In imitation of the Jacobins and the Girondists at Paris, they established clubs in the capital and in the principal towns throughout the provinces, in which the measures of Government were daily canvassed, and the most violent language constantly used to keep up the fervor of the public mind. Many of them acquired a fatal celebrity in the future history of the revolution. At the same time, all restrictions on the press being removed, a host of journals sprang up in the capital, which vied with each other in the propagation of the most violent revolutionary sentiments.[1]

[1] Martignac, i. 206, 207; Ann. Hist. iii. 420.

78. Legislative measures.

The measures of the Government soon gave tokens of their influence. Swift as had in 1789 been the march of revolution in France, swifter still was now its advance in Spain. Before the Cortes had even assembled, the junta and clubs of Madrid had dictated decrees to the nominal Government, which had effectually secured the supremacy of the democratic party. Some of them were worthy of unqualified admiration; others were of the most perilous tendency. Among the first, were decrees abolishing the Jesuits and the Inquisition, and all April 4. monuments and emblems which bore reference to them, and establishing an entire freedom of the press. In the last category must be placed the decrees which followed, abolishing all exclusive privileges, and investing in April 12. the nation all seignorial jurisdictions; April 24. the institution of national guards, with their officers chosen by the election of the privates, agreeably to the constitution of 1812; and one, declaring that the taking of all monastic vows should be suspended until the meeting of the Cortes, and that, in the mean time, *no alienation of any part of the monastic property should be valid.* The last enactment was of the most sinister augury, the more especially as the necessities of the exchequer had been noways diminished by the recent convulsions, and the property of the church in Spain was estimated at eighteen thousand millions of reals. Meanwhile honors, gratuities, and pensions were showered on the generals and officers of the army in the island of Leon, which had made the revolution; and all idea of prosecuting the expedition to South America having been abandoned, an invitation was sent to the insurgent states to send deputies, in terms of the constitution, to the Cortes; and in the mean time thirty *Suppliants*, or substitutes, were chosen among the South Americans resident in the Peninsula.[2]

[2] Ann. Hist. iii. 420, 421; Martignac, i. 211, 212, 223.

79. Meeting of the Cortes: its composition.

The elections were conducted with great regularity, and the Cortes met on the 9th July. Elected by universal suffrage during the first fervor of the revolution, its members presented that strange assemblage, and exclusion of various important classes, which invariably result from a uniform and single system of suffrage. Not a single grandee of Spain was elected; very few of the noblesse or landholders; only three bishops. Advocates, attorneys, factors, merchants, generals and military officers, who had risen to eminence by the revolution, and were ardently attached to its fortunes, constituted a decided majority. Generals Quiroga and O'Daly, and the other chiefs of the army of Leon, were amongst its ranks: Riego was only absent, because, having been appointed to the command of the army in the Isle of Leon, he could not be spared from its ranks. The conservative party, or the one attached to old institutions, was almost unrepresented. Navarre, and a few remote and obscure parts of New Castile, had alone returned members in that interest, and their number was so small that they had no weight in the assembly, and from the very outset were stigmatized by the name of *Serviles*.[1] Universal suffrage had done its work: it had established, as it invariably does, class government of the very worst kind, that of an ignorant and irresponsible majority.

[1 Martignac, i. 224, 225; Ann. His. iii. 422.]

Disorders meanwhile had broken out in the provinces, which sufficiently demonstrated that, however popular in the great and seaport towns, the revolutionary régime was any thing but agreeable to the inhabitants of the country. At Saragossa a disturbance arose, in the attempt of five or six hundred peasants to throw down the pillar of the constitution, which was only put down by General Haxo, with two regiments of infantry and cavalry, and a battery of artillery, with the loss of twenty lives, and triple that number wounded. The consequences were serious. The Marquis Alazan, governor of the province, brother of the famous Palafox, was deprived of his command, which was bestowed on Riego, his wife was arrested, and sixty monks were thrown into prison to await their trial before a military commission. Shortly after an insurrection broke out in the mountains of Galicia, near the confines of the Portuguese province of Entre Douro e Minho. A junta, styled "the apostolical," was elected, with the device "Religion and the King." Crowds of peasants flocked round the sacred standard. The royalists passed the Minho, and advanced toward St. Iago, where they hoped to be joined by numerous partisans. Their number soon amounted to three thousand; but they were worsted in several encounters with the regulars near Zuy on the Minho, and at length dispersed. Among the papers of their chiefs, which were seized, were letters which proved that they were in correspondence with secret royalist committees in Aragon, Andalusia, Old Castile, and the capital itself.[2]

80. Disorders in the provinces.

May 14.

June 15.

July 7.

[2 Ann. His. iii. 424, 425.]

On the night before the assembling of the Cortes, an event happened of evil augury as to its future career. A part of the body-guard attached to liberal principles broke into the royal palace, under pretext, which was wholly unfounded, that a number of *Serviles* had assembled there to offer the king their services, and murdered a faithful officer who withstood their entrance. So far there was nothing remarkable; such tragedies are almost invariably the accompaniment of civil dissension. But what followed proved the impotence of the law; and that the majority, as in America, had now become so powerful that no crime committed in their interest could be brought to punishment. The fact of the murder was notorious, it had been committed by the assassins with their official scarfs on; the persons implicated in it were well known; but so far from being punished, they were all acquitted on a mock trial, and immediately promoted.[1]

81. Murder of one of the body-guard, and reward of the murderers.

[1 Martignac, i. 224, 225.]

The session of the Cortes was opened with great pomp by the king on the 9th July, in presence of the queen and whole *corps diplomatique*. The sovereign again took the oath to the Archbishop of Seville, the first President of the Cortes, who addressed his Majesty in a speech which terminated with these words: "The most virtuous of nations will forgive its injuries, pardon the outrages it has received, establish its constitutional government, and preserve in all its purity its holy religion. The distrust, the seeds of discord, the fears, the odious suspicions, which the perfidious have so long sought to inspire in the best of kings, will cease, and all will unite around his throne by a fraternal alliance, which will secure the public peace, produce abundance, and prove the source of every social blessing." The king pronounced a speech which re-echoed these warm anticipations and benevolent intentions. It will appear in the sequel how, on either side, these promises were fulfilled and these anticipations realized.[2]

82. Opening of the Cortes. July 9.

[2 An. Hist. iii. 426.]

One of the most important public documents presented to the Cortes was a report on the state of the army, which gave a graphic picture of its deplorable condition, and revealed the main cause of the revolutionary spirit with which it was animated. The minister reported that, including the guard, its entire effective strength was only 53,705 men, in lieu of 87,000, its strength on paper; and 7085 cavalry mounted. The whole was in the most deplorable state of nudity and destitution. The clothing of the infantry for the most part *had not been renewed since* 1814; only seven regiments of cavalry were dressed in any thing like homogeneous uniform; various dresses clothed the remainder, all worn out. The artillery was crazy and broken down, the arsenals empty. The entire cost of the army was 352,607,000 reals (£3,500,000), being more than half the revenue of the monarchy, and yet every branch of the service was deeply in arrear of their pay. No less than 38,000,000 reals (£380,000) was due to the cavalry, and £150,000 to the infantry. The report announced that the constitution had been accepted at Puerto Rico, St. Domingo, and Cuba, but that the war, "fomented by the stranger," still lingered on the continent of America, to which, since 1815, forty-two thousand men had been dispatched from Old Spain. Here is the secret of the Spanish revolution; it is to be found in the destitution of the exchequer, and ruin of the external commerce of the kingdom, in consequence of the South American revolution. Had the trade of Cadiz and Corunna been as flourishing as it was prior to 1810, and the Spanish troops been paid, clothed, fed, and

83. Report on the state of the army. July 15.

lodged, like the English soldier, there would have been no revolution; the king, with the general consent of the nation, would have reigned like his fathers, and Riego, unknown and guiltless, would have died a natural death.

<small>84. Majority of quent years of the galleys, imprison- the Cortes: ment, or exile, had confirmed in their its leaders.</small> The majority of the Cortes was composed of the liberals of 1812, whom six subse-
principles, and inspired with an ardent thirst of vengeance against their oppressors. It was no wonder it was so; the royal government now experienced the retribution due for its severities, and had leisure to lament the failure to act in that magnanimous spirit which, by forgiving error, might have caused it to be abjured. But although the composition of the majority was such as presaged violent and destructive measures at no distant period, its leaders were men of enlarged views and great capacity, whose statesmanlike wisdom at first imposed a considerable check upon its excesses. In the front rank of the leaders must be placed MARTINEZ DE LA ROSA, a man of great ability and uncommon oratorical powers; and CALATRAVA, an orator less brilliant, but more argumentative, and a statesman more experienced in public affairs. The MARQUIS TORENO also, a nobleman of the most enlarged views, who had studied with advantage, and learned the action of representative governments by traveling in foreign countries, lent the aid of his extensive knowledge and profound reflection. If any thing could warrant the hope of a prudent use of power in a body constituted as the Cortes was, it was its being directed by such men. But there were others of a different stamp, whose influence ere long increased, and at length became irresistible from the combined influence of the clubs and the press. Among these were soon remarked Gasco, Philippe Navarro, Romero, Alpuente, and Moreno, the Jacobins of the revolution.

<small>1 Martignac, I. 223, 226; Ann. Hist. iii. 428, 429.</small> Their party at first did not number above a sixth of the whole Cortes; but, as is too often the case in such circumstances, they in the end acquired its entire direction.[1]

<small>85. Suppression of the Jesuits, and measures regarding entails.</small> The first measures of the Cortes, though not of a violent or sanguinary character, were nevertheless obviously calculated to increase the democratic influence and action in the country. The *Afrancesados*, who awaited their fate in Biscay in deep distress, were restored to their property, but not to their offices, pensions, or honors; the sixty-
<small>Sep. 21.</small> nine of the old Cortes were included in the amnesty, but, with the exception of the Marquis of Mattaflorida, declared incapable of holding any election or public office. The decree of the former Cortes and of the king against the Jesuits was adopted, with certain modifications. An important law was also passed restricting the entails, which had so long operated to the prejudice of Spanish agriculture. They were prohibited in future absolutely in landed estates, and permitted only in payments out of land, as right of superiority, or of the manor, to the extent of 20,000 ducats for grandees, 40,000 for persons enjoy- <small>Oct. 12.</small> ing title, and 20,000 for private individ-
uals. No entail was admitted below 6000 ducats. These were steps, and important ones, in the right direction; and if the leaders of the revolution had limited themselves to such practical reforms, they would have deserved well of their country and of the human race.[1] <small>1 An. Hist. iii. 430, 432, 439; Martignac, I. 230, 231.</small>

But in the midst of these beneficent labors, the dreadful evil of embarrassment of the finances still made itself felt, and with increasing severity, from the cessation of speculation and confidence which had arisen from the revolution. The loss of the revenue derived directly from South America by the produce of the mines, and indirectly by the stoppage of the commercial intercourse with the revolted colonies, rendered abortive all attempts to pay the interest of the debt and carry on the current expenses of the nation from its domestic resources.* In this extremity the Spanish Cortes did what the Constituent Assembly had done before them; they <small>Oct. 1.</small> suppressed all the monasteries except eight, and confiscated their property to the service of the state; the monks and nuns, 61,000 in number, turned out, received small pensions varying from 100 to 400 ducats (£20 to £80). Already the clubs had be- <small>Oct. 14.</small> come so formidable that a decree was passed closing their sittings, which remained a dead letter. Tithes were abolished, both in the hands of the clergy and lay proprietors, but the half of them was kept up as a direct contribution for the service of the state.[2] <small>2 An. Hist. iii. 440, 443; Rapport du Comte Toreno; Martignac, I. 230, 231.</small> Even after all these extraordinary revolutionary resources had been taken into the exchequer, the budget exhibited a deficit of 172,000,000 of reals (£1,720,060), being about a fourth of the annual revenue,† which was provided for by a loan of £2,000,000, negotiated with Lafitte and the bankers on the liberal side in Paris.

<small>86. Financial measures.</small>

But meanwhile the Government, the creature of military revolution, was subjected to the usual demands and insults consequent on such an origin. They found ere long that the prætorian guards in the Isle of Leon were as imperious, and as difficult of management, as their predecessors in the camp which have overawed the masters of the world. Incessant were the efforts made by Riego, who had now the command of that force, to keep alive the spirit of revolution among the troops; but as it rather declined, and rumors of an intention to separate the army began to reach the Isle of Leon, Riego hastened to Madrid, to support by

<small>87. Tumult at Madrid, and dismissal of Riego.</small>

<small>* According to a report presented to the Cortes by the Commission of Finance, on 22d October, the National Debt consisted of—

Reals.	Francs.	£.
142,220,572,391 or	3,839,580,000 or	140,000,000

The whole revenues of Spain were not equal to the discharge of the interest of this debt annually.—*Rapport*, Oct. 22, 1850. *Annuaire Historique*, iii. 440.

† The budget proposed by the Cortes exhibited—

From all sources	530,394,271 reals, or	£5,304,000
An expenditure of	702,807,000	7,028,600
Deficit	172,408,033	£1,724,000

which was provided for by a loan of 200,000,000 reals, or £2,000,000.—*Ann. Hist.* iii. 443.</small>

his presence the revolutionary clubs against the Government, which was suspected of leaning to moderate ideas. He arrived there in the end of August, and for a week was the object of general adulation. He was surrounded by the club Lorrenzini, by the influence of which the minister-at-war was removed, and succeeded by Don Gastano Valdes. In the middle of it he visited the theatre, where an audience from the clubs, vehemently excited, called for a party air, the *Tragala Perro*, which had been composed in hatred of the noblesse during the fervor at Cadiz; and Riego himself, standing up surrounded by his whole staff, joined in the chorus. This open insult to the nobility and the Government led to a fearful tumult in the theatre, in the course of which Riego openly resisted the police and other authorities; and next day the clubs were all in a tumult, and the banners so well known in the French Revolution were seen in the great square—"The Constitution or Death." The Government, however, was not deterred. The troops remained faithful to their duty: large bodies, with artillery loaded with grape-shot, were stationed around the square of the Puerto del Sol, where the mobs were assembled; and the revolutionists, seeing themselves mastered, were compelled to submit. On the following day a decree of the Cortes put the clubs under a strict surveillance, closed the Lorrenzini, and Riego was deprived of his command in Galicia, and sent into exile at Oviedo. At the same time the army in the Isle of Leon was broken up; but to keep the troops in good humor, and insure obedience to the decree, large gratuities and pensions were voted to the troops, according to their rank and periods of service. Riego and Quiroga for their share got a pension of 84,000 reals each (£840), equivalent to about £1500 in Great Britain.[1]

Aug. 29.

Sept. 3.

Sept. 4.

[1] Martignac, i. 234, 249; Ann. Hist. iii. 432, 435.

This vigorous step was attended by an immediate schism in the popular party. Arguelles and Quiroga, who had been foremost in resisting the clubs, were soon denounced as traitors and apostates; and Riego, for a short time, was the rallying-cry of the seditious in the provinces. If this victory had been followed up with vigor and perseverance, the downward progress of the revolution might have been arrested, and Spain saved unutterable calamities. But it was not so: the press continued as violent as ever; the clubs resumed their ascendant, and the progress of anarchy became unrestrained. The Cortes had passed the decree, despoiling the religious houses for the advantage of the state, already mentioned, and it was brought to the king to adhibit his signature in terms of the constitution, which declared that necessary for it to become a law. Instead of doing so, he wrote at the bottom the words prescribed for his refusal. He was perfectly entitled to do so, as much as the Cortes was to present to him the project of the law. It was on the *third* presenting only in successive sessions that he was constrained to accept. But it is not in the nature of democracy to admit of any compromise, or tolerate any bridle, how gentle soever, in its career. The clubs were instantly in motion; the cry of a counter-revolution was heard. Frightful crowds of the lowest of the populace, yelling and vociferating vengeance in the most violent manner, paraded the streets, and converged toward the arsenal which contained all the arms and ammunition. The report spread that the troops would not act against the insurgents; that the life of the king was in danger. Intimidated and overawed, the ministers counseled submission, and renewed their intreaties to the king to sanction the law. He long resisted; but overcome at last by the increasing danger, and their assurance that the troops could not be relied on, he affixed his signature, and immediately after set out from Madrid for the Escurial.[1]

88. Closing of the session, and rupture with the king. Nov. 16.

[1] Martignac, i. 246, 248; Ann. Hist. iii. 443, 444.

The victory thus gained over the king was not attended by the advantages which had been anticipated. In some places in and around the great towns, as of Valencia and Barcelona, the people broke in tumultuous crowds into the monasteries, forcibly expelled the monks and nuns, and it was with difficulty that the heads of the houses were rescued from their hands. At Valencia, the archbishop, besieged by a furious mob in his palace, on account of an anathema which he had fulminated against the sale of the ecclesiastical estates, was only rescued from death by being embarked in the night for Barcelona, where, on landing, he encountered similar dangers. But in the rural districts, especially Galicia, Leon, Navarre, Asturias, Old Castile, and Aragon, the decree against the priests met with a very different reception, and was found to be incapable of execution. Transported with indignation at the thoughts of the hospitable doors, where they had so often been fed in adversity, being closed against them, and their reverend inmates being turned adrift upon the world without house or home to shelter them, the people rose in crowds and forcibly prevented the execution of the decree. Between the resistance of the people in some districts, and the cupidity of their own agents in others, the treasury derived scarcely any aid from this great measure of spoliation. It was exactly the same in France in 1789; it will be so in similar circumstances to the end of the world. When Government takes the lead in iniquity, it soon finds it impossible to restrain the extortions of inferior agents: it is like a woman who has deviated from virtue attempting to control the manners of her household.[2]

89. Reception of the decree against the priests in Spain.

[2] An. Hist. iii. 411,445; Martignac, i. 248, 251.

Meanwhile the king, shut up in the Escurial, refused to be present at the closing of the session of the Cortes, which terminated on the 9th November; and in secret meditated an attempt to extricate himself from the meshes in which he was enveloped. To effect this, the support of the military was indispensable; and with that view the king, of his own authority, and without the concurrence of any of his ministers, which, by the constitution, was required to legalize the appointment, promoted General Carvajal to the situation of Captain-general of New Castile, in room of the constitutional General Vigodet, who held that important command. A warm altercation ensued between

90. Illegal appointment of General Carvajal by the king. Nov. 16.

the two generals when the order to cede the command was produced, which ended by Vigodet declaring that he would retain the command till superseded by a general legally appointed. The intelligence of this rash step on the part of the king soon transpired: the clubs immediately met and commenced a warm agitation; the committee of the Cortes met, and declared its sittings permanent; the ministers were in constant consultation; and in the clubs and agitated crowds in the streets, it was openly announced that a counter-revolution had been resolved on, and that *dethronement* had become now indispensable. Anxious to avoid such an extremity, the ministers sent in their collective resignation to the king; and the permanent commission of the Cortes, and municipality of Madrid, sent deputations to the Escurial, with grave and severe remonstrances against the illegal step which had been taken. The irresolute and inconsistent character of the king immediately appeared. No sooner were the addresses read than he declared he had no idea he was doing an unconstitutional thing in the appointment of General Carvajal, that he revoked it; that he would dismiss the Count Miranda, the grand-master of his household, and his confessor, Don Victor Paez, and within three days would re-enter his capital.[1]

¹ An. Hist.
iii. 416, 447;
Martignac,
i. 253, 254;
Ann. Reg.
1820, 229,
230.

He arrived, accordingly, on the 21st, accompanied by the queen, who was in a very feeble state of health, surrounded, by a crowd shouting vociferous revolutionary cries, through a double line of National Guards, and amidst cries of "Viva el Constitution!" Suddenly a child was raised up above the crowd, with the book of the constitution in its hand, which it was made to kiss with fervor. A thousand cries, and the most fearful threats of vengeance, accompanied the incident; and when the king inquired what it was, he was informed it was the son of General Lacy come to demand justice against his father's murderers. Overcome with terror, and almost stupefied with emotion, the king, with feeble steps and haggard looks, re-entered the palace, and immediately shut himself up in his apartment. The most sinister presentiments were felt. Terror froze every heart. The striking resemblance of the procession which had just terminated to that of Louis XVI. from Versailles to Paris in 1789, struck every mind; and men shuddered to think how short an interval separated that melancholy journey from the 21st January, when the martyr king ascended the scaffold.[2]

91.
Return of the king to Madrid.
Nov. 21.

² An. Hist.
iii. 449;
Martignac,
i. 225, 227,
Ann. Reg.
1820, 230.

The victory of the revolutionists was now complete, and they were not slow in improving it to the utmost advantage. General Riego, so recently in disgrace, was appointed Captain-general of Aragon; Velasco, the late governor of Madrid, who had been dismissed from his office for his supineness on occasion of Riego's riot in the theatre, was appointed Governor of Seville; Mina was made Captain-general of Galicia; Lopez Baños, of Navarre; Don Carlos Espiñosa, of Old Castile; Arco-Aguerro, of Estremadura;

92.
Victory of the Revolutionists.

the Duque del Infantado, President of the Council of Castile; and all the persons of moderation in the Government were sent into exile from the capital. These were all men, not only of approved courage, but of the most determined revolutionary principles. The whole subordinate officers, civil as well as military, were selected from the same party; so that the entire authority in the kingdom had, before the end of the year, passed into the hands of the supporters of the new order of things. The clubs resumed their former activity, and increased in vigor and audacity in the metropolis; and with them were now associated a still more dangerous body of allies in the *secret societies* of the provinces. The ancient and venerable institution of freemasonry, formed for the purposes of benevolence, and hitherto unstained by those of party, was now perverted to a different object, and converted into a huge Jacobin Society, held together by secret signs and oaths; and along with it was associated a new institution of a still more dangerous and pernicious tendency.[1]

¹ Martignac, i. 259, 261; Ann. Hist. iii. 449; Ann. Reg. 1820, 230, 232.

This was a society, which assumed the title of "*Franc-Communeros.*" Their principles were those of the Socialists, in their widest acceptation; their maxims, that universal equality was the birthright of man, and that nothing had hitherto so much impeded its establishment as the false and hypocritical ideas of philanthropy and moderation by which the reign of despots had been so long prolonged. In pursuance of these principles, they were bound by their oath, on entering the society, to obey all mandates they received from its superior officers, whatever they were, and however contrary to the laws of the state; and they engaged "to judge, condemn, *and execute* every individual, without exception, including *the king* or his successors, who might abuse their authority." So far was this power of self-judging and lynch law carried, that it led to serious disturbances, particularly in Asturias and Galicia, in the end of November and December, which were not suppressed without serious bloodshed; while in Madrid the agitation was so violent that one of the clubs was shut up by order of Government, while the whole garrison was called out to enforce the order; and the king, trembling for his life, no longer ventured to leave his own palace. An incident soon occurred which showed how well-founded his apprehensions were, and gave a pitiable proof of the state of degradation to which the royal authority was reduced. The king at length went out in his carriage, which was speedily surrounded by an insulting mob, which, from furious cries, proceeded to assail the royal vehicle and guards with showers of stones. Indignant at such conduct, the guards wheeled about, charged the assailants, wounded several, and dispersed the rest. Instantly a furious mob got up, which surrounded the barrack to which the guard had retired, and insisted upon the obnoxious men being delivered up to them. This was done; they were thrown into prison and detained there long, though their conduct was so evidently justifiable that they were not

93.
New society for execution of lynch law.

brought to trial; and the king, on the representation of his ministers that the sacrifice could no longer be averted, was obliged to dismiss his whole guard, and confine himself to his own palace.[1]

¹ Martignac, i. 264, 267; Ann. Reg. iii. 450, 451.

94. Identity of recent history of Spain and Portugal.

PORTUGAL evidently was intended by nature to form part of the same monarchy as Spain. The Pyrenees, which separate them both from all the rest of Europe; the ocean, which encircles both their shores, and opens to them the same commerce and maritime interests; the identity of soil and climate which they both enjoy in the old hemisphere, the vast colonies they had acquired in the new, the homogeneous nature of the races and nations from which they were both descended, and the similarity of manners and institutions which both, in consequence, had established, have caused their history, especially in recent times, to be almost identical. The tyranny of the Spanish government, the patriotic resistance of the heroic house of Braganza, even entire centuries of jealousy or war, have not been able to eradicate these seeds of union so plentifully sown by the hand of nature. Like the English and Scotch, they yearned to each other, even when severed by political discord, or engaged in open hostility; happy if, like them, they had been reunited in one family, and one pacific sceptre restored peace to the whole provinces of the Peninsula.

95. Revolution at Oporto. Aug. 23.

It was not to be expected that so very important an event as the Spanish Revolution of 1820, overturning as it did, by military revolt, an aged throne, and establishing a nominal monarchy and real democracy in its stead, was to fail in exciting a corresponding spirit, especially among the military in the sister kingdom. But, in addition to this, there were many circumstances which rendered revolution in favor of a constitutional form of government more natural—it might almost be said unavoidable—in Portugal than in Spain. Long habits of commercial intercourse, close alliance between the two countries, glorious victories in which the two nations had stood side by side, had inspired the Portuguese with an ardent, it might almost be said an extravagant, admiration of British liberty and institutions. They had seen the probity of English administration, and contrasted it with the corruptions of their own; they ascribed it all to the influence of English institutions, and thought they would exchange the one for the other, by adopting a representative form of government; they had seen the valor of British soldiers, and thought liberty would in like manner render them invincible. A conspiracy, which proved abortive, headed by General Freyre, in 1817, had already given proof how generally these ideas influenced the army; and three additional years of government by a Regency at Lisbon, without the lustre or attractions of a court to enlist the selfish feelings on the side of loyalty, had given them additional strength, and rendered the whole population of the seaports and army ripe for a revolt. The consequence was, that when it broke out, on the night of the 23d August, it met with scarcely any resistance. The whole military commenced the revolt; the people all joined them; a junta, consisting of popular leaders, was established, and a constitutional government proclaimed.[1]

¹ Aug. 23. Ann. Hist. iii. 471, 474; Ann. Reg. 1820, 232, 233.

96. Which is followed by a revolution at Lisbon. Sept. 15.

When the English, retiring from their long career of victory, withdrew from Portugal, Marshal Beresford, who had trained their army and led it to victory, was left at its head, and about a hundred English officers, chiefly on the staff or in command of regiments, remained in Portugal. Aware of the crisis which was approaching, Marshal Beresford had, in April, embarked for Rio Janeiro, to lay in person before the king a representation of the discontents of the country, and the absolute necessity of making a large and immediate remittance to discharge the pay of the troops, which had fallen very much into arrears. Many of the English officers, however, were at Oporto when the insurrection broke out; and as *their* fidelity to their oaths was well known, they were immediately arrested and put into confinement, though treated with the utmost respect. Meanwhile the insurrection spread over the whole of the north of Portugal, and the Conde de Amarante, who had endeavored to make head against it in the province of Tras-os-Montes, was deserted by his troops, who joined the insurgents, and obliged to fly into Galicia. The Regency at Lisbon, on the 29th August, published a fierce proclamation, denouncing the proceedings at Oporto, and declaring their resolution to subvert them. But they soon had convincing proof that their authority rested on a sandy foundation. The 15th September, the anniversary of the delivery of the Portuguese territory from Junot's invasion in 1808, had hitherto always been kept as a day of great national and military rejoicing in Portugal. On this occasion, however, the Regency, distrustful of the fidelity of their troops, forbade any military display. The soldiers had been ordered to be confined to their barracks, when, at four in the afternoon, the 18th regiment, of its own accord, marched out, headed by its officers, and, making straight for the great square of the city, drew up there in battle array, amidst cries of "Viva el Constitution." They were soon joined by the 16th regiment from the castle, the 4th from the Campo d'Ourique, the cavalry, the artillery, and ere long by the whole of the garrison. All, headed by their officers, and in full marching order, were assembled in the square, amidst cheers from the soldiers and deafening shouts from the people. No resistance was any where attempted; nothing was seen but unanimity, nothing heard but the "vivas" of the soldiery, and the huzzas of the multitude. The halls of the Regency were thrown open, and a new set of regents appointed by the leaders of the revolt by acclamation; and having accomplished the revolution, the soldiers returned at ten at night, in parade order, to their barracks, as from a day of ordinary festivity.[2]

² Ann. Reg. 1820, 231, 235; Ann. Hist. iii. 473, 475.

Aug. 28.

Universal enthusiasm ensued for some days, and the unanimity of the people proved how

VOL. I.—P

general and deep-seated had been the desire for political change and a representative government, at least among the military and the citizens of the towns. The entire country followed, as is generally the case in such instances, the example of the capital; the constitution was every where proclaimed, and the former persons in authority were superseded by others attached to the new order of things. On the 1st October, the Oporto Junta entered the capital, and immediately fraternized in the most cordial way with the Junta already elected there. The British officers were every where dispossessed of their commands, and put under surveillance, but treated with equal kindness and consideration. After a debate, which was prolonged for several days, it was decreed that the two Juntas should be united into one composed of two sections—one charged with the ordinary administration, and the other with the steps necessary for assembling the Cortes; and Count Palmella was dispatched on a special embassy to Brazil, to lay before the king an account of the events which had occurred, and assure his Majesty of the continued loyalty of the Portuguese to the royal family.[1]

<small>97. Establishment of a joint regency at Lisbon. Oct. 6.</small>

<small>[1] Ann. Hist. iii. 475, 476; Ann. Reg. 234, 235.</small>

In the midst of these events, Marshal Beresford returned from Brazil to Lisbon, in the Vengeur of 74 guns, charged with a message from the king to the former junta. Being informed by a fisherman, as he approached the coast, of the revolution, and subversion of the former authorities, he made no attempt to force his way in, but requested permission to land as a private individual, as he had many concerns of his own to arrange. This, however, was positively refused: he was forbid on any account to approach the harbor; the guns were all loaded, and the artillerymen placed beside them to enforce obedience to the mandate. Beresford expostulated in the warmest manner, but in vain; and as the agitation in the city became excessive as soon as his return was known, it was intimated to him that the sooner he took his departure for England the better. During all this time the shores were strictly guarded, and no precaution omitted which could prevent any communication with the Vengeur. At length Beresford, finding he could not open any correspondence with the new Junta, sent them the money he had received at Rio Janeiro for the pay of the troops, and returned to England in the Arabella packet; while the Vengeur proceeded on its destination up the Mediterranean.[2]

<small>98. Return of Marshal Beresford, who is forced to go to England.</small>

<small>[2] Ann. Reg. 1820, 237; Ann. Hist. iii. 426, 427.</small>

Such was the return which the Portuguese nation made to the British for their liberation from French thraldom, and the invaluable aid they had rendered them during six successive campaigns for the maintenance of their independence! A memorable, but, unhappily, a not unusual instance of the ingratitude of nations, and the immediate disregard of the most important services when they are no longer required, or when oblivion of them may be convenient to the parties who have been benefited.

<small>99. Effect of the banishment of the British.</small>

Above a hundred officers accompanied Marshal Beresford to England; and the effects of the absence of this nucleus of regular administration soon appeared in the measures of Government. The two Juntas came to open rupture in regard to the manner in which the Cortes was to be convoked. The Lisbon maintained it should be done according to the ancient forms of the constitution; but this was vehemently opposed by the Oporto Junta, which was composed of ardent democrats, who asserted that these antiquated forms were far too aristocratical, and that the public wishes would never be satisfied with any thing short of the immediate adoption of the *Spanish* constitution. Few knew what that constitution really was; but it instantly was taken up as a rallying-cry by the extreme democratic party. Still the Junta of Lisbon held out, upon which Silviera, who was at the head of the violent revolutionists, and had great influence with the troops, surrounded the Palace of the Junta with a body of soldiers, who, by loud shouts and threats, instantly extorted a decree, adopting *in toto* the Spanish constitution, and appointing one deputy for every thirty thousand inhabitants, to be elected by universal suffrage.[1]

<small>Nov. 11.</small>

<small>[1] Ann. Hist. iii. 478, 480; Ann. Reg. 1820, 236, 237.</small>

So far the victory of the revolutionists was complete, but the step had been too violent; neither the public nor the majority of the army were, on consideration, inclined to go into such violent measures. The incorporations (*Gremios*) and magistrates protested against the proceedings, and a majority of the officers in the army came round to the same sentiments. A hundred and fifty officers in the army, and nearly all the civil authorities, resigned their situations. The consequences were soon felt. On the 17th November a general council of officers was held, at which Colonel Castro Sepulveda, who was at the head of the moderate party, labored so assiduously to convince them of their error, that, after a debate of six hours, resolutions were passed to the effect that the state of public opinion in the capital required that those who had resigned should resume their situations; that the election of the Cortes shall be made according to the Spanish system, but no other part of the Spanish constitution adopted till the Cortes had met and considered the subject. The reaction was now complete: upon these resolutions being intimated to the officers of the late Government who had resigned, they resumed their functions. Silviera was, with the general concurrence of the people, ordered to quit the city in two hours, which he did, amidst loud acclamations, and the ascendency of the moderate party was for a time established. But it was for a time only. The fatal step had been taken, the irrecoverable concession made. The resolution that the Cortes should be elected on the Spanish principle, which was a single chamber and universal suffrage, and that there should be a member for every thirty thousand inhabitants, necessarily threw the power into the hands of the multitude, and precluded the possibility of any thing like a stable or free constitution being formed.[2]

<small>100. Reaction, and adoption of more moderate measures.</small>

<small>[2] Ann. Hist. iii. 481; Ann. Reg. 1820, 237, 238; Diario de Lisbon, Nov. 18, 1820.</small>

101. Commencement of reforms in Italy.

ITALY was not long in catching the destructive flame which had been kindled, and burned so fiercely, in the Spanish peninsula. The career of reform was begun in Piedmont on the 25th February, 1820, by a decree of the King of Sardinia, which created a commission composed of the most eminent statesmen and jurisconsults, to examine the existing laws, and consider what alterations should be made to bring them into harmony with the institutions of other countries and the spirit of the age; and even in the realm of Naples, the germ of practical improvement had begun to unfold itself. The excessive increase of the land-tax, which had in some places risen to thirty-three per cent, had tended to augment in that country the general discontent, which in the inhabitants of towns, and the more intelligent of those in the country, had centred in an ardent desire for representative institutions, which they regarded as the only effectual safeguard against similar abuses in time to come. The government of Murat, and the society of the French officers during eight years, had confirmed these ideas, and augmented the importance for these institutions. This desire had been fanned into a perfect passion in Sicily by the experiment which had been made of a representative government of that country by the English during the war, which was in the highest degree popular with the liberal leaders. But it had been found by experience to be so alien to the character and wants of the rural inhabitants, that it fell to the ground of its own accord after the withdrawal of the English troops on the peace; and the only trace of the constitutional régime which remained was the ominous word "*uno budgetto*," a money account, which had been imported from their Gothic allies into the harmonious tongue of the Italian shores.[1]

¹ Colletta, Historia di Napoli, 1780, 1825, ii. 330, 340; Ann. Hist. iii. 488.

102. Breach of the king's promise of a constitution. July 25. May 1815.

Ferdinand the king had, in accordance with the declared wishes of the most intelligent part of his subjects, announced the acceptance by the Government of a constitutional régime during the crisis which preceded the fall of Napoleon and conclusion of the war. Before leaving the Sicilian shores to reoccupy the throne of his fathers, on the dethronement of Murat in 1815, he had issued a proclamation, in which he announced "*The people will be the sovereign*, and the monarch will only be the depositary of the laws, which shall be decreed by a constitution the most energetic and desirable." These words diffused universal satisfaction, and, like Lord William Bentinck's celebrated proclamation to the Genoese in the preceding year, were regarded with reason as a pledge of the future government under which they were to live.* But it soon appeared that these promises, like those of the German sovereigns during the mortal agony of 1813, were made only to be broken. What-

ever the individual wishes of Ferdinand may have been, he was overruled by a superior influence which he had no means of withstanding. By a secret article of the treaty between Austria and Naples, concluded in 1815, it was expressly stipulated that "his Neapolitan majesty should not introduce in his government any principles irreconcilable with those adopted by his Imperial majesty in the government of his Italian provinces."[1]

¹ Ann. Reg. 1820, 233; Ann. Hist. iii. 488; Colletta, ii. 330, 312; Treaty, Nov. 24, 1815; Recueil Diplomatique, iii. 224.

103. Progressive but slight reforms already introduced.

The hands of the King of Naples were thus tied by an overwhelming power, which he had not the means, even if he had possessed the inclination, to resist. All that could be done was to introduce local reforms, and correct in a certain degree local abuses; and some steps toward a representative government had already been taken in this way. Provincial and municipal assemblies had been authorized, which had commenced some reforms and suggested others, and were in progress of collecting information from practical men as to the real wants and requirements of the country. But these slow and progressive advances by no means suited the impatience of the ardent Italian people, and least of all, of that energetic and enthusiastic portion of them who were enrolled in the SECRET SOCIETIES which already overspread that beautiful peninsula, and have ever since exercised so important an influence on its destinies.[2]

² Colletta, ii. 338, 311; Ann. Hist. iii. 488; Ann. Reg. 1820, 238.

104. Origin of secret societies.

Secret societies banded together for some common purpose are the natural resources of the weak against the strong, of the oppressed against the oppressors. It is the boast, and in many respects the well-founded boast, of free nations, that by removing the necessity which has produced it, they alone have succeeded in eradicating this dreadful evil from the social system. Where men are permitted to combine openly, and the constitution affords a legitimate channel of complaint, the necessity of secret associations is removed, and with that removal their frequency is much abated. Yet it is not altogether removed: the desire to compass even legitimate ends by unlawful means sometimes perpetuates such societies when the necessity for them no longer exists; and the Ribbonism of Ireland and trades-unions of England remain a standing reproof against free institutions, and a lasting proof that the enjoyment of even a latitudinarian amount of liberty sometimes affords no guarantee against the desire to abuse its powers. In Italy, however, at this time, the despotic nature of the institutions had given such societies a greater excuse —if any thing can ever excuse the banding together of men by secret means and guilty acts, to overturn existing constitutions.

105. Their origin and previous history.

The CARBONARI of Italy arose in a very different interest from that to which their association was ultimately directed. They were founded, or perhaps taken advantage of, by Queen Caroline, on occasion of the French invasion of Naples in 1808; and it was by their means that the resistance was organized in the Abruzzi and

---

* "De' cinque fogli del re, scritti in Messina dal 20 al 24 maggio erano i sensi: pace, concordia, oblio delle passate vicende; vi traluceva la modesta confessione de' propri torti; parlavasi di leggi fondamentali dello stato, di libertà civile, di formali guarentigie; e così vi stava adombrata la costituzione senza proferirnesi il nome."—COLLETTA, *Historia di Napoli*, ii. 264.

Calabria, which so long counterbalanced the republican influence in the southern parts of the Peninsula. Subsequently they were made use of by Murat at the time of the downfall of Napoleon, to promote his views for the formation of a great kingdom in Italy, which should be free from Tramontane influence, and restore unity, independence, prosperity, and glory to the descendants of the former masters of the world. Being directed now to a definite practicable object, which had long occupied the Italian mind, which had been the dream of its poets, the aspiration of its patriots—which it was hoped would rescue it from the effects of the "fatal gift of beauty" under which it had so long labored, and terminate a servitude which clung to it conquering or conquered—this association now rapidly increased in numbers, influence, and the hardihood of its projects. It continued to grow rapidly during the five years which succeeded the fall of Napoleon and re-establishment of the Bourbon dynasty in Naples; and as the desires of peace had come in place of the passions of war, it had grown up so as to embrace considerable portions of the members, and by far the greater part of the talent and energy of the State. It had comparatively few partisans in the rural districts, among which ancient influences still retained their ascendency; but in the towns, among the incorporations, the universities, the scholars, the army, and the artists, it had nearly spread universally; and it might with truth be said, that among the 642,000 persons who in Italy were said to be enrolled in its ranks, were to be found nearly the whole genius, intelligence, and patriotism of the land.¹

¹ Colletta, ii. 340, 345; Idem, Cinque Jours de l'Histoire de Naples, pp. 35. Ann. Hist. iii. 488, p. 228, 299.

Governed both by princes of the house of Bourbon, and intimately connected for centuries by political alliance, intermarriage of families, and similarity of manners, Naples had for long been influenced in a great degree by the political events of Spain. Upon a people so situated, actuated by such desires, and of so excitable a temperament, the example of the Spanish revolution operated immediately, and with universal force. The Carbonari over the whole Peninsula were speedily in motion, to effect the same liberation for it as had already been achieved without serious effusion of blood in Spain; and as it was known that the Franc-Communeros of that country had played an important part in its revolution, sanguine hopes were entertained that they might be equally successful in their patriotic efforts. Their great reliance was on the army, many of the higher officers of which were already enrolled in their ranks, and which it was hoped would be generally influenced by the example and rewards obtained by the insurrectionary host in the island of Leon. These hopes were not disappointed; on the 2d July, Morelli and Menichini—the one a simple lieutenant in the army, the other a priest in the town of Nola, but who both held important situations in the society of the Carbonari—assembled the soldiers of the former's troop, raised the cry of "God, the King, and the Constitution;" fraternized with the National Guard, who joined in the same sentiments; and with their united force marched upon Avellino, the chief town of the province, in the hope of inducing its inhabitants to join their cause. This was not long in being effected. Concilli, who commanded the militia of that town, joined the popular cause; Morelli and he proclaimed the Constitution amidst unanimous shouts, and Concilii was, by acclamation, declared the head of the patriotic force and the Riego of Naples.¹

106. Commencement of the Neapolitan revolution.

July 2.

¹ Colletta, ii. 346, 347; Ann. Hist. iii. 489, 490.

The news of the insurrection at Nola, followed as it was immediately by the defection of the garrison of Avellino, threw the court of Naples into the utmost consternation, and General Pepe and Campana, who had the command at Salerno, received orders to march without delay on the latter town, while all the disposable force at Naples was ordered to advance in support. But vain are all attempts to extinguish revolt by soldiers who themselves are tainted with the spirit of insurrection. General Carascosa, who commanded the troops which came up from Naples, was no sooner in presence of the insurgents who were marching on Salerno, than he found his men so shaken that he was constrained to retire, to prevent them from openly joining their ranks. The revolutionists advanced accordingly to Salerno, which they occupied in force; and the intelligence of their approach excited such a ferment in Naples that it soon became evident that the maintenance of the government had become impossible. A large body of the principal officers in the garrison waited on GENERAL PEPE, and entreated him to put himself at the head of the insurrection, assuring him of the support of the entire army. He yielded without difficulty to their entreaties; and taking the command of a regiment of horse in Naples which had declared for the constitutional cause, he set out amidst loud cheers for the headquarters of the insurgents, whom he joined at Salerno, where he was immediately saluted by acclamation General-in-chief.²

107. Defection of General Pepe and the garrison of Naples.

² Colletta, ii. 348, 349; Ann. Hist. iii. 490, 492.

Every day now brought intelligence of fresh defections. The whole regiments in the garrison of Naples declared for the constitution, and every post announced the junction of some new garrison to the cause of the insurgents. Numerous crowds constantly surrounded the palace, and with loud cries and threats demanded the instant proclamation of the constitution. The students, the professors, the municipality, the whole intelligent classes, loudly supported the demand; and the king, without guards or support of any kind, moral or physical, found himself constrained to yield to their demands. Anxious to gain time, he consented, after some negotiation, to resign his authority into the hands of his son, the Duke of Calabria, whom he declared his Vicar-general, with the unlimited authority of "Alter ego." The prince immediately issued a proclamation declaring his acceptance of the Spanish Constitution, under certain conditions; but

108. The king yields, and swears to the constitution.

* "Vincitrice o vinta sempre asserva."

the silence of the king still excited the alarm of the popular party, and at length his majesty himself issued a proclamation, in which he ratified the promise made by his son, and engaged to accept the Spanish Constitution, under the reservation of such alterations as the national representation legally convoked might find it necessary to adopt.* The prince, at the same time, issued a decree declaring his unconditional acceptance of the Spanish Constitution as promulgated by His Most Catholic Majesty on the 7th March; and the king two days after solemnly took the oath in presence of all the civil and military authorities of the kingdom.† The whole authority in the kingdom immediately passed into the hands of the revolutionists. General Pepe was declared Commander-in-chief instead of the Austrian General Nugent, who was dismissed. General Felangieri was appointed Governor of Naples; the ministry was entirely changed, and a new one, composed of ardent liberals, appointed; a junta of fifteen persons nominated to control the Government, and the whole appointments solemnly confirmed by the king. Great popular rejoicings and a general illumination testified the universal joy at these rapid changes; but it augured ill for the stability of the new order of things, or its adaptation to the people by whom it was adopted, that they had *to send to Spain for a copy of the Constitution* to which they had all sworn fealty.¹

July 7.

¹ Colletta, ii. 368, 371; Ann. Hist. iii. 491, 495; Ann. Reg. 1820, 240.

109. Causes which prepared revolution in Sicily.

While military treason was thus overturning monarchy in Naples, and blasting the growth of freedom, by establishing a constitution utterly at variance with the habits, capacities, or interests of the great majority of the people, and not understood by ten in a million of the inhabitants, the progress of insurrection was still more rapid in Sicily, where, as already mentioned, a constitutional monarchy had been established by the English during their occupation in the latter years of the war, and the people, generally speaking, were more practically acquainted with the working of a free constitution. The English institutions had been abolished when they withdrew from the kingdom—unlike the Code Napoleon, which, founded on the matured wisdom of the Roman law, every where survived the fall of his dynasty. The government, however, had established municipal councils, elected by the more respectable classes, declared any additional imposts illegal without the consent of the States-General of the realm, and issued some salutary decrees for the limitation of the excessive evils of entails. But these practical reforms did not in the least answer the wishes of the Sicilian revolutionists, who, even more than the Neapolitans, sighed for the establishment of representative institutions, and ardently desired instantly to separate from Naples, and get the command of the country by adopting the Spanish Constitution. The first news of the revolution at Naples excited a great sensation; and this was fanned into a perfect tumult when the official intelligence arrived on the 14th of the acceptance of the constitution by the king. They had no thought, however, of remaining subject to his government. In the Sicilian mind, as in the Irish, personal freedom and revolution are inseparably connected with insular independence; and the first impulse of patriotism ever has been to detach themselves from the dominant power which has ruled, and, as they think, oppressed them.¹

July 14.

July 14.

¹ Colletta, ii. 376, 377; Ann. Hist. iii. 496, 498; Ann. Reg. 1820, 241.

The following day, July 15, happened to be the great national festival of the Sicilians—that of St. Rosalie—when, even in ordinary times, all business is suspended, and the whole inhabitants devote themselves to festivity and joy. It was held on this occasion with more than wonted splendor and animation at Palermo, the capital of the island. Early in the morning, the committees of the Carbonari were in activity, the bands of the revolutionists in motion; cries of "Viva la Costituzione Spagnuola!—Viva l'Independenza!" were universal; and the inhabitants even of an opposite way of thinking were compelled to adopt cockades of the national color (yellow), with the Sicilian eagle; and a trifling incident having excited their resentment against General Church, an Englishman, who still retained the command of the place, he was attacked, and his house pillaged. General Naselli, who commanded the Neapolitan troops in the island, in vain endeavored, by yielding to the movement, to moderate its excesses. The populace, having once tasted of the pleasures of pillage, and become excited by the passions of revolution, became wholly ungovernable, and proceeded to the most deplorable excesses. They advanced in tumultuous bodies to the three forts of La Sancta, Castellamare, and Palermo Reale, which commanded the city; and as the troops, having received no orders how to act, made scarcely any resistance, the populace made themselves masters of the forts and the whole arsenals they contained, from which they armed themselves, and immediately commenced an indiscriminate pillage.²

110. Revolution in Palermo. July 15.

² Colletta, ii. 378, 379; Ann. Hist. iii. 499; Ann. Reg. 1820, 241.

---

* "La costituzione del regno delle Due Sicilie sara la stessa adottata per il regno delle Spagne nell' anno 1812, e sanzionata da S. M. Cattolica nel marzo di questo anno; salve le modificazioni che la rappresentanza nazionale, costituzionalmente convocata, credera di proporre per adattarla alle circostanze particolari dei reali dominii." Francesco, *Vicaris*. July 6, 1820.—COLLETTA, *Storia di Napoli*, ii. 361.

† The oath taken by the Prince Vicar-general was as follows: "In quanto alla costituzione di Spagna, oggi ancora nostra, io giuro (e alzò la voce più daquel che importava l'essere udito) di serbarla illesa, ed all' uopo di fenderla col sangue."—COLLETTA, ii. 368, 369.

The oath of the king, taken on the 13th in presence of all the authorities of the kingdom, was still more solemn: "'Io Ferdinando Borbone, per la grazia di Dio e per la costituzione della monarchia napoletana, re, col nome di Ferdinando I. del regno delle Due Sicilie, giuro in nome di Dio e sopra i Santi Evangeli che difendero e conservero' . . . . . . (seguivano le basi della costituzione: poi diceva), 'Se operassi contra il mio giuramento, e contra qualunque articolo di esso, non dovrò essere ubbidito; ed ogni operazione con cui vi contravvenissi, sara nulla e di nessun valore. Così facendo, Iddio mi ajuti e mi proteggga; altrimenti, me ne dimandi conto.' Il profferrio giuramento era scritto. Finito di leggerlo, il re alzò il capo al cielo, fissò gli occhi alla croce e spontaneo disse: 'Onnipotente Iddio che collo sguardo infinito leggi nell' anima e nell' avvenire, se io mentissi o se dovrò mancare al giuramento, tu in questo istante derizi sul mio capo i fulmini della tua vendetta.'"—COLLETTA, ii. 370, 371.

Alarmed at the consequences of the movement they had in the first instance encouraged, Naselli and the nobles now endeavored to restrain the excesses of the populace. They appointed a junta of fifteen persons armed with full powers to restore order; and then having rallied the troops, succeeded, on the following day, in regaining possession of the forts which had been lost on the preceding. But the revolutionists, now infuriated by wine, and rendered desperate by the loss of the forts, proceeded to the prisons, which had been with difficulty defended on the preceding day, broke open the doors, burst through the barriers, and, amidst frightful yells on both sides, liberated eight hundred galley-slaves, who instantly joined their ranks. Encouraged by this great reinforcement, they proceeded, amidst revolutionary cries and shouts of triumph, to assail the troops which were concentrated on the Piazza del Castello, to the number of seventeen hundred. Assailed on all sides by a highly excited multitude twenty thousand strong, armed with the weapons they had won on the preceding day, and led on by a fanatic monk named Vaglcia, the troops were soon broken, and immediately a frightful massacre ensued. Prince Catolica, who had, in the first instance, declared in favor of the cause of independence, but subsequently united with the troops to coerce the excesses of the people, was inhumanly massacred, his head put on a pike in the centre of the city, and his four quarters exposed in four of its principal streets. Prince Aci and Colonel Sanzas, who had resisted the seizure of the artillery in the forts, shared the same fate; and General Naselli, who was besieged in the governor's palace, with great difficulty made his escape by a back way with a hundred soldiers, and, reaching the harbor, set sail in the utmost consternation for Naples. Nearly the whole remainder of the troops, fifteen hundred in number, were put to death; the whole Neapolitans in Palermo, to the number of six thousand, were thrown into prison; a new junta, composed of the most ardent revolutionists, was appointed by the populace; and during the remainder of the day and following night the town was abandoned to pillage, and all the horrors of a fortress taken by assault.[1]

III.
Frightful massacre in Palermo, July 16.

[1] An. Reg. 1820, 500, 501; Ann. Reg. 1820, 244; Colletta, ii. 378, 379.

The first care of the new junta, as is generally the case in such instances, after the victory has been gained, was to coerce the excesses of the unruly allies by whom it had been achieved. The galley-slaves were with some difficulty persuaded to give up their arms, a general amnesty for all offences was proclaimed, and they all receive 1 a free pardon upon condition of leaving the city; the whole murders and robberies of the preceding day were hushed up, and their perpetrators declared to have deserved well of their country; the most prominent of them received golden medals; the monk Vaglcia, was declared a colonel in the national army, and the Piazza del Castello, where the troops had been massacred, was directed to be called "Piazza della Vittoria." More efficient means were taken to assert the national independence, and restore the order which had been so fearfully disturbed. A national guard was established, and soon acquired in Palermo a tolerable degree of efficiency; circulars were sent to the other towns in the island, inviting them to join the patriots in its capital, and a deputation of eight persons was sent to Naples to arrange the terms of an accommodation, on the footing of the political independence of Sicily.[1]

112.
First measures of the new junta.

[1] An. Reg. 1820, 241; Ann. Hist. iii. 501; Colletta, ii 379, 380.

But the republicans of Naples were by no means inclined to these sentiments; and the revolutionists of Sicily soon found, as those of Ireland had done in the days of Cromwell, that whatever changes the elevation of the people to power may produce in the measures of government, it makes none in the ambition by which it is animated, and that a democratic rule is even more hard to shake off than a monarchical. So far from being inclined to agree to a separation of the two governments, the popular leaders at Naples were determined to uphold the union, and animated with the most intense desire to take vengeance on the Sicilians for the frightful atrocities with which the revolution had commenced. When the deputation from Sicily approached, it was only allowed to come to Procida, an island in the Bay of Naples; and the first question asked, was whether they recognized King Ferdinand, which having been answered in the affirmative, the negotiation commenced; but it soon broke off upon discovering that the *sine quâ non* of the Sicilian deputies was a separate parliament and constitution for themselves. "Repeal of the Union" was their watchword, which was answered in equally loud terms from the Parthenopeian shores, "Unity and Indivisibility of the Constitution." So far from acquiescing in the demand for a separation, the Neapolitan government made the most vigorous preparations for asserting their supremacy by force, and reducing the sanguinary and rebellious Sicilians to entire subjection.[2]

113.
Failure of the negotiations with Naples.

[2] Colletta, ii. 384, 385; Ann. Hist. 501, 502, Ann. Reg. 1820, 241, 242.

In the beginning of September, General Floridan Pepe, brother to the generalissimo at Naples, landed at Malazzo in Sicily, four leagues from Palermo, at the head of four thousand men; and though he met with some opposition he easily overcame it, and in a few days appeared before the gates of the capital. Its inhabitants were nearly reduced to their own resources, for the other boroughs in the island, horror-struck, and terrified at the frightful excesses of which Palermo had been the theatre, hung back, and had forwarded none of the required contingents for the support of the cause of separation in that city. The guerrillas which infested his flanks, composed almost entirely of the liberated galley-slaves, who dreaded the reimposition of their fetters, having been cleared away, the attack on the forces of Palermo began in good earnest on the 3d and 4th of September. They at first attempted to keep the field, but their raw levies proved no match for the regular troops of Naples. Defeated with serious loss in several encounters, their forces were soon shut up in Palermo; and the principal towns in the island having sent in their adhe-

114.
Suppression of the insurrection in Palermo. Oct. 5.

Sept. 3.

sion to General Pepe, and the regular troops in the garrisons, which still held out for the royal cause, having joined their forces to his, the junta of Palermo became convinced that the contest was hopeless, and were disposed to lend an ear to an accommodation. To facilitate and enforce it, Pepe moved forward on the 25th of September to the very gates of the city. He then renewed his propositions; but the violent party in the city had now regained the ascendancy, and dispossessed their own junta; the flag of truce was fired on, and the people seemed prepared for a desperate resistance. But it was seeming only. On the next day the Neapolitan forces succeeded in penetrating into the city by the royal park, and the Neapolitan flotilla in the roads drew near, and prepared to second Pepe by a general bombardment. The most furious republicans, now convinced that further resistance was hopeless, and could end only in the destruction of themselves and their city, listened to terms of accommodation. Pepe humanely acceded to their offer of submission, and, to save the city from the horrors of an assault, withdrew his troops from the posts they had won within its walls. The populace, seeing the troops withdraw, ascribed it to fear, and recommenced hostilities; but the retribution was immediate and terrible. On the 27th the bombardment commenced, and with the most dreadful effect. The town was soon on fire in several places, and the infuriated mob, passing from one extreme to another, ere long craved peace in the most abject terms. A capitulation was concluded on the 5th, and General Pepe was put in possession of the forts. The Neapolitan constitution was proclaimed, a new junta named, and the Prince of Palermo appointed to its head.[1]

Sept. 25.
Sept. 26.
Sept. 27.

[1 Colletta, ii. 355, 357; Ann. Hist. iii. 504, 505; Ann. Reg. 1820, 241, 242.]

Hitherto every thing had succeeded to a wish with the Neapolitans, but they soon found that great difficulties remained behind. The question of separation was not yet decided; the second article of the capitulation had provided that that difficult matter should be decided by a majority of votes in the Sicilian parliament legally convoked. This article, as well it might, was extremely ill received at Naples; the capitulation was annulled, as having been entered into by General Pepe without any authority to leave the question of separation unsettled. He was dismissed from his command, which was conferred on General Colletta. He was soon reinforced by six thousand troops from Calabria, with the aid of which he reduced Palermo to entire subjection, disarmed the inhabitants, and imposed on the city a heavy military contribution, which had a surprising effect in cooling their revolutionary ardor. Hostilities immediately ceased through the whole island, and the Sicilians soon found, to their cost, that they had gained little by their change of masters, and that their revolutionary rulers at Naples were more difficult to deal with than their former feeble monarch had been.[2]

115.
Renewal of hostilities.
Oct. 15.

[2 An. Hist. iii. 505, 506; Ann. Reg. 1820, 242; Colletta, ii. 358, 359.]

By the Spanish Constitution, now adopted as that of Naples, there was to be one deputy for every thirty thousand inhabitants, which gave seventy-four deputies for Naples, and twenty-four for Sicily; the inhabitants of the former being 5,052,000, of the latter 1,681,000. The electors were anxiously adjured in a proclamation to choose wise and patriotic representatives—a vain recommendation in a country recently convulsed by the passions and torn by the desires of a revolution. The deputies were such as in these circumstances usually acquire an ascendency—violent democrats, village attorneys, revolutionary leaders of the army, a few professors and literary men, and some renegade priests. The report of the Minister of Foreign Affairs announced that all the great powers had refused to recognize the revolutionary changes at Naples; that of the Minister of the Interior signalized the numerous abuses which had prevailed in the internal administration of the kingdom, and which it was proposed to remedy, and recommended the sale of a large part of the national domains to meet the deficiencies of the exchequer; that of the Minister at War, the measures which were in progress for providing for its external defense. This consisted in a regular army of 52,000 men, movable, national guards 219,000 strong, and an immovable one of 400,000 men. But these forces existed on paper only, notwithstanding all the efforts of the Carbonari;[1] the recruiting went on extremely slow; disorder and corruption pervaded every branch of the public administration; and, distrustful of all the vaunted means of national defense, all eyes were already turned to the congress of the allied powers at Troppau, where it was evident the real destiny of the revolution would be determined.

116.
Meeting of the Neapolitan parliament. October 1.

[1 Colletta, iii. 399, 403; Ann. Hist. iii. 506, 507; Ann. Reg. 1820, 242.]

The Roman States were too near, and too closely connected with the Neapolitan, not to participate in their passions, and in some degree share their destinies. Disturbances accordingly took place at an early period in the pontifical dominions; but they began in a very peculiar class, whose efforts for liberation proved of as little value as their assistance was discreditable to the liberal cause. On the night of the 4th September a revolt broke out in the great depôt of galley-slaves at Civita Vecchia, where sixteen hundred convicts of the worst description were confined. At seven in the evening a low murmur was heard in the principal depôt, and immediately a general insurrection commenced. The irons were broken, and by sheer strength and the weight of numbers the barriers were burst through, and the infuriated multitude rushed with frightful cries into the outer parts of the inclosure. The troops arrived, and the galley-slaves immediately invited them to fraternize with them, calling out "Long live the republic! Join with us, and to-morrow we shall establish a republic in Civita Vecchia, and all will be right." But the troops were not convinced that all would be right with the aid of such allies; they did their duty: several volleys fired at point-blank distance spread terror among their ranks, and at length, at seven next morning, the insurrection was suppressed, though not without considerable bloodshed. This outbreak was con-

117.
Insurrection of the galley-slaves in Civita Vecchia. Sept. 4.

nected with a much more considerable conspiracy in Rome and Beneventum, which, although suppressed in the capital by the vigilance of the police, succeeded in the latter town, and for a time severed it from the Ecclesiastical States.¹

A more serious insurrection soon after ensued in PIEDMONT, which, from its close vicinity to France, the long service of its troops with the armies of that power, and the martial spirit of its inhabitants, has always been more swift to share in the revolutionary spirit, and more sturdy in maintaining it, than any other of the Italian states. Like Spain and Portugal, the desire for free and representative institutions had there come to animate the breasts of the officers in the army, and nearly the whole of the educated and intelligent classes of the people. The Carbonari numbered not only the whole of the ardent and enthusiastic, but by far the greater part of the intelligence and patriotism in the state. Unhappily, their information and experience were not equal to their vigor and spirit, and by at once embracing the Spanish Constitution they entangled themselves in all the evils and difficulties with which that absurd and perilous system was environed.

On the 11th January some young students appeared at the theatre of Andennes, in the district of Novarrais, wearing the red cap of liberty, and by the violence of their conduct occasioned a tumult, which was only suppressed next day by four companies of the guards from Turin, which were marched from that capital under the command of its governor. But though suppressed on this occasion, the revolutionary spirit was far from being extinct, and it soon broke out under more serious circumstances, and in a far more influential class. In the end of February, on the representation of the Austrian minister that they were engaged in a conspiracy to chase the Imperialists from Italy, several noblemen, leaders of the liberal cause, were arrested in Piedmont, and conducted to the citadel of Finistrelles. This was the signal for a general movement, which it appears was embraced by the highest officers in the army, and principal nobles in the state, to whose conspiracy for the establishment of a constitutional government the Prince of Carignan, the heir-apparent to the throne, was no stranger.² He at first engaged to co-operate in their designs, but soon after, despairing of success, he drew back, and counseled the abandonment, or at least postponement, of the undertaking. But the conspirators were too far advanced to recede, and the advance of the Austrians toward Naples convinced them that not a moment was to be lost if they were ever to strike a blow for the independence of Italy.

On the morning of the 4th March symptoms of revolt appeared in some regiments stationed on and near Verulli, but the conspirators failed in their object then, from the majority of the troops holding out for the royal cause. But on the 16th the constitution of Spain was openly proclaimed at Alessandria, by Count Parma and Colonel Regis, who permitted such of the troops as were opposed to the movement to return to their homes, which a great number of them, including nearly all the mountaineers from Savoy, accordingly did. With the aid of such as remained, however, and a body of ardent students, the leaders got possession of the citadel of that important fortress, and immediately hoisted the *Italian* tricolor flag—green, red, and blue. No sooner was the intelligence of this important success received in Turin than the whole Carbonari and conspirators were in motion. Cries of "Viva il Re!" and "Viva la Costituzione!" were heard on all sides from a motley crowd of soldiers and students who surrounded the royal troops, who were not permitted to act against them, and probably would not have done so if ordered. Emboldened by this inaction, and hearing every hour of some fresh insurrection of the troops in the vicinity, the conspirators, on the following day, ventured on still more decisive measures, which proved entirely successful. Captain Lesio, setting out early from Turin, raised the regiment of light-horse at Pignerol, who moved toward the heights of Carmagnuola, shouting "Death *to the Austrians!*"¹ Their arrival at Turin, joined to the alarming intelligence received of similar insurrections in other quarters, decided the governor of the capital, the Chevalier di Varns, to evacuate the town with the few troops which still adhered to the royal cause. This was immediately done; the citadel and forts were taken possession of by the liberals, and the Spanish Constitution proclaimed amidst the combined shouts of the military and people.

On receiving intelligence of this alarming and successful insurrection, the king, who was at the chateau of Monte-Calveri, in the neighborhood, hastened to Turin, and a cabinet council was hurriedly assembled to consider what should be done in the circumstances.

At first it was intended by the monarch to put himself at the head of the guards and march upon Alessandria, which was regarded as the head-quarters of the insurrection; and a proclamation was issued denying the statements which had been spread abroad that Austria had demanded the disbanding of the Piedmontese troops and the occupation of the fortresses. But the accounts which rapidly arrived from all quarters of the general defection of the troops, rendered this a hopeless undertaking. The guards themselves were not to be relied on. Crowds, which there was no means of dispersing, collected on all sides, exclaiming, "Viva la Costituzione!" The military sent against them joined in the shouts, or remained passive spectators of the tumult. In this extremity a fresh council was held of the king's ministers, and it was there proposed to proclaim the constitution of France as a sort of *mezzotermine* between monarchy and a republic. But matters had gone too far to admit now of such a compromise.² While the council was sitting in the palace, and a vast crowd, with the military in their front, filled the great square adjacent, three guns were heard from the citadel, which announced that it had fallen into the hands of the conspirators; and soon the tricolor flag, hoisted on the ramparts, amidst loud cheers from all parts of the city, announced that the triumph of the insurgents was complete.

<small>121. Resignation of the king, and proclamation of the Prince of Carignan as regent, and the Spanish Constitution. March 13.</small>

Upon receiving this stunning intelligence, the king dispatched the Prince of Carignan to the citadel to ascertain the objects and demands of the conspirators. He found an immense crowd on the glacis, shouting "Viva il Re—Viva la Costituzione di Spagna!" and the troops in dense masses on the ramparts responding to the cries. The Prince was received by the garrison with the honors of war, and every demonstration of respect; but the demand was universal for the Spanish Constitution. "Our hearts," said they, "are faithful to the king, but we must extricate him from his fatal councils: war with Austria, and the constitution of Spain—that is what the situation of the country and the people require." With this answer the prince returned to the palace, where a long conference took place between the princes of the royal family and the cabinet. It was animated in the extreme, and continued through the whole night. The king was firm; resolved not to be unfaithful to his engagements with his allies or the cause of royalty, he took the resolution to abdicate in favor of the next heir, who was less implicated in the one, and might feel less reluctant to forego the rights of the other. This determination was immediately acted upon. Early on the morning of the 13th, the royal family, under a large escort, set out from Turin for Nice, and a proclamation was issued by the Prince of Carignan, declaring that he had been appointed regent of the realm. The change of government was immediately notified to the foreign ministers, the regent installed in full sovereignty, and the constitution of Spain proclaimed amidst universal acclamation, without the vast majority knowing what they had adopted or were shouting about.[1]

<small>[1] Revolution Piedmontain, 74, 79; Ann. Hist. iv. 341, 343, Ann. Reg. 1821, 238, 239.</small>

<small>122. General character of the revolutions of 1820.</small>

Such was the Revolution of 1820, in the Spanish and Italian peninsulas, and which more or less extended its influence over all Europe. Commencing with military treason, it ended with robbery, massacre, and the insurrection of galley-slaves. Nothing durable or beneficial was to be expected from such a commencement, "non tali auxilio nec defensoribus istis." It was characterized, accordingly, throughout, by impassioned conception and ephemeral existence: violent change, disregard of former usage, inattention to national character, oblivion of the *general* national interests. Designed and carried into execution by an active and energetic, but limited and special class of the people, it exhibited, in all the countries where it was established, the well-known features of class legislation; and by the establishment of class representation of the very worst kind—universal suffrage—it insured at no distant period its own downfall. It will appear in the sequel how sudden and violent the reaction was, how quickly the newly-raised fabric yielded to the aroused indignation of mankind, and how galling, and heavy, and lasting were the chains of servitude which, from the failure of this ill-judged attempt at liberation, were imposed upon the people.

In truth, all revolutions which, like that of Spain, and its imitations in Portugal, Naples, Sicily, and Piedmont, are brought about by a single and limited class of society, involve in themselves the principles of their own speedy destruction. They may be propped up for a time by the aid of foreign powers politically interested in the establishment of such institutions; but even with such external aid they can not long endure; without it, they at once fall to the ground. The reason is, that the constitution which they establish, being founded on the principle of opposition to all that has preceded it, the growth of centuries, is soon found to be wholly unsuited to the national disposition and necessities; and having been brought about by the efforts of a single class, it is calculated only for its interests, and proves destructive to those of all the other classes. There was no need of the bayonets of Austria or France to overturn the revolutions of the two peninsulas. Left to themselves, they would speedily have perished from their experienced unsuitableness to the circumstances of the countries. The only revolutions which ever have or ever can terminate in durable institutions, are those which, brought about, like that of Great Britain in 1688, by an unbearable tyranny which has for a time united *all* classes for its overthrow, are limited to the change requisite to guard against the recurrence of that tyranny, avoid the fatal evil of class legislation, the invariable result of class revolution, and make no further change in the institutions or government of the state, the growth of centuries, and the creation of the national wants, than is necessary to secure their unimpaired continuance.

<small>123. What caused their speedy overthrow?</small>

<small>124. What should the military do in such circumstances?</small>

What, it is often asked, are the military to do when called on by the government to act against insurgents demanding a change in the national institutions? Are they to imbrue their hands in the blood of their fellow-citizens, guilty of no other offense but that of striving to obtain the first of human blessings, that of civil liberty? The answer is, "Certainly," if they would secure its acquisition for themselves and their children. Freedom has been often won by the gradual pressure of pacific classes on the government; it never yet was secured by the violent insurrection of armed men. To be durable, it *must* be gradually established: its builders must be the pacific citizens, not the armed soldiers: it never yet was won by the sudden revolt of the military. The only effect of the success of such an insurrection is an increase in the strength and means of oppression in the ruling power—the substitution of the vigor of military for the feebleness of monarchical, or the infatuation of priestly government. Riego and Pepe were the real murderers of freedom in the Spanish and Italian peninsulas, for they overturned the national constitution to establish military rule, and blasted the cause of liberty by the excesses which came to be committed in its name.

CHAPTER VIII.

RUSSIA AND POLAND, FROM THE PEACE OF 1815 TO THE ACCESSION OF NICHOLAS IN 1825.

1. Vast growth and extent of Russia, America, and British India in recent times.

GREAT as have been the changes, marvelous the events, of recent times, in all countries, the most wonderful have occurred in different and distant parts of the world, where they exceed every thing not only witnessed by contemporaries, but recorded by history of former periods. We are too near them to measure their proportions with the eye; future times, which hear of them at a distance with the ear, or are witnesses, after the lapse of ages, of their effects, will more correctly estimate their relative magnitude and importance. The simultaneous growth of the Russian power in Europe and Asia, of the United States in America, and of the British empire in India and Australia, stand forth pre-eminent in this age of wonders. Great changes in human affairs—the overthrow of aged, the rise of youthful empires—the realization of the dreams of the Crusaders—the dwindling away of the Mohammedan faith, the boundless extension of the Christian—the restoration of a European and civilized empire on the shores of the Euxine—vast transplantations of mankind to the East and the West—the rolling back of the tide of civilization to the land of its birth—the peopling of a new world with the race of Japhet—are obviously connected with, or the direct consequence of, these events. The effects they have produced will always be regarded as a decisive turning-point in the annals of mankind; not less memorable than the overthrow of the Roman Empire—not less prolific of consequences than the Reformation in Europe, and the discovery of America. Nor have the gifts of Providence been wanting to aid in the mighty movement, and carry it out in accordance with the welfare and happiness of mankind. If to the age of Columbus it gave the compass and the art of printing, to that succeeding Napoleon it gave steam navigation, railway communication, and the electric telegraph; and if the activity of the former period was stimulated by the grant to man of the silver mines of Potosi and Mexico, the enterprize of the latter was still more powerfully aroused by the discovery of the gold-laden fields of California and Australia.

2. Increase of Russia by the treaties of 1814 and 1815.

Vast and powerful as the Russian empire was when its children, in emulation of those of Numantium, applied the torch to the palaces of Moscow, or carried their victorious arms to the heights of Montmartre and the banks of the Seine, it had not then attained half the influence and importance which it has since acquired. The victory of Alexander doubled his power—the overthrow of Napoleon halved his enemies. Independent of the immense increase of influence and importance, which necessarily and immediately resulted from the destruction of the vast armament which Napoleon had marshaled for its destruction, and the proud pre-eminence conceded to it in the diplomatic negotiations of Vienna, the physical resources and territorial extent of Russia had been enormously augmented during, and by the results of, the struggle. It was hard to say whether it had prospered most from victory or defeat. The carnage of Eylau, the overthrow of Tilsit, led only to the incorporation of Finland with its vast dominions, the acquisition of a considerable territory from its ally Prussia, the consolidation of its power in the Caucasus and Georgia, and the incorporation of Wallachia and Moldavia, and extension of its southern frontier to the Danube. And although, during the first agonies of the French invasion, these valuable provinces were in part abandoned, and the Pruth was fixed on as the boundary in the mean time of the empire, yet it was at the time evident, what the event has since abundantly proved, that this unwonted retirement of the Russian eagle was for a time only; and that their march toward Constantinople, conquering and to conquer, was destined to be not permanently arrested.

3. Important acquisition of Russian the grand-duchy of Warsaw.

But the great and lasting acquisition of Russia, from the results of the war, was that of the GRAND-DUCHY OF WARSAW. This important territory, which brings the Russian outposts within a comparatively short distance of both Vienna and Berlin, and renders the influence of its diplomacy irresistible in eastern Europe, was virtually annexed to Russia by the treaty of Vienna in 1815; for although, by the strenuous efforts of Lord Castlereagh and M. Talleyrand, its immediate incorporation with the dominions of the Czar was prevented, yet this was done only by its establishment as a state nominally independent, but really part of his vast territories. The grand-duchy of Warsaw was erected into a separate state, but the Emperor Alexander was at its head; his brother, the Grand Duke Constantine, was his viceroy, and Russian influence was predominant in its councils. A constitutional monarchy, and the form at least of representative institutions, were, by the strenuous efforts of France and England, established at Warsaw; but it was the form only. National habits and character proved stronger, as is ever the case, than diplomatic changes; freedom was found to be unavailing to a nation when it was conferred, not by domestic effort, but by foreign intervention; and the prosperity communicated to the Poles by the vigor of Russian rule, and the organization of Russian power, proved only an addition to the strength of Russia, when, after an unsuccessful and ill-judged revolt, the grand-duchy was formally incorporated with her dominions.

The grand-duchy of Warsaw, which the treaty of Vienna in this manner handed over to Russia, contained, in 1846, 4,865,000 inhabitants; it extends over 47,000 square geographical miles (about half more than Ireland), the people being thinly scattered over it, at the rate of 100 to the square mile; and the land under cultivation within its limits amounts to 5,444,000 *dessiatines*, or 14,000,000 English acres, being at the rate only of 1.12 dessiatine (three acres) to each inhabitant.* As the soil is generally rich, every where level, and for the most part capable of yielding the finest wheaten crops, it is evident that the inhabitants might be five times their present amount, not only without any diminution, but with a great and durable increase in their comfort and well-being. But the character of the Poles, like that of the Celts, ardent, enthusiastic, and daring, but gay, volatile, and *insouciant*, had rendered these gifts of nature of little avail, and retained the nation in a state of internal poverty and external weakness, when the means of attaining the reverse of both were within their power. Great part of the country was overshadowed by dark forests of fir; vast swamps extended along the margin of the rivers, and formed morasses and lakes in the interior, which chilled the atmosphere around; and even where cultivation had crept into the wilderness, it was in such a rude and imperfect manner as bespoke rather the weakness of savage than the powers of civilized man.[1]

4. Statistics of the grand-duchy of Warsaw.

¹ Tegob. Etudes sur la Russie, i. 111, 119; Haxthausen, Stat. de la Russie, i. 227.

The new kingdom of Poland, on the throne of which the Emperor of Russia was placed, was proclaimed at Warsaw on the 20th June, 1815. It consisted of the grand-duchy of Warsaw, as it existed in the time of Napoleon, with the exception of the city and little territory of Cracow, which was erected into a separate republic, the salt mines of Wielicza, which were ceded to Austria, and the grand-duchy of Posen, which was set apart to Prussia. Still the portion left for Russia was very great, and formed an immense addition to its already colossal strength; for it brought its dominions almost into the centre of Europe, and left the capitals of Austria and Prussia within ten days' march of its frontiers, without a fortified town or defensible frontier between. It added, too, the military strength of a warlike race, celebrated in every age for their heroic exploits, to the Russian standards—men whom Napoleon has characterized as those of all Europe who most readily become soldiers. They formed at this time a willing and valuable addition to the Muscovite legions, for the Poles clung to this little kingdom, as a nucleus from which might arise the restoration of their lost nationality; and the benevolent dispositions and known partiality for Poland of the Emperor Alexander inspired the warmest hopes that this long-wished-for result might take place. The strength and vigor which were ere long communicated to the new kingdom by the Russian administration, caused the country rapidly to prosper in the most remarkable manner in all its material interests; while the shadow, at least, of representative institutions, which was obtained for it by the efforts of Lord Castlereagh at the Congress of Vienna, flattered the secret hope that, with its lost nationality, the much-loved liberties of Poland might one day be restored.¹

5. Establishment of the kingdom of Poland. June 20, 1815.

¹ Malte Brun, Geog. Univ. vi. 505; Biog. Univ. des Hommes Viv. ii. 227.

The GRAND DUKE CONSTANTINE, who was placed as viceroy at the head of the government of this infant kingdom, was one of those strange and *bizarre* characters which occur but seldom in history, and can be produced only by a temporary, and, in some degree, fortuitous blending of the dispositions of various races, and the feelings produced by different states of society. The second son of the Emperor Paul I. and the celebrated Empress Catherine, he was born on the 8th May, 1779, and christened Constantine, from the design of that aspiring potentate to place him on the throne of Constantinople, and restore the Byzantine empire, as an appanage of the imperial house of Russia. He was married on 26th February, 1796, to a princess of the house of Saxe-Coburg; but the marriage proved unfortunate, and was soon followed by a separation. The savage manners and despotic inclinations of the Grand Duke were speedily felt as insupportable by a princess accustomed to the polished and considerate manners of European society.* He soon after entered on the career of arms, and in it from the very first he greatly distinguished himself. His first essay in real warfare was in 1799, under Suwarroff, on the banks of the Po, where his daring character and headlong valor were very conspicuous. Subsequently he joined the allied army, at the head of his splendid regiment of cuirassiers, in the plains of Moravia in 1805; and by the glorious charges, in which he defeated the best regiments of the imperial guard, and captured an eagle, had all but changed the face of Europe on the field of Austerlitz.² Subsequently he arrested the triumphant march of Napoleon at Eylau, and nearly closed his career amidst the snows of Poland. He went through the whole campaigns of 1812, 1813, and 1814 in Russia, Germany, and France, and attended the victorious march of his countrymen from Moscow to Paris.† He did not accompany them to London, but attended the Congress of Vienna, from whence he proceeded to take possession of his new kingdom in June, 1815.³

6. Biography of the Grand Duke Constantine.

² Hist. e. Europe. e. xl. §§ 130, 131.

³ Biog. des Hommes Viv. ii. 227.

His character and habits but ill-qualified him for the task. Born on the confines of Europe and Asia, inheriting the Tartar blood, warmed by the Slavonian temperament, his Oriental character had never yielded to the manners or civilization of Europe. He was an emblem of the nations of which he was so nearly the head: refinement had never penetrated the interior—the delicacy and graces of polished manners were on the surface only. His countenance, which was

7. His character.

* The Russian *dessiatine*, by which all their land is measured, contains 2¾ acres nearly, the acre being .37 of a dessiatine.

* The author has been informed by a lady, to whom the Grand Duchess herself recounted it, that, in some of his fits of passion, he used to make her rise during the night, and lie across the threshold of the door of their apartment.

† The author met him frequently there in 1814, and the chief traits in this description are taken from his own observation.

strongly characterized by the Tartar features, and severely marked by the small-pox, was ill-favored and ungainly; but his manners were polished in society, and no one, when so inclined, could be more winning and attractive. But the real disposition was widely different; he had nothing mild or gentle in his temperament. He rivaled Richard Cœur-de-Lion in his valor in the field, but he surpassed him also in the vehemence with which he ruled the cabinet, and the acts of tyranny by which both his public administration and private life were characterized. Violent, capricious, and irritable, he could never brook contradiction, and when inflamed by passion, indulged his vehement disposition by frightful and disgraceful acts of cruelty. He was an untamed savage, armed with the power and animated by the imperious disposition of an Eastern sultan, imperfectly vailed over by the chivalrous manners of modern Europe. Yet was the savage not destitute of generous sentiments; he could occasionally do noble things; and though the discipline he maintained in his troops was extremely severe, yet it was redeemed, and their affections won, by frequent acts of kindness. The close of his public career was very remarkable, and afforded a memorable proof of what is the real vanquisher of the savage dispositions of man, and how love can melt even the most ferocious bosoms. Such was the influence which a Polish lady of charming and fascinating manners acquired over him, that he sacrificed for her the most splendid prospects which the world could offer; and it will appear in the sequel that "all for love, or the world well lost," was, to the astonishment of Europe, realized by an Oriental prince, the heir to the greatest empire in Christendom.¹

¹ Biog. des Hom. Viv. ii. 227, 228; Personal knowledge.

8. His first acts of administration, and training of the army.

As might have been expected from a prince of such a character and habits, his chief attention was concentrated on the army. On the 11th December, 1815, when the annexation of Poland to the Russian crown was seriously contested in the Congress of Vienna, Constantine addressed to it an animated proclamation, in which he recounted with truth and deserved pride their glorious deeds in arms, their fidelity in misfortune, their inextinguishable love of their country, and called on them to rally round the emperor as its only bulwark.*

* "Réunissez-vous autour de votre drapeau ; armez vos bras pour défendre votre Patrie, et pour maintenir son existence politique. Pendant que l'Empereur Alexandre prépare l'heureux avenir de votre pays, montrez-vous prêts à soutenir ses nobles efforts. Les mêmes chefs qui, depuis vingt ans, vous ont conduits sur le chemin de la gloire, sauront vous ramener l'Empereur apprécier votre valeur. Au milieu du désastre d'une guerre funeste, il a vu votre honneur survivre à des événements qui ne dépendaient pas de vous. De hauts faits d'armes vous ont distingués dans une lutte dont le but souvent vous était étranger ; à présent que vos efforts ne seront consacrés qu'à la Patrie, vous serez invincibles. Soldats et guerriers de toutes les armes, donnez les premiers l'exemple de l'ordre qui doit régner chez tous vos compatriotes. Dévouement sans bornes envers l'Empereur, qui ne veut que le bien de votre Patrie, amour pour son auguste personne, obéissance, concorde ; voilà le moyen d'assurer la prospérité de votre pays, qui se trouve sous la puissante Égide de l'Empereur. C'est par là que vous arriverez à l'heureuse situation, que d'autres peuvent vous promettre, mais que lui seul peut vous procurer. Sa puissance et ses vertus vous en sont garant."—*Biographie des Hommes Vivants*, ii. 229.

On the 24th of the same month he presided at a solemn meeting of the Senate, at which the new constitution was read, and proclaimed with great solemnity. The prospect of the restoration of their country, of its resuming its place in the family of Europe, the known affection with which the emperor regarded Poland, and the generous deeds toward it by which his reign had already been signalized, the hope of the restoration of their liberties by means of the constitution which had been promulgated, diffused a universal enchantment, and for a brief season made the Poles forget the long-continued misfortunes of which their country had been the theatre.¹

Dec. 24.

¹ Biog. des Hom. Viv. ii. 228.

Great material prosperity followed the junction of the Polish and Russian crowns, and vast advantage to both countries. The very cessation of the jealousy and hostility which had so long subsisted between them, and the opening of the vast market of Muscovy to Polish industry, was of itself an immense advantage. Add to this the termination of the long anarchy of Polish democracy, and the substitution of the steady rule of a regular government, which, however despotic, was strong, uniform, and consistent, for the ceaseless dissensions and senseless jealousies of their stormy national assemblies. Warsaw, which, in 1797, contained only 66,572 inhabitants, and at the accession of Alexander less than 80,000, rapidly increased in splendor and opulence, and in 1842 numbered 140,000 souls. The industry of the country made sensible progress with the preservation of peace, and the steady market opened for agricultural produce both in the warehouses of Dantzic and in the consumption of the capital. Its revenue had augmented before 1830 by more than a third, and the seeds even of manufacturing prosperity had begun to germinate on its soil. The entire kingdom, which in 1815 could number only a hundred weaving looms, had come, in 1830, to contain six thousand, which manufactured annually seven million yards of cloth. All other rude fabrics had advanced in a similar proportion; but capital was still chiefly accumulated in the hands of the Jews, who amounted in Warsaw alone to twenty-seven thousand, and were to be found at the head of nearly all the industrial establishments in the kingdom. Nor was public instruction neglected; on the contrary, it was extended in the most remarkable manner during the pacific rule of the Russian emperor. Schools of every description had been established at Warsaw, and in various parts of the kingdom, which were crowded by the ardent youth of that impassioned land. The scholars, who were only a few hundreds in 1815, had risen in the capital alone in 1830 to 3700, and over the whole kingdom to 35,000, which was in the proportion of 1 to 130 souls, while in the neighboring realm of Russia it was only 1 to 280.²

9. Great advantage to Poland from its union with Russia.

² Malte Brun, Geog. Univ. vi. 528, 530 ; Tegoborski, i. 422.

But as it was to the military force of this new kingdom that the attention of the viceroy and the government was chiefly directed, so it was there that the most rapid changes and the most extraordinary progress took place.

10. Great increase of its military strength.

It would pass for incredible, were it not attested by undoubted evidence, and accounted for by the singular aptitude of the Poles for military instruction, and the extraordinary skill of the Russians in military organization. The Polish army, though it never exceeded forty thousand men—less than one in a hundred of the entire population—soon became, under the tuition of Constantine, one of the most formidable in Europe, from its incomparable state of discipline and equipment. The viceroy was extremely anxious on this subject, and rigorous to a fault in exacting the most ceaseless attention to the smallest minutiæ of dress and discipline. Though second to none in the hardihood with which he headed his chivalrous guards in a charge, it was on the trifling splendor of pacific display that he was chiefly set. He often said, after seeing his guards defile behind, "What a pity it is to go to war!—*it dirties their dress; it spoils soldiers.*" To such a degree of perfection did he bring them in these respects, that when, in October, 1816, the Emperor Alexander passed them in review at Warsaw, he was so struck with their martial air, exact discipline, and splendid appearance, that he embraced his brother several times in their presence. But they were not mere carpet knights who thus charmed the greatest military monarch in the world by their appearance: none showed, when the hour of trial arrived, that they were more equal to the duties and penetrated with the spirit of real soldiers. When the disastrous revolt of 1830 arrived, and the little kingdom of Poland strove to detach itself from its colossal neighbor, its fortresses of Modlin and Zamosc were in such a state of defense, and its army so efficient, that for ten months it maintained a doubtful conflict with its gigantic foe, and in the end was only subdued by the aid of Prussia[1]—a memorable instance of devoted though mistaken patriotism, and of the glorious destiny which awaited Poland, if its sons had had the sense to establish a stable government, and their heroic courage and military spirit had not been rendered nugatory by the insane divisions and democratic selfishness of former times.

[1] Biog. des Hom. Viv. ii, 228; Malte Brun, vi. 529, 530.

11. Failure of the representative system in Poland.

The powers of western Europe acted naturally and in a liberal spirit in stipulating, for the fragment of the Polish nation embraced in the new kingdom, constitutional privileges and a representative government, and the Emperor Alexander not less so in conceding them. But they proved worse than useless in practice; and their entire failure adds another to the numerous instances which history affords of the extreme danger of transplanting institutions suitable to one race and state of society to men inheriting a different blood, and in a different stage of political existence. Not less stormy and unmanageable by ordinary means, or any appeals to reason, than their ancient diets, where eighty thousand horsemen discussed the affairs of state in the plains of Volo, the new Assembly united to it the selfishness, interested motives, and corruption which are the gangrenes of the representative system, even in the most highly-advanced and polished societies. They were seldom convoked, and, when assembled, more than once abruptly dissolved. Poland flourished under the Russian rule prior to the calamitous revolt in 1830, not in consequence of her representatives, but in spite of them. No salutary or useful measures are to be traced to their influence; and they drew forth from no common man, the Emperor Nicholas, the following, it is to be feared, as applied to that people, just condemnation: "I understand a republic; it is a clear and sincere government, or at least it may be so; I understand an absolute government, since I am the chief of such an order of things; but I do not understand a representative monarchy. It is the government of falsehood, fraud, and corruption: I would retreat to the wall of China rather than adopt it. I have been a representative monarch; and the world knows what it has cost me declining to submit to the exigencies of that infamous government. I disdained the usual means of managing such assemblies: I would neither purchase votes nor corrupt consciences, nor seduce some to corrupt others. I disdained such methods, as not less degrading to those who yield to, than disgraceful to him who employs them, and I have paid dear for my sincerity; but God be praised, I have done, and forever, with that form of government." Thirty years ago, these words would have passed for the violent declamation of a despotic prince, abusing any institutions which put a restraint upon his own power; but time has since then taught us many lessons: we have seen the representative system working in France, Ireland, and some parts of England.[1]

[1] Le Marquis de Custine, La Russie en 1839, ii. 46, 47.

12. Great influence of Russia.

Strengthened by this great accession of power and territory, which brought their advanced posts into the heart of Europe, within a hundred and eighty miles both of Vienna and Berlin, Russia now assumed the place which she has ever since maintained as the undisputed arbiter of eastern Europe. Happy if she does not also become the mistress of the west, and the endless divisions of its aspiring inhabitants are not in the end extinguished by the unity of her advancing power. Great as are the physical resources of Russia, and rapidly as they have recently increased her influence, the prestige of her name, the dread of her strength, have increased in a still greater proportion. Men looked with a sort of superstitious awe on an empire which had never receded for centuries—which, secured in rear by the snows of the polar circle, had stretched its mighty arms almost to the torrid zone; which numbered the Vistula, the Amour, the Danube, and the Euphrates among its frontier streams, and already boasted of possessing a seventh of the habitable globe within its dominions. Nor had the events of recent times weakened this undefined impression; Napoleon's words had proved true, that Russia was backed "by two invincible allies, time and space:" foreign assault was hopeless against a state which had repelled the invasion of five hundred thousand men; and no empire, how strong soever, seemed capable of withstanding a power which, beginning its career of victory with the burning of Moscow, had terminated it by the capture of Paris.

What has augmented in the most remarkable degree this moral influence, is the prudence and wisdom with which it has been exercised. Never impelled by senseless ambition on the part of its rulers, or frantic passions among its people, the policy of Russia for two centuries has been eminently moderate and judicious. Its rulers are constantly actuated by the lust of conquest, but they never precipitate the moment of attack; conscious of their own strength, they await calmly the moment of action, and then appear with decisive effect. Like a great man in the conduct of life, they are never impelled by the thirst for immediate display which is the torment and bane of little minds, but are satisfied to appear when circumstances call them forth, aware that no effort will then be required to prove their superiority. Their conquests, how great soever, seem all to have been the result of necessity; constantly, in reality, aggressive, they have almost always *appeared*, in serious warfare, on the defensive. The conquest of Finland in 1808, the result of the treaty of Tilsit, is the only one for the last century in which its cabinet was avowedly and ostensibly the aggressors. While this prudent policy disarms their neighbors, and induces them to rely on the supposed moderation and magnanimity of the government, it adds immensely to their own strength when the moment of action has arrived. Every interval of peace is attended by a rapid growth of their internal resources, and its apparent leisure is sedulously improved by the government in preparing the means of future conquest. No senseless cry for economy, no "ignorant impatience of taxation," paralyzes their strength on the termination of hostilities, and makes them lose in peace the whole fruits of conquest in war. Alike in peace as in war, at home and abroad, their strength is constantly rolling on; like a dark thunder-cloud, a hundred and fifty thousand men, ready for instant action, constantly overhang in Poland eastern Europe; and every state within reach of their hostility is too happy to avert it by submission. When the storm broke on Hungary in 1849, it at once extinguished the conflagration which had set Europe in flames.*

13. Great wisdom of its external policy.

The secret of this astonishing influence of Russia in European politics, is not merely her physical resources and rapid growth, great as it will immediately appear both are, but the *unity of purpose* by which the whole nation is animated. Like that of individuals in private life, this is the great secret of national success; it is not so much superiority in means, as their persevering direction to one object, which is the spring to which in both it is mainly to be ascribed. The ceaseless direction of Roman energy to foreign conquest gave Rome the empire of the world; that of the French to the thirst for glory and principle of honor, conferred on them the lead in continental Europe; that of the English to foreign commerce and domestic industry, placed in their hands the sceptre of the waves. Not less persevering than any of these nations, and exclusively directed to one object, rivaling the ancient masters of the world in the thirst for dominion, and the modern English in the vigor with which it is sought, the whole Russians, from the emperor on the throne to the serf in the cottage, are inspired with the belief that their mission is to conquer the world, and their destiny to effect it. Commerce is in little esteem among them; its most lucrative branches are in the hands of the Germans, who overspread its towns as the Jews do those of Poland. Agriculture, abandoned to the serfs, is regarded only as the means of raising a rude subsistence for the cultivators, and realizing a fixed revenue for the proprietor. Literature is in its infancy, law considered as an inferior line; but war is cultivated with the utmost assiduity, and vast schools, where all subjects connected with it are taught in the most approved manner and with the latest improvements, are constantly attended by two hundred thousand of the best young men in the empire. The ablest among them are selected for the diplomatic service, and hence the great talent by which that profession in Russia is ever distinguished; but the whole remainder are turned into the army, where they find themselves at the head of ignorant but bold and hardy men, not less inflamed than themselves with the thirst for foreign conquest—not less impressed with the idea that to them is destined the sceptre of the world.

14. Their unity of purpose.

The physical circumstances of Russia are such as to justify, in a great degree, these anticipations. Its population in Europe consisted in 1850 of 62,088,000 souls, and in Asia of 4,638,000 more; in all, 67,247,000, and including the army, 68,000,000. It is now (1853) not less than 70,000,000. Of this immense mass no less than 60,500,000 are the inhabitants of the country, and engaged in cultivation, and only 5,388,000 the indwellers in towns, and engaged in their industrial pursuits, the remainder being nomads, or in the army. This enormous proportion of the cultivators to the other classes of society—*twelve to one*—at once indicates the rude and infantine state of civilization of the immense majority of the inhabitants, and demonstrates in the clearest manner the utter groundlessness of those apprehensions regarding the increasing difficulty of raising subsistence for the increasing numbers of mankind in the later stages of society, which in the early part of this century took such general hold of the minds of men. For while, in the immense and fertile plains of Russia, twelve cultivators only raise food for themselves and their families and one inhabitant of towns, and perhaps an equal number of consumers in foreign states— that is, six cultivators feed themselves and *one other member of society*—in Great Britain, by the census of 1841, the number of persons engaged in the cultivation of the soil was to the remaining classes of society as one to seven nearly; and yet the nation was self-supporting. In other words, the power of labor in raising food was above *forty times greater*, in proportion to the population in the old and densely-peopled, than the young and thinly-peopled state. The same truth has been exemplified in America, where, by the census of 1841, the cultivators over the whole Union are to the other classes

15. Statistics of the empire: its population.

---

* The Russian army which invaded Hungary in 1849 was 161,500 strong.—GEORGEY's *Memoirs of the War in Hungary*, ii. 142.

of society as *four*, and beyond the Alleghany Mountains as *eight to one*; facts which demonstrate that so far from population, as Mr. Malthus supposes, pressing in the later stages of society on subsistence, subsistence is daily acquiring a greater and more decisive ascendency over population.[a]

16. Great rapidity of increase of the Russian population.

The rapidity with which this immense body of men increases in numbers is as important in a political point of view as it is formidable to the rest of Europe. The annual present addition to the population has been from 1840 to 1850, as one to a hundred, and that notwithstanding the fearful ravages of the cholera, which in 1847 caused a decrease of 296,000.[†] This average increase will cause a duplication of the population in seventy years, being as nearly as possible the rate of increase in the British empire for thirty years prior to 1846; since that time the prodigious drain of the emigration, which has now reached the enormous amount of 365,000 a year, has occasioned an annual decline, probably only temporary, of from 200,000 to 250,000. It is greater than that of any other state in Europe, Prussia alone excepted, which is increasing at such a rate as to double in fifty-two years; but far from equaling that of the United States of America, which for two centuries has regularly doubled

[a] Koepper's Population de la Russie en 1838, 22; Tegoborski, i. 130, 132, 193.

its inhabitants every twenty-four years, aided, it is true, by a vast immigration from Europe, which has latterly risen to the enormous amount of 550,000 a year[1].

But the formidable nature of this increase, which, if it remains unchecked, will bring Russia, in seventy years, to have 140,000,000 of inhabitants, or about *half* of the whole population of Europe at this time, which is estimated at 280,000,000, arises from the vast and almost boundless room which exists in its immense possessions for future augmentation. Such is the extent of its territory, that, great as its population is, it is at the rate less than 30 the square mile for Russia in Europe, while in Great Britain it is at the rate of 220, and in France of 171. If Russia in Europe were peopled at the rate of Great Britain and Ireland, it would contain 500,000,000 souls—a number by no means impossible, if the vast extent of waste land in the Highlands of Scotland, and the mountains of Cumberland and Wales, not less sterile than the fir forests of the north of Russia, is taken into account.[c] Its entire superficies is 2,120,000 square geographical miles, while that of Great Britain and Ireland is 120,340; that of France, 207,252; that of Austria, 257,830; that of Prussia, 107,958; facts which, even more than its present number of inhabitants, demonstrate the prodigious capabilities which it contains, and the destinies to which it is ultimately called.[2]

[1] Tegob. i. 88, 92, 93; Koepper, Mem. sur la Population de Russie.

17. Great room for future increase in its inhabitants.

[c] Schnitzler, Russie, Pologne, et Finland, 238; Tegoborski, i. 98, 99.

What renders a people, advancing at such a rate, and possessed of such resources, in a peculiar manner formidable, is the unity of purpose and feeling by which the whole of the immense mass is animated. It is a common opinion in western Europe that a people inhabiting so vast and varied a territory can not by possibility remain united, and that Russia broken up, as it must ere long be, into a number of separate dominions, will cease to be formidable to the other powers of Europe. There never was a greater mistake. To reason thus is to fall into the usual error of supposing that all mankind are placed in the same circumstances, and actuated by the same desires. There have been many insurrections and revolts in Russia, but none which ever pointed in the most remote degree either to a change in the form of government, or to a separation of one part of the country from the other. It is in its Polish conquests alone that this passion has been felt. Even when the Russians have appeared in revolt, as they have often done, it was ever in obedience to the impulse of loyalty: they combated the Czar in the name of another Czar,

18. Unity of feeling in the whole empire.

* By the census of 1840, the proportion of cultivators to all other classes in the United States of America stood thus:

Agricultural.................. 3,717,756
All other classes............. 1,078,660

Or about 3½ to 1. Beyond the Alleghany Mountains they were:

Agricultural.................. 2,092,255
All other classes............. 257,751

Or about 8 to 1 in the basin of the Mississippi, the garden of the world. On the other hand, in Great Britain, by the census of 1831 and 1841, the families respectively engaged in agriculture and other pursuits stood thus:

	1831.	1841. Great Britain and Ireland.
Agricultural......	961,134	3,343,974
All other pursuits..	2,453,941	23,482,115

Or 7 to 1 in the latter period only. And yet, down to this period, the nation was, to all practical purposes, self-supporting—the importation of wheat having been for forty years back not only trifling but declining, and in some years nothing at all. Average of wheat imported yearly:

AVERAGES.		SINGLE YEARS.			
Years.	Quarters.	Years.	Quarters.	Years.	Quarters.
1800 to 1810	600,468	1808	—	1833	82,341
1810 to 1820	458,578	1815	—	1834	64,363
1820 to 1830	534,992	1819	122,133	1835	28,483
1830 to 1835	398,507	1820	31,279	1836	24,876
		1821	2	1837	244,087
		1822			

—*Vide* PORTER's *Progress of the Nation*, 3d edition, 139, 140; *History of Europe*, chap. xc. 31; and *American Census*, 1840.

†
	Population.	Excess of births over deaths.		In 100.
1840	50,231,000	393,000	....	.8
1841	50,626,000	344,000	....	.6
1842	50,910,000	842,000	....	1.7
1843	51,782,000	972,000	....	1.9
1844	52,754,000	755,000	....	1.4
1845	53,509,000	583,000	....	1.1
1846	54,092,000	538,000	....	1
1847	54,630,000	296,000 decr. (cholera)	....	.5

—TEGOBORSKI, i. 88.

	Population in 1851.	Proportion to sq. mile going.
British Isles............	27,435,315	220
France.................	35,690,000	171
Prussia................	16,576,000	150
Austria................	38,286,000	148
Russia in Europe.......	62,000,000	30

—TEGOBORSKI, i. 99.

The population of Great Britain and Ireland, however, was only 27,435,315 by the census of 1851, but that was in consequence of the Irish famine, 1846, and emigration ever since, so that the rate for it must be taken at what it was in 1845.

not knowing which was the right one, as the Scotch Highlanders did the Hanoverian family in the name of the Stuarts. The principle of cohesion is much stronger in Russia than it is in the British dominions, infinitely more so than in the United States of America. England and France may be subjugated, or broken into separate states, before the integrity of Russia is threatened; and many rival republics will be contending for the superiority on the Trans-atlantic plains, while Muscovites are still slumbering in conscious strength and patient expectation under the sceptre of the Czar.

19. Reason of this unity. Their Asiatic habits and religious feelings.

The cause of this remarkable, and, to the other states of Europe, most formidable unity of feeling in the Russian dominions is to be found, in the first place, as that of all great national peculiarities is, in the original character and disposition of the race. The Russians are not, it is true, encamped on the plains of Scythia as the Turks have been for four centuries on those of the Byzantine Empire; they have taken root in the soil, they constitute its entire inhabitants, and are now devotedly attached to it by the possession of its surface and the labors of agriculture. But they are not on that account less Oriental in their ideas, feelings, and habits; on the contrary, it is that very circumstance, joined to their agricultural pursuits, which renders them so formidable. They unite the devotion and singleness of purpose of Asia to the industry and material resources of Europe. It is incorrect to say that the Russians, like the inhabitants of England or France, are generally loyal, and only occasionally seized with the disturbing passions of revolution or religion. They are loyal at all times, and in all places, and under all circumstances. They can never be brought to combat the Czar but in the name of the Czar. Devotion to the throne is so interwoven with the inmost feelings of their hearts that it has become part and parcel of their very being; it is as universal as the belief in God or a future state is in other countries. No disturbing or rival passions interfere with the unity of this feeling, which is sublime from its universality, and respectable from its disinterestedness. The Czar is at once their temporal sovereign, their supreme chief, whose will is law in all temporal affairs, and the head of their church, under the ægis of whose protection they alone hope for entrance into paradise in the world to come. The Patriarch of Constantinople is, properly speaking, the head of the Greek Church, but he is a foreigner, and at a distance; the real ecclesiastical authority resides in the Czar, who appoints all the bishops; and his brows are surrounded, in Levesque, Histoire de Russie, v. 64, 95. their eyes, at once with the diadem of the sultan and the tiara of the pontiff.¹

20. Unity of interest in the empire.

This unity of feeling—the result of the combination, in the same people, of the Asiatic principle of passive obedience in temporal, and the Roman Catholic one of unity of belief in religious concerns—has been much enhanced in Russia by the entire identity of material interests over every part of the empire. Other nations are partly agricultural, partly manufacturing, partly commercial; and experience has proved that not the least serious causes of internal division are to be traced to the varied and conflicting interests of these different classes of society. But in Russia no such cause of division exists. The empire is, speaking in general terms, wholly agricultural. Its seaports are only emporiums for the sale of its rude produce; its merchants, its grain and hemp factors; its manufacturers, the clothers of its rural population; its nobles, the persons enriched by their labors. So inconsiderable is the urban population—only a twelfth of the rural—that it can secure no sort of influence in the state; and such as it is, its most lucrative professions are chiefly in the hands of foreigners. St. Petersburg itself has, including the garrison, which is never less than 60,000 men, only 470,000 inhabitants; but for the court, it would soon sink below 100,000; Moscow, 319,000—neither greater than Manchester or Glasgow at this moment.* If this extremely small proportion of the urban to the rural population is prejudicial to the national wealth, by depriving the state of the great hives of industry which in other states are the nurseries of capital, it is eminently favorable to the unity of feeling which pervades the empire. The Russians have the two strongest bonds of cohesion which can exist in a state—identity of religious belief, and unity of temporal interests.

21. General insufficiency of the schools to produce enlightenment.

The Empress Catherine took some steps toward introducing schools into her vast dominions; and great establishments for the young of both sexes excite the admiration of travelers both at St. Petersburg and Moscow. But she did so, only that her vanity might be gratified by the praise of the philosophers of western Europe; for she at the same time wrote to one of her favorites that if they were general through the empire, neither he nor she would long remain where they then were.† Catherine was right; the unbounded authority of the Czar, both as the temporal sovereign of the state and the head of the church, is based on the general ignorance which prevails. Before the light of knowledge the vast fabric would insensibly melt away, but with it would disappear at the same time the internal solidity and external strength of the empire. The Emperor Alexander did much to establish schools in his dominions; but as they were all either in the hands of the sovereign or the Church, they did little to enlighten the general mind, save in the military art, in which they kept it on a level with, if not superior to, any country of Europe. The schools, other than the government ones, which are mere military academies, being entirely in the

* Population in 1840 of—

St. Petersburg	470,202	Rigga	59,960
Moscow	319,068	Cronstadt	54,747
Warsaw	140,474	Wilna	54,499
Odessa	60,055	Toula	54,735
Astrakan	45,938	Kiev	47,424
Kazan	44,304	Woronije	43,860

—TEGOBORSKI, i. 122, 123.

† "Mon cher Prince,—Ne vous plaignez pas de ce que les Russes n'ont pas le désir de s'instruire. Si j'institue des écoles, ce n'est pas pour nous; c'est pour l'Europe, où il faut maintenir notre rang dans l'opinion: mais du jour où nos paysans voudraient s'éclairer, ni vous ni moi nous ne resterions à nos places."—CATHERINE, Impératrice, au Gouverneur de Moscow, 8 June 1772; DI CUSTINE, La Russie en 1839, ii. 115.

hands of the clergy, who are themselves, with some bright exceptions, the most uninformed of the community, little is to be expected for the training of the general mind from the spread of education, as it is at present constituted.

22. The clergy.
There is no nation in the world more profoundly impressed with religious feelings than the Russians, and yet there is none to which the Gospel has less been preached. The Bible is to them a sealed book, for not one in a hundred can read; preaching is unknown, for it would not be understood; form is all in all. Repeated genuflexions at passing the image of a saint, invariable crossing themselves before eating, and attendance at church to witness a few ceremonies around the altar on Sunday, form, in general, the whole of their devotional practices. In truth, the vast majority of the people are in so backward a state as to civilization, that they could neither understand doctrines nor apprehend precepts apart from the influence of the senses. Like all rude nations, they are deeply impressed with religious feelings; but it is the religion which enters by the eye rather than the ear, and is nourished by visible objects, not abstract ideas. Paintings of Scriptural subjects are to be seen in all directions, and are the objects of the most superstitious devotion to the entire people; for they think that the prohibition in the Commandments is only against *graven*, not painted images; and that, provided only the *surface is flat*, it is lawful to fall down and worship it. The clergy are a very numerous body in the empire—they amounted, in 1829, to 243,000; and being allowed to marry, their children are still more numerous, and having nearly all received the elements of education, they constitute the chief class from whom the numerous civil *employés* of government are drawn.* They are little elevated, either in instruction, station, or circumstances, above the peasants by whom they are surrounded, whose virtues and vices they in general share; but among the higher prelates, appointed by the emperor, are to be found men, as in the elevated diplomatic circles, second to none in the world in piety and zeal, and learning.¹

¹ Custine's Russia, iii. 276, 279.

23. Rank in Russia the Tchinn.
Titles and estates are hereditary in Russia, but not rank—a curious distinction, little understood in western Europe, where they are invariably united, but highly characteristic of its social system, and important in its social and political effects on the inhabitants. It is this distinction which has crushed the feudal system in that country, and placed society on an entirely different basis—half European, half Asiatic— from any of the other states founded by the conquerors who overthrew the Roman empire. Peter the Great was the author of the system which is called the *Tchinn*, and by its establishment he effected a greater revolution in the destinies of the empire than by the destruction of the Strelitzes. The whole people were by this strange but vigorous lawgiver divided into fourteen classes, corresponding to the grades in the army, and something analogous to the centuries into which, for the purposes of taxation and election, the Romans, in the days of the Republic, were divided. Each of these classes has certain privileges peculiar to itself, which are not enjoyed by the one below it: the lowest class, which is immediately above the serfs, is invested with the single privilege of not being beaten except by judicial authority; and to insure the enjoyment of this privilege, and prevent strangers from in ignorance invading it, every person in that class is obliged to have his number placarded above his door. All the inferior *employés* of government, and persons charged with subaltern duties in the administration, belong to this class. Every person who becomes a soldier acquires its privileges when he puts off his uniform and obtains his discharge. As to the serfs, they are left in the condition that our peasants were by Magna Charta— any one may beat them at pleasure.¹

¹ Custine, ii. 311, 312. Malt. Brun, vi. 415, 417.

24. Great power given by the Tchinn.
This singular organization of society, which pervades all ranks in Russia, from the Czar downward, augments to a most enormous degree the power of the sovereign, for it places the personal rank and privileges of every individual in the realm at his disposal. By a stroke of the pen the Czar can degrade every individual in the empire, whatever his descent, or family, or titles may be, from his rank, deprive him of all the privileges belonging to it, and cast him down to the very lowest class immediately above the serfs. With equal facility he can elevate any person to a class in which he was neither born, nor to which he is entitled by any distinction or services rendered to the state, and thus place him in a rank superior to any, even the very highest noble in the land. The rank thus conferred is personal only; it does not descend with the holder's titles or estates to his heirs; it is given by the sovereign, held of, and may at any moment be resumed by him. An awful example of the exercise of this power by the Czar is sometimes given, who, in flagrant cases, degrades a colonel at the head of his regiment, or a civil governor in the seat of his authority—has him flogged in presence of those so recently subjected to his authority, and instantly sent off in one of the cars provided for convicts to Siberia. It is these terrible instances of severe, but, in so despotic a state, necessary justice, often falling like a flash of lightning on the highest functionaries, and in the most unforeseen manner, which inspires so universal a dread of the power of the Czar, and causes his mandates to be obeyed like the laws of the Almighty or the decrees of fate, which mortals must accept and submit to in trembling silence. It has given rise to the common opinion that rank in Russia is military only, and depends on the position held in the army. This is in appearance true

---

* The clergy are thus divided, which shows how vast a preponderance the Greek Church enjoys:—viz.

Greek Church	223,000
United Greeks	7,000
Roman Catholics	6,000
Mahommedan	6,000
Reformed	400
	243,000

The whole are married, or capable of being so, except the Roman Catholic priests. The entire persons belonging to the clergy and their families, forming the *clergy class*, amounted, in 1829, to 900,000, and are now above a million of souls.—MALTE BRUN, vi. 421.

VOL. I.—2

but not really so; for in no country are civil gradations more firmly established or scrupulously observed than in Russia. They are *abreast* of the steps in military rank, and confer the same rights, but they do not confer steps in the army; hence a hair-dresser or tailor sometimes has the rank of a major-general, but he could not command a company. At the head of the Tchinn was long placed Field-marshal Paskewitch, the conqueror of Persia and Poland, and governor of Warsaw; at its foot the whole postillions and couriers in the empire.[1]

¹ Malte Brun, vi. 409, 412; Custine, ii. 312, 315.

25. *Caste of the nobles.*
This organization of society betrays its Eastern origin: it recalls the castes of Egypt and Hindostan, with this difference, that the rank is personal, and entirely dependent on the emperor's will—not hereditary, as with them, and naturally descending, like the color of the skin, from parent to child. As such, it confers an influence on the sovereign unknown even on the banks of the Nile or the Ganges. The class of nobles is very numerous; it embraced in 1829 no less than 389,542 individuals. It need hardly be said that a great portion of this class are destitute of property; but such as are so, for the most part find a refuge in the ample ranks of the army. Some of them are possessed of enormous fortunes, and when not trained to civil or military duties in the diplomatic or military line, they for the most part spend their lives in St. Petersburg or Moscow, where a great proportion of them, even to the most advanced age, are engaged in an incessant round of profligacy and pleasure. It exceeds any thing witnessed, at least on the surface, either in Paris or London; for passion, relieved from the pressure of public opinion, and too distant to fall under the coercion of the emperors, riots without control, and to a degree which would not be tolerated in the societies of western Europe. Democratic desires, with all their inconveniences, have this good effect, that they provide for the decorum of society, and check those gross instances of license which at once degrade and corrupt it. They render every man a spy on his neighbor, and the espionage of no arbitrary sovereign is so willingly and effectually exercised; for though no man likes to have a restraint imposed on his own passions, every one is willing to have it fastened upon those of his neighbor.[2]

² Custine, iii. 357, 361; Malte Brun, vi. 413.

26. *Of the bourgeois and trading classes.*
The trading or *bourgeois* class, which composes several ranks of the Tchinn, is made up in Russia, so far as the higher persons in it are concerned, for the most part, of foreigners. The portion of it drawn from the nation is composed of persons entirely emancipated, or of those who, still serfs, and not attached to the soil, and have commuted their obligation of personal service into the payment of a certain annual sum called the *obrok*, generally ten or twelve rubles a year (£1 12s. 6d. or £1 18s.). This latter class is very numerous; it contains no less than 14,000,000 of souls, including the families of the semi-emancipated serfs. They can not, however, leave their trade or force the purchase of their freedom on their master against his consent, and the obrok is generally raised as their supposed gains augment. This is perhaps the very best way in which the step, always difficult, sometimes dangerous, can be made from slavery to freedom, because it makes the gaining of the habits of industry precede the cessation of its compulsion, and renders man capable of being free before he becomes so. The peasants on the domains of the Crown, though engaged in the labors of agriculture, are substantially in the same situation; they pay their obrok or capitation-tax, and enjoy the whole remaining fruits of the soil they have cultivated, or of the manual labor. Their number is very great; it amounts to no less than 7,938,000 individuals of the male sex. The trading classes are all arranged in separate guilds or corporations, in which they enjoy considerable privileges—in particular, those of being exempt from personal chastisement, and the obligation to serve in the army, and to pay the capitation-tax, and having courts of their own where their matters in dispute are determined, as in the Saxon courts of the Heptarchy, by a jury of their peers. This arrangement of the trading classes in separate guilds or fraternities, enjoying certain privileges, and bound together by community of interest, is the very best that human wisdom ever devised to improve the condition and habits of the industrious classes, because it tends to establish an aristocracy among them, which at once elevates their caste and protects their labor, and tends to prevent that greatest of all social evils, *equality among the poor;* which, as it destroys their influence, inevitably ends in the equality of despotism.[1]

¹ Malte Brun, vi. 412, 415.

27. *The serfs: their number and condition.*
The last class in Russia is that of the SERFS or peasants, the property of their masters, who are by the law attached to the soil, and, for the most part, engaged in the labors of agriculture. Their number is immense: they amounted in Russia in Europe alone to 10,865,993 males in 1834, and in 1848 they had increased to 11,938,000, being as nearly as possible one-half of the entire population engaged in the cultivation of the soil.* It is a total mistake, however, to suppose that this immense body of men are slaves in our sense of the word—that is, in the state in which the negroes till recently were in the West India islands, or as they still are in the Southern States of America. They are the property, indeed, of their masters; they are sold with the estate, and can not leave it without his consent; and the property in them, as in the West Indies till of late, constitutes the chief part of its value.² But they enjoy several important immunities, which go far to assuage the bitterness of servitude, and render it doubtful whether, in the existing state of Russian society, they could be so well off under any other circumstances.

² Schnitzler, ii. 272; Custine, iii. 371, 380; Tegoborski, i. 311, 312.

* Peasants in Russia slaves in 1848 11,938,182
Free peasants, viz.:
Free peasants and Odnovoirsy. 2,395,070
Crown peasants.............. 9,209,200
Crown colonists.............. 150,000
Newly emancipated............ 146,550
                                   ————
                                   11,900,820
—TEGOBORSKI, i. 320.

28.
Privileges and advantages they enjoy.

They are sold with the estate, but they can not, without their own consent, be sold without it—a privilege of incalculable value, for it prevents the separation of husband and wife, parent and child, and the tearing up of the slave from the home of his fathers, which constitutes the last drop in the cup of his bitterness. By a ukase of the Emperor Paul in 1797, who, in this instance at least, proved himself a real father to his people, every slave or peasant subject to forced labor on his master's account, is permitted during three days in the week to work on his own. By a ukase of the present emperor, slaves are even permitted to hold small pieces of land on their own account, though in their master's name; and if he attempts to interfere with their enjoyment of the fruits, he is liable to be restrained by an order from the governor of the province. In addition to this, the master is obliged to maintain the slave in sickness or old age—an obligation which is always and willingly discharged, for a very sufficient reason, that the great extent of waste land in his possession, or surplus produce in his hands, in general enables the master to discharge the duty without feeling it as a burden.[1] It results from these circumstances that the condition of the serf is, generally speaking, so far as rude comfort goes, equal or superior to that of any peasantry in Europe, and that even the best-conditioned cultivators in its western states would find something to envy in the constant food and secure position of a Russian serf.[2]

[1] Schnitzler, i. 216, 229; Tegoborski, i. 316, 329; Studien Haxthausen über Russland, i. 174.

29.
The Tieglo: its advantages and evils.

There is a very curious institution, almost universal among the serfs of Russia, which betrays their Eastern origin, and has done more than any other circumstance to mitigate the severity of slavery among them. It savors of the village system so firmly rooted in all the northern parts of Hindostan, and recalls the days when the whole lands of Palestine were allotted afresh every half century to the Jews in ancient times. It is called the *Tieglo*, and consists in this: All the peasants of Russia or of Spain live in villages; isolated cottages, the glory and mark of English and Swiss freedom, are unknown. Each village has a certain portion of land allotted to it by the emperor, if the lands hold of the Crown, or by their lord, if of a subject, and which they labor on their own account for the subsistence of themselves and their families. Another portion of the estate is cultivated by the serfs, under the *corvée*, on their master's account. As the waste land in general bears so great a portion to that under cultivation, both portions are very extensive, and there is room and to spare for future increase.[1] The land allotted to the peasants is not divided into separate portions as it would be in England, where, in some places, "each rood has its man," but is all put at the disposal of the entire village community, which, in its turn, becomes responsible for the whole charges and obligations incumbent on its members.

[1] Haxthausen, Stud. über Russland, i. 169, 178; Tegob. i. 328, 331.

30.
Way in which it is carried into effect.

A certain number of the elders of the village make the partition of the lands among all the householders, and it is generally done with great care and circumspection, according to the necessities and capabilities of each inhabitant. The lot awarded to each is in proportion to the numbers which he has to feed, and the arms he can bring to aid in the cultivation of its furrows. When a son marries during the lifetime of his father, he applies for and obtains a separate portion for himself, which he labors on his own account, and which is augmented in proportion as his family increases. On the other hand, if it declines, his lot is proportionally contracted; and if he dies without children, it is given to some other by the little senate of the village. Inequality in the richness of the soil, or difficulties in its cultivation, are carefully weighed and compensated by the grant of a larger or smaller portion of ground. If the land at the disposal of the community exceeds the wants of its inhabitants, the surplus is divided among such of her peasants as have the largest stock of cattle and implements of husbandry, who are proportionally burdened with a share of the charges of the community. On the other hand, if the land falls short, a portion of the community hives off like a swarm of bees, and settles in some government or province where there is enough, and where they are always sure of a cordial welcome, for they bring with them industry, wealth, and cultivation. So firmly is this system established in Russia—as, indeed, it is generally in the East—and so suitable is it to the circumstances of the people, that, although it has many inconveniences, and checks the improvement of agriculture by the sort of *community of land* which it establishes, and its frequent repartition, the peasants resolutely resist any attempt at its removal and limitation, and cling to it as the great charter which secures to them all the means of living and bringing up their children. In some instances it has been given up, and the land permanently allotted to each inhabitant; but they have almost always recurred to the old system, as the only one fitted to their circumstances. It is so; it almost realizes the aspirations of the Socialists of Paris, as it did those of the Spartans; and it is a curious circumstance, indicating how extremes meet, that the nearest approximation that ever has been made in modern Europe to the visions of the Communists, is amidst the serfs, and under the Czar of Russia.[2]

[2] Haxthausen, i. 164, 178; Tegob. i. 330, 331.

A very simple reason chains the peasants in the greater part of Russia to the conditions of

* The Marquis Custine, any thing but a eulogist of Russian institutions and manners, gives the following account of the appearance of the old serfs, released from labor for life, sitting at the doors of their cottages: "Je ne puis m'empêcher de trouver un grand charme à l'ignorance, lorsque j'en vois le fruit dans la physionomie céleste des vieux paysans russes. Ces patriarches modernes se reposent noblement au déclin de leur vie; travailleurs exempts de la corvée, ils se débarrassent de leur fardeau vers la fin du jour et s'appuyent avec dignité sur le seuil de la chaumière qu'ils ont rebâtie plusieurs fois, car sous ce rude climat la maison de l'homme ne dure pas autant que sa vie. Quand je ne rapporterais de mon voyage en Russie, que le souvenir de ces vieillards sans remords, appuyés contre les portes sans serrures, je ne regretterais pas la peine que j'ai prise pour venir voir des créatures si différentes de tous les autres paysans du monde. La noblesse de la chaumière m'inspire toujours un profond respect."—De Custine, *Voyage en Russie*, iv. 10. Would the inmates of our workhouses present an equally agreeable spectacle?

feudal servitude; it is necessity. Slavery is the condition of existence. Writers in England are, for the most part, strangely misled on this subject by what they see around them. They behold their own farmers living in comfort, often rising to affluence, each on his own possession, and they ask why should not a similar state of things arise in Russia? They forget that the English farmer has a county bank near him, to furnish him with the means of improvement; a canal or a railway at his door, to transport his produce to market—an unfailing vent in numerous great towns for its disposal; ample means of purchasing the most approved implements, and learning the best methods of cultivation in the publications to which he has access. In all these respects the situation of the Russian peasant is not analogous, but a contrast. Situated in the midst of a vast and thinly-peopled wilderness, he is fortunate if he is only three or four hundred miles from any seaport, thirty or forty miles from any considerable town. Canals or railways there are none; banks are unknown, and if established, he has no security to offer for advances; his capital is confined to the ax which he carries on his shoulder, and the plow which he steers with his hands. Instead of the mild climate which enables country labor to go on, country animals to pasture in the open fields, during the greater part of the winter, he is doomed to inactivity during eight months in the year by three or four feet of snow upon the ground, and compelled to make the most of a brief summer to gather stock to live on during a long and dreary winter. How are animals to be fed, the wages of freemen paid, markets found, or freemen to exist, under such circumstances? Withdraw the capital of the landowners; throw the slaves upon their own resources, or the imaginary wages of labor in the present state of society, and the human race would perish, in a great part of Russia, as fast as, from the want of some similarly protective system, it has recently melted away in Ireland. The first winter would gather many millions to their fathers.[1]

M. Haxthausen, whose very interesting work has thrown such light on the rural economy and agricultural population of Russia, has enumerated three particulars in which the peasants of that country differ from those of western Europe, and which render any general and compulsory enfranchisement of the serfs extremely perilous, if not impossible. 1. The mass of disposable capital available to carry on cultivation by means of free laborers, paid by day's wages, bears no sort of proportion either to the wants of the inhabitants or the immense extent of arable land which requires to be cultivated. 2. In a great part of the empire the existing value of the product of the soil, if sold, so far from enabling the cultivators to pay any rent, would not even cover the expenses of cultivation. 3. In the remoter provinces, or where seaports are distant and money scarce, the only possible mode of paying a rent is by rendering forced labor legal, for there are no means of turning the rude produce into money. A similar necessity has been felt in similar circumstances in other countries. Witness the services in kind, and obligations to render rent in labor, formerly universal, still known in the remoter parts of Scotland. Accordingly, it has been often found in Russia that peasants whom the proprietors, from motives of humanity, or in imitation of the emperor, have put under the obrok system, and who enjoy the entire fruits of their labor after paying a certain annual sum, are much less at their ease than the old serfs, and they in general leave the cultivation of their fields to seek a less laborious existence in towns. In many instances, such has been their suffering from having incurred the destitution of freedom, that they have returned to their masters, and requested to be again made serfs. In general, it has been observed that emancipation has not succeeded, except in circumstances where easy modes of earning subsistence in other ways exist; and hence M. Haxthausen judiciously concludes that the liberation of the serfs should never be made a general or compulsory measure in Russia, but should be left to the wants and interests of each locality.[1]

It is not to be supposed from this, however, that slavery in Russia is not both a very great social evil, and eminently dangerous to the rest of Europe, and that he would not be the best friend of both who could devise and establish a method for its gradual and safe abolition. Probably that method is to be found only in the progressive rise of towns and spread of manufactures, which, by rendering the obrok system more general, should give the slaves the means of purchasing and the masters the desire of selling freedom to them. It is not easy to see, however, how this safe and wise method, which is analogous to the way in which it imperceptibly died out in the states of western Europe, is to spread generally in a country of such enormous extent as Russia, possessing eighteen times the area of Britain and Ireland, in Europe alone, intersected by few rivers, and for the most part so far distant from the seacoast. Its inhabitants seem chained by their physical circumstances to the system of compulsory labor for an indefinite course of years. This system provides amply, and better than any other under such circumstances could, for their subsistence, and the gratification of the animal wants of life; but it provides for nothing more. No gradation of rank can exist among the laboring classes while it continues; all are equally well fed, and equally ill civilized. The spread of knowledge, the extrication of genius, the growth of artificial wants, are alike impossible. If this state of matters is a great evil to the inhabitants of this empire, what is it to the rest of Europe, when it promotes the growth of a population of sixty millions, doubling every seventy years, and all nearly equally supplied with the physical, and destitute of the intellectual food of man? Perhaps the only safeguard against the encroachments of such a colossus, directed in politics and war with consummate ability, is to be found in the growth of a similar colossus, similarly directed, on the other side; and it would be a curious object for the contemplation of philosophy in future times, if the barbarism of infant could be stopped only by that of aged civilization, and the ambition of the Czar, heading the strength of the desert, was first checked by the ambition of the emperor leading forth the forces induced by the Communist doctrines of Paris.

34. Foreign conquest ever forced upon Russia by its climate.

Marquis Custine says, that in Russia we are perpetually reminded of two things —the absence of the Sun and the presence of Power. Both are equally important alike in their social and external effects; perhaps the last is the necessary consequence of the first. A very simple reason makes, and ever must make, the Russians desirous above all things of escaping out of their own country; it is the severity of its climate. Those who live in a country where the snow covers the ground for eight months in the year, and the long nights of winter are illuminated only by the cold light of the aurora borealis, long with inexpressible ardor for the genial warmth and sunny hills of the south, where the skies are ever blue, the sun ever shines, and nature teems with the luxuriance of tropical vegetation. The shores of the Bosphorus, the Golden Horn, the dome of St. Sophia, are not only the secret dream of ambition to every Russian, but the undoubted object of their expectation. "I do not wish Constantinople," said Nicholas; "my empire is already too large; but I know that I or my successors must have it: you might as well arrest a stream in its descent from a mountain, as the Russians in their advance to the Hellespont."[1] The habits which necessity has given to them, permanently fit, and ever must fit them for foreign conquest. Their life is a continual conflict with the severity of nature; actual warfare, as to the Roman soldiers, is felt chiefly as a relaxation from the rude but invigorating discipline of peace. What are the hardships of a campaign to men who never knew the luxury of beds, whose food is black bread and water, who sleep ever on the hard bench or cold ground, and know no pleasure save the simple ones of nature, and the exciting ones of conquest? When the north ceases to communicate vigor to the frame, hardihood to the habits, and ambition to the soul, Russia will cease to be a conquering country, but not till then.

[1] Schnitzler, ii. 247.

35. Fear the universal principle of government in Russia.

The presence of Power is not less universally felt in Russia than the absence of the sun. It is not merely that the Czar is despotic, that his will constitutes law, and that he is the master without control of the lives, liberties, and fortunes of all his subjects—the same system is continued, as is always the case in such circumstances, through every inferior grade in society. What the emperor is in his council or his palace, every inferior prefect or governor is within the limits of his territory, over his vast dominions. Despotism is the general system, force the constant weapon of authority, fear the universal basis of government. Gross acts of maladministration, indeed, are often made the subject of immediate and terrible punishment; the efforts of government are unceasing to find them out, and the justice of the Czar implacable when they are clearly established. But it may easily be conceived that in a country of such enormous extent, where the machine of government is so complicated, and no free press exists to signalize its abuses, these instances are the exception, not the rule. Power is, in general, undetected in its abuses, or supported in its measures. So universal is the dread of authority in Russia, that it has moulded the national character, determined the national tastes, and even formed the national manners. Obedience is universal, from the Empress on the throne to the humblest serf in his log-house. All do not what they like, or what they would have themselves chosen, but what they are ordered and expected to do. Dissimulation is universal: if they are not happy, they pretend to be so, to avoid the reality of sorrow which awaits expressed discontent. The present Empress—a woman of high spirit and the most captivating manners—is sinking under the incessant labor of amusing and being amused; the fortunes even of the greatest nobles or highest functionaries are wasting away under the enormous expenses imposed on or expected of them by the court. All must exert themselves incessantly, and to the uttermost, to keep up with the demand of authority, or conceal the vexation, ennui or discontent which, in reality, is preying upon their bosoms.[1]

[1] Custine, and in passim.

36. General use of corporeal chastisement.

Clark, the celebrated English traveler, says that there is not a second in Russia, during the day or night, that a blow is not descending on the back or shoulders of some Russian peasant. Notwithstanding a considerable softening of manners since the time when the description was given, it is still precisely applicable. Corporeal chastisement of their slaves is permitted to masters, without any other authority but their own; and, except in the classes in the Tchinn, who are exempt from that penalty, it is the great engine of authority with all intrusted with judicial power. The punishment of death is abolished by law in all cases except high treason; but such is the severity of the corporeal inflictions authorized, that it would be a mercy if it was restored. When a man receives a sentence of above a hundred strokes with the knout, the executioner understands what is meant; by striking at a vital place, he in mercy dispatches him at the third or fourth. The police officers lay hold of disorderly persons or malefactors in the streets, and beat them, without the formality of a trial, in the severest manner, without their cries exciting any attention among those who witness it, who, glad that the tempest has not fallen on their shoulders, quietly pass by without either observation or surprise. The nobles and higher classes of the Tchinn are exempt from such chastisement; but Siberia is constantly hanging over their heads, the most effectual of all bastinadoes to the mind; and the prisons resound with the cries of those upon whom the punishment of flogging for crime, or at the instance of their masters, is inflicted. The frightful screams of the sufferers under these inflictions leave the most melancholy impression on the minds of such as have heard them; they recall the horrors of slavery among the boasted republican institutions of America.[1]

57. Character which these circumstances have imprinted on the Russians.

It is this constant recurrence to force, and the frequency and severity of corporeal punishments in Russia, which has imprinted at once its regular methodical aspect on the march of government, and their supple character and extraordinary powers of dissimulation on the people. Like a well-disciplined regiment, in which the lash is the constant object of apprehension, every thing goes on silently and smoothly in Russia. Nothing retards or checks the machine of government; riots or disturbances of any sort are unknown; resistance is never thought of, or, if attempted, is speedily suppressed by the strong arm of power. The country resembles rather a vast army obeying the directions and coerced by the authority of a single general-in-chief, than a great community actuated by separate interests and impelled by various passions. As a necessary consequence of this irresistible force of power and necessity of submission, the character of the Russians has been modified in a most essential degree. Originality or independence of thought is in a great degree unknown; where these qualities exist, as doubtless they must in many breasts, they are carefully concealed, as the most dangerous qualities which the possessor can discover. Like the Greeks under the Mussulman yoke, the Russians have become perfect adepts in all the arts by which talent eludes the force of authority, and astuteness escapes the discoveries of power. They are admirably skilled in the use of flattery, and, like all persons initiated in that dangerous art, passionately desirous of praise themselves. The Americans do not exceed them in their thirst for national, —the French in their passion for individual praise—the certain proof in both of the secret consciousness of very serious defects. Those who feel none, do not desire the balm. They are most skillful imitators; and their powers of dissimulation are universally admitted to exceed those of the most accomplished courtiers or skillful diplomatists in western Europe.

58. Causes which have led to this character.

It was not thus in former days: this dissimulation and address is a contrast to the manliness and simplicity of early times. The Slave originally, like a rude and barbarous savage, was bold, intrepid, and outspoken, pitiless to his enemies, but simple, kind, and guileless to his friends; and such is still the character of the Cossacks, and of those distant tribes which have not felt the crushing influence of the central government. The principles of freedom had strongly taken root among them, and at a time when all the nations of western Europe were sunk in slavery, a republic flourished in Novgorod the Great, which rivaled for centuries the energy, in its fall it equaled the heroism, of the republics of Greece and Rome. It was the dreadful irruption of Bati and the Tartar hordes in the fourteenth century, who overran the whole eastern and southern countries of the empire, and for three long centuries kept them in a state of cruel servitude, which induced this disposition upon them; they assumed the character because they were subjected to the lot of slaves. During those disastrous centuries the Poles joined their arms to the Tartars; and the Muscovites, assailed on all sides, and driven to their last fastnesses, were fain to avoid utter destruction by the most abject submission. Ivan IV. first extricated them from this dreadful yoke; he won for them Kazan, Astracan, and the boundless realms of Siberia, but it was only to subject them to a tyranny almost as terrible as that from which they had escaped, and which won for him the lasting surname of the Terrible. Severe as it was, his yoke was cheerfully borne for half a century, because it averted the still more dreadful oppression of the Tartars; and when Peter the Great, a century after, sought to gain for them a place in the European family, he found the Muscovites prepared to submit to any mandates, and ready to be moulded by any will which assumed their direction. Let us not boast of the independent character and fearless disposition of the English peasantry, but rather thank the Almighty, who, in the encircling ocean, has given them a barrier against their enemies. Had the circumstances of both been different—had the Russians been located in Yorkshire, and the Anglo-Saxon on the banks of the Volga—who will affirm that the character of the two nations, despite the all but indelible influence of race, would not have been exchanged?[1] *

[Karamsin, Histoire de Russie, v. 447, 448.]

39. Great effect of the distances in Russia.

The Emperor Nicholas has often said that "its distances are the scourge of Russia;" and considered with reference to the march of civilization, it is obvious that the observation is well founded. It is difficult, indeed, to conceive how civilization can spread generally in a country of such enormous extent, possessing such slender means, natural or artificial, of internal communication, with so few seaports, and these few, for the most part, blocked up half the year with ice. At the accession of Peter the Great, Russia possessed only one seaport (Archangel), on the White Sea; and it was the pressing want of a great harbor to connect it with the commerce and ideas of western Europe which made him lavish such sums, and waste such an enormous amount of human life, in the construction of St. Petersburg. The same want is still felt with unmitigated severity in the interior. Civilization meets with grievous impediments in a country entirely flat, without minerals or coal to stimulate manufactures, covered with snow half the year, in great part shaded by forests, with few navigable rivers, and still fewer canals or rail

---

* "L'orgueil national s'anéantit parmi les Russes: ils eurent recours aux artifices qui suppléent à la force chez les hommes condamnés à une obéissance servile; habiles à tromper les Tartares, ils devinrent aussi, plus savants dans l'art de se tromper mutuellement; achetant des barbares leur sécurité personnelle, ils furent plus avides d'argent et moins sensibles aux injures et à la honte: exposés sans cesse à l'insolence des tyrans étrangers, il se pourrait que le caractère actuel des Russes conservât quelques-unes des taches dont l'a souillé la barbarie des Mongols. Le soutien des boyards ayant disparu, il fallait obéir au souverain sous peine d'être regardé comme traitre ou comme rebelle: et il n'existe plus aucune voie légitime de s'opposer à ses volontés, en un mot on vit naître l'autocratie."—KARAMSIN, Histoire de Russie, v. 44; vi. 351.

roads, distant from any harbor, and necessarily chained by physical necessity, over great part of its extent, to rude agricultural labor during the whole year. The situation of the basin of the Mississippi, of surpassing fertility, and intersected in every part by a vast net-work of navigable rivers, which descend from the Alleghanies on the one side and the Rocky Mountains on the other, is not a parallel but a contrast to that of Muscovy; and if we would rightly appreciate the advantages which Great Britain has derived, and Ireland might have derived, from its insular situation, compact provinces, numerous harbors, and mineral riches, we have only to contemplate what Russia has suffered from the want of them.

40. Civilization depends entirely on the higher ranks.

It results necessarily from these circumstances, that as much as Russia abounds to overflowing in the elements of physical, is she weak in the materials of intellectual strength: and that if a great destiny awaits her, as it plainly does, it is to be found in the conquest of the bodies, not the subjugation of the souls of men. Civilization depends entirely on and flows from the higher ranks; there is none of the ascending pressure from below which constitutes so important an element in the society of western Europe. In the very highest ranks it exists in the most refined and captivating form, and one of the many contrasts which strike a stranger most in that extraordinary country, is the strange contrasts which exist between the manners, habits, and tastes of the nobility and those of the great body of the people. After traversing hundreds of leagues over a country imperfectly cultivated, overrun by forests or swamps, and tilled in the places which the plow has reached by ignorant serfs, the astonished traveler finds himself suddenly landed in an enchanted palace, where the last refinements of European civilization are to be met with, where the finest copies of the Greek statues adorn marble halls of surpassing magnificence, where the choicest gems of Titian or Raphael enchant the eye, in drawing-rooms enriched with all the luxury of Ormolu and Sèvres, and beautiful women, arrayed in the last Parisian fashion, alternately fascinate the mind by conversation on the most celebrated novels or operas of the day, or charm the senses by the finest melodies of Mozart or Beethoven. It is this strange and startling combination of rudeness with refinement, of coarseness with elegance of taste, of barbarity with the last delicacies of civilization, in one class, with the first attempts at improvement in those beneath it, which strikes the traveler at every step in Russia. Diderot long ago said that "the Russians were rotten before they were ripe;" but it would be more just to say that they are ripe in one class before they are even beginning to form fruit in those below it.

41. Strong imitative turn of the Russians.

The Russians are essentially an imitative people, and they have carried talent in this respect to a length unequaled in any other age or country of the world. Their manners, their fashions, their arts, their luxuries, their architecture, their painting, are all copied from those of western Europe. Like the inhabitants of all northern countries, they are passionately fond of traveling, for this plain reason, that they seek in foreign countries gratifications they can not find in their own. They make good use of the opportunities they thus enjoy: they are well known as the most lavish patrons of art both in France and Italy, and they carry back with them to their deserts not only the finest specimens of ancient statuary or modern painting, but the most refined taste for their beauties, and correct appreciation of their excellences. Their architecture, in all but the very oldest structures of the empire, is all copied from the Greek or Roman; it is the Parthenon of Athens, the Pantheon of Rome, at every step. In the Kremlin alone, and some of the oldest structures of Nijni and great Novgorod, is to be seen the ancient and native emanations of Russian genius before it was crushed by the barbarism of the Tartars, or nipped in the bud by the imitative passion of Peter the Great. The eye of the traveler is fascinated by these long lines of pillared scenery interspersed with monuments and obelisks; but after a time it palls on the senses, from its very richness and uniformity: it is felt to be an exotic unsuited to the climate, and which can not take root in the soil; and the imagination sighs for the original architecture of the English cathedrals and the Moorish Alhambra, which mark the native-born conceptions of the Gothic and Arabian conquerors of the world.

42. Military strength of Russia.

But if western Europe has little to fear from the rivalry of Russian art or the flights of Russian genius, it is otherwise with the imitation of the MILITARY ART, which has been carried to the very highest point in the Muscovite armies. The army consisted in 1840 of 72 regiments of infantry, 24 of light cavalry, 90 batteries of foot and 12 of horse artillery. Each regiment consists of 7 battalions of 1000 men each; so that the infantry alone, if complete, would contain above 500,000 men. The guards, which are composed of the *élite* of the whole male population of the empire, consist of 12 regiments of infantry, 12 of cavalry, 12 batteries of foot and 4 of horse artillery, which are always kept complete. Besides this, there are 24 regiments of heavy reserve cavalry, and 12 batteries of reserve horse artillery, and the corps of the Caucasus, Orenburg, Siberia, Finland, and the interior, which contain 100 battalions of 1000 men each, 40 regiments of cavalry, and 36 batteries of cannon. Besides these immense forces, the emperor has at his disposal 164 regiments of Cossacks, each containing 800 warriors, of whom 56 come from the steppes of the Don, and are superior to any troops in the world for the service of light cavalry. If these immense forces were all complete, they would contain above 800,000 infantry, 250,000 horses, and 100,000 artillerymen. But the ranks are very far, indeed, from being complete; and in no country in the world is the difference so great between the numerical force of an army on paper and its effective muster in the field. The reason is, that numerous officers in every grade have an interest in representing the force as greater than it really is; as they draw pay and rations for the whole, and appropriate such as is allotted to the non-existing to themselves. Still, after making every allowance for these great deficiencies, it is not going too far to assert that Russia, when her strength is fully called forth, could produce 400,000 infantry, 100,000 cavalry, and 50,000 artillerymen for service beyond her own frontier, though the distances of the empire are so great that it would require more than a year to bring even the half of this immense force to bear on any point in Europe or Asia.[1]*

¹ Marmont, Voyages, i. 181, 182; State Hem, 48 S.; Londonderry, Russia, ii. 136, 139.

43. The military colonies. A very curious and interesting part of the institutions of Russia is to be found in the MILITARY COLONIES, which are established in several of the southern provinces of the empire. They owe their origin to the Emperor Alexander, who, being struck with the protection which similar establishments on the frontiers of Transylvania had long afforded to the Austrians and Hungarians in warding off the predatory incursions of the Mussulman horse, resolved in 1817 to found colonies of the same sort in several parts of his dominions. The system was extended and improved, under the able guidance of General de Witt, in the southern provinces in 1821. Several divisions of veterans, regular cavalry, were colonized in this manner, and a floating population of seventy thousand wandering tribes settled on certain districts allotted to them. The principle of these establishments is, that an immense tract of arable and pasture land is divided among a certain number of leading colonists, who are married, and for the most part have families, each of whom holds his lands, like the military tenants of former days in Europe, under the obligation of maintaining constantly a horseman and horses completely equipped, and providing for his maintenance. In return, he is entitled to the labor of the cavalier, when not actually in the field. In addition to these horsemen, who are constantly ready for service, there are a much greater number of substitutes, or *suppléans*, as they are called, who also are trained to the use of arms, and being all expert horsemen, are ready at a moment's warning to take the principal's place if he is killed or disabled for active service. All the children of the colony are trained to military service, and are bound to serve, if required, twenty-two years, after which they obtain their discharge and a grant of land to themselves. The whole are subjected to the most rigorous military discipline, and regulated by a code of laws entirely for themselves. At first the children were brought up somewhat after the Spartan fashion, being taken from their parents at the early age of eight years, and bred exclusively at the military schools;[1] but this was found to be attended with so many evils that the system was essentially modified by various regulations established by the Emperor Nicholas between 1829 and 1831. At present the military colonies form a sort of permanent cantonment of a part of the army, and they can, at a moment's warning, furnish 100,000 soldiers, fully drilled and equipped, capable of being raised by the *suppléans* and principal colonists to 250,000 men.

¹ Malte Brun, vi. 410, 411; Marmont, Voyages, i. 193, 215; Schnitzler,

The COSSACKS, so well known during the war with Napoleon, form another sort of military colony on a still greater scale. Their lands are of immense extent, embracing fifty-seven thousand square geographical miles—about two-thirds of the entire area of Great Britain, and incomparably more level and fertile. They are all held under the obligation of furnishing, when required, the whole male population of the country capable of bearing arms for the service of the emperor. They constantly furnish 100,000 men, distributed in 164 regiments, to the imperial forces. So strong, however, is the military spirit among them, and so thoroughly are they all trained from infancy to the duties of horsemanship, that if summoned to his standard, they could easily furnish double this force, either for the defense of the country or the purposes of aggressive warfare. Glory, plunder, wine, and women, form irresistible attractions, which impel the the entire nation into the career of conquest. It is their immense bodies of horse, more nearly resembling the hordes of Timour or Genghis Khan than the regular armies of western Europe, which constitute the real strength of the Czar; and as their predatory and roving habits never decline, and can not do so from the nature of the country which they inhabit, while their numbers are constantly and rapidly increasing, it is easy to foresee how formidable they must ere long become to the liberties of the other states of Christendom.[2]

44. The Cossacks.

² Bremner, Russia, ii. 432, 446; Enorowsky, Poland, 74, 75; Malte Brun, vi. 402, 403.

What renders the Russian armies the more formidable is the extreme ability with which they are trained, disciplined, and commanded. Whatever may be thought of the inferiority, in an intellectual point of view, of a nation where only 1 in 280 is at the entire schools of the state of any description, the same can not be said of their military training, which is conducted on the most approved system, and in the most efficient manner. All the improvements in arms, tactics, accoutrements, evolutions, or discipline, which experience or science has suggested to the other nations of Europe, are, with the rapidity of the electric telegraph, transmitted to Russia, and taught in the military schools which train its youth for their duties in the field, or adopted in its vast arrays. The Russian army, according-

45. The admirable discipline and equipment of the army.

* RUSSIAN ARMY, August, 1853:

	Men.	Guns.	Horses.
Guards.............	60,296	116	17,100
Grenadiers........	47,178	112	8,900
1st corps..........	59,178	112	8,800
2d do..............	59,178	112	8,800
3d do..............	59,178	112	8,800
4th do.............	59,178	112	9,400
5th do.............	59,178	112	8,800
6th do.............	59,178	112	8,800
Reserve Horse....	33,979	96	35,760
Active............	496,521	996	99,160
Caucasian.........	133,508	176	16,188
Finland...........	13,880	16	1,360
Orenburg..........	21,000	24	10,480
Siberia...........	28,100	24	10,000
	196,488	240	37,868
Grand total.......	693,309	1,236	137,028

—United Service Journal, Aug. 1853, 426.

ly, exhibits a combination of physical strength and intellectual power—of the energy of the desert and the resources of civilization, of the unity of despotism and the vigor of democracy—which no other country in modern times can exhibit, and to find a parallel to which we must go back to the Roman legions in the days of Trajan or Severus. The ranks of the infantry are recruited by a compulsory levy, generally, in time of peace, of five in a thousand—of war, of two or three in a hundred; but the cavalry, in a country abounding so much in nomad tribes, and where, in many vast districts, the whole male population nearly live on horseback, is in great part made up by voluntary enrollment; and as the whole rising talent of the empire is drawn into the military or diplomatic lines, it may easily be conceived what a formidable body, under such direction, the military force of the empire must become. Every soldier is entitled to his discharge after twenty-two years' service in the line, or twenty in the guards; and he leaves the ranks a freeman, if before he was a serf—a privilege which goes far to diminish the hardship of the compulsory levy on the rural population. The weakness of the army consists in the want of integrity in its inferior officers, which is as conspicuous in general as the honor and patriotism of its generals and commanders: the necessary consequence of the want of a class of gentry from which they can alone be drawn.[1]

[1] Malte Brun, vi. 412, 413; Bremner, ii. 376; Schnitzler.

46. Russian navy.

The navy, like the army in Russia, is maintained by a compulsory levy, which amounts in time of peace to 33,000 men. The fleet consists of thirty ships of the line and twenty-two frigates in the Baltic, and of sixteen sail of the line and twelve frigates in the Black Sea, carrying in all 6000 guns. These large forces give the Czar, in a manner, the command of those two inland seas, which can not be regarded in any other light but as vast Russian lakes. But as the sailors who man them are accustomed only to navigate a sea shut up with ice during half the year, or to plow the comparatively placid waters of the Euxine, they could never contend in the open sea with those who have been trained in the storms of the German Ocean, or braved the perils of the Atlantic. Still, as the Russian sailors, like their soldiers, are individually brave, and stand to their guns, as well as point them, as steadily as any Englishman, they may eventually prove formidable even to the colossal maritime strength of England; the more especially when it is recollected that Cronstadt is within a fortnight's sail of the mouth of the Thames; that the fleet is constantly kept manned and afloat in summer, by the compulsory levy; that thirty thousand soldiers are habitually put on board those in the Baltic, to accustom the crews to their conveyance to distant quarters; and that the interests of Great Britain and Russia in the East so frequently come into collision, that several times during the last thirty years they have been on the eve of a rupture, once with France and Russia united against England.[2]

[2] Malte Brun, vi. 410; Brem. ii. 375, 376; Schnitzler, ii. 176.

The revenue of Russia, though not considerable compared with that of France or England, is perfectly adequate to the maintenance of its vast establishments, from the high value of money and low rate of pay of nearly all the public functionaries, civil and military, in the empire.

47. Revenue of Russia.

It amounts to 460,000,000 paper roubles, or 500,000,000 francs (£20,000,000), and is raised chiefly by, 1st, A capitation-tax of four francs (3s. 6d.) on every male inhabitant, that of serfs being paid by their masters; 2d, A tax on the capital of merchants, ascertained by their own disclosure, checked by judicial authority; 3d, The revenues of the Crown demains, with the obrok paid by the emancipated serfs, who are very numerous; 4th, The custom-house duties by sea and land, which, on articles of foreign manufacture, are for the most part very heavy; 5th, The stamp-duties, which on sales of heritable property amount to an ad valorem duty of 5 per cent.; 6th, A duty on spirituous liquors and salt; 7th, The imperial duties on the mines of gold and platina, which are daily becoming more productive, from the great quantities of these valuable metals, now amounting to £3,000,000 annually, which are worked out in the Ural and Atlas mountains. It can not be said that any of these taxes are peculiarly oppressive, or such as weigh on the industry or capital of the nation; but they produce, when taken together, a sum which is very large in a country where the value of money is so high, and the standard of comfort so low, that the common soldiers are deemed to be adequately remunerated by a pay which, after the deductions for rations and other necessaries are made, leaves them scarcely a halfpenny a day to themselves.[3]*

[3] Schnitzler, ii. 276, 280; Malte Brun, vi. 406, 408.

48. Positions of the principal armies.

As the distances in Russia are so prodigious that it takes at least a year and a half to gather up its mighty strength, the principal armies are permanently disposed in positions where they may be comparatively near the probable scene of military operations, and best favor the designs of the diplomatic body. The first army, 112,000 strong, is composed of three corps, and stationed in Poland and the adjacent frontiers of Russia: it is intended to overawe the discontented in the former country, and hang like a thunder-cloud on the rear of Austria and Prussia. The second army, also 112,000 strong, is cantoned in the southern provinces of the empire, between Odessa and the Danube; it is destined to intimidate the Turks, and give weight to the ceaseless diplomatic encroachments of Russia at Constantinople. The third, which musters 120,000 combatants, is stationed as a reserve at Moscow, Smolensko, and in the central provinces of the empire; it is intended to reinforce either of the great armies on the frontier which may require to be supported,

---

* The Emperor Nicholas, since his accession to the throne, has labored assiduously to diminish the public expenses and check the frauds continually practiced in the distribution of the national revenue. In his own household and guards he has effected a reduction, with no diminution of splendor, of no less than 67,500,000 paper rubles. The expenses of the kitchen and cellar were reduced at once from 600 paper rubles to 200 a day. By similar economies in every department he was enabled to carry on the costly war in Turkey and Russia, in 1827 and 1828, without any sensible increase to the public debt. In 1830 it amounted in all to 1,360,000,000 francs, or £52,000,000.—SCHNITZLER, Hist. Int., ii. 184-186.

and is advanced nearer to the scene of active operations the moment that hostilities commence. In addition to this, there are never less than 60,000 men, including the guards, at St. Petersburg, and 40,000 on the Caucasus, or in the province of Georgia to the south of it. These immense forces may all be rendered disposable without weakening any garrison or military station in the interior. They are, however, so far separated from each other that it requires a long time to concentrate them on any one point, or produce the imposing array of 160,000 warriors, whom Alexander, in 1815, reviewed on the plains of Vertus in Champagne.[1]

<small>1 Hist. of Europe, c. xcv. § 26. Schnitzler, Historic Int. de la Russie, ii. 3, 4.</small>

<small>49. General corruption in Russia.</small>
Montesquieu long ago said that honor is the principle of a monarchy, and virtue of a republic. Both are true, in a certain sense, of society generally, though not of every individual of which it is composed; for though few are willing to practice these virtues themselves, yet all are ready to exact them of their neighbors. Public opinion inclines to the right side, because it is founded on our judgment of others; private acts often to the wrong, because they are prompted by our own inclinations. If we are to form our opinion from the example of Russia, we should be forced to conclude that the principle of despotism is CORRUPTION. This arises from the selfish desire of gain in individuals being unchecked by the opinion of those who, as they do not participate in, are not biased by it; and from the immensity of the empire, and the innumerable number of functionaries employed, rendering all the vigilance of the emperor and of the higher officers of state inadequate to check the general abuses which prevail. Doubtless there are many men in the highest situations, both civil and military, in Russia, who are as pure and honorable as any in the world; but they are the exceptions, not the rule. Generally speaking, and as a national characteristic, the functionaries in Russia are corrupt. The taking of bribes is general; justice is too often venal; the chiefs of the police, on the most moderate salaries, soon accumulate large fortunes; and even elevated functionaries are often not proof against the seductions of a handsome woman, or a magnificent Cashmere shawl for their wives or daughters.* The Emperor Alexander, in a moment of irritation at some great dilapidations which he had discovered in the naval stores, said, "If they knew where to hide them, they would steal my ships of the line; if they could draw my teeth without waking me, they would extract them during the night."[2]

<small>2 Schnitzler, Histoire Int. de la Russie, ii. 415, ii. p. 2.</small>

No words can convey an idea of the extent to which this system of pillage, both on the public and on individuals, prevails on the part of those intrusted with power in Russia; those practically acquainted with the administration of affairs in Great Britain may approach to a conception of its magnitude, from the strenuous efforts constantly making to introduce the same system into the British dominions, when the vigilant eye of Parliament and Government is for any considerable time averted. It is the great cause of the unexpected reverses or trifling successes which have so often attended the Russian arms on the first breaking out of fresh hostilities. So universal and systematic had been the fraud of the whole functionaries connected with the armies, that they are often found, when they take the field, to be little more than half the strength which was represented on paper, and on which the cabinet relied in commencing the campaign. When Nicholas declared war against Turkey in 1827, he relied on Wittgenstein's army in the south being, as the returns showed, 120,000 strong; but it was never able to bring 60,000 sabres and bayonets into the field: and when the army approached the Danube, he found, to his utter dismay, that the wood for the bridges, which were represented as already thrown over the Danube, was *not even cut* in the forests of Bessarabia.[1]

<small>50. Enormous abuses which prevail.</small>

<small>1 Schnitzler, Hist. Int. de la Russie, ii. 184, 185.</small>

Sometimes, indeed, the enormous abuses that are going on are revealed to the emperor, and then the stroke of justice falls like a thunderbolt from heaven on the head of the culprit; but these examples are so rare in comparison with the enormous number of dilapidations which are going on in every direction, that they produce no lasting impression. Like the terrible railway accidents which frequently occur in England, or steamboat explosions in America, they produce general consternation for a few days, but are soon forgotten. Occasionally, too, the malversation is found to involve such elevated functionaries, that the tracing of guilt or its punishment are alike impossible. At a review in April, 1826, soon after his accession to the throne, four men, dressed as peasants, with great difficulty succeeded in penetrating to the Emperor Nicholas, near his magnificent palace of Tsareko-Selo, and revealed to him an enormous system of dilapidation of the public naval stores which was going on at Cronstadt, where cordage, anchors, and sails belonging to the Crown were publicly exposed at the bazaar, and purchased at a low price by foreigners. Nicholas instantly ordered an officer with three hundred men to surround the bazaar; and upon doing so, ample proofs of the truth of the charges were discovered. Orders were given to prosecute the delinquents with the utmost rigor, and the imperial seal was put on the dilapidated stores; but the culprits were persons of great consideration; in the night of the 21st of June following, a bright light was seen from St. Petersburg to illuminate the western sky, and in the morning it was cautiously whispered that the bazaar had been totally consumed by fire, and with it the whole evidence of the guilt of the accused

<small>51. Striking instances of this corruption.</small>

<small>* On the accession of the Emperor Nicholas in 1826, it was discovered that in sixteen governments of Russia out of no less than 2749 ukases, or decrees of the Senate, passed, 1821 had remained unexecuted; in the single government of Kourak 600 lay buried and unknown in the public archives. In the same year there were 2,850,000 causes in dependence in the different tribunals of the empire, and 127,000 persons under arrest. The Senate decides annually 40,000 causes on an average; in 1825 the number was 60,000; which sufficiently proves that the vast majority must have been decided in absence, or without any consideration.—SCHNITZLER, Histoire Int. de la Russie, ii. 171, 175, 176.</small>

The *Gazette* of St. Petersburg made no mention of the fraud, or of the conflagration by which its punishment had been prevented.[1]

As a set off to this inherent vice and consequent weakness in the Russian empire, there is one most important source of strength which is every day contrasting more strongly with the opposite cause of decline operating in western Europe. Emigration among them is very general: in no country in the world is a larger proportion of the population more able and prepared, on the slightest motive, to locate themselves in fresh habitations. Armed with his hatchet on his shoulder—his invariable auxiliary—the Muscovite peasant is often inclined to leave his log-house and his fields, and carve out for himself fresh ones in some distant or more fertile forest. Followed by his flocks, his mares, and his herds, the Cossack or the dweller on the steppes is ever ready to exchange the pasture of his fathers for that of other lands. But there is this vital difference between these migrations and the emigration of western Europe—they are *internal* only; they do not diminish, they augment the strength of the state. From the British islands, at this time, an annual stream of 350,000 emigrants, nearly all in the prime of life, issues, of which two-thirds settle in the wilds of America;[*] and from Germany the fever of moving has, since the revolution of 1848, become so violent that 100,000 annually leave the Fatherland. It is needless to say that such prodigious drains, springing out of the passions and necessities of civilization, can not go on for any length of time without seriously weakening the strength and lessening the population of western Europe. But the very reverse of all this obtains in Russia, for there the movement is all within; what is lost to one part of the empire is gained to another, and a rate of increase approaching the Transatlantic appears, not in a distant hemisphere, but on the plains of the Ukraine and the banks of the Volga. Nor will it for long be otherwise, for the remote situation of the Russian peasants renders them ignorant of other countries, and averse to the sea; while their poverty precludes them from moving, except with their hatchets to a neighboring forest, or their herds to an adjoining steppe.

To this it must be added that the introduction of the free-trade system into Great Britain has already given a very great impulse to agricultural industry in Russia, where it is advancing as rapidly as it is declining in the British Islands. As this change has arisen from the necessary effect of the wealth, civilization, and advanced years of the British empire, so there is no chance of its undergoing any alteration, and it must come every day to evince a more powerful influence on the relative strength and fortunes of the two empires. Even before the free-trade system had been two years established in Great Britain, it had, despite the rude system of agriculture there prevalent, nearly doubled the exportation of grain from the harbors of Russia,[*] and tripled its value, while it has caused the production of cereal crops in the British Islands to decline 4,000,000 of quarters. The effect of such a continued and increasing augmentation on the one side, and decline on the other, can not fail ere long to exercise a powerful influence on the fortunes and relative strength of the two empires; and when it is recollected that the increase is given to a young and rising, and the drain taken from an old and stationary state, it may easily be foreseen how important in a short time the difference must become.

What, then, is the destiny of Russia?—for a destiny, and that a great one, she evidently has. Her rapid growth and ceaseless progress through all the mutations of fortune in the adjoining states clearly bespeak not only consummate wisdom of general internal direction, but the evolutions of a mighty design.[†] She is probably not intended to shine in the career of civilization. Her sons will not, at least for long, rival the arts of Italy or the chivalry of France, the intellect of England or the imagination of Germany. There will be no Shakspeares or Miltons, no Racines or Corneilles, no Tassos or Raphaels, no Schillers or Goethes, amidst the countless millions of her boundless

---

* EXPORTATION ON AN AVERAGE OF THREE YEARS, OF WHEAT, BARLEY, AND OATS FROM RUSSIA.

Years.	Tchetwerts.	Value in Roubles.	In Pounds Sterling.
1824–62	3,398,127	11,913,200	£1,970,000
1827–29	7,486,012	24,191,500	4,031,500
1830–32	11,324,731	39,407,400	6,566,000
1833–35	9,244,266	10,357,900	1,722,900
1836–38	7,510,299	31,873,200	5,312,200
1839–41	8,864,364	47,753,900	7,958,900
1842–44	8,685,907	40,131,100	6,680,000
†1845–47	14,349,986	115,483,700	19,262,100

—Tengoborski, i. 250.

Captain Larcom has reported that the wheat produce of Ireland has declined 1,500,000 quarters since 1845; and the return of sales in the market towns of England indicates a diminished production of wheat alone in Great Britain of at least 2,500,000 quarters more.

† Free trade in England.

† TABLE SHOWING THE INCREASE OF RUSSIA SINCE 1462.

Epochs.	Extent in Sq. Germ. Miles, 16 to an Eng.	Population. Approximate.
Under Ivan III., in 1462	18,200	6,000,000
At his death, in 1505	37,437	10,000,000
At the death of Ivan IV., in 1584	25,165	12,000,000
(Conquest of Kazan, Astracan, Siberia.)		
At the death of Michael I., in 1645	254,361	12,500,000
At the accession of Peter the Great, in 1689	263,000	15,000,000
At his death, in 1725	273,815	20,000,000
At the accession of Catherine II., in 1763	319,538	25,000,000
At her death, in 1796	331,819	36,000,000
At the death of Alexander, in 1825	367,494	53,000,000
Under Nicholas, in 1829	373,000	55,000,000
Under Nicholas, in 1852	376,000	70,000,000

—Malte Brun, vi. 380.

---

* EMIGRATION FROM THE BRITISH ISLES.

Year.	Number of Emigrants.	Excess of Births over Deaths.	Total Annual Decrease.
1850	280,484	240,000	40,484
1851	335,966	240,000	95,966
1852	368,764	250,000	118,764

Total in three years, 985,214 .... 730,000 255,214

—*Emigration Report*, March 1853. The annual increase of the births over the deaths is about 230,000; so that, when the emigration is taken into view, there is an annual decline of 120,000 or 130,000 in the entire population. This appeared in the census of 1851. Though the great emigration had only recently begun, it showed a decline in Great Britain and Ireland, taken together, of 600,000 souls since 1845; in Ireland, taken singly, of 2,000,000.— See Census 1851, and *ante*, c. 1, § 58.

territory; but there may be—there will be—an Alexander, an Attila, a Timor. Literature, science, the arts, are the efflorescence of civilization; but in the moral, not less than in the physical world, efflorescence is succeeded by decline, the riches of the harvest border on the decay of autumn. There is a winter in nations as well as in seasons; the vulture and the eagle are required to cleanse the moral not less than the physical world. If the glories of civilization are denied to Russia, she is saved from its corruption; if she does not exhibit the beauties of summer, she is not stained by its consequent decay. Hardened by suffering, inured to privation, compelled to struggle eternally with the severities of climate, the difficulties of space, the energy of the human character is preserved entire amidst her ice and snows. From thence, as from the glaciers of the Alps, the destroying but purifying streams descend upon the plenty of the vales beneath. Russia will evidently conquer Turkey, and plant her eagles on the dome of St. Sophia; she will do what the Crusaders failed in doing—she will rescue the Holy Shrines from the hands of the Infidels. But that, though an important part, is not the whole of her destiny. Still, when the Cross is seen triumphant over the wide expanse of the Lower Empire, will her millions remain in their snowy deserts, invigorated by necessity, hardened by suffering, panting for conquest. She is never destined to be civilized, save for the purposes of war; but she is destined to do what intellect and peace can never do. Scythia will forever remain what it has been from the earliest times—THE STOREHOUSE OF NATIONS, THE SCOURGE OF VICIOUS CIVILIZATION.

55. Two different people in Russia.

It has been well observed, that the great difficulty in Russia is, that it contains, in a manner, *two different people;* the one on a level with the most highly civilized states of Europe, the other, at the utmost, only fashioned to civilization by the police. The Marquis Custine says, "it contains a society half barbarous, but restrained in order by fear;" and though that is by no means true of the first people, it is strictly so of the last. The interests, feelings, and desires of these two different people are irreconcilable; an impassable abyss separates them. That which the first desires with the most passionate ardor, is a matter of indifference or unintelligible to the other. The highly-educated classes, acquainted with the society, familiar with the literature, impregnated with the ideas of western Europe, often sigh for its institutions, its excitements, its freedom. The immense mass of the peasantry, the great majority of the trading classes, repel such ideas as repugnant to their feelings, at variance with their habits, subversive of their faith. The first long for parliaments, elections, constitutional government, a national literature, a free press; the latter are satisfied to go on as their fathers did before them, with their Czar, their bishops, their popes—obeying every mandate of government as a decree of the Most High; desiring, knowing nothing beyond their village, their fields, their steppe. For which of these different people is the Emperor to legislate? for the enlightened few or the ignorant many; for the three hundred thousand travelled and highly-polished nobles, or the seventy millions of simple and unlettered peasants? Yet must institutions of some kind be established, legislation of some sort go on; and the great difficulty in Russia is, that the one class in secret desires what the other in sincerity abominates, and what would be beneficial to the former would prove utter ruin to the latter.[1]

[1] Schnitzler, ii. 44; 45: Custine, iii. 95.

This great difficulty, by far the most serious which exists in Russian society, was much aggravated after the termination of the war by the feelings with which the *officers* of the army returned from the fields of their conquest and their fame. In the hard-fought campaigns of Germany and France they had stood side by side with the ardent youth of the Teutonic universities, whose feelings had been warmed by the fervor of the Tugendbund, whose imaginations had been kindled by the poetry of Körner; at the capture of Paris they had seen the world in transports at the magnanimous words of the Czar in praise of liberal institutions; many of them had shared in his reception in London, and witnessed the marvelous spectacle of a free people emerging unscathed from a contest, from which they themselves had been extricated only by committing their capital to the flames. Immense was the influence which these circumstances came ere long to exercise on the highly-educated youth of Russia, speaking French and English as well as natives, associating with the very highest society of these nations, and contrasting the varied excitements and intellectual pleasures at their command, with the stillness and monotony, save from physical sensations, of their own fettered land. They saw civilization on its bright side only: they had basked in its sunshine, they had not felt its shade. They returned home, as so many travelers do, to the cold regions of the north, discontented with their own country, and passionately desirous of a change. These sentiments were dangerous; their expression might consign the utterer at once to Siberia: they were shrouded in silence, like a secret passion in the female heart from a jealous husband; but like all other emotions, they only became the more violent from the necessity of being concealed, and came in many noble breasts entirely to absorb the mind, to the exclusion of all objects of pacific interest or ambition.[2]

56. Liberal ideas with which the troops returned from France and Germany.

[2] Schnitzler, ii. 45, 49; Custine, iii. 95, 99.

Ignorant of the spread of passions which were destined ere long to cause the earth to quake beneath his feet, and carried away by the intoxicating incense which the loudly expressed admiration of the world had lavished upon him at Paris, the Emperor Alexander returned to St. Petersburg in 1814, after his magnificent reception in London, with a mind set rather on vast projects for the pacification of the world, the extirpation of war, and the spread of the sway of the Gospel in every land, than the establishment of any safe or practicable reforms in his own. His benevolence was great, his heart large, his imagination warm; but his practical acquaintance with men was small, and he aimed rather at reforming man-

57. First steps of Alexander, on his return to Russia in 1814.

kind at once by the ukases of despotism, than putting matters in a train for the slow and almost imperceptible growth of real improvement, working through the changed habits and desires of the people. He re-entered his capital after his long absence on the 24th July, and his arrival, after such marvelous events as had signalized his absence, was prepared to be celebrated by extraordinary demonstrations of joy. By an order from the Emperor they were all stopped. "The events," said he to the governor of St. Petersburg, "which have terminated the bloody wars of Europe, are the work of the Most High; it is before Him alone that it behoves us to prostrate ourselves."[1]

[1 Schnitzler, i. 73, 75; Biog. Univ. lvi. 180, 181, (Alexandre).]

59. His beneficent measures.

He refused the title of "the Blessed," which the Senate had decreed should be conferred upon him. His first care was to efface, so far as possible, the traces of the war; his next, to grant a general pardon to all the persons, of whom there were many, who had, during its continuance, been drawn into traitorous correspondence with the enemy. He remitted the capitation tax to the peasants in the provinces which had suffered the most from invasion, and opened at Berlin and Konigsberg banks, where the notes of the Bank of Russia which had been given in payment during the war were retired from the holders at the current rate of exchange. Soon after, he concluded a peace with the Sultan of Persia, by which, in consideration of a very large district of country ceded to Russia, he promised his aid in supporting the son whom the Shah might design for his successor. By this treaty the Russians acquired the whole important country which lies between the Black Sea and the Caspian, and became masters of the famous gates of Derbend, which so often in former ages had opened to the Tartars an entrance into Southern Asia.[2]

[2 Biog. Univ. lvi. 181, 182 (Alexandre).]

A full account has already been given of the part which Russia took in the Congress of Vienna and the acquisition of Poland in a former work;[3] and of the magnanimous sentiments which Alexander displayed at the Congress of Aix-la-Chapelle in this.[4] Two important alliances, destined to influence materially the international relations of Europe, were concluded during this period. The first was the marriage of his sister, the Grand Duchess Ann, to the Prince of Orange, which took place when he visited Brussels and the field of Waterloo in September, 1815; the second, the conclusion of the arrangements for the marriage of his brother Nicholas, who has since become emperor, to Charlotte, Princess of Prussia, who is still Empress of Russia, which was solemnized some years after. From thence he proceeded to Warsaw, where he concluded the arrangements for the establishment of the kingdom of Poland, and left General Zayonchek, a Pole by birth, in command as viceroy. He returned to St. Petersburg on 13th December, having, by this acquisition of territory and family alliances, extended the Russian

59. Marriage of Alexander's sister to the Prince of Orange, and of the Grand Duke Nicholas to the Princess of Prussia.

[3 Hist. of Europe, 1789-1815, c. xcvi. §§ 53, 69.]

[4 Ante, c. vi. §§ 69, 70.]

Sept. 19, 1815.

July 13, 1817.

influence in a direct line, and without any break, over the whole north of Europe, from the Niemen to the Rhine. Thus was the Netherlands restored to its proper position and rank in Continental affairs; instead of being the outwork of France against Europe, it became the bulwark of Europe against France.[1]

[1 Ann Reg 1815, 101. Biog. Univ. lvi. 185; Biog. des Hommes Vivantes, iv 512.]

Consumed with the desire to heal the wounds of war, and convince himself with his own eyes of the necessities of the districts for which succor was petitioned, Alexander gave himself only a few months' repose at St. Petersburg. His life, for the next ten years to his death, was more than half spent in traveling, and flying with almost incredible rapidity from one part of his vast dominions to another. The postillions, urging their horses to the utmost speed, carried him over the rough roads of Russia at the rate of seventeen miles an hour; wrapt in his cloak, meditating acts of justice, dreaming of projects of philanthropy, the Czar underwent, for days and nights together, with almost incredible patience, the exhausting fatigue. Hardly was his departure from St. Petersburg heard of, when the thunder of artillery announced his arrival at Moscow, Warsaw, or Odessa. But although Alexander thus wasted his strength and passed his life in traversing his dominions, his heart was elsewhere. The great events of Paris had got possession of his imagination; the Holy Alliance, the suggestions of Madame Krudener, occupied his thoughts; and he dreamed more of his supposed mission as the apostle of peace, the arbiter of Christendom, than of his duties as the Czar of Russia, the supreme disposer of the lives and liberties of sixty millions of men.[2]

60. Incessant travels of Alexander from 1815 to 1825.

[2 Schnitzler, i. 75; Biog. Univ. lvi. 185.]

The heart of the emperor, however, was too warm, his disposition too benevolent, for him not to feel keenly the sufferings of his subjects, and engage in any measures that appeared practicable for their relief. Various beneficent acts signalized the pacific years of his reign; but they were such as went to relieve local distress, or induce local advantage, rather than to stimulate the springs of industry over his whole empire, or remove the causes which obstructed civilization over its vast extent. In August, 1816, he visited Moscow, then beginning to rise from its ashes, and in a touching manifesto, which evidently came from the heart, testified his profound sympathy for the sufferings induced by its immortal sacrifice. At the same time, he set on foot or aided in the establishment of many valuable undertakings in different parts of the empire. He rebuilt, at a cost of 160,000 rubles, the bridge over the Neva; he took the most efficacious measures for restoring the naval forces of the empire, which had been unavoidably neglected during the pressure of the war—several ships of the line were begun both at Cronstadt and Odessa; no less than 1,500,000 rubles was advanced from the treasury to set on foot several new buildings in the two capitals; the completion of the splendid façade of the Admiralty; the building of a normal school for the training of teachers; an imperial lyce-

61. Various beneficent measures introduced by him.

Aug. 25, 1816.

um, in which the imperial founder ever took a warm interest; and several important regulations adopted for the encouragement of agriculture and the establishment of colonies in desert districts. The finances of the empire engaged his special and anxious attention. By a ukase, dated 16th April, 1817, he devoted to the payment of the debts contracted during 1812 and 1813, which were still in floating assignats, 30,000,000 rubles annually out of the imperial treasury, and a like sum out of the hereditary revenue of the Crown. At the same time he advanced 30,000,000 rubles to establish a bank specially destined for the support of commerce; and decreed the "Council of Public Credit," which, by its constitution, presented the first shadow of representative institutions. Such was the effect of these measures, that when the emperor opened a subscription for a large loan, to enable him to retire a proportion of the floating, and reduce considerably the immense mass of paper assignats in circulation, at an advance of 85 rubles paid for 100, inscribed as 6 per cent. stock, 30,000,000 was subscribed the first day, and before the end of the year 33,000,000 more—in all, 63,000,000—which enabled the Government to retire a similar amount of assignats.[1] *

April 16, 1817

[1] Ann. Hist. i. 277, 278; Biog. Univ. lvi. 185.

Alexander was sincerely and deeply interested in the prosperity of Poland, to which he was attached, not only by the brilliant additions which it made to the splendor and influence of the empire, but by the more tender feelings excited by the Polish lady to whom he had been so long and deeply attached. The sufferings of the country had been unparalleled, from the events of the war, and the enormous exactions of the French troops: the population of the grand-duchy of Warsaw, which, before it commenced, had been 3,300,000, had been reduced at its close to 2,600,000 souls. The country, however, had prospered in the most extraordinary degree during the three years of peace that it had since enjoyed; new colonists had been invited and settled from the neighboring states of Germany; and industry had flourished to such an extent that the state was now able to maintain, without difficulty or contracting debt, a splendid army of forty thousand men, which, clothed in the Polish uniform, and commanded by Polish officers, and following the Polish standards, was almost worshiped by the people as the germ of their reviving nationality.[2] The emperor arrived at Warsaw on the 13th March, and immediately the Polish standard was hoisted on the palace amidst the thunder of artillery and cheers from every human being in the city.

62. His arrival at Warsaw in 1818.

[2] Ann. Hist. i. 270, 271; Biog. Univ. lvi. 186.

The diet opened on the 27th of March, and the speech of the emperor, which was listened to with the deepest attention, was not only prophetic of peace and happiness to Poland, but memorable as containing evidence of the views he at that period entertained for the regeneration and freedom of mankind. After having expatiated on the advantages of a constitutional régime, he added, "With the assistance of God, I hope *to extend its salutary influence to ALL the countries intrusted to my care.* Prove to the contemporary kings that liberal institutions, which they pretend to confound with the disastrous doctrines which in these days threaten the social system with a frightful catastrophe, are not a dangerous illusion, but that, reduced in good faith to practice, and directed in a pure spirit toward conservative ends and the good of humanity, they are *perfectly allied to order, and the best security for the happiness of nations.*" Such were the sentiments and intentions of the Czar, while yet influenced by the illusions of 1814, and before the brilliant and benevolent dream had been dissipated by the military treason and social revolutions of southern Europe in 1820. When such words came from such lips, and every thing around bespoke order and peace, and the reviving nationality of Poland, it need not be said that all was unanimity and hope in the Diet, and its sittings were closed, after a short session of thirty days, without a dissenting voice on any question of general interest having been heard in the assembly.[1]

63. Alexander's memorable speech to the Diet March 27, 1818.

[1] An. Hist. i. 270, 271, 275; Biog. Univ. lvi. 185, 186.

From Warsaw, which he left on the 20th April, the emperor proceeded to Odessa, after traversing, with the utmost rapidity, the fertile plains and verdant turf of the Ukraine, where, as their poets say, the "sky is ever blue, the air clear, and storms and hurricanes are unknown." In Odessa he beheld, with astonishment, the rapid progress and rising importance of a city which, under the fostering care of government, and the wise direction of the Duke de Richelieu, had sprung up, as if by enchantment, on the edge of the wilderness, become the emporium of the south, and realized all that the genius of Virgil had fancied of the fabled rise of Carthage under the sceptre of Dido. He there assisted at the launching of a seventy-four, laid down an 110-gun ship, and evinced at once his sympathy with the sufferings of humanity, by erecting a monument to the celebrated Howard, who had died, in 1790, in the neighborhood of that city, and his admiration of his virtues, by subscribing to the erection of one in Paris to Malesherbes, the generous and intrepid defender of Louis XVI. He there appointed also a government commission, specially intrusted with the duty of watching over and aiding the settlement of colonists in Bessarabia and the southern provinces of the empire, of whom vast numbers had already begun to flock from the neighboring states; and, passing by Moscow to the north, he there met the King of Prussia, with whom he returned to St. Petersburg, where magnificent rejoicings attended the union of the two sovereigns. Hardly were they concluded when he set out

64. Journey of Alexander to his southern provinces.

---

* The *public debt* of Russia, on 1st January, 1818, stood thus :—

Foreign (Dutch loan)............ 99,600,000 florins.
Bank assignations............... 214,201,184 rubles.
In silver....................... 3,344,690 do.
In gold......................... 18,520 do.

                              Rubles.
Paid off in 1817—Capital........ 13,863,000
     ...   Interest....... 16,171,000

— *Ann. Historique*, i. 277.

for Aix-la-Chapelle, where his generous interposition, in conjunction with the Duke of Wellington, in favor of France, already mentioned,¹ was attended with such happy results; and from thence returned to St. Petersburg, and concluded an almost incessant journey of two thousand leagues, devoted, without a day's intermission, to the interests of humanity.²

<small>¹ Ante, c. vi. 44 63, 66.</small>

<small>² An. Hist. i. 278, 279; Biog. Univ. lvi. 186</small>

<small>65. His efforts for the enfranchisement of the peasants.</small>

Although Alexander's mind was not of the most penetrating character, and his practical knowledge of mankind was small, his intentions were all of the most generous, his feelings of the most philanthropic kind. He had already, by several ukases, completed the enfranchisement of the peasants on the Crown domains; and at Mittau, on his way to Aix-la-Chapelle, he had assisted at a very interesting ceremony—that which completed by a solemn act, the entire liberation of the serfs of Courland, Esthonia, and Livonia, the provinces of the empire next to Germany, by the voluntary act of the nobles, who, in this instance, had anticipated the wishes of the emperor. He had also, in the same year, published a ukase, which accorded several important immunities to the peasants of Merick, whose miserable condition had forcibly arrested his attention in passing through that province on his way from Warsaw to Odessa. He opened the year 1819 by a still more important step, because it was one of general application, and of vast influence on the social training of the nation. This was a ukase which extended to serfs in every part of the empire, and to whomsoever pertaining, the right, hitherto confined to the nobles and merchants, of establishing themselves as manufacturers in any part of the empire, and relieving them from the capitation tax during four years. At the same time he took a step, and a very material one, in favor of public instruction, by completing the organization of universities at Moscow, Wilna, Alo, St. Petersburg, Karkow, and Kazan; and of religious freedom, by taking the Lutheran and Calvinist clergy and flocks under the imperial protection, and establishing in the capital an Episcopal chair for the clergy of those persuasions.³

<small>Sept. 24, 1818.</small>

<small>³ An. Hist. i. 279, 280, ii. 358; Biog. Univ. lvi. 186.</small>

<small>66. Transactions of 1819.</small>

The finances of the empire, in the following year, exhibited the elasticity which might have been expected from the continuance of peace, and the wise measures for the reduction of the floating debt adopted in the preceding year. The sinking fund had withdrawn from circulation 80,000,000 paper rubles (£4,000,000) in the preceding year; and specie, to the number of 26,000,000 silver rubles (£1,600,000), had issued from the mint in the same time—a quantity greater than had been coined during the ten preceding years. The deposits and discounts at the bank recently established exhibited a large and rapid increase. The Lancasterian system of instruction was extended by the emperor even to Siberia, and normal schools established at St. Petersburg to train teachers for the principal towns, from which alone the light of knowledge could radiate to the country. In the autumn of this year the emperor visited Archangel, which had not been honored by the presence of the sovereign for a hundred and seventeen years; and from thence he issued a decree, authorizing the levy of two men in every five hundred, which produced a hundred and eighty thousand soldiers—the first levy which had taken place since the war. At the same time, measures were taken for colonizing the army cantoned in Bessarabia, above a hundred thousand strong; and steps adopted for establishing the army on the Polish frontier in like manner. The design of the emperor, which was a very magnificent one, was to encircle the empire with a zone of military colonies, stretching from the Black Sea to the Baltic, where the soldiers might acquire dwellings, and pursue the labors of agriculture, like the Roman legions, while still guarding the frontiers, and connect them with similar establishments of a pastoral kind on the frontiers of Persia and Tartary, where the vigilance of the Cossacks guarded from insult the vast steppes which run up to the foot of the Caucasus.¹

<small>¹ An. Hist. ii. 359, 360.</small>

<small>67. Expulsion of the Jesuits.</small>

The year 1820 commenced with a very important step—the entire expulsion of the Jesuits from Russia. They had already, in consequence of their intrigues, been banished in 1815 from St. Petersburg and Moscow, but their efforts to win over proselytes to their persuasion had since that time been so incessant and harassing, that they were now finally expelled from the whole empire.* Provision was made for their maintenance in the mean time, and every precaution taken to render the measure as gentle in its operation as possible. Certainly, as the Roman Catholics, like most other sects, regard theirs as the only true faith, and all others as heresies, it can be no matter of surprise, still less of condemnation, that they every where make such strenuous efforts to gain proselytes and reclaim souls, as they deem it, on the eve of perdition, to the bosom of the Church. But as other persuasions are equally convinced that their own is the true form of worship, they can not be surprised, and have no right to complain, if their every where aggressive attitude is met by a corresponding defensive one; and if these states, without seeking to convert them to their faith, seek only to adopt measures that may secure their own.²

<small>² An. Hist. iii. 296, 297 ; Biog. Univ. lvi. 297, Ukase, March 23, 1820.</small>

The time, however, had now arrived when the views of the emperor, heretofore so liberal and indulgent, were to undergo an entire change, when the illusions of 1814 were to be dispelled, and Russia, instead of being, as it had been for many years, at the head of the move-

<small>* "Les Jésuites quoique suffisamment avertis par l'un ander/esson qu'ils avaient encourue, ne changèrent pas ns manières de conduite. Il fut bientôt constaté par les rapports des autorités civiles qu'ils continuaient à attirer dans leur communion les élèves du rit orthodoxe, places au collège de Mohilow à Saratof et dans la Sibérie. Le Moniteur des Cultes se unique point de signaler ces transgressions au Père Général de l'ordre, des l'année 1815. Ces Administrations furent inutiles. Loin de s'abstenir, à l'instance de l'église dominante, de tout moyen de séduction et de conversion, les Jésuites continuèrent à semer le trouble dans les colonies du rit Protestant, et se poussèrent jusqu'à la violence pour soustraire les enfants Juifs à leurs parents."—Ukase, 25 Mars 1820. Annuaire Historique, iii, 296, 297.</small>

ment party in Europe, was to become its most decided opponent. Already the emperor had been warned by anonymous letters and various mysterious communications, as well as by reports from the secret police, of the existence of a vast conspiracy, which embraced several of the leading officers in the armies both of Poland and the Danube, and nobles of the highest rank and consideration in St. Petersburg. The object of the conspirators was stated to be to dethrone and murder the emperor, imprison the other members of the imperial family, and establish a constitutional monarchy on the footing of those of western Europe. For long the emperor gave no credit to these warnings; he could not believe that an army which, under himself, had done such great things, and had given him personally such proofs of entire devotion, could have so soon become implicated in a traitorous project for his destruction. But the military revolution in Spain, Portugal, and Naples, in the early part of the year 1820, opened his eyes as to the volcano on which possibly his empire might be resting; and the events in Poland ere long left no doubt that the danger was rapidly approaching his own dominions.[1]

marginalia: 68. Great changes in the emperor's mind from the revolution of 1820.
1 Schnitzler, ii. 1, 32; Ann. Hist. iii. 300, 302.

The Polish Diet opened in September, and the emperor, who assisted at it in person, in the Polish uniform, and surrounded with Polish officers, was received with enthusiasm: the city was illuminated on his arrival, and at several reviews the troops of the national army evinced the most loyal feelings. The exposition of the minister exhibited the most flattering appearance; the population had increased to 3,468,000, being no less than a million since the termination of the war; agriculture, manufactures, the finances, were in the most flourishing state. But what is material prosperity, beneficent government, to a country infested with the fever of revolution? It soon appeared, when the Diet proceeded to real business, with what species of spirit they were animated. On a proposition to amend the criminal law, brought forward by the ministers, a violent opposition broke forth in the chamber, on the ground that the proposed mode of trial was not by jury; and it was rejected by 120 votes to 3. Another proposal of government, for certain changes in the Senate, was also rejected by a large majority. It was evident that the Diet was animated with the wild spirit of Polish equality, not merely from their measures, but from the extreme violence of the language which they used, and that they would be as difficult to manage as the old *comitia*, where any member, by the exercise of his *liberum veto*, might paralyze the whole proceedings. Alexander was profoundly affected; he saw at once the depth of the abyss which yawned beneath his feet, if these ideas, as in Spain and Naples, should gain possession of the army, the main prop of the throne in his despotic realms; and he closed the Diet with a speech, in which his apprehensions and indignation expressed in the most striking manner.[2]*

marginalia: 69. Violent scene, and dissolution of the Polish Diet, Sept. 28.
2 Ann. Hist. iii. 304, 306.

This incident exercised an important influence on the affairs of Europe in general, for the emperor at this period was on his way to the Congress of Troppau, where the recent revolution in the Spanish and Italian peninsulas, and the alarming state of affairs in France, were to be taken into consideration. As this congress was called chiefly in consequence of the suggestions of the Emperor Alexander, and was the first practical application of the principles of the Holy Alliance of which he was the author, it belongs more properly to the annals of Russia than Germany, within whose bounds it was held. The Emperor of Austria, whose terror at the alarming situation of Italy was extreme, arrived there on the 18th October; the Emperor of Russia joined him there on the 20th. Indisposition prevented the King of Prussia from coming till the 7th November, but he was represented by the hereditary prince his son. Prince Metternich and M. Gentz on the part of Austria; Count Nesselrode and Capo d'Istria on that of Russia; Prince Hardenberg and Count Bernstorf on that of Prussia; Count Caraman, the French Embassador at Vienna, and Sir Charles Stuart, the English Embassador there, represented the several powers. The events in Italy and Spain had excited the greatest alarm among all the parties assembled, and the most vigorous measures were resolved on; and although the English government did not take an active part in their deliberations, it did not formally oppose the measures resolved on.[3]

marginalia: 70. Congress of Troppau: Oct. 20, 1820.
Oct. 20.
3 Ann. Hist. iii. 512, 513; Biog. Univ. lvi. 127.

So great was the importance of the topics discussed at the Congress of Troppau, and so various the interests of the powers there assembled, that in former days it would in all probability have led to a general war. But the remembrance of past strife was too recent, the terror of present revolutions too great, to permit of any serious divergence of opinion or measures taking place. From the very outset the Emperor Alexander, whose apprehensions were now fully awakened, declared that he was prepared to second with all his forces any measures which the Emperor of Austria might deem necessary for the settlement and pacification of Italy. At the same time the march of the Austrian troops toward the south of Italy continued without intermission, and a holograph letter was dispatched from the

marginalia: 71. Congress of Troppau: its resolutions.

important de développer et d'affermir vos institutions nationales, vous pouvez facilement apprendre de combien vous en êtes rapprochés. Interrogez votre conscience, et vous saurez si dans le cours de vos discussions, vous avez rendu à la Pologne tous les services qu'elle attendait de votre sagesse, ou si, au contraire, entraînés par des séductions trop communes de vos jours, et minoçant un espoir qu' aurait réalisé une prévoyante confiance, vous n'avez pas retardé dans son progrès l'auvre de la restauration de votre Patrie. Cette grave responsabilité pesera sur vous. Elle est la sûreté nécessaire de l'indépendance de vos suffrages. Ils sont libres, mais une intention pure doit toujours les déterminer. La mienne vous est connue. Vous avez reçu le bien pour le mal, et la Pologne est remontée au rang des états. Je persévérerai dans mes desseins à son égard, quelle que soit l'opinion qu'on puisse se former sur la manière dont vous venez d'excuser vos prorogations."—*Discours de l'Empereur Alexandre à Varsovie, 1/13 Octobre, 1820, à la clôture de la Diète Polonaise. Annuaire Historique, iii. 616.*

* "Parvenus au terme où s'arrêtent aujourd'hui les travaux qui doivent vous conduire par degrés vers ce but

assembled sovereigns to the King of Naples, inviting him to join them in person at a new congress, to be held at Laybach in Styria. A minister sent from Naples on the part of the revolutionary government was refused admission; and the views of the assembled monarchs on the late revolutions were announced in several semi-official articles, published in the Vienna papers, which, even more than their official instruments, revealed their real sentiments.[1]*

The congress, to be nearer the scene of action, was soon after transferred to Laybach, where the Emperor of Austria arrived on the 4th January, and the Emperor of Russia on the 7th. The King of Prussia was hourly expected; and the King of Naples, whom the revolutionary government established in his dominions did not venture to detain at home, came on the 8th. So much had been done at Troppau in laying down principles, that nothing remained for Laybach but their practical application. The principle which Alexander adopted, and which met with the concurrence of the other sovereigns, was that the spirit of the age required liberal institutions, and a gradual admission of the people to a share of power; but that they must flow from the sovereign's free will, not be forced upon him by his subjects; and, therefore, that no compromise whatever could be admitted with revolutionists either in the Italian or Spanish peninsulas. In conformity with this determination, there was signed, on 2d February, 1821, a treaty, by which it was stipulated that the allied powers should in no way recognize the revolutionary government in Naples; and that the royal authority should be re-established on the footing on which it stood prior to the insurrection of the army on 5th July, 1820. To carry their resolution into effect, it was agreed that an Austrian army should, in the name of Austria, Russia, and Prussia, be put at the disposition of the King of the two Sicilies; that, from the moment of its passing the Po, its whole expenses should be at the charge of that kingdom, and that the Neapolitan dominions should be occupied by the Austrian forces during three years, in the same manner, and on the same conditions, as France had been by the army under the Duke of Wellington. England and France were no parties to this treaty, but neither did they oppose it, or enter into any alliance with the revolutionary states. They simply remained neuter, passive spectators of a matter in which they were too remotely interested to be called on practically to interfere, but which they could not theoretically approve. Lord Castlereagh contented himself with declaring that Great Britain could take no part in such transactions, as they were directly opposed to the fundamental laws of his country.[1]*

This deserves to be noted as a turning point in the modern history of Europe. It marks the period when separate views and interests began to shake the hitherto firmly cemented fabric of the Grand Alliance; and Great Britain and France, for the first time, assumed a part *together* at variance with the determination of the other great powers. They had not yet come into actual collision, much less open hostility; but their views had become so different, that it required not the gift of prophecy to foresee that collision was imminent at no distant period. This was the more remarkable, as England had been, during the whole of the revolutionary war, the head and soul of the alliance against France, and strenuously contended for the principle, that though no attempt should be made to force a government against their will on the French people, yet a coalition of the adjoining powers had become indispensable to prevent them from forcing their institutions upon other states. The allied governments commented freely on this great change of policy, and observed that England was very conservative as long as the danger was at her own door, and her own institutions were threatened by the contagion of French principles;[2] but that she became very liberal when the danger was removed to a more distant quarter, and the coun-

---

Side notes:
Nov. 20.
[1] An. Hist. iii. 514, 515. Aperçu des resultats des conferences de Troppau, ibid. iii. 639.

72.
Congress of Laybach. Jan. 8, 1821.

Feb. 2.

1 Treaty, Feb. 2, 1821, Ann. Hist. iii. 642. Lord Castlereagh's Despatch, Jan. 19, 1821; Ib. ii. 689.

73.
Reflections on the discussion among the allied powers.

2 Le Comte de Nesselrode au Comte de Staekelberg, Jan. 31, 1821; Ann. Hist. ii. 692, 693.

---

* "On a acquis la conviction que cette revolution, produite par une serie egarée et execitée par des soldats indisciplines, suivie d'un renversement violent des institutions legitimes, et de leur remplacement par un systeme d'arbitraire et d'anarchie, est non-seulement contraire aux principes d'ordre, de droit, de morale, et de vrai bien-être des peuples, tels qu'ils sont établis par les monarques, mais de plus incompatible par ses resultats inevitables avec le repos et la securite des autres etats Italiens, et par consequent avec la conservation de la paix en Europe. Penetres de ces verites, les Hauts Monarques ont pris la ferme resolution *d'employer tous leurs moyens* afin que l'etat actuel des choses dans le royaume des Deux-Siciles, produit par la revolte et la force, soit detruit, mais cependant S. M. le Roi sera mis dans une position telle qu'il pourra determiner la constitution future de ses etats d'une maniere compatible avec sa dignité, les interets de son peuple, et le repos des etats voisins."—*Observateur Autrichien.*

* "Le système des mesures proposées serait, s'il était l'objet d'une reciprocité d'action, diametralement opposé aux lois fondamentales de la Grande-Bretagne, mais lors même que cette objection decisive n'existerait pas, le gouvernement Britannique n'en jugerait pas moins, que les principes qui servent de base à ces mesures, ne peuvent être admis avec quelque sureté comme systèmes de loi entre les nations. Le gouvernement du roi pense que l'adoption de ces principes sanctionnerait inevitablement, et pourrait amener par la suite, de la part des souverains moins bienveillants, une intervention dans les affaires interieures des etats, beaucoup plus frequente et plus etendue que celle dont il est persuadé que les augustes personnages ont l'intention d'user, ou, qui puisse se concilier avec l'interet general, ou avec l'autorite reelle, et la dignite des souverains independants. Quant à l'affaire particulière de Naples, le gouvernement Britannique n'a pas hesite, des le commencement, à exprimer fortement son improbation de la manière dont cette Revolution s'est effectuée, et des circonstances dont elle paraissait avoir été accompagnée, mais en même temps, il declara expressement aux differentes cours alliees, qu'il ne croyait pas devoir, ni même conseiller une intervention de la part de la Grande-Bretagne. Il admit toujours que d'autres etats Europeens, et specialement l'Autriche, et les puissances Italiennes, pouvaient juger que les circonstances etaient differentes relativement à eux, et il declara que son intention n'etait pas de prejuger la question en ce qui pouvait les affecter, ni d'intervenir dans la marche que tels etats pourraient juger convenable d'adopter pour leur propre sureté; pourvu toutefois, qu'ils fussent disposes à donner toutes les assurances raisonnables que, leurs vues n'etaient, en dangers vers des objets d'agrandissement, ni vers la subversion du systeme territorial de l'Europe, tel qu'il a été etabli par les derniers traités."—Castlereagh, *Depeche Circulaire, addressé aux Ministres de S. M. Britannique pour les cours Etrangeres*, 14 Jan. 1821. Ann. Hist. royu. ii. 698, 699.

tries threatened were Italy, southern Germany, or France itself.*

To fix the just principles, and define the limits of the right of intervention, is unquestionably one of the most difficult problems in politics, and one fraught with the most momentous consequences. If the right is carried out to its full extent, incessant warfare would, in civilized communities in different stages of civilization, be the inevitable destiny of the species; for every republican state would seek to revolutionize its neighbors, and every despotic one to surround itself with a girdle of absolute monarchies. Each party loudly invokes the principle of non-intervention, when its opponents are acting on the opposite principle, and as certainly follows their example, when an opportunity occurs for establishing elsewhere a regime conformable to its own wishes or example. Perhaps it is impossible to draw the line more fairly than by saying, that no nation has a right to interfere in the internal concerns of another nation, unless that other is adopting measures which threaten its own peace and tranquillity; in a word, that intervention is only justifiable when it is done for the purposes of self-defense. Yet is this a very vague and unsatisfactory basis on which to rest the principle; for who is to judge when internal tranquillity is threatened, and external intervention has become indispensable? It is much to be feared that here, as elsewhere, in the transactions of independent states, which acknowledge no superior, much must depend on the moderation of the stronger; and that "might makes right" will be the practice, whatever may be the law of nations, to the end of the world. But one thing is clear, that it is with the democratic party that the chief—indeed, of late years, the entire—blame of intervention rests. The monarchical powers have never moved since 1789 but in self-defense. Every war which has desolated Europe and afflicted humanity since that time has been provoked by the propagandism of republican states; if left to themselves, the absolute monarchs would have been too happy to slumber on, reposing on their laurels, weighed down by their debt, recovering from their fatigue.

It was the circumstance of the three powers which had signed the Holy Alliance appearing banded together to crush the revolution in Italy, which caused that Alliance to be regarded as a league of sovereigns against the liberties of mankind, and to become the object of such unmeasured obloquy to the whole liberal party throughout the world. There never was a greater mistake. The Holy Alliance became a league, and it proved a most efficient one, against the progress of revolution; but it was not so at first. It was forced into defensive measures by the aggressions of its political antagonists in Spain and Italy. Not one shot has been fired in Europe, nor one sabre drawn, from any contest which it commenced, though many have been so from those into which it has been driven. In truth, this celebrated Alliance, which was the creation of the benevolent dreams of the Emperor Alexander, and the mystical conceptions of Madame Krudener, was, as already explained, a philanthropic effusion, amiable in design, but unwise in thought, and incapable of application in a world such as that in which we are placed.¹

It is evident, however, that it was impossible for England to have acted otherwise than as she did on this occasion, and that the line which Lord Castlereagh took was such as alone befitted the minister of a free people. Being the representative of a country which had progressively extorted its liberties from its sovereigns, and at length changed the dynasty on the throne to secure them, he could not be a party to a league professing to extinguish popular resistance: placed at a distance from the theatre of danger, the plea of necessity could not be advanced to justify such a departure from principle. He took the only line which, on such an occasion, was consistent with his situation, and dictated by a due regard to the national interest;—he abstained from taking any part in the contest, and contented himself with protesting against any abuse of the pretension on which it was rested.

The contest in Italy was of very short duration. The revolutionists proved incapable of defending themselves against an Austrian army, little more than half of their own strength; they were formidable only to their own sovereign. The Minister at War announced to the parliament at Naples, on the 2d January, that the regular army amounted to fifty-four thousand men, and the national guards to a hundred and fifty thousand more; that the fortresses were fully armed and provisioned, and in the best possible state of defense; and that every thing was prepared for the most vigorous resistance. But already serious divisions had broken out in the army, especially between the guards and the troops of the line; and dissensions of the most violent kind had arisen between the leaders of the revolt, especially the Cardinal Ruffo and the chiefs of the Carbonari. The consequence was, that when the moment of action arrived, scarce any resistance was made. On 8th February a courier from Laybach announced at Naples that all hope of accommodation was at an end, and that the sovereigns assembled there would in no shape recognize the revolutionary authorities at Naples. The effect of

---

* "La Révolution de Naples a donné au monde un exemple, aussi instructif que déplorable, de ce que les nations ont à gagner, lorsqu' elles cherchent les reformes politiques dans les voies de la rébellion. Ourdie en secret par une secte, dont les maximes impies attaquent à la fois la religion, la morale, et tous les liens sociaux; exécutée par des soldats traitres à leurs sermens; consommée par la violence, et les menaces dirigées contre le souverain légitime, cette Révolution n'a produit que l'anarchie et la disposition militaire qu'elle a renforcée, au lieu de l'affaiblir, en creant un régime monstreux, incapable de servir de base a un gouvernement quel qu'il soit, incompatible avec tout ordre public, et avec les premiers besoins de la société. Les souverains alliés, ne pouvant, des le principe se tromper sur les effets inevitables de ces funestes attentats, se deciderent sur-le-champ à ne point admettre, comme legal, tout ce que la revolution et l'usurpation avaient pretendu établir dans le Royaume de Naples; et cette mesure fut adoptée par la presque totalité des gouvernements de l'Europe."—LE COMTE NESSELRODE au COMTE DE STACKELBERG, Ambassadeur à Naples, Laybach, 19 (31) Jan. 1821. Ann. Historique, ii. 603.

this announcement was terrible; it did not rouse resistance—it overpowered it by fear. In vain the assembly ordered fifty thousand of the national guards to be called out, and moved to the frontier; nothing efficient was done—terror froze every heart. The ministers of Russia, Austria, and Prussia, left Naples; the presence of ten French and eight English sail of the line in the bay rather excited alarm than inspired confidence. On the 4th February, General Frimont published from his head-quarters at Padua a proclamation, announcing that his army was about to cross the Po, to assist in the pacification of Italy; and on the following day the troops, nearly fifty thousand strong, commenced the passage of that river at five points between Cremona and St. Benedetto.[1]

¹ Colletta, ii. 419, 424; Ann. Hist. iv. 319, 320.

78. Unresisted march of the Austrians toward Naples. Feb. 21.

The march of the Austrian army met with so little opposition that the events which followed could not be called a campaign. When they arrived at Bologna, the troops were separated into two divisions; one of which, under the command of Count Walmoden, crossed the Apennines, and advanced, by Florence and Rome, by the great road to Naples; while the other moved by the left to the sea-side, and reached Ancona. The first corps passed Rome, without entering it, on February 28th; the second occupied Ancona on the 19th. Meanwhile the preparations of the Neapolitans were very extensive, and seemed to presage a serious resistance. Their forces, too, were divided into two corps; the first of which, forty thousand strong, under General Carascosa, occupied the strong position of St. Germans, with its left on the fortress of Gaeta, within the Neapolitan territory; while the second, under General Pepe, of thirty thousand, chiefly militia, was opposed to the corps advancing along the Adriatic, and charged with the defense of the Abruzzi. But it was all in vain. Pepe, finding that his battalions were disbanding, and his troops melting away before they had even seen the enemy, resolved to hazard an attack on the Austrians at Reidi. But no sooner did they come in sight of the German vanguard, consisting of a splendid regiment of Hungarian cavalry, than a sudden panic seized them. The new levies disbanded and fled, with the cry of "*Tradimento; salvearsi chi può!*" The contagion spread to the old troops. Soon the whole army was a mere mob, every one trying to outrun his neighbor. Cannon, ammunition, standards, were alike abandoned. Pepe himself was carried away by the torrent, and the Abruzzi were left without any defense but the impediments arising from the wreck of the army, whose implements of war strewed the roads over which it had fled.[2]*

² Colletta, ii. 435-438; Ann. Hist. iv. 322, 325.

* "Vacillarono le nostre giovani bande, si ritirarono le prime, non procederono le seconde, si confusero le ordinanze. Ed allora avanzò prima lentamente, poscia incalzando i passi, ed alfine in corsa un superbo reggimento di cavalleria Ungherese, si che nell' aspetto del crescente pericolo le milizie civili, nuove alla guerra, trepidarono, fuggirono, strascinarono coll' impeto e coll' esempio qualche compagnia di più vecchi soldati, si ruppero gli ordini, si udirono le voci di *tradimento, e salvearsi chi può*; scomparve il campo.—Proseguirono nella succedente notte i disordini dell' esercito; Antrodoco fu abbandonata; il General Pepe seguiva i fuggitivi.—Miserando spettacolo!"

This catastrophe was a mortal stroke to the insurrection; for, independent of the moral influence of such a discreditable scene succeeding the warm appeals and confident predictions of the revolutionists, the position of their main army, and on which alone they could rely for the defense of Naples at St. Germans, under Carascosa, was liable to be turned by the Abruzzi, and was no longer tenable. The broken remains of Pepe's army dispersed in the Apennines, and sought shelter in its fastnesses; some made their appearance in Naples, where they excited universal consternation. In this extremity the parliament, assembled in select committee, supplicated the Prince Vicar to mediate between them and the king; and, above all, to arrest the march of the Austrian troops. But it was all in vain. The Imperial generals, seeing their advantage, only pressed on with the more vigor on the disorderly array of their opponents. Walmoden advanced without opposition through the Abruzzi. Aquila opened its gates on the 10th March, its castle on the 12th; and Carascosa, seeing his right flank turned by the mountains, gave orders for his troops to retire at all points from the position they occupied on the Garigliones. This was the signal for a universal dissolution of the force. Infantry, cavalry, and artillery, alike disbanded and fled. A few regiments of the royal guard alone preserved any semblance of military array, and the main Austrian army advanced without opposition toward Naples, where terror was at its height, securities of all sorts unsalable, and the revolutionary government powerless. Finding further resistance hopeless, Carascosa made the Prince Vicar, who had set out to join the army, return to Naples; and on the 20th of March a suspension of hostilities was agreed on, the condition of which was the surrender of Capua and Aversa to the Imperialists. This was followed by the capitulation of Naples itself, a few days after, on the same terms as that of Capua. The Austrians entered on the following day, and were put in possession of the forts; while Carascosa, Pepe, and the other chiefs of the insurrection, obtained passports, which were willingly granted by the conquerors, and escaped from the scene of danger. Sicily, when the revolution had assumed so virulent a form, submitted, after a vain attempt at resistance, shortly after; and the king, on the 12th May, amidst general acclamations, re-entered his capital, now entirely garrisoned, and under the control of the Austrian troops.[1]

79. Subjugation of Naples, and return of the king.

March 10.

March 20.

March 23.

March 24.

May 12. ¹ Colletta, ii. 444, 455; Ann. Hist. iv. 329, 333.

It was during these events, so fatal to the cause of revolution in Naples, that the old government was overturned in Piedmont, and the standard of treason hoisted on the citadel of Turin. The account of that important but ill-timed event, which took place on the 13th March, has been already given, as

80. Movement of the insurgents in Piedmont. March 13.

gettate le armi e le insegne; le macchine di guerra, fatto inciampo al fuggire, rovesciate, spezzate; gli argini, le trincere, opere di molte menti e di molte braccia, aperte, abbandonate; ogni ordine scomposto; esercito poco innanzi spaventoso al nemico, oggi visto in ludibrio."—Colletta (a liberal historian), ii. 437, 438.

forming the last in the catalogue of revolutionary triumphs which followed the explosion in Spain.¹ As it broke out at the very time when the Neapolitan armies were dissolving at the sight of the Hungarian hussars, and only ten days before Naples opened its gates to the victors, it was obviously a hopeless movement, and the only wisdom for its promoters would have been to have extricated themselves as quietly and speedily as they could from a contest now plainly become for the time hopeless. But the extreme revolutionary party, deeming themselves too far committed to recede, determined on the most desperate measures. War was resolved on by the leaders of the movement at Alessandria, which had always been the focus of the insurrection, and a ministry installed to carry it into execution; but the Prince Regent escaped in the night from Turin, with some regiments of troops, upon whom he could still rely, to Novarra, where the nucleus of a royal army began to be formed, from whence, two days after, he issued a declaration renouncing the office of Prince Regent, and thus giving, as he himself said, "now and forever, the most respectful proof of obedience to the royal authority." This made all persons at Turin who were still under the guidance of reason aware that the cause of revolution was for the present hopeless. Symptoms of returning loyalty appeared in the army; and Count de la Tour, who was secretly inclined to the royalists, resolved to retire to Alessandria, with such of the troops as he could rely on, to await the possible return of better times; and orders were given to that effect.²

¹ Ante, c. vii. § 118.

March 21.

March 23.

² An. Hist. iv. 346, 349.

Meanwhile the allied sovereigns at Laybach were taking the most vigorous measures to crush the insurrection in Piedmont. The Emperor of Austria instantly ordered the formation of a corps of observation on the frontier of that kingdom, drawn from the garrisons in the Lombard-Venetian provinces; and the Emperor of Russia directed the assembling of an army of 100,000 men, taken from the armies of the South and Poland, with instructions to march direct towards Turin. Requisitions were made to the Helvetic cantons to take precautionary measures against a conflagration which threatened to embrace the whole of Italy. Before this resolution, however, could be carried into effect, intelligence was received that the queen's regiment of dragoons had left Novarra amidst cries of "Vive la Constitution!" This news so elevated the spirits of the insurgents that the orders to retire to Alessandria were countermanded, and on the following day they issued from the seat of government a proclamation, in which, after declaring that the king was a captive in the hands of Austria, and that the Prince Vicar had been deceived, they called on the Piedmontese to take up arms, promising them "the succor of the Lombards and the support of France." This appeal had little effect; the intelligence of the unresisted march of the Austrians toward Naples froze every heart in the capital. At Genoa, however, the popular determination

81.
Meeting of the Allies, and fresh revolution in Genoa.

March 21.

was more strongly evinced. A proclamation of the governor, calling on the people to abandon the constitution and submit themselves to the former government, led to a fresh commotion, in which he narrowly escaped with his life, and which was only appeased by the appointment of a junta of government composed of the most decided popular chiefs. The intelligence of this fresh insurrection greatly raised the spirit of the leaders at Turin, and the preparations for war in the capital were continued with unabated zeal by the government.¹

March 24.

¹ An. Hist. iv. 352, 353.

But it was too late: the fate of the Piedmontese revolution had been determined in the passes of the Abruzzi. Already, on the requisition of Charles Felix, the deposed king, a corps of Austrians, fifteen thousand strong, had been assembled, under Count Bubna, on the Ticino, the bridges over which had been broken down, to prevent any communication with the insurgents. General Latour, meanwhile, the governor of Turin, seeing the cause of the revolution hopeless, and wishing to avoid the interference of foreigners, was taking measures to restore the royal authority there without the intervention of the Austrians; and a large part of the army, especially the royal carabineers, were already disposed to second him. But his designs were discovered and frustrated by the Minister at War, a staunch revolutionist, who caused several regiments known to be most attached to the constitution to come to Turin, where they had a skirmish with the carabineers, which ended in two-thirds of the latter body leaving the capital and taking the road to Novarra, where eight thousand men were already assembled round the royal standard.² The knowledge of their strength, which nearly equaled that of the troops on the other side, and of the certain support of the Austrians, made the members of the junta lend a willing ear to the proposals of the Count Mocenigo, the Russian minister, who suggested, in the name of the emperor, a submission to the king on the condition of a general amnesty, and the hope of a constitution which should guarantee the interests of society.

82.
Increasing difficulties of the insurgents.

² Comte Sta Rosa, Evenemens en Piemont, 147; Ann. Hist. iv. 350, 352.

But, as often happens in such convulsions, the ardor of the extreme and enthusiastic of the insurgents defeated all the efforts of the more moderate of their party, and left to the Piedmontese the exasperation of civil war and the bitterness of foreign subjugation. The majority of the junta continued to hold out; and their eyes were not opened to the declining circumstances of their cause even by the disbanding of several battalions of the militia, who, instead of joining the general rendezvous at Alessandria, left their colors and returned home. At length, seeing no prospect of an accommodation, the Count de la Tour, who had joined the royal army at Novarra, and was at its head, having concerted measures with the Austrian general, advanced to Vercelli. Here, however, he was met by a considerable body of the insurgents, and not deeming himself in sufficient strength to encounter them, he fell back to Novarra, where he was

83.
Total defeat of the insurgents at Agogna. April 8.

joined, on the 7th April, by the Austrians, who had crossed the Ticino at Buffalora and Mortera. Their junction, which took place at two in the morning of the 8th, was unknown to the insurgents, who, driving the light troops of the royalists before them, appeared, at ten in the morning, in front of the bastions of the place, anticipating its speedy capture, and an easy victory. But they were soon undeceived. Suddenly a terrible fire of grape and musketry opened from the bastions; as the smoke cleared away, the Austrian uniform and schakos were seen above the parapets, and the insurgents found themselves engaged with the combined Austrian and Piedmontese forces, nearly triple their own, supported by the guns of the place. The effect of this unexpected apparition was immense upon the spirits of the assailants, who immediately fell back toward Vercelli. The retreat was conducted at first with more order than could have been expected, as far as the bridge of Agogna, at the entrance of a long defile formed by the chaussée, where it traverses the marshes. There, however, the rear-guard was charged vigorously by the Austrian horse, and thrown into confusion; the disorder rapidly spread to the troops engaged in the defile, who were already encumbered with their artillery and baggage-wagons; and ere long the whole dispersed, and sought their homes, leaving their cannon, baggage, and colors to the enemy.[1]

April 8.

[1] Ann. Hist. iv. 335, 336.

This affair terminated the war, although it had cost only a few killed and wounded to the defeated party; so swift had been their flight that very few prisoners were taken. The junta at Turin, upon hearing of this defeat, gave orders to evacuate the capital, and fall back to Genoa, where they declared they would defend themselves to the last extremity. But it is seldom, save in a single city, that the cause of an insurrection can be maintained after a serious defeat. The constitutionalists melted away on all sides; every one hastened to show not only that he was loyal now, but had been so throughout, and in the worst times. Finding the case hopeless, the junta surrendered their powers, on the day following, to a committee of ten, invested with full power to treat. They immediately sent a deputation to General la Tour, offering him the keys of the capital, and entreating that it should be occupied only by the national troops. This was agreed to, and it was promised that the Austrians should not advance beyond Vercelli. On the 12th, General la Tour, surrounded by a brilliant staff, and followed only by the national troops, made his public entrance into Turin, where the royal authority was immediately re-established. The revolutionary journals disappeared; the clubs were closed; and the public funds, which had lately been at 69, rose to 77. On the following day, the Austrian troops took possession of Alessandria, and other fortresses on the frontier; and as the old king, Victor Emmanuel, persisted in his resolution to abdicate after he had become a free agent, and his sincerity could no longer be suspected, his brother, the Duke de Genevois, assumed the title, and began to ex-

81. Submission of the capital, and termination of the war. April 8.
April 9.
April 12.
April 19.

ercise the powers of royalty. A commission was appointed to examine the conduct of the chiefs of the insurrection; the leaders had, for the most part, escaped into France; but the effects of forty-three were put under sequestration, and themselves executed, happily only in effigy.[1]

[1] Ann. Hist. iv. 357, 359, 370.

The violent repression of the revolution in Italy, by the Austrian bayonets, was followed by a great variety of harsh and oppressive measures on the part of the conquerors, which augured ill for the peace of the peninsula in future times. A general disarmament of all the provinces of the Neapolitan territories where Austrian soldiers had been assassinated was decreed, and enforced by domiciliary visits; the whole irregular corps, raised since 5th July, 1820, were disbanded; foreign journals loaded with such heavy taxes as amounted to a prohibition; and the most rigorous inquiry made into the books, many of them highly dangerous, which had been put into the hands of the young at schools. The king, on his return, published a decree, engaging to "stifle all personal resentment, and make the nation forget, in years of prosperity, the disastrous events which have stained the last days of Neapolitan history;" but within three days after, measures of severity began. Four courts-martial were constituted, to take cognizance of the military who had taken part in the revolts which ended in the revolution, and several of the leading deputies of the assembly were sent into confinement in Austria. By a decree on July 1, which commented, in severe but just terms, on their treacherous conduct, the army, which had been the chief instrument of the revolution, was disbanded, and reorganized anew on a different footing.[*] The finances were found to be in so deplorable a condition, that loans to the amount of 3,800,000 ducats (£850,000) alone enabled the king to provide for immediate necessities, and heavy taxes were levied to enable him to carry on the government. Finally, a treaty was signed on 28th October, by which it was stipulated that the army of occupation should consist of forty-two thousand men, including seven thousand cavalry, besides the troops stationed in Sicily; and that it should remain in the Neapolitan territory for three years, entirely at the charge of its inhabitants.[2]

85. Violent reaction in Italy.
April 12.
May 15.
July 1.

[2] Colletta, ii. 459, 481. Treaty, Oct. 28, 1821; Ann. Hist. iv. 651.

Piedmont did not fare better, after the dis-

---

[*] "L'armée est la principale cause de ces maux. Factieuse, ou entretenue par des factions, elle nous a abandonnés au moment du danger; et nous n'a par la, privés des moyens de prévenir les malheureuses conséquences d'une revolution. S'étant livrée à une secte qui detruit tous les liens de la subordination, et de l'obeissance, l'armée, après avoir trahi ses devoirs envers nous, s'est vue incapable de remplir les devoirs que la révolte avait voulu lui imposer. Elle a opéré elle-même sa destruction, et les chefs qu'elle s'etait donnés, n'ont fait que presider à sa dissolution; elle n'offre plus aucune garantie necessaire à l'existence d'une armée: le bien de nos états exige cependant l'existence d'une force protectrice, nous avons ete obligés de la demander à nos Alliés; ils l'ont mise à notre disposition. Nous devons pouvoir à son entretien, mais nous ne pouvons pas faire supporter à nos sujets, le pesant fardeau des frais d'une armée qui n'existe plus, parce qu'elle n'a pas su exister. Ces motifs nous ont determinés à dissoudre l'armée, à compter du 24 Mars de cette année."—*Decret, 1 Juillet, 1821. Annuaire Historique, iv. 364.*

solution of the revolutionary forces, than Naples had done. The prosecutions against the principal authors of the revolt, both civil and military, were conducted with vigor, and great numbers of persons were arrested, or deprived of their employments. Happily, however, as the whole chiefs of the conspiracy had escaped into France, there were no capital executions, except among a few of the most guilty in the army. To tranquilize the fears of Austria, and give stability to the restored order of things in Piedmont, a treaty between the two powers was concluded on the 26th July, by which it was stipulated that an imperial force of twelve thousand men should continue in occupation, until September, 1822, of Stradella, Voghera, Tortona, Alessandria, Valencia, Coni, and Vercelli. Its pay, amounting to 500,000 francs (£20,000) a month, and its maintenance, extending to thirteen thousand rations daily, was to be wholly at the charge of the Piedmontese government. A general amnesty, disfigured by so many exceptions as to render it applicable only to the mass of the insurgents, was published on 30th September; and a few days after, a very severe decree was fulminated against the secret societies, which had brought such desolation and humiliation on Italy. The king made his public entry into Turin shortly after, assumed the reins of government, and appointed a royalist ministry; but every one felt that it was a truce only, not a peace, which had been established between the contending parties, and that beneath the treacherous surface there lurked the embers of a conflagration which would break out with additional violence on the first favorable opportunity.[1]

The Emperor Alexander found, on his return to St. Petersburg after the closing of the Diet of Warsaw, that the danger had reached his own dominions, and infected even the guards of the imperial palace. During his absence in Poland a serious mutiny occurred in the splendid regiment of the guards called Semenoff, which had been established by Peter the Great, and was much esteemed by the present emperor. It was occasioned by undue severity of discipline on the part of the colonel, who was a Courlander by birth, and enamored of the German mode of compelling obedience by the baton. The regiment openly refused to obey orders, broke the windows of its obnoxious colonel, and was only reduced to obedience by the courage and *sang froid* of the governor of St. Petersburg, General Milaradowitch, at whose venerated voice the mutineers were abashed, and retired to their barracks. It was ordered by the Czar to be dissolved, and the officers and men dispersed through other regiments, and the most guilty delivered over to courts-martial. The St. Petersburg papers all represented this mutiny as the result merely of misgovernment on the part of its colonel, and unconnected with political events; but its succeeding so rapidly the military revolutions in Spain and Naples led to an opposite opinion being generally entertained, and it had no slight influence in producing the vigorous resolutions taken at the congresses of Troppau and Laybach against the insurgents in the south of Europe. This impression was increased by the emperor in the following year, after his annual journey to the southern provinces, after the usual great reviews of the army there, returning abruptly to St. Petersburg.[1]

In truth, Alexander was now seriously alarmed, and the suspicions which he had conceived as to the fidelity of his troops, and the dread of insurrection, not only embittered all the remaining years of his life, but materially modified his external policy. This appeared in the most decisive manner in his conduct in regard to the Greek revolution, which began in this year, and which will form the interesting subject of a subsequent chapter of this History. Every thing within and without eminently favored a great and decisive movement in favor of the Greeks, on whose behalf, as co-religionists, the warmest sympathy existed among all classes in the Russian empire. The army was unanimous in favor of it, and at a great review of his guards, fifty thousand strong, in September, 1821, at Witepsk, the feelings of the soldiers were so strong on the subject that, amidst unbounded demonstrations of enthusiastic loyalty, they could not be prevented from giving vent to their warlike ardor in favor of their Greek brethren. The news of the insurrection of Prince Ipsilanti in Moldavia reached the emperor at Laybach, and such was the consternation of the European powers at the revolutions of Spain and Italy at that period, that no serious opposition was to be apprehended to any measures, how formidable soever, which he might have proposed, against the Turks, or even their entire expulsion from Europe. But that very circumstance determined the Czar, in opposition to the declared wish of both his army and people, to disavow the insurrection. He saw in it, not, as heretofore, a movement in favor of the Christian faith, or an effort for religious freedom, but a revolutionary outbreak, similar to those of Spain and Italy, which he could not countenance without departing from his principles, or support without the most imminent risk of the contagion spreading to his own troops. He returned for answer, accordingly, to the earnest application for aid from the insurgent Greeks, " Not being able to consider the enterprise of Ipsilanti as any thing but the effect of the excitement which characterizes the present period, and of the inexperience and levity of that young man, he had given orders to the Minister of the Interior to disapprove of it formally." The consequence was that the insurrection was crushed, and a great number of the heroic youths who had taken up arms in defense of their faith perished under the sabres of the Mussulmans.[2]*

---

* The Emperor Alexander, in a highly-interesting conversation with M. de Chateaubriand at Verona in 1823, explained the views on this important subject : " Je suis bien aise," said he, " que vous soyez venu à Vérone, afin de rendre temoignage à la verité. Auriez-vous cru, comme le disent nos ennemis, que l'Alliance n'est qu'un mot qui ne sert qu'à couvrir des ambitions ? Cela eut pu être vrai dans l'ancien etat des choses ; ne is il s'agit bien aujourd'hui de quelques interets particuliers, quand le

89. Extension of the Russian empire in North America.

This year the already gigantic empire of Russia received a huge addition by the appropriation of a vast territory opposite Kamtchatka, on the northwestern coast of America. Several settlements of the Russians, chiefly for the purpose of fishing and the fur-trade, had already been made on this desert and inhospitable coast from the opposite shores of Asia, which, in the immensity of the wilderness, had scarcely been noticed even by the United States, most interested in preventing them. They were for the most part made on the shores which had been discovered by Captain Cook and Vancouver, so that, on the footing of priority of discovery, the best claim to them belonged to Great Britain. But England already possessed an enormous territory, amounting to four million square miles, of which scarce a tenth was capable of cultivation, and her government was indifferent to the settlement of Russians on the coast of the Pacific. The consequence was that they were allowed quietly to take possession, and on the (16) 28th September the Czar issued a ukase defining the limits of the Russian territory in America, which embraced twice as much as the whole realm of France. The ukase also confined to Russian subjects the right of fishing along the coast from Behring Straits to the southern cape of the island of Onroff, and forbade all foreign vessels to fish within a hundred miles of the coast, under pain of confiscation of their cargo. These assumed rights have not hitherto been called in question, but as the Anglo-Saxons in America are as aspiring as the Muscovites, and growing even more rapidly, it is not likely that this will long continue; and it is not impossible that the two great races which appear to divide the world are destined to be first brought into collision on the shores of the Pacific.[1]

Sept. 28, 1821.

[1] Ukase, Sept. 28, 1821; Ann. Hist. iv. 304, 305; Biog. Univ. lvi. 189.

90. Suppression of freemasons' and other secret societies. Oct. 15.

The increasing jealousy of the Czar at liberal opinions, and the secret societies by which it was attempted to propagate them in his dominions, was evinced in the same year by a decree suppressing the order of Freemasons throughout the whole of his dominions. In spite, however, of every precaution that could be taken, the secret societies continued and multiplied; and it was ere long ascertained that they embraced not only many of the first nobles in the country, but, what was far more dangerous, several of the officers high in the army, and even in the imperial guard. Obscure intimations of the existence of a vast conspiracy were frequently sent to the government, but not in so distinct a form as to enable them to act upon it until 1823, when a ukase was issued, denouncing, under the severest penalties, all secret societies, especially in Poland; and a number of leaders of the "Patriotic Society," in particular Jukasinsky, Dobrogoyski, Machynicki, and several others, chiefly Poles, were arrested, and sent to Siberia. It was hoped at the time that the danger was thus removed, but it proved just the reverse. The seizure of these chiefs only served to warn the others of the necessity of the most rigorous secrecy, and gave additional proof, as it seemed to them, of the necessity for a forcible reformation in the state. The secret societies rapidly spread, especially among the highest in rank, the first in patriotic spirit, and the most generous in feeling, both in the civil and military service; a melancholy state of things, when those who should be the guardians of order are leagued together for its overthrow, but the natural result of a state of society such as then existed in Russia, where the power of the sovereign, entirely despotic, was rested on the blind submission of the vast majority of the nation, and a longing for liberal institutions and the enjoyment of freedom existed only in a very limited circle of the most highly-educated classes, but was felt there in the utmost intensity.[1]

Aug 18, 1823.

[1] Ann. Hist. vi. 381, 383; Biog. Univ. lvi. 189; Schnitzler, Hist. Int. de la Russie, i. 90, 91.

monde civilisé est en péril. Il ne peut plus y avoir de Politique Anglaise, Française, Prussienne, Autrichienne. Il n'y a plus qu' une politique générale qui doit, pour le salut de tous, être admise en commun par les peuples et les rois. C'est à moi de me montrer le premier convaincu des principes, sur lesquels j'ai fondé l'Alliance. Une occasion s'est présentée, le soulèvement de la Grèce. Rien sans doute ne garanissait être plus dans mes intérêts, dans ceux de mon peuple, dans l'opinion de mon pays qu' une guerre religieuse contre la Turquie; mais j'ai cru remarquer, dans les troubles du Péloponèse, le signe revolutionnaire, dès lors je me suis abstenu. Que n'a-t-on fait pour rompre l'Alliance! On a cherché tour à tour à me donner des provocations; on a blessé mon amour-propre; on m'a outragé ouvertement. On me connaissait bien mal, si l'on a cru que mes principes ne tenaient qu'à des vanités, ou pouvaient céder à des ressentiments. Non, je ne me separerai jamais des monarques auxquels je me suis uni. Il doit être permis aux Rois, d'avoir des alliances publiques, pour se défendre contre les sociétés secrètes. Qu' est-ce qui pourrait me tenter? Qu' ai-je besoin d'accroître mon empire? La Providence n'a pas mis à mes ordres huit cent mille soldats, pour satisfaire mon ambition; mais pour protéger la religion, la morale, la justice; et pour faire régner ces principes d'ordre, sur lesquels repose la société humaine."—CHATEAUBRIAND, Congres de Vérone, i. 221, 222.

91. General failure of the emperor's philanthropic projects.

The desponding feelings of the Czar, occasioned by the discovery that his efforts for the amelioration of his country were only met by secret societies banded together for his destruction, was much aggravated by the failure of some of his most favorite philanthropic projects. In many of the provinces in which the peasants had received from the sovereign or their lords the perilous gift of freedom, they had suffered severely from the change. The newly enfranchised peasants, in many places, regretted the servitude which had secured to them an asylum in sickness or old age. In the province of Witepsk, where the change had been carried to a great extent, they refused to pay the capitation-tax imposed on them in lieu of their bondage, alleging that they had not the means of doing so; and besieged the empress-dowager, who was known to adhere to old ideas, with the loudest complaints on the "fatal gift" which they had received. So serious did the disorders become among the new freemen, that they were only appeased by the quartering of a large military force on the disturbed districts. Russia suffered even more than the other countries of Europe, in this and the preceding year, from the depreciation of prices, which fell with unmitigated severity on the holders of the immense stores of its rude produce. Banks, by order of the emperor, were established in many places to relieve the distresses of the surcharged proprietors, but they did not meet with general success; and the advances meant to stimulate industry, were too often applied only to feed luxury or minister to depravity.[1]

[Marginal: ¹ Ann. Hist. xii. 319, 321 ; Tegoborski, ii. 373.]

The external transactions of Russia in regard to the Congress of Verona, the Greek revolution, and the Turkish war, will be recounted more suitably in the chapters which relate to those important subjects. But there are a few internal events in Russia which deserve notice before the melancholy period when Alexander paid the common debt of mortality. The first of these was the dreadful inundation at St. Petersburg, in November, 1824. The emperor had just returned from a visit to Orenburg, and the south-eastern provinces of his empire, to his palace at Tzarskocelo near St. Petersburg, when a terrible hurricane arose, which, sweeping over the whole of the Baltic, strewed its shores with wrecks, and inflicted the most frightful devastation on all the harbors with which it is studded. But the catastrophe at the capital was so frightful, that for some hours it was menaced with entire destruction, and all but accomplished a remarkable prophecy, made to Peter the Great when he commenced its construction, that it would one day perish under the waves of the Baltic.[1]*

[Marginal: 92. Dreadful flood at St. Petersburg.]
[Marginal: ¹ Schnitzler, Hist. Int. i. 85; Ann. Hist. vii. 386, 387.]

To understand how this happened, it is necessary to obtain a clear idea of the local circumstances and situation of St. Petersburg. When Peter selected the islands at the mouth of the river Neva, which, descending from the vast expanse of the Lake Ladoga, empties itself in a mighty stream into the Baltic, for the site of his future capital, he was influenced entirely by the suitableness of its situation for a great harbor, of which he severely felt the want, as Archangel, on the frozen shores of the White Sea, was the only port at that period in his dominions. Carried away by this object, which, no doubt, was a very important one, he entirely overlooked the probable unhealthiness of the situation, where a metropolis rested like Venice on marshy islands, the highest part of which was only elevated a few feet above the branches of the river with which they were surrounded; the extreme cold which must ensue in winter from the close proximity of enormous ice-fields,² and the probability of its being exposed to the greatest danger from a sudden rising of the waters of the river owing to a high wind of long continuance blowing in the waters of the Baltic,

[Marginal: 93. Description of the situation of St. Petersburg.]
[Marginal: ² An. Hist. vii. 386; Schnitzler, i. 81.]

and back those which usually flow from the Lake Ladoga. It was this which had previously occurred on more than one occasion, and which now threatened the capital with destruction.

Regardless of these dangers, and of the enormous consumption of human life which took place during the building of the city, from the unhealthiness of the situation, which is said to have amounted to a hundred thousand persons, the Czar drove on the work with the impetuosity which formed so leading a feature in his character, and at length the basis of a great city was laid amidst the watery waste. On the spongy soil and low swamps, which had previously encumbered the course of the Neva, the modern capital arose. Vast blocks of granite, brought from the adjacent plains of Finland, where they are strewed in huge masses over the surface, faced the quays; palaces were erected, of more fragile materials, on the surface, within the isles; and the Perspective Newski is perhaps now the most imposing street in Europe, from the beauty of its edifices and the magnitude of its dimensions. The splendid façade of the Admiralty, the Winter Palace of the emperor, the noble Cathedral of St. Isaac—the statue of Peter the Great, resting on a single block of granite of 1800 tons weight—the noble pillar of Alexander, formed of a single stone of the same material, the largest in the world, combined in a single square, now overpower the imagination of the beholder by their magnificence, and the impression they convey of the power of the sovereign by whose energy these marvels have been made to spring up amidst the watery wilderness. But the original danger, arising from the lowness of the situation, and its liability to inundations, still continues. Great as it is, the power of the Czar is not so great as that of the Baltic waves. From the main channel, where the Neva majestically flows through superb quays of granite, surmounted by piles of palaces, branch off, as from the great canal at Venice, numerous smaller streams, forming by their intersection so many isles, some covered with streets, and forming the most populous quarters; others adorned by beautiful villas and public gardens, the recreation of the citizens during their brief but brilliant summer. But these canals open so many entrances for the floods of the Neva or waves of the Baltic to penetrate into every part of the city. None of it is elevated in its foundations more than a few feet above the ordinary level of the water, and the spectator shudders to think that the rise of the flood, even in a small degree, may threaten the entire city with destruction.[1]

[Marginal: 94. Continued.]
[Marginal: ¹ Custine, i. 26; Schnitzler, i. 83, 84, 85.]

This was what in effect happened at this time. On several former occasions the river had been much swollen: once, immediately before the birth of the present emperor, it was ten feet above its ordinary level. But Nov. 19, this was as nothing compared to the 1824. terrible inundation which now presaged his death. All the 19th of November the wind blew from the south west with terrific violence, and brought the Baltic waves in such a prodigious mass to the mouth of the Neva that its

[Marginal: 95. Great inundation of St. Petersburg. Nov. 19, 1824.]

---

* A curious incident, highly characteristic of Peter, occurred at this time. "When the foundation of his new capital was commencing on the desolate islands of the Neva, which are now covered by the fortress of Cronstadt and the superb palaces of St. Petersburg, Peter observed, by accident, a tree marked at a considerable height from the ground. He called a peasant of Finland, who was working near, and asked him 'what the mark was for?' 'It is the highest level,' replied the peasant, 'which the water reached in the inundation of 1680.' 'You lie' cried the Czar in a fury; 'what you say is impossible;' and seizing a hatchet, he with his own hands cut down the tree, hoping thereby to extinguish alike all memory of the former flood, and guard against the recurrence of a similar calamity."—SCHNITZLER, i. 85, 26.

waters were made to regorge, and soon the quays were overflowed, and the lower parts of the city began to be submerged. This at first, however, excited very little attention, as such floods were not uncommon in the end of autumn; but the alarm soon spread, and terror was depicted in every visage, when it rapidly ascended and spread over the whole town. By half past ten the water in the Perspective Newski was ten feet deep; in the highest parts of the city it was five. The Neva had risen four fathoms above its ordinary level, and, worse still, it was continuing to rise. The whole inhabitants crowded to the upper stories of the houses. Despair now seized on every heart; the reality of the danger came home to every mind; the awful scenes of the Deluge were realized in the very centre of modern civilization. At Cronstadt a ship of the line was lifted up from a dry dock, and floated over the adjacent houses into the great square. At eight in the morning the cannon of alarm began to be discharged. The terrible warning, repeated every minute, so unusual amidst the ordinary stillness of the capital, proved the terror which was felt by government, and augmented the general consternation. Ships torn up from their anchors; boats filled with trembling fugitives; stacks of corn borne on the surface of the waves from a great distance; cattle buffeting with the torrent, intermingled with corpses of persons drowned, or at their last gasp, imploring aid; and immense quantities of furniture, and movables of every description, were floated on to the most intricate and secluded parts of the city. The waters continued to rise till four in the afternoon, and every one imagined that all who could not save themselves in boats would be drowned. The rush was dreadful, accordingly, into every vessel that could be seized on, and numbers perished in striving to get on board. At five in the evening the wind fell, and the water sunk as rapidly as it had risen, and by the next morning the Neva had returned to its former channel. The total loss occasioned by the wind and the inundation was estimated at 100,000,000 rubles (£4,000,000); five hundred persons perished in the waves, and twice that number, sick or infirm, were drowned in their houses. Such had been the violence of the wind and flood, that when the waters subsided they were found to have floated from their place cannons weighing two tons and a half.[1]

[1] Schnitzler, i. 86, 87; Ann. Hist. vii. 386, 387; Gazette de St. Petersburg, Nov. 20, 21, 1824.

At the sight of this terrible calamity, which for a time seemed to bid defiance to the utmost human efforts, the Czar in despair stretched forth his hands to Heaven, and implored that its anger might fall upon his own head, and spare his people. He did not, however, neglect all human means of mitigating the calamity. Throwing himself into a bark, he visited in person the quarters most threatened, distributed the troops in the way most likely to be serviceable, and exposed himself to death repeatedly in order to save his people. All would have been unavailing, however, and the city totally destroyed, if the wind had not mercifully abated, and the waters of the Neva found their usual vent into the Baltic. Munificent subscriptions followed the calamity; the emperor headed the list with fifty thousand pounds. The most solid houses were impregnated with salt, and in a manner ruined; and a severe frost which set in immediately after, before the water had left the houses, augmented the general suffering by filling them with large blocks of ice. Even the most solid granite was exfoliated, and crumbled away before spring, from the effects of the frost on the humid structures. The people regarded this calamity as a judgment of Heaven for not having assisted their Christian brethren during their recent and frightful persecutions from the Turks—the emperor as a punishment for sins of which he was more immediately concerned in his domestic relations.[1]

96. Noble charity of the emperor and nobles.

[1] Schnitzler, i. 89, 91; Ann. Hist. vii. 386, 388.

The year 1824 was marked by a ukase ordering a levy of two in five hundred males over the whole empire—a measure which brought 120,000 men to the imperial standards. As this measure was adopted during the contest in Greece, and when all thought was turned toward the liberation of its inhabitants from the Ottoman yoke, it was obeyed with alacrity, and even enthusiasm. The persons drawn took their departure as for a holy war, amidst the shouts of their relations and neighbors; and from them, in great part, were formed the redoubtable bands which in a few years carried the Russian eagles to Varna, Erivan, and Adrianople. A dangerous revolt in the same year broke out in the province of Novgorod, owing to the peasants having been misled into the belief that the emperor had given them their freedom, and that it was withheld by their lords, which was only crushed by a great display of military force and considerable bloodshed. It was the more alarming, from its being ascertained that the conspiracy had its roots in the military colonies recently established in the southern provinces. The financial measures adopted in 1820 and 1822, for withdrawing a large part of the assignats from circulation, were continued with vigor and success—a circumstance which, of course, made a progressive rise in the value of money, and fall in that of produce, and added much to the general distress felt among the class of producers. Already the ruble was worth 50 per cent. more than it had been a few years before. A treaty was signed on the 27th April between Russia and the United States, which settled the respective limits of their vast possessions in North America: the line of demarcation was fixed at 64° north latitude; all to the north was Russian, all to the south American; and the reciprocal right was secured to the inhabitants of both countries, of fishing on each other's coasts, navigating the Pacific, and disembarking on places not occupied, but for the purpose only of trade with the inhabitants, or supplies for themselves.[2]

97. Internal measures of 1824, and settlement of the boundaries of Russian America. Aug. 27.

[2] Schnitzler, Hist. Int. i. 92; Treaty, April 17, 1824; Ann. Hist. vii. 389, 644.

When, in 1793, the Empress Catherine deemed it time to select a spouse for her grandson, Alexander, she cast her eyes on the family of the Grand Duke of Baden, who at that time had three daughters, gifted with all the virtue and graces, and much of the beauty of their sex. They all made splendid alliances. The eldest became Queen of Sweden; the youngest, Queen of Bavaria; the second, Empress of Russia. Married on 9th October, 1793, to the young Alexander, then only sixteen years of age, when she was fifteen, she took, according to the Russian custom, the name of Elizabeth Alexejiona instead of her own, which was Louise-Marie-Auguste, under which she had been baptized. The pair, though too young for the serious duties of their station, charmed every eye by the beauty of their figures, and the affability of their manners. But the union, however ushered in by splendid prognostications, proved unfortunate: it shared the fate of nearly all in every rank which are formed by parental authority, before the disposition has declared itself, the constitution strengthened, or the tastes formed. The young empress was gifted with all the virtues and many of the graces of her sex. Her countenance, though not regular, was lightened by a sweet expression; her hair, which she wore in locks over her shoulders, beautiful: her figure was elegant, and her motions so graceful that she seemed to realize the visions of the poet, which made the goddess reveal herself by her step.* In disposition she was in the highest degree amiable and exemplary, self-denying, generous, and affectionate. But with all these charms and virtues she wanted the one thing needful for a man of a thoughtful and superior turn of mind: she was not a companion. She had little conversation, few ideas, and none of that elasticity of mind which is necessary for the charm of conversational intercourse. Hence even the earliest years of their marriage were productive of no lasting ties; they seldom met, save in public; and the death of their two only children, both of whom were daughters, deprived them of the enduring bond of parental love.[1]

No one need be told that conjugal fidelity is of all others the virtue most difficult to practice on the throne, and that it is never so much so as to sovereigns of the most energetic and powerful minds. Ardent in one thing, they are not less so in another; of few, from Julius Cæsar to Henry IV., can it be said that they are, like Charles XII.,

" Unconquered lords of pleasure and of pain."

Alexander was not a sensualist, and he had not the passion for meretricious variety, which so often in high rank has disgraced the most illustrious characters. But his mind was ardent, his heart tender, and he had the highest enjoyment in the confidential *épanchements* which, rarely felt by any save with those of the opposite sex, can never be so but with them—by sovereigns whose elevation keeps all of their own at a distance. Before many years of his married life had passed, Alexander had yielded to these dispositions; and the knowledge of his infidelities completed the estrangement of the illustrious couple. "Out of these infidelities arose," says M. de Chateaubriand, "a fidelity which continued eleven years." Alexander, however, suffered in his turn by a righteous retribution the pangs of jealousy. The object of his attachment (a married Polish lady of rank) had all the beauty, fascination, and conversational talent which have rendered her countrywomen so celebrated over Europe, and to which even the intellectual breast of Napoleon did homage; but she had also the spirit of coquetry and thirst for admiration which has so often turned the passions they have awakened into a consuming fire. Unfaithful to duty, she had proved equally so to love: the influence of the emperor was, after a long constancy, superseded by a new attachment; and the *liaison* between them was already broken, when a domestic calamity overwhelmed him with affliction. Meanwhile the empress, who had left Russia, and sought solace in foreign traveling, mourned in silence and dignified retirement the infidelity of her husband—the blasting of her hopes. Yet even then, under a calm and serene air, and the cares of a life entirely devoted to deeds of beneficence, was concealed a heart wasted by sorrow, but faithful to its first attachment. "How often," says the annalist, "was she surprised in tears, contemplating the portrait of that Alexander, so lovable, yet so faithless!"[2]

From this irregular connection had sprung three children, two of which had died in infancy. But the third, Mademoiselle N., a child gifted with all the graces and charms of her mother, though in delicate health, still lived, and had become the object of the most passionate affection to her father. It became necessary to send her to Paris, for the benefit of a milder climate and the best medical advice; and during her absence, the emperor, a solitary hermit in his palace, but thirsting for the enjoyments of domestic life, sought a temporary respite to his anxiety in frequenting the houses of some highly respectable families in middle life, for the most part Germans, to whom his rank was known, but where he insisted upon being treated as an ordinary guest. There he often expressed his envy at the happiness which reigned in those domestic circles, and sighed to think that the Emperor of all the Russias was compelled to seek, at the hearth of others, that felicity which his grandeur or his faults had denied him at his own. But the hand of fate was upon him: he was to be pierced to the heart through the fruit of his own irregularities. His daughter, who was now seventeen, had returned from France, apparently restored to health, and in all the bloom of youth and beauty. She was engaged to be married, with the entire consent of her father: the magnificent trousseau was ordered at Paris, but when it arrived at St. Petersburg she was no more.[3] So sudden was the death of the young *fiancée*, that it occurred when the emperor was out at a review of his guards. An aid-de-camp, with a melancholy ex-

---

* " Et vera incessu patuit Dea."—VIRGIL.

pression, approached, and requested leave to speak to him in private. At the first words he divined the whole: a mortal paleness overspread his visage, and, turning up his eyes to heaven, he struck his forehead and exclaimed, "I receive the punishment of my sins!"

<small>101. Reconciliation of the emperor and empress.</small> These words were not only descriptive of the change in the emperor's mind in the latter years of his life, but they presaged, and truly, an important change in his domestic relations, which shed a ray of happiness over his last moments. His mind, naturally inclined to deep and mystical religious emotions, had been much affected by the dreadful scenes which he had witnessed at the inundation of St. Petersburg, and this domestic bereavement completed the impression that he was suffering, by the justice of Heaven, the penalty of his transgressions. Under the influence of these feelings, he returned to his original dispositions; and that mysterious change took place in his mind, which so often, on the verge of the grave, brings us back to the impressions of our youth. He again sought the society of the empress, who had returned to St. Petersburg, was attentive to her smallest wishes, and sought to efface the recollection of former neglect by every kindness which affection could suggest. The change was not lost upon that noble princess, who still nourished in her inmost heart her first attachment; and the reconciliation was rendered complete by the generous tears which, in sympathy with her husband's sorrow, she shed over the bier of her rival's daughter. But she, too, was in an alarming state of health; long years of anxiety and suffering had weakened her constitution, and the physicians recommended a change, and return to her native air. But the empress declared that the sovereign must not die elsewhere but in her own dominions, and she refused to leave Russia. They upon this proposed the Crimea; but Alexander gave the preference of TAGANROG. The emperor fixed his departure for the 13th September, 1825, some days before that of the empress, in order to prepare every thing for her reception. Though his own health was broken, as he had not recovered from an attack of erysipelas, he resolved upon running the risk of the journey; an expedition of some thousand miles had no terrors for one the half of whose life was spent in traveling.¹

<small>¹ Madlle. Choiseul Gouffier, 381, 386; Schnitzler, i. 105.</small>

<small>102. Solemn service in the cathedral of Notre Dame de Kazan. Sept. 13.</small> Sincerely religious to the extent even of being superstitious, the emperor had a presentiment that this journey was to be his last, and that he was about to expire beside the empress, amidst the flowery meads and balmy air of the south. Impressed with this idea, he had fixed his departure for the 1st September (old style, 13th), the day after a solemn service had been celebrated in the cathedral of Kazan, on the translation of the bones of the great Prince Alexander Newski from the place of his sepulture at Vladimir to that holy fane on the banks of the Neva. On every departure for a long journey, the emperor had been in the habit of repairing to its altar to pray; but on this occasion he directed the metropolitan bishop in secret to have the service *for the dead* chanted for him when he returned on the following morning at four o'clock. He arrived there, accordingly, next day at that early hour, when it was still dark, and was met by the priests in full costume as for the burial service, the service of which was chanted as he approached. He drove up to the cathedral by the magnificent street of Perspective Newski in a simple calèche drawn by three horses abreast, without a single servant, and reached the gate as the first streaks of light were beginning to appear in the eastern sky. Wrapped in his military cloak, without his sword, and bareheaded, the emperor alighted, kissed the cross which the archbishop presented to him, and entered the cathedral alone, the gates of which were immediately closed after him. The prayer appointed for travelers was then chanted; the Czar knelt at the gate of the rail which surrounded the altar, and received the benediction of the prelate, who placed the sacred volume on his head, and, receiving with pious care a consecrated cross and some relic of the saint in his bosom, he again kissed the emblem of salvation, "which gives life,"* and departed alone and unattended, save by the priests, who continued to sing till he was beyond the gates of the cathedral the chant, "God save thy People."¹

<small>¹ Oertel, Derniers Jours d'Alexandre, 54, 69; Schnitz. i. 105, 110.</small>

<small>103. His departure from the cathedral.</small> The archbishop, called in the Greek Church "the Seraphim," requested the emperor, while his traveling carriage was drawing up, to honor his cell with a visit, which he at once agreed to do. Arrived at this retreat, the conversation turned on the *Schimnik*, an order of peculiarly austere monks, who had their cells in the vicinity. The emperor expressed a wish to see one of them, and immediately the archbishop accompanied him to their chief. The emperor there found only a small apartment furnished with deal boards, covered with black cloth, and hung with the same funeral garb. "I see no bed," said the emperor. "Here it is," said the monk; and, drawing aside a curtain, revealed an alcove, in which was a coffin covered with black cloth, and surrounded with all the lugubrious habiliments of the dead. "This," he added, "is my bed; it will ere long be yours, and that of all, for their long sleep." The emperor was silent, and mused long. Then suddenly starting from his reverie, as if recalled to the affairs of this world, he bade them all adieu with the words, "Pray for me and for my wife." He ascended his open calèche, the horses of which bore him toward the south with their accustomed rapidity, and was soon out of sight; but he was still uncovered when the carriage disappeared in the obscure gray of the morning.²

<small>² Oertel, 60, 61; Schnitz. i. 110, 114.</small>

<small>104. His arrival at Taganrog.</small> Alexander made the journey in twelve days; and as the distance was above fifteen hundred miles, and he was obliged to stop at many places, he must have gone from a hundred and fifty to two hundred miles a day. He was fully impressed with the idea of his approaching death the whole way, and often asked the coachman

---

* A term consecrated in the Russian Church.

"if he had seen the wandering star?" "Yes, your majesty," he replied. "Do you know what it presages? Misfortune and death: but God's will be done." Arrived at Taganrog, he devoted several days to preparing every thing for the empress, which he did with the utmost solicitude and care. She arrived ten days after, and they remained together for some weeks, walking and driving out in the forenoon, and conversing alone in the evening with the utmost affection, more like newly-married persons than those who had so long been severed. The cares of empire, however, ere long tore the emperor from this charming retreat; and on the urgent entreaty of Count Woronzoff, governor of the Crimea, he undertook a journey in that province. He set out on the 1st November; Nov. 1. and during seventeen days that the expedition lasted, alternately admired the romantic mountain scenery and beautiful sea views, rivaling those of the Corniche between Nice and Genoa, which the route presented. At Ghirai, however, on the 10th, after Nov. 10. dinner, when conversing with Sir James Wylie, his long-tried and faithful medical attendant, on his anxiety about the empress, who had just heard of the death of the King of Bavaria, her brother-in-law, he mentioned, as if accidentally, that he felt his stomach deranged, and that for several nights his sleep had been disturbed. Sir James felt his pulse, which indicated fever, and earnestly counselled the adoption of immediate remedies. "I have no need of you," replied the emperor, smiling, "nor of your Latin pharmacopœia—I know how to treat myself. Besides, my trust is in God, and in the strength of my constitution." Notwithstanding all that could be said, he persisted in his refusal to take medicine, and even continued his journey, and exposed himself to his wonted fatigue on horseback when returning along the pestilential shores of the Putrid Sea.[1]

[1] Schnitzler, i. 120, 124; Ann. Hist. viii. 373, 374; Sir James Wylie, 37, 41.

He returned to Taganrog on the 17th, being the exact day fixed for that event before his departure; but already shivering fits, succeeded by cold ones, the well-known symptoms of intermittent fever, had shown themselves. The empress, with whom he shared every instant that could be spared from the cares of empire, showed him the most unremitting attention, and by the earnest entreaties of his physician he was at length prevailed on to take some of the usual remedies prescribed for such cases. For a brief space they had the desired effect; and the advices sent to St. Petersburg of the august patient's convalescence threw the people, who had been seriously alarmed by the accounts of his illness, into a delirium of joy. But these hopes proved fallacious. On the 25th the symptoms suddenly became more threatening.[2] Extreme weakness confined him to his couch, and alarming dispatches from General Diebitch and Count Woronzoff augmented his anxiety, by revealing the existence and magnitude of the vast conspiracy in the army, which had for its object to deprive him of his throne and life. "My friend," said he to Sir James Wylie, "what a frightful design! The mon-

105. His last illness. Nov. 17.

[2] Wylie, 76, 79; An. Hist. viii. 374, 375; Schnatzler, i. 132, 134.

sters—the ungrateful! when I had no thought but for their happiness."*

The symptoms now daily became more alarming, and the fever assumed the form of the bilious or gastric, as it is now called, and at last showed the worst features of the typhus. His physicians then, despairing of his life, got Prince Volkonsky to suggest the last duties of a Christian. "They have spoken to me, Wylie," said the emperor, "of the communion; has it really come to that?" "Yes," said that faithful counselor, with tears in his eyes; "I speak to you no longer as a physician, but as a friend. Your Majesty has not a moment to lose." Next day the emperor confessed, and with the empress, who never for an instant, day or night, left his bedside, received the last communion. "Forget the emperor," said he to the confessor; "speak to me simply as a dying Christian." After this he became perfectly docile. "Never," said he to the empress, "have I felt such a glow of inward satisfaction as at this moment; I thank you from the bottom of my heart." The symptoms of erisypelas in his leg now returned. "I will die," said he, "like my sister," alluding to the Grand Duchess of Oldenburg, who had refused Napoleon at Erfurth, and afterward died of that complaint. He then fell into a deep sleep, and wakened when it was near mid-day, and the sun was shining brightly. Causing the windows to be opened, he said, looking at the blue vault, "What a beautiful day!"† and feeling the arms of the empress around him, he said tenderly, pressing her hand, "My love, you must be very fatigued." These were his last words. He soon after fell into a lethargic sleep, which lasted several hours, from which he only wakened a few minutes before he breathed his last. The power of speech was gone; but he made a sign to the empress to approach, and imprinted a last and fervent kiss on her hand. The rattle was soon heard in his throat. She closed his eyes a few minutes after, and, placing the cross on his bosom, embraced his lifeless remains for the last time. "Lord!" said she, "pardon my sins; it has pleased thy omnipotent power to take him from me."[1] ‡

106. And death. Nov. 26.

Dec. 1.

[1] Schnitzler, i. 134, 136; Wylie, 79, 82; Ann. Hist. viii. 374, 375.

---

* "Le monarque dit un jour à M. Wylie, 'Laissez-moi, je sais moi-même, ce qu'il me faut: du repos, de la solitude, de la tranquillité.' Un autre jour, il lui dit: 'Mon ami, ce sont mes nerfs qu'il faut soigner; ils sont dans un desordre épouvantable.' 'C'est un mal,' lui repliqua Wylie, 'dont les rois sont plus souvent atteints que les particuliers.' 'Surtout dans les temps actuels,' répliqua vivement Alexandre! 'Ah' j'ai bien sujet d'être malade.' Enfin, étant en apparence sans aucune fièvre, l'Empereur se tourna brusquement vers le docteur, qui était seul présent. 'Mon ami,' s ceria-t-il, 'quelles actions, quelles epouvantables actions:' et il fixa sur le médecin un regard terrible et incomprehensible."—*Annuaire Historique*, viii. 37, note.

† "Light—more light!" the well-known last words of Goethe, as noticed by Bulwer in his beautiful romance, "My Novel." Those who have witnessed the last moments of the dying, know how often a request for, or expressions of satisfaction for light, are among their last words.

‡ The empress addressed the following beautiful letter to her mother-in-law on this sad bereavement: "Maman, votre ange est au ciel, et moi, je végète encore sur la terre. Qui aurait pensé que moi, faible malade, je pourrais lui survivre! Maman, ne m'abandonnez pas, car je suis absolument seule dans ce monde de douleurs. Notre cher defunt a repris son air de bienveillance, son sourire me prouve qu'il est heureux, et qu'il voit des choses plus

107. And funeral.

The body of the emperor, after being embalmed, was brought to the Church of St. Alexander Newski at Taganrog, where it remained for some days in a *chapelle ardente*, surrounded by his mourning subjects, and was thence transferred, accompanied by a splendid cortège of cavalry, Cossacks, and artillery, after a long interval, to the cathedral of St. Peter and St. Paul, in the citadel of St. Petersburg, where his ancestors were laid. The long journey occupied several weeks, and every night, when his remains were deposited in the church of the place where the procession rested, crowds of people, from a great distance around, flocked to the spot to kneel down, and kiss the bier where their beloved Czar was laid.

March 10. The body reached St. Petersburg on the 10th of March, but the interment, which was conducted with extraordinary magnificence in the cathedral, did not take place till the 25th. The Grand Duke Nicholas (now become emperor), with all the imperial family, was present on the occasion, and a splendid assembly of the nobility of Russia and diplomacy of Europe. There was not a heart which was not moved, scarce an eye that was not moistened with tears. The old grenadiers, his comrades in the campaigns in Germany and France, and who bore the weight of the coffin when taken to the grave, wept like children; and he was followed to his last home by his faithful servant Ilya, who had driven the car from Taganrog, a distance of fifteen hundred miles, and who stood in tears at the side of the bier, as his beloved master was laid in the tomb.[1]

¹ Gazette de St. Petersburg, March 26, 1826; Schnitzler, ii. 235, 214; Ann. Hist. ix. 337, 338.

108. Death and burial of the empress. May 16.

The Empress Elizabeth did not long survive the husband who, despite all her sorrows, had ever reigned supreme in her heart. The feeble state of her health did not permit of her accompanying his funeral procession to St. Petersburg, which she was passionately desirous to have done; and it was not till the 8th May that she was able to leave Taganrog on her way to the capital. The entire population of the town, by whom she was extremely beloved, accompanied her for a considerable distance on the road. Her weakness, however, increased rapidly as she continued her journey; grief for the loss of her husband, along with the sudden cessation of the anxiety for his life, and the want of any other object in existence, proved fatal to a constitution already weakened by long years of mourning and severance. She with difficulty reached Belef, a small town in the government of Toule, where she breathed her last, serene and tranquil, on the 16th May. Her remains were brought to St. Petersburg, where she was carried to the cathedral on the same car which had conveyed her husband, and laid beside him on the 3d July. Thus terminated a marriage, celebrated thirty years before with every prospect of earthly felicity, and every splendor which the most exalted rank could confer. "I have seen," said a Russian poet, "that couple, he

July 3.

beautiful as Hope, she ravishing as Felicity. It seems only a day since Catherine placed on their youthful heads the nuptial crown of roses; soon the diadems were mingled with thorns; and too soon, alas! the angel of death environed their pale foreheads with poppies, the emblem of eternal sleep."[1]

¹ Schnitzler, ii. 263, 266; Ann. Hist. ix. 311, 342.

109. His character.

Had Alexander died shortly after the first capture of Paris in 1814, he would have left a name unique in the history of the world, for seldom had so great a part been so nobly played on such a theatre. It is hard to say whether his fortitude in adversity, his resolution in danger, or his clemency in victory, were then most admirable. For the first time in the annals of mankind, the sublime principles of forgiveness of injuries were brought into the governments of nations in the moment of their highest excitement, and mercy in the hour of triumph restrained the uplifted hand of justice. To the end of the world the flames of Moscow will be associated with the forgiveness of Paris. But time has taken much from the halo which then environed his name, and revealed weaknesses in his character well known to his personal friends, but the existence of which the splendor of his former career had hardly permitted to be suspected. He had many veins of magnanimity in his character, but he was not a thoroughly great man. He was so, like a woman, by impulse and sentiment, rather than principle and habit. Chateaubriand said, "Il avait l'âme forte, mais le caractère foible." He wanted the constancy of purpose and perseverance of conduct which is the distinguishing and highest mark of the masculine character.

110. His failings.

Warm-hearted, benevolent, and affectionate, he was without the steadiness which springs from internal conviction, and the consistency which arises from the feelings being permanently guided by the conscience and ruled by the reason. He was sincerely desirous of promoting the happiness of his subjects, and deeply impressed with a sense of duty in that respect; but his projects of amelioration were not based upon practical information, and consequently, in great part, failed in effect. They savored more of the philanthropic dreams of his Swiss preceptor La Harpe than either the manners, customs, or character of his own people. At times he was magnanimous and heroic, when circumstances called forth these elevated qualities; but at others he was flexible and weak, when he fell under influences of a less creditable description. Essentially religious in his disposition, he sometimes sank into the dreams of superstition. The antagonist of Napoleon at one time came to share the reveries of Madame Krüdener at another. Affectionate in private life, he yet broke the heart of his empress, who showed by her noble conduct on his death-bed how entirely she was worthy of his regard. His character affords a memorable example of the truth so often enforced by moralists, so generally forgot in the world, that it is in the ruling power of the mind, rather than the impulses by which it is influenced, that the distinguishing mark of character is to be looked for; and that no

belles qu' ici-bas. Ma seule consolation dans cette perte irréparable est, que je ne lui survivrai pas, j'ai l'espérance de m'ounir bientôt a lui."—L'IMPÉRATRICE MARIE FOEDOROVNA, 2 Dec., 1825.

amount of generosity of disposition can compensate for the want of the firmness which is to control it.

The death of Alexander was succeeded by events in Russia of the very highest importance, and which revealed the depth of the abyss on the edge of which the despotic sovereigns of Europe slumbered in fancied security. It occasioned, at the same time, a contest of generosity between the two brothers of Alexander, Constantine and Nicholas, unexampled in history, and which resembles rather the fabled magnanimity with which the poets extricate the difficulties of a drama on the opera stage, than any thing which occurs in real life. By a ukase of (5) 16th April, 1797, the Emperor Paul had abolished the right of choosing a successor out of the imperial family, which Peter the Great had assumed, and established forever the succession to the crown in the usual order, the males succeeding before the females, and the elder in both before the younger. This settlement had been formally sanctioned by the Emperor Alexander on two solemn occasions, and it constituted the acknowledged and settled law of the empire.[1] As the late emperor had only two daughters, both of whom died in infancy, the undoubted heir to the throne, when he died, was the Grand Duke Constantine, then at Warsaw, at the head of the government of Poland. On the other hand, the Grand Duke Nicholas, the next younger brother, was at St. Petersburg, where he was high in command, and much beloved by the guards in military possession of the capital. In these circumstances, if a contest was to be apprehended, it was between the younger brother on the spot endeavoring to supplant the elder at a distance. Nevertheless it was just the reverse. There was a contest, but it was between the two brothers, each endeavoring to devolve the empire upon the other.[2]

Intelligence of the progress of the malady of Alexander was communicated to Constantine at Warsaw, as regularly as to the empress-mother at St. Petersburg; and it was universally supposed that, as a matter of course, upon the demise of the Czar, to whom he was only eighteen months younger, he would succeed to the throne. The accounts of the death of the reigning sovereign reached Warsaw on the 7th December, where both Constantine and his youngest brother, the Grand Duke Michael, were at the time. The former was immediately considered as emperor by the troops, and all the ministers and persons in attendance in the palace, though he shut himself up in his apartment for two days on receiving the melancholy intelligence. But to the astonishment of every one, instead of assuming the title and functions of empire, he absolutely forbade them; declared that he had resigned his right of succession in favor of his younger brother Nicholas; that this had been done with the full knowledge and consent of the late emperor; and that Nicholas was now emperor. And in effect, on the day following, the Grand Duke Michael set out for St. Petersburg, bearing holograph letters from Constantine to the empress-mother and his brother Nicholas, in which, after referring to a former act of renunciation in 1822, deposited in the archives of the empire, and which had received the sanction of the late emperor, he again, in the most solemn manner, repeated his renunciation of the throne.[1]*

To understand how this came about, it is necessary to premise that the Grand Duke Constantine, like his brother Alexander, had been married, at the early age of sixteen, by the orders of the Empress Catherine, to the Princess Julienne of Saxe-Coburg, a house which has since been illustrated by so many distinguished marriages into the royal families of Europe. The marriage, from the very first, proved unfortunate; the savage manners of the Grand Duke proved insupportable to the princess; they had no family; and at the end of four years they separated by mutual consent, and the Grand Duchess returned with a suitable pension, to her father in Germany. The Grand Duke was occupied for twenty years after with war, interspersed with temporary *liaisons;* but at length, in 1820, when he was viceroy of Poland, his inconstant affections were fixed by a Polish lady of uncommon beauty and fascination. She was Jeanne Grudzinska, daughter of a count and landed proprietor at Pistolaf, in the district of Bromberg. So ardent was the passion of Constantine for the Polish beauty, that he obtained a divorce from his first wife on 1st April, 1820, and immediately espoused, though with the left hand, the object of his present passion, upon whom he bestowed the title of Princess of Lowicz, after a lordship in Masovia which he gave to her brother, and which had formerly formed part of the military appanage bestowed by Napoleon upon Marshal Davoust.[2]

The marriage of Constantine, however, was with the left hand, or a *morganatic* one only; the effect of which was, that, though legal in all other respects, the sons of the marriage were not grand dukes, and could not succeed to the throne; nor did the princess by her marriage become a grand duchess.

---

* The letter to the empress-mother was in these words: "Habitué dès mon enfance, à accomplir religieusement la volonté, tant de feu mon père que du defunt empereur, ainsi que celle de V. M. I.; et me renfermant maintenant encore dans les bornes de ce principe, je considère comme une obligation, de céder mon droit à la puissance, conformément aux dispositions de l'acte de l'empire sur l'ordre de succession dans la famille impériale, à S. A. I. le Grand-duc Nicolas et à ses héritiers." In the letter, of the same date, to the Grand Duke Nicholas, Constantine thus expressed himself: "Je regarde comme un devoir sacré: de prier très-humblement V. M. I. qu'elle daigne accepter de moi, tout le premier, *mon serment de sujétion et de fidélité*; et de me permettre de lui exposer que, n'élevant mes yeux à aucune dignité nouvelle, ni à aucun titre nouveau, je désire de conserver seulement celui de Césarowitch, dont j'ai été pour mes services, par feu notre père. Mon unique bonheur sera toujours que V. M. I. daigne agréer les sentimens de ma plus profonde vénération, et de mon dévouement sans bornes; sentimens dont j'offre comme gage, plus de trente années d'un service fidèle, et du zèle le plus pur qui m'anime envers L. L. M. les empereurs mon père et mon frère de glorieuse mémoire. C'est avec les mêmes sentimens que je ne cesserai jusqu'à la *fin de mes jours de servir V. M. I., et ses descendants dans mes fonctions et ma place actuelle.*"—CONSTANTIN, *à l'impératrice* MARIE *et au Grand-duc* NICOLAS, 8th December, 1825. SCHNITZLER, *Hist. Int. de la Russie*, i. 190–191.

But in addition to this, Constantine had come under a solemn engagement, though verbal, and on his honor as a prince only, to renounce his right of succession to the crown in favor of his brother Nicholas; and it was on this condition only that the consent of the emperor had been given to his divorce. In pursuance of this engagement he had, on the (14) 26th January, 1822, left with his brother, the Emperor Alexander, a solemn renunciation of his right of succession, which had been accepted by the emperor by as solemn a writing, and a recognition of Nicholas as heir to the throne. The whole three documents had been deposited by him in a packet sealed with the imperial arms, endorsed, "Not to be opened till immediately after my death, before proceeding to any other act,"¹ with Prince Pierre Vassiluvitch Lapoukhine, President of the Imperial Council.*

Jan. 26, 1822.

¹ Schnitzler, i. 162, 163.

The intelligence of the death of Alexander arrived at St. Petersburg on the 9th December, in the morning, at the very time when the imperial family were returning thanks, in the chapel of the palace, to Heaven for his supposed recovery, which the dispatches of the preceding day had led them to hope for. The first thing done was, in terms of the injunction of Alexander, to open the sealed packet containing Constantine's resignation. As soon as it was opened and read, the Council declared Nicholas emperor, and invited him to attend to receive their homage. But here an unexpected difficulty presented itself. Nicholas positively refused to accept the throne. "I am not emperor," he said, "and I will not be so at my brother's expense. If, maintaining his renunciation, the Grand Duke Constantine persists in the sacrifice of his rights, but in that case only, will I exercise my right to the throne." The Council remained firm, and entreated him to accept their homage; but Nicholas positively refused, alleging, in addition, that as Constantine's renunciation had not been published or acted upon during the lifetime of the late emperor, it had not acquired the force of a law, and that he was consequently emperor, and if he meant to renounce, must do so afresh, when in the full possession of his rights. The Council still contested the point; but finding the Grand Duke immovable, they submitted with the words, "You are our emperor; we owe you an absolute obedience; since, then, you command us to recognize the Grand Duke Constantine as our legitimate sovereign, we have no alternative but to obey your commands." They accordingly declared Constantine emperor. Their example determined the Senate; and the guards, being drawn up on the place in front of the Winter Palace, took the usual oath to the Cesarowitch as the new emperor. The motives which determined Nicholas to take this step were afterward stated in a noble proclamation on his own accession to the throne.¹*

115. Nicholas refuses the crown, and proclaims Constantine. Dec. 9.

¹ Ann. Hist. ix. 3+1; Schnitzler, i. 168, 169.

Matters were in this state, when the Grand Duke Constantine being proclaimed emperor, and recognized by all the authorities at St. Petersburg, when the Grand Duke Michael arrived there, with the fresh renunciation by the former of his rights, after the death of the late sovereign had been known to him. Nothing could be more clear and explicit than that renunciation, concerning the validity of which no doubt could be now entertained. Nevertheless Nicholas persisted in his generous refusal of the throne, and, after a few hours' repose, dispatched the Grand Duke Michael back to Warsaw, with the intelligence that Constantine had already been proclaimed emperor. He met, however, at Dorpat, in Livonia, a courier with the answer of Constantine, after he had received the dispatches from St. Petersburg, again positively declining the empire, in a letter addressed "To his Majesty the Emperor." Nicholas, however, still refused the empire, and again besought his brother to accept it. The interregnum continued three weeks, during which the two brothers—a thing unheard of—were mutually declining and urging the empire on the other! At length, on the 24th December, Nicholas, being fully persuaded of the sincerity and legality of his brother's resignation, yielded to what appeared the will of Providence, mounted the throne of his fathers, and notified his accession to all the sovereigns of Europe, by whom he was immediately recognized.²

116. Contest of generosity between the two brothers, and Nicholas mounts the throne. Dec. 24.

² Ann. Hist. ix. 75, 76; Pièces Historiques; Schnitzler, i. 192, 194; Nesselrode aux Puissances Étrangères, 13 (25) Dec. 1825.

---

* "Ne reconnaissant en moi, ni le génie, ni les talents, ni la force necessaire pour être jamais élevé a la dignité souveraine, a laquelle je pourrais avoir droit par ma naissance, je supplie V. M. I. de transferer ce droit a celui a qui il appartient après moi, et d'assurer ainsi pour toujours la stabilité de l'empire. Quant a moi, j'ajouterai par cette renonciation, une nouvelle garantie et une nouvelle force a l'engagement que j'ai spontanément et solennellement contracté, a l'occasion de mon divorce avec ma premiere épouse. Toutes les circonstances de ma situation actuelle, me portent de plus en plus a cette mesure, qui prouvera à l'empire et au monde entier la sincerité de mes sentiments. Daignez, sire, agreer avec bonté ma prière, daignez contribuer a ce que notre auguste mere veuille y adherer; et sanctionnez-la de votre assurance imperiale. Dans la sphere de la vie privée, je m'efforcerai toujours de servir d'exemple a vos fidèles sujets; a tous ceux qu' aime l'amour de notre chere Patrie."—CONSTANTIN à l'Empereur, St. Petersbourg, 14 (26) Jan., 1822. The acceptance of the emperor of this renunciation was simple and unqualified, and dated 2 (14th) Feb., 1822. The Emperor added a manifesto in the following terms, declaring Nicholas his heir: "L'acte spontanée par lequel notre frere puiné, le Cesarowitch et Grand-duc Constantin, renonce a son droit sur le trône de toutes les Russies, est, et demeurera, fixe et invariable. Ledit Acte de Renonciation sera, pour que la notorie en soit assurée, conserve a la Grande Cathédrale de l'Assomption a Moscow, et dans les trois hautes administrations de notre Empire, au Saint Synode, au Conseil de l'Empire, et au Senat Dirigeant. En consequence de ces dispositions, et conformement a la stricte teneur de l'acte sur la succession au trône, est reconnu pour notre héritier, notre second frère le Grand-duc Nicolas. ALEXANDRE."—Journal de St. Petersbourg, No. 150. SCHNITZLER, i. 163, 164.

* "Nous n'eumes ni le désir, ni le droit, de considerer comme irrevocable cette renonciation, qui n'avait point été publiée lorsqu'elle eut lieu; et qui n'avait été convertie en loi. Nous voulions aussi manifester notre respect pour la premiere loi fondamentale de notre Patrie, sur l'ordre invariable de la succession au trône. Nous cherchions uniquement a garantir de la moindre atteinte la loi qui régle la succession au Trône, a placer dans tout son jour la loyauté de nos intentions, et de preserver notre chere Patrie, même d'un moment d'incertitude, sur la personne de son legitime souverain. Cette determination, prise dans la pureté de notre conscience devant le Dieu qui lit au fond des cœurs, fut benie par S. M. l'Imperatrice Marie, notre mere bien-aimée."—Proclamation, 25 Dec., 1825; Journal de St. Petersbourg, No. 150. SCHNITZLER, i. 169, 170.

But while every thing seemed to smile on the young emperor, and he was, in appearance, receiving the reward of his disinterested and generous conduct, in being seated, by general consent, on the greatest throne in the world, the earth was trembling beneath his feet, and a conspiracy was on the point of bursting forth, which ere long involved Russia in the most imminent danger, and had well-nigh terminated, at its very commencement, his eventful reign. From the documents on this subject which have since been published by the Russian Government, it appears that, ever since 1817, secret societies, framed on the model of those of Germany, had existed in Russia, the object of which was to subvert the existing Government, and establish in its stead representative institutions and a constitutional monarchy. They received a vast additional impulse upon the return of the Army of Occupation from France, in the close of 1818, where the officers, having been living in intimacy, during three years, with the English and German officers, and familiar with the liberal press of both countries, as well as of Paris, had become deeply imbued with republican ideas, and enthusiastic admirers of the popular feelings by which they were nourished, and of the establishments in which they seemed to end. The conspiracy was the more dangerous that it was conducted with the most profound secrecy, embraced a number of the highest nobles in the land, as well as military officers, and had its ramifications in all the considerable armies, and even in the guards at the capital. So strongly was the danger felt by the older officers of the empire, who were attached to the old régime, that one of them said, on the return of the troops from France, "Rather than let these men re-enter Russia, I would, were I emperor, throw them into the Baltic."[1]

117. Account of the conspiracy against him

1 Rapport de la Commission d'Enquête, Dec. 14 (26), 1-25; Ann. Hist. ix. 7, 80, 82-3; Schnitzler, i. 200. n. 7, 14.*

The conspiracy was divided into two branches, each of which formed a separate society, but closely connected by correspondence. The directing committee of both had its seat at St. Petersburg, and at its head was Prince Troubetzkoi—a nobleman of distinguished rank, but more ardor than firmness of character, who was high in the emperor's confidence—Ryleif, Prince Obolonsky, and some other officers in the garrison, besides sixty officers in the guards. The second society, which was much more numerous, and embraced a great number of colonels of regiments, had its chief ramifications in the army of the south on the Turkish frontier, then under the command of Count Wittgenstein. At the head of this society were Captain Nikita Mouravieff, Colonel Pestel, and Alexander Mouravieff, whose names have acquired a melancholy celebrity from the tragedy in which their efforts terminated. These men were all animated with a sincere love of their country, and were endowed with the most heroic courage. Under these noble qualities, however, were concealed, as is always the case in such conspiracies, an inordinate thirst for elevation and individual ambition, and an entire ignorance of the circumstances essential to the success of any enterprise, having for its object the establishment of representative institutions in their country. They were among the most highly educated and cultivated men in the Russian empire at the time; and yet their project, if successful, could not have failed to reduce their country to anarchy and throw it back a century in the career of improvement and ultimate freedom. So true it is that the first thing to be inquired into, in all measures intended to introduce the institutions of one country into another, is, to consider whether their political circumstances and national character are the same. The conspiracy was headed by the highest in rank and the first in intelligence, because it was on them that the chains of servitude hung heaviest. "Envy," says Bulwer, "enters so largely into the democratic passion, that it is always felt most strongly by those who are on the edge of a line which they yet feel to be impassable. No man envies an archangel."[1]

118. Details on the conspiracy.

1 Rapport, 14 (26) Déc. 1825; Ann. Hist. ix. 80; Documents Historiques, Partie 2.

Information, though in a very vague way, had been communicated to the late emperor of these societies; but it was not suspected how deep-seated and extensive they in reality were, or how widely they had spread throughout the *officers* of the army. The privates were, generally speaking, still steady in their allegiance. Wittgenstein, however, and Count de Witt, had received secret but authentic accounts of the conspiracy at the time of Alexander's journey to Taganrog, and it was that information, suddenly communicated during his last illness, which had so cruelly aggravated the anxiety and afflicted the heart of the Czar. The project embraced a general insurrection at once in the capital and the two great armies in Poland and Bessarabia; and the success of similar movements in Spain and Italy inspired the conspirators with the most sanguine hopes of success. The time had been frequently fixed, and as often adjourned from accidental causes; but at length it was arranged for the period of Alexander's journey to Taganrog, in autumn, 1825. It was only prevented from there breaking out by the appointment of Wittgenstein to the command of the army of the south, whose known resolution of character rendered caution necessary; and it was then finally resolved it should take place in May, 1826. The conspirators were unanimous as to an entire change of government, and the adoption of representative institutions; but there was a considerable division among them, at first, what was to be done with the emperor and his family. At length, however, as usual in such cases, the more decided and sanguinary resolutions prevailed, and it was determined to put them all to death.[2]

119. Information given of the conspiracy to Alexander.

2 Rapport, 14 (26) Déc. 1825; Ann. Hist. ix. 81, 82; Doc. Hist. Ibid. 383; Schnitzler, ii. 87, 91.

The death of Alexander at first caused uncertainty in their designs; but the long continuance of the interregnum, and the strange contest between the two brothers for the abandonment of the throne, offered unhoped-for chances of success, of which they resolved to avail themselves. To divide the army, and avoid shock-

120. Plans of the conspirators.

ing, in the first instance at least, the feelings of the soldiers, it was determined that they should espouse the cause of Constantine; and as he had been proclaimed emperor by Nicholas and the Government, it appeared an easy matter to persuade them that the story of his having resigned his right of succession was a fabrication, and that their duty was to support him against all competitors. As Nicholas seemed so averse to be charged with the burden of the empire, it was hoped he would renounce at once when opposition manifested itself, and that Constantine, supported by their arms, would be easily got to acquiesce in their demands for a change of government. Their ulterior plans were, to convoke deputies from all the governments; to publish a manifesto of the Senate, in which it was declared that they were to frame laws for a representative government; that the deputies should be summoned from Poland, to insure the unity of the empire, and in the mean time a provisional government established.[1] Constantine was to be persuaded that it was all done out of devout feelings of loyalty toward himself.

[1 An. Hist. ix. 385; Rappert, 26 Dec. 1825; Ibid. p. 82, 81; Doc. Hist.]

121. Continued.

In contemplation of these changes, the greatest efforts had been made for several days past to gain the regiments of the guards, upon whose decision the success of all previous revolutions had depended; and they had succeeded in gaining many officers in several of the most distinguished regiments, particularly those of Preobrazinsky, Simonoffsky, the regiments of Moscow, the bodyguard grenadiers, and the corps of marines. Information, though in a very obscure way, had been conveyed to Nicholas, of a great conspiracy in which the household troops were deeply implicated, and in consequence of that the guard had not been called together; but it was determined that, on the morning of the 26th, the oath of allegiance should be administered to each regiment in their barracks. The Winter Palace, where the emperor dwelt, was intrusted to the regiment of Finland and the sappers of the guard, instead of the grenadiers-du-corps, to whom that charge was usually confided, and all the posts were doubled. But for that precaution, incalculable evils must have arisen. In truth, the danger was much greater, and more instant, than was apprehended. Prince Troubetzkoi, Ryleif, and Prince Obolonsky, the chiefs of the conspiracy, had gained adherents in almost every regiment of the guards, especially among the young men who were highest in rank, most ardent in disposition, and most cultivated in education; and the privates could easily be won, by holding out that Constantine, who had already been proclaimed, was the real Czar, and that their duty required them to shed their blood in his defense.[2]

[2 Schnitzler, i. 201, 202; Ann. Hist. ix. 385, 386.]

122. A revolt is decided on by the conspirators. Dec. 24.

Matters were brought to a crisis by the return of the Grand Duke Michael from Livonia with the intelligence of the final refusal of the throne by Constantine. It was then determined to act at once; and Troubetzkoi was named dictator—a post he proved ill qualified to fill, by his want of resolution at the decisive moment. The emperor published a proclamation on the 24th December, in which he recounted the circumstances which had compelled him to accept the empire, and called on the troops and people to obey him; and on the same day a general meeting of the conspirators was held, at which it was determined to commence the insurrection without delay. It was agreed to assassinate the emperor. "Dear friend," said Ryleif to Kakhofski, "you are alone on the earth; you are bound to sacrifice yourself for society; disembarrass us of the emperor." Jakoubovitch proposed to force the jails, liberate the prisoners, and rouse the refuse of the population by gorging them with spirits; but these extreme measures were not adopted. Orders were sent to the army of the south, where they reckoned on a hundred thousand adherents, to raise the standard of revolt. On the following evening, very alarming intelligence was received, in consequence of which it was agreed immediately to adopt the most desperate measures. They learned that they had been betrayed, and information sent to government of what was in agitation; thus their only hope now was in the boldness of their resolutions. "Una spes victis nullam sperare salutem." "We have passed the Rubicon," said Alexander Bestoujif, "and now we must cut down all who oppose us." "You see," said Ryleif, "we are betrayed; the court is partly aware of our designs, but they do not know the whole. Our forces are sufficient; our scabbards are broken; we can no longer conceal our sabres. Have we not an admirable chief in Troubetzkoi?" "Yes," answered Jakoubovitch, "*in height*"—alluding to his lofty stature. At length all agreed upon an insurrection on the day when the oath should be tendered to the troops.[1]

[1 Schnitzler, i. 213, 216; Ann. Hist. ix. 385, 386]

123. Commencement of it. Dec. 26.

On the morning of the 26th, the oath was taken without difficulty in several of the first regiments of the guards, especially the horse-guards, the chevalier guards, and the famous regiments Preobrazinsky, Simoneffsky, Imailoffsky, Pauloffsky, and the chasseurs of the guard. But the case was very different with the regiment of Moscow, the grenadiers of the body-guard, and the marines of the guard. They were for the most part at the devotion of the conspirators. The troops were informed that Constantine had not resigned, but was in irons, as well as the Grand Duke Michael; that he loved their regiments, and, if reinstated in authority, would double their pay. Such was the effect of these representations, enforced as they were by the ardent military eloquence of the many gifted and generous young men who were engaged in the conspiracy from patriotic motives,* that the men tumultuously broke their ranks, and, with loud hurrahs, "Constantine for ever!"

* Alexander Bestoujif, brother of Michael Bestoujif, one of the leaders of the revolt, addressed the following prayer to the Almighty, as he rose on the eventful day: "Oh God! if our enterprise is just, vouchsafe to us thy support; if not, thy will be done to us." It is difficult to know whether to admire the courage and sincerity of the men who braved such dangers, as they conceived, for their country's good, or to lament the blindness and infatuation which led them to strive to obtain for it institutions wholly unsuited for the people, and which could terminate in nothing but temporary anarchy and lasting military despotism.—SCHNITZLER, i. 221, note.

rushed into their barracks for ammunition, from whence they immediately returned with their muskets loaded with ball. They were just coming out when an aid-de-camp arrived with orders for the officers to repair forthwith to the head-quarters of the general (Frederick) and the Grand Duke Michael. "I do not acknowledge the authority of your general," cried Prince Tchechipine, who commanded one of the revolted companies, and immediately he ordered the soldiers to load their pieces. At the same instant Alexander Bestoujff discharged a pistol at General Frederick himself, who was coming up, and wounded him on the head. He fell insensible on the pavement, while Tchechipine attacked General Chenchine, who commanded the brigade of the guard, of which the regiment of Moscow formed a part, and stretched him on the ground by repeated blows of his sabre. In a transport of enthusiasm at this success, he with his own hand snatched the standard of the regiment from the officer who bore it, and, waving it in the air, exclaimed aloud, "Constantine forever!" The soldiers loudly answered with the same acclamation, and immediately the greater part of the regiments, disregarding the voice of their superior officers, Colonel Adlesberg and Count Lieven, who held out for Nicholas, moved in a body forward from the front of their barracks, and took up a position on the Grand Place behind the statue of Peter the Great. There they were soon joined by a battalion of the marines of the guard, who had been roused in a similar manner by Lieutenant Arbouzoff, and by several companies of the grenadiers of the body-guard. By ten o'clock, eighteen hundred men were drawn up in battle array on the Place of the Senate, behind the statue, surrounded by a great crowd of civilians, most of whom were armed with pistols or sabres; and the air resounded with cries of "Constantine forever!"¹

¹ Schnitzler, i. 222, 223.

124. Heroic conduct of Nicholas on the occasion.

The die was now cast, and the danger was so imminent, that, if there had been the slightest indecision at head-quarters, the insurrection would have proved successful, and Russia have been delivered over to the horrors of military license and servile revolt. But in that extremity Nicholas was not awanting to himself; he won the empire by proving he was worthy of it. He could no longer reckon on his guards, and without their support a Russian emperor is as weak as with it he is powerful. At eleven he received intelligence that the oath had been taken by the principal officers in the garrison, and it was hoped the danger was over; but in a quarter of an hour news of a very different import arrived—that an entire regiment of horse-artillery had been confined to their barracks, to prevent their joining the insurgents, and that a formidable body of the guards in open revolt were drawn up on the Place of the Senate. He instantly took his resolution, and in a spirit worthy of his race. Taking the empress, in whom the spirit, if not the blood, of Frederick the Great still dwelt, by the hand, he repaired to the chapel of the palace, where, with her, he invoked the blessing of the Most High on their undertaking. Then, after addressing a few words of encouragement to his weeping but still courageous consort, he took his eldest son, a charming child of eight years of age, by the hand, and descended to the chief body of the yet faithful guards, stationed in front of the palace, and gave orders to them to load their pieces. Then presenting the young Grand Duke to the soldiers, he said, "I trust him to you; yours it is to defend him." The chasseurs of Finland, with loud acclamations, swore to die in his cause; and the child, terrified at their cheers, was passed in their arms from rank to rank, amidst the tears of the men. They put him, while still weeping, into the centre of their column, and such was the enthusiasm excited that they refused to give him back to his preceptor, Colonel Moerder, who came to reclaim him.¹* "God knows our intention," said they; "we will restore the child only to his father, who intrusted him to us."

¹ Schnitzler, i. 224, 225; Ann. Hist. ix. 367, 368.

Meanwhile Nicholas put himself at the head of the first battalion of the regiment Preobrazinsky, which turned out with unheard-of rapidity, and advanced toward the rebels, supported by the third battalion, several companies of the grenadiers of Pauloffsky, and a battalion of the sappers of the guard. On the way he met a column proceeding to the rendezvous of the rebels. Advancing to them with an intrepid air, he called out in a loud voice, "Good-morning, my children!"—the usual salutation of patriarchal simplicity of the emperors to their troops. "Hourra, Constantine!" was the answer. Without exhibiting any symptoms of fear, the emperor, pointing with his finger to the other end of the Place, where the insurgents were assembled, said, "You have mistaken your way; your place is there with traitors." Another detachment following them, to which the same salute was addressed, remained silent. Seizing the moment of hesitation, with admirable presence of mind, he gave the order, "Wheel to the right—march!" with a loud voice. The instinct of discipline prevailed, and the men turned about and retraced their steps, as if they had never deviated from their allegiance to their sovereign.²

125. Nicholas advances against the rebels.

² Schnitzler, i. 227, 228.

The rebels, however, reinforced by several companies and detachments of some regiments which successively joined them, were by one

---

* What a scene for poetry or painting!—realizing on a still greater theatre all that the genius of Homer had prefigured of the parting of Hector and Andromache:

"Thus having spoke, the illustrious chief of Troy
Clasped his fond arms to clasp the lovely boy,
The babe clung crying to his nurse's breast,
Scared at the nodding plume and dazzling crest.
With secret pleasure each fond parent smiled,
And Hector hastened to relieve his child;
The glittering terrors from his brow unbound,
And placed the beaming helmet on the ground;
Then kissed the child, and, lifting high in air,
Thus to the gods preferred a father's prayer:
O Thou! whose glory fills the ethereal throne,
And all ye deathless powers, protect my son!
Grant him, like me, to purchase just renown,
To guard the Trojans, to defend the crown;
Against his country's foes the war to wage,
And rise the Hector of the future age.
So, when triumphant from successful toils,
Or heroes slain, he bears the reeking spoils,
Whole hosts may hail him with deserved acclaim,
And say this chief transcends his father's fame;
While, pleased amidst the general shouts of Troy,
His mother's conscious heart o'erflows with joy."

Pope's *Iliad*, vi. 595, 610.

o'clock in the afternoon above three thousand strong, and incessant cries of "Hourra, Constantine!" broke from their ranks. The ground was covered with snow, some of which had recently fallen; but nothing could damp the ardor of the men, who remained in close array, cheering, and evincing the greatest enthusiasm. Loud cries of "Long live *the Emperor* Constantine!" resounded over the vast Place, and were repeated by the crowd, which, every minute increasing, surrounded the regiments in revolt, until the shouts were heard even in the imperial palace. Already, however, Count Alexis Orlof had assembled several squadrons of his regiment of horse-guards, and taken a position on the Place in front of the mutineers; and the arrival of the emperor, with the battalion of the Preobrazinsky regiment and the other corps from the palace, formed an imposing force, which was soon strengthened by several pieces of artillery, which proved of the greatest service in the conflict that ensued. Of the chiefs of the revolt, few had appeared on the other side. Troubetzkoi was nowhere to be seen; Colonel Boulatoff was in the square, but concealed in the crowd of spectators awaiting the event. Ryleif was at his post, as was Jakoubovitch; but the former, not seeing Troubetzkoi, could not take the command, and lost the precious minutes in going to seek him. Decision and resolution were to be found only on the other side, and, as is generally the case in civil conflicts, they determined the contest.¹

126. Forces on both sides, and irresolution of the chiefs of the revolt.

¹ Schnitzler, i. 230, 232.

Deeming the forces assembled sufficient to crush the revolt, the generals who surrounded the emperor besought him to permit them to act; but he long hesitated, from feelings of humanity, to shed the blood of his subjects. As a last resource, he permitted General Milaradowitch, the governor of St. Petersburg, a noble veteran, well known in the late war, who had by his single influence appeased the mutiny in the guards in the preceding year, to advance toward the insurgents, in hopes that his presence might again produce a similar effect. Milaradowitch, accordingly, rode forward alone, and when within hearing, addressed the men, in a few words, calling on them to obey their lawful sovereign, and return to their duty. He was interrupted by loud cries of "Hourra, Constantine!" and before he had concluded, Prince Obolonsky made a dash at him with a bayonet, which the veteran, with admirable coolness, avoided by wheeling his horse; but at the same instant Kakhof-ki discharged a pistol at him within a few feet, which wounded him mortally, and he fell from his horse.² "Could I have believed," said the veteran of the campaign of 1812, "that it was from the hand of a Russian I was to receive death?" "Who," said Kakhofski, "now speaks of submission?" Milaradowitch died the following morning, deeply regretted by all Europe, to whom his glorious career had long been an object of admiration.

127. Death of Milaradowitch.

² Schnitzler, i. 232, 233; Ann. Hist. ix. 387.

The emperor, notwithstanding this melancholy catastrophe, was reluctant to proceed to extremities; and perhaps he entertained a secret dread as to what the troops he commanded might do, if called on to act decisively against the insurgents. A large part of the guards were there ranged in battle array against their sovereign: what a contest might be expected if the signal was given, and the chevalier guards were to be ordered to charge against their leveled bayonets! Meanwhile, however, the forces on the side of Nicholas were hourly increasing. The sappers of the guard, the grenadiers of Pauloffsky, the horse-guards, and the brigade of artillery, had successively come up; and the Grand Duke Michael, who acted with the greatest spirit on the occasion, had even succeeded in ranging six companies of his own regiment, the grenadiers of Moscow, the leaders of the revolt, on the side of his brother. Still the emperor was reluctant to give the word; and as a last resource, the Metropolitan Archbishop, an aged prelate, with a large part of the clergy, were brought forward, bearing the cross and the sacred ensign, who called on them to submit. But although strongly influenced by religious feelings, the experiment failed on this occasion: the rolling of drums drowned the voice of the Archbishop, and the soldiers turned his gray hairs into derision. Meanwhile the leaders of the revolt, deeming their victory secure, began to hoist their real colors. Cries of "Constantine *and the Constitution!*" broke from their ranks. "What is that?" said the men to each other. "Do you not know," said one, "it is the empress (Constitoutzia)?" "Not at all," replied a third; "it is the carriage in which the emperor is to drive at his coronation."¹

128. The Archbishop also fails in reducing the mutineers.

¹ Schnitzler, i. 233, 234; Bremner, Russia, ii. 127

At length, having exhausted all means of pacification, the emperor ordered the troops to act. The rebels were attacked in front by the horse-guards and chevalier guards, while the infantry assailed them in flank. But these noble veterans made a vigorous resistance, and for a few minutes the result seemed doubtful. Closely arrayed in column, they faced on every side; a deadly rolling fire issued from the steady mass,

129. The emperor gains the victory.

* "'Hear me, good people: I proclaim, in the name of the king, free pardon to all excepting—' 'I give thee fair warning,' said Burley, presenting his piece. 'A free pardon to all but—' 'Then the Lord grant grace to thy soul!' with these words he fired, and Cornet Richard Grahame fell from his horse. He had only strength to turn on the ground, and exclaim, 'My poor mother!' when life forsook him in the effort. 'What have you done?' said one of Balfour's brother officers. 'My duty,' said Balfour firmly. 'Is it not written, Thou shalt be zealous even to slaying? Let those who dare *now* speak of truce or pardon.'"—*Old Mortality*, chap. viii. How singular that the insurrection of St. Petersburg in 1825 should realize, within a few hours, what the bard of Chaos had conceived in song and the Scottish novelist in prose, at the distance of twenty-five centuries from each other, and what a proof of the identity of human nature, and the deep insight which those master-minds had obtained into its inmost recesses, that a revolt in the capital of Russia in the nineteenth century should come so near to what, at such a distance of time and place, they had respectively prefigured.

* "The leaders of the revolt, however, had different ideas of what they, at all events, understood by the movement. On loading his pistols on the morning of that eventful day, Boulatoff said, 'We shall see whether there are any Brutuses or Rieges in Russia to-day.' Nevertheless, he failed at the decisive moment: he was not to be found on the Place of the Senate."—*Rapport sur les Événements, &c.*, 26 Dec. p. 125, and SCHNITZLER, i 232, note

and the cavalry in vain strove to find an entrance into their serried ranks. The horsemen were repulsed; Kakhofski with his own hand slew Colonel Strosler, who commanded the grenadiers; and Kuchelbecker had already uplifted his arm to cut down the Grand Duke Michael, when a marine of the guard on his own side averted the blow. Jakoubovitch, charged with dispatching the emperor, eagerly sought him out, but, in the *melée* and amidst the smoke, without effect. The resistance, however, continued several hours, and night was approaching, with the rebels, in unbroken strength, still in possession of their strong position. Then, and not till then, the emperor ordered the cannon, hitherto concealed by the cavalry, to be unmasked. The horsemen withdrew to the sides, and showed the muzzles of the guns pointed directly into the insurgent square; they were again summoned to surrender, while the pieces were charged with grape, and the gunners waved their lighted matches in the now darkening air. Still the rebels stood firm; and a first fire, intentionally directed above their heads, having produced no effect, they cheered and mocked their adversaries. Then the emperor ordered a point-blank discharge, but the cannoneers refused at first to fire on their comrades, and the Grand Duke Michael, with his own hand, discharged the first gun. Then the rest followed the example, and the grape made frightful gaps in the dense ranks. The insurgents, however, kept their ground, and it was not till the tenth round that they broke and fled. They were vigorously pursued by the horse-guards along the quays and through the cross streets, into which they fled to avoid their bloody sabres. Seven hundred were made prisoners, and several hundred bodies remained on the Place of the Senate, which were hastily buried under the snow with which the Neva was overspread. By six o'clock the rebels were entirely dispersed; and the emperor, now firmly seated on his throne, returned to his palace, where the empress fell into his arms, and a solemn *Te Deum* was chanted in the chapel.[1]

¹ Schnitzler, i. 237, 239; Ann. Hist. ix. 389, 390; Golovine, La Russie sous Nicholas I., i. 26.

130. Seizure of the leaders of the conspiracy, and generous conduct of Nicholas to the privates.

Of all the conspirators during this terrible crisis, Jakoubovitch had alone appeared at the post assigned him. Troubetskoi, whose firmness had deserted him on this occasion, sought refuge in the hotel of the Austrian embassador, Count Libzeltern, but, on the requisition of the emperor, he was brought from that asylum into his presence. At first he denied all knowledge of the conspiracy; but when his papers were searched, which contained decisive proof not merely of his accession to it, but of his having been its leader, he fell at the emperor's feet, confessed his guilt, and implored his life. "If you have courage enough," said Nicholas, "to endure a life dishonored and devoted to remorse, you shall have it; but it is all I can promise you." On the following morning, when the troops were still bivouacked, as the evening before, on the Place of the Senate, and the curious crowds surveyed at a distance the theatre of the conflict, the emperor, accompanied by a single aid-de-camp, rode out of the palace to review those who had combated for him on the preceding day. Riding slowly along their ranks, he thanked them for their fidelity, and promised them a considerable augmentation of pay, as well as the usual largesses on occasion of the accession of a new emperor. He then proceeded to the regiments which had revolted, and granted a pardon alike politic and generous. To the marines of the guard, who had lost their colors in the conflict, he gave a fresh one, with the words, "You have lost your honor; try to recover it." The regiment of Moscow, in like manner, received back its colors, and was pardoned on the sole condition that the most guilty, formed into separate companies, should be sent for two years to expiate their fault in combating the mountaineers of the Caucasus. The emperor promised to take their wives and children under his protection during their absence. These generous words drew tears from the veterans, who declared themselves ready to set out on the instant for their remote destination.[1]

¹ An. Hist. ix. 391, 392; Schnitzler, i. 242, 247.

But although all must admit the justice of these sentiments—and indeed it was scarcely possible to act otherwise with men who were merely misled, and who resisted the Czar when they thought they were defending him—a very different course seemed necessary with the leaders of the revolt, who had seduced the soldiers into acts of treason through the very intensity of their loyalty. All the chiefs were apprehended soon after its suppression, and the declarations of the prisoners, as well as the papers discovered in their possession, revealed a far more extensive and dangerous conspiracy than had been previously imagined. The emperor appointed a commission to investigate the matter to the bottom, and on the 31st he published a manifesto, in which, after exculpating the simple and loyal-hearted soldiers who were drawn into the tumult, he denounced the whole severity of justice against the leaders, "who aimed at overturning the throne and the laws," subverting the empire,

131. Appointment of a commission of inquiry. Dec. 29.

* "Deux classes d'hommes ont pris part à l'événement du 14 (26) Decembre, evénement qui, peu important par lui-même, ne l'est que trop par son principe et par ses conséquences. Les uns, personnes égarées, ne savaient pas ce qu'ils faisaient; les autres, véritables conspirateurs, voulaient abattre le Trône et les lois, bouleverser l'empire, amener l'anarchie, entraîner dans le tumulte les soldats des compagnies séduites, qui n'ont participé à ces attentats, ni de fait, ni d'intention: une enquête sévère m'en a donné la preuve; et je regarde, comme un premier acte de justice, comme ma première consolation, de les déclarer innocents. Mais cette même justice défend d'epargner les coupables. D'après les mesures deja prises, le châtiment embrassera dans toute son étendue, dans toutes ses ramifications, un mal dont le germe compte des années; et j'en ai la confiance, elles le detruiront jusque dans le sol sacré de Russie; elles feront disparaître cet odieux mélange de tristes verités et de soupçons gratuits, qui répugne aux ames nobles; elles tireront à jamais, une ligne de démarcation entre l'amour de la Patrie et les passions revolutionnaires, entre le désir du mieux et la fureur des bouleversements; elles montreront au monde, que la nation Russe, toujours fidèle à son souverain et aux lois, repousse les secrets efforts de l'anarchie, comme elle a repoussé les attaques ouvertes de ses ennemis déclarés; elles montreront comme on se délivre d'un tel fleau; elles montreront que ce n'est point, pourtant, qu'il est indestructible."—*Proclamation*, 29th December, 1825; Schnitzler, i. 255-296—said to have come from the pen of the celebrated historian Karamsin, who died shortly after.

and inducing anarchy." A commission was accordingly appointed, having at its head the Minister at War, General Talischof, president; the Grand Duke Michael; Prince Alexander Gallitzin, Minister of Public Instruction; General Chernichef, Aid-de-camp General, and several other members, nearly all military men. There were only two civilians, Prince Alexander Gallitzin and M. Blondof.[1]

[1] Schnitzler, i. 258, 260.

132. Its composition and report

From a commission so composed, the whole proceedings of which were private, there was by no means to be expected the same calm and impartial inquiry which might be looked for from an English special commission which conducted all its proceedings in public, and under the surveillance of a jealous and vigilant press. But nevertheless their labors, which were most patient and uninterrupted, continuing through several months, revealed the magnitude and frightful perils of the conspiracy, and the abyss on the edge of which the nation had stood, when the firmness of Nicholas and the fidelity of his guards saved them from the danger. Their report—one of the most valuable historical monuments of the age, though of necessity, under the circumstances in which it was drawn up, one-sided to a certain degree—unfolds this in the clearest manner: and although no judicial investigation can be implicitly relied on which is not founded on the examination of witnesses on *both* sides, in public, yet enough which can not be doubted has been revealed, to demonstrate how much the cause of order and real liberty is indebted to the firmness which on this momentous occasion repressed the treasonable designs which in such an empire could have terminated only in the worst excesses of anarchy.[2]

[2] Rapport, May 30, 1826, Ann. Hist. ix. 79, 112.

133. Leaders of the revolt in the army of the south.

Before the commission had well commenced their labors, a catastrophe occurred in the south which afforded confirmation strong of the extent of the conspiracy and the magnitude of the danger which had been escaped. The great armies both of the south and west were deeply implicated in the designs of the rebels, and it was chiefly on their aid that the leaders at St. Petersburg reckoned in openly hoisting the standard of revolt. It was in the second army (that of the south) that the conspiracy had the deepest roots, and Paul Pestel was its soul. He was son of an old officer who had been governor-general of Siberia, and had gained his company by his gallant conduct at the battle of Arcis-sur-Aube, in France, in 1814. He was colonel of the regiment of Vietka in 1825, when the revolt broke out, and his ability and pleasing manners had made him an aid-de-camp of the commander-in-chief, Count Wittgenstein. He was inspired with a strong horror at oppression of any kind; but the other conspirators said it was only till he was permitted to exercise it himself.[3] He was a declared republican, but Ryleif said of him, "He is an ambitious man, full of artifice—a Bonaparte, and not a Washington." He had great resolution, however, and power of eloquence, and those qualities had procured for him unbounded influence among his comrades.

[3] Schnitzler, ii. 9, 13; Rapport, May 30, 1826, p. 74.

134. And in that of the west.

In the first army, stationed on the Polish frontier, the conspiracy had ramifications not less extensive. At its head, and in that force, were two brothers, Serge and Matthew Mouravieff-Apostol, the first of whom was a colonel of the regiment of Tchernigof; the second a captain in that of Semenof. Their father, who was nephew of the preceptor of Alexander, had been educated with that prince, by whom he was tenderly loved; and he was one of the few Russians of family, at that period, who engaged in literary pursuits. He had translated the *Clouds* of Aristophanes into Russian; and his *Travels in Tauris*, published at St. Petersburg in 1825, revealed the extent and accuracy of his classical knowledge. He had composed a beautiful sonnet, in Greek verse, on the death of Alexander, which he had also translated into Latin. His two sons, on whom he had bestowed the most polished education, had been brought up abroad, where they had imbibed the liberal ideas, and vague aspirations after indefinite freedom, at that period so common in western Europe. They returned to Russia deeply imbued with republican ideas, and in good faith and with benevolent views, but without any practical knowledge of mankind, or any fixed plan of reform, or what was to be established in its stead, entered into the project for the overthrow of the government. A third leader was a young man named Michael Bestoujif-Rumine, an intimate friend of Pestel, and who formed the link which connected the two Mouravieffs with the projects of the conspirators in the capital, and in the army of the south.[1]

[1] Schnitzler, ii. 17, 21; Ann. Hist. ix, 329, 330.

135. Arrest of the Mouravieffs, and outbreak of the conspiracy in the Army of Poland.

When the papers of the persons seized at St. Petersburg, on the 26th December, were examined, it was discovered that the two Mouravieffs were deeply implicated in the conspiracy, and orders were sent to have them immediately arrested. The orders, however, got wind, and they sought safety in flight, but were arrested, on the 18th January, in the burgh of Trilissia, by Colonel Ghebel, whose painful duty it was to apprehend one of his dearest friends. Informed of their arrest, a number of officers of the Society of United Sclavonians surrounded the house in which they were detained by Ghebel, and rescued them, after a rude conflict, in which Ghebel fell, pierced by fourteen wounds. Delivered in this manner, the Mouravieffs had no safety but in a change of government. Serge Mouravieff succeeded in causing his regiment to revolt, by the same device which had proved so successful at St. Petersburg, that of persuading them to take up arms for their true Czar, Constantine. The leaders of the conspiracy, amidst the cries of "Hourra, Constantine!" tried to introduce the cry of "Long live the Sclavonic Republic!" but the soldiers could not be brought to understand what was meant. "We are quite willing," said an old grenadier, "to call out, 'Long live the Sclavonic Republic;' *but who is to be our emperor?*" The officers spoke to them of liberty, and the priests read some passages from the Old Testament, to prove that democracy was the form of government most agreeable to the Almighty; but the soldiers constantly answered, "Who is to be emperor—Constantine or Nicholas Paulovitch?" So strong was this impression, that Mouravieff, by his own admission, was obliged to give over speaking of liberty or republics, and to join in the cry of "Hourra, Constantine!"¹

¹ Rapport Officiel, May 30, 1826, p. 134; Schnitzler, ii. 24, 26, 29. Ann. Hist. ix. 329, 330.

It was now evident that the common men were at heart loyal, and that it was by deception alone that they had been drawn into mutiny. Taking advantage of their hesitation, Captain Koglof, who commanded the grenadiers, harangued his men, informing them that they had been deceived, and that Nicholas was their real sovereign. "Lead us, captain," they exclaimed; "we will obey your orders." He led them, accordingly, out of the revolted regiment, without Mouravieff venturing to oppose any resistance. Reduced by this defection to six companies, that regiment was unable to commence any offensive operations. Mouravieff remained two days in a state of uncertainty, sending in vain in every direction in quest of succor. Meanwhile, the generals of the army were accumulating forces round them in every direction; and though numbers were secretly engaged in the conspiracy, and in their hearts wished it success, yet as intelligence had been received of its suppression at St. Petersburg, none ventured to join it openly. The rebels, obliged to leave Belain-Tzerskof, where they had passed the night, were overtaken, on the morning of the 15th, on the heights of Ostinofska. Mouravieff, nothing daunted, formed his men into a square, and ordered them to march, with their arms still shouldered, straight on the guns pointed at them. He was in hopes the gunners would declare for them; but he was soon undeceived. A point blank discharge of grape was let fly, which killed great numbers. A charge of cavalry quickly succeeded, which completed their defeat. Seven hundred were made prisoners, among whom were Matthew and Hippolyte Mouravieff, and the chief leaders of the revolt; and a conspiracy, which pervaded the whole army, and threatened to shake the empire to its foundation, was defeated by the overthrow of six companies and fifty men killed and wounded. The unhappy Mouravieff, father of the rebels, saw himself deprived of his three sons at one fell swoop. "Nothing remained," he said, "but for him to shroud his head under their ashes."²

136. Its suppression. Jan. 12.

² Rapport Officiel, May 30, 1826, 24, 130. Ann. Hist. 1826, p. 81, 130; Schnitzler, ii. 30, 34.

The commission which had been appointed to try the insurgents at St. Petersburg extended its labors to the conspiracy over the whole empire, and traced its ramifications in their whole extent. It can not be said that their proceedings were stained with unnecessary cruelty; for of so great a number of conspirators actually taken in arms against the Government, or whose guilt was established beyond a doubt, five only, viz., Colonel Pestel, Ryleif, Colonel Serge Mouravieff, Bestougif-Rumine, and Kakhofski, were sentenced to death. While thirty-one others, originally sentenced to death, had their sentences commuted to exile, accompanied with hard labor, for life or for long periods, in Siberia. They formed a melancholy list; for among them were to be found several men of the highest rank and noblest feelings in Russia, the victims of mistaken zeal and deluded patriotism. Among them were Prince Troubetzkoi, Colonel Matthew Mouravieff-Apostol, Colonel Davidof, General Prince Serge Volkonsky, Captain Prince Stehpine Boslowsky, and Nicholas Tourguneff, councillor of state. One hundred and thirty others were sentenced to imprisonment and lesser penalties.¹

137. Sentences on the conspirators.

¹ Jugement, July 14, 1826; An. Hist. viii. 112, 113.

The conspirators who were selected for execution met their fate in a worthy spirit. They faced death on the scaffold with the same courage that they would have done in the field. Their original sentence was to be broken on the wheel; but the humanity of the emperor led him to commute that frightful punishment, and they were sentenced to be hanged. This mode of death, unusual in Russia, was keenly felt as a degradation by men who expected to meet the death of soldiers. Ryleif, the real head of the conspiracy, and the most intellectual of all its members, acknowledged that his sentence was just, according to the existing laws of Russia; but he added, that, having been deceived by the ardor of his patriotism, and being conscious only of pure intentions, he met death without apprehension. "My fate," said he, "will be an expiation due to society." He then wrote a beautiful letter to his young wife, in which he conjured her not to abandon herself to despair, and to submit, as a good Christian, to the will of Providence, and the justice of the emperor. He charged her to give his confessor one of his golden snuff-boxes, and to receive from him his own last blessing from the scaffold.² Nothing shook Pestel's courage; he maintained to the last his principles and the purity of his intentions. All received and derived consolation from the succors of religion.

138. Their conduct on the eve of death.

² Schnitzler, ii. 303, 305.

There had been no capital sentence carried into execution in St. Petersburg for eighty years; and in all Russia but few scaffolds had been erected for death since the reign of the Empress Elizabeth, a century before. The knowledge that five criminals, all of eminent station, were about to be executed, excited the utmost consternation in all classes; and Government wisely kept secret the exact time when the sentence was to be carried into effect. At two in the morning of the 25th July, however, a mournful sound was heard in every quarter of the city, which presaged the tragedy which was approaching: it was the signal for every regiment in the capital to send a company to assist at the melancholy spectacle. Few spectators, save the military, were present, when, on the edge of the rampart of the citadel, was seen dimly through the twilight which preceded the morning, a huge gallows, which froze every heart with horror. The rolling of drums was soon heard, which announced the approach of the thirty-one criminals condemned to death, but whose lives had been spared, who were led

139. Their execution. July 25.

out, and on their knees heard their sentence of death read out. When it was finished, their epaulets were torn off, their uniform taken off their backs, their swords broken over their heads, and, dressed in the rude garb of convicts, they were led away to undergo their sentence in the wilds of Siberia. Next came the five criminals who were to be executed: they mounted the scaffold with firm steps, and in a few minutes the preparations were adjusted, and the fatal signal was given. Pestel and Kakhofski died immediately; but a frightful accident occurred in regard to the other three. The ropes broke, and they were precipitated, while yet alive, from a great height into the ditch beneath. The unhappy men, though severely bruised by their fall, reascended the scaffold with a firm step. The spectators hoped they were about to be pardoned; but this was not so, for the emperor was absent at Tsariko-Velo, and no one else ventured to give a respite. "Can nothing, then, succeed in this country," said Rylief—"not even death!" "Woe to the country," exclaimed Serge Mouravieff, "where they can neither conspire, nor judge, nor hang!" Bestoujif-Rumine was so bruised that he had to be carried up to the scaffold; but he, too, evinced no symptoms of trepidation. This time fortunately the rope held good, and in five minutes a loud rolling of drums announced that justice was satisfied, and the insurrection terminated.[1]

[1] Schnitzler, ii. 304, 307; Custine, ii. Lettres, 14, 29, 31.

It is impossible to recount these details without the most melancholy feelings— feelings which will be shared to the end of the world by all the generous and humane, who reflect on capital executions for political offenses. The peculiar and harrowing circumstance in such cases is, that the persons upon whom the extreme punishment of the law is thus inflicted are sometimes of noble character—men actuated by the purest patriotism, who, in a heroic spirit, sacrifice themselves for their country, and, as they conceive, the good of mankind. Even when, as in this, as in most other instances, such conspiracy could terminate only in disaster, and its suppression was a blessing to humanity, and a step in the march of real freedom, it is impossible to avoid feeling respect for the motives, however mistaken, of the persons engaged in it, and admiration for the courage with which they met their fate. The ends of justice, the cause of order, is more advanced by the humanity which, in purely political offences, remits or softens punishment, than by the rigor which exacts its full measure. The state criminal of one age often becomes the martyr of the next, the hero of a third; and the ultimate interests of society are never so effectually secured as when, by depriving treason of the halo of martyrdom, it is allowed to stand forth to the memory of futurity in its real colors.[*]

140. Reflections on this event.

[*] Rylief, who was a man of fine genius, in his remarkable poem, entitled *Voenarofski*, expressed his firm confidence in the irresistible march of freedom in these words, which he put into the mouth of an Ataman of the Cossacks: "That which in our dream seemed a dream of heaven, was not recorded on high. Patience! Let us await till the colossus has for some time accumulated its wrongs—till, in hastening its increase, it has weakened itself in striving to embrace the half of the earth. Allow it; the heart swollen with pride, parades its vanity in the rays of the sun. Patience! the justice of Heaven will end by reducing it to the dust. In history, *God is retribution*; He does not permit the seed of sin to pass without its harvest." SCHNITZLER, ii. 309.

But if the fate of these gallant though deluded men must ever excite very mixed feelings in every generous bosom, there is one subject connected with their companions in suffering, which must ever awaken the most unbounded interest and admiration. The convicts who were banished to Siberia were for the most part of high rank and noble family; many of them were married, and their wives, of equal station in society, had moved in the very first circles in St. Petersburg. The conduct of these ladies, on this terrible crisis, was worthy of eternal admiration. When their husbands set off on their long and painful journey of three thousand miles into the interior of Siberia, seated on wooden chariots without springs, and often exposed to the insults and assaults of the populace, they did not go alone. These noble women, who were themselves entirely innocent, and were offered the protection of the emperor, and all the luxuries of the elevated circles in which they had been born and lived, if they would remain behind, unanimously refused the offer, and insisted upon accompanying their husbands into exile. They bore without repining, even with joy, the mortal fatigues of the long and dreary journey in open carts, and all the insults of the populace in the villages through which they passed, and arrived safe, supported by their heroic courage. To accustom themselves to the hardships they were to undergo, they voluntarily laid aside in their palaces at St. Petersburg, some weeks before their departure, the splendid dresses to which they had been accustomed, put on instead the most humble garments, and inured their delicate hands to the work of peasants and servants, on which they were so soon to enter. "Thou shalt eat thy bread with the sweat of thy brow" became their resolution, as it is the ordinary lot of humanity. The Princess Troubetzkoi, the Princess Serge Volkonsky, Madame Alexander Mouravieff, Madame Nikitas Mouravieff (née Tchenciehef), and Madame Narisichkine (née Ronovnitsyne), the two last of the noblest families in Russia, were among the number of those who performed this heroic sacrifice to duty. History may well preserve their names with pride; it is seldom that in either sex it has such deeds to recount.[1]

141. Noble conduct of the Princess Troubetzkoi and the other wives of the convicts.

[1] Schnitzler, ii. 309, 311; Custine, iii. 29, 30.

It is some consolation to know that the generous self-sacrifice did not even in this world go without its reward. A sense of duty, the courage which often springs up with misfortune, the consciousness of suffering together, softened the horrors of the journey to such a degree that before it was concluded they had come to be contented, even happy, and it would have been deemed a misfortune to have been turned back.[*] Their ultimate destination was the village of Tchitinsk, on the Ingoda river, beyond the lake Baikal, and not far removed from the frontiers

142. Condition of the exiles in Siberia.

[*] One of the traveling companions of one of those mothers overheard her say to her daughter, who had been petulant on the journey, "Sophie, if you don't behave better, you shan't go to Siberia."—SCHNITZLER, ii. 310.

of China. The climate there is somewhat less severe than in the same latitude in other parts of Siberia; and the humanity of the emperor permitted a few articles of comfort to be introduced, which softened the asperities of that deep solitude. Tchitinsk, where they were all assembled, became a populous colony, an oasis of civilization in the midst of an immense desert. The forced labor of the convicts extended only to a few hours a day; some slender comforts, and even luxuries, were stealthily introduced; and a library containing a few books, permitted by the police, enlivened the weary hours of solitude by the pleasures of intellectual recreation. But the simple duties of their situation left them little leisure for such amusements, and the regular routine of humble life, if it deprived them of the excitement, at least saved them from the torment of ennui, the bane and punishment of civilized selfishness. Many of them tasted a happiness, in this simple and patriarchal existence, to which they had been strangers amidst all the splendors of St. Petersburg. The Princess Troubetzkoi had been on distant terms with her husband before his banishment, and she had no family; but misfortune did that which prosperity had failed to effect—they were drawn together by suffering in common; they lived contentedly together in their humble cottage, and she is now the happy mother of five children.[1]

[1] Schnitzler, ii. 311, 313; Custine, iii. 29, 31.

142. Generous conduct of the emperor to the relatives of the convicts.

The emperor behaved generously to the families and relations of such as had suffered either death or exile for their political offenses. So far from involving them in any species of responsibility, he in many cases did much to relieve them from the consequences of that which they had already undergone in the punishment of those who were dear to them. He gave 50,000 rubles (£2500) to the father of Pestel, with a valuable farm on one of the domains of the crown, and appointed his brother, a colonel in the chevalier guards, one of his own aids-de-camp. He was extremely anxious to relieve the distresses of Ryleif's widow, who had been left in very destitute circumstances, and sent repeatedly to inquire into her necessities; but this high-minded woman, proud of her suffering, refused all his proffered kindness, and said the only favor she asked of him was to put her to death, and lay her beside her husband. Unknown to her, he caused relief to be conveyed to her children, with whose maintenance and education he charged himself. But to the women who had accompanied their husbands into exile he showed himself inexorable; he thought that by so doing they had adopted their crimes, instead of extenuating it by the opposite virtues. After undergoing fifteen years of exile in their appointed place of banishment, the Princess Troubetzkoi earnestly petitioned the emperor for a removal, not into Russia, but to a place where the climate was milder, and she might obtain the rudiments of education for their children, and be near an apothecary to tend them when ill. She wrote a touching letter to the emperor, which concluded with the words, "I am very unhappy; nevertheless, if it was to do over again, I would do the same."

But her petition was sternly refused. "I am astonished that you venture to speak to me," said he to the lady who ventured to present it, "in favor of a family which has conspired against me."[1]

[1] Custine, iii. 31, 41; Schnitzler, ii. 313, 316.

144. Expiatory ceremony on the Place of the Senate. July 21.

According to an established usage in Russia, a solemn religious ceremony was performed on the termination of the great contest with the principles of anarchy which had signalized the emperor's accession to the throne. "On the spot," said the emperor in another proclamation, "where seven months ago the explosion of a sudden revolt revealed the existence of a vast conspiracy which had been going on for ten years, it is meet that a last act of commemoration—an expiatory sacrifice—should consecrate on the same spot the memory of the Russian blood shed for religion, the throne, and the country. We have recognized the hand of the Almighty, when He tore aside the vail which concealed that horrible mystery: it permitted crime to arm itself in order to assure its fall. Like a momentary storm, the revolt only broke forth to annihilate the conspiracy of which it was the consummation."* In conformity with these ideas, the whole garrison of St. Petersburg, sixty thousand strong, was on the morning after the execution of the conspirators assembled on the Place of the Senate, where the mutineers had taken their station. The emperor issued from the Church of the Admiralty, which is the centre of St. Petersburg, led by the Metropolitan Archbishop, clad in his pontifical robes, and accompanied by the Empress and Prince Charles of Prussia, her brother. A solemn thanksgiving was then performed at the altar, and the priests, descending from the steps, scattered holy water over the soldiers, the people, and the pavement of the square. When the purification was completed, the bands of all the regiments struck up a hallelujah; and the discharge of a hundred guns announced that the expiation was concluded and the crime effaced.[2]

[2] Schnitzler, ii. 318, 320; Journal de St. Petersbourg, July 27, 1826.

145. Great reforms in all departments introduced by the emperor.

Nicholas made, in one important respect, a noble use of his victory. During the course of the long investigation which took place into the conspiracy, great part of which was conducted by the emperor in person, ample revelations were made, not merely in regard to the extent and ramifications of the conspiracy, but to the numerous social and political evils which had roused into such fearful activity so large a portion of the most intrepid

---

* The address contained these words, applicable to all ages and people: "May the fathers of families by this sad example be led to pay proper attention to the moral education of their children. Assuredly it is not to the progress of civilization, but to the vanity which is the result of idleness and the want of intelligence—to the want of *real education*—that we are to ascribe that licentiousness of thought, that vehemence of passion, that *half-knowledge, so confused and perilous*, that thirst after extreme theories and political visions, which begin with demoralizing and end by ruining. In vain will the Government make generous efforts, in vain will it exhaust itself in sacrifices, if the *domestic education* of the people does not second its views and intentions, if it *does not pour into the hearts the germs of virtue*."—*Journal de St. Petersbourg*, July 24, 1826, No. 16; and SCHNITZLER, ii. 316.

and patriotic of the higher classes. The leaders, who were examined by the emperor, unfolded without reserve the whole evils which were complained of, in particular the dreadful corruption which pervaded every branch of the administration, and the innumerable delays and venality which obstructed or perverted the course of justice in every department.* He was so horror-struck by the revelations which were made, that for a long time he despaired of success in the attempt to cleanse out so vast and frightful an Augean stable; and his spirits were so affected by the discoveries made, that gloom pervaded the whole court for a long time after his accession. But at length he rose superior to the difficulties with which he was environed, and boldly set about applying a remedy, in the only true and safe method, by cautious and practical reform.[1]

[1] Ann. Hist. ix. 334; Schnitzler, ii. 135, 138.

146. Great legal reforms of the emperor.

His first care was to dispatch circulars to all the judges and governors in the empire, urging them in the most earnest way to the faithful discharge of their duty, under the severest penalties, and inculcating in an especial manner the immediate decision of the numerous cases in arrear before them, both in regard to persons and property. With such success was this attended, that out of 2,850,000 processes depending in the beginning of 1826, nearly all had been decided before the end of that year; and out of 127,000 persons under arrest, there remained only 4900, in the beginning of 1827, in custody. The change was so great and satisfactory, that it was with reason made the subject of a special congratulation from the emperor to the Minister of Justice. Some of the laws which pressed with most severity on the Cossacks and the southern provinces were repealed. But the grand defect, which struck the emperor in the internal administration of Russia, was the want of any regular code of laws in the hands of all the judges, accessible to all, according to which justice might be uniformly administered in all the governments. This was the more essential, since, as already noticed, in a great proportion of the governments the ukases of the emperors had never reached the judges. Great part, indeed, were what may be termed private ukases, being addressed to individuals, not the Senate, and yet binding on the whole community. They formed, as was well observed at the time, "a hidden code of laws yet ruling the empire." To remedy this great defect, a complete collection of the ukases, which formed, like the rescripts of the Roman emperors, the laws of Russia, was formed, printed, and codified by the order of Nicholas. The great work proved to be one of immense labor; but by the vigilant attention and incessant energy of the emperor, it was completed in a surprisingly short space of time. The printing commenced on the 1st May, 1828, and was concluded on 1st April, 1830. It then embraced 35,993 ukases or acts, of which 5075 had been pronounced since the accession of the present emperor, and the collection which was sent to all the judges amounted to fifty-six large quarto volumes. In addition to this, Nicholas undertook, and successfully carried through, a still more difficult undertaking—viz., the construction of a uniform code, forming a complete system of law, out of the enormous and often heterogeneous materials. This gigantic undertaking, akin to the Institutes and Pandects of Justinian, was completed in seven years more, and now forms the "*sood*" or body of Russian law. Thus had Nicholas the glory, after having rivaled Cæsar in the courage with which he had suppressed military revolt, of emulating Justinian in the zeal with which he prosecuted legal reforms. Yet must his antagonists not be denied their share in the honor due to the founders of the august temple; for if the emperor raised the superstructure, it was the blood of the martyrs which cemented the foundations.[1]

[1] Ann. Hist. ix. 342; Schnitzler, ii. 131, 140.

147. Crime of the insurgents.

Yet was the crime of these generous but deluded men great, and their punishment not only necessary, but just. The beneficial results which followed their insurrection were accidental only, and arose from its defeat; had it been suppressed by other hands, or proved successful, it could not have failed to have induced the most terrible calamities. Met and crushed by Ivan the Terrible or the Empress Catherine, it would have drawn yet closer the bands of tyranny on the state, and thrown it back for centuries in the career of real freedom. No man had a right to calculate on the suppression of the revolt being immediately followed on the part of the conqueror by the compilation of the Pandects. It was utterly impossible that a military revolt, of which a few officers only knew the object, into which the private soldiers had been drawn by deceit, and to which the common people were entire strangers, could, if successful, terminate in any thing but disaster. Even the Reign of Terror in France would have been but a shadow of what must have ensued in the event of success; the proscriptions of Marius and Sylla, the slaughter of Nero, the centralized unmitigated despotism of the Lower Empire, could alone have been looked for. Benevolent intentions, generous self-devotion, patriotic spirit, are neither alone sufficient in public men, nor do they afford, even in the light of morality, an adequate vindication of their acts, if the laws are infringed. It is the first duty of those who urge on a movement to consider

---

* While the conspirators avowed that their designs ultimately involved the destruction of the emperor and his family, and expressed the deepest contrition for that offense, they at the same time portrayed with courage and fidelity the social evils which consumed their country, and had induced them to take up arms. Many of them, Ryleif and Bestoujf in particular, evinced a noble spirit in misfortune. "I knew before I engaged in it," said the former to the emperor, "that my enterprise would ruin me, but I could no longer bear to see my country under the yoke of despotism: the seed which I have sown, rest assured, will one day germinate, and in the end bear fruit." "I repent of nothing I have done," said Michel Bestoujf; "I die satisfied, and soon to be avenged." The emperor was so struck with the courage of his answers, and the hideous revelations which he made in regard to the abuses of the public administration, that he said to him, "I have the power to pardon you; and if I felt assured you would prove a faithful servant, I would gladly do so." "That, sire!" said he, "is precisely what we complain of, the emperor can do every thing, and there is no law In the name of God, let justice take its course, and let the fate of your subjects not in future depend on your raptures or the impressions of the moment." They were noble men who, in presence of the emperor, and with the ax suspended over their heads, could express such sentiments in such language.—SCHNITZLER, ii. 134, 135.

is what it must terminate, and whether the instruments by which it is to be accomplished are capable of performing the new duties required of them, if successful. Nations have seven ages, as well as man; and he is their worst enemy, who, anticipating the slow march of time, inflames childhood with the passions of youth, or gives to youth the privileges of manhood.

148. Coronation of the emperor and empress at Moscow. Aug. 22 (Sept. 3). The coronation of the emperor and empress took place, with extraordinary pomp, at Moscow on the 22d August (3d September) in the same year. The youth and beauty of the two sovereigns, the dreadful contest which had preceded their accession to the throne, the generous abnegation of self by which the mutual renunciation of the throne by the two imperial brothers had been characterized, gave an extraordinary interest to the august spectacle, and crowds of the most distinguished strangers from every part of Europe flocked together to witness it. The entry of their imperial majesties took place on the 5th August (17th), the emperor riding between the Grand Duke Michael and Prince Charles of Prussia; the empress followed in a magnificent chariot, drawn by eight horses, having her son, the heir of the empire, by her side. Enthusiastic acclamations burst from the immense crowd, which advanced several miles on the road to St. Petersburg to meet them. Moscow exhibited the most splendid spectacle. All traces of the conflagration of 1812 had disappeared, magnificent buildings had arisen on every side, and the quarters which had suffered most from its ravages could now be traced only by the superior elegance and durability of the *stone* structures, by which the former wooden palaces and buildings had been replaced. On the 15th, when, according to the custom of Russia, a great religious ceremony took place, an unexpected event threw the people into transports of joy. The emperor appeared, holding with his right hand the Grand Duke Constantine, who had arrived the evening before in Moscow, and with his left the Grand Duke Michael. Shouts of joy arose from the assembled multitude, but the cry which resounded above all, "Hourra, Constantine!" at first startled the emperor; he had heard it on the Place of the Senate on the 26th December. It was but for a moment, however, and his countenance was soon radiant with joy, when that prince was the first to do him homage, and threw himself into his arms. The universal acclamations now knew no bounds, the reality of the self-sacrifice was demonstrated; future concord was anticipated from the happy union in the imperial family. Splendid reviews of fifty thousand of the guards and chosen troops of the empire, and a hundred and sixty guns, succeeded, and the coronation took place on the day fixed, 22d August (3d September), in the cathedral of Moscow, with circumstances of unheard-of magnificence and splendor. The Grand Duke Constantine was the first to tender his homage to the new sovereign.[1]

[1] Ann. Hist. ix. 353, 356; Schnitzler, ii. 350, 357.

Nicholas I., who, under such brilliant circumstances, and after the display of such invincible resolution, thus ascended the throne of Russia, and whom subsequent events have, in a manner, raised up to become an arbiter of Eastern Europe, is the greatest sovereign that that country has known since Peter the Great; in some respects he is greater than Peter himself. Not less energetic in character and ardent in improvement than his illustrious predecessor, he is more thoroughly national, and he has brought the nation forward more completely in the path which nature had pointed out for it. Peter was a Russian only in his despotism: his violence, his cruelty, his beneficence, his ardor for improvement, his patriotic ambition, were all borrowed from the states of western Europe. As these states were greatly further advanced in the career of civilization than his was, his reforms were in great part premature, his improvements abortive, his refinements superficial. He aimed at doing by imperial, what so many ardent men have endeavored to effect by democratic despotism—to ingraft on one nation the institutions of another, and reap from the infancy of civilization the fruits of its maturity. The attempt failed in his hands, as it has ever done in those of his republican imitators, as it will do in those of their successors, whether on the throne or in the tribune, to the end of the world. His civilization was all external merely; it made a brilliant appearance, but it did not extend beneath the surface, and left untouched the strength and vitals of the state. He flattered himself he had civilized Russia, because he ruled by a police which governed it by fear, and an army which retained it in subjection by discipline.

149. Character of the emperor Nicholas, and parallel between him and Peter the Great.

Nicholas, on the other hand, is essentially Russian in all his ideas. He is heart and soul patriotic, not merely in wish, but in spirit and thought. He wishes to improve and elevate his country, and he has done much to effect that noble object; but he desires to do so by developing, not changing the national spirit, by making it become a first Russia, not a second France or England. He has adopted the maxim of Montesquieu, that no nation ever attained to real greatness but by institutions in conformity with its spirit. He is neither led away by the thirst for sudden mechanical improvement, like Peter, nor the praises of philosophers, like Catherine, nor the visions of inexperienced philanthropy, like Alexander. He has not attempted to erect a capital in a pestilential marsh, and done so at the expense of a hundred thousand lives; nor has he dreamt of mystical regeneration with a visionary sybil, and made sovereigns put their hands to a holy alliance from her influence. He neither corresponds with French atheists nor English democrats; he despises the praises of the first, he braves the hostility of the last. His maxim is to take men as they are, and neither suppose them better nor worse. He is content to let Russia grow up in a Russian garb, animated with a Russian spirit, and moulded by Russian institutions, without the aid either of Parisian communism or British liberalism. The improvements he has effected in the government of his dominions have been vast, the triumphs with which his external policy have been attended

150. He is essentially Russian.

unbounded; but they have all been achieved, not in imitation of, but in opposition to, the ideas of western Europe. They bespeak, not less than his internal government, the national character of his policy. But if success is the test of worldly wisdom, he has not been far wrong in his system; for he has passed the Balkan, heretofore impervious to his predecessors; he has conquered Poland, converted the Euxine into a Russian lake, planted the cross on the bastions of Erivan, and opened through subdued Hungary a path to Constantinople.

Nature has given him all the qualities fitted for such an elevated destiny. A lofty stature and princely air give additional influence to a majestic countenance, in which the prevailing character is resolution, yet not unmixed with sweetness. Like Wellington, Cæsar, and many other of the greatest men recorded in history, his expression has become more intellectual as he advanced in years, and became exercised in the duties of sovereignty, instead of the stern routine of military discipline. Exemplary in all the relations of private life, a faithful husband, an affectionate father, he has exhibited in a brilliant court, and when surrounded by every temptation which life can offer, the simplicity and affections of patriarchal life. Yet is he not a perfect character. His virtues often border upon vices. His excellences are akin to defects. Deeply impressed with the responsibility of his situation, his firmness has sometimes become sternness, his sense of justice degenerated into severity.* He knows how to distinguish the innocent from the guilty, and has often evinced a noble and magnanimous spirit in separating the one from the other, and showing oblivion of injury, even kindness to the relatives of those who had conspired against his throne and life. But toward the guilty themselves he has not been equally compassionate. He has not always let the passions of the contest pass away with its termination. He is an Alexander the Great in resolution, but not in magnanimity. He wants the last grace in the heroic character—he does not know how to forgive.

151.
His personal appearance and failings.

* "It is in regard to political offenses of a serious dye, however, that this severity chiefly applies. In lesser matters, relating to order and discipline, he is more indulgent, and at times generous. At his coronation at Moscow, his eyes met those of General Paskewitch, who had severely upbraided him for some military error at the head of his regiment some years before. 'Do you recollect,' said he, with a stern air, 'how you once treated me here?' The wind has turned; take care lest I return you the like.' Two days after, he appointed him General-in-Chief."—SCHNITZLER, ii. 356.

A striking proof of the emperor's simplicity of character is recorded by the Marquis Custine, who had frequent and confidential conversations with him. Speaking of his conduct on the revolt of 26th December, he said: "'J'ignorais ce que j'allais faire, j'étais inspiré.' 'Pour avoir de pareilles inspirations,' disait le Marquis, 'il faut les mériter.' 'Je n'ai fait rien d'extraordinaire,' répliqua l'Empereur; 'j'ai dit aux soldats, retournez à vos rangs; et au moment de passer le regiment en revue, j'ai crié, a genoux. Tous ont obéi. Ce qui m'a rendu fort, c'est que l'instant auparavant, j'étais résigné à la mort. Je suis reconnaissant du succés, je n'en suis pas fier; je n'y ai aucun mérite.' 'Votre majesté,' répliqua Custine, 'a été sublime dans cette occasion.' 'Je n'ai pas été sublime,' répondit l'empereur, 'je n'ai fait que mon métier. En pareille circonstance, nul ne peut savoir ce qu'il dira; on court au-devant du peril, sans se demander comment on s'en tirera.'"—LE MARQUIS DE CUSTINE, Russie en 1839, ii. 40, 41, 57. Lamartine has frequently said in society, in reference to his conduct when he persuaded the people to lay aside the red flag at Paris, on the revolution of 1848, "J'étais sublime ce jour-là." Such is the difference between the simplicity of the really magnanimous and the self-love of those in whom it is deformed by overweening and discreditable vanity. I have heard this anecdote of Lamartine from two ladies of high rank, both of whom heard him use the expression on different occasions in reference to his own conduct, which was really noble and courageous on that day.

CHAPTER IX.

ROYALIST REACTION IN FRANCE.

FRANCE FROM THE COUP D'ETAT OF 5TH MARCH, 1819, TO THE ACCESSION OF THE PURELY ROYALIST MINISTRY IN DECEMBER, 1821.

1. Great evils of France at the close of 1816.

THERE is no instance in the whole records of history of a country which so rapidly recovered from the lowest point of depression, as France did in the interval from the close of 1816 to the beginning of 1820. Every conceivable ill which could afflict a state seemed to have accumulated around it at the commencement of that period. Its capital was taken, its government overturned, its sovereign a dethroned captive, its army defeated and disbanded, and eleven hundred thousand armed men in possession of its territory. Contributions to an enormous and unheard-of extent had been imposed upon its inhabitants; the armed multitude lived at free quarters among them, and were supported by exactions coming from their industry; and about sixty millions sterling of indemnities had been levied on them for the allied powers or their subjects. Such was the bequest of the Revolution to France. The inclemency of nature had united with the rigor of man to waste the devoted land. The summer and autumn of 1816 had been beyond all example cold and stormy; the harvest had proved extremely deficient, and prices risen in many places to a famine level. It seemed impossible for human malignity to conceive a greater accumulation of disasters, or for human ability to devise any mode of rendering them bearable.

2. Rapid flow of prosperity which succeeded them in the next year.

Nevertheless it proved otherwise, and the resurrection of France was as rapid as had been her fall into the abyss of misfortune. Three years only had elapsed, and all was changed. Plenty had succeeded to want, confidence to distrust, prosperity to misery. The Allies had withdrawn, the territory was freed; the contributions were paid or provided for, the national faith had been preserved entire. All this had been purchased by a cession of territory so small that it was not worth speaking of. The public funds were high in comparison of what they had been; and though the loans necessary to furnish the Government with the funds to make good its engagements had been contracted at a very high rate of interest, yet the resources of the country had enabled its rulers to pay it with fidelity and exactness, and strengthened their credit with foreign states. The simple preservation of peace—a blessing so long unknown to France—had effected all these prodigies, and worked wonders in the restoration of the national industry. Agriculture, relieved from the wasting scourge of the conscription, had sensibly revived; the husbandman every where sowed in hope, reaped in safety; and the benignity of Providence, which awarded a favorable harvest in 1818 and 1819, filled the land with plenteousness. Great improvements had in many places been introduced into this staple branch of the national industry. The division of property, which always induces a great increase in the amount of labor applied to the cultivation, had not as yet been attended by its subsequent effect—an exhaustion of its productive powers; and the six millions of proprietors succeeded in extracting a considerable increase of subsistence from the fields. New and valuable trees had been planted in the woods; and horticulture, to which a large part of the country near the great towns was devoted, had made rapid strides by the introduction of the improved style of English gardening. Population had largely advanced since the peace; but no want was experienced among the inhabitants. Commerce had every where revived, latterly it had come to flourish to an extraordinary degree. The animation on the roads in the interior, on the canals which conveyed merchandise, and in the seaport towns, proved how largely the means of consumption had increased among the inhabitants.[1]

[1] Lac. ii. 319, 322.

3. Brilliant appearance of Paris.

The capital, in an especial manner, had shared in the general prosperity, and gave unequivocal proof of its reality and extent. The concourse of strangers attracted by its celebrity, its monuments, its galleries, its theatres, and its other attractions, was immense; and their great expenditure consoled the Parisians for the national reverses which had paved the way for their arrival. The Russians and English, their most formidable and persevering enemies, were in an especial manner conspicuous in this lucrative immigration. Under the influence of such extraordinary stimulants, Paris exhibited an unwonted degree of affluence: the brilliant equipages and crowded streets bespoke the riches which were daily expended, while the piles of splendid edifices arising on all sides exceeded any thing previously witnessed in the brightest days of its history, and added daily to the architectural beauties it presented.[2]

[2] Personal observation.

4. Exports, imports, and revenue of France during this period.

Statistical facts of unquestionable correctness and convincing weight attested the reality and magnitude of this change. The exports, imports, and revenue of the country had all gone on increasing, and latterly in an accelerated ratio. The imports, which in 1815 (the last year of Napoleon's reign) had been only 199,467,660 francs, had risen, in 1817, to 332,000,000, and in 1821 they had advanced to 355,591,877 francs. The exports also had risen considerably; they had increased from 422,000,000 to 464,000,000 francs.* The amount of revenue levied during these years could not, by possibility, afford a true index to the real state of the country, from the enormous amount of the contributions to the allied powers; but in those items in which an increase was practicable, or which indicated the greater well-being of the people, the improvement was very conspicuous. So marked a resurrection of a country and advance of its social condition, in so short a period, had perhaps never been witnessed; and it is the more remarkable, from its occurring immediately after such unprecedented misfortunes, and from the mere effect of an alteration in the system and policy of Government.

5. Thorough establishment of representative institutions in France.

Add to this, that France had now, for the first time in its entire history, obtained the full benefit of representative institutions. The electors of the Chamber of Deputies were few in number—indeed, not exceeding 80,000 for the whole country—but they represented the national feelings so thoroughly, that their representatives in parliament had not only got the entire command of the state, but they expressed the national wishes as faithfully as eight millions could have done. If there was any thing to be condemned on the part of Government, it was that it had yielded too rapidly and immediately to the wishes of the people, whatever they were at the moment. The Royalist reaction of 1815; the subsequent leaning to liberal institutions; the *coup d'état* of September 5, 1816; the great creation of peers in March, 1819, had all been done in conformity with the wishes, and in obedience to the fierce demands, of the majority at the time. Weak from the outset, in consequence of the calamitous circumstances under which it was first established, and deprived at length of all support from external force, the Government had no alternative throughout but to conform, in every material step, to the national will, and for good or for evil inaugurate the people at once in the power of self-government. To such a length had this been carried, that at the close of the period the king had come to an entire rupture with his Royalist supporters, and thrown himself without reserve into the arms of the Liberal and anti-monarchical party.

It might reasonably have been expected that these great concessions would have conciliated the Constitutional party, who were now not only in possession of the blessings of freedom, but the sweets of office, and that they would have done their utmost to support a Government which had conferred such advantages upon their country and themselves. Yet it was just the reverse. With every concession made to them, their demands rose higher, their exasperation became greater; the press was never so violent, the public effervescence so extreme, as when the Government was opposing the least resistance to the popular will; and at length the danger became so imminent, from the increasing demands of the Liberals and the menacing aspect of the legislature, that the king, from sheer necessity, and much against his will, was driven into a change of system, and return to a monarchical administration.

6. Which have no effect in conciliating the Liberal party.

The new Ministry appointed when the Liberals were in the ascendant, being not altogether confident in their stability, and having come to an open rupture with the Royalists, did every thing in their power to increase their popularity, and conciliate the democratic party, upon whom they exclusively depended. Various measures of great utility, and attended by the very best consequences, were set on foot, which have been felt as beneficial even to these times. To them we owe the first idea of an exhibition of the works of national industry, which was fixed for the 25th August, 1819, to be followed by a similar one every two years afterward, and which was attended with such success that it gave rise, in its ultimate effects, to the magnificent Great Exhibition in London, in the year 1851. A Council-General of Agriculture was established, consisting of ten members, of whom the Minister of the Interior was President, which was to correspond with and direct affiliated societies all over the kingdom. In the choice of its members the most laudable impartiality was shown, and the Duke de la Rochefoucauld, the head of the Royalist nobility, was the first person on the list, followed by the Dukes of Choiseul and Liancourt, who were equally distinguished by their opposition to the present Government. A Council-General of Prisons was established, and the attention of the philanthropist directed to the unhappy convicts, a class of sufferers who had been alike neglected amidst the declamations of the Republic and the glories of the Empire. To aid them in their philanthropic labor, a society was formed, under the direction of the Minister of the Interior, which, under the title of the "Royal Society of Prisons," was soon actively engaged with projects for the improvement of prison discipline, and moral and religious instruction of the inmates. Great solicitude was

7. Popular acts of the new Ministry.

---

* EXPORTS AND IMPORTS AND REVENUE OF FRANCE, FROM 1815 TO 1821.

Years.	Imports.	Exports.	Revenue Ordinary.	Revenue Extraordinary.	Total Revenue.
	Francs.	Francs.	Francs.	Francs.	Francs.
1815	199,467,664	422,147,776	729,154,571	147,163,661	876,318,232
1816	242,698,753	547,706,917	878,903,354	157,801,000	1,036,801,354
1817	332,371,593	461,049,387	899,813,624	370,499,896	1,270,312,550
1818	335,571,188	502,281,083	937,751,487	476,329,198	1,414,080,625
1819	291,518,246	460,232,224	895,386,818	41,271,966	936,658,784
1820	335,069,566	543,112,774	933,439,553	5,798,510	939,238,063
1821	355,591,857	450,788,843	928,515,558	7,436,491	935,653,049
1822	368,990,533	427,679,156	937,427,670	16,493,592	953,921,262

—*Statistique de la France Commerce Extérieur*, p. 9. Ibid., *Administration Publique*, 116, 121.

evinced for the advancement of primary instruction; and in no former period, either of the Republic or the Empire, had a greater number of improvements been effected in that important department of public instruction.¹ Finally, the attention of the Government was directed, in an especial manner, to the administration of justice, and the numerous abuses which prevailed in the delay generally incurred in bringing prisoners to trial; and a circular issued by M. de Serres, the Minister of Justice, deserves a place in history, from the admirable spirit which it breathes on a subject hitherto unaccountably neglected by all the parties who had been successively called to the helm of affairs.*

<small>¹ Lac. ii. 323, 336, Cap. vi. 145, 155. Circulaire aux Préfets, ii. 271.</small>

8. *Return of Maret and many other of the proscribed to France.*

At the same time, nearly the whole persons banished for their accession to the conspiracy of the Hundred Days received permission to return to their country. Maret, Duke of Bassano, the principal author of that revolt, obtained it, and after his return the same indulgence could scarcely be refused to inferior delinquents. The king never refused forgiveness to any application from any of his Ministers; rarely to any respectable inferior application. By these means, in a few months nearly all the proscribed persons, excepting the actual regicides, had returned to their country, and these were so few in number, and for the most part so old and infirm, that their absence or presence, except as an example, and indicating the triumph or defeat of a principle, was almost equally an object of indifference.²

<small>² Cap. vi. 156, 158; Lac. ii. 317, 321.</small>

9. *Increasing strength of the Liberals, and resistance to the Government.*

Notwithstanding this indulgent administration, and substantial benefits conferred on France by the Government of the Restoration, it was daily becoming more unpopular, and the general discontent had now reached such a height as seriously to menace its existence. Three elections remained to complete the last renewal of the Chamber, and the persons elected, M. Daunou, Saint-Aignan, and Benjamin Constant, were all leaders of the extreme democratic party. Nor was the hostility to the Ministers confined to electoral contests. In the Chamber itself the most violent and systematic resistance was made to every proposal of the Government; and every concession they made, so far from disarming the opposition, only rendered it more virulent and persevering. The press was never so violent and undisguised in its attacks on the administration; and to such a length did its hostility proceed, that before two months had elapsed from the *coup d'état* creating sixty new peers in the democratic interest, Ministers found it necessary to bring forward a lasting law regarding the press, to be a bridle on its excesses.

10. *Law regarding the press. April 21.*

Although this law was a great concession to the popular party, and placed the liberty of the press upon a better basis than it had ever been, since the Restoration gave freedom to France, it excited the most violent opposition in both Chambers and in the public press. It abolished the censorship—an immense step in the progress of real freedom—and declared that offenses against the laws for restraining its excesses should be tried by juries. This was evidently laying the only true foundation for entire freedom on this subject; but the enactment which it also contained, that the proprietors of newspapers should find security to meet fines or claims of damages which might be awarded against them, gave rise to the most violent opposition, both in the legislature and the public journals. "The press is strangled," was the universal cry; "give us back the censorship." Yet—markworthy circumstance—the proposal passed into a law; the resistance was overcome; of the whole journals, not one perished from inability to find caution; but the violence and vehemence of the press became greater than ever. In truth, in an age of intelligence and strong political excitement, it is impossible to restrain the press; and the enactments of the legislature, be they what they may, are of little consequence, for they ere long become a dead letter. During the whole of the stormy discussion which took place on this subject, the Royalists took no part, confining themselves to the urging an amendment, declaring offenses against religion punishable; which was agreed to. They desired freedom of discussion as the only means of achieving their return to power; but they were ashamed of the allies who aided them at the moment in the attempt. The project passed ultimately into a law by a majority of eighty-five; the numbers being a hundred and forty-three to fifty-eight; and thus the Restoration might justly boast of having obtained for France the inestimable blessing of a real liberty of the press, to which no approach ever had been made during either the Revolution or the Empire.¹

<small>¹ Cap. vi. 161, 164; Lac. ii. 307; Ann. Hist. ii. 83, 88, 110; Moniteur, April 22, 1819.</small>

11. *Debate on the return of the proscribed persons.*

A still more vehement debate took place on a matter which was anxiously pressed on the king by the whole extreme left of the Chamber, and all their supporters in the public press—viz, the general and unqualified return of the proscribed persons. From the state of maturity to which the project for the overthrow of the Bourbons had arrived, this was a matter of very great importance; for the exiles whom it was proposed to get back would be the very first to become its leaders. The Ministers resisted the attempt to force such a measure upon the king; they had some in-

<small>* "Des réclamations nombreuses ont signalé dans ces derniers temps divers abus dans l'Instruction des Procédures criminelles. Ces plaintes peuvent n'être pas exemptes d'exagération. Il paraît cependant que plusieurs ne sont que trop fondées. Elles ont porté sur la facilité, la légèreté même, avec laquelle sont faites les arrestations. 2. Sur une prolongation ou un application abusive de l'Interdiction aux prevenus de communiquer. 3. Enfin, sur la négligence apportée dans l'Instruction des procès. Je crois donc utile de retracer sur chacun de ces points les principes, à la stricte application desquels vous devez sans cesse rappeler les Procureurs du Roi, les Juges d'Instruction, et chacun des agents judiciaires qui vous sont subordonnés. . . . Attachez-vous à imprimer fortement cette vérité aux Magistrats Instructeurs que la *célérité dans les Informations* est pour eux un devoir impérieux, et qu'ils se chargent d'une grande responsabilité lorsque, sans une nécessité évidente, ils la prolongent au delà du temps suffisant pour faire régler la Compétence, et statuer sur la Préconisation en Connaissance de Cause."—*Circulaire aux Préfets*, 24th April, 1819. *Circulaire aux Préfets*, ii. 271.</small>

formation as to the danger which impended over the monarchy, and thought justly, that if the sovereign was driven into such a general measure, it would take away all credit for acts of grace conferred upon individuals.[1] M. de Serres, on this occasion, broke forth into an eloquent declamation, the termination of which made an immense sensation, and contributed, in an essential manner, to alienate the democratic leaders from the crown, and reveal the secret hostility with which they were actuated against it.

<small>1 Cap. vi. 170, 171; Ann. Hist. ii. 228, 229.</small>

<small>12. Speech of M. de Serres on the subject.</small>
"In the petitions which have been presented," said M. de Serres, "it is particularly to be observed, that there is no question as to individuals exiled for a time under the law of 12th January, 1816, but of *all* the proscribed individuals in a mass. They include not only the regicides, but the family of Bonaparte himself. When the deplorable day of the 20th March, 1815, appeared, in the midst of the profound consternation of all good citizens, and the frantic joy of a few agitators; when, from the confines of Europe and Asia to the shores of the ocean, Europe ran to arms, and France was invaded by millions of foreign soldiers; when it was despoiled of its fortune, its monuments, and in danger of having its territory reft away, every one felt that the first duty of every good citizen was to defend the crown by severe measures against fresh aggressions. Then arose the question, whether the individuals who had concurred in the vote for the death of Louis XVI. should be removed from the French territory; and every one knows with what perseverance the royal clemency struggled against the proposition for their banishment. Many men, known by their boundless devotion to the royal cause, and to the principles of a constitutional monarchy, maintained that a universal and unqualified amnesty should be pronounced. But it was otherwise decided; and having been so, the decision was irrevocable. The extreme generosity of the king might engage individuals to abstain from voting; but when once the law was passed, it was evidently impossible, without doing violence to the strongest moral feelings, without inflicting a fatal wound on the royal authority in the eyes of France and Europe, to urge the king to restore to the country the assassins of his brother, his lawfully crowned predecessor.[2] It is necessary, therefore, to make a distinction between the individuals struck at by the law of January, 1816. In the irrevocable category should be placed the family of Bonaparte and the regicide voters. The rest are only exiled for a time. To conclude in one word—the regicides, *never*; as to those exiled for a time, entire confidence in the goodness of the king."

<small>2 Ann. Hist. ii. 230, Moniteur, May 18, 1819; Cap. vi. 171, 173.</small>

<small>13. Immense sensation produced by this debate.</small>
The expression used by M. de Serres, *jamais* (never), made an immense sensation. It at once separated the extreme Left from the Ministry, and, by the exasperation which it produced, revealed their secret designs. So great was the ferment that, in the report of his speech in the *Moniteur*, it was deemed necessary to add a qualifying expression, to the effect that, although the regicides could never claim a return, they might hope for it from the clemency of the king, in consideration of age and infirmities.* But this qualification produced no impression. The unqualified words had been spoken by the minister in his place in the Chamber, and were taken as a decisive indication of the intentions of Government. The exasperation of the extreme Liberals, accordingly, continued unabated, and was so strongly expressed in the contemporary journals in their interest, that both M. de Serres and M. Decazes began to hesitate in regard to the possibility of carrying on the government by the support of such allies. A schism, attended in the end with important effects, was beginning in the Cabinet, and to this period is to be referred the commencement of an alteration in the sentiments of the leading members of administration, which ultimately led to a change of government.[1]

<small>1 Cap. vi. 174, 175; Lac. ii. 316, 317.</small>

Open war being now declared between the Government and the Liberal press, and all restraints upon the latter being taken away by the removal of the censorship, there was no end to the violence with which Ministers were assailed by the democratic party. All that they had done was forgotten: what it was feared they would do alone was considered. The *coup d'état*, which had changed the Electoral Law, and promised soon to give them the command of the Chambers—the creation of peers, which had already given them a majority in the upper chamber—were never once mentioned: the word "jamais" alone resounded in every ear. The most unbounded benefits conferred on their country and themselves were forgotten in the denial of an amnesty to a few hoary Jacobins, stained with every atrocity which could disgrace humanity. Three-fourths of the public press was leagued together against the Government, and poured forth its venom daily with a vigor and talent which bore down all opposition. The *Courrier*, which was supported by the Doctrinaire party, and adorned by the talents of M. Guizot, Royer-Collard, and Kerratry, proved in this strife no match for the *Constitutionnel*, which then first attained its immense circulation, and in which M. Thiers was beginning his eventful career. The Royalist journals, in which M. Chateaubriand and Hyde Neuville exerted their talents, were supported with greater genius and eloquence than the Liberal, and strongly confirmed the minority, which agreed with them in their opinion of the present downward progress of things; but their voices were those of a minor ity only of the entire population. The majority, upon the whole, was decidedly with the Liberals, and they were more vehement in their attacks on the Government than they had been on the Royalist administration. A popular party which is suspected of an intention of stopping in the career of concession, soon becomes the object of more inveterate hostility than that which had always opposed it.[2]

<small>14. Increasing violence and exasperation of the press.</small>

<small>2 Lac. ii. 330, 331. Cap. vi. 175, 190; Lam. vi. 213, 214.</small>

---

* "A l'égard des régicides jamais, sauf, comme je l'ai dit, les tolérances accordées par la clémence du roi a l'âge et eux infirmités."—*Moniteur*, May 18, 1819; *Ann Hist* ii. 230.

As these ulcerated feelings arose from disappointed ambition rather than patriotic feeling, they were in no degree abated by the general prosperity which prevailed, and which proved how much, as a whole, the Government of the Restoration had deserved the support and affections of the country. The budget of 1819 presented a striking and most gratifying contrast to those which had preceded it, and proved the immensity of the relief which the Congress of Aix-la-Chapelle, and the evacuation of the territory, had procured for the French nation.* The estimated expenses of the year were only 889,200,000 francs, being a reduction of nearly 300,000,000 francs from those of the preceeding year, which had amounted to 1,154,000,000 francs. In the expense of the year, independent of the cessation of the payments to the Allies, there was a reduction of 15,000,000 francs. The Government had good reason to congratulate itself upon the exposition of its financial situation: nothing nearly so favorable had been presented since the Revolution; for here was a reduction of £12,000,000 a year, effected, not by contributions exacted from other countries, or any reduction in the national armaments, but simply by successful diplomatic arrangements with foreign states, and the moderation on the part of their rulers which the policy of the French Government had inspired.¹

¹ An. Hist. ii. 161, 163; Cap. vi. 191, 193.

^{16.} Preparations for the election of 1819.

All eyes, in the autumn of this year, were fixed on the annual election for filling up the fifth of the Chamber, which by law was vacated and renewed every season. Already the evils of these annual elections had come to be severely felt; and the expression of the approach of the "Electoral Fever" had become as common as, in after days, that of the approach of the cholera was to be. Ministers felt strongly the importance of the ensuing election, and exerted themselves to the utmost to gain popularity before it came on. The king visited frequently the magnificent exhibition of the productions of native industry, which was held in the Louvre, and was prodigal of those flattering expressions of which he was so accomplished a master: not a manufacturer withdrew without believing that he had captivated the royal taste. Crosses of the Legion of Honor were profusely bestowed, but yet with discernment, and without regard to party; and the circulars to the prefects earnestly inculcated the utmost lenity in prosecution of offenders, and diligence in encouraging every object of social improvement. The prosecution of the assassins of Marshal Brune was authorized, if they could be discovered; the proscribed returned in crowds from Belgium; while, to conciliate the Royalists, the concordat with the court of Rome was modified; bulls were given to the new French bishops; and the sacred ceremonies frequently announced the installation of a new bishop in his diocese. A million of francs (£40,000) was devoted to the establishment of new parish priests; while, to evince their impartiality, three new Protestant ministers were endowed at the same time with the Catholic bishops; and the presidents of the electoral colleges were all chosen from the Centre of the Assembly, and taken from men of moderation and respectability.¹

¹ Cap. vi. 216, 219.

It was all in vain; and the elections of 1819, which had an important effect on the destinies of the monarchy, afford another example of the truth exemplified by so many passages of contemporary history—that in periods of excitement, when the passions are violently roused, moderate men are assailed on both sides, and it is the extremes on either who alone prove successful. All that the king and the ministers had done for the Liberal party—and it was not a little—went for nothing; or rather, they only encouraged them to rise in their demands, and return representatives who would extort what they wished from the Government. The Royalists in many places coalesced with them to throw out the ministerial candidates: their journals openly advised them to do so, inculcating the doctrine, "Better the Jacobins than the Ministerialists; for the Jacobins will bring matters to a crisis." In truth, however, the crisis was nearer than they imagined, and it was brought on very much by their policy. Five-and-thirty extreme Liberals were returned, fifteen Ministerialists, and only four Royalists. Among those whom the Liberals returned were GENERAL FOY, the most distinguished popular orator of the Restoration, and two extreme Jacobins, whose appearance in the returned lists excited universal consternation—M. Lambrecht, and the ABBÉ GRÉGOIRE, the Jacobin and constitutional bishop of Blois, whose name was identified with several of the worst acts of the Convention.²

^{17.} Their result; election of the Abbé Grégoire.

² Cap. vi. 216, 220; Lac. ii. 330, 335; Lam. vi. 221, 222.

The Abbé Grégoire, who had left the Church of Rome during the Revolution, and received in return from the civil authorities the bishopric of Blois, had not actually voted for the death of Louis XVI., having been absent on a mission at the time; but he had given several subsequent votes, which evinced his approval of that great legislative murder. His language had always been violent and immeasured against royalty and the Bourbons; and no one had spread brief sarcastic sayings against them more widely, or done more to injure their cause with the great body of the people, with whom stinging epithets or bold assertions often prevail more than sound argument or truth in the statement of facts. A mute senator under the Empire, he had possessed good sense enough to abstain from joining in the movement which followed the return of Napoleon from Elba, which prevented his being included in the sentence of banishment pronounced against those concerned in that event, and paved the way for his return as a member of the Chamber of Deputies.

^{18.} Biography of the Abbé Grégoire.

* The budget of 1819 stood thus:—

	Francs.
Interest of public debt	232,600,000
Civil list and royal family	34,000,000
Foreign Affairs	8,000,000
Justice	17,460,000
Interior	102,700,000
War	192,750,000
Marine	45,200,000
Miscellaneous	257,000,000
	889,210,000 or £35,450,000

—*Annuaire Historique*, ii. 161.

He had never been wholly faithless to the cause of Christianity, though he had to that of the court of Rome, in whose service he had been; and there were many men in the Convention. But it was impossible to find one more personally obnoxious to the Bourbons, or whose return was considered a more decided triumph by the party which aimed at their overthrow.[1]

[1 Lam. vi. 222, 223; Cap. vi. 227, 229.]

19. General Foy; his biography.

GENERAL FOY, a far nobler and superior character, though not so much dreaded at the time, proved a much more formidable enemy in the end to the Government of the Restoration. Born at Havre in 1775, he had early served under Dumourier, Pichegru, and Dampierre in the legions of the Revolution. Subsequently he was wounded by the side of Desaix, in one of the campaigns in Germany; and he served under Massena in the campaign of Zurich in 1799. He early evinced, however, an independent spirit, and devoted his leisure hours, in the intervals of his campaign, to the study of law and social questions. He refused to sign the servile addresses which were sent by the troops with whom he acted to Napoleon, fell, in consequence, under the imperial displeasure, and was sent to Spain to expiate his offense in the dreadful campaigns in that country. To this circumstance we owe his very interesting account of the early campaigns in that memorable war. He joined the Bourbons in 1811; but, without being implicated, like so many others, in the revolt of 1815, he hastened to the scene of danger when the independence of France was menaced; and none combated with more gallantry both at Quatre-Bras and Waterloo. In 1815, he returned to private life, on the disbanding of the army, and employed his leisure hours in writing the annals of his campaigns.[2]

[2 Lam. vi. 225, 227; Biog Univ. lxiv. 288, 291.]

20. M. de Serres.

The only man in the Chamber, who, on the Ministerial side, was capable of balancing the power of General Foy on the Liberal, was M. DE SERRES. He was in every sense a very eminent man, and seemed to have inherited the spirit of Mirabeau without being stained by his vices, and enlightened by experience and subsequent events. He was fitted by nature, if any man was, to have brought about the marriage of the hereditary monarchy with the liberty of the Revolution, which that great man, in the close of his career, endeavored to effect, but which his own violence at that period had contributed to render impossible. A Royalist by descent, born on 12th March, 1776, of a noble family in Lorraine, he had, in the first instance, served with the other emigrants in the army of the Prince of Condé against the Revolution. But his inclination led him to peaceful studies rather than warlike pursuits, and he returned to France on occasion of Napoleon's amnesty in 1801, and began his studies for the bar. Such, however, at that period, from long residence abroad, was his ignorance of his own language, that he required to study it as a foreign tongue. He made his *début* at the provincial bar of Metz, and in a few years had distinguished himself so much that in 1811 Napoleon appointed him public prosecutor there, and soon after President of the Imperial Court at Hamburg. In that situation he remained till 1814, when, having declared his adhesion to the Bourbons on the fall of Napoleon, he was appointed President of the Royal Court at Colmar, a situation which he held when he was named deputy for that department in 1815. With that commenced his parliamentary and ministerial career.[1]

[1 Biog. Univ. lxxxv. 133, 134.]

21. His character.

His principles were Royalist from birth and early impressions, and he was of a religious disposition; but when his reason was fully developed, his opinions inclined to the Liberal side, and then he readily fell into the alliance of the Royalist Liberals, of whom M. Decazes was the head, and which Louis XVIII. adopted as the basis of his government. He was more remarkable for the power of his eloquence, and the commanding flow of his oratory, than the consistency of his political conduct. His soul was ardent, his imagination rich, his words impassioned, his elocution clear and emphatic. He was thus the most powerful debater, the most brilliant orator on the ministerial side, and was put forward by them on all important occasions as their most valuable supporter. Such was the force of his language, and the generous liberality of his sentiments, that he not only never failed to command general attention, but often to elicit the warmest applause from both sides of the Chamber—an intoxicating but dangerous species of homage, to which the consistency of more than one very eminent man, on both sides of the Channel, has fallen a sacrifice. His previous life and known principles still obtained for him the applause of the Royalists, while the new-born liberality of his sentiments extorted the cheers of the Liberals on the left. Thus his parliamentary influence at the moment was extensive—more so, perhaps, than that of any other man; but it was not likely to be durable. Mere talent, how great soever, will not long secure the suffrages of any body of men, least of all an assembly in which ambition is the ruling principle of action in the great majority. Both sides applaud him so long as both hope to gain him, but when his decision is once taken, the party which he has abandoned becomes his bitterest enemy. Wisdom of thought and consistency of conduct, though often exposed to obloquy at the time, are the only secure foundation for lasting fame, because they alone can lead to a course upon which time will stamp its approval.[2]

[2 Lam. vi. 211.]

22. Conversation of Louis XVIII and the Count d'Artois on the election.

The result of the elections, and in an especial manner the return of the Abbé Grégoire, acted like a clap of thunder on Louis XVIII. and M. Decazes, to whose Electoral Law it was obviously to be ascribed. It was no longer possible to shut their eyes to the danger. Every successive election, since the *coup d'état* of September 5, 1816, had proved more unfavorable than the preceding, and the last had turned out so disastrous, both in the general results and the character of the individuals returned, that not a doubt could remain that the next would give a decided majority in the Chamber to the declared enemies of the Bourbon family. Immense was the sensation which these untoward results produced at the Tuileries; and the evidence of facts was now too clear and convincing for the king any longer to shut his eyes to the inferences deducible from them. On the evening of the day when intelligence had been received of the return of the Abbé Grégoire, the Count d'Artois thus addressed Louis: "Well my brother, you see at last whither they are leading you." "I know it, my brother," replied the king, softening his voice, and in an under-tone, "I know it, and will provide against it." Confidence was by these words immediately re-established between the heir-apparent and the throne. A long and cordial conversation ensued between the two brothers, in the course of which it was agreed that an Electoral Law, which had induced such a succession of defeats to the Government and insults to the throne, evidently required to be altered. The very same evening M. Decazes received orders to prepare a new electoral bill. The minister saw that his master's mind was made up, and at once agreed to do so. M. de Serres, whose early prepossessions and imaginative turn of mind inclined him to the same side, and even to magnify the approaching dangers, readily fell into the same views, and M. Portal, the Minister of Marine, adopted them also. On the other hand, the President, General Dessolles, General Gouvion St. Cyr, War Minister, and Baron Louis, the Finance Minister, were decidedly in favor of the existing system; so that the Cabinet was divided on the subject, as well as the country.[1]

^{1 Lam. vi. 227; Cap. vi. 234, 235, Lac. ii. 339.}

23. Change in the Ministry.

When a division had taken place in the Cabinet on so vital a subject as the Electoral Law, it was impossible that it could be adjusted without a change in the composition of the Ministry. The king and M. Decazes, aware of the danger of showing symptoms of division in their own camp, in presence of an enterprising and insatiable enemy, made great efforts to avert the rupture, and labored hard to convince the Liberal members of the administration that no change involving principle was contemplated, but only such a modification in details as circumstances had rendered necessary. But the ministers adverse to a change stood firm, and resolved to resign rather than enter into the proposed compromise. On the other hand, the king was fortified in his view of the case by the accession of M. Pasquier, who laid before him a very able memoir, in which the dangers of the present law were clearly pointed out, and its further maintenance was shown to be inconsistent with the existence of the monarchy. The Liberal journals, made aware of the danger of their chiefs, sounded the alarm in the loudest possible notes, and praised General Dessolles, General Gouvion St. Cyr, and Baron Louis to the skies, as the sole patriotic ministers, and the only ones who had the interest of the people and the support of the national liberties really at heart. But it was all in vain. The king's mind was made up; the danger was too obvious and pressing to be any longer disregarded; and as no compromise was found to be practicable, the result was a great and important change in the Ministry. M. Decazes was sent for by the king, and declared President of the Council. He reserved for himself the situation of Minister of the Interior, for which his talents and habits peculiarly qualified him. M. Pasquier was appointed Minister of Foreign Affairs; General Latour Maubourg, Minister-at-War; and M. Roy, Finance Minister.[1]

^{1 Cap. vi. 235, 254; Lam. vi. 228, 229; Lac. ii. 339.}

24. Violent attacks on the new Ministry by the press.

It was comparatively a matter of little difficulty to make a change in the Ministry, but it was not so easy to see how the alteration was to be supported in the Chamber, or rendered palatable to the public press, in both of which Liberal principles were in the ascendant. Every thing depended on the Centre of the Assembly, and to secure its support the new Cabinet Ministers had been taken from its ranks; and to gain time for the parties to arrange themselves, the opening of the Chambers was adjourned to the 29th November. But meanwhile, both the journals and the pamphleteers on the Liberal side, now freed from the restraints of the censorship, commenced a war to the knife with the new Ministry. M. Decazes, so recently the object of general idolatry as long as he headed the movement, was instantly assailed with the most virulent reproaches; none are so much so as public men who change their line, or are unfaithful to their principles, especially when the change conduces, as in this instance it did, to their own advantage. Nor were publications awanting of a higher stamp, and which had greater weight with persons of thought and reflection. In particular, M. de Staël, son of the illustrious authoress, in a pamphlet of great ability, defended the contemplated change in the Electoral Law, pointed out the evils of the existing system, and proposed, to remedy them, the duplication of the Chamber of Deputies, elections by arrondissements and chief places, and a renewal of the entire Chamber every five years, instead of the annual renewal of a fifth. The Doctrinaires, including M. de Staël, M. Guizot, and M. de Broglie, tendered their powerful support to the new Cabinet, demanding only, as a guarantee for its sincerity, two portfolios, one for M. Royer-Collard, and one for M. de Broglie or M. de Barante.[2]

^{2 Cap. vi. 256, 259; Lam. vi. 228, 229.}

25. King's speech at opening the session. Nov. 29.

The king's speech, at the opening of the Chamber on November 29, gave tokens of the apprehensions with which the royal mind was inspired, and of the change of policy which was in contemplation. "In the midst," said he, "of the general prosperity, and surrounded by so many circumstances calculated to inspire confidence, there are just grounds for apprehension which mingle with our hopes, and demand our most serious attention. A vague but real disquietude has seized every mind; pleased with the present, every one asks pledges for its duration: the nation enjoys, in a very imperfect way, the fruits of legal government and peace; it fears to see them reft from it by the violence of faction; it is terrified by the too undisguised expression of its designs. These fears and wishes point to the necessity of some additional guarantee for repose and tranquillity. Impressed with these ideas, I have reverted to the subject which has so much occupied my thoughts, which I wished to realize, but which requires to be matured by experience, and enforced by necessity before it is carried into execution. Founder of the charter, to which are attached the whole interests of my people and my family, I feel that if there is any amelioration which these great interests require, and which should modify some regulating forms connected with the charter, in order the better to secure its power and action, it rests with me to propose it. The moment has come when it is necessary to fortify the Chamber of Deputies, and withdraw it from the annual action of party, by securing it a longer endurance, and one more in conformity with the interests of public order and the exterior consideration of the state. It is to the devotion and energy of the two Chambers, and their cordial co-operation with my government, that I look for the means of saving the public liberties from license, confirming the monarchy, and giving to all the interests guaranteed by the charter the entire security which we owe to it."¹

¹ Moniteur, Nov. 30, 1819; Ann. Hist. iii. 2, 3.

26. Comparative strength of parties in the Chamber.

It was impossible that words could announce more explicitly a change of policy adopted by the king and the Government; but the result of the first division in the Chamber proved that the extreme Left, reduced to itself, could not disturb its movements, and that, if the Centre supported Ministers, they would be able to carry through their measures. In the division for the president, M. Lafitte, who had all the extreme Liberal strength, had only sixty-five votes, while M. Ravez, who was supported by the Centre and Right, had a hundred and five, and M. de Villèle by the Right alone, seventy-five. This sufficiently proved where the majority was to be found; but that it could not be relied on to support any change in the Electoral Law was proved by the division on the address, on which Ministers were defeated by a majority of one, the numbers being a hundred and eight to a hundred and seven. The new address, drawn up by the commission which the majority had nominated, bore, "Why weaken our hopes, and the calmness of our felicity, by unnecessary fears? The laws are every day meeting with an easy execution; nowhere is the public tranquillity disturbed; but it is no doubt true that a vague disquietude has taken possession of the public mind, and the factions, which attempt no concealment of their projects and their hopes, endeavor to corrupt public opinion, and they would plunge us into licentiousness, in order to destroy our liberties."²

² An. Hist. iii. 3, 4; Moniteur, Dec. 2, 1819; Cap. vi. 270, 271.

27. Designs of the Liberals in Paris.

It was too true that the factions made no attempt to conceal their projects, and the impunity with which they were permitted to carry them on in face of day afforded the clearest proof of the weakness of the Government. The following account of the secret associations at this time in Paris, and of their designs, is given by a distinguished writer, who himself has since been, for a brief season, their principal leader: "At this period," says Lamartine, "the opposition, obliged to avoid the light of day, took refuge in secret societies. The spirit of conspiracy insinuated itself into them, under the color of liberal opinions. Public associations were formed, to defend, by all legal means, the liberty of thought, of opinion, and of the press. MM. de Lafayette, d'Argenson, Lafitte, Benjamin Constant, Gevaudeau, Mechin, Gassicourt, de Broglie, and others, impressed the course of public action. M. de Lafayette, in his hôtel, held meetings of still more secret and determined committees. Every defensive arm gained by our institutions to public freedom, became, in their hands, an aggressive arm for the purposes of conspiracy. Secret correspondences were established between the persons proscribed at Brussels and the malcontents in Paris. They spoke openly of changing the dynasty. The King of the Netherlands, it was said, secretly favored their projects, and hoped to elevate his house on the ruins of the Bourbons. Negotiations were attempted between the Prince of Orange, the proscribed persons, and Lafayette. The threads of the conspiracy extended into Germany, Italy, Spain, Piedmont, and Naples. The spirit of freedom which had roused Europe against Napoleon, seeing itself menaced in France, every where prepared to defend itself. CARBONARISM was organized in Italy, anti-monarch liberty at Cadiz, and a general union in the universities of Germany. One of the young members of that sect, the student Sand, assassinated, in cold blood, Kotzebue, who formerly enjoyed an extensive popularity, but who was supposed to be sold to Russia."⁴

⁴ Lam. vi. 219, 220.

A full account of these important changes in Europe has already been given; but their influence was great and decided on the measures of Government at Paris. It was no longer a question, whether the Electoral Law should be modified—the only point was, to what extent. The Cabinet, in conjunction with M. de Broglie, M. Guizot, M. Vilmain, and the Doctrinaires, drew up a bill, the heads of which were—1st, That the Chamber should be renewed entire every five or seven years, and not a fifth every year as at present; 2d, That the number of its members should be considerably augmented; 3d, That the colleges of arrondissement as they now stood should be broken into smaller divisions. The Doctrinaires agreed to support this bill with their whole weight from the Centre of the Chamber, and it was hoped it would pass. But great delay took place in adjusting the details, and the Liberals took advantage of the time thus gained to rouse the country against the Government. Petitions against the Ministers were got up in all quarters, and the violence of the press exceeded any thing ever witnessed since the days of the Convention. In vain were prosecutions instituted against the delinquents: the juries, in the face of the clearest evidence, constantly acquitted the persons brought before the tribunals. Caulincourt openly saluted Napoleon as Emperor in his writings, and Béranger lent to his cause the fascination of genius and the charms of poetry. The intelligence daily received of the progress of the revolution in Spain, and the fermentation in Germany and Italy, added to the general excitement; and the Napoleonists, deeming the reat-

28. New Electoral Law proposed by the Government.

ization of their hopes approaching, every where struck the chord which still vibrated so powerfully in the hearts of the French; and the mighty image of the Emperor, long banished from the lips, but treasured in the hearts of men, again seemed to arise in gloomy magnificence on the extreme verge of the distant ocean.[1]

Lam. vi. 223, 225; Cap. vi. 277, 281; Lac. ii. 347, 353.

29. Electoral law finally agreed on by the Government.

The project ultimately agreed on for the modification of the Electoral Law was one founded in wisdom, and which, by providing a remedy against the great danger of the existing system—the *uniform representation*, and consequent preponderance of one single class in society—promised to establish it in France on the only basis on which it can ever be beneficial or of long duration in an old and mixed community. It obtained the concurrence both of the Royalists and the Doctrinaires. It was agreed that the Chamber of Deputies was to be composed of 430 members, instead of 260, the present number—258 being returned by the colleges of arrondissements, and 172 by the colleges of departments. The colleges of arrondissements were to appoint the electors of the colleges of departments *among those who paid 1000 francs (£40) of annual taxes;* the half of all taxes, to make up the quota, was to be of land-tax; the elections were to be made by inscriptions on a bulletin; the 172 departmental deputies were to be elected immediately; the Chamber to go on without renewal in any part for seven years. The material thing in this proposed law was, that *a different class* of electors was introduced for the colleges of departments—viz., persons paying 1000 francs of annual taxes, instead 300, which constituted the franchise at present.[2]

2 Cap. vi. 290, 292; Lam. vi. 235, 237.

30. Violent opposition of the Liberals.

The project no sooner got wind than the Liberals sounded the alarm. The violence of the press became insupportable. Assassination was openly recommended; Brutus and Cassius, Sand and Carlisle, Riego and Quiroga the leaders of the Spanish revolution, were lauded to the skies as the first of patriots. In a pamphlet by Saint Simon it was asserted that the murder of the king, of the Duke d'Angoulème, and the Duke de Berri, would be less to be deplored than that of the humblest mechanic, because persons could more easily be found to act the part of princes than of common workmen. But, dangerous as these publications were, all attempts to check them proved entirely nugatory; for neither weight of evidence nor magnitude of delinquence had the slightest effect in inducing the juries to convict. The contest ere long assumed the most virulent aspect; the Government and Royalists felt that they had no chance of saving the monarchy but by a change in the Electoral Law; and the Liberals and revolutionists were resolute to prevent, at all hazards, any change in the present law, which promised so soon to subvert it.[3]

3 Cap. vi. 293, 294; Lam. vi. 237, 238; Lac. ii. 353.

These open incitements to assassination were not long of leading to the desired result; and a deplorable event plunged the royal family and Royalists in grief, and caused such consternation in the general mind as for a time made the balance incline in favor of conservative principles. The DUKE DE BERRI, second son of the Count d'Artois, had now become the chief hope of the royal family, because it was from him alone that a continuance of the direct line of succession could be looked for. This circumstance had given an importance to his position and an interest in his fate which could not otherwise have belonged to it. He was more gifted in heart and disposition than in external advantages. His figure was short, his shoulders broad, his lips thick, his nose *retroussé;* every thing in his appearance indicated a gay and sensual, rather than an intellectual and magnanimous disposition. But the sweetness of his smile, and the cordiality of his manner, revealed the native benevolence of his disposition, and speedily won every heart among those who approached him. He had all the hereditary courage of his race, and had sighed all his life for a share of the military fame which surrounded his country in a halo of glory, but from which his unfortunate position as a prince of the exiled family, and in arms against his compatriots, necessarily excluded him. He was not free from the foibles usual in princes in whom luxury has enhanced and idleness has afforded room for the gratification of the passions; but he caused them to be forgotten by the generous qualities with which they were accompanied. Constant in love, faithful in friendship, eager for renown, thirsting for arms, if he had not acquired military fame, it was not owing to any lack of ambition to prove himself the worthy descendant of Henry IV., but to the circumstances of his destiny, which had condemned him to inaction.[1]

31. The Duke de Berri.

1 Lam. vi. 239, 241; Biog. Univ. lvii. 82.

32. His biographical character.

Being the youngest of the princes of the blood, he came to play a more important part on the Restoration. He was the bridge of communication between the pacific family of the Bourbons and the army; and being himself passionately attached to the career of arms, he took to the soldiers as his natural element. He anxiously cultivated the friendship of the marshals, the generals, the officers—even the private soldiers attracted a large share of his attention; and before his career was cut short by the hand of an assassin, he had already made great progress in their affections. On the return of Napoleon from Elba, he was invested with the command of the army which was assembled round Paris; and when the retreat to Flanders was resolved on, he commanded the rear-guard, and by his personal courage and good conduct succeeded in escorting his precious charge in safety to the frontier, without having shed the blood of a Frenchman. At Bethune he advanced alone against a regiment of cavalry, and by his intrepid bearing imposed upon them submission. On the return to Paris after Waterloo, he continued his military habits, and many happy expressions are recorded of his, which strongly moved the hearts of the soldiers. He had been very kindly received by the inhabitants of Lisle, on the retreat to Ghent; and having been sent there after the second Restoration, the mutual transports were such, that on leaving them he said, "Henceforth it is between us for life and death." At the barracks in Paris, having one day fallen into conversation with a veteran of the Imperial army, he asked him why the soldiers loved Napoleon so much? "Because he always led us to victory," was the reply. "It was not very difficult to do so with men such as you," was the happy rejoinder of the prince, which proved that, besides the spirit, he had in some degree the felicity of expression of Henry IV. On the 28th March, 1816, a message from the king to both Chambers announced that the Duke de Berri was about to espouse CAROLINE MARY, eldest daughter of the heir to the crown of Naples—an event which was hailed with every demonstration of joy both by the Legislature and the people of France. The Chambers spontaneously made him a gift of 1,500,000 francs (£60,000), but he declared he would only accept to consecrate it to the departments which had suffered most during the dreadful scarcity of that year—a promise which he religiously performed. The marriage proved an auspicious one. The young princess won every heart by the elegance of her person and the engaging liveliness of her manner; and she gave proof that the direct line of succession was not likely to fail while her husband lived. The two first children of the marriage, the eldest of whom was a prince, died in early infancy; but the third, Princess Mary, who afterwards became Duchess of Parma, still survived, and the princess had been three months *enceinte* when the hand of an assassin deprived her of her husband, and induced a total change in the prospects and destinies of France. Never were severed married persons more tenderly attached, or on whose mutual safty more important consequences to the world were dependent.¹

> Chateaub.
> Mort. du
> Duc de
> Berri,
> Œuv. xvi.
> 282; Lam.
> vi. 239, 241.
> Lac. ii. 356,
> 356; Biog.
> Univ. lvm.
> 83, 84.

There lived at Paris at that time a man of the name of Louvel, whose biography is only of interest as indicating by what steps, and the indulgence of what propensities, and what opinions, men are conducted to the most atrocious crimes. He had been born at Versailles, in 1787, of humble parents, who made their bread by selling small-wares to the retainers of the palace. He had received the first rudiments of education, if education it could be called, amidst the fêtes of the Convention, where regicides were celebrated as the first of patriots, and the operatic worship of the theo-philanthropists, where universal liberation from restraint was preached as the obvious dictate and intention of nature. Solitary in his disposition, taciturn in his habits, he revolved these ideas in his mind without revealing them to any one, and they fermented so in his bosom that when Louis XVIII. landed at Calais, in 1814, he endeavored to get to the pier to assassinate him the instant he set foot on the soil of France. For several years after, he was so haunted by the desire to become a regicide, or at least signalize himself by the murder of a prince, that he was forced to move from place to place, to give a temporary distraction to his mind; and he went repeatedly to St. Germain, St. Cloud, and Fontainebleau to seek an opportunity of doing so. He was long disappointed, and had hovered about the opera for many nights, when the Duke de Berri was there, in hopes of finding the means of striking his victim, when, on the 13th February, 1820, chance threw the long-wished-for opportunity in his way.¹

> ¹ Lam. vi.
> 244, 247.
> Lac. ii. 356,
> 357.

On that day, being the last of the carnival, the Duke de Berri was at the opera with the princess; and Louvel lurked about the door, armed with a small sharp poniard, with which he had previously provided himself. He was at the door when the prince entered the house, and might have struck him as he handed the princess out of the carriage; but a lingering feeling of conscience withheld his hand at that time. But the fatal moment ere long arrived. During the interval of two of the pieces, the Duke and Duchess left their own box to pay a visit to that of the Duke and Duchess of Orleans, who, with their whole family, destined to such eventful changes in future times, were in a box in the neighborhood. On returning to her own box, the door of another one was suddenly opened, and struck the side of the Duchess de Berri, who, being apprehensive of the effects of any shock in her then delicate situation, expressed a wish to the prince to leave the house and return home. The prince at once agreed, and handed the Duchess into her carriage. "Adieu!" cried she, smiling to her husband, "we shall soon meet again." They parted, but it was to be reunited in another world. As the prince was returning from the carriage to the house, Louvel, who was standing in the shade of a projecting part of the wall, so still that he had escaped the notice both of the sentinels on duty and the footmen of the Duke, rushed suddenly forward, and seizing with his left arm the left shoulder of the prince, struck him violently with the right arm on the right side with the poniard. So instantaneous was the act that the assassin escaped in the dark; and the Duke, who only felt, as is often the case, a violent blow, and not the stab, put his hand to the spot struck. He then felt the hilt of the dagger, which was still sticking in his side; and being then made aware he had been stabbed, he exclaimed, "I am assassin ated; I am dead; I have the poniard; that man has killed me!"²

> ² Lam. vi.
> 233, 235;
> Lac. ii. 359,
> 360; Biog.
> Univ. lvm.
> 84, 85.

34.
Assassination of the Duke de Berri.

The princess was just driving from the door of the opera-house when the frightful words reached her ear. She immediately gave a piercing shriek, heard above all the din of the street, and loudly called out to her servants to stop and let her out. They did so, and the moment the door was opened, before the steps were let down, she sprung out of the carriage and clasped her husband in her arms, who was covered with blood, and just drawing the dagger from his side. "I am dead!" said he; "send for a priest. Come, dearest!—let me die in your arms." Meanwhile the assassin, in the first moments of terror and agitation, had made his escape, and he had already reached the arcade which branches off from the Rue de Richelieu, under the spacious arches of the Bibliothèque du Roi, when a waiter in a coffee-house, named Pauloise, hearing the alarm, seized, and was still writhing

35.
His last moments.

with him, when three gendarmes came up, and having apprehended, brought him back to the door of the opera-house. He was there nearly torn in pieces by the crowd, which was inflamed with the most violent indignation; but the gendarmes succeeded with great difficulty in extricating him, being fearful that the secrets of an extended conspiracy would perish with him. Meanwhile the prince had been carried into a little apartment behind his box, and the medical men were arriving in haste. On being informed of the arrest of the assassin, he exclaimed, "Alas! how cruel is it to die by the hand of a Frenchman!" For a few minutes a ray of hope was felt by the medical attendants, and illuminated every visage in the apartment; but the dying man did not partake the illusion, and fearing to augment the sufferings of the princess by the blasting of vain expectations, he said, "No! I am not deceived: the poniard has entered to the hilt, I can assure you. Caroline, are you there?" "Yes," exclaimed the princess, subduing her sobs, "and will never quit you." His domestic surgeon, M. Bougon, was sucking the wound to restore the circulation, which was beginning to fail. "What are you doing?" exclaimed the prince: "for God-sake, stop; perhaps the poniard was poisoned."

<sup>1 Lam. vi.
4, 257;
Derniers
Moments
du Duc de
Berri, 32,
42. Biog.
Univ. lxviii.
64.</sup>

The Bishop of Chartres, his father's confessor, at length arrived, and had a few minutes' private conversation with the dying man, from which he seemed to derive much consolation. He asked for his infant daughter, who was brought to him, still asleep. "Poor child!" exclaimed he, laying his hand on her head, "may you be less unfortunate than the rest of your family." The chief surgeon, Dupuytren, resolved to try, as a last resource, to open and enlarge the wound, to allow the blood, which had begun to impede respiration, to flow externally. He bore the operation with firmness—his hand, already clammy with the sweat of death, still clasping that of the Duchess. After it was over, he said, "Spare me any further pain, since I must die." Then caressing the head of his beloved wife, whose beautiful locks had so often awakened his admiration, "Caroline," said he, "take care of yourself, for the sake of our infant which you bear in your bosom." The Duke and Duchess of Orleans had been in the apartment from the time the prince was brought in, and the king, the Duke d'Angoulême, and the rest of the royal family, arrived while he was still alive. "Who is the man who has killed me?" said he: "I should wish to see him, in order to inquire into his motives: perhaps it is some one whom I have unconsciously offended." The Count d'Artois assured him that the assassin had no personal animosity against him. "Would that I may live long enough to ask his pardon from the king," said the worthy descendant of Saint Louis. "Promise me, my father—promise me, my brother, to ask of the king the life of that man."

36. His last moments.

<sup>2 Lam. vi.
259, 261,
Biog. Univ.
lvii. 65,
Derniers
Moments
du Duc de
Berri, 45,
51.</sup>

But the supreme hour soon approached: all the resources of art could not long avert the stroke of fate. The opening of the wound had only for a brief period relieved the accumulation of blood within the breast, and symptoms of suffocation approached. Then, on a few words interchanged between him and the Duchess, two illegitimate children which he had had in London, of a faithful companion in misfortune, and whom both had brought up at Paris with the utmost kindness, were brought into the room. As they knelt at his side, striving to stifle their sobs in his bloody garments, he said, embracing them with tenderness, "I know you sufficiently, Caroline, to be assured you will take care, after me, of these orphans." With the instinct of a noble mind, she took her own infant from Madame de Gontaut, who held it in her arms, and, taking the children of the stranger by the hand, said to them, "Kiss your sister." The prince confessed soon after to the Bishop of Chartres, and received absolution. "My God," said he, at several responses, "pardon me, and pardon him who has taken my life." It was announced that several of the marshals had arrived, eager to testify their interest and affliction. "Ah!" he exclaimed, "I had hoped to have shed my blood more usefully in the midst of them for France." But still the pardon of his murderer chiefly engrossed his thoughts. When the trampling of the horses on the pavement announced the approach of the king, he testified the utmost joy; and when the monarch entered the apartment, his first words were, "My uncle, give me your hand, that I may kiss it for the last time;" and then added with earnestness, still holding the hand, "I entreat of you, in the name of my death, the life of that man." "You are not so ill as you suppose," answered Louis; "we will speak of it again." "Ah!" exclaimed the dying man, with a mournful accent, "you do not say Yes; say it, I beseech you, that I may die in peace." In vain they tried to turn his thoughts to other subjects. "Ah!" said he, with his last breath, "the life of that man would have softened my last moments! If, at least, I could depart with the belief that the blood of that man would not flow afterwy death." With these words he expired, and his soul winged its way to heaven, having left the prayer for mercy and forgiveness as its last bequest to earth.¹

37. His death.

<sup>1 Lam. vi.
263, 264;
Biog. Univ.
lviii. 65,66;
Derniers
Moments
du Duc de
Berri, 64,
72.</sup>

No words can convey an idea of the impression which the death of the Duke de Berri produced in France. Coming at a time of increasing political excitement, when the minds of men were already shaken by a vague disquietude, and the apprehension of great and approaching but unknown change, it excited a universal consternation. The obviously political character of the blow struck magnified tenfold its force. Leveled at the heir of the monarchy, and the only prince from whom a continuance of the direct line of succession could be hoped, it seemed at one stroke to destroy the hopes of an heir to the throne, and to leave the nation a prey to all the evils of an uncertain future and a disputed succession. Pity for the victim of political fanaticism, admiration for the magnanimity and lofty spirit of his death, mingled with apprehensions for themselves, and a mortal terror of the revolutionary convulsions which

38. Immense sensation which it produced.

might be expected from a repetition of the blows of which this was the first. The public consternation manifested itself in the most unequivocal ways. All the theatres—and that, in Paris, was a decisive symptom—were closed. The balls of the carnival were interrupted; and it was decreed by the Government, with the general consent of the people, that the opera-house should be removed from the spot where the execrable crime had been committed, and an expiatory monument erected on its site. But these changes did not adequately express the public feelings. They exhaled in transports of indignation against the rashness of the ministries whose measures had brought matters to such a point, and the incapacity of the police, which had permitted the crime to be committed; and it was loudly proclaimed, that an entire change of government and measures had become indispensable, if the monarchy was to be saved from perdition.[1]

[1] Lam. vi. 264, 266. Lac. ii. 366, 359; Biog. Univ. lvii. 83.

33. Chateaubriand's words on the occasion.

"The hand," said Chateaubriand, "which delivered the blow is not the most guilty. Those who have really assassinated the Duke de Berri are those who, for four years, have labored to establish democratic laws in the monarchy; those who have banished religion from our laws; those who have recalled the murderers of Louis XVI.; those who have heard, with indifference, impunity for regicides discussed at the tribune; those who have allowed the journals to preach up the sovereignty of the people, insurrection, and murder, without making any use of the laws intended for their repression; those who have favored every false doctrine; those who have rewarded treason and punished fidelity; those who have filled up all employments with the enemies of the Bourbons, and the creatures of Bonaparte; those who, pressed by the public indignation, have promised to repeal a fatal law, and have done nothing during three months, apparently to give the Revolutionists time to sharpen their poniards. These are the true murderers of the Duke de Berri. It is no longer time to dissemble; the revolution we have so often predicted has already commenced, and it has already produced irreparable evils. Who can restore life to the Duke de Berri, or give us back the hopes which love and glory had wound up with his august person? Surprise is expressed that a poniard should have been raised; but the real subject of wonder is, that a thousand poniards have not been leveled at the breasts of our princes. During four years we have overwhelmed with rewards those who preach up an agrarian law, a republic, and assassination; we have excited those who have nothing against those who have something; him who is born in a humble class against him to whom misfortune has left nothing but a name; we have permitted public opinion to be disquieted by phantoms, and represented a part of the nation as set on re-establishing rights forever abolished, institutions forever overturned. If we are not plunged in the horrors of external or civil war, it is not the fault of the administration which has just expired."[2]

[2] Chateaub. Feb. 18, and March 3, 1820.— Œuvres, xi. 286, 291.

When language so violent as this was used in the midst of the crisis, by so distinguished a writer as the Viscount Chateaubriand, it may be supposed that inferior authors were still more impassioned in their strictures. The clamor became so violent that no ministry could stand against it. An untoward incident, which occurred while the Duke de Berri yet lived, tended to augment the public feeling on the subject. Entering the room in which Louvel was detained, M. Decazes was seized with a sudden suspicion that the dagger might have been poisoned; and thinking, if so, an antidote might be applied, and possibly the life of the prince saved, he had whispered in his ear. "Miserable man! a confession remains for you to make, which may save the life of your victim, and lessen your crime before God. Tell the truth sincerely to me, and me alone—was the dagger poisoned?" "It was not," replied the assassin coldly, with the accent of truth. The words spoken on either side were not heard; but the fact of M. Decazes having whispered something to Louvel, during his first interrogatory, became known, and was seized upon and magnified by all the eagerness of faction. It was immediately bruited abroad that the minister had enjoined silence to the assassin, and thence it was concluded he had been his accomplice. So readily was this atrocious calumny received in the excited state of the public mind, and so eagerly was it seized upon by the vehemence of faction, that next day M. Clausel de Coussergues, a Royalist of the extreme Right, a respectable man, but of an impassioned temperament and credulous disposition, said in the Chamber of Deputies, "There is no law which prescribes the mode of impeaching ministers; but justice requires it should be done in public sitting, and in the face of France. I propose to the chamber to institute a prosecution against M. Decazes, Minister of the Interior, as accomplice in the assassination." The Chamber revolted against such an accusation, and only twenty-five voices supported it. General Foy said, "If such an event is deplorable for all, it is in an especial manner so for the friends of freedom, since there can be no doubt that their adversaries will take advantage of this execrable crime to wrest from the nation the liberties which the king has bestowed upon it, and which he is so anxious to maintain."[1]

40. General indignation against M. Decazes.

[1] Lam. vi. 268, 273; Cap. vi. 305, 306; Ann. Hist. iii. 32, 33.

From the moment when the Duke de Berri breathed his last, the king foresaw the immense advantage it would give to the ultra-Royalists, and the efforts they would make to force him to abandon the system of government and the public servants to whom he was so much attached. "My child," said he to M. Decazes next day, "the *ultras* are preparing against us a terrible war; they will make the most of my grief. It is not your system that they will attack—it is mine; it is not at you their blows are leveled—it is at me." "Should your Majesty," answered M. Decazes, "deem my retiring for the good of your service, I am ready to resign, though grieved to think my retreat will lead to such fatal consequences."

41. The king resolves to support him.

"I insist upon your remaining," replied the monarch; "they shall not separate you from me." Then, after weeping in common over the deplorable event which had altered the destinies of France, and let loose the parties who tore its entrails with such fury against each other, they agreed on the measures to be adopted in consequence;¹ and these were, that the Chamber of Peers should be summoned as a supreme court to try the assassin of the Duke de Berri; and that laws, restrictive of the license of the press, and giving the Government extraordinary powers of arrest, and modifying the Electoral Law, should be introduced into the Lower Chamber.

But how determined soever the king might be to support his favorite minister and system of government, the tide of public feeling soon became so strong that it was impossible to resist it. The terrible words of M. de Chateaubriand regarding M. Decazes in the *Conservateur*, "His feet have slipped in blood," vibrated in every heart. The accusation against him, though quashed in the Chamber of Deputies, and repudiated by every unprejudiced mind, still hung over him in general opinion. People did not believe him guilty, but he had been openly accused, and no proof of his innocence had been adduced. The agitation of the public mind was indescribable, and soon assumed such a magnitude as portended great changes, and is always found, for good or for evil, to be irresistible. The terrible nature of the catastrophe—its irreparable consequences on the future of the monarchy—the chances of future and unknown dangers which it had induced, were obvious to every apprehension. Every one trembled for his fortune, his life; a few for the public liberties. The Liberals became subdued and downcast, the Royalists vehement and exulting. Matters were at last brought to a crisis by a conversation which ensued between the king and the principal members of the royal family. The Count d'Artois demanded the dismissal of the prime minister, and a change in the system of government. "We are hastening to a revolution, sire," said the Duchess d'Angoulême, "but there is still time to arrest it. M. Decazes has injured the Royalists too deeply for any accommodations to take place between them: let him cease to be a member of your Cabinet, and all will hasten to tender to you their services." "I do not suppose," replied the king, "that you propose to force my will: it belongs to me alone to determine the policy of my government." "It is impossible for me," rejoined the Count d'Artois, "to remain at the Tuileries when M. Decazes, openly accused of the murder of my son, sits at the council: I beseech you to allow me to retire to Compiègne." The Duchess d'Angoulême united her instances to those of the Count d'Artois, and at length the king, dreading a total rupture of the royal family, said, "You are determined on it: well, we shall see you all shall be satisfied."²

When M. Decazes heard of the result of this conference, he saw it was no longer possible to maintain his position, and he accordingly sent in his resignation. The king, deeply affected, felt himself constrained to receive it. "My child," said he, "it is not against you, but against me that the stroke is directed. The Pavillon Marsan would deprive me of all power. I will not have M. de Talleyrand; the Duke de Richelieu alone shall replace you. Go and convince him of the necessity of his agreeing to the sacrifice which I demand of him. As for you, I shall show these gentlemen that you have in noways lost my confidence." The Duke de Richelieu accordingly was commissioned to form a ministry, but he evinced the utmost repugnance at undertaking the task, and it was only at the earnest solicitation of the king, and as a matter of patriotic duty, that he at length agreed. M. Siméon was made Minister of the Interior, and M. Portalis under-secretary to the Minister of Justice. No other changes were made in the Cabinet; and M. Decazes was appointed embassador at London, with magnificent allowances. He was so far from losing his influence, however, by his departure, that the king corresponded with him almost daily after he was settled in London. The Duke de Richelieu made the absolute and unconditional support of the Royalists a condition of his taking office, and this the Count d'Artois engaged to secure;¹ and as a pledge of the cordiality of the alliance, M. Capelle, his private secretary, was made principal secretary to the Minister of the Interior. The Ministry therefore was materially modified by the introduction of Royalist members, though it still retained, as a whole, its Liberal character. But a still more material change took place at this period in the private disposition of the king, owing to a change of favorites, which materially influenced his policy during the remainder of his reign.

Although the age and infirmities of the king prevented him from becoming the slave of the passions which had disgraced so many of his race, and his disposition had always made him more inclined to the pleasures of the table than to those of love, yet he was by no means insensible to female charms, and extremely fond of the conversation of elegant and well-informed women. He piqued himself, though neither young nor handsome, upon his power of rendering himself agreeable to them in the way which he alone desired, which was within the limits of Platonic attachment. He had a remarkable facility in expressing himself, both verbally and in writing, in elegant and complimentary language toward them: he spent several hours every day in this refined species of trifling, and prided himself as much on the turn of his flattery in notes to ladies, as on the charter which was to give liberty to France and peace to Europe. Aware of this disposition on the part of the sovereign, the Royalists, in whose saloons such a person was most likely to be found, had for long been on the look-out for some lady attached to their principles, who might win the confidence of Louis, and insensibly insinuate her ideas on politics in the midst of the complimentary trifling or unreserved confidence of the boudoir. Such a person was found in a young and beautiful woman then in Paris, who united a graceful exterior to great powers of conversation, and an entire command of diplomatic tact and address; and to her influence the future policy of his reign is in a great degree to be traced.[1]

[1] Lam. vi. 279, 280.

45. The Countess Du Cayla.

Madame, the Countess Du Cayla, was the daughter of M. Talon, who held a respectable position in the ancient magistracy of France, and had taken an active part, in concert with Mirabeau and the Count de la Marche, in the intrigues which preceded the Revolution. He was said to be possessed of some valuable papers, implicating Louis XVIII., then Count of Provence, in the affair for which the Marquis de Favras suffered death in 1789, and these had descended after his decease to his daughter. She had been brought up in the school of diplomacy under Madame Campan, and was intimate both with the Empress Joséphine, and Hortense Queen of Holland, since Duchess of St. Leu. She was married early in life to an old man of fortune, whose temper was soon found to be incompatible with her own, and having separated from him, without reproach, after the French fashion, she was living without scandal in the family of the Prince of Condé, with whose natural daughter, the Countess de Rully, she was intimate, when the Royalist leaders cast their eyes upon her as a person likely to confirm their ascendency in the royal councils.[2]

[2] Lam. vi. 281, 282.

46. Her first interview with Louis, which proves successful.

The Viscount de la Rochefoucauld was the person intrusted with the management of this delicate affair, and he did so with great tact and address. He first impressed upon the young and charming countess that she would confer inestimable services on the cause of religion and her country if she would take advantage of the gift of pleasing which Providence had bestowed upon her, and reclaim the sovereign to the system of government which would alone secure the interests of his religion, his people, or his family.* The mind of Madame Du Cayla, as her published letters demonstrate, at once pious and tender, and endowed with a reach of thought equal to either Madame de Sévigné or the Princess des Ursins, readily embraced the duty thus assigned to her by the political party to which she was attached. "It was necessary," said she afterward, playfully, "to have an Esther for that Ahasuerus." The next point was to throw her in the king's way, and this was easily brought about by the unfortunate circumstances in which she was placed. Her husband, with whom she had come to open rupture, at once claimed her fortune, and insisted upon obtaining delivery of her children; and the disconsolate mother solicited an interview with Louis, to throw herself at his feet, and solicit his interest and support in the difficult circumstances in which she was placed. The king granted it, and the result was entirely successful. Dazzled by her beauty, captivated by her grace, impressed by her talents, melted by her tears, the king promised to aid her to the utmost of his power, and invited her to a second interview. So great was the ascendency which her genius and charms of manner soon gave her, that she became necessary to the monarch, who spent several hours every day in her society, without any of the scandal arising which in ordinary cases follows such interviews. Great was the effect of this secret influence on the future destinies of France, especially after the removal of M. Decazes to London had removed the chief counterpoise on the other side.[1]

[1] Lettres de Madame Du Cayla, 39, 94; Lam. vi. 281, 296.

47. Character of M. Decazes.

Thus fell, never again to rise, M. Decazes; for though he was appointed embassador to London, and retained the confidence of the king, yet he never again formed part of the Ministry, and his career as a public man was at an end. It is impossible to deny that he was possessed of considerable abilities. No man raises himself from a humble station to the rule of empire, without being possessed of some talents, which, if they are not of the first order, are at least of the most marketable description. It is generally characters of that description which are most successful in maintaining themselves long at the head of affairs. Genius anticipates the march of events, and is often shipwrecked because the world is behind its views; heroism recoils from the concessions requisite for success, and fails to conquer, because it disdains to stoop. It is pliant ability which discerns the precise mode of elevation, and adopts the principles requisite for immediate success. M. Decazes had this pliant ability in the very highest degree. Discerning in character, he at once scanned the king's disposition, and perceived the foibles which required to be attended to in order to gain his confidence. Able in the conduct of affairs, he made himself serviceable in his employment, and attracted his notice by the valuable information which he communicated, both in his own department and that of others. Energetic and ready in the tribune, he defended

* "Louis a besoin d'aimer ceux à qui il permet de le conseiller, son cœur est pour moitié dans la politique. Madame de Balbi, M. Duvarny, M. de Blacas autrefois, M. Decazes aujourd'hui, sont les preuves encore vivantes de cette disposition de sa nature. Il faut lui plaire pour avoir le droit de l'influencer. Des femmes illustres par leur crédit, utile ou funeste, sur le cœur et sur l'esprit de nos rois, ont tour à tour perdu ou sauvé la royauté en France et en Espagne. C'est d'une femme seule aujourd'hui que peut venir le salut de la religion et de la monarchie. La nature, la naissance, l'éducation, le malheur même, semblent vous avoir designée pour ce rôle. Voulez-vous être le salut des princes, l'âme du roi, l'Esther des royalistes, la Mauténon femme et irréprochable d'une cour qui se perd et qu'une femme peut reconduire et sauver? Demandez au roi une audience sous prétexte d'implorer sa protection dont vous avez besoin pour vous et pour vos enfants. Montrez-lui comme par hasard ces trésors de grâce, de bon sens, et d'esprit que la nature vous a prodigués, non pour l'oubli en la retraite, mais pour l'entretien d'un roi appréciateur passionné, des dons de l'âme; charmez-le par une première conversation; retournez quand il vous rappellera; et quand votre empire inaperçu sera fondé dans un attachement par les habitudes, employez peu à peu cet empire à détourner de son conseil le favori dont il est fasciné, et à réconcilier le roi avec son frère, avec les princes, et à lui faire adopter de concert, dans la personne de M. de Villèle, et de ses amis, un ministère à la fois royaliste et constitutionnel qui retienne le trône à plomb sur la base monarchique, et qui prévienne les prochaines catastrophes dont le trône est menacé."—*Paroles de M. de la Rochefoucauld à Madame la Comtesse Du Cayla.* LAMARTINE, *Hist. de la Restauration*, vi. 290, 292.

the ministerial measures with vigor and success against the numerous attacks with which they were assailed.

48. Merits of his measures as a statesman.

He acquired the surprising ascendency which he gained over the mind of the king mainly by studying his disposition, and proposing measures in the Cabinet which were in a manner the reflection of those which he perceived were already contemplated in the royal breast; but the temporary success which they met with proved that both had correctly discerned, if not the ultimate consequences of their measures, at least the immediate signs of the times. The Royalists justly reproach him with having established, by the royal authority, an electoral system of the most democratic character, and thrown himself into the arms of the Liberals, who made use of the advantage thus gained to undermine the monarchy. But, in justice to him, it must be recollected that the working of representative governments was then very little understood, and the practical results of changes, now obvious to all, were then only discerned by a few; that his situation was one surrounded with difficulties, and in which any false step might lead to perdition; and that if the course he pursued was one which entailed ultimate dangers of the most serious kind on the monarchy, it was, perhaps, the only one which enabled it to shun the immediate perils with which it was threatened. In common with the king, his leading idea was reconciliation; his principle, concession; his policy, to disarm opposition by anticipating its demands. This view was a benevolent and amiable one, but unfortunately more suited to the Utopia of Sir Thomas More than the storm-beaten monarchy of the Bourbons; and experience has proved that such a policy, in presence of an ambitious and unscrupulous enemy, only postpones the danger to aggravate it.

49. Division of parties in the Assembly after M. Decazes' fall.

The Assembly, by the fall of M. Decazes, and the infusion of Royalist members into the Cabinet, was divided differently from what it had hitherto been. The intermediate third party was extinguished by the fall of M. Decazes. Royalists and Liberals now formed two great parties which divided the whole Assembly between them—the Centre all adhered to the Right or Left. This circumstance rendered the situation of the Ministry more perilous in the outset, but more secure in the end; it was more difficult for them to gain a majority in the first instance, but, once gained, it was more likely to adhere permanently to them. It is a great evil, both for Government and Opposition, to have a third party between them, the votes of which may cast their balance either way; for it imposed upon both the necessity of often departing from their principles, and avoiding immediate defeat by permanently degrading themselves in the eyes of the country. The Doctrinaires all retired with their chief, M. Decazes, but they voted on important questions with the new Ministry; and the abilities of M. Guizot, M. de Staël, M. de Barante, and M. de Saint Aulaire, who formed the strength of that party,[1] were too well known not to make their adhesion a matter of eager solicitation

[1] Cap. v. 334, 337; Lam. vi. 312, 314; Lac. ii. 291, 294.

and no slight manœuvring, on both sides of the Assembly

Two painful scenes took place before the measures of the new Ministers were brought forward in the Chamber of Deputies—the funeral of the Duke de Berri, and the trial and execution of his assassin. The body of the prince was laid in state for several days in the Louvre, and afterward carried with every possible magnificence to the ancestral but now untenanted vaults of Saint-Denis. The king, accompanied by the Duke and Duchess of Angoulême, attended the mournful ceremony, which was celebrated with every circumstance of external splendor which could impress the imagination, and every reality of woe which could melt the heart:

50. Funeral of the Duke de Berri, and execution of Louvel, March 14.

"When a prince to the fate of a peasant has yielded,
  The tapestry waves dark in the dim-lighted hall;
With scutcheons of silver the coffin is shielded,
  And pages stand mute by the canopied pall;
Through the courts at deep midnight the torches are gleaming,
In the proudly-arched chapel the banners are beaming,
Far adown the long aisles sacred music is streaming,
  Lamenting a chief of the people should fall."

Such was the emotion of the Duchess d'Angoulême at witnessing such a scene in such a place, that she sunk senseless on the pavement. One only ray of hope remained to the royal family, arising from the situation of the Duchess de Berri, which gave hopes that an heir might yet be preserved for the monarchy, and the hopes of the assassin blasted. That fanatical wretch was brought to trial, and condemned on the clearest evidence, fortified by his own confession. He admitted the enormity of his crime, but still insisted that on public grounds it was justifiable.* His answers, when interrogated, evinced the deplorable atheism in which the dreams of the Revolution ended. "I was sometimes a Catholic," said he, "sometimes a theophilanthropist." "Do you not fear the Divine justice?" asked the Prévost de Montmorency. "God is a mere name," replied the assassin. He was executed on the 7th June, and evinced on the scaffold the same strange indifference which had characterized his demeanor ever since the murder.[1]

[1] Moniteur, June 8, 1820; Ann. Hist. iii. 129; Lac. ii. 363, 391.

The first measures of the new Ministers were directed to the prosecution of the measures prepared by the former ones, arming Government with extraordinary powers of arrest, and restraining the licentiousness of the press. Much difficulty was at first experienced in arranging terms of accommodation with the Royalists on the right, so as to secure a majority in the Chambers, but at length the terms were agreed on; and these were, that the powers of arrest were to be conferred on Government for a limited period, that the press was to be restrained, and that a new electoral law was to be introduced, restoring the double step in elections. Nothing could equal the vehemence with which these laws were assailed

51. Ministerial measures of the session. Argument against the first.

* "C'était une action horrible, c'est vrai," disait Louvel, "quand on tue un autre homme: cela ne peut passer pour vertu, c'est un crime. Je n'y aurais jamais été entraîne sans l'intérêt que je prenais à la nation suivant moi; je croyais bien faire suivant mon idée."—Moniteur, June 4, 1820; Procès de Louvel, 37.

by the Opposition, when they were introduced. That on the law of arrest was the first that came under discussion. "It belongs to the wisdom of the Chambers," said General Foy and Benjamin Constant, "to defend a throne which misfortune has rendered more august and more dear to fidelity. Let us beware lest, in introducing a law more odious than useful, we substitute for the present public grief other grounds of discontent which may cause the first to be forgotten. The prince whom we mourn pardoned with his dying breath his infamous assassin. Let us take care that the example of that sublime death is not lost for the nation, the royal family, and the public morality; that posterity may not reproach us with having sacrificed the public liberties on a hecatomb at the funeral of a Bourbon.

"The abyss of a counter-revolution is about to open: a system is announced which will attack successively all our rights, all the guarantees which the nation sighed for in vain in 1789, and hailed with such gratitude in 1814. The régime of 1788 is to be revived by the three laws which are proposed at the same time, the first reviving *lettres de cachet*, the second establishing the slavery of the press, the third fettering the organs of freedom whom it sends to the Chamber. Experience has demonstrated in every age, and more especially in the disastrous epoch of the Revolution, that if a government once yields to a party, that party will not fail soon to subjugate it. The present time affords a proof of it. The barrier, feeble and tottering as it was, which the Ministry opposed to the counter-revolution, shakes, and is about to be thrown down. Perhaps the Ministry does not at this moment foresee it; but all the laws which you are called on now to pass, will be turned to the profit of the counter-revolution, and that principle is to be applied to the proposed law, compared to that of 1817. That which in 1817 was, from the pressure of circumstances, merely irregular, will in 1820 be terrible; that which in 1817 was only vicious in principle, will in 1820 become terrible in its application."

52. *Continued.*

¹ An. Hist. iii. 61, 81. Lac. ii. 397, 398.

On the other hand, it was answered by the Duke de Richelieu and the Duke de Fitz-james, on the part of the Government: "Is it possible that any one can be so blind to existing circumstances, and the dangers which menace the state and the royal family? Does any one persist in asserting that the assassination of the 13th February is an isolated act? Have the persons who assert this been shut up in their houses for the last six months? What! are those ferocious songs, repeated night after night with such perseverance that the indulgent police have at length come to pretend that they do not hear them, nothing?—those songs which commenced on the very night of the assassination, and which they had the effrontery to repeat under the windows of the Duchess de Berri herself! What! those placards, those menaces, those anonymous letters —not to us, who are accustomed to, and disregard them, but to her for whom they know we are disposed to sacrifice a thousand times our lives—those execrable threats against a bereaved father, whose grief would have melted tigers, but has only increased the thirst for blood in our revolutionary tigers. What! those medals, struck with the name of Marie Louise and her son—their images sent every where through the kingdom, and now paraded even in the capital; those clubs, in which they count us on our benches, and have a poniard ready for each of our breasts; the coincidence of what passes in the nations around us with what we witness in our interior—the assassination by Sand, the attempted assassination of Thistlewood, repetitions abroad of what was going on in our interior—homicide and regicide converted into virtues, and recommended as deeds worthy of eternal glory. What! Spain become the prey of a military faction, and of acts of treason which have dishonored the name of a soldier. Are these not proofs of a conspiracy extending over all western Europe, which is advancing with rapid strides toward its maturity?" So obvious were these dangers, that, notwithstanding a vehement outcry in both houses, the proposed law was passed by considerable majorities, the numbers in the Chamber of Deputies being 134 to 113; in the Peers, 121 to 86!¹

53. *Answer by the Government.*

¹ An. Hist. iii. 61, 82. Lac. ii. 399, 400. Cap. vi 345, 356.

The law re-establishing the censorship of the press excited a still more violent storm in the Chambers. As a prelude to it, the most extraordinary ferment took place in the public journals, which nearly unanimously assailed the proposed measure with a degree of vehemence unexampled even in those days of rival governments and desperate party contests. On the one hand, it was said by M. Manuel, M. Lafayette, and M. Camille-Jourdan: "The censorship is essentially partial; it has always been so, and it is impossible it should be otherwise, for it is absolute government in practice. You have already suspended individual liberty, and you are now about to add to the rigor of arbitrary detention by the censure, for you render it impossible for the Ministers to be made aware of their error. You ask for examples of the abuse of the censorship; they are innumerable: the most arbitrary spirit prevailed when it was last established, for they erased even the speeches of your own colleagues, when they were in defense against attacks. To what do you aspire with these ill-timed attempts at repression? To extinguish the volcano? Do you not know that the flame is extending beneath your feet, and that, if you do not give it an adequate means of escape, it will occasion an explosion which will destroy you all? While the liberty of Europe is advancing with the steps of a giant, and when France wishes, and ought to be at the head of that great development of the dignity and faculties of man, a government, to whom, indeed, hypocrisy can no longer be objected, is endeavoring to drag you into a backward course, and to widen more and more the breach which already yawns in the nation. Whither are we tending? You accumulate *lettres de cachet* and censors! I am no panegyrist of the English government, but I do not believe that any minister could be found so bold as to propose,

51. *Censorship of the press. Arguments against it by the Opposition.*

in that country, at the same time, the censorship of the press, and the suspension of the Habeas Corpus Act.

"To prevent is not to repress, say the partisans of the censorship. Never was a more deplorable illusion. To subject the journals to such fetters is to strike at the liberty of the press in its very heart. The liberty of the periodical press is the life-blood of freedom. Vigilant advanced guards, ever-wakeful sentinels, their sheets are to representative governments what language is to man. They serve as the medium of communication between distant places, whose interests are the same; they leave no opinion without defense, no abuse in the shade, no injustice without an avenger. The Government is not less aided by its efforts. The Ministry know beforehand what it has to hope or to fear; the people, who are their friends, and who their enemies; and to them we owe that early communication of intelligence, and that rapid expression of wishes, which is an advantage which nothing else can supply. Attack openly the liberty of the press, or respect that of the public journals; but recollect that the charter has not separated them, and that it has withdrawn both alike from every species of censorship. This is not a question of principle; it is a question of life or death. We have arrived at that point, that if our personal freedom, the liberty of the press, and the liberty of elections, are taken away, the charter has become a mockery, the constitutional monarchy is at an end. Nothing remains for us but anarchy or despotism. Power will rest with the strongest; and if so, woe to the feeble majority in this Chamber which now directs it. Nothing can long remain strong which is not national. Do not denationalize the throne; if you do so, your majority will soon be broken to pieces."¹

On the other hand, it was contended by Baron Pasquier and Count Siméon: "It is books, and not pamphlets, which have enlightened the world. Cast your eyes on the condition to which the unrestricted liberty of the journals has brought society, and every where you will see the passions roused to the highest degree, hatreds envenomed, the poniards of vengeance sharpened—and the horrible catastrophe which we all deplore is a direct consequence of it. Consider the character of that crime: one special character distinguishes it, and that is fanaticism. But what sort of fanaticism? Every age has had its own, and ours is not less clearly defined than that which, two hundred years ago, sharpened the dagger of Ravaillac. It is not now the pulpit, it is the journals which encourage fanaticism; it is no longer religious, but political. Where are the organs of that fanaticism which threatens to tear society in pieces to be found? By whom is it cherished, flattered, exalted? Who can deny that it is the journals and periodical publications that do this? Men eminent for their talents, respectable for their virtues, influential from their position, have not disdained to descend into this arena, and to employ their great abilities to move the people. Others, borrowing every mask, have learned and employed every art to turn to their advantage the most shameful projects, the most infamous objects which the heart of man can harbor. Such is the government of journals; powerful to destroy, they are powerless to save. They have destroyed the Constitution of 1791, which gave them liberty; they destroyed that Convention which made the world tremble.

"We are told that the liberty of the press is the soul of representative governments. Doubtless it is so; but it is not less true than the licentiousness of the press is its most mortal enemy. I do not hesitate to assert there is no political system sufficiently strong to bear the attacks which it has now come to organize among us. Possibly the time may come when, as in England, it may be practicable to establish fully the liberty of the press among us; but unquestionably that time has not yet arrived. The event we all deplore, the universal *débâcle* of violence which has succeeded it, is a sufficient proof of this. In the mean time, Government, without the aid of extraordinary powers, can not command a remedy for these evils; it has not, and should not have, any influence over the tribunals; the dependence of magistrates would degrade, unsuccessful prosecutions weaken it; verdicts of juries, so powerful on public opinion, might destroy it. In a word, it is necessary to supply the deficiency of *repressive*, by augmenting the strength of *preventive* checks; and this can only be done by the censorship. It is in vain to object to such a power, that it may be converted into the arm of a party. Doubtless it might be so; but that party is the party of France—of the Bourbons—of the charter of freedom. That party must be allowed to triumph, for it is that of regular government. The time has arrived when we must say to the people, 'The danger with which you are menaced does not come from your governors; it comes from yourselves—from the factions, in whose eyes nothing is fixed, nothing sacred, and which, abandoned to their senseless furies, would not scruple to trample every law under their feet. It is from them that we must wrest their arms, under pain of perishing in case of failure, for they aim at nothing short of universal ruin.'"¹

The Doctrinaires, who felt that their influence was mainly dependent on strength of intellect, and dreaded any restriction upon its expression, almost all voted against the Government on this occasion in the Chamber of Deputies; and in the Peers, M. de Chateaubriand, whose ardent genius revolted at the idea of restraint, was also ranged against them. The Right Centre, however, with that exception, nearly unanimously adhered; and the result showed how nearly the parties were balanced, now that the Chamber was divided into two only. In the Peers the numbers were 106 to 104; in the lower house, 136 to 110.² It is remarkable that, on so vital a point for public freedom, the majority was so much greater in the Commons than the Peers. On the day after the final division in the Chamber of Deputies, a commission was appointed by the Minister of the

Interior to examine all periodical journals before their publication, and the censorship came into full operation.

<small>59. Reflections on this subject.</small> Experience has confirmed the assertion here made, that no government has ever been established in France, since the Revolution, which has been able to stand for any length of time against the unrestricted assaults of the public press. Whether it is from the vehemence and proneness to change in the French character, or from the absence of that steadying mass of fixed interests, which, like the fly-wheel in the machine, steadies its movements, and restrains the actions of the moving power, the fact is certain. No dynasty or administration has ever existed for any length of time, which had not contrived somehow or other to restrain the violence of the periodical press. There is more here than a peculiarity of national temperament, to which, on this side of the Channel, we are so apt to ascribe it. It points to a great truth, of general application and lasting importance to mankind—that is, that the public press is only to be relied on as the bulwark either of freedom or good government, where classes exist in society, and interests in the state, which render the support of truth a matter of immediate profit to those engaged in the great work of enlightening or directing the public mind. Individuals of a noble and lofty character will, indeed, often be found who will sacrifice interest to the assertion of truth, but they are few in number; and though they may direct the thinking few, they can not be expected, in the first instance at least, to have much influence on the unthinking many. The ability of those engaged in the public press is in general very great; but it is like the ability of the bar—it is employed to support the views which suit the interests of its clients, and more occupied with objects of present interest than with those of ultimate importance. Those who live by the people must please the people. There is no security so complete alike for stable government and public freedom as a free press, when great interests on *both sides* exist in society, and the national talent is equally divided in pleading their cause respectively. But where, either from the violence of previous convulsions, or any other cause, only *one* prevailing interest is left in society, the greater part of the public press at once ranges itself on its side: the other is never heard; or, if heard, never attended to. The chains are thrown over the minds of men, and a free press becomes, as in republican America, the organ of the mandates of a tyrant majority; or, as in imperial France, the instrument of a military despotism.

<small>60. Alarming state of the country, and defensive measures of Government.</small> Government soon found that the decree directed against the periodical press had neither extinguished the freedom of thought nor taken away the arms of faction. The journals, being fettered by the censorship, took refuge in pamphlets, which were not subjected to it, and Paris soon was overrun with *brochures* which assailed Government with the utmost fury, and, on the plea that it had departed from the constitutional régime, indulged in the most uncontrolled violence of language. Not the Ministry merely, the dynasty was openly assailed; and then, for the first time, there appeared decisive evidence of the great conspiracy which had been organized in France against the Bourbons. As long as the electoral system was established on such a footing as gave them a near prospect of dispossessing the Crown by legislative means, this conspiracy was kept in abeyance; but now that a quasi-Royalist Ministry was in power, and there was a chance of a change in the Electoral Law which might defeat their projects, they became entirely undisguised in their measures, and openly menaced the throne. In these arduous circumstances the conduct of Government was firm, and yet temperate. Prosecutions were instituted against the press, which, in some instances, were successful, and in some degree tended to check its licentiousness. The army, moreover, was firm, and could be relied on for the discharge of its duty;[1] which was the more fortunate and meritorious on its part, that a great portion of its officers were veterans of Napoleon's army, and that the greatest efforts had been made by the Liberal party to seduce both them and those on half-pay into the treasonable designs which were in contemplation. Aware of the approach of danger, the Minister of War drew the Royal Guard nearer to Paris, and arranged its station so that in six hours two thirds of its force might be concentrated at any point in the capital which might be menaced.

<small>1 Cap. vii. 1, 7, 12; Lac. ii. 403, 405.</small>

<small>61. Denunciation of the secret government.</small> An untoward circumstance occurred at this juncture, which, although trivial in ordinary times, now considerably augmented the difficulties of Government. A magistrate at Nimes, M. Madier, a respectable but injudicious and credulous man, presented a petition to the Chamber of Deputies, in which he stated that, some days after the death of the Duke de Berri, two circulars had been sent to Nimes, not from the Minister of the Interior, but from the Royalist committee, denouncing M. Decazes, and directing the Royalists to organize themselves as for ulterior events.* It was evident from the tenor of these circulars, which without doubt had emanated from the Royalist committee at Paris, that they related only to electioneering preparations, in the event of a dissolution of the Chambers taking place in consequence of the change of Ministry; and that when the retreat of M. Decazes was secured, nothing more was intended to be done. But this petition and the revelation of the Royalist circulars served as an admirable handle to the Liberal party, who pointed to it as a proof of a secret government, which counteracted all the measures of the responsible one, and was preparing the entire ruin of the public liber-

---

<small>* "Ne soyez ni surpris ni effrayés quoique l'attentat du 13 Février n'ait pas amené sur-le-champ la chute du Favori; agissez comme s'il était déjà renvoyé. Nous l'arracherons de ce poste si on ne consent pas à l'en bannir; en attendant, organisez-vous; les avis, les ordres, l'argent ne vous manqueront pas." Another—"Nous vous demandons il y a peu de jours une attitude imposante, nous vous recommandons aujourd'hui le calme, nous venons de remporter un avantage décisif en faisant chasser Decazes: de grands services peuvent vous être rendus par le nouveau ministère: il faut bien vous garder de lui inspirer des sentimens hostiles."—CAPEFIGUE, v. 11.</small>

ties. Vehement debates followed on the subject in the Chamber of Deputies, in the course of which the "factious personage" near the throne, from whom they all emanated, was openly denounced, and a motion was even brought forward for an address to the Crown to dismiss the new Ministers. The proposal was negatived, but the object was gained; the public mind was agitated, and the people were prepared to embrace the idea that the continuance of the Ministry was inconsistent with the preservation of the public liberties.¹

[margin: ¹ Ann. Hist. id. 217, 219; Cap. vii. 15, 21; Lac. ii. 402, 407.]

It was in this agitated state of the public mind that Ministers were charged with the arduous duty of bringing forward their new law of election—the most dangerous and exciting topic which it was possible for them to broach, but which was made an indispensable condition of the Royalist alliance with the Centre in support of the Government. No small difficulty was experienced, however, in effecting a compromise on the subject, and adjusting a project in which the coalescing parties might agree; but at length, by the indefatigable efforts of M. Siméon, M. Pasquier, and M. Mounier, the terms were agreed to on both sides, and were as follows: Two classes of colleges of electors—one of the departments, the other of the arrondissements. The electoral college of each department was to consist of a fifth part of the whole electors paying the highest taxes; the electoral colleges of the arrondissements were to consist of the whole remainder of the electors having their domicile within their limits. The electoral colleges of the arrondissements named by a simple majority as many candidates as the department was entitled to elect; and the college of the department chose from among them the deputies to send to the Chamber. This project was imperfect in its details, and drawn up in haste; but it tended to remove the grand evil of the existing system—the election of the whole Chamber by one uniform class of electors; and as such it was promised the support of the Doctrinaires and a large part of the Centre of the Assembly.²

[margin: 62. Ministerial project of a new electoral law.]

[margin: ² Cap. vii. 26, 27.]

The discussion was brilliant and animated in both Chambers, and called forth the very highest abilities on either side. On the side of the Opposition it was contended by M. Royer-Collard, M. Lafayette, and General Foy: "The charter has consecrated the Revolution by subjecting it to compromise; it is it which has given us all our liberties—the liberty of conscience, which is expressly guaranteed by it; and equality, which is guaranteed by representative institutions. The Chamber of Deputies is the guarantee of the charter. That is a proposition which no one will be so bold as to dispute. Take away the Elective Chamber, and power resides alone in the Executive and the Chamber of Peers; the nation becomes retrograde—it becomes a domain, and is possessed as such. Take away the guarantees promised by the charter, and you turn that instrument against itself; or, what is even worse, you render it an object of derision, alike against the sovereign who granted and the people who received it. If the Government had persisted in its intention of revising the charter, it would have experienced less opposition than in this attempt, which is pretending to uphold the charter, to undermine its most important provisions. It is not because the charter has given this one the title of Baron, another that of Bishop, that it is the idol of the nation; it is because it has secured liberty of conscience and personal freedom that it has become so, and that we have sworn fidelity to it. Now we are virtually absolved from our oaths—the aristocracy is secretly undermining both the nation and the throne. Can you doubt it, when you recollect the contempt and derision it has cast on that glorious standard with which such recollections are associated—that standard which, we do not hesitate to repeat, is that of public freedom?

[margin: 63. Argument against it by the Opposition.]

"In vain may the proposed law be passed, and even for a time carried into execution; the public feeling will extinguish it, wear it out, destroy it by resistance; it never will become the law of France. Representative government will not be wrested from you; it is stronger than the will of its adversaries. By a *coup d'état* of 18th Fructidor* you may transport men; you can not transport opinions. Our old parliaments were not so robust as a representative assembly; they did not speak in the name of France, but they sometimes defended the public liberties, and the eloquent and courageous remonstrances which they laid at the foot of the throne resounded through the nation. The ministry of Louis XV. wished to overthrow them: he was conquered. The parliaments, for a moment subdued, raised themselves again amidst the public acclamations; and the ephemeral puppets with whom they had filled their benches disappeared forever. Thus will vanish the Chamber of Privilege.

[margin: 64. Continued.]

"You strive in vain against an irresistible torrent. You are under the iron hand of necessity. So long as equality is the law of society, equal representation is imposed upon it in all its energy and purity. Ask from it no concessions; it is not for it to make them. The representative government is itself a guarantee. As such it is called on to demand concessions, not to make them. Be not surprised, therefore, that it is partial to the new order of things—it exists only to insure the triumph of the charter. Would you obtain its support?—Embrace its cause. Separate right from privilege. Affection is the true bond of societies. Study what attracts a nation, what it repudiates, what it hopes, what it fears; in a word, show yourself a part of it, and you will be popular. During eight centuries, this has been the secret of the English aristocracy. Legitimacy is the idea the most profound, and withal the most fruitful, which has penetrated modern society. It renders evident to all in a visible and immortal image the idea of right, that noble appanage of the human race; of right, without which there would be nothing on earth, but a life without dignity, and a death without hope. Legitimacy belongs to us more than any other nation, for no other nation possesses it in such

[margin: 65. Continued.]

---

* In 1797, when the Directory was overturned.

purity as ourselves, or can point to so illustrious a line of great and good princes.

"Rivers do not flow back to their sources: accomplished facts are not restored to nonentity. A bloody Revolution had changed the face of our earth; on the ruins of the ancient society, overturned with violence, a new society had raised itself, governed by new maxims and new men. Like all conquerors, I say it in its presence, that society was barbarous: it had neither received, in its origin nor in its progress, the true principle of civilization—right. Legitimacy, which alone had preserved the ark of our salvation, could alone restore it to us: it has restored it. With the royal race, right has reappeared; every day has been marked by its progress in opinions, manners, and laws. In a few years we have recovered the social doctrines which we had lost. Right has succeeded to power. Legitimacy on the throne has become the guarantee of the general ascendant of law. As it is the ruling principle in society, good faith is its august character; it is profaned if it is lowered to astuteness or devoured by fraud. The proposed law sinks the legitimate monarchy to the level of the government of the Revolution, by resting it on fraud. The project of the proposed law is the most fatal which has ever come out of the councils of kings since those, of fatal memory, which overturned the family of the Stuarts. It is the divorce of the nation from its sovereign."[1]

[sidenote: 66. Concluded.]

[sidenote: 1 Ann. Hist. iii. 105, 125; Moniteur, May, 18–30, 1820, Lac. ii. 413, 415; Cap. vii 30, 35.]

On the other hand, it was contended, on the part of the Government, by M. de Serres, M. Siméon, and M. Villèle: "We are reminded of two periods—the days of our Revolution and the present time. History will judge the first, and it will judge also the men who were engaged in it. But I can not dissemble what the strange speech of M. Lafayette obliges me to declare, that he put himself at the head of the men who attacked the monarchy, and in the end overturned it. I am convinced that generous and elevated sentiments animated him; but, inspired by these feelings, is it surprising to him that men attached by principle and duty to that monarchy should have defended it before it fell? He should be just enough not to impute to the victims of those times all the evils of a Revolution which has pressed so heavily on themselves. Have these times left in the mind of the honorable member some mournful recollections, many useful lessons? He should have known—many a time he must have felt, with death in his heart and blushes on his face—not only that, after having once roused the masses, their leaders have no longer the power to restrain them, but that they are forced to follow, and even to lead them.

[sidenote: 67. Answer by the Ministerialists.]

"But let us leave these old events, and think of our present condition, and the questions which are now before us. What chiefly weighs with me is the declaration made by General Lafayette, that he has entered these walls to make oath to the *constitution* (he has not said *the king* and the constitution), and that that oath was reciprocal; that the acts of the legislature—your acts—have violated the constitution, and that he

[sidenote: 68. Continued.]

is absolved from his oath! He declares this in the name of himself and his friends; he declares it in the face of the nation! He adds to this declaration an éloge, as affected as it is ill-timed, of colors which can not now be regarded as any other colors but those of rebellion. The scandal which I denounce, so far from being repented of, has been renewed a second time in the tribune. What, I ask, can be the motive for such conduct? If insensate persons, excited by such language criminally imprudent, proceed to acts of sedition, on whose head should fall the blood shed in rebellion, or in extinguishing it by the hands of the law? And when a man, who himself has precipitated the excesses of the people, saw their fury turned against himself—when that man, respectable in many respects, uses language of which his own experience should have taught him the danger, are not his words to be regarded as more blamable than if they came from an ordinary man? The honorable member, who should be so well aware of the danger of revolutionary movements, now pretends to be ignorant of them. With the same breath he pronounces a glowing eulogium on the cause of rebellion, and declares, in his own name and that of his colleagues, that he considers himself absolved from his oath of fidelity to the charter; he proclaims the sovereignty of the people, which is, in other words, the right of insurrection. Is not such an appeal an incitement to rebellion? And does not that point to your duty in combating an opposition animated by such principles?

"The Electoral Law of 1817 has lost, since it was carried into execution, the most important of its defenders. It has been the cause of the present crisis in society. The same Ministers who formerly proposed, who subsequently have been compelled to defend it, convinced by experience, animated by a sense of duty, now come forward to propose its modification. The very Chamber of Peers which voted its adoption has risen up against it. Sixty peers were created to vanquish the resistance to it in that Chamber; a hundred would be required to insure its continuance. It is no wonder it is so, for the law of 1817 failed in the chief object of representative institutions. It excluded the masses alike of property and numbers. What renders it in an especial manner dangerous is, that the limited homogeneous class to which it has confined the franchise becomes every year, by the annual elections, more grasping, more selfish, more exclusive. So evident has this danger become, that if the present change is not carried, the friends of liberty will be compelled themselves to bring forward a modification of the law in the interest of freedom.

[sidenote: 69. Continued.]

"France will never bear for any time a homogeneous representation, as the proposer of the existing law at one time supposed it would; unmistakable proofs of the general revolt against such a system arise on all sides. Besides, in the present state of things, the existence of a revolutionary faction among us—of a faction irreligious, immoral, the enemy of restraint, the friend of usurpation—has been demonstrated beyond the possibility of a doubt. It speaks in the jour-

[sidenote: 70. Continued.]

nals, it sits in the directing committees; this conviction is forced upon all the Ministers, not merely by their reason, but their official information. I predict to the honorable members who are now the allies of that faction, that they will in the end sink under its attacks, and that they will disappear from the Chamber the moment they venture to resist it. Public opinion has already repudiated both the faction and the Electoral Law which supports it. Horror struck at the spectacle of a regicide returned to the Chamber, real public opinion has become alarmed alike at the principle of that law and its consequences.

"It has become indispensable to alter the mode of election, since we see faction straining to support it, from a conviction that it throws the greatest influence into the lowest class of proprietors—to the very class which has the least interest in the soil. The law proposed, by restoring to the larger proprietors a portion of that influence of which the existing law has deprived them, gives a share in the choice of deputies to those who are most interested in upholding it. The law will never be complete and safe till the electoral power is made to rest on the entire class of proprietors, and is intrusted by them to a smaller body, chosen from among those who pay the greatest amount of assessments; and whose list, accessible to all, and from its very nature shifting and changeable, can never constitute a privileged class, since those who fall within it to-day may be excluded from it to-morrow. In the political system pursued since the Restoration is to be found the seat of the evil which is devouring France. Under the existing law a constant system of attack against the existing dynasty is carried on. Lofty ambitions arrested in their course, great hopes blasted, fanaticism ever rampant, have coalesced together; the conspiracy was at first turned—it has now sapped the foundations of the throne—it will soon overturn it. At Lyons, as at Grenoble, cast down but not destroyed, it ever rises again more audacious than ever, and menaces its conquerors. Intrenched in the law of elections as its last citadel, it threatens its conquerors. It is determined to conquer or die. It is no longer a matter of opinion which it agitates, 'to be or not to be, that is the question.' The uniform suffrage has placed the monarchy at the mercy of a pure democracy."[1]

71. Concluded.

1 Moniteur, June 1–19, 1820; Ann. Hist. iii. 102, 125; Lac. ii. 420, 423; Cap. vii. 35, 37.

So sensible were the Liberal chiefs of the weight of these arguments, and of the large proportion of enlightened opinion which adhered to them, that they did not venture to meet them by a direct negative, but endeavored to elude their force by an amendment. It was proposed by Camille-Jourdan, and was to this effect, "That each department shall be divided into as many electoral arrondissements as there are deputies to elect for the Chamber; that each of these arrondissements shall have an electoral college, which shall be composed of the persons liable to taxes, having their political domicile in the arrondissement, and paying three hundred francs of direct contribution; that every electoral college shall nominate its deputy directly." Though this was represented by him as a compromise, it in reality was not so; for, by perpetuating the uniform suffrage and direct representation, it continued political power exclusively in the hands of the most democratic portion of the community, the small proprietors. It received, accordingly, the immediate and enthusiastic support of the whole Liberal party; the democratic press was unanimous in its praise; and so nearly were parties balanced in the Chamber, that the amendment was carried *against* Government by a majority of *one*, the numbers being a hundred and twenty-eight to a hundred and twenty-seven. The balance was cast by M. de Chauvelin, who, though grievously ill, was carried into the Chamber, and decided the question by his vote. He was conveyed home in triumph by a vociferous mob, and became for a brief period the object of popular idolatry. The revolutionists were in transports, and every where anticipated the immediate realization of their hopes, by the defeat of the Government on so vital a question.[1]

72. Camille-Jourdan's amendment carried.

1 Cap. vii. 37, 38; An. Hist. iii. 129.

In this extremity, Ministers made secret overtures to the chiefs of the Doctrinaires, whose numbers, though small, were yet sufficient to cast the balance either way in the equally divided assembly. This overture proved entirely successful. A fresh amendment was proposed by M. Boin and M. Convoisier on their part, and supported by the whole strength of the Government, the Right, and their adherents in the Centre. It was to this effect, that the Chamber of Deputies was to consist "of two hundred and fifty-eight members chosen by the arrondissements, and a hundred and seventy-two by the departments; the latter being chosen, not by the *whole electors*, but by *a fourth of their number, composed of those who paid the highest amount of taxes.*" This was an immense change to the advantage of the aristocracy; for not only did it add a hundred and seventy members to this Chamber, but it added them of persons chosen by a fourth of the electors for each department paying the highest assessment: in other words, by the richest proprietors. Nevertheless, so gratified were the Doctrinaires by getting quit of the much-dreaded double mode of election, or so sensible had they in secret become of its dangerous tendency, that they agreed to the compromise; and M. de Boin's amendment was carried by a majority of *five*, the numbers being a hundred and thirty to a hundred and twenty-five. Only five members were absent from the entire Chamber—an extraordinary circumstance, proving the unparalleled interest the question had excited. This victory was decisive; the waverers came round after it was gained; and the final division on the question showed a majority of ninety-five for Government.[2]

73. The amendment of M. Boin is carried by Government.

2 Moniteur, June 13, 1820, Ann. Hist. iii. 128, 153

It soon appeared that this vehement strife in the Chamber was connected with still more important designs out of doors —that they were linked with the revolutions in progress in Spain, Portugal, and Italy; and that it was not without an ulterior object that Lafayette had

74. Disturbances in Paris. June 5

invoked the tricolor flag, and thrown down the gauntlet, as it were, to the monarchy. No sooner was the news of the decisive vote in favor of the principle of the new law known in the capital than the most violent agitation commenced. M. Manuel and M. Benjamin Constant published an inflammatory address to the young men at the university and colleges; and the sinister omen of crowds collecting in the streets indicated the secret orders and menacing preparations of the central democratic committee. Seditious cries were heard; and so threatening did affairs soon appear, that the military were obliged to disperse them by force; and in the tumult a young student of law, named Lallemand, was shot, and died soon after. This unhappy event augmented the general excitement; the mobs assembled in still greater force, and the Government took serious precautions. The posts were every where doubled; the guards were drawn into Paris; large bodies of infantry and cavalry were stationed on the bridges in the Place Carrousel, and around the Chamber of Deputies; and proclamations were placarded in all directions, forbidding all assemblages of persons even to the number of three.[1]

<small>¹ Moniteur, June 6, 1820; Ann. Hist. iii. 130, 136; Lam. vi 322, 324.</small>

75. Which become serious. June 6.

This proclamation was met by a counter one from the democratic committee, which was affixed to the gates of all the colleges and schools, calling on the young men to meet and avenge their comrade who had been slain. They did so accordingly; and, marching two and two, so as to avoid the literal infringement of the order of the police, formed a column of above five thousand persons, armed with large sticks and sword-canes, which debouched upon the Place Louis XV., directly in front of the palace of the legislative body. The gates of the Tuileries and gardens were immediately closed, and the huge mass was driven, by repeated charges of cavalry, who behaved with the most exemplary forbearance, out of the Place. They immediately marched along the Boulevards toward the Faubourg St. Antoine, where the immense masses of workmen, so well known in the worst days of the Revolution, were already prepared to receive them; and, returning from thence with numbers now swelled, by the idle and excited from every coffee-house, to between thirty and forty thousand men, moved toward the Place de Grève and Hôtel de Ville. The head of the column, however, was met on the way by a strong body of the gendarmerie-à-cheval, which charged and dispersed it, upon which the whole body took to flight. Thirty or forty were made prisoners, and immediately lodged in custody.[2]

<small>² Moniteur, June 7, 8, 1820, Ann. Hist. iii. 133, 135; Lam. vi. 324.</small>

76. Loud declamation on the subject in the Chamber of Deputies.

It may be readily imagined what use was made of these untoward events by the unscrupulous and impassioned leaders of the Liberal party in the Chamber of Deputies. The loudest and most vehement complaints were made against all concerned in the repression of the riots—the Ministers, for having ordered the measures which led to their suppression; the military, gendarmerie, and police, for having executed them. Although the conduct of all the three had been prudent, forbearing, and exemplary in the highest degree, yet they were all overwhelmed by the most unmeasured obloquy. Not a whisper was breathed against the leaders or followers of the seditious assemblages, which had not only for days together kept the metropolis in alarm, but seriously menaced the monarchy. Still less was it observed by these impassioned declaimers, that a revolt of so serious a kind had been stifled with the loss of a single life. "Blood," exclaimed M. Lafitte, "has never ceased, during eight days, to flow in Paris; a hundred thousand of its peaceable citizens were charged, sabred, and trampled under the hoofs of horses yesterday by the cuirassiers. The indignation of the capital is at its height; the agitation of the people is hourly increasing; tremble for the morrow." "Here is the blade of a sabre broken by a cut," exclaimed M. de Corcelles, holding up the fragment with a theatrical air. "Blood flows, and you refuse to hear us; it is infamous." The Ministers ably and energetically defended their measures; and the violence of the two parties became so great that the president, in despair, covered himself, and broke up the meeting.[1]

<small>¹ Lam. vi. 325, 327; Ann. Hist. iii. 139, 142</small>

77. Their suppression.

These violent appeals, however, failed in the desired result, and their failure contributed more than any other circumstance to produce that adhesion of the Doctrinaires to the proposed electoral law, as modified by M. Boin, which led to its being passed into a law. A suppressed insurrection never fails, for the time at least, to strengthen the hands of government. In the present instance, the influence of that repression was enhanced, not only by the patience and temper of the armed force employed, and moderation of the Government in the subsequent prosecutions, but by another circumstance of decisive importance—*the military had faithfully adhered to their duty.* The utmost efforts had been made to seduce them, and failed of success. All the hopes of the insurgents were rested on their defection, and their steadiness made them despair of the cause. The leaders of the revolt saw that their attempt had been premature, that the military had not been sufficiently worked upon, and that the attempt must be adjourned. They let it die away accordingly at the moment, reserving their efforts for a future period. Although the crowds continued to infest the streets for several days, and great efforts were made at the funeral of Lallemand—who was buried with much solemnity, in presence of some thousand spectators, on the 9th—yet the danger was evidently past. The capital gradually became tranquil; the large majority of 95 in the Chamber of Deputies, on the last reading of the bill, passed almost without notice; and it was passed by a majority of 95 in the Peers, the numbers being, 141 to 56. The Government behaved with exemplary moderation, it may even be said timidity, in repressing this revolt. It was known that money had circulated freely among the insurgents, and it was known from whom it came.[2] But it was deemed more prudent, now that the insurrection had been surmounted, not to agitate the public mind by

<small>² An. Hist. iii.139,161; Lam. vi 325, 327. Cap vii 47, 49.</small>

Vol. I.—U

the trial of its leaders, and no further prosecutions were attempted. It will appear in the sequel what return they made for this lenity, when the crisis of 1830 arrived.

This was the great struggle of the year, because it was a direct effort to supplant the Bourbon dynasty on the one hand, and establish it more firmly in the legislature on the other. Every thing depended on the troops: if they had wavered when the insurgents marched on the Hôtel de Ville, on June 6th, it was all over, and 1820 would have been 1830. The remaining objects of the session, which involved the comparatively trifling matters of the public welfare or social happiness, excited scarcely any attention. The budget was voted with scarce any opposition. The gross revenue of the year was 8,741,087,000 francs; the net income, deducting the expense of collection, 739,712,000 francs, which showed a cost of above £5,000,000 in collecting an income of £30,000,000, or nearly 17 per cent.—a very large proportion, but which is explained by the circumstance of the direct taxes, forming above a third of the whole, being exigible from above five millions of separate little proprietors. The expenditure was estimated at 511,871,000 francs, exclusive of the interest of the debt. Every branch of the public revenue exhibited symptoms of improvement, and the most unprecedented prosperity pervaded the country.[1] It is a singular circumstance, but highly characteristic of the real motives which actuated the Liberal opposition at this period, that this era of unexampled social well-being was precisely the one which they selected for most violently agitating the public mind for an overthrow of the monarchy and change of the dynasty, by whom alone those blessings had been introduced.*

[78] The budget.

[1] Ann. Hist. iii. 175, 192.

Convinced, from the unsuccessful issue of this attempt, that they had no chance of success in their attempts to overthrow the Government, unless they could enlist the military on their side, the Liberal leaders, after the prorogation of the Chamber, bent their whole efforts to that object. It is now known who they were; subsequent success has made them boast of their attempts; they are no longer afraid to admit their treason. "M. Lafayette," says Lamartine, "declared to his friends that open force could now alone overturn the Government, which had declared war against the equality of classes." Emissaries despatched from this centre set out to sound the departments and the troops. The parliamentary opposition of M. Lafitte and Casimir Perier unconsciously aided the conspirators, who were grouped around Lafayette, d'Argenson, Manuel, Corcelles, Roy, and Merilhou. That conspiracy found innumerable accomplices, without the need of affiliating them, in the half-pay officers, the remains of Napoleon's army, in the small number of Republicans, in the Bonapartists—as numerous as the discontented—in the holders of the domains of the emigrants, who were every day more apprehensive of the loss of their heritages, and of the influence of those who were now protected by the Government.[1]

Numerous as this band of conspirators was, it was not on them alone that their leaders totally, or even chiefly, rested. The great object was to seduce the military actually in arms; for long experience had taught the French that it is by them that all social convulsions in their country are, in the last resort, determined. They were not long in finding a few desperadoes who were willing to execute their designs. A captain in the Legion de la

[79] Military conspiracy, headed by Lafayette.

[80] Their designs, and efforts to corrupt the troops.

[1] Lam. vi. 329.

* The Budget of 1820 and 1821 stood thus:

RECEIPTS.

	1820. Francs nett.	1821. Francs nett.
Direct taxes	311,773,780	325,035,159
Indirect ditto	140,000,000	191,566,300
Registrations	147,000,000	158,986,500
Woods	14,000,000	17,047,400
Customs and salt	86,000,000	111,113,000
Postes	12,097,000	23,790,710
Lottery	9,000,000	14,000,000
Retained from salaries	5,600,000	5,600,000
Miscellaneous	14,712,970	15,433,970
Total nett	739,712,750	740,566,105
Expense of collection	134,375,130	136,871,925
Total gross	874,087,880	877,437,880

EXPENDITURE.

	1820. Francs nett.	1821. Francs nett.
Interest of public debt	188,341,000	189,052,764
Sinking fund	40,000,000	40,000,000
King and Royal Family	34,000,000	34,000,000
Justice	17,460,000	17,959,500
Foreign affairs	7,850,000	7,855,000
Interior	102,240,000	109,060,800
War	184,750,000	179,736,600
Marine	45,200,000	52,970,000
Finances and miscellaneous	115,880,000	119,572,000
	739,712,750	747,206,664

From a statement laid before the Chamber by the Minister of Finances, it appeared that the produce of the sinking fund, which, in 1816, was 20,000,000, and in 1817 was increased to 40,000,000, had been highly gratifying. It was as follows:

	Sums applied. Francs.	Annuities bought up. Francs.
1816	20,439,724	1,782,765
1817	43,084,946	3,322,114
1818	51,532,333	3,673,642
1819	67,094,682	4,354,776

And from a statement laid before the Chamber by the celebrated economist M. Ganilh, it appeared that *before* the Revolution the public burdens stood thus:

	France.
Total taxes	585,000,000

Of which the direct taxes were—

	Francs.	f. s.
On realized property	250,000,000, or 8 1-40 per cent
Industry and commerce	30,000,000, or 1 1-20 "
Consumers	304,000,000, or 10 1-2 "

After the Revolution in 1820 they stood thus:

	Francs.
Total revenue and taxes	875,941,663
Of which raised by taxes	Francs. 800,712,600
Of which the land paid	288,000,000, or 9 francs 16 cents
Taxed capital money	154,000,000, or 9 " 16 "
Industry and commerce	56,000,000, or 1 " 16 "
Consumers	302,116,300, or 8 " 16 "

So that the taxes on land, industry, and fixed capital had increased *a third*, and those on consumption had remained the same, though their amount per head diminished, from the increase of population, in the intervening period, from 25,000,000 to 30,000,000 souls.—*Ann. Hist.* iii. 175, 198, 200; and iv. 661, 663.

Meurthe, in garrison at Paris, named Nantil, a half-pay colonel, named Sauzet, and a colonel of the disbanded Imperial Guard, named Mazaire, agreed to act as leaders. Their plan was to surprise the fortress of Vincennes, to corrupt the regiments in Paris, to rouse the faubourgs and the schools, and with the united forces march on the Tuileries. A great number of the half-pay generals of the Empire—in particular, Generals Pajol, Bacheluz, Merten, Maransin, Lafitte, and superior officers in retirement—were engaged in the conspiracy, the object of which was to dethrone the Bourbons. On that they were all agreed, but on ulterior measures there was great difference of opinion. Lafayette desired to proclaim a republic or a constitutional monarchy, whose interests were identical with those of the Revolution, and who might be "fettered by the bonds of a representative democracy." The great majority wished to proclaim Napoleon II., hoping to restore with him the days of glory, of promotion, and plunder. Lafayette indulged a sanguine hope that, as Napoleon's son was in the hands of the Austrians, who would not allow him to accept the proffered crown, it would become a matter of necessity to bestow on him the dictatorship, of which he had enjoyed a foretaste in 1790, and of which he had dreamed in 1815. The day of rising was fixed for 19th August: Nantil was to raise his legion, and head the attack; Lafayette went to his château of Lagrange to rouse his department, and aid in the assault on Vincennes; M. d'Argenson went to Alsace to array in arms its numerous republicans; and M. de Coreelles was charged with organizing the revolt in the great and populous city of Lyons.[1]

[1 Lam. vi. 328, 330; Cap. vii. 62, 63; Lac. iii. 6-9, 429.]

§ 81. Which fails by accident. Aug. 19.

An accidental circumstance prevented this deeply laid design from being carried into effect. On the day before it was to have taken place, an explosion of powder, from fortuitous causes, took place in the castle of Vincennes, and this led to the military and police being assembled in considerable numbers in that important fortress. Their presence led the conspirators to suppose that their designs were discovered, which was really not the case, for they were not fully developed till long afterward. Information had, however, been given to Government, by some of the officers upon whom unsuccessful attempts had been made, of a plot to overturn the Government, and the whole Ministers, in consequence, were summoned to the Duke de Richelieu's on the morning of the 19th. From the information there laid before them, it was resolved to remove the Legion de la Meurthe, which was most disaffected, from Paris to the frontiers, and the suspected officers were arrested in their barracks early in the forenoon by officers of the police. M. de Latour Maubourg, the War Minister, was himself present when this was done. No resistance was attempted; the common soldiers were astonished, not irritated; it was their officers, not themselves, who were privy to the conspiracy. Before night, the Legion de la Meurthe marched out for Landrecies in a state of tumult and indiscipline, which recalled the description given by Tacitus of the Roman legions in the mutiny which Germanicus repressed. Several of their officers were arrested on the march. Nantil, and the principal leaders of the conspiracy, however, made their escape.[1]

[1 Lam. vi. 329, 331; Cap. vii. 66, 67; Lac. iii. 8, 9.]

Government acted with the utmost lenity in the prosecutions consequent on this abortive revolt. Lists of the persons implicated in it had been furnished to the Ministry, and they comprised most of the leaders of the Liberal party in Paris. M. Lafayette and M. Manuel were at its head. Ministers, however, recoiled from the idea of openly coming to a rupture of an irreconcilable kind with the chiefs of a party strong in the Chambers, strong in popular support, strong, as had recently appeared, in the affections of a part at least of the army. It was doubtful how far—however clear the moral evidence might be—the complete measure of legal proof could be obtained against the real but half-vailed leaders of the conspiracy. It was deemed more expedient, therefore, to proceed only against the inferior agents, and even against them in the most lenient manner. They were sent for trial to the Chamber of Peers, by whom a few, after a long interval, were convicted, and sentenced to secondary punishments, and several acquitted. But ten years afterward, the real leaders were revealed in those who received the rewards of treason, at a time when none dared call it by its right name.[2]

[§ 82. Lenity shown in the prosecutions.]

[2 Lac. iii. 9, 12, Cap. vii. 67, 68; Lam. vi. 330, 333.]

While conspiracies so serious and widespread were in progress to overthrow the dynasty of the Bourbons, Providence appeared in an extraordinary manner to have interposed in their behalf; and an event occurred which, beyond any which had yet occurred, elevated the hopes of their partisans throughout the country. The Duchess de Berri, notwithstanding the dreadful shock received from the murder of her husband, went successfully through the whole period of her pregnancy, and on the night of the 20th September was safely delivered of a son, who was christened Henry Duke of Bordeaux. As by the Salic Law males only can succeed to the throne of France, and the infant which the duchess bore was the last hope of continuing the direct line of succession, the utmost pains were taken to secure decisive evidence of the child really being of the royal line. The moment the duchess was seized with her pains, she desired that Marshal the Duke of Albufera (Suchet) should be sent for, and she had the courage and presence of mind, after the delivery was over, to insist that the umbilical cord should not be cut till the marshal with his own eyes had been satisfied with the reality of the birth and the sex of the infant. Several of the Guard, besides the usual attendants on the princess, were also eye-witnesses to the birth. The old king hastened to the apartment on the first alarm, and when the infant was presented to him, said, "Here is a fine Duke de Bordeaux: he is born for us all;" and taking a few drops of the wine of Pau, which according to old tradition had anointed the lips of Henry IV. before he had received his mother's milk, did

[§ 83. Birth of the Duke of Bordeaux. Sept. 20.]

the same to his infant descendant. Then taking a glass, he filled it, and drank to the health of the duchess. "Sire!" she replied, "I wish I knew the song of Jean d'Albert, that everything should be done here as at the birth of Henry IV."¹

No words can convey an idea of the transports into which the Royalists were thrown over all France by this auspicious event; and even those of the opposite parties could not resist feeling the influence of the general enthusiasm. There was something in the birth of the infant—the last remnant of a long line of kings, and who had been born in so interesting and almost miraculous a manner after his father's death—which spoke to every heart. The general enthusiasm exceeded even that felt at the birth of the king of Rome, ten years before—for Napoleon might have had many other sons—but no one, save this infant, could transmit in the direct line the blood of Henry IV. and Louis XIV. to future generations. It had been announced that twelve cannon-shots should announce the birth of a daughter, twenty-four of a son. When the guns began to fire, all Paris was roused, and in speechless anxiety watched the successive discharges; but when the thirteenth report announced that an heir to the monarchy had been born, the transports were universal. The telegraph speedily conveyed it to every part of France, and the thirteenth gun in all the fortresses and harbors announced the joyful intelligence to the people. One would have supposed, from the universal joy, that France had but one heart, one soul —so strongly had the romantic and interesting circumstances of the birth wrought upon the public mind. Congratulatory addresses from every part of the country poured in to the king and the duchess, and the grace of her manner and felicity of her answers added to the general enchantment. A protest, in the name of the Duke of Orléans, was published in the London papers, though disavowed by that prince; but he asked the important question solemnly of the Duke of Albufera—"M. le Maréchal," said he, "you are a man of honor; you were a witness of the accouchement of the Duchess de Berri. Is she really the mother of a boy?" "As certainly as your royal highness is father of the Duke de Chartres," replied the Marshal. "That is enough, M. le Maréchal," rejoined the duke; and he immediately went with the duchess to congratulate the happy mother, and salute the infant who might one day be their king. At the same time, the Duchess de Berri gave proof that she was animated with the sublime spirit of forgiveness shown on his death-bed by her husband, by requesting and obtaining the pardon of two men, named Gravin and Bonton, sentenced to death for an attempt on her life, or that of her child, which she did in terms so touching that they deserve a place even in general history. Her conduct at this period was so generous and noble, that the Emperor Alexander expressed his admiration of it in a touching epistle addressed with his own hand to the princess.¹

The birth of the Duke de Bordeaux, which afforded so fair a prospect of continuing the direct line of succession, confirming the dynasty of the Bourbons, and establishing the peace of Europe, was too important an event not to awake the general sympathy and interest of the European powers. Congratulations were received from all quarters: that from the Emperor Alexander was peculiarly warm and cordial. The *corps diplomatique* of Paris expressed a noble sentiment on this occasion in the words. "Providence has awarded the greatest possible blessing to the paternal tenderness of your Majesty. The child of grief, of regrets, of tears, is also the *child of Europe*—he is at once the guarantee and the pledge of the repose and peace which should follow so many agitations." This expression revealed the feeling of the European powers: it was, that the elder branch of the Bourbons was the sole pledge for the peace of Europe, and that the new-born infant was the bond which was to unite its rulers. The Emperor Alexander wrote to Louis—"The birth of the Duke of Bordeaux is an event which I consider as most fortunate for the peace of Europe, and which affords just consolation to your family. I pray your Majesty to believe that I adopt the title of the 'child of Europe,' which the diplomatic body has already bestowed upon him." Promotions, honors, and gratifications were bestowed in the most liberal manner in France: the crown debtors were nearly all liberated from prison; most of the political offenders pardoned; immense sums bestowed in charity; and a great creation of the order of the *Cordon Bleu* attested at once the gratitude and liberality of the sovereign.²

But though these circumstances argued favorably for the stability of the dynasty, and the consequent peace of Europe, symptoms were not awanting of a divergence of opinion, which portended divisions that might prove fatal in future times. It was with the Doctrinaires that the rupture first took place. This party, which afterward, from the talents of some of its members, became so celebrated, had already become important, from its position between the two great parties which divided the state, and its power, by inclining to either side, to give a preponderance to either. The conduct of the leaders of this party during the session, if not decidedly hostile to the Ministry, had been equivocal;

---

* "Sire! comme je ne puis voir le Roi aujourd'hui, je lui écris pour lui demander la grâce de deux malheureux qui ont été condamnés à mort pour tentative contre ma personne. Je serais au désespoir qu'il pût y avoir des Français qui mourussent pour moi: l'ange que je pleure demandait en mourant la grâce de son meurtrier, il sera l'arbitre de ma vie; me permettez-vous, mon oncle, de l'imiter, et de supplier votre Majesté d'accorder la grâce de la vie à ces deux infortunés? L'auguste exemple du Roi nous a habitués à la clémence; daignera-t-il permettre que les premiers instants de l'existence de mon Henri, de mon cher fils, de votre, du fils de la France, soient marqués par un pardon? Excusez, mon cher oncle, la liberté que j'ose prendre de vous ouvrir mon cœur; dans toutes les occasions votre indulgente bonté m'y a encouragée. Je supplie le Roi d'excuser ma hardiesse, et de croire au respect profond avec lequel je suis," &c.—*Caroline Duchesse de Berri au Roi de France*, 28 Sept., 1820.

and the increasing leaning of Government to the Royalist side, since the great reaction consequent on the death of the Duke de Berri, had rendered the position which they still held under the Administration precarious and painful. At the same time Government could not dispense with the support of the Royalists, for it was by their aid alone that the majorities, slender as they were, in the Chamber of Deputies had been obtained. The Doctrinaires had become sensible of the great error into which they had fallen in supporting the *coup d'état* of 5th September, 1816, which changed the Electoral Law; and it was by the secession of a part of their members from the Liberal ranks that the amendment of M. Boin, which again changed it, had been carried. But on other points they were decidedly opposed to the Government as now constituted; and the divergence before the close of the session had become so evident, that neither the security of the one party, nor the character of the other, would admit of their longer remaining united. The Duke de Richelieu, accordingly, at the instigation of M. Lainé, who had been much hurt by a speech of M. Royer-Collard on the budget, took his resolution, in which he was unanimously supported by the Cabinet; and the *Moniteur*, in announcing, after the close of the session, the names of the Council of State, omitted those of Royer-Collard, Guizot, Barante, Camille-Jourdan, and Mirbel. Four prefects, who were known to belong to the same party, were dismissed from office. At the same time, the Duke de Richelieu had several conferences with M. de Villèle and M. Corbière, on the conditions of a cordial union with the Royalist party.[1]

¹ Cap. vii. 55, 58; Lam. vi. 337, 338.

87. Views of the Doctrinaires.

Although the great abilities of the persons thus dismissed from the Government deprived them of very powerful support, especially in debate, yet in truth the severance was unavoidable, for there was an irreconcilable difference between them. It arose from principle, and an entirely different view of the most desirable structure of society, or of what was practicable under existing circumstances. The Doctrinaires were conservative in their views, but they were so on the principles of the Revolution. They adored the equality which was at once the object of its ambition, and the victory it had achieved. They thought it was possible, on the basis of absolute equality, to construct the fabric of constitutional monarchy and regulated freedom. They wished a hierarchy, but it was one, not of rank, or territories, or fortune, but of talent; and, being conscious of great abilities in themselves, they indulged the secret hope that under such a system they would rise to the power and eminence which they were conscious their capacity deserved. They had the natural jealousy which intellectual always feels of political power, and felt the utmost repugnance at the restoration of those distinctions in society which tended to re-establish the ancient supremacy of rank or fortune. In a word, they were the philosophers of the Revolution; and philosophers, when they are not the sycophants, are always jealous of nobles.

The Royalists, on the other hand, were set upon an entirely different set of objects. They were as well aware as the Doctrinaires that the old régime could not be re-established, that feudality was forever abolished, and that general liberty was at once the birth-right and greatest blessing of man. But they thought it could only be secured by the continuance of the monarchy, and that constitutional government was impossible without the reconstruction of a territorial nobility and ecclesiastical hierarchy, who might be at once a support of the throne and a check upon its power. Absolute equality, according to them, was the best possible foundation for Eastern despotism, but the worst for European freedom; you might as well construct a palace out of the waves of the ocean, as a constitutional monarchy out of the absolute equality of classes. Infidelity had been the principle of the Revolution in matters of belief; the only foundation for the monarchy was to be found in the restoration of the influence of the ancient faith. The centralization of all power in the capital by the system of the Revolution, and the destruction of all power in the provinces by the division of property, threatened, in their view, the total destruction of public freedom, and would leave France no other destiny but that of an armed democracy or an irresistible despotism. The sequel of this history will show which of these sets of opinions was the better founded; in the mean time, it is obvious that they were wholly irreconcilable with each other, and that no harmonious cabinet could by possibility be constructed out of the leaders of such opposite parties.*

88. Views of the Royalists.

* M. de Chateaubriand, in an article in the *Conservateur*, on 30th Nov., 1819, has well explained the views and intentions of the Royalists at this period, and subsequent events have rendered his words prophetic: "Voila donc les Royalistes au pouvoir, fermement resolus à maintenir la charte; tout leur edifice sera posé sur ce fondement; mais, au lieu de bâtir une democratie, ils élèveront une monarchie. Ainsi leur premier devoir, comme leur premier soin, serait de changer la loi des elections. Ils feraient en même temps retrancher de la loi de recrutement le titre VI.,† et rendraient ainsi à la couronne, une des plus importantes prerogatives. Ils retabliraient dans la loi sur la liberté de la presse le mot 'Religion,' qu'a leur honte eternelle, de pretendus hommes d'Etat en ont banni. Ministres! vous fondez une legislation, et elle produira des mœurs conformes à vos regles.

"Apres la modification des lois capitales, les Royalistes proposeraient les lois les plus monarchiques, sur l'organisation des communes et sur la Garde Nationale. Ils n'imiteraient le systeme de centralisation; ils rendraient une puissance salutaire aux conseils generaux. Creant, partout, des aggregations d'interets, ils les substitueraient à ces individualités trop favorables à l'etablissement de la tyrannie. En un mot, ils reconquerraient l'aristocratie, troisieme pouvoir qui manque à nos institutions, et dont l'absence pendant le frottement dangereux que l'on remarque aujourd'hui entre la puissance royale et la puissance populaire. C'est dans cette vue, que les Royalistes solliciteraient les substitutions en faveur de l'aînée. Ils chercheraient à arreter, par tous les moyens legaux, la division des proprietés, division qui, dans trente ans, en reduisant la loi agraire, nous fera tomber en democratie farcée.

"Une autre mesure importante serait encore prise par l'administration Royaliste. Cette administration demanderait aux Chambres, tant dans l'intérêt des acquereurs que dans celui des anciens proprietaires, une juste indemnité pour les familles qui ont perdu leurs biens dans le cours de la Revolution. Les deux espèces de proprietes qui existent parmi nous, et qui créent, pour ainsi dire, deux peuples sur le moment, sont la grande plaie de la France. Pour la guerir, les Royalistes n'auraient que le merite de faire revivre la proposition de M. le Marechal Macdonald; 'On apprend tout dans les camps Français la justice comme la gloire.'"—*Conservateur*, 30 Nov., 1819, and *Œuvres de M. Chateaubriand*, xx. 270, 271.

† That regulating the promotion of officers irrespective of the Crown.—*Ante*, ch. vi. § 47.

The great military conspiracy, which was to have broken out on 19th August, had its ramifications in the provinces, and in several places the disturbances which ensued required to be coerced by open force. At Brest, M. Ballart, the deputy, was openly insulted by the populace, and the national guard evinced such symptoms of disaffection that it required to be dissolved. At Saumur, M. Benjamin Constant was threatened by the scholars of the military school for cavalry. Every thing indicated the approach of the most fearful of all contests—a contest of classes. The exasperation of parties, as usual in cases where they are nearly balanced, was extreme; the Royalists were excited by the prospect of ere long attaining power, the Liberals exasperated at the thoughts of losing it. The ruling principle with the Duke de Richelieu, and which had directed the distribution of the honors of the *Cordon Bleu*, had been to form a new hierarchy, drawn from all classes, around the throne, and thus to interest in its support alike the Liberals, Imperialists, and Royalists. This maxim had been acted upon with great discrimination and success; but now the violent exasperation of parties, and the ascertained conspiracies in the army, rendered it advisable to adopt still more vigorous measures of conciliation, and those resolved on were the following.[1]

marginal: Disturbances in the provinces. Internal measures of the Government.
marginal: 1 Cap. vii. 110, 112; Lam. vii. s. 9.

A new organization was given to the household of the king, which embraced a considerable extension. It was divided into six departments, the heads of four of which were great officers of the Crown, and the other two great officers of the household.* The king regulated these departments entirely himself, and never would permit any interference on the part of his Cabinet Ministers. He said, and not without reason, that as he left them the disposal of all the offices of the state, they might leave him the patronage of his own household. In filling up the situations, however, he carried out to its full extent the system of fusion, on which he was so much bent. M. de Lauriston was put at the head of the household, in reward of his military services, and recent activity in suppressing the disturbances in Brest. His devotion to the royal family, good sense, and discernment, justified the choice. But so far did the king go in his desire to conciliate all parties, that he appointed General Rapp, a brave and distinguished, but rough and homespun veteran of Napoleon's, Grand Master of the Wardrobe. The old soldier, however, soon showed, that if he had been bred in camps, he could take on, late in life, if not the polish, at least the address of courts; for, on occasion of the death of Napoleon, which soon after ensued,[2] having been gently chid by the king for the extreme grief which he manifested, he replied: "Ah! Sire, I owe him every thing—even the happiness of serving your Majesty."

marginal: 90. Changes in the household. Nov. 1, 1820.
marginal: 2 Cap. vii. 113, 115; Lac. iii. 20.

A more important change was adopted soon after, which tended, more than any thing else, to the prolonged existence of the dynasty of the Restoration. This was an entirely new organization of the army. The object of the former division of the troops into departmental legions had been, to destroy the disaffected spirit of the Imperial army, by breaking up the regiments from whose *esprit de corps* its continuance was chiefly to be apprehended; and the measure had in a great degree been attended with success. But the military conspiracy of August 19, and the certain information obtained that a considerable part of the army had been privy to it, proved that the new regulations, recently introduced, regarding promotion in the army, which determined it by certain fixed rules, irrespective of the choice of the sovereign, was fraught with danger, and might, at some future period, prove fatal to the monarchy. M. Latour-Maubourg, accordingly, felt the necessity of a change of system; and he presented a report to the king, stating a variety of considerations, which, however just, were not the real ones,* which determined the alteration he proposed—a return to the old system. According to his recommendation, a new ordonnance was issued, which re-established the army, very much on the footing on which it had stood prior to the great change introducing departmental legions in 1815. The infantry was divided into eighty regiments, of which sixty were of the line, and twenty light infantry. Each regiment consisted of three battalions, and each battalion of eight companies; each company of three officers and eighty sub-officers and soldiers. Thus each regiment, including field-officers, consisted of two thousand and ten men, and the whole foot-soldiers of a hundred and sixty-one thousand men.[1] Fourteen états-majors, six legions, and between two thousand and three thousand officers, were put on half-pay. No change was made on the guards or cavalry, the spirit of which was known to be sufficiently good. The ordonnance experienced no resistance in any quarter; very much in consequence of its gratifying the soldiers, by ordering the resumption of the old blue uniform, associated with so many recollections—a change which induced them to hope, at no distant period, for the restoration of the tricolor cockade.

marginal: 91. New organization of the army.
marginal: Oct. 27, 1820.
marginal: 1 Moniteur, Oct. 28, 1820; Ann. Hist. iii. 233, 234; Ordonnance, Oct. 27, 1820.

---

* Viz.: "De la grande Aumônerie, du grand Maître, du grand Chambellan, du grand Ecuyer, du grand Veneur, du grand Maître des Cérémonies. Le grand Veneur et le grand Maître des Cérémonies étaient grands officiers de la maison; les autres, grands officiers de la couronne."—*Histoire de la Restauration*, vii. 114.

* "Que l'appel sous les drapeaux des jeunes soldats donnait lieu, dans le système des legions, à des dépenses considérables, par la nécessité de les diriger sur les legions de leur département, qui en était souvent placé à une grande distance; or en diminuant la distance à parcourir, on obtenait avec une réduction dans les dépenses, l'avantage de compter moins de déserteurs. Dans certaines legions le nombre des sujets capables est si grand, que l'avancement qui leur est dévolu, n'offre pas assez de chances pour les retenir au service, tandis que dans d'autres legions on est totalement dépourvu de bons sous-officiers; et puis, à la guerre, ou dans le cas d'une expédition lointaine un événement malheureux pèserait tout entier sur la population militaire de quelques départements, et rendrait impossible, pour longtemps, la réorganisation de leur corps."—*Rapport de M. de Gouvion St. Cyr.* CAPEFIGUE, *Histoire de la Restauration*, vii. 115, 116.

92. Ordonnance regarding public instruction. Nov. 1, 1820.

A change not less important, both in its effects and as indicating the altered disposition of the Government, was made by the Minister of the Interior in the important matter of public instruction. An ordonnance of the king re-established the "Secretaries General" of schools, which had been abolished in 1816. These officers were erected into a royal commission, of which M. Corbière soon became the head; and their duty was to exercise a superintendence over the system of education pursued, and the works read, in all the schools of the kingdom. As they virtually came in place of the old university of Napoleon, and discharged its functions, so they were divided into its departments, and resumed its costume.[1] The object of this measure, as that of Napoleon had formerly been, was to bring public opinion into harmony with the existing dynasty and system of government by moulding the minds of the rising generation. An academy of medicine was soon after created by the king, and several stringent regulations passed, the object of which was to restrain the turbulent and refractory spirit which, in the late tumults, had manifested itself in Paris in the students of law and physic.[2]

[1] Vide Hist. of Europe, c. i. ᛟ 76, 79.

[2] An. Hist. iii. 232, 233; Moniteur, Dec. 21, 1820.

93. The king's circular to the electors. Oct. 25.

All these matters, however, though most momentous in their ultimate effects, yielded in importance to the elections, upon the result of which the fate of the Ministry, in a great measure, depended, and which were this year of the greater importance, that they would indicate, for the first time, the working of the new Electoral Law upon the composition of the Legislature. At a Cabinet Council assembled to consider this question, M. Pasquier stated, that the circumstances appeared to be so grave that a circular should be written by the king to the electors, explaining his views, and the course which he was desirous they should adopt on the occasion. Louis caught up the idea; and, to render the royal intervention still more apparent, he proposed that M. Pasquier should draw up the address, that he should correct it, copy it over with his own hand, and sign it, and that *lithographic copies of the royal autograph should be sent to every elector in the kingdom.* This was accordingly done, and a hundred thousand copies thrown off and circulated for that purpose.*

This is a very curious circumstance, strongly indicative of how little the first elements of constitutional government were understood in France. They were destitute of what must ever be the basis of the fabric—the power of *self-direction*. Both the Royalists and the Liberals were aware of this, and neither wished to alter it. They regarded the people as a vast army, which would best discharge its duties when it obeyed with docility the voice of its chiefs; they had no conception of the chiefs obeying the voice of the army. Sad and irremediable effect of the destruction of all intermediate ranks and influence by the Revolution, which left only the executive standing erect, in awful strength, amidst the level surface of the people. Of the two, however, the Royalists were the most likely, if they had been permitted to do so, to prepare the people for the exercise of constitutional rights; because they desired to restore the nobility, hierarchy, and provincial incorporations, by whom a public opinion and rural influence, capable of counter-balancing the executive, might be formed: but it is more than doubtful whether the attempt could have been successful; because, in their insane passion for equality, the nation would not permit the foundation even of the edifice to be laid.[1]

[1] Cap. vii. 119, 120.

94. Result of the elections favorable to the Royalists.

At length the elections came, and were more favorable to the Royalists than their most sanguine hopes could have anticipated. They demonstrated not only the magnitude of the change made on the constituency by the late change in the Electoral Law, but the reaction which had taken place in the public mind from the birth of the Duke of Bordeaux, and improved prospects of the Bourbon dynasty. Not merely were the whole new members elected for the departments chosen for the first time by the fourth of the whole who paid the highest amount of taxes—one hundred and sixty in number—with a few exceptions, on the Royalist side, but even those for the arrondissements, of whom a fifth, according to the existing law, were changed, proved, for the first time since the *coup-d'état* of 5th September, 1816, on the whole favorable to their views. Out of forty-six to be chosen to fill up the fifth, twenty-seven were Royalists and only seventeen Liberal. On the whole, the Royalists had now, for the first time since 1815, obtained a decided preponderance in the popular branch of the legislature. Passionately desirous of victory in civil equally as military contests, the majority of the French in any conflict invariably, irrespective of principle, range themselves on the side of success. The principle, so strong in England, of *dogged resistance to victorious power*, is almost unknown among them. Louis XVIII. was terrified at the success of the friends of the monarchy.[2] "We shall be overwhelmed, M. de Richelieu," said he; "can you possibly restrain

[2] Lac. iii. 20, 21; Cap. vii. 120.

[3] Ann. Hist. iii. 231, 232.

* "Une liberté forte et légitime, fondée sur des lois émanées de son amour pour les Français, et de son espérance des temps, était assurée à ses peuples: 'Ecartez des fonctions de député,' ajoutait-il, 'les fauteurs de troubles, les artisans de discordes, les propagateurs d'injustes défiances contre mon gouvernement. Il depend de vous d'assurer le repos, la gloire et le bonheur de notre commune patrie; vous en avez la volonté, manifestez-la par vos choix. La France touche au moment de recevoir le prix de tous ses sacrifices, de voir ses impôts diminués, les charges publiques allégées; et ce n'est pas quand tout fleurit et tout prospère, qu'il faut nourrir dans les mains des factieux, et livrer à leurs desseins pervers, les arts, l'industrie, la paix des familles, et une félicité que tous les peuples de la terre envient. Vos députés choisis parmi les citoyens, amis sincères et zélés de la charte, devoués au trône et a la patrie, affermiront avec moi l'ordre sans lequel nulle société ne peut exister; et j'affermirai avec eux ces libertés que deux fois je vous ai rendues, et qui ont toujours en pour asile le trône de mes aïeux.'"—*Louis XVIII. aux Electeurs*, 25 October, 1820.

Annuaires Historiques, iii. 231; and CAPEFIGUE, *Histoire de la Restauration*, vii. 119, 121. The idea of Louis XIV., "L'etat, c'est moi," is very apparent in this proclamation of his descendant, notwithstanding all the lessons of the Revolution.

such a majority?" We have the word of Monsieur," replied the Minister; "and at all events, it was indispensable above all to save the monarchy."

95. Effect of the change in the Assembly.

This great change in the composition of the popular deputies proved decisively how much the long-continued ascendency of the Liberals had been owing to the fatal effects of a constituency founded on one *uniform qualification*, which the *coup-d'état* of 5th September, 1816, had introduced. The Royalists and their adherents in the Centre were now fully two-thirds of the Assembly; and this majority was formidable, not only from its number, but from its ardent and uncompromising character. Now was seen how little crime advances any cause; deeply did the Liberals mourn the murder of the Duke de Berri. Among the new deputies were upward of sixty of the old Chamber of 1815, whom the change in the law had since excluded from the Chamber, and who had nursed in solitude their opinions, and become confirmed in their prejudices. M. de Peyronnet, who had been king's advocate at Bourges, was returned, but he was cautious and reserved at first, and far from presaging the eminence which as Minister he afterwards attained. M. Dudon, who had commenced his official career rather unfortunately, soon rose to eminence, chiefly from the great facility of speaking which he possessed, and the energy with which he defended any cause which he espoused. General Donnadieu, who had become known by the prompt suppression of the insurrection at Grenoble, and the exaggeration and violence with which it was followed, acquired distinction also, from the intrepidity of his thoughts and the fearlessness of his language. He was able and energetic in his ideas, but impetuous and declamatory in his language—a peculiarity very common with military men, when they become orators or authors, and one which sensibly impedes their influence. An ultra-Royalist, he included the whole Ministry in his long-cherished hatred of M. Decazes, and did not advert to the rapid modification toward Royalist principles which it was undergoing. The Liberals beheld with satisfaction those feuds among their adversaries, and loudly applauded General Donnadieu in his diatribes against the administration of the Duke de Richelieu.[1]

[1] Cap. vii. 128, 131; Lac. iii. 20, 21.

96. Accession of Villèle, &c. to the Ministry.

The first public proof of the leaning of the Ministry toward the Royalists — which, in truth, had become unavoidable from the composition of the Chambers—was given by the appointment of M. de Chateaubriand to the embassy at Berlin, which he accepted, at the special request of the Duke de Richelieu. It was arranged between the Royalist chiefs and the Premier that M. de Villèle and M. de Corbière should, at the same time, be taken into the administration; but there was some difficulty in finding, at the moment, places for men of their acknowledged talents and weight in the legislature. It was got over by the moderation of M. de Villèle, who, set on higher objects of ambition, stooped to conquer. "Do something for Corbière: a place in the king's Council is enough for me." It was arranged accordingly that M. Lainé should, in the mean time, cede the port-folio of Public Instruction to M. de Corbière, and that M. de Villèle should be admitted without office into the Cabinet; but the appointment did not appear in the *Moniteur* till after the session commenced. The only condition which M. de Villèle made on entering the Cabinet, was that a new Municipal Law should be introduced by the Government, which was done accordingly.[1]

[1] Mem. de Chateaubriand, vii. 276, 279; Cap. vii. 131, 132.

97. Speech of the king, and answer of the Chambers.

The Chambers met on the 20th December, and the speech of the king, which was delivered in the hall of the Louvre bearing the name of Henry IV., on account of the health of his majesty not permitting him to go to the Palace of the Legislative Body, earnestly counseled moderation and unanimity. "Every thing announced," said he, "that the modifications introduced into our electoral system will produce the desired results. Whatever adds to the influence and consideration of the legislature, adds to the authority and dignity of my crown. By strengthening the relations necessary between the monarch and the Chambers, we shall succeed in forming such a system of government as a great monarchy such as France will require in all time to come. It is to accomplish these designs that I would see the days prolonged which Providence may accord to me; and, to insure this great object, desire that you may reckon on my firm and invariable will, and I on your loyal and constant support." The address was, as usual, an echo of the speech; but it terminated with expressions which revealed the ruling feelings of the majority, and furnish the key to nearly the whole subsequent career of the Royalist administration in France. "To fortify the authority of religion, and purify morals by a system of education at once Christian and monarchical; to give to the armed force that organization which may secure tranquillity within and peace without; to improve all our institutions which rest on the charter, and are intended to protect our liberties—such are the well-known intentions of your majesty, and such also are our duties. We will pursue these ameliorations with the moderation which is the accompaniment of strength; we will obtain them by patience, which is the act of awaiting in patience the fruits of the beneficial changes already introduced. May Heaven, measuring the years of your Majesty by the wishes and prayers of your people, cause to dawn on France those happy and serene days which are presaged by the birth of a new heir to the throne."[2] "You have expressed," said the monarch in reply, "my intentions, and your answer is a pledge that you will second them. I repeat it: if I wish to prolong my days, it is to consolidate the institutions I have given to my people. But whatever may be the intentions of Providence, let us never forget our constitutional maxim, 'The king never dies in France.'"

[2] An. Hist. iv. 2, 3; Doc. Hist. App. 585; Cap. vii. 145.

Although these expressions and allusions seemed to presage an important and perhaps eventful session, yet it proved otherwise, and the session passed over with fewer legislative measures of importance than any which had curred since the Restoration. The reason was that the Royalist majority was so decided that the strife of party was over, while, at the same time, as they were still in a minority in the Cabinet, they could not bring forward those measures on which their leaders were set, with a view to modify the general frame and influence of Government. The initiation of laws still belonged to the king's Ministers: the opposition could only introduce their ideas by amendments, which, however, often assumed the importance of original propositions. An important bill in its practical effects, though not so much so in appearance, was introduced and carried, to determine the boundaries of electoral districts. It was intended to increase the Royalist influence, and did so most effectually. Great difficulty was experienced in arranging the details of the municipal law which had been promised to M. de Villèle, but at length M. Mounier succeeded in drawing one which met the views of both parties. But being founded on a compromise, it was really acceptable to neither; and it experienced so much resistance in the Chamber that after a prolonged discussion it was at length withdrawn. The king said on this occasion, "I had abandoned the rights of the crown; the Chambers would not permit it: I have learned a lesson."[1]

[margin: 98. Measures of the session, fixing the boundaries of the electoral districts.]

[1] An. Hist. iv. 44, 51; Cap. vii. 149, 151.

The strength of the Royalists in the Chamber made Ministers feel the necessity of bringing forward some measure in support of the Church, upon which they were so anxiously set. They did so accordingly, and the law they proposed gave the king power to establish twelve new bishoprics, and to raise considerably the salaries of the clergy in those situations where it might be deemed necessary. The report of the commission, to whom the matter was referred, bore "that religion, resting between the two concordats of 1801 and 1817, without any solid basis, was reduced with its ministers to the most deplorable state, to which the legislature is not sufficiently alive. The absolute absence of religion in the country districts is an evil to which no other is comparable. Civilization is the perfection of the laws—very different from politeness, which is the perfection of the arts—and is nothing but Christianity applied to the legislation of societies." The law met with very violent opposition from the Liberal party in the Chamber, but it passed by a majority of more than two to one—the numbers being 219 to 105; a result which sufficiently indicated the vast change which the recent changes in the Electoral Law had made in the popular branch of the legislature.[2]

[margin: 99. Law for additional ecclesiastical endowments.]

[2] An. Hist. iv. 96, 110; Cap. vii. 151, 152.

The return of peace, and opening of its harbors to the commerce of all nations, had produced, though in a lesser degree, the same effect in France as in Great Britain. Importation had increased to a degree which excited alarm; and the grain districts loudly demanded some restrictions upon foreign importation, as a protection to native industry. In the course of the discussion, M. de Villèle stated, that the annual consumption of France was 160,000,000 hectolitres of grain; that the crop of 1819 had exceeded that amount by a tenth; notwithstanding which 1,400,000 hectolitres, or about 1-100 of the annual consumption, had been imported; while the exportation had only been 538,000 hectolitres; leaving a balance of 862,000 hectolitres introduced when not required. The import duty paid on these 862,000 hectolitres was 2,573,000 francs. The importation came chiefly from Odessa, America, and Egypt. The regulations proposed and adopted in consequence were chiefly of a local character, throwing restrictions on the importation of foreign grain, by limiting the number of places where it might be received. But the increased importation, even under the considerable protecting duty which existed in France, is a valuable illustration of the eternal law, that the old and rich state is always undersold in the productions of subsistence by the poor one, as much as it undersells the latter in the production of manufactures.[1]*

[margin: 100. Modifications in the corn-laws.]

[1] An. Hist. iv. 75, 89, 567.

A law, which excited much more attention, though not of so much real importance, was brought forward by Government for an indemnity to the Imperial donataries. These were the marshals, generals, and others whom, as explained in a former work, Napoleon had endowed, often richly, out of the revenues of Italy, Germany, and other countries over which his power extended, during the spring-tide of his fortunes,[2] but who, by the reflucnce of his dominion to the limits of Old France, had been entirely bereaved of their possessions, and were reduced to great straits in consequence. The distresses of these persons had been such, that they obtained a slight relief from the Treasury by the finance law of 1818, but now it was proposed to give them a durable indemnity. As many of these persons were of the highest rank, and their names associated with the most glorious epochs of the Empire, the proposal excited a very great sensation, and was loudly applauded by the Imperial party, who were to profit by it. The intention of Government was to make this grant to the time-honored relics of the Imperial régime a precedent for the great indemnity which they meditated to the emigrants and others who had been dispossessed of their estates by the Revolution; for after the Liberals had unanimously supported grants from the public funds for the relief of their chiefs who had lost their possessions by the calamities of war, it was not easy to see on what principle they could oppose a similar

[margin: 101. Law for the indemnity of the Imperial donataries.]

[2] Hist. of Europe, c. l. § 52.

---

* The price of wheat at Odessa was, on an average, this year—which was there one of scarcity—12 francs; freight to Marseilles, 3 francs 50 cents, and the import duty 5 francs 50 cents; in all 20 francs (16s.) the hectolitre, or 48s. the quarter. The usual price at Odessa was 4 francs the hectolitre, which corresponds to about 12 francs (10s.) the quarter. Exportation was permitted in France by the law of 14th December, 1814, only when the price in the frontier departments was 23 francs for the best wheat, 21 francs for the second, and 19 francs for the third, which showed that the average cost of production was above the highest of these sums. The import duty was 5 francs 50 cents the hectolitre, but even at this high import duty the influx of foreign grain from America, Odessa, and the Nile had caused a ruinous fall of prices in all the southern provinces.—*L'Annuaire Historique*, iv. 75.

grant to the sufferers under the confiscations of the Revolution. The Royalists, however, did not see this, or they had no faith in the existing Ministry carrying out this design, as Marshal Macdonald, who introduced the project in 1814, had intended, and it met accordingly with the most impassioned resistance from the Right of the Assembly. No words can describe the indignation of the Royalists when they heard the names of the chief persons to be benefited by the new law, embracing the principal leaders of the Napoleonist party, and those most deeply implicated in the conspiracy of 1815.* "It is," said M. Duplessis, "a reward for conspirators." The indemnity proposed was an inscription on the Grand Livre—in other words, the gift of so much stock in the Five per Cents, bearing date 22d Sept., 1821, in certain fixed proportions. The bill underwent many amendments in committee; but at length, after great hesitation, indicative of weakness on the part of Ministers, it passed as originally proposed by a majority of 203 to 125.¹

^{1 An. Hist. iv. 115, 128; Cap. vii. 148, 149.}

102. Law regarding the censorship of the press.

The question of the censorship of the press still remained, which afforded as regular a subject for the encounter of parties in France as that of Catholic Emancipation did in England. Although the Ministry was now of so mixed a character that it might reasonably have been supposed that both sets of journalists, having each something to hope from the Government, would support it, yet it proved otherwise; and there is no period in the whole annals of the Restoration when the press was more violent, or parties were more exasperated against each other. Perhaps this was unavoidable: the effect of the change in the Electoral Law was now evident, and a party in possession of power is never so exasperated as when it sees the reins gradually but perceptibly slipping from its hands. The Minister of the Interior accordingly, Count Siméon, brought forward a project for continuing the censorship, alleging, in justification of the proposal, that it had during the past year been so gently exercised, that no fair discussion had ever been interfered with, but intemperate abuse alone excluded. The commission, however, to which the matter was referred, reported against the project, and Government, in the Chamber itself, were defeated on an amendment proposed by M. Courtarvel, on the part of the Liberals, that the restriction should continue only three months after the commencement of the session of 1821. Thus modified, however, the proposal passed into a law in the Deputies by a majority of 214 to 112; in the Peers, by 83 to 45.²

^{2 An. Hist. iv. 180, 191, 195.}

103. Speech of M. Pasquier on the occasion, July 6th.

This debate was chiefly memorable for the first open declaration of opinion on the part of Ministers, which revealed an irreconcilable division of opinion and approaching rupture in the Cabinet. "If the censorship," said M. Pasquier, "has been useful, it has been chiefly in what relates to foreign affairs, and certainly it has rendered great services, in that respect, not only to France, but to Europe. We are accused of having enmities and partialities; yes, I admit I have a repugnance to those men, to whatever party they belong, who wish to trouble, or, without intending it, do trouble, the tranquillity of our country, who disunite minds when they should be united. I have a repugnance to the men who, too often exhuming from the tomb the revolutionary maxims, would gladly make them a means of destroying the felicity we enjoy, perverting the rising generation, and bringing upon their heads the evils which have so long desolated us. I have a repugnance to the men who, by odious recriminations, generally unjust, always impolitic, furnish arms and auxiliaries to those whom I have designated. As I distrust every usurpation, I have a repugnance to a small body of men who would claim exclusively for themselves the title of Royalists—who would wish to monopolize for themselves the sentiments which belong to the French nation; and who would every day contract a circle which it is for the interest of all should be expanded. Still more have I a repugnance to the same men, when they evince too clearly the design of making of a thing so sacred as royalty, and the power which emanates from it, the instruments of their passions, their interests, or their ambition. I have a repugnance to these men, but chiefly because I feel assured that if they obtained all that they desire, they would make use of the power they have acquired for no other end but to gratify private interests, and that we should thus see them reproduce, by the successive triumph of their petty ambition, that system of government which, in the years preceding the Revolution, had done such mischief to France."¹

^{1 Moniteur, July 8, 1821. Ann. Hist. iv. 187; Cap. vii. 157, 158.}

104. Increasing irritation of parties, and difficulties of the Ministry.

When sentiments such as these were expressed by the Minister for Foreign Affairs, in language so unmeasured in regard to a body of men who formed part of the Ministry, who had a majority in both Chambers, and whose support was essential to their existence, it was evident that the dissolution of the Government was at hand. The difficulties of Ministers and the irritation of parties increased rapidly after the session of the legislature terminated. The Count d'Artois and the Royalists were dissatisfied that, when they had a majority in the Chambers, they had not one in the Ministry, and that M. Polignac and Peyronnet had not seats in the Cabinet. They condemned also, in no measured terms, the conduct of the Government, which, after having obtained, by the revelations made in the course of the trial of the conspirators of August 19th, decisive evidence of the accession of the Liberal leaders, especially Lafayette and Manuel, to the design of overthrowing the Government, let them escape untouched, and chastised even the inferior delinquents only with subordinate penalties." "M.

---

*They were, MM. Jean-Bon Saint-André, Jean de Bry, Quinette, General Hullin, Labedoyere, Marshal Ney, Count d'Estur, General Lefevre-Desnouettes, General Gilly, General Mouton-Duvernet, General Clauzel, Count de Laborde, General Excelmans, the Duke of Bassano, General Lamarque, Baron Méchin.—CAPEFIGUE, Hist. de la Restauration, vii. 149.

* "Dans le procès des troubles du mois de juin le pouvoir ministériel avait reculé devant un système de pénalité trop forte, trop afflictive. De tous ces débats c'est ressortie la certitude qu'il existait un comité actif, dirigeant,

de Richelieu is an honest man, but weak; M. de Serres, uncertain; M. de Pasquier, a Bonapartist in disguise; M. Portal, worst of all, a Protestant; M. Roy, a representative of the Hundred Days; M. Siméon, the minister of the *Emperor Jérôme*; M. Mounier, secretary to the usurper." Such was the language of the Royalists, and the Liberals and Doctrinaires were not behind them in vehemence. In particular, M. Guizot published a pamphlet entitled, "On the Restoration of the Present Ministry," which made a great noise, chiefly by the graphic picture it presented of their difficulties and divisions. The bland temper and moderate disposition of the Duke de Richelieu was sorely tried by these accumulated attacks on every side; and, on his return from the embassy in London, he complained to M. Decazes on the subject. "I wonder you are surprised," said he: "they betrayed me, they will betray you; it is their part to do so: it is impossible to act with them."¹

¹ De la Restauration, etc du Ministère Actuel, par M. Guizot, 34, 42; Cap. vii. 161, 165, 173.

At length matters came to such a pass that M. de Villèle and M. Corbière, finding they could no longer preserve terms with the Royalists on the one hand, and the semi-liberal Ministry on the other, resigned their situations shortly before the parliamentary session came to a close. Chateaubriand retired with them, greatly regretted, from the embassy at Berlin. Negotiations upon this were opened with Monsieur and the Royalist chiefs, who wished to retain the Duke de Richelieu as premier, but demanded the Ministry of the Interior for M. de Villèle, the creation of a Ministry of Public Instruction for M. Corbière, the embassy at London for M. de Chateaubriand, and another embassy for M. de Vitrolles. The Cabinet offered the Ministry of the Marine to M. de Villèle, but held firm for retaining M. Mounier in the Ministry of the Interior, by far the most important for political influence of any in the Government. The negotiations broke off on this vital point, and Ministers, without the support of the Right, ventured to face the next session. In their expectations, however, of being able to go on without their support, they soon found themselves mistaken. The elections of 1821 considerably augmented the Royalist majority, already so great, and on the first division in the Chamber the latter were victorious by an immense majority. The speech of the Crown was studiously guarded, so as if possible to avoid a division; but in the answer of the Chamber to the king, a passage was inserted at which both the monarch and the Duke de Richelieu took mortal offense, as seeming to imply a doubt of their patriotism and honor.² The king returned a severe answer to

105. Rupture with the Royalists, and fall of the Richelieu Ministry.

the address," and is was for a time thought the triumph of the minister was complete; but this hope proved fallacious. The Duke de Richelieu found his situation so painful, with a decided majority hostile to him in the Chamber, that, after some conference with the Count d'Artois, in which it was found impossible to come to an understanding, he resolved on resigning with all his colleagues, which was accordingly done on the 13th of December.¹

¹ Cap. vii. 220, 247; Ann. Hist. iv. 205, 240; Moniteur, December 15, 1821.

According to established usage, the Duke de Richelieu advised the king whom to send for, to form the new Ministry, and he of course recommended M. de Villèle. There was no difficulty in forming a Government; the near approach of the crisis had been so long foreseen, that the Royalists had their arrangements all complete. M. de Villèle was President of the Council and Minister of Finance; M. de Peyronnet, Secretary of State and Minister of Justice; Viscount Montmorency, Minister for Foreign Affairs; M. Corbière, Minister of the Interior; Marshal Victor, of War; the Marquis Clermont-Tonnerre, of the Marine. In addition to this, the ex-ministers, M. de Serres, General Latour-Maubourg, Count Siméon, Baron Portal, and M. Roy, were appointed members, as usual on such occasions, of the Privy Council; and, in addition, Latour-Maubourg was appointed Governor of the Invalides. The Ministerial revolution was complete; the Royalists were in entire possession of the government, and the change in all subordinate, as well as the principal offices, was thorough and universal. The king would probably never have consented to so entire a revolution, had he possessed the bodily or mental vigor which he did in the earlier parts of his reign. But this was very far from being the case. His health, which had been long declining, had now become so feeble that his life was almost despaired of; and he had fallen into that state of dependence on those around him, which such a state of debility generally produces. To a monarch who was not able to rise from his chair, who was wheeled about the room, and required to be tended almost with the care of an infant, the influence of Monsieur, the Duchess d'Angoulême, and the Countess Du Cayla, was irresistible. Louis, in fact, had almost resigned the reigns of government to his brother. He regarded his reign as having terminated with the retirement of the Duke de Richelieu. "At last," said he, "M. de Villèle triumphs: I know little of the men who are entering my Council along with him;² I believe, however, that they have good sense enough not to follow blindly all the follies of the Right. For the rest, I consider myself annihilated from this moment; I undergo the usual fate of constitutional monarchs: hitherto, at least, I

106. The new Ministry.

² Moniteur, Dec. 15, 1821; Ann. Hist. iv. 212; Cap. vii. 247.

---

² "Dans l'exil et la persécution, j'ai soutenu mes droits, l'honneur de ma race et celui de mon français; en le trône, entouré de mon peuple, je m'indigne à la seule pensée que je puisse jamais sacrifier l'honneur français et la dignité de ma couronne. J'aime à croire que la plupart de ceux qui ont voté cette adresse n'en ont pas presenti toutes les expressions—s'ils avaient eu le temps de les apprécier, ils n'eussent pas souffert une supposition que, comme Roi, je ne dois pas caractériser."—*Moniteur*, 20th Nov., 1820. CAPEFIGUE, vii. 237.

---

¹ Dont les chefs et les projets étaient connus. Comment des lors les Royalistes pouvaient-ils s'expliquer cette insouciance et cette faiblesse qui s'arrêtaient devant certains noms propres? La Correspondance de M. de Lafayette avec Goyet de la Sarthe revelait les desseins et les plans revolutionnaires; pourquoi ne pas la déposer comme pièce principale d'un acte d'accusation?"—CAPEFIGUE, *Hist. de la Restauration*, vii. 161.

² "Nous nous félicitons, Sire, de vos relations constamment amicales avec les puissances étrangères; dans la juste confiance qu'une paix si précieuse n'est point altérée par des sacrifices incompatibles avec l'honneur de la nation et avec la dignité de la Couronne."—*Moniteur*, 30th Nov., 1821. Ann. Hist. iv. 259.

have defended my crown; if my brother casts it to the winds, it is his affair."

107. Reflections on this event. The fall of M. de Richelieu's administration, and the accession of a purely Royalist Government, was so great a change in France, that it was equivalent to a revolution. Nothing appears so extraordinary as that such an event should have taken place, in consequence of a parliamentary majority, so soon after the period when the tide of Liberal opinions set in so strongly in the nation that two successive *coups d'état* had been deemed necessary by the Government, in September 1816 and March 1819, to mould the two branches of the legislature in conformity with it. But many similar examples of rapid change of opinion, and the setting in of entirely opposite flood-tides of opinion, are to be found both in the previous and subsequent annals of that country; and they are not without a parallel both in the ancient and recent history of this. Whoever studies the changes of public opinion in the reign of Charles II., which within a few years led to the frightful judicial massacres of the Papists, and the inhuman severities of the Rye-House Plot—or recollects that the same nation which brought in Sir Robert Peel by a majority of 91 in 1841, in the House of Commons, to support Protection, ten years afterward obliged Lord Derby to abandon it—will see, that, though the variations of opinion in Great Britain are not quite so rapid as in France, they are not less remarkable, nor less decisive in their results.

108. Great effects of the change in the Electoral Law. No doubt, the great change in the Electoral Law of France, carried through with so much difficulty by the Duke de Richelieu's administration, contributed largely to this result. The new principle introduced by that law, of giving the departmental electors representatives of their own in the Chamber, and of having them chosen, not by the electors generally, but by a fourth of their number who paid the highest amount of taxes, was a great change, not merely in its numerical results, upon the composition of the Chamber, but in the principle of representation itself. It was a return from the principle of the Revolution, which was that of a mere representation of *numbers*, to the general ancient representative system of Europe, which was that of *classes*. It was an abandonment of the principle of *uniform representation*, the most pernicious which can possibly be ingrafted on the constitutional system, because it tends at once to introduce class government, and that of the very worst, because the most irresponsible kind. Some one class inevitably, under such a system, acquires the majority in the elections and in the legislature; and the moment it does so, and feels its strength, it commences and carries through a series of measures calculated for its own benefit, without the slightest regard to the effect they may have upon the interest of other classes, or the general prosperity of the state. The only way to check this is to introduce into the legislature the representatives of other classes, *elected under a different suffrage*, and thus prevent the selfishness of one class from becoming paramount, by permitting the selfishness of another class to combat it.

109. Defects of the representative system in France. But although the introduction of the hundred and sixty departmental members, elected by "les plus imposés," was a most important step, and one in the right direction, yet another step was wanting to give the French nation a proper representation. This was a representation of numbers. To base the whole legislature upon them is doubtless to introduce class government of the worst kind; but it is also a great mistake, which in the end may be attended with fatal consequences, to exclude them from the representation altogether. The interests of labor are not only not identical with those of moneyed wealth, but they are often adverse to it: the sequel of this history will place this beyond a doubt, with respect to the British islands. The condition of the great body of the working classes may not only be noways benefited, but essentially injured, by a representation resting entirely on property, especially of a commercial kind; because measures injurious to their welfare may be passed into law by the class which alone is represented. As the representative system of the Restoration in France, even when amended by the act of 1820, contained no provision whatever for the representation of the working classes, by allowing no vote except to those paying at least 300 francs yearly of direct taxes, it was wanting in a most important element both of utility and general confidence. It will appear in the sequel how large a share this defect had in inducing the great catastrophe which, ten years afterward, proved fatal to the dynasty of the Restoration.

110. Undue ascendency of the Parti-Prêtre. Connected with this great defect in the French representative system was another circumstance, attended in the end with consequences not less disastrous. This was, that, while labor was unrepresented, religion was too much represented. This was the natural, and, in truth, unavoidable result of the irreligious spirit of the Revolution; the reaction was as violent as the action; its opponents conceived, with reason, that it could be combated only with the weapons and with the fervor of the ancient faith. The class of considerable proprietors, in whom a decided majority of the Chamber of Deputies was now vested, was attached to this party from principle, tradition, and interest. But although it is impossible to over-estimate the salutary influence of religion on human society, it unhappily does not equally follow that the ascendency of its professors in the legislature is equally beneficial. Experience has too often proved that the *Parti-Prêtre* is perhaps the most dangerous that can be intrusted with the administration of affairs. The reason is, that those who direct are not brought into contact with men in the actual business of life, and they deem it their duty to be regulated, not by expedience, or even practicability, but solely by conscience. This disposition may make courageous martyrs, but it produces very bad legislators; it is often noble in adversity, but always perilous in prosperity. Power is the touchstone which the Romish Church has never been able to withstand, as suffering is the ordeal from which it has never failed to emerge, surrounded by a halo of glory.

The danger of this party holding, as they now did, the reins of power, supported by a large majority in both Chambers, was much increased by the circumstance, that, though the peasants in the country were, for the most part, under the influence of the ancient faith, it was held in abhorrence by the majority of the working classes in the great towns, who were, at the same time, without any legal channel whereby to make their feelings influential in the legislature, but in possession of ample resources to disturb the established government.

<small>111. Cause of the reaction against Liberal institutions.</small> Although the change in the Electoral Law was the immediate cause of the majority which the Royalists now got in the Chamber, yet the real and ultimate cause is to be looked for in circumstances of wider extension and more lasting effects. It was the violence and crimes of the Liberal party over Europe which produced the general reaction against them. It was the overthrow of government in Spain, Portugal, Naples, and Piedmont, and the absurd and ruinous institutions established in their stead, which alarmed every thinking man in France; the assassination of the Duke de Berri, the projected assassination of the Cabinet Ministers in London, the attempted insurrection in the streets of Paris, opened the eyes of all to the means by which the hoped-for change was to be effected. The alteration in the Electoral Law in France was itself an effect of this change in the public mind; for it took place in a Chamber heretofore decidedly liberal. A similar modification had taken place in the views of the constituency, for the Royalists were now, for the first time for five years, in a majority in the arrondissements with regard to which no change had been made. It is Louvel, Thistlewood, and Riego, who stand forth as the real authors of this great reaction in Europe, and of the long stop to the progress of freedom which resulted from it—a memorable instance of the eternal truth, that no cause is in the end advanced by means at which the general mind revolts, and that none are such sufferers from the effects of crime as those for whose interest it was committed.

While France was thus under going the political throes and changes consequent <small>112. Death of Napoleon. May 5.</small> on its great Revolution, and the forcible change of the dynasty which governed it, and at the very moment when the infant prince was baptized who, it was hoped, would continue the ancient race of the Bourbon princes, that wonderful man breathed his last upon the rock of St. Helena who had so long chained the destinies of the world to his chariot-wheels. Since his transference, by the unanimous determination of the allied sovereigns, to that distant and melancholy place of exile, he had alternately exhibited the grandeur of a lofty, the weaknesses of a little, and the genius of a highly-gifted mind. He said at Fontainebleau, when he took leave of his faithful guards, that what "they had done together he would write;"[1] and <small>1 Hist. of Europe, c. lxxxix. § 26.</small> he had fulfilled the promise, in part at least, with consummate ability. It is hard to say whether his fame does not now rest nearly as much on his sayings and thoughts recorded at St. Helena, as on all the mighty deeds which he achieved in Europe. Yet even here, and when his vast genius alternately revealed the secrets of the past, and pierced the depths of the future, the littleness of a dwarf appeared in striking contrast to the strength of a giant. He was irritable, jealous, and spiteful, not less than able, discriminating, and profound; his serenity was disturbed by his being addressed with the title of General, or attended, at a distance, by an English orderly in the course of his rides; and exaggeration, falsehood, and envy, appeared in his thoughts and writings, not less than genius, capacity, and depth. His character, as revealed by misfortune, that touchstone of the human heart, affords the most striking proof of the truth of Dr. Johnson's observation, that no man ever yet raised himself from a private station to the government of mankind, in whom great and commanding qualities were not blended with littlenesses which would appear inconceivable in ordinary men.

Without doubt, it must ever be a matter of deep regret to every generous mind, <small>113. Reflections on his captivity.</small> and to none so much as to the inhabitants of Great Britain, that it was necessary to impose any restraint at all on the latter years of so great a man. How much more grateful would it have been to every honorable mind, to every feeling heart, to have acted to him as Xerxes did, in the first instance at least, to Themistocles, and in the spirit to which he himself appealed when he said, that he placed himself on the hearth of the "greatest, the most powerful, and the most persevering of his enemies." But there was this essential difference between the two cases—Themistocles, when he took refuge in the dominions of the great king, had not given his word and broken it. Napoleon had been treated with signal lenity and generosity when, after having devastated Europe by his ambition, he was allowed the splendid retirement of Elba; and the only return he made for it was, to invade France, overturn Louis XVIII., and cause his kingdom to be overrun by a million of armed men. He had signed the treaty of Fontainebleau, and the first thing he did was to break it.* When chained to the rock of St. Helena, he was still an object of dread to the European powers; his name was more powerful than an army of a hundred and fifty thousand men; he was too great to be forgotten, too little to be trusted. Every imaginable precaution was necessary to prevent the escape of a man who had shown that he regarded the faith of treaties only till it was his interest to break them; and of whom it had been truly said by exalted gen-

---

<small>* The author is well aware of the ground alleged by the partisans of Napoleon for this infraction, viz., that the payments stipulated by the treaty had not been made by the French Government to him. But supposing that there was some foundation for this complaint, it could afford no justification for so desperate and outrageous an act as invading France, without the slightest warning or declaration of war, and overturning the Government. The excessive pecuniary difficulties under which France at that period labored, owing to the calamities in which he himself had involved and left her, were the cause of this backwardness in making some of the payments; and the last man in the world who had any title to complain of them was the person whose insatiable ambition had caused them all.</small>

ins, that "his cocked hat and great-coat, placed on a stick on the coast of Brittany, would cause Europe to run to arms from one end to another."¹

Great was the sensation excited in Europe, and especially England, by the publication of the St. Helena memoirs, and the loud and impassioned complaints made of the alleged harsh treatment of the exiled Emperor by the English authorities. They were re-echoed in Parliament by Lord Holland and the leaders of the Opposition, and even the most moderately disposed men were led to doubt the necessity of the rigid precautions which were adopted, and to regret that more generous feelings had not been shown to a fallen enemy. Time, however, has now exercised its wonted influence over these mournful topics: it has demonstrated that the conduct of the English Government toward their illustrious captive was not only, in the circumstances, unavoidable, but highly liberal and considerate; and so clearly is this demonstrated, that it is now admitted by the ablest and most impassioned of the French historians of the period.* England bore the whole brunt of the storm, because she was in the front rank, and held the Emperor in her custody; but she did not act singly in the matter—she was only the executor of the general resolutions of the Allies. These were to treat Napoleon with all the respect and consideration due to his rank, but under such precautions as should render his escape a matter of impossibility. The conduct of his partisans, to which he was no stranger, added to the necessary rigor of these precautions; for several plots were formed for his escape, and only failed of success by the vigilance of the military and naval authorities on the island. Yet, even in the presence of these difficulties, the indulgence with which he was treated was such as now to excite the surprise of the most impassioned historians of the Revolution. The account shall be given in the words of the ablest and most eloquent of their number.²

"The sum of 300,000 francs (£12,000) a year," says Lamartine, "often added to by additional grants, was consecrated by the English Government to the cost of the table of the little court of the exiled Emperor. Bertrand the marshal of the palace, his wife and son; M. and Madame de Montholon, General Gourgaud and Dr. O'Meara; the valet-de chambre Marchand, Cypriani maitre-d'hôtel, Prérion chief of office, Saint-Denys, Noverras, his usher Santini, Rousseau keeper of the plate, and a train of valets, cooks, and footmen, formed the establishment. A library, ten or twelve saddle-horses, gardens, woods, rural labors, constant and free communication at all times between the exiles, correspondence under certain regulations with Europe, receptions and audiences given to travelers who arrived in the island, and were desirous to obtain an audience of the Emperor—such were the daily amusements of Longwood. Pickets of soldiers under the command of an officer watched the circuit of the building and its environs; a camp was established at a certain distance, but out of sight of the house, so as not to offend the inmates. Napoleon and his officers were at liberty to go out on foot or on horseback from daybreak to nightfall, and to go over the whole extent of the island accompanied only by an officer at a distance, so as to prevent all attempt at escape. Such was the respectful captivity which the complaints of Napoleon and his companions in exile styled the dungeon and martyrdom of St. Helena."¹ To this it may be added, that the entire establishment at St. Helena was kept up by the English Government on so splendid a scale that it cost them £400,000 a year; that Champagne and Burgundy were the daily beverage—the best French cookery the fare of the whole party; that the comfort and luxuries they enjoyed were equal to those of any duke in England; and that, as the house at Longwood had been inconvenient, the English Government had provided, at a cost of £40,000, a house neatly constructed of wood in London, which arrived in the island two days after the Emperor's death. Such were the alleged barbarities of England toward a man who had so long striven to effect her destruction, and who had chastised the hostility of Hofer by death in the fosse of Mantua, of Cardinal Pacca by confinement amidst Alpine snows in the citadel of Fenestrelles, and the supposed enmity of the Duke d'Enghien by massacre in the ditch of Vincennes.²⁸

But all this was as nothing as long as Mordecai the Jew sat at the king's gate. In the first instance, indeed, the bland and courteous manners of Sir Pulteney Malcolm, who was intrusted with the chief command, softened the restraints of captivity, and made the weary hours pass in comparative comfort; but he was unfortunately succeeded by Sir Hudson Lowe, whose manners were far less conciliating.

* "Après la crise de 1815, lorsque l'Europe, encore une fois menacée par Napoléon, crut nécessaire de prendre une mesure de précaution qui empêchât une seconde tourmente, Sainte-Hélène fut choisie comme prison d'état. Les puissances durent arrêter un système de surveillance à l'egard du prisonnier, car elles craignaient par-dessus tout le retour de Napoléon. L'Angleterre pourvut largement à ses besoins; la table seule de Napoléon coûtait à la Trésorerie 12,000 livres sterling. Il y a quelque chose qui dépasse mes idées, quand j'examine le grandiose du caractère de Napoléon, et sa vie immense d'administration et de batailles; c'est cet esprit qui s'arrête tant à Sainte-Hélène aux petites difficultés d'étiquette. Napoléon boude si l'on s'assied en sa présence, et si l'on ne le traite pas de Majesté, et d'Empereur; il se drape perpetuellement; il ne voit pas que la grandeur est en lui et non dans la pourpre et de vains titres. A Austerlitz, au conseil d'Etat, Napoléon est un monument de granit, et de bronze; a Sainte Hélène, c'est encore un colosse, mais paré d'un costume de cour."—CAPEFIGUE, *Histoire de la Restauration*, vii. 209.

* The allowance of wine to the establishment at Longwood was as follows, a fortnight:

	Bottles
Vin ordinaire	84
Constantia	7
Champagne	14
Vin de Grave	21
Teneriffe	84
Claret	140
	350

And besides, forty-two bottles of porter. A tolerable allowance for ten grown persons, besides servants.—See *Parliamentary Debates*, xxxv. 1159. The total cost of the table was £12,000 a year.—*Ibid.*, 1158.

A gallant veteran, who had accompanied the army of Silesia, in the quality of English commissioner, through its whole campaign in France, he was overwhelmed with the sense of the responsibility under which he labored, in being intrusted with the custody of so dangerous a captive; and he possessed none of the graces of manner which so often, in persons in authority, add to the charms of concession, and take off the bitterness of restraint. The obloquy cast on Sir Colin Campbell, in consequence of having been accidentally absent from Elba when the Emperor made his escape, was constantly before his eyes. He does not appear to have exceeded his instructions; and certainly the constant plots which were in agitation for Napoleon's escape, called for and justified every imaginable precaution. But he was often unreasonably *exigeant* on trifles of no real moment to the security of the Emperor's detention; and his manner was so unprepossessing, that, even when he conferred an indulgence, it was seldom felt as such. Napoleon, on his part, was not a whit behind the governor of the island in irritability or unreasonable demands. He seemed anxious to provoke outrages, and his ideas were fixed on the effect the account of them would produce in Europe. He was in correspondence with the leading members of the English Opposition, who made generous and strenuous efforts to soften his captivity; and he never lost the hope that, by the effect these representations would make on the British people, and on the world, his place of confinement might be altered; and, by being restored to Europe, he might succeed in playing over again the game of the Hundred Days. All his thoughts were fixed on this object, and it was to lay a foundation for these complaints that he affected to take offense at every trifle, and voluntarily aggravated the inconveniences of his own position. Montholon said truly to Sir Hudson Lowe, "If you had been an angel from heaven, you would not have pleased us."[*]

¹ Forsyth's Napoleon at St. Helena, iii. 334, 337; Lam. vi. 416, 417.

The truth is, none of the parties implicated in the treatment of Napoleon at St. Helena have emerged unscathed out of the ordeal through which they have passed since his death; and the publication of the papers of Sir Hudson Lowe, by Mr. Forsyth, has placed this beyond a doubt. The British government was the first to blame: its conduct in the main, and in all essential articles, was indulgent and considerate; but in matters of lesser real moment, but still more important to a person of Napoleon's irritable disposition, their instructions were unnecessarily rigid. Admitting that after his stealthy evasion from Elba it was indispensable that he should be seen daily by some of the British officers, and attended by one, beyond certain prescribed limits, where was the necessity of refusing him the title of Emperor, or ordering every thing to be withheld which was addressed to him by that title? A book inscribed "Imperatori Napoleon" might have been delivered to him without his detention being rendered insecure. A copy of Coxe's *Marlborough*, presented by him to a British regiment which he esteemed, might have been permitted to reach its destination, without risk of disaffection in the British army.¹ It is hard to say whether most littleness was evinced by the English government refusing such slight gratifications to the fallen hero, or by himself in feeling so much annoyed at the withholding the empty titles bespeaking his former greatness. It is deeply to be regretted, for the honor of human nature, which is the patrimony of all mankind, that he did not bear his reverses with more equanimity, and prove that the conqueror of continental Europe could achieve the yet more glorious triumph of subduing himself.

117. All parties were wrong regarding his treatment at St. Helena.

¹ Forsyth, iii. 277, 279.

For a year before his death he became more tractable. The approach of the supreme hour, as is often the case, softened the asperities of previous existence. He persisted in not going out to ride, in consequence of his quarrel with the governor of the island, who insisted on his being attended by an officer beyond the prescribed limits; but he amused himself with gardening, in which he took great interest, and not unfrequently, like Dioclesian, consoled himself for the want of the excitements of royalty, by laboring with his own hands in the cultivation of the earth. The cessation of riding exercise, however, to one who had been so much accustomed to it, proved very prejudicial. This, to a person of his active habits, coupled with the disappointment consequent on the failure of the revolutions in Europe, and the plans formed for his escape, aggravated the hereditary malady in the stomach, under which he labored, and in spring 1821 caused his physicians to apprehend danger to his life.²

118. Change in Napoleon before his death.

² Forsyth, iii. 190, 195; Ann. Hist. iv. 215, 216; Lam. vi. 416, 417; Chateaub. Mem. vii. 160, 163.

The receipt of this intelligence caused the English government to send directions for his receiving every possible relief and accommodation, and even, if necessary, for his removal from the island. But these humane intentions were announced too late to be carried into effect. In the beginning of May he became rapidly worse; and on the evening of the 5th, at five minutes before six, he breathed his last. A violent storm of wind and rain at the same time arose, which tore up the trees in the island by their roots—it was amidst the war of the elements that his soul departed. The howling of the wind seemed to recall to the dying conqueror the roar of battle, and his last words were: "Mon Dieu—La Nation Française—Tête d'armée." He declared in his testament, "I die in the Apostolic and Roman religion, in the bosom of which I was born, above fifty years ago." When he breathed his last, his sword was beside him, on the left side of the couch; but the cross, the

119. His death, May 5.

---

[*] "En lisant attentivement les correspondances et les notes étrangères a tout prétexte, entre les familiers de Napoléon et de Hudson Lowe, on est confondu des outrages, des provocations, des invectives, dont le captif et ses amis insultent a tout propos le gouverneur. Napoléon en ce moment cherchait à émouvoir par des cris de douleur la pitié du parlement anglais et à fournir un grief aux orateurs de l'opposition contre le ministère, afin d'obtenir son rapprochement de l'Europe. Le désir de provoquer des outrages par des outrages, et de présenter en suite ces outrages comme des crimes au Continent, transpire dans toutes ces notes. Il est évident que le gouverneur, souvent irrité, quelquefois inquisiteur, toujours inhabile, se sentait lui-même victime de la responsabilité."—LAMARTINE, *Hist. de la Restauration*, vi. 416, 417.

emblem of peace, rested on his breast. The child of the Revolution, the Incarnation of War, died in the Christian faith, with the emblem of the Gospel on his bosom! His will, which had been made in the April preceding, was found to contain a great multitude of bequests, but two in an especial manner worthy of notice. The first was a request that his body "might finally repose on the banks of the Seine, among the people he had loved so well;" the second, a legacy of 10,000 francs to the assassin Cantillon, who, as already noticed,* had attempted the life of the Duke of Wellington, but had been acquitted by the jury, from the evidence being deemed insufficient. He died in the 53d year of his age, having been born on the 5th February, 1768.¹

¹ Ann. Hist. iv. 216, 217; Forsyth, iii. 281, 287; Antomarchi, Derniers Mom. de Napoleon, ii. 239, 246, 312.

120. His funeral.

Napoleon had himself fixed upon the place in the island of St. Helena where he wished, in the first instance at least, to be interred. It was in a small hollow, called Slanes Valley, high up on the mountain which forms the island, where a fountain, shaded by weeping willows, meanders though verdant banks. The *tchampas* flourished in the moist soil. "It is a plant," says the Sanscrit writings, "which, notwithstanding its beauty and perfume, is not in request, because it grows on the tombs." The body, as directed by the Emperor, lay in state in a "chapelle ardente," according to the form of the Roman Catholic Church, in the three-cornered hat, military surtout, leather under-dress, long boots and spurs, as when he appeared on the field of battle, and it was laid in the coffin in the same garb. The funeral took place on the 9th May. It was attended by all the military and naval forces, and all the authorities in the island, as well as his weeping household. Three squadrons of dragoons headed the procession. The hearse was drawn by four horses. The 66th and 20th regiments, and fifteen pieces of artillery, formed part of the array, marching, with arms reversed, to the sound of mournful music, and all the touching circumstances of a soldier's funeral. When they approached the place of sepulture, and the hearse could go no further, the coffin was borne by his own attendants, escorted by twenty-four grenadiers of the two English regiments who had the honor of conveying the immortal conqueror to his last resting-place. Minute-guns, during the whole ceremony, were fired by all the batteries in the island. The place of sepulture was consecrated by an English clergyman,† according to the English form, though he was buried with the Catholic rites.² Volleys of musketry and discharges of artillery paid the last honors of a nation to their noble antagonist. A simple stone of great size was placed over his remains, and the solitary willows wept over the tomb of him for whom the earth itself had once hardly seemed a fitting mausoleum.

² Ann. Hist. iv. 217; Forsyth, iii. 296, 298; Antomarchi, ii. 180, 192.

* Ante, chap. vi. § 73.   † The Rev. Mr. Vernon.

The death of Napoleon made a prodigious sensation in Europe, and caused a greater change of opinion, especially in England, than any event which had occurred since that of Louis XVI. There was something in the circumstances of the decease of so great a man, alone, unbefriended, on a solitary rock in the midst of the ocean, and in the contrast which such a reverse presented to his former grandeur and prosperity, which fascinated and subdued the minds of men. All ranks were affected, all imaginations kindled, all sympathies awakened by it. In England, in particular, where the antipathy to him had been most violent, and the resistance most persevering, the reaction was the most general. The great qualities of their awful antagonist, long concealed by enmity, misrepresented by hatred, misunderstood by passion, broke upon them in their full lustre, when death had rendered him no longer an object of terror. The admiration for him in many exceeded what had been felt in France itself. The prophecy of the Emperor proved true, that the first vindication of his memory would come from those who in life had been his most determined enemies. Time, however, has moderated these transports; it has dispelled the illusions of imagination, calmed the effervesence of generosity, as much as it has dissipated the prejudices and softened the rancor of hostility. It has taken nothing from the great qualities of the Emperor; on the contrary, it has brought them out in still more colossal proportions than was at first imagined. But it has revealed, at the same time, the inherent weaknesses and faults of his nature, and shown that "the most mighty breath of life," in the words of genius, "that ever had animated the human clay, was not without the frailties which are the common inheritance of the children of Adam."

121. Immense sensation it excited in Europe.

With Napoleon terminated, for the present at least, the generation of ruling men —of those who impress their signet on the age, not receive its impression from it. "He sleeps," says Chateaubriand, "like a hermit at the extremity of a solitary valley at the end of a desert path. He did not die under the eye of France; he disappeared on the distant horizon of the torrid zone. The grandeur of the silence which shrouds his remains, equals the immensity of the din which once environed them. The nations are absent, their crowds have retired." The terrible spirit of innovation which has overspread the earth, and to which Napoleon had opposed the barrier of his genius, and which he for a time arrested, has resumed its course. His institutions failed, but he was the last of the great existences. The shadow of Napoleon rises on the frontier of the old destroyed world, and the most distant posterity will gaze on that gigantic spectre over the gulf into which entire ages have fallen, until the appointed day of social resurrection.¹

122. He was the last of the men who rule their age.

¹ Chateaub. Mem. vii. 168, 171.

CHAPTER X.

DOMESTIC HISTORY OF ENGLAND, FROM THE PASSING OF THE CURRENCY ACT OF 1819 TO THE DEATH OF LORD LONDONDERRY IN 1822.

1. Difference of the objects of the Liberal party in France and England.

The contest between parties in France was directed to different ends, and was of an entirely different character from that in Great Britain. At Paris the object was to overthrow a dynasty, in London it was to gain a subsistence. The contest in the one country was political, in the other it was social. All the discontented in France, however much disunited upon ulterior objects, were agreed in their hatred of the Bourbons, and their desire to dispossess them. The multitude of ambitions which had been thwarted, of interests injured, of glories tarnished, of prospects blasted, by the disasters in which the war had terminated, and the visions which it had overthrown, rendered this party very numerous and fearfully energetic. In England, although there were, doubtless, not a few, especially in the manufacturing towns, who desired a change of government, and dreamed of a British or Hibernian Republic, the great majority of the discontented were set upon very different objects. The contest of dynasties was over: no one thought of supplanting the House of Hanover by that of Stuart. Few, comparatively, wished a change in the form of government: there were some hundred thousands of ardent republicans in the great towns; but those in the country who were satisfied, and desired to live on under the rule of King, Lords, and Commons, were millions to these. But all wished, and most reasonably and properly, to live comfortably under their direction; and when any social evils assumed an alarming aspect, or distress prevailed to an unusual degree among them, they became discontented, and lent a ready ear to any demagogue who promised them, by the popularizing of the national institutions, a relief from all the evils under which the country labored.

2. Difference in the causes which produced discontent in the two countries.

From this difference in the prevailing disposition and objects of the people in the two countries, there resulted a most important distinction in the causes which, on the opposite sides of the Channel, inflamed the public mind, or endangered the stability of existing institutions. In France, the objects of the opposition in the Chambers, the discontented in the country, being the subversion of the Government and a change of dynasty, whatever tended to make the people more anxious for that change, and ready to support it, rendered civil war and revolution more imminent. Hence, general prosperity and social welfare, ordinarily so powerful in allaying discontent, were there the most powerful causes in creating it; because they put the people, as it might be said, into fighting-trim, and inspired them, like a well-fed and rested army, with the ardor requisite for success in hazardous enterprises. In England, on the other hand, as the contest of dynasties was over, and the decided republicans who aimed at an entire change of institutions were comparatively few in number, nothing could enlist the great body of the people, even in the manufacturing towns, on the side of sedition, but the experience of suffering. So strong, however, is the desire for individual comfort, and the wish to better their condition, in the Anglo-Saxon race, that general distress never fails to excite general disaffection, at least in the great cities; and whatever tends to induce it, in the end threatens the public tranquillity. Thus, in France at that period, at least, general prosperity augmented the danger of revolution; in England, it averted it.

3. Great effects of the change in the monetary laws.

A cause, however, had now come into operation, which, more than any other recorded in its modern annals, produced long-continued and periodically-returning distress among the British people; and at length, from the sheer force of suffering, broke the bonds of loyalty and patriotism, and induced a revolution attended with lasting and irremediable consequences on the future prospects of the empire. It need not be said what that cause was: a great alteration in the monetary laws, ever affecting the life-blood of a commercial state, is alone adequate to the explanation of so great an effect. The author need not be told that this is a subject exceedingly distasteful to the great bulk of readers; he is well aware that the vast majority of them turn over the pages the moment they see the subject of the currency commenced. He is not to be deterred, however, by that consideration from entering upon it. All attempts to unfold the real history of the British empire, during the thirty years which followed the peace, will be nugatory, and the views they exhibit fallacious, if this, the main-spring which put all the movements at work, is not steadily kept in view. History loses its chief utility, departs from its noblest object, when, to avoid risk to popularity, it deviates from the great duty of furnishing the materials for improvement: the nation has little shown itself prepared for self-government, when in the search of amusement it forgets inquiry. Enough of exciting and interesting topics remain for this history, and for this volume, to induce even the most inconsiderate readers to submit for half an hour to the elucidation of a subject on which, more than on any other, their own fortunes and those of their children depend. It may the more readily be submitted to at this time, as this is the turning-point of the two systems, and the subject now explained need not be again reverted to in the whole remainder of the work.

VOL. I.—X

The great father of political economy has well explained the principles of this subject; and was himself more than any other man alive to their importance. "Gold and silver," says Adam Smith, like every other commodity, vary in their value, are sometimes cheaper, sometimes dearer, sometimes of easier, and sometimes of more difficult purchase. The quantity of labor which any particular quantity of these can purchase or command, or the quantity of other goods it will exchange for, depends always upon the fertility or barrenness of the mines which happen to be known about the time when such exchanges are made. The discovery of the abundant mines of America reduced, in the sixteenth century, the value of gold and silver in Europe to *about a third of what it had formerly been*. As it cost less labor to bring those metals from the mine to the market, so when they were brought there, they could purchase or command less labor; and this revolution in their value, though perhaps the greatest, is by no means the only one of which history gives some account. But as a measure of quantity, such as the natural foot, fathom, or handful, which is continually varying in its own quantity, can never be an accurate measure of the value of other commodities; so a commodity which is itself continually varying in its own value, can never be an accurate measure of the value of other commodities."[1]

¹ Wealth of Nations, book i. c 5.

5. Great effects of any variation in the value of the standard of value.

If debts, taxes, and other encumbrances, could be made at once to rise or fall in their amount, according to the fluctuation of the medium in which they are to be discharged, any changes which might occur in the exchangeable value of that medium itself would be a matter of little practical importance. But the experience of all ages has demonstrated that this is impossible. The transactions of men, when they become at all extensive or complicated, absolutely require some fixed known standard by which they are to be measured, and their discharge regulated, without anything else than a reference to that standard itself. It never could be tolerated that every debtor, after having paid his debt in the current coin of the realm, should be involved in a dispute with his creditor as to what the present value of that current coin was. Hence the necessity of a fixed standard; but hence also the immense effects of any material alteration in the value of that standard, and the paramount necessity, so far as practicable, of preventing any considerable fluctuations in it. If the standard falls in value, the weight of all debts and encumbrances is proportionally lessened, because a lesser quantity of the produce of labor is required for their discharge; if it rises, their weight is proportionally augmented, because a larger quantity is required for that purpose. So great is the effect of any considerable change in this respect, that it has occasioned, and can alone explain, the greatest events in the intercourse of nations of which history has preserved a record.

The great contest between Rome and Carthage, which Hannibal and Scipio conducted, and Livy has immortalized, was determined by a decree of the Senate, induced by **necessity**, which postponed the payment of all obligations of the public treasury in specie to the conclusion of the war, and thereby created an inconvertible paper currency for the Roman empire.[a] More even than the slaughter on the Metaurus, the triumph of Zama, this decree determined the fate of the ancient world, for it alone equipped the legions by whom those victories were gained. Rome itself, saved in its utmost need by an expansion, sunk in the end under a still greater contraction of the national currency. The supplies of specie for the Old World became inadequate to the increasing wants of its population, when the power of the emperors had given lasting internal peace to its hundred and twenty millions of inhabitants. The mines of Spain and Greece, from which the chief supplies were obtained at that period, were worked out, or became unworkable, from the exactions of the emperors; and so great was the dearth of the precious metals which thence ensued, that the treasure in circulation in the Empire, which in the time of Augustus amounted to £380,000,000, had sunk in that of Justinian to £80,000,000 sterling; and the golden *aureus*, which in the days of the Antonines weighed 118 grains, had come, in the fifth century, to weigh only 68,[1] though it was only taken in discharge of debts and taxes at its original and standard value. As a necessary consequence of so prodigious a contraction of the currency, without any proportional diminution in the numbers or transactions of mankind, debts and taxes, which were all measured in the old standard, became so overwhelming that the national industry was ruined; agriculture disappeared, and was succeeded by pasturage in the fields; the great cities were all fed from Egypt and Libya; the revenue became irrecoverable; the legions dwindled into cohorts, the cohorts into companies; and the six hundred thousand men, who guarded the frontiers of the Empire in the time of Augustus, had sunk to one hundred and fifty thousand in that of Justinian — a force wholly inadequate to its defense.[2]

6. Examples of this from former times.

[1] Greaves on Ancient Coins, i. 329, 331.

[2] Gibbon's Rome, c. iv. 42, 71, Milman's edit.; Alison's Essays, iii 442.

---

[a] "Hortati censores, ut omnia perinde agerent, tocarent *ac si pecunia in œrario esset; neminem nisi bello confecto, pecuniam ab œrario petiturum esse.*"—LIV. lib. xxiv. cap. 18.—On one occasion, when in a party in London, composed chiefly of Whigs, opponents of Mr. Pitt's Currency Act of 1797, the dangerous effects of this measure were under discussion, the late Lord Melbourne, whose sagacity of mind was equal to his charm of manner, quoted this passage from memory. "The censors," says Arnold, "found the treasury unable to supply the public service. Upon this, trust moneys belonging to widows and minors, or to widows and unmarried women, were deposited in the treasury; and whatever sums the trustees had to draw for were paid by the quarter in bills on the banking commissioners, or *triumviri mensarii*. It is probable that these bills were actually *a paper currency*, and that they circulated as money, on the security of the public faith. In the same way, the government contracts were also paid in paper; for the contractors came forward in a body to the censors, and begged them to make their contracts as usual, promising *not to demand payment till the end of the war*. This must, I conceive, mean that they were to be paid in orders upon the treasury, which orders were to be converted into cash when the present difficulties of the government should be at an end."—ARNOLD, ii. 267. This was just an inconvertible paper currency, and its issue, after the battle of Cannæ, saved the Roman empire.

7. Discovery and wonderful effects of a paper currency.

What rendered this great contraction of the circulating medium so crushing in the ancient world was, that they were wholly unacquainted, except for a brief period during the necessities of the second Punic War, with that marvelous substitute for it—a paper currency. It was the Jews who first discovered this admirable system, to facilitate the transmission of their wealth amidst the violence and extortions of the middle ages; and it is, perhaps, not going too far to assert that, if it had been found out, and brought into general use, at an earlier period, it might have averted the fall of the Roman Empire. The effects of a scarcity of the precious metals, therefore, were immediately felt in the diminished wages of labor and price of produce, and increasing weight of debts and taxes. A paper currency, adequately secured and duly limited, obviates all these evils, because it provides a REPRESENTATIVE of the metallic currency, which, when the latter becomes scarce, may, without risk, be rendered a SUBSTITUTE for them. Thus the ruinous effects of a contraction of the circulating medium, even when most violent, may be entirely prevented, and the industry, revenue, and prosperity of a country completely sustained during the utmost scarcity, or even entire absence, of the precious metals. It was thus that the alarming crisis of 1797, which threatened to induce a national bankruptcy, was surmounted with ease, by the simple device of declaring the Bank of England notes, like the treasury bonds in the second Punic War, a legal tender, not convertible into cash till the close of the war; and that the year 1810, when, from the demand for gold on the Continent, there was scarcely a guinea left in this country, was one of general prosperity and the greatest national efforts recorded in its annals.

8. Advantages of a paper circulation, duly limited.

As paper may with ease be issued to any extent, either by Government or private establishments authorized to circulate it, it becomes an engine of as great danger, and attended with as destructive effects, when it is unduly multiplied as when it is unduly contracted. It is like the blood in the human body, whose circulation sustains and is essential to animal life: drained away, or not adequately fed, it leads to death by atrophy; unduly increased, it proves fatal by inducing apoplexy. To preserve a proper medium, and promote the circulation equally and healthfully through all parts of the system, is the great object of regimen alike in the natural frame and the body politic. Issued in overwhelming quantities, as it was in France during the Revolution, it induces such a rise of prices as destroys all realized capital, by permitting it to be discharged by a mere fraction of its real amount; contracted to an excessive degree, either by the mutations of commerce or the policy of Government, it proves equally fatal to industry, by lowering the money price of its produce, and augmenting the weight of the debts and taxes with which it is oppressed.

A paper currency, when perfectly secure, and hindered by the regulations under which it is issued from becoming redundant, may not only, in the absence of gold and silver, supply its place, but in its presence almost supersede its use. "If," says Adam Smith, "the gold and silver in a country should at any time fall short, in a country which has wherewithal to purchase them, there are more expedients for supplying their place than almost any other commodity. If provisions are wanted, the people must starve; if the materials for manufacture are awanting, industry must stop; but if money is wanted, barter will supply its place, though with a good deal of inconvenience. Buying and selling upon credit, and the different dealers compensating one another once a month or year, will supply it with less inconveniency. A well-regulated paper money will supply it, *not only without inconveniency, but in some cases with some advantage.*"[1] Experience may soon convince any one [Weather Nations, b. 4, c. i.] that this latter observation of Mr. Smith is well founded, and that a duly regulated paper is often more convenient and serviceable than one entirely of specie. Let him go into any bank at a distance from London, and he will find that they will give him sovereigns to any extent without any charge; but that for Bank of England notes, or a bill on London, they will, in one form or other, charge a premium; and if he has any doubt of the superior convenience of bank-notes over specie for the transactions of life, he is recommended to compare traveling in England with £500, in five English notes, in his waistcoat pocket, with doing so in France with the same sum in Napoleons in his portmanteau.

9. What is the standard of value?

The question is often asked, "What is a pound?" and Sir Robert Peel, after mentioning how Mr. Locke and Sir Isaac Newton had failed, with all their abilities, in answering it, said that he could by no possible effort of intellect conceive it to be any thing but a certain determinate weight of gold metal. Perhaps if his valuable life had been spared, and he had seen the ounce of gold selling in Australia at £3 to £3 10s. instead of £3 17s. 10½d., the mint price, he would have modified his opinion. In truth, a pound is an *abstract measure of value*, just as a foot or yard is of length; and different things have at different periods been taken to denote that measure according as the conveniency of men suggested. It was originally a pound weight of silver; and that metal was till the present century the standard in England, as it still is in most other countries. When gold was made the standard, by the Bank being compelled by the Act of 1819 to pay in that metal, the old word, denoting its original signification of the less valuable metal, was still retained. During the war, when the metallic currency disappeared, the pound was a Bank of England pound-note: the standard was thus paper—for gold was worth 28s. the pound, from the demand for it on the Continent. Since California and Australia have begun to pour forth their golden treasures, the standard has practically come again to be silver, as the precious metal which is least changing in value at this time. The proof of this is decisive; the ounce of gold is selling for £3 to £3 10s. at Melbourne; gold is measured by silver, not silver by gold. In truth, different things at different times are taken to express the much-coveted abstract standard; and what is always taken is that article in general circulation which is most steady in value and most generally received.

10. Vast effect of variations in the currency.

None but those practically acquainted with the subject can conceive how powerfully, and often rapidly, an extension or contraction of the currency acts upon the general industry and fortunes of the country. All other causes, in a commercial state, sink into insignificance in comparison. "The judicious operations of banking," says Mr. Smith, "enable the trader to convert his dead stock into active and productive stock. The first forms a very valuable part of the capital of the country, which produces nothing to the country. The operation of banking, by substituting paper in room of a great part of the gold and silver, enables the country to convert a great part of dead stock into active and productive stock—into stock which produces something to the country. The gold and silver money which circulates in any country may very properly be compared to a highway, which, while it circulates and carries to market all the grass and corn of the country, does not itself produce a single pile of either. The judicious operations of banking enable the country to convert, as it were, a great part of its highways into good pastures and corn-fields, and thereby increase considerably the annual produce of its land and labors."[1]

[1] Wealth of Nations, b. ii. c. 2.

To this it may be added, that so great is the effect of an increase of the paper circulation, and consequently of the expansion of the credit, industry, and enterprise of a commercial state, that a country which has dead stock, as Mr. Smith says, of the value of twenty thousand millions, may find the value of all its articles of merchandise enhanced or diminished fifty per cent. by the expansion or contraction of the currency to the extent of ten millions sterling. Such an addition or subtraction is to be compared, not to the entire amount of its realized wealth, but to the amount of that small portion of it which forms its circulating medium, upon which its prosperity depends; just as the warmth of a house is determined, not by the quantity of coals in the cellar, but by what is put upon the fires. Such an addition to the wealth of a state may be as nothing to the value of its dead stock, but it is much to the sum total of its circulating medium.

11. When this contraction of the currency acts upon effect takes place.

It is not in the general case *immediately* that this great effect of an expansion or contraction of the currency acts upon the price of the produce and the remuneration of the labor of the country: months may sometimes elapse after the augmented issues go forth from the bank before their effects begin to appear upon prices and enterprise; years, before these effects are fully developed. But these effects are quite certain in the end: an expansion never fails by degrees to stimulate, a contraction to depress. The reason of the delay in general is, that it takes a certain time for the augmented supplies of money and extended credit to flow down from the great reservoirs in the metropolis, from whence it is first issued, to the country banks which receive it, and through them upon their different customers, whose speculation and industry it develops. There is no immediate connection between augmented supplies of money, whether in gold, silver, or paper, and a rise in the price of commodities, or between their diminution and a fall; it is by the gradual process of stimulating enterprise, and increasing the demand for them in the one case, and diminishing it in the other, that these effects take place; and either is the work of time. When matters approach a crisis, however, and general alarm prevails, any operations on the currency are attended with effects much more rapidly, and sometimes instantaneously. Several instances of this will appear in the sequel of this history.

12. Vast importance of an inconvertible currency as a regulator of prices.

As the increase or diminution of the currency in any considerable degree is thus attended with such incalculable effects upon the industry, enterprise, and prosperity of every country which is largely engaged in undertakings, it becomes of the last importance to preserve its amount *as equal as may be*, and to exclude, if possible, all casual or uncalled-for expansions or contractions. Such variations are fatal to prudent enterprise and legitimate speculation, because they induce changes in prices irrespective altogether of the judgment with which they were undertaken, against which no wisdom or foresight can provide, and which render commercial speculations as hazardous, and often ruinous, as the gaming-table. They are injurious in the highest degree to the laboring classes, because they encourage in them habits of improvidence and lavish expenditure at one time, which are inevitably succeeded by depression and misery at another. They often sweep away in a few months the accumulated savings of whole generations, and leave the nation with great undertakings on its hands, without either credit or resources to carry them on. Their effects are more disastrous than those of plague, pestilence, and famine put together, for these, in their worst form, affect only an existing generation; but commercial crises extend their ravages to distant times, by sweeping away the means of maintaining the future generations of man.

13. A currency based on the precious metals is always liable to fluctuations.

No currency which is based exclusively upon the precious metals, or consists of them, can possibly be exempt from such fluctuations, because, being valuable all over the world, these are always liable to be drained away at particular times by the mutations of commerce or the necessities of war in the neighboring states. A war between France and Austria occasioning a great demand for gold on the Continent; a bad harvest in England rendering necessary a great exportation of it to bring grain from Poland or America; a revolution in France; three weeks' rain in August in England—events, unhappily, nearly equally probable—may at any time induce the calamity True, the precious metals will always in the end be attracted to the centre of wealth and commerce; but before they come back, half the traders and manufacturers in the country may be rendered bankrupt. Any interruption of the wonted issues of cash to them is like the stopping the issuing of rations to an army, or food to a people. The only possible way of averting so dire a calamity, is either by having had such immense treasures of gold and silver in the country, that they are adequate to meet any possible strain which may come upon them, and may fairly be considered inexhaustible; or by having some currency at home not convertible into specie, but which, issued in moderate quantities, and under sufficient safeguards against excess, may supply its place, and do its work during its temporary absence. Of the first, Great Britain and the whole civilized world afforded in 1852 a memorable example, when the vast and newly-discovered treasures of California and Australia diffused animation and prosperity over every nation; the second was illustrated by England in 1797 and 1810, when not a guinea was left in the country, but every difficulty was surmounted by the moderate issue of an inconvertible paper, which, without becoming excessive, was adequate to the wants of the community.

14. Concurring causes which brought about the bill of 1819.
The bill of 1819, which re-established cash payments, and thereby rendered the national currency, with the exception of £14,000,000, which the Bank was authorized to issue upon securities, entirely dependent on the retention of the precious metals in the country, was brought about by a singular but not unnatural combination of causes. In the first place, there was the natural reaction of the human mind against the enormous evils which had arisen in France from the abuse of the system of assignats, the quantities of which issued exceeded at one time £700,000,000 sterling, and caused such a rise of prices as swept away nearly the whole realized capital of the country. In the next place, there was the natural dread on the part of all the holders of realized wealth of such a continued elevation of prices as might lessen the exchangeable value of their fortunes, and in some degree deprive them of their inheritances or the fruits of their toil. Thirdly, the whole persons engaged in manufactures—a large and increasing class—were impressed with the same ideas, from the experience which the opening of the harbors had afforded them, since the peace, of the great difference between the money wages of labor and prices of raw material on the Continent, where money was scarce, because its inhabitants were poor, and England, where it was plentiful, because they were rich, and the necessity of contracting the currency in order to lower prices, especially of raw material and labor, and enable them better to compete with their Continental rivals. The Whigs, as a party, naturally and unanimously adhered to the same opinion. They did so, because Mr. Pitt and Lord Castlereagh had supported the opposite system, on the principle of Mr. Tierney: "The business of the Opposition *is to oppose every thing*, and turn out the Government." Lastly, the political economists, struck with the obvious dangers of great variations in prices, of which recent times had afforded so many examples, formed the same opinion, from an idea that, gold being the most precious of all metals, and the most in request in all countries and ages, no circulation could be considered as safe or lasting except such as was built upon that imperishable foundation. These circumstances, joined to the weight and abilities of Mr. Huskisson, Mr. Horner, and the Bullion Committee, who had recommended the resumption of cash payments, and of Mr. Peel, who had recently embraced their views, and the general ignorance of the greater part of the community on the subject, produced that "chaos of unanimity" which, as already mentioned, led to the resolutions introducing it being adopted by the House of Commons without one dissenting voice.[1]

¹ Ante, c iv. § 78.

15. Danger of a currency entirely rested on a metallic basis.
A chaos of unanimity, however, which confounds parties, obliterates old impressions, and is followed by new alliances, is seldom in the end attended by advantages; on the contrary, it is in general the herald of misfortune. As it arises from the judgment of men being obliterated for a season, by the pressure of some common passion or apprehension, so it ends in their interests being confounded in one common disaster. The great danger of considering paper as the *representative* of gold and silver, not, when required, a *substitute* for them, consists in this, that it tends necessarily to *multiply or diminish them both at the same time*; a state of things of all others the most calamitous, and fraught with danger to the best interests of society. When gold and silver are plentiful abroad, and they flow in large quantities into this country, from its being the best market which the holders of those metals can find for them, they, of course, accumulate in large quantities in the banks, especially the Bank of England, which being obliged to take them at a fixed price, often above the market value, of course gets the largest proportion. It pays for this treasure with its own paper, which thus augments the circulation, already, perhaps, too plentiful from the affluence of the precious metals. Then prices rise, money becomes easy, credit expands, and enterprises often of the most absurd and dangerous kind are set on foot, and are generally for a brief period attended with great profit to the fortunate holders of shares. When a change arrives—as arrive it must, from this rapid increasing of the currency both in specie and paper at the same time, and the precious metals are as quickly withdrawn to other countries, probably to pay the importations which the preceding fever had brought into the country—the very reverse of all this takes place. The banks, finding their stock of treasure daily diminishing, take the alarm; discounts cease, credits are contracted; the greatest mercantile houses are unable to obtain even inconsiderable advances, and the nation is left with a vast variety of speculations and undertakings on hand, without either funds or credit to bring them to a successful issue.

16. True system.
The true system would be just the reverse. Proceeding on the principle that the great object is to equalize the currency, and with it prices and speculation, it would *enlarge* the paper currency when the precious metals are withdrawn and credit

is threatened with stoppage, and proportionally contract it when the precious metals return, and the currency is becoming adequate without any considerable addition to the paper. In this way, not only would the immense danger of the gold and paper being poured into the circulation at the same time be avoided, but a support would be given to credit, and an adequate supply of currency provided for the country when its precious metals are drained away, and a monetary crisis is at hand. A few millions, secured on Government credit, not convertible into cash, judiciously issued by Government commissioners when the exchanges are becoming unfavorable and money scarce, would at any time arrest the progress of the most dreadful monetary crisis that ever set in upon the country. That of 1793 was stopped by the issue of Exchequer bills; that of 1797 by suspending cash payments; that of 1825 was arrested, as will appear in the sequel, by the accidental discovery and issue of two millions of *old bank-notes* in the Bank of England, when their treasure was all but exhausted; that of 1847 was at once stopped by a mere letter of the Premier and Chancellor of the Exchequer, authorizing the suspension of cash payments. The *prospect* even of a currency which was to be a substitute for gold, not a representative of it, at once arrested the panic, and saved the nation. Such an expedient, when intrusted to Government commissioners, and not to bankers or interested parties, is comparatively safe from abuse; and it would at once put an end to that fluctuation of prices and commercial crises, which have been the constant bane of the country for the last thirty years.*

In addition to these dangers with which the resumption of cash payments and the establishment of a paper currency—the representative, not the substitute for gold, and therefore de-

pendent on the retention of the precious metals —must always be attended, there were peculiar circumstances which rendered it eminently hazardous, and its effects disastrous, at the time it was adopted by the English government. The annual supply of the precious metals for the use of the globe, which, as already mentioned, had been on an average, before 1810, ten millions sterling, had sunk, from the effects of the revolution in South America, to little more than two millions.¹ The great paper currency guaranteed by all the allied powers, issued so plentifully during 1813 and 1814, and which had circulated as cash from the banks of the Rhine to the wall of China, had been drawn in, in conformity with the Convention of London of 30th September, 1813; and the Continent had never yet recovered from the contraction of credit and shortcoming of specie consequent on its disappearance, and on the cessation of the vast expenditure of the war. The loans on the Continent, in the years following its termination, had been so immense, that they had ruinously contracted the circulation, and destroyed credit. The fall of prices in consequence, and from the good harvest of 1818, had been as great in Germany after the peace as in Great Britain, and the cabinets of Vienna, Berlin, and St. Petersburg, were as much straitened for money in the beginning of 1819 as the French government.²

17. Peculiar dangers with which the resumption of cash payments was attended.

¹ Ante, c. i. § 36.

² Ante, c. vi. § 76.

In addition to this, the strain on the money market at Paris, in the close of 1818 and commencement of 1819, had been so dreadful that a monetary crisis of the utmost severity had set in there, which had rendered it a matter of absolute necessity, as already mentioned, for the French government to solicit, and the allied cabinets to grant, a prolongation of the term for payment of the immense sums they were required to pay, by the treaty of Aix-la-Chapelle, as the price of the evacuation of their territory, which was extended, by a convention in December 1818, from nine to eighteen months.³ It was not surprising that such a financial crisis should have taken place on the Continent at this time, for the loans negotiated by its different governments in the course of 1817 and 1818 amounted to the enormous sum of £38,600,000,† of which £27,700,000 was on ac-

18. Strain on the money market, from the immense loans on the Continent.

³ Ante, c. i. § 76.

---

* Adam Smith clearly saw the advantages of an inconvertible paper currency issued on such principles, and on such safeguards against abuse. "The government of Pennsylvania," says he, "without amassing any treasure, invented a method of lending, *not money, indeed*, but what is equivalent to money, to its subjects. By advancing to private people at interest, and upon land security to double the value, paper bills of credit, to be redeemed fifteen years after their date, and in the mean time made transferable from hand to hand like bank-notes, and declared by act of Parliament to be a legal tender in all payments by one inhabitant of the province to another, it raised a moderate revenue, which went a considerable way toward defraying the expenses of that orderly and frugal government. The success of an expedient of this kind must depend on three circumstances: first, upon the demand for some other instrument of commerce besides gold and silver money, or upon the demand for such a quantity of consumable stock as could not be had without *sending abroad the greater part of their gold or silver money in order to purchase it*; secondly, upon the good credit of the government which makes use of the expedient; thirdly, upon the *moderation with which it is used*, the whole value of the paper bills of credit never exceeding that of *the gold and silver money* which would have been necessary for carrying on their circulation, had there been no paper bills of credit. The same expedient was upon different occasions adopted by several other American States; but from want of this moderation, it produced in the greater part of them much disorder and inconvenience."—*Wealth of Nations*, book v. chap. 2. This is the true principle which should regulate the issue of inconvertible paper, its main use serving as a substitute for gold and silver, not as a representative of it, to be used chiefly where the precious metals are drawn away, and never exceeding *the amount of them which would have been required to conduct and facilitate its real transactions*. The moderation of Pennsylvania was a prototype of the wisdom of the English; the extravagance of the other American colonies, of the madness of France in the use of this powerful agent for good or for evil during the subsequent revolutionary war.

† FALL OF PRICES OF WHEAT ON THE CONTINENT FROM 1817 TO 1819.

	March 1817.		September 1819.
Vienna	114s. 0d.	...	19s. 6d.
Munich	151s. 0d.	...	21s. 5d.
Norway	81s. 10d.	...	55s. 3d.
Venice	99s. 6d.	...	29s. 4d.
Lisbon	117s. 0d.	...	34s. 2d.
Fiume	88s. 11d.	...	29s. 9d.
Udine	99s. 6d.	...	31s. 7d.

The bad harvest of 1816 was the cause of the high prices in 1817, but the prodigious fall in 1819 was due mainly to the pressure on the money market.—TOOKE *On Prices*, ii. 93, 94, and authorities there quoted.

‡ LOANS RAISED IN EUROPE IN 1817 AND 1818.

France	£27,700,000
Prussia	2,800,000
Austria	3,600,000
Russia	4,500,000
	£38,600,000

—*Appendix to Lords' Com. on Cash Payments*, 1819, p. 424.

count of France. At least three-fourths of these loans were undertaken in London and Amsterdam by Messrs Baring and Hope; and as the whole sums they had to pay up under them required to be remitted in specie, the drain which in consequence set in upon the Bank of England was so severe that its accumulated treasure, which in October, 1817, had been £11,914,000, and in February, 1818, £10,055,460, had sunk, on 31st August, 1818, to £6,363,160, and on 27th February, 1819, was only £4,184,000.[1]

[1 Tooke On Prices, ii. 54-96.]

19. Great prosperity of England in end of 1818 and spring of 1819, from extension of its currency.

It was the suspension of cash payments by the Bank of England in 1817 and 1818, which, as already mentioned, alone enabled this country to prosper during this terrible crisis, which was acting with such severity upon other states, and occasioning so fearful a drain on its own metallic resources. But that suspension had not only, by providing it with an adequate internal currency, averted the catastrophe so general at that time on the Continent, but had given it at the very same time an extraordinary degree of prosperity. "In consequence," says Mr. Tooke, "of the great fall in the French funds, combined with the great and sudden fall of the prices of grain on the Continent, extensive failures occurred in Paris, Marseilles, and other parts of France, as also in Holland and in Hamburg, in 1818, *before any indication had appeared of discredit, or of any pressure on the money market of this country.* A loan had also been negotiated in 1818 for the Russian government, the payments for a large proportion of which were made in bullion exported from this country, thus adding greatly to the pressure on the money market, and at the same time exhibiting the phenomenon of prices falling rapidly on the continent of Europe —much more rapidly than here—while bullion was flowing there from hence."[1] It is not surprising that it was so; for the Continental states, during 1817 and 1818, had no paper adequate to sustain their industry during the scarcity of money, owing to the immense pressure on their money market, whereas England enjoyed in the highest degree that advantage. The paper circulation of Great Britain had greatly increased during the drain on the precious metals, and compensated for their want, and in the last of these years had reached £48,000,000 in England alone, a higher amount than in any year of the war. Hence the prosperity in this country which coexisted with the most serious pressure and distress on the Continent."

[1 Tooke, ii. 95.]

20. Great internal prosperity of the country.

The consequences of this abundant supply of the currency in Great Britain had been an extraordinary degree of prosperity to the country in the last months of 1818 and first of 1819, accompanied by a corresponding and a too sudden start in speculations of every sort. It was so great, and the change so rapid, that it was made the subject of special congratulation and notice in the speech from the throne.† Statistical facts demonstrate how great a start had at the same time taken place in all our principal articles of imports and manufactures, and in the general rise of prices of all sorts. The former had more than doubled, the latter advanced fully 50 per cent., as shown in the following Table from Tooke *On Prices,* ii. 61, 62:

IMPORTS INTO GREAT BRITAIN.

Years.	Silk.	Wool.	Cotton.	Manufactures.	Tallow.	Linseed.	Colonial Produce.
	lb.	lb.	lb.	Tons.	Tons.	Qrs.	£
1816	1,137,922	8,117,864	93,920,055	18,473	20,858	76,892	26,374,920
1817	1,177,693	14,715,843	124,912,968	22,863	19,298	162,759	29,916,330
1818	2,101,618	26,405,486	177,282,158	35,020	27,149	237,141	35,819,798

The unavoidable consequence was, that prices were high, but not unreasonably so: they had not advanced so as to afford grounds to fear a reaction. Wheat, on an average of 1819, was at 72s., while during the scarcity of 1817 it had been 116s., and at the lowest point of the great fall of spring 1816, 52s. And that the imports, how great and increased soever, as compared with the distressed years which had preceded it, were not excessive, or running into dangerous speculation, is decisively proved by the fact that the imports and exports of Great Britain in 1818, as compared to its population and revenue, were not half what they have since become, not only without risk of collapse, but with the most general and admitted prosperity. In a word, the British empire, in the whole of 1818 and commencement of 1819, was beginning to taste the blessed fruits of peace and prosperity; and industry, vivified and supported by a currency at once adequate and duly limited, was flourishing in all its branches, and daily discovering new channels of profit and enterprise, at the very time when the scarcity of money on the Continent was involving all classes in unheard-of disasters.‡

* CIRCULATION OF BANK OF ENGLAND AND COUNTRY NOTES.

Years.	Bank of England.	Country Banks.	Total.
1816	£27,013,620	£15,096,000	£42,109,620
1817	27,397,900	15,894,000	43,291,900
1818	27,771,070	20,507,000	48,278,070
1819	25,227,100	15,701,328	40,928,428

—ALISON'S *Europe,* chap. xcvi., Appendix.

† "The Prince Regent has the greatest pleasure in being able to inform you that the trade, commerce, and manufactures of the country are in a most flourishing condition. The favorable change which has so rapidly taken place in the internal circumstances of the United Kingdom, affords the strongest proof of the solidity of its resources. To cultivate and improve the advantages of our present situation will be the object of your deliberations."—PRINCE REGENT's Speech, Jan. 21, 1819; *Parliamentary Debates,* xxxix. 21.

‡ This opinion was strongly expressed by the most intelligent persons at the time. "Both trade and manufactures are in a flourishing condition, and likely to improve still further. There appears to be little speculation beyond the regular demands of the different markets, men without capital finding it almost impossible to procure credit; so that there is now no disposition to force a trade, and

But these flattering prospects were of short duration, and Great Britain was soon doomed to experience, in all its bitterness, the disastrous effects of an ill-judged and worse-timed contraction of the currency. At the moment when the annual supplies of the precious metals for the use of the globe had been reduced, by the South American revolution, to a fourth of their former amount—when the coin annually issued from the English mint had in consequence sunk to only £1,500,000 a year*—when the drains of gold on the Bank, to meet the gigantic loans contracted for in this country for the Continental powers, and pay for the immense importations of the year, had reduced the treasure in the Bank from £12,000,000 to £3,500,000, and when the large mercantile transactions recently entered into in this country, and the general prosperity and activity which prevailed, imperatively required, instead of a contraction, a great increase of the currency, Parliament, *without one dissenting voice*, passed an act, requiring the Bank of England, at no distant period,[1] to resume cash payments, thereby rendering the currency dependent on the retention of gold—the very thing which, in the circumstances of the country, could not be retained.†

21 Disastrous contraction of the currency.

[1] Ante, c. iv. § 7s.

The effects of this extraordinary piece of legislation were soon apparent. The industry of the nation was speedily congealed, as a flowing stream is by the severity of an arctic winter. The alarm became universal—as wide-spread as confidence and activity had recently been. The country bankers, who had advanced largely on the stocks of goods imported, refused to continue their support to their customers, and they were in consequence forced to bring their stock into the market. Prices in consequence rapidly fell—that of cotton, in particular, sunk in the space of three months to half its former level. The country bankers' circulation was contract-

22. Its effects on the Bank issues.

ed by no less than five millions sterling; the entire circulation of England fell from £48,278,000 in 1818, to £40,928,000 in 1820; and in the succeeding year it sunk as low as £34,145,000. Nothing in this disastrous contraction of the currency, at a period when its expansion was so loudly called for, sustained the national industry, or averted a general bankruptcy, but the fortunate circumstance that the obligation on the Bank to pay in specie was, by the Act of 1819, only to commence on the 1st Febuary, 1820;* and this enabled that establishment, in the preceding autumn, when the crash began, not only not to contract its issues, but even in a slight degree to increase them.†

The effects of this sudden and prodigious contraction of the currency were soon apparent, and they rendered the next three years a period of ceaseless distress and suffering in the British islands. The accommodation granted by bankers diminished so much, in consequence of the obligation laid upon them of paying in specie when specie was not to be got, that the paper under discount at the Bank of England, which in 1810 had been £23,000,000, and in 1815 not less than £20,660,000, sunk in 1820 to £4,672,000, and in 1821 to £2,676,000!‡ The effect upon prices was not less immediate or appalling. They sunk in general, within six months, to half their former amount, and remained at that low level for the next three years. [See Note (1) on opposite page.] Imports sunk from nearly £36,000,000 in 1818, to £29,769,000 in 1821; exports from £45,000,000 in the former year, to £35,000,000 in the latter. §

23. And on prices of all commodities.

* BANK AND BANKERS' NOTES.

Years	Bank of England.	Country Bankers.	Total.	Money Coined and Issued at the Mint
	£.	£.	£.	£.
1818	27,771,000	20,507,000	48,278,070	3,458,652
1819	25,227,100	15,701,328	40,928,428	1,270,817
1820	23,569,150	10,576,245	34,145,395	1,787,233
1821	22,471,450	8,256,180	30,727,630	9,954,444
1822	18,172,170	8,416,430	26,588,600	5,388,217

—Parliamentary Papers quoted in ALISON's *Europe*, chap. xcvi.; Appendix to TOOKE *On Prices*, ii. 129.

Mr. Sedgewick, of the Stamp Office, estimates the contraction of country bank-notes as follows:—

1819	£15,284,491
1820	11,767,391
1821	8,414,281
1822	8,067,260
1823	8,798,277

—TOOKE *On Prices*, ii. 128.

† CIRCULATION OF THE BANK OF ENGLAND.

		Bullion.
27th February, 1819	£25,126,970	£4,184,620
31st August, 1819	25,252,790	3,595,360

—TOOKE *On Prices*, ii. 96.

‡ PAPER UNDER DISCOUNT AT THE BANK OF ENGLAND.

1808	£12,950,100	1814	£13,363,475
1809	18,127,597	1815	20,660,000
1810	23,070,000	1819	6,515,000
1811	15,199,032	1820	3,883,600
1812	17,610,950	1821	2,676,700
1813	14,514,744	1822	2,662,000

—TOOKE *On Prices*, ii. 381–383.

	Exports, Declared Value.	Imports.
§ 1818	£45,180,150	£35,845,340
1819	34,252,251	29,681,640
1820	35,569,677	31,515,222
1821	35,823,127	29,769,122
1822	36,176,597	29,432,376

—ALISON's *Europe*, chap. xcvi., Appendix.

---

no injurious competition to procure orders, and consequently wages are fair and reasonable."—Lord SHEFFIELD to Lord SIDMOUTH, 17th Dec., 1818; *Sidmouth's Life*, iii. 242.

* MONEY COINED AND ISSUED AT THE MINT.

1817	6,771,595
1818	3,458,652
1819	1,270,817
1820	1,787,233
1821	7,954,444

—PORTER's *Parl. Tables*. ALISON's *Europe*, chap. xcvi., Appendix.

† Lord Eldon, however, had strongly opposed it in the Cabinet, and wished the project postponed for two years.—TWISS's *Life of Lord Eldon*, ii. 329. Mr. WARD (Lord Dudley) said—"Those that are near the scene of action are not less surprised than you are at the turn the Bullion question has taken. Canning says it is the greatest wonder he has witnessed in the political world."—Earl of DUDLEY's *Letters*, 222. The truth is, Ministers at the period were very weak, and had sustained several defeats in the House of Commons, particularly on the Criminal Law, and they did not venture to face the Opposition on the Bullion question. Lord Liverpool, at the period it was first broached in the Cabinet, wrote to Lord Eldon in allusion to their difference of opinion on the subject: "After the defeats we have already experienced during this session, our remaining in office is a positive evil. It confounds all the ideas of government in the minds of men. It disgraces us personally, and renders us less capable every day of being of any real service to the country now. It, therefore, things are to remain as they are, I am quite clear that there is no advantage in any way in our being the persons to carry on the public service."—Lord LIVERPOOL to Lord ELDON, May 10, 1819; *Eldon's Life*, ii. 329.

Distress was universal in the latter months of the year 1819, and that distrust and discouragement was felt in all branches of industry, which is at once the forerunner and the cause of disaster. The Three per Cents, which had been at 79 in January, gradually fell, after the Bank Restriction Act passed, to 65 in December; and the bankruptcies, which had been 86 in January, rose in May to 178; the total in the year was 1499, being an increase of 531 over the preceding year.[1]

24. Rapid increase of disaffection in the country.

The effects of this panic, and consequent distress, especially in the manufacturing districts, speedily appeared; and the demagogues were not slow to turn to the best account this unexpected turn of fortune in their favor. Mr. Cobbett said afterward, that the moment he heard in America of the resumption of cash payments in Great Britain, he prepared to return to this country, as he felt certain that the cause of Reform in Parliament could not long be averted; and the result proved that he had correctly scanned the effects of that measure. The disaffected, under the direction of their able and intelligent leaders, changed the direction of their tactics. They no longer confined their operations to the breaking of mills or destruction of machinery; political changes became their object; and their method of effecting them was by making displays of vast multitudes of men, in a certain degree disciplined, and closely banded together in feeling. At a great meeting of 30,000 or 40,000 persons, which took place at Glasgow on 16th May, called to petition the Prince Regent for relief and means to emigrate to Canada, an amendment was proposed, and carried by an overwhelming majority, that no good was to be expected but from annual parliaments, universal suffrage, vote by ballot, and diminished taxation. They now, for the first time, assumed the name of RADICAL REFORMERS, and began to use, as their war-cries, the necessity of annual parliaments, universal suffrage, vote by ballot, and the other points which have since been combined in what is called the People's Charter. The leaders of the great meetings which took place, much to their credit, strenuously inculcated upon the people the necessity of keeping the peace, and abstaining from all acts of intimidation and outrage; and, considering the immense multitudes who were congregated together, amounting often to

---

(From TOOKE On Prices, ii. 390, 397, 429.)

(1) PRICES OF THE UNDERMENTIONED ARTICLES IN THE YEAR, AND WHEAT IN DECEMBER OF EACH YEAR.

Year.	Wheat, per qr.		Cotton, per lb.		Iron, per ton.		Rice, per ton.		Silk, per lb.		Tea, per lb.		Wool, per lb.		Sugar, per cwt.		Beef, per lb. too
	s.	d.	s.	d.	£.	s.	s.	s.	s.	d.	s.	d.	s.	d.	s.	s.
1818	80	8	2	0	9	0	45		39	6	3	1	- 6	0	70		100
1819	66	3	1	11	8	10	43		30	0	2	10	6	0	66		115
1820	54	6	1	5	9	0	32		24	5	2	4	3	6	58		130
1821	49	0	1	1	7	10	36		21	0	2	4	3	3	58		115
1822	38	1	1	0	6	10	33		25	1	2	5	3	6	42		80

* Mr. Tooke, whose industry and talents entitle his opinions to the highest respect, has labored hard to show that the contraction of the currency in 1819 had no connection with the distress of that and the three following years, but that it is entirely to be ascribed to overtrading, and in this opinion he is followed by Miss Martineau. With what success their arguments are founded may be judged of by the facts above stated. Mr. Tooke's arguments are based upon an idea which every one acquainted with the real working of commerce knows to be fallacious—that the effects of monetary changes, if real, upon prices, must be immediate, and, therefore, as he finds the Bank issues a shade higher in August, 1819, than they had been in February of that year, he concludes that there was no contraction to account for the distress, and that it arose entirely from overtrading.—(TOOKE On Prices, ii. 96, 113.) He takes no account of the prodigious drain on the metallic currency which brought the bullion in the Bank down from £12,000,000 to £3,500,000, nor of the contraction of £5,000,000 in the country bankers' issues, from the passing of the act. But, in truth, his notion that there is an immediate connection between currency and prices if there is any, is entirely erroneous. Sometimes, doubtless, the effect is very rapid, but in general it is the work of time. If a sudden panic is either produced or arrested by legislative measures, the effect may be instantaneous; but in other cases it is by slow degrees, and by working through all the ramifications of society, that a contraction or expansion of the currency acts upon the interests of society. If five millions additional are thrown into the money market, or gradually withdrawn, it by no means follows that there is to be an instantaneous effect on prices. The effect takes place gradually, in consequence of the extended speculations and undertakings which are set on foot in the one case, or ruined or contracted in the other. The effect of the contraction of the currency, which began in 1819, continued through the whole three following years, till it was arrested by an expansion of it in 1823, which soon landed the nation in another set of dangers on the opposite side. The speculation of 1818 was doubtless considerable, and would probably, in any event and with the best regulated currency, have led to a check and a temporary fall of prices, just as an abundant harvest for a season lowers the price of grain. But it is quite chimerical to suppose that the long-continued distress, from 1819 to 1823, was owing to the importations of 1818. If they were excessive, that evil would speedily check itself, and restore prices to their average and healthful state. But that they were not excessive, and should not, if the currency had been let alone, have terminated in any thing like disaster, is decisively proved by the fact that they were not half as great, relatively to the population of the empire, as they have since become in years not only unaccompanied by disaster, but marked by the most unequivocal prosperity. This distinctly appears from the following table of exports and imports:—

Years.	Exports—official value.	Imports—official value.	Population of Great Britain and Ireland.
1818	£42,700,524	£35,845,310	
1819	35,534,176	29,684,640	20,500,000
1820	38,395,625	31,515,222	
1823	43,804,372	34,591,260	
1824	48,785,551	36,056,551	22,000,000
1825	47,166,020	42,660,954	
1834	73,821,550	49,362,811	
1835	78,376,731	48,911,542	23,500,000
1836	85,229,837	57,023,867	
1844	131,564,503	75,441,555	
1845	134,599,116	85,281,955	27,500,000
1846	132,288,315	75,958,874	
1847	125,907,063	90,921,806	

—PORTER's Parl. Tables; and ALISON's Europe, Appendix, chap. cxvi.

It is true, several of these prosperous years terminated in disaster; but that was the necessary effect of the system of currency established in the empire, which rendered periods of disaster as necessary the followers of prosperity as night is of day.

34,000 and 40,000 persons, it was surprising how generally the directions were followed. Aware from the symptoms in the political atmosphere of an approaching storm, but wholly unconscious that it had proceeded from their own acts, Government strengthened themselves by the admission of the Duke of Wellington into the Cabinet as Master-General of the Ordnance, on his return from the command of the Army of Occupation in 1819.[1]

[1] Martineau, i. 225; Life of Lord Sidmouth, iii. 245, 248; Ann. Reg. 1819, 104, 106.

25. Meeting at Peterloo, Aug. 16, 1819.

These political meetings were general in all the manufacturing towns of England and Scotland during the whole summer of 1819, and the leading topics constantly dwelt on were the depression of wages and misery of the poor, which were invariably ascribed to the Corn Laws, the weight of taxation, the influence of the boroughmongers, or holders of nomination boroughs, and the want of any representation of the people in Parliament. The speeches, which were often eloquent and moving, acquired additional force from the notorious facts to which they could all refer, which were too expressive of the general distress which prevailed. No serious breach of the peace occurred till the 16th of August, 1819, when a great assemblage took place at *Peterloo*, near Manchester. As it was known that multitudes were to come to that meeting from all the towns and villages in that densely-peopled locality, great apprehensions were entertained by the local authorities, and extraordinary precautions taken to prevent a breach of the peace, in conformity with a circular from the Home Office on 7th July, which recommended the utmost vigilance on the part of the local magistracy, and the adoption of prompt and vigorous measures for the preservation of the public tranquillity. The yeomanry of the county of Cheshire, and a troop of Manchester yeomanry, were summoned; and the military, consisting of six troops of the 15th Hussars, two guns, and nearly the whole of the 31st regiment, were also on the spot and under arms. A large body of special constables was sworn in, and, armed with their batons, surrounded the hustings where the speakers were to be placed.[2]

[2] Ann. Reg. 1819, 105, 106; Martineau, i. 233; Life of Lord Sidmouth, iii. 234, 237; Mr. Joliffe's Letter.

26. Great excitement, and objects of the meeting.

The avowed object of the first proposed meeting, which had been called by regular advertisement, was to elect "a representative and legislatorial attorney" to represent the city of Manchester, as had already been done at Birmingham, Stockport, Leeds, and other places. This meeting was called for the 9th August; but as the magistrates, feeling such an object to be illegal, had intimated it would be dispersed, the next or adjourned meeting, which was called for the 16th, was simply to petition for a reform in Parliament. Drilling had been practised in many places in all the country round; and large bodies of men had met on the hills between Lancashire and Yorkshire, in the gray of the morning, to go through their evolutions, though without having any arms. The consequence was, that they marched into Manchester from every direction for thirty miles around, six abreast, with bands of music and colors flying. On these were inscribed, "No Corn Laws;" "Annual Parliaments;" "Universal Suffrage;" "Vote by Ballot;" "Equal Representation or Death;" "Liberty or Death;" "God armeth the Patriot,"—with a figure of Wallace. Two bands of female reformers were among them, one numbering 150 members, with light blue silk flags: they added much interest and excitement to the scene. Mr. Hunt was the person who was to address the multitude, and before he arrived on the ground it was computed that 60,000 persons were assembled, chiefly from places around Manchester, a large proportion, as usual in such cases, being women, and not a few children.[1]

[1] Life of a Radical, ii. 197, 204; Martineau, i. 228, 230; Life of Lord Sidmouth, iii. 254, 258.

27. Its dispersion by the military.

The magistrates of Manchester, deeming such a meeting for such an object to be illegal, resolved to prevent it by arresting Mr. Hunt, its avowed leader, before the proceedings had begun. He arrived about noon in an open carriage, and made his way with some difficulty to the hustings erected on the centre of the ground, amidst cheers which rent the air. A warrant was immediately made out to arrest him, and put into the hands of Mr. Nadin, the chief constable, with orders to execute it immediately. He declared, however, that he could not do so; which was evidently the case, as the crowd was so dense that it was physically impossible to force a passage through the throng up to the hustings. Upon this they directed the military to be called up to clear the way—and notes were dispatched to the commanders of the yeomanry and the military to advance to the support of the civil officers who were to execute the warrant. The Manchester yeomanry were nearest at hand, and, coming up, adopted the unlucky resolution of advancing two by two at a walk. A loud shout was set up when they appeared, and as they continued to move on, they were speedily detached from each other, hemmed in, and some of them unhorsed. Upon seeing this, the commanding officer of the hussars said to Mr. Hutton, the chief magistrate, "What am I to do?" "Do you not see they are attacking the yeomanry?—disperse the crowd," was the answer. Upon this the word "Forward" was given; the hussars came up at a trot, and, forming on the edge of the throng, the trumpet sounded the charge, and the horsemen, advancing, wheeled into line, and speedily drove the multitude before them. The dense mass of human beings forced forward was instantly thrown into the most dreadful alarm; numbers were trod down, and some suffocated by the pressure; and although the hussars acted with the utmost forbearance, and struck in general only with the flat side of their sabres, yet four or five persons, including one woman, were pressed to death, and about twenty injured by sabre wounds. About seventy persons in all were more or less hurt during this unhappy affray, including one special constable ridden over by the hussars, and one yeoman struck from his horse by a stone from the mob.[2] Mr. Hunt and ten of his friends were arrested and committed, first on a charge of high treason, and after-

[2] Mem. of Lord Sidmouth, iii. 256, 261; Martineau, i. 229, 234; Mr. Joliffe's Account.

ward of conspiring to alter the law by force and threats; and several men were wounded by a discharge from the foot-soldiers, when violently assailed by the mob when conveying the prisoners to jail.

28. Noble conduct of Lord Sidmouth on the occasion.

Lord Sidmouth, to whom, as Home Secretary, the first intelligence of this unhappy affair was sent, acted in the noblest manner on the occasion. Perceiving at once that a crisis of no ordinary kind had arrived, and that the conduct of the magistrates in ordering the dispersion of the crowd before any acts of violence had been committed, would be made the subject of unbounded obloquy, and probably great misrepresentation, on the part of the popular press, he at once determined to take his full share of the responsibility connected with it; and accordingly, before there was time to call together the entire Cabinet to deliberate on the subject, he conveyed, with the concurrence of the Prince Regent, the law-officers of the Crown, and such of the Cabinet as could be hastily got together, the royal approbation for the course pursued on the occasion.* In doing this, he acted on the principle which "he considered an essential principle of government, namely, to acquire the confidence of the magistracy, especially in critical times, by showing a readiness to support them in all honest, reasonable, and well-intended acts, without inquiring too minutely whether they might have performed their duty a little better or a little worse."[1] His conduct on this occasion, though attacked with the utmost vehemence at the time, earned the support of all men really acquainted with the necessary action of government in a popular community, as it must command the admiration of every right-thinking man in all time coming.†

[1 Life of Sidmouth, iii. 262.]

29. Result of Hunt's trial.

The generosity of Lord Sidmouth's conduct is wholly irrespective of the real merits of the conduct of the magistracy on this occasion; nay, it becomes greater, if, after the act was done, and could not be undone, he voluntarily interposed the shield of his responsibility, to shelter those whose conduct may be considered as open to some exception. Mr. Hunt was afterward indicted, along with Johnson, Moorhouse, and seven others, before the Manchester Grand Jury, for seditious conspiracy, who found true bills against them all. They traversed, in English law phrase—that is, got the trial postponed till the next assizes—in order to give the public effervescence time to subside; and they were ultimately tried before Mr. Justice Bayley at York, and, after a long and most impartial trial, which lasted eleven days, and which Mr. Hunt himself had the candor to call "a magnificent specimen of British justice," Hunt, Johnson, Healy, and Bamford, were convicted of conspiracy to get up a seditious meeting, and "alter the government by force and threats." The case was afterward carried to the Court of King's Bench, by which the verdict was affirmed, and Hunt sentenced to two years and a half, the others to one year's imprisonment in Ilchester jail; which sentences were carried into full execution.[1] The verdicts of the coroner's inquest on the persons killed in the Manchester affray were of such a kind as amounted to casual death, or justifiable homicide, with the exception of one, which, after having been long protracted, was quashed by the Court of King's Bench on the ground of irregularity, from the coroner not having, with the jury, inspected inspected the body, as by law directed.*

[April, 1820.]

[1 Trial of Hunt, &c., at York, March 16, 1820, State Trials; An. Reg. 1820, 849; App. to Chron. and Chron. 147.]

30. Reflections on the impolicy of allowing such meetings.

The judgment of these high authorities leaves no room for doubt as to the illegality of the meeting at Manchester by the English law; and very little reflection is required to show that it was a proceeding of such a kind as in no well-regulated community should now be tolerated. So long, indeed, as the great majority of the manufacturing towns and districts were unrepresented in Parliament, there was a plausible—it may be a just—reason assigned for allowing such meetings, that there was no other way in which the people could make known their wishes to the legislature. But since the Reform Act has passed, and every considerable place is fully represented in Parliament, and a legal channel has been provided for the transmission of the popular will to Government, this plea can no longer be advanced. Such meetings are now simply dangerous and pernicious, without being attended with one countervailing advantage. Too large and promiscuous either for deliberation or discussion, they tend only to inflame passion and multiply

---

* "The Prince Regent desires me to convey to your lordship his approbation and high commendation of the conduct of the magistrates and civil authorities at Manchester, as well as the officers and troops, both regular and yeomanry cavalry, whose firmness and effectual support of the civil powers preserved the peace of the town upon that most critical occasion. His Royal Highness entertains a favorable sense of the forbearance of Lieutenant Colonel L'Estrange in the execution of his duty, and bestows the greatest praise upon the zeal and alacrity manifested by Major Trafford and Lieut.-colonel Townsend, and their respective corps. I am, &c.
"H. BLOOMFIELD.
"To the Lord Viscount Sidmouth."
—Lord Sidmouth's Life, iii. 262.

† "To attack the executive for supporting the magistracy on such an occasion, appears to me perfectly senseless. How can it be supposed that any magistrate will act unless assured of support—nay, unless supported with a high hand? Assuredly as the executive shrinks from encouraging, approving, and supporting the magistracy, there will be an end of all subordination."—LORD SHEFFIELD to Lord SIDMOUTH, Nov. 1, 1819; Sidmouth's Life, iii. 263.

* Lord Eldon said, in the debates which followed in the House of Lords, "When I read in my law books that numbers constitute force, and force terror, it is impossible to say that the Manchester meeting was not an illegal one."—Parl. Deb., 23d Nov., 1819; HANSARD, xli. 38. This is undoubtedly true; but it may be observed, that it is impossible the law on this point can be on a more unsatisfactory footing, and that it is high time it should be at once defined, by act of Parliament, what is an illegal meeting, independent of actual commenced violence. Who is to be the judge of what inspires terror, and in whom? In a dozen old men or old women, or a dozen intrepid young men? Between these two extremes, infinite diversities of opinion will be found to exist; no two witnesses will agree, no two juries will arrive at the same conclusion. The practical result is, that no man, as the law now stands, can say with certainty what is an illegal meeting; and every magistrate, if he gives orders to disperse it, places himself at the mercy of a subsequent jury, who may be called on to determine whether the circumstances were such as to have inspired terror in a reasonable mind, as to which, it is a mere chance what opinion they form. The only security for the magistrate in such cases is, to wait till the danger has become so imminent that a tolerable unanimity of witnesses may be hoped for before orders to act are given.

misrepresentation. Their purpose really is not to express opinion, but to inspire terror; it is by the display of their physical numbers, not their intellectual strength, that they hope to gain their object. As such, they tend to uproot the very foundations of government, which must always be laid in the loyalty and submission of the great body of the people. They are always on the edge of violence, if they do not actually commence it; and if they are not actually treasonable, they may be rendered such at no distant period. In all considerable towns in the empire, where such meetings are in use to be held, there are rooms capable of holding at least as many as can possibly hear the speakers; the press will next morning convey their sentiments to the whole nation; and if the display of numbers is desired, the petition or resolutions agreed to may be presented to Parliament, supported by a million of signatures.

31. And on the conduct of the magistrates.

The conduct of the magistrates on this unhappy occasion, though not illegal, appears to have been more open to exception in point of prudence; and though properly and courageously approved of by the Government at the time, it should by no means be followed on similar occasions. They had not issued any proclamation before, warning the meeting that its object was illegal, and that it would be dispersed by force; nor, indeed, could such a proclamation have been issued, as the avowed object of the meeting to petition for a reform in Parliament was legal. The banners carried, though in some instances inflammatory and dangerous, could hardly be called, upon the whole, seditious. "God save the King," and "Rule Britannia," had been played by the bands without any signs of disapprobation from the meeting; and though they had in part marched in military array, they had no arms except a few pikes, had numbers of women and children among them, and had attempted no outrage or act of violence. They had not commenced the proceedings when the dispersion began, so that nothing had been said on the spot to justify it. The Riot Act had been read from the window where the magistrates were, but the hour required to justify the dispersion of a peaceable assembly had not elapsed. The highest authorities have taught us that the meeting was illegal, from its menacing and dangerous character; but the point is, was it *expedient* at the moment, when no warning had been given of its illegality, to disperse it by force?* True, the warrant to arrest Hunt and his friends could not be executed but by military force; but where was the necessity of executing it at all in the presence of the multitude? Could they not have been observed by the police, and arrested in the evening, or at night, after they had dispersed, when no tumult or disorder was to be apprehended? Had the crowd proceeded to acts of violence or depredation, they could not have been too quickly or vigorously charged by the military; but while yet pacific and orderly, and when no seditious resolutions had been proposed, *they* at least were innocent, whatever their leaders may have been. In a word, the conduct of the magistrates, though legal, seems to have been ill-judged, and their measures inexpedient. But great allowance must be made for unprofessional men suddenly placed in such trying circumstances; and as their error, if error there was, was one of judgment only, there can be but one opinion on the noble and intrepid course which Government pursued on the occasion.¹*

¹ Parl. Deb. xli. 365, 369.

32. Seditious meetings in other quarters.

It soon appeared how little effect the violent suppression of the Manchester meeting had in preventing assemblages of a similar or still more alarming description throughout the country. Meetings took place at Birmingham and Leeds, in Westminster, York, Liverpool, Bristol, and Nottingham, attended by great multitudes, at which flags representing a yeoman cutting at a woman were displayed, with the word "Vengeance" inscribed in large letters, and resolutions vehemently condemning the Manchester proceedings were adopted. A meeting of the Common Council of London was held on 9th September, when a petition was voted to the Prince Regent, condemning the conduct of the magistrates and yeomanry,

* Lord Eldon appears, at first at least, to have been of this opinion, for he wrote to his brother, Sir William Scott, soon after hearing of it: "Without all doubt the Manchester magistrates must be supported; but they are very generally blamed here. For my part, I think if the assembly was *only an unlawful assembly*, that task will be *difficult enough in sound reasoning*. If the meeting was an overt act of high treason, their justification was complete." He then goes on to say he thought it was an overt act of treason.—Lord ELDON to Sir W. SCOTT; *Eldon's Life*, ii. 355.

* In truth, in all such cases, what the magistrate has chiefly to consider is, not what is, strictly speaking, legal merely, but what will bear the efforts of misrepresentation and the ordeal of public opinion. Many things are legal which must often not be attempted by those intrusted with authority; many things illegal, in those subjected to it, which must yet be sometimes tolerated. The following rules to guide the magistrate in such difficult circumstances may perhaps be of use to those who are liable to be called on to act under them, and have been the result of some experience and much reflection on the part of the author: 1st. If a meeting, evidently treasonable or seditious, or obviously tending to a breach of the peace—as to choose a provisional government, or to levy war on the Government, or to train without proper authority, or to have an Orange procession among Ribbonmen—is announced, to meet it by a counter-proclamation denouncing it as illegal; but not to do this unless the illegality or danger is manifest, and the magistrate is prepared, and has the force to act decidedly if his admonition is disregarded. 2d. If, in defiance of the proclamation, the meeting is held or the procession attempted, to stop it as gently as possible by force, the magistrate being always himself at the head of the civil or military force which may be employed. 3d. If a meeting, not called for treasonable or seditious purposes, takes place, but threatening to the public peace, to assemble in the vicinity as large a civil and military force as he has at his disposal, but place them out of sight, and never let them be exposed passively either to the insults or the seductions of the people. 4th. If acts of violence, as breaking into houses, setting fire to them, or assaulting or robbing individuals, are attempted, to charge the mob instantly, the magistrate taking his place beside the commanding officer, and taking on himself the entire responsibility; but not to give orders to act till the felonious acts are so clear and decided as to leave no doubt of the impending danger, and to be capable of being proved, in defiance of misrepresentation, by numerous witnesses. 5th. If the leaders are to be arrested, but nothing illegal has yet been done by the multitude, to have the warrant ready, but not to attempt to execute it till they have dispersed, taking the precaution, however, to have the speeches listened to, or taken down by persons who can be relied on. 6th. If acts of decided felony have been commenced, to act *at once*, without waiting for the hour required to elapse by the Riot Act, and though it has not been read, the object of that Act being to render illegal a legal and peaceable, not to justify the dispersion of a violent and illegal assembly.

and praying for inquiry; and at Paisley a meeting of the most violent and seditious character was held, which led to still more serious results. The magistrates of the burgh and sheriff of the county had there very properly issued a proclamation, denouncing the proposed meeting as illegal, and warning the public that it would be dispersed by force; but notwithstanding this, the people met on a common near the town, and entered it in great force, with colors, bearing seditious devices, flying, and music sounding. They were met by the sheriff and magistrates, who seized the colors, and warned the people to disperse. This led to a violent tumult, in the course of which several shops were broken into and pillaged, and order was not restored till the military had been brought from Glasgow, and twenty of the ringleaders seized. In Yorkshire a meeting was held, on a requisition to the high sheriff, signed by Lord Fitzwilliam, the lord-lieutenant of the West Riding of the county, and many other noblemen and gentlemen, where resolutions strongly condemnatory of the Manchester proceedings were adopted. For his share in that proceeding, Lord Fitzwilliam was immediately removed from his high office by order of Government, to the great regret of the friends of that highly-respected nobleman; but the divergence of opinions between him and the Administration had become such that it was impossible they could longer act together.¹

¹ Ann. Reg. 1819, 109, 111; Sidmouth's Mem. iii. 208, 304.

33. Augmentation of the Chelsea pensioners.

Great inconvenience had been experienced throughout all these disturbances, occurring simultaneously in so many different and distant quarters, from the want of any adequate military force to overawe the disaffected and preserve the public peace. A serious riot occurred at Ely, in the course of which the rioters got possession of, and kept for some time, the little town of Littleport, and the only force to oppose to them was eighteen dragoons. The like force was all that could be collected to oppose an insurrection at Derby. When the disturbance broke out at Paisley in the end of September, and the most pressing request for more troops was sent by Sir Thomas Bradford, the Commander-in-Chief in Scotland, the only mode of answering it was by sending a regiment from Portsmouth, and supplying its place by one from Guernsey. The Commander-in-Chief, with the exception of the Guards, who could not with safety be moved from London, had not a single regiment at his disposal, when applications for protection were coming in from all quarters, and yet Parliament was ringing with declamations about the undue increase of the military force of the country. In this extremity Government adopted the wisest course which could have been followed, by calling out the most efficient of the pensioners, and arranging them in veteran battalions—a measure which, at a cost of only £500,000 a year, added nearly 11,000 men to the military force of the kingdom. Lord Sidmouth was indefatigable in pursuing this object, as well as in augmenting the number and strength of the yeomanry force throughout the country; and so ceaseless and energetic were his efforts in both respects, that the Prince Regent observed, with equal truth and justice, "He is the Duke of Wellington on home service." At the same time that illustrious commander, who now, on his return from the Continent, commenced that career of administrative reform and amelioration which, not less than his military career, entitle him to the gratitude and admiration of his country, addressed a letter to Lord Sidmouth, of lasting value to all magistrates and officers placed in similar circumstances.¹*

Oct. 29.

¹ Ann. Reg. 1819, 111; Sidmouth's Life, iii. 290, 294.

Parliament met on the 23d November, and of course there was special allusion in the Speech from the Throne to the seditious practices which had unfortunately become so prevalent in the country. There were no congratulations on the prosperity of the country, or the general well-being of the working classes. On the contrary, the speech contained an emphatic admission of deep distress in several branches of industry.† It is not surprising that Ministers alluded to the distress which pervaded several branches of manufacturing industry, for from the papers laid before Parliament, to justify the measures of repression which were proposed, it appeared that wages in the cotton manufacture had sunk *a half* within the last eight months, and in most other trades in the same proportion—a fact speaking volumes both as to the real cause

31. Meeting of Parliament, and measures of Government. Nov. 23.

---

* "I strongly recommend to you to order the magistrates to carry into execution, without loss of time, the law against training, and to furnish them with the means of doing so. Do not let us be again reproached with having omitted to carry the laws into execution. By sending to Carlisle and Newcastle 700 or 800 men, cavalry and infantry, and two pieces of cannon, or, in other words, two of this movable column, the four would be more than sufficient to do all that may be required. Rely upon it, that, in the circumstances in which we are placed, *impression on either side is every thing*. If, upon the passing of the training law, you prevent training, either by the use of force or the appearance of force, in the two places above mentioned, you will put a stop at once to all the proceedings of the insurgents. *They are like conquerors; they must go forward; the moment they stop they are lost.* Their adherents will lose all confidence, and by degrees every individual will relapse into their old habits of loyalty or indifference. On the other hand, the moment the loyal see there is a law which can prevent these practices, and means and inclination and determination to carry it into execution, they will regain courage, and will do every thing which you can desire. In my opinion, if you send the troops, and order that the law shall be carried into execution, you will not be under the necessity of using them; and the good effect of this will be felt not only in these towns, but over all England. Observe also, that if training is continued after the passing of the law, which it will be unless you send a force to prevent it, the insurgents will gain a very important victory."—WELLINGTON to Lord SIDMOUTH, Dec. 11, 1819; *Sidmouth's Life*, iii. 293.

† "The seditious practices so long prevalent in several parts of the manufacturing districts of the country, have been continued with increased activity since you were last assembled. They have led to proceedings incompatible with the public tranquillity, and with the peaceful habits of the industrious classes of the community; and a spirit is now fully manifested utterly hostile to the constitution of this kingdom, and aiming not only at the change of those political institutions which have hitherto constituted the pride and security of the country, but at the subversion of the rights of property, and of all order in society. . . . . Some depression still continues to exist in certain branches of our manufactures, and I deeply lament the distress felt by those who more immediately depend upon them; but this depression is in a great measure to be ascribed to the embarrassed situation of other countries, and I earnestly hope it will be found to be of a temporary nature."—PRINCE REGENT'S Speech, 23d Nov., 1819; *Ann. Reg.* for 1819, 116, 117.

which at this particular period had rendered the efforts of the demagogues so successful in disturbing the population, and the futility of the ideas of those who ascribed the distress which prevailed to the excess of importations, which could have had no other effect but a beneficial one on the manufactures for the export sale, by diminishing the price at which the raw material and the subsistence for the workmen would be purchased.¹*

<small>¹ Parl. Deb. xl. 1, 5, 422; Ann. Reg. 1819, 132.</small>

As soon as the debates on the Address, which were unusually long and stormy, but which terminated in large ministerial majorities in both houses, were over, Lord Sidmouth in the House of Lords, and Lord Castlereagh in the Commons, introduced the new measures which the Cabinet had deemed essential to meet the exigencies of the times. They were four in number, and, with the addition of two others not immediately connected with the public disturbances, were long famous in England under the name of the *Six Acts*. By the first, all training or practicing military exercises, by persons not authorized by Government, was prohibited, and persons engaged in it were declared liable to punishment by fine, or imprisonment not exceeding two years. By the second, justices of the peace were authorized to issue warrants in certain counties of England and Scotland, to search for arms or other weapons dangerous to the public peace, on a sworn information. By the third, the court was authorized, in the event of the accused allowing judgment to go by default, to order the seizure of all copies of a seditious or blasphemous libel, to be restored if the person accused was afterward acquitted; and for the second offense banishment might be inflicted. By the fourth, no more than fifty persons were to be allowed to assemble, except in borough or county meetings called by the magistrate; and the carrying of flags or attending such meetings armed was prohibited, and extensive powers given to justices of peace or magistrates for dispersing them. In addition to this, a bill was introduced by the Lord Chancellor, to prevent traversing or postponing of the trial, in cases of misdemeanor, to subsequent assizes; and another in the Commons by Lord Castlereagh, subjecting newspapers to certain stamps, and to prevent the abuses arising from the publication of blasphemous and seditious libels. The first and third of the first four acts alone were permanent; the second and third were temporary only in their endurance, and have long since expired. The bills were all strenuously resisted, with the exception of the first, in both houses, but were passed by large majorities—that in the Commons, on the Seditious Meetings Bill, being 223, the numbers 351 to 128; in the Lords, on the same bill, 97, the numbers being 135 to 38. In regard to the Training Act, however, which is still in force, a much greater degree of unanimity prevailed. Several members

<small>35. Lord Sidmouth's Acts of Parliament. Nov. 29.</small>

of both houses usually opposed to Government, but officially acquainted with the state of the country, added their testimony to its necessity; and that the practice of training was then generally prevalent has since been admitted by the Radical leaders, and their ablest historical advocates.¹*

<small>¹ Parl. Deb. xli. 675, 677, 1295; Ann. Reg. 1819, 133, 134; Lord Sidmouth's Mémoires, iii. 302, 303.</small>

A curious but instructive circumstance took place when the Radical leaders were brought up for examination before the Privy Council, into the presence of those whom they had been taught to regard as of a cruel and unrelenting disposition, and the bitterest enemies of the people. "The simple-minded men who had followed Hunt were surprised," says Miss Martineau, "when brought into the presence of the Privy Council, at the actual appearance of the rulers of the land, whom they had regarded as their cruel enemies. They found no cruelty or ferocity in the faces of the tyrants²—Lord Castlereagh, the good-looking person in a plum-colored coat, with a gold ring on the little finger of his left hand, on which he sometimes looked while addressing them: Lord Sidmouth, a tall, square, and bony figure, with thin and gray hairs, broad and prominent forehead, whose mild and intelligent eyes looked forth from their cavernous orbits; his manners affable, and much more encouraging to freedom of speech than had been expected."³ "How often," says Thiers, "would factions the most opposite be reconciled, if they could meet and read each other's hearts." On the other hand, Hunt was far from exhibiting the constancy in adversity which, in every age, has animated the patriot and the hero. He was alternately querulous and depressed—elated by popular applause, but sadly cast down when the intoxicating draught was taken from his lips. In this there is nothing surprising; rectitude of intention is the principle which animates the patriot, who is sustained by its consciousness when aiding the people often against their will. Vanity is the prevailing passion of the demagogue, and his spirits sink the moment the exciting influence is withdrawn.⁴

<small>36. Impression made on the Radicals.</small>

<small>² Martineau, i. 246.</small>

<small>³ Bamford's Life of a Radical, i. 106.</small>

<small>⁴ Martineau, i. 246, 247.</small>

The beginning of the year 1820 was marked by two events which strongly riveted the attention of the nation, and had a beneficial general effect in reviving those feelings of loyalty, which, though sometimes forgotten, are never extinct in the breast of the English people. The Duke of Kent, the father of our present gracious Sovereign, had accompanied the Duchess and his infant daughter, the future Sovereign of Great Britain, to Sidmouth in Devonshire, for the benefit of change of air. There he was unfortunately exposed to wet and cold on the 13th

<small>37. Death of the Duke of Kent. Jan. 13.</small>

<small>* "In all the great stations of the cotton manufacture, as Manchester, Glasgow, Paisley, the rate of wages had fallen on an average more than *one half*. This depression might be traced through the last twenty years to measures of *political economy*."—Lord LANSDOWNE'S Speech, Dec. 1, 1819; Parl. Deb. xiii. 422.</small>

<small>* "There is, and can be, no dispute about the fact of military training; the only question is in regard to the design or object of the practice. Numerous informations were taken by the Lancashire magistrates, and transmitted to Government in the beginning of August." Bamford, the Radical annalist, assures us it was done solely with a view to the great meeting on the 16th August at Manchester.—See Miss MARTINEAU, i. 227; BAMFORD'S *Life of a Radical*, i. 177, 180.</small>

January, which brought on a cough and inflammation of the lungs, which, notwithstanding the most active treatment, terminated fatally on the 23d of the same month. He was interred, with the usual solemnities, at Windsor on 7th February. This prince took little share in public life; and the rigorous discipline which he had found it necessary to enforce in the army, in his earlier years, when in command, had at the time given rise to considerable discussion. But he had survived this temporary unpopularity, as really estimable characters seldom fail to do; and in his latter years he possessed alike the respect of the nation and the warm affection of his personal friends. Personally intrepid, as his race have ever been, he possessed at the same time the kindness of heart and charm of manner, which in all, but in none so much as those of exalted station, are the main foundation of lasting affection. In politics he inclined to the Liberal side, as his brother the Prince Regent and the Duke of Sussex had so long done; but he had little turn for political contentions, and shrouded himself in preference in the seclusion and enjoyments of private life. Deeds of beneficence, or the support of institutions of charity, of which he was a munificent patron, alone brought him before the eye of the public; but in private, no one was more kindly in his disposition, or had secured by acts of generosity a wider or more attached circle of friends.[1]

[1] An. Reg. 1820, 6; Hughes, vi. 403.

38. Death of George III. Jan. 28.

The death of the Duke of Kent was speedily followed by that of his father, who had so long swayed the sceptre of the realm. Toward the end of January, the health of George III., which had hitherto been surprisingly preserved during his long and melancholy mental alienation, rapidly sunk, his strength failed, his appetite left him, and it became evident that the powers of nature were exhausted. At length, at half-past eight on the 28th January, he breathed his last; and the Prince Regent, as George IV., formally ascended the throne, of which, during ten years, he had discharged the duties. On Monday the 31st, the new sovereign was proclaimed with the usual formalities at the Palace, Temple Bar, Charing Cross, and other places; the members of Parliament were sworn in, and both houses immediately adjourned to the 17th February.[2]

[2] Ann. Reg. 1820, 7; Hughes, vi. 411.

39. Deep impression which his death made on the country.

Although he had lived nearly ten years in retirement, and the practical discharge of the functions of royalty by the sovereign who succeeded him had so long withdrawn him from the public gaze, the death of George III. made a profound impression on the British heart. The very circumstances under which the demise had taken place added to the melancholy interest which it excited, and the feelings with which the bereavement was regarded by the people. Nearly the whole existing generation had grown up during his long reign of sixty years; there was no one who had not been accustomed to regard the 4th of June, the well-known birth-day of the sovereign, as a day of rejoicing; no one could form an idea of a king without the aged form which still flitted through the halls of Windsor occurring to the mind. The very obscurity in which his last days had been shrouded, the mental darkness which had prevented him from being conscious of the surpassing glories of the close of his reign, the malady which had secluded him from the eyes of his affectionate people, added to the emotion which his death occasioned. Old feelings were revived, former affections, long pent up, gushed forth, and flowed without control. The realization of the catastrophe, though not of the sorrows, of Lear on the theatre of the world, profoundly affected every heart. The king had survived all his unpopularity; he had lived down the bitterest of his enemies. When the eloquent preacher quoted the words of Scripture, "And Joseph asked them of their welfare, and said, Is your father well? the old man of whom ye spake, is he yet alive? And they answered, Our father is yet alive. And they bowed their heads, and made obeisance,"[*] all felt that now, as in the days of the patriarchs, the same affections of a people to their common father were experienced. The removal of the aged king from this earthly scene made no change in the political world; it was unfelt in the councils or cabinets of princes; but, like a similar bereavement in private life, the circle of the domestic affections was for a season drawn closer, from the removal of one who had shared in its brightness. Nor did it lessen the emotion felt on this event, that it occurred at the time when the mighty antagonist of the departed sovereign was declining in distant and hopeless captivity, and that while George III. slept to death in the solitude of his ancestral halls, Napoleon was dying a discrowned exile in the melancholy main.

The French said, in the days of their loyalty, "The king is dead—long live the king!" Never was the value of this noble maxim more strongly felt than on the present occasion. The death of the king, preceded as it had been by that of the Princess Charlotte, the heiress of the throne, the age and circumstances of the sovereign who had just ascended it, and the situation of the other members of the royal family, had long awakened a feeling of disquietude as to the succession to the monarchy. The Duke of York, now the heir-apparent, was married, had no family, and the duchess was in declining health; the Duke of Clarence, the next in succession, was advanced in years, and although he had had children, they had all died in infancy or early youth. The successors to the crown, after the present sovereign, whose health was known to be in a precarious condition, were, a prince from whom no issue could now be expected, and, after him, an infant princess. Many were the gloomy apprehensions entertained of the eventual consequences of such a state of things, at a time when Europe was convulsed by revolutionary passions, and vigor and capacity on the throne seemed, in an especial manner, requisite to steer the monarchy through the shoals with which it was surrounded. But how often does the course of events deviate from what was once anticipated, and Providence, out of seeming disaster, educe the means of future salvation! Out of

40. Birth of Queen Victoria. May 23, 1819.

[*] Sermon on the Jubilee, 1810, by Rev. A. Alison.—Sermons, i. 412.

this apparently untoward combination of circumstances arose an event of the last importance in after times to the British empire. George IV. reigned just ten years after his accession to the throne, the Duke of Clarence only seven; and his demise opened the succession to our present gracious sovereign, then an infant in the arms, who, uniting the courage and spirit of her Plantagenet and Stuart, to the judgment and integrity of her Hanoverian ancestors, has reunited, in troubled times, all hearts to the throne, and spread through her entire subjects the noble feelings of disinterested loyalty. The sequel of this history will show of what incalculable importance it was that, at a time when every crown in Europe was shaking on the brow of its wearer, and the strongest monarchies were crumbling in the dust, a Queen should have been on the British throne, whose virtues had inspired the respect, while her intrepidity had awakened the admiration of all her subjects, and who, like her ancestress Queen Mary, was regarded with warmer feelings of chivalrous devotion than any king, how eminent soever, could have been; for toward her, to all that could command respect in the other sex were united

——— "the gallantry of man
In lovelier woman's cause."

41. Alarming illness of George IV.

The English were soon made aware on how precarious a footing the succession to the throne was placed, and how soon they might have to mourn a second death among their monarchs. Hardly had the new king ascended the throne, when he was seized with a violent attack of inflammation in the chest, which was the more alarming, from its being the same complaint which had so recently proved fatal to the Duke of Kent. For several days his life was in imminent danger, and almost despaired of; but at length the strength of his constitution, and the skill of his physicians, triumphed over the virulence of the disease, and the alarming symptoms disappeared. He long continued, however, very weak, from the copious bleedings which he had undergone; and when his royal father was laid in the grave at Windsor, on the 16th February, the highest in station was absent, and the Duke of York was chief mourner.[1]

[1] Ann. Reg. 1820,17,18; Hughes, i. 405, 406.

42. Ominous questions regarding the omission of Queen Caroline's name in the Liturgy.

Parliament met again, after the prorogation, on the 17th February. By the Constitution, the House of Commons must be dissolved within six months after the demise of the king, and the state of the public business rendered it advisable that this should take place as soon as possible, in order to get it over by the ordinary time of prorogation. It was indispensable, however, for Ministers to obtain some votes in supply before the House was dissolved; and, in doing so, they received early warning of a serious difficulty which awaited them at the very threshold of their career as ministers of the new monarch. Hitherto Queen Caroline had been prayed for in the Liturgy as the Princess of Wales. But as the king was determined never, under any circumstances, to acknowledge her as Queen of England, it was deemed indispensable to make a stand at the very

Feb. 12.

outset; and, accordingly, her name was omitted in the Liturgy by an order of the Privy Council. This gave rise to an ominous question in the House of Commons a few days after. Mr. Hume asked, on the 18th February, whether the allowance of £35,000 a year, hitherto made to her Royal Highness, was to be continued; and Lord Castlereagh having answered in the affirmative, no further notice of the subject took place, though Mr. Brougham, her chief legal adviser, was present, and had made a violent attack on the Government. But on the 21st, when a motion was made that the House should resolve itself into a committee of supply, Mr. Hume again introduced the subject, and said that, without finding fault with any exercise of the prerogative, on the part of the sovereign, as head of the Church, he might be permitted to ask why an address of condolence and congratulation had not been voted to her Majesty on her accession to the throne, and to express his regret at the manner in which she had been treated. Was she to be left a beggar upon the Continent, and the Queen of England to be thrown a needy suppliant on the cold charity of foreign princes? Something definite should be fixed in regard to the future provision for her.[1]

Feb. 18.

[1] Ann. Reg. 1820, 25, 26; Parl. Deb. xli. 1606, 1608, 1621, 1623.

43. Remarkable speech of Mr. Brougham.

The speech of Mr. Brougham on this occasion was very remarkable, and seemed to presage, as he was the Queen's Attorney-general, a more favorable issue to this unhappy division than could have been at first anticipated. He deemed it unnecessary to lay any stress on the omission of her name in the Liturgy, or her being called by the King's ministers in this debate an "exalted personage" instead of Her Majesty. Was she not the wedded wife of the sovereign? What she was called could not alter her position one way or other. These are trifles light as air, which can never render her situation either precarious or uncertain. If the advisers of the Crown should be able to settle upon her what was necessary to maintain her rank and dignity out of the civil list, there would be no need to introduce her Majesty's name. He had refused to listen to any surmise; he had shut his ears to all reports; he knew nothing of any delicate investigations; but if any charge was preferred against her Majesty, he would be prepared to meet it alike as her Majesty's confidential adviser, and as an independent member of Parliament.[2]

[2] Parl. Deb. xli. 1616; Ann. Reg. 1820, 27.

44. Cato Street conspiracy. Thistlewood's previous life.

Nothing further followed on this conversation, and Parliament, having been prorogued to the 13th March, was next day dissolved, and writs issued for the election of a new Parliament to meet on 27th April. But ere it could assemble the nation was horror-struck by the discovery of one of the most atrocious murderous conspiracies that ever disgraced the annals of mankind, and which was only prevented from ending in the massacre of the whole Cabinet by the timidity or treachery of one of the members of the gang, who revealed the plot to the Government. This was the CATO STREET CONSPIRACY, which may well take its place beside the worst outbreaks of Italian crime, and showed to what frightful extremities the English mind, when violently excited by political passions, is capable of being led. The author of the plot was Arthur Thistlewood, who was born in 1770, had received a tolerable education, and had served both in the militia and in a West India regiment. He soon, however, resigned his commission, and, notwithstanding the war, succeeded in making his way to Paris, where he arrived shortly after the fall of Robespierre. He there embraced all the extravagant ideas which the Revolution had caused to germinate in France, and he returned to England firmly persuaded that the first duty of a patriot was to massacre the Government, and overturn all existing institutions. He was engaged in Watson's conspiracy, already

[1 Ante, c. iv. § 65.] mentioned,[1] and, like him, acquitted in the face of distinct proof, chiefly from the indictment having been laid for high treason, which was straining a point, instead of conspiracy and riot, as to which the evidence was clear. On his acquittal he sent a challenge to Lord Sidmouth, for which he was handed over to the civil authorities, by whom he was sentenced to a year's imprisonment. He came out of prison at its expiration thirsting for vengeance, and burning with revolutionary passions, at the very time when the "Manchester massacre," as it was called, had

[2 Ann. Reg. 1820, 29; Hughes, vi. 408; Martineau, i. 212.] excited such a ferment in the country, and he immediately engaged himself in the furtherance of a conspiracy, the object of which was to murder the Ministers and overturn the Government.[2]

He soon succeeded, in that period of excitement, in collecting a band of conspirators as determined and reckless as himself—men fit, indeed, "to disturb the peace of the whole world," though certainly not to "rule it when 'tis wildest." Ings, a butcher; Davidson, a creole; Brunt and Tidd, shoemakers, were his principal associates, but with them were collected forty or fifty more, who were to be employed in the execution of their designs. They met twice a day, during February, in a hired room near Gray's Inn Lane, and their first design was to murder the king, but this was soon laid aside for the massacre of his ministers, who were to be dispatched separately in their own houses. On Saturday, February 19th, their plans were arranged. Forty men were to be set apart for these detached murders, and whoever faltered in the great work was to atone for it with his life; while a detachment was, at the same time, to seize two pieces of artillery stationed in Gray's Inn, and six in the artillery ground. The Mansion House was to be immediately attacked, and a provisional government established there, the Bank assaulted, and London set on fire in several places. But this design was modified, in consequence of information given by Edwards, one of their number, who after-

45. Design of the conspirators. Feb. 19.

[1 Thistlewood's Trial, 37, 45; Ann. Reg. 1820, 30, 31; Martineau, i. 212.] ward revealed the conspiracy, that the whole Cabinet was to dine at Lord Harrowby's in Grosvenor Square.[1] Thistlewood immediately proposed to murder them all at once when assembled there, which was assented to: "for," said he, "as there has not

been a dinner for so long, there will no doubt be fourteen or sixteen there; and it will be *a rare haul to murder them all together.*"

In pursuance of this plan, two of the conspirators were stationed in Grosvenor Square to see what was going on there; and a room was taken above a stable in Cato Street, off the Edgeware Road, where the conspirators were to assemble on the afternoon of the 22d February, when the dinner at Lord Harrowby's was to take place. The only access to this room, which was large enough to hold thirty persons, was by a ladder, which led up to a trap-door, and there, at six in the evening, Thistlewood, and twenty-four of the conspirators, fully armed, were assembled. It was arranged that one of the conspirators was to call at Lord Harrowby's with a note when the party were at dinner, and on the door being opened the whole were to rush in, murder the Ministers, and as trophies of their success bring out the heads of Lord Sidmouth and Castlereagh, for which purpose bags were provided. Meanwhile the cavalry barracks in King Street, Portman Square, were to be set on fire by throwing fire-balls into the straw depôt, and the Bank and Mansion House attacked by those left in the city. Every thing was in readiness, arms and ammunition provided, fire-balls prepared, the treasonable proclamation ready, and at half-past seven the conspirators were arming themselves in the Cato Street loft by the light of two small candles. But meanwhile Ministers had information of their designs from the information of Edwards, who had revealed the whole conspiracy, and instead of dining at Lord Harrowby's they dined together privately in Downing Street. The preparations for the dinner at Lord Harrowby's, however, were allowed to proceed without any interruption, and a party of fourteen police, under that able police magistrate, Mr. Birnie, proceeded to the place of rendezvous, where it had been arranged they were to be supported by a detachment of the Coldstream Guards. The Guards, however, were not ready to start instantly when Birnie called with the police at their barracks, and in consequence, thinking not a moment was to be lost, that intrepid officer hastened on with his fourteen policemen alone.[*]

46. Their final plans.

[1 Thistlewood's Trial, 56, 64; Ann. Reg. 1820, 32, 33; Martineau, i. 212, 213.]

---

[*] The delay in getting the detachment of Foot Guards ready when Birnie called at the barracks with the police, was not owing to any want of zeal or activity on the part of that gallant corps, the detachment of which, under their noble leader, Captain Fitzclarence, behaved with the utmost spirit, and rendered essential service in the affray when they did come up. It arose from a different meaning being attached by military men and civilians to the words, "ready to turn out at a moment's warning." The former understood these words to mean, "ready to take their places in file, and be told off," when ordered to do so; the latter, ready to *face about and march straight out of the barrack gate*. The difference should be known, and is often attended with important consequences. In this instance, if the Guards had been drawn up and told off in the barrack-yard, and marched out with Birnie the moment he arrived, the whole conspirators would at once have been taken in the loft, and perhaps no lives lost. They had been ordered to be in readiness to start at a moment's warning, but some little time was lost in putting them in their places and telling off. Another instance will occur in the sequel of this history, where a similar misunderstanding as to the meaning of these words between the magistrates and military occasioned the loss of five lives.

538   HISTORY OF EUROPE.   [CHAP. X.

47.
Conflict in
the dark in
the Cato
Street loft.
Feb. 22.

The first of the police who ascended the trap-stair was an active and brave officer, named Smithers, who, the moment he got to the top of the ladder, called on the conspirators to surrender. As they refused to do so, he advanced to seize Thistlewood, and was by him run through the body and immediately fell. The lights were instantly extinguished, and a frightful conflict began in the dark between the police officers and the gang, in the course of which some dashed headlong down the trap-stair, and others, including Thistlewood, made their escape by the back windows of the loft. At this critical moment the Foot Guards, thirty in number, came up with fixed bayonets, and, hastening in double-quick time to the door of the stable, arrived there as some of the conspirators were rushing out. Captain Fitzclarence, who was at their head, advanced to seize the sentinel at the door, who instantly aimed a pistol at his head, the ball of which was averted by his covering Sergeant Logge, whom it wounded. Fitzclarence upon this ordered his men to follow him into the stable, himself leading the way. He was met by a mulatto, who aimed a blow at him with a cutlass, which one of the soldiers warded off with his musket. Both these men were made prisoners. They then mounted the ladder, and five men were secured in the loft, making, with those previously taken by the police, nine in all. The rest, in the darkness and confusion, had escaped, among whom was Thistlewood; but a reward of £1000 having been offered for his apprehension, he was made prisoner the following morning in his bed.[1]

1 Trial of Thistlewood, 65, 74; Ann. Reg. 1820, 32, 33; App. to Chron. 935, 940; Hughes, vi. 410, 411.

48.
Execution of the conspirators.
May 1.

The Ministers, whose lives had been saved by the discovery of this conspiracy, returned thanks publicly at St. Paul's a few days after, and the whole respectable classes in the country were horror-struck at the intelligence. Thistlewood, Ings, Tidd, Brunt, and Davidson, were arraigned for high treason on the 17th of April, found guilty, and sentenced to death, on proof which, though consisting in part of the testimony of two of the conspirators who were taken as king's evidence, was so confirmed by the police officers, military, and others engaged in the capture, that not a doubt could exist of their guilt. Five were sentenced to transportation for life, and one, after sentence, received a free pardon. Indeed, so far from denying their guilt, Thistlewood and Brunt gloried in it at their trial, alleging that assassination was fully justifiable in the circumstances, and that it was a fit retribution for the high treason committed against the people by the Manchester massacre.* They were executed on the 1st May, in presence of an immense crowd of spectators, many of whom evinced a warm sympathy with their fate. They behaved with great firmness in their last moments, exhibiting that mixture of stoicism and ruffianism so common in persons engaged in political conspiracies. All attempts to awaken them to any sense of religion or feelings of repentance failed, except with Davidson. "In ten minutes," said Ings, as he ascended the scaffold, "we shall know the great secret." The frightful process of decapitation, prescribed by the English law for cases of high treason, was executed, it is to be hoped for the last time, on their lifeless remains, amidst the shudders of the crowd, who were more horror-struck with this relic of ancient barbarity than impressed with the guilt of the criminals.[1]

1 Hughes, vi. 411; An. Reg. 1820, 32; Ap. to Chron. 946, 949; Martineau, i. 243.

49.
Disturbances in Scotland and north of England.

Hardly had the nation recovered from the shock arising from this atrocious conspiracy, and its dreadful punishment, when a fresh alarm of a more serious and wide-spread nature broke out in the north. Notwithstanding the powers given to the magistrates to suppress military training by the late act, it still continued through the whole winter in the West Riding of Yorkshire, Lancashire, Durham, and the neighborhood of Glasgow. All the vigilance of the magistrates was unable to detect or suppress these alarming practices, which evidently presaged, at no distant period, a general insurrection against the Government. It was at first fixed for the 1st November, but adjourned then, and on various other occasions, in consequence of the preparations not being complete. Meanwhile the midnight training went on without intermission on the hills and moors, sometimes in one place, sometimes in another, so as to elude discovery or pursuit; and at length, all things being conceived to be in readiness, the insurrection was arranged to take place on the 2d April. The large military force, however, which was stationed in Lancashire and Yorkshire prevented any serious outbreak in that quarter, and it ended in an assembly of three hundred malcontents near Huddersfield, who dispersed on the rumor of the approach of a body of cavalry.[2] But in Scotland affairs became more serious, and revealed at once the precipice on the brink of which the nation stood, and the extraordinary sway which the leaders of the move-

2 Ann. Reg. 1820, 36, 37; Hughes, vi. 412; Martineau, i. 245.

* "High treason was committed against the People at Manchester, but justice was closed against the mutilated, the maimed, and the friends of those who were upon that occasion indiscriminately massacred. The Prince, by the advice of his Ministers, thanked the murderers, still reeking in the gore of their victims. If one spark of honor, if one spark of independence still glimmered in the breasts of Englishmen, they would have risen as one man. Insurrection then became a public duty, and the blood of the victims should have been the watchword for vengeance on their murderers. Albion is still in the chains of slavery. I quit it without regret. I shall soon be consigned to the grave; my body will be immured beneath the soil where I first drew breath. My only sorrow is, that the soil should be a theatre for slaves, for cowards, and for despots. I disclaim any personal motives. My every principle was for the prosperity of my country. My every feeling, the height of my ambition, was for the welfare of my starving countrymen. I keenly felt for their miseries; but when their miseries were laughed at, and when, because they dared to express those miseries, they were inhumanly massacred and trampled upon, my feelings became too intense, and I resolved on vengeance! I resolved that the lives of the instigators should be required to the souls of the murdered innocents."—Thistlewood's Address before receiving sentence.

"Lords Castlereagh and Sidmouth have been the cause of the death of millions. I conspired to put them out of the world, but I did not intend to commit high treason. In undertaking to kill them and their fellow-ministers, I did not expect to save my own life; but I was determined to die a martyr in my country's cause, and to avenge the innocent blood shed at Manchester."—Brunt's Speech before receiving sentence; Ann. Reg. 1820, 946, 947; Appendix to Chronicle.

ment had obtained over the working classes in the manufacturing districts.

50. Insurrection in Scotland. April 2.
On Sunday morning, April 2d, a treasonable proclamation was found placarded over all the streets of Glasgow, Paisley, Stirling, and the neighboring towns and villages, in the name of a provisional government, calling on the people to desist from labor; on all manufacturers to close their workshops; on the soldiers to remember the glorious example of the Spanish troops; and on all friends of their country to come forward and effect a revolution by force, with a view to the establishment of an entire equality of civil rights. Strange to say, this treasonable proclamation, unsigned, proceeding from an unknown authority, was widely obeyed. Work immediately ceased; the manufactories were closed from the desertions of their workmen; the streets were filled with anxious crowds eagerly expecting news from the south; the sounds of industry were no longer heard; and two hundred thousand persons in the busiest districts of the country were thrown at once into a state of compulsory idleness by the mandates of an unseen and unknown power. Never was there a clearer proof how powerful an engine fear is to work upon the human heart—how much its influence is extended by the terror being awakened from a source of which all are ignorant. How true are the words of Tacitus, "*Omne ignotum pro magnifico;*" and how well founded was the boast of Marat, that with three hundred determined bravoes he would govern France, and cause three hundred thousand heads to fall.[1]

[1] Scotch State Trials, i. 40; Ann. Reg. 1820, 35, 37; Hughes, vi. 412, 413; Personal observation.

51. Outbreak of the insurrection, and its suppression. April 3.
Fortunately at this juncture the energy of Government, and the spirit of the untainted parts of the country, were adequate to encounter the danger. Volunteer and yeomanry corps had shortly before been formed in various districts; regiments 800 strong had been raised in Edinburgh and Glasgow, entirely clothed at their own expense. Squadrons of yeomanry had been formed in both towns, and they came forward at the approach of danger with the most praiseworthy alacrity. At 2 P.M. on April 3, summonses were dispatched to the Edinburgh squadron, which was 99 strong, to assemble in marching order; at 4 P.M. 97 were at the appointed rendezvous, and set out for Glasgow.* Volunteer and yeomanry corps rapidly poured into that city; in a few days 5000 men, of whom 2000 were horse, with eight guns, were assembled in it. The crown-officers hastened to Glasgow, and directed the proceedings. This great demonstration of moral and physical strength extinguished the threatened insurrection. The expected movement in England did not take place; the appointed signal of the stopping of the London mail in vain was looked for: a tumultuous body of insurgents, which set out from Strathaven, in Lanarkshire, melted away before they arrived in Glasgow; another between Kilsyth and Falkirk was encountered at Bonnymuir by a detachment of fourteen hussars and fourteen of the Stirlingshire yeomanry, totally defeated, and nineteen of their number made prisoners. Before the week had elapsed the danger was over; the insurgents saw they were over-matched; a rigorous search for arms in Glasgow revealed to them their weakness; numerous arrests paralyzed all the movements of the leaders, and sent numbers into voluntary exile; the people gradually resumed their avocations; and this outbreak, which at first had appeared so threatening, was terminated with the sacrifice only of two men executed at Stirling, one at Glasgow, and seven or eight transported. But the rebellious spirit of the manufacturing districts was suppressed in a far more effectual and better way, which neither caused blood to flow nor a tear to fall. They were morally slaughtered; the strength of their opponents, their own weakness, was evinced in an unmistakable manner. The ancient spirit and loyalty of the Scotch was shown in the most striking manner on this occasion; the flower of the youth in all the counties ranged themselves in arms around the standard of their country; and Sir Walter Scott, whose chivalrous spirit was strongly roused by these exciting events, boasted, in the pride of his heart, that at a public dinner of 800 gentlemen in Edinburgh, presided over by the Marquis of Huntly, there were gentlemen enough assembled to have raised 50,000 men in arms.[1]*

[1] Personal knowledge. Ann. Reg. 1820, 37, 39; Scotch State Trials, ii. 100, 234; Hughes, vi. 414, 415.

52. Death and character of Mr. Grattan.
Parliament met, after the general election, on 21st April. Its result had made no material difference in the respective strength of parties, but, if any thing, strengthened the ministerial ranks—the usual result of public disturbances, which awaken men to a sense of the necessity of supporting the Government, whatever it is, which is intrusted with the duty of repressing them. One distinguished member of the House, however, Mr. GRATTAN, never took his seat in the new Parliament, and expired soon after the session commenced. He was the last of that bright band of patriots, who, warmed into life by the great struggle for Irish independence in 1782, when the chains in which that country had so long been held by England first began to be broken, were, after the Union, transferred to the British Parliament, which they caused to resound with strains of eloquence rarely before heard within its walls.[2]

June 6.

[2] An. Reg. 1820, 142; 143; Martineau, i. 263.

---

* The author has much pleasure in recording this just tribute to a fine and spirited corps, in the ranks of which some of the happiest days of his life have been spent. The Edinburgh squadron at that time, which was the successor of that in which Sir Walter Scott had served, and has immortalized, contained several young men destined to distinguished eminence; among others, the present Lord Justice Clerk, Hope; Mr. Patrick Tytler, the historian of Scotland; Mr. Lockhart, since editor of the *Quarterly Review*; and Mr. Francis Grant, since so eminent as a painter in London.

* "We have silenced the Scottish Whigs for our time, and, I think, drawn the flower of Scotland round the King and Constitution. Laterally I do not exceed the mark, when Lord Huntly, our Cock of the North, as he is called, presided over 800 gentlemen, there was influence and following enough among us to raise 50,000 men, property enough to equip and pay them for a year, young men not unacquainted with arms enough to discipline them, and one or two experienced generals to command them. I told this to my Whig friends who were bullying me about the popular voice—and added, they might begin when they liked, we were as ready as they."—SIR WALTER SCOTT to Lord Sidmouth, 17th February, 1821; *Sidmouth's Life*, iii. 343.

He was not so luminous in his exposition of facts as Pitt, nor so vehement in his declamation as Fox; but in burning thoughts, generous feelings, and glowing language, he was sometimes superior to either. Occasional passages in his speeches, when quoted or repeated, are perhaps the finest and most imaginative pieces of eloquence in the English language. It was justly observed by Sir James Mackintosh, in moving a new writ for Dublin, which he had long represented, that he was perhaps the only man recorded in history who had obtained equal fame and influence in two assemblies differing from each other in such essential respects as the English and Irish Parliaments. Forty years before his death, he had been voted a grant to purchase an estate, by the Irish Parliament, in consideration of his eminent national services, a thing unknown in an individual not connected with the public establishments. He had been a warm supporter of the Union, hoping, as he himself expressed it, that Ireland, instead of receiving laws from England, should henceforth take an equal share with her in legislating for the united empire. It is only to be regretted that his genius, great as it was, had been through life chiefly directed to an unattainable object. The independence of Ireland was the chief aspiration of his mind, and he lived to see that it was hopeless. He said, in his figurative and beautiful language, "I have sat by its cradle, I have followed its hearse." Hence his name, with the exception of the Union and the shackles burst in 1782, is linked with no great legislative improvement in his native country—for Catholic emancipation, of which he was the strenuous and able advocate, has failed, by the admission of its warmest supporters, to prove such. It is remarkable that the Irish or Celtic character, gifted, often beyond the Anglo-Saxon, with the brightest imaginative qualities, has in general been found deficient in that practical turn and intuitive sagacity which is necessary to turn them to any good purpose; and that, amidst all our admiration of their genius, we are too often reminded of the elegant allegory told of the Duke of Orleans, that every fairy invited to his christening sent him a gift of person, genius, or fortune; but that one old fairy, to whom no invitation had been given, sent one fatal present — that he should be unable to make any use of them.[1]

One of the first measures adopted by Government, with the sanction of Parliament, was the increase of the yeomanry force, which was so much augmented that before the end of the year it amounted to nearly 35,000 men, all animated with the best spirit, and for the most part in a surprising state of discipline and efficiency. Without doubt, it takes above a year to make a good horse soldier; but it often excites the wonder of military officers how quickly men of intelligence and spirit, such as usually compose the yeomanry corps, if previously able to ride, acquire the rudiments of skill even in the cavalry service; and still more, how *quickly their horses learn it.* The Duke of Wellington recommended that the militia should be called out throughout the kingdom; but this was thought not advisable, probably because it was doubtful how far, in the manufacturing districts, such a force could be relied on. Two thousand men, however, were added to the marines, which rendered disposable an equal amount of the regular force stationed in the garrison seaport towns. Such was the vigor of Lord Sidmouth in following up the measures for the increase of the yeomanry force, that the king happily said of him, "If England is to be preserved England, the arrangements he has made will lead to that preservation." Without doubt, the powerful volunteer force, organized especially in the manufacturing districts at this period, and the decisive demonstration it afforded of moral and physical strength on the part of the Government, was the chief cause of Great Britain escaping an alarming convulsion, at the time when the spirit of revolution was proving so fatal to monarchy in so many of the Continental states.[1]

The revenue for the year fell considerably short of what had been anticipated, the natural consequence of the general distress which prevailed in the country. Mr. Alderman Heygate, who had so strenuously resisted the resumption of cash payments in the preceding year, did not fail to point out the contraction of the currency as the main cause of that deficiency.* Great disputes as usual took place as to the real amount of the revenue, as compared with the expenditure; but it appeared upon the whole evident that the revenue, had fallen above a million short of what had been anticipated, and that instead of the expected real sinking fund of £5,000,000, no reduction in the public debt had taken place, as the unfunded debt had decreased £2,000,000, and the funded debt increased by exactly the same sum. The revenue for 1820 and 1821 exhibited,† without any change in taxation, and the most strenuous efforts at economy on the part of Government, decisive evidence of the

---

* "Let the House contrast the quantity of the circulating medium which was floating in the country in May, 1818, with the amount in circulation in the same month in the present year. In the issue of Bank of England notes there had been a diminution of £4,000,000; in the issue of country bank-notes there had been a diminution of £5,000,000. The total diminution in that short period had been £9,000,000, a sum amounting to more than one-sixth of the whole circulation of the country. The state of the exchange during that period had been almost uniformly in our favor, but not a single piece of gold had made its appearance to replace the notes which had been withdrawn. Three-fourths of the distress of the country was to be ascribed to the haste with which so large a proportion as £9,000,000 had been withdrawn from the circulation."—Mr. HEYGATE's *Speech*, June 19, 1820; *Parl. Debates*, i. 1178, new series.

† The revenue of Great Britain and Ireland for 1820 and 1821 stood thus:—

INCOME.

	1820—Nett.	1821—Nett.
Customs	£10,743,189	£11,475,259
Excise	28,622,248	28,941,629
Stamps	6,794,866	6,853,086
Lands Assessed, including Ireland	8,313,148	8,192,301
Post Office	1,692,636	1,621,326
Lesser Imposts	1,323,893	1,731,231
Hereditary Revenue	127,820	130,077
	£57,304,650	£58,108,855
Loans from Sinking Fund	17,292,544	13,833,783
Total	£74,597,193	£71,937,638
Of which was Irish Revenue	3,905,299	3,672,179

laboring state of the finances of the country, and took away all hopes of making, during peace, any serious impression on the public debt. The details are of little practical importance in a work of general history; but the result is so, as demonstrating how entirely the effects had corresponded to what had been predicted as to the effects of the currency bill passed so unanimously in the preceding year by both Houses of Parliament.[1 Parl. Deb. i. 1170, 1174.]

56. Important subjects of debate in this session. The Parliamentary debates of 1820 embrace fewer topics than usual of general moment, in consequence of the engrossing interest of the proceedings regarding the Queen, to be immediately noticed. But three subjects of lasting importance were brought forward—namely, that of general education, introduced by Mr. Brougham; the disfranchisement of Grampound, by LORD JOHN RUSSELL; and Free Trade, by Mr. Wallace of the Board of Trade. On the first point it is superfluous to give the speeches, even in an abbreviated form, because the subject is one upon which the minds of all men are made up. It is no more necessary to prove that the sun's rays will give light and warmth, than that the lamp of knowledge will illuminate and humanize the mind. But the subject, as all others in which the feelings of large bodies of men are warmly interested, is beset with difficulties; and Mr. Brougham's speech was replete with valuable information on it. His project, which was for the establishment, as in Scotland, of a school, maintained by the public funds, in every parish, failed chiefly from its proposing to connect the schools with the Established Church, which at once lost for it the support of all the Dissenters. But the facts which he had collected were of lasting value in the great cause of moral and social improvement.[2 Martineau, i. 265.]

EXPENDITURE.

	1820.	1821.
National Debt and Sinking Fund	£47,070,927	£47,130,171
Unfunded Debt, Ireland	1,819,219	2,219,602
Civil List, &c.	2,134,213	2,268,940
Civil Government, Scotland	132,080	133,077
Lesser Payments	438,339	476,873
Navy	6,387,799	5,913,879
Ordnance	1,401,585	1,337,923
Army	8,926,423	8,932,779
Miscellaneous	2,616,700	3,870,042
Foreign Loans, &c.	50,357	48,464
	£71,067,648	£72,361,756

NATIONAL DEBT.

Unfunded Debt	£37,012,433	£36,211,726
Debt Redeemed by Sinking Fund to 5th January, 1821	399,560,101	399,358,419
Unredeemed Debt at ditto	772,066,898	795,312,767
Annual Interest:		
Funded Debt	31,450,128	31,450,128
Sinking Fund	16,649,514	16,649,514

—Ann. Reg. 1821, 251, 271; and 1822, 319, 325.

* " No scheme of popular education can ever become national in this country, which gives the management of schools and appointment of masters to the Church, while Dissenters constitute a large proportion of the inhabitants in almost every district, and especially in the most populous, where the Dissenters bear their full share in such education as already exists. This difficulty was immediately fatal to Mr. Brougham's measure, and has been so in every scheme proposed in succeeding years; the members of the Established Church insisting on direct religious instruction as a part of the plan, and the Dissenters refusing to subject their children to the religious instruction of the Church, or to pay for a system from which their children are necessarily excluded."—MISS MARTINEAU's *Thirty Years of Peace*, i. 265.

57. Statistics on education in England and Wales, by Mr. Brougham. According to Mr. Brougham's statement, there were then 12,000 parishes or chapelries in England; of these, 3500 had not a vestige of a school, endowed or unendowed, and the people had no more means of education than the Hottentots or the Caffres. Of the remainder, 3000 had endowed schools, and the remaining 5500 were provided only with unendowed schools, depending entirely on the casual and fleeting support of the parents of the children attending them. The number of children annually receiving education at all the schools, week-day and Sunday, was 700,000, of whom only 600,000 were at day-schools, where regular attendance was given and discipline enforced. Fifty thousand were estimated as the number educated at home, making in all 750,000 annually under tuition of one sort or another, which, taking the population of England at 9,540,000, the amount by the census of 1811, was about *one-fifteenth* of the whole population.

But in reality the population of England was proved, by the census taken in the succeeding year, to be considerably greater than he supposed, for it amounted to no less than 11,260,000, besides 470,000 in the army, navy, and mercantile sea-service. Thus the real proportion receiving education was not more than *one-seventeenth* of the entire population; a small figure for a country boasting so great an amount of intelligence and civilization, for in many countries with less pretensions in these respects the proportion was much higher. In Scotland the proportion at that period was between one-ninth and one-tenth; in Holland it was one-tenth; in Switzerland, one-eighth; in Prussia, one-tenth; in Austria, one-eleventh. In France—to its disgrace be it said—the proportion was still one-twenty-eighth only, though 7200 new schools had been opened in the last two years. But though England presented a much more favorable aspect, yet there the deficiency was very great; for the total children requiring education were about 1,000,000, and as 750,000 only were at any place of education, it followed that 250,000 persons, or a quarter of the entire juvenile population, were yearly growing up without any education whatever.[1 Parl. Deb. ii. 61, 65, June 28, 1820; Ann. Reg. 1820, 50, 51.]

58. Difficulties of this subject, and necessity of an assessment. It is abundantly evident from these facts, and the same has been proved in other countries, that no reliance can be placed on the voluntary system for the support of education, and that unless the means of instruction are provided at the public expense, the education of the people will always be in a most unsatisfactory state, and its blessings in a considerable portion of society wholly un-

* Mr. Brougham stated that in endowed schools 165,432 children were educated, and 490,000 in unendowed, besides 11,000 who might be allowed for the unendowed schools in 150 parishes, from which no returns had been obtained. Of this number 53,000 were at dame schools, where only the rudiments of education were taught. Small as the proportion of educated children was, it had only become such as it was of late years, for of the total educated about 200,000 were in 1820 Lancasterian schools, which only began to be established in 1803, so that before that time not more than one-twentieth, of the population was annually receiving instruction.—*Ann. Reg.* 1820, 50

known. Whatever ministers to the physical necessities or pleasures of the people is easily rendered self-supporting, but it is otherwise with what tends to their moral improvement or social elevation. These can never be safely left to private support, for this plain reason, that a large portion of society, and that the very one which most stands in need of them, is wholly insensible to their value, and will pay nothing for their furtherance. Had the property which once belonged to the Church still remained in its hands, and been righteously administered, it might have solved the difficulty, because it was adequate to the gratuitous support of the whole religious and educational institutions requisite for the country. But as so large a part of it had been seized on by private cupidity, and been alienated from the Church at the Reformation, this precious resource was lost, and nothing remained but assessment, and there the difficulty at once is felt.

59. Its difficulties, and attempts at their solution.

At first sight, it appears easy to solve the difficulty by simply establishing a school-rate in every parish, to be collected along with the poor-rate and prison-rate, and which, at a trifling cost to the community, would afford to the children of all adequate means of instruction. This was what Lord Brougham proposed in England, and which has been long established with great success in America. But a difficulty, which has hitherto been found insurmountable, lies at the very threshold in this country, which is the more serious that it arises from the combined sincere convictions and selfish jealousies of the ministers of religion and their zealous followers. What religion is to be taught? Is it to be the Episcopalian, Catholic, or Dissent? If the last, which Dissent, for their name is legion? So great is this difficulty, that it has hitherto been found insurmountable both in England or Ireland, and caused all attempts at a general system of education to fail. Each sect not only gives no support to any attempt to establish any general system of education connected with any other sect, but meets it with the most strenuous opposition. Nor is this surprising, for each considers its own tenets and forms the ones most conducive to temporal well-being—and not a few, the only portals to eternal salvation.

60. Probable mode of solving it.

Scotland is the exception. Its parochial schools were established in 1696, when the fervor of the Reformation in a community as yet only agricultural had produced an unusual degree of unanimity on religious subjects, and the burden was laid entirely on the landholders. No *general* school-rate could by possibility succeed now, in the divided state of the religious world in that country. The difficulty might perhaps be solved by simply levying a rate, and dividing it in each parish, for the support of schools, in proportion to the number of families belonging to each considerable persuasion; and possibly this is the way in which alone the difficulty can ultimately be overcome. In urban parishes, at least, where the evils of want of education for the poor are most strongly felt, it would be easy to establish in every school a room or rooms, in which the elements of secular education are taught to all, while in an adjoining apartment the children of the different persuasions are in succession instructed on religious subjects by their respective religious teachers. A general rate might be levied on all for the support of the teachers in the first; a special rate on those professing each persuasion for the instruction in the last. This is done in several schools in manufactories in Scotland, and is generally practiced in America with perfect success. The system appears complicated, but it is perhaps the only way in which the difficulties connected with the subject can be obviated, or a general assessment for educational purposes be reconciled with the sincere and therefore respectable, scruples of the serious portion of the community.[1]

[1] Tremanhare's America, 56, 57, 64.

61. What is to be done with the educated classes?

But supposing this difficulty surmounted, another, and a yet more formidable one, remains behind, to the magnitude of which the world is only beginning to awaken. When the people are educated, what is to be done with them? How is the country to get on when so many more are trained to and qualified for intellectual labor than can by possibility find a subsistence, even by the most successful prosecution of any of its branches? How is the constantly increasing multitude of well-educated persons, armed with the powers of intellect, stimulated by the pressure of necessity, not restrained by the possession of property, to be disposed of, when no possible means of providing for them but by physical labor, which they abhor, can be devised? How are they to be prevented, in periods of distress, from becoming seditious, and listening to the suggestions of the demagogues who never fail to appear in such circumstances, who tell them that all their distresses are owing to the faulty institutions of society, and that under the reign of "Liberty, Equality, and Fraternity," they will all disappear before the ascending power of the people? How, in such circumstances, is the balance of the different classes of society to be preserved, and the great, but inert, and comparatively unintellectual mass of the rural population to be hindered from falling under the dominion of the less numerous, but more concentrated, more wealthy, and more acute inhabitants of towns? If they do become subjected to them, what is that but class-government of the worst and most dangerous, because the most numerous and irresponsible kind? And what is to be expected from it, but the entire sacrifice of the interests of the country, by successive acts of the legislature, to those of towns? England has already felt these evils, but not to the degree that she otherwise would, from the invaluable vent which her numerous colonies have afforded to her surplus educated and indigent population: in America they have been wholly unknown, because the Far West has absorbed it all.

62. Effect of education in leading to the discussion of mankind.

These observations are not foreign to a work of general history: its subsequent volumes will be little more than a commentary on this text. And without anticipating the march of events, which will abundantly illustrate them, it may be observed that the maintenance of despotic institutions in a country of advancing intelligence is impossible; that as knowledge is power, so knowledge will obtain power; that the wisdom of government with a people growing in information, is gradually and cautiously to admit them to a share in its duties; that the only way to do this with safety, is by the representation of *interests*, not *numbers*, the latter being class-government of the worst kind; and that, with all that, safety must mainly be looked for in the providing ample outlets for the indigent intelligence of the state in colonial settlements. It is impossible it should be otherwise, for it is by the force of education that the destinies of the species are to be worked out by the voluntary acts of free agents. The desires consequent on information, with their natural offspring, democratic ambition, are the great moving powers of nature; and in the last days of man, as in the first, it is by eating of the fruit of the tree of knowledge that he is torn up from his native seats, and impelled by the force of his own desires to obey the Divine precept to overspread the earth and subdue it.

63. Disfranchisement of Grampound, and transfer of its members to Yorkshire.

Another subject, destined in the end to be attended with paramount importance, though its moment was not perceived at this time, was at the same time introduced into Parliament, and showed how closely the growing intelligence of an era is connected with the desire for an extension of political power. This was PARLIAMENTARY REFORM. Lord John Russell on 9th May introduced the subject by proposing three resolutions: 1. That the people were dissatisfied with the representation; 2. That boroughs convicted of bribery should be disfranchised; and, 3. That their members should be transferred to some populous place not represented. Grampound had been convicted of bribery in the last election, on so extensive a scale that it appeared in evidence that "perhaps there might be *two or three electors* who had *not* received bribes." The bill disfranchising the borough passed without any opposition, but a great division of opinion arose as to the place to which the members for it should be transferred. In the bill, as it originally stood, it was proposed that they should be transferred to Leeds; but the aristocratic party, in both Houses, inclined to give them to some rural district, where their influence might be more easily exerted. The bill was not pushed through all its stages this session, in consequence of the proceedings against the Queen absorbing the whole attention of the legislature; but it was revived in the next, and, as it passed the Commons, the franchise was conferred on Leeds. In the Lords, however, this was altered, and the members were bestowed on the county of York. With this alteration the Reform party were far from being satisfied; but they wisely agreed to it, and the bill, thus amended, passed into a law. Thus was the foundation laid of the great fabric of parliamentary reform, ten years before the empire was shaken to the centre by the superstructure being raised. Even at this early period, however, the opening made awakened very serious alarms in many able persons, who afterward became leaders of the Whig party.* Happy would it have been for the nation if it had been regarded by the opposite parties as a question of social amelioration, not political power, and the use that was practicable had been made of the progressive and just reforms which might have been founded on the disfranchisement of the boroughs convicted of corruption, instead of the wholesale destruction of the majority of their number.[1]

[1] An Reg 1820, 46, 47; Parl. Deb. v. 604, 624, 696, 974.

64. Rise of free trade ideas among the merchants, and Lord Lansdowne's declaration on the subject.

The doctrine of FREE TRADE, afterward so largely acted upon by the British legislature, first began at this time to engross the thoughts not only of persons engaged in commerce and manufactures, but of the heads of the Government. On 8th May, Mr. Baring presented a petition on this subject from the merchants of London; and on the 16th, Mr. Kirkman Finlay, a Glasgow merchant, equally remarkable for the extent of his transactions and the liberality of his views, brought forward a petition from the Chamber of Commerce of Glasgow, which set forth, in strong terms, the evils arising from the restricted state of the trade with China and the East Indies, and the advantages over British subjects which the Americans enjoyed in that respect; and urged the repeal of the Usury Laws, and the reduction or removal of the duties on the importation of several foreign commodities. These views were so favorably received in both Houses of Parliament, that Lord Lansdowne was encouraged, a few days after, to bring forward a motion for the appointment of a committee to take into consideration the means of extending our foreign commerce. He dwelt, in an especial manner, on the inconveniences to which the trade of the country was now exposed by the numerous duties which restricted it in every direction, and argued that, "whatever brought the *foreign* merchant to this country, and made it a general mart for the merchandise of the world, was beneficial to our trade, and enriched the industrious population of our ports. Such freedom of transit would allow an assortment of cargoes for foreign markets, and thus extend our trade in general. The import duties on Baltic timber should be removed, for they cost us annually £500,000 more for our ships and houses than

---

* In October, 1819, after the Grampound Disfranchisement bill had first been introduced into Parliament, Mr. Ward, afterward Lord Dudley, wrote to the Bishop of Llandaff: "All I am afraid of is, that by having the theoretical defects of the present House of Commons perpetually dinned into their ears, the well-intentioned and well-affected part of the community should at last begin to suppose that *some reform* is necessary. Now, I can hardly conceive *any reform* that would not bring us within the whirlpool of democracy, toward which we should be attracted by an irresistible force, and in an hourly accelerated ratio. But I flatter myself there is wisdom enough in the country to preserve us long from so great an innovation." In April, 1820, he again wrote: "When I see the progress that reform is making, not only among the vulgar, but persons, like yourself, of understanding and education, clear of interested motives and party fanaticism, my spirits fail me. I wish I could persuade myself that the first day of reform will not be the first of the English Revolution." In February, 1821, he writes, "Mackintosh would keep the nomination boroughs; for my part, I am content with the constitution as it stands."—LORD DUDLEY's *Letters*, 220, 247, 277.

if we bought it from the north of Europe. The duties on French wines also should be lowered, to augment the trade with that country, and the trade with India entirely thrown open. As a proof of the superior value of the free trad to the East to that of the East India Company, it is sufficient to observe, that the former has 61,000 tons of shipping and 4720 seamen while the latter employs only 20,000 tons and 2550; and our trade to America, which, at the period of the independence of that country, was only £3,000,000, has now swelled to the enormous amount of £20,000,000 a year."[1]

[1] An. Reg. 1820, 83. So. Parl. Deb. i. 436, &c.

Lord Liverpool made a very remarkable speech in reply; memorable as being the first enunciation, on the part of Government, of the principles of free trade, which, half a century before, had been promulgated by Quesnay in France, and Adam Smith in Great Britain. "It must be admitted," he observed, "that there has been a great falling off in our foreign trade in the last year; for our exports have declined no less than £7,200,000 in the year 1819, compared with the average of the three preceding years. It is of importance to examine in what branches of our trade so great and alarming a diminution has occurred. It is not in any great degree in our intercourse with the Continent; with it the decline has been only £600,000. The great decrease has been in our trade with the East Indies and the United States of America; with the latter alone there was a falling off in the last, compared with the three preceding years, of no less than £3,500,000. The general doctrines of freedom of trade, viewed in the abstract, are undoubtedly well founded; but the noble marquis (Lansdowne) who introduced the subject is too experienced a statesman not to qualify them in their application to this country. It is impossible for us, or any country in the world, except, perhaps, the United States of America, to act unreservedly upon that principle.

65. Lord Liverpool's memorable speech in reply.

"If we look to the general principles of trade and commerce, we must, at the same time, look to our law concerning agriculture. We shall there see an absolute prohibition of the importation of great part of foreign agricultural produce, and heavy duties on the remainder. Under the operation of these laws, we can not admit free trade to foreign countries. We will not take their cattle, nor their corn, except under heavy duties; how can we expect them to take our manufactures? With what propriety may not those countries say to us, 'If you talk big of the advantages of free commerce, if you value so highly the principles of your Adam Smith, show your sincerity and your justice by the establishment of a reciprocal intercourse. Admit our agricultural produce, and we will admit your manufactures.' Your lordships know it would be impossible to accede to such a proposition. We have risen to our present greatness under the opposite system. Some suppose that we have risen in consequence of that system; others, *of whom I am one*, believe we have risen in spite of that system. Whichever of these hypotheses be true, certain it is we have risen under a very different system from that of free and unrestrained trade. It is utterly impossible, with our debt and taxation, even if they were but half their existing amount, that we can suddenly adopt the principles of free trade. To do so would be to unhinge the whole property in the country; to make a change in the value of every man's possessions, and in none more so than those of agriculture, the very basis of our opulence and power.

66. Continued.

"I was one of those who, in 1815, advocated the Corn Bill. In common with all the supporters of that measure, I believed it expedient to give an additional protection to the agriculturist. I thought that, after the conclusion of a twenty years' war, and the unlimited extent to which speculation in agriculture had been carried, and the comparatively low price at which corn could be raised in several countries of the Continent, great distress would ensue to all persons engaged in the cultivation of the land. I thought the Corn Bill should be passed then, or not at all. Having been passed, it should now be steadily adhered to; for nothing aggravates the difficulties of all persons engaged in cultivation so much as alterations in the laws regarding importation. While, therefore, I advocate going into a committee, with a view to removing many of the restrictions and prohibitions affecting our foreign and colonial trade, I must at the same time state that, as a general measure, absolute freedom of trade can not be established. In agricultural productions, and several branches of our manufactures, protection must be adhered to. It might have been better had it been otherwise from the beginning, and each country had attended only to those branches of manufacture in which it has natural advantages; but, as matters stand, we can not, save under large exceptions, attempt to retrace our steps. I do not believe the change in the currency has had *any connection* with the general distress which has since unhappily prevailed."[1]

67. Concluded.

[1] Parl. Deb. i. 596,599—corrected by Lord Liverpool.

This subject of agricultural distress was anxiously pressed on both Houses of Parliament during this session; and the petitions relating to the subject were so numerous, and stated facts of such importance and startling magnitude, that although Government opposed the appointment of a committee to inquire into the subject, it was carried by a majority of 150 to 101. It met, accordingly, collected a great deal of valuable evidence and information, and, as will appear in the sequel, published a most important report. But what is chiefly of moment in this stage of the inquiry is the opinions delivered by three very remarkable men, well qualified to judge of the subject, and on the justice of whose views subsequent experience has thrown an imperishable light. These were Mr. Brougham, Mr. Huskisson, and Mr. Ricardo; and the quotations, brief as they shall be, from their speeches, present the kernel, as it were, of that great debate with the issue of which the future fate of the empire was indissolubly wound up.[2]

68. Appointment of a committee to inquire into agricultural distress.

[2] An. Reg. 1820, 76.

It was observed by Mr. Brougham: "Agriculture is in an especial manner entitled to protection, both because many public burdens press unequally upon it, and because much poor land has been brought into cultivation, which could not be thrown back to its former state without immense misery to individuals, as well as injury to the public. A manufacturer erects a huge building in a parish, in which the production of two articles is carried on—*cotton and paupers;* and although this manufactory may yield to the proprietor £30,000 a year, yet he is only rated for poor-rates at £500 a year, the value of his buildings; while his poor neighbor, who rents land to that amount, is rated at the same, though his income, so far from being equal to the manufacturer's, is not a fourth part even of his rent. Besides this, there are the bridge-rates, the county-rates, the church-rates, and many other blessings, heaped on that favored class the agriculturalists. They, of course, must not raise their voices against such a distribution of these imposts, nor for a moment be heard to contend for an equality of burdens with the other classes of the community.

69. Opinion of Mr. Brougham on this subject.

"It is said that it is an erroneous policy to purchase corn dear at home, when it can be bought at a much cheaper rate abroad; and the only effect of this, it is added, is to lead men to cultivate bad land at a very great expense. This may possibly be true in the abstract; but the question we have now to consider is not whether, at such an expense, you ought to bring bad land into cultivation, but whether, having encouraged the cultivation of that land, we should now allow it to run to waste? The circumstances in which the country has been placed have been such, that even the worst land has been eagerly cultivated and brought in at an immense expense. It has been drained, hedged, ditched, manured, and become part of the inheritance of the British people. The capital expended in these improvements has been irrecoverably sunk in the land: it has become part and parcel of the soil, and was the life and soul of the cultivators and a large part of our inhabitants. Is it expedient to allow this inheritance to waste away, this large capital to perish, and with it the means of livelihood to so large a part of our people?

70. Continued.

"Some time ago there were several vessels in the harbor of London laden with wheat, which, but for the Corn Laws, might have been purchased for 37s. a quarter. On the principle on which the Corn Laws are opposed, this corn ought to have been purchased, because it was cheaper than any which we can grow; but then, if that principle were acted upon, what would be the consequence? The inevitable result would be, that, in the next season, seven or eight millions of acres would be thrown out of cultivation, and the persons engaged in it out of employment. Is there any man bold enough to look such a prospect in the face? What does the change amount to? To this, and nothing more, that we would inflict a certain calamity on the cultivator and landlord, in order to enable the consumer to eat his quartern loaf a penny cheaper. Can the destruction of so large a portion of the community be considered as a benefit, because another gained by it? There is no philosopher or political economist who has ever ventured to maintain such a doctrine. The average of imports of wheat for the last five years have been 477,138 quarters. This is formidable enough of itself, but what is it to what may be anticipated under a free trade in grain?"*

71. Concluded.

¹ Parl. Deb. i. 686, May 30, 1820; An. Reg. 1820, 69, 70.

On the other hand, it was maintained by Mr. Ricardo, on the part of the Freetraders: "The agriculturists argue that they are entitled to a remunerating price for their produce, forgetting that what is remunerating must vary according to circumstances. If, by preventing importation, the farmer is induced to expend his capital on land not suited for the production of grain crops, you voluntarily, and by your own act, raise the price by which you are remunerated, and then you make that price a ground for again prohibiting importation. Open the ports, admit foreign grain, and you drive this land out of cultivation; a less remunerating price will then do for the more productive soils. You might thus have fifty remunerating prices, according as your capital was employed on productive or unproductive soils. It becomes the legislature, however, not to look at the partial losses which would be endured by a few who could not cultivate their land profitably at a diminished price, but to the general interests of the nation. It is better to have a greater quantity of produce at a low price than a lesser at a large price, for the benefit to the

72. Answer by Mr. Ricardo.

* Mr. Huskisson, who followed on the same side, made several most important observations, which subsequent events have rendered prophetic. He observed, "that he still retained the same views on this question which he had held in 1815, when the present Corn Law was passed. In the first place, he considered that during a long series of years, by circumstances over which the country had no control, an artificial protection had been afforded to agriculture, which had forced a great mass of capital to the raising of corn which would not otherwise have been applied to that object. If an open trade in corn had been then allowed, a great loss of the capital thus invested, and a great loss to the agricultural part of the community, would have been occasioned. It was considered that 80s. the quarter was the price which would remunerate the the farmer, and he had voted for it accordingly. The second reason was, that, in its peculiar circumstances, it was of great importance to this country not to be dependent on foreign countries for a supply of food. It is an error to say there will be suffering on both sides, if the country which raised corn for us attempted to withhold the supply. So there would; but would the contest be an equal one? To the foreign nation the result would be a diminution of revenue or a pressure on agriculture. To us the result would probably be revolution and the subversion of the state. Let it be recollected that America, during the late war, despite its dependence on agriculture, and its sensitiveness to the voice of the people, actually submitted to an embargo with a view to incommode us by cutting off our supply of grain. A great power, like that of Napoleon, might compel a weak neutral to close its harbors, and thus starve us into submission, without suffering any inconvenience itself. The third ground on which he had consented to the modification of the principle of free trade, was the situation of Ireland, which had previously received encouragement from our demand, to withdraw which would have been most injurious to that country. To give a superior cultivation to the fertile land of that most fertile country, and to turn British capital into it, would ultimately tend, in a most material degree, to increase the resources and revenue of the empire. Since the passing of the Corn Laws the imports from Ireland had increased every year."—*Parl. Debates,* new series, i. 678, 679. One of the most curious things in history is the clear and lucid way in which the result of measures under discussion is often foretold, the entire insensibility which is at the time shown to the prediction, and its ultimate complete accomplishment.

producer is the same, and that to the consumer is much greater.

"By cheapening food the people will be enabled at once to purchase a larger quantity of it, and an additional supply of other conveniences or luxuries. The high price of provisions diminishes at once the profits of capital and the comforts of the workmen he employs. What constitutes the greater part of the price of manufactured articles? The wages of labor. Diminish those wages, by lessening the cost of the subsistence which must always form its principal ingredient, and you either augment the profits of capital, or extend the market for its produce by lessening its cost. Either of these would be a great benefit to our manufacturing population. The agriculturists say that they are able to supply the whole inhabitants of the country with food, and they demand heavy duties to enable them to feel secure in their efforts to do so. But the answer to all their demands is plain. You can grow these articles, it is true; but we can purchase them cheaper than you can grow them. Is it expedient to force cultivation on your inferior soils at a loss to yourselves? All principle is against it. They might as well urge in France, that, as they can grow sugar from beet-root at a cost greater than it can be raised in the West Indies, therefore you should load West Indian sugar in that country with prohibitory duties.

74. Concluded.
"Again it is said, as shipowners and various classes of manufacturers are protected, the agriculturists should be the same. In truth, however, these protections are of no use whatever, either to the country or the branches of industry which are protected. Take any branch of trade you please; let it be in the most flourishing state, and enjoying the best possible prospects; surround it with prohibitory duties, and you will soon see it languish and decline. The reason is, that the stimulus to human industry, the spur to human exertions arising from necessity, has been taken away. Even if the trade protected were thereby benefited, it could only be at the expense of the rest of the community; and all that is said on the other side about the injustice of benefiting one class at the expense of another, here turns against themselves.

Countervailing duties, if adopted in one country, will soon be followed in others, and thence will arise a war of tariffs, which will cripple, and at last destroy all commerce whatever. The interests of the agriculturists and of the other classes of the community might, indeed, be identified, provided we were restrained from all intercourse with other nations; but this is impossible in a country such as ours, which carries on an extensive commercial intercourse with foreign countries. The price of grain may be altered either by alterations in the currency, which will raise it along with all other articles, or by legislative restrictions, which will alter it alone. The first alteration may not be injurious, because it affects all alike. The latter necessarily must be so, because it lowers at once both the profits of stock and the wages of labor."[1]

[1] Parl. Deb. i. 671, 674.

Such was the commencement of this great debate, which for the next quarter of a century almost constantly convulsed the nation, and certainly never was pleaded on both sides with greater force or by more consummate masters. One important consideration, however, was omitted on both sides, from statistical researches having not as then brought it to light, though it now stands forth in the brightest colors. This is the infinitely superior value of our home or colonial trade to that of the grain-growing countries from whom we import food, and the extreme impolicy, even with a view to the interest in the end of the manufacturers themselves, of discouraging the former to encourage the latter. So great is this disproportion, that it would pass for incredible, if not established by the unerring evidence of statistical facts.* Our manufacturers still find their best customers in the men who cultivate the adjoining fields. Notwithstanding the great extent of our foreign commerce, the manufactures consumed in the home market are still double in value those consumed in all foreign markets put together: our own husbandmen take off fifty times the amount of our manufactures per head which those of the grain-growing countries do, from whom we now derive so large a part of our subsistence; and small as is the number of their inhabitants to those of the rest

75. Additional facts since discovered on this subject.

* Exports from Great Britain in 1850.

	Exports. Declared value.	Population.	Rate per head.
Russia	£1,289,794	66,000,000	£0 0 3¾
Prussia	503,531	16,000,000	0 0 7
France	2,028,463	34,000,000	0 0 10
British America	3,813,707	2,500,000	1 10 0
West Indies	2,201,032	972,000	2 14 0
Australia	2,807,356	538,000	5 17 0
Total British Colonies	19,517,039	115,675,000	0 4 9
United States of America	14,362,976	25,000,000	0 13 8
British Colonies and Descendants	£33,880,015	140,675,000	£0 4 8
All the rest of the World	40,668,707	830,000,000	0 1 0
Manufactured for Home Market	£74,448,722 130,000,000	27,000,000	£5 0 0

—*Parliamentary Papers*, 1851.

Excluding the native population of India, which is 109,000,000, and supposing they consume £5,000,000 worth of the £7,000,000 of exports to British India, the exports to British native colonial population, which is about 6,000,000, will be £14,000,000, or £2 5s. a head, against 1s. a head for all the rest of the world.

of the world, our exports to our own colonies, emancipated and unemancipated, are nearly equal to those to all the rest of the world put together.

76. Commencement of the troubles about the Queen.

These, and all other social questions, how momentous soever, were cut short in this Parliament by the proceedings against the Queen, which entirely engrossed the attention of the legislature and the interest of the people during the whole remainder of the year, and not only seriously shook the Ministry, but violently agitated the nation. This unhappy Princess, the second daughter of the sister of George III., and of the illustrious House of Brunswick, had been married early in life to the Prince of Wales, now the reigning Sovereign, without their ever having seen each other, or possessing the smallest acquaintance with each other's tastes, habits, or inclinations. It is the melancholy fate of persons in that elevated sphere in general to have marriages imposed upon them as a matter of state-necessity, without the slightest regard to their wishes or happiness; and great is the domestic misery to which this necessity too often leads. But the peculiar circumstances of this case rendered the situation of the royal pair beyond the ordinary case of crowned heads calamitous. The Prince at the time of his marriage was deeply attached to, and had been married, though without the consent required by the Marriage Act, and of course illegally, to another lady of great personal and mental attractions. The Princess, to whom he was afterward compelled to give his hand, though possessed of great liveliness and considerable talent, and no small share of personal charms, was totally unsuited to his tastes, and repugnant to his habits. The consequence was, that both parties were inspired with a mutual aversion from the moment they first met; the marriage ceremony was gone through, but it was more a form than any thing else; after the first few days they never met in private, and after the birth of the Princess Charlotte, no hope remained of any further issue to continue the direct line of succession to the throne.[1]

[1] Lord Malmesbury's Diaries, iii. 116, 211.

77. Sketch of her late prior to this period.

The Princess, after her separation from her husband, lived chiefly at Blackheath, and there Mr. Perceval, afterward Prime Minister, was for long her principal adviser; but Mr. Canning also shared her society, and has recorded his opinion of the liveliness of her manner, and the charms of her conversation; and Sir Walter Scott has added his testimony to the flattering opinion. It was scarcely possible that a Princess of a lively manner, fond of society, and especially of that of young and agreeable men, and living apart from her husband, should escape the breath of scandal, and it would probably have attached to her notwithstanding the utmost decorum and propriety on her part. Unfortunately, however, the latter qualities were precisely those in which the Princess was most deficient; and without going the length of asserting that her conduct was actually criminal, or that she retaliated in kind on her husband for his well-known infidelities, it is sufficient to observe that the levity and indiscretion of her manners were such as to awaken the solicitude of her royal parents; and that a "delicate investigation" took place, the particulars of which have never been disclosed, and upon the import of which the only observation which can safely be made is, that no public proceedings were adopted in consequence of it.[1]

[1] Hughes, vi. 422; Martineau, i. 251.

78. Her conduct abroad, and proceedings in consequence of it.

When the Continent was opened to British travelers after the peace, the Princess of Wales, to the great relief of her royal spouse, went abroad, with a separate allowance of £35,000 a year, and for several years little was heard of her in this country, except her occasional appearance at a foreign court. It appeared, however, that, unknown to the public, her conduct was strictly watched; confidential persons of respectability were sent abroad to obtain evidence; and, from the information received, Government conceived themselves called upon to send instructions to our embassadors and ministers at foreign courts, that they were not to give her any official or public reception; and if she were received publicly by the sovereign, they were not to be present at it. This, with her formal exclusion from the English court, which had been previously pronounced, rendered her situation abroad very uncomfortable; and to put an end to it, and get matters arranged on a permanent footing, Mr. Brougham, who had become her confidential adviser, proposed to Lord Liverpool, in June, 1819, though without the knowledge of her Royal Highness, that, on condition of her allowance of £35,000 a year, which she at present enjoyed, being secured for her by act of Parliament or warrant of the Treasury for life, instead of being, as at present, dependent on the life of the Prince Regent, she should agree to remain abroad during the whole remainder of her life. The Ministers returned a favorable answer to this application; and it was no wonder they did so, for it went to relieve them from an embarrassment which all but proved fatal to the Administration. The Prince strenuously contended for a divorce, as not only justified, but called for, in the circumstances, which, he maintained, were such as would entitle any private subject to that remedy. The Cabinet opposed this, as likely to lead to a very serious agitation in the present disturbed state of the public mind. At length they came to a compromise, to the effect that, if she remained abroad, no further proceedings of any sort should be adopted against her Royal Highness; but that, if she returned to England, they would accede to the Prince's wishes.[2]

[2] Hughes, vi. 422; Ann. Reg. 1820, 123, 124; Eldon's Life, ii. 362.

79. Omission of the Queen's name in the Liturgy, and her return to England.

Matters remained in this position, in a kind of lull, during the remainder of the life of George III. But when that monarch died, in February, 1820, and the strong step of omitting her Majesty's name in the Liturgy was taken, matters were brought to a crisis. The new Queen loudly exclaimed, that such an omission was a direct imputation on her honor, which could not for a moment be submitted to; and that she would return to England instantly to vindicate her character. The King, learning this, as obstinately contended for an immediate divorce, in the event of her carrying her threat into execution; and as his Ministers refused to accede to this, they tendered their resignation, and attempts were made to form a new ministry, of which Lord Wellesley was to be the head. These failed; and it was at length agreed that, if the Queen returned, proceedings were to be immediately commenced against her. Attempts were, however, again made to avert so dire an alternative; it was even proposed to increase her allowance to £50,000 a year, provided she agreed to take some other name or title than that of Queen, and not to exercise any of the rights belonging to that character. These proposals were formally transmitted to Mr. Brougham, as her Majesty's principal law-officer, on the 15th April, and approved of by him. The indignant feelings and impetuous disposition of the Queen, however, rendered all attempt at accommodation fruitless. She was much incensed, in February, by being refused a guard of honor as Queen of England; and no sooner did she hear of the omission of her name in the Liturgy, than she took the bold resolution of returning immediately to this country, alleging that England was her real home, and to it she would immediately fly. However we may regret this resolution, and deplore the unfortunate results to which it led, we can not but admire the spirit of a Princess who thus braved the utmost dangers, it might be to her life, in vindication of her honor, or fail to admit that, in whatever else Queen Caroline was awanting, it was not in the courage hereditary in her race.[1] *

^{March 16.}

^{1 Ann. Reg. 1820, 127, 129; Lord Dudley's Letters, 254; Letter of the Queen, March 16, 1820.}

80. Her landing in England, and enthusiastic reception.

She was met by Mr. Brougham and Lord Hutchinson, who in vain endeavored to get her to accede to the King's offer of £50,000 a year, provided she would remain abroad, and not assume the title or duties of the Queen of England. She indignantly rejected the proposal, as an insult to her honor and a stain upon her character; and having dismissed Bergami, her alleged paramour, at St. Omer, she landed at Dover on the afternoon of the 6th June. No words can adequately describe the universal enthusiasm which her arrival excited among the great bulk of the people. They had previously been prepared for her reception by the publication of her letters complaining of the treatment she had experienced, and she had been expected almost daily for several weeks past. The courage and decision displayed by her Royal Highness on this trying occasion excited general admiration, and was hailed as a

convincing proof of her innocence. The spectacle of a Queen deserted by her husband, calumniated, as it was thought, by his Ministers, threatened with trial, it might be death, if she set her foot on British ground, braving all these dangers in vindication of her innocence, awakened the warmest sympathy of the multitude, in whom noble deeds seldom fail to excite the most enthusiastic feelings. Pity for her supposed wrongs, united with admiration of her real courage, and the fine expression of Mr. Denman, that if she had her place at all in the Prayer-Book, it was in the supplication "for all who are desolate and oppressed," found a responsive echo in the British heart.[1]

^{1 Martineau, i. 252; Ann. Reg. 1820, 131, 132; Lord Dudley's Letters, 226.}

That these were the feelings of the vast majority of the British people, who hailed the arrival of the Queen with such enthusiastic feelings, is beyond a doubt; and it was honorable to the nation that they were so general. But the Radical leaders, who fanned the movement, were actuated by very different and much deeper views. Better informed than the multitude whom they led, they had no confidence in the ultimate vindication of the Queen's innocence; but, so far from being deterred by that circumstance, they built on it their warmest hopes, and considered it as a reason for the most strenuous efforts. Innocent or guilty, they could not but gain by the investigation, and the agitation to which it would infallibly lead:

81. Views of the Radical leaders on the occasion.

"Careless of fate, they took their way,
Scarce caring who might win the day;
Their booty was secure."

If her innocence were proved, they would gain a triumph over the King, force upon him a wife whom he could not endure, overturn his Ministers, and perhaps shake the monarchy: if her guilt, they would gain the best possible ground for declaiming on the corruption which prevailed in high places, and the monstrous nature of those institutions which gave persons of such character the lead in society. The views they entertained, and the hopes by which they were animated, have been stated by one of the ablest of their number, whose voluminous writings and sterling sense have given him a lasting place in British annals.[2] Lord Eldon, more correctly, as the event proved, foresaw the issue of the crisis, when he wrote at the time, "Our Queen threatens to approach England; if she can venture, she is the most courageous lady I ever heard of. The mischief, if she does come, will be infinite. At first, she will have extensive popularity with the multitude; in a few short weeks or months, she will be ruined in the opinion of all the world."[2]

^{2 Twiss's Life of Eldon, ii. 363; Ann. Reg. 1820, 139, 140; Hughes, vi. 427, 429.}

* "I have written to Lord Liverpool and Lord Castlereagh, demanding to have my name inserted in the Liturgy of the Church of England, and that orders be given to all British embassadors, ministers, and consuls, that I should be acknowledged and received as Queen of England; and after the speech made by Lord Castlereagh in the House of Commons, in answer to Mr. Brougham, I do not expect to receive further insult. I have also demanded that a palace may be prepared for my reception. England is my real home, to which I shall immediately fly."—Queen CAROLINE, March 16, 1820; Ann. Reg 1820, p. 131. "Her promptitude and courage," said Lord Dudley at the time, "confounded her opponents, and gained her the favor of the people. Whatever one may think of her conduct in other respects, it is impossible not to give her credit for these qualities."—Lord DUDLEY's Letters, 254.

² " 'The people, in their sense of justice,' says Cobbett, 'went back to the time when she was in fact turned out of her husband's house, with a child in her arms, without blame of any sort having been imputed to her; they compared what they had heard of the wife with what they had seen of the husband, and they came to their determination accordingly. As for an related to the question of guilt or innocence, they did not care a straw; but they took a large view of the matter; they went over her whole history; they determined that she had been wronged, and they resolved to uphold her."—COBBETT's Life of George IV, 425.

The reception which the Queen met with was such as might swell her heart with exultation, and flatter the Radicals into the hope of an approaching subversion of the Government. Nothing like it had been witnessed since the restoration of Charles II. An immense multitude awaited her arrival at the harbor of Dover; the thunder of artillery from the castle, for the first and *last time*, saluted her approach; the road to London was beset with multitudes eager to obtain a glimpse of her person. She entered the metropolis, accompanied by two hundred thousand persons. Night and day her dwelling was surrounded by crowds, whose vociferous applause of herself and her friends was equaled by their vituperation of the King, and threats against his Ministers. Government were in the utmost alarm; meetings of Ministers were held daily, almost hourly. Their apprehensions were much increased by symptoms of insubordination being manifested in one of the regiments of the foot-guards stationed in the Mews barracks at Charing Cross, which, although ostensibly grounded on the inconveniences and crowded state of their barracks, were strongly apprehended to be connected with the excited feelings of the populace in the metropolis, with whom the household troops were in such constant communication. The Duke of Wellington was sent for, and by his presence and courage succeeded in restoring order, and next morning the disaffected troops were sent off in two divisions to Portsmouth. The night before the last division marched, however, an alarming mob collected round the gates of the barracks, calling on the troops to come out and join them; and they were only dispersed by a troop of the life-guards, called out by Lord Sidmouth in person.

82 Enthusiastic reception of the Queen at Dover and in London

1 Ann. Reg. 1820, 139, 143; Martineau, i. 251; Sidmouth's Life, iii. 330, 331.

After the Queen's arrival in London, an attempt was made by her able advisers, Messrs. Brougham and Denman, to renew the negotiation, and prevent the disclosures, painful and discreditable to all concerned, to which the threatened investigation would necessarily lead. The basis of the proposal was to be, that the King was to retract nothing, the Queen admit nothing, and that she was to leave Great Britain with an annuity, settled upon her for life, of £50,000 a year. It failed, however, in consequence of her Majesty insisting on the insertion of her name in the Liturgy and a reception at foreign courts, or at least some one foreign court, in a manner suitable to her rank. On the first point the King was immovable; on the last, the utmost length he would go, was to agree to notify her being legally Queen of England to some foreign court, leaving her reception there to the pleasure of that court. The utmost mutual temper and courtesy were evinced by the commissioners on both sides, who were no less persons than Lord Castlereagh and the Duke of Wellington on the part of his Majesty, and Messrs. Brougham and Denman on that of the Queen. But all attempts at adjustment of the differences were unsuccessful, and on the 19th June it was formally announced in both Houses of Parliament that the negotiation had failed, and on the 4th July, the secret committee of the Lords, to whom it had been referred, reported "that the evidence affecting the honor of the Queen was such as to require, for the dignity of the Crown and the moral feeling and honor of the country, a solemn inquiry." The Queen next day declared, by petition to the Lords, her readiness to defend herself, and praying to be heard by counsel; and soon after Lord Liverpool brought forward, in the House of Lords, the famous Bill of Pains and Penalties, which, on the narrative of improper and degrading conduct on the part of her Majesty, and an adulterous connection with a menial servant named Bartelomeo Bergami, proposed to dissolve the marriage with his Majesty, and deprive her of all her rights and privileges as Queen of England.

83 Failure of the negotiations, and commencement of the inquiry.

July 4.

July 5.

1 Protocol, June 15, 16, 1820; Ann. Reg. 1820, 159, 161; Parl. Deb. ii. 167, 207, 218.

The die was now cast, and the trial went on in good earnest. But who can paint the scene which ensued, when the first of British subjects was brought to trial before the first of British assemblies by the most powerful of British sovereigns! Within that august hall, fraught with so many interesting recollections, where so many noble men had perished, and innocence had so often appealed from the cruelty of man to the justice of Heaven; where Anne Boleyn had called God to witness, and Queen Catherine had sobbed at severance from her children; where Elizabeth had spoken to the hearts of her people, and Anne had thrilled at the recital of Marlborough's victories; whose walls were still hung with the storied scene of the destruction of the Armada—was all that was great and all that was noble in England assembled for the trial of the consort of the Sovereign, the daughter of the house of Brunswick! There was to be seen the noble forehead and serene countenance of Castlereagh—the same now, in the throes of domestic anxiety, as when he affronted the power of France, and turned the scales of fortune on the plains of Champagne; there the Roman head of Wellington, still in the prime of life, but whose growing intellectual expression bespoke the continued action of thought on that constitution of iron. Liverpool was there, calm and unmoved, amidst a nation's throes, and patiently enduring the responsibility of a proceeding on which the gaze of the world was fixed; and Sidmouth, whose courage nothing could daunt, and whose tutelary arm had so long enchained the fiery spirit which was now bursting forth on every side. There was Eldon, whose unaided abilities had placed him at the head of this august assembly, and who was now called to put his vast stores of learning to their noblest use— that of holding the scales of justice, even against his own strongest interests and prepossessions; and there was Copley, the terror of whose cross-examination proved so fatal on the trial, and presaged the fame of his career as Lord Chancellor. There was Grey, whose high intellectual forehead, big with the destinies of England, bespoke the coming revolution in her social state; and Lansdowne, in whom suavity of manner and dignity of deportment adorned, without concealing, the highest gifts of elo-

84. Scene which ensued on the trial.

quence and statesmanship. There were Brougham and Denman, whose oratorical powers and legal acuteness were sustained by a noble intrepidity, and who, in now defending the illustrious accused against the phalanx of talent and influence by which she was assailed, apparently to the ruin of their professional prospects, worthily won a seat on the Woolsack, and at the head of the King's Bench of England. Lawrence there gazed on a scene more thrilling and august than the soul of painting had ever conceived; and Kean studied the play of passions as violent as any by which he had entranced the world on the mimic stage. And in the front of all was the Queen of England, a stranger, childless, reviled, discrowned, but sustained by the native intrepidity of her race, and gazing undaunted on the hostility of a nation in arms.*

<small>85. Progress of the trial, and its difficulties.</small> The trial—for trial it was, though disguised under the name of a Bill of Pains and Penalties—went on for several months; and day after day, during that long period, was the public press of England polluted by details, which elsewhere are confined to the professed votaries or theatres of pleasure. Immense was the demoralizing influence which the production of these details exercised upon the nation, which laid before the whole people scenes, and familiarized them with ideas, which had hitherto been confined to the comparatively few, whom traveling had made acquainted with the license of foreign manners. It does not belong to history to bring them again to light; they repose in decent obscurity, accessible to few, in the *Parliamentary Debates*, and have come to be forgotten even by the licentious, to whom at the time they were a subject of such unbounded gratification. Suffice it to say, that the facts sworn to by the witnesses for the prosecution were of such a nature as to leave no doubt of the guilt of the accused, if the evidence was to be relied on; but that there the case was beset by the greatest difficulties. Most of the witnesses were Italians, upon whose testimony little reliance could be placed; some of them were involved in such contradictions, or broke down so under cross-examination, that they required to be thrown overboard altogether. The principal of them, Theodore Majocchi, the Princess's valet, pretended ignorance, on cross-examination, of so many things which he obviously recollected, that his answer to the questions, "*Non mi ricordo*," has passed into a proverbial expression known all over the world, to express the culpable concealment of known truth by a perjured witness. Yet did the conduct of the Queen herself afford reason to suspect that he had something material to reveal; for when his name was called out by the clerk, as the first witness, she started up, gave a faint cry, and left the House.[1]

<small>1 Hughes, vi. 442; Ann. Reg. 1820; App. to Chron. 996, Marineau, i. 297.</small>

Mr. Brougham thus closed his eloquent opening of the defense for her Majesty, justly celebrated as one of the finest specimens of British forensic eloquence: "Such, my Lords, is the case before you! Such is the evidence in support of this measure— evidence inadequate to prove a debt, impotent to deprive of a civil right, ridiculous to convict of the lowest offense, scandalous if brought forward to support the highest charge which the law knows, monstrous to stain the honor and blast the name of an English queen. What shall I say, then, if this is the proof by which an act of judicial legislation, a parliamentary sentence, an *ex post facto* law, is sought to be passed against this defenseless woman? My Lords, I pray you to pause; I do earnestly beseech you to take heed. You are standing on the brink of a precipice— then beware! It will go forth as your judgment, if sentence shall go against the Queen. But it will be the only judgment you ever pronounced, which, instead of reaching its object, will return, and bound back upon those who gave it. Save the country, my Lords, from the horrors of this catastrophe—save yourselves from this peril. Rescue that country of which you are the ornaments, but in which you can flourish no longer, when severed from the people, than the blossom when cut off from the roots and the stem of the tree. Save that country that you may continue to adorn it—save the Crown, which is in jeopardy—the aristocracy, which is shaken—the altar, which must totter with the blow which rends its kindred throne! You have said, my Lords—you have willed—the Church and the King have willed —that the Queen should be deprived of its solemn service. She has, instead of that solemnity, the heart-felt prayers of the people. She wants no prayers of mine; but I do here pour forth my humble supplications at the throne of mercy, that that mercy may be poured down upon the people, in a larger measure than the merits of its rulers may deserve, and that your hearts may be turned to justice."[1]

<small>[86. Peroration of Mr. Brougham's defense.]</small>

<small>1 Speech of Mr. Brougham, i. 227, 228; Parl. Deb. III. 210.</small>

Such was the effect of this splendid speech, and such the apprehensions felt in a large part of the House of Peers of the hourly-increasing agitation out of doors, that it is generally thought, by those best acquainted with the feelings of that assembly, that if the vote had been taken at that moment, the Queen would have been entirely acquitted. Mr. Brougham himself intended to have done this, after having merely presented her maid Mariette Bron for examination. But she was not to be found: and the case went on with most able arguments by Mr. Denman and Mr. Williams, followed by evidence led at great length for her Majesty, and powerful replies by the Attorney and Solicitor General. The speech of the first (Sir Robert Gifford) was in an especial manner effective—so much so, that the Radical leaders gave up the case for lost, and Cobbett threw off 100,000 copies of an answer to it.[2] It was not the evidence for the prosecution which had this effect, for it was of so suspicious a kind that little reliance could be placed on it, but what was elicited, on cross-examination, from the English officers on board the vessel which conveyed her Majesty to the Levant, men of integrity and honor, of

<small>87. Queen's defense, and failure of the bill.</small>

<small>2 Life of George IV., 447.</small>

<small>* The reader of Macaulay's incomparable *Essay on Warren Hastings* need not be told what model was in the author's eye in this paragraph; but no one can feel so strongly as he does the futility of all attempts to rival that noble picture.</small>

whose testimony there was not a shadow of suspicion. Without asserting that any of them proved actual guilt against her Majesty, it cannot be disputed that they established against her an amount of levity of manner and laxity of habits, which rendered her unfit to be at the head of English society, and amply justified the measures taken to exclude her from it. The result was, that on the 6th November, the second reading of the bill was carried by a majority of 28, the numbers being 123 to 95, which was equivalent to a finding of guilty. In committee, when the divorce clause came forward, it was sustained by a majority of 129 to 62, the Opposition having nearly all voted for the clause, with the view of defeating the bill in its last stage. This proved successful; for on the third reading, on 10th November, the majority sunk to NINE, the numbers being 108 to 99. Upon this, Lord Liverpool rose and said, that with so slender a majority he could not think of pressing the measure further, and withdrew the bill.¹

¹ Parl. Deb. iii. 1726, 1743; Ann. Reg. 1820, 184, 190.

68. General transports of the people.

No words can convey an adequate idea of the general transports which prevailed through the British Islands when the intelligence of the withdrawal of the bill was received. London was spontaneously, though partially, illuminated for three successive nights—those who did not concur in the general joy, and they were many, joining in the festivity from a dread of the sovereign mob, and of the instant penalty of having their windows broken, which in general followed any resistance to its mandates. Edinburgh, Dublin, Manchester, Liverpool, and all the great towns, followed the example. For several days the populace in all the cities of the empire seemed to be delirious with joy; nothing had been seen like it before since the battle of Waterloo; nothing approaching to it after, till the Reform Bill was passed. Addresses were voted to the Queen, from the Common Council of London, and all the popular constituencies in the kingdom; and her residence in London was surrounded from daybreak to night by an immense crowd, testifying in their usual noisy way the satisfaction they felt at her victory. Yet, amidst all these congratulations, the position of her Majesty was sensibly deteriorated even by the completeness of her triumph.²

² Ann. Reg. 1820, 192, 193; Cobbett's Life of Geo. IV., 417, 419; Hughes, vi. 417.

69. Rapid reaction of public opinion.

Being now secure of her position, and independent of the support of the populace, she ceased to court them, and this speedily cooled their ardor in her cause. They complained that she was now always encircled by a coterie of Whig ladies, and no longer accessible to their deputations. When the struggle was over and the victory gained, the King and his Ministers defeated, and the Queen secured in her rank and fortune, they began to reflect on what they had done, and the qualities of the exalted personage of whom they had proved themselves such doughty champions. They called to mind the evidence in the case, which they had little considered while the contest lasted, and they observed, not without secret misgivings, the effect it produced on the different classes of society.

They saw that the experienced hesitated at it, the serious shunned it, the licentious gloated over it. The reaction so usual in such cases, when the struggle is over, ensued; and, satisfied with having won the victory, they began to regret that it had not been gained in a less questionable cause. As has often been the case in English history, old feelings revived when recent ones were satiated; and, strange to say, the most popular years of the reign of George IV. were those which immediately followed the greatest defeat his Government had experienced.¹

¹ Hughes, vi. 447; Ann. Reg. 1820, 193; Martineau, i. 260; Twiss's Life of Eldon, ii. 412.

70. Consternation of the Ministry, who resolve to remain at their posts.

The Ministers, however, who were not aware of the commencement of this reactionary feeling, and looked only at their public position as the King's Government, felt most acutely the defeat they had undergone. It all but overturned the Administration; and, with men of less nerve and resolution at its head, it unquestionably would have done so. But Lord Liverpool, Lord Castlereagh, and Lord Sidmouth, resolved to remain at their posts, conscious that to desert their Sovereign at this crisis would be nothing less than for his generals to abandon him in the day of battle. They were well aware that they were at the moment the most unpopular men in the British dominions; they were never seen in the street without being reviled by the mob; and anonymous letters every day threatened them with death, if the proceedings against her Majesty were not abandoned.² They paid no regard to these threats, and walked or drove to the House every day as if nothing had occurred; and the people, admiring their courage, abstained from actual violence.† Division, as might naturally have been expected, ensued in the Cabinet, and more than one resignation was tendered to his Majesty; but one only—that of Mr. Canning, as President of the Board of Control—was accepted, who was suc-

² Life of Sidmouth, iii. 332, 340; Twiss's Life of Eldon, ii. 398, 404, 405.

* "The Whig faction flocked round the Queen, directly after the abandonment of the bill, and her lawyers, who now called themselves her constitutional advisers, belonged to that faction who thought to get possession of power by her instrumentality, she having the people at her back. But the people, who hated this faction more than the other, the moment they saw it about her, troubled her with no more addresses. They suffered her to remain very tranquil at Brandenburg House; the faction agitated questions concerning her in Parliament, concerning which the people cared not a straw; what she was doing soon became as indifferent to them as what any other person of the royal family was doing; the people began to occupy themselves with the business of obtaining a Parliamentary reform; and her way of life, and her final fate, soon became objects of curiosity, much more than interest, with the people."—COBBETT's Life of George IV., 451.

† "Matters here are in a very critical state. Fear and faction are actively, and not unsuccessfully, at work; and it is possible we may be in a minority and the fate of the Government determined in a very few days."—Lord SIDMOUTH to Mr. BATHURST, 27th October, 1820. "I cannot describe to you how grievously I suffer, and have suffered, on account of the dangerous and deplorable situation in which our country, the King's Government, and indeed all of us, have been placed—a situation from which I profess to see no satisfactory or safe deliverance."—Ditto to ditto, 28th October, 1820. "One day, at this time, when Lords Castlereagh and Sidmouth were walking through Parliament Street, they were violently hooted at by the mob. 'Here we go,' said Lord Sidmouth, 'the two most popular men in England.' 'Yes,' replied Lord Castlereagh, 'through a grateful and admiring multitude.'"—Life of Sidmouth, iii. 330, 333.

ceeded by Mr. Bragge Bathurst, and the Government, as a body, ventured to weather the storm.

The result showed that they were right, and had not miscalculated the effect of just and courageous conduct on the English mind. Though liable to occasional fits of fervor, which for the time have often looked like national insanity, the English mind, when allowed time for reflection, and not precluded from thinking by the pressure of suffering, rapidly in general regains its equilibrium, and never so much so as after a decisive victory. In the present instance, the change in the public feeling was so rapid and remarkable, that it attracted the notice of the King himself, and his Ministers felt no difficulty in meeting Parliament.* Nor is it surprising that this was so; for reflection soon taught the nation that their zeal, how generous and honest soever, had been exerted on an unworthy object; that the Queen was by no means the immaculate character they supposed; and that however culpable and heartless the King's conduct had been to her in the outset of her married life, latterly at least the principal fault had been on her side; in truth, also, be the fault where it may, her habits abroad had been such as rendered her unfit to be placed at the head of English society. The trial, they saw, was of her own seeking; she was offered the title of Queen, and a handsome provision abroad; and they could not regard without regret the enthusiasm which had prevailed in favor of a woman whom the highest court in the kingdom, upon evidence the force of which all must feel, had virtually pronounced guilty. The battle had been a drawn one: the people could pride themselves on their victory; the Ministers on the evidence by which they had justified their proceedings; and both parties having thus something to gratify their self-love, their mutual irritation was lessened, and reconciliation resulted from a proceeding which presaged at first irreparable alienation.

92. Meeting of Parliament, and first proceedings.

Parliament met, after being prorogued in the end of November, on the 23d January, and Ministers were able to congratulate the country with reason on the improved condition of the people, and more contented temper of the public mind. In truth, the change in both respects was most remarkable; and Ministers, who had anticipated a narrow division, if not a defeat, on the question of the Queen, and their conduct in regard to her, were, to their surprise, supported by large majorities in both Houses, which on 6th February rose to 146 in the Commons. This great victory in a manner terminated the contest of parties on that painful subject. It was now evident that the long proceedings which had taken place on the Queen's trial, and the weighty evidence which had come out against her, had completely changed the public opinion on the subject, and that even the Radicals must look out for some fresh subject of complaint in their attempts to overturn the Government.[1]

[1] Parl. Deb. iv. 460, 507; Ann. Reg. 1821, 15, 21.

93. Debates on foreign affairs.

Such a subject would, but for the manly and judicious course adopted by the Government, have been afforded by the course which foreign affairs had taken at this period. The revolutions in Spain, Portugal, Naples, and Piedmont, and the ferment in Germany, had deeply agitated the public mind. It was hard to say whether the hopes these events had awakened in one party, or the fears in another, were most preponderant. All observed, many hoped, some feared, from them. The Congresses of Laybach and Troppau, of which an account has already been given,[2] which had been assembled avowedly to consider the course to be adopted by the great Continental powers in regard to these portentous events, afforded a fertile field for eloquent declamation on the part of the Liberal leaders; and Lord Grey in the Upper House, and Sir James Mackintosh in the Lower, in moving for the production of papers relative to these events, took occasion to inveigh strongly against the dangerous attempts, evidently making by the Continental powers, to stifle the growth of freedom, and overturn constitutional monarchies in all the lesser states around them. Ministers resisted the motion, but declared at the same time that the English Government were no parties to these congresses, and that they had officially notified to the powers there assembled their dissent from the principles and right of interference there advanced. It was known that this statement was well founded, and Parliament, satisfied with having obtained such an assurance from the Government, and with the strong declaration of English feeling from the Opposition, supported Ministers in both Houses by large majorities.[3]

[2] Ante, c. viii. § 70.
[3] Ann. Reg. 1821, 102, 104.

94. Sir James Mackintosh's efforts to improve the criminal law.

Sir James Mackintosh continued in this Parliament, as he had done in the last, his able and indefatigable efforts to obtain a relaxation of the monstrous severities and anomalies of the English criminal code. His increasing success, though not unmixed with checks, demonstrated that public opinion was rapidly changing on this important subject, and that the time was not far distant when, practically speaking, the punishment of death would not be inflicted in any case except deliberate murder, in which, both on the authority of the Divine law, and every consideration of human justice, it never should be abrogated. As this blessed change has now for above ten years been practically in operation, it is superfluous to enumerate all the steps by which it was effected. Suffice it to say, therefore, that it was by the efforts of Sir Samuel Romilly, and after him of Sir James Mackintosh, that the necessity of this great reform was first impressed on the public mind, and by the adoption of their principles by Sir Robert Peel when he became Home Secretary, that it was on a large scale carried into effect. The only thing to be regretted is, that when

---

* "It is clear beyond dispute, from the improvement of the public mind, and the loyalty which the country is now every where displaying, if properly cultivated and turned to the best advantage by Ministers, that the Government will thereby be enabled to repair to the country and to me those evils, of the magnitude of which there can be but one opinion."—GEORGE IV. to Lord ELDON, Jan. 9, 1821; TWISS's *Life of Eldon*, ii. 413.

the penalty of death was so justly taken away for so many offenses, care was not taken at the same time to increase the certainty and enlarge the efficiency of secondary punishments; and that from the long-continued neglect by the colonial secretaries of the obvious expedient of always mingling, in due proportion, the streams of gratuitous Government with forced penal emigration, the country has in a great measure lost the immense advantage it might otherwise have derived from the possession of such outlets for its surplus population and dangerous crime; and that the colonies have been led to regard with horror, and strive to avert, a stream which, duly regulated, might, and certainly would, have been hailed as the greatest possible blessing.

95. Mr. Canning's striking speech on Catholic Emancipation.

Mr. Plunkett, on the 28th February, brought forward a motion regarding Roman Catholic Emancipation, and it soon became evident, that if the mantle of Romilly had descended on Mackintosh, that of Grattan had fallen on the shoulders of Plunkett. As this subject will be fully discussed in a subsequent part of this volume, when the passing of Catholic Emancipation is narrated, it would be superfluous to give the arguments advanced on both sides; but there is one speech in the Commons, and one in the Lords, from which brief extracts must be given, from the importance of the sentiments which they conveyed. Mr. Canning was the most eloquent supporter, Mr. Peel the most determined opponent, of the measure. "We are," said the former, "in the enjoyment of a peace, achieved in a great degree by Catholic arms, and cemented by Catholic blood. For three centuries we have been erecting mounds, not to assist or improve, but to thwart nature; we have raised them high above the waters, where they have stood for many a year frowning proud defiance on all who attempted to cross them; but, in the course of ages, even they have been nearly broken down, and the narrow isthmus now formed between them stands between

"Two kindred seas,
Which, mounting, viewed each other from afar,
And longed to meet."

Shall we, then, fortify the mounds which are almost in ruins? or shall we leave them to moulder away by time or accident?—an event which, though distant, must happen, and which, when it does, will only confer a thankless favor—or shall we at once cut away the isthmus that remains, and float on the mingling waves the ark of our common constitution?" ¹

¹ Parl. Deb. iv. 1311.

96. Answer by Mr. Peel.

On the other hand, it was argued by Mr. Peel, in words which subsequent events have rendered prophetic: "I do not concur in the anticipation that the emancipation of the Catholics would tend to re-establish harmony in the state, or smooth down conflicting feelings. I do not wish to touch prospectively upon the consequences of intemperate struggles for power. I do not wish to use language which may be construed into a harsh interpretation of the acts and objects of men who proceed in the career of ambition, but I must say this much, that if Parliament admits an equal capacity for the possession of power between Protestant and Catholic in this respect, they will have no means of considering the state of the population, of securing that equal division of power which is, in my opinion, essential to the stability of the existing form of government. The struggle between the Catholic and Protestant will be violent, and the issue doubtful. If they were to be sent forth together as rival candidates, with an equal capacity for direct parliamentary representation, so far from seeing any prospect of the alleviation of points of political differences, I can only anticipate the *revival of animosities now happily extinct*, and the continuance, in an aggravated form, of angry discussions, now happily gliding into decay and disuse. If, in consequence of this alteration of the constitution, the duration of Parliament should be reduced from seven to three years, then will the frequent collision of Catholic and Protestant furnish a still greater accession of violent matter to keep alive domestic dissension in every form in which it can be arrayed, against the internal peace and concord of the empire. These are my honest sentiments upon this all-important question, uninfluenced by any motive but an ardent anxiety for the durability of our happy constitution." ¹

¹ Parl. Deb. iv. 1002, 1003.

97. Which is carried in the Commons, and lost in the Peers.

This debate is memorable for one circumstance—it was the first occasion on which a majority was obtained for Catholic Emancipation. The second reading was carried by a majority of 11, the numbers being 254 to 243; and this majority was increased, on the third reading, to 19, the numbers being 216 to 197. The bill, accordingly, went into committee, and passed the Commons; but it was thrown out, on the second reading, by a majority of 39 in the House of Lords, the numbers being 159 to 120. On this occasion the Duke of York made a memorable declaration of his opinion on this subject. "Educated," said his Royal Highness, "in the principles of the Established Church, I am persuaded that her interests are inseparable from those of the constitution. I consider it as an integral part of the constitution. The more I hear the subject discussed, the more am I confirmed in the opinion I now express. Let it not be supposed, however, that I am an enemy to toleration. I should wish that every sect should have the free exercise of its religion, so long as it does not affect the security of the established, and as long as its members remained loyal subjects. *But there is a great difference between allowing the free exercise of religion and the granting of political power.* My opposition to this bill arises from principles which I have embraced ever since I have been able to judge for myself, and which I hope I shall cherish to the last hour of my life." This decisive declaration on the part of the heir-apparent of the throne, whose early accession seemed likely from the health of the reigning Sovereign, produced a very great impression, and carried the popularity of his Royal Highness to the highest point. He became the object of enthusiastic applause at all the political meetings of persons attached to the Established Church, at which the singular coincidence in number of the thirty-nine peers who threw out the bill

April 17, 1821.

Vol. I.—Z

and the thirty-nine articles of the Church of England, never failed to be observed on, and elicit unbounded applause.[1]

[margin: 1 Parl. Deb. v. 282, 736.]

[margin: 98. Lord John Russell's motion for Parliamentary Reform.]

Lord John Russell, about the same time, brought forward a bill for a gradual and safe system of Parliamentary Reform. It was founded on resolutions, that there were great complaints on the subject of the representation of the people in Parliament; that it was expedient to give such places as had greatly increased in wealth and population, and at present were unrepresented, the right of sending members to serve in Parliament; and that it should be referred to a committee to consider how this could be done, without an inconvenient addition to the number of the House of Commons; and that all charges of bribery should be effectually inquired into, and, if proved, such boroughs should be disfranchised. The motion was rejected by a majority of 31, the numbers being 156 to 125; but the increasing strength of the minority, as well as weight of the names of which it was composed, indicated the change of general opinion on the subject, and might have warned the supporters of the existing system of the necessity of consenting to a safe and prudent reform, if any thing could convince men who are mainly actuated by the desire to retain, or the thirst to obtain, political power.[2]

[margin: 2 Parl. Deb. v. 622, 623.]

[margin: 99. Appointment of a committee to inquire into agricultural distress, March 7.]

The various branches of manufactures, during this year, exhibited a marked and gratifying improvement; but in agriculture the prevailing distress was not only unabated, but had become greater than ever, and, in truth, had now risen to such a height that it could no longer be passed over in silence. On 7th March, Mr. Gooch brought forward a motion for the appointment of a committee to inquire into agricultural distress; and in the course of the debate Mr. Curwen observed, "In the flourishing days of the empire, the income of the nation was £400,000,000, and the taxation was £80,000,000 annually. At present the income is only £300,000,000, yet the taxation was nearly the same. In what situation was the farmer? The average of wheat, if properly taken, was not more than 62s. a quarter; the consequence of which was, that the farmer lost 3s. by every quarter of wheat which he grew. On the article of wheat alone, the agricultural interest had lost £15,000,000, and on barley and oats £15,000,000 more. In addition to this, the value of farming stock had been diminished by £10,000,000; so that in England alone there was a diminution of £40,000,000 a year. The diminution on the value of agricultural produce in Scotland and Ireland can not be less than £15,000,000; so that the total loss to the agriculturists of the two islands can not be taken at less than £55,000,000. This is probably a quarter of the whole value of their productions; and as their taxation remains the same, it has, practically speaking, been increased twenty-six per cent. also."[3] The truth of these statements, how startling soever, was so generally known,

[margin: 3 Parl. Deb. iv. 1147, 1151.]

that Government yielded; and a committee was appointed to inquire into the causes of agricultural distress, which made a most valuable report in the next session of Parliament.

[margin: 100. Bank Cash Payment Bill.]

Great light was thrown upon the causes of this distress in a debate which took place, shortly after, on a bill of little importance, introduced by Government, authorizing the Bank, if they chose, to resume cash payments on 1st May, 1821, instead of May, 1822, as had been provided by the bill of 1819. The reason assigned by the Chancellor of the Exchequer for giving the Bank this option was, that they had, at a very heavy expense to themselves, accumulated a very great treasure, and that the paper circulation of the country had been so much contracted that cash payments might be resumed with safety. He stated that, "in June, 1819, the issues of the Bank amounted to £25,600,000; and they had been progressively diminished, till now they were only £24,000,000. The country bankers had drawn in their notes in a still greater proportion. Above four millions had been withdrawn from the circulation in less than two years—a state of things which amply justifies the present proposal to give the Bank the option of issuing gold coin, if they thought fit, a year sooner than by law provided."[1]

[margin: 1 Parl. Deb. iv. 1315, 1316.]

[margin: 101. Mr. Baring's speech on the subject.]

The effects of the contraction of the currency, thus made the subject of boast by the Chancellor of the Exchequer, were thus stated by Mr. Baring in the same debate: "In looking at this question, it is very material to consider what is the state of the country in this the sixth year of peace. Petitions are coming in from all quarters, remonstrating against the state of suffering in which so many classes are unhappily involved, and none more than the agricultural class. When such is the state of the country in the sixth year of peace, and when all the idle stories about over-production and under-consumption, *and suchlike trash*, have been swept away, it is natural to inquire into the state of a country placed in a situation without a parallel in any other nation or time. No country before ever presented the continuance of so extraordinary a spectacle as that of living under a progressive increase in the value of money, and decrease in the value of the productions of the people. It appears clear that, from the operations of the altered currency, we have loaded ourselves, not only with an immense public debt, but also with an *increased debt between individual and individual*, the weight of which continues to press upon the country, and to the continuance of which pressure no end can be seen.

[margin: 102. Continued.]

"The real difficulty is to meet the increased amount of debts of every sort, public and private, produced by the late change in the currency. It is an observation than which nothing can be more true, that an alteration in the value of the currency is what nobody, not even the wisest, generally perceive. They talk of alteration in the price of bread and provisions, never reflecting that the alteration is not in the value of these articles, but in that of the currency in which they are paid. To talk of the alteration of the value of money being three, five, or six per cent. is mere trifling. What we now are witnessing is the exact converse of what occurred during the war, from the enlarged issue of paper, and over the whole world from the discovery of the mines of Mexico and Peru. The misfortune is, in reference to agriculture, that what is a remunerating price at one time becomes quite the reverse at another. Formerly it was thought that 50s. a quarter was a remunerating price, but that is not the case now. What is the reason of that? It is occasioned by the altered currency, and by the produce of this country coming into contact with the commodities from all parts of the world, at a time when the taxes, debts, and charges which the farmer has to meet have undergone no alteration. His products did not bring their former price, while his private debts remained at their original amount. Besides this, there is the great mortgage of the National Debt, which sweeps over the whole country, and renders it impossible for the farmer to live on prices which formerly were considered a fair remuneration. The difficulties of the country, then, arise from this, that you have brought back your currency to its former value, so far as regards your income; but it remains at its former value, so far as regards your expenditure." Weighty, indeed, are these remarks, which subsequent events have so fully confirmed, and which came then from the first merchant in the world, who afterward conferred honor on, instead of receiving it from, the title of Ashburton.¹

^{t Parl. Deb.
iv. 1318,
1322.}

103. Vehement demand for a reduction of taxation.

The increased weight of debts and taxes, coinciding with the diminished incomes arising from the contracted currency, produced its natural and usual effect in inducing an additional pressure on Government for the reduction of taxation. Mr. Hume* brought this subject before the House of Commons, and the whole finances of the country underwent a more thorough investigation than they had ever previously done. His labors embraced chiefly the expenses of the offices connected with the army, navy, and ordnance departments; and there can be no doubt that he rendered good service by exposing many abuses that existed in these departments; and a committee was appointed to inquire into the subject. In consequence of the universal complaint of agricultural distress, Mr. Western brought forward a bill to repeal the malt duties, which was carried, on the first reading, by a majority of 24, the numbers being 149 to 125. It was thrown out, however, on the second reading; and so productive is this tax, and so widely is its weight diffused over the community, that its repeal has never yet been carried. The majority on the leave to bring in the bill, however, was an ominous circumstance, characteristic of the depression of the agricultural interest; and members were so impressed with it that they deemed it expedient to yield on a subordinate point, and the agricultural horse-tax was accordingly repealed this session.¹

^{1 Ann. Reg.
1821, 84,
100.}

The committee on agricultural distress presented their report on 18th June. It was a most elaborate and valuable document, as it bore testimony to the fact established before the committee, that "the complaints of the petitioners were founded in fact, in so far as they represented that, at the present price of corn, the returns to the owners of occupied land, after allowing growers the interest of investments, were *by no means adequate to the charges and outgoings;* but that the committee, after a long and anxious inquiry, had not been able to discover any means calculated immediately to relieve the present distress." * It is by no means surpris-

101. Agricultural committee reports, and state of the consumption of articles of luxury.

---

* The returns obtained by Mr. Hume presented the following comparative statement of the British army, exclusive of the troops in India, in 1792 and 1821 respectively, viz.:

1792.	Men.
Regulars in Great Britain—Infantry and cavalry	15,919
Do. Ireland	12,000
Colonies	17,323
Artillery	3,730
Marines	4,425
Total regulars	53,397
Militia disembodied	33,110
	86,507

1821.	Men.
Regulars in Great Britain—Cavalry and infantry	27,552
Do. Ireland	20,778
Do. Colonies	32,476
Artillery	7,872
Marines	8,000
Colonial troops—Cape	452
Do. Ceylon	3,606
Recruiting Establishment	497
Total regulars	101,539
Disembodied militia—England	55,692
Do. Ireland	22,472
Yeomanry—Great Britain	36,291
Do. Ireland	30,786
Volunteer infantry	6,931
Great Britain—Veterans disembodied	10,000
East India Company's regiment	750
Total irregulars	162,328
Grand Total	263,867

—Parl. Papers, No. 363, 1821; Parl. Deb., v. 1362.

* "So far as the pressure arises from superabundant harvests, it is beyond the application of any legislative provision; so far as it is the result of the increased value of money, it is not one peculiar to the farmer, but extends to many other classes. That result, however, is the more severely felt by the tenant, in consequence of its coincidence with an overstocked market. The departure from our ancient standard, in proportion as it was perjudicial to all creditors of money, and persons dependent on a fixed income, was a benefit to the active capital of the country; and the same classes have been oppositely affected by a return to that standard. The restoration of it has also embarrassed the landholder, in proportion as his estate has been encumbered with mortgages, and other fixed payments assigned on it during the depreciation of the currency. The only alleviation for this evil is to be looked for in such a gradual reduction of the rate of interest as may lighten the burdens on the landed interest. At present the annual produce of corn, the growth of the United Kingdom, is, upon an average crop, equal to our present consumption, and that, with such an average crop, the present import prices, below which foreign corn is by law altogether excluded, are fully sufficient, more especially since the change in the currency, to secure to the British farmer the complete monopoly of the home market. The change in the value of our money is virtually an advance upon our import prices; and the result of every such advance, supposing prices not to undergo a corresponding rise in other countries, must but expose this country to greater and more grievous fluctuations in price, and the business of the farmer to greater fluctuation and uncertainty. Protection can not be carried further than monopoly, which the British farmer has completely enjoyed for the last two harvests, the ports having been almost constantly shut against foreign imports during thirty months."—*Commons' Report*, June 18, 1821; Parl. Deb., v. 81, Appendix.

ing that it was so; for as their difficulties all arose from the contraction of the currency, it was impossible they could be removed till that contraction was alleviated, a thing which the great majority of the legislature was resolved not to do. It is remarkable that at the very same time Lord Liverpool demonstrated in the House of Lords, that the *general consumption* of the country, in articles of comfort and luxury, had considerably increased in the last year.¹ This fact is important, as affording an illustration of the observation already made² as to the eternal law of nature, that the division of labor and improvement of machinery, capable of indefinite application to manufacturing industry, have no tendency to cheapen the production of the subsistence of man, and consequently that the first and the last to suffer from a contraction of the currency, and enhancement of the value of money, are the classes engaged in the cultivation of the soil.²

¹ Ante, c. i. §§ 41, 42.

² Ann. Reg. 1821, 73; Commons' Report, June 18, 1821; Parl. Deb. v. 79, App.

105. Increase of the desire for reform among the agriculturists.

This long-continued and most severe depression in the price of agricultural produce, coupled with the reiterated refusals of Parliament to do any thing for their relief, at length came to produce important political effects. It spread far and wide among the landowners and farmers, who in every age had been the firmest supporters of the throne, the conviction that they were not adequately represented in Parliament, and that no relief from their sufferings could be anticipated, until, by a change in the composition of the House of Commons, their voice was brought to bear more directly and powerfully upon the measures of Government. Every thing was favorable: all the world was at peace; trade had revived; the seasons were fine; importation was prohibited, and had ceased. Nevertheless prices were so low that it was evident that a few more such years would exhaust all their capital, and reduce them to beggary. Reform had become indispensable, if they would avoid ruin. Now, accordingly, for the first time, the desire for parliamentary reform spread from the towns, where it had hitherto prevailed, to the rural districts, and gave token of an important change in this respect in the landed interest; and the ablest of the historians of the time in the Radical interest has borne testimony to the fact that, but for the change in the currency, the alteration of the constitution never could have taken place.†

	Average of three years ending January, 1820.	Year 1821.
* Beer, barrels	5,356,000	5,509,000
Candles, lb.	79,816,000	88,350,000
Malt	23,289,000	24,511,000
Salt	1,936,000	1,981,000
Soap, lb.	69,174,000	73,765,000
Spirits	5,047,000	6,575,000
Tea	22,186,000	22,542,000
Sugar	3,117,000	3,413,000

—Ann. Reg., 1821, 73.

† "In the beginning of 1822," says Miss Martineau, "every branch of manufacturing industry was in a flourishing state; but agriculture was depressed, and complaints were uttered at many county meetings, both before and after the meeting of Parliament. These incessant groanings, wearisome to the ears, and truly distressing to the hearts, were not borne idly to the winds. The complainers did not obtain from Parliament the aid which they desired, but they *largely advanced the cause of Parliament-*

Lord Castlereagh, to whom the mutability of the populace was well known, had prophesied, at the close of the proceedings against the Queen, that "in six months the King would be the most popular man within his dominions." This prediction was verified to the letter. The symptoms of returning popularity were so evident, that his Majesty, contrary to his inclination and usual habits, was prevailed on by his Ministers to appear frequently in public, both in the parks and principal theatres, on which occasions he was received with unbounded applause. This favorable appearance induced Government to determine on carrying into effect the coronation, which had been originally fixed for August in the preceding year, but had been postponed in consequence of the proceedings against the Queen, and the disturbed state of the public mind which ensued. Her Majesty, who was not aware that her popularity had declined as rapidly as that of her royal spouse had increased, was so imprudent as to prefer a claim, both to the King and the Privy Council, to be crowned at the same time as Queen Consort. The Council, however, determined that she was not entitled to demand it as a matter of right, and that in the circumstances they were not called on to concede it as a matter of courtesy; and her demand was in consequence refused. Upon this the Queen applied to the Duke of Norfolk, as Earl-Marshal of England, and the Archbishop of Canterbury, for a place in the Abbey at the coronation; but as they were subject to the King in Council in this matter, the petition was of course refused, though in the most courteous manner. Upon this her Majesty declared her resolution to appear personally at the coronation, and deliver her protest into the King's own hand. This determination, being known, diffused a general apprehension that a riot would ensue on the occasion; and to such a degree did the panic spread, that places to see the procession, which previously had been selling for ten guineas, were to be had on the morning of the ceremony for half-a-crown, and all the troops in London and the vicinity were assembled near Westminster Abbey to preserve the peace.¹

106. Coronation of George IV. July 19.

¹ Hughes, vi. 469, 470; Ann. Reg. 1821, 124, 125; Martineau, i. 259.

ary reform. If the agricultural interest had been in a high state of prosperity from 1820 to 1830, *the great question of reform in Parliament must have remained much longer afloat than it actually did,* from the inertness or opposition of the agricultural classes, who, as it was, were sufficiently discontented with Parliament to desire a change. Extraordinary as this may appear, when we look only to the preponderance of the landed interest in the House at that time, we shall find, on looking abroad through the country, that it was so. Such politicians as Cobbett presented themselves among the discontented farmers, and preached to them about the pressure of the debt, a bad system of taxation, a habit of extravagant expenditure, and of a short method of remedying these evils by obtaining a better constitution of the House of Commons. It was no small section of the agricultural classes that assisted in carrying the question at last; and it would be interesting to know how many of that order of reformers obtained their convictions through the distress of these years."—MARTINEAU's *Thirty Years of Peace,* i. 267. At that period the author, whose head was then more full of academical studies than political speculations, frequently stated it in company as a problem in algebra, easy of solution, "Given the Toryism of a landed proprietor, required to find the period of want of rents which will reduce him to a Radical reformer." He little thought then what momentous consequences to his country and the world were to ensue from the solution of the problem.

The ceremony took place accordingly, but it soon appeared that the precautions and apprehensions were alike groundless. This coronation was memorable, not only for the unparalleled magnificence of the dresses, decorations, and arrangements made on the occasion, but for this circumstance—it was the LAST where the gorgeous but somewhat grotesque habiliments of feudal times appeared, or will ever appear, in the realm of England. All that the pomp of modern times could produce, or modern wealth purchase, joined to the magnificence of ancient costume, were there combined, and with the most imposing effect. The procession, which moved from the place where it was marshaled in Westminster Hall to the Abbey; the ceremony of coronation within the Abbey itself, which had seen so many similar pageants from the earliest days of English story; the splendid banquet in the Hall, where the Champion of England, in full armor, rode in, threw down his gauntlet to all who challenged the King's title, and backed his harnessed steed out of the Hall without turning on his sovereign, were all exhibited with the most overpowering magnificence. Sir Walter Scott, whose mind was so fraught with chivalrous images, has declared that "a ceremony more august and imposing in all its parts, or more calculated to make the deepest impression both on the eye and the feelings, can not possibly be conceived. The expense, so far as it is national or personal, goes directly and instantly to the encouragement of the British manufacturer. It operates as a tax on wealth, and consideration for the benefit of poverty and industry—a tax willingly paid by one class, and not less acceptable to the other, because it adds a happy holiday to the monotony of a life of labor."[2]

[107. Ceremony on the occasion.]

[1 Sir Walter Scott's Description, Edinburgh Chronicle, July 23, 1821; Ann. Reg. 1821, 337, 346; Hughes, vi. 471, 472; App. to Chron.]

Men whose names have become immortal, walked—some of them, alas! for the last time—in that magnificent pageant. There was Wellington, who grasped in his hand the baton won on the field of Vittoria, and bore by his side the sword which struck down Napoleon on the plains of Waterloo, and whose Roman countenance, improved but not yet dimmed by years, bespoke the lofty cast of his mind; there Lord Castlereagh, who had recently succeeded to the title of Londonderry, in the magnificent robes of the Garter, with his high plumes, fine face, and majestic person, appeared a fitting representative of the Order of Edward III.; and there was the Sovereign, the descendant of the founder of the Garter, whose air and countenance, though almost sinking under the weight of magnificence and jewels, revealed his high descent, and evinced the still untarnished blood of the Plantagenets and Stuarts. Nor was female beauty wanting to grace the splendid spectacle, for all the noblest and fairest of the nobility of England, the most lovely race in the world, were there, and added the lustre of their diamonds, and the still brighter lustre of their eyes, to the enchantment of the matchless scene.[2]

[108. Aspect of Wellington, Londonderry, and George IV.]

[2 Sir Walter Scott, ut supra; Hughes, vi. 473.]

But the first and highest lady in the realm was not there; and the disappointment she experienced at being refused admittance was one cause of her death, which soon after ensued. The Queen, with that resolution and indomitable spirit which, for good or for evil, has ever been the characteristic of her race, though refused a ticket, resolved to force her way into the Abbey, and witness, at least, if she was not permitted to take part in, the ceremony. She came to the door, accordingly, in an open barouche, drawn by six beautiful bays, accompanied by Lord and Lady Hood and Lady Anne Hamilton, and was loudly cheered by the populace as she passed along the streets. When she approached the Abbey, however, some cries of an opposite description were heard; and when she arrived at the door, she was respectfully, but firmly, refused admittance by the door-keeper, who had the painful duty imposed on him of denying access to his sovereign. She retired from the door, after some altercation, deeply mortified, amidst cries from the people, some cheers, but others which proved how much general opinion had changed in regard to her. Such was the chagrin she experienced from this event, that, combined with an obstruction of the bowels that soon after seized her, mortification ensued, which terminated fatally in little more than a fortnight afterward. The ruling passion appeared strong in death. She ordered that her remains should not be left in England, but carried to her native land, and buried beside her ancestors, with this inscription, "Here lies Caroline of Brunswick, the injured Queen of England."[1]

[109. The Queen is refused admittance: her death. Aug. 7.]

[1 Ann. Reg. 1821, 347, 348; App. to Chron.; Hughes, vi. 473, 474; Martineau, i. 260.]

Before the death of the Queen was known, the King had made preparations for a visit to Ireland, and it was not thought proper to interrupt them. On Saturday, 11th August, his Majesty embarked at Holyhead, and on the following afternoon landed at Howth in the Bay of Dublin, where he was received with the loudest acclamations, and the most heartfelt demonstrations of loyalty, by that warm-hearted and easily-excited people. They escorted him with the most tumultuous acclamations to the vice-regal lodge, from the steps of which he thus addressed them: "This is one of the happiest days of my life. I have long wished to visit you. My heart has always been Irish; from the day it first beat, I loved Ireland, and this day has shown me that I am beloved by my Irish subjects. Rank, station, honors, are nothing; but to feel that I live in the hearts of my Irish subjects, is to me exalted happiness." These felicitous expressions diffused universal enchantment, and, combined with the graceful condescension and dignified affability of manner which the Sovereign knew so well to exhibit when inclined to do so, roused the loyalty of the people to a perfect enthusiasm. For the week that he remained there, his life was a continued triumph: reviews, theatres, spectacles, and entertainments, succeeded one another in brilliant succession; and after a short sojourn at Slanes Castle,[2] the

[110. King's visit to Ireland. Aug. 12.]

[2 Ann. Reg. 1821, 129, 131; App. to Chron.; Hughes, vi. 474, 475.]

seat of the Marquis of Conyngham, he returned to England, and soon after paid a visit to Hanover, where he was received in the same cordial and splendid manner.

111. Funeral of the Queen, and dismissal of Sir R. Wilson from the army.

The funeral of the Queen took place on the 14th August, at the very time when the King was receiving the impassioned demonstrations of loyalty on the part of his Irish subjects; and it caused a painful and discreditable scene, which led to the dismissal of one of the most gallant officers in the English army from the service which his valor and conduct had so long adorned. It had been directed by her Majesty that her body, as already mentioned, should be taken to Brunswick to be interred. Anxious to avoid any rioting or painful occurrence in conveying the body from Brandenberg House, where she died, to the place where it was to be embarked, Romford in Essex, Ministers had directed that the hearse which conveyed the body, with attendants suitable to her rank, should proceed by a circuitous route through the north suburbs of London and the new road to Islington. The direct road to Romford, however, lay through the city; and the people were resolved that the procession should go that way, that they might have an opportunity of testifying their respect to the illustrious deceased. As the orders of the persons intrusted with the direction of the procession were to go the other way, and they attempted to do so, the populace formed in a close column twenty deep, across the road at Cumberland Gate, and after a severe conflict, both there and at Tottenham Court Road, in the course of which two men were unfortunately killed by shots from the Life-Guards, the procession was fairly forced into the line which the people desired, and proceeded through the city in great pomp, amidst an immense crowd of spectators, with the Lord Mayor and civic authorities at its head, the bells all tolling, and the shops shut.¹

¹ An. Reg. 1821, 126, 127; App. to Chron.; Hughes, vi. 471, 475; Martineau, i. 261.

112. Dismissal of Sir R. Wilson from the army.

The procession reached Romford without further interruption, and the unhappy Queen was at length interred at Brunswick on August 23d. But the occurrence in London led to a melancholy result in Great Britain. Sir Robert Wilson, who had remonstrated with the military on occasion of this affray, and taken an active part in the procession, though not in the riot, and the police magistrate who had yielded to the violence of the populace, and changed the direction of the procession, were both dismissed, the first from the service, the last from his situation. However much all must regret that so gallant and distinguished an officer as Sir Robert Wilson should have been lost, even for a time, to the British army, no right-thinking person can hesitate as to the propriety of this step. Obedience is the first duty of the armed force; it acts, but should never deliberate. He who tries to make soldiers forget their duty to their sovereign, or sets the example of doing so, fails in his duty to his king, but still more to his country; for the cause of freedom has been often thrown back, but never yet was, in the end, promoted by military revolt; and it was not a time to provoke such a catastrophe in Great Britain, when military revolution had just proved so fatal to the cause of liberty not less than of order in southern Europe.¹ *

¹ Hughes, vi. 475, 476, Ann. Reg. 1821, 128.

113. Changes in the Cabinet.

Notwithstanding the favorable state of general feeling in the country, and the improved condition of the manufacturing classes, Ministers felt that their position was insecure, and that it was highly desirable to obtain some further accession of strength, both in the Cabinet and the House of Commons. The continued and deep distress of the agricultural interest had not only led to several close divisions in the preceding session in the House of Commons, but occasioned several public meetings, where the voice of that class had made itself loudly heard. They had actually resigned upon his Majesty's demand for a divorce; they had been all but shipwrecked on the Queen's trial; and on occasion of the late riots at her funeral, he had let fall some alarming expressions as to the way in which that delicate affair had been conducted. It was deemed indispensable, therefore, to look out for support; and the Grenville party—a sort of flying squadron between the Ministerialists and Liberals, but who had hitherto always acted with the Whigs—presented the fairest prospect of an alliance. Proposals were made accordingly, and accepted. Lord Grenville, the head of the party, was disabled by infirmities from taking an active part in public life, and could not be lured from his retreat; but the Marquis of Buckingham was made a duke; Mr. Wynne, President of the Board of Control; and Mr. H. Wynne, envoy to the Swiss Cantons. This coalition gained Ministers a few votes in the House of Commons; but it was of more importance as indicating, as changes in the Cabinet generally do, the commencement of a change in the system of government. The admission of even a single Whig into the Cabinet indicated the increasing weight of that party in the country, and as they were favorable to the Catholic claims, it was an important change. Lord Eldon, *ultimus Romanorum*, presaged no good from the alliance. "This coalition," he said, "will have consequences very different from those expected by the members of the administration who brought it about. I hate coalitions."²

² Twiss's Life, ii. 446; Life of Sidmouth, iii. 382; Ann. Reg. 1821, 4, 5; Hughes, vi. 482.

114. Retirement of Lord Sidmouth, who is succeeded by Mr. Peel, as Home Secretary.

A still more important change took place at the same time, in the retirement of Lord Sidmouth from the onerous and responsible post of Home Secretary. A life of thirty years in harness, oppressed with the cares of official life, had nearly exhausted the physical strength, though they had by no means dimmed the mental energy of this conscientious and intrepid statesman; and though no decline in his faculties was perceptible to those around him, he felt that the time had arrived when he should withdraw from the cares and responsibility of office, and dedicate

---

* Sir R. Wilson was afterward restored to his rank in the army, and was for some years Governor of Gibraltar; but his military decorations, bestowed by the English Government, were never restored.

his remaining years to the enjoyment of his family, to which he was strongly attached, and his duties to his Maker. He deemed it a fitting opportunity to take such a step, when the internal situation of the country was so tranquil that the public service could sustain no detriment by his withdrawing from it; for had it been otherwise, he would, at any hazard to his own health or life, have remained at his post.* He was succeeded in his arduous duties by a much younger man, Mr., afterward Sir ROBERT PEEL, one of greater abilities, and whose mind was more in harmony with the spirit of the age, but not of greater energy and integrity, and by no means of equal moral courage. Lord Sidmouth's abilities, though not of the highest order, were of the most useful kind, and his administrative talents stood forth pre-eminent. His industry was indefatigable, his energy untiring, his intrepidity, both moral and physical, such as nothing could quell. He steered the vessel of the state, during the anxious years which succeeded the close of the war, through all the shoals with which it was beset, with exemplary vigor and undaunted courage; and it was not a little owing to his resolution that the crisis was surmounted in 1820, which proved fatal to the cause of liberty and order in so many other states.[1]

[Marginal: 1 Lord Sidmouth to Bishop Huntingford, Nov. 11, 1821; Sidmouth's Life, iii. 388, 390.]

115. Lord Wellesley appointed Viceroy of Ireland, and change in the government there.

This parliamentary coalition was attended with still more important changes in Ireland, for there it commenced an entire alteration in the system of government, which has continued, with little interruption, to the present day. As the Protestants, ever since the Revolution, had been the dominant party in that island, and the Catholics were known to be decidedly hostile both to the British government and alliance, the Viceroy, and all the officers of state who composed its government, had hitherto been invariably stanch Protestants; and Lord Talbot, the present Viceroy, and Mr. Saurin, the Attorney-general, were of that persuasion. But as the Cabinet itself was now divided on the subject of concession of the Catholic claims, it was thought necessary to make a similar partition in the Irish administration. Accordingly, Marquis Wellesley, a decided supporter of the Catholics, was made Lord-lieutenant in room of Lord Talbot; Mr. Saurin, the champion of the Orange party, made way for Mr. Plunkett, the eloquent advocate of the Catholic claims in the House of Commons; and Mr. Bushe, also a Catholic supporter, was made Solicitor-general; while, on the principle of preserving a balance of parties, Mr. Goulburn, a stanch Protestant, was appointed Secretary to the government. Great expectations were formed of the beneficial effects of this conciliatory policy, which, it was hoped, would continue the unanimity of loyal feeling which had animated the country during the visit of the Sovereign. But these hopes were miserably disappointed; party strife was increased instead of being diminished by the first step toward equality of government, and the next year added another to the innumerable proofs which the annals of Ireland have afforded, that its evils are social, not political, and are increased rather than diminished by the extension to its inhabitants of the privileges of free citizens.[1]

[Marginal: 1 Pearce's Memoirs of Wellesley, iii. 316, 317; Ann. Reg. 1822, 7; Hughes, vi. 460.]

Entirely agricultural in their habits, pursuits, and desires—solely dependent for their subsistence on the fruits of the soil, and without manufactures, mines, fisheries, or means of livelihood of any sort, save in Ulster, except that derived from its cultivation—the possession of land, and the sale of its produce, was a matter of life or death to the Irish people. The natural improvidence of the Celtic race, joined to the entire absence of all those limitations on the principle of increase which arise from habits of comfort, the desire of rising, or the dread of falling, in the world—and the interested views of the Catholic priesthood, who encouraged marriage, from the profits which bridals and christenings brought to themselves—had overspread the land with an immense and redundant population, which had no other means of livelihood but the possession and cultivation of little bits of land. There were few laborers living on paid wages in any of the provinces of Ireland; in Leinster, Munster, and Connaught, where the Celtic race and Catholic creed predominated, scarcely any. Of farmers possessed of capital, and employing farm-servants, there were in the south and west none. Emigration had not as yet opened its boundless resources, or spread out the garden of the Far West for the starving multitudes of the Emerald Isle. They had no resources or means of livelihood, but in the possession of little pieces of land, for which they bid against each other with the utmost eagerness, and from which they excluded the stranger with the most jealous care. Six millions of men, without either capital or industry, shut up within the four corners of a narrow though fruitful land, were contending with each other for the possession of their patches of the earth, like wolves inclosed within walls for pieces of carrion, whose hostility against each other was only interrupted by a common rush against any hapless stranger who might venture to approach their bounds, and threaten to share their scanty meal.[2]

[Marginal: 116. Cause of the wretchedness of Ireland.]

[Marginal: 2 Pearce's Life of Wellesley, iii. 348; Ann. Reg. 1822, 14; Marquis Wellesley to Mr. Secretary Peel, Jan. 29, 1823.]

Experience has abundantly proved, since that time, what reason, not blinded by party, had already discovered—what were the real remedies for such an alarming and disastrous state of things, and what alone could have given any lasting relief. These were, to furnish the means of emigration, at the public expense, to the most destitute of the peasants of the country, and form roads, canals, and harbors, to facilitate the sale of the produce of such as remained at home. Having in this way got quit of the worst and most dangerous part of the population, and lessened the competition for small farms among such as were still there, an opening would have been afforded for farmers, possessed of capital

[Marginal: 117. What would have relieved the country, and its neglect.]

---

* "The truth is, it was *because* my official bed had become a bed of roses, that I determined to withdraw from it. When strewn with thorns, I would not have left it."—*Sidmouth's Life*, iii. 399.

and skill, from England and Scotland, to occupy the land of those who had been removed to a happier hemisphere; and with them the religion, industrial habits, and education of the inhabitants of Great Britain, might gradually, and in the course of generations, have been introduced. But, unfortunately, party ambition and political delusion blinded men to all these rational views, which went only to bless the country, not to elevate a new party to its direction. Faction fastened upon Ireland as the arena where the Ministry might be assailed with effect; Catholic emancipation was cherished and incessantly brought forward, as the wedge, the point of which, already inserted, might be made, by a few hard strokes, to split the Cabinet in pieces; and while motions on this subject, involving the entry of sixty gentlemen into Parliament, enforced by the eloquence of Canning and Plunkett, and resisted by the argument of Peel, never failed to attract a full attendance of members on both sides of the House, Mr. Wilmot Horton's proposals regarding emigration, the only real remedy for the evils of the unhappy country, and involving the fate of six millions, were coldly listened to, and generally got quit of by the House being counted out.

118. Ruinous effect of the contraction of the currency upon Ireland.

But it was not merely by sins of omission that the legislature, at this period, left unhealed the wounds, and unrelieved the miseries, of Ireland. Their deeds of commission were still more disastrous in their effects. The contraction of the currency, and consequent fall of the prices of agricultural produce fifty per cent, fell with crushing effect upon a country wholly agricultural, and a people who had no other mode of existence but the sale of that produce. This had gone on now for nearly three years; and its effect had been, not only to suck the little capital which they possessed out of the farmers, but in many instances to produce a deep-rooted feeling of animosity between them and their landlords, which was leading to the most frightful disorders.* All the agrarian outrages which have in every age disgraced Ireland have arisen from one cause—the contests for pieces of land, the dread of being ejected from them, and jealousy of any stranger's interference. It is no wonder it is so; for to them it is a question, not of change of possession, but of life or death.¹ The ruinous fall in the price of agricultural produce of all sorts had rendered the payment of rents, at least, in full, wholly impossible, and had led, in consequence, to measures of severity having been in many instances resorted to. Distrainings had become frequent; ejections were beginning to be resorted to, and the landlords were fain

¹ Pearce's Memoirs of Wellesley, iii. 337; Ann. Reg. 1822, 14, 15; Marquis Wellesley to Secretary of State, Jan. 14, 1822.

* "I request your attention to the suggestions which I have submitted for the more effectual restraint of this system of mysterious engagements, formed under the solemnity of secret oaths, binding his Majesty's liege subjects to act under authorities not known to the law, nor derived from the State, for purposes undefined, not disclosed in the first process of initiation, nor until the infatuated novice has been sworn to the vow of unlimited and lawless obedience."—Marquis WELLESLEY to Mr. Secretary PEEL, Jan. 22, 1823; Life of Wellesley, iii. 360.

to introduce a set of Scotch or English farmers, who might succeed in realizing those rents which they had enjoyed in former days, but saw no longer a chance of extracting from their Celtic tenantry.

This was immediately met by the usual system of resistance on the part of the existing occupants of the soil; and on this occasion it assumed a more organized and formidable appearance than it had ever previously done. Over the whole extent of the three disturbed provinces a regular system of nocturnal outrage and violence was commenced, and carried on for a long time with almost entire impunity. Houses were entered in the night by bands of ruffians with their faces blackened, who carried off arms and ammunition, and committed outrages of every description; the roads were beset by armed and mounted bodies of insurgents, who robbed every person they met, and broke into every house which lay on their way; and to such a length did their audacity reach, that they engaged, in bodies of five hundred and a thousand, with the yeomanry and military forces, and not unfrequently came off victorious. Even when, by concentrating the troops, an advantage was obtained in one quarter, it was only at the expense of losses in another; for the "Rockites," as they were called, dispersed into small bodies, and, taking advantage of the absence of the military, pursued their depredations at a distance. No less than two thousand men assembled in the mountains to the north of Bandon, and their detachments committed several murders and outrages; and five thousand mustered together, many of them armed with muskets, near Macroom, and openly bid defiance to the civil and military forces of the country.¹

119. Progress of the agrarian disturbances in Ireland.

¹ Pearce's Life of Wellesley, iii. 324, 335, 349, 361; Lord Wellesley to Mr. Secretary Peel, Jan. 29, 1823; Ann. Reg. 1822, 10.

These frightful and alarming outrages commanded the early and vigilant attention of the Lord-lieutenant. Not content with sending immediate succor, in men and arms, to the menaced districts, he prepared and laid before Government several memorials on the measures requisite to restore order in the country, in which, as the first step, a great increase in the police establishment of the country was suggested.* At the same time the greatest exertions were made to reconcile parties, and efface party distinctions at the Castle of Dublin. Persons of respectability of all parties shared in the splendid hospitality of the Lord-lieutenant; Orange processions and

120. Lord Wellesley's able conduct and impartiality.

* One authentic document may convey an idea of the general state of Ireland, with the exception of the Protestant province of Ulster, at this period. "The progress of this diabolical system of outrage, during the last month, has been most alarming; and we regret to say that we have been obliged, from want of adequate force, to remain almost passive spectators of its daring advances, until at length many have been obliged to convert their houses into garrisons, and others have sought refuge in the towns. We can not expect individuals to leave their houses and families exposed, while they go out with patrolling parties; and to continue in such duty for any length of time, is beyond their physical strength, and inconsistent with their other duties."—(Memorial of twenty eight Magistrates of County Cork.) Annual Register, 1822, p. 9.

commemorations were discouraged; the dressing of King William's statue in Dublin, a party demonstration, was prohibited; and every effort made to show that Government was in earnest in its endeavors to appease religious dissensions, and heal the frightful discord which had so long desolated the country. But the transition from a wrong to a right system is often more perilous than the following out of a wrong one. You alienate one party without conciliating the other; so much more deep is recollection of injury, than gratitude for benefits in the human breast. Marquis Wellesley's administration, so different from any thing they had ever experienced, gave the utmost offense to the Orange party, hitherto in possession of the whole situations of influence and power in the country. To such a length did the discontent arise, that the Lord-lieutenant was publicly insulted at the theatre of Dublin, and the riot was of so serious a kind as to give rise to a trial at the next assizes.[1]

¹ Ann. Reg. 1822, 14, 16, 55; Pearce's Life of Wellesley, iii. 348, 351; Lord Wellesley to Mr. Secretary Peel, Jan. 29, 1823.

121. Dreadful examples in the disturbed districts.

Dreadful but necessary examples were made, in many of the disturbed districts, of the most depraved and hardy of the depredators. So numerous had been the outrages, that although the great majority of them had been perpetrated with impunity, yet great numbers of prisoners had been made—prisoners against whom the evidence was so clear that their conviction followed of course. In Cork, no less than 366 persons awaited the special commission sent down in February to clear the jail, of whom thirty-five received sentence of death. Several of these were left for immediate execution. Similar examples were made in Limerick, Tipperary, and Kilkenny, where the assizes were uncommonly heavy; and by these dreadful but necessary examples the spirit of insubordination was, by the sheer force of terror, for the time subdued. One curious and instructive fact appeared from the evidence adduced at these melancholy trials, and that was, that the principal leaders and most daring actors in their horrid system of nocturnal outrage and murder, were the persons who had been cast down from the rank of substantial yeomen, and reduced to a state of desperation by the long-continued depression in the price of agricultural produce.[2]*

² Ann. Reg. 1822, 30, 31.

122. Dreadful famine in the south and west of Ireland. April, 1823.

But ere long a more dreadful evil than even these agrarian outrages broke out in this unhappy land; and the south and west of Ireland was punished by a calamity the natural consequence, in some degree, of its sins, but aggravated to a most frightful extent by a visitation of Providence. The disturbed state of the country during the whole of 1822 had caused the cultivation of potatoes to be very generally neglected in the south and west, partly from the numbers engaged in agrarian outrages, partly from the terror inspired in those who were more peaceably disposed. In addition to this, the potato crops in the autumn of 1822 failed, to a very great degree, over the same districts; and though the grain harvest was not only good, but abundant, yet this had no effect in alleviating the distresses of the peasantry, because the price of agricultural produce was so low, and they had been so thoroughly impoverished by its long continuance, that they had not the means of purchasing it. Literally speaking, they were starving in the midst of plenty. The consequence was, that in Connaught and Munster, in the spring of 1823, multitudes of human beings were almost destitute of food; and the nocturnal disturbances ceased, not so much from the terrors of the law, as from the physical exhaustion of those engaged in them. What was still worse, the sufferings of the present had extinguished the hopes of the future; and the absorption of three-fourths of the seed-potatoes, in many places, in present food, seemed to presage a still worse famine in the succeeding year. In these melancholy and alarming circumstances, the conduct of Government was most praiseworthy, and was as much distinguished by active and well-judged benevolence as it had previously been by impartial administration, and the energetic repression of crime. Five hundred thousand pounds were placed at the disposal of the Irish government by the English cabinet; and roads, bridges, harbors, and such objects of public utility, were set on foot wherever they seemed practicable. But this melancholy calamity called forth a still more striking proof of British kindness and generosity, and afforded proof how thoroughly Christian charity can obliterate the fiercest divisions, and bury in oblivion the worst delinquencies of this world. England forgot the sins of Ireland; she saw only her suffering. Subscriptions were opened in every church and chapel of Great Britain; and no less than £350,000 was subscribed in a few weeks, and remitted to Dublin, to aid the efforts of the local committees, by whom £150,000 had been raised for the same benevolent purpose. By these means the famine was stayed, and the famishing multitude was supported, till a favorable crop, in the succeeding year, restored the usual means of subsistence.[1]*

¹ Pearce's Memoirs of Wellesley, iii. 123, 312, 311; Ann. Reg. 1822, 33, 37; Sir D. Baird to Sir H. Taylor, June 24, 1822.

* "The authors of the outrages consisted of three classes; 1. Many farmers had advanced their whole capital in improvements upon the land. These men, by the depression of farming produce, had been reduced from the rank of substantial yeomen to complete indigence, and they readily entered into any project likely to embroil the country, and, by the share of education which they possessed, unaccompanied by any religious sentiments, became at once the ablest and least restrained promoters of mischief. 2. The second consisted of those who had been engaged in the Rebellion of 1798 and their disciples. 3. The third consisted of the formidable mass of ignorance and bigotry which was diffused through the whole south of Ireland."—*Annual Register*, 1822, p. 30, 31.

* "The distress for food, arising principally from the want of means to purchase it, continues to prevail in various districts; and the late accounts from the south and west are of the most afflicting character. Colonel Patrickson, whose regiment (the 43d) has recently relieved the 57th in Galway, reports the scenes which that town presents to be truly distressing. Hundreds of half-famished wretches arrive almost daily from a distance of fifty miles, many of them so exhausted by want of food that the means taken to restore them *fail of effect from the weakness of the digestive organs, occasioned by long fasting*."—Sir D. Baird to Sir H. Taylor, 24th June, 1822; *Memoirs of Lord Wellesley*, iii. 313, 314.

In June, 1822, there were in Clare alone 99,639 persons subsisting on daily charity; in Cork, 122,000; in Limerick, 29,000, out of a population not at that period exceeding 67,000.—*Ann. Reg.*, 1822, p. 40.

Those awful scenes, in which the visitations of Providence were mingled with the crimes and punishment of man—and both were met, and could be softened only, by the unwearied energy of Christian benevolence—excited, as well they might, the anxious attention of Government and the British Parliament. Whatever the remote causes of so disastrous a state of things might be, it was evident that nothing but vigorous measures of repression could be relied on in the mean time. Justice must do its work before wisdom commenced its reform. Unfortunately only the first was energetically and promptly done; the last, from political blindness and party ambition, was indefinitely postponed. Lord Londonderry (Lord Castlereagh) introduced into the Lower House two bills, one for the suspension of the Habeas Corpus Act until the 1st August following. This was strongly resisted by the Opposition, but agreed to by a large majority, the numbers being 195 to 68. The Insurrection Act, which authorized the Lord-lieutenant, upon application of a certain proportion of the magistrates of a district, to declare it by proclamation in a state of insurrection—and in that event gave extraordinary powers of arrest to the magistrates of all persons found out of their houses between sunset and sunrise, and subjected the persons seized, in certain events, to transportation—was next brought forward, and passed by a large majority, the numbers being 59 to 15. Two other bills were also passed, the one indemnifying persons who had seized gunpowder without legal authority since 1st November, and the other imposing severe restrictions on the importation of arms and ammunition. The lawless state of the country, and the constant demand of the nocturnal robbers for arms, rendered these measures absolutely necessary in this as they have been in every other disturbed period of Irish history, and the powers thus conferred were immediately acted upon by the Lord-lieutenant. A still more efficient measure of repression was adopted by a great increase of the police, who were brought to that state of vigor and efficiency which they have ever since maintained.[1]

123. Suspension of the Habeas Corpus Act, and Insurrection Act.

[1] Hughes, vi. 481; An. Reg. 1822, 26, 34.

The Catholic claims were in this session of Parliament again brought forward by Mr. Canning, in the form of a motion to give them seats in the House of Peers, and enforced with all the eloquence of which he was so consummate a master.* They were as strongly opposed by Mr. Peel, who repeated his solemn assurances of indelible hostility to the claims of that body. The progressive change in the public mind on this question was evinced in the increasing majority in the Commons, which this year rose to 12; the numbers being 235 to 223, the largest the Catholics had yet obtained in Parliament. The bill, as was anticipated, was thrown out, after a keen debate, in the House of Lords, by a majority of 42, the numbers being 171 to 129. But as the Cabinet was divided upon the subject, and its ablest members spoke in favor of the Catholic claims, and as the House of Commons, by having the command of the public purse, have the real command of the country, these divisions were justly considered by the Catholic party as decisive triumphs in their favor, and as presaging, at no distant period, their admission into both branches of the legislature.[1]

124. Divisions on the Catholic claims. April 30.

[1] Ann. Reg. 1822, 56, 67.

Another question—that of parliamentary reform—made a still more important stride in this session of Parliament; and the increasing numerical strength of the majority, as well as the weight of the names of which it was composed, indicated in an unequivocal manner the turn which events were ere long to take on that vital question. Several important petitions had been presented on the subject, both from boroughs and counties, and Lord John Russell was intrusted with the motion. He dwelt in a peculiar manner on the increasing intelligence, wealth, and population of the great towns, once obscure villages, which were unrepresented, and the impossibility of permanently excluding them from the share to which they were entitled in the legislature. Mr. Canning as decidedly opposed him, resting his defense of the constitution on the admirable way in which it had practically worked, and the incalculable danger of substituting for a system which had arisen out of the wants, and moulded itself according to the wishes of the people, one more specious in theory—one which, on that very account, would in all probability be found on trial to be subject to some fatal defect in practice. As the arguments on this all-important question will be fully given in a future volume, they need not be here anticipated; but the peroration of Mr. Canning's splendid reply deserves a place in history, as prophetic of the future career both of the noble mover and of the country.[2]

125. Increasing strength of the minority on parliamentary reform. April 29.

[2] Parl. Deb. vii. 84, 135.

"Our lot is happily cast in the temperate zone of freedom—the clime best suited to the development of the moral qualities of the hu-

* On this occasion Mr. Canning made a very happy use of the late imposing ceremony of the coronation, the splendor of which was still fresh in the minds of his auditors. "Do you imagine," said he, "it never occurred to the representatives of Europe, that, contemplating this imposing spectacle, it never occurred to the embassadors of Catholic Austria, or Catholic France, or of states more bigoted, if any such there be, to the Catholic religion, to reflect that the moment this solemn ceremony was over, the Duke of Norfolk would become deprived of the exercise of his privileges among his fellow-peers—stripped of his robes of office, which were to be laid aside, and hung up until the distant the if a very distant?) day, when the coronation of a successor to his present and gracious sovereign should again call him forth to assist at a similar solemnization? Thus, after being exhibited to the peers and people of England, to the representatives of princes and nations of the world, the Duke of Norfolk, highest in rank among the peers, the Lord Clifford, and others like him, representing a long line of illustrious and heroic ancestors, appeared as if they had been called forth and furnished for the occasion, like the lustres and banners that flamed and glittered in the scene; and were to be, like them, thrown by as useless and temporary formalities: they might, indeed, bend the knee and kiss the hand; they might bear the train and rear the canopy; they might perform the offices assigned by Roman pride to their barbarian forefathers, 'Purpurea tollant aulœa Britanni;' but with the pageantry of the hour their importance faded away as their distinction vanished: their humiliation returned, and he who headed the procession to-day could not sit among them as their equal to-morrow."—CANNING'S Speech, 30th April, 1822; Parl. Deb., vii. 232, 233.

man race, to the cultivation of their faculties, and to the security as well as improvement of their virtues—a clime not exempt, indeed, from variations in the elements, but variations which purify while they agitate the atmosphere which we breathe. Let us be sensible of the advantages which it is our happiness to enjoy. Let us guard with pious care the flame of genuine liberty—that fire from heaven, of which our constitution is the holy depository; and let us not, for the chance of rendering it more intense and more brilliant, impair its purity or hazard its extinction. That the noble lord will carry his motion this evening, I have no fear; but with the talents which he has already shown himself to possess, and with, I hope, a long and brilliant parliamentary career before him, he will no doubt renew his efforts hereafter. Although I presume not to expect that he will give any weight to observations or warnings of mine, yet on this, probably the last opportunity I shall have of raising my voice on the question of parliamentary reform,* while I conjure the House to pause before it consents to adopt the proposition of the noble lord, I cannot help adjuring the noble lord himself to pause before he again presses it upon the country. If, however, he shall persevere, *and if his perseverance shall be successful*, and if the results of that perseverance shall be such as I can not help anticipating, his be the triumph to have precipitated these results, be mine the consolation that, to the utmost and the latest of my power, I have opposed them." The motion was thrown out by a majority of 105 only—the numbers being 269 to 164.†

<small>*Parl. Deb. vii. 135.*</small>

<small>126. Peroration of Mr. Canning's speech.</small>

Sir James Mackintosh continued his benevolent and important efforts this year for the reformation of our criminal law, and contrasted with great effect the state of our code, which recognized two hundred and twenty-three capital offenses, with that of France, which contained only six. In this country, the convictions in the first five years after 1811 were five times greater in proportion to the population than in France; in the second five years they were ten times greater. "This increase," he added, "though in part it might be ascribed to the distress under which the country had groaned, and continued to groan, was also in part caused by the character of our penal code. The motion to take the subject into serious consideration next session was carried by a majority of 117 to 101. There can be no doubt that this was a step in the right direc-

<small>127. Sir James Mackintosh's motion regarding the criminal law.</small>

tion, and paved the way for those important changes in the criminal law of England which Mr. Peel soon after introduced. But the result has shown that it was a mistake to ascribe the superior rapidity in the increase of crime in Great Britain, as compared to France, to the severity of our penal laws; for the same disproportion has continued in a still greater degree since the punishment of death was taken away, practically speaking, from all offenses except deliberate murder. The truth is, that, like the disturbed state of Ireland, the increase of crime arose mainly from the general distress which had prevailed, with very few exceptions, since the peace; and the errors on this subject afford only another illustration of the truth which so many passages of contemporary history illustrate, that the great causes determining the comfort, conduct, and tranquillity of the working classes are to be found in those which, directly or indirectly, affect the wages of labor.¹

<small>¹ Ann. Reg. 1822, 82, 91.</small>

But these material distresses had increased, and were increasing with a rapidity which outstripped all calculation, and had now reached a height which compelled investigation, and threatened to bear down all opposition. The great fall in the price of the whole articles of agricultural produce, which had gone on without intermission from the monetary bill of 1819, and had now reached 50 per cent. on every product of rural labor, had, at length, spread to every other species of manufacture. All, sharing in the influence of the same cause, exhibited the same effect. The long continuance of the depression, and its universal application to *all* articles of commerce, excluded the idea of its being owing to any glut in the market, or any excess in trading in particular lines of business, and furnished a valuable commentary on the predictions of Mr. Ricardo and Mr. Peel, that the change of prices could not by possibility exceed 3 per cent."² This subject accordingly engaged the repeated and anxious consideration of both Houses of Parliament; it was made the topic of repeated and luminous debates of the very highest interest and importance, and it forced at length a change of the utmost moment in our monetary system, which for the next three years entirely changed our social condition, and induced another set of dangers the very reverse of those under which the nation for the three preceding years had been laboring.

<small>128. Great fall in the price of all sorts of produce.</small>

<small>² Ante, c. iv. § 74, note.</small>

This important debate was opened by Mr. Brougham on the 8th of February, who in a powerful speech demonstrated the extreme distress of the agricultural class, in connection with the heavy load of poor-rates and local taxes with which they were exclusively burdened. The motion he made for the consideration of the burdens peculiarly affecting agriculture was negatived by a majority of 212 to 108; but this was brought about only by Lord Londonderry, on the part of the Govern-

<small>129. Measures for the relief of the agricultural classes.</small>

<small>* Mr. Canning at this period expected to proceed immediately to India, as Governor-general, a prospect which was only changed by his being soon after appointed Foreign Secretary.</small>

<small>† Lord John Russell on this occasion brought forward a very curious and important statement in regard to the newspapers published in the three kingdoms in 1782, 1790, and 1821, which clearly indicated the necessity of a concession to the great towns, where their principal readers were to be found. It was as follows:</small>

	1782.	1790.	1821.
England	50	60	135
Scotland	8	27	31
Ireland	3	27	56
London—Daily	9	14	16
" Twice a week	9	7	8
" Weekly	0	11	32
British Islands	0	0	6

<small>—Ann. Reg. 1822, p. 69.</small>

<small>* Prices of Wheat in December of each year, from 1818 to 1822.</small>

	s. d.		s. d.
1818	80 8	1821	49 0
1819	66 3	1822	38 11
1820	51 6	—Tooke On Prices. ii. 393

ment, engaging to introduce some measures for the relief of that interest. On the 15th of the same month his lordship redeemed his pledge, by introducing the measures of relief proposed by Government, which were, the repeal of the annual malt-tax, which produced £1,000,000 a year, and the advance of £1,000,000 in Exchequer bills to the landed proprietors on security of their crops, until the markets improved. In the course of his speech on this subject Lord Londonderry remarked, and satisfactorily proved, that no diminution of taxation to any practicable amount could afford any adequate relief to the agricultural classes; and it was no wonder it was so, for the utmost extent of any such relief, supposing it conceded, could not have amounted to more than six or seven millions yearly, whereas their difficulties arose from a depression in the value of their produce, which could not be estimated at less than sixty or seventy millions.[1]

[1 Ann. Reg. 1822, 98, 101.]

130. Detailed measures of Government for the relief of the agriculturists.

Lord Londonderry's plan was laid before Parliament, with the report of the committee on agricultural distress, which had been agreed to early in the session without opposition, and was replete with valuable information and suggestions.* The leading resolutions proposed were, that whenever the average price of wheat shall be under 60s. a quarter, Government shall be authorized to issue £1,000,000 on Exchequer bills to the landed proprietors on the security of their crops; that importation of foreign corn should be permitted whenever the price of wheat shall be at and above 70s. a quarter; rye, peas or beans, 46s.; barley, 35s., and oats, 25s.: that a sliding-scale should be fixed, that for wheat being under 80s. a quarter, 12s.; above 80s. but under 85s., 5s.; and above 85s., only 1s. Greatly lower duties were proposed for colonial grain, with the wise design of promoting the cultivation and securing the fidelity of their dependencies. They were as follows: For colonial grain—wheat at and above 59s., rye, &c., 39s., barley 36s., and oats 20s.; subject to certain moderate rates of duty. Mr. Huskisson and Mr. Ricardo proposed other resolutions, which were, however, negatived; and Lord Londonderry's resolutions, with the exception of the first, regarding the Exchequer bills, which was withdrawn,[2] were agreed to by large majorities in both Houses, and passed into law.

[2 Ann. Reg. 1822, 98, 107.]

The great debate of the session, however, came on on 11th June, when Mr. Western moved for the appointment of a committee to consider the effect of the act 59 Geo. III., c. 14 (the Bank Cash-Payments Bill), on the agriculture, commerce, and manufactures of the United Kingdom. The motion was negatived, after a long debate, by a majority of 194 to 30. This debate was remarkable for one circumstance—Lord Londonderry spoke against the motion, with the whole Ministers, and Mr. Brougham in support of it. It led, as all motions on the same subject have since done, to no practical result, as the House of Commons has constantly refused to entertain any change in the monetary policy adopted in 1819; but it is well worthy of remembrance, for it elicited two speeches, one from Mr. Huskisson in support of that system, and one from Mr. Attwood against it, both of which are models of clear and forcible reasoning, and which contain all that ever has or ever can be said on that all important subject.[1]

131. Motion of Mr. Western on the currency. June 11.

[1 Ann. Reg. 1822, 108, 121; Parl. Deb. vii. 678, 1027.]

Mr. Huskisson argued—"The change of prices which has undoubtedly taken place is only in a very slight degree to be ascribed to the resumption of cash payments. To that measure we were in duty bound, as well as policy, for all contracts had been made under it. Even if it had been advisable not to revert to a sound currency, the irrevocable step has been taken, and the widest mischief would ensue from any attempt to undo what has been done. It is said on the other side, that it would be for the benefit of all classes that the value of money should be gradually diminished, and that of all other articles raised. What is this but the system of Law the projector, of Lowndes, and of many others? But it is one to which, it is to be hoped, this country will never lend its sanction. It is, in truth, the doctrine of debtors; and still more of those who, already being debtors, are desirous of becoming so in a still greater degree.

132. Mr. Huskisson's arguments in support of the existing system.

"The foundation of the plan on the other side is, that the standard of value in every country should be that which is the staple article of the food of its inhabitants; and therefore wheat is fixed upon, as it is the staple article of the food of our people. At that rate, potatoes should be the standard in Ireland, rice in India, maize in Italy. To what endless confusion in the intercourse of nations would this lead! Who ever heard of a potato standard? It does not, in the slightest degree, obviate the objection, that you propose to make the currency not of wheat, but of gold, as measured by that standard. How can a given weight of gold, of a certain fineness, and a certain denomination, which in this country is now the common measure of all commodities, be itself liable to be varied in weight, fineness, or denomination, according to the exchangeable value of any other commodity, without taking from gold the quality of being money, and transferring it to that other commodity? All that you do is, in fact,

133. Continued.

---

* The committee reported that the prices of wheat for six weeks preceding 1st April, 1822, the date of their report, had been—

	s.	d.
March 16	45	11
" 9	46	10
" 2	46	11
Feb. 23	47	7
Highest price in 1822	50	7

"And that the quantity sold, both of wheat and oats, between 1st November and 1st March has, under these prices, very considerably exceeded any quantity sold in the preceding twenty years. That it is impossible to carry protection further than monopoly, and this monopoly the British grower has possessed for more than three years, which is ever since February, 1819, with the exception of the ill-timed and unnecessary importation of somewhat more than 700,000 quarters of oats, which took place during the summer of 1820. It must be considered further, that this protection, in consequence of the increased value of our currency, and the present state of the corn market, combined with the prospect of an early harvest, may in all probability remain uninterrupted for a very considerable time to come."—Commons' Report on Agriculture, 1st April, 1822; Annual Register, 1822, p. 438, 441.

to make wheat the currency, and gold its representative, as paper now is of gold. But to say that one commodity shall be the currency, and another its standard, betrays a confusion of ideas, and is, in fact, little short of a contradiction in terms.

"Again, it is said we ought to measure the pressure of taxation by the price of corn; and we are reminded that, as in 1813, wheat was at 108s. 7d., and the taxes £74,674,000, 13,733,000 quarters of wheat were sufficient for their payment; while in the present year, the price being 45s., nearly double that amount of quarters are necessary to pay the reduced taxes of £54,000,000. But observe to what this system of measuring the weight of taxes by the price of wheat, or any other article save gold itself, would lead. The year 1817 was a prosperous year, for the taxes were reduced to £55,836,000, and wheat having risen to 94s. 9d., it follows that 11,786,000 quarters were sufficient for the payment of its taxes. Was this actually the case? If distress, bordering upon famine—if misery, bursting forth in insurrection, and all the other symptoms of wretchedness, discontent, and difficulty, are to be taken as symptoms of pressure upon the people, then is the year 1817 a year which no good man would ever wish to see the like again. On the other hand, the years 1815 and 1821, being the years of the severest pressure of taxation, according to this new mode of measuring its amount, are among the years when the laboring parts of the community have had least reason to complain of their situation.

134. Continued.

"The proposition now boldly made is for a depreciation of the standard of the currency. How strange must be the condition of this country, if it can only prosper by a violation of national faith, and a subversion of private property; by a measure reprobated by all statesmen and all historians; the wretched and antiquated resource of barbarous ignorance and arbitrary power, and only known among civilized communities as the last mark of a nation's weakness and degradation! Would not such a measure be a death-blow to all public credit, and to all confidence in private dealings between man! If you once, in an age of intelligence and enlightenment, consent, under the pressure of temporary difficulty, to lower the standard, it will become a precedent which will immediately be resorted to on every future emergency or temporary pressure, the more readily as credit, and every other more valuable resource, on which the country has hitherto relied, will be at an end. If the House entertain such a proposition by vote, the country will be in alarm and confusion from one end of it to another. All pecuniary transactions will be at an end; all debtors called on for immediate payment; all holders of paper will instantly insist for coin; all holders of gold and silver be converted into hoarders! Neither the Bank, nor the London bankers, nor the country bankers, could survive the shock! What a scene of strife, insolvency, stagnation of business, individual misery, and general disorder, would ensue! All this would precede the passing of the proposed bill; what would it be after it had become a law?"[1]

135. Concluded.

[1] Parl. Deb. vii. 878, 823.

"The fall of prices," said Mr. Attwood in reply, "has not been confined to any one article, nor has it been of passing nature, as all are which arise from over-production or a glut in the market. It has been uniform and progressive since the monetary act of 1819 was passed, embracing all commodities, extending over all periods. Who ever heard of a fall in prices, arising from over-production, enduring for three years? It is invariably terminated in six or eight months, by the production being lessened. In the present instance all the leading articles of commerce have undergone a similar reduction, and in all it has continued without abatement during that long period. Wheat, which in the year 1818 was 84s., is now selling at 47s., showing a reduction of 37s., or 45 per cent. Iron, in 1818, was £13 the ton; it is now £8, being a fall of 40 per cent. Cotton, in 1818, was 1s. the pound; it is now 6d., being a fall of 50 per cent. Wool, which in 1818 was selling at 2s. 1d., now sells for 1s. 1d., being a reduction of 50 per cent. These are the great articles of commerce, and the average of the fall upon them is 45 per cent., being exactly the reduction on the price of grain. This is recommended to the consideration of those who tell us of over-production and an excessive cultivation of corn-land. Mr. Tooke has compiled a table exhibiting the fall between May 1818 and May 1822, and the fall is the same in all the articles, with the exception of indigo. The fall, therefore, is not peculiar to agriculture; it is universal, and has embraced every article of industry, every branch of commerce. How trade or production could by possibility be carried on with a profit, while a fall of such magnitude was going forward, it is for the supporters of the opposite system to explain.

136. Reply by Mr. Attwood.

"This fall of prices must have been produced by one of two causes: either the quantity of all commodities has increased, or the quantity of all money has diminished. One of these must of necessity have occurred, for the proportion is altered. Are we to believe that great changes have suddenly taken place in the productive powers of nature, or the resources of art, so as to account for this sudden and universal fall of prices? Is it likely that production in all branches of industry, agricultural and manufacturing, would go on for three years constantly increasing in the face of a constantly diminishing price? The thing is evidently out of the question. It is the quantity of money that must have been reduced. That this has really been the case is sufficiently proved by authentic documents, which show distinctly where the deficiency is to be found.

137. Continued.

"The circulation of the country rests entirely upon that of the Bank of England; and its notes in circulation, immediately preceding the Act of 1819, and the fall of prices, were, at an average, from twenty-nine to thirty millions. That was the amount in circulation for the last half of 1817 and first of 1818. If we take the circulation in the middle of each quarter, which Mr. Harman states is the fairest mode of striking the average, it will appear that the diminution of the circulation has been nearly a third. Nothing can be more regular, gradual, and uni-

138. Continued.

form than the contraction of the currency immediately preceding and accompanying the great reduction in the rate of prices.* It was altogether a forced and systematic contraction. It did not take place in consequence of the fall of prices; it preceded it. It worked silently but incessingly through every branch of industry, till it had reduced them all to the same miserably low level. It was not effected by means of any lessened demand for bank-notes; on the contrary, it took place in the midst of a constantly increasing demand for them, when population was rapidly augmenting, general peace prevailed, and the growing commerce and transactions of men were daily rendering more necessary an enlargement of the circulating medium by which they were to be carried on. The requisitions made to the Bank by the mercantile community were less at the time of its greatest circulation, in the last half of 1817, than they had been at any subsequent period when the circulation has been so fearfully contracted. The Bank is now under greater advances to merchants with a circulation of only £23,000,000 than it was when its circulation was £30,000,000. The reduction in the circulation, therefore, has taken place in consequence of no decline in the demands of the mercantile community, but solely and entirely from the forced but yet regular and persevering measures of the Bank directors to reduce its circulation, first in preparation for, and next in consequence of, the Cash Payments Bill of 1819.

139. Continued.
"The reduction of prices has been in a much greater proportion than the contraction of the currency. The bank-notes have been diminished by about a fourth, but prices of every article have fallen a *half*. This is a very important fact, for it indicates how powerfully—much more so than could have been expected—a reduction in the amount of the currency affects prices, and through them the resources of all the producing classes in the community. The same is observable in regard to grain, or meat, or any other article in universal and daily use: a failure of the crop to the extent of a fourth or fifth doubles prices, and often more. It is not difficult to discover the cause of this anomaly. The bank-notes do work far beyond their amount in value: they conduct and turn over the whole transactions of the country. The payment of taxes and dividends, and all the innumerable transactions between man and man, are done by their means. A diminution of their number, by lessening credit and the means of purchase or speculation over the whole community, affects prices far more extensively than the nominal amount of this diminution, for it affects the power of buying among all the persons through whose hands the notes pass in their circulation through the community.

140. Continued.
"In addition to this, there are a great many payments which do not fall with a diminution on the circulating medium of the community. The great and burdensome charges of the nation remain the same, however much the currency may be contracted and prices fall. The taxes, the interest of mortgages and bonds, jointures to widows, provisions to children, poor-rates, life insurances, and the like, undergo no diminution. Nay, there are several articles of consumption, as salt, tea, malt, sugar, and some others of equal importance, in which the tax bears so great a proportion to the price of the article, that its price can not fall in any perceptible degree from a diminution in the demand. These heavy fixed burdens, and extensive articles of consumption, require the same amount of bank-notes for their discharge or payment under a reduced as amidst a plentiful circulation. Thus the whole effects of the reduction in the circulating medium are run into, and act upon, the sale of those articles of commerce in which a reduction of price is practicable; and as they are not half the entire expenditure of the nation, the effect upon them is proportionally greater. It is like a man with a fixed income, say £1000 a year, who is burdened with fixed payments to the extent of £600, being deprived of one-half of the remainder, or £200. Though that reduction is only of *a fifth* of his entire income, it will draw after it a reduction of that part of his expenditure over which he has a control to the extent of *a half*; and if he does not draw in to that amount, he will very soon become bankrupt.

141. Continued.
"The repayment of the Bank advances by Government has been the measure on which this reduction in the quantity of money, and the consequent increase in its value, was founded. Since 1817, no less than £15,000,000 has been repaid to the Bank by Government. When the Bank got these repayments they did not reissue them again, as they had been accustomed to do in former days, but they retained them in their coffers, and thereby withdrew them from circulation. These proceedings have produced a regular progressive reduction of prices, irrespective altogether of any excess in the production. If the Bank were to advance again this £15,000,000, or any considerable part of it, to Government, and were enabled to do so by the necessary alteration in the Act of 1819, the effect would be an immediate return to the scale of prices which existed in 1818 and during the war.

142. Concluded.
"Such is the evil under which we are now laboring, and which will suffer no abatement so long as the causes which produced it continue in operation. We have been occupied with changes in our pecuniary system, and it is precisely since they

---

* AMOUNT IN CIRCULATION OF ALL NOTES.

August 16, 1817	£30,100,000
November 13	29,400,000
February, 1818	28,700,000
May, 1818	28,000,000
August, 1818	26,600,000
November, 1818	26,000,000
February, 1819	25,600,000
May, 1819	23,900,000
August, 1819	26,000,000
November, 1819	24,600,000
February, 1820	24,000,000
May, 1820	23,900,000
August, 1820	24,400,000
November, 1820	23,400,000

Amount of £5 Notes and upward.

November, 1817	£19,600,000
November, 1818	16,900,000
November, 1819	15,100,000
November, 1820	15,300,000
November, 1821	14,800,000
May 1822	14,600,000

were commenced that our difficulties have been experienced. To enhance the value of money, to raise the price of gold, we have lowered that of all other commodities, while at the same time we have left the great payments of the nation raised from the sale of these commodities! Strange, indeed, would it be if such a system was not to have produced the general and long-continued distress which we see around us. The reduction effected in the amount of money in circulation has been nearly one-half of that employed in supporting agricultural, commercial, and manufacturing industry. Hence these classes are unable to obtain much more than half the return they obtained for their industry before the alteration took place, and yet all their great money engagements remain the same! This is the origin of that state of things which in its result leaves the land-owner without rent, the merchant without profit, the laborer without employment or wages, which revolutionizes property, and disorganizes all the different relations and interests of society."[1]

[1 Parl. Deb. vii. 898, 925, 906, 1007.]

143. Repeated defeats of Ministers in the House of Common

Dr. Arnold said that Sir Robert Peel "would yield to pressure on every thing *except the currency.*" It is not surprising it was so; for determination to adhere on that one point necessarily drew after it concession on every other. The distress produced by the general fall of all prices 50 per cent. had become such among the producing classes, that no combination of the leaders of the opposite parties, and no efforts on the part of Ministers, were able any longer to avert its effects. It was in the loud and fierce demand for a reduction of taxation that the public voice, in the House of Commons, first made itself heard in an unmistakable manner. Several ominous divisions, presaging total defeat in the event of any further resistance to the demands of the country in this particular, took place in the early period of the session. A motion by Mr. Calcraft, for the progressive diminution of the salt-tax, by taking off a third in each of the next three years, was only thrown out by a majority of *four*, the numbers being 169 to 165. This near approach to a defeat was the more remarkable, that Lord Londonderry and the Chancellor of the Exchequer had loudly declared that this tax was essential to the maintenance of the Sinking Fund, and that its repeal would be the signal for the entire abandonment of that fund. This doubtful conflict was soon followed by decided defeats. On the very next day, on a motion made by Sir John Osborne, for a reduction of two of the junior lords of the Admiralty, Ministers were left in a minority of 54, the numbers being 182 to 128. This was soon after followed by another defeat, on the motion of Lord Normanby for the reduction of one of the two joint Postmasters-general, which was only thrown out by a majority of 25, the numbers being 184 to 159. The same motion, put in a different form, was, in a subsequent period of the session, carried against Ministers by a majority of 15, the numbers being 216 to 201.[2]

Feb. 28.
March 1.
March 13.

[2 Parl. Deb. vi. 861, 881, 1111, vii. 312; Ann. Reg. 1822, 145.]

These disasters were sufficient to convince Ministers that, however ignorant they might be of the real source of their difficulties, and however tenacious they might be of the monetary bill of 1819, the distresses of the country had become such that relief, in some form or another, was indispensable; and that, if they would not give it in the form of measures calculated to raise the remuneration of industry, they *must* give it in the form of a reduction of its burdens. The effect of the shake they had received soon appeared in the financial measures which, in a subsequent period of the session, they brought forward. Although, in February, Lord Londonderry had declared that the retention of the salt-tax was indispensable to the upholding of the Sinking Fund to the level of £5,000,000, which the House had solemnly pledged itself, in 1819, to maintain inviolate, he was yet compelled to bring forward, on 24th May, a motion for its reduction from 15s. a bushel to 2s., which occasioned a loss to the revenue of £1,300,000 a year. This was followed by a reduction of the war-tax on leather, which occasioned a further loss of £600,000 a year. The tonnage-duty and Irish hearth-tax were also abandoned, which produced between them £400,000 yearly. These great reductions, amounting, with the annual malt-tax, which brought in £1,500,000 a year, and which Government had announced their intention of abandoning at an early period of the session, amounted together to £3,500,000 a year, being half a million more than the amount of the new taxes, imposed in 1819, to keep up the Sinking Fund to £5,000,000 yearly.[1] There can be no doubt that the taxes thus removed were judiciously selected, as they were those which bore most heavily on the laboring classes of the community; and still less that their distress had become such as to render a considerable reduction of the taxes pressing on them indispensable; for, measured in quarters of wheat, their true standard, the poor-rates of England were now *twice* as heavy as they had been in 1812.* But the necessity of removing these taxes, and thereby abandoning the very foundation of the Sinking Fund, afforded the most decisive evidence both how wide-spread the distress had become, and how entire a revolution it had already induced in the financial system and policy of the country.[2]

144. Great reductions of taxation introduced by Ministers.

May 24.

[1 Ante, c. iv. 81.]

[2 An. Reg. 1822, 147; Parl. Deb. vii. 148; Hughes, vi. 407, 1413; 496.]

145. The budget.

The budget was brought forward on the 1st July, and its leading feature was the reduction of the Sinking Fund from £13,000,000 to £7,500,000, by appropriating £5,500,000 to the current service of the year. This signal and calamitous departure from the form even of our former policy, in this vital particular, was sought to be justified by the Chancellor of the Exchequer on various grounds; but it was evident that it was im-

---

* POOR-RATES PAID IN MONEY AND QUARTERS OF WHEAT.

Year.		Quarters of wheat.
1811	£6,656,105	1,440,445
1814	5,418,846	1,792,255
1821	6,959,249	2,557,763
1822	6,358,702	2,910,440

—Hughes, vi. 495; Alison's *Europe*, chap. cvi., Appendix.

posed upon him by sheer necessity, and was a direct abandonment of the solemn resolution to maintain a real surplus of £5,000,000 over the expenditure, which Parliament had unanimously adopted only three years before; for, as the nominal Sinking Fund was reduced to half its former amount, it was plain that the real redemption of debt was virtually abandoned. The expenditure of the present year, however, as the great reduction of taxation made in the course of it had not taken effect, was nearly £5,000,000 below the income, leaving that sum applicable to the diminution of debt—a striking and melancholy proof of what the resources of the country really were at this period, had the ruinous contraction of the currency not imposed upon the present and all future governments the necessity of remitting the indirect taxes, by which alone the Sinking Fund could be maintained. It is not surprising it was so. A hundred millions a year is not cut off from the remuneration of productive labor, in a country the source from which its entire wealth must be drawn, without producing lasting effects upon its financial situation and ultimate destiny.[1]

[1] An. Reg. 1822, 149, 151; Parl. Deb. vii. 1414, 1434.

146. Reduction of the 5 per cents.

Two measures, the one of the most unquestionable, the other of very doubtful wisdom, were brought forward during this session of Parliament, and carried into effect. The first of these was the reduction of the navy 5 per cents. to 4 per cent. About £156,000,000 stood in this species of stock; consequently, any reduction in the interest payable on it was a very great relief to the national finances. The condition proposed to the holders was, that for every £100 of their existing stock they should be inscribed for £105 in a new stock bearing 4 per cent. interest. Those who signified their dissent before 1st March, 1823, were to be paid off. So high were the Funds, however, that those who took advantage of this were only 1373, and the stock they held amounted to £2,605,978—not a fiftieth part of the entire stock; so that the measure was carried into execution with the most complete success. The entire saving to the nation, including that effected by a similar saving on the Irish 5 per cents, was no less than £1,230,000 a year—a very great sum, and which affords the clearest proof of the justice of the observations made in a former work,* as to the impolicy of the system which Mr. Pitt so long pursued, of borrowing the greater part of the public debt in the 3 instead of the 5 per cents.; for if the whole debt had been borrowed in the latter form, the reduction effected in the annual interest this year would not have been £1,200,000, but above £6,000,000 sterling.[1]

[1] An. Reg. 1822, 127, 129; Parl. Deb. vi. 666, 679.

147. Equalization of the Dead Weight, and military and naval pensions.

The next great financial measure of the session, upon which a more doubtful meed of praise must be bestowed, was that, as it was commonly called, for the equalization of the *Dead Weight*. This was a measure by which the burden of the naval and military pensions, most justly bestowed upon our gallant defenders during the late war, was equalized for more than a generation to come, by being spread, at an equal amount, over the present and the future. This burden amounted to nearly £5,000,000 a year; and although, as the annuitants expired, its amount would diminish, and at the end of forty or fifty years would be a mere trifle, yet that prospect proved but a poor resource to the present necessities of a needy Chancellor of the Exchequer. In these circumstances, when the difficulties of Government to make head against present exigencies were so great, the expedient was thought of, of granting a fixed annuity, for forty-five years *certain*, to parliamentary commissioners, who, in consideration of that, were to undertake the burden of the varying existing annuities. The effect of this, of course, was to diminish in a great degree the burden in the outset, and proportionally augment it in the end.[2]

[2] An. Reg. 1822, 128, 137.

148. Details of the measure.

Government in the first instance received £4,900,000 from the commissioners, and paid out only £2,800,000, thereby effecting a present saving of £2,100,000. But this was gained by authorizing the commissioners to sell as much of the fixed sum of £2,800,000 a year, which was directed to be paid to them out of the Consolidated Fund, as might be necessary to enable them to meet the excess of present payments over the income received; and of course it had the effect of rendering the dead weight as much heavier than it otherwise would have been at the close of the period, as it had been lightened at its commencement. This project received the sanction of both branches of the legislature, as did a supplementary measure throwing the burden of superannuated allowances on the holders of offices under Government, by stopping off their salaries a sum adequate to insuring for its amount, which effected a saving of £370,000 a year. These two measures effected a reduction of present expenses to the amount of nearly £2,500,000 a year, but, like the reduction of

* INCOME AND EXPENDITURE OF THE YEAR 1822.
INCOME—Nett.

Customs	£12,923,420
Excise	28,976,344
Stamps	6,880,494
Taxes	7,517,643
Post-Office	2,049,326
Lesser Payments	1,451,341
Total Taxes	£59,798,568
Loans‡	11,872,155
Grand Total	£71,670,724

EXPENDITURE.

Charges of Collection	£5,688,691
Interest on Funded Debt	29,400,897
Interest on Unfunded Debt	1,430,596
Naval and Military Pensions	1,400,000
Civil List and Expenses	1,057,000
Army	7,608,973
Navy	4,915,642
Navy Pensioners	246,000
Ordnance	1,007,821
Miscellaneous	2,105,797
Lesser Payments	529,961
Surplus applicable to Debt	4,915,529
Grand Total	£60,102,711

—Parliamentary Paper in *Annual Register*, 1823, p. 215-217.

‡ The loans to discharge Exchequer Bills.

* Vide *History of Europe*, chap. xii. § 62. The difference of the interest paid in the 3 and the 5 per cents., seldom exceeded a *quarter* per cent.—Ibid. chap. xii. § 64, note.

the 5 per cents, by increasing the burden of the nation in future times; for the first, at this moment, is adding above £1,500,000 to the annual charges of the nation above what it otherwise would have been, and the last has added seven millions by the 5 per cent. bonus given to the holders of stock to the amount of the national debt.[1]

<small>1 An. Reg. 1822, 136, 149; Parl. Deb. vi. 751, 783, vii. 739, 759.</small>

<small>149. Important Small Notes Bill.</small>
Amidst so many measures which attracted general attention, and had become indispensable, from the necessitous state of the public exchequer, one of the greatest importance was quietly introduced into the legislature. Ministers had not the manliness to confess they had been wrong in the course they had adopted in regard to the bill compelling cash payments in 1819, or perhaps they were aware that the influence of the moneyed interest in the House of Commons was too strong to render it possible for them openly and avowedly to recede from that system. But they did so almost secretly, perhaps unconsciously, in the most effective way. Lord Londonderry alone had the sagacity to perceive, and the courage to avow, the real nature of the measure introduced, and the evils it was intended to obviate. "He did not treat it," said Sir JAMES GRAHAM, a statesman subsequently well known, "as a question of fluctuation of prices, of want of means of consumption, or of superabundant harvests. The noble marquis (Londonderry) said plainly and directly, 'This is a question of currency: *the currency of the country is too contracted for its wants, and our business is to apply a remedy.*'"[2]

<small>2 Sir James Graham on June 3, 1828, Parl. Deb.; and Tooke On Prices, ii. 127, 128.</small>

<small>150. Its provisions.</small>
The remedy applied was most effectual, and entirely successful, so far as the evils meant to be remedied were concerned. By the Act of 1819 it had been provided that the issuing of small notes by the Bank of England or country banks should cease on 1st May, 1823, and it was the necessity of providing against this contingency which was one great cause of the contraction of the currency. On 2d July, however, Lord Londonderry introduced a bill permitting the issue of £1 notes to continue for *ten years longer*, and declared the £1 notes of the Bank of England a legal tender every where except at the Bank of England. This, coupled with the grant of £1,000,000 Exchequer bills, which Government were authorized to issue in aid of the agricultural interest, had a surprising effect in restoring confidence and raising prices; and by doing so, it repealed, so long as it continued in operation, the most injurious parts of the Act of 1819. It will appear in a subsequent chapter how vast was the effect of this measure, what a flood of temporary prosperity it spread over the country, and in what a dismal catastrophe, from the necessity of paying all the notes at the Bank itself in gold, it ultimately terminated. Yet so ignorant were the legislature of the effects of this vital measure, and so little attention did it excite, that the second reading of it was carried in a house of forty-seven members only in the Commons; and while so many hundred pages of *Hansard* are occupied with debates on reduction of expenditure and similar topics, which at the utmost could only save the nation a few hundred thousands a year, this measure, which restored at least eighty millions a year to the remuneration of industry in the country, does not in all occupy two pages, and can only be discovered by the most careful examination in our parliamentary proceedings.[1]

<small>1 Part. Deb. vii. 1454, 1662; Stat. 3 Geo. IV., c. 172.</small>

<small>151. Six acts relating to commerce and navigation.</small>
Six very important acts were passed this session of Parliament at the instance of Mr. Wallace, the President of the Board of Trade, for removing the shackles which fettered the trade and navigation of the country, and improving their facilities. These acts opened a new era in our commercial legislation —the era of unrestricted competition and free trade in shipping. As such they are highly deserving of attention; but their provisions will come with more propriety to be considered in a subsequent chapter, when taken in connection with the RECIPROCITY SYSTEM in maritime affairs, then introduced by Mr. Huskisson. At present, it is sufficient to observe the date of the commencement of the new system being the same with that of so many other changes in our social system and commercial policy, and when the general cheapening of articles of all sorts had rendered a general reduction of all the charges, entering into however remotely soever into their composition, a matter of absolute necessity.[2]

<small>2 An. Reg. 1822, 123, 127.</small>

<small>152. Visit of the king to Edinburgh. Aug. 15.</small>
Parliament rose on the 6th August, and the king proceeded shortly after on a visit to Edinburgh, which he had never yet seen. He embarked with a splendid court at Greenwich on board the Royal George yacht on the 10th August, and arrived in Leith Roads in the afternoon of the 15th. No sovereign had landed there since Queen Mary arrived nearly three hundred years before. The preparations for his Majesty's reception, under the direction of Sir Walter Scott, were of the most magnificent description, and the loyal spirit of the inhabitants of Scotland rendered it interesting in the highest degree. The heart-burnings and divisions of recent times were forgotten; the Queen's trial was no more thought of; the Radicals were silent. The ancient and inextinguishable loyalty of the Scotch broke forth with unexampled ardor; the devoted attachment they had shown to the Stuarts appeared, but it was now transferred to the reigning family. The clans from all parts of the Highlands appeared in their picturesque and varied costumes, with their chieftains at their head; the eagle's feather, their well-known badge, was seen surmounting many plumes; two hundred thousand strangers from all parts of the country crowded the streets of Edinburgh, and for a brief period gave it the appearance of a splendid metropolis.[3]

<small>3 An. Reg. 1822, 179, 180; Personal observation.</small>

<small>153. Particulars of the royal visit.</small>
The entry of the Sovereign into the ancient city of his ancestors was extremely striking. The heights of the Calton Hill, and the cliffs of Salisbury Crags, which overhang the city, were lined with cannon, and ornamented with standards; and from these batteries, as well as

the guns of the Castle, and the ships in the roads, and Leith Fort, a royal salute was fired as the monarch touched the shore. The procession passed through an innumerable crowd of spectators, who loudly and enthusiastically cheered, up Leith Walk, and by York Place, St. Andrew Square, and Waterloo Place, to Holyrood House, where a levée and drawing-room were held a few days after. On the night following, the city was illuminated, and the guns of the Castle, firing at ten at night, realized the sublimity without the terrors of actual warfare. At a magnificent banquet given to the Sovereign by the magistrates of Edinburgh in the Parliament House, at which the Lord Provost acted as chairman, and Sir Walter Scott as vice-chairman, the former was made a baronet, with that grace of manner and felicity of expression for which the King was so justly celebrated. A review on Portobello sands exhibited the gratifying spectacle of 3000 yeomanry cavalry, collected from all the southern counties of Scotland, marching in procession before their Sovereign. Finally, the King, who during his residence in Scotland had been magnificently entertained at Dalkeith Palace, the seat of the Duke of Buccleuch, embarked on the 27th at Hopetoun House, the beautiful residence of the Earls of Hopetoun, where he conferred the honor of knighthood on Henry Raeburn, the celebrated Scottish artist, and arrived in safety in the Thames on the 30th, charmed with the reception he had met with, and having left on all an indelible impression of the mingled dignity and grace of his manners, and felicity of his expressions.[1]

¹ An. Reg. 1822, 179, 180; Personal observation.

151. Death of Lord Londonderry. Aug. 12.
His return was accelerated by a tragical event, which deprived England of one of her greatest statesmen, and the intelligence of which arrived amidst these scenes of festivity and rejoicing. Lord Londonderry, upon whose shoulders, since the retirement of Lord Sidmouth, the principal weight of government, as well as the entire labor of the lead in the House of Commons, had fallen, had suffered severely from the fatigues of the preceding session, and shortly after exhibited symptoms of mental aberration. He was visited in consequence by his physician, Dr. Bankhead, at his mansion at North Cray in Kent, by whom he was cupped. Some relief was experienced from this, but he continued in bed, and the mental disorder was unabated. It was no wonder it was so: Romilly and Whitbread had, in like manner, fallen victims to similar pressure on the brain, arising from political effort. On the morning of the 12th August, Dr. Bankhead, who slept in the house, being summoned to attend his lordship in his dressing-room, entered just in time to save him from falling. He said, "Bankhead, let me fall on your arms—'tis all over," and instantly expired. He had cut his throat with a penknife. The coroner's inquest brought in a verdict of insanity. His remains were interred on the 20th in Westminster Abbey, between the graves of Pitt and Fox. The most decisive testimony to his merits was borne by some savage miscreants, who raised a horrid shout as the body was borne from the hearse to its last resting-place in the venerable pile; a shout which, to the disgrace of English literature, has since been re-echoed by some whose talents might have led them to a more generous appreciation of a political antagonist, and their sex to a milder view of the most fearful of human infirmities.[1]*

¹ Ann. Reg. 1822, 180; 182; Martineau, i. 287; Hughes, vi. 502.

Chateaubriand has said, that while all other contemporary reputations are declining, that of Mr. Pitt is hourly on the increase. The same is equally true of Lord Londonderry; the same ever has, and ever will be, true of the first and greatest of the human race. Their fame with posterity is founded on the very circumstances which, with the majority of their contemporaries, constituted their unpopularity; they are revered, because they had wisdom to discern the ruinous tendency of the passions with which they were surrounded, and courage to resist them. The reputation of the demagogue is brilliant, but fleeting, like the meteor which shoots athwart the troubled sky of a wintery night; that of the undaunted statesman, at first obscured, but in the end lasting like the fixed stars, which, when the clouds roll away, shine forever the same in the highest firmament. Intrepidity in the rulers of men is the surest passport to immortality, for it is the quality which most fascinates the minds of men. All admire, because few can imitate it.

155. His character.

> "Justum et tenacem propositi virum
> Non civium ardor prava jubentium,
> Non voltus instantis tyranni
> Mente quatit solida neque Auster,
> Dux inquieti turbidus Hadriæ,
> Nec fulminantis magna manus Jovis:
> Si fractus illabatur orbis,
> Impavidum ferient ruinæ."

Never was there a human being to whom these noble lines were more applicable than to Lord Londonderry. His whole life was a continual struggle with the majority in his own or foreign lands; he combated to subdue and to bless them. He began his career by strenuous efforts to effect the Irish Union, and rescue his native country from the incapable legislature by which its energies had so long been repressed. His mature strength was exerted in a long and desperate conflict with the despotism of revolutionary France, which his firmness, as much as the arm of Wellington, brought to a triumphant issue; his latter days in a ceaseless conflict with the revolutionary spirit in his own country, and an anxious effort to uphold the dignity of Great Britain, and the independence of lesser states abroad. The un-

156. Its indomitable firmness.

* "The news of Lord Londonderry's death struck the despots of Europe aghast upon their thrones—news which was hailed with clasped hands and glistening eyes by aliens in many a provincial town of England, and with imprudent shouts by conclaves of patriots abroad. There are some now, who in mature years can not remember without emotion what they saw and heard that day. They could not know how the calamity of one man—a man amiable, winning, and generous in the walk of daily life—could penetrate the recesses of a world but as a ray of hope in the midst of thickest darkness. This man was the screw by which England had riveted the chains of nations. The screw was drawn, and the immovable despotism might now be overthrown. There was abundant reason for the rejoicing which spread through the world on the death of Lord Londonderry, and the shout which rang through the Abbey when his coffin was taken from the hearse was natural enough, though neither decent nor humane."—Miss Martineau, i. 287, 288.

compromising antagonist of Radicalism at home, he was at the same time the resolute opponent of despotism abroad. If Poland retained, after the overthrow of Napoleon, any remnant of nationality, it was owing to his persevering and almost unaided efforts; and at the very time when the savage wretches who raised a shout at his funeral were rejoicing in his death, he had been preparing to assert at Verona, as he had done to the Congresses of Laybach and Troppau, the independent action of Great Britain, and her non-accordance in the policy of the Continental sovereigns against the efforts of human freedom.

157. His policy in domestic affairs.

His policy in domestic affairs was marked by the same far-seeing wisdom, the same intrepid resistance to the blindness of present clamor. He made the most strenuous efforts to uphold the Sinking Fund, that noble monument of Mr. Pitt's patriotic foresight: had those efforts been successful, the whole national debt would have been paid off by the year 1845, and the nation *forever* have been freed from the payment of thirty millions a year for its interest.* He resisted with a firm hand, and at the expense of present popularity with the multitude, the efforts of faction during the seven trying years which followed the close of the war, and bequeathed the constitution, after a season of peculiar danger, unshaken to his successors. The firm friend of freedom, he was on that very account the resolute opponent of democracy, the insidious enemy which, under the guise of a friend, has in every age blasted its progress, and destroyed its substance. Discerning the principal cause of the distress which had occasioned these convulsions, his last act was one that bequeathed to his country a currency adequate to its necessities, and which he alone of his Cabinet had the honesty to admit was a departure from former error. Elegant and courteous in his manners, with a noble figure and finely-chiseled countenance, he was beloved in his family circle and by all his friends, not less than respected by the wide circle of sovereigns and statesmen with whom he had so worthily upheld the honor and the dignity of England.

158. Political changes in progress, from the resumption of cash payments.

Three years only had elapsed since the great monetary change of 1819 had been carried into effect, and already it had become evident that that was the turning-point of English history, and that an entire alteration would ere long be induced in its external and internal policy. Changes great, decisive, and irremediable, had already occurred, or were in progress. The cutting off of a hundred millions a year from the remuneration of industry, agricultural and manufacturing, while the public and private debts remained the same, had changed the whole relations of society, altered all the views of men. Reduction in expenditure, when so great a chasm had been effected in income, was the universal cry. In 1819, the House of Commons had solemnly resolved that the Sinking Fund should under no circumstances be reduced below £5,000,000 a year, and laid on £3,000,000 of indirect taxes to bring it up to that amount; but already the system was abandoned, taxes to the amount of £3,500,000 had been repealed in a single year, and the doctrine openly promulgated by Government, which has since been so constantly acted upon, that the nation should instantly receive the full benefit of a surplus income in a reduction of taxation, instead of a maintenance of the Sinking Fund. The fierce demand for a reduction of expenditure, which made itself heard in an unmistakable manner even in the unreformed House of Commons, had rendered it indispensable to reduce the land and sea forces of the state to a degree inconsistent with the security of its vast colonial dependencies, and the maintenance of its position as an independent power.

159. Internal changes arising from the same cause.

Changes still more important in their ultimate effects were already taking place in the social position and balance of parties in the state. The distress in Ireland—a purely agricultural state, upon which the fall of 50 per cent. in its produce fell with unmitigated severity—had become such that a change in the system of government in that country had become indispensable; and the altered system of Lord Wellesley presaged, at no distant period, the admission of the Roman Catholics into the legislature, and the attempt to form a harmonious legislature out of the united Celt and Saxon—the conscientious servant of Rome, and the sturdy friend of Protestant England. The wide-spread and deep distress of the manufacturing classes, and the inability of the legislature to afford them any relief, had rendered loud and threatening the demand for reform in those great hives of industry, while the still greater and more irremediable sufferings of the agriculturists had shaken the class hitherto the most firmly attached to existing institutions, and diffused a very general opinion that things could not be worse than they were, and that no alleviation of the evils under which the country labored could be hoped for till the representation of the people was put on a different footing. Lastly, the general necessity of cheapening every thing, to meet the reduced price of produce, had extended itself to freights, and several acts had already passed the legislature which foreshadowed the repeal of the Navigation Laws, and the abandonment of the system under which England had won the sceptre of the seas, and a colonial empire which encircled the earth. The dawn of the whole future of England is to be found in these three years.

160. Lord Londonderry was the last of the real rulers of England.

The Marquis of Londonderry was the last minister in Great Britain of the rulers who really governed the state; that is, of men who took counsel only of their own ideas, and imprinted them on the internal and external policy of their country. Thenceforward statesmen were guided on both sides of the Channel, not by what they deemed right, but what they found practicable; the ruling power was found elsewhere than either in the cabinet or the legislature. Querulous and desponding men, among whom Chateaubriand stands foremost, perceiving this, and comparing the past with the present, concluded that this was because the period of greatness

* Vide *History of Europe*, chap. xli. sect. 21, where this is demonstrated, and the calculation given.

had passed, because the age of giants had been succeeded by that of pigmies; and that men were not directed, because no one able to lead them appeared. But this was a mistake; it was not that the age of great men had ceased, but the age of great causes had succeeded. Public opinion had become irresistible—the press ruled alike the cabinet and the legislature on important questions; where the people were strongly roused, their voice had become omnipotent; on all it gradually but incessantly acted, and in the end modified the opinions of government.

161. Increased ascendant of the rulers of thought.

The *Vox Populi* is not always, at the moment, the *Vox Dei*: it is so only when the period of action has passed, and that of reflection has arisen—when the storms of passion are hushed, and the whisperings of interest no longer heard; but when the still small voice of experience speaks in persuasive tones to future generations of men, it will be shown whether the apparent government of the many is more beneficial in its effects than the real government of a few; but this much is certain, that it is their *apparent* government only. Men seek in vain to escape from the first of human necessities—the necessity of being governed by establishing democratic institutions. They do not change the direction of the many by the few; by the establishment of these they only change the few who direct. The oligarchy of intellect and eloquence comes instead of that of property and influence; happy if it is in reality more wise in its measures and far-seeing in its policy than that which it has supplanted. But it is itself directed by the leaders of thought: the real rulers of men appear in those who direct general opinion; and the responsibility of the philosopher or the orator becomes overwhelming when he shares with it that of the statesman and the sovereign.

162. Simultaneous outbreak of the revolutionary spirit in different countries.

No doubt can remain, upon considering the events in the memorable years 1819 and 1820 in Europe, that they were the result of a concerted plan among the revolutionists in Spain, France, Italy, Germany, and England; and that the general overthrow of governments, which occurred in 1848, had been prepared, and was expected, in 1820. The slightest attention to dates proves this in the most decisive manner. The insurrection of Riego at Cadiz broke out on 1st January, 1820—that at Corunna on 24th February in the same year—the king was constrained to accept the Constitution on 7th March; Kotzebue was murdered in Germany on 21st March; the revolution of Naples took place on 7th March, that of Piedmont on 7th June; the Duke de Berri was assassinated on 13th March; *émeutes* in Paris, which so nearly overturned the Government, broke out on 7th June, the military conspiracy on 19th August; the assassination of the English Cabinet was fixed for 19th February by the Cato Street conspirators;

April 3, 1820.
the insurrection at Glasgow took place on 3d April. So many movements of a revolutionary character, occurring so near each other in point of time, in so many different countries, demonstrates either a simultaneous agency of different bodies acting under one common central authority, or a common sense of the advent of a period in an especial manner favorable to the designs which they all had in contemplation. And when it is recollected that the Chambers of France had, by the operation of the *coups d'état* of 5th September, 1816, and March, 1819, been so thoroughly rendered democratical that the dethronement of the king and establishment of a republic, by vote of the legislature, was with confidence anticipated when the next fifth had been elected for the Chamber of Deputies, and that distress in Great Britain had become so general, by the operation of the monetary law of 1819, that insurrectionary movements were in preparation in all the great manufacturing towns, and had actually broken out in several—it must be confessed, that a more favorable time for such a general outbreak could hardly have been selected.

163. Different characters of the revolts in the different states.

And yet, although these revolutionary movements were obviously made in pursuance of a common design, and for a common purpose, yet the agents in them, and the parties in each state to which their execution was intrusted, were widely different. In Great Britain, they were entirely conducted by the very lowest classes of society; and although they met with apologists and defenders more frequently than might have been expected in the House of Commons, and from a portion of the press, yet no person of respectability or good education was actually implicated in the treasonable proceedings. The *whole* respectable and influential classes were ranged on the other side. But the case was widely different on the Continent. The French revolutionists embraced a large part of the talent, and by far the greater part of the education of the country; and it was their concurrence, as the event afterward proved, which rendered any insurrectionary movement in that country so extremely formidable. In Spain and Portugal, the principal merchants in the seaport towns, the most renowned generals, and almost the whole officers in the army, were engaged on the revolutionary side, and their adhesion to its enemies in the last struggle left the throne without a defense. In Italy, the ardent and generous youth, and nearly the whole educated classes, were deeply imbued with Liberal ideas, and willing to run any hazard to secure their establishment; and nearly the whole youth educated at the German universities had embraced the same sentiments, and longed for the period when the Fatherland was to take its place as the first and greatest of representative governments. Such is the difference between the action of the revolutionary principle upon a constitutional and a despotic monarchy, and such the security which the long enjoyment of freedom affords for the continuance of that blessing to future times.

CHAPTER XI.

ENGLAND, FRANCE, AND SPAIN, FROM THE ACCESSION OF VILLELE IN 1819 TO THE CONGRESS OF VERONA IN 1822.

1. Divergence of France and England in regard to the Spanish Revolution.

FRANCE and England, since the peace of 1815, had pursued separate paths, and their governments had never as yet been brought into collision with each other. Severally occupied with domestic concerns, oppressed with the burdens or striving to heal the wounds of war, their governments were amicable, if not cordially united, and nothing had as yet occurred which threatened to bring them into a state of hostility with each other. But the Spanish revolution ere long had this effect. It was viewed with very different eyes on the opposite sides of the Channel. Justly proud of their own constitution, and dating its completion from the Revolution of 1688, which had expelled the Stuarts from the throne—for the most part ignorant of the physical and political circumstances of the Peninsula, which rendered a similar constitution inapplicable to its inhabitants, and deeply imbued with the prevailing delusion of the day, that forms of government were every thing, and differences of race nothing—the English had hailed the Spanish revolution with generous enthusiasm, and anticipated the entire resurrection of the Peninsula from the convulsion which seemed to have liberated them from their oppressors. These sentiments were entirely shared by the numerous and energetic party in France, which aimed at expelling the Bourbons, and restoring a republican form of government in that country. But for that very reason, opinions diametrically opposite were entertained by the supporters of the monarchy, and all who were desirous to save the country from a repetition of the horrors of the first Revolution. They were unanimously impressed with the belief that revolutionary governments could not be established in Spain and Italy without endangering to the last degree the existing institutions in France; that the contagion of democracy would speedily spread across the Alps and the Pyrenees; and that a numerous and powerful party set upon overturning the existing order of things, already with difficulty held in subjection, would, from the example of success in the neighboring states, speedily become irresistible.

2. Peculiar causes which augmented this divergence.

This divergence of opinion and feeling, coupled with the imminent danger to France from the convulsions in the adjoining kingdoms, and the comparative exemption of Great Britain from it, in consequence of remoteness of situation, and difference of national temperament, must inevitably, under any circumstances, have led to a difference in the policy of the two countries, and seriously endangered their amicable relations. But this danger was much increased in France and England at this period, in consequence of the recent events which had occurred in the Peninsula, and the character of the men who were then placed, by the prevailing feeling in the two countries, at the head of affairs. Spain and Portugal were the theatre of Wellington's triumphs; they had been liberated by the arms of England from the thraldom of Napoleon; they had witnessed the first reverses which led to the overthrow of his empire. The French beheld with envy any movement which threatened to increase an influence from which they had already suffered so much; the English, with jealousy any attempt to interrupt it. In addition to this, the two Ministers of Foreign Affairs on the opposite sides of the Channel, when matters approached a crisis, were of a character and temperament entirely in harmony with the ideas of the prevailing influential majority in their respective countries, and both alike gifted with the genius capable of inflaming, and destitute of the calmness requisite to allay, the ferment of their respective people.

3. Character of Mr. Canning.

GEORGE CANNING, who was the Foreign Minister that was imposed upon the King of England, on Lord Londonderry's death, by the general voice of the nation, rather than selected by his choice, and who took the lead, on the British side, in the great debate with France which ensued regarding the affairs of the Peninsular was one of the most remarkable men that ever rose to the head of affairs in Great Britain. Of respectable but not noble birth, he owed nothing to aristocratic descent, and was indebted for his introduction to Parliament and political life to the friendships which he formed at college, where his brilliant talents, both in the subjects of study and in conversation, early procured for him distinction.*

---

* George Canning was born in London on 11th April, 1770. He was descended from an ancient family, which, in the time of Edward III., had commenced with a mayor of Bristol, and had since been one of the most respected of the county of Warwick. His father, George Canning, the third son of the family, was called to the bar, but being a man of more literary than legal tastes, he never got into practice, and died in 1771 in very needy circumstances, leaving Mrs. Canning, an Irish lady of great beauty and accomplishments, in such destitution that she was obliged for a short time to go on the stage for her subsistence. Young Canning was educated at Eton out of the proceeds of a small Irish estate bequeathed to him by his grandfather, and there his talents and assiduity soon procured for him distinction. He joined there several of his schoolfellows in getting up a literary work, which attained considerable classical eminence, entitled the *Microcosm*. Mr. Canning was its avowed editor, and principal contributor. In 1788, in his eighteenth year, he left Eton, already preceded by his literary reputation, and was entered at Christ Church, Oxford. The continued industry and brilliant parts which he there exhibited gained for him the highest honors, and, what proved of still more importance to him in after-life, the friendship of many eminent men, among whom was Lord Hawkesbury, who afterward became Earl of Liverpool. On leaving Oxford he entered Lincoln's Inn, but rather with the design of strengthening his mind by legal argument than following the law as a profession. He there formed an acquaintance with Mr. Sheridan, which soon ripened into a friendship that continued through life.

oratorical and literary talents such as he possessed till in acquiring distinction at a university, though still greater powers and more profound capacity rarely do attain it. Bacon made no figure at college; Adam Smith was unknown to academic fame; Burke was never heard of at Trinity College, Dublin; Locke was expelled from Cambridge. On the other hand, there has been scarcely a great orator or a distinguished minister in England for a century and a half whose reputation did not precede him from the university into Parliament. The reason is, that there is a natural connection between eminence in scholarship and oratorical power, but not between that faculty and depth of thought; both rest upon the same mental faculties, and can not exist without them. Quickness of perception, retentiveness of memory, a brilliant imagination, fluent diction, self-confidence, presence of mind, are as essential to the debater in Parliament as to the scholar in the university. Both are essentially at variance with the solitary meditation, the deep reflection, the distrust of self, the slow deductions, the laborious investigation, the generalizing turn of mind, which are requisite to the discovery of truth, and are invariably found united in those destined ultimately to be the leaders of opinion. The first set of qualities fit their possessors to be the leaders of senates, the last to be the rulers of thought.

When Mr. Canning first entered Parliament, the native bent of his mind, and the aspirations which naturally arise in the breast of one conscious of great intellectual power and destitute of external advantages, inclined him to the Liberal side. But as its leaders were at that period in opposition, and Mr. Canning did not possess an independent fortune, they generously advised him to join the ranks of Mr. Pitt, then in the midst of his struggle with the French Revolution. He did so, and soon became a favorite *élève* of that great man. It was hard to say whether his poetry in the *Anti-Jacobin*, or his speeches in Parliament, contributed most to aid his cause. Gradually he rose to very high eminence in debate—an eminence which went on

4. His peculiar style of eloquence.

His literary and oratorical distinction was much enhanced by the brilliant appearances he made in several private societies in London, and this led to his introduction into public life. Mr. Pitt, having heard of his talents as a speaker and writer, sent for him, and in a private interview stated to him that, if he approved of the general policy of Government, arrangements would be made to procure him a seat in Parliament. Mr. Canning declared his concurrence in the views of the minister, acting in this respect on the advice of Mr. Sheridan, who dissuaded him from joining the Opposition, which had nothing to offer him. Mr. Canning's previous intimacies had been chiefly with the Whigs; and, like Pitt and Fox, he had hailed the French Revolution at its outset with unqualified hope and enthusiasm. He was returned to Parliament in 1793 for the close borough of Newport, in the Isle of Wight, entering thus, like all the great men of the day, public life through the portals of the nomination boroughs.

His first speech was on the 31st January, 1794, in favor of a loan to the King of Sardinia; and it gave such promises of future talent that he was selected to second the Address. In spring 1796 he was appointed Under-Secretary of State for Foreign Affairs; and on 1st March, 1799, delivered a speech against the slave-trade, which has deservedly obtained a place in his collected speeches. At this time he became the most popular contributor to the *Anti-Jacobin Review*, of which Mr. Gifford was the editor. His pieces are chiefly of the light, sportive, or satirical kind, and contributed to check, by the force of ridicule, the progress of French principles in the country. In 1799 he delivered two brilliant speeches in favor of the union with Ireland, which led to his afterward becoming the warm and consistent advocate of the Catholic claims in Parliament; and in 1801 went out of office with Mr. Pitt. He did not oppose Mr. Addington's administration, but neither did he support it, and wisely discontinued almost entirely his attendance in Parliament during its continuance. In July, 1800, he married Miss Joan Scott, daughter and co-heiress of General Scott, who had made a colossal fortune chiefly at the gaming-table. This auspicious union greatly advanced his prospects. Her fortune, which was very large, made him independent, her society happy, her connections powerful; for her eldest sister had recently before married the Marquis of Titchfield, eldest son of, and who afterward became, Duke of Portland.

In spring 1803, Mr. Canning took a leading part in the series of resolutions condemnatory of the conduct of ministers, which led to the overthrow of Mr. Addington's administration, and on the return of Mr. Pitt to power was appointed Treasurer of the Navy, an office which he held till the death of that great man, in December, 1805. On the accession of the Whigs to office he was of course displaced, and became an active member of that small but indefatigable band of opposition which resisted Mr. Fox's administration. Such was the celebrity which he thus acquired, that when the Tories returned to power, in April, 1807, he was appointed Secretary of State for the Foreign Department, and for the first time became a Cabinet Minister.

In this elevated position he not only took the lead in conducting the foreign affairs of the country, but was the main pillar of administration in resisting the attacks with which it was assailed, particularly on the Orders in Council and the Copenhagen expedition. The breaking out of the Spanish war in May, 1808, and the active part which Great Britain immediately took in that contest, gave him several opportunities for the display of his eloquence in the generous support of Liberal principles and the independence of nations, of which through life he had been the fervent supporter. To the vigor of his counsels in the cabinet, and the influence of his eloquence in the senate, is, in a great degree, to be ascribed the energetic part which England took in that contest, and its ultimately glorious termination. He conducted the able negotiation with the Emperors Alexander and Napoleon, when, after the interview at Erfurth in 1808, they jointly proposed peace to Great Britain; and the complicated diplomatic correspondence with the American government relative to the affair of the Chesapeake, and the many points of controversy concerning maritime rights which had arisen with the people of that country. In all these negotiations his dispatches and state papers were a model of clear, temperate, and accurate reasoning. Subsequent to this he became involved in a quarrel with Lord Castlereagh, arising out of the failure of the Walcheren expedition in 1809, and Mr. Canning's attempts to get him removed from the Ministry, which terminated in a duel, and led to the retirement of both from office at the very time when the dangers of the country most imperatively called for their joint services. He did not, however, on resigning, go into opposition, but continued an independent member of Parliament; and it was after this that he made his celebrated speech in support of the Bullion Report—a speech which displays at once the case with which he could direct his great powers to any new subject, however intricate, and the decided bias which inclined him to Liberal doctrines.

At the dissolution of Parliament, in the close of 1812, Mr. Canning stood for Liverpool, on which occasion he made the most brilliant and interesting speeches of his whole career; for they had less of the fencing common in Parliament, and more of real eloquence in them than his speeches in the House of Commons. In 1814 he was sent into a species of honorable banishment as ambassador at the court of Lisbon, from whence he returned in 1816; and in the beginning of 1817 he was appointed President of the Board of Control on the death of the Earl of Buckinghamshire. In the spring of 1820 he sustained a severe loss by the death of his eldest son George, who expired on the 31st March. Overwhelmed with this calamity, and desirous to be absent during the discussions on the Queen, he took but little part in public affairs during 1821 and 1822, during which years he resided chiefly in France and Italy; but the capacity he evinced as President of the Board of Control, coupled with a secret desire on the part of the Prince Regent to get him removed from the Cabinet, pointed him out as a fit person to be appointed Governor-general of India, which situation he had agreed to accept, and even attended the farewell dinner of the East India directors on his appointment, when the unexpected death of Lord Londonderry, and the general voice of the public on the 20th August, in a manner forced him upon the Government as Foreign Secretary.—*Memoir of Mr. Canning*, i. 29. *Life and Speeches*, vol. i.

continually increasing till he obtained the entire mastery of the House of Commons, and commanded its attention to a degree which neither Mr. Burke, Mr. Pitt, nor Mr. Fox had done. The reason was, that his talents were more completely suited to the peculiar temper and average capacity of that assembly: they neither fell short of it, nor went beyond it. Less philosophical than Burke, less instructive than Pitt, less impassioned than Fox, he was more attractive than any of them, and possessed in a higher degree the faculty, by the exhibition of his varied powers, of permanently keeping alive the attention. He neither disconcerted his audience by abstract disquisition, nor exhausted them by statistical details, nor terrified them by vehemence of declamation. Alternately serious and playful, eloquent and fanciful, sarcastic and sportive, he knew how to throw over the most uninteresting subjects the play of fancy, and the light of original genius. Whatever the subject was, he touched it with a felicity which no other could reach. He never rose without awakening expectation, nor sat down without exciting regret. Gifted by nature with a poetic fancy and a brilliant imagination, an accomplished scholar, and a felicitous wit, he knew how to enliven every subject by the treasures of learning, the charms of poetry, and the magic influence of allusion. At times he rose to the very highest strains of eloquence; and if the whole English language is searched for the finest detached passages of splendid oratory, they will be found in the greatest number in his collected speeches.

5. His defects.

If Mr. Canning's reach of thought and consistency of conduct had been equal to these brilliant qualities, he would have been one of the very greatest statesmen, as unquestionably he was one of the first orators that England ever produced. But unfortunately this was very far from being the case; and he remains a lasting proof that, if literary accomplishment is one of the most important elements in oratorical power, it is very far from being the same in statesmanlike wisdom. Perhaps they can not co-exist in the same mind. Mr. Burke himself, the greatest of political philosophers, was by no means an equally popular speaker—his voice seldom failed to clear the House of Commons. Mr. Canning had too much of the irritability of genius in his temper, of the fervor of poetry in his thought, of the restlessness of ambition in his disposition, to be, when intrusted with the direction of affairs, either a safe or a judicious statesmen. Passionately fond of popularity, accustomed to receive its incense, and reap at once the rewards of genius by the admiration which his brilliancy in conversation, his versatility in debate, awakened, he forgot that immediate applause is in general the precursor, not of lasting fame, but of dangerous innovation and permanent condemnation. He mistook the cheers of the multitude for the voice of ages. He forgot the reproof the Greek philosopher, when his pupil was intoxicated with the applause of the mob; "My son, if you had spoken wisely, you would have met with no such approbation." Hence he yielded with too much facility to the bent of the age in which he was called to power; he increased, instead of moderating, its fervor. His career as a statesman, in mature life, is little more than a contrast to his earlier speeches as a legislator. He was the first of that school, unfortunately become so numerous in later times, who sacrifice principle to ambition, and climb to power by adopting the principles which they have spent the best part of their life in combating. Unbounded present applause never fails to attend the unlooked-for and much-prized conversion. Time will show whether it is equally followed by the respect and suffrages of subsequent ages.

6. Viscount Chateaubriand.

Mr. Canning rose to power in England, by embodying in the most effective and brilliant form the spirit and wishes of his country at the time: as Napoleon said of himself, "Il marchait toujours avec l'opinion de cinq millions d'hommes." By a singular coincidence, another man of similar talents and turn of mind at the same time was elevated by the influence of the ruling party at the moment in France to the direction of its foreign affairs, and, equally with his English rival, embodied the ideas and wishes of the ruling majority on the other side of the Channel. VISCOUNT CHATEAUBRIAND has attained to such fame as a writer, that we are apt to forget that he was also a powerful statesman; that he ruled the foreign affairs of his country during the most momentous period which had elapsed since the fall of the empire; and achieved for its arms a more durable, if a less brilliant conquest than the genius of Napoleon had been able to effect. Like Mr. Canning, he was a type of the "literary character." Mr. Disraeli could not, in all history, discover two men whose productions and career evince in more striking colors its peculiarities, its excellences, and defects. His imagination was brilliant, his disposition elevated, his soul poetical. Descended of an ancient and noble family—bred in early life in a solitary chateau in Brittany, washed by the waves of the Atlantic, the gloomy imagery which first filled his youthful mind affixed a character upon it which subsequently was rendered ineffaceable by the disasters and sufferings of the Revolution.* He had the

* FRANCOIS RENÉ DE CHATEAUBRIAND was born on 4th September, 1769, the same year with Marshal Ney, and which Napoleon declared was his own. His mother, like those of almost all eminent men recorded in history, was a very remarkable woman, gifted with an ardent imagination and a wonderful memory, qualities which she transmitted in great perfection to her son. His family was very ancient, going back to the tenth century; but, till immortalized by Francois Réné, they lived in unobtrusive privacy on their paternal acres. After receiving the rudiments of education at home, he was sent at the age of seventeen into the army; he was engaged in the campaign of 1792, under the Prince of Condé, and the Prussians under the Duke of Brunswick, against Dumouriez. He there, as he was marching along in his uniform as a private, with his knapsack on his back, accidentally met the King of Prussia. Struck with his appearance, the king asked him where he was going. "Wherever danger is to be found," was the reply of the young soldier. "By that answer," said the king, touching his hat, "I recognize the noblesse of France." His regiment soon after revolted, in consequence of which he resigned his commission, and came to Paris, where he witnessed the storming of the Tuileries on 10th August, 1792, and the massacres in the prisons on 2d September. Many of his nearest relations, in particular his sister-in-law Madame de Chateaubriand, and his sister, Madame Rosambo, were executed along with Malesherbes, shortly before the fall of Robespierre. Obliged now to leave France to avoid death himself, he escaped to and took refuge in England, where he lived for some years in extreme poverty and

spirit of chivalry in his soul, but not the gayety of the troubadour in his heart. Generous, high-minded, and disinterested in the extreme, he was so inured in youth to the spectacle of woe, that it was stripped of most of those terrors which render it so appalling to less experienced sufferers. Like the veteran who has seen his comrades for years fall around him, the image of death had been so often before his eyes, that it had ceased to affect his imagination. He was ever ready at the call of duty, or the impulse of chivalrous feeling, to imperil his life or his fortune even in behalf of a cause which was obviously hopeless. "Fais ce que tu dois, advienne ce que pourra," was his maxim, as it ever has been, and ever will be, of the really great and noble in every age and country. He evinced this intrepidity alike in braving the hostility of Napoleon in the zenith of his power, on occasion of the murder of the Duke d'Enghien, and in opposing the government of the Restoration, when it sought, in its palmy days, to impose shackles on the freedom of thought; and in adhering to it with noble constancy amidst a nation's defection, when it was laid in the dust on the accession of Louis Philippe.

Chateaubriand's merits as an author—by far the most secure passport he has obtained to immortality—will be considered in a subsequent chapter, which treats of the literature of France during the Restoration. It is with his qualities as an orator and a statesman that we are here concerned, and they were both of no ordinary kind. Untrained in youth to parliamentary debate, brought for the first time, in middle life, into senatorial contests, he had none of the facility or grace of Mr. Canning in extempore debate. This was of the less consequence in France, that the speeches delivered at the tribune were almost all written essays, with scarcely any alter-

7. His merits as an orator.

obscure lodgings in London, supporting himself entirely by his pen, and, like Johnson, often scarce able, even by its aid, to earn his daily meal. He there wrote his first and least creditable work, the *Essai Historique*, many passages in which prove that even his ardent spirit had for a time been shaken by the infidelity and dreams of the Revolution.

But he soon awakened to better feelings, and regained amidst suffering his destined and glorious career. Tired of his obscure and monotonous life, and disconcerted by the issue of a love affair in England, he set out for America with the Quixotic idea—indicative, however, of a mind as aspiring as that of Columbus—of discovering by land the long-sought northwest passage to the Pacific. He failed in that attempt, for which, indeed, he was possessed of no adequate means; but he saw the Falls of Niagara, dined with Washington; and in the solitudes of the Far West inhaled the spirit, while his eye painted on his mind the scenes, of savage nature. Many of the finest descriptions and allusions which adorn his works are drawn from the scenes which then became impressed on his memory; and, combined with those of the East, which he afterward visited, constitute not the least charm of his writings. Finding that there was nothing to be done in the way of geographical discovery, with his limited means, in America, he returned to England in 1798, from whence, on the pacification of France, on the fall of the Directory and accession of Napoleon, he returned to Paris, and began his literary career.

He was now in the thirty-second year of his age, and the mingled ardor, information, and poetic fervor of his mind appeared in their full perfection in the works which he gave to the public. *Attala* and *René*, a romance, of which the scene was laid in, and the characters drawn from America, exhibited in the most brilliant form the imagery, ideas, and scenery of the Far West, seen through the eyes of chivalrous genius; while the *Génie du Christianisme* presented, on a larger scale, and in an immortal work, the combined fruits of study, observation, and experience, in illustrating the blessings which Christianity has conferred upon mankind. Such was the celebrity which these works almost immediately acquired, that they attracted the attention of Napoleon, who was anxious to enlist talent of all kinds in his service. He sent for Chateaubriand accordingly, and offered him the situation of Minister to the Republic of the Valais, as a first step in diplomatic service. He at once accepted it; but ere he had time to set out on his proposed mission, the murder of the Duke d'Enghien occurred, and while all Europe was in consternation at that dreadful event, he had the courage, while yet in Paris, to brave the Emperor's wrath by resigning his appointment.

His friends trembled for his life in the first burst of Napoleon's fury; but he was sheltered by the Princess Eliza, and having made his escape from Paris, he turned his steps to the East, the historic land on which, from his earliest years, his romantic imagination had been fixed. He visited Greece and Constantinople, the isles of the Ægean and the stream of the Jordan, Jerusalem and Cairo, the pyramids, Thebes, and the ruins of Carthage. From this splendid phantasmagoria he drew the materials of two other great works, which appeared soon after his return to Paris; *Les Martyrs*, which embodied the most striking images which had met his eye in Greece and Egypt, and the *Itinéraire de Paris à Jérusalem*, which gave the entire details of his journey. The wrath of Napoleon having now subsided, as it generally did after a time, even when most strongly provoked, he was allowed to remain at Paris, which he did in privacy, supporting himself by literary contributions to the few reviews and journals which the despotism of the Emperor permitted to exist, and by the sale of his acknowledged works, until 1814, when, as the approach of the Allies gave rational hopes of the restoration of the Bourbons, he composed in secrecy, and published within a few days after their entry into Paris, his celebrated pamphlet, *Bonaparte et les Bourbons*, which had almost as powerful an effect as the victories of the Allies in bringing about the restoration of the exiled family.

On the accession of Louis XVIII. parties were too much divided, and the influence of Talleyrand was too paramount, to allow of his being admitted into the Government, but, with his usual fidelity to misfortune, he accompanied Louis during the Hundred Days to Ghent, where he powerfully contributed by his pen to keep alive the hopes of the Royalists, and hold together the fragments of their shipwrecked party. On the second restoration the real or supposed necessity of taking Fouché into power made him decline any office under Government, although he was, at the earnest request of the Count d'Artois, created a peer of France in 1815. Subsequently the principles and policy of M. Decazes and the Duke de Richelieu were so much at variance with those which he professed, and had consistently maintained through life, that he not merely kept aloof from the Government, but became an active member of the Royalist Opposition, which, as usually happens in such cases, occasionally found themselves in a strange temporary alliance with their most formidable antagonists on the Liberal side. As they were in a minority in both Chambers, their only resource was the press, of the freedom of which Chateaubriand became an ardent supporter, as well from the consciousness of intellectual strength as from the necessities of his political situation. This added as much to his literary fame as it diminished his popularity with Government. Power has an instinctive dread, under all circumstances, of the unrestrained exercise of intellectual strength. He only obtained, under the semi-liberal administration of the Restoration, the temporary appointment of an embassy to Prussia; and it was not till the Royalists in good earnest succeeded to power, on the downfall of the Duke de Richelieu's second administration, that he was appointed embassador to London, in the beginning of 1822, a situation which, in the following year, was exchanged for that of Minister for Foreign Affairs, which brought him into direct collision with Mr Canning, in one of the most interesting and momentous periods of the history of France and England. He held that situation only for two years; he had too much of the pride of intellect in his mind, of the irritability of genius in his disposition, to be a practicable minister under another leader. His noble and disinterested conduct in refusing the portfolio of Foreign Affairs on the accession of Louis Philippe, and preferring exile and destitution to power and rule obtained by the sacrifice of principle and honor, will form an interesting, and, for the honor of human nature, redeeming episode in a subsequent volume of this History.—*Mémoires d'Outre-Tombe*, par M. le Vicomte de CHATEAUBRIAND, vols. i. to viii.; and *Biographie des Hommes Vivants*, ii. 144–149.

ation made at the moment. But, independently of this, his turn of mind was essentially different from that of his English rival. It was equally poetical, brilliant, and imaginative, but more earnest, serious, and impassioned. The one was a high-bred steed, which, conscious of its powers, and reveling in their pacific exercise, canters with ease and grace over the greensward turf; the other, a noble Arab, which toils have inured to privation, and trained to efforts over the sterile desert, and which is any day prepared to die in defense of the much-loved master or playmates of its childhood. Many of his speeches or political pamphlets contain passages of surpassing vigor, eloquence, and pathos; but we shall look in vain in them for the light touch, the aërial spirit, the sportive fancy, which have thrown such a charm over the speeches of Mr. Canning.

8. His character as a statesman.

As a practical and consistent statesman, we shall find more to applaud in the illustrious Frenchman than the far-famed Englishman. It was his good fortune, indeed, not less than his merit, which led to his being appointed Minister of Foreign Affairs in France at the time when its external policy was entirely in harmony with his recorded opinions through life. Mr. Canning's evil star placed him in the same situation, when his policy was to be directly at variance with those of his. But, unlike Canning, Chateaubriand showed on other occasions, and on decisive crises, that he could prefer consistency, poverty, and obloquy, to vacillation, riches, and power. His courageous defense of the liberty of the press alone prevented his obtaining a minister's portfolio during the ministry of the Duke of Richelieu. His generous adherence to the fallen fortunes of Henry V. caused him to prefer exile, poverty, and destitution, to the Ministry of Foreign Affairs, which he was offered on the accession of Louis Philippe.[1] He was in general to be found in direct opposition to the ruling majority, both in numbers and influence, around him—the sure sign of a powerful and noble mind. Power came for a brief season to him, not he to power; he refused it when it could be purchased only at the expense of consistency.

1 Chateaubriand, Memoires, viii. 372.

9. His defects.

Yet with all these great and lofty qualities, Chateaubriand was far from being a perfect character, and many of his qualities were as pernicious to him as a statesman as they were valuable to him as a romance or didactic writer. He had far too much of the irritability of genius in his temper—that unfortunate peculiarity which is so often conspicuous where the force of intellect is not equal to the brilliancy of imagination, and which so generally disqualifies imaginative writers from taking a permanent lead in the government of mankind. He had a great store of historical knowledge at command, but it was of the striking and attractive more than the solid and the useful kind; and there is no trace, either in his speeches or writings, of his having paid any attention to statistics, or the facts connected with the social amelioration of mankind. In that respect he was decidedly inferior to Mr. Canning, who, although not inclined by nature to that species of information, was yet aware of its importance, and could at times, when required, bring out its stores with the happiest effect. Above all, he was infected with that inordinate vanity which is so peculiarly the disgrace of the very highest class of French literature, and which, if it at times sustained his courage in the most trying circumstances, at others led him into the display of the most puerile weaknesses, and renders his memoirs a melancholy proof how closely the magnanimity of a great can be connected with the vanities of a little mind.

10. M. de Villele.

M. DE VILLELE, who was the head of the new and purely Royalist Ministry which succeeded the second one of the Duke de Richelieu, and who played so important a part in the subsequent history of the Restoration, was a very remarkable man.* He had no natural advantages,

* JOSEPH DE VILLELE was born at Toulouse in 1773, of an ancient Languedoc family. He entered, at a very early age, the service of the marines, and, under M. de St. Felix, served long in the Indian seas. On the breaking out of the revolutionary war, the crew of the vessel in which he was revolted against their officers, who held out faithfully for their captive king, and in consequence he was brought, with M. de St. Felix, a prisoner into the Isle of France, where the latter escaped and was sheltered by a courageous friend, while the revolutionary authorities in the island put a price on his head. M. de Villele was acquainted with the place of his retreat, and as this was known, he was seized, thrown into prison, and threatened with instant death if he did not reveal it; but neither menaces nor offers could prevail upon him to be unfaithful to his friend. Meanwhile M. de St. Felix, informed of his danger, voluntarily quitted his retreat, and surrendered himself to the revolutionary authorities, by whom he was brought to trial along with M. de Villele. The latter, however, defended himself with so much courage, ability, and temper, that he excited a general interest in his behalf, which led to his acquittal. As he could not rejoin his vessel, which was entirely under the guidance of revolutionary officers, he remained in the island, where his amiable manners, and the universal esteem in which he was held among its inhabitants, procured for him the hand of the daughter of a respectable planter, and with it a considerable fortune. He fixed his residence in consequence there; made himself acquainted with its local affairs; and from the attention which he bestowed upon them, and the ability he displayed, he was elected a member of the colonial legislature, and obtained nearly its entire direction.

He returned to France, in 1807, with a moderate fortune, and fixed his residence at his paternal estate of Marville, near his native town of Toulouse, where he devoted himself to agricultural pursuits, without losing sight of the colonial interests, of which he had become so entire a master. In 1814, when the Bourbons were first restored, he evinced the strength of his Royalist principles by the publication of a pamphlet, in which he protested against the charter as an unwarrantable encroachment on the rights of the crown. His conduct subsequently, on the return of Napoleon from Elba, was so courageous, that it attracted the notice of the Duke of Angoulême, who recommended him to the king for the situation of mayor of Toulouse, which he accordingly obtained. His conduct in that capacity was so firm, temperate, and judicious, that it procured for him the esteem of all classes of citizens, and led to his being chosen, in a short time after, to represent that city in the Chamber of Deputies. He did not rise, like a meteor, to sudden eminence there, but slowly acquired confidence, and won the ascendency which is never in the end denied to men who save their more indolent but not less impassioned associates the labor of thinking and the trouble of study. He did not shine by his eloquence or fervor at the tribune, but by degrees won respect and confidence by the information which his speeches always displayed, the moderation by which they were distinguished, and the thorough acquaintance which they evinced with the pressing wants and material interests of the dominant middle class of society. It was easy to see how much he had profited by the salutary misfortunes which had rendered him for so many years a planter in the Isle of France. Thenceforward his biography forms part of the history of France. —*Biographie des Hommes Vivants*, v. 511, 513; and LAMARTINE's *Histoire de la Restauration*, vii. 9, 11.

either of rank, family, or person. What he became he owed to the native vigor of his mind, and the practical force of his understanding, and to them alone. Diminutive in figure, thin in person, and in his later years almost emaciated, with a stoop in his shoulders, and a feeble step, he was not qualified, like Mirabeau or Danton, to overawe popular assemblies by a look. His voice was harsh—even squeaking; and a nasal twang rendered it in a peculiar manner unpleasant. The keenness of his look, and penetration of his eye, alone revealed the native powers of his mind. When speaking, he generally looked down, and was often fumbling among the papers before him—the most unfortunate habit which a person destined for public speaking can possibly acquire. But all these disadvantages, which, in the case of most men, would have been altogether fatal, were compensated, and more than compensated, by the remarkable powers of his mind. Thought gave expression to his countenance, elocution supplied the want of voice, earnestness made up for the absence of physical advantages. Intelligence revealed itself in spite of every natural defect. His auditors began by being indifferent; they soon became attentive; they ended by being admirers. A clear and penetrating intellect, great powers of expression, its usual concomitant, a just and reasonable mind, and an enlightened understanding, were his chief characteristics. He did not carry away his audience by noble sentiments and eloquent language, like Chateaubriand; nor charm them by felicitous imagery and brilliant ideas, like Canning; but he succeeded in the end in not less forcibly commanding their attention, and often more durably directed their determinations. The reason was, that he addressed himself more exclusively to their reason: the considerations which he adduced, if less calculated to carry away in the outset, were often more effective in prevailing in the end, because they did not admit of a reply. He was a decided Royalist in principle; but his loyalty was that of the reason and the understanding, not the heart and the passions, and, therefore, widely different from the unreflecting violence of the *ultras*, or the blind bigotry of the priests. He was a supporter of the monarchy, because he was convinced that it was the form of government alone practicable in and suited to the necessities of France; but he was well aware of the difficulties with which it was surrounded, from the interests created by, and the passions evolved during, the Revolution; and it was his great object to pursue such a moderate and conciliatory policy as could alone render such a system durable.[1]

His penetrating understanding early perceived that, in this view, the most pressing of all considerations was the management of the finances. Aware that it was the frightful state of disorder in which they had become involved which had been the immediate cause of the Revolution, he anticipated a similar convulsion from the recurrence of similar difficulties, and saw no security for the monarchy but in such a prudent course as might avoid the embarrassments which had formerly proved so fatal. He saw not less clearly that, as the territorial aristocracy had been destroyed, and the Church shorn of its whole temporal influence, during the Revolution, it was neither by the sentiments of honor which thrilled the hearts of the nobility, nor the pious devotion which conciliated the power of the Church in the olden time, that attachment to the throne was now to be secured. The land, divided among four millions of little proprietors, the majority of whom could not read, had ceased to maintain an influential body in the state; literary talent, all-powerful in directing others, had no separate interests save that of consequence and place for its possessors, and its energies were directed to the support of the wishes of the really ruling class in society. It was in the burgher class that power was now in reality vested; and it was by attention to their interests and wishes that durability, either for any administration or for the monarchy itself, was to be secured. Economy in expenditure, diminution of burdens, were the great objects on which they were set; no argument was so convincing with them, no appeal so powerful, as that which promised a reduction of taxation. Penetrated with these ideas, M. de Villèle, from the outset of his parliamentary career, devoted himself, in an especial manner, to the subject of finance, and by his close attention to it, and the store of statistical information which his vast powers of application enabled him to accumulate, and his retentive memory to bring forth on every occasion, he soon acquired that superiority in debate which ultimately led to his being placed at the head of the Government. He was, in every sense, the man of the age; but he was the man of that age only. He had no great or enlarged ideas: he saw the present clearly, with all its necessities; but he was blind to the future, with its inevitable accessories. His mind had, in the highest perfection, the powers of the microscope, but not of the telescope. He felt skilfully in with, and worked out admirably, present ideas; but he was not their director, and never could have become the ruler of ultimate thought.[1]

[1 Cap. vii. 259, 260; Lam. vii.; b, 11; Lac. iii. 191, 192.]

M. de Villèle was the life and soul of the new Ministry, but he had several coadjutors, who, though not of equal capacity, were yet important in their several departments. M. de Corbière, in the important situation of Minister of Finance, displayed qualities, not only of the most suitable, but the most marketable kind. Though of good family, he was essentially bourgeois in his character; he had its virtues, its industry, its perseverance, but at the same time its contracted views, selfishness, and jealousy. The aristocracy was not less the object of his animosity, than it was of the most democratic shopkeeper in the Faubourg St. Antoine. His morals were austere, his probity universally known; his manners harsh, his conversation cynical; respected by all, he was beloved by none; but he was a favorite with the Liberal deputies, and possessed great weight in the Chamber, because he was the enemy of their enemy—the noblesse. No

[12. M. de Corbière, M. Mathieu de Montmorency, M. de Peyronnet, Victor.]

11. His peculiar turn of mind, and course of policy.

contrast could be more striking than the Minister of Foreign Affairs, M. Mathieu de Montmorency, exhibited. Born of the noblest family in France, inheriting from his historic ancestors their courage, their elevation of mind, and grace of manner, he had united to these qualities of the olden time the liberal ideas and enlarged views of modern society. Carried away, like so many of the young noblemen of the day, by the deceitful colors of the Revolution, he had at first been the warm supporter of its doctrines; and when their fatal tendency had been demonstrated by experience, he fled from France, and consoled himself on the banks of the Leman Lake with the intellectual conversation of Madame de Staël, the fascinating grace of Madame Récamier. Latterly, he had become devout, and was the steady supporter of the *Parti-Prêtre*; but he did not possess the habits of business or practical acquaintance with affairs requisite for his office, and was more fitted to shine in the saloons than the cabinet of the Foreign Office. M. de Peyronnet, the Minister of Justice, had been a barrister who had distinguished himself by his courage at the side of the Duchess of Angoulême at Bordeaux in 1815, and by his ability in pleading the cause of Madame Du Cayla, when claiming her children and fortune from her inexorable husband. His talent was remarkable, his fidelity to the royal cause undoubted, his zeal great, his firmness equal to any emergency. But his prudence and capacity were not equal to his resolution; and it was already feared, what the result too clearly proved to be the case, that he might ruin the royal cause while wishing to save it. Finally, Marshal Victor, Duke of Belluno, in the important situation of Minister at War, presented a combination of qualities of all others the most important for a ministry of the Restoration. A plebeian by birth, a soldier of fortune who had raised himself by his courage and capacity, a marshal of Napoleon, he conciliated the suffrages of the Liberals; a resolute character, a determined minister, a faithful Royalist, a man of intrepidity and honor, he carried with him the esteem and respect of the aristocratic party.¹

¹ Lam. vii. 12, 17; Cap. vii. 253, 257; Lac. iii. 193, 193.

13. Law regarding the press.

The first difficulty of the new Ministry was with the laws regarding the press, and this, situated as they were, was a difficulty of a very serious kind. The administration of the Duke de Richelieu had been overthrown, as is usually the case with a legislature divided as that of France was at that period, by a coalition of extreme Royalists and extreme Liberals, who for the moment united against their common enemy, the moderate Centre. But now that the victory was gained, it was not so easy a matter to devise measures which should prove acceptable to both. The first question which presented itself was that of the press, the eternal subject of discord in France, and, like that of Catholic emancipation in England, the thorn in the side of every administration that was or could be formed, and which generally proved fatal to it before any considerable period had elapsed. It was the more difficult to adjust any measure which should prove satisfactory, that the former Ministry had been mainly overthrown by the press, and M. Chateaubriand, who held a distinguished place in the new appointments, had always been the ardent supporter of its liberty, and owed his great popularity mainly to his exertions in its behalf. Nevertheless, it was obviously necessary to do something to check its licentiousness; the example of successful revolution in Spain, Portugal, Naples, and Piedmont, was too inviting not to provoke imitation in France; and it was well known to the Government that the secret societies, which had overturned every thing in those countries, had their affiliated branches in France. It was foreseen also, what immediately happened, that the great majority of the journals, true to the principle "to oppose every thing, and turn out the ministry," would speedily unite in a fierce attack upon the new administration. The necessity of the case prevailed over the dread of being met by the imputation of inconsistency, or the lingering qualms of the real friends of freedom of discussion; and a law was brought forward, which, professing to be based on the charter, in reality tended to abridge the liberty of the press in several most important particulars.¹

¹ Lac. iv. 222, 223; Cap. vii. 278, 279; Ann. Hist. v. 6, 7.

14. Its stringent provisions.

By this law, which was brought forward by M. de Peyronnet on the 2d January, it was enacted that no periodical journal could appear without the king's authority, excepting such as were in existence on the 1st of January, 1822; the delinquencies of the press were declared to fall exclusively under the jurisdiction of the royal courts, which decided without a jury; they were authorized to suspend, and, in serious cases, suppress any journal which published a series of articles contrary to religion or the monarchy; the pleadings were permitted to be in private, in cases where the court might be of opinion that their publication might be dangerous to order or public morality. In the event of serious offenses against the law, during the interval of the session of the Chambers, the king was authorized to re-establish the censure by an ordonnance, countersigned by three ministers; but this power was to be transitory only, and was to expire, if, within a month after the meeting of the Chambers, it was not converted into a law. There can be no doubt that these provisions imposed very great restrictions upon the press, and, by withdrawing the offenses regarding it from the cognizance of juries, rendered the punishment of them more expeditious and certain. Still, as it did not re-establish the censorship, and left untouched publications exceeding twenty leaves, it did not infringe upon the most valuable part of public discussion, that which was addressed to the understanding, however galling it might be felt by that which was most dangerous, being addressed to the passions.²

² Cap. vii. 278, 280; Ann. Hist. v. 6, 7; Lac. iii. 222, 223.

15. Discussion on it.

The "Gauche" in the Chambers, the Liberals in the country, rose up at once, and *en masse*, upon the project of a law being submitted to the deputies. "It," said it, "is the slavery of the press, the entire suppression of its freedom, which you demand. Better live in Constantinople than in France, under such a government." Nothing could exceed the violence with which the project was assailed, both by the Opposition in the Chambers and the press in the country. M. de Serres on this occasion rejoined the ranks of the Liberals, from which he had so long been separated: he distinguished himself by an eloquent speech against that part of the project which proposed to withdraw offenses against the laws of the press from the cognizance of juries. "The mask has fallen," said he; "we are presented with a law destructive of the liberty of the press—one which, under pretense of saving our institutions, in reality subverts them. The proposed law strikes at the root of representative institutions, for it goes to destroy intelligence in those who are to exercise them. What is the present condition of society? Democracy overwhelms us like a spring-tide. Legitimate monarchy has nothing to fear from a power which places the press under its safeguard; it is our adversaries who have exposed it to its real danger, by holding out its liberty as inconsistent with monarchical institutions. The press is a social necessity which it is impossible to uproot. The proposed law tends to destroy its utility by subjecting it to arbitrary restrictions. In vain, however, do you attempt this: its power will resist all your attacks, and only become the more dangerous from being directed against the throne, not the ministers who abuse its powers." "We wish the charter," replied M. Castelbajac in a voice of thunder, "but still more we wish the king; we wish for liberty, but it is liberty without license: unrestrained freedom of discussion is another word for anarchy: the law presented to us is peculiarly valuable, for it brings back this difficult subject to the principles of the charter. Respect religion, the laws, the monarch—such are the laws which order demands; the liberty of the press can only be maintained by the laws which prevent its abuse. Such repression is the soul of real freedom." It is doubtful how, under ordinary circumstances, this difficult matter might have been determined; but the example of the ruin of monarchy in the adjoining states proved all-powerful with the majority in both Houses—the majority, however, a curious circumstance, being greater in the Commons than the Peers. In the former it was 82, the numbers being 219 to 137; in the latter 41, they being 124 to 83.[1]

[1] Ann. Hist. v. 51, 76, 80; Cap. vii. 2d, 29th; Lac. iii. 225, 228.

This victory on the part of the administration was immediately followed by a general organization of secret societies over all France, and the turning of the energy of democratic ambition into the dangerous channel of occult conspiracy. Ever since the second Restoration and the Royalist severities of 1815, these societies had existed in France, and many of the leading men of Opposition were initiated in them, but the events of this stormy year gave them redoubled activity and importance. The example of government overturned, and the Liberals universally installed in power in Spain and Italy, was sufficient to turn cooler heads than the ardent republicans of France. The *Carbonari* of Italy established corresponding societies over all the country, with the same signs, the same oaths, the same objects, the same

16. Rise of the Carbonari and secret societies in France.

awful denunciations of vengeance, in the event of the secrets of their fraternity being revealed. The existence of these societies, which were the chief means by which the revolutions of 1820 were brought about, was strenuously denied at the time, on both sides of the Channel, while the designs of the conspirators were in progress; but they have been fully revealed since 1830, when they were entirely successful. Every one was then forward to claim a share in the movement which had placed a new dynasty on the throne, and which none then dared call treason.[1]

[1] Lam. vii. 20, 21; Cap. vii. 301, 302; Vaulabelle, des Sociétés Secrètes, i. 30.

This most perilous and demoralizing system was first introduced from Italy into France in the end of 1820, and the autumn of the succeeding year was the time when it attained its highest development, and when it became a formidable power in the state. Nothing could be conceived more admirable for the object to which it was directed, or better calculated to avoid detection, than this system. It was entirely under the direction of a central power, the mandates of which were obeyed with implicit faith by all the initiated, though, who composed it, or where it resided, was unknown to all save a very few. Every person admitted into the ranks of the Carbonari was to provide himself with a musket, bayonet, and twenty rounds of ball-cartridge. All orders, resolutions, and devices were transmitted verbally; no one ever put pen to paper on the business of the association. Any revelation of the secrets or objects of the fraternity was punished with death, and they had bravoes ready at any time to execute that sentence, which was pronounced only by the central committee, or to assassinate any person whom it might direct. The members were bound by the most solemn oaths to obey this invisible authority whatever it might enjoin, without delay, hesitation, consideration, or inquiry. The association borrowed the illusions of the melodrama to add to the intensity of its impressions: it had, like the German, its *Geheim-gericht* nocturnal assemblages, its poniards, directed against the breast, its secret courts of justice, its sentences executed by unknown hands. It was chiefly among the students at colleges, the sub-officers in the army, and the superior classes of mechanics and manufacturers, that this atrocious system prevailed, and it had reached its highest point in the end of 1821. It has since spread across the Channel, and those who are acquainted with the machinations of the Ribbonmen in Ireland, and the worst of the trades-unions in Great Britain, will have no difficulty in recognizing features well known to them, perhaps by dear-bought experience.[1]

17. Rise of Carbonarism in France.

[1] Vaulabelle, Sociétés Secrètes, 19, 37; Cap. vii. 301, 305; Lam. vii. 21, 22.

M. Lafayette,* Manuel, and d'Argenson were

* "Cette fois, M. Lafayette, pressé sans doute par les années qui s'accumulaient, et craignant que la mort ne lui ravît, comme à Moïse, la terre promise de la liberté, avait manqué à son rôle de tribun légal, à son caractère, à son serment civique de député, à ses habitudes d'opposition en plein jour; et il avait consenti, au risque de la sécurité de sa vie, et de sa conscience, à devenir le moteur, le centre, et le chef d'une ténébreuse conspiration. Toutes les sociétés secrètes des ennemis des Bourbons, et le Carbonarisme qui les résumait toutes en ce moment, jaillirent de ses menées, et aboutissaient à lui."—LAMARTINE, *His-*

18.
Abortive conspiracy at Béfort. January 1, 1822.

at the head of these secret societies in France, and they had attained such an extent and consistency in the end of 1821 that it was thought the time for action had arisen, the more especially as the revolutions of Spain and Naples, which were mainly their work, had strongly excited men's minds, and the accession of the Royalist Ministry in France threatened danger if the execution of their measures was any longer delayed. It was determined to make an outbreak in several different places at once, in order to distract the attention of Government, and inspire a belief of the conspiracy having more extensive ramifications than it really had. Saumur, Thouars, Béfort, Nantes, Rochelle, and Toulon, were the places where it was arranged insurrections should take place, and to which the ruling committee at Paris transmitted orders for immediate risings. So confident were they of success, that General Lafayette set out from Paris to Béfort, to put himself at its head, and only turned back when near that town, on hearing that it had broken out, and failed of success. Béfort, in effect, was so filled with conspirators, and they were so confident of success, that they at length were at no pains to conceal their designs, and openly armed themselves with sabres and pistols, and mounted the tricolor cockade. The vigor and vigilance of the governor, however, and the fidelity of the garrison, caused the attempt to miscarry. M. de Tourlain, the governor, was shot by one of them; but the rest, including M. de Corcelles and Carrel, fled on the road to Paris, and met General Lafayette a few leagues from the gate, just in time to cause him to turn back to his chateau of La Grange, near that capital. Such was the energy with which the Carbonari removed all traces or proofs of the conspiracy, that Colonel Pailhis Tellier, and two or three others, who had been caught in the very act, alone were brought to justice, and escaped with the inadequate punishment of three years' imprisonment.¹

¹ Lam. vii. 36, 40; Cap. vii. 394,393; Lam. iii. 233, 231.

19.
Berton's conspiracy at Thouars. Feb. 23.

A more serious insurrection broke out, toward the end of February, at Thouars, where general Berton was at the head of the conspirators. In the night of the 23d February he set out from Parthenay, and surprised Thouars, where he made prisoners the brigade of gendarmerie, and published a proclamation declaring the establishment of a provisional government, composed of Generals Foy, Demarcay, and Lafayette, M. Benjamin Constant, Manuel, and d'Argenson, at Paris. He next attempted an attack upon Saumur, but in that he was foiled by the intrepidity of the mayor, at the head of a body of young Royalists, at the military school, and the commander of the castle. Obliged to retreat, the insurgents soon lost heart, and dispersed; and Berton himself sought

refuge in the marshes of Rochefort, where he was at length arrested, along with several of his accomplices. Their guilt was self-evident; they had made themselves masters of Thouars, and proclaimed a provisional government. Six of the leaders, including Berton and a physician, Caffé, were sentenced to death; but the lives of all were spared, at the intercession of the Duchess d'Angoulême, excepting the two last. Caffé anticipated the hands of justice by committing suicide in prison; but Berton was brought to the scaffold, and died bravely, exclaiming with his last breath, "Vive la France! Vive la liberté!"¹

¹ Ann. Hist. v. 87, 90; Lac. iii. 235, 237, 253; Lam. vii.56, 58; Cap. vii. 311, 312.

20.
Conspiracy of La Rochelle.

Still more important consequences followed a conspiracy at Rochelle. It originated at Paris, on the instigation of General Lafayette, who directed a young and gallant man, named Bories, a sub-officer in the 45th regiment, to proceed from Pau, with some of the privates of his regiment, whom he had enrolled in the ranks of the Carbonari, to that city, in order, with the aid of the affiliated there, to get up a revolt. They were betrayed, however, before the plot could be carried into execution, by one of their accomplices, at the very time when they were concerting with the emissaries of General Berton a joint attack upon Saumur. Most important articles of evidence were found upon them, or from the information to which their apprehension led; among others, the cards cut in two, and the poniards, marked with their number in the *vente* or lodge, which had been put into their hands by Lareche, an agent of Lafayette. From the declarations of these prisoners, and others apprehended with them, a clew was obtained to the whole organization of the Carbonari in France, ascending, through various intermediate stages, to the central committee in Paris, presided over by Lafayette himself. These revelations were justly deemed of such importance that the trial of the accused was transferred to the capital, and conducted by M. Marchangy, the King's Advocate, himself. The oath taken by the affiliated bound them to face any peril, even death itself, in support of liberty, and to abandon, at a moment's warning, their own brothers by blood to succor their brethren among the Carbonari.* The object of the association was to overturn the existing government in every country, and establish purely republican forms of government. To carry it into complete effect, there was a central committee of three persons at Paris, whose mandates were supreme, and which all the inferior lodges throughout the kingdom were bound instantly, and at all hazards, to obey; and subordinate committees of nine members, whose mandates were equally supreme within their respective districts.² A more formidable conspiracy never was brought to light, or one more calculated, if successful, to tear society in pieces, and elevate the most ambitious and unscrupulous characters to its direc-

² Procès de Bories, &c.; Ann. Hist. v. 777, 802; Lam. vii. 46, 47.

---

¹ère de la Restauration, vii. 26. See also, to the same effect, CAPEFIGUE, *Histoire de la Restauration*, vii. 308. The chiefs of this dark conspiracy were General Lafayette and his son, M. Manuel, Dupont de l'Eure, M. d'Argenson, Jacques Koehler, Comte Thiard, General Taragre, General Corbineau, M. de Lascelles, and M. Merilhou. General Lafayette was by all acknowledged to be the head and soul of the conspiracy.—LAMARTINE, *Hist. de la Restauration*, vii. 29, 30.

* The oath was in these terms: "Je jure de tenir avant toute chose à la liberté ; d'affronter la mort en toutes les occasions pour les Carbonari ; d'abandonner au premier signal le trésor de mon propre sang, pour aider et secourir mes frères."—*Annuaire Historique*, v. 777

tion. It is melancholy to think that Lafayette, d'Argenson, Manuel, and the leaders of the Liberal party in the legislature, were at the head of such a perilous and destructive association.*

21.
Their trial and execution.

Bories and his associates made a gallant defense when brought to trial; and the former melted every heart by the noble effort which he made, when the case had obviously become desperate, to draw to himself the whole responsibility of the proceedings, and exculpate entirely his unhappy associates. "You have seen," said he, in the conclusion of his address to the jury, "whether the evidence has produced any thing which could justify the severity of the public prosecutor in my instance. You have heard him yesterday pronounce the words, 'All the powers of oratory will prove unavailing to withdraw Bories from public justice;' the King's Advocate has never ceased to present me as the chief of the plot: well, gentlemen, I accept the responsibility—happy if my head, in falling from the scaffold, can save the life of my comrades." The trial, which took place at Paris, lasted several days, during the course of which the public interest was wound up to the very highest pitch, and every effort was made, by crowds surrounding the court-house, anonymous threatening letters to the jury, and other means, to avert a conviction. But all was unavailing; Bories, Gouben, Pommier, and Rautre, were convicted, and sentenced to death. They received the sentence with calmness and intrepidity. Determined to make a great example of persons deeply implicated in so wide-spread and dangerous a conspiracy, Government was inexorable to all applications for mercy. An effort was made, with the approbation of Lafayette, to procure their escape by corrupting the jailer; he agreed, and the money was raised, and brought to the prison gates; but the persons in the plot were seized by the police at the very moment when it was counting out. As a last resource, twelve thousand of the Carbonari of Paris bound themselves by an oath to station themselves behind the files of gendarmes who lined the streets as the accused were led to execution, armed with poniards, and to effect their deliverance by each stabbing one of the executors of the law. They were on the streets, accordingly, on the day of execution, and the unhappy men went to the scaffold expecting every moment to be delivered. But the preparations of Government were so complete that the conspirators were overawed; not an arm was raised in their defense; and the assembled multitude had the pain of beholding four gallant young men, the victims of deluded enthusiasm, beheaded on the scaffold, testifying with their last breath their devotion to the cause for which they suffered.¹

¹ Procès de Bories, &c.; Ann. Hist. v. 776, 807; Lam. vii. 45, 47; Lac. ia. 262, 264.

22.
Reflections on these events.

It is impossible to read the account of four young men suffering death for purely political offenses, under a Government founded on moderation and equity, without deep regret, and the warmest commiseration for their fate. Yet must justice consider what is to be said on the other side, and admit the distinction between persons openly levying regular war against their sovereign, who may be perhaps entitled to claim the right of prisoners taken in external warfare, and those who, like these unhappy young men, belong to secret societies, having for their object to overturn Government by murder, and sudden and unforeseen outbreaks, vailed in their origin in studious obscurity. It is the very essence of such secret societies to be vailed in the deepest darkness, and to accomplish their objects by assassination, fire-raising, and treason. Every man who enters into them surrenders his conscience and freedom of action to an unseen and unknown authority, whose mandates he is bound instantly to obey, be they what they may. He is never to hesitate to plunge a dagger in the heart of his king, his father, his wife, his benefactor, or his son, if the orders of this unseen authority require him to do so. Such institutions convert the society which they regulate into a disciplined band of bravoes, ready to murder any man, burn any house, fire any arsenal, or commit any other atrocious act that may be enjoined. It is impossible to hold that death is too severe a penalty for the chiefs who establish in any country so atrocious and demoralizing a conspiracy; and the example of the Ribbonmen in Ireland, and some of the trades' unions in Great Britain, too clearly prove to what abominable excesses, when once established, they inevitably lead. The only thing to be regretted is, that these chiefs so often escape themselves, while the penalty of the law falls upon their inferior and less guilty agents. But their guilt remains the same; and it was not the less in this instance that these chiefs were Lafayette, Manuel, d'Argenson, Benjamin Constant, and the other leaders of the Liberal party in France, whose declamations were so loud in the legislature in favor of the great principles of public morality.*

---

* "Il existe à Paris un grand comité d'orateurs, qui entretient des correspondances avec tous les départements. Il y a dans chaque département, un comité de neuf membres, dont l'un est président.

"Ce comité correspond avec ceux de l'arrondissement, et avec le grand comité. Il y a dans chaque arrondissement un comité composé de cinq membres, dont l'un est président.

"Les chevaliers de l'ordre doivent être pris: 1. Parmi les jeunes gens instruits des villes et des campagnes. 2. Les étudiants des collèges, et des écoles de droit, de médecine et d'autres. 3. Les anciens militaires réformés, retraités ou à demi-solde. 4. Les possesseurs de biens nationaux. 5. Les gros propriétaires dont les opinions sont parfaitement connues. 6. Ceux qui professent les arts libéraux, avocats, médecins, et autres. 7. Les sous-officiers de l'armée active, rarement les officiers, à moins qu'ils n'aient donné des preuves non équivoques de leur manière de penser.

"Le récipiendaire sera instruit verbalement de l'existence de la société, du but qu'elle se propose, ensuite il prêtera le serment suivant:

"Je jure d'être fidèle aux statuts de l'ordre des chevaliers de la liberté. Si je viens à les trahir, la mort sera ma punition.

"C. signifie chevalier; V., vente; V. H., haute vente; V. C., vente centrale; V. P., vente particulière; P., Paris; B. C., bon cousin."—Procès de Bories, &c., No. ix. Annuaire Historique, v. 801, 802.

* It is fully admitted now by the French historians of both parties, that these men were the the chiefs of the Carbonari in France, and that the statements of M. Marchangy on the subject, in the trial of the Rochelle prisoners, were entirely well founded: "Le réquisitoire de M. de Marchangy restera comme un monument de vérité historique et de courage; son tableau du carbonarisme n'était point un roman, comme on le disait alors, mais de l'histoire, comme on l'avoue aujourd'hui. Il avait parfaitement pénétré dans le mystère des sociétés secrètes; il en avait compris la portée et les desseins."—CAPEFIGUE.

23. Insurrection at Colmar, Marseilles, and Toulon. July 1.

The insurrections at Béfort, Thouars, and La Rochelle were not the only ones that Lafayette and the Carbonari committee projected, and tried to carry into execution during this eventful year. A few days after the outbreak at Béfort had failed, Colonel Caron, a half-pay officer, deeply implicated in their designs, with the aid of Roger, another discontented ex-military man, attempted to excite an insurrection in a regiment of dragoons stationed at Colmar. It in effect received him with cries of "*Vive Napoléon II.!*" and Caron led them from village to village for some time trying to excite an insurrection; but they every where failed, and the regiment which had revolted, seeing the affair was hopeless, ended by arresting him, and delivering him over to the police, who were all along privy to the design. He was brought, after the manner of Napoleon, before a military council, by whom he was condemned, and shot in one of the ditches of the citadel of Colmar. Similar attempts, attended with no better success, were made about the same time at Marseilles and Toulon, but they were all frustrated by the vigilance of the police and military, and terminated in similar judicial tragedies, which every friend of humanity must deeply regret, but which were absolutely necessary to extinguish the mania for secret societies and conspiracies which had so long been the scourge of France, and had been encouraged in so flagitious a manner by the Liberal leaders in the Chamber of Deputies, and Lafayette, Manuel, and Koechlin, the central chiefs at Paris. Happily the failure of these conspiracies, and the executions, had the desired effect, and France, during the remaining years of the Restoration, was freed from a political disease of all others the most fatal to public morality and the ultimate interests of general freedom.[1]

[1] Ann. Hist. v. 210, 216; Lam. vii. 46, 62.

24. Budget of 1822.

The interest excited by these events diminished the importance of the parliamentary proceedings in this year: it was useless to attempt legislative measures when the Liberal leaders were every day expecting the Government to be overturned, and a republican régime established, of which they themselves were to be installed as the primary leaders. Thus, after the grand discussion on the restriction of the press, which lasted six weeks, had terminated, the parliamentary history of France, during the remainder of the session, exhibits nearly a blank. The budget alone called forth an animated discussion, and the details which the Finance Minister brought forward on this subject proved that the country was in as prosperous a condition, so far as its material interests were concerned, as it was in a disturbed one, as regards its political feelings and passions. From these details it appeared that the revenue of the year 1823 was estimated at 909,130,000 francs (£36,450,000), and the expenditure at 900,475,000 francs (£36,025,000), leaving a surplus of above 8,000,000 francs, or £320,000. The vote of the supplies for 8000 Swiss in the army was the subject of impassioned invective on the part of the Liberal Opposition; they dreaded a repetition, on a similar crisis, of the fidelity of 10th August, 1792. The revenue of 1822 was 915,591,000 francs (£36,600,000); the expenditure 882,321,000 francs (£35,960,000), leaving a surplus of 33,270,000 francs (£1,320,000) disposable in the hands of Government. To what object they destined this large surplus was obvious from the magnitude of the sums voted for the army, which amounted to 250,000,000 francs (£10,000,000), from a supplementary credit for 13,000,000 francs (£520,000), put at the disposal of the Minister of Finance, and a levy of 40,000 men for the army, authorized by an ordonnance on 20th November.[1]

[1] Ann. Hist. v. 623, 639; Ordonnance Nov. 20, 1822; Moniteur, Nov. 21.

The annual election of the fifth of the Chamber, in the autumn of this year, indicated the great change which the law of the preceding had made in the constituency, and the increased ascendency of property and superior education which the *classifying* the electors into colleges of the arrondissements and the departments, and the throwing those paying the highest amount of direct taxes in the department into the latter, and forming it of them exclusively, had occasioned. In the colleges of arrondissements, the Royalists gained twenty-eight seats, the Liberals seventeen; in the colleges of departments, the former had twenty-four, the latter only five.[*] Thus, upon the whole, the gain was thirty to the monarchical party. So considerable an acquisition, and, still more, the fact of the majority being decided in both colleges, proves that the result was owing to more than the change, great as it had been, in the Electoral Law; and that the example of successful revolutions in the two adjoining peninsulas,[2] and the numerous plots which had broken out in various parts of their

25. Favourable result of the elections to the Royalists.

[2] Ann. Hist. v. 259, 260; Cap. vii. 330, 331.

[*] The election showed the following results:

	Voted.	Total Electors.
Voted in the Colleges d'Arrondissement	13,804	16,930
For Royalist candidates	9,058	—
For Liberal	5,751	—
Voted in Colleges de Département	3,158	4,126
For Royalist candidates	2,418	—
For Liberal	740	—

—*Annuaire Historique*, v. 260.

Histoire de la Restauration, vii. 312. "Le voile longtemps épais par la dissimulation parlementaire des orateurs de 1822 à 1829, qui couvrirent des conspirations actives du nom d'opposition loyale et inoffensive, s'est déchiré depuis 1830. Les meneurs, les plans, les complots, les instigateurs, les acteurs, les sièges, les victimes de ces conspirations ont apparu dans toute la franchise de leurs rôles. Les Casernes, les sociétés secrètes, les prisons, les échafauds mêmes, ont parlé. Sous cette opposition à haute voix, et à visage découvert, qui luttait contre les ministres, en affichant le respect et l'inviolabilité de la royauté des Bourbons, on a vu quelles trames obscures et implacables s'ourdissaient pour la renverser, les unes au profit de Napoléon II., les autres au profit de la république, celles-ci au profit des prétoriens subalternes, celles-là au profit d'un Prince étranger, d'autres au profit d'un Prince de la Maison Royale, d'autres enfin au hasard de toutes les anarchies pouvant élever ou engloutir de téméraires dictateurs comme M. de La Fayette. *Nous-mêmes nous avons reçu d'acteurs principaux, une partie de ces mystérieuses confidences.* Nous empruntons le reste à des historiens initiés par eux-mêmes ou leur parti à ces conspirations, ou ils furent confidents, instruments, ou complices: surtout à un historien consciencieux, exacte, et pour ainsi dire juridique, M. de Vaulabelle, témoignage d'autant moins récusable que son jugement sur la Restauration sont plus sévères, et que son opinion et ses sentiments conspirent involontairement avec les opinions et les sentiments des conspirateurs, pour lesquels il réclame 'a gloire et la reconnaissance devant la postérité.'"—LAMARTINE, *Histoire de la Restauration*, vii. 21, 22.

own country, had brought a large portion of the holders of property, who formerly were neutral, or inclined to be Liberal, to vote with the monarchical party.

26. State of public opinion.

Notwithstanding these favorable appearances in the elections, and the indication they afforded of the state of opinion in the wealthier classes, in whom the suffrage was exclusively vested, the tone of general feeling was very much opposed to this; and the results of the elections tended only to augment the discontent generally felt in the towns, at least in the middle classes of society. These important classes, who alone had emerged unscathed from the storms of the Revolution, were extremely ambitious of enjoying the powers and the freedom of self-government, and felt proportionate jealousy of an administration which was based on aristocratic influences, and closely connected with the ultra party in the Church. It was the latter circumstance which, more than any other, tended to depopularize the Government of the Restoration, and in its ultimate results induced its fall. The reason was, that it ran counter to the strongest passion of the Revolution, and the one which alone had survived in full vigor all its convulsions. That passion was the desire of *freedom of thought*—the strongest wish of emancipated man—the source of all social improvement, and all advances in science, literature, or art, but the deadly enemy of that despotism of opinion which the Romish Church had so long established, and sought to continue over its votaries. The Royalists committed a capital mistake in allying themselves with this power—the declared and inveterate enemy of all real intelligence, and therefore the object of its unceasing and unmeasured hostility. Those best acquainted with the state of France during the Restoration are unanimous in ascribing to this circumstance the increasing unpopularity of Government during its later years, and its ultimate fall." And—markworthy circumstance!—at the very same time, it was in the support of the clergy, and the identity of feeling between them and the vast majority of the educated classes of society, that the British government found their firmest bulwark against the efforts of the revolutionists—a clear proof that there is no real antagonism, but, on the contrary, the closest national alliance between the powers of thought and the feelings of devotion, and that it was the ambition and despotism of the Church of Rome that alone set them at variance with each other. The French Revolution, in all its phases, was mainly a reaction against the revocation of the Edict of Nantes; and had Louis XIV. not sent half a million of innocent Protestants into exile, his descendants would not have been now suppliants in foreign lands.[1]

[1] Cap. vii. 322, 323.

While France and England were thus with difficulty struggling with the fresh outbreak of the revolutionary passions which had resulted from the overthrow of the government in Spain, the monarch of that country was sinking fast into that state of impotence and degradation which in troublous times is the invariable precursor of final ruin. After the humiliation experienced in the affair of the guards at Madrid, which has been recounted in a former chapter,[1] the king perceived that a vigorous effort had become necessary to vindicate his fallen power, and he resolved to make it in person. He came suddenly, accordingly, into the hall of the Council of State, when its members (a sort of permanent Cortes) were assembled, and in a long and impassioned speech detailed the series of humiliations to which his Liberal Ministry had subjected him. He painted his authority set at nought, his complaints disregarded, his dignity sacrificed. He recounted the long course of suffering which he had undergone, and concluded with declaring that the limits of human endurance had been reached, and that he was resolved to deliver himself from his oppressors. Stupefied at this sudden outbreak, the Council directed the Ministers to be called in, that they might be heard in their defense; but when they arrived, instead of vindicating themselves, they commenced an attack upon the king, recapitulated all his violent and illegal acts, and even accused him of having violated his oath, and conspired to overturn the constitution. Furious at this unexpected resistance to his authority, the king rushed out of the hall, and signed an order for the immediate arrest of his Ministers. But his attendants and family represented to him in such strong colors the extreme peril of such a step, of which no one could foresee the consequences, that the order, before it could be executed, was revoked, and the Ministers remained in power. But as the king's secret intention had now been revealed, the seeds of irreconcilable jealousy had been sown between him and his Ministers; and the executive, torn by intestine divisions, ceased to be any longer the object either of respect or apprehension to the ambitious Liberals, who were rapidly drawing to themselves the whole power and consideration in the state.[2]

27. Attempted restoration of the royal authority at Madrid. Sept. 1821.

[1] Ante, c. vii. § 112.

[2] Martignac, i. 268, 270; Ann. Hist. iv. 438, 439.

The result soon appeared. The session of the Cortes opened on 1st March, 1821, and the king, who had adopted from his Ministers his opening speech, added to it several sentences of his own composition. In the first part of it he astonished the Royalists by an unequivocal approbation of the revolutions of Naples and Piedmont, blamed the King of Naples for having gone to the congress of sovereigns at Laybach, and openly condemned the threatened invasion of the Neapolitan States by the Austrian forces. The Liberals were in transports; they could scarcely believe their own ears; the king seemed at last to have identified himself in good earnest with the cause of revolution, and loud applause testified the satisfaction of the majority at the sentiments which had proceeded from the throne. But what was their surprise when, after this concession to the democracy, the king suddenly began on a new key, and, raising his voice as he came to the sentences composed by himself or his secret advisers, recapitulated the repeated attempts made to represent him as insincere

28. Opening of the Cortes, and dismissal of the Ministers. March 1, 1821.

* "Religieux par nature, je dis avec douleur, ce qui fit le plus de mal à la Restauration, ce fut précisément cette idée qu'on parvint à inculquer au peuple, que les Bourbons s'identifiaient avec le clergé."—CAPEFIGUE, *Histoire de la Restauration*, vii. 322.

in his career as a constitutional sovereign, the insults to which, in his person and his government, he had so often been subjected—"insults," he added, "to which he would not be subjected if the executive power possessed the energy which the constitution demands, and which, if continued, will involve the Spanish nation in unheard-of calamities." The audience were stupefied by these unexpected words; the Ministers felt themselves struck at; they recollected the former scene in the Council of State, and, deeming themselves secure of victory if they held out, in the same evening they, in a body, tendered their resignations.[1]

[1] Ann. Hist. iv. 439, 440; Lac. iii. 320, 321; Martignac, i. 275, 276.

29. Conduct of the Cortes, and appointment of a new Ministry.

With so little foresight or discretion were the king's measures pursued, that though it might have been anticipated that a resignation of Ministers would follow such an outbreak, no arrangements whatever had been made for appointing their successors. For several days the country remained without a government, during which the capital was in the most violent state of agitation; the clubs resounded with declamations, the journals were in transports of indignation, and the hall of the Cortes was the scene of the most violent debates. They carried, by a large majority, a resolution, that the late ministers had deserved well of the nation, and, in proof of their gratitude, settled on each of them a pension of 60,000 reals (£600). To allay the tempest he had so imprudently conjured up, the king requested the Cortes to furnish him with a list of the persons whom they deemed fit for the situation; but they refused to do so, alleging that the responsibility of choosing his ministers rested with the king. At length he made his choice, and he was compelled to choose them among the Liberal leaders. Among them was Don Ramon Felix, who had long been imprisoned (since 1814) for his violent conduct, who was appointed minister of the Transmarine Provinces; and Don Eusebio Bardaxi, who had been Minister of Foreign Affairs to the Cortes at Cadiz, was reinstated in the same office.[2]

[2] An. Hist. iv. 441, 445; Martignac, i. 278, 281.

30. Effect produced in Spain by the crushing of the revolution in Italy.

It was now evident that the king had not in reality the choice of his ministers; and in order to conciliate the majority, he addressed a message of condolence to them on the overthrow of the revolution in Naples and Piedmont, which soon after ensued, and promised the fugitives from these countries a safe asylum in Spain, where, in effect, great numbers of them soon after arrived, and were very hospitably received. These external events produced a very deep impression in Spain; for the hopes of the Liberals had been unbounded upon the first outbreak of these convulsions, and their depression was proportionally great upon their overthrow. They produced, as usual in such cases, a fresh burst of the revolutionary passion over the whole country. Terror, as it had done in France when the advances of the Duke of Brunswick into Champagne induced the massacre in the prisons of Paris, produced cruelty; and the actions of the secret societies occasioned a measure so extraordinary, and of such extent, that nothing in the whole annals of history is to be compared to it.

31. Extraordinary outbreak of revolutionary fury in the east of Spain.

At once, and at the same moment, in all places, a vast number of individuals, of both sexes, and of all ranks and classes of society, chiefly on the east coast of Spain, who were suspected of a leaning to the monarchical party, were arrested, chiefly during the night, hurried to the nearest seaport by bands of armed men acting under the orders of self-constituted societies, and put on shipboard, from whence they were conveyed, some to the Balearic Islands, and some to the Canaries, according to the caprice of the imperious executors of the popular will. There was no trial, no legal warrant of arrest, no conviction, no condemnation. With their own hands, of their own authority, under their own leaders, the people executed what they called justice upon their enemies. Several hundred persons—many of them of high rank—were in this manner torn from their families, hurried into exile, without the hope of ever returning, chiefly from Barcelona, Valencia, Corunna, Carthagena, and the neighborhood of these towns. With such secrecy was the measure devised, with such suddenness carried into execution, that no resistance was any where either practicable or attempted; and the unfortunate victims of this violence had scarcely awakened from the stupor into which they had been thrown by their seizure, when they found themselves at sea, on board strange vessels, surrounded by strange faces, and sailing they knew not whither! The annals of the Roman proscriptions, of Athenian cruelty, of French atrocity, may be searched in vain for a similar instance of general, deliberate, and deeply-devised popular vengeance.[1]

[1] Martignac, i. 284, 290; Ann. Hist. iv. 453, 454.

32. Revolutionary laws passed by the Cortes. April 14.

Deeds of violence on the side of the populace seldom fail to find apologists. The illegal seizure and deportation of such a number of persons at the same time in various parts of Spain was a public and notorious event, which could not be concealed; while the secrecy with which it had been devised, and the suddenness with which it had been executed, indicated the work of occult and highly dangerous societies. It was accordingly made the subject of discussion in the Cortes, but the turn which the debate took was very curious, and eminently characteristic of the slavish cowardice which successful revolutionary violence so often induces. No blame whatever was thrown on the authors or executors of this atrocious proceeding; not one of them was even accused, though they were as well known as the commanders of the provinces where the violence had occurred. The whole blame was thrown on the judges and civil authorities in the provinces, whose supineness or dilatory conduct in bringing the enemies of the people to justice had obliged them, it was said, to take the affair into their own hands. All that was done, to avert similar acts of violence by self-constituted authorities in future, was to pass two laws, worthy to be placed beside those constituting the revolutionary tribunal at Paris in point of atrocity. By the first of these the

Vol. I.—B b

punishment of *death* was decreed against all persons who should be convicted of offenses against either religion or the constitution; and by the second, those charged with such offenses were to be arrested by the armed force, and brought before a council of war chosen out of the corps which had ordered the arrest. This judgment was to be pronounced in six days, to be final and without appeal, and carried into execution, if confirmed, by the military governor of the province within forty-eight hours. And the only reparation made to the transported victims was, that government, when they learned the places to which they had been conveyed, secretly brought some of them back, one by one, to their own country.[1]

[1 An. Hist. iv. 452, 453; Martignac, i. 293, 294.]

29. Barbarous murder of the priest Vinuesa.—May 3.

As the military force of Spain was entirely in the hands of the Liberals—at least so far as the officers were concerned—and it had been the great agent which brought about the Revolution, these sanguinary laws, in effect, put all at the mercy of the revolutionists, by whom, as by the Jacobin clubs at Paris, death to any extent, and under no limitation, might with impunity be inflicted on their political opponents or personal enemies. But the proceedings of the courts-martial, summary and final as they were, appeared too slow for the impatient wrath of the populace; and an instance soon occurred in which they showed that, like the Parisian mob, they coveted the agreeable junction, in their own persons, of the offices of accuser, judge, and executioner. A fanatic priest, named Vinuesa, had published at Madrid a crazy pamphlet recommending a counter-revolution. For this offense he was brought before the court intrusted with the trial of such cases at Madrid, and sentenced to ten years of the galleys—a dreadful punishment, and the *maximum* which law permitted for crimes of that description. But this sentence, which seemed sufficient to satisfy their most ardent passions, was deemed inadequate by the revolutionists. "Blood, blood!" was the universal cry. On the day following, an immense crowd assembled in the Puerto del Sol, the principal square of Madrid, where a resolution was passed that they should themselves execute the sentence of death on their victim. This was at noon; but so deliberate were the assassins, and so secure of impunity, that they postponed the execution of the sentence till four o'clock. At that hour they reassembled, after having taken their *siesta*, and proceeded to the prison-doors. Ten soldiers on guard there made a show of resistance, but it was a show only. They soon submitted to the mandates of the sovereign people, and withdrew. The doors of the prison were speedily broken open; the priest presented himself, with a crucifix in his hand, and in the name of the Redeemer prayed for his life. His entreaties were disregarded; one of the judges of the Puerto del Sol advanced, and beat out his brains with a sledge-hammer as he lay prostrate before them on the pavement of his cell.[2]

May 4.

[2 Martignac, i. 295, 296; Ann. Hist. iv. 454.]

Barbarous and uncalled-for as this murder was, it has too many parallel instances in cruelty, aristocratic and democratic, in all ages and in all countries. But what follows is the infamy of Spain, and of the cause of revolution, and of them alone. Having dispatched their victim in prison, the mob proceeded, with loud shouts, to the house of the judge who had condemned him to ten years of the galleys, with the intention of murdering him also; but in this they were disappointed, for he had heard of his danger, and escaped. In the evening the clubs resounded with songs of triumph at this act of popular justice; the better class of inhabitants trembled in silence; the violent revolutionists were in ecstasies. Martinez de la Rosa had the courage in the Cortes to denounce the atrocious act, but a great majority drowned his voice and applauded it. The press was unanimous in its approbation of the glorious deed. To commemorate it for all future times, an *order of chivalry* was instituted by the assassins, entitled the *Order of the Hammer*, which was received with general applause. Decorations consisting of a little hammer, for those who were admitted into it, were prepared, and eagerly bought up by both sexes; and to the disgrace of Spain be it said, the insignia of an order intended to commemorate a deliberate and cold-blooded murder were to be seen on the breasts of the brave and the bosoms of the fair.[1]

31. Institution of the Order of the Hammer.

[1 Martignac, i. 297, 299.]

This cruel act, and still more the general approbation with which it was received in the clubs, and by the press of Madrid, opened the eyes of the better and more respectable classes over the whole country to the frightful nature of the abyss into which all the nation, under its present rulers, was hurrying. A reactionary movement broke out in Navarre, at the head of which was the curate Merino, already well known and celebrated in the war with Napoleon. He was soon at the head of eight hundred men, with which, after having been successful in several encounters, he was marching on Vittoria, when he was met and defeated at Ochandiano by the captain-general of the province. Four hundred prisoners were made, and sent to Pampeluna; the chiefs—nearly all priests or pastors—were immediately executed. Taking advantage of the consternation produced by these events, the king ventured on the bold step of appointing Don Pablo Murillo, the celebrated general under Wellington in the war with Napoleon,—the undaunted antagonist of Bolivar in that of South America—to the situation of captain-general at Madrid. Murillo was very unwilling to undertake the perilous mission, but at length, at the earnest solicitation of the king, who represented that he was his last resource against the revolution, he agreed to accept it.[2]

35. Insurrection in Navarre, and appointment of Murillo at Madrid.

[2 Ann. Hist. iv. 454, 455; Martignac, i. 300, 304.]

The knowledge of Murillo's firm and resolute character had for some time a considerable effect in overawing the factions in the capital; for though the army was the focus of the revolution, such was known to be his ascendency with the troops, that it was feared, under his orders, they would not hesitate to act in support of the royal authority. But unhappily his influence did not

36. Proceedings of the Cortes.

extend over the Cortes, and the proceedings of that body were daily more and more indicative of the growing ascendency of an extreme faction, whose ideas were inconsistent, not merely with monarchical, but with any government whatever. The clubs in Madrid, as they had been during the first Revolution at Paris, were the great centres of this violent party, and it was through them that the whole press had been ranged on the democratic side. Fatigued with a perpetual struggle with their indefatigable adversaries in the Cortes, the galleries, the clubs, and the press, the moderate party in the legislature at length gave way, and submitted to almost every thing which their adversaries chose to demand of them. So far did this yielding go, that they consented to pass a law which entirely withdrew the clubs from the cognizance both of the government and the magistrates; forbade any persons in authority to intrude upon the debates; and by declaring the responsibility of the president for what there took place, in effect declared the irresponsibility of every one else. So obvious was the danger of this law, that the king, in terms of the constitution, and relying on the support of Murillo, refused his sanction. A few days after he did the same with a law which passed the Cortes, tending to deprive the chief proprietors of a considerable part of their seignorial rights.¹

¹ Martignac, i. 314, 315, 316; Ann. Hist. iv. 409.

The finances were daily falling into a more deplorable condition; the necessary result of the unsettled state of the kingdom, and the extreme terror regarding the future which pervaded all the more respectable classes, from the violence of the Cortes and the absence of any effective control upon their proceedings. Though a half of the tithes of the clergy had been appropriated to the service of the state, and half only left for the support of the Church, the budget exhibited such a deficit that it became necessary to authorize a loan of 361,800,000 reals (£3,600,000), being more than half the whole revenue of the state; but such was the dilapidated state of public credit, that, notwithstanding the utmost efforts of the Liberals, only a fourth part of the sum was subscribed by the end of the year.² Insurrections were constantly breaking out in the provinces, which were only suppressed by the armed force, and a great effusion of blood. No sooner were they put down in one quarter than they broke out in another; and the country, as in the war with Napoleon, was infested by guerrilla bands, who plundered alike friend and foe. In the midst of this scene of desolation and disaster, the king, on 30th June, closed the sitting of the Cortes, with a speech composed by his Ministers, in which he pronounced the most pompous eulogium on the wisdom, justice, and magnanimity of their proceedings; the flourishing state of the finances, and the general prosperity which pervaded all parts of the kingdom.³

37
Deplorable state of the finances, and measures regarding them.

² Ann. Hist. iv. 457, 458; Martignac, i. 316, 317.

The event soon showed how far these praises of the revolutionary régime were well founded. Ever since the murder of the priest Vinuesa, it had been the practice of the mobs in Madrid to assemble every evening under the windows of such persons as were suspected of anti-revolutionary principles, and there sing the *Traga la Perro*, the *Marseillaise* of the Spanish revolution, accompanied in the chorus with the strokes of a hammer on a gong, to put them in mind of that tragic event. In the beginning of August, an unhappy prisoner, charged with anti-revolutionary practices, and condemned to the galleys, was lying imprisoned in a convent, awaiting the execution of his sentence, along with the soldiers apprehended some months before on the charge of assaulting the people, while dispersing the mob who insulted the king in his carriage, as narrated in a former chapter.¹ It was determined in the club of the Fontana d'Oro that they should all be executed summarily in prison; and bands were already formed for this purpose, when Murillo appeared with a body of troops and dispersed the assassins. This prompt vindication of the law occasioned the most violent ebullition of wrath in the clubs, and it was resolved to act more decidedly and with greater force on the next occasion. Accordingly, on the 20th August an immense crowd assembled around the convent where the soldiers were confined, singing the *Traga la Perro*, and beating the hammers as usual; and when the guard interfered, and tried to make them disperse, they were surrounded and overpowered. Informed of the danger, Murillo hastened to the spot with a strong body of troops, and, drawing his sword, charged the mob, who immediately dispersed.²

38
Fresh tumults in Madrid. August 2.

¹ Ante, c. vii. § 112.

Aug. 20.

² Ann. Hist. iv. 460, 461; Martignac, i. 329, 330.

This fresh act of vigor completed the exasperation of the Liberals at the intrepid general who had coerced their excesses. Next morning the clubs resounded with declamations against the bloody tyrant who had dared to insult the majesty of the sovereign people; the journals were unanimous in their condemnation of his conduct; seditious crowds uttering menacing cries were formed, and every thing indicated an approaching convulsion. Conscious of the rectitude and integrity of his conduct, and desirous of allaying a ferment which threatened in its results to compromise the throne, Murillo anticipated the sentence of the clubs, and resigned his command, declaring, at the same time, he would not resume it till he was cleared of the charges brought against him. This courageous act produced an immediate reaction in public opinion in his favor; and the accusation against him being proved, on examination, entirely groundless, he resumed his functions with general approbation.³

39
Resignation of General Murillo.

³ Martignac, i. 331, 332; Ann. Hist. iv. 461, 462.

Meanwhile the secret societies, styled in Spain "*Communeros*," which had gone so far to shake society to its centre in France, had spread equally to the south of the Pyrenees. Violent as the proceedings of the open

40
The secret societies, of Communeros.

---

* The expenditure was 756,211,217 reals, or £7,560,000
  The revenue .... 675,000,000 " or 6,750,000

  Deficit .... 81,211,217 " or £810,000
  —Budget, 1821; Annuaire Historique, iv. 459.

Liberals in possession of the government at Madrid had been, they were nothing compared to the designs formed by these secret associations, which were, not merely the destruction of the monarchy and of the Cortes, but the establishment of a republic on the basis of an equal division or community of property, and all the projects of the Socialists. The oath taken by these political fanatics bound them, as elsewhere, to obey all the mandates of the chiefs of the association at the peril of their lives, and to put at their disposal their swords, property, and existence.* This tremendous association had its chief ramifications in Madrid, Barcelona, Saragossa, Corunna, Valencia, and Carthagena; and it was by their agency that the extraordinary measure of seizing and transporting such a number of persons in these cities had recently been effected. Murillo was well aware of the secrets and designs of these conspirators, and was in possession of a number of important papers establishing them. It was mainly to get these papers out of his hands, as well as on account of his known resolution of character, that the public indignation was so strongly directed against him on occasion of his conduct in repressing the recent disturbances in Madrid.¹

¹ Martignac, 326, 327.

41. Riego's plot at Saragossa, and his arrest, Sept. 18.

Riego, who, as already mentioned, had been reinstated in his command in Arragon after having been temporarily deprived of it, was closely connected with the clubs in Saragossa, and was suspected by the government, not without reason, of having lent himself to their extravagant designs. His principal associate was a French refugee named Montarlot, who employed himself at Saragossa in writing proclamations which were sent across the Pyrenees, inviting the French troops to revolt and establish a republic. Government having received intelligence of the conspiracy, took the bold step of ordering Moreda, the political chief at Saragossa, to arrest Riego. He was apprehended, accordingly, as he was returning to that city from a tour in the provinces, where he had been haranguing and exciting the people, and conducted a prisoner to Lerida. Immense was the excitement which this event produced among the Liberals over all Spain. His bust was carried at the head of a triumphal procession through Madrid; the clubs resounded with declamations; the press was unanimous in denying his criminality; and to give vent to the public transports, a picture was painted, intended to be carried in procession through the streets, representing Riego in the costume which he wore on occasion of the revolt in the island of Leon, holding in one hand the Book of the Constitution, and overturning with the other the figures of Despotism and Ignorance.¹

¹ Martignac, i. 339, 340; Ann. Hist. iv. 465, 466.

The moment was decisive. Anarchy or law must triumph; and the victory of the former was the more to be apprehended, as it was known that the military were undecided, and that some regiments had openly declared they would take part with the insurgents. But in this crisis Murillo was not wanting to himself or the cause with which he was intrusted. Having assembled the civic guard, he harangued them on the necessity of crushing the advance of the factions; and having previously given orders to the military to stop the procession, he put himself at the head of the national guard to support them. The revolutionists, however, declared that they would proceed with the procession carrying the picture; and when they arrived at the *Puerto del Sol*, the royal guard stationed there refused to stop them; and the regiment of Saguntum, stationed in another part of the city, broke out of their barracks to advance to their support. All seemed lost; but then was seen what can be done by the firmness of one man. Murillo advanced at the head of the national guard; San Martin, his intrepid associate, seized the picture with his own hands, which he threw down on the ground; and at the same time Murillo charged the head of the procession with the bayonet. Struck with consternation at a resistance which they had not anticipated, the mob fled and dispersed, and Madrid was for the time delivered from the efforts of a faction, which threatened to involve the country in anarchy and devastation.²

42. Suppression of the tumults thence arising at Madrid.

² Martignac, i. 341, 343; Ann. Hist. iv. 463.

In the midst of these civil dissensions, a fresh scourge broke out in Spain, which threatened to involve the country in the evils, not merely of political troubles, but of physical destruction. The yellow fever appeared in the end of July in Barcelona, and by the middle of August it had made such progress that all the authorities quitted the town, and a military cordon was established within two leagues of the walls around it. In spite of this precaution, or perhaps in consequence of the greater intensity which it occasioned to the malady in the infected districts, the disease soon appeared in various quarters in the rear of the cordon, particularly Tortosa, Mequinenza, and Lerida. By the middle of October, when the fever was at its height, 9000 persons had been cut off by it in Barcelona alone, out of a population not at that period exceeding 80,000 persons, and 300 died every day. So terrible a mortality struck terror through every part of Spain; and the French government, under pretense of establishing a sanitary cordon, assembled an army of 30,000 men on the eastern frontier of the Pyrenees, but which was really intended chiefly to prevent communication between the revolutionary party in the Spanish towns and the secret societies in France. In the midst of these

43. Yellow fever at Barcelona. Sept. Oct.

---

* "Je jure de me soumettre sans réserve à tous les décrets que rendra la confédération, et d'aider en toute circonstance, les chevaliers *Communeros*, de mes biens, de mes ressources, et de mon épée. Et si quelque homme puissant, ou quelque tyran, voulait, par la force ou d'autres moyens, détruire en tout ou en partie la confédération, je jure en union avec les confédérés de défendre, les armes à la main, tout ce que j'ai juré, et comme les illustres *Communeros* de la bataille de Villalar, de mourir plutôt que de céder à la tyrannie ou à l'oppression. Je jure si quelque chevalier *Communero* manquait en tout ou en partie à son serment, *de le mettre à mort*, dès que la confédération l'aura declaré traître; et si je viens à manquer à tout ou partie de mes serments sacrés, je me déclare moi-même traître, méritant que la confédération me condamne à une mort infâme; que les portes et les grilles des châteaux et des tours me soient fermées, et pour qu'il ne reste rien de moi après mon trépas, que l'on me brûle, et que l'on jette mes cendres au vent."—*Engagement des Communeros. Sur la Révolution d'Espagne*—MARTIGNAC, i. 325, 326.

alarms, physical and moral, two classes of the people alone were insensible to the peril, and hastened, at the risk of their lives, to the scene of danger. The French physicians flocked over of their own accord to the theatre of pestilence, and brought to its alleviation the aid of their science and the devotion of their courage; and the Sisters of Charity appeared in the scenes of woe, and were to be seen, amidst the perils of the epidemic, by the bedside of the sick, and assisting at the supreme unction of the dying. Their exertions were not unavailing in alleviating individual distress; and the cool weather having set in, the epidemic gradually abated, and by December had entirely disappeared, but not before it had cut off 20,000 persons in Barcelona, out of 80,000; and in Tortosa six out of twelve thousand inhabitants.[1]

¹ Ann. Hist. iv. 467, 469; Martignac, i. 347, 349.

41. Fresh agitation.

The terrors of the epidemic did not allay for any considerable time the political agitation of Spain. The club of the Fontana d'Oro resounded with declamations, of which the arrest of Riego was the principal subject; and its orators declared "that the political atmosphere would never be purified but by the blood of twelve or fifteen thousand inhabitants of Madrid." The Government felt itself unable to coerce these excesses; and the extreme democrats in the provinces, seeing the impotence of the executive, erected themselves, with the aid of self-constituted juntas, into separate powers, nearly as independent of the central government at Madrid as they had been during the war with Napoleon. Saragossa continued the theatre of such violent agitations that Moreda, the intrepid officer who had arrested Riego, was obliged, on the summons of the municipality and clubs, to resign his post and retire. At Cadiz, the Government dismissed General Jauregui, and having appointed the Marquis de la Reunion, a nobleman of moderate principles, to the command, the Liberals refused to receive him. The Baron d'Andilla having upon this been substituted in his room, he too was rejected, and General Jauregui, a noted Liberal, who was entirely in their interest, forcibly retained in his post. The municipality and people of Seville, encouraged by this example of successful resistance, revolted also against the central authority; and Manuel de Velasco, the captain-general, and Escovedo, the political chief of the province, addressed the king in the same style as the Liberals at Cadiz, and caused their names to be inscribed in the national guard of the city, "in order to die at their post, if necessary, in defense of their country." Nor was Valencia in a more tranquil condition, for General Elio, a gallant veteran of the war, the former governor of the province, had been condemned to death by the revolutionary authorities in that city, as having acted in 1814 against the Constitution of 1812, and the sentence having not as yet been executed, the clubs resounded with incessant declamations, demanding his instant execution.[2]

² Ann. Hist. iv. 455, 470, 471; Martignac, i. 353, 355.

Matters had now come to such a pass that the Government at Madrid saw they had no alternative but to take a decided line, or to abdicate in favor of the provincial authorities. They accordingly transmitted orders to Baron d'Andilla to proceed to Cadiz and take the command. But they soon found that their real power was confined to the walls of Madrid. The authorities at Cadiz continued Jauregui in the command, refused to admit the baron within their gates, put the city in a posture of defense, and sent orders to all the towns in Andalusia to stop and arrest him wherever he might appear. The same thing was done at Seville, where General Moreno Davix, sent from Madrid to assume the command, was stopped at Ecija, on his way to that city, and sent back. Meanwhile Meria at Corunna, who had been replaced by General Latré, sent from Madrid, revolted, and having secured the garrison in his interest, expelled Latré, and declared himself independent of the central government. But Latré was not discouraged. He raised the militia of the province of Galicia, which was thoroughly loyal, and appearing with an imposing force before the gates of Corunna, compelled Meria to surrender and depart to Seguenza, the place assigned for his exile. At the same time troubles broke out in Estremadura, Navarre, and Old Castile, where guerrilla bands appeared, ravaged the country, and rendered all collection of the revenue impossible. To such straits was the treasury in consequence reduced, that the Minister of Finance was obliged to open a fresh loan of 200,000,000 reals (£2,000,000) in foreign states, which was only in part obtained, and that at a most exorbitant rate of interest.[1]

45. Refusal of Cadiz and Seville to receive the king's governors, and the revolt at Corunna.

¹ Memorias de General Mina, ii. 375, 389; Martignac, i. 356 357; Ann. Hist. iv. 470, 471.

The distracted state of the country rendered an early and extraordinary convocation of the Cortes necessary, in the hope of obtaining that moral support from its votes which was sought in vain in the affections of the country. It met accordingly on the 25th November, and the king, in his opening speech, deeply deplored the events at Cadiz, and earnestly invoked the aid of the Cortes to support him in his endeavor to cause the royal authority to be respected." The Cortes, in reply, appointed two commissioners, one charged with preparing an answer to the royal address, the other, with considering what was to be done to support the royal authority. The reports were presented on the 9th December, and although drawn in the most cautious style, and with the anxious wish to avoid giving offense to the Liberals, they did so most effectually, for they bore that the authorities at Seville and Cadiz should be brought to trial—a resolution which was adopted by the Cortes by a majority of 130 to 48. This decision excited the most violent animosity in the clubs, the journals, and the coffee-houses: cries of " Long live Riego!

46. Opening of an extraordinary Cortes. Nov. 25.

Dec. 9.

* " C'est dans la plus profonde amertume de mon cœur, que j'ai appris les derniers événements de Cadiz, où, sous le prétexte d'amour pour la constitution, on l'a foulée aux pieds en méconnaissant les droits qu'elle m'accorde. J'ai ordonné a mes secrétaires d'etat de présenter aux Cortès, la nouvelle d'un événement aussi fâcheux, dans la confiance interne qu'ils coopéreront avec energie, d'accord avec mon gouvernement, à faire en sorte que les prérogatives de la couronne, ainsi que les libertés publiques, qui sont une de ses garanties, soient conservées intactes."—*Discours du Roi*, 25th Nov., 1821. *Moniteur*, 2d Decembre, 1821. *Ann. Hist.*, iv. 471, 472.

Down with the Ministers! down with the Serviles!" were heard on all sides; and so completely were the majority of the Cortes intimidated by these proceedings, that a few days after an amendment was carried by a majority of 104 to 59, which bore, "that *as the Ministers did not possess the moral force* requisite to conduct the affairs of the nation, they implored the king to adopt the measures imperatively called for by such a state of public affairs."¹

Dec. 14.
¹ Ann. Hist. ii. 476, 477; Martignac, i. 359, 367.

47. Contradictory resolutions of the Cortes.
This vote of want of confidence in Ministers coming so soon after a solemn condemnation of their adversaries, indicated in the clearest manner the prostration of the executive and disastrous state of the monarchy, reeling like a sinking ship alternately before one wind and another. Immense was the general exultation in the great cities at this direct vote of censure on Ministers. The authorities at Cadiz and Seville were so encouraged by it that they carried their audacity so far as openly to bid defiance to the Cortes and the king, and sent an address to the latter, stating that they would receive or execute no order or appointment from the king till the present Ministers were dismissed. On this occasion the Cortes rescinded virtually their last resolution: their *amour propre* was wounded by this open defiance of their authority; and after a long and stormy debate, in which the leading orators on the Liberal side took part with the Government, it was determined by a majority of 112 to 36 that all those who had signed this seditious address should be prosecuted.²

Dec. 23.
² Martignac, i. 366, 370; Ann. Hist. iv. 477, 479.

48. Irresolute conduct of the king, and royalist insurrection in the north.
Being now supported by the Cortes, and sure of the protection of a part, at least, of the military, the king, had he possessed firmness adequate to the undertaking, had a fair opportunity for asserting the royal authority, and rousing the vast majority of the country to check the urban faction which had turned the revolution into such a downward channel. But he had no consistency in his character, and was as vacillating in his acts as the Cortes in their votes. Hardly was his authority in some degree reinstated by this last vote of the Cortes, than he gave the factions a triumph by dismissing four of his Ministers, the most decided in the intrepid conduct which had lately been pursued. Two others resigned, so that one only remained and continued in the new administration, which was composed entirely of the most moderate of the patriots of 1812. This act of weakness renewed the resistance of Cadiz and Seville at the very time when the vote of the Cortes had disarmed it. Meanwhile, insurrections of an opposite character, in favor of religion and the monarchy, broke out, and were daily gaining ground in Navarre, Arragon, Galicia, and Biscay, and the year closed with Spain torn in all quarters—it was hard to say whether most by the furious democrats of the cities in the south, or the hardy royalists of the valleys in the north.³

³ An. Hist. iv. 480, 482; Martignac, i. 367, 372.

The action of the secret societies styled *Comuneros* and *Descamisados* ("communists" and "shirtless") became more violent and dangerous when the elections for the new Cortes, which had to take place in the first month of 1822, drew near. To counteract their influence, which was daily becoming more formidable, Martinez de la Rosa, Toreno, Calatrava, and some of the other moderate Liberals, set up another society, styled "The Society of the Friends of the Constitution," or of "the King." It at first met with some success; but, as usual in times of vehement excitement, it soon declined, and was no more heard of. When the passions are excited, moderation is considered on all sides as a species of common enemy, and nothing has any chance of influence but such associations as, by alimenting, inflame them. The evils of a licentious press, of the unrestrained right of presenting petitions to the Cortes, and of the extreme violence in the clubs, at length became so flagrant that the Government submitted three laws for their repression to the legislature. As they proposed to impose very effectual checks on these evils, they were resisted with the whole strength of the anarchists, and gave rise to serious disturbances in Madrid, which still further impaired the royal authority, and proclaimed its weakness.¹

49. Proposed laws against the press and patriotic societies.
Jan. 21, 1822.
¹ An. Hist. v. 408, 413; Martignac, i. 374, 377.

50. Riots in Madrid on the passing of a bill against the press.
These proposals came to be discussed in the Cortes under very peculiar circumstances. The resignation of the former ministers had been accepted, but their successors had not been appointed—the places were vacant. The leading orators on the Liberal side then conceived hopes that they might be selected as their successors, and to improve their chances of success, they, for the most part, joined in the debate in favor of the proposed laws. Martinez de la Rosa and Toreno particularly distinguished themselves in this manner, and a motion made by Calatrava, to throw out at once the whole three proposed laws, was rejected by the narrow majority of 90 to 84. This unexpected result inflamed the clubs and the anarchists to the very greatest degree; every means to excite the public mind were instantly adopted without reserve; and so successful were they in rousing the passions of the multitude, that a furious crowd surrounded Toreno as he left the hall of the Assembly after the decisive vote, pursued him with groans and hisses to his own house, which they broke into, and wounded some of the domestics. Toreno escaped by a back door, upon which the crowd proceeded with loud shouts to the house of Martinez de la Rosa, which they were proceeding to attack, when Murillo and San Martin arrived with a body of cavalry, by whom the mob was dispersed, amidst the most violent cries and imprecations. The laws against the offenses of the press, and against the seditious petitions, were adopted by considerable majorities. It was observed that the whole deputies from South America, about thirty-eight in number, voted on all these occasions with the Opposition, which swelled their ranks to eighty, or nearly the half of the Cortes. The extraordinary session closed on the 12th February, having, during

its long and momentous sittings, effected great changes, exhibited many acts of courage, and, on the whole, done less to pull down the entire fabric of society than might have been expected from the excited state of the public mind when it was elected, and the universal suffrage on which it was founded.[1]

[1] An. Hist. v. 415, 419; Martignac, i. 379, 380.

51. Composition of the new Cortes.
The new Cortes was elected under darker auspices, and the incurable vices of the electoral system developed themselves in stronger colors. The kingdom was distracted in all its parts when the elections took place; in some by the triumph of the Liberals, in others by the efforts of the Royalists. The former had been everywhere active, and in most places successful; the latter had in great part abstained from voting, to avoid all responsibility in the formation of a legislature which they plainly foresaw would terminate only in disaster. In some places, especially Granada, open violence was employed at the elections; the multitude broke into the place of voting, and by force imposed their favorites on the electors. But, in general, open violence did not require to be resorted to; the clubs and universal suffrage rendered it unnecessary. The extreme Liberals got everything their own way. The result was soon apparent. In the whole Cortes there was not one single great proprietor or bishop. The noblesse were represented only by a few nobles of ruined fortunes and extreme democratic opinions: the Duke del Parque, a leading orator at the Fontana d'Oro, was the only grandee in the assembly. The majority was composed of men who had signalized themselves by opposition to the Government during the sitting of the last Cortes—governors who had taken part with the people, and refused to execute the laws or obey the injunctions of the Government; magistrates who had betrayed their trust, soldiers who had violated their oaths. Among the most dangerous of these characters, who readily found a place in the new legislature, were the monk Riego, who had been proscribed in 1814, and had since been involved in every seditious movement; Manuel Bertrand du Lys, a man of the most violent temper and extreme principles; Galiano, a brilliant orator but rebellious magistrate, who was under accusation as such when he was elected; Burnaga, a leading speaker at the Fontana d'Oro; Escovedo, the chief of the revolt at Seville, also saved from prosecution by his return; finally, Riego, also delivered from trial by being made a member of the legislature, and who was immediately chosen its president. Uniformity of qualification had done its usual work; it had practically *disfranchised every class except the very lowest intrusted with the suffrage*, which, as the most numerous, gained nearly all the returns, and the government of the country was intrusted to the uncontrolled direction of the most ignorant, the most dangerous and the most unbitious class of the community.[2]

[2] Martignac, i. 381, 385; Ann. Hist. v. 419, 420.

52. New Ministry.
The first duty of the king, before the new Cortes met, was to fill up the six vacant places in the Administration; and as the temper of the new assembly was not fully known, the moderate party obtained the appointments. Martinez de la Rosa was Prime Minister, and had the portfolio of foreign affairs, and the choice of his colleagues. Aware of the difficulty of conducting the government in presence of a Cortes of which Riego had been chosen president, he long refused the perilous post, and only yielded at length to the earnest solicitation of the king. Don Nicolas Garotti, an ex-professor of law in Valencia, was appointed Minister of Justice; Don José de Alta Mira of the Interior; Don Diego Clormneneros, Director of the Royal Academy of History, Colonial Minister; Don Philippe Sierra-Pambley to the Finances; Brigadier Balanzat, Minister at War; Don Jacinti Romorate for the Marine. These persons all belonged to the Moderate party—that is, they were the first authors of the revolution, but had been passed in the career of innovation by their successors. It was a circumstance characteristic of the times, and ominous to the nobility, that two of the most important ministers—those of Justice and the Interior—were professors in universities.[1]

[1] An. Hist. v. 419; Martignac, i. 385, 386.

53. Opening of the Cortes, and disastrous state of the finances.
The Cortes opened on the 1st March; and the opening speech, and reply of the President Riego, were more auspicious than could have been anticipated, and promised returning prosperity to the country. The report of the Finance Minister was the first to dispel these flattering illusions. It exhibited a deficit of 197,428,000 reals (£1,974,000), which required to be covered by loans; and as no money could be got in the country, they required to be borrowed in foreign states.* They were nearly all got, though at a very high rate of interest, in London; the prospect of high profits, and the belief in the stability of popular institutions, inducing our capitalists to shut their eyes to the obvious risks of lending their money to such unstable governments as those which then ruled in the Peninsula. This circumstance deserves to be especially noted, as the commencement of numberless disasters both to the Peninsula and this country. It gave a large and influential body of foreign creditors *an interest in upholding the revolutionary government in the Peninsula*, because no other one would recognize the loans it had contracted. Their influence was soon felt in the public press both of France and England, which, with a few exceptions, constantly supported the cause of revolution in Spain and Portugal; and to this circumstance more than any other the long and bloody civil wars which distracted both nations, and the entire ignorance which pervaded this country as to their real situation, are to be ascribed.[2]

[2] Ann. Hist. v. 421, 422; Martignac, i. 383, 384.

54. General dissensions in Spain.
The entire divergence of opinion between the Cortes and the Government was not long of proclaiming itself. The Cortes insisted that the execution of the royal decrees should be intrusted to

---

* The public accounts for the year 1822 were—
Receipts .... 664,162,000 reals, or £6,664,000
Expenditure ..... 861,591,000 " or 8,615,000

Deficit .... 197,428,000 " or 1,974,280
—*Finance Report*, March, 12, 1822; *Ann. Hist.*, v. 421, 423.

the authorities in the Isle of Leon and Seville, who had revolted against the Government. This was resisted by the administration, and the division led to animated and impassioned debates in the legislature. But while these were yet in progress, disorders broke out in every part of the country, which were not only serious in themselves, but presaged, at no distant time, a universal civil war in the country. The extreme leaders, or "Exaltados," as they were called, were in such a state of excitement that they could not be kept from coming to blows in all the principal towns of the kingdom. At Barcelona, Valencia, Pampeluna, and Madrid itself, bloody encounters took place between the military, headed by the magistrates of municipalities, on the one side, and the peasantry of the country and royalists, led on by the priests, on the other. "Viva Riego! Viva el Constitucion!" broke out from the ranks on one side; "Viva Murillo! Viva el Rey Assoluto!" resounded on the other. Riego was the very worst person that could have been selected to moderate the Cortes in such a period of effervescence. Himself the leader of the revolution, and the acknowledged chief of the violent party, how was it possible for him to restrain their excesses? "I call you to order," said he to a deputy who was attacking that party in the assembly; "you forget I am the chief of the Exaltados."—"To refuse to hear the petitioners from Valencia," said another, "is to invite the people to take justice into their own hands in the streets." To such a length did the disorders proceed that the Cortes appointed a committee to inquire into them, which reported that the state of the kingdom was deplorable. The King's Ministers were ordered, by the imperious majority in that assembly, to the bar of the Cortes, to give an account of their conduct; the military were as much divided as the people; and under the very eye of the legislature a combat took place between the grenadiers of the guard, who shouted, "Viva Murillo!" and the regiment of Ferdinand VII., who replied, "Viva Riego!" which was only ended by a general discharge of musketry by the national guards, who were called out, by which several persons, including the standard-bearer of the guard, were killed. Intimidated by these disorders, which he was wholly powerless to prevent, the king left Madrid, and went to Aranjuez, from whence he went on to pass Easter at Toledo; and his departure removed the only restraint that existed on the excesses in the capital.[1]

March 24.

1 Martignac, i. 391, 393; Ann. Hist. v. 424, 425.

55. Proceedings of the Cortes, and progress of the civil war.

The first proceedings of the Cortes related to the trial of various persons on the Royal side who had taken a part in the late tumults. It was never thought of prosecuting any person on the Liberal. A committee of the Cortes, to whom the matter was referred, reported that the ex-Minister of War, Don Sanchez Salvador, and General Murillo, should be put on their trial; and the resolution was adopted by the assembly as to the former, and only rejected as to the latter by a narrow majority. A new law also was passed, submitting offenses of the press to the decision of the juries, which, in the present state of the country, was securing for them alternately total impunity, or subjecting them to vindictive injustice. A bill was also brought in, and passed, for the reduction of the ecclesiastical establishment, which was certainly excessive, notwithstanding all the reforms which had taken place. It was calculated that, when it came into full operation, it would effect a reduction of 73,000 ecclesiastics, and 600,000 reals (£6000) a day. The knowledge that these great changes were in progress, which went to strike so serious a blow at the influence and possessions of the Church, tended to augment the activity and energy of the royalist party in the provinces. The civil war soon became universal; the conflagration spread over the whole country. Every considerable town was wrapt in flames, every rural district bristled with armed men. In Navarre, Quesada, at the head of six hundred guerrillas, was in entire possession of the country up to the gates of Pampeluna, and although often driven by the garrison of that fortress into the French territory, yet he always emerged again with additional followers, and renewed the war, and united with the Royalists in Biscay. In Catalonia, Misas led a band of peasants, which soon got the entire command of the mountain district in the north; while the Baron d'Erolles, well known in the War of Independence, secretly, in the south of the province, organized a still more formidable insurrection, which, under the personal direction of Antonio Maranon, surnamed the "Trappist," soon acquired great influence. This singular man was one of the decided characters whom revolution and civil war draw forth in countries of marked native disposition.[1]

1 Martignac, i. 396, 398; Ann. Hist. v. 427, 428.

56. The Trappist: his appearance and character, and followers.

Originally a soldier, but thrown into the convent by misfortunes, in part brought on by his impetuous and unruly disposition, the Trappist had not with the cowl put on the habits, or become endued with the feelings of the Church. He carried with him into the cloister the passions, the desires, and the ambition of the world. He was now about forty-five years of age—a period of life when the bodily frame is, in strong constitutions, yet in its vigor, and the feelings are steadily directed rather than enfeebled by age. His eye was keen and piercing, his air confident and intrepid. He constantly wore the dress of his order, but beneath it burned all the passions of the world. Arrayed in his monkish costume, with a crucifix on his breast and a scalp on his head, he had pistols in his girdle, a sabre by his side, and a huge whip in his hand. Mounted on a tall and powerful horse, which he managed with perfect address, he galloped through the crowd, which always awaited his approach, and fell on their knees as he passed, and dispensed blessings to the right and left with the air of a sovereign prince acknowledging the homage of his subjects. He never commenced an attack without falling on his knees, to implore the protection of the Most High; and, rising up, he led his men into fire, shouting, "Viva Dio! Viva el Rey!" In April, 1822, he was at the head of a numerous band of men, animated by his example, and electrified by his speeches. Monks, priests, peasants, smugglers, curates, landowners, hidalgos, were to be seen, side by side, in his bands, irregularly armed, scarcely disciplined, but zealous and hardy, and animated with the highest degree of religious enthusiasm. Their spirit was not so much that of the patriot as of the crusader; they took up arms, not to defend their homes, but to uphold the Roman Catholic faith. Individually brave, they met death, whether in the field or on the scaffold, with equal calmness; but their want of discipline exposed them to frequent reverses when brought into collision with regular troops—which, however, were soon repaired, as in the wars of Sertorius, the Moors, and Napoleon, by the unconquerable and persevering spirit of the peasantry.[1]

_{1 Martignac, i. 398, 401; Ann. Hist. v. 428.}

57. Desperate assault of Cervera. May 18.
The insurgents, after a variety of lesser successes, had made themselves masters of Cervera, where they had established their head-quarters. The Trappist, after sustaining several gallant actions, was driven back into that town by General Bellido, who attacked him with three regiments drawn out of Lerida, and on the 18th May made a general assault on the town. To distract the enemy, he set it on fire in four different places, and in the midst of the conflagration, which spread with frightful rapidity, his troops rushed in. The Trappist made a gallant and protracted defense; but after a conflict of ten hours' duration, from house to house, and from street to street, his men were driven out with great slaughter, though with heavy loss to the victors. Twelve hundred of the Royalists fell or were made prisoners, among whom were one hundred and fifty monks, and nearly half the number of the Constitutional troops were lost. The Trappist himself escaped with a few followers to the mountains, where his powerful voice soon assembled a second band, not less gallant and devoted than that which had perished amidst the ruins and flames of Cervera.[2]

_{2 Ann. Hist. v. 428, 429; Martignac, i. 401, 402; Moniteur, May 25, 1822.}

58. Defeat of Misas. May 26.
Meanwhile Misas, who had been driven into France, re-entered Spain, drew together several desultory bands to his standard, and carried the war to the very gates of Barcelona. He was attacked, however, by the regular troops in that fortress, driven back to Puycerda, where he was utterly routed, and the remains of his band driven back a second time into France, where they again found an asylum—an ominous circumstance for the republican régime in Spain. But in other quarters the Royalists appeared with indefatigable activity: Galicia was almost entirely, in its mountain districts, in their hands; Navarre was overrun by their adherents; and in the neighborhood of Murcia, Jaimes, a noted partisan, had again raised his standard and drawn together a considerable number of followers. The king, meanwhile, was at Aranjuez, and on the 30th May, being the day of his fête, an immense crowd of peasants assembled in the gardens of the palace shouting "El Rey Assoluto!" which was caught up and repeated by the soldiers of the guard. The national guard upon this was called out by the Liberal authorities, and dispersed the crowd; in the course of which one of them drew his sabre against the Infant Don Carlos, and was with difficulty saved by that prince from the fate which awaited him at the hands of the enraged soldiery. On the same day a still more serious tumult broke out at Valencia, where a great mob assembled, shouting, "Long live Elio!—Down with the Constitution!" and proceeded to the citadel where that general still lay in prison, having never been brought to trial. They got possession of the stronghold by the aid of the garrison by which it was held, but were immediately invested there by the national guard and remainder of the garrison of the place, and being without provisions, they were soon obliged to surrender. The victors now proceeded to Elio's dungeon, shouting "Death to Elio!" and his last hour seemed to have arrived; but he was reserved for a still more mournful end. A little gold which he had about him occupied the first attention of the assassins, and meanwhile the address of the commander of the place got him extricated from their hands and conveyed to a place of safety.[1]

_{1 Ann. Hist. v. 434, 435; Martignac, i. 409, 411.}

59. Severe laws passed by the Cortes. June 3.
The intelligence of these events worked the Cortes up to a perfect fury; and in the first tumult of passion they passed several decrees indicating their extreme exasperation, and which contributed in a great decree to the sanguinary character which the civil war in the Peninsula soon afterward assumed, and has unhappily ever since maintained. It was decreed that "all towns, villages, and rural districts, which should harbor or give shelter to the factious, should be treated as enemies with the whole rigor of military law; that those in which there were factious juntas should be subjected to military execution; that every convent in which the factions were found should be suppressed, and *its inmates put at the disposal of the political authorities.*" Such extreme measures necessarily produced reprisals on the other side, and led to a war where quarter was neither given nor taken. A few days after, a decree was passed putting 20,000 of the militia on permanent duty, and establishing national guards throughout the kingdom on the same footing as in France during the Revolution—that is, with the officers of every grade appointed by the privates. They at the same time summoned the Ministers to their bar to give an account of the state of the kingdom, and supplicated the king in the most earnest terms to change his advisers, and intrust every thing to the Liberal party—a demand which he had the address in the mean time to evade.*

June 4.

June 16

---

* "Que le peuple voue le pouvoir confie a des hommes qui aiment les libertés publiques, que la Nation Espagnole voue que le titre et les vertus du véritable patriote sont le seul droit, le seul chemin, pour monter jusqu'à Votre Majesté, pour meriter la faveur, et pour obtenir les honneurs qu'elle peut accorder, et que toute la rigueur de la justice et l'indignation du roi retombent sur les méchants qui osent profaner son nom auguste et sacré, pour opprimer la patrie et la liberté. Les Cortès supplierant V. M. instamment, pour faire cesser les craintes auxquelles nous sommes livrés, et prévenir les maux que nous avons indiqués, de vouloir bien ordonner que la milice nationale volontaire soit immédiatement augmentée et armée dans tout le royaume. En même temps les Cortès espèrent que V. M. fera connaître à tout gouvernement étranger qui, directement ou indirectement, voudrait prendre part à

his part was soon apparent; for a few days after, on a representation by the Ministers of the alarming and distracted state of the kingdom, the Cortes themselves saw the necessity of conferring upon them the extraordinary powers which the public exigencies imperiously demanded.[1]

[margin: 1 Ann. Hist. v. 432, 435, 437. Martignac, i. 412, 413.]

In truth the state of the country had now become such, that such a measure could no longer be delayed if the shadow even of peace and tranquillity was to be preserved in the kingdom. The Royalists in the north, far from being discouraged by their reverses, were daily increasing in numbers and audacity, and, sheltered by the mountain ridges which in that quarter intersect Spain in every direction, they had come to extend their ramifications over half the kingdom. Eguia, Nuñez, and Quesada, who had taken refuge in France after the disaster at Cervera, issued from thence a proclamation in the name of the Royalist provisional government in which they offered 160 reals (32s.) to every Spaniard who should repair, armed and in uniform, to the head-quarters of the Army of the Faith at Roncesvalles before the end of the month. This proclamation put every part of Navarre, Biscay, and the north of Catalonia on fire. In a few days Quesada was at the head of fifteen hundred men, with which, ascending the Pass of Roncesvalles, he entered the valley of Bastan; and as General Lopez-Bañios, with the regular troops from l'ampeluna, which had been considerably reinforced, succeeded in cutting him off from France and Biscay, he boldly threw himself into Arragon, where nearly the whole rural population joined him. Meanwhile a still more important success was gained in Catalonia, where Miralles, Romagosa, and the Trappist, having united their forces, to the amount of five thousand men, suddenly moved upon La Sue d'Urgel, a fortified town on the frontier, in which were deposited large stores of artillery and ammunition. Encouraged by their partisans within the town, the Royalists in a few days ventured upon an assault by escalade. The attempt was made at dead of night: the Trappist, with a huge cross in one hand and his whip in the other, was the first man of the assaulting columns that ascended the ladders; and, after a sanguinary contest of several hours' duration, the whole forts and town were taken, with sixty pieces of cannon, sixteen hundred muskets, and large stores of ammunition. Great part of the garrison were, in retaliation for the massacre at Cervera, and subsequent decrees of the Cortes prohibiting quarter, put to death without mercy.[2]

[margin: 60. Great extension of the civil war.]
[margin: June 11.]
[margin: June 15.]
[margin: June 21.]
[margin: 2 Ann. Hist. v. 438, 439; Martignac, i. 414, 415.]

This great success, by far the most important which had yet attended the Royalist arms, gave an entirely new character to the war, by diffusing universal encouragement among their partisans, and giving them a base of operations, the muniments of war, and a secure place of refuge in case of disaster. It in a manner stilled the passions of the Cortes, which, after voting extraordinary powers to the Ministry to meet the danger, was prorogued, shortly after the intelligence was received, without opposition. Even before the session was closed, however, several quarrels, attended with bloodshed, of sinister augury, had taken place between the royal guards and the national guards of the capital; and the budget exhibited a melancholy proof of the deplorable state of destitution to which the treasury had been reduced by the distrust and convulsions consequent on the Revolution.* Though the army had been reduced to 62,000 men from 80,000, and the expense of the navy from 104,000,000 reals (£1,040,000) to 80,000,000 reals (£800,000), it was found necessary to contract a loan of 102,000,000 reals (£1,020,000), to cover the ordinary expenses calculated on for 1823. The interest of the debt contracted by the Cortes since 1820 amounted to 65,586,000 reals (£655,800), and the interest of the national debt was no less than 148,894,000 reals (£1,488,000), although three-fifths of it had been held as extinguished by Church confiscation, and of what remained no less than 2,069,333,613 reals (£20,693,336) had been set down *without interest*, as having been also provided for by the Church property confiscated to the state, which was estimated at eight milliards of reals or £80,000,000 sterling.[1]

[margin: 61. Deplorable state of the Spanish finances. June 30.]
[margin: 1 Finance Moniteur Exposé, June 21, 1822; Ann. Hist. v. 440, 441.]

Such a state of the Spanish finances said but little either of the benefits which the nation had derived from the revolutionary régime during the three years it had endured, or of the resources either in warlike preparations or national credit to meet the difficulties with which it was on every side beset. But the march of events was so rapid as to outstrip the convulsions inevitable under such a state of the national finances, and induce a crisis much sooner than might have been expected from the comparatively slow progress of pecuniary embarrassment. On the very day on which the Cortes was prorogued a melancholy event occurred, which brought matters to a crisis. An immense crowd assembled and accompanied the king's carriage from the hall of the Cortes to the palace, part shouting "Viva el Rey Netto! Viva el Rey Assoluto!" part "Viva Riego! Viva Libertade." To such a length did the mutual exasperation proceed that it reached and infected the royal guard itself, which was nearly as much divided and inflamed; and

[margin: 62. Riot in Madrid, and death of Landsbura. June 30.]

---

* The entire debt of Spain in 1822 was thus disposed of by the finance committee of this session of the Cortes:

	Reals.	£
Total Debt	14,020,572,591	140,205,725
Extinguished by confiscation of church and charitable funds by decrees of the Cortes	8,459,896,260	84,598,962
Remained	5,560,676,331	55,606,763
Of which bore no interest	2,069,333,613	20,693,336
Remained bearing interest	3,491,342,718	34,913,427

—*Finance Commissioners' Report*, June 21, 1822; *Annuaire Historique*, v. 440, 441.

[footnote: nos affaires domestiques, que la Nation n'est pas dans le cas de recevoir des lois; qu'elle a des forces et des ressources pour se faire respecter, et que si elle a su défendre son independance et son roi avec gloire, c'est avec la même gloire et avec de plus grands efforts encore qu'elle saura toujours défendre son roi et sa liberté."—*Adresse des Cortes au Roi*, 24th May, 1822; Ann. Hist., v. 433, 434.]

as Landaburu, an officer of the guard, of decided Liberal feelings, endeavored to appease the tumult among his men, Martignac, he was shot in the breast, and instantly expired.[1]

[1: Ann. Hist. v. 412, 413; Martignac, i. 416, 417.]

63. Commencement of the strife between the guard and the garrison. June 30.

This atrocious murder, for such it really was, though disguised under the name of a homicide *in rixa*, excited the most violent feelings of indignation among the Liberals of all classes in Madrid; for however willing to excuse such crimes when committed by, they were by no means equally tolerant of them when perpetrated on, themselves. The whole city was immediately in a tumult; the militia of its own accord turned out, the troops of the line and artillery joined them; the municipality declared its sitting permanent, and every thing presaged an immediate and violent collision between the Court and royal guard on the one side, and the Cortes, soldiers of the line, and militia, on the other. The night passed in mutual suspense, both parties being afraid to strike the first blow; and next day nothing was done, except an order on the part of the king to have the murderers of Landaburu punished, and a decree settling a pension on his widow. Meanwhile the royal guard, against which the public feeling in the metropolis was so violently excited, remained without orders, and knew not how to act. Being more numerous and better disciplined than the regiments in the garrison, and in possession of all the principal posts, it might with ease have made itself master of the park of artillery in the arsenal—an acquisition which would have rendered it the undisputed master of the city. Had Napoleon been at its head, he would at once have done so; the seizure of the park of artillery near Paris by Murat, under his orders, on occasion of the revolt of the Sections in October, 1795, determined the contest there in favor of the Directory.[2] But there was no Napoleon in Spain; and the indecision of the Government, by leaving the guard without orders, exposed them to destruction, and lost the fairest opportunity that ever occurred of reinstating, without foreign aid, the royal authority.[3]

July 1.

[2: Hist. of Europe, chap. xix. § 60.]
[3: Ann. Hist. v. 441, 445; Martignac, i. 418, 419.]

64. Departure of the royal guard from Madrid. July 1.

Two of the six battalions of which the guard was composed were on service at the king's palace; the remaining four were in barracks, detached from each other, in the city. Fearful of being shut up there by the troops of the line and militia, they took the resolution, of their own accord, of leaving the capital and encamping in the neighborhood—a resolution which was carried into effect, without tumult or opposition, at nightfall on the 1st July. Meanwhile the most energetic preparations were made by the municipality to meet the crisis which was approaching, and a fresh corps, called the "Sacred Battalion," was formed of volunteers, consisting for the most part of the most desperate and energetic revolutionary characters, who threatened to be even more formidable to their friends than their enemies. The Government and permanent deputation of the Cortes were in consternation, and fearing alike the success of either of the extreme parties now arrayed against each other, they sought only to temporize, and if possible effect an accommodation between them. Murillo, who, as captain-general of New Castile, had the entire command of the military and militia in the province, was the natural chief upon whom it devolved to make head against the insurrection. He was distracted by opposite feelings and duties, for, in addition to his other appointments, the king had recently named him commander of the guard; and it was hard to say whether he should attend to his public duties, as the head of the armed force in the capital, or the whisperings of his secret inclinations, which led him to devote himself to the personal service of the king.[1]

[1: An. Hist. v. 446, 447; Martignac, i. 420, 422; Ann. Reg. 1822, 211, 242.]

65. Progress of the negotiations with the insurgents. July 1–7.

Riego was clear to attack the guards instantly, and in person urged that advice on Murillo. "Who are you?" asked the general, with an ironical expression. "I am," he replied, "the deputy Riego." "In that case," replied the general, "you may return to the congress; you have nothing to do here." Six days passed in fruitless negotiations, in the course of which, however, the Liberals gained a decided advantage; for the Sacred Battalion, during the night of the 3d, got possession of the park of artillery at St. Gol, which proved of the utmost importance in the contest which ensued. The royal treasury, meanwhile, was empty, and so low had the credit of the Government fallen that no one in Madrid would advance it a real. Public anxiety was much increased, during this period of suspense, by the intelligence that a regiment of carabineers had revolted in Andalusia, that several corps of militia had joined it, and that their united force was advancing into La Mancha, to join the insurgent guards in the capital, amidst cries of "Viva el Rey Assoluto." Meanwhile the opposite forces were in presence of each other in the neighborhood of the Royalist camp, and frequent discharges of musket-shots from the outposts at each other kept the public in an agony of apprehension, from the belief that the impending conflict had commenced. In effect, a combined movement was soon found to be in preparation; for early on the morning of the 7th, while it was yet dark, the guards broke up in silence and the best order, and advanced rapidly to the capital. They effected their entrance, without difficulty, by a barrier which was not guarded, and when within the city divided into three columns. The first advanced to take possession of the park of artillery posted at the gate of St. Vincent, the second to the Puerta del Sol, the third to the Place of the Constitution.[2]

[2: Martignac, i. 427, 428; Ann. Hist. v. 454, 455; Ann. Reg. 1822, 242.]

66. Attack of the guard on Madrid, and its defeat. July 7.

From the secrecy with which this movement was executed, and the success with which, in the first instance it was attended, it was evident that it was the result of a well-laid design; and if it had been carried through with as much resolution as it was planned with ability, it would in all probability have met with success, and might have altered the whole course of the revolution. But one of those panics so frequent in nocturnal enterprises seized two of the columns when they came in contact with the enemy, and caused the whole undertaking to terminate in disaster. The corps directed to attack the park of artillery never reached its destination. Assailed by a few musket-shots from the Sacred Battalion as they approached the gate of St. Vincent, they turned about, fled out of the town, and disbanded in the wood of La Monda. The second column was more successful; it gained possession of the Puerta del Sol, after a vigorous resistance from a body of cavalry stationed there to guard the entrance. But instead of moving on to the general point of rendezvous in the Place of the Constitution, it marched to the palace to rally the two battalions of the guard stationed there. The third reached the Place of the Constitution without opposition; but there they found Murillo, Ballasteros, Riego, and Alava, at the head of the militia, and two guns. Though met by a brisk fire, both from the troops and the artillery, they replied by a vigorous and well-sustained discharge of musketry, and forced their way into the square, where they maintained themselves for some time with great resolution. But at length, hearing of the rout of the corps destined for the attack of the artillery, and discouraged by the non-arrival of the corps which had gained the Puerta del Sol, but gone instead to the palace to obtain the aid of the battalions in guard there, who were under arms ready to succor them, they broke their ranks and retreated in disorder toward the palace, closely followed by Ballasteros, who with his guns kept up a destructive fire on their ranks. At length the whole guard, with the exception of the corps which had disbanded, found itself united in front of the palace, but in a state of extreme discouragement, and in great confusion. There they were speedily assailed by ten thousand militia, with a large train of artillery, who with loud shouts and vehement cries crowded in on all sides, and had already pointed their guns from all the adjacent streets on the confused mass, when the white flag was hoisted, and intelligence was received that the guard had surrendered.[1]

¹ An. Hist. v. 454, 455; Ann. Reg. 1-22, 242, 243; Martignac, i. 429, 431.

This ill-conducted attempt to reinstate the royal authority had the usual effect of all such efforts when terminating in miscarriage: it utterly destroyed it. The 7th July, 1822, was as fatal to the crown in Spain as the 10th August, 1792, had been to that of Louis in France. The permanent committee of the Cortes, which had been entirely unconnected with these events, immediately took the direction, and tacitly, without opposition, usurped the entire powers of Government. Their first care was that of the guards, who had laid down their arms without any regular capitulation. The committee compelled the king to impose upon the four battalions which had combated the hard condition of a surrender at discretion; the two at the palace, which had not fought, were to retire from Madrid with their arms, but without ammunition, to distant quarters assigned them, after delivering up the murderers of Landabura. The two last battalions departed in silence, armed and downcast;

67. Destruction of the royal guard. July 7.

but the four others, foreseeing in a surrender at discretion only a snare to involve them in destruction, adopted at the eleventh hour the desperate resolution of resistance. Determined to sell their lives dearly, they opened a general volley on the corps of militia which advanced to disarm them, and, instantly leveling bayonets, charged in close column down the street leading to the nearest gate of the city. All opposition was quickly overthrown, and the entire column succeeded in forcing its way out of the town, closely pursued, however, by two squadrons of the regiment of Almanza, some companies of militia, the Sacred Battalion, and a few guns. They sustained great loss during the pursuit, which was continued until nightfall without intermission. A considerable body of them scaled the walls of the *Casa del Campo*, a country palace of the king, and for some time resisted the pursuers; but being destitute of provisions, they were obliged to surrender, to the number of 360 men and 9 officers, at two on the following morning. Such of the remainder as were unwounded escaped. The entire loss of the guard in these disastrous days was 371 killed, 700 wounded, and 600 prisoners; and the brilliant corps which a few days before seemed to hold the destinies of Spain in their hands, disappeared forever from its annals. Conducted with more skill, led with greater courage, they might, with half the loss, have re-established the monarchy and averted the French invasion.[1]

¹ An. Hist. v. 457, 459; Ann. Reg. 1-22, 243, 244; Martignac, i. 431, 433.

The same day which witnessed the destruction of the royal guard at Madrid, was marked by the suppression of the military revolt in the south of Spain. The Royalist carabineers and their adherents were attacked in the neighborhood of Montero by General O'Donoghu, at the head of a greatly superior body of Constitutional troops, and completely routed. The fugitives escaped to the vicinity of Ciudad Real, where they were again attacked on the 16th, and obliged to surrender. About the same time a conspiracy of a totally different character was discovered and defeated at Cadiz. This had been set on foot by Don Alphonso Gueriera, Don Ramon Ceruti, and a number of others, the chiefs of the ultra-revolutionary party in that city, the object of which was to depose all the constituted authorities, proclaim a republic, and divide among themselves all its places and emoluments. The civil and military authorities in the island of Leon, having received intelligence of the plot, and having put the garrison and militia under arms, apprehended the whole conspirators without opposition on the night of the 9th July.[2]

68. Defeat of the insurgents in Andalusia and Cadiz.

July 16.

² An. Reg. 1822, 245; Ann. Hist. v. 459, 460; Martignac, i. 432, 435.

These repeated successes utterly prostrated the royal authority in Madrid, and deprived the king of the shadow of respect which had hitherto belonged to him. The violent party, supported by the clubs, the press, and the secret societies, became omnipotent. For some days the king remained shut up in his palace without ministers; his former ones had resigned, and no one in such

69. Change of Ministry, and complete triumph of the revolutionists.

a crisis was willing to incur the danger of becoming their successors. At length the absolute necessity of having some government prevailed over the terrors of those offered the appointments, and a new ministry was appointed, consisting, as might be expected in such circumstances, entirely of the leaders of the extreme Liberal party. The king, wholly powerless, agreed to every thing demanded of him, provided he were allowed to leave Madrid, and take up his residence at St. Ildefonso, which was agreed to. San Miguel, formerly chief of the staff to Riego during the revolution in the island of Leon, was made Minister of Foreign Affairs, with the lead in the Cabinet; Lopez-Baños, another chief of the Isle of Leon, was appointed Minister at War; and M. Gasco, one of the most violent members of the Opposition, in the last Cortes, of the Interior; M. Benicio Navarro, another deputy of the same stamp, received the portfolio of Justice; and M. Mariano, Egon, and Cassay, of the Finances and the Marine respectively. The triumph of the extreme Liberals was complete; their adherents, and those of the most determined kind, filled all the offices of Government.[1]

¹ Martignac, i. 436, 437; Ann. Hist. v. 460. Ann. Reg. 1822, 216.

70. The new Ministry, and provincial appointments.

The first care of the new Cabinet was to make an entire change in the royal household, and to banish, or deprive of their commands, all the leading men of the country whose sentiments were not in accordance with their own. Murillo, notwithstanding the determined stand he had made at the head of the Constitutional troops against the royal guard, was deprived of his offices of Captain-general and Political Chief at Madrid, which were bestowed on General Copons, a stanch revolutionist; Quiroga was made Captain-general of Galicia, and Mina of Catalonia. The Duke del Infantado, the Marquis las Amarillas, General Longa, and several other noblemen, who, although Liberals, were known to belong to the Moderate party, were exiled, some to Ceuta, some to the Canaries; and in the palace an entire change took place. The Duke de Montemart, Major d'Uomo, Count Toreno, and the Duke de Belgide, were dismissed; and the Marquis de Santa-Cruz, General Palafox, and Count Onaté, substituted in their room. In a word, the extreme party was every where triumphant; the Jacobins of the Revolution, as is usually the case when the malady is not checked, had supplanted the Girondists.[2]

² Ann. Hist. v. 461, 462; Martignac, i. 437, 438.

71. Murder of Colonel Geoffeux.

It soon appeared what the new Government was to be, and whether the Jacobin successors of France in their thirst for blood. The soldiers of the guard who had been implicated in the murder of Landabaru had already been condemned to death, but the revolutionists demanded, with loud cries, the head of Colonel Geoffeux, an officer of the guard, and who, although neither connected with the death of that man, nor the revolt of the guards, as he was with the two battalions which remained at the palace, was known to entertain decided Royalist sentiments, and as such was selected as the object of popular indignation.

He was arrested accordingly at Butrago, when on his way back to France, of which he was a native. When taken, his name was not known, and a falsehood might have saved him; but when asked who he was, he at once answered, "Geoiffeux, first-lieutenant in the guard." He was immediately brought back to Madrid, taken before a court-martial, and condemned to death. His character, however, was generally esteemed, his innocence known. His courage on his trial excited universal admiration; sympathy was warmly excited in his behalf, and even the revolutionary municipality was preparing a petition in his favor. The anarchists feared lest their victim should escape; the clubs, the press, the mob in the street, were put in motion, and the innocent victim was led out to death. His courage on the scaffold made even his enemies blush with shame, and shed a lustre on the cause for which he suffered. General Copons, who, as military commander at Madrid, had confirmed the sentence, soon afterward gave the clearest proof of its illegality by declaring the tribunal which had tried him incompetent in the case of some other officers charged with a similar offense, who were not marked out for destruction; a decision which excited so great a clamor in reference to the former trial, that he was obliged to resign his appointment.[1]

¹ Martignac, i. 440, 441; Ann. Hist. v. 462.

72. Second trial and execution of Elio.

Elio was the next victim. This distinguished general and intrepid man had been three years in prison, charged with alleged offenses committed when in command at Valencia; but though convicted by the revolutionary tribunal, he had never been executed: so flagrant and obvious was the iniquity of punishing a military commander for acts done in direct obedience to the orders of Government. The cry for his blood, however, was now so vehement that he was again brought to trial, not on the former charges, but for alleged accession to the riot of 30th May, when an attempt, as already mentioned, had been made by a Royalist mob to effect his liberation from prison. The absurdity of charging him with participation in that affray, when at the time he was a close prisoner, carefully watched under military guard in the citadel, made as little impression on his iniquitous accusers as did his patriotic services and glorious career. No small difficulty was experienced in finding military officers who would descend to the infamy of becoming his judicial murderers. The Count d'Almodavar, the Captain-general, resigned his office to avoid it; Baron d'Andilla, appointed in his stead, feigned sickness to escape. None of the generals or colonels in Valencia would sit on the commission; and they were at last obliged to take for its president a lieutenant-colonel, named Valterra. Every effort was made to suborn or falsify evidence, but in vain. The cannoneers accused of being concerned in the plot for his liberation were offered their lives if they would declare they had been instigated by Elio; none would consent to live on such terms. An alleged letter was produced by the general to his sister, avowing his participation in the offense; it was proved *he had no sister.* The accused had no counsel, but he defended himself with courage

Aug. 28.

and spirit for two hours. Even Valterra long hesitated to sign a conviction wholly unsupported by evidence, but the revolutionists were inexorable. The municipality threatened to make Valterra responsible with his head if he did not instantly sign the conviction; the clubs resounded with declamations; a furious mob surrounded the court-house; he trembled and obeyed. Elio was led out to the scaffold, erected on a public promenade with which he had embellished Valencia during his government. He died with the courage which had marked his life, firm in his religious and political principles, and praying for the forgiveness of his murderers.¹

¹ Ann. Hist. v. 463; Ann. Reg. 1822, 247; Martignac, i. 447, 445.

Meanwhile, the civil war in the northern provinces assumed a more regular and systematic aspect, by the solemn installation of a regency at Seo d'Urgel on the 14th September, consisting of the Archbishop of Tarragona and the Baron d'Erolles, which appointed ministers to all the offices of state, and professed to administer the government of the state in the name of Ferdinand VII. *during his captivity.* It soon found itself at the head of an imposing force; a considerable park of field artillery had been collected, uniforms and arms in great quantities purchased, officers for a powerful army had repaired to the royal standard, and twenty thousand men were enrolled under their banners. No less than four hundred and fifty towns and villages in the northern provinces had overturned the pillar of the constitution. Already, on the 23d July, Mequinenza had been carried, and the garrison, four hundred strong, massacred with savage cruelty, in revenge for the slaughter at Cervera. Lerida and Vich were threatened, and the whole of Catalonia, with the exception of the fortresses, had fallen into the hands of the Royalists. In Navarre, Quesada had been defeated by Lopez-Bañoz, who surprised his troops by a nocturnal attack; but he retreated to Roncesvalles, where his dispersed men rejoined his standard; reinforcements poured in from Biscay, and he was soon in a situation to resume the offensive, and establish himself in a fortified camp at Irati, where he maintained himself during the whole remainder of the campaign. The regency issued proclamations in the name of the king, in which they declared null all his acts since he had been constrained to accept the Constitution of 1812, called on the troops to abandon the standard of treason, and engaged to establish a constitutional monarchy based on the ancient laws and customs of the state.²*

73. Civil war in the northern provinces. August 14.

July 23.

July 3.

² Ann. Hist. v. 465, 466; Ann. Reg. 1822, 248; Martignac, 445, 446.

* The proclamation of the Baron d'Erolles bore: "We, too, wish for a constitution, a fixed law to govern the state; but we do not wish it to serve as a pretext for license, or to take crime for its ally. After the example of their ancestors, the people, *legally assembled*, shall enact laws adapted to their manners and to the times in which they live. The Spanish name shall recover its ancient glory, and we shall live, not the vile slaves of factious anarchists, but subject to the laws which we ourselves shall have established. The king, the father of his people, will swear as formerly to the maintenance of our liberties and privileges, and we shall thus have him legally bound by his oath."—*Proclamation of Baron d'Erolles*, 18th August, 1822; Ann. Reg. 1822, p. 249.

The government at Madrid was seriously alarmed at these successes of the Royalists in the north; the establishment of a regular government in the name of the king at Seo d'Urgel, in particular, struck them with consternation. They acted with vigor to make head against the danger. Mina, appointed captain-general of the seventh military division, which comprehended the whole of Catalonia and part of Arragon, repaired to his post in the beginning of September, and having drawn together a considerable force at Lerida, advanced toward Cervera on the 7th September. It was high time he should do so, for the Constitutional forces had recently before been defeated in an attempt upon Seo d'Urgel by the Baron d'Erolles, and driven back with great loss into Lerida. The Trappist, who had received orders to penetrate into Navarre in order to effect a junction with Quesada, after sustaining a severe check on the 19th from Zarco del Valle, had succeeded in rallying his troops in the mountains, and joined Quesada on the 23d. Their united force defeated a division of the enemy at Benavarra, commanded by Tabuenca, who was shot in cold blood. From thence they proceeded against Jaca, an important fortress on the frontier commanding one of the chief passes into France; but they failed in the attempt, and retired to the mountains.¹

74. Vigorous measures of the revolutionary government.

Aug. 19.

Aug. 19.

Aug. 23.

Sept. 18.

¹ Ann. Hist. v. 468, 469; Martignac, i. 447; Ann. Reg. 1822, 251.

These alternative victories and defeats, in which success was nearly equally balanced between the contending parties, and cruelty was unhappily practiced alike by both, determined nothing. The arrival of Mina, however, speedily altered the face of affairs, and, combined with the destruction of the royal guard at Madrid, and the general establishment of the most violent revolutionary authorities in all parts of the country where the Royalists were not in force, caused the balance to incline decisively to the Liberal side. He first laid seige to Castelfollit, a considerable town on the river Bregas, which he took after a siege of six days. Five hundred of the garrison escaped before the assault; the rest were put to the sword after having surrendered. The town was sacked, burned, and totally destroyed. This was done, although Mina himself, in a proclamation after the assault, said, "The defense had been long, firm, and obstinate; the garrison had performed prodigies of valor and acts of heroism equal to the most noble which history has recorded." This frightful massacre diffused the utmost consternation in Catalonia, which was not a little increased by a proclamation issued immediately after,* in which Mina threatened the same fate

75. Capture of Castelfollit, and savage proclamation of Mina.

Oct. 24.

Oct. 25.

* "1. Every town or village which shall yield to a band of rebels, amounting in number to less than one-third of its population, shall be sacked and burnt.

"2. Every town or village which shall surrender to a band of rebels, greater in number than one-third of the inhabitants, and the greater part of which inhabitants shall join the insurgents, shall also be sacked and burnt.

"3. Every town or village which shall furnish succor or the means of subsistence to rebels of any kind, who do not present themselves in a force equal to a third of the inhabitants, shall pay a contribution of one thousand Catato all who should still resist the Liberal forces, offering a free pardon to such as should desert with their arms before the 20th of November. The cruel resolution to put all to the sword who were found in arms contending against the Liberal forces, was too faithfully executed. All, whether monks, priests, peasants, or soldiers, were shot in cold blood, after having surrendered.[1]

Upon receiving intelligence of the fall of Castelfollit, the Baron d'Erolles hastened to unite himself to the remains of the garrison, with five thousand men whom he had collected in the mountains. Mina advanced to meet him: the opposite forces met between Tora and Sanehaga, and the Royalists were surprised and totally defeated. From thence Mina advanced to Balaguer, and its garrison, one thousand strong, fearing the fate of that of Castelfollit, evacuated the place, and withdrew to the mountains on his approach. Quesada, a few days before, had been worsted in an encounter with Espinoza in Navarre, his corps, three thousand five hundred strong, dispersed in the mountains, and he himself obliged to take refuge in Bayonne. In Old Castile the curate Merino had about the same time been defeated, and his band dispersed near Lerma. The Royalist cause seemed every where desperate, and the regency at Urgel, despairing of being able to maintain their ground in Spain, had evacuated that town, and taken refuge in Puycerda, close to the French frontier. The Trappist, after vainly endeavoring to make head against greatly superior forces, now concentrated against him in Catalonia, had been obliged also to take refuge within the French frontier, and had repaired Toulouse, where he was the object of almost superstitious veneration and dread; and the Baron d'Erolles himself, closely followed by Mina, was obliged to accept battle from his indefatigable pursuer, and being defeated, and his corps dispersed, had also found an asylum within the friendly lines of France. The sole strongholds now remaining to the Royalists in the north of Spain, in the end of November, were the forts of Urgel and Mequinenza, which were immediately invested by Mina; and although the guerrilla contest still continued in the mountains, every thing like regular warfare was at an end throughout the Peninsula.[2]

[1] Ann. Reg. 1822, 251; Martignac, i. 447, 449; Ann. Hist. v. 469; Memorias del Espoz-y-Mina, iii. 5, 12.

76. Continued disasters of the Royalists, and flight of the regency from Urgel.

Nov. 3.
Oct. 27.
Oct. 28.
Nov. 10.
Nov. 29.
Nov. 28.

[2] Ann. Hist. v. 494, 496; Ann. Reg. 1822, 252, 253; Memorias del Espoz-y-Mina, iii. 24, 32.

Ionian livres, and the members of the municipality shall be shot.

"4. Every detached house in the country, or in any town or village which may be abandoned on the approach of the Constitutional troops, shall be sacked, pulled down, or burnt

"5. The municipal councilors, magistrates, and curés, who shall, being within three hours' march of my headquarters, neglect to send me daily information of the movements of the rebels, shall be subjected to a pecuniary contribution; and if serious disadvantage shall arise from the neglect of this duty, they shall be shot.

"6. Every soldier from the rebel ranks who shall present himself before me, or one of my generals of division, before 20th November next, shall be pardoned.
"MINA."

—*Annual Register*, 1822, p. 251.

CHAPTER XII.

CONGRESS OF VERONA—FRENCH INVASION OF SPAIN—DEATH OF LOUIS XVIII.

1. Great effect produced by these successes of the Liberals.

These decisive successes on the part of the Spanish revolutionists demonstrated the immense advantages they possessed from the command of the Government, the army, the treasury, and the fortified places, and rendered it more than doubtful whether, with all the support which the rural population could give it, the Royalist cause would ever be able, without external aid, to prevail. Experience had now sufficiently proven, that however individually brave, ardent, and indefatigable the detached corps of the Royalists might be, and however prolonged and harassing the warfare they might maintain in the mountains, they could not venture beyond their shelter without incurring the most imminent hazard of defeat. It was impossible to expect that a confused and undisciplined band of priests, monks, curés, peasants, hidalgos, and smugglers, hastily assembled together, in general without artillery, always without magazines or stores, could make head against regular armies issuing out of fortresses amply supplied with both, and conducted by generals trained in the campaigns of Wellington. Immense was the impression which these successes produced on both sides of the Pyrenees. There was no end to the exultation of the Liberals, in most of the French and Spanish towns, at victories which appeared to promise a lasting triumph to their cause. Great as they had been, they were magnified tenfold by the enthusiasm of the Liberals in the press of both countries; it was hard to say whether the declamations of their adherents in the Spanish Cortes or the French Chamber of Deputies were the most violent. On the other hand, the Royalists in both countries were proportionally depressed. A ghastly crowd of five or six thousand fugitives from the northern provinces had burst through the passes of the Pyrenees, and escaped the sword of their pursuers only by the protection of a nominally neutral but really friendly territory. They were starving, disarmed, naked, and destitute of every thing, and spread, wherever they went, the most heart-rending accounts of their sufferings. They had lost all in the contest for their religion and their king—all but the remembrance of their wrongs and the resolution to avenge them.[1]

[1] An. Hist. v. 497, 498; Martignac, i. 452, 453.

2. Effect of these events in France and Europe.

These events made the deepest impression upon the Government and the whole Royalist party in France. The exultation of the Liberals in Paris, and the open Io Pæans sung daily in the journals, filled them with dismay. The conviction was daily becoming stronger among all reflecting men, that however calamitous the progress of the revolution had been to Spain, and however much it threatened the cause of order and monarchy in both countries, it could not be put down without foreign interference, and that the Royalists, in combating it, would only ruin themselves and their country, but effect nothing against the organized forces of their enemies. The question was one of life or death to the French monarchy; for how was royalty to exist at Paris if cast down at Madrid? The necessity of the case can not be better stated than in the words of a celebrated and eloquent but candid historian of the Liberal school. "Whatever," says Lamartine, "may have been the faults of the Government of the Restoration at that period, it is impossible for an impartial historian to disguise the extreme danger against which Louis XVIII. and his ministers had to guard themselves from the revolutions in the adjoining countries of Spain, Portugal, Naples, and Piedmont, from which the contagion of military revolutions and secret societies had spread into the armies, the last support of thrones. It was not the cause of the French Bourbons which tottered, it was that of all kings and of all thrones. Even more, it was the cause of all the ancient institutions which were sapped in all the south of Europe by the new ideas and institutions. The north itself—Germany, Prussia, Russia—felt themselves penetrated in their inmost veins by that passion for a renewal of things, that pouring of youthful blood into the institutions, that participation of the people in the government, which is the soul of modern times. Entire nations, which had slept for centuries in their fetters, gave symptoms of returning life, and even on the confines of Asia hoisted the signal of the resurrection of nations. All was the work of seven years of peace, and of the freedom of thought in France.

3. Lamartine's observations on the subject.

"The Bourbons had given freedom to the press and to the tribune in their country; and that liberty of thought, re-echoed from Paris and London in Spain, Italy, and Greece, had occasioned the explosion of the revolutionary elements which had been accumulating for centuries in the capitals of those countries. By a natural rebound, these revolutions—restrained at Naples and Turin, fermenting and combating in Greco-Moldavia and Wallachia, triumphant and exasperated in Spain—reacted with terrible effect on the press, the tribune, the youth, and the army of France. The Constitution proclaimed at Cadiz, which left only the shadow of royalty, which surpassed in democracy the constitution of 1791 in France, and which was nothing in reality but a republic masked by a throne, threw into the shade the Charter of Louis XVIII. and the mixed constitution of Great Britain. Revolutionary France blushed for its timidity in the career of innovation in presence of a nation which, like the Spanish, had achieved, at the first step, the realization of all the visions of the philosophy of 1789; which had established freedom of worship in the realm of the Inquisition, vindicated the land from the priesthood in a state of monastic supremacy, and dethroned kings in a nation where absolute royalty was a dogma, and kings a faith. Every audacious step of the revolution at Madrid was applauded, and proposed to the imitation of the French army. The most vehement speeches of the orators in the Cortes, the most violent articles in the revolutionary journals, were reprinted and eagerly read in France; the insurrection, the anarchy of the Spanish revolution, were the subject of enthusiasm in Paris; every triumph of the anarchists at Madrid over the throne or the clergy was publicly celebrated as a triumph by the French revolutionists. Spain was on the verge of a republic; and a republic proclaimed on the other side of the Pyrenees could not fail to overturn the Bourbons in France. Europe was slipping from beneath the monarchies; all felt it, and most of all the revolutionists of Paris. Was it possible that the Bourbons and their partisans should alone not perceive it? War was declared between their enemies and themselves; the field of battle was Spain: it was there they must conquer or die. Who can blame them for having not consented to die?"[1]

[1] Lamartine, Histoire de la Restauration, vii. 64, 66.

4. Opposite views which prevailed in Great Britain.

But while the considerations here so eloquently set forth demonstrate the absolute necessity of French intervention in Spain, and vindicate the steps they took accordingly, there were many reasons, equally cogent and well-founded, which caused a very different view to be taken of the subject in Great Britain. The first of these was the general, it may be said invariable, sympathy of the English with any other people struggling for freedom, and their constant conviction that the cause of insurrection is that of justice, wisdom, and ultimate happiness. This is not a mere passing conviction on the part of the inhabitants of this country—it is their firm and settled belief at all times, and in all places, and under all circumstances. No amount of experience of ruin in other states, or suffering in their own, from the effect of such convulsions, is able to lessen their sympathy for the persons engaged in them, or shake their belief in their ultimately beneficial consequences. Justly proud of their own freedom, and tracing to its effects the chief part of the grandeur and prosperity which this country has attained, they constantly think that if other nations could win for themselves similar institutions, they would attain to an equal degree of felicity. They never can be brought, generally speaking, to believe that there is an essential difference in race, physical circumstances, and degree of civilization, and that the form of government which is most beneficial in one situation is utterly ruinous in another. Their sympathy is always with the rebels; their wishes, in the outset at least, for the people and against the government. This was the case in 1789, when nearly all classes in Great Britain were carried away by the deceitful dawn of the French Revolution, and Mr. Pitt himself hailed it with rapture; and the same disposition led them, with a few exceptions of reflecting men, to augur well of the Spanish revolution, and to sympathize warmly with its fortunes.

In addition to this, there was another circumstance, strongly rooted in the national feelings, which rendered the thoughts of any French intervention in Spain peculiarly obnoxious to every person actuated by patriotic dispositions in Great Britain. Spain had been the battle-field of England and France during the late war; it had been the theatre of Wellington's victories—the most glorious victories her arms had ever gained. The last time the French ensigns had been seen in the Pyrenees was when they were retiring before the triumphant host which the English general led in pursuit; the last time the English flag had waved in Roncesvalles was when they were preparing to carry a war of retaliation into the heart of France. To think of all this being reversed; of a hundred thousand French retracing their steps as conquerors through those defiles where they had so lately fled before a hundred thousand English, Spaniards, and Portuguese, was insupportable. Most of all did it appear so, when the invading host was now thought to be arrayed in the cause of despots against the liberties of mankind, and the defensive bands of the Spanish were united in the great cause of civil freedom and national independence.

5. Repugnance to French intervention.

Add to this another consideration, not so obvious to the general feelings of the multitude, influenced by present impressions, but perhaps still more cogent with the far-seeing statesman, guided by ultimate results. England had repeatedly, during the course of the eighteenth century, been brought to the brink of ruin by the superiority of the French and Spanish fleets, taken together, to her own; the admirable skill of her admirals, the heroic resolution of her seamen, had alone enabled her to make head against the odds. The fatal error committed by the Tories, in the days of Marlborough, in allowing the Spanish crown to remain on the head of a Bourbon prince, had become apparent to all reflecting men: it was equalled only by the error of the Whigs, in the days of Wellington, in doing their utmost to allow it to remain on the head of a brother of Napoleon. The "family compact" in either case might prove fatal to the independence of Great Britain. Such a compact was in an especial manner to be dreaded, if it became an alliance of feeling and interest, not less than blood and cabinets; and a Bourbon king, restored to his throne by the arms of a Bourbon prince, was thrown into a close alliance with our hereditary enemies by identity of cause and necessity of situation, not less than family connection and the danger of common enemies.

6. Danger of a renewal of the family compact between France and Spain.

These considerations must ever be entitled to respect, for they were founded on the generous feelings, a sincere, though perhaps mistaken zeal for the happiness of mankind, and a just appreciation of our political situation, and the dangers which might ultimately come to threaten our independence. But in

7. Influence of the South American and Spanish bondholders.

addition to this there were others less entitled to respect, because based entirely on selfish desires, but not on that account the less likely to guide the opinions and form the wishes of a powerful portion of society. Influenced partly by their constant sympathy with revolutionary efforts, and partly by the thirst for the extravagant gains offered for loans by the rulers of revolutionary states, the capitalists of England had largely embarked in adventures connected with the independence of South America. The idea of "healthy young republics" arising in those immense regions, and equaling those of North America in rapidity of growth and extent of consumption of our manufactures, influenced some; the prospect of seven, eight, and nine per cent., offered for loans, and for a few years regularly paid, attracted others; the idea of the cause of liberty and independence spreading over the whole of the New World carried away a still greater multitude. No one doubted that these young republics, which had been mainly rescued from the colonial oppression of Spain by the sympathizing arms of England, and the valor of Wellington's disbanded veterans, would speedily become powerful states, in close alliance, political and commercial, with Great Britain, paying with regularity and thankfulness the ample interest due upon their debts, consuming an immense and daily increasing amount of our manufactures, and enriching in return the fortunate shareholders of the mining companies that were daily springing up, with a large share of the riches of Mexico and Peru.

8. Immense extent of the Spanish and South American loans.
The sums expended by the capitalists of Great Britain in advances to the revolutionary governments of the Peninsula and their revolted colonies were so great as almost to exceed belief. They were stated by Lord Palmerston, in his place in Parliament, at £150,000,000 between 1820 and 1850; and a considerable part of this immense sum had been advanced before the end of 1822. Payment of the interest even of those vast loans was thought, and not without reason, to be entirely dependent on support being given the revolutionary governments in the Peninsula and South America. It was well known that the independence of the revolted colonies had been mainly secured by the insurrection of the army assembled in the island of Leon, which had also overturned the monarchy of Spain; and it was expected, with reason, that the utmost exertions would be made by the royal government, if once restored, to regain their sway over regions with which so lucrative a commerce was wound up, and from which so large a part of the royal revenues was derived. Great fears were entertained, which were afterward amply justified by the event, that the king, if restored to unrestricted authority, would not recognize the loans contracted by the Cortes, nearly the whole of which had been supplied from London. Influenced by these considerations, the large and powerful body of English capitalists implicated in these advances, made the greatest efforts, by means of the press, public meetings, and detached publications, to keep alive the enthusiasm in regard to Spanish freedom and South American independence; and with such success were their efforts attended, that the people of England were kept almost entirely in the dark as to the real nature and ultimate results of the contest in both hemispheres, and the enthusiasm in their favor was all but universal.

9. Views of the Cabinet and Mr. Canning on the subject.
A feeling so general, and supported by so many heart-stirring recollections and warm anticipations, could not fail, in a country enjoying the popular form of government which England did, to communicate itself to the House of Commons; and so powerful was the current, that it is probable no ministry could have been strong enough to withstand it. But, in addition to this, there were many circumstances at that period which rendered any resistance to the popular wishes in this respect impossible. The Ministry, which had narrowly escaped shipwreck on the question of the queen's trial, was only beginning to recover its popularity, and the king, who had so long labored under the load of unpopularity, had for the first time recently experienced, in Dublin and Edinburgh, the intoxication of popular applause. It was not the time to check these favorable dispositions, by running counter to the national wishes on a great question of foreign policy. Add to this, that the Cabinet itself was divided on the subject, and a considerable portion, probably a majority, were inclined to go along with the popular views regarding it. Mr. Canning, in particular, who, on Lord Londonderry's death, had exchanged the office of Governor-general of India, to which he had been appointed, for the still more important one of Foreign Secretary, was an ardent supporter of these views. He was actuated in this alike by sentiment, ambition, and necessity. His feelings had originally led him to take part with the Whigs; and although on his entrance into public life, he, by the advice of their leaders, joined Mr. Pitt, and became one of the most ardent opponents of the French Revolution, yet it was its excesses, not its original principles, which he condemned. His first inclinations never deserted him through life. The steady supporter of Catholic emancipation, he had also warmly embraced the new views in regard to freedom of trade which were then beginning, not only to prevail in Parliament, but to influence Government. During his keen contest for Liverpool, he had been thrown much among, and been on the most intimate terms with, the leading merchants of that city, and become acquainted with all their sanguine expectations as to the immense benefits which would accrue to this country from the establishment of South American independence. A steady supporter of Wellington during the war, the idea of the work he had achieved being undone, and French influence re-established in the Peninsula, was utterly abhorrent to his mind: a politician influenced rather by feeling and impulse than reasoning and reflection, he did not see that the cause he was now so anxious to support in Spain was precisely the same as that which he had formerly so energetically combated in France. Finally, he was ambitious, and a great career lay open before him; he was the man of the people, and they had placed him in power; he was the champion of England, and his present

greatness, as well as future renown, was wound up with the maintenance of its interests and the furtherance of its desires.

10. Congress of Verona agreed on by all the powers.
When views so utterly opposite were entertained on a great question of European politics, upon which it was indispensable that a decision should be immediately adopted by the powers most immediately interested, and by whose amity the peace of the world had hitherto been preserved, it was not surprising that the other powers should have become anxious for the result, and eagerly sought after every means of avoiding the dreaded rupture. If England and France came to blows on the Spanish question, it was obvious to all that a desperate European strife, possibly equaling the last in duration and blood, would be the result. For although the military strength of France, backed by that of the Northern powers, was obviously far greater than that of Spain supported by Great Britain and Portugal, yet who could say how long this would last, and how soon an outbreak at Paris might overturn the Government there, and array the strength of France on the side of revolution? The throne of Louis XVIII. rested on a volcano; any day an eruption of the fires smouldering beneath the surface might blow it into the air; and if such a catastrophe should occur, what security was there either for the independence of other nations, or the ability of the Northern powers to withstand the advances of revolution supported by the united strength of France and England? These considerations were so obvious, that they forced themselves on every mind; and in order to avert the danger, a congress was resolved on, and VERONA fixed on as the place of its assemblage.

11. Members of the Congress there.
It was originally intended that Lord Londonderry, then Foreign Minister, should himself have proceeded to this important congress; but his unhappy death rendered this impossible, and the Duke of Wellington was appointed to go in his stead. It was thought with justice that England, in an assembly where the leading object of deliberation would be the French intervention in Spain, could not be so appropriately or efficiently represented as by the illustrious warrior who had effected its liberation from the thraldom of Napoleon. He was accompanied by Lord Strangford, the English embassador at Constantinople, the present Marquis of Londonderry, and Lord Burghersh. France was represented by her Foreign Ministers, M. de Montmorency, M. de la Ferronnay, who was highly esteemed by the Emperor Alexander, at whose court he was embassador, and M. de Chateaubriand, who was admired by all the world, and who, at his own request, had left the situation of embassador at London to share in the excitement and deliberation of the Congress. From his known semi-liberal opinions, as well as his great reputation, he was selected to be in some degree a check on M. de Montmorency, who was the representative of the extreme Royalists in France, and might, it was feared, unnecessarily precipitate hostilities. The Emperor Alexander was there in person, accompanied by Nesselrode, M. de Takicheff, M. de Strogonoff, his embassadors at Vienna and Constantinople, and Count Pozzo di Borgo. Capo d'Istria, on account of his known interest in the Greek insurrection, was absent. Metternich, who soon became the soul of the negotiations, was there on the part of Austria, with Count Lebzeltern, the embassador at St. Petersburg; and Prussia was represented by its veteran diplomatists, Prince Hardenberg and Count Bernstorff. Florence was at first thought of as the place of meeting; but at the request of the Emperor Alexander it was exchanged for Verona, on account of the latter city being a sort of midway station between Spain and Greece, the two countries which it was foreseen would principally occupy the attention of the Congress.[1]

[1] Cap. vii. 365, 373; Lam. vii. 94, 96; Lac. iii. 407, 408; Chateaubr. and, Congrès de Vérone, i. 17, 22.

12. Description of Verona.
Verona, a city celebrated alike in ancient and modern times, is situated at the foot of the Alps, at the place where the Adige, after forcing its way through the defile of Chiusa, immortalized by Dante, first emerges into the smiling plain of Lombardy. It is chiefly known to travelers from its noble amphitheatre, second only to the Coliseum in solidity and grandeur, and the interior of which is still as perfect as when it was filled with the admiring subjects of the Roman emperors. Its situation, at the entrance of the great defile which leads from Germany into Italy, has rendered it the scene since that time of many memorable events, when rival generals contended for the mastery of the Empire, and the Gothic hordes descended from the north to slake their thirst for spoil with the riches of the fairest part of Europe. The great contest between Otho and Vitellius, which Tacitus has immortalized,[2] was decided under its walls; the hordes of Alaric, the legions of Theodoric, defiled through its gates; and it was from thence that Napoleon set out at the head of the redoubtable grenadiers who decided the terrible strife between France and Austria on the dikes of Arcola. Nor is the charm of imagination wanting to complete the interest of these historic recollections, for it contains the tomb of Juliet, and has been immortalized by the genius of Shakspeare.[*] The modern city presents an interesting assemblage of the relics of ancient and modern times; for if the stately remains of its amphitheatre carry us back to the days of the Roman emperors, its fortified bridges, curious arches, and castellated towers, remind us not less forcibly of the times of Gothic strife; while its spacious squares, elegant piazzas, and decorated theatres, bespeak the riches and luxury which have grown up with the peace of modern society.[3]

[2] Tacitus, Hist. ii. 30, 34.
[3] Personal observation.

13. Views of the different powers at the opening of the Congress.
Before going to Verona, M. de Montmorency repaired to Vienna, where he had several confidential interviews with M. de Metternich. Their views were entirely in unison; and as it was anticipated that the intentions of the cabinet of Berlin would be mainly influenced by those of the Emperor Alexander, who was known to have the utmost dread of the military revolts of Southern Europe, it was

[*] See "The Tomb at Verona," a fragment, but one of the most interesting of the many interesting monuments of Sir E. B. Lytton's genius.

with reason expected that the resolutions of the assembled powers would be all but unanimous. England, indeed, it was well known, would be strongly opposed to any armed intervention of France in the Peninsula; but, oppressed as she was with debt, and absorbed in pacific objects, it was not anticipated that she would draw the sword in its behalf, in opposition to the declared resolution of all the great powers on the Continent; and the extreme division of opinion in Spain and Portugal themselves, on the subject of the revolution, encouraged the hope that their governments would fall to the ground of themselves, without the necessity of military operations. Yet, notwithstanding the favorable circumstances which augured so well for vigorous measures, the Cabinet of Louis XVIII. was much divided on the subject. The king himself, with M. de Villèle, his Prime Minister, strongly inclined to a pacific policy, and deprecated war as a last resource to be avoided as long as possible.[1]

[1] Cap. vii. 373, 376; Lac. iii. 405, 4 7, Lam. vii. 96, 99.

11. Brilliant assemblage of princesses and courtiers at Verona.

Verona exhibited, when the Congress opened within its walls, even more than the usual union of rank, genius, celebrity, and beauty, which are usually attracted by such assemblages. The Empress of Austria was present, the ex-Empress Marie-Louise was there, and enjoyed the happiness of being again united to her august family; but the brilliant dream of her life had already passed away, and the widow of Napoleon had sunk into the obscure wife of her own chamberlain. The Queen of Sardinia, with the princesses her daughters, the princesses of Tuscany, Modena, and several of the German powers, embellished the saloons by their beauty, or adorned them by their charms. Never had any town in Italy exhibited such a combination of every thing that could distract the thoughts of the diplomatists, or dazzle the eyes of the multitude. The principal actors and actresses from Paris and Vienna had arrived, and added by their talents to the general enchantment; splendid balls succeeded each other in rapid succession, intermingled with concerts, in which the genius of Rossini shone forth with the highest lustre. In the midst of all this pomp and splendor, the business of diplomacy proceeded abreast of that of amusement; the embassadors were as much occupied as the chamberlains; and a hidden but most formidable power—that of the Jesuits, and the extreme religious party —carried on a series of intrigues destined to produce the most important results.[2]

[2] Lac. iii. 40s, 411; Cap. vii. 373, 375.

15. Treaty for the evacuation of Piedmont and Naples. Dec. 14, 1822.

The first matter brought under the consideration of the Congress was the insurrection in Greece, and the complicated relations of Russia and the Porte; but they must be reserved for a subsequent chapter, when that important subject will be fully discussed. The state of Piedmont next came under discussion, and as it presented much fewer difficulties, it was soon adjusted. The King of Sardinia declared that the time had now arrived when the state of his dominions was so satisfactory that he could dispense with the presence and protection of the auxiliary Austrian force. The allied sovereigns acceded to his request for its removal, and a treaty was in consequence concluded, by which it was stipulated that the Austrian troops should begin to evacuate his territories on the 31st December, and that the evacuation should be completed by the delivery of the fortress of Alessandria on the 30th September, 1823. By a separate convention, concluded at the same time, it was agreed that the auxiliary Austrian force which occupied Naples and Sicily, and which was supported entirely at the cost of their inhabitants, should be reduced by seventeen thousand men.[1]

[1] Treaty, Dec. 14, 1822; Ann. Hist. v. 707; Cap. vii. 375, 376.

16. Resolution of the Congress regarding the slave-trade.

A strenuous and most praiseworthy attempt was made by the Duke of Wellington, under Mr. Canning's instructions, to procure some resolution from the allied powers against the slave-trade. He stated, in his note on this subject, that of the eight powers who, in 1815, had signed a declaration against that atrocious traffic, and expressed a desire to "put a period to a scourge which had so long desolated Africa, disgraced Europe, and afflicted humanity," seven had passed laws with the design of prohibiting their subjects entirely from engaging in it; but Portugal and Brazil continued to carry it on to an unprecedented extent. To such a length was this trade now pushed, that during seven months of the year 1821 above 38,000 human beings had been torn from the coast of Africa, and thrown into hopeless and irremediable slavery; and from the month of July, 1820, to that of October, 1821, no less than 352 vessels had entered the rivers of Africa, to the north of the equator, to buy slaves, each of which could carry 500 or 600 slaves, which would, if they were all filled, imply a transportation of nearly 200,000 human beings. Great part of this detestable traffic was stated to be carried on under the French flag. Notwithstanding these appalling facts, which could neither be denied nor controverted, the resistance on the part of the French government to any decisive measure which might exclude them from a share of this lucrative commerce was so great, that all that Great Britain could obtain from the Congress was a vague declaration from the five great powers, "that they have never ceased, and will never cease, to regard the slave-trade as a traffic which has too long desolated Africa, disgraced Europe, and afflicted humanity; and that they are ready, by all means in their power, to concur in all measures which may insure and accelerate the entire and final abolition of that commerce.["2]

[2] Wellington's Note, Nov. 24, 1822; Reponce de Chateaubriand, Nov. 26, 1822; Resolutions des Congrès, Nov. 28, 1822; An. Hist. v. 700, 707.

17. Note of England regarding South American independence.

Another subject was brought under the notice of the Congress by Great Britain, upon which the views of its Cabinet and of that of the Tuileries were still more at variance, and which presaged great and lasting changes in both hemispheres. This was the all-important one of SOUTH AMERICAN INDEPENDENCE. The Duke of Wellington presented a note to the Congress, in which it was stated, "The connection subsisting between the subjects of his Britannic Majesty and the other parts of the globe has for long rendered it necessary for him to recognize the existence *de facto* of governments formed in different places, so far as was necessary to conclude treaties with them; the relaxation of the authority of Spain in her colonies in South America has given rise to a host of pirates and adventurers—an insupportable evil, which it is impossible for England to extirpate without the aid of the local authorities which occupy the adjacent coasts and harbors; and the necessity of this co-operation can not but lead to the recognition *de facto* of a number of governments of their own creation." Veiled under a desire to suppress the undoubted evil of piracy, this was an attempt indirectly to obtain from the Congress some act or declaration amounting to a recognition of the independence of South America. The other powers, accordingly, saw the object, and immediately took the alarm. Austria answered, "that England was perfectly entitled to defend her commercial interests from piracy; but as to the independence of the Spanish colonies, Austria would never recognize it, so long as his Christian Majesty had not formally renounced the rights of sovereignty heretofore exercised over these provinces." Prussia and Russia answered the note in the same terms; and in a long and able note, drawn by M. de Chateaubriand, on the part of France—"In so grave a question, France feels that Spain should, in the first instance, be consulted as sovereign *de jure* of these colonies. France concurs with England in holding that, when intestine troubles have long prevailed, and the law of nations has thereby been practically abrogated, on account of the weakness of one of the belligerent powers, natural right resumes its empire. She admits that there are inevitable prescriptions of some rights, and that, after a government has long resisted, it is sometimes obliged to yield to overbearing necessity, in order to terminate many evils, and prevent one state from alone reaping advantages in which other states are entitled to participate. But to prevent the jealousies and rivalries of commerce, which might involve governments against their will in hostilities, some general measure should be adopted; and perhaps it would be possible to reconcile the interests of Spain, of its colonies, and of the European states, by a measure which, founded on the broad basis of equality and reciprocity, might bring into harmony also the rights of legitimacy and the necessities of policy." The proposed measure, as a matter of course, came to nothing; but the circumstance of its being broached at all proved what adverse interests were arising in the world, and the seeds of what divisions were germinating beneath the treacherous surface of the European alliance.¹

¹ Chateaubriand, Congrès de Vérone, i. 89, 91.

18. Instructions of M. de Villèle to M. de Montmorency regarding Spain.

But all these subjects of division, important and pregnant with future changes as they were, yielded to the Spanish question, for the solution of which the Congress had been assembled, and which required immediate decision. The instructions of M. de Villèle on this subject were very cautiously worded, and intended, above all, to avoid the appearance of France requesting from the other powers *instructions* how to act in the affairs of the Peninsula. They bore, "We have not determined to make war on Spain; the Cortes would carry Ferdinand back to Cadiz rather than suffer him to be conducted to Verona. The situation of France is not such as to oblige us to ask for permission for a war of invasion, as Austria was at Laybach; for we are under no necessity of declaring war at all, nor of asking for succor to carry it on if we do; and we could not admit of it, if it should lead to the passage of foreign troops through our territory. The opinion of our plenipotentiaries upon the question of what the Congress should determine on in regard to Spain is, that *France is the sole power which should act with its troops, and that it must be the sole judge of when it is necessary to do so.* The French plenipotentiaries must never consent that the Congress should prescribe the conduct which France should pursue in regard to Spain. They should accept of no pecuniary succor nor aid from the passage of troops through our territory. They should be firm in considering the Spanish question in its general aspect, and endeavor to obtain from the Congress a contingent treaty, honorable and advantageous to France, either for the case of a war between herself and Spain, or for the case of the powers recognizing the independence of South America.¹

¹ Chateaubriand, Congrès de Vérone, i. 102, 104.

On the other hand, the instructions of England to her plenipotentiary were equally decided, and such as apparently to render almost unavoidable a rupture between the two powers. Lord Londonderry, before his death, had drawn up a note for our plenipotentiaries, which repudiated, in the strongest manner, any interference in the domestic concerns of Spain.* Mr. Canning had only been forty-eight hours in office when he was called on to give his instructions to the Duke of Wellington, who was appointed successor to that lamented nobleman as the plenipotentiary of England; but he had no difficulty in at once drawing them up. His private inclination, not less than his public duty, led him to adhere to the line marked out by Lord Londonderry. His instructions to Wellington, accordingly, on this point were, "If there be a determined project to interfere, by force or by menace, in the present struggle in Spain, so convinced are his Majesty's Ministers of the uselessness and danger of any such interference, so objectionable does it appear to them in principle,² as well as utterly impracticable in execution, that, when the necessity arises—or, I would rather say, when an opportunity presents itself—I am to instruct

19. Mr. Canning's instructions to Duke of Wellington. Sept. 27, 1822.

² Mr. Canning's Instructions to Wellington, Sept. 27, 1822; Ann. Reg. 1822, 97; Public documents, and Ann. Hist. v. 683.

* "With respect to Spain, there seems nothing to add to, or vary, in the course of policy hitherto pursued. Solicitude for the royal family, observance of our engagements with Portugal, and a rigid abstinence from any interference in the internal affairs of that country, must be considered as forming the limits of his Majesty's policy."—Marquis LONDONDERRY's Instructions, transferred to the Duke of Wellington, Sept. 14, 1822. Annual Register, 1822, p. 96. (Public Documents.)

your Grace at once frankly and decidedly to declare, that to *any such interference his Majesty will not be a party.*"

20. Measures adopted by the majority of the Congress on the subject.

When instructions so directly at variance were given to the English and French plenipotentiaries upon a great public question, on which an instant decision required to be taken by the powers immediately concerned, it need not be said that the peace of Europe was seriously threatened. In effect, the divergence of opinion upon this point, as well as the ulterior one of recognizing the independence of the revolted colonies in South America, was so great, that it probably would have been broken, and a calamitous war ensued, if the other powers had been less unanimous and decided than they were in supporting the French view of the necessity of an armed intervention. The Emperor Alexander, from the first, both officially through his plenipotentiaries, and privately in society, expressed his opinion in the strongest manner on this subject, and declared his readiness to support any measures which France might deem essential for its safety. Prussia adopted the same views: the obligations contracted in 1813 rendered no other course practicable to the Cabinet of Berlin. Austria was more doubtful: Metternich had a mortal dread of the northern Colossus, and in secret urged M. de Villèle to adopt no measures which should give the Emperor of Russia a pretext for again moving his troops across Germany. But as he was fully impressed with the danger to Europe from the revolutionary principles acted upon in Spain, and he had himself coerced them in the most vigorous manner in Italy, he could not ostensibly deviate from the other Continental powers on a subject so vital to their common welfare. Accordingly, after several conferences, in the course of which the Duke of Wellington strongly insisted on the necessity of limiting their interference with Spain to resistance to its external aggressions or attempts at propagandism, but not attempting any armed interference with its domestic concerns, the matter came to this, that the Duke of Wellington *refused to sign the procès verbaux* of the conference, when the opinions of the other powers were expressed in favor of an intervention, in certain events, in the Peninsula.[1]

[1] Procès Verbal, Oct. 20, and Nov. 17, 1822; Ann. Hist. v. 683; Chateaubriand, Congrès de Vérone, i. 104, 129.

21. Questions proposed by France, and answers of the Continental powers and England.

The mode of deliberating on this subject was very peculiar, but well calculated to cut short the usual evasions and subterfuges of diplomatic intercourse. France, through its minister, proposed three questions to the Congress, which were as follows: "1. In case France should find herself under the necessity of recalling her embassador from Madrid, and interrupting all diplomatic relations with Spain, are the great powers disposed to adopt similar steps, and to break off their intercourse with that country also? 2. If war should break out between France and Spain, in what way, and by what acts, would the great powers give France their moral support, in such a manner as to inspire a salutary terror into the revolutionists of all countries? 3. What, in fine, are the intentions of the great powers in regard to the extent of the material succor which they are disposed to give to France, in case, on her requisition, such assistance might appear necessary?" To these questions "the three Continental powers answered, on the 30th October, that they would follow the example of France in respect to their diplomatic relations; that they would take the same attitude which France took; and that they would give all the succor of which it might stand in need. A treaty was to fix the period and mode of that co-operation." The Duke of Wellington answered, on the part of Great Britain, "that having no information as to the causes of this misunderstanding, and not being in a situation to form a judgment on the hypothetical case put, it was impossible for him to answer any of the questions." It was afterward agreed that, instead of a joint note being prepared by the four Continental powers, and signed by their respective plenipotentiaries, each should address a separate note to the Cabinet of Madrid of the same general import, but containing in detail the views by which they were severally actuated; which was accordingly done; while the Duke of Wellington addressed a note to the Congress, stating the reasons why his Government abstained from any such intervention.[1*]

[1*] Wellington's Memorandum, Nov. 12, 1822, and Questions of France; Ann. Hist. v. 684, 686.

* The notes of the four Continental powers were all of the same import; that of Prussia was the most explicit, and was in these terms: "The Prussian Government sees with grief the Spanish Government enter upon a career which menaces the tranquillity of Europe; it recollects the title to the admiration of the world which the Spanish nation has given during so many ages, and the heroic perseverance with which it has triumphed over the ambitious and oppressive efforts of the usurper of the throne of France. The moral state of Spain is such at present, that the foreign powers must necessarily find themselves disturbed by it. Doctrines subversive of all social order are there openly preached and protected; daily insults against all the sovereigns of Europe fill its journals with impunity. The clubs of Spain have their emissaries in all quarters, to associate with their dark designs conspirators in every country against the public order and the legitimate authority. The inevitable effect of these disorders is seen in the interruption of the relations between France and Spain. The irritation to which it gives rise is such as to inspire the most serious alarm as to the preservation of peace between the two countries. That consideration itself would suffice to determine the united sovereigns to break silence on a state of things which from day to day threatens to compromise the tranquillity of Europe. It is not for foreign powers to determine what institutions answer best for the character, manners, and real necessities of the Spanish nation; but it belongs to them undoubtedly to judge of the effects which experience has taught them such changes produce upon themselves, and to fix their determination and future position in regard to Spain on these considerations."—CHATEAUBRIAND, *Congrès de Vérone*, i. 130, 131.

On the other hand, the Duke of Wellington, in his note to the Continental sovereigns, said, "The origin, circumstances, and consequences of the Spanish Revolution, the existing state of affairs in Spain, and the conduct of those who have been at the head of the Spanish Government, may have endangered the safety of other countries, and may have excited the uneasiness of the Governments whose Ministers I am now addressing, and those Governments may think it necessary to address the Spanish Government upon the topics referred to in their dispatches. But I would request those Ministers to consider whether the measures now proposed are calculated to allay the irritation against France, and to prevent a possible rupture, and whether they might not with advantage be delayed to a later period. They are certainly calculated to irritate the Government of Spain; to afford ground for a belief that advantage has been taken of the irritation which subsists between that Government and France to call down

22. Views of what had occurred in this Congress.

The business of the Congress at Verona was now concluded, and it had turned out entirely to the advantage of France; for not only had she gained the consent of all the Continental states to the policy which she deemed it expedient to adopt, but, what was of equal importance, she had been allowed to remain the judge of that policy: the other powers had agreed to follow in her wake, not take the lead. For the first time for a very long period, England found herself isolated on the Continent, and doomed to be the impotent spectator of operations which she neither approved of nor could prevent. Without following out further the thread of the negotiations, which were now substantially decided, it is more material to show what were the secret views of the French diplomatists in this, for them, auspicious state of affairs. "The dispatch of M. de Montmorency," said Chateaubriand to M. de Villèle, "will show you the conclusion of the affair of Spain, which has turned out entirely as you wished. This evening we are to have a conference, to determine on the mode of making known the sentiments of the Alliance to Europe. Russia is marvellously favorable; Austria is with us on this, though on other points inclined to the English policy; Prussia follows Austria. The wish of the powers is decidedly pronounced for a war with Spain. It is for you, my dear friend, to consider whether you ought not to seize the occasion, perhaps unique, to replace France in the rank of military powers; to restore the white cockade in a war, in short, almost without danger, to which the opinions of the Royalists and the army strongly incline. There is no question of the occupation of the Peninsula, but of a rapid movement which would restore power to the true Spaniards, and take away from you all disquietude for the future. The last dispatches of M. Lagarde prove how easy that success would be.[1] All continental Europe would be for us; and if England took umbrage, she would not even have time to throw herself on a colony. As to the Chambers, success covers every thing. Doubtless commerce and the finances would suffer for a moment, but nothing great can be done without some inconvenience. To destroy a focus of Jacobinism, to re-establish a Bourbon on the throne by the arms of a Bourbon—these are results which outweigh all considerations of a secondary nature."

[1] Chateaubriand to M. de Villèle, Verona, Oct. 31, 1822, Congrès de Verone, t. 144, 145.

23. Views of M. de Villèle and Louis XVIII.

But while M. de Chateaubriand, M. de Montmorency, and the war party, were with reason congratulating themselves on the success of France at the Congress, very different views were entertained by Louis XVIII. and M. de Villèle at Paris. They were sincerely pacific in their ideas, and, not without reason, extremely apprehensive of the possible consequences of a war with Spain. It was not external, but internal, danger that they dreaded. They were well aware that Spain, in its distracted state, would be wholly unable to withstand the arms of France, if these arms were united; but who could answer for this unanimity prevailing in a war of opinion, when the French troops grouped round the white flag were to be met by the Spanish arrayed under the tricolor standards? The recent disasters of the Royalists in Spain had shown how little reliance was to be placed on their support in any serious conflict; and was there no reason to apprehend that, if the arms and the Liberal press of England were engaged on the side of the republicans in the Peninsula, a convulsion fatal to the reigning dynasty might ensue to the south of the Channel? These considerations weighed much both with the king and his Prime Minister; and although, on his return from the Congress, M. de Montmorency was made a duke, yet grave doubts were still entertained whether it was either prudent or safe to go into the measures agreed on by the Congress. They were confirmed in these opinions by the Duke of Wellington, who, on his way back from Verona, had a long and confidential interview with Louis XVIII. at Paris, in which he represented to him in the strongest manner the extreme danger which France would run in the event of a rupture, both from internal dissension and the loss of the alliance and moral support of England. The great personal influence of the Duke of Wellington, the services he had rendered to the royal cause, and the obvious weight of his arguments, produced such an effect, that they had well-nigh overturned every thing done at Verona, and detached France from the alliance of the Continental sovereigns.[1] *

[1] Lam. vii. 107, 108; Cap. viii. 5, 7.

24. Secret correspondence of M. de Villèle and M. de Lagarde.

The first effect it produced was to overturn M. de Montmorency, and place M. de Chateaubriand in his stead. So uneasy was the king at what the Duke of Wellington had represented, that he demanded a distinct explanation from M. de Montmorency of the causes of complaint which he had against the Spanish government. The latter replied, "that

---

upon Spain the power of the Alliance, and thus to embarrass still more the difficult position of the French Government. His Majesty's Government is of opinion, that to animadvert upon the internal transactions of an independent state, unless such transactions affect the essential interests of his Majesty's subjects, is inconsistent with those principles on which his Majesty has invariably acted on all questions concerning the internal concerns of other countries: that such animadversions, if made, must involve his Majesty in serious responsibility if they should produce any effect, and must irritate if they should not; and if addressed as proposed, to the Spanish Government, are likely to be injurious to the best interests of Spain, and to produce the worst consequences upon the probable discussion between that country and France. The King's Government must therefore decline to advise his Majesty to hold a common language with his allies upon this occasion; and it is so necessary for his Majesty not to be supposed to participate in a measure of this description, and calculated to produce such consequences, that his Government must equally refrain from advising his Majesty to direct that any communication should be made to the Spanish Government on the subject of its relations with France."—Duke of WELLINGTON'S *Note to the Allied Powers*, 20th November, 1822; *Annual Register*, 1822, p. 101. (Public Documents.)

* The duke's instructions on this occasion were as follows: "The Duke of Wellington may declare openly to his Majesty the King of France, that the Government of His Britannic Majesty has always been opposed to any foreign intervention in the internal affairs of Spain. The Spanish Government has given no cause of complaint to any power, and the defects of its constitution are a matter of internal politics, with which no foreign power has any title to interfere."—Mr. CANNING'S *Memorandum to the Duke of Wellington*, Nov. 4, 1822; CAPEFIGUE, viii. 5, 6.

the causes of difference between France and Spain were not of so precise a kind as to admit of an exact and special definition; that a new state of things had been formed by the relations of the two countries; that the opinions in the ascendant in Spain were such as to endanger his Majesty's dominions, and that France would rather incur all the risks of war than expose itself to the inconveniences of the other alternative." Meanwhile the journals in the interest of the respective ministers commenced a violent contest on the subject, the *Journal des Débats* maintaining the necessity of preserving peace, the *Quotidienne* the imperative duty of going to war. In this state of division, both in respect of public opinion and in his own Cabinet, the king, with the concurrence of M. de Villèle, adopted the questionable step of opening, through the Prime Minister, a secret correspondence with M. de Lagarde, the embassador at Madrid, unknown to the Foreign Minister, in which he recommended a conciliatory course of policy, entirely at variance with what had been agreed upon at the Congress, and very nearly in accordance with the views of England on the subject. The idea of Louis XVIII., and which flattered his secret vanity, was, that Ferdinand VII. should follow his example, and *give a constitution to his subjects*, which might establish a representative monarchy in harmony with that existing to the north of the Pyrenees. It never occurred to him that, without the support of the allied bayonets, that constitution never would have been accepted in his own dominions.[1]

[1] Cap. viii. 7, 10; Lam. vii. 107, 108.

* The note of M. de Villèle approved of by Louis XVIII. set forth—" Since the revolution which occurred in Spain in April, 1820, France, regardless of the dangers with which she herself was threatened by that revolution, has used its best endeavors to draw closer the bonds which unite the two kings, and to maintain the connections which unite the two people. But the influences which had led to the changes in the Spanish monarchy have become more powerful than the changes themselves, as it was easy to foresee would be the case. A constitution which King Ferdinand had neither recognized nor accepted in resuming his crown, was imposed upon him by a military insurrection. The natural consequence of that has been, that every discontented Spaniard has conceived himself entitled to seek by the same method an order of things more in harmony with his opinions and principles, and the use of force has caused it to be regarded as a right. Thence the movement of the guard at Madrid, the appearance of armed corps in different parts of Spain. The provinces adjoining France have been the principal theatre of that civil war. Thence arose the necessity on the part of France to take measures for its own security. The events which have taken place since the establishment of the army of observation at the foot of the Pyrenees have sufficiently justified the foresight of his Majesty in forming it. The precautions of France have appeared just to its allies; and the Continental powers have adopted the resolution to unite themselves to her, if it should become necessary, to maintain her dignity and repose. France would have been contented with a resolution at once so friendly and honorable to her; *but Austria, Prussia, and Russia* have deemed it necessary to add to that act of the Alliance a manifestation of their own sentiments. Diplomatic notes have in consequence been addressed to the representatives of these powers at Madrid, who will follow the instructions of their respective courts. As for you, M. le Comte, you will say that the government of the king is intimately united with his allies in the firm determination to *repel* by every means the revolutionary principle; and that it participates equally strongly with them in the desire which they feel that the noble Spanish nation may find a remedy *of itself* for the evils which afflict it—evils which are of a kind to disquiet the governments of Europe, and impose upon them precautions always painful. You will assure them that the people of the Peninsula, restored to tranquillity, will always find in their neighbors sincere and loyal friends. The succor of all kinds which France can dispose of in favor of Spain will always be offered to insure its happiness and increase its prosperity; but you will declare at the same time, that France will relax in none of *its protective measures* so long as Spain shall be torn by factions. His Majesty's government will not hesitate to recall you from Madrid, and to seek for guarantees in more effective dispositions, if its essential interests continue to be compromised, and if he loses all hope of an amelioration, which he still hopes from the sentiments which have so long united the French and Spaniards in the love of their kings and of a wise liberty."—*Le President du Conseil du Ministres au M. le Comte* DE LA GARDE, *Ambassadeur à Madrid*, Paris, 25th Dec., 1822; LACRETELLE, *Histoire de la Restauration*, iii 477-479. *Pièces Justificatifs.*

As soon as M. de Montmorency was made acquainted with this secret intrigue, which virtually superseded him in his own department in the most important branch of state policy, he insisted on a meeting of the Cabinet being called. The point submitted to them was, whether a decided note prepared by M. de Montmorency, in accordance with what had been agreed on at Verona, and to which his personal honor as well as the faith of France stood pledged, should be forwarded to Madrid, to supersede the conciliatory and temporizing one prepared by M. de Villèle? A majority of the council approved of M. de Montmorency's note; in particular, Peyronnet and Clermont-Tonnerre were energetic in its support. The Duke of Belluno (Victor) strongly advocated the same side. He represented the state of opinion in the army, which he as war minister had peculiar means of knowing; that the example of the Spanish revolution was extremely dangerous for the throne of France; that the impression it had already produced upon the soldiers might prove prejudicial to the tranquillity of the country; that it was absolutely necessary to act, to extirpate by force that mania for military revolutions; that the army was well affected, and would become, in a campaign, devoted to the Bourbons, but that it was extremely dangerous to leave it at rest on the frontier. "Nothing," he added, "is so easy of corruption *as a body of troops in a state of inaction:* when they advance, they become animated with one spirit, and are incapable of treachery." On the other hand, M. de Villèle, M. de Lauriston, and M. de Corbière argued in favor of the pacific note, as likely to conciliate matters, and avoid the serious risks of a war of opinion, which might involve all Europe in conflagration. The matter was still in suspense, and the issue doubtful, when Louis cut the matter short by declaring that the note of M. de Villèle appeared to him to express with more prudence than that of M. de Montmorency the opinion of his Cabinet. The consequence was, that M. de Montmorency tendered his resignation, which was accepted; and M. de Chateaubriand, whose public opinion rather than the private favor of the monarch had already designed for his successor, was appointed in his stead.[1]

25. Debate on it in the Cabinet, and resignation of M. de Montmorency, who is succeeded by M. de Chateaubriand.

[1] Cap. viii. 11, 14; Lam. vii. 108, 109.

Although, however, M. de Chateaubriand was borne forward to the portfolio of foreign affairs by a movement in the Cabinet which implied an entire change of national policy on the vital question now at issue between France and Spain, yet no such alteration in

26. The warlike preparations of France continue.

effect took place; and he was compelled, nothing loth, to fall into the system of his predecessor. The pacific note drawn up by M. de Villèle, and approved of by Louis XVIII., was sent to M. de Lagarde, at Madrid, on the 25th December, soon after the more decided notes of the other Continental powers had been presented; but the warlike preparations were not for a moment suspended, and the march of troops to the foot of the Pyrenees continued without intermission. In truth, the current of public opinion in France ran so strongly in favor of war, that, like similar transports which have prevailed in other countries on similar occasions, it was irresistible, and, for good or for evil, must work out its destined effects. The war party in the legislature, always strong, had been greatly augmented by the result of the annual election of a fifth in the preceding autumn, and it now comprehended five-sixths of the entire Chamber of Deputies. On this occasion, too, for the first time since the Restoration, it carried a vast majority of the French nation with it. All classes concurred in demanding hostilities. The Royalists felt their blood roused at the prospect of strife, as the war-horse does at the sound of the trumpet. The army rejoiced at the prospect of a contest, and joyfully wended their way to the Pyrenees, hoping to efface the disgrace of Baylen and Vittoria; the peasants trusted that the days of the Empire and of glory were about to return, and the fields of Spain to be laid open to their ambition or their plunder; the mercantile classes and shopkeepers apprehended, indeed, a diminution of their profits from a rupture of peace, and approved the cautious policy of M. de Villèle, but they were not in sufficient strength to withstand the general current. The revolutionists and democrats in secret were not disinclined to hostilities; they hoped that the troops, when brought into collision with the tricolor standard, would desert their colors, and that, in an attempt to restore the throne of another monarch, Louis would lose his own.[1]

[1] Cap. vii. 23, 25; Lam. vii. 111, 112.

The British government, however, aware of the division on the subject which prevailed in the French cabinet, and of the aversion of the king to war, did all that was possible to avert hostilities. Sir William A'Court, the ambassador at Madrid, received instructions to exert himself to the utmost to procure such a modification of the Constitution from the Cortes itself as might take away all pretext for French interference; and Lord Fitzroy Somerset was, in the first week of January, dispatched from Paris by the Duke of Wellington, in order to co-operate in the same object. All their efforts, however, were in vain. The Spanish government, with that confidence in itself, and insensibility to external danger, which is so characteristic of the nation, obstinately refused to make any concession, or modify the Constitution in the smallest particular. The consequence was, that the ambassadors of Russia, Prussia, and Austria, after having delivered their respective notes as agreed on at the Congress, withdrew from Madrid; and although the French minister remained behind, and with Sir W. A'Court continued his good offices, yet they came to nothing; and ere long M. de Chateaubriand dispatched a note to M. de Lagarde,* recapitulating all the grounds of complaint which France had against Spain, and directing him forthwith to demand his passport. This was accordingly done, and the rapid concentration of forces on the Pyrenees left no doubt that war in good earnest was approaching.[1]

27. Failure of the negotiations at Madrid, and departure of the French ambassador. Jan. 18.

[1] Duke of Wellington to Lord Fitzroy Somerset, Jan. 6, 1823; Ann. Hist. vi. 705; Lam. vii. 113, 114; Cap. viii. 36, 39.

The French Chambers met on the 28th January, and the speech of the king, delivered with great solemnity to a crowded assembly, resounded like a clap of thunder throughout Europe. "France owed to Europe a prosperity which no nation can ever obtain but by a return to religion, legitimacy, order, and true liberty. It is now giving that salutary example; but the Divine justice permits that, after having made other nations long feel the terrible effects of our discord, we should ourselves be exposed to the dangers arising from similar calamities in a neighboring kingdom. I have tried," said the king, in a firm accent, "every thing to secure the peace of my people, and to preserve Spain herself from the last misfortunes; but all in vain. The infatuation with which my efforts have been rejected at Madrid leaves little hope of the possibility of maintaining peace. I have ordered the recall of my minister. A hundred thousand men, commanded by a prince of my family (the Duke d'Angoulême), are ready to march, invoking the God of St. Louis to preserve the throne of Spain to a descendant of Henry IV., to save that fine kingdom from ruin, and reconcile it to Europe. Should war prove inevitable, I shall use my best endeavors to restrict its circle and abridge its duration; it shall only be undertaken to conquer that peace which the present state of Spain renders impossible. Let Ferdinand VII. be free to give to his people the institutions which they can never hold but

28. Speech of the king at the opening of the Chambers. Jan. 28.

* "Le Gouvernement Espagnol rejetant toute mesure de conciliation; nonseulement il ne montrait aucun espoir de l'amélioration que l'on pourrait attendre des sentiments qui avaient, pendant si longtemps, uni les Espagnols et les Français; mais il allait jusqu'à exiger que la France retirât son armée d'observation, et expulsât les étrangers qui lui avaient demandé asile. La France n'est pas accoutumée à entendre un pareil langage, et elle ne le pardonne à son auteur qu'en considération de l'exaspération qui regne en Espagne. Quiconque est le pied sur le territoire français est libre, et jouit des droits d'une hospitalité inviolable. Les victimes des commotions qui agitaient l'Espagne s'y étaient réfugiées, et étaient traitres avec tous les égards dus au malheur. L'Espagne s'est-elle conduite d'une plus mauvaise manière envers la France? Nonseulement elle a donné asile à des hommes coupables, condamnés par les tribunaux, mais encore elle leur a promis des emplois dans ses armées. La confusion qui regne en Espagne actuellement est préjudiciable à quelques-uns de nos plus grands intérêts. Sa Majesté avait désiré que son ministre pût rester à Madrid après le départ des ambassadeurs d'Autriche, de Prusse, et de Russie; mais ses derniers vœux n'ont pas été écoutés; sa dernière espérance a été déçue; le mauvais genie des révolutions préside imaintenant aux conseils de l'Espagne, tout espoir est éloigné; comme l'expression des sentiments les plus modérés ne nous attire que de nouvelles provocations, il ne peut convenir, M. le comte, à la dignité du roi, et à l'honneur de la France, que vous restiez plus longtemps à Madrid. En conséquence, veuillez demander vos passe-ports pour vous-même et toute votre legation, et partez sans perdre de temps immédiatement après qu'ils vous auront été remis."—*M. de Chateaubriand à M. le comte de Lagarde*, Paris, Jan. 5, 1853; CAPEFIGUE, *Histoire de la Restauration*, vi. 37, 38.

of Lyons, and which, in assuring the repose, will dissipate the just disquietudes of France; from that moment hostilities shall cease. I venture to take in your presence, gentlemen, that solemn engagement. I have consulted the dignity of my crown, the honor and security of France. We are Frenchmen, and we shall always be united to defend such interests."¹

<small>Discours du Roi, Jan. 28, 1823; Moniteur, Jan. 29, 1823; Ann. Hist. vi. 668.</small>

28.
King of England's speech at opening of Parliament. February 4.

Such was the war-cry of the Royalists in France, and the aristocratic party throughout Europe, against the Spanish revolution, in the composition of which the fervent genius and poetic mind of M. de Chateaubriand appeared tempered by the statesmanlike caution of M. de Villèle. It was first responded to on this side of the channel, in the king's speech, delivered by commission, at the opening of Parliament on 4th February. "Since you last met," it said, "his Majesty's efforts have been unceasingly exerted to preserve the peace of Europe. Faithful to the principles which his Majesty has promulgated to the world, as constituting the rules of his conduct, his Majesty declined being a party to any proceedings at Verona which could be deemed an interference in the internal concerns of Spain on the part of foreign powers. And his Majesty has since used, and continues to use, his most anxious endeavors and good offices to allay the irritation unhappily subsisting between the French and Spanish governments, and to avert, if possible, the calamity of a war between France and Spain. Discussions have been long pending with the Spanish government respecting depredations committed on the commerce of his Majesty's subjects in the West Indian seas, and other grievances, and those discussions have terminated in an admission by the Spanish government of the justice of his Majesty's complaints, and in an engagement for satisfactory reparation."²

<small>² Ann. Reg. 1823, 4, 5; Parl. Deb. viii. 1, 2.</small>

30.
Reply of the Spanish government. March 1.

The official reply of the Spanish Government to the French declaration was not given till the opening of the session of the ordinary Cortes on 1st March. "The Continental powers," said Ferdinand's ministers, "have raised their voice against the political institutions of that country which has conquered its independence at the price of its blood. Spain, in solemnly answering the insidious accusations of these powers, has rested on the principle that its fundamental laws can be dictated only by itself. That clear and luminous principle cannot be attacked but by sophisms supported by the force of arms; and those who have recourse to these methods in the nineteenth century give the most complete proof of the injustice of their cause. His most Christian Majesty has declared that a hundred thousand French shall come to regulate the domestic affairs of Spain, and correct our institutions. When did soldiers receive the mission of correcting laws? In what code is it written that military invasions are the precursors of the felicity of people? It would be unworthy of reason to attempt the refutation of such antisocial errors; and it does not become a constitutional king of Spain to make an apology for the national cause, in order to defend it against those who cover themselves with the vail of the most detestable hypocrisy to trample under foot all sentiments of shame. I hope that the energy and perseverance of the Cortes will furnish the best reply to the speech of his most Christian Majesty; I hope that, firm in their principle, they will continue to march in the path of their duty—that they will always remain the Cortes of the 9th and 11th January, worthy of the nation which has intrusted to them its destinies. I hope, in fine, that reason and justice will be not less powerful than the genius of oppression and servitude. The nation which enters into negotiation with an enemy whose bad faith is known is already subdued: to receive the law from one who pretends to impose it with arms in his hand is the greatest of ignominies. If war is an evil without a remedy, the nation is magnanimous: it will combat a second time for its independence and its rights. The path of glory is not unknown to it, and the sacrifices it requires will be cheerfully made. The removal of my person, and of the Cortes, into a place less exposed to military operations will defeat the projects of our enemies, and prevent the suspension of acts of the Government which should be known in every part of the monarchy."¹*

<small>¹ Discours du Roi, Madrid, March 1, 1823; Ann. Hist. vi. 715.</small>

31.
M. Hyde de Neuville's address in reply to the speech of the king.

M. Hyde de Neuville, in the address of the Chamber of Deputies, which he prepared in answer to the speech from the throne, even exceeded M. de Chateaubriand in warlike zeal. "Faction," said he, "has at length lost the hope of impunity. France has shown to Europe how public misfortunes repair themselves. Destined by Providence to close the gulf of revolution, the king has tried every thing which can give security to his people, and save Spain from the consequences of a revolution induced by a body of perjured soldiers. A blind obstinacy has rendered them deaf to the counsels of the chief of the Bourbons. Sire! we are Frenchmen; no sacrifice

---

* The best statement of the Spanish side of the question is contained in a previous state paper, by M. Miguel, the Foreign Secretary, to the Russian minister.

"1. La nation Espagnole est gouvernée par une constitution reconnue solennellement par l'empereur de toutes les Russies, dans l'année 1812.

"2. Les Espagnols amis de leur patrie qui ont proclamé, au commencement de 1812, cette constitution, renoncée par la violence de 1814, n'ont point été parjures, mais ils ont la gloire que personne ne peut souiller, d'avoir été les organes du vœu général.

"3. Le roi constitutionnel des Espagnols jouit du libre exercice des droits que lui donne le code fondamental, et tout ce qu'on allègue au contraire de cette assertion est une invention des ennemis de l'Espagne qui la calomnient pour l'avilir.

"4. La nation Espagnole ne s'est jamais mêlée des institutions ni du régime intérieur, ni d'aucun autre.

"5. Et le remède à apporter aux maux qui peuvent l'affliger, n'intéresse qu'elle seule.

"6. Ces maux ne sont pas l'effet de la constitution, mais nous viennent des ennemis qui veulent la détruire.

"7. La nation Espagnole ne reconnaîtra jamais à aucune puissance le droit d'intervenir ni de se mêler de ses affaires.

"8. Le gouvernement de sa Majesté ne s'écartera pas de la ligne que lui tracent son devoir, l'honneur national, et son adhésion invariable au code fondamental juré dans l'année 1812."—E. S. Miguel, Circulaire addressée par le Ministre des affaires étrangères à Madrid aux chargés d'affaires pour les cours de Vienne, Berlin, et St. Pétersbourg, 9th January, 1823; Ann. Hist., vi. 698.

will be regarded by your people which may be necessary to sustain the dignity of your crown, the honor and dignity of France. It is your part to conquer peace by stifling anarchy, to restore liberty to a prince of your blood, to deliver from oppression a people who will aid you to break their chains. Your army is courageous and faithful; that army, which knows how to repel the cowardly invitation to revolt, starts forward with ardor under the *Fleur-de-lis* standard at your voice; it has not taken up, it will not take up arms, but to maintain social order, and to preserve from a fatal contagion our country and our institutions." This address was carried by a majority of 109, the numbers being 202 to 93, and presented to the king amidst unbounded acclamations on the 9th February.[1]

¹ *Moniteur*, Feb. 10, 1823; Ann. Hist. vi. 30, 33.

32. Speech on the war in the House of Commons by Mr. Brougham, Feb. 4.

It was in the debates on the subject, however, in the Chamber of Deputies of France and the English Parliament, that the subject was brought out in its true colors; and in these mighty assemblies, from whence their voices rolled over the globe, the great Parliamentary leaders, on either side, adduced every consideration which could by possibility be urged upon it. Mr. Canning, in consequence of his recent appointment as Foreign Secretary, was not in the House when the debate came on, but his place was ably filled by his antagonist, Mr. Brougham, who, in a speech of extraordinary power and vigor, untrammeled by the restraints of office, gave vent to English opinion on the subject. He said that he "joined with the mover of the address, and with every man who deserved the name of Briton, in abhorrence and detestation at the audacious interference of the allied powers in the internal affairs of Spain; a detestation equaled only by contempt for the hypocrisy by which their principles had been promulgated to the world. The communication made in the king's speech will be tidings of joy and a signal for exultation for England; it will spread joy and exaltation over Spain, will be a source of comfort to all other free states, and will bring confusion and dismay to the Allies, who with a pretended respect for, but a real mockery of, religion and morality, make war upon liberty in the abstract, endeavor to crush national independence wherever it is to be found, and are now preparing with their armed hordes to carry their frightful projects into execution.

"The internal situation of the country is certainly one of deep distress, especially so far as regards that most important and useful branch of the community, the farmers; and I am the last man who would not recommend continued and unsparing economy in every department; but the time has now come, when, to assert our principles and maintain our independence, not only no further diminution, but probably a great increase, of our naval and military establishments has become indispensable. Our intervention, in some shape, will probably be found to be unavoidable; and if war is once begun, perhaps, for the protection of our old ally Portugal, it must be carried on with the whole strength of the empire. I am rejoiced that the ominous words 'strict neutrality' did not escape from the lips of either the mover or seconder of the address. A state of declared neutrality on our part would be nothing less than a practical admission of those principles which we all loudly condemn, and a license to the commission of the atrocities which we are all unanimous in deprecating. It is obviously the duty of his Majesty's Ministers, with whom the whole House on this occasion will be ready to co-operate, in certain events to assist the Spaniards—a course which we, though most averse to war, must be the first on this occasion, and to avert greater evils, to support.

33. Continued.

"To judge of the danger of the principles now shamelessly promulgated, let any one read attentively, and, if he can, patiently, the notes presented by Austria, Prussia, and Russia, to the Spanish government. Can any thing more absurd or extravagant be conceived? In the Prussian note the Constitution of 1812, restored in 1820, is denounced as a system 'which, confounding all elements and all power, and assuming only the principle of a permanent and legal opposition to the Government, necessarily destroyed that central and tutelary authority which constitutes the essence of the monarchical system.' The Emperor of Russia, in terms not less strong, called the constitutional government of the Cortes 'laws which the public reason of all Europe, enlightened by the experience of ages, has stamped with the disapprobation of the public reason of Europe.' What is this but following the example of the autocrat Catherine, who first stigmatized the constitution of Poland, and then poured in her hordes to waste province after province, and finally hewed their way to Warsaw through myriads of unoffending Poles, and then ordered *Te Deum* to be sung for her success over the enemies of Poland? Such doctrines, promulgated from such quarters, are not only menacing to Spain; they threaten every independent country; they are leveled at every free constitution. Where is the right of interference to stop, if these armed despots, these self-constituted judges, are at liberty to invade independent states, enjoying a form of government different from their own, on pretense of the principle on which it is founded being not such as they approve, or

34. Continued.

---

* M. Hyde de Neuville, one of the most brilliant and distinguished characters of the Restoration, had devoted to the exiled family, when in misfortune, his youth, his fortune, and put in hazard his life. Descended from English ancestry, he had inherited from his Cavalier forefathers that generous devotion to the royal family which in them had become a species of worship, to which honor, religion, and country alike summoned, and to which exile and the scaffold seemed only the appropriate sacrifice. During the Republic and the Empire he was actively engaged in all the conspiracies for the restoration of the Bourbons. During the latter years of the Empire, when all hopes of a restoration seemed lost, and Europe could no longer present a safe asylum, he took refuge in America, where he learned to mingle respect for popular freedom with a devoted respect to the principles of loyalty to the sovereign. Returning to France in 1814 with the exiled princes, he was elected deputy for Berry, his native province; and in the Chamber he soon signalized himself among the Royalists by his ardent loyalty, coupled with a manly eloquence and decision of character, which bespoke the man of action as well as the orator. His noble figure, martial air, and erect carriage—his numerous adventures, the dungeons he had occupied, his persecutions, his exile—threw an air of romance about his character, and augmented the influence due to his loyalty, eloquence, and courage.—LAMARTINE, *Hist. de la Rest.*, vii. 122, 123.

which they deem dangerous to the frame of society established among themselves?

25. Continued.
"It is true, there have been civil war and bloodshed in Spain, but how have they been excited? By an ally. They were produced by those cordons of troops which were stationed along the frontiers armed with gold and steel, and affording shelter and assistance to those in whose minds disaffection had been excited by bribery. It is true, blood has been shed; but what blood was it? Why, it was the blood of persons who attacked the existing Government, which Alexander and all the Allies had recognized in 1812, and who were repulsed in direct rebellion against the Royal authority. As well might the people, Parliament, and Crown of England be charged with causing blood to flow, because the sentinels at St. James's fired on some persons attempting to force the palace or assassinate the king. And who is it that uses this monstrous language? It is Russia, a power only half-civilized, that with all her colossal mass of physical strength is still as much Asiatic as European, whose principles of policy, both foreign and domestic, are completely despotic, and whose practices are almost entirely Oriental and barbarous. Its language is, when unvailed, nothing but this—'We have hundreds of thousands of hired mercenaries, and we will not stoop to reason with those whom we would insult and enslave.'

36. Continued.
"It is impossible not to admire the equal frankness with which this haughty language has been met by the Spanish government; the papers which it sent forth were plain and laconic. They said, 'We are millions of freemen, and will not stoop to reason with those who would enslave us.' They hurled back the menaces upon the head which uttered it, little caring whether it were Goth, Hun, or Calmuck, with a frankness that outwitted the craft of the Bohemian and defied the ferocity of the Tartar. If they found all the tyrants of the earth leagued against them, they might console themselves with the reflection, that wherever there was an Englishman, either of the Old or New World—wherever there was a Frenchman, with the exception of that miserable little band which now for the moment swayed the destinies of France, in opposition to the wishes and sentiments of its liberal and gallant people—a people who, after wading through the blood of the Revolution, were entitled, if any ever were, to enjoy the blessings of freedom—wherever there breathed an Englishman or a true-born Frenchman, wherever there existed a free heart and a virtuous mind, there Spain had a natural ally, and an unalienable friend.

37. Continued.
"When the allied powers were so ready to interfere in the internal concerns of Spain, because they were afraid of its freedom, and when the most glaring attempts were made in all their state papers to excite rebellion among its inhabitants, what is so easy as to retort upon them with the statement of some of their domestic misdeeds? What was to hinder the Spaniards to remind the Prussian monarch of the promises which, in a moment of alarm, he made to his subjects of giving them a free constitution, and to ask him what has come of the pledges then given to his loyal and gallant subjects, by whose valor he has regained his lost crown? Might they not ask whether it would not have been better to have kept these promises, than to have kept on foot, at his people's cost, and almost to their ruin, a prodigious army, only to defend him in violating them? Could any thing have been more natural than to have asked the Emperor of Austria whether he, who professed such a regard for strict justice in Ferdinand's case, when it cost him nothing, had always acted with equal justice toward others when he himself was concerned? that, before he was generous to Ferdinand, he should be just to George, and repay some part of the £20,000,000 he had borrowed of him, and which alone had enabled him to preserve his crown? Might he not be called to account for the noble and innocent blood he had shed in the Milanese, and the tortures, stripes, and dungeons he had inflicted on the flower of his subjects in his Italian provinces? Even the Emperor Alexander himself, sensitive as he was at the sight of blood flowing in a foreign palace, might call to mind something which had occurred in his own. However pure in himself, and however fortunate in having agents equally innocent, was he not descended from an illustrious line of ancestors, who had with exemplary uniformity dethroned, imprisoned, and slaughtered husbands, brothers, children? Not that he could dream of imputing these enormities to the parents, sisters, or consorts; but it somehow happened that those exalted and near relations never failed to reap the whole benefit of the atrocities, and had never, in one single instance, made any attempt to bring the perpetrators of them to justice.

28. Continued.
"I rejoice that the Spaniards have such men only to contend with. I know there are fearful odds when battalions are arrayed against principles; but it is some consolation to reflect, that those embodied hosts are not aided by the talents of their chiefs, and that all the weight of character is happily on the other side. It is painful to think that so accomplished and enlightened a prince as the King of France should submit to make himself the tool of such a junta of tyrants. I would entreat him to reflect on the words of the most experienced statesman, and one of the greatest philosophers of antiquity, in his recently discovered work, *De Republica*—'Non in ulla civitate, nisi in qua summa potestas populi est, ullum domicilium libertas habet.' When called on to combat one of the most alarming conspiracies that ever man was exposed to, he had recourse only to the Roman constitution; he threw himself on the good-will of his patriotic countrymen; he put forth only the vigor of his own genius, and the vigor of the law; he never thought of calling in the assistance of the Allobroges, Teutones, or Scythians of his day. And now I say, that if the King of France calls in the modern Teutones, or the modern Scythians, to assist him in this unholy war, judgment will that moment go forth against him and his family, *and the dynasty of Gaul will be changed at once and forever*.

29. Concluded.
"The principles on which this band of congregated despots have shown their readiness to act are dangerous in the extreme, not only to free, but to every

independent state. If the Czar were met with his consistory of tyrants and armed critics, it would be in vain for the Ulema to plead that their government was one of the most sacred and venerable description; that it had antiquity in its favor; that it was replete with 'grand truth;' that it had never listened to 'the fatal doctrines of a disorganized philosophy;' and that it had never been visited by any such things as 'dreams of fallacious liberty.' In vain would the Ulema plead these things; the '*three gentlemen* of Verona' would pry about for an avenue, and when it suited his convenience to enter, the Czar would be at Constantinople, and Prussia would seek an indemnity in any province England might possess adjacent to their territory. It behoves every independent state to combine against such monstrous pretensions. Already, if there is any force in language, or any validity in public documents, we are committed to the defensive treaties into which we have entered. If Spain is overrun by foreign invaders, what will be the situation of Portugal? And are we not bound, by the most express treaty, as well as by obvious interest, to defend that ancient ally? Above all things, we ought to repeal, without delay, the Foreign Enlistment Bill—a measure which ought never to have been passed. Let us, in fine, without blindly rushing into war, be prepared for any emergency; speak a language that is truly British, pursue a policy which is truly free; look to free states as our best and natural allies against all enemies whatever; quarreling with none, whatever be their form of government; keeping peace whenever we can, but not leaving ourselves unprepared for war; not afraid of the issue, but calmly determined to brave its hazards; resolved to support, amidst any sacrifice, the honor of the crown, the independence of the country, and every principle considered most valuable and sacred among civilized nations."[1]

[1 Parl.Deb. vm. 46, 61.]

40. Mr. Canning adopts the principle of non-interference. Feb 24.

This animated and impassioned harangue contained the sentiments merely of an individual, who, how eminent soever, did not in the general case of necessity implicate any one but himself, or, at most, the political party to which he belonged. But on this occasion it was otherwise. Mr. Brougham's speech was not merely the expression of his own or his party's opinion; it was the channel by which the feelings of a whole nation found vent. The cheers with which it was received from both sides of a most crowded House, the vast impression it made on the country, the enthusiasm it every where excited, proved, in the clearest manner, that it carried the universal mind with it. Mr. Canning was not in the House when this important debate occurred, having vacated his seat upon his appointment as Foreign Minister, and not been yet again returned; but he gave his sanction to the principles it contained on 24th February, when he observed,[2] "I am compelled in justice to say that, when I entered upon the office I have the honor to fill, I found the principles on which the Government was acting reduced into writing, and this state paper formed what I may be allowed to call the po-

[2 Lord Londonderry's Memoir; Ante, c. xii, § 19.]

litical creed of Ministers. Upon the execution of the principles there laid down, and upon it alone, is founded any claim I may have to credit from the House." And again, on 14th April, in the debate on the Spanish negotiation, he said, "I cast no blame upon those who, seeing a great and powerful nation eager to crush and overwhelm with its vengeance a less numerous, but not less gallant people, are anxious to join the weaker party. Such feelings are honorable to those who entertain them. The bosoms in which they exist, unalloyed by any other feelings, are much more happy than those in which that feeling is chastened and tempered by considerations of prudence, interest, and expedience. I not only know, but absolutely envy, the feelings of those who call for war, for the issue of which they are not to be responsible; for I confess that the reasoning by which the war against Spain was attempted to be justified appears to me to be much more calculated than the war itself to excite a strong feeling against those who had projected it. There is no analogy between the case of England in 1793 and France in 1823. What country had Spain attempted to seize or revolutionize, as France did before our declaration of 19th November, 1792? England made war against France, not because she had altered her own government, or even dethroned her own king, but because she had invaded Geneva, Savoy, and Avignon; because she had overrun Belgium, and threatened to open the mouth of the Scheldt, in defiance of treaties; and because she openly announced, and acted upon, the determination to revolutionize every adjoining state. But this country is not prepared to give actual and efficient support to Spain; absolute *bonâ fide* neutrality is the limit to which it is prepared to go in behalf of a cause to which its Ministers can never feel indifferent."[1]

[1 Parl. Deb. viii. 242, 890, 895.]

41. M. de Chateaubriand's reply in the French Chambers.

On the other hand, it was maintained by M. de Chateaubriand in the French Chamber, in a speech worthy of himself and of these great antagonists: "Has a government of one country a right to interfere in the affairs of another? That great question of international law has been resolved by different writers on the subject in different ways. Those who incline to the natural right, such as Bacon, Puffendorf, Grotius, and all the ancients, maintain that it is lawful to take up arms in the name of the human race against a society which violates the principles on which the social order reposes, on the same ground on which, in particular states, you punish an individual malefactor who disturbs the public repose. Those again who consider the question as one depending on civil right, are of opinion that no one government has a right to interfere in the affairs of another. Thus the first vest the right of intervention in duty, the last in interest. I adopt in the abstract the principles of the last. I maintain that no government has a right to interfere in the affairs of another government. In truth, if this principle is not admitted, and above all by people who enjoy a free constitution, no nation could be in security. It would always be possible for the corruption of a minister or the ambition of a king to attack a state which attempted to ameliorate its condition. In many cases wars would be multiplied; you would adopt a principle of eternal hostility—a principle of which every one would constitute himself judge, since every one might say to his neighbor, Your institutions displease me; change them, or I declare war.

"But when I present myself in this tribune to defend the right of intervention in the affairs of Spain, how is an exception to be made from the principle which I have so broadly announced? It is thus: When the modern political writers rejected the right of intervention, by taking it out of the category of natural to place it in that of civil right, they felt themselves very much embarrassed. Cases will occur in which it is impossible to abstain from intervention without putting the state in danger. At the commencement of the Revolution, it was said, 'Perish the colonies rather than one principle,' and the colonies perished. Shall we also say, 'Perish the social order,' rather than sacrifice a principle, and let the social order perish? In order to avoid being shattered against a principle which themselves had established, the modern jurists have introduced an exception. They said—'No government has a right to interfere in the affairs of another government, *except in the case where the security and immediate interests of the first government are compromised.*' I will show you immediately where the authority for that exception is to be found. The exception is as well established as the rule; for no state can allow its essential interests to perish without running the risk of perishing itself. Arrived at that point of the question, its aspect entirely changes; we are transported to another ground; I am no longer obliged to combat the rule, but to show that the case of the exception has accrued for France.

"I shall frequently have occasion, in the sequel of this discourse, to speak of England; for it is the country which our honorable antagonists oppose to us at every turn. It is Great Britain which singly at Verona has raised its voice against the principle of intervention; it is that country which alone is ready to take up arms to defend a free people; it is it which denounces an impious war, at variance with the rights of nations—a war which a small, servile, and bigoted faction undertakes, in the hope of being able to burn the Charter of France after having torn in pieces the Constitution of Spain. Well, gentlemen, England is that country; it alone has respected the rights of nations, and given us a great example. Let us see what England has done in former days.

"That England, in safety amidst the waves, and defended by its old institutions —that England, which has neither undergone the disasters of two invasions, nor the overturnings of a revolution of thirty years, conceives it has nothing to fear from the Spanish revolution, is quite conceivable, and no more than was to be expected. But does it follow from that, that France enjoys the same security, and is in the same position? When the circumstances were different—when the essential interests of Great Britain were compromised—did it not—justly, without doubt

42. *Continued.*

43. *Continued.*

44. *Continued.*

—depart from the principles which it so loudly invokes at this time? England, in entering on the war with France, published in 1793 the famous declaration of Whitehall, from which I read the following extract: 'The intention announced to reform the abuses of the French government, to establish personal freedom and the rights of property on a solid basis, to secure to a numerous people just and moderate laws, a wise legislature, and an equitable administration—all these salutary views have unhappily disappeared. They have given place to a system destructive of all public order, sustained by proscriptions, exiles, and confiscations without number, by arbitrary imprisonments without number, and by massacres the memory of which alone makes us shudder. The inhabitants of that unhappy country, so long deceived by promises of happiness, everlastingly renewed at every fresh accession of public suffering, the commission of every new crime, have found themselves plunged in an abyss of calamities without example.

"'Such a state of things can not exist in France without involving in danger the countries which adjoin it, without giving them the right, and imposing on them the duty, of doing every thing in their power to arrest an evil which subsists only on the violation of all laws which unite men in the social union. His Majesty has no intention of denying to France the rights of reforming its laws; never will he desire to impose by external force a government on an independent state. He desires to do so now only because it has become essential to the repose and security of other states. In these circumstances, he demands of France—and he demands it with a just title—to put a stop to a system of anarchy, which has no power but for evil, which renders France incapable of discharging the first duties of government, that of repressing anarchy and punishing crime, which is daily multiplying in all parts of the country, and which threatens to involve all Europe in similar atrocities and misfortune. He demands of France a legitimate and stable government, founded on the universally recognized principles of justice, and capable of retaining nations in the bonds of peace and friendship. The king engages beforehand instantly to stop hostilities, and give protection to all those who shall extricate themselves from an anarchy which has burst all the bonds of society, broken all the springs of social life, confounded all duties, and made use of the name of Liberty to exercise the most cruel tyranny, annihilate all charters, overturn all property, and deliver over entire provinces to fire and sword.'

"It is true, when England made that famous declaration, Louis XVI. and Marie Antoinette were no more. I admit that Marie-Josephine is as yet only a captive; that her tears only have been caused to flow. Ferdinand is still a prisoner in his palace, as Louis XVI. was in his before being led to the Temple and the scaffold. I have no wish to calumniate the Spaniards, but I can not esteem them more than my own countrymen. Revolutionary France gave birth to a Convention; why should not revolutionary Spain do the same? England has murdered its

45. *Continued.*

46. *Continued.*

Charles I., France its Louis XVI.; if Spain follows their example, a series of precedents in favor of crime will be established, and a body of jurisprudence of people against their sovereigns.

"England herself has admitted the principle for which I contend, in recent times. She has conceded to others the right for which she contended herself. She did not consider herself entitled to interfere in the case of the Italian revolution, but she judged otherwise for Austria; and accordingly Lord Castlereagh, while repudiating the right of intervention in that convulsion claimed by Austria, Prussia, and Russia, declared expressly, in his circular from Laybach of 19th January, 1821—'It must be clearly understood that no government can be more disposed than the British to maintain the right of any state or states to intervene when *its immediate security or essential interests* are seriously compromised by the transactions of another state.' Nothing can be more precise than that declaration; and Mr. Peel has not been afraid to say on a late occasion in the House of Commons, that Austria 'was entitled to interfere in the affairs of Naples, because that country had adopted the Spanish Constitution:' no one can contest the right of France to interfere in those of Spain, when it is menaced by that Constitution itself.

"Can any one doubt that we are in the exceptional case—that our interests are essentially injured by the Spanish revolution? Our commerce is hampered by the suffering consequent on that convulsion. We are obliged to keep vessels of war in the American seas, which are infested by pirates who have sprung out of the anarchy of Europe; and we have not, like England, maritime forces to protect our ships, many of which have fallen into their hands. The provinces of France adjoining Spain are under the most pressing necessity to see order re-established beyond the Pyrenees. Our consuls have been menaced in their persons, our territory three times violated; are not their 'essential duties' compromised? And how has our territory been violated? To massacre a few injured Royalists, who thought themselves in safety under the shadow of our generous country. We have been obliged, in consequence, to maintain a large army of observation on the frontier; without that, our southern provinces could not enjoy a moment's security. That state of semi-hostility has all the inconveniences of war without the advantages of peace. Shall we, in obedience to the partisans of peace, withdraw the army of observation? Certes, we are not yet reduced to the necessity of flying before the chevaliers of the Hammer, or giving place to the Landabarian bands. England herself has recognized the necessity of our army of observation, for the Duke of Wellington said at the Congress of Verona, 'Considering that a civil war has been lighted on the whole extent of the frontier which separates the two kingdoms, no one can contest the necessity of establishing the army of observation.'

"It was not I who spoke first of the *moral contagion*, but since it has been mentioned by our adversaries, I confess that it is the most serious and alarming of all the dangers. Is any one ignorant that the revolutionists of Spain are in correspondence with our own? Have they not by public proclamations invited our soldiers to revolt? Have they not threatened to bring down the tricolor flag from the summit of the Pyrenees, to restore the son of Bonaparte? Do we not know the plots, the conspiracies of those traitors who have escaped from the hands of justice in this country, and now pretend to invade us in the uniform of the brave, unworthy to cover their treacherous hearts? Can a revolution which rouses in us such passions, and awakens such recollections, ever fail to compromise our essential interests? Can it be said to be shut up in the Peninsula, when it has already crossed the Pyrenees, revolutionized Italy, shaken France and England? Have the occurrences at Naples and Turin not sufficiently proved the danger of the moral contagion? And let it not be said the revolutionists in these states adopted the Constitution of the Cortes on account of its excellence. So far from that being the case, the first thing they were obliged to do, after having adopted the Spanish Constitution, was to appoint a commission to examine what it was. Thus it soon passed away, as every thing does which is foreign to the customs of a country. Ridiculous from its birth, it expired in disgrace between an Austrian corporal and an Italian Carbonari.

"Whence this extraordinary passion for England, and praise of its constitution, which has suddenly sprung up among us? A year has not elapsed since the boulevards were covered with caricatures, which insulted in the grossest manner every thing connected with London. In their love of revolution, the same persons have forgotten all their hatred for the soldiers who were fortunate at Waterloo: little does it signify what they have done, provided now they aid them in supporting the revolutionists of Spain against a Bourbon. How has it happened that the Allies, now so much the object of animadversion, were not then regarded in the same light? Where was their jealousy of the Continental powers when they paraded with so much satisfaction their approval of the *coup d'état* of 5th September, which revolutionized the legislature; or the prosecutions of the Royalists, which shook the foundation of the throne? Who heard then of the dignity of France, or its being unworthy of her to seek support in the approbation of foreign states? When we had no army—when we were counted as nothing in the estimation of foreign states—when little German states invaded us with impunity, and we did not venture to utter a complaint—no one said that we were slaves. But now, when our military resurrection has astonished Europe—now, when we raise a voice in the councils of kings which is always attended to—now, when new and honorable conventions expiate those in which we expiated our victories, we are now for the first time told that we are placing our necks under a humiliating yoke.

"I admit at once, France has no title to intermeddle in the internal concerns of Spain. It is for the Spaniards to determine what species of constitution befits them. I wish them, from the bottom of my heart, liberties commensurate to their morals, institutions which may put their virtues beyond the reach of fortune or the caprice of men. Spaniards! It is no enemy of yours who thus speaks; it is he who had predicted the return of your noble destinies, when all believed you forever disappeared from the scene of the world.* You have surpassed my predictions; you have rescued Europe from a yoke which the most powerful empires had sought in vain to break. You owe to France your misfortunes and your glory; she has sent you these two scourges, Bonaparte and the Revolution. Deliver yourselves from the second, as you have delivered yourselves from the first.

"As to the Ministers, the speech of the Crown has traced the line of their duties.

52. Concluded. They will never cease to desire peace, to invoke it from the bottom of their hearts, to listen to every proposition compatible with the honor and security of France; but it is indispensable that Ferdinand should be free; it is necessary that France, at all hazards, should extricate itself from a position in which it would perish more certainly than from all the dangers of war. Let us never forget that, if the war with Spain has, like every other war, its inconveniences and perils, it has also for us this immense advantage: it will have created an army; it will have caused us to resume our military rank among nations; it will have decided our emancipation, and re-established our independence. Something was perhaps awanting to the entire reconciliation of Frenchmen; that something will be found beneath the tent; companions in arms are soon friends; and all recollections are lost in the remembrance of a common glory. The king, that monarch so wise, so pacific, so paternal, has spoken. He has thought that the security of France and the dignity of the Crown rendered it imperative on him to have recourse to arms, after having exhausted the counsels of peace. He has declared his wish that a hundred thousand men should assemble under the orders of a prince who, at the passage of the Drome showed himself as valiant as Henry IV.[1] With generous confidence he has intrusted the guard of the white flag to the captains who have triumphed under other colors. They will teach him the path of victory; he has never forgotten that of honor."[2]

[1] Ante, c. iii. § 87.
[2] Ann. Hist. vi. 38, 40; Lam. vii. 129, 137; Moniteur, February 15, 1823.

53. Immense sensation produced by this speech. This splendid speech made a prodigious sensation in France, greater perhaps than any other since the days of Mirabeau. It expressed with equal force and felicity the inmost and best feelings of the Royalists; and those feelings were on this occasion, perhaps for the first time, in unison with the sentiments of the great majority of Frenchmen. The nation had become all but unanimous at the sound of the trumpet. The inherent adventurous and warlike spirit of the Franks had reappeared in undiminished strength at the prospect of war. Chance, or the skillful direction of Government, had at last found an object in which all classes concurred—in which the ardent loyalty of the Royalist coincided with the buoyant ambition of the people. In vain the Liberal chiefs, who anticipated so much from the triumph of their allies beyond the Pyrenees, and dreaded utter discomfiture from their defeat, endeavored to turn aside the stream, and to envenom patriotic by party feelings. The attempt wholly failed: the Chambers were all but unanimous in favor of the war; and their feelings were re-echoed from Calais to the Pyrenees.[1]

[1] Lam. vii. 136, 137; Ann. Hist. vi. 34, 41.

54. M. Talleyrand's speech on the war. M. Talleyrand made a remarkable speech on this occasion, which deserves to be recorded, as one of the most unfortunate prophecies ever made by a man of ability on the future issue of affairs. "It is just sixteen years to-day," said he, "since I was called by him who then governed the world to give him my advice on the struggle in which he was about to engage with Spain. I had the misfortune to displease him because I revealed the future—because I unfolded the misfortunes which might arise from an aggression as unjust as it was inexpedient. Disgrace was the reward of my sincerity. Strange destiny!—which now, after so long an interval, leads me to give the same counsels to a legitimate sovereign! It is my part, who have had so large a share in the double Restoration—who, by my efforts, I may say by my success, have wound up my glory and my responsibility entirely with the alliance between France and the house of Bourbon—to contribute as much as lies in my power to prevent the work of wisdom and justice from being compromised by rash and insane passions." When this counsel on the Spanish war is compared with the result which occurred a few months afterward, the difference is sufficiently striking. Talleyrand, with his sagacity and experience, proved a more fallacious counselor than Chateaubriand, with his poetry and romance. Wisdom was found in the inspirations of genius rather than the deductions of experience. The reason is, that Talleyrand thought the result would be the same, because it was an attack by France on Spain, forgetting that the circumstances were materially different, and that the Bourbon invasion had that in its favor which in that of Napoleon was altogether awanting—viz., the support of the great body of the people. A memorable example of the important truth, that events in history are not to be drawn into a precedent unless the material circumstances attending them are similar; and that it is in the faculty of discerning where that similarity exists that the highest proof of political wisdom is to be found.[2]

[2] Lam. vii. 120; Ann. Hist. vi. 34, 35.

55. Vote of credit of 100,000,000 francs. The enthusiasm of the Chamber of Deputies in favor of the war did not evaporate merely in vehement harangues from the tribune; substantial acts testified their entire adhesion to the system of the Government. They voted, by a very large majority, a supplementary credit of

* M. de Chateaubriand alluded to the following passage in his Génie du Christianisme, published in 1803: "L'Espagne, séparée des autres nations, présente encore à l'historien un caractère plus original. L'espèce de stagnation de mœurs dans laquelle elle repose, lui sera peut-être utile un jour; et lorsque les peuples européens seront usés par la corruption, elle seule pourra reparaître avec éclat sur la scène du monde, parce que le fond des mœurs subsiste chez elle."—Génie du Christianisme, partie iii. t. iii. c. 4.

100,000,000 francs (£4,000,000) for carrying on the war, to be put at the disposal of the minister. The state of the revenue this year was very flattering, and demonstrated how rapidly the national resources were augmenting under the influence of the peace, freedom, and security of property which France was enjoying under the mild rule of the Bourbon princes.*[1]

[1 Ann. Hist. vi. 39, 40.]

56. Affair of M. Manuel, in the Chamber of Deputies; his speech.

In the course of the debate on this grant, an incident occurred, which, in a more unfavorable state of the public mind, might have overturned the monarchy. M. Manuel was put forward by the Opposition to answer the speech of M. Chateaubriand, he being the orator on the Liberal side whose close and logical reasoning, as well as powers of eloquence, were deemed most capable of deadening the sensation produced by the splendid oration of the Foreign Minister. He said, in the course of his speech—"The Spaniards, it is said, are mutually cutting each other's throats, and we must intervene to prevent one party from destroying the other. It is without doubt a singular mode of diminishing the horrors of civil war, to superinduce to them those of foreign hostilities. But suppose you are successful. The insurrection is crushed in Spain; it is annihilated; the friends of freedom have laid down their arms. What can you do? You can not forever remain in the Peninsula; you must retire; and when you do so, a new explosion, more dangerous than the former, will break forth. Consult history: has ever a revolution in favor of civil liberty been finally subdued? Crushed it may be for the moment; but the genius which has produced it is imperishable. Like Antæus, the giant regains his strength every time he touches the earth.

57. Continued.

"The civil war which recently raged in Spain was mainly your own work; the soldiers 'of the faith' only took up arms in the belief they would be supported by you. How, then, can you find in the consequences of your own acts a justification of your intervention? Can you justify deeds of violence by perfidy? You say you wish to save Ferdinand and his family. If you do, beware of repeating the same circumstances which, in a former age, conducted to the scaffold victims for whom you daily evince so warm and legitimate an interest. Have you forgotten that the Stuarts were only overturned because they sought support from the stranger; that it was in consequence of the invasion of the hostile armies that Louis XVI. was precipitated from the throne? Are you ignorant that it was the protection accorded by France to the Stuarts which caused the ruin of that race of princes? That succor was clandestine, it is true; but it was sufficient to encourage the Stuarts in their resistance to public opinion; thence the resistance to that opinion, and the misfortunes of that family—misfortunes which it would have avoided if it had sought its support in the nation. Need I remind you that the dangers of the royal family have been fearfully aggravated when the stranger invaded our territory, and that revolutionary France, feeling the necessity of defending itself by new forces and a fresh energy—"[1]

[1 Ann. Hist. vi. 72, 73; Lam. vii. 161, 163.]

58. Storm in the Chambers.

At these words a perfect storm arose in the Chamber. "Order, order!" was shouted on the Right; "this is regicide justified and provoked." "Expulsion, expulsion!" "Let us chase the monster from our benches!" exclaimed a hundred voices. The president, M. Ravez, seeing the speaker had been interrupted in the midst of a sentence, and that the offence taken arose from a *presumed* meaning of words which were to follow, not of what had actually been used, hesitated with reason to act upon such speculative views, and contented himself with calling M. Manuel to order. So far were the Royalists from being satisfied with this moderate concession, that they instantly rose up in a body, surrounded the president's chair with loud cries and threats, demanding that the apologist of regicide should be instantly expelled from the Chamber; while one of them, more audacious than the rest, actually pulled M. Manuel from the tribune, and, mounting in his stead, demanded in a stentorian voice the vengeance of France on the advocate of assassins. Meanwhile M. Manuel, conscious that the sentence which had been interrupted, if allowed to be completed, would at once dispel the storm, was calm and impassible in the midst of the uproar; but that only made matters worse with the infuriated majority; and at length the president, finding all his efforts to appease the tumult fruitless, gave the well-known signal of distress by covering his head, and broke up the meeting.[2]

[2 Ann. Hist. vi. 70, 73; Moniteur, Feb. 27, 1823; Lam. vii. 162, 163.]

59. Expulsion of M. Manuel.

This scene had already been sufficiently violent, and indicative of the risks which the representative system ran in France from the excitable temper of the people; but it was as nothing to that which soon after ensued. The Royalists, when the meeting was dissolved, rushed in a body out of the Chamber, and broke into separate knots, to concert ulterior operations; while the Liberals remained on their benches, in the midst of which M. Manuel wrote a letter to the president, in which he stated how the sentence which had been interrupted was to have been concluded, and contended for his right to finish the sentence, and then let its import be judged of by the Chamber.* The sitting was resumed, to consider this explanation; but a heated Royalist from the south, M. Forbin des Essarts, instantly ascended the tribune, and demanded the expulsion of the orator

---

* It exhibited a surplus of 42,915,907 francs (£1,680,000), so that the extraordinary credit only required to be operated upon to the extent of 57,054,093 francs (£2,310,000).—Budget, 1823. *Annuaire Historique*, vi. 29, 40.

* " 'Je demandais si on avait oublié qu'en France la mort de l'infortuné Louis XVI. avait été précédée par l'intervention armée des Prussiens et des Autrichiens, et je rappelais comme un fait connu de tout le monde que c'est alors que la France révolutionnaire, sentant le besoin de se défendre par des forces et une énergie nouvelles.' C'est ici que j'ai été interrompu. Si je n'eusse pas été, ma phrase eut se prononcer ainsi:—'Alors la France révolutionnaire, sentant le besoin de se défendre par des forces et une énergie nouvelles, mit en mouvement toutes les masses, exalta toutes les passions populaires, et au risque de terribles excès et une déplorable catastrophe ou même d'une généreuse résistance.'"—M. MANUEL au Président, 26th Feb. 1823. *Annuaire Historique*, vi. 108. *Moniteur*, 27th Feb.

"who had pronounced such infamous expressions, seeing no rules of procedure could condemn an assembly to the punishment of hearing a man whose maxims and speech recommended or justified regicide." M. Manuel attempted to justify himself; but he was again interrupted by the cries of the Royalists, and the president, hoping to gain time for the passions to cool, adjourned the sitting to the following day. But in this hope he was disappointed, as is generally the case when consideration succeeds after the feelings have been thoroughly roused. What is called reflection is then only *listening to the re-echo of passion;* one only voice is heard, one only key is touched, one only sentiment felt. A lover, who is contending with himself, rises from his sleepless couch confirmed, not shaken, in his prepossessions. During the night, a formal motion for the expulsion of the supposed delinquent, for the remainder of the session, was prepared by M. de la Bourdonnaye, the acknowledged leader of the extreme Royalists; and although the justice or shame of the Chamber permitted M. Manuel to be heard in his defense, and the debate was more than once adjourned, to enable the numerous speakers, who inscribed their names on the tribune, to be heard on the question, the torrent was irresistible. The determination of the Royalists only increased with the effervescence of the public mind; and, amidst agitated crowds which surrounded the Assembly on all sides, and under the protection of squadrons of cavalry, the expulsion of M. Manuel, during the remainder of the session, was voted, on the evening of 4th March, by a majority of fully two to one, the whole Centre coalescing with the Right. The agitation which prevailed rendered it impossible to take the vote otherwise than by acclamation.[1]

March 4.
[1] Ann. Hist. vi. 90, 106; Moniteur, March 5, 1823; Lam. vii. 169, 181.

60. Dramatic scene at his expulsion.

The exclusion of a single member, during the remainder of a single session, was no very serious injury to a party, or blow leveled at the public liberties; but the passions on both sides were so strongly excited by this imprudent abuse of power by the Royalist majority, that the Liberals resolved to resist it to the very uttermost. It was determined to compel the majority to use force for his expulsion; and the recollection of the risk which ensued to the throne from the dragging of M. d'Eprémenil from the Parliament of Paris, at the commencement of the first Revolution,[2] was of sinister augury as to the effects of enforcing the present decree by similar means. The Government, however, was firm, and resolved, at all hazards, to carry the decree of the Chamber into execution. Every preparation was accordingly made to overawe, and, if necessary, to subdue resistance. The Liberal leaders, however, were determined to have a scene, and, instead of yielding obedience to the decree of the Chamber, M. Manuel appeared next morning in the Hall, and took his seat. When invited by the president to retire without disturbance, he replied, "I told you yesterday I would only yield to force; I come to make good my word," and resumed his seat. The president then desired the Assembly to evacuate the hall, and retire into their respective apartments, which was immediately done by the whole Right and Centre, but the entire Left remained in their places, grouped around Manuel. Presently the folding-doors opened, and the chief of the bar-officers, followed by a numerous staff of his colleagues, advanced, and read to Manuel the decree of the Chamber. "Your order is illegal," replied he; "I will not obey it." The peace-officers then retired, and the anxiety in the galleries, and the crowd around the Chamber, arose to the highest point, for the "measured step of marching men" was heard in the lobby. Presently the folding-doors again opened, and a detachment of national guards and troops of the line, with fixed bayonets, slowly entered, and drew up in front of the refractory deputy. The civil officer then ordered the sergeant of the national guard, M. Morrier, to execute the warrant; but, overcome by the violence of the crisis, and the cries of the deputies around Manuel, he refused to obey. "Vive la Garde Nationale!" instantly burst in redoubled shouts from the opposition benches; "Honneur à la Garde Nationale!" was heard above all the din in the voice of Lafayette. But the difficulty had been foreseen and provided for by the Government. The national guard and troops of the line were instantly withdrawn, and thirty gendarmes, under M. de Foucault, an officer of tried fidelity and courage, were introduced, who, after in vain inviting Manuel to retire, seized him by the collar, and dragged him out, amidst vehement gesticulations and cries from the Left, which were heard across the Seine.[1]

[1] Lam. vii. 181, 182; Ann. Hist. vi. 107, 109; Moniteur, Mar. 5, 1823.

61. General enthusiasm excited by the Spanish war.

These dramatic scenes, so well calculated to excite the feelings of a people so warm in temperament as the French, might, under different circumstances, have overturned the monarchy, and induced in 1823 the Revolution of 1830. They were followed next day by a solemn protest, signed by sixty deputies who had adhered to M. Manuel in the struggle, among which the signatures of General Lafayette, General Foy, and M. Casimir Perier appeared conspicuous. But no other result took place. The public mind is incapable of being violently excited by two passions at the same time; if the national feelings have been roused, the social ones are little felt. It was a perception of this truth which caused the Empress Catherine to say, at the commencement of the French Revolution, that the only way to combat its passions was to go to war.[2] The din, great as it was, caused by the dragging M. Manuel out of the Chamber of Deputies, was lost in the louder sound of marching men pressing on to the Pyrenees. The civic strife was heard of no more after it had terminated; nothing was thought of but the approaching conflict on the fields of Spain. Incessant was the march of troops toward Bayonne and Perpignan, the two points from which the invasion was to be made. The roads were covered by columns of infantry, cavalry, and artillery, moving forward toward the Spanish frontier, in the finest order, and in the highest spirits; and the warlike enthusiasm of the

[2] Hist. of Europe, c. xiii. § 7.

French, always strong, was roused to the very highest pitch, by the prospect of vindicating the tarnished honor of their arms on the fields of Castile, and re-entering Madrid as conquerors. The Duke of Angoulême set out from Paris, to take the command of the army, on the 15th March; and as war was no longer doubtful, the anxiety on both sides arose to the very highest pitch.[1]

<small>March 15. [1] Lam. vii. 188, 194; Ann. Hist. vi. 108, 112; Moniteur, March 16, 1823; Cap. vii. 120, 126, 145, 146.</small>

<small>62. Preparations of the Liberals to sow disaffection in the army.</small>

On their side, the Liberals, both in France and Spain, were not idle. Their chief reliance was on the presumed disaffection of the French army; for they were well aware that if they remained united, the forces of Spain, debased by misgovernment, and torn by civil war, would be unable to oppose any effectual resistance to their incursion. The most active measures, however, were taken to sow the seeds of disaffection in the French army. Several secret meetings of the Liberal chiefs in Paris took place, in order to concert the most effectual means of carrying this design into execution; and it was at first determined to send M. Benjamin Constant to Madrid to superintend the preparations on the revolutionary side, it being with reason supposed that his great reputation and acknowledged abilities would have much influence with the revolutionists in Spain, and be not without its effect on the feelings of the French soldiery. But this design, like many others formed by persons who are more liberal of their breath than their fortunes, failed from want of funds. Benjamin Constant, whose habits of expense were great, and his income from literary effort considerable, refused to undertake the mission unless not only his expenses were provided for, but an indemnity secured to him, in the event of failure, for the loss of his fortune and the means of repairing it, which his position in Paris afforded. This, however, the Liberals, though many of them were bankers or merchants, possessed of great wealth, declined to undertake; the Duke of Orleans was equally inexorable; and the consequence was, that Constant refused to go, and the plan, so far as he was concerned, broke down. All that was done was to send a few hundred political fanatics and refugees, who were to be under the command of Colonel Fabvier, and who, though of no importance as a military reinforcement, might, it was hoped, when clothed in the uniform of the Old Guard, and grouped round the tricolor standard, shake the fidelity of the French soldiers on the banks of the Bidassoa. Their first step was to issue a proclamation in the name of *Napoleon II.* to the French soldiers, calling on them to desert their colors, and join the revolutionary host, a proceeding which amply demonstrated, if it had been required, the necessity of the French intervention.[2]*

<small>[2] Lam. vii. 195, 197; Chateaubriand, Congrès de Vérone, i. 252, 254. Cap. vii. 147, 148.</small>

While hostilities were thus evidently and rapidly approaching on the Continent, and the dogs of war were held only in the leash, ready to be let loose at a moment's warning, to desolate the world, England, indignant and agitated, but still inactive, remained an anxious spectator of the strife. Never were the feelings of the nation more strongly roused, and never would a war have been entered into by the Government with more cordial and enthusiastic support on the part of the people. This is always the case, and it arises from the strength of the feelings of liberty which are indelibly engraven on the minds of the Anglo-Saxon race. Their sympathy is invariably with those whom they suppose to be oppressed; their impulse to assist the insurgents against the ruling power. They would support the colonies of all countries, *except their own*, in throwing off their allegiance to the parent state: those who attempt the same system in regard to their own, they regard as worse than pirates. They consider revolution a blessing to all other countries except England: there the whole classes possessed of property are resolute to oppose to it the most determined resistance. They think, with reason, they have already gone through the ordeal of revolution, and do not need to do so a second time; other nations have not yet passed through it, and they can not obtain felicity until they have.

<small>63. Feelings of Mr. Canning and the English people at this crisis.</small>

Mr. Canning, whose temperament was warm, his sympathy with freedom sincere, and his ambition for his country and himself powerful, shared to the very full in all these sentiments. No firmer friend to the cause of liberty existed in the British dominions at that eventful crisis, and none whose talents, eloquence, as well as political position, enabled him to give it such effectual support. In truth, at that period it may be said that he held the keys of the cavern of Æolus in his hands, and that it rested with him to unlock the doors and let the winds sweep round the globe. But

<small>64. Views of Mr. Canning at this juncture.</small>

<small>* "Vainqueurs de Fleurus, de Iena, d'Austerlitz, de Wagram, vous laisserez-vous aller à leurs insinuations perfides ! Scellerez-vous de votre sang, l'infâme dont on veut vous couvrir, et la servitude de l'Europe entière ! Obéirez-vous à la voix des tyrans, pour combattre contre vos droits, au lieu de les défendre ; et ne viendrez-vous dans nos rangs que pour y apporter la destruction et la mort, lorsqu'ils vous sont ouverts pour la liberté sainte qui vous appelle du haut de l'enseigne tricolore qui flotte sur les monts Pyrenées, et dont elle brûle d'ombrager encore une fois vos nobles fronts couverts de tant d'honorables cicatrices ! Braves de toute arme de l'armée française, qui conservez encore dans votre sein l'étincelle du feu sacré ! c'est à vous que nous faisons un généreux appel ; embrassez avec nous la cause majestueuse du peuple, contre celle d'une poignée d'oppresseurs ; la Patrie, l'honneur, votre propre intérêt le commandent ; venez, vous trouverez dans nos rangs tout ce qui constitue la force, et des compatriotes, des compagnons d'armes, qui jurent de défendre jusqu'à la dernière goutte de leur sang, leurs droits, la liberté, l'indépendance nationale. Vive la liberté ! Vive Napoléon II. ! Vivent les braves!" —CHATEAUBRIAND, *Congrès de Vérone*, i. 254, 255.

In the *Observateur Espagnol* of 1st Oct., 1822, before the Congress of Verona was opened, it was said—"L'epée de Damoclès qui est suspendue sur la tête des Bourbons, va bientôt les atteindre. Nos moyens de vengeance sont de toute évidence. Outre la vaillante armée espagnole, n'avons-nous pas dans cette armée sanitaire dix mille chevaliers de la liberté, prêts à se joindre à leurs anciens officiers, et à tourner leurs armes contre les oppresseurs de la Patrie? N'avons-nous pas cent mille de ces chevaliers dans l'intérieur de ce royaume, dont vingt cinq mille au moins dans l'armée, et plus de mille dans la garde royale? N'avons-nous pas pour nous, cette haine excusable, que les neuf dixièmes de la France ont vouée à d'exécrables tyrans!"—*L'Observateur Espagnol*, 1st Oct., 1822.</small>

though abundantly impelled (as his private conversations and correspondence at this period demonstrate) by his ardent disposition to step forward as the foremost in this great conflict, yet his experience and wisdom as a statesman, joined to the influence of Mr. Peel, who threatened to resign if an active intervention was attempted, restrained him from taking the irrecoverable step, and preserved the peace of the world when it appeared to be most seriously menaced." Resolutely determined to abstain from all intervention in the affairs of Spain, and to do his utmost to prevent France from taking that step, he was not the less determined to abstain from actual hostilities, and to keep aloof from the conflict so long as it was confined to continental Europe. He had too vivid a recollection of what the last Peninsular war had been, to engage without absolute necessity in a second; and if he had been otherwise inclined, the majority of the Cabinet would not have supported him.[1]†

[1] Marcellus, Politique de la Restauration, 151, 152; Canning's Life, 334; Martineau, i. 226.

* "Leave the Spanish revolution to burn itself out within its own crater. You have nothing to apprehend from the eruption, if you do not open a channel for the lava through the Pyrenees. It is not too late to save the world from a flood of calamities. The key to the floodgate is yet in your hands; unlock it, and who shall answer for the extent of devastation? 'The beginning of strife is as the letting out of waters.' So says inspired wisdom. Genius is akin to inspiration; and I pray that it may be able on this occasion to profit by the warning of the parable, and pause."—Mr. CANNING to M. de CHATEAUBRIAND (confidential), 27th January, 1823 ; Congrès de Vérone, i. 475.

"Well, then, to begin at once with what is most unpleasant to utter: You have united the opinions of this whole nation as one man against France. You have excited against the present sovereign of that kingdom the feelings which were united against the usurper of France and Spain in 1808. Nay, the consent, I grieve to say, is more perfect now than on that occasion; for then the Jacobins were loth to inculpate their idol; now they and the Whigs and Tories, from one end of the country to the other, are all one way. Surely such a spontaneous and universal burst of national sentiment must lead any man, or any set of men, who are acting in opposition to it, to reflect whether they are acting quite right. The Government has not on this occasion led the public—quite otherwise. The language of the Government has been peculiarly measured and temperate; so much so, that the mass of the nation was in suspense as to the opinion of Government till it was actually declared; and that portion of the press usually devoted to them was (for reasons perhaps better known on your side of the water than on ours) turned in a directly opposite course."—Mr. CANNING to Viscount CHATEAUBRIAND, 7th February, 1823 ; Congrès de Vérone, i. 475.

† "J'apprends à l'instant, et de très-bonne source, qu'avant-hier, dans un conseil secret des Ministres, M. Canning a prétendu qu'on ne pouvait lutter contre l'opinion générale, et que cette opinion demandait impérieusement de secourir l'Espagne. M. Peel a déclaré, alors, que l'honneur de l'Angleterre, l'intérêt de ses institutions et de son commerce étaient de maintenir une stricte neutralité ; et il a terminé en disant que si une conduite opposée à celle que l'Angleterre avait toujours suivie envers la Révolution, venait à être adoptée, il devait à sa conscience, de se retirer du ministère aussitôt. Ce jeune ministre l'a emporté. La grande majorité du conseil s'est réunie à lui, et M. Canning a décidé au nombre."—M. MARCELLUS, Chargé d'Affaires à Londres, à M. de CHATEAUBRIAND, 2e Février, 1823 ; MARCELLUS, 152.

Notwithstanding the divergence on political subjects of their opinions, which the opposite sides they espoused on the Spanish question much augmented, Mr. Canning and M. de Chateaubriand had the highest admiration for each other, and mutually lamented the circumstances which had drawn them out of the peaceful domain of literature to the stormy and fleeting arena of politics. The inmost thoughts of the former were revealed in the following conversation at this period with M. Marcellus, for whom he had a very high regard. "C'est donc à cette petite poussière de la tombe que vont aboutir inévitable-

The peculiar position of Mr. Canning at this period has never been so well described as by one who knew him intimately, and had become, as it were, the depositary of his inmost thoughts. "Let us not deceive ourselves," said M. Marcellus, "in regard to Mr. Canning. Still undecided, he is yet in suspense between the monarchical opinions, which have made his former renown, and the popular favor which has recently borne him forward to power; but as he attends, above all, to the echo of public opinion, and spreads his sails before the wind which blows, it is easy to foresee to which side he will incline. An élève of Pitt, Tory down to this time, he will become half a Whig, and will adopt the democratic principles if they appear to be in the ascendant. His secret inclinations lead him to the aristocracy, and even the high opposition society; he is feared rather than beloved by the king; but the people are with him. The people, dazzled by his talents, have put him where he is; and the people will support him there as long as he obeys their wishes."[1]

65. Portrait of Mr. Canning, by M. Marcellus.

[1] M. Marcellus to M. de Chateaubriand, London, Jan. 20, 1823 ; Marcellus, 120.

Mr. Canning at this period was decidedly of opinion that the Peninsular war, if once commenced, would be of very long duration—as long, possibly, as that with revolutionary France. "When I speak," said he, "of the dangers of war to France, do not suppose I undervalue her resources or power. She is as brave and strong as she ever was before; she is now the richest, the most abounding in resources, of all the states in Europe. Hers are all the sinews of war, if there be the disposition to employ them. You have a million of soldiers, you say, at your call: I doubt it not; and it is double the number, or thereabouts, that Bonaparte buried in Spain. You consider 'un premier succès au moins comme

66. His opinion as to the probable duration of the war.

ment nos inutiles efforts. Qu'ai-je gagné à tant de combats? De nombreux enemis, et mille calomnies. Tantôt retenu par le défaut d'intelligence de mes partisans, toujours gêné par le déplaisir du Roi, ne pouvant rien exécuter, rien essayer même de ce qu'une voix interne et solennelle semble me dicter. Je le disais recemment dans ma tristesse ; je me prends quelquefois pour un oiseau des hauteurs qui, loin de voler sur les hauteurs et sur les précipices des montagnes, ne vole que sur des marais, et rase à peine le sol. Je me consume sans fruit dans des discussions intestines, et je mourrai dans un accès de découragement, comme mon prédécesseur et mon malheureux ennemi Lord Castlereagh. Combien de fois n'ai-je pas été tenté de fuir loin des hommes, l'ombre même du pouvoir, et de me réfugier dans le sein des lettres, qui ont nourri mon enfance, seul abri véritablement inaccessible aux mensonges de la destinée. La littérature est pour moi plus qu'une consolation, c'est une espérance et un asile. Je l'ai en outre toujours considérée comme la franc-maçonnerie des gens bien élevés. C'est à ce signe qu'en tout pays la bonne compagnie se distingue et se reconnaît. Ne vaudrait-il pas mieux pour M. de Chateaubriand et pour moi, que nous n'eussions jamais, ni l'un ni l'autre, approché de nos lèvres la coupe empoisonnée de ce pouvoir qui nous enivre, et nous donne des vertiges ! La littérature nous eût rapprochés encore, mais cette fois sans arrière-pensée, et sans amertume, car il est comme moi l'amant des lettres, et bien mieux que moi il protège de ses préceptes. Combien de fois n'ai-je pas voulu abandonner le monde politique si turbulent, la société des hommes si méchants, pour me vouer tout entier à la retraite et à mes livres, seuls amis qui ne se trompent jamais.

'Oh God! oh God!
How weary, stale, flat, and unprofitable
Seem to me all the uses of this world !' "
—MARCELLUS, Politique de la Restauration, 25, 26.

certain.' I dispute it not. I grant you a French army at Madrid; but I venture to ask, What then, if the King of Spain and the Cortes are by that time where they infallibly will be—in the Isle of Leon? I see plenty of war, if you once get into it; but I do not see a legitimate beginning to it, nor an intelligible object. You would disdain to get into such a war through the side door of an accidental military incursion. You would enter in front, with the cause of war on your banners: and what is that cause? It is vengeance for the past, and security for the future—a war for the modification of a political constitution, for two Chambers, for the extension of legal rights. That passes my comprehension. You are about to enter, and you believe the war will be short: I believe otherwise, and I am bordering on old age. In 1793, Mr. Pitt, with the 'patriot's heart, the prophet's mind,' declared to me that the war then declared against a great people in a state of revolution would be short; and that war outlived Mr. Pitt."[1]

[Margin: ¹ Mr. Canning to Chateaubriand, Jan. 21, 1823, Congrès de Vérone, i. 453; Marcellus, 17.]

67. Views of George IV. and the Duke of Wellington on the subject.

These anticipations were not peculiar to Mr. Canning at that time; they were shared by probably nine-tenths of the educated classes, and probably ninety-nine hundredths of the entire inhabitants of Great Britain. Yet were there not awanting those in the most elevated rank who were not carried away by the general delusion, and anticipated, very nearly as it turned out, the real march of events. "Do not allow yourself," said George IV. to M. Marcellus, "to be dazzled by our representative system, which is represented as so perfect. If it has its advantages, it has also its inconveniences; and I have never forgot what a king and a man of talent said to me: 'Your English constitution is good only to encourage adventurers, and discourage honest men.' For the happiness of the world, we should not wish any other people to adopt our institutions. That which succeeds admirably with us would have very different success elsewhere. Every country does not bear the same fruits, nor the same minerals beneath its surface. It is the same with nations, their temperament, and character. Reflect on this, my dear Marcellus: my conviction on the subject is unalterable; I wish you to know that you have the king on your side. It is my part to be so; and when my Ministers become Radicals, I may be excused if, on my side, I become an ultra-Royalist." The Duke of Wellington, at the same period, thus expressed himself at the Foreign Office, when the chance of a parliamentary majority on the question of war was under discussion with Lord Liverpool and Mr. Canning: "I am not so *au fait* of parliamentary majorities as my colleagues, but I know Spain better than them. Advance without delay, without hesitation, and you will succeed. There is no majority, believe me, to be compared to cannon and a good army." With these words he took his hat and went out. "The words," said Lord Liverpool, "of a man of war, but not of a statesman." "The Duke of Wellington," rejoined Mr. Canning, "thinks himself always on the field of battle; and yet he has himself put a period to the bloody era of conquest. He understands nothing of constitutional dominations, *which are yet the only ones which now have any chance of duration*."[1] *

[Margin: ¹ Marcellus, 33, 37, 41.]

68. Difficulties of the French at the entrance of the campaign.

The war which divided in this manner the opinions of the most eminent men and the strongest heads of Europe, at length began in good earnest. The Duke d'Angoulême, as already noticed, left Paris for the army on 15th March. At the very threshold, however, of his career, an unexpected difficulty presented itself. Inexperienced for the most part in actual warfare, from the peace of eight years which had now continued, the commissaries and civil functionaries attached to the French army were in a great measure ignorant of the vast scale on which, when a hundred thousand men are to be put in motion, supplies of every sort must be furnished. Considerable magazines of corn had been formed at Bayonne and other places on the frontier; but, by a strange oversight, nothing had been done to provide forage for the horses, and the means of transport were wholly awanting. A hundred millions of francs (£4,000,000) had been placed at the disposal of the general-in-chief for the purchase of provisions on the march to Madrid—for Napoleon's system of making war maintain war was no more to be thought of—but no correspondence had been opened with the persons along the route who were to furnish the supplies. In these circumstances, it seemed impossible for the troops to move forward; and so great was the alarm produced in Paris by the reports transmitted by the Duke d'Angoulême when he reached head-quarters, that Government took the most vigorous measures to apply a remedy to the evil. The Minister of War (Victor) was directed, by an ordonnance of 23d March, to proceed immediately to the army, invested with ample powers, and the title of Major-general; all the soldiers who had obtained leave of absence down to the 31st December, 1822, were recalled to their standards; and a law was brought forward by the interim war-minister (Count Digeon) to authorize the king to call out, in the course of the present year, the conscripts pertaining to the year 1823, who, by the existing law, would not be required before the spring of 1824.[2]

[Margin: ² Ann. Hist. vi. 139, 140; Lam. vii. 190, 200; Cap. vii. 152, 154.]

* At this juncture the following highly interesting conversation took place between Mr. Canning and M. Marcellus: "A quoi bon," disait M. Canning, "soutenir un principe qui prête tant à la discussion, et sur lequel vous voyez que nous sommes enfin, vous et moi, si peu d'accord? Un Bourbon va au secours d'un Bourbon! Vous reveillez ainsi en nous mille souvenirs d'inimitié, l'invasion de Louis XIV. en Espagne, l'inabilité de nos efforts pour éloigner sa puissante dynastie du trône de Madrid. Jugez-en quand un roi donne au peuple les institutions dont le peuple a besoin, quel a été le procédé le l'Angleterre? Elle expulsa ce roi, et mit à sa place un roi d'une famille alliée sans doute, mais qui se trouve ainsi non plus; un fils de la royauté confiant dans les droits de ses ancêtres, mais le fils des institutions nationales, tirant tous ses droits de cette seule origine. Puisque Ferdinand, comme Jacques II., résiste aux volontés de sa nation, appliquons la méthode anglaise à l'Espagne. Qu'en résulte-t-il? L'expulsion de Ferdinand. Écoutez-moi; cet exemple peut s'étendre jusqu'à vous. Vous n'ignorez pas qu'un désordre du dogme de légitimité *presque pareille à la nôtre se lève et couve en France en ce moment*. Vous savez quel progrès elle fait dans le parti d'une opposition prétendue modérée. *La tête à couronner est là*."—MARCELLUS, 19, 20.

These measures, however, though calculated to provide for the future, had no influence on the present; they would neither feed the starving horses, nor drag along the ponderous guns and baggage-wagons. In this extremity, the fortune of the expedition, and with it the destiny, for the time at least, of the Restoration, was determined by the vigor and capacity of one man (M. OUVRARD)—a great French capitalist, who had concluded a treaty with the King of Spain, which secured to him in 1805 the treasures of the Indies, and which, after having enabled Napoleon to fit out the army which conquered at Austerlitz, excited his jealousy so violently as for the time occasioned Ouvrard's ruin.[1] He stepped forward, and offered—on terms advantageous to himself, without doubt, but still more advantageous to the public—to put the whole supplies of the army on the most satisfactory footing, and to charge himself with the conveyance of all its artillery and equipages. The necessity of the case, and the obvious inefficiency of the existing commissaries, left no time for deliberation; the known capacity and vast credit of M. Ouvrard supported his offer, how gigantic soever it may have at first appeared; and in a few days a contract was concluded with the adventurous capitalist, whereby the duty of supplying entire furnishings for the army was devolved on him. By the influence of the Duchess d'Angoulême, and the obvious necessity of the case, the contract was ratified at Paris; and although it excited violent clamors at the time, as all measures do which disappoint expectant cupidity, the event soon proved that never had a wiser step been adopted. The magic wand of M. Ouvrard overcame every thing; his golden key unlocked unheard-of magazines of every sort for the use of the troops; in a few days plenty reigned in all the magazines, the means of transport were amply provided, and confidence was re-established at head-quarters. So serene was the calm which succeeded to the storm, that the discord which had broken out in the Duke d'Angoulême's staff was appeased; General Guilleminot, who had been suspended from his command, was restored to the confidence of the commander-in-chief; Marshal Victor, relinquishing his duties as major-general, returned to the war-office at Paris; and the army, amply provided with every thing, advanced in the highest spirits to the banks of the Bidassoa.[2]

60.
Which are obviated by M. Ouvrard.

[1] Hist. of Europe, c. lxii. § 10, 13.

[2] Ann. Hist. vi. 153, 140, 376; Cap. vii. 151, 155; Lam. vii. 201, 205.

The preparations on both sides were of the most formidable description, and seemed to prognosticate the long and bloody war which Mr. Canning's ardent mind anticipated from the shock of opinions, which was to set all Europe on fire. The forces with which France took the field were very great, and, for the first time since the catastrophe of Waterloo, enabled her to appear on the theatre of Europe as a great military power. Wonderful, indeed, had been the resurrection of her strength under the wise and pacific reign of Louis XVIII. The army assembled at Bayonne for the invasion of Spain by the Western Pyrenees mustered ninety-one thousand combatants. It was divided into four corps, the command of which was intrusted with generous, but, as the event proved, not undeserved confidence, to the victorious generals of Napoleon. The first corps, under the command of Marshal Oudinot, with Counts d'Autichamp and Boront under him, was destined to cross the Bidassoa, and march direct by the great road upon Madrid. The second, which was commanded by Count Molitor, was destined to support the left flank of the first corps, and advance by the Pass of Roncesvalles and the Valley of Bastan upon Pampeluna. Prince Hohenlohe commanded the third corps, which was to protect the right flank of the first, and secure its rear and communications during the advance to Madrid from the Bidassoa. The fourth corps, under the orders of the Duke of Cornigliano (Marshal Moncey), was to operate, detached from the remainder of the army, in Catalonia; while the fifth, under the orders of General Count Bordesol, composed of a division of the guard under Count Bourmont, and of two divisions of cavalry, was to form the reserve of the grand army—but, in point of fact, it was almost constantly with the advanced posts.[1]

70.
Forces, and their disposition on both sides.

[1] Ann. Hist. vi. 374, 377.

The Spanish forces intended to meet this political crusade were not less formidable, so far as numerical amount was considered; but they were a very different array if discipline, equipments, and unanimity of feeling were regarded as the test. They consisted of 123,000 men, of whom 15,000 were cavalry, and a new levy of 30,000, who were thus disposed. In Biscay, opposite to the Bidassoa, were 20,000, under Ballasteros; in Catalonia, under Mina, 20,000; in the centre, 18,000 under d'Abisbal; in Galicia, 10,000; in garrison, in the fortresses, 52,000. The forces on either side were thus not unequal in point of numerical amount; but there was a vast difference in their discipline, organization, and equipment. On the French side these were all perfect, on the Spanish they were very deficient. Many of the corps were imperfectly disciplined, ill fed, and worse clothed. The cavalry was in great part ill mounted, the artillery crazy or worn out, the commissariat totally inefficient. Penury pervaded the treasury; revolutionary cupidity had squandered the resources of the soldiers, scanty as they were. Above all, the troops were conscious that the cause they were supporting was not that of the nation. Eleven-twelfths of the people, including the whole rural population, were hostile to their cause, and earnestly prayed for its overthrow; and even the inhabitants of Madrid and the seaport towns, who had hitherto constituted its entire support, were sensibly cooled in their ardor, now that it became a hazardous one, and called for sacrifices instead of promising fortune.[2]

71.
The Spanish forces.

[2] Rapport aux Cortes, Jan. 1, 1823; Ann. Hist. vi. 379, 380.

On the 5th of April, the French were grouped in such force on the banks of the Bidassoa, that it was evident a passage would be attempted on the following day. The French ensigns had last been seen there on 7th October, 1813, when the passage was forced by the Duke of Wellington. In anticipa-

72.
Theatrical scene at the passage of the Bidassoa.

tion of this movement, the Spaniards had made great preparations.[1] A considerable force was drawn up on the margin of the stream; but it was not on them that the principal reliance of their commanders was placed. It was on the corps of French refugees bearing the uniform of the Old Guard, and clustered round the tricolor flag, that all their hopes rested. Colonel Fabvier, however, who commanded them, found the array very different from what he expected. He had been promised a corps of eight hundred veterans of Napoleon in admirable order; he found only two hundred miserable refugees, half-starved, who had been involved in the conspiracies of Saumur and Befort, and found in Spain an asylum for their crimes. They were clothed, however, in the old and well-known uniform, with the huge bear-skins of the grenadiers of the Guard on their heads; the tricolor flag waved in the midst of them, and as the French advanced posts approached the bridge, they heard the Marseillaise and other popular airs of the Revolution chanted from their ranks. The moment was critical, for the French soldiers halted at sight of the unexpected apparition, and gazed with interest on the well-known and unforgotten ensigns. But at that moment General Vallin, who commanded the advanced guard, galloped to the front, and ordered a gun to be discharged along the bridge. The first round was fired over the heads of the enemy, in the hope of inducing them to retire; and the refugees, seeing no shot took effect, thought the balls had been drawn, and shouted loudly, "Vive l'Artillerie!" Upon this, General Vallin ordered a point-blank discharge, which struck down several; a third round completed their dispersion, and the passage was effected without further resistance. Louis XVIII. did not exaggerate the importance of this decisive conduct on this critical occasion, when, on the general who commanded on the occasion being presented to him after the campaign was over, he said, "General Vallin, your cannon-shot has saved Europe."[2]

[1] Hist. of Europe, c. lxxxiii. § 12.
[2] Lam. vii. 206, 207; Ann. Hist. v. 377, 379; Moniteur, April 12, 1853.

73. Progress of the French, and their rapid success.

This bold act was decisive of the fate of the campaign. The French army having effected their passage, their right wing, after a sharp action, drove back the garrison of St. Sebastian within the walls of that fortress, and established the blockade of the place; while the centre, supported by the whole reserve, in all 40,000 strong, pushed on rapidly on the great road to Madrid. On the 10th they reached Tolosa, on the 11th Villareal, and on the 17th their columns entered Vittoria in triumph, amidst an immense concourse of inhabitants and unbounded joy and acclamation. How different from the ceaseless booming of the English cannon, which rung in their ears when they last were in that town, flying before the bloody English sabres on 21st June, 1813! At the same time, with the left wing, Oudinot crossed the Ebro and advanced to Burgos, after having made himself master of l'ancorbo; and the extreme right, under Quesada, composed of Spanish auxiliaries, reached Bilboa, which

April 10-17.

opened its gates without opposition. Every where the French troops were received as deliverers; as they advanced, the pillars of the Constitution were overthrown, the revolutionary authorities dispossessed, and the ancient régime proclaimed amidst the acclamations of the people. The invaders observed the most exact discipline, and paid for every thing they required—a wise policy, the very reverse of that of Napoleon—which confirmed the favorable impression made on the minds of the Spaniards. The ancient animosity of the people of France and Spain seemed to be lulled; even the horrors of the late war had for the time been buried in oblivion; three years of revolutionary government had caused them all to be forgotten, and hereditary foes to be hailed as present deliverers.[1]

[1] Ann. Hist. vi. 381, 282; Moniteur, Feb. 16, 1823; Cap. vii. 153, 155.

The main body of the French army, encouraged by this flattering reception, advanced with vigor, and that celerity which in all wars of invasion, but especially those which partake of the nature of civil conflict, is so important an element in success. Resistance was nowhere attempted, so that the march of the troops was as rapid as it would have been through their own territory. The guards and first corps entered Burgos on the 9th May, where they were received with the utmost enthusiasm, and thence proceeded in two columns toward Madrid—the first, under the generalissimo in person, by Aranda and Buytrago; the latter by Valladolid, where the reception of the troops was if possible still more flattering. At the latter place, where head-quarters arrived on the 17th May, a flag of truce arrived from the Conde d'Abisbal, who had been left in command at Madrid by the Cortes, they having retired toward Seville, taking the king a prisoner with them. In vain had the monarch declared he would not abandon his capital; the imperious Cortes forced him away, and he set out accordingly under an escort or guard of 6000 men, leaving Madrid to make the best terms it could with the conqueror. Saragossa, Tolossa, and all the towns occupied by the French in the course of their advance, instantly, on their approach, overturned the pillar of the Constitution, reinstated the Royalist authorities, and received the invaders as deliverers. Literally speaking, the Duke d'Angoulême advanced from Irun to Madrid amidst the acclamations of the people, and under triumphal arches. Nor was the success of the French less decisive in Upper Catalonia, where the retreat of Mina and the Constitutional troops was so rapid that Moncey in vain attempted to bring them to action; and within a month after the frontiers had been crossed, nearly all the fortified places in the province, except Barcelona and Lerida, had opened their gates and received the French with transports.[2]

74. Advance of the Duke d'Angoulême to Madrid.

May 9.

May 17.

May 15.

[2] Ann. Hist. vi. 384, 387; Lam. vii. 225, 226.

Nothing could be more agreeable to the Duke d'Angoulême than the offer on the part of the Conde d'Abisbal and the municipality of Madrid to capitulate on favorable terms, and accordingly he at once agreed to every

75. Advance of the French to Madrid. May 24.

thing requested by them. It was agreed that General Zayas should remain with a few squadrons to preserve order in the capital till it was occupied by the French troops, which was arranged to take place on the 24th May. The guard left, however, proved inadequate to the task; the revolutionists, who were much stronger in Madrid than in any other town the French had yet entered, rose in insurrection, and d'Abisbal only saved his life by flying in disguise, and taking refuge with Marshal Oudinot. The moment was critical, for Madrid was in a state of great excitement, and a spark might have lighted a flame which, by rousing the national feelings of the Spaniards, might, as in 1808, have involved the whole Peninsula in conflagration. But at this decisive moment the wisdom of the Duke d'Angoulême and his military counselors solved the difficulty, and at once detached the extreme revolutionary from the patriotic party. M. DE MARTIGNAC, a young advocate of Bordeaux, destined to celebrity in future times, drew up a proclamation,[*] which the prince signed, which soothed the pride of the Castilians, gratified the feelings of the Royalists, and disarmed the wrath of the revolutionists. Every thing was accordingly arranged in concord for the entry of the prince generalissimo and his army on the morning of the 24th.[1]

¹ Ann. Hist. vi. 389, 392; Lam. vii. 226, 227; Moniteur, June 1, 2, 1823.

76. Entry of the Duke d'Angoulême into Madrid.

Early on the morning of that day an immense crowd issued from the gate by which it was understood the prince was to make his entry, with boughs of trees and garlands of flowers in their hands, and every preparation as for a day of festivity and rejoicing. The windows were all hung with tapestry or rich carpeting; the handsomest women in their gala-dresses were there, and beautiful forms adorned with chaplets of flowers graced the spectacle. Precisely at nine, the Duke d'Angoulême, surrounded by a brilliant staff, made his appearance at the gate of Recolletts, where a triumphal arch had been erected, at the head of the guards and reserve; while Marshal Oudinot at the same time entered by the gate of Segovia, from which side he had approached at the head of his corps. Both were received with the loudest demonstrations of joy, amidst the acclamations of the people, the ringing of bells, and the heart-stirring strains of military music. The general enthusiasm was increased by the splendid appearance of the troops, their martial air, the exact discipline and perfect order they every where maintained. They were saluted with loud acclamations in all the streets through which they passed, and in the evening a general illumination gave vent to the universal joy. Never was seen so clear a proof that revolutions are brought about by bold and turbulent minorities overriding supine and timorous majorities. The universal joy equaled that of the Parisians, when their Revolution was closed by the entrance of the Emperor Alexander and allied sovereigns on 31st March, 1814.[1]

¹ Ann. Hist. vi. 392, 393; Moniteur, June 2, 1823.

Well aware of the importance of following up with all possible rapidity the important advantages thus gained, the Duke d'Angoulême did not repose on his laurels. Two columns, one commanded by General Bordesoult, the other by General Bourmont, set out immediately in pursuit of the revolutionary forces, which, taking the king a prisoner along with them, were hastening by forced marches toward Seville. So rapid was their flight, that the French troops endeavored in vain to come up with them. Bordesoult, who with eight thousand men followed the direct road from Madrid by Aranjuez to Seville, never got sight of their retiring columns; and although a show of resistance was made to Bourmont, who with an equal force took the road to Badajoz, at Talavera de la Reyna, yet it was but a show. The enemy retreated as soon as the French troops, aided by the Spanish Royalists, appeared in sight. A corps of fifteen hundred men was attacked and routed near Santa Cruz by General Dino; another of equal size dispersed near the mountains of Villiers the next day by the same general, and three hundred prisoners taken; the bridge of Arzobisbo was seized two days after; and on the same day General Bordesoult, who had never fired a shot, arrived at Cordova, beyond the Sierra-Morena, where, the moment the revolutionary troops withdrew, a vehement demonstration, accompanied with the most enthusiastic ebullition of joy, took place in support of the Royalist cause.[2]

77. Advance of the French into Andalusia.

June 9.
June 10.
June 11.

² Moniteur, June 24, 1823; Ann. Hist. vi. 396, 398.

Meanwhile the Cortes, whose sole power consisted, as often was the case in the days of feudal anarchy, in the possession of the person of the sovereign, had established themselves at Seville, where a show of respectability was still thrown over their

78. Proceedings of the Cortes, and deposition of Ferdinand VII.

---

* "Espagnols! Avant que l'armée française franchît les Pyrénées, j'ai declaré a votre genereuse nation que nous n'étions pas en guerre avec elle. Je lui ai annoncé que nous venions comme amis et auxiliaires l'aider à relever ses autels, à delivrer son roi, à retablir dans son sein la justice, l'ordre, et la paix. J'ai promis respect aux propriétes, sûreté aux personnes, protection aux hommes paisibles. L'Espagne a ajouté foi à mes paroles. Les provinces que j'ai parcourues ont reçu les soldats français comme des frères, et la voix publique vous aura appris s'ils ont justifié cet accueil, et si j'ai tenu mes engagements. Espagnols! si votre roi etait encore dans la capitale, la noble mission que le roi mon oncle m'a confiée, et que vous connaissez tout entière, serait déjà prête a s'accomplir. Je n'aurais plus, après avoir rendu le monarque à la liberté, qu'à appeler sa paternelle sollicitude sur les maux qu'a soufferts son peuple, sur le besoin qu'il a de repos pour le present, et de securité pour l'avenir. L'absence du roi m'impose d'autres devoirs. Dans ces conjonctures difficiles, et pour lesquelles le passé n'offre pas d'exemple à suivre, j'ai pensé que le moyen le plus convenable et le plus agréable au roi, serait de convoquer l'unique conseil suprême de la Castille, et le conseil suprême des Indes, dont les hautes et diverses attributions embrassent le royaume et ses possessions d'outremer, et de confier aux grands corps independans par leur élévation, et par la position politique de ceux qui les composent, le soin de designer, eux-mêmes, les membres de la régence." And on the day after his entrance, as the two councils did not conceive themselves authorized by the laws to appoint a regency, but only to recommend one to the French commander-in-chief, to act during the captivity of Ferdinand VII., he nominated, on their recommendation, as members of the regency, the Duke del Infantado, the Duke de Montemart, the Baron d'Erolles, the Bishop of Urina, and Don Antonio Gomez Calderon, who on 4th June issued a proclamation as the Council of Regency to the Spanish nation.—*Annuaire Historique*, vi. 721, 722, Appendix.

proceedings by the presence of the English embassador, who followed the captive monarch in his forced peregrinations. This circumstance, joined to the presence of a considerable English squadron in the bay of Cadiz, led for some time to the belief that the English government, which had evinced so warm a sympathy for the cause of the revolution, would at length give it some more effectual support than by eloquent declamations in Parliament. But these hopes soon proved illusory. It was no part of the policy of the English Cabinet to go beyond the bounds of a strict neutrality; and even the liberal ardor of Mr. Canning had been sensibly cooled by the sight of the unresisted march of the French troops to Madrid, and the decisive demonstrations afforded that the cause of the revolution was hateful to nine-tenths of the Spanish people. Even if he had been otherwise inclined, the violence of the Cortes themselves, which increased rather than diminished with the disasters which were accumulating round them, ere long rendered any further alliance impossible. On hearing of the approach of the French forces, they proposed to the king to move with them to Cadiz, so as to be beyond the reach of the French troops and the Royalist reaction. The king, however, who foresaw the approaching downfall of the revolutionary government, and had heard of the rapid approach of his deliverers, positively refused, after repeated summonses, to leave Seville.* Upon this the Cortes held an extraordinary meeting, in which, on the motion of M. Galliano, they declared the king deposed, appointed a provisional regency to act in his stead, and, now no longer attempting to disguise his captivity, forced him and the royal family into carriages, which set out attended by eight thousand men for Cadiz, where they arrived three days afterward.† Only six members of the Cortes had courage enough to vote against the motion for deposing the king: Señor Arguelles, and all the influential members, were found in the majority. The English embassador, Sir W. A'Court, refused to accompany the deposed monarch, and remained at Seville, from whence he went to Gibraltar to await the orders of his Government.¹

June 10.

June 11.

June 12.

¹ Ann. Hist. vi. 410, 411; Lam. vii. 298, 299.

This violent act completed the ruin of the Cortes and the cause of the revolution in Europe, and immediately subverted it in Spain. No sooner had the last of the revolutionary troops taken their departure on the evening of the 12th for Cadiz, than a violent reaction took place in Seville, which soon extended to all the towns in Spain that still adhered to the cause of the revolution. Vast crowds assembled in the streets, shouting "Viva el Rey Assoluto! Viva Ferdinand! Viva el Inquisition!" Disorders speedily ensued. Several of the Liberal clubs were broken open and pillaged, and the pillars of the Constitution were broken amidst frantic demonstrations of joy. Two days after, a corps of the revolutionists under Lopez-Baños entered the city, engaged in a frightful contest in the streets with the Royalists, in the course of which two hundred of the latter perished; and having gained temporary possession of its principal quarters, he proceeded to plunder the churches of their plate, with which he set out for Cadiz; but finding the road in that direction occupied by General Bordesoult, he made for the confines of Portugal with his booty, where he joined a corps of revolutionists under Villa Campa. Two days after, General Bourmont entered Seville, where he permanently re-established the royal authority; and the forces of the Cortes, abandoning Andalusia on all sides, took refuge within the walls of Cadiz, where twenty thousand men, the last stay of the revolution, were now assembled. Every where else the cause of the revolution crumbled into dust. General Murillo, who commanded at Valencia, passed over with half his forces to the Royalists; Ballasteros, after sustaining a severe defeat at Carabil, was obliged to capitulate, with seven thousand men, to the French. Carthagena, Tarragona, and all the other fortresses, with the exception of Barcelona, Corunna, and Ferrol, soon after opened their gates, and ere long there remained only to the Liberal leaders the forces shut up within the walls of Cadiz and Barcelona, and a few guerrillas, who, under Mina, still prolonged the war in the mountains of Catalonia.¹

79. Violent reaction at Seville, and over all Spain. June 13.

June 18.

¹ Memorias del General Espoz-y-Mina, ii. 170, 176; Lam. vii. 228, 229; Ann. Hist. vi. 413, 415; Cap. vii. 202, 203.

Still the position of the revolutionists in Cadiz was strong, for the fortress itself had been proved in the late war to be impregnable; the inhabitants were zealous in their support; and the principal leaders and officers of the garrison of twenty thousand men were so deeply implicated in the cause, that they had no chance of safety but in the most determined resistance. Above all, the command of the person of the king and the royal family, for whose lives the most serious apprehensions were entertained, gave them the means of negotiating with advantage, and in a manner imposing their own terms on the conquerors. Ferdinand, though nominally restored to his functions, in order to give a color to their proceedings, was in reality detained a close prisoner in the palace, or rather prison, in which he was lodged, and not allowed to walk out even on the terrace of his abode, except under a strong guard, and within very narrow precincts. Meanwhile Riego issued from the Isle of Leon, as he had done during the re-

80. State of affairs in Cadiz.

---

* "La députation des Cortès a représenté de nouveau à sa Majesté, que sa conscience ne pouvait être compromise ou blessée en cette matière; que s'il pouvait être en qualité d'homme, il n'était comme roi constitutionnel aupé à aucune responsabilité; qu'il ne fallait que se ranger à l'avis de ses conseillers et des représentants du peuple, sur qui reposait le fardeau de la responsabilité pour le salut du pays. Le roi ayant signifié à la députation qu'il avait sa réponse, et la mission donnée à celle-ci étant remplie, il ne lui restait qu'à déclarer aux Cortès qu'il ne jugeait pas la translation convenable."—*Procès Verbal des Cortès,* 10th June, 1823; *Annuaire Historique,* vi. 409, 410.

† "Je prie les Cortès, qu'en conséquence du refus de sa Majesté de mettre sa personne royale et sa famille en sûreté à l'approche de l'invasion de l'ennemi, il soit déclaré que le cas est arrivé de regarder sa Majesté comme étant dans un état d'empêchement moral prévu par l'article 187 de la constitution, et qu'il soit nommé *une régence provisoire* qui sera investie seulement pour le cas de, ou pendant la translation de la plénitude du pouvoir exécutif."—*Proposition de M.* GALLIANO, *11th June, 1823; Annuaire Historique,* vi. 410.

vain in 1820, to endeavor to rouse the inhabitants of the mountains in the rear of the French armies; and every preparation was made within the walls for the most vigorous defense. But all felt that the cause was hopeless. The more moderate members of the Cortes had withdrawn and taken refuge in Gibraltar; and even the violent party of Exaltados, who still inculcated the necessity of prolonging the contest, did so rather from the hope of securing favorable terms of capitulation for themselves, than from any real belief that it could much longer be maintained.[1]

<small>1 Lam. vii. 229, 230; Ann. Hist. vi. 435, 437.</small>

§1. Advance of the Duke d'Angoulême into Andalusia, and decree of Andujar.

Encouraged by the favorable reports which he received on all sides of the defeat or dispersion of the Revolutionists, and the general submission to the royal authority, the Duke d'Angoulême resolved to proceed in person with the great bulk of his forces to Andalusia, in order to bring the war at once to a close by the reduction of Cadiz. He set out, accordingly, on the 18th July, from Madrid, taking with him the guards and reserve, and leaving only four thousand men to garrison the capital. The Regency had issued a decree annulling all the acts of the revolutionary government since the Constitution had been forced upon the king on 7th March, 1820, contracted a considerable loan, and made some progress in the formation of a Royalist corps, to be the foundation of a guard; but the extreme penury of the exchequer, the inevitable result of the political convulsions of the last three years, rendered its equipment very tardy. Meanwhile, disorders of the most serious kind were accumulating in the provinces; the Royalist reaction threatened to be as serious as the revolutionary action had been. In Saragossa fifteen hundred persons had been arrested and thrown into prison by the Royalists, and great part of their houses pillaged; and similar disorders, in many instances attended with bloodshed, had taken place in Valencia, Alicante, Carthagena, and other places which had declared for the royal cause. Struck with the accounts of these atrocities, which went to defeat the whole objects of the French intervention, and threatened to rouse a national war in Spain, the Duke d'Angoulême published on the 8th August, at Andujar, the memorable proclamation bearing the name of that place, one of the most glorious acts of the Restoration, and a model for all future times in those unhappy wars which originate in difference of political or religious opinion.[2]

July 18.

June 18.

Aug. 8.

<small>2 Cap. vii. 202, 203; Lam. vii. 231; An. Hist. vi. 437, 438.</small>

By this ordonnance it was declared, "that the Spanish authorities should not be at liberty to arrest any person without the authority of the French officers; the commanders-in-chief of the corps under the orders of his royal highness were instantly to set at liberty all persons who had been arbitrarily imprisoned from political causes, and especially those in the militia, who were hereby authorized to return to their homes, with the exception of such as after their enlargement might have given just cause of complaint. The commanders-in-chief of the corps were authorized to arrest every person who

§2. Its provisions

should contravene this decree; and the editors of periodical publications were put under the direction of the commanders of corps." Though this ordonnance was dictated by the highest wisdom as well as humanity, seeing it put a stop at once to the Royalist reaction which had become so violent, and threatened such dangerous consequences, yet as it took the government in a manner out of the hands of the Spanish authorities, and seemed to presage a prolonged military occupation of the country, it excited the most profound feelings of indignation at Madrid, and among the ardent Royalists over the whole country. With them, loyalty to their sovereign was identical with thirst for the blood of his enemies. The whole members of the Regency sent in their resignations, and were only prevailed on to withdraw them by explanations offered of the real object of the ordonnance; and the diplomatic body made remonstrances, which were only appeased in the same manner.[1]*

<small>1 Cap. vii. 204, 205; An. Hist. vi. 437; Ordonnance d'Andujar, August 8, 1823; Moniteur, Aug. 24; Ann. Hist. vi. 724.</small>

The condition of Spain at this time was such as to call forth the utmost solicitude, and threatened the most frightful consequences. The war still lingered in Galicia, where Sir R. Wilson had appeared, accompanied, not, as was expected, by ten thousand men, but by a single aide-de-camp; and a harassing guerrilla warfare was yet kept up by Mina, and the forces under his command in Catalonia. The Royalists in Madrid had been in a state of the highest exultation, in consequence of a rumor which had obtained credit, that the king had been set at liberty, when the decree of Andujar fell upon them like a thunderbolt, and excited universal indignation. The same was the case in all the provinces. Such is the force of passion and the thirst for vengeance in the Spanish character, that nothing inflames it so violently as being precluded from the gratification of these malignant feelings. The army employed in the blockade of Pampeluna prepared and signed an address to the Regency, in which this wise decree was denounced as worse than any act of Napoleon's.† In such an excited state of the public mind, no central authority could be established. All recognized the Regency at Mad-

§3. Violent irritation of the Royalists in Spain.

<small>* "Jamais l'intention de S. A. R. ne fut d'arrêter, le cours de la justice dans les poursuites pour des délits ordinaires sur lesquels le magistrat doit conserver toute la plénitude de son autorité; les mesures prescrites dans l'ordre du 8 Août n'ont d'autre objet que d'assurer les effets de la parole du prince, par laquelle il garantissait la tranquillité de ceux qui, en la foi de promesses de S. A. R., se séparent des rangs des ennemis. Mais en même temps, l'indulgence pour le passé garantit la sévérité avec laquelle les nouveaux délits seront punis, et conséquemment les commandants français devront non-seulement laisser agir les tribunaux ordinaires auxquels il appartient de punir suivant la rigueur des lois, ceux qui, à l'avenir, se rendront coupables de désordres et de désobéissance aux lois, mais encore ils devront agir d'accord, avec les autorités locales, pour toutes les mesures qui pourront intéresser la conservation de la paix publique."—Lettre du Général Guillemenot à la Régence à Madrid, 26th August, 1823; Annuaire Historique, vi. 724.

† "Un attentat qui n'osa pas commettre le tyran du monde, doit être réprimé à l'instant, quelles qu'en soient les conséquences, et dussions-nous être exposés aux plus grands dangers. Que l'Espagne soit couverte de cadavres plutôt que de vivre avilie par le déshonneur, et de subir le joug de l'étranger."—Adresse de l'armée de Navarre à la Régence, 20th August, 1823; Annuaire Historique, vi. 441.</small>

ril; none obeyed it. Provincial juntas were rapidly formed, as in the commencement of the war in 1809, composed of the most violent Royalists, who soon acquired the entire direction of affairs within their respective provinces. The surrender of Corunna on 13th August, followed by the capitulation of all the Liberal corps in the province, and that of San Sebastian, Ferrol, and Pampeluna, soon after terminated the war in the north and west of Spain, and hostilities continued only in Catalonia and round the walls of Cadiz.¹

Aug. 13.
Aug. 27.

¹ Ann. Hist. vi. 436, 442; Lam. vii. 230, 231; Cap. vii. 204, 205.

84.
Progress of the siege of Cadiz.

In this distracted state of the country, it was plain that nothing could produce concord but the authority of the sovereign, and to effect his liberation the whole efforts of the Duke d'Angoulême were directed. The siege of Cadiz had been undertaken in good earnest, but it was no easy matter to prosecute it with effect. The distance of the nearest points on the bay from the city was so considerable that nothing but bombs of the largest calibre and the longest range could reach it, and the dykes which led across it into the fortress were defended by batteries of such strength that all attempts to force the passage were hopeless. Two thousand pieces of cannon, and ammunition in abundance, were arrayed in defense of the place. A grand sortie, undertaken to drive the French from their posts around the bay, led to a warm action, and was at length repulsed with the loss to the besieged of seven hundred men. About the same time the Minister at War, Don Sanchez Salvador, cut his throat after having burned all his papers. He left a writing on his table, in which he declared that he did so "because life was every day becoming more insupportable to him, but that he descended to the tomb without having to reproach himself with a single fault." The approach of the prince-generalissimo soon led to more important operations. His first care was to send a letter to the President of the Cortes, expressing the anxious wish of the French government that "the King of Spain, restored to liberty and practicing clemency, should accord a general amnesty, necessary after so many troubles, and give to his people, by the convocation of the ancient Cortes, a guarantee for the reign of justice, order, and good administration; an act of wisdom to which he pledged himself to obtain the concurrence of all Europe." But to this noble and touching letter, the Cortes, with the mixture of pride and obstinacy which seems inherent in the Spanish character, returned an answer in such terms as rendered all hope of pacific adjustment out of the question.²*

July 16.

July 14.

Aug. 17.

² Lettre du Duc d'Angoulême, Aug. 17, 1823, et Reponse des Cortes, Aug. 18; Ann. Hist. vi. 449, 450.

Continued hostilities being thus resolved on, the French engineers directed all their efforts against the fort of the Trocadero. This outwork of Cadiz, situated on the land side of the bay, is placed at the extremity of a sandy peninsula running into it, and was of great importance as commanding the inner harbor, and enabling the mortar batteries of the besiegers to reach the city itself. It had been fortified, accordingly, with the utmost care—was mounted with fifty pieces of heavy cannon, garrisoned with seventeen hundred men; and as a ditch, into which the sea flowed at both ends, had been cut across the peninsula, the fort stood on an island, with a front of appalling strength toward the land. Against this front the whole efforts of the French were directed; the approaches were pushed with incredible activity, and on the 24th the first parallel had been drawn to within sixty yards of the ditch. A tremendous fire was kept up from the batteries of the assailants on the works of the place during the six following days, and on the 31st the cannonade was so violent as to induce the garrison to apprehend an immediate assault. The day, however, passed over without its taking place, and the Spaniards began to raise cries of victory. But their triumph was of short duration. Early on the morning of the 31st, while it was still dark, the assaulting column, consisting of fourteen companies, defiled in silence out of the trenches, and stood within forty paces of the enemy's batteries. With such order and regularity was the movement executed, that the besiegers were not aware of their having emerged from the trenches till just before the rush commenced. They were seen, however, through the gray of the morning as they were beginning to move, and a violent fire of grape and musketry was immediately directed against the living mass. On they rushed, disregarding the fire, plunged into the ditch, with the water up to their arms, and ascending the opposite side under a shower of balls, broke through the chevaux-de-frise, and mounted the ramparts with the utmost resolution. The Spaniards stood their ground bravely, and for some minutes the struggle was very violent, but at length the impetuosity of the French prevailed. Great numbers of the Spaniards were bayoneted at their guns; the remainder fled to fort St Louis, the last fortified post on the peninsula. There, however, they were speedily followed by the French, who scaled the ramparts and carried every thing before them. By nine o'clock the conquest was complete—the entire peninsula had fallen into the hands of the victors, with all its forts and artillery. The Duke d'Angoulême exposed himself, in this brilliant affair, to the enemy's fire, like a simple grenadier; and the Prince of Carignan, eldest son of the King of Sardinia, was one of the first of the forlorn hope who mounted the breach. Strange destiny of the same prince to be within two years the leader of a democratic revolt in his own country, and a gallant volunteer with the assaulting party of the Royalist army which combated it!¹

85.
Assault of the Trocadero. August 31.

¹ Moniteur, August 5; Ann. Hist. vi. 452, 453; Lam. vii. 232, 233; Duke d'Angoulême's Despatches, August 1, 1823.

Disaster also attended the operations of Riego, who had left the Isle of Leon in order to

* "Le roi est libre; les meilleurs de l'Espagne viennent tous de l'invasion; l'établissement des anciennes Cortés est aussi incompatible avec la dignité de la couronne qu'avec l'état actuel du monde, la situation politique des choses, les droits, les usages, et le bien-être de la union espagnole. Si S. A. R. abusait de la force, elle serait responsable des maux qu'elle pourrait attirer sur la personne du roi, sur la famille royale, et sur cette cité bien meritante."—Reponse des Cortes, 18th August, 1823; Annuaire Historique, vi. 429.

collect the scattered bands of the Liberals in the mountains of Granada and Andalusia, and operate in the rear of the French army. The Cortes, who were too glad to get quit of him, gave him the command of all the troops he could collect: he eluded the vigilance of the French cruisers, and disembarked at Malaga on the 17th August with ample powers, but no money. He there took the command of two thousand men who remained to Zayas in that place, and soon made amends for his want of money by forced contributions from the whole merchants and opulent inhabitants of the place, without excepting the English, whom he imprisoned, transported, and shot without mercy, if they withstood his demands. The loud complaints which they made throughout all Europe went far to open the eyes of the people of England to the real tendency of the Spanish revolution.

On the 3d September he set out from Malaga at the head of two thousand five hundred men, carrying with him the whole plate of the churches and of all the respectable inhabitants in the place, and made for the mountains, with the view of joining the remains of the corps of General Ballasteros, which he effected a few days after. He was closely followed by Generals Bonnemaine and Loverdi, whom Molitor had detached from Granada in pursuit. Though the troops of Ballasteros had capitulated, and passed over to the Royalist side, yet they were unable to stand the sight of their old ensigns and colors, and, like the soldiers of Napoleon at the sight of the imperial eagles, they speedily fraternized with their old comrades. Cries of "Viva el Union! Viva Riego! Viva la Constitucion!" were heard on all sides, and Ballasteros himself, carried away by the torrent, found himself in Riego's arms. Concord seemed to be established between the chiefs, and they dined together, apparently in perfect amity; but in reality the seeds of distrust were irrevocably sown between them. Ballasteros quietly gave orders to his troops to separate from those of Riego: the latter, penetrating his designs, made the former a prisoner, but was compelled to release him by his officers. Discord having now succeeded to the temporary burst of unanimity, the two armies were separated, and the greater part of Riego's two best regiments deserted in the night, and joined Ballasteros' troops. The expedition had entirely failed, and, instead of raising the country in the rear of the French army before Cadiz, nothing remained to Riego but to seek by hill-paths to effect a junction with Mina, who still maintained a desultory warfare in the mountains of Catalonia.[1]

He set out accordingly with two thousand men; but destitute of every thing, and unable to convey their heavy spoil with them, the march proved nothing but a succession of disasters. Bonnemaine, who closely followed his footsteps with a light French division, came up with him on the heights near Jaen, and after a short action totally defeated him, with the loss of five hundred of his best troops. The day following he was again assailed with such vigor that his troops, no longer making even a show of resistance, dispersed on all sides, leaving their chief himself attended only by a few followers, who still adhered with honorable fidelity to his desperate fortunes. Riego himself was wounded, and in that pitiable state fled, accompanied only by three officers, toward the Sierra-Morena. Exhausted by fatigue, he was obliged to rest at a farm-house near Carolina d'Arguellos, where he was recognized, and information sent to his pursuers of his retreat, by whom he was arrested. Conducted under a strong escort to Andujar, he was assailed by a mob with such violent imprecations and threatening gesticulations, that the French garrison of the place were obliged to turn out to save his life. As M. de Coppons, an officer of Marshal Moncey's staff, covered him with his body at the hazard of his life, he said, "The people who are now so excited against me— the people who, but for the succor of the French, would have murdered me—that same people last year, on this very spot, bore me in their arms in triumph: the city forced upon me, against my will, a sabre of honor: the night which I passed here the houses were illuminated: the people danced till morning under my windows, and prevented me, by their acclamations, from obtaining a moment of sleep."[1]

These repeated disasters, and the accounts received from all quarters of the general submission of the country, at length convinced the Cortes of the hopelessness of the contest in which they were engaged. They got Ferdinand, accordingly, to sign a letter to the Duke d'Angoulême, in which he requested a suspension of arms, with a view to the conclusion of a general peace. The duke replied, that it was indispensable, in the first instance, that the king should be set at liberty, but that, as soon as this was done, "he would earnestly entreat his Majesty to accord a general amnesty, and to give of his own will, or to promise, such institutions as he may deem in his wisdom suitable to their feelings and character, and which may seem essential to their happiness and tranquillity." The Cortes, upon this, asked what evidence he would require that the king was at liberty? To which the duke answered that he would never regard him as so till he saw him in the middle of the French troops. This answer broke off the negotiation, and soon after the arrival of Sir R. Wilson revived the hopes of the besieged, who still clung to the expectation of English intervention. But these hopes proved fallacious; and ere long the progress of the French was such that further resistance was obviously useless. On the 20th, a French squadron of two ships of the line and two frigates opened a heavy fire on the fort of Santa Petri, on the margin of the bay, and with such effect, that on preparations being made for an assault, the white flag was hoisted, and the place capitulated on condition of the garrison being permitted to retire to Cadiz. From the advanced posts of the Trocadero and Santa Petri thus acquired, a bombardment of the town itself was three days after commenced, while the ships in the bay kept up a fire with uncommon vigor on the batteries on the sea-side. The effect of this bombardment, which brought the reality of war to their homes, was terrible. The regiment of San Marcial, heretofore deemed one of the steadiest in support of the Revolution, revolted, and was only subdued by the urban militia. Terror prevailed on all sides; cries of "Treason!" became general; every one distrusted his neighbor; and that universal discouragement prevailed which is at once the effect and the forerunner of serious disaster.[1]

<small>1 Ann. Hist. vi. 467, 468; Lam. vii. 233, 234.</small>

<small>89. Subdued at length by so many calamities, the special commission of the Cortes entered in good earnest into negotiations. In a special meeting, called on the 28th September, a report was laid before the Cortes by the Government, which set forth that all their means of defense were exhausted, that no hope of intervention on the part of England remained, and that it was indispensable to come to terms with the enemy. The Cortes, accordingly, declared itself dissolved the same day; and the king sent a message to the Duke d'Angoulême, declaring that he was now at liberty; that he was making dispositions to embark at Port Santa Maria; that he had engaged to disquiet no one on account of his political conduct; and that he would reserve all public measures till he had returned to his capital. Three days afterward, accordingly, on the 1st October, every preparation having been completed, and the king having published a proclamation, in which he promised a general amnesty, and every thing the Constitutionalists wished, the embarkation of the king and royal family took place at Santa Maria with great pomp, and amidst universal acclamation, and the thunder of artillery from all the batteries, both on the French and Spanish side of the bay.[*] The embarkation was distinctly seen from the opposite coast, where the Duke d'Angoulême, at the head of his troops, and surrounded by a splendid staff, awaited his arrival; and every eye watched, with speechless anxiety, the progress of the bark which bore the royal family of Spain from the scene of their captivity, and with them restored, as was hoped, peace and happiness to the entire Peninsula.[2]</small>

Deliverance of the king, and dissolution of the Cortes. Septem. 28.

Oct. 1.

<small>2 Ann. Hist. vi. 471, 474; Lam. vii. 235, 236.</small>

Trained by long misfortunes, not less than the precepts of his confessors, to perfect habits of dissimulation, Ferdinand, even when rowing across the bay, kept up the mask of generosity. He conversed with Valdez and Alava, who accompanied him, down to the last moments, of the gratitude which he felt to them; of the need in which he stood of experienced and popular ministers to guide him in his new reign; he invited them to trust to his magnanimity—to land with him, and quit forever a city where their kindness to him would be imputed to them as a crime. They distrusted, however, the sincerity of the monarch, and as soon as the royal family landed, pushed off from the shore. "Miserable wretches!" exclaimed the king, "they do well to withdraw from their fate!" The Duke d'Angoulême received the king kneeling, who immediately raised him from the ground, and threw himself into his arms. The thunder of artillery, waving of standards, and cheers of the troops, accompanied the auspicious event, which, in terminating the distraction of one, seemed to promise peace to both nations. But from the crowd which accompanied the royal cortège to the residence provided for them, were heard cries of a less pleasing and ominous import—"Viva el Rey! Viva el Religion! Muera la Nacion! Mueran los Negros!"[3]

90. Scene at his deliverance. October 1.

<small>1 Lam. vii. 236, 237, 241; Ann. Hist. vi. 471, 472; Cap. vii. 208, 209.</small>

The first act of the king on recovering his liberty was to publish a proclamation, in which he declared null all the acts of the Government which had been conducted in his name from 7th March, 1820, to 1st October, 1823, "seeing that the king had been during all that period deprived of his liberty, and obliged to sanction the laws, orders, and measures of the revolutionary government." By the same decree he ratified and approved every thing which had been done by the regency installed at Oyarzun, on the 9th April, 1822, and by the regency established at Madrid on the 26th May, 1823, "until his Majesty, having made himself acquainted with the necessities of his people, may be in a situation to give them the laws and take the measures best calculated to insure their happiness, the constant object of his solicitude." In vain the Duke d'Angoulême counseled measures of moderation and humanity: the voice of passion, the thirst for vengeance, alone were listened to. An entire change of course took place in the king's household; the Duke del Infantado was placed at its head, and the Regency in the mean time continued in its functions. The dissolution of the Cortes and deliverance of Ferdinand put an end to the war; for the disaffected, however indignant, had no longer a head to which they could look, or an object for which they were to contend. Before the end of October all the fortresses which still held out for the revolutionary government had hoisted the royal flag, and all the corps which were in arms for its support had sent in their adhesion to the new Government.[2]

91. First acts of the new Government.

<small>2 Ann. Hist. vi. 474, 476; Lam. vii. 237, 239, 250; Cap. viii. 208.</small>

A great and glorious career now lay before Ferdinand, if he had possessed magnanimity sufficient to follow it. The revolution had been extinguished with very little effusion of blood; the angry passions had not been awakened by general massacres; the revolutionary government had been overturned as easily, and with nearly as little loss of life, as the royal authority at Paris, by the taking of the Bastile on 14th June, 1789. The

92. Loud calls on Ferdinand for moderation and clemency.

<small>* "Le roi promet l'oubli complet et absolu de ce qui est passé, la reconnaissance des dettes contractées par le gouvernement actuel, le maintien des grades, emplois, traitements et honneurs, militaires ou civils, accordés sous le régime constitutionnel, declarant d'ailleurs de sa volonté libre et spontanée, sur la foi de la parole royale, que s'il fallait absolument modifier les institutions politiques actuelles de la monarchie, S. M. adopterait un gouvernement, qui pût faire le bonheur de la nation, en garantissant les personnes, les propriétés, et la liberté civile des Espagnols."—*Proclamation du Roi Ferdinand, 30th September, 1823; Annuaire Historique, vi. 471, 472.</small>

<small>* "Long live the King! Long live Religion! Death to the Nation! Death to the Liberals!"</small>

king had pledged his royal word to an absolute and unconditional amnesty. Clemency and moderation were as easy, and as loudly called for, in the one case as the other; and if this wise and generous course had been adopted, what a long train of calamities would have been spared to both countries! The revolutionists and the king had alike many faults to regret, many injuries to forgive; and it would have been worthy of the first in rank and the first in power, to take the lead in that glorious emulation. But unhappily, in the Spanish character, the desire for vengeance and the thirst for blood are as inherent as the spirit of adventure and the heroism of resistance; and amidst all the declamations in favor of religion, the priests who surrounded the throne forgot that the forgiveness of injuries is the first of the Christian virtues. The consequence was, that the royalist government took example from the revolutionary in deeds of cruelty; the reaction was as violent as the action had been; and Spain was the victim of mutual injuries, and torn by intestine passions for a long course of years, until the discord ceased by the exhaustion of those who were its victims.

Riego was the first victim. Cries were heard,
93. Sentence of Riego. which showed how profound was the indignation and wide-spread the thirst for vengeance in the Spanish mind. The first step taken was to bring him to trial. No advocate could be found bold enough to undertake his defense; the court was obliged to appoint one to that perilous duty. During the whole time the trial was going on, a furious crowd surrounded the hall of justice with cries of "Muera Riego! Muera el Tradidor! Viva el Rey Assoluto!" His conviction followed as a matter of course, and he was sentenced to death amidst the same shouts from an excited audience, whom even the solemnity of that awful occasion, and the very magnitude of the offense with which the prisoner was charged, could not overawe into temporary silence.[1]

[1] An. Hist. vi. 481, 482; Lam. vii. 261, 262.

His execution took place a few days afterward, and under circumstances peculiarly shocking, and which reflected the deepest disgrace on the Spanish government. Stript of his uniform, clothed in a wrapper of white cloth, with a green cap, the ensign of liberty, on his head, he was placed with his hands tied behind his back, on a hurdle drawn by an ass, in which he was conveyed, surrounded by priests, and with the *Miserere* of the dying unceasingly rung in his ears by a chorister, to the place of execution. The multitude gazed in silence on the frightful spectacle. The memorable reverse of fortune, from being the adored chief of the revolution to becoming thus reviled and rejected, for a moment subdued the angry passions. Arrived at the foot of the scaffold, which was constructed upon an eminence in the Plaza de la Cebada, forty feet high, so as to be seen from a great distance, he received absolution for his crimes, and was lifted up, still bound, pale and attenuated, already half dead, to the top of the scaffold, where the fatal cord was passed round his neck, and he was launched into eternity.[2] A monster in the human form

94. His execution. Nov. 7.

[2] Lam. vii. 263, 264; Ann. Hist. vi. 483; Moniteur, Nov. 14, 1823.

gave a buffet to his countenance after death; a shudder ran through the crowd, which was soon drowned in cries of "Viva el Rey! Viva el Rey Assoluto!"

The King and Queen of Spain made their triumphal entry into Madrid six days after that melancholy execution, amidst an immense crowd of spectators, and surrounded by every demonstration of joy. Their majesties were seated on an antique and gigantic chariot, twenty-five feet high, which was drawn by a hundred young men elegantly attired, surrounded by groups of dancers of both sexes, in the most splendid theatrical costumes, whose operatic display elicited boundless applause from the spectators. The spirit of faction appeared to be dead; one only feeling seemed to animate every breast, which was joy at the termination of the revolution. But it soon appeared that, if the convulsions had ceased, the passions it had called forth were far from being appeased. The long-wished-for amnesty, so solemnly promised by the king before his liberation at Cadiz, and which would have closed in so worthy a spirit the wounds of the revolution, had not yet been promulgated, and it was looked for with speechless anxiety by the numerous relatives and friends of the persons compromised. For several days after the king's arrival in the capital it did not make its appearance, and meanwhile arrests continued daily, and were multiplied to such a degree that the prisons were soon overflowing. At length the public anxiety became so great that the Government were compelled to publish the amnesty on the 19th. It contained, however, so many exceptions, that it was rather a declaration of war against the adverse party than a healing and pacific measure. It excepted all the persons who had taken a leading part in the late disturbance, and their number was so great that it was evident it laid the foundation of interminable discords and certain reaction. On the 2d December, the list of the new Ministry appeared, constructed, as might have been expected, from amongst the persons who had been most instrumental in promoting the return to the ancient régime.† The Duke del Infantado was dismissed from the presidency of the Privy Council, which was bestowed on Don Ignace Martinez de la Rosa; and the council itself was composed of ten persons, all devoted Royalists. At the same time, however, on the urgent representation of Count Pozzo di Borgo, who bore a holograph letter of the Emperor of Russia on the subject, a pledge was given of an intention to revert to more moderate councils, by the dismissal of Don Victor Laez, the organ of the violent apostolic party, from the important office of confessor to the king, who was succeeded by a priest of more reasonable views.[1]

95. Entry of the king and queen into Madrid. Nov. 13.

Nov. 19.

Dec. 2.

[1] Moniteur, Dec. 10, 1823; Cap. vii. 205, 213; Ann. Hist. vi. 485, 486.

* The same thing was done to the beautiful head of Charlotte Corday after she had been guillotined.—See *History of Europe*, former series, chap. xii. § 78. How identical is the passion of party and the spirit of vengeance in all ages and countries!

† Marquis Casa-Irugo, Premier and Foreign Affairs; Don Narcisso de Heredia, Minister of Grace and Justice; Don José de la Cruz, War; Don Luis Lopez-Ballasteros, Finances; Don Luis-Maria Salazar, Marine and Colonies —*Annuaire Historique*, vi. 481.

The revolution was now closed, and the royal government re-established in Spain, supported by ninety thousand French soldiers, in possession of its principal fortresses, and so disposed as to be able at once to crush any fresh revolutionary outbreak. But it is not by the mere cessation of hostilities that the passions of revolution are extinguished, or its disastrous effects obliterated. Deplorable to the last degree was the condition of Spain on the termination of the civil war, and deep and unappeasable the thirst of vengeance with which the different parties were animated against each other. The finances, as usual in such cases, gave woeful proof of the magnitude of the general disorder, and the extent to which it had sapped the foundations alike of public and private prosperity. In the greater part of the provinces the collection of revenue had entirely ceased; where it was still gathered, it came in so slowly as not to deserve the name of a national revenue. The 5 per cents were down at 16; loans attempted to be opened in every capital of Europe found no subscribers. The effects of the clergy, the revenues of the kingdom offered in security of advances, failed to overcome the terrors of capitalists. Recognition of the loans of the Cortes was every where stated as the first condition of further accommodation, and this the disastrous state of the finances rendered impossible, for they were wholly inadequate to meet the interest of these. The only activity displayed in the kingdom was in the mutual arrest of their enemies by the different parties; the only energy, in preparing the means of wreaking vengeance on each other. But for the presence of the French army, they would have flown at each other's throats, and civil war would in many places have been renewed. Peace and protection were every where experienced under the white flag; and so general was the sense of the absolute necessity of its shelter, that no opposition was made any where to a convention by which it was stipulated that for a year longer thirty-five thousand French troops should remain in possession of the principal Spanish fortresses.[1]

96. Distracted and miserable state of Spain.

Dec. 18.

[1] Ann. Hist. vi. 487, 488; Lam. vii, 201; Cap. viii. 210, 213.

97. State of Portugal during this year. Royalist insurrection.

Portugal has in recent times so entirely followed the political changes of Spain, that in reading the account of the one you would imagine you are perusing that of the other. The parties were the same, the objects of contention the same, their alternate triumphs and disasters the same. In the early part of the year the Cortes were still all-powerful, and a long lease of power was presaged for the constitutional government. When the French invasion of Spain appeared certain, an army of observation was formed on the frontier without opposition. But civil war soon appeared. On the 23d of February, the Conde d'Amarante, at Villa-Real, raised the standard of insurrection, and published a proclamation, in which he called on all loyal subjects to unite with him in "delivering the country from the yoke of the Cortes, the scourge of revolution, the religion of their enemies, and to rescue the king from captivity." The proclamation was received with enthusiasm; in a few days the whole province of Tras-os-Montes was in arms, several regular regiments joined the Royalist standard, and in the beginning of March a formidable force appeared on the banks of the Douro. There, however, they were met by the Constitutional generals at the head of eight thousand men; and after a variety of conflicts with various success, in the course of which the Conde d'Amarante was often worsted, the Royalists were driven back into Tras-os-Montes with considerable loss, from whence Amarante was fain to escape into Spain, where he joined the curate Merino, who had hoisted the white flag, with four thousand men in the neighborhood of Valladolid. The insurrection seemed subdued, and the session of the Cortes concluded amidst Io Pæans and congratulatory addresses on the part of the Constitutionalists.[1]

Feb. 23.

March 18.

April 4. [1] Ann. Hist. vi, 498, 501; Ann. Reg. 1823, 170.

But these transports were of short duration; the French invasion speedily altered the aspect of affairs, not less in Portugal than in Spain. On the 27th May, one of the regiments in the army of observation on the frontier raised the cry of "Viva el Rey!" and on the following night the Infant Don Miguel, the acknowledged head of the royalist party, escaped from Lisbon, and joined the revolted corps at Villa-Franca. The prince immediately published a proclamation, in which he declared that his object was to free the nation from the shameful yoke which had been imposed on it, to liberate the king, and give the people a constitution exempt alike from despotism and license. A great number of influential persons immediately joined him, and the Court at Villa-Franca became a rival to that at Lisbon. On the 29th, Sepulveda, with part of the garrison of Lisbon, declared for the royal cause; and the Cortes, which had assembled, was thrown into the utmost consternation by the same cry being repeated in various quarters of the city. At length the infection spread to the royal guard; cries of "Viva el Rey Assoluto!" broke from their ranks; the cockades of the Constitution were every where torn off and trampled under foot, and the king himself, who had come out to appease the tumult, was obliged to join in the same cry, and to detach the Constitutional cockade from his breast. In the evening a proclamation was published, dated from the royalist head-quarters, in which he announced a change of government and modification of the constitution. The Cortes was dissolved on the 2d of June; on the same day a proclamation was published, denouncing in severe terms the vices of the revolutionary system; and two days after the counter-revolution was rendered irrevocable by the king moving to the Royalist head-quarters at Villa-Franca. Three days after, he returned in great pomp to Lisbon, where he was received with universal acclamations; the Ministry was changed; the Infant Dom Miguel was declared generalissimo of the army, the Count de Palmella appointed Premier and Minister of Foreign Affairs, and the whole Cabinet composed of royalist chiefs. Every thing immediately re-

98. Royalist counter-revolution. May 27.

May 31.

June 2.

June 5.

turned into the old channels; the revolutionary authorities all sent in their adhesion or were dismissed and to the honor of Portugal be it said, the counter-revolution was completed without bloodshed, and no severer penalties than the exile from Lisbon of thirty of the most violent members of the Cortes, and the loss of office by a few of the Liberal chiefs.[1]

[1] Ann. Reg. 1823, 178, 190. Ann. Hist. vi. 504, 512.

99. Triumphant return of the Duke d'Angoulême to Paris. Dec. 2.

The return of the Duke d'Angoulême, and the greater part of his army, after this memorable campaign, was a continual triumph. It was no wonder it was so; it had proved one of the most remarkable recorded in history. In less than six months, with the loss of only four thousand men, as well by sickness as the sword, with an expenditure of only 200,000,000 francs (£8,000,000), they had subdued and pacified Spain, delivered the king, arrested the march of revolution, and stopped the convulsions of Europe. The campaigns of Napoleon have no triumphs so bloodless to recount. Great preparations had been made in Paris to receive them in a manner worthy of the occasion. On the 2d December, the anniversary of the battle of Austerlitz, the prince made his triumphal entry into Paris on horseback, at the head of the *élite* of his troops, surrounded by a splendid staff, among whom were to be seen Marshals Oudinot, Marmont, and Lauriston, General Bordesoult, the Duke de Guiche, and Count de la Rochejaquelein. The aspect of the troops, their martial air and bronzed visages, recalled the most brilliant military spectacles of the Empire. They passed under the magnificent triumphal arch of Neuilly, finished for the occasion, and thence through the Champs Elysées to the Tuileries, through a double line of national guards, and an immense crowd of spectators, who rent the air with their acclamations. The municipality and chief public bodies of Paris met the prince at the barrier de l'Etoile, and addressed him in terms of warm but not undeserved congratulation on his glorious exploits.* The prince, modestly bowing almost to his charger's neck, replied, "I rejoice that I have accomplished the mission which the king intrusted to me, re-established peace and shown that nothing is impossible at the head of a French army." Arrived at the Tuileries, he dismounted, and hastened to the king, who stood in great pomp to receive him. "My son," said the monarch with solemnity, "I am satisfied with you;" and, taking him by the hand, he led him to the balcony, where an immense crowd, with redoubled acclamations, testified their sympathy with the scene.[1]

[1] Lam. vii. 267, 270; Ann. Hist. vi. 242, 244.

100. Offer of assistance by Russia to France rejected.

This triumphant career of the French army in Spain was viewed with very different eyes by the powers in Europe most interested in the issue. The Emperor of Russia, who had warmly supported the project of the intervention at Verona, and anxiously watched the progress of the enterprise, offered to move forward his troops from the Vistula to the Rhine, and to cover the eastern frontier of France with his armed masses. Mr. Canning, justly alarmed at so open an assertion of a right of protectorate over Europe, strongly opposed the proposal. "France," said he, "conceiving her safety menaced, and her interests compromised, by the existing state of things in the Peninsula, we have not opposed her right to intervene; but she should only act singly, and the strictest neutrality should be observed by the other powers. If, in defiance of all stipulations, the European cabinets should act otherwise, England would feel herself constrained to enforce the observance of existing engagements, and would at once consider the cause of Spain as her own." M. de Chateaubriand cordially seconded these remonstrances, and respectfully declined the proffered succor—

"Non tali auxilio, nec defensoribus istis."

The armed intervention of Russia was thus averted by the union of the two western powers; and as the revolution of Portugal threatened the influence of England in that country, Mr. Canning and the Prince de Polignac, the French embassador in London, came to an understanding that France was not to interfere between the Cabinet of St. James's and its ancient ally.[3]

[3] Cap. vii. 209, 214.

101. Views of Mr. Canning in recognizing the republics of South America.

It was with undisguised vexation that Mr. Canning beheld the triumphant progress of the French arms in Spain; and deeming, with reason, the throne of the Bourbons greatly strengthened, and the influence of France on the Continent in a great degree re-established by the successful issue of the campaign, he resolved upon a measure which should re-establish the balance, and at the same time, as he hoped, materially benefit the commercial interests of England. This was the RECOGNITION OF THE REPUBLICS OF SOUTH AMERICA. His intention in this respect had been long before divined by the able diplomatist who conducted the French interests in London;* and

* "'Nos vœux vous suivaient à votre départ,' lui dit le préfet de Paris, 'nos acclamations vous attendaient à votre heureux retour. Depuis trente ans, le nom de guerre n'était qu'un cri d'effroi, qu'un signal de calamités pour les peuples; la population des états envahis, comme celle des états conquérants, se précipitant l'une sur l'autre, offraient aux yeux du sage, un spectacle lamentable. Aujourd'hui la guerre relève les nations abattues sur tous les points d'un vaste empire. Elle apparaît humaine, protectrice et généreuse, guerrière sans peur, conquérante sans vengeance. Votre vaillante épée, à la voix d'un puissant Monarque, vient de consacrer le noble et le légitime emploi de la valeur et des armes. Les trophées de la guerre, devenus la consolation d'un peuple opprimé, le volcan de la Révolution fermé *pour jamais*, la réconciliation de notre patrie cimentée aux yeux du monde, la victoire rendue à nos marins comme à nos guerriers, et la gloire de tous les enfants de la France confondue dans un nouveau faisceau; tels sont, Monseigneur, les résultats de cette campagne, telle est l'œuvre que vous avez accomplie.'"—*Moniteur*, Dec. 3, 1823.

* "Il est temps de jeter un regard sérieux sur l'avenir, et sur le dangereux ministre qui est venu se placer à la tête des destinées de l'Angleterre. Il nous faut sa chute ou sa conversion. Il ne tombera pas; ses ennemis n'ont pu l'exiler sur le trône des Indes. M. Peel, jeune, ferme, et populaire, s'avance sans impatience vers le ministère, *qui ne peut lui manquer un jour*. Lord Wellington, guerrier peu redoutable *sur le champ de l'intrigue*, a dû céder aux talents et à l'habileté de M. Canning. Il ne tombera pas; il faut donc pour nous qu'il change de conduite, et que de Briton qu'il est, il se fasse Européen; faites reluire à ses yeux l'éclat d'une grande gloire diplomatique: assemblez un nouveau congrès, qu'il vienne y traiter, à son tour, des intérêts de l'Orient, des colonies *Américaines*, de nos quatre dernières révolutions créées en deux ans, la Grèce, l'Italie, le Portugal, l'Espagne! Que l'Europe le couvre de faveurs! Inaccessible à l'or,

we now possess the history of his views from the best of all sources—his own recorded statement. "When the French army," said he, "was on the point of entering Spain, we did all we could to prevent it; we resisted it by all means short of war. We did not go to war, because we felt that, if we did so, whatever the result might be, it would not lead to the evacuation of Spain by the French troops. In a war against France at that time, as at any other, you might perhaps have acquired military glory; you might perhaps have extended your colonial possessions; you might even have achieved, at a great loss of blood and treasure, an honorable peace; but as to getting the French out of Spain, that is the one object which you would certainly not have accomplished. Again, is the Spain of the present day the Spain whose puissance was expected to shake England from her sphere? No, sir; it was quite another Spain: it was the Spain within whose dominions the sun never sets; it was 'Spain *with the Indies*' that excited the jealousies and alarmed the imagination of our ancestors. When the French army entered Spain, the balance of power was disturbed, and we might, if we chose, have resisted or resented that measure by war. But were there no other means but war for restoring the balance of power? Is the balance of power a fixed and invariable standard; or is it not a standard perpetually varying as civilization advances, and new nations spring up to take their place among established political communities?

102. Continued. "To look to the policy of Europe in the time of William and Anne, for the purpose of regulating the balance of power in Europe at the present day, is to disregard the progress of events, and to confuse dates and facts, which throw a reciprocal light upon each other. It would be disingenuous not to admit that the entry of the French army into Spain was, in a certain sense, a disparagement—an affront to the pride, a blow to the feelings, of England; and it can hardly be supposed that the Government did not sympathize on that occasion with the feelings of the people. But, questionable or unquestionable as the act might be, it was not one which necessarily called for our direct and hostile opposition. Was nothing then to be done?—was there no other mode of resistance but by a direct attack upon France, or by a war undertaken on the soil of Spain? What if the possession of Spain might be rendered harmless in rival hands—harmless as regarded us, and valueless to the possessors? Might not compensation for disparagement be obtained, and the policy of our ancestors vindicated, by means better adapted to the present time? If France occupied Spain, was it necessary, in order to avoid the consequences of that occupation, that we should blockade Cadiz? No: I looked another way; I sought materials for compensation in another hemisphere. Contemplating Spain such as our ancestors had known her, I resolved that, if France had Spain, it should not be Spain 'with the Indies.' *I called the New World into existence, to redress the balance of the Old.*"[1]

[1 Parl. Deb. xvi. 394, 395.]

103. Mr. Canning did not give independence to South America, but only acknowledged it.

It is one of the most curious truths apparent from history, how identical are the impulses of the human mind, at all times and in all countries, in similar circumstances, and how insensible men are to the moral character of actions when pursued for their own benefit, to which they are sensibly alive when undertaken for the advantage of others. The English had loudly exclaimed against the iniquity of the Northern powers in pretending to preserve the balance of power in the east of Europe, by dividing the spoils of Poland among each other; and they dwelt on the selfishness of Austria, in after times, which held out the Russian acquisition of Wallachia and Moldavia a sufficient ground for giving them a claim to Servia and Bosnia; but they thought there was nothing unjustifiable in our upholding the balance of power in the West, not by defending Spain against France, but by sharing in its spoils, and loudly applauded the minister who proposed to seek compensation for the French invasion of the Peninsula, by carving for British profit independent republics out of the Spanish dominions in South America, at the very time when he professed the warmest interest in its independence. But be the intervention of England in South America justifiable or unjustifiable, nothing is more certain than that neither its merit nor its demerit properly belongs to Mr. Canning. The independence of Columbia was decided by a charge of English bayonets on the field of Carabobo, on 14th June, 1821, more than a year before Mr. Canning was called to the Foreign Office.[2] It was the ten thousand British auxiliaries, most of them veterans of Wellington, who sailed from the Thames, the Mersey, and the Clyde, under the eye of Lord Castlereagh, in 1818, 1819, and 1820, who really accomplished the emancipation of South America. Mr. Canning did not call the New World into existence, he only recognized it when already existing.[3]

[2 Hist. of Europe, c. lxvii. § 73.]
[3 Hist. of Europe, c. lxvii. § 69.]

104. Recognition of the South American republics by Mr. Canning.

There can be no doubt, however, that this recognition was of essential importance to the infant republics, and that it was the stability and credit which they acquired from it which enabled them to fit out the memorable expedition which in the next year crossed the Andes, and at the foot of the cliffs of Ayacucho achieved the independence of Peru.[4] Mr. Canning's measures, when he had once determ-

[4 Hist. of Europe, c. lxvii. §§ 76, 77.]

---

il ne l'est pas à la louange : enfin reconnoîtr<unreadable> le avec mes anciennes opinions monarchiques, et pardonnez-moi si, malgré mon jeune âge, je parle si librement avec vous des plus hauts intérêts de mon pays."—M. MARCELLUS à M. DE CHATEAUBRIAND, 17th December, 1822. "Ne comptez pas sur l'Angleterre. Elle se refusera a toute mesure même pacifique, et cachera sous l'apparence de quelques demandes sans force réelle, son indifférence profonde des intérêts purement continentaux. Ce système de séparation ou d'égoisme est imposé a M. Canning par ses amis, et surtout par son intérêt. Cet intérêt même peut le pousser à des concessions d'opinion personnelle, qu'on n'eut jamais obtenues du Marquis de Londonderry. Ainsi on le verra reconnaître la Colombie pour gagner le commerce, épouser la cause des Noirs pour plaire au Parlement, puis suspendre son action jusqu'ici favorable à la réforme catholique. Enfin il fera tout pour accroître cette popularité à laquelle il devra son maintien, comme il lui doit son élévation."—M. MARCELLUS à M. DE CHATEAUBRIAND, Londres, 3 Octobre, 1832; MARCELLUS, *Politique de la Restauration*, 96; and LAMARTINE, *Histoire de la Restauration*, vii. 222.

ined on neutralizing the efforts of France in this way, were neither feeble nor undecided. On the 26th February, 1823, he obtained from the British government, by order in council, a revocation of the prohibition to export arms and the muniments of war to Spain*—a step which called forth the loudest remonstrances from the French minister in London at the time.† This was soon after followed by still more decisive measures. On 16th April, Lord Althorpe brought forward a motion, in the House of Commons, for the repeal of the Act of 1819, which prohibited British subjects from engaging in foreign military service, or fitting out, in his Majesty's dominions, without the royal license, vessels for warlike purposes; and although this proposal was thrown out by a majority of 216 to 110, yet the object was gained by the proof afforded of the interest which the cause of the insurgent colonies excited in this country. In June, Mr. Canning refused to recognize the Regency established at Madrid after the entry of the Duke d'Angoulême; and in July, on a petition from some respectable merchants in London engaged in the South American trade, he agreed to appoint consuls to Mexico, Columbia, Peru, Chili, and Buenos Ayres. His language on this occasion was manly, and worthy of a British minister. "We will not," said he, "interfere with Spain in any attempts she may make to reconquer what were once her colonies, but we will not permit any third power to attack them, or to reconquer them for her; and in granting or refusing our recognition, we shall look, not to the conduct of any European power, but to the actual circumstances of these countries." And when Prince Polignac, the French minister in London, applied for explanations on the subject, and urged the expedience of establishing, in concert with the other European powers, monarchical states in South America, Mr. Canning's reply was, that "however desirable the establishment of a monarchical form of government in any of those provinces might be, his Government could not take upon itself to put it forward as a condition of their recognition."¹

¹ Parl. Deb. x. 712; Martignac, i. 299; Ann. Reg. 1823, 27, 145, 146; Canning's Life, 331.

105. Effects of this measure on British interests.

Thus was achieved, mainly in consequence of the French invasion of Spain, the recognition of the independence of the South American republics. Whether they were fitted for the change—whether the cause of liberty has been advanced, or the social happiness of mankind advanced, by the substitution of the anarchy of independence for the despotism of old Spain, and whether British interests have been benefited by the alteration—may be judged of by the fact, that while the exports of Spain to her colonies, before the war of independence began, exceeded £15,000,000 sterling, the greater part of which consisted of British manufactures, conveyed in Spanish bottoms, the whole amount of our exports to these colonies is now (1852), thirty years after their independence had been established, only £5,000,000; and that the republic of *Bolivia*, called after the liberator Bolivar, has entirely disappeared from the chart of British exports.

106. M. de Chateaubriand's designs in regard to the South American states.

But whatever opinion may be formed on this point, one thing is clear, that M. de Chateaubriand has furnished a better vindication of the British intervention in South America than any consideration of commercial advantages could have done. It appears from a revelation in his memoirs, that Mr. Canning only anticipated his own designs upon these vast possessions of Spain, and that, instead of British consuls negotiating with independent republics, he contemplated monarchical states under Bourbon princes. "Cobbett," says he, "was the only person in England at that period who undertook our defense, who did us justice, who judged calmly both of the necessity of our intervention in Spain, and of the view which we had to restore to France the strength of which it had been deprived. Happily he did not divine our entire plan—which was *to break through or modify the treaties of Vienna, and to establish Bourbon monarchies in South America*. Had he discerned this, and lifted the vail, he would have exposed France to great danger, for already the alarm had seized the cabinets of Europe."¹

¹ Congrès de Vérone, i. 358.

107. Speech of Mr. Canning at Plymouth. Sept. 14.

The great danger which there was at that period of Europe being involved in a general war, and the ardent feelings which Mr. Canning had on the subject, can not be better illustrated than by a speech which he made at Plymouth in the autumn of this year, memorable alike from the sentiments it conveyed and the beauty of the language in which they were couched. "Our ultimate object," said he, "is the peace of the world; but let it not be said

---

* EXPORTS IN 1852 FROM GREAT BRITAIN TO

Chili	£1,167,494
Brazil	3,164,394
Peru	1,024,007
Buenos Ayres	837,538
Mexico	366,026
Venezuela	273,733
Central America	260,602
Uruguay	615,418
New Granada	502,728

Total to South American republics .. £5,046,982
—Parl. Paper, 17th July, 1853.

EXPORTS IN 1809 FROM SPAIN TO

Porto Rico	£2,750,000
Mexico	5,250,000
New Granada	1,450,000
Caraccas	2,150,000
Peru and Chili	2,875,000
Buenos Ayres and Potosi	875,000
	£15,200,000

—HUMBOLDT, *Nouvelle Espagne*, iv. 153, 154.

---

* "As far as the exportation of arms and ammunition was concerned, it was in the power of the Crown to remove any inequality between France and Spain simply by an order in council. Such an order was accordingly issued, and the prohibition of exporting arms and ammunition to Spain was taken off."—Mr. CANNING's *Speech*, April 16, 1823; *Parl. Deb.*, viii. 1051. It was prohibited since 1819, both to Spain and the colonies, on the remonstrance of the Spanish government.—*Ante*, chap. iv. sect. 95.

† "Hier je me suis plaint, et très-vivement, de la permission d'exporter en Espagne toutes armes et munitions de guerre; permission que le ministre vient de donner, de son propre mouvement, en révoquant l'arrêt qui s'y oppose. Des marches importants d'armes et de munitions se traitent; des banquiers, membres influents de la Chambre des Communes, sont entrés dans ces spéculations que le gouvernement encourage de la manière la plus manifeste."—M. MARCELLUS à M. de CHATEAUBRIAND, Londres, 28th Feb., 1823; MARCELLUS, 151.

we cultivate peace, either because we fear, or because we are not prepared for war: on the contrary, if, eight months ago, the Government did not hesitate to proclaim that the country was prepared for war, if war should unfortunately be necessary, every month of peace that has since passed has made us so much the more capable of exertion. The resources created by peace are the means of war. In cherishing these resources, we but accumulate those means. Our present repose is no more a proof of inability to act than the state of inertness and inactivity in which I have seen those mighty masses that float in the waters above your town, is a proof they are devoid of strength, and incapable of being fitted for action. You well know, gentlemen, how soon one of those stupendous masses, now reposing on their shadows in perfect stillness—how soon, upon any call of patriotism or necessity, it would assume the likeness of an animated thing, instinct with life and motion—how soon it would ruffle, as it were, its swelling plumage—how quickly it would put forth all its beauty and its bravery, collect its scattered elements of strength, and awake its dormant thunders! Such as is one of those magnificent machines when springing from inaction into a display of its strength—such is England herself: while apparently passive and motionless she silently caused the power to be put forth on an adequate occasion."[1]

[1] Ann. Reg. 1823, 146, 147.

108. The election of 1824, and strength of the Royalists.

The usual effects of success appeared in the result of the elections which took place for the renewal of the fifth of the Chamber in the autumn of 1823. Nearly all were in favor of the Royalists, who had now acquired a decisive preponderance in the Chamber, sufficient to set at defiance the united strength of the Liberals and Centre. Several appointments were made at this time, all of extreme Royalists, indicating the acknowledged supremacy of that party in the legislature. M. de Villèle skilfully availed himself of this favorable state of affairs to contract a loan of 413,980,981 francs (£16,400,000) with the house of Rothschild and Co., which, in exchange for it, received an inscription on the *Grand Livre* for 23,114,000 francs yearly (£920,000); in other words, they took the stock created at 89.55 per cent. This advantageous loan—by far the most favorable for Government which had been made since the Restoration—put the treasury entirely at ease, and enabled Government to clear off all the outstanding debts connected with the Spanish war. Encouraged by this eminently favorable state of the public mind, M. de Villèle resolved on a dissolution of the Chamber, which was done by an ordonnance on 24th December. The colleges of arrondissements were by the ordonnance appointed to meet on the 25th February, those of the departments on the 6th March. They met accordingly, and the result was entirely favorable to the Royalists. In Paris, the centre of the Liberal party, and where they had hitherto in general obtained all the twelve seats, they succeeded in returning only General Foy, M. Casimir Perier, and Benjamin Constant. So entire was the defeat of the Opposition, that over all France they succeeded, out of 434 elections, in gaining only fifteen seats in the colleges of arrondissements, and two in those of departments—in all, seventeen—an astonishing result in a country so recently torn by popular passions, and indicating at once the great change in the composition of the legislature which the institution of the colleges of departments had made, and the overwhelming influence of military success on a people so essentially warlike in their disposition as the French. Such was the effect of these circumstances on the public funds, that notwithstanding the great loan contracted for by Rothschild, and which was not yet fully paid into the treasury, the Five per Cents rose in the beginning of March to 104.80, an elevation which they had never even approached for half a century.[1]

Dec. 24.

[1] Moniteur, March 6, 1824. Ann. Hist. vii. 6, 7; Cap. viii. 216, 222; Lam. vii. 270, 274.

109. Great effect which this had on the future destinies of France.

To all appearance the Government of the Restoration was now established on the most solid of all bases on which a constitutional throne can rest, for an overwhelming majority in its favor had at last been obtained even in the popular branch of the legislature. Yet so closely are the seeds of evil interwoven with those of good in the complicated maze of human affairs, that out of this very favorable state of affairs arose the principal causes which in the end occasioned its fall. It induced a result—fatal in a free state—that of making Government consider themselves safe if they could command a majority in the Chamber of Deputies; a very natural opinion in men accustomed to look to its votes as determining the fate of administrations, and even of dynasties, but of all others the most dangerous, if the period arrives, as it must do in the course of time, when the public mind is strongly excited, and the popular representatives do not respond to its mutations. This tendency revealed itself in the very first measures of the new legislature.[2]

[2] Lam. vii. 276, 277; Cap. viii. 220, 224, Ann. Hist. vii. 8, 9.

110. Meeting of the Chambers, and measures announced in the royal speech. March 23.

The Chambers met on the 23d March, and the king's speech congratulated the country with reason on the eminently auspicious circumstances under which they were assembled. "The triumph of our arms," said the monarch, "which has secured so many guarantees for order, is due to the discipline and bravery of the French army, conducted by my son with as much wisdom as valor." At these words, loud cries of "Vive le Roi! Vive le Duc d'Angoulême!" arose on all sides; but subjects more likely to elicit difference of opinion were next introduced. After stating the inconveniences which experience had proved resulted from the annual election of a fifth of the Chamber, it announced an intention of introducing a bill for extending the duration of the legislature to *seven years*, subject to the king's right of dissolution; and another for the purpose of "providing the means of repaying the holders of Government annuities, or converting their rights into a claim for sums annually, more in accordance with the present state of other transactions; an operation which can not fail to have a beneficial influence on commerce and agriculture, and will enable Government, when it is carried into effect, to diminish the public burdens, and close the last wounds of the Revolution."[1]

[marginal note: 1 Discours du Roi, March 23, 1824, An. Hist. vii. 8.]

These words announced the two important measures of the session, which were immediately brought forward by Government. So obvious were the advantages, at first sight at least, of the first, that the Cabinet were unanimous on the subject. The sagacious and practical M. de Villèle, and the ardent and enthusiastic M. de Chateaubriand, alike gave it their cordial support. It was argued in support of this measure, "that the time had now arrived when it had become practicable to remove the great difficulty with which the Bourbons had had to contend since the Restoration. That difficulty was the want of a fixed majority in the Chamber of Deputies, upon which Government could rely for the support of their measures. The inevitable consequence of this was, that any thing like a consistent system of government was impossible. The king was obliged to take his ministers at one time from the Liberal, at another from the Royalist side; a single vote might compel an entire change in the system of administration, both external and internal; one session might undo every thing, how beneficial soever, which the preceding session had done. The effect of this was not only to deprive Government of any thing like a fixed or consistent character, but to keep alive party ambition and the spirit of faction in the legislature, from the near prospect which was constantly afforded to either party of dispossessing their antagonists, and seating themselves in power. Add to this, that the annual renewal of a fifth of the Chamber kept the people in a continual ferment, and aggravated the evils of corruption and undue influence, by concentrating the whole efforts of parties annually on a fifth only of the entire electors. And as to the danger of the legislature ceasing to represent public opinion, that was greater in appearance than reality, because, as the king had the power of dissolution, he could at any time give the people an opportunity of making any change on this which they might desire."[2]

[marginal note: 2 An. Hist. vii. 88, 94, Lam. vii. 276, 277; Cap. viii. 265, 271.]

[marginal note: 112. Argument on the other side.]

Strong as these arguments were, and powerfully as they spoke to a Government now, for the first time for ten years, in possession of a decided majority in the popular branch of the legislature, there were considerations on the other side, less pressing at the moment, but perhaps still more important in the end. "The change," it was answered, "proposes to repeal a vital part of the Charter, which expressly provides for the annual renewal of a fifth of the Chamber, and, contrary to the whole principles of representative government, goes to introduce an entire change into the constitution. The great, the lasting danger to be apprehended from the alteration is, that it tends to make the king independent of the popular voice, and may bring his legislature into such discredit with the nation as, in troubled times, may induce the most terrible convulsions, in pacific, totally destroying its utility. What is the use, where is the moral influence, of a legislature which is at variance with the great body of the nation? A senate which is merely to record the decrees of an emperor, in order to take from him their responsibility, may be a convenient appendage of despotism, but it is no part of the institutions of a free people. But the legislature, if elected for seven years certain, without any means of infusing into it, during that long period, any new blood, any fresh ideas, runs the most imminent hazard of degenerating into such an instrument of despotism. In vain are we told that the monarch may dissolve it, and thus bring in another more in harmony with the general opinion at the moment. What security have we that he will adopt this wise and temperate course? Is it not next to certain that he will do just the reverse? If the crown is at issue with the people upon some question which strongly interests both, is it probable that the Government will adopt the course of dissolving a legislature which is favorable to its views, and introducing one which is adverse to them? As well may you expect a general to disband his faithful guards, and raise a new body of defenders from the ranks of his enemies. And what is to be expected from such a blind reliance of the Crown on an immovable legislature, but such an accumulation of discontent and ill-humor in the nation, as can not fail, on the first occasion when the passions of the people are strongly excited, to overturn the monarchy?"[1]

[marginal note: 1 An. Hist. vii. 171, 203; Moniteur, May 30, 1823.]

Notwithstanding the strength of these arguments, the justice of which was so fatally verified by the event, the proposed bill, which fixed the duration of the Chamber at seven years, passed both branches of the legislature by large majorities, the numbers in the Deputies being 292 to 87, in the Peers 117 to 64.[2]

[marginal note: 2 Ann. Hist. vi. 104, 203.]

The next great measure of the session encountered a more serious opposition, and was ultimately unsuccessful. The project of Government, which was brought forward by the Finance Minister on 5th April, was to take advantage of the present high rate of interest, to convert the 5 per cents into 3 per cents, taking the latter at 75. They had made arrangements with the leading bankers in Paris to advance the requisite funds to pay off such of the public creditors as should decline to submit to the reduction, the lenders of the money receiving the new 3 per cents stock at the same rate. This measure, it was calculated, would effect a reduction in the annual charge of the debt of 30,000,000 francs (£1,200,000), and at the same time would establish the credit of Government and the nation on the most solid foundation, by demonstrating the trust of the leading capitalists in the integrity of its administration, and the magnitude of its resources; while, by effecting so great a diminution of the public burdens, it might pave the way for ulterior measures, which would close the last wounds of the Revolution.[3]

[marginal note: 113. Law for the reduction of interest of the national debt.]

[marginal note: 3 An. Hist. vii. 36, 37; Moniteur, April 6 & 7, 1823; Cap. viii. 283, 285.]

It was ascertained at this time that there were 250,000 persons in France holders of Gov-

114
Which is passed by the Deputies, but thrown out by the Peers.

ernment annuities, of whom more than a half held right to only 500 francs (£20) a year or under. The public funds were thus the great savings-bank of the nation; and it might easily have been foreseen, what the event soon proved, that the proposal to reduce their incomes would excite the most violent commotions. Nothing, accordingly, could exceed the violence with which it was assailed, both in the legislature and in the public journals; and every day that the discussion lasted, the public excitement became greater. Such, however, was the influence of Government in the Royalist Chamber, that, after a prolonged discussion, and having encountered the most violent opposition, it passed the Deputies, on the 3d May, by a majority of 238 to 145. But the result was different in the Peers, where, on the 31st July, it was thrown out by a majority of 34, the numbers being 128 to 94. It was particularly observed, that M. de Chateaubriand, though holding the situation of Foreign Secretary, did not speak in favor of the ministerial project, and that several of his party, both in the Peers and Commons, voted against it.[1]

[1] Moniteur, May 4 and August 1, 1823; Ann. Hist. vii. 65, 168.

115
Reflections on this decision. Difference of the English and French funds.

In forming an opinion on this decision, it is necessary to distinguish between the situation of the holders of stock in the English and French funds. In the former, where the whole debt has been contracted by money advanced at different times to Government, it is impossible to dispute that, if a succeeding administration are in a situation to repay the capital sum borrowed, the holder of the stock has no reason to complain. In this country, accordingly, various parts of the public debt have at different times undergone a reduction of interest, without the slightest complaint, or imputation of injustice to Government. But the case is widely different in France. There the public debt consisted almost entirely of *perpetual annuities* or "*rentes*," as they are called, which were contracted by Government for no principal sum advanced at any one time, but as a compensation for the bankruptcies, spoliations, and confiscations of the Revolution, when two-thirds of the national debt were swept away, or in consideration of sums advanced to extricate Government from its embarrassments, or to effect the liberation of the territory in 1818. It was an essential condition of all such advances and arrangements, that the annuity was to be *perpetual*, and it was the understanding that it was to be such which constituted its principal marketable value. To transfer to these holders of rents the principles rightly applied to the English loans of capital was obviously unjust, and therefore there seems to be no doubt that the decision of the House of Peers on this momentous question was consonant to justice.[2]

[2] Lam. vii. 277, 278; Cap. viii. 303, 305.

116
Splendid position of M. de Chateaubriand.

The rejection of this law gave the utmost satisfaction in Paris, and was celebrated by bonfires in the streets, and all the noisy ebullitions of popular rejoicing. It led to one result, however, of a very important character, and which, in its ultimate results, was eminently prejudicial to the Government of the Restoration. M. de Chateaubriand was not personally agreeable to Louis XVIII., and he was the object of undisguised jealousy to the whole administration. This is noways surprising; genius always is so. Power hates intellectual influence, mediocrity envies renown, ambition dreads rivalry. Obsequious talent, useful ability, is what they all desire, for they aid without endangering them. In truth, since the successful issue of the Spanish war, the position of Chateaubriand had become so commanding that it overbalanced that of the Prime Minister himself. He united in his own person the political influence of Mr. Canning, and the literary fame of Sir Walter Scott. This was more than human nature could bear; a similar combination of political and military power had roused the jealousy which proved fatal to Marlborough. The conduct of Chateaubriand and his friends, on the question of reduction of the *rentes*, had indicated a desire to court popularity, which was suspected, not without reason, to spring from a secret design to supplant the Prime Minister.

117
His dismissal, and that of Marshal Victor.

M. de Villèle saw his danger, and resolved to anticipate the blow. The day after the vote in the Peers on the *rentes*, M. de Chateaubriand received a notification, in the coldest terms, from M. de Villèle, that his services were no longer required at the Foreign Office; and, to make the dismissal the more galling, it was sent by a common menial. The portfolio of Foreign Affairs was bestowed on M. de Damas; and at the same time the office of Minister at War was given to M. Clermont-Tonnerre, in room of Marshal Victor, who received his dismissal. Chateaubriand, who was very ambitious, and, with all his great qualities, inordinately vain, felt his fall keenly; he had not manliness enough to act a noble part on the occasion; he avenged the minister on the throne; and the pen which had mainly contributed to the restoration of the Bourbons, became one of the most powerful agents in bringing about their fall.[1]

[1] Chateaubriand, Mem. d'Outre Tombe, vii. 457,462, Lam. vii. 287, 292; Cap. viii. 307, 312.

118
Statistics of France in this year.

The remainder of the session presented nothing worthy of notice in general history but the budget, which exhibited the most flattering appearances. From the papers laid before the Chamber, it appeared that the total revenue of the state in 1823 was 1,123,456,000 francs (£40,120,000), including 100,000,000 (£4,000,000) borrowed for the Spanish war, and for 1824, only 905,306,653 francs (£36,800,000), in consequence of the cessation of hostilities. The expenditure in the first year was 1,118,025,169 francs (£40,020,000), and in the second 904,731,000 (£36,240,000), leaving in each year a trifling balance of income over expenditure. The public debt in 1823 was 2,700,726,000 francs (£115,000,000); the army mustered 230,000 combatants, the navy 49 ships of the line and 31 frigates.[2]

[2] Ann. Hist. vii. App. 594, 627.

During this year Louis XVIII. lived, but did not reign. His mission was accomplished; his work was done. The reception of the Duke d'Angoulême and his triumphant host at the Tuileries was the last real act of his eventful career; thenceforward the royal functions, nominally his own, were in reality performed by others. It must be confessed he could not have terminated his reign with a brighter ray of glory. The magnitude of the services he rendered to France can only be appreciated by recollecting in what state he found, and in what he left it. He found it divided, he left it united; he found it overrun by conquerors, he left it returning from conquest; he found it in slavery, he left it in freedom; he found it bankrupt, he left it affluent; he found it drained of its heart's blood, he left it teeming with life; he found it overspread with mourning, he left it radiant with happiness. An old man had vanquished the Revolution; he had done that which Robespierre and Napoleon had left undone. He had ruled France, and showed it could be ruled, without either foreign conquest or domestic blood. Foreign bayonets had placed him on the throne, but his own wisdom maintained him on it. Other sovereigns of France may have left more durable records of their reign, for they have written them in blood, and engraven them in characters of fire upon the minds of men; but none have left so really glorious a monument of their rule, for it was written in the hearts, and might be read in the eyes of his subjects.

[119. Reign of Louis XVIII. draws to a close.]

This arduous and memorable reign, however, so beset with difficulties, so crossed by obstacles, so opposed by faction, was now drawing to a close. His constitution, long oppressed by a complication of disorders, the result in part of the constitutional disorders of his family, was now worn out. Unable to carry on the affairs of state, sinking under the load of government, he silently relinquished the direction to M. de Villèle and the Count d'Artois, who really conducted the administration of affairs. Madame Du Cayla was the organ by whose influence they directed the royal mind. The pomp of the court was kept up, but Louis was a stranger to it; he sat at the sumptuous table of the Tuileries, but his fare was that of the hermit in his cell. He presided at the councils of his Ministers, but took little part in their deliberations. His only excitement consisted in frequent excursions in his carriage, which was driven with the utmost speed; the rapidity of the motion restored for a brief season his languid circulation. He felt, says Lamartine, the same pleasure in these exercises that a captive does in the presence of the sun. During the summer of 1824 he was manifestly sinking, and he knew it; but no symptoms of apprehension appeared in his conversation or manner. "Let us put a good face upon it," said he to M. de Villèle, "and meet death as becomes a king." The Minister, however, was more aware than he was how much the public tranquillity depended on his life; and to prevent alarm on the subject being prematurely excited, the liberty of the press was by royal edict provisionally suspended, by re-establishing the censure. The people felt the motive, and had delicacy enough to acquiesce in silence in the temporary restraint. Soon after, the influence which now

[120. His declining days.]

[Aug. 15.]

gained possession of the government appeared in another ordonnance, which created a new ministry, that of "Ecclesiastical Affairs," which was bestowed on Count Frayssenous, Bishop of Hermopolis, Grand-master of the University. As he was a man of ability, and the acknowledged representative of the *Parti Prêtre*, this appointment was of sinister augury for the tranquillity of the succeeding reign.[1]

[Aug. 26]
[1 Ann. Hist. vii. 300, 301; Lam. vii. 308, 312.]

The declining days of this monarch were chiefly spent in conversation, an exercise of the mind in which he took the greatest delight, as is generally the case with those whose intellectual faculties in advanced years remain entire, but who are debarred by increasing infirmities from continuing the active duties of life. "His natural talent," says Lamartine, "cultivated, reflective, and quick, full of recollections, rich in anecdotes, nourished by philosophy, enriched by quotations, never deformed by pedantry, rendered him equal in conversation to the most renowned literary characters of his age. M. de Chateaubriand had not more elegance, M. de Talleyrand more wit, Madame de Staël more brilliancy. Never inferior, always equal, often superior to those with whom he conversed on every subject, yet with more tact and address than they, he changed his tone and the subject of conversation with those he addressed, and yet was never exhausted by any one. History, contemporary events, things, men, theatres, books, poetry, the arts, the incidents of the day, formed the varied text of his conversations. Since the suppers of Potsdam, where the genius of Voltaire met the capacity of Frederick the Great, never had the cabinet of a prince been the sanctuary of more philosophy, literature, talent, and taste."[2]

[121. His great powers of conversation.]

[2 Lam. vii. 310, 311.]

Though abundantly sensible of the necessity of the support of religion to the maintenance of his throne, and at once careful and respectful in its outward observances, Louis was far from being a bigot, and in no way the slave of the Jesuits, who in his declining days had got possession of his palace. In secret, his opinions on religious subjects, though far from sceptical, were still farther from devout: he had never surmounted the influence of the philosophers who, when he began life, ruled general opinion in Paris. He listened to the suggestions of the priests, when they were presented to him from the charming lips of Madame Du Cayla; but he never permitted themselves any nearer approach to his person. As his end was visibly approaching, this circumstance gave great distress to the Count d'Artois and Duchess d'Angoulême, and the other members of the royal family, who were deeply impressed with religious feelings, and dreaded the king's departing this life without having received the last benediction of the church. They could not, however, for long induce him to send for his confessor; and to attain the object, they were at last obliged to recall to court Madame Du Cayla, who had found her situation so uncomfortable, from the cold reception she experienced from the royal family, that she had re-

[122. His religious impressions in his last days.]

tired from the palace. She came back accordingly, and by her influence Louis was persuaded to send for the priest, and after confessing received supreme unction. "You alone," said he, taking her hand and addressing Madame Du Cayla, "could venture to address me on this subject. I will do as you desire: Adieu! We will meet in another world. I have now no longer any concern with this."[1]

[margin: 1 Lam. vii. 314, 394.]

At length the last hour approached. The extremities of the king became cold, and symptoms of mortification began to appear; but his mind continued as distinct, his courage as great as ever. He was careful to conceal his most dangerous symptoms from his attendants. "A king of France," said he, "may die, but he is never ill;" and around his death-bed he received the foreign diplomatists and officers of the national guard, with whom he cheerfully conversed upon the affairs of the day. "Love each other," said the dying monarch to his family, "and console yourselves by that affection for the disasters of our house. Providence has replaced us upon the throne; and I have succeeded in maintaining you on it by concessions which, without weakening the real strength of the Crown, have secured for it the support of the people. The Charter is your best inheritance; preserve it entire, my brothers, for me, for our subjects, for yourselves;" then stretching out his hand to the Duke de Bordeaux, who was brought to his bedside, he added, "and also for this dear child, to whom you should transmit the throne after my children are gone. May you be more wise than your parents." He then received supreme unction, thanked the priests and his attendants, and bade adieu to all, and especially M. Decazes, who stood at a little distance, but whose sobs attracted his notice. He then composed himself to sleep, and rested peaceably during the night. At daybreak on the following morning the chief physician opened the curtains to feel his pulse; it was just ceasing to beat. "The king is dead," said he, bowing to the Count d'Artois—"Long live the king!"[2]

[margin: 2 Lam. vii. 394, 397; Ann. Hist. vii. 302, 303; Cap. viii. 375, 383.]

[margin: 123. His death. Sept. 16.]

[margin: 124. Character of Louis XVIII.]

Louis XVIII., who thus paid the debt of nature, after having sat for ten years on the throne of France, during the most difficult and stormy period in its whole annals, was undoubtedly a very remarkable man. Alone of all the sovereigns who have ruled its destinies since the Revolution, he succeeded in conducting the Government without either serious foreign war or domestic overthrow. In this respect he was more fortunate, or rather more wise, than either Napoleon, Charles X., or Louis Philippe; for the first kept his seat on the throne only by keeping the nation constantly in a state of hostility, and the two last lost their crowns mainly by having attempted to do without it. He was no common man who at such a time, and with such a people, could succeed in effecting such a prodigy. Louis Philippe aimed at being the Napoleon of peace; but Louis XVIII. really was so, and succeeded so far that he died king of France. The secret of his success was, that he entirely accommodated himself to the temper of the times. He was the man of the age—neither before it, like great, nor behind it, like little men. Thus he succeeded in steering the vessel of the state successfully through shoals which would have in all probability stranded a man of greater or less capacity. The career of Napoleon illustrated the danger of the first, that of Charles X. the peril of the last.

In addition to this tact and judgment which enabled him to scan with so much correctness the signs of the times, and choose his ministers and shape his measures accordingly, he had many qualities of essential value in a constitutional monarch, who must always be more or less guided by others. His intellect was clear, his memory great, his observation piercing. Though he formed strong opinions from his own judgment, he was ready to listen to considerations on the opposite side; often yielded to superior weight in argument, and even, when unconvinced, knew how to yield when circumstances rendered it expedient to do so. He was humane and benevolent; few monarchs surmounted so many rebellions with so little effusion of blood; and the rare deeds of severity which did occur during his reign were forced upon him, much against his will, by the strength of the public voice, or the violence of an overwhelming parliamentary majority. He had his weaknesses, but they were of a harmless kind, and did not interfere with his public conduct. Though oppressed in later years with the corpulence hereditary in his family, and the victim of gout and other painful diseases, he was abstemious in the pleasures of the table, and generally dined amidst the sumptuous repasts of the Tuileries on two eggs and a few glasses of wine. A constitutional coldness, and the infirmities to which he was latterly a victim, preserved him from the well-known weaknesses to which his ancestors had so often been the slaves; but he yielded to none of them in appreciation of the society of elegant and cultivated women, and devoted all his leisure hours, perhaps to a blamable extent, to their society, or the daily correspondence he kept up with them. But he did not permit their influence to warp his judgment in affairs of state, and never yielded to it so readily as when employed in pleading on behalf of the unfortunate.

[margin: 125. His private qualities and weaknesses.]

The final issue of the Spanish revolution affords the clearest illustration of the extreme danger and inevitable tendency of the military treachery and revolt in which it took its rise. No one can doubt that the cause of freedom in the Peninsula, and in Europe, was essentially and deeply injured by the revolt of Riego and Quiroga in the Isle of Leon in 1820, which at the time was hailed with such enthusiasm by the whole friends of freedom in the Old and New World. It was not merely from the strong and general reaction to which it of necessity gave rise that this effect took place; the result was equally certain, and would have been still more swift, had the triumph of the revolutionists continued uninterrupted. Military treason, Prætorian revolt, even when supported at the time by the voice of a vast majority of the people, can never in the end terminate in any thing but destruction

[margin: 126. Political inferences from the result of the Spanish revolution.]

to the cause for which it is undertaken, for this plain reason, that, being carried into effect by the strongest, it leaves society without any safeguard against their excesses. This accordingly was what took place in Spain; it was the triumph of the revolutionists which, by destroying liberty, rendered inevitable their fall. The Royalist reaction, and desolating civil war to which it gave rise, preceded, not followed, the invasion of the French. It arose from the oppressive measures of the Government appointed by the military chiefs, who had been the leaders of the revolt. It was Riego, not the Duke d'Angoulême, who was the real murderer of liberty in Spain. It was the same in England. No one supposes that either the Long Parliament or Cromwell were the founders of British liberty; what they induced was, the military tyranny which made all sigh for the Restoration. No cause ever yet was advanced by treachery and treason, least of all in the armed defenders of law and order. So true are the words of Wieland, placed in an inscription on the hero's sword:—

"Vermess sich kerner untugendlich,
Diess schwertes anzumuthen sich;
Treuegeht uber alles
Untrue schandet alles!"*

127.
Great merit of the French expedition into Spain in 1823.

The French invasion of Spain in 1823 was a model of combined energy and moderation, and affords an apt illustration of observations made in another work as to the consequences which might have resulted from a more vigorous action on the part of the allied powers in their invasion of Champagne in 1792.¹ Denied and passed over in silence by the Liberal and Napoleonist historians, who had an object in keeping out of view its merits, it was in reality an expedition which reflected equal honor on the government which planned, and the generals and soldiers who executed it. Undertaken in support of Royalist principles, and to overcome a revolutionary convulsion, it partook of the dangerous character which more or less belongs to all wars of opinion; and had it been conducted with less vigor and moderation, it would infallibly have lighted a flame which would have involved Europe in conflagration. Jealousy of France was inherent in the Spanish character; it burned as fiercely in the breasts of the Royalists as the Liberals; a spark might have set the whole country on fire. A cruel massacre, such as that of Murat at Madrid, on 2d May, 1808—an act of perfidy, like that which has forever disgraced the name of Napoleon at Bayonne—would at once have caused the entire nation to run to arms. England, in such an event, could never have remained a passive spectator of the strife, and probably a new Peninsular war would have arisen, rivaling in blood and devastation that which Wellington had brought to a glorious termination. But by advancing with vigor and celerity at once to the capital—by paying for every thing, and avoiding the execrable system of making war maintain war—by disclaiming all intention of territorial aggrandizement, and generously proclaiming an entire amnesty for political offences, they succeeded in detaching the revolutionary party from the vast majority of the nation, and effecting that which Napoleon, during six campaigns, sought in vain to accomplish. Little blood was shed in Spain, because the wisdom of the measures adopted required little to be shed; and never was eulogium more just than the generous one pronounced on it by Mr. Canning, who said, "Never was so much done at so little cost of human life."¹ ¹ Ann. Hist. vi. 480, 481.

128.
It had nearly established the throne of the Restoration.

So great was the advantage gained by the government of the Restoration, in consequence of the glorious issue of this campaign, that it went far to establish it on a lasting foundation. But for the blind infatuation which, under the direction of the priests, guided the Government of Charles X., it in all probability would have done so. The prophecy of Chateaubriand had been fulfilled to the letter. The Royalists and Republicans had forgot their animosities under the tent; the reign of Louis XVIII. terminated in a state of peace and unanimity which could not possibly have been hoped for at its commencement. So strong is the military spirit in the French people, so ardent and inextinguishable their thirst for war, that when these passions are once roused, they obliterate for the time every other, and unite parties the most opposite, and feelings the most discordant, in the eager pursuit of the ruling national desire. Napoleon himself could not have preserved his throne but for the whirl in which his incessant wars kept the minds of his people. Louis XIV. was, till he became involved in misfortune, the most popular monarch who ever sat upon the throne of France; and if circumstances had admitted of either Charles X. or Louis Philippe going to war, and emerging victorious from its dangers, it is not going too far to assert that the family of one or other of them would still have been in possession of it.

129.
The French invasion of Spain was justifiable.

No doubt can now remain that the French invasion of Spain, against which public feeling in this country was so strongly excited at the time, was not only a wise measure on the part of the Bourbon government, but fully justifiable on the best principles of international law. The strength of this case is to be found, not in the absurdity and peril of the Spanish constitution, or even the imminent hazard to which it exposed the royal family in that country, and the entire liberties and property of the country; it is to be found in the violent inroads which the Spanish revolutionists and their allies to the north of the Pyrenees were making on France itself, and the extreme hazard to which its institutions were exposed in consequence of their machinations. Ever since the Spanish revolution broke out, France had been kept in a continual ferment: the second in succession to the throne had been murdered, and his consort, when *enceinte* of an heir to the monarchy, attempted to be murdered, by political fanatics: military conspiracies in great numbers had been got up to imitate the example of the soldiers in the Isle of Leon, and overturn the government; Paris

* "Scatheless held by virtue's shield,
Dare alone this sword to wield;
God shall bless the faithful hand—
Ruin waits the faithless brand!"

had been convulsed by an attempted revolution; France was covered with secret societies, having Lafayette, Benjamin Constant, Manuel, and all the Liberal leaders in the Chamber of Deputies, at their head, the object of which was to overthrow the Government by means of murder, treason, and revolt; and a band of desperadoes had been collected on the Pyrenees, under the tricolor flag, who openly invited the French soldiers to fraternize with them, throw off the yoke of the Bourbons, and rally round the standard of Napoleon II. When such measures were in progress, it was evident that the safety of France, and the preservation of its institutions, were seriously menaced, and that its Government was warranted in taking steps to extinguish so perilous a volcano in the neighboring state, by the strongest of all reasons—that of self-preservation.

130. Was the English intervention in behalf of South American justifiable.¹

It is more difficult to find grounds to vindicate the intervention of England in favor of the insurgent colonies in South America, which was done in so efficacious a manner, and from the success of which consequences of such incalculable importance have ensued to both hemispheres. Nothing can be clearer, indeed, than that when the colonies of Spain had become *de facto* independent, and Spain was obviously unable to reassert her dominion over them, we were warranted in treating with them as independent powers, and sending consuls to their chief towns to guard British mercantile interests. If our intervention had been limited to this, the most scrupulous public morality could not have objected to the course pursued. But we not only did this—we did a great deal more, and of a much more questionable character. We repealed the laws against foreign enlistments; permitted expeditions of eight and ten thousand men, many of them Wellington's veterans, to sail from the Thames under the very eye of Government; and advanced immense sums by loan, to enable the insurgent states to prolong the contest. It was by these means, *and these alone*, that the conflict was ultimately decided in favor of the colonies, and against the mother country. The decisive battle of Carabobo was gained entirely by British battalions and a charge of the British bayonet.¹

¹ Hist. of Europe, c. lxvii. §§ 60, 72.

What was the justification for this armed and powerful intervention? Was the freedom of England menaced by the re-establishment of Spanish authority in South America? Confessedly it was not: the hope of commercial advantages, the vision of a vast trade with the insurgent states, was the ruling motive. But commercial advantages will not constitute legal right, or vindicate acts of injustice, any more than the acquisition of provinces will justify an unprovoked invasion. It sounds well to say you will call a new world into existence to redress the balance of the old; but if that new world is to be carved out of the dominions of an allied and friendly power, it is better to leave it to itself. England saw very clearly the iniquity of this insidious mode of proceeding when it was applied to herself, when Louis XVI. allowed covert succors to the American insurgents to sail from the French harbors, and the Americans sent some thousand sympathizers to aid the Canadian revolt in 1837. She loudly denounced it when the Americans allowed an expedition to sail from New Orleans, in 1852, to revolutionize Cuba; and she exclaimed against the Irish democrats, who petitioned the French revolutionary Government, in 1848, to recognize a Hibernian republic in the Emerald Isle. But what were the two last but following her example? She sees the mote in her neighbor's eye, but can not discover the beam in her own. It will appear in the sequel of this history whether England in fact derived any benefit, even in a commercial point of view, from this great act of disguised aggression; whether the cause of freedom and the interests of humanity were really advanced by it; and whether the greatest calamities, public and private, its inhabitants have ever undergone, may not be distinctly traced to its consequence

131. Its ultimate disastrous effects to England.

END OF VOL. I.

www.ingramcontent.com/pod-product-compliance
Lightning Source LLC
Chambersburg PA
CBHW032000300426
44117CB00008B/844